CASES AND MATERIALS ON

CONTRACTS: MAKING AND DOING DEALS

Fifth Edition

■ ■ ■

David G. Epstein
George E. Allen Chair Professor of Law
University of Richmond

Bruce A. Markell
Professor of Bankruptcy Law and Practice
Northwestern Pritzker School of Law

Lawrence Ponoroff
Dean & Professor of Law
Michigan State University College of Law

AMERICAN CASEBOOK SERIES®

WEST ACADEMIC PUBLISHING

444 Cedar Street, Suite 700
St. Paul, MN 55101
1-877-888-1330

Printed in the United States of America

ISBN: 978-1-63460-648-6

To Libby and Charlie Epstein—world's greatest grandchildren.

DGE

To Emily, fur-ever.

BAM

To my wife, Monica, and in memory of her father and my friend, James E. Moses.

LP

PREFACE TO THE FIFTH EDITION

The Fifth Edition of MADD brings some inevitable changes, a little refreshening, and some new materials. However, we have tried to retain the basic organizational structure and conversational tone of past editions because, in our view, they worked well and made the book popular with students.

Over the years we have received a lot of feedback from professors who have adopted the book and from students who have used it. That feedback has not always been universally positive, but we beam when we get a note from a law student at a school other than one of our own saying, "thank you." We try to take this feedback, particularly the constructive criticism, to heart each time we prepare a new edition, and this edition is no different. So we thank our loyal faculty adopters and their students.

Among the changes from the last edition of MADD, this edition features:

- A new feature called "Questions Before the Case." These questions are intended to focus the students on what to look for or bear in mind *as they read each case*, as opposed to only raising questions after they've finished reading. We've kept, however, questions at the end of each case which are designed to push students' understanding.
- We have expanded our treatment of arbitration both in the Remedies chapter—as it pertains to commercial arbitration—and in our discussion of the defense of unconscionability—in connection with consumer arbitration.
- We have revised and expanded our treatment of electronic contracting as this area of the law continues to grow and develop.
- As seems to be the case with all of the earlier editions, we have re-organized the Remedies chapter, this time so as to conclude rather than start with equitable remedies. We've also reorganized our chapter on post-formation excuse, dropping some dud cases (thanks, Markell . . . .) and adding some newer, hopefully more interesting ones.
- We have tried to make the book more manageable by a combination of (1) eliminating some cases that did not really add a lot to what had already been covered (thanks again, Markell), (2) substituting shorter cases that made the point just as well as the longer cases they replaced (thanks

Epstein), and (3) more vigorously editing some existing cases (thanks Ponoroff).

- In addition to the foregoing, we are always on the lookout for cases—particularly newer cases—that will serve as better learning vehicles than the ones we have used in the past. We found a few of them as well.

In order to minimize the burden on law students (and to those misguided instructors tasked with Contracts against their will), all of the cases have been edited to one degree or another. With the occasional exception of long string citations or parenthetical references to pleadings in the case (which we just unceremoniously excised), three asterisks (* * *) have been inserted in place of any portion of a case opinion that has been omitted. We also eliminated formatting references that may have been part of the original version of the case but added nothing to understanding. Finally, in some instances we have re-numbered the footnotes in a case—though not the actual content of the notes themselves. Footnotes that we, as editors, have inserted are referenced by an asterisk rather than a number.

Each edition of the book has witnessed a change in professional circumstances for at least one of us (as we've all seemed to have had difficulty in holding down a job!) and this time is no different. Markell has moved from Florida State to the Northwestern Pritzker School of Law. Apparently determining that he hadn't been punished enough, Ponoroff has moved from the University of Arizona to the Michigan State University College of Law in order to take on his third deanship. Remarkably, Epstein, historically the most peripatetic of the three of us, remains happily ensconced at Richmond Law.

Epstein would like to thank his University of Richmond students who, every year, act surprised when he wears a chicken suit to class, and, more important, don't tell the Dean when he uses some of the seven dirty words that you used to not be able to say on television https://www.youtube.com/watch?v=kyBH5oNQOS0), although now you can on television but not. . . . Epstein also thanks Karen Berry, the "administrative assistant" who is always cheerful even though she is "responsible" for Epstein and at least ten other faculty members whose mommas did not teach them to share. Markell expresses his appreciation to Lauren Pope and Brian Mochoruk (who undertook to scrub the text of typographical and other silly errors, all the while gently reminding Markell of the reality of being a modern law student), and to all his demanding students at Northwestern. Ponoroff does his own work and thanks no one. However, we would all like to thank our friends at West Academic Publishing for their support and encouragement.

Our goal when we first went to work on this book nearly 20 years ago was to produce materials that would be not only instructive but that would also be enjoyable to use (or at least as enjoyable as a law book can be) for both students and instructors. Whether we've achieved that lofty goal is for you the reader to decide. However, we have loved working on this book from day one; we have loved teaching from it over the years; and we have even come to tolerate one another. We very much hope that all of you enjoy the book as much as we do. We also hope the students who use the book will at the end of the semester, be able to say: "You know, Contracts was my favorite subject"! Let us know how it goes.

DAVID G. EPSTEIN
BRUCE A. MARKELL
LAWRENCE PONOROFF

Richmond, Chicago, East Lansing
March 2018

SUMMARY OF CONTENTS

TABLE OF CONTENTS

TABLE OF CASES

The principal cases are in bold type.

CASES AND MATERIALS ON

CONTRACTS: MAKING AND DOING DEALS

Fifth Edition

CHAPTER 1

WHAT ARE WE GOING TO BE DOING IN THIS COURSE?

■ ■ ■

1. INTRODUCTION

You're probably excited about law school. We were. And you're probably concerned that Contracts is going to be boring. We were concerned that Contracts was going to be our most boring class, and one of us was right in thinking that. If, however, that is what you're thinking, then you're wrong. The students who have used the past four editions of the book have used many adjectives in describing the book. "Boring" was not among those many adjectives. Not even when describing Markell's part of the book. Not even the Pierces (http://www.metrolyrics.com/boring-lyrics-the-pierces.html) who are very easily bored would use the word "boring" in describing this book.

You will learn about Contracts mostly by reading real cases, selected not only to show you rules of contract law, but also the roles that lawyers play in contract law. Our first case involves the question of whether a surrogate parenting agreement that grants custody of the child to the father and his wife is enforceable. The Probate and Family Court judge's answer is that the agreement is enforceable. On appeal, the justices on the Supreme Judicial Court of Massachusetts decide that the Probate and Family Court judge (a law school graduate whom we can assume knows a hell of a lot more law than you do) came up with the *wrong* answer. The Supreme Judicial Court of Massachusetts's opinion in *R.R. v. M.H.*, edited and reproduced below, explains the reasons that the Supreme Judicial Court of Massachusetts concludes "the surrogacy agreement is not enforceable."

In reading this judicial opinion (and all of the other "cases" in this book), you should be asking yourself, "Self, why am I reading this case"? If after reading *R.R v. M.H.* your answer to that question is, "Self, I was reading this case to learn that in Massachusetts, surrogate parenting contracts are unenforceable," then: (1) your answer is too broad, and (2) your answer is too narrow, and (3) you should not ask the registrar of your law school whether you can just skip first year law school courses and get to the second and third year courses where professors don't "cold call" on students and the grades are all "A" or "A–," with only the occasional "B+"

QUESTIONS BEFORE THE CASE*

1. You can sell a car; you can sell a house; can you sell a baby? Is this case about the sale of a baby?
2. Was there a "contract" in this case?

R.R. v. M.H.

Supreme Judicial Court of Massachusetts
426 Mass. 501, 689 N.E.2d 790 (1998)

WILKINS, CHIEF JUSTICE.

* * * [W]e are concerned with the validity of a surrogacy parenting agreement between the plaintiff (father) and the defendant (mother). Both the mother and the father are married but not to each other. A child was conceived through artificial insemination of the mother with the father's sperm, after the mother and father had executed the surrogate parenting agreement. The agreement provided that the father would have custody of the child. During the sixth month of her pregnancy, and after she had received funds from the father pursuant to the surrogacy agreement, the mother changed her mind and decided that she wanted to keep the child.

The father thereupon brought this action and obtained a preliminary order awarding him temporary custody of the child. * * * The judge's order granting the preliminary injunction is before us on her report of the propriety of that order which was based in part on her conclusion that the father was likely to prevail on his assertion that the surrogacy agreement is enforceable. * * * This court has not previously dealt with the enforceability of a surrogacy agreement.

The Facts

The baby girl who is the subject of this action was born on August 15, 1997, in Leominster. The defendant mother and the plaintiff father are her biological parents. The father and his wife, who live in Rhode Island, were married in June 1989. The wife is infertile. Sometime in 1994, she and the father learned of an egg donor program but did not pursue it because the procedure was not covered by insurance and had a relatively low success rate. Because of their ages (they were both in their forties), they concluded that pursuing adoption was not feasible. In April 1996, responding to a

---

* The questions preceding this, and every other, case in the book are intended to focus your thinking as you read the case. We call them "framing questions." They are intended to keep you from wandering too far adrift from the main point or points of the case. Keep them in mind as you read each case and don't try to answer them until *after* you've read the case. Eds.

newspaper advertisement for surrogacy services, they consulted a Rhode Island attorney who had drafted surrogacy contracts for both surrogates and couples seeking surrogacy services. On the attorney's advice, the father and his wife consulted the New England Surrogate Parenting Advisors (NESPA), a for-profit corporation that helps infertile couples find women willing to act as surrogate mothers. They entered into a contract with NESPA in September 1996, and paid a fee of $6,000.

Meanwhile, in the spring of 1996, the mother, who was married and had two children, responded to a NESPA advertisement. She reported to NESPA that her family was complete and that she desired to allow others less fortunate than herself to have children. The mother submitted a surrogacy application to NESPA. The judge found that the mother was motivated to apply to NESPA by a desire to be pregnant, in order to earn money, and to help an infertile couple.

In October, Dr. Angela Figueroa of NESPA brought the mother together with the father and his wife. They had a seemingly informative exchange of information and views. The mother was advised to seek an attorney's advice concerning the surrogacy agreement. Shortly thereafter, the mother, the father, and his wife met again to discuss the surrogacy and other matters. The mother also met with a clinical psychologist as part of NESPA's evaluation of her suitability to act as a surrogate. The psychologist, who also evaluated the father and his wife, advised the mother to consult legal counsel, to give her husband a chance to air his concerns, to discuss arrangements for contact with the child, to consider and discuss her expectations concerning termination of the pregnancy, and to arrange a meeting between her husband and the father and his wife.[2] The psychologist concluded that the mother was solid, thoughtful, and well grounded, that she would have no problem giving the child to the father and that she was happy to act as a surrogate. The mother told the psychologist that she was not motivated by money, although she did plan to use the funds received for her children's education. The mother's husband told the psychologist by telephone that he supported his wife's decision.

The mother signed the surrogate parenting agreement and her signature was notarized on November 1. The father signed on November 18. The agreement stated that the parties intended that the "Surrogate shall be inseminated with the semen of Natural Father" and "that, on the birth of the child or children so conceived, Natural Father, as the Natural Father, will have the full legal parental rights of a father, and surrogate will permit Natural Father to take the child or children home from the hospital to live with he [*sic*] and his wife." The agreement acknowledged that the mother's parental rights would not terminate if she permitted the

[2] Her husband had had a vasectomy in 1994 and did not have sexual relations with the mother after October 1996.

father to take the child home and have custody, that the mother could at any time seek to enforce her parental rights by court order, but that, if she attempted to obtain custody or visitation rights, she would forfeit her rights under the agreement and would be obligated to reimburse the father for all fees and expenses paid to her under it. The agreement provided that its interpretation would be governed by Rhode Island law.

* * *

The agreement provided for compensation to the mother in the amount of $10,000 "for services rendered in conceiving, carrying and giving birth to the Child." Payment of the $10,000 was to be made as follows: $500 on verification of the pregnancy; $2,500 at the end of the third month; $3,500 at the end of the sixth month; and $3,500 at the time of birth "and when delivery of child occurs." The agreement stated that no payment was made in connection with adoption of the child, the termination of parental rights, or consent to surrender the child for adoption. The father acknowledged the mother's right to determine whether to carry the pregnancy to term, but the mother agreed to refund all payments if, without the father's consent, she had an abortion that was not necessary for her physical health. The father assumed various expenses of the pregnancy, including tests, and had the right to name the child. The mother would be obliged, however, to repay all expenses and fees for services if tests showed that the father was not the biological father of the child, or if the mother refused to permit the father to take the child home from the hospital. The agreement also provided that the mother would maintain some contact with the child after the birth.

The judge found that the mother entered into the agreement on her own volition after consulting legal counsel. There was no evidence of undue influence, coercion, or duress. The mother fully understood that she was contracting to give custody of the baby to the father. She sought to inseminate herself on November 30 and December 1, 1996. The attempt at conception was successful.

The lawyer for the father sent the mother a check for $500 in December 1996, and another for $2,500 in February. In May, the father's lawyer sent the mother a check for $3,500. She told the lawyer that she had changed her mind and wanted to keep the child. She returned the check uncashed in the middle of June. The mother has made no attempt to refund the amounts that the father paid her, including $550 that he paid for pregnancy-related expenses.

Procedure

Approximately two weeks after the mother changed her mind and returned the check for $3,500, and before the child was born, the father commenced this action against the mother seeking to establish his paternity, alleging breach of contract, and requesting a declaration of his rights under the surrogacy agreement. Subsequently, the wife's husband was added as a defendant. The judge appointed a guardian *ad litem* to represent the interests of the unborn child. Proceedings were held on aspects of the preliminary injunction request (now resolved) and on the mother's motion to determine whether surrogacy contracts are enforceable in Massachusetts.

On August 4, 1997, the judge entered an order directing the mother to give the child to the father when it was discharged from the hospital and granting the father temporary physical custody of the child. She did so based on her determination that the father's custody claim was likely to prevail on the merits of the contract claim, and, if not on that claim, then on the basis of the best interests of the child. The mother was granted the right to frequent visits.

On August 13, 1997, the judge reported the propriety of her August 4 order which, as we have said, was based in part on her conclusion that the surrogacy contract was enforceable. * * *

Other Jurisdictions

A significant minority of States have legislation addressing surrogacy agreements. Some [state statutes] simply deny enforcement of all such agreements. Some States have simply exempted surrogacy agreements from provisions making it a crime to sell babies. * * * A few States have explicitly made unpaid surrogacy agreements lawful. * * *

There are few appellate court opinions on the enforceability of traditional surrogacy agreements. * * * The best known opinion is that of the Supreme Court of New Jersey in *Matter of Baby M.,* 109 N.J. 396, 537 A.2d 1227 (1988), where the court invalidated a compensated surrogacy contract because it conflicted with the law and public policy of the State. The *Baby M* surrogacy agreement involved broader concessions from the mother than the agreement before us because it provided that the mother would surrender her parental rights and would allow the father's wife to adopt the child. The agreement, therefore, directly conflicted with a statute prohibiting the payment of money to obtain an adoption and a statute barring enforcement of an agreement to adoption made prior to the birth of the child. The court acknowledged that an award of custody to the father was in the best interests of the child, but struck down orders terminating the mother's parental rights and authorizing the adoption of the child by the husband's wife. The court added that it found no "legal prohibition against surrogacy when the surrogate mother volunteers, without any payment, to act as a surrogate and is given the right to change her mind and to assert her parental rights."

Discussion

1. *The governing law.* The agreement before us provided that "Rhode Island Law shall govern the interpretation of this agreement." No party has argued that Rhode Island law has any application to the issues before us.[7] We are, in any event, not concerned with "the interpretation of this agreement," but rather with the legal significance, if any, of its provisions. The child was conceived and born in Massachusetts, and the mother is a Massachusetts resident, all as contemplated in the surrogacy arrangement. The significance, if any, of the surrogacy agreement on the relationship of the parties and on the child is appropriately determined by Massachusetts law.

2. *General Laws c. 46, § 4B.* The case before us concerns traditional surrogacy, in which the fertile member of an infertile couple is one of the child's biological parents. Surrogate fatherhood, the insemination of the fertile wife with sperm of a donor, often an anonymous donor, is a recognized and accepted procedure. If the mother's husband consents to the procedure, the resulting child is considered the legitimate child of the mother and her husband. G.L. c. 46, § B. Section 4B does not comment on the rights and obligations, if any, of the biological father, although inferentially he has none. In the case before us, the infertile spouse is the wife. No statute decrees the consequences of the artificial insemination of a surrogate with the sperm of a fertile husband. This situation presents different considerations from surrogate fatherhood because surrogate motherhood is never anonymous and her commitment and contribution is unavoidably much greater than that of a sperm donor.[10] * * *

3. *Adoption statutes.* Policies underlying our adoption legislation suggest that a surrogate parenting agreement should be given no effect if the mother's agreement was obtained prior to a reasonable time after the child's birth or if her agreement was induced by the payment of money. Adoption legislation is, of course, not applicable to child custody, but it does provide us with some guidance. Although the agreement makes no reference to adoption and does not concern the termination of parental rights or the adoption of the child by the father's wife, the normal expectation in the case of a surrogacy agreement seems to be that the father's wife will adopt the child with the consent of the mother (and the father). Under G.L. c. 210, § 2, adoption requires the written consent of the father and the mother but, in these circumstances, not the mother's husband. Any such consent, written, witnessed, and notarized, is not to be

---

[7] It appears that Rhode Island does not have statutes similar to those in Massachusetts which, as will be seen, provide us guidance.

[10] A situation which involves considerations different from those in the case before us arises when the birth mother has had transferred to her uterus an embryo formed through in vitro fertilization of the intended parents' sperm and egg. This latter process in which the birth mother is not genetically related to the child (except coincidentally if an intended parent is a relative) has been called gestational surrogacy.

executed "sooner than the fourth calendar day after the date of birth of the child to be adopted." That statutory standard should be interpreted as providing that no mother may effectively agree to surrender her child for adoption earlier than the fourth day after its birth, by which time she better knows the strength of her bond with her child. Although a consent to surrender custody has less permanency than a consent to adoption, the legislative judgment that a mother should have time after a child's birth to reflect on her wishes concerning the child weighs heavily in our consideration whether to give effect to a prenatal custody agreement. No private agreement concerning adoption or custody can be conclusive in any event because a judge, passing on custody of a child, must decide what is in the best interests of the child

Adoptive parents may pay expenses of a birth parent but may make no direct payment to her. *See* G.L. c. 210, § 11A; 102 Code Mass. Regs. § 5.09 (1997). Even though the agreement seeks to attribute that payment of $10,000, not to custody or adoption, but solely to the mother's services in carrying the child, the father ostensibly was promised more than those services because, as a practical matter, the mother agreed to surrender custody of the child. She could assert custody rights, according to the agreement, only if she repaid the father all amounts that she had received and also reimbursed him for all expenses he had incurred. The statutory prohibition of payment for receiving a child through adoption suggests that, as a matter of policy, a mother's agreement to surrender custody in exchange for money (beyond pregnancy-related expenses) should be given no effect in deciding the custody of the child.

4. *Conclusion.* The mother's purported consent to custody in the agreement is ineffective because no such consent should be recognized unless given on or after the fourth day following the child's birth. In reaching this conclusion, we apply to consent to custody the same principle which underlies the statutory restriction on when a mother's consent to adoption may be effectively given. Moreover, the payment of money to influence the mother's custody decision makes the agreement as to custody void. Eliminating any financial reward to a surrogate mother is the only way to assure that no economic pressure will cause a woman, who may well be a member of an economically vulnerable class, to act as a surrogate. It is true that a surrogate enters into the agreement before she becomes pregnant and thus is not presented with the desperation that a poor unwed pregnant woman may confront. However, compensated surrogacy arrangements raise the concern that, under financial pressure, a woman will permit her body to be used and her child to be given away.

There is no doubt that compensation was a factor in inducing the mother to enter into the surrogacy agreement and to cede custody to the father. If the payment of $10,000 was really only compensation for the mother's services in carrying the child and giving birth and was unrelated to custody of the child, the agreement would not have provided that the mother must refund all compensation paid (and expenses paid) if she should challenge the father's right to custody. Or would the agreement have provided that final payment be made only when the child is delivered to the father? We simply decline, on public policy grounds, to apply to a surrogacy agreement of the type involved here the general principle that an agreement between informed, mature adults should be enforced absent proof of duress, fraud, or undue influence.

We recognize that there is nothing inherently unlawful in an arrangement by which an informed woman agrees to attempt to conceive artificially and give birth to a child whose father would be the husband of an infertile wife. We suspect that many such arrangements are made and carried out without disagreement.

If no compensation is paid beyond pregnancy-related expenses and if the mother is not bound by her consent to the father's custody of the child unless she consents after a suitable period has passed following the child's birth, the objections we have identified in this opinion to the enforceability of a surrogate's consent to custody would be overcome. Other conditions might be important in deciding the enforceability of a surrogacy agreement, such as a requirement that (a) the mother's husband give his informed consent to the agreement in advance; (b) the mother be an adult and have had at least one successful pregnancy; (c) the mother, her husband, and the intended parents have been evaluated for the soundness of their judgment and for their capacity to carry out the agreement; (d) the father's wife be incapable of bearing a child without endangering her health; (e) the intended parents be suitable persons to assume custody of the child; and (f) all parties have the advice of counsel. The mother and father may not, however, make a binding best-interests-of-the-child determination by private agreement. Any custody agreement is subject to a judicial determination of custody based on the best interests of the child.

The conditions that we describe are not likely to be satisfactory to an intended father because, following the birth of the child, the mother can refuse to consent to the father's custody even though the father has incurred substantial pregnancy-related expenses. A surrogacy agreement judicially approved before conception may be a better procedure, as is permitted by statutes in Virginia and New Hampshire. A Massachusetts statute concerning surrogacy agreements, pro or con, would provide guidance to judges, lawyers, infertile couples interested in surrogate parenthood, and prospective surrogate mothers.

We do not reach but comment briefly on the mother's argument that the agreement was unconscionable. She actively sought to become a surrogate and entered into the surrogacy agreement voluntarily, advised by counsel, not under duress, and fully informed. Unconscionability is not apparent on this record.

A declaration shall be entered that the surrogacy agreement is not enforceable. Such further orders as may be appropriate, consistent with this opinion, may be entered in the Probate and Family Court.

So ordered.

QUESTIONS, NOTES, AND CONNECTIONS

1. Questions about the facts of this case

   1.1. What was the mother's "best" fact; that is, the fact that you would emphasize if you were representing the mother?

   1.2. What is the father's best fact?

   1.3. Was the agreement process in *R.R. v. M.H.* fair? Was that relevant to the court's decision? Should it be?

   1.4. Show me the money! Did the agreement require the genetic father to make payments to the mother? Was that relevant to the court's decision? Should it be?

   1.5. Show me the kid! Was it in the best interests of the child to remain with her birth mother? Was that relevant to the specific question the court answered; i.e., the enforceability of the surrogacy agreement? Should it be? What happened to the kid?

2. Questions about the law

   2.1. Do adoptions involve contracts? Did this case involve an adoption? If not, why did the court discuss adoption statutes?

   2.2. The court noted that "surrogate fatherhood, the insemination of the fertile wife with the sperm of a donor, often an anonymous donor, is a recognized and accepted procedure." Assume that Epstein enters into an artificial insemination agreement whereby: (i) he provides sperm,* (ii) Clare Danes pays Epstein $10,000, and (iii) Clare Danes will have custody of any child that results from her artificial insemination. Epstein later changes his mind about relinquishing custody rights. Would this court find such a surrogacy agreement unenforceable?

   2.3. Another medically-accepted surrogacy procedure involves implanting the embryo created by the egg and sperm of a man and woman in another woman. To illustrate, eggs from J.R. were

---

* We understand that Epstein is old; *really* old. And, yes, there is a contracts concept that you may have learned about in an undergraduate Business Law course that undergraduate Business Law teachers call "impossibility." We will deal with that concept later, but for now, forget about it so it doesn't interfere with the question we are currently posing.

artificially inseminated with sperm from J.F. and then implanted in D.B. who subsequently gave birth. J.R., the "egg donor" was paid $2,500 and D.B., the gestational surrogate, was paid $20,000 by J.F. and his wife. If the agreements for such a gestational surrogacy arrangement were similar to the agreement in *R.R. v. M.H.*, would the Supreme Judicial Court of Massachusetts find the agreements unenforceable? How about if the agreement between J.F. and D.B. provided that "D.B. will not attempt to form a parent-child relationship with any child conceived pursuant to the contract, and will institute proceedings upon the birth of any child to terminate her parental rights"? *See* J.F. v. D.B.*, 116 Ohio St.3d 363, 879 N.E.2d 740 (2007).

3. Notes

3.1. According to Professor Gillian Hadfield, "contract pregnancy" raises two difficult policy questions.

> The first is a public-law question and is concerned with whether, as a society, we should permit individuals to contract for the conception of a child and the allocation of parental status. This question raises the specter of commodification, and feminists grapple with the implications for children, women and sexuality of the use of market mechanisms to structure childbirth and parenting. The second question is a private-law contract puzzle. It is concerned with whether in a given case in which the birth mother refuses to relinquish her parental status and in the absence of public-law prohibition, contract law should find that the birth mother has a contractual obligation to release the child. Further, the second question asks whether any breach of this obligation should be remedied with an order of specific performance as opposed to an order for compensation.

Gillian K. Hadfield, *An Expressive Theory of Contract: From Feminist Dilemmas to a Reconceptualization of Rational Choice in Contract Law*, 146 U. Pa. L. Rev. 1235, 1240 (1998). Professor

* "See" does not mean that you are really supposed to go see these cases. "See" is an "introductory signal" that indicates that "the cited authority directly states or clearly supports the proposition." *See* (sic) THE BLUEBOOK: A UNIFORM SYSTEM OF CITATIONS R. 1.2(a) at 22–23 (Columbia Law Review Ass'n et al. eds., 19th ed. 2010). All of you will actually see "the Bluebook" in your first year of law school (and your second and third years of law school if you "make law review"). A law professor with a typical law professor-like sense of humor once described the Bluebook as the "Bible of citation form" or even the "Kama Sutra of legal citation." It is at once "Divine Word" and Divine Comedy, holy writ and sexual manual rolled in one. (Yes, that is why they say "Make love, not law review"). Gil Grantmore, *The Death of Contra*, 52 STAN. L. REV. 889, 890 (2000) (The use of the phony name, Gil Grantmore, is another example of what passes for humor in stuff written by law professors; it is a "spoof" of the name of a "famous," and dead, law professor, Grant Gilmore who (while still alive) wrote a book entitled THE DEATH OF CONTRACT.)

Richard Epstein of University of Chicago Law School has answers for Professor Hadfield's policy questions: unless there is fraud or duress, there should be "full contract enforcement" for surrogacy contracts. Richard A. Epstein, *Surrogacy: The Case For Full Contractual Enforcement*, 81 Va. L. Rev. 2305 (1995).

We will reconsider *R.R. v. M.H.* and Professor Hadfield's questions and the other Professor Epstein's answer when we consider contract law reasons for not enforcing an agreement in Chapter 3 and how courts enforce contracts in Chapter 6.

3.2. Professor Heidi Anderson has blogged about *R.R. v. M.H.* and a similar situation involving Jason Patric (Markell and Ponoroff are counting on Epstein's students to explain to him who Jason Patric is). Here it is if you want to take a look:

http://lawprofessors.typepad.com/contractsprof_blog/2013/02/a-modern-twist-on-rr-v-mh-and-statutory-interpretation.html.

3.3. A recent decision by the Wisconsin Supreme Court provides a nice counterpoint to *R.R. v. M.H.* In *Rosecky v. Schissel,* 833 N.W.2d 634 (2013), the Roseckys (Marcia and David) entered into a so-called Parentage Agreement (the "PA") with the Schissels (Monica and Corey), under the terms of which Monica (for an unstated consideration) was to become pregnant through artificial insemination using David's sperm, and the parties agreed that legal and physical custody of the child would be with the Roseckys and that the Schissels would disclaim all parental rights. The suit ensued after the couples had a falling out and Monica reneged on her obligations under the PA. After determining that Wisconsin statutes did not provide a specific answer as to the enforceability of the PA, the Court considered whether the contract was unenforceable on grounds of public policy, as Monica argued. Ultimately, the Court concluded that, aside from the provision regarding termination of parental rights, the PA was a valid, enforceable contract. As part of its reasoning, the Court reiterated the importance of the principle that "individuals should have the power to govern their own affairs without governmental interference," and that "enforcement of surrogacy agreements promotes stability and permanence in family relationships because it allows for the intended parents to plan for the arrival of their child, reinforces the expectations of all parties to the agreement, and reduces contentious litigation that could drag on for the first several years of the child's life."

Is *Rosecky* a rejection of the holding in *R.R.*?

4. **You Be the Lawyer!**

   If you had been the lawyer representing the birth father and his wife in *R.R. v. M.H.* in negotiating and drafting the surrogate parenting agreement with the birth mother, what would you have done differently?

5. Connections

   Before *R.R. v. M.H.* we asked you to ask yourself, "Why am I reading this case"? Throughout the book, as you read new cases, we also want you to ask yourself, "Self, how does this case relate to other cases I've read"? Obviously, you can't answer the latter question now because *R.R. v. M.H.* is the only case you've read.

   The reason we suggest you do this, beginning after you read another case and from then on, is that, at the end of the semester when you take the final exam (on which your grade in the course and probably your entire future will depend), what your professor will want to see is not whether you can simply regurgitate the rules of contract law, but rather whether you can *integrate* the materials covered over the course of the semester and apply them in a thoughtful and coherent manner. In other words, although we have tried to edit the cases and other materials so that you are learning contracts one concept at a time, what you will be expected to do on the final is combine and synthesize these materials. We hope our occasional "connections" sections will assist you in this endeavor.

---

2. WHAT IS A CONTRACT?

People often use the word "contract" to refer to the writing that embodies the agreement or deal. For example, Epstein, Markell, and Ponoroff each has a piece of paper signed by them and signed by the lovely Pamela Siege Chandler on behalf of West Academic Publishing Company in which Epstein, *et al.* agree to write a wonderful Contracts book for West and West agrees to pay them $60 for each copy of the book sold.* People think of such a piece of paper as being a "contract."

But the piece of paper is not a "contract." At least it is not a "contract" as we will be using the word "contract." At most, the piece of paper is a memorialization of the contract between Epstein, Markell, and Ponoroff, on the one hand, and West, on the other.

---

* That is why your law school casebooks are so expensive—obscenely high royalties paid to professor/authors.

In law school (and usually in the practice of law), a contract is a promise or set of promises that the law will enforce. Epstein, *et al.*, promise to write a book; West promises to pay royalties. That is the contract.

To state the obvious (we hope), there are thus two key elements to the existence of a contract:

(1) a promise or promises, AND

(2) enforcement.

Let's briefly consider "promise" first. A "promise" is a commitment as to the happening or non-happening of some future event: "I promise I will paint your house" or "I promise I will not sell my 1973 Cadillac to anyone else for ten days."

"Enforcement" means legal enforcement—an award of damages or some other order by a court of law. Not all promises are legally enforceable. In some instances, the making of a promise creates a moral obligation but not a legal obligation.

Because there can be no promise unless there is also someone to whom the promise is made, any contract inevitably involves a legal relationship between at least two parties. Moreover, more often than not, each of the parties will be bound by reciprocal promises to one another. This is because the only reason A may have made a promise to B—A was willing to give up $10,000—was that B promised in return to sell her car to A. Therefore most contracts involve *exchange* relationships where A's promise was motivated by the return promise from B, which, in turn, was induced by A's promise. We will, in this course, be concerned primarily with *exchange transactions*. This is because under the English common law system, from which our own law of contracts evolved, courts are (except in special circumstances) unwilling to enforce a promise unless something is given or promised in return. More technically put, an enforceable promise must be supported by *consideration*.

The promise, "I'll sell you my car for $10,000," if accepted, is enforceable. The promise, "I'll give you my car next Tuesday," is not, because nothing was given or promised in return and the *nudum pactum* (naked promise) is not enforceable under traditional principles of contract law. As should be obvious to you, contract law, and the doctrine of consideration, derive from and, in turn, serve the needs of trade and commerce. A market-driven economy relies heavily on direct, bilateral exchanges between private parties to allocate economic resources, and our law of contracts developed to facilitate these transactions. It is not as if contract law is irrelevant or indifferent to promises made in non-commercial settings, such as social or familial situations, but it is true that contract law is less concerned with those promises and, as we will see contract law operates less elegantly when applied in those non-commercial settings.

At bottom, contract law exists to satisfy the basic impulse—to which most people subscribe—that the reasonable expectations excited by a promise, if and when disappointed without legal excuse, are entitled to recompense in a court of law. Nevertheless, because not all promises can be enforced, there is considerably less agreement today on when, and, in particular, the reasons *why*, the coercive power of the state should be brought to bear to enforce certain broken promises. Is it to ensure fairness and promote justice? Because of the moral obligation attendant to the making of any promise? Or is it simply to promote commerce and aggregate social wealth? No one can answer these questions for you, but how *you* answer the question has enormous implications for deciding which promises ought to be enforced and which not. Consider these thoughts from Professor Farnsworth about wanting to make a commitment and regretting being committed.

E. ALLAN FARNSWORTH, *CHANGING YOUR MIND: THE LAW OF REGRETTED DECISIONS*

13–14, 16–18, 24, 26–27 (1998)

[T]he function of promising is usually very different from the function of resolving. While you make a resolution with a view to self-control, you most often make a promise with a view toward self-interest. You make it in order to get what you want from someone else whose self-interest is in having your commitment in return. You make it as part of an exchange in which you swap your commitment for something that you want. * * *

Complete freedom to renege on your promises would make it difficult for you to deal with others by lowering your worth in their eyes. Keeping your resolutions may be of little concern to others, but keeping your promises is an altogether different matter. Who would swap for your promises if you were free to renege on them?

To be sure, even if the law imposed no restraints you might honor your promises because of extralegal restraints. Some of these restraints are external: You might fear diminished standing among peers, harm to reputation, impairment of relationships, or loss of future opportunities. * * * Other restraints are internal: you might be moved by a sense of integrity, acquired by upbringing, education, or introspection. Why else do we use the word "honor" in this connection? * * *

For the law the question is not *why* do you honor your promises but *when* should you be restrained from reneging on your promises. Since extralegal restraints cause some promisors to honor their promises quite without regard to what the law requires, the law has an impact in restraining promisors only to the extent they would otherwise renege.

Even though you wanted to be committed at the time you made your promise, you may in hindsight wish you were not. Rare is the promisor who has never felt regret—the sensation that comes from such hindsight. * * *

Promises are made in the face of an uncertain future. Even if your promise reflected your existing preferences, so that you had no cause for regret, you might nevertheless have cause for regret after the passage of time. For this there are two possible reasons.

First, because you were poor at predicting external circumstances, you may find that they have changed and you made an improvident decision. Because contracts are devices for dealing with uncertainty by allocating risks of future changes, courts have tended to be markedly less paternalistic [i.e., intervene to allow you out from your promise] when faced with excuses based on improvident decisions than when confronted with excuses based on uninformed decisions. * * *

Second, because you were poor at predicting your preferences, you may find they have changed even though external circumstances have not, and that you have made an obsolete decision. * * *

Country-music star, Willie Nelson, when asked about his four marriages, replied, "I've changed. I'm not the same guy that was married to this person or that person. * * * [E]ach of my wives was married to a different person."[37] But contract law is not so forgiving. Even a financial disaster that not only alters one's preferences but leaves one unable to perform is dismissed as mere "subjective impossibility, that is, impossibility that is personal to the promisor and does not inhere in the nature of the act performed" and so is no excuse.[38]

* * *

To sum up, only rarely will a court allow you to change your mind and renege on a binding promise, though there is a trend toward tolerance of reneging and in this sense toward paternalism.

Professor Farnsworth's comments underscore the reasons why, once each party has voluntarily made a promise to the other, the law holds the parties to their promises, regardless of what might happen in the future that makes one of those promises more burdensome or less advantageous than originally contemplated. This idea is what we mean when we use the phrase "freedom of contract"—expressing the policy that parties are free to

---

37 60 Minutes, April 20, 1997 (CBS).

38 *B's Co. v. B.P. Barber & Assocs.*, 391 F.2d 130, 137 (4th Cir. 1968).

bargain about the terms of their deal, but once the deal is struck there is no turning back. But how far does this principle of freedom of contract extend? Consider that question often as you read the cases in this book. But before reading the cases in the book (or any more of this introductory stuff), please consider:

WHICH OF THE FOLLOWING LOOKS LIKE A CONTRACT TO YOU, A LAW STUDENT WHO HAS NOT YET HAD EVEN ONE DAY OF CONTRACTS?

1. Subaru Sales, Inc. (S) and B sign a document that provides, *inter alia*, that "S, party of the first part, is hereby selling and B, party of the second part, is hereby buying a 2014 Subaru Legacy for $25,000." S delivers the car and title to B, and B writes a check for $25,000.

2. Same facts as #1 above, except that the document does not include the word "hereby" or the phrases "party of the first part" and "party of the second part."

3. On September 9, the partners of X law firm and the partners of Y law firm sign a document that provides that the two firms will merge, effective October 10, with the new firm to be called XY.

4. S asks F if he wants to buy her Contracts notes for $100. F responds that he does if he can get the notes before Friday. S says that she will deliver the notes by Friday.

5. O, a Tucson resident who owns a second home in Florida, sends the following e-mail to P, a house painter in Florida. "Will pay you $1,000 for painting my house in Florida, with the work to be completed by November 25." P responds immediately by e-mail, "Great. Will paint your house and will complete the work before November 25."

6. Same facts as #5 above, except that P does not respond by email but instead paints O's house and completes the work by November 25.

7. T's lease with L expires next month. L sends T the following fax transmission: "I will renew the lease for two more years, with no increase in rent."

3. WHY DO LAWYERS AND LAW STUDENTS NEED TO KNOW ABOUT CONTRACTS AND CONTRACT LAW?

In a free market economy, contracts and contractual relationships permeate almost every aspect of day-to-day life. Perhaps nobody has put it quite so well as Sir Henry Maine who, at the end of the nineteenth century, observed that, "The movement of the progressive societies has hitherto been a movement from status to contract."* We each make numerous contracts of every stripe every year; for example, when we lease an apartment, open a checking account, buy a car, subscribe for cellular phone service, or sign our student loans. Not surprisingly, therefore, contract law and enforcement touch virtually every field of legal practice, from intellectual property to labor law to real estate. For this reason, every lawyer must be conversant with, and every law student must have exposure to, the basic rules and principles of contract law.

Ultimately, however, contract law is economic in focus and orientation. Business and commercial dealings and relationships in this country and, for that matter, throughout the free world are fundamentally contractual in nature. "Contracts" is the area of law that facilitates trade and commerce by setting forth the rules governing economic exchanges and enforcement of commercial obligations. It is important to recognize that businesspeople and companies relate to the rest of the world through their contracts, including contracts with employees, customers, suppliers, lenders, and many others. Indeed, most forms of business transaction, whether a big corporate merger or the routine purchase of office supplies, involve at their core a *contract* between two or more parties; that is to say, each of these parties has undertaken a legally binding performance obligation to the other in order to secure some desired reciprocal performance in return.

As should be apparent to you already, the law of "contracts" applies to an exceedingly wide array of transactions in an equally wide variety of settings. Having said this, however, it is also important to point out that certain types of contracts involve special rules because of the unique nature of the relationship involved. For example, if you plan to study labor law, there is a complex statutory framework governing labor/management agreements that you will have to master. Likewise, insurance contracts, government contracts, and consumer credit contracts are the subject of detailed regulatory schema that address the special concerns and issues that arise in each of those areas. However, even the special rules governing these particular kinds of contracts are built upon the basic principles of common law contracts and, in many instances, rely on those principles to fill the gaps where the applicable legislation is silent. Thus, it is the study of those basic rules and principles that this course and book are devoted to

* HENRY SUMNER MAINE, ANCIENT LAW 141 (New Universal Library ed. 1905).

because no lawyer worth her salt, whatever her area of expertise, can function effectively in ignorance of them.

---

4. WHERE DOES CONTRACT LAW COME FROM?

Contract law has a long history. Ancient Rome had its own form of contract law. Roman contract law influenced the development of contract law in England in medieval times. And, English contract law, in turn, influenced the development of American contract law.

Even today, lawyers and judges continue to use terms and concepts derived from Roman law and early English common law, such as *quantum meruit*, *assumpsit*, etc. Obviously, the particular problems and more general policy concerns in 21st century America are different from those in ancient Rome, or medieval England or even 18th century America. Thus, there are challenges in adapting long-accepted contract concepts to 21st century deals involving matters such as e-commerce, technology licensing or (as in our very first case) surrogate parenting agreements. The first step, however, is to develop an appreciation for the historical antecedents of contemporary American contract law.

A. ENGLISH COMMON LAW ORIGINS AND THE EVOLUTION OF *ASSUMPSIT*

E. ALLAN FARNSWORTH, *THE PAST OF PROMISE: AN HISTORICAL INTRODUCTION TO CONTRACT*

69 COLUM. L. REV. 576, 592–98 (1969)

The view that promises are not generally enforceable, which started from the premise of Roman law that a mere agreement did not beget an action, was held by the common law. Its choice was scarcely surprising. It accorded well with the procedural niceties of common law courts, where recovery was not to be had unless the claim could be fitted within one of the established forms of action; and it suited the status-oriented society of the Middle Ages, which was anything but conducive to the flowering of promise. Furthermore, there was no great pressure for enforceability as contracts were not a significant part of the business of the common law courts. * * *

The challenge that faced [the courts in developing a general basis for the enforcement of promises] was to work within the framework of the forms of action, first to develop exceptions as the Romans had done, and then to so fashion these exceptions as ultimately to achieve what the

Romans had never achieved—a general theory of contract. This challenge was met by the common law courts in the course of the fifteenth and sixteenth centuries. * * * The achievement was all the more remarkable in view of the fact that when this development began, the English law of contracts was little more advanced than that of many primitive societies. How was it brought about?

The common law courts found the answer in the law of torts. They had already recognized that liability in tort arose when a person undertook (*assumpsit*) to perform a duty and then performed it in such a way as to cause harm. Suit could be brought on the special variety of trespass on the case that came to be known as assumpsit. At the beginning of the fifteenth century it was available only where there had been misfeasance in performance of the undertaking. This example was given in 1436: "If a carpenter makes a covenant with me to make me a house good and strong and of a certain form, and he makes me a house which is weak and bad and of another form, I shall have an action of trespass on my case."[74] In such cases of misfeasance it was not hard to justify liability in tort. But might not the same remedy lie when there had merely been nonfeasance, a failure to perform the undertaking? At first the answer was no. In 1410 it was said: "Certainly it would lie [if the carpenter had built the house badly], because he would then answer for the wrong which he had done, but when a man makes a covenant and does nothing under that covenant, how can you have an action against him without a deed?"[75]

Nevertheless, by the second half of the fifteenth century there was a growing tendency among the common law judges to make the first major extension in the action of assumpsit by enforcing such promises even where there had been only nonfeasance. * * * But some limits had to be placed on what promises would be enforced, for the judges were not about to allow "that one shall have trespass for any breach of covenant in the world."[76] The courts were therefore forced to find a test to distinguish instances where nonfeasance was actionable from those where it was not. Since the misfeasance cases that had originally given rise to the action in assumpsit were characterized by a detriment incurred by the promisee in reliance on the promise, it was natural to formulate an analogous test and to allow enforcement where the promisee had changed his position on the faith of the promise, and had been consequently damaged by its nonperformance.

* * *

As the sixteenth century drew to a close, however, the common law courts, conscious of the expanding jurisdiction of Chancery and anxious to preserve their own powers, made a second major extension of the action of

74 Y.B. 14 Hy. VI, at 18. 3 W. Holdsworth [A History of English Law] 430 [(4th ed. 1936)].

75 Y.B. Mich. 11 Hy. IV, pl 60, 3 W. HOLDSWORTH, *supra* note [74], at 433–34.

76 Y.B. Hil. 3 Hy. VI, pl. 33, 3 W. HOLDSWORTH, *supra* note [74], at 435.

assumpsit. Thus it was held that a party who had given only a promise in exchange for the other's promise had, nonetheless, suffered a detriment by having his freedom of action fettered, since he was in turn bound by his own promise. * * *

On this ground the extension of the action of assumpsit to include the mere exchange of promises can be justified.

The action was to experience yet one more important extension. The procedure in actions of assumpsit, in which the plaintiff was entitled to a jury trial, was more favored by creditors than that in actions of debt, in which the defendant could resort to wager of law.* The next step in the common law's development of the law of contract was to permit assumpsit to supplant debt. By the middle of the sixteenth century, it had been recognized that an action in assumpsit could be brought against a defendant who, being already indebted (*indebitatus*), expressly undertook (*assumpsit*) to pay a particular sum. This action was called one in "*indebitatus assumpsit*", to distinguish it from the older "special assumpsit." Toward the end of the century, it began to be held that a debt alone, without a subsequent express promise, would support such an action. The final triumph of this view came at the beginning of the seventeenth century in Slade's case in which, on a jury finding that "there was no other promise or assumption, but only the said bargain,"[83] all the judges of England resolved "that every contract executor imports in itself an assumpsit."[84] The creditor was at last assured of the benefits of jury trial in place of wager of law and was freed of the technicalities of pleading in debt.

B. CLASSICAL ERA OF AMERICAN CONTRACT LAW

LAWRENCE M. FRIEDMAN, *CONTRACT LAW IN AMERICA*

17–18, 20–22 (1965)

Quite clearly, Anglo-American law now pays more attention to contract than medieval English law ever did. The rise of contract to legal prominence is fairly recent. Blackstone's classic exposition of the common law was written shortly before the American Revolution; in it, only a few

* The debt form of action permitted the defendant to invoke the archaic "wager of law" as the method of trial, instead of trial by jury. Under this system, the party accused of owing a debt could avoid liability by reciting a scripted oath, in effect swearing he did not owe such debt, and supporting his own oath with those of certain hired "oath sayers" who, for a price, would swear that the defendant's testimony was unperjured. The plaintiff was not permitted to cross-examine the oath sayers, meaning that if the defendant was prepared to lie under oath, he could in fact get away with it. Eds.

83 Slade's Case, 4 Co. Rep. 92 b, 76 Eng. Rep. 1074 (Q.B. 1602).

84 *Id.* at 1077.

short sections include contract, while the special doctrines of real-property law fill almost the whole of one of the four books of the *Commentaries* and color much of the rest. * * * The nineteenth century was very different. Even in the lawyer's narrow sense, the law of contract swelled into one of the main branches of legal learning. There were no important treatises on the law of contracts published until the nineteenth century; the appearance then of such works was a sure sign that the lawyers saw bread-and-butter importance to the field. When Christopher Columbus Langdell [Dean of the Harvard Law School] in the 1870s undertook to reform legal education and to establish the case method of instruction, he began the career of the law school case-book with a volume on contracts. In the mid-twentieth century the subject remains an immutable pillar of the first-year curriculum of every law school.

* * *

The law of contract is, therefore, roughly coextensive with the free market. Liberal nineteenth-century economics fits neatly with the law of contracts so viewed. It, too, had the abstracting habit [of removing from the realm of concern all particularities concerning persons and subject-matter]. In both theoretical models—that of the law of contracts and that of liberal economics—parties could be treated as individual economic units which, in theory, enjoyed complete mobility and freedom of decision. * * * The correspondence between law and economic theory was never exact. Contract law was not a book written by Adam Smith. Nobody purposely sat down to turn contract law into an applied branch of liberal economics. But a free market developed, and grew; the law of contract was the legal reflection of that market and naturally took on its characteristics. Contract was abstract; the free market was abstract; and the two institutions directed behavior along similar channels.

C. DEMISE OF CLASSICAL PRINCIPLES OF CONTRACT LAW

"Classical contract law," of which Professor Friedman speaks, flourished more or less from 1850 through 1940, holding at its core the first principle of *freedom of contract* and the corollary of that principle, *pacta sund servanda* (promises are to be kept). But what do we mean by "freedom of contract"? The phrase encompasses the notion that private bargains, freely and voluntarily entered into, should be enforced without reservation and certainly blind to the identities of the parties or the relative equities of their positions under the contract. This judicial "hands-off" approach reflected the bias, consistent with the pervading economic theory of the day, that the good of the economy, and ergo society as a whole, would best be served by allowing tough, rugged individualists to bargain it out in the marketplace free from interference or regulation by the state except in extreme cases of fraud, duress, or illegality.

Under the classical principles of contract law, it was not perceived as the role of the courts to review, rewrite, or evaluate the underlying fairness of the deal; the role of the courts was simply to ensure that a bargain had been struck and, if so, to enforce it; nothing less and certainly nothing more. This ensured the stability, predictability, and certainty on which business relied and efficient commercial relations depended. Of course, these principles only existed in idealized form; the reality of contract law and enforcement was always a more complex and nuanced phenomenon. Nevertheless, as you will see, the principles that govern contractual relations today bear only the faintest resemblance to the principles that exemplified classical contract law just over one hundred years ago.

In the main, the second half of the twentieth century witnessed a number of changes in contracts doctrine, but none more important than the removal by both legislative and judicial intervention of various issues that had previously been left to the realm of private bargain of the parties. In effect, as to these matters, freedom of contract has been, if not eliminated, at least curtailed. Professor Grant Gilmore, in his famous work titled THE DEATH OF CONTRACT 95–96 (1974), neatly summed up the reasons for this evolution in contract law theory and doctrine as follows:

> As we look back on the nineteenth century theories, we are struck most of all, I think, by the narrow scope of social duty which they implicitly assumed. No man is his brother's keeper; the race is to the swift; let the devil take the hindmost. For good or ill we have changed all that. We are now all cogs in a machine, each dependent on the other. The decline and fall of the general theory of contract and, in most quarters, of laissez-faire economics may be taken as remote reflections of the transition from nineteenth century individualism to the welfare state and beyond.

There are any number of social, cultural, and economic factors and attitudes that can be identified as contributing to the demise of classical contract law and the erosion of unbridled freedom of contract. Among the most significant, however, has been the increasing complexity and interdependency of our economic system. The growth of large, powerful corporations and other commercial enterprises, coupled with the perfection of the "standard printed form," has meant that the relative equality in bargaining strength and position that was the unstated assumption on which the principle of freedom of contract was predicated no longer reflects the reality of many exchange transactions in contemporary society. This has led courts to take a much more activist role in monitoring the fairness of contractual relationships, particularly where there is a significant disparity in bargaining power between the parties. The hard and fast rules of contract doctrine that tended to confine the discretion of the court in earlier times has in general given way to more open-ended and flexible standards that leave significant room for courts to do particularized justice in individual cases.*

A drawback, arguably, of this trend in the law has been some loss in the certainty, predictability, and stability of contractual relationships. Unlike the era when the policy of freedom of contract reigned supreme, parties can no longer be sure that their bargains, freely and voluntarily entered into, will be enforced. Business and commerce rely on clear rules, as much if not more than they do on the content of those rules. Consider the court's statement in *Shreve v. Cheesman,* 69 F. 785, 791 (8th Cir. 1895): "It is universally conceded that it is often more important that rules [affecting property rights] should be certain and changeless than that they should be right. Men engaged in active business buy and sell in reliance on them." Do you agree with this statement? How much certainty should be sacrificed in the interests of justice? Need one always come at the expense of the other?

Regulation of bargain relationships, and the waning deference to private autonomy, goes far beyond post hoc judicial review of the fairness of existing contracts. Congress and the state legislatures have also gotten into the act, wholly removing certain types of contracts from the realm of general principles of contract law. As we noted earlier, today, labor contracts, insurance contracts, consumer credit agreements, and others are the subject of comprehensive statutory enactments that regulate in detail the form and terms of the contract, as well the permissible scope of what the parties may or may not bargain over by private agreement.

Other statutes create rights in one party to the agreement that the party did not himself bargain for. For example, recognizing that people caught unaware in their homes by a slick, experienced salesman might end up agreeing to buy something (encyclopedias or a vacuum cleaner) that they really didn't want, the Federal Trade Commission, acting under authority of a federal law, adopted a regulation (an administrative rule) giving consumers in door-to-door sales transactions a three-day "cooling off period" during which they retain the right to cancel the deal even though they signed a "binding contract." 16 C.F.R. § 429 (effective June 7, 1974). In still other cases, a statute may limit the permissible scope of negotiations. For instance, today, parties are free to negotiate over and reach agreement on the rate of interest that one party will have to pay the other in a loan transaction, but only to a point because their agreement is subject to applicable state (or federal) law governing usury. Therefore, even though knowingly and voluntarily agreed to, a promise to pay a usurious rate of interest will simply not be enforced. Likewise, some states restric

* *See generally* P.S. ATIYAH, THE RISE AND FALL OF FREEDOM OF CONTRACT (1979).

the ability of employers to negotiate for and include non-competition covenants in an employment contract upon the employee's termination from service. Unlike many of the rules of contract law which can be "contracted around" if the parties so choose,* these legislative prescriptions cannot be altered by the parties. This is because they represent a form of external regulation of the exchange relationship, typically imposed because of social judgments about either the need to protect parties to contract relationships or the need to protect society as a whole from certain types of conduct.

Despite these legislative incursions into the law of private bargain in certain transactions, our focus in this book remains largely on the general body of principles comprising "contract law" that have been developed over several hundred years by courts employing the common law style of reasoning and analysis. We believe this is appropriate because, even with respect to statutory law, the courts still play a pivotal role in the development of the law. Unlike the application of legislative codes in civil law jurisdictions, where judicial decisions tend to have little impact or effect except upon the litigants to the particular case under decision, in a common law system when a court decides a specific case by interpreting and applying a governing statutory provision, it may also be placing its own *gloss* on that rule. Often, that gloss becomes part of the law and, thus, may affect the interests of litigants in future cases.

D. SOURCES OF MODERN CONTRACT LAW

For most of our history, the basic rules and principles of contract law derived and evolved from a wide variety of cases decided by the English courts with some but relatively few statutory modifications. This is what's known as "common law." Common law is the legal system that evolved out of the Anglo-American tradition. It is found in most English speaking countries. The common law system is to be contrasted with the *civil law* tradition, the legal system, which prevails in European, South American, and most Asian countries. The civil law, which is a Code-based system, can also be found in Louisiana because of the state's Spanish and French heritage.

Of course, the common law courts did not act wholly without structure. They were, in the first instance, guided by the principle of *precedent* and influenced to a considerable degree by other bodies of law such as Roman law, Canon Law and, particularly, The Law Merchant, which was a

* Because it is impossible for the parties to address every aspect of their relationship in detail, an important function of contract law is to supply the rule that will apply in the absence of specific agreement of the parties. These rules are sometimes called "default" rules to contrast them from other kinds of rules which are mandatory or "immutable."

separate system of rules that developed (reaching its heyday during the sixteenth century) in England to govern commercial transactions, largely administered by local mercantile authorities. The law of contracts that was imported into the American legal system was essentially this common law of contracts as it existed at the end of the eighteenth century.

As noted in the section immediately above, beginning early in the twentieth century, a trend developed, which continues to the present day, to *codify* our laws, including the law of contracts. The first major codification effort was the Uniform Sales Act, patterned on its English predecessor of 1893, which was approved by the National Conference of Commissioners on Uniform State Laws (the NCCUSL) in 1906. Professor Samuel Williston, also the author of a major treatise on contract law, was the principal draftsperson of the Uniform Sales Act, which was eventually adopted by over thirty states.

The Uniform Sales Act was eventually replaced by the Uniform Commercial Code (the U.C.C.), a much more comprehensive statute governing a wide range of commercial transactions. Contracts involving the sale of goods are the subject of Article 2 of the U.C.C. The U.C.C., the first official text of which was approved in 1952, was the product of a joint effort by the NCCUSL and the American Law Institute (the ALI). The U.C.C. has enjoyed near-universal acceptance in the states (Louisiana, the only civil law jurisdiction in the U.S., has now adopted most of the U.C.C., although not Article 2).

Since its inception, the U.C.C. has been the subject of continuing revision and modernization. In 1987, for example, a whole new Article dealing with personal property leases, Article 2A, was approved and has received widespread adoption. In 2003, a completely new Article 2 was proposed, but it was not adopted by any state

The Code's Permanent Editorial Board, established by the joint sponsors of the U.C.C. in 1961 to promote uniform state enactment and interpretation of the Code, is responsible for evaluating the operation of the Code in the various states and determining when revisions to the various Articles may be appropriate. With each such revision, a new official text of the uniform version of the Code is promulgated. The most current official text, and the one we refer to when citing to Code provisions (except for Article 2) in this book, is the 2008 Official Text.

The primary architect of the U.C.C., and the principal draftsperson of Article 2, was Karl Llewellyn. The statute very much reflects his normative view of law, and those of a generation of legal scholars roughly classified together as *Legal Realists*. The realists were decidedly pragmatic. They rejected the idea of law as a "science." Instead they believed that the law was a tool to serve societal and economic interests and, therefore, legal rules should be crafted to conform to people's expectations of how the law *ought* to work. The realist attitude about the role of the commercial law is evident in section 1–103(a) of Article 1 of the Code, which broadly sets forth the purposes of the U.C.C. as intending "to simplify, clarify, and modernize the law governing commercial transactions; to permit the continued expansion of commercial practices through custom, usage and agreement of the parties; and to make uniform the law among the various jurisdictions."

The U.C.C. has been very influential even in transactions that do not fall within its broad scope. Article 2 supplies the governing law only if the subject matter of the contract involves a transaction in goods. Nevertheless, Article 2 has had a profound effect upon the development of contract law in non-sale of goods cases, such as contracts involving real estate or services of one kind or another. This is because courts will frequently look to the provisions of Article 2, and even apply those provisions by analogy, in deciding non-sale of goods cases.

The second major development in contract law in the last century has been the *Restatements of Contracts*, developed under the aegis of, and published by, the American Law Institute. The American Law Institute was founded in 1923 "to promote clarification and simplification of the law and its better adaptation to social needs, to secure the better administration of justice, and to carry on scholarly and scientific legal work." Its membership is composed of distinguished judges, lawyers, and law teachers.* Work on the first *Restatement of Contracts* began in 1923, and the final version was approved in 1932. Professor Williston was the Reporter for the project. Among his advisors was Professor Arthur Corbin, the author of another major treatise on contract law. Professors Williston and Corbin's views about, and approach to, contract law are frequently contrasted. Williston was much inclined to see the law as fixed and immutable. Sometimes described as a *positivist* view of law, Williston tended to regard law as a closed system of rules that could be consistently applied to resolve any fact situation. Professor Corbin's approach to contract law was much less mechanical and formalistic. A principal figure in the legal realist movement, Corbin was willing to accept a much greater degree of indeterminacy in the law than Williston in order to assure a just or fair result. Corbin felt that the hard and fast rules of contract law needed to be applied much more flexibly, tempered by the prevailing norms, mores, and attitudes of the social and economic milieu in which the rules operated. Thus, Corbin was open to incorporating into the law broad, open-ended considerations of ethics and justice.

At this writing *Restatement of Consumer Contracts* has been drafted by the American Law Institute, but has not yet been approved. This proposed Restatement focuses on aspects of the law unique to consumer

* As all three of your authors are members of the ALI, it also includes some less than distinguished law teachers.

contracts and on regulatory techniques that are prominently applied in consumer-protection law.

The enormous pace of new developments in contract law in the quarter century following adoption of the first *Restatement* led to the decision in the early 1960s to begin work on the *Restatement (Second) of Contracts*, with Professor Robert Braucher serving as Reporter. Professor Alan Farnsworth replaced Professor Braucher in 1971, after Braucher was appointed to the Supreme Judicial Court of Massachusetts. Work on the *Restatement (Second)* was finally completed in 1981. Heavily influenced by Corbin's perspective on the law, as well as by the U.C.C., the *Restatement (Second)* took a decidedly conscious turn from its predecessor, placing a much greater emphasis on protecting parties' detrimental *reliance* on promises and forsaking bright-line rules for more flexible, open-ended standards.

It is important to realize that the *Restatements*, unlike the U.C.C., do not have the force of law. No state legislature has enacted a *Restatement*. Instead, they reflect a systemic distillation of the prevailing rules and principles of the common law of contracts, albeit sometimes with a deliberative normative twist, into a single code-like document. Thus, while very influential in judicial decision making because of the prestige of the American Law Institute and the individuals selected to work on these projects, a court is not bound to apply the *Restatement* if it believes the applicable rule is wrong or, more likely, not in accord with the common law in that jurisdiction.

While contract law is predominantly state law, there are federal laws relating to specific matters of federal concern, such as interstate commerce or the procurement of goods and services by federal governmental units and agencies. Moreover, the trend toward codification of the law of contracts has not been limited to domestic law. In 1980, the United Nations Commission on International Trade submitted a draft of the *Convention on Contracts for the International Sale of Goods* (*CISG*), which governs in the case of contracts between citizens of ratifying nations. The United States formally ratified *CISG* in 1986, and it came into force on January 1, 1988 after being ratified by 11 countries.* Finally, in 1994, the International Institute for the Unification of Private Law (UNIDROIT) announced its *Principles of International Commercial Contracts*, reflecting rules derived from both civil and common law legal systems that might desirably apply to international contracts. Not a formal treaty, which would require adoption by member-nations, the *UNIDROIT Principles* are more like a *Restatement*, although they may be made applicable to a transaction by agreement of the parties. They can also be referred to by an international

* Today, more than 70 nations have ratified the CISG.

tribunal as an authoritative source of rules for resolving a dispute between parties from different countries.

E. LAW AND EQUITY: ORIGINS AND CURRENT IMPORT IN CONTRACT

In medieval England, a litigant unhappy with the decision of the law courts (courts of common plea), could always appeal to the King as the ultimate "fount of justice." Resolution of such petitions was delegated by the sovereign to the Chancellor—typically a clergyman and not a lawyer—and by the 15th century a separate Court of Chancery had developed as a rival to the common law courts. Dispensing "equitable jurisdiction," for a time these courts were neither bound by precedent nor any fixed body of rules or principles. Each court system had its own set of substantive and procedural rules

The story of the conflict between the common law and the Chancery courts is part and parcel of the larger story of the long struggle for hegemony between Parliament and the Crown in the 18th and 19th centuries. Eventually, law and equity in England were fused in a single court system by the Judicature Acts of the 1870's, although equity continued to exist as a separate branch of law.

As noted earlier, our law of Contracts derives from these English law origins as part of the "reception" of English common law as it existed at the time of the founding of the Republic into the states of the United States. Thus, many U.S. states also had both courts of law and courts of equity for a time. Gradually, most states merged the powers of law and equity into a single court system. Likewise, the federal courts possess both legal and equitable powers, such that all claims may now be brought in a single "civil action."

Despite the combination of law and equity for purposes of the administration of justice, the distinction between the two systems of rules continues to be a matter of some consequence in contract law. This is principally evident in the set of remedies that each offers. The traditional common law remedy for breach of contract is money damages, which represents a charge against the defendant's property. Equitable remedies, on the other hand, are enforced through injunctive relief, such as "specific performance, representing an order to the person to do or not do something under threat of the contempt sanction. Equitable remedies trace their lineage to the formerly separate "equity" component of our legal tradition. As a general rule, today, a party is not entitled to equitable relief unless her remedies at law—money damages—are "inadequate," which is to say cannot make her whole.

It should also be noted, as we will in Chapter 7, that when a court exercises its equitable jurisdiction, it has much greater flexibility to take into account considerations of "fairness" and "morality," than is true when the court is simply applying legal rules. Finally, the right to trial by jury is not available when the relief sought by the litigant is equitable in nature. Rather, the judge, as "successor to the chancellor," will serve as the trier of fact and decide in his or her discretion whether to grant relief and to what extent.

Although the much of the distinction between law and equity may be seen as a historical anachronism, some will argue that it still serves an important in function by moderating the harshness that can at times result from the strict application of legal rules. By contrast, those that tend to view the law through the prism of economic efficiency will typically argue that the exercise of judicial discretion is more likely than not to introduce uncertainty costs that would not exist if focus was limited to the expressed intention of the parties. What do you think? More importantly, what will you think when the course is over? Do let us know.

---

5. WHAT IS THE LAWYER'S ROLE IN CONTRACT LAW?

Two parties considering entering into a contractual relationship are initially under no obligation to, and have no rights against, one another. Instead, unlike in most areas of law, they have the opportunity, subject only to relatively minimal restriction, to define by agreement what their rights and obligations will be. That is to say, the essence of contractual liability is that it is a consensual form of liability. This notion is reflected in that still core contract law principle of *freedom of contract*. Freedom of contract means that the parties are free to establish their corresponding rights and duties by private bargain. By the same token, the principle of freedom of contract implies its corollary, namely, the principle of freedom *from* contract, which means that neither party is obligated to conclude a deal with the other. Thus, either party may elect to break off negotiations at any point prior to the formation of a binding contract. How does the lawyer fit into this dynamic?

The permutations are innumerable. In the case of large, sophisticated business parties, the lawyer's role tends to be more purely legal; giving advice relating to legal issues and considerations, and drafting the definitive documentation of the transaction. With smaller business clients and individuals, the lawyer will perform these functions as well, but in addition often will also be consulted on the business points of the deal. In both instances, the role of the lawyer is predominantly a *planner* and not an *adversary*. Moreover, while the lawyer is always looking out first and foremost for the interests of her client in the transaction, in many contractual settings there is a substantial identity of interests between the parties and a common or shared desire to achieve a mutually satisfactory accommodation of those interests. This is particularly so in situations where the parties anticipate a long-term mutually advantageous relationship, such as, for example, a partnership arrangement. In some of these cases, with the consent of the parties, the lawyer may actually represent both parties. This will, however, preclude the lawyer's representation of either party individually should there be a falling out in the future because such representation would constitute a conflict of interest and a violation of the lawyer's ethical obligations. However, even when the parties approach one another at arms-length and have their own separate counsel, the lawyers' objectives are often to reach reasonable accommodation on the key points of negotiation rather than solely to maximize their respective client's interests at the expense of the other party. In short, the role is much more collaborative in nature than is ordinarily true of the lawyer's role in representing a party once a dispute has broken out under a contract.

It is also important to recognize that lawyers encounter contracts in virtually all aspects of practice. "Contracts" does not itself represent a discrete area of legal practice in the same way, for example, we might speak of a criminal or a personal injury law practice. Rather, contract law and contractual relationships transcend many different areas of practice, but, in particular, form the foundation of the commercial law. Whether the transaction being handled by the lawyer at any particular moment involves a real estate conveyance, a corporate combination, a financing arrangement, or an employment or agency relation, more often than not the key to the deal is an acceptable contractual arrangement. Thus, the "hired gun" image typically associated with the lawyer in the traditional litigation model is simply inaccurate (if not inappropriate) in the contract negotiation and formation stage of the deal.

Perhaps the most critical lawyer responsibility at this stage is the responsibility for *drafting* the actual written terms of the transaction. Even when contracts are "custom drafted," the lawyer will inevitably begin by retrieving an agreement from a prior deal to use a form. This is because most contracts will contain what has come to be referred to as *boilerplate.* The term boilerplate is used to refer to contractual provisions and language that are routinely included as part of any agreement. There is nothing wrong with boilerplate if it fits, but the draftsperson who includes boilerplate from a form without consciously considering its applicability and appropriateness in the current transaction runs the risk of doing her client a grave disservice.

On other occasions, the lawyer will be faced with a contract where there is no opportunity to participate in the drafting of the proposed agreement. This is because the client will have been presented with a "take it or leave it" deal. In the area of consumer transactions, for example, since World War II businesses have increasingly come to rely upon the standard printed form, representing the only basis on which the merchant will do business with a prospective customer. If you'd like to test this assertion, go down to a new car dealership. Decide on the make and model you'd like and negotiate a price. Then tell the salesperson that you'll draft the contract up that evening and be back in the morning. Now, watch his or her reaction. But what's wrong with you drafting the contract rather than using the dealership's form? In truth, nothing's "wrong" with it, it just "ain't gonna happen."

If you're forced to do business on the dealer's form, how valid is the principle of freedom of contract in these circumstances? Should the courts take a different attitude toward enforcement in consumer cases? As a practical matter, how many of these kinds of contracts do you suppose are actually reviewed by lawyers before they're signed? We haven't actually counted, but we think bloody few.

Even in the non-consumer or commercial setting, oftentimes the parties will not approach one another from a position of equal bargaining strength. In these situations, the party in the superior position may insist the deal be done on its terms or not at all. For instance, how much opportunity do you suppose that the average worker has to negotiate the terms of his or her employment arrangements? In these cases, a lawyer counseling a client plays a somewhat different role. Because there will be very little opportunity to control the terms of the contract, the lawyer's job is to help the client understand the risk so that the client can intelligently decide whether to take the job or look for one that offers greater security.

All of the cases in this book consist of deals that went bad. That's why there was a lawsuit. We think it might be useful for you to ask yourself from time-to-time what you, as the lawyer for one of the parties to the deal might have done differently to have, if not avoided the problem, at least better protected your client's interest. Just in case you forget to ask yourself that question, sometimes, we will do so, in a "You Be the Lawyer!" section following many of the cases. Remember, freedom of contract means not only considerable freedom for the party to the contract to affect the terms and conditions of the deal, but considerable freedom for the party's lawyer to help structure the transaction in a manner that best serves the client's interest.

6. WHAT IS A FIRST YEAR COURSE IN CONTRACTS?

Contracts will not only be your favorite first year subject, it will also be your easiest. Part of what makes contracts the easiest first year course is that you have already done contracts—apartment leases, automobile purchases, employment agreements, etc. And, part of what makes contracts the easiest first year course is that it only covers eight somewhat related, overlapping* questions:

1. Is there a deal?
2. Was there the necessary consideration or consideration substitute?
3. Is there some reason based on the agreement process or the terms of the agreement not to enforce the agreement?
4. What are the terms of the deal?
5. When is someone who made an enforceable deal excused from doing what she agreed to do because of some post-agreement occurrence or non-occurrence?
6. How does the law enforce a deal?
7. What are the alternatives to contracts and contract law?
8. When can someone assert legal rights because of a deal made by others?

Indeed, contract law is so easy that, when you get out of law school, you will re-learn (learn?) everything that you need to know about contracts for the bar exam in six to nine hours of lecture in a bar review course (which will probably be taught by Epstein, who has been teaching bar review since the Civil War).

Why then do law schools spend four to nine months on contracts instead of just six to nine hours? The six to nine hours of bar review coverage of contract law helps prepare you for two days of fairly predictable contract law questions from bar examiners. The four to nine months of law school coverage of contracts helps prepare you for a career of unpredictable contracts questions and assignments from clients, judges, and other lawyers in your law firm—a career of writing contracts so as to minimize if not eliminate later problems, and a career of resolving those problems that contract drafting did not eliminate.

As a part of that preparation, your teacher will regularly ask unpredictable questions—questions different from the questions in the

* In the world of practicing law, most of your work assignments will involve more than one of these eight questions. In the world of learning law, we will, to the extent possible, consider these questions in this order, one question at a time.

book, and different from the questions that you anticipated. And, you will find that most of your professors' questions in law school (like most of the questions from clients, judges, and other lawyers in the "real world") do not have simple answers—or even answers at all.

In dealing with these questions, you will discover the importance of:

1. *Knowing vocabulary*

   Contract law has its own vocabulary. This vocabulary includes familiar words with new meanings. For example, a "contract" is more than just an agreement; an "offer" is similar but not identical to a proposal; "acceptance" is a special form of response to an offer; and "consideration" has a meaning that is even more "special." And it is a vocabulary with lots of new terms and phrases, such as "rescission," "impracticability," "executory contract," "parol evidence," and "promissory estoppel."

2. *Understanding cases and the "case method"*

   Most contract law in law school comes from the written opinions of judges in decided cases. This is commonly called "common law."

   American courts, with the partial exception of state courts in Louisiana, follow the English common law tradition. Louisiana and most of the rest of the world operate under a civil law system. In a civil law system, the legislature makes the laws and courts basically interpret and apply these legislative enactments. Legislatures in a common law system also enact laws, like U.C.C. Article 2, which are interpreted and applied by courts.

   The essential difference between a common law system and a civil law system is that in a common law system courts also make law. A common law court's decision not only resolves the specific dispute between the parties but also becomes a part of the law in that court that is to be applied when similar disputes arise in the future.

   In other, new, words, a common law system is based on "*stare decisis*," *i.e.*, judicial adherence to past decisions that are "precedents." A law dictionary defines "precedent" as "a decided case that furnishes a basis for determining an identical or similar case that might arise later, or a similar question of law."*

* BRYAN A. GARNER, A DICTIONARY OF MODERN LEGAL USAGE 680 (2d ed. 1995).

A big part of the practice of law is reading judicial opinions to determine which cases are "precedent" that will affect how the court will decide "your" case. And so, learning to read cases is a big part of law school. This is sometimes referred to as the "case method," and we largely follow that approach in this book.

The case method is not, however, without its limitations. To begin with, lawyers don't decide cases, judges do. Therefore, by just reading appellate opinions you do not learn a great deal about the lawyering process. Furthermore, the appellate decision is just the tip of the iceberg in what was a real dispute between real parties that eventually ended up in litigation, *i.e.*, having to be resolved by a judge or jury. However, the reality is that in the vast majority of settings in which lawyers act, they serve as problem-solvers, not progenitors. The true measure of a good lawyer is the ability to plan in advance and in a manner that avoids or at least minimizes the likelihood of problems arising in the future. Therefore, throughout this book we also consider the role of the lawyer and ask you not only how you might have handled the case, but also what you might have done differently to avoid the problem in the first place.

The other major problem with the case method is that it tends to inculcate in students new to the area the false impression that most rules of contract law are ambiguous and that most contract disputes are resolved by trial. In fact, the vast majority of contractual obligations are simply performed without incident. This is in part because many of the rules of contract law and liability are in fact clear and unambiguous. Moreover, when disputes do occur, the vast majority of those are settled amicably by the parties either without the necessity for litigation or prior to trial if suit is actually filed. Finally, as we discuss at the end of this chapter, contract disputes are increasingly resolved by private arbitration, mediation, and other forms of alternative dispute resolution. While the pivotal role that a lawyer plays in the formal adjudicatory process is well-known and understood, the advice and assistance of counsel is often equally critical in the negotiation of private settlements or resolution through informal dispute resolution mechanisms.

3. *Distinguishing the role of trial courts and appellate courts*

This book is filled with cases, mostly appellate decisions. A lawsuit begins in a trial court. The trial court hears testimony from the witnesses and arguments from the attorneys as to what the relevant facts are, what the relevant law is, and how the law should be applied to the facts. The trial court then makes a decision.

After the trial court has made its decision as to who "wins" and who "loses," the losing party makes a decision as to whether to incur the additional costs of an appeal. In making that decision, the losing party's attorney knows that an appellate court will reverse the trial court's decision if, through her briefs and oral argument, she can convince a majority of the judges on the appellate court that the trial court got the law "wrong." That is to say, an appellate court does *de novo* review of questions of law.

Appellate review of a factual basis for the trial court's decision is much more limited. Since an appellate court does not hear new testimony or consider new evidence, it will generally defer to the factual findings made by the trial court. The trial court's resolution of factual disputes will be reversed on appeal only if "clearly erroneous." Accordingly, most appeals and most appellate court opinions focus on questions of law.

Think about what this means about the cases that you will be studying in law school. The cases in this book and your other casebooks involve questions of law sufficiently close and unclear that someone was willing to incur the costs of litigating the questions in a trial court and then again on appeal.

Virtually all of the cases in the book have been edited by us, your authors. That is to say, we have omitted certain portions of the courts' discussion from the actual decisions that we considered extraneous or simply not relevant for our purposes. Indeed, sometimes we edited a case simply to make it more readable for you. In any event, whenever you see three asterisks ("* * *"), that is our signal to you that we have deleted some material from the opinion as actually reported.

4. *Recognizing what you are supposed to learn in this class*

Here is what Professor Clark Byse, the inspiration for Professor Kingsfield in the movie *The Paper Chase*, told his contracts students at Harvard (and later Boston University) in their very first class meeting:

> On the first day of the class on Contracts, there is a temptation to lecture because, as Adlai Stevenson said

> when he was the speaker at a college commencement, "This is a wonderful opportunity, for there is so much that I, a man in his fifties, have learned in my lifetime that would be of great value to you in your early twenties." At this point, Mr. Stevenson paused, shook his head slightly, and said in a mournful tone, "But it would do no good for me to tell you those things, for what is important and lasting in life must be learned—by action, by participation, rather than by passive absorption." So never forget that the emphasis in this class is on what and how you think, not on what some judge or treatise writer or your instructor thinks. My function is to assist you to develop your lawyerly skills and understanding of the institution of Contract and of the legal process and the role of law in our society. Developing those skills and understanding can and will be an exciting experience for some. For others, the experience at times may be frustrating, even unpleasant. Some will enjoy being called on and speaking in class. For others, speaking in front of 100 hearers may be embarrassing, even painful—something to be avoided at all costs. To those who dread being called on, I say, Relax. We are all in this together, to learn, to improve ourselves. Of course, mistakes will be made. This is why there are erasers on pencils. There is nothing wrong about making a mistake. What would be wrong is not learning from one's mistakes.

Clark Byse, *Introductory Comments to the First-Year Class in Contracts,* 78 B.U. L. REV. 59 (1998).

5. *Considering competing policies*

While our common law system is based on judicial adherence to precedent, courts can and do avoid following earlier cases. Often, courts "distinguish" earlier decisions, meaning they conclude that the earlier case was sufficiently dissimilar to the present case that its precedent is not controlling. Less often, a court decides in a later case that the rule it established in an earlier decision should no longer be followed.

In such instances, courts turn to "policy." For example, contract law should be fair. **Equitable.** Contract law should apply even-handedly to all members of society. **Consistent.** Contract law should be certain so that businesses and individuals can act accordingly. **Predictable.** Contract law should reflect our free market economy. **Freedom of contract.**

While most of us would have trouble challenging any of these policies in the abstract, all of us will have trouble this year in reconciling these policies in particular situations. That was true in our very first case, *R.R. v. M.H.*, where "freedom of contract" took it on the chin.

Now, you think you have finally gotten all of this "introductory stuff" out of the way, and you almost have, but before we move on to Chapter 2 and all of the great cases to come, we want to say one more word about the lawyer's role in contract law, which entails how parties sometimes attempt to avoid the formal litigation process entirely.

---

7. THE LAWYER'S ROLE IN CONTRACT LAW REVISITED—ARBITRATION

The remainder of this book is filled with cases that arose when one party sued another in court. This is where much of our law of contracts has traditionally been, and will continue to be, made—in decided and published judicial decisions. However, it is important to realize that most actual contract disputes are disposed of by other means. It has always been the case that, in many instances, the parties will "settle" their dispute by some form of negotiated agreement reached either before a lawsuit is filed, or after filing but before a final judgment is rendered by a court. Recent decades, however, have also witnessed the rise of so-called "alternative dispute resolution" (ADR) mechanisms whereby the parties will agree to have their disputes resolved by submittal to a private legal regime instead of instituting a lawsuit in court.

A. ARBITRATION IN CONSUMER CONTRACTS

Arbitration provisions are frequently utilized by businesses in standard printed form consumer contracts to deprive the computer purchaser, cell phone user, bank or brokerage customer, etc. of effective recourse to a court of law in the event the consumer is aggrieved in some fashion by the vendor's conduct. This has resulted in considerable criticism over the use of so-called "mandatory arbitration clauses."*

While arbitration *provisions* are frequently utilized, arbitration itself is not. According to Professor Rory Van Loo, "arbitrators rarely handle

---

* *See, e.g., Davis v. Chase Bank USA, NA,* 299 Fed.Appx. 662, 2008 WL 4832998 (9th Cir. 2008) (refusing to enforce an arbitration provision in a consumer contract of adhesion in a setting in which the party with superior bargaining power has carried out a scheme to deliberately cheat large numbers of customers out of individually small sums of money).

consumer disputes. By way of illustration, the American Arbitration Association—the leading non-profit provider of arbitration—adjudicates fewer than 1,500 consumer cases annually. In contrast, the online marketplace e-Bay alone internally handles 60 million disputes each year between buyers and sellers. Comcast's customer service department has over a million customer touch points each day. The main institutional actor in the private consumer legal system is not the arbitration tribunal, but the consumer-facing corporation."*

Mandatory arbitration provisions in consumer contracts arguably dissuade victims from pursuing claims due to cost and accessibility. Significantly, mandatory arbitration in consumer contracts can also eliminate the use of class action lawsuits as a mechanism for vindicating consumers' rights. When arbitration is a required mechanism from the start, rather than a voluntary way to settle disputes with consumers and workers, it can give companies a free pass for low quality and abusive practices. When the risk of being held accountable is low, there is less incentive for companies to do the right thing. In addition, because arbitrators are likely to want to do business with a company in the future, they have a built-in reason to side with the company over the consumer.

Because of the special problems of arbitration in consumer agreements, we return to the topic in the chapter of the book—Chapter 4—dealing with contract defenses, and specifically unconscionability

---

B. ARBITRATION IN COMMERCIAL CONTRACTS

Increasingly, parties to complex commercial deals, who enjoy significant mutual bargaining power, will agree voluntarily in their contract to submit any disputes to private adjudication through arbitration in lieu of suit in a public court. Unlike other forms of ADR, such as conciliation and mediation, arbitration is typically "binding." This means that the parties have agreed to live with the private arbitrator's decision and forego virtually any opportunity for judicial review of the arbitrator's decision.

Why are sophisticated commercial parties so eager to eschew conventional civil litigation in favor of private arbitration? Most commonly, large companies express the conviction that arbitration represents a more cost effective and expeditious way for resolving their disputes. Reasons for this include more limited discovery than in typical judicial proceedings and avoidance of crowded dockets. Other characteristics of arbitration—frequently cited by proponents as to why that form of conflict resolution

* Rory Van Loo, The Corporation as Courthouse, 33 YALE JOURNAL ON REGULATION 547 (2016).

produces more predictable and satisfactory results—include having the matter: (1) resolved by expert decision makers rather than a judge who may have no background in the subject matter of the dispute; (2) decided in a proceeding that is basically confidential rather than available as a matter of public record; and (3) determined solely on the substantive merits of the dispute without concern about the precedential effect of the decision on future litigants.

Arbitration clauses are particularly common in international transactions, and the use of arbitration in these contracts is facilitated by a number of international conventions, such as the Convention on the Recognition and Enforcement of Foreign Arbitral Awards (the "New York Convention"). Rather than face dispute resolution in a foreign tribunal with unknown procedures and of uncertain reliability, parties to these deals often prefer the ability to select a neutral forum in a prescribed location for arbitration conducted in accordance with established and understood rules and procedures.

On the other hand, arbitration is not without its critics. Some contend that, as it has grown more formalized, arbitration has become nearly as inflexible, costly, and time-consuming as going to court. There is also concern over the availability of good commercial arbitrators, the accountability of private arbitrators, and the perceived tendency of many arbitrators to avoid "all or nothing" judgments in favor of "cutting the baby in half" or "compromise" decisions. It has also been pointed out that the limits on discovery posited as an advantage of arbitration can also deprive parties of the opportunity to investigate and establish valid claims.

In the United States, federal and state arbitration statutes establish broad policies favoring enforcement of written agreements to arbitrate. The Uniform Arbitration Act, originally approved in 1955, was eventually adopted by 49 states. That Act was revised in 2000 by its sponsoring agency, the National Conference of Commissioners on Uniform State Laws and the Revised Uniform Arbitration Act has already been adopted by 19 states and approval is pending in another two states. Section 6 of the Revised UAA provides:

> An agreement contained in a record to submit to arbitration any existing or subsequent controversy arising between the parties to the agreement is valid, enforceable, and irrevocable except upon a ground that exists at law or in equity for the revocation of a contract.

The Federal Arbitration Act ("FAA"), 9 U.S.C. §§ 1–15 was enacted by Congress in 1925. It governs arbitration agreements in maritime transactions and contracts involving interstate commerce. Section 2 of the FAA holds that such agreements "shall be valid, irrevocable, and enforceable, save upon such grounds as exist at law or in equity for the revocation of any contract." The FAA further provides that "[a] party aggravated by the alleged failure, neglect, or refusal of another to arbitrate under a written agreement for arbitration may petition any United States district court * * * for an order directing that such arbitration proceed in the manner provided for in such agreement." *Id.* § 4. The court should then "stay the trial of the action until such arbitration has been had in accordance with the terms of the agreement." *Id.* § 3.

When determining whether to compel a party to arbitrate a dispute under the FAA, a district court may not review the merits of the dispute, but instead must limit its inquiry to: 1) whether a valid agreement to arbitrate exists, and, if it does, 2) whether the agreement encompasses the dispute at issue. Moreover, like the Revised UAA, the FAA broadly endorses the enforceability of agreements to arbitrate future as well as existing disputes. Finally, the FAA has been interpreted to preempt state laws that would limit the enforcement of an arbitration provision in a contract subject to the FAA.

The concomitant to the broad enforceability of private arbitration agreements is strict statutory limitations on judicial review of arbitration awards. By and large, an arbitration award will only be overturned if it can be shown that there was some fundamental unfairness in the process. In other words, a review on the merits for errors of fact or law is rare. This deference to the arbitrator's award is seen as necessary to ensure the values of speed and respecting party autonomy in the choice of decision makers. It does, however, also mean that the traditional mechanism for addressing serious errors on appeal at the trial level that exists in the case of conventional litigation is scarified when the parties agree to resolution by means of a private arbitrator or panel of arbitrators in an extra-legal adjudicatory process.

This final point has important implications for lawyers advising clients in the planning, negotiating, and drafting stages of a contract. To what extent do the actual or perceived advantages of arbitration—rapidity, cost, privacy, and less formality—outweigh the risks of placing so much authority for conflict management and resolution in a private arbitrator? Can these risks be controlled to some extent by designating the timing, duration, and procedure that will govern in the event arbitration of a dispute under the contract becomes necessary? These are not questions that we can answer here nor is there any single "right" answer in every case. Rather, working with his or her client, and carefully assessing that client's needs in the particular transaction at issue, these are issues lawyers must think about, because good lawyering entails not only the ability to respond to conflict after it arises, but also the skill to prospectively manage conflict resolution at the onset of the deal.

We return to mandatory arbitration in commercial contracts in the chapter of the book—Chapter 7—dealing with remedies (how the law enforces the deal). So stay tuned, campers, more fun ahead.

CHAPTER 2

HAS YOUR CLIENT MADE A DEAL?

■ ■ ■

The first of the eight general questions that we will be considering in this course is whether your client has made an agreement—whether there is a deal. It is in the very nature of our system of contract law that an individual can decline to deal with another, and even walk away from unconcluded negotiations, without liability. So, how do you know whether and when your client has made a deal?

In most situations there will be little doubt that an agreement was reached *or* that it was not. For example, in our first case, *R.R. v. M.H.*, there was no dispute over the fact that the parties had made a deal. Rather, the issue in that case was whether it was an agreement the court should enforce.

Remember, then, from *R.R. v. M.H.*, that just because we have an *agreement* does not mean we have a *contract*—an agreement that the law recognizes by way of enforcement. The question of whether an agreement is enforceable is one we take up in Chapters 3 and 4. Later chapters explore how we determine and enforce the terms of the deal. But, if there is no agreement, there's not much point in talking about anything else. Let's begin by considering the question of how you know whether your client has made a deal.

The question of whether there was an agreement typically arises in situations in which there have been various conversations and negotiations between two persons, one of whom now contends that an agreement was reached, and the other of whom disagrees. We need to read the cases in this chapter to gain an understanding of when parties cross the line from "mere negotiations"—from which either party may walk away without liability—to "agreement"—which may commit the parties to mutual performance obligations under threat of liability for breach.

---

1. DETERMINING MUTUAL ASSENT

It is frequently said that an agreement is formed when there is a "meeting of the minds" between the parties on all of the essential terms of the proposed transaction. But that phrase is a misnomer. Hopefully, the phrase "meeting of the minds" will never be uttered by you, because, in fact, there is really no way to determine whether there was a meeting of the minds—short of a Vulcan mind meld.

As we'll see in the next three cases, the question of whether the parties have made a deal is determined not by ascertaining whether this so-called "meeting of the minds" occurred, but rather by answering the question of whether there was a manifestation of *mutual assent*. In reading these three cases, ask yourself, "Self, what are the policy considerations which explain or justify this approach for ascertaining mutual assent?"

QUESTION BEFORE THE CASE

Was there a "meeting of the minds" in this case?

LUCY V. ZEHMER

Supreme Court of Virginia
196 Va. 493, 84 S.E.2d 516 (1954)

BUCHANAN, J.

This suit was instituted by W. O. Lucy and J. C. Lucy, complainants, against A. H. Zehmer and Ida S. Zehmer, his wife, defendants, to have specific performance of a contract by which it was alleged the Zehmers had sold to W. O. Lucy a tract of land owned by A. H. Zehmer in Dinwiddie county containing 471.6 acres, more or less, known as the Ferguson farm, for $50,000. J. C. Lucy, the other complainant, is a brother of W. O. Lucy, to whom W. O. Lucy transferred a half interest in his alleged purchase.

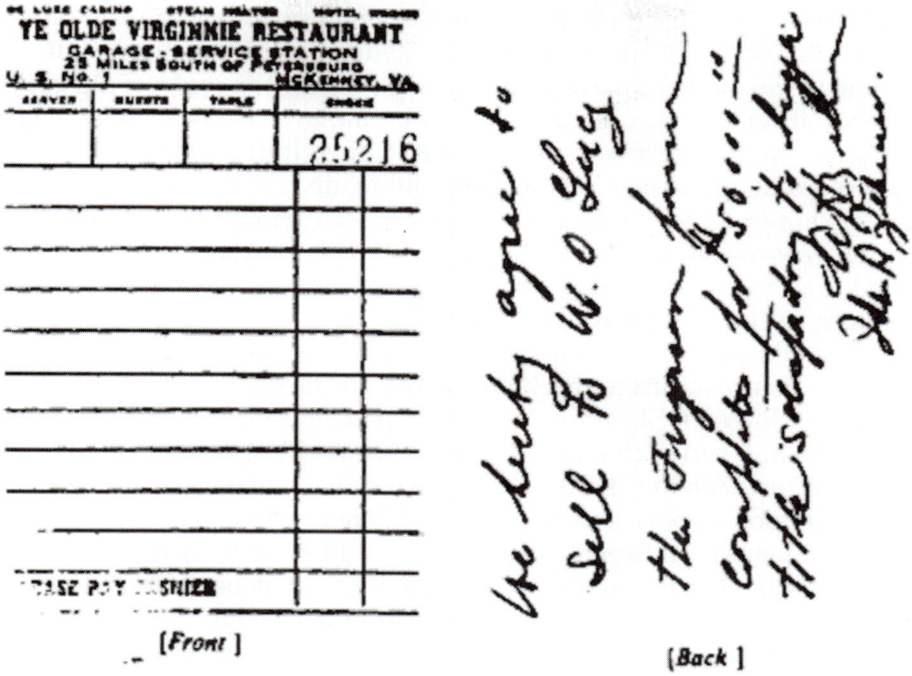

Lucy Contract

The instrument sought to be enforced was written by A. H. Zehmer on December 20, 1952, in these words: "We hereby agree to sell to W. O. Lucy the Ferguson Farm complete for $50,000.00, title satisfactory to buyer," and signed by the defendants, A. H. Zehmer and Ida S. Zehmer.

The answer of A. H. Zehmer admitted that at the time mentioned W. O. Lucy offered him $50,000 cash for the farm, but that he, Zehmer, considered that the offer was made in jest; that so thinking, and both he and Lucy having had several drinks, he wrote out "the memorandum" quoted above and induced his wife to sign it; that he did not deliver the memorandum to Lucy, but that Lucy picked it up, read it, put it in his pocket, attempted to offer Zehmer $5 to bind the bargain, which Zehmer refused to accept, and realizing for the first time that Lucy was serious, Zehmer assured him that he had no intention of selling the farm and that the whole matter was a joke. Lucy left the premises insisting that he had purchased the farm.

Depositions were taken and the decree appealed from was entered holding that the complainants had failed to establish their right to specific performance, and dismissing their bill. The assignment of error is to this action of the court.

W. O. Lucy, a lumberman and farmer, thus testified in substance: He had known Zehmer for fifteen or twenty years and had been familiar with the Ferguson farm for ten years. Seven or eight years ago he had offered Zehmer $20,000 for the farm which Zehmer had accepted, but the agreement was verbal and Zehmer backed out. On the night of December 20, 1952, around eight o'clock, he took an employee to McKenney, where Zehmer lived and operated a restaurant, filling station and motor court. While there he decided to see Zehmer and again try to buy the Ferguson farm. He entered the restaurant and talked to Mrs. Zehmer until Zehmer came in. He asked Zehmer if he had sold the Ferguson farm. Zehmer replied that he had not. Lucy said, "I bet you wouldn't take $50,000.00 for that place." Zehmer replied, "Yes, I would too; you wouldn't give fifty." Lucy said he would and told Zehmer to write up an agreement to that effect. Zehmer took a restaurant check and wrote on the back of it, "I do hereby agree to sell to W. O. Lucy the Ferguson Farm for $50,000 complete." Lucy told him he had better change it to "We" because Mrs. Zehmer would have to sign it too. Zehmer then tore up what he had written, wrote the agreement quoted above and asked Mrs. Zehmer, who was at the other end of the counter ten or twelve feet away, to sign it. Mrs. Zehmer said she would for $50,000 and signed it. Zehmer brought it back and gave it to Lucy, who offered him $5 which Zehmer refused, saying, "You don't need to give me any money, you got the agreement there signed by both of us."

The discussion leading to the signing of the agreement, said Lucy, lasted thirty or forty minutes, during which Zehmer seemed to doubt that Lucy could raise $50,000. Lucy suggested the provision for having the title examined and Zehmer made the suggestion that he would sell it "complete, everything there," and stated that all he had on the farm was three heifers.

Lucy took a partly filled bottle of whiskey into the restaurant with him for the purpose of giving Zehmer a drink if he wanted it. Zehmer did, and he and Lucy had one or two drinks together. Lucy said that while he felt the drinks he took he was not intoxicated, and from the way Zehmer handled the transaction he did not think he was either.

December 20 was on Saturday. Next day Lucy telephoned to J. C. Lucy and arranged with the latter to take a half interest in the purchase and pay half of the consideration. On Monday he engaged an attorney to examine the title. The attorney reported favorably on December 31 and on January 2 Lucy wrote Zehmer stating that the title was satisfactory, that he was ready to pay the purchase price in cash and asking when Zehmer would be ready to close the deal. Zehmer replied by letter, mailed on January 13, asserting that he had never agreed or intended to sell.

Mr. and Mrs. Zehmer were called by the complainants as adverse witnesses. Zehmer testified in substance as follows:

He bought this farm more than ten years ago for $11,000. He had had twenty-five offers, more or less, to buy it, including several from Lucy, who had never offered any specific sum of money. He had given them all the same answer, that he was not interested in selling it. On this Saturday night before Christmas it looked like everybody and his brother came by there to have a drink. He took a good many drinks during the afternoon and had a pint of his own. When he entered the restaurant around eight-thirty Lucy was there and he could see that he was "pretty high." He said to Lucy, "Boy, you got some good liquor, drinking, ain't you?" Lucy then offered him a drink. "I was already high as a Georgia pine, and didn't have any more better sense than to pour another great big slug out and gulp it down, and he took one too."

After they had talked a while Lucy asked whether he still had the Ferguson farm. He replied that he had not sold it and Lucy said, "I bet you wouldn't take $50,000.00 for it." Zehmer asked him if he would give $50,000 and Lucy said yes. Zehmer replied, "You haven't got $50,000 in cash." Lucy said he did and Zehmer replied that he did not believe it. They argued "pro and con for a long time," mainly about "whether he had $50,000 in cash that he could put up right then and buy that farm."

Finally, said Zehmer, Lucy told him if he didn't believe he had $50,000 "you sign that piece of paper here and say you will take $50,000.00 for the farm." He, Zehmer, "just grabbed the back off of a guest check there" and wrote on the back of it. * * *

After Zehmer had, as he described it, "scribbled this thing off," Lucy said, "Get your wife to sign it." Zehmer walked over to where she was and she at first refused to sign but did so after he told her that he "was just needling him [Lucy], and didn't mean a thing in the world, that I was not selling the farm." Zehmer then "took it back over there * * * and I was still looking at the dern thing. I had the drink right there by my hand, and I reached over to get a drink, and he said, 'Let me see it.' He reached and picked it up, and when I looked back again he had it in his pocket and he dropped a five dollar bill over there, and he said, 'Here is five dollars payment on it.' * * * I said, 'Hell no, that is beer and liquor talking. I am not going to sell you the farm. I have told you that too many times before.' "

Mrs. Zehmer testified that when Lucy came into the restaurant he looked as if he had had a drink. When Zehmer came in he took a drink out of a bottle that Lucy handed him. She went back to help the waitress who was getting things ready for next day. Lucy and Zehmer were talking but she did not pay too much attention to what they were saying. She heard Lucy ask Zehmer if he had sold the Ferguson farm, and Zehmer replied that he had not and did not want to sell it. Lucy said, "I bet you wouldn't take $50,000 cash for that farm," and Zehmer replied, "You haven't got $50,000 cash." Lucy said, "I can get it." Zehmer said he might form a company and get it, "but you haven't got $50,000.00 cash to pay me tonight." Lucy asked him if he would put it in writing that he would sell him this farm. Zehmer then wrote on the back of a pad, "I agree to sell the

Ferguson Place to W. O. Lucy for $50,000.00 cash." Lucy said, "All right, get your wife to sign it." Zehmer came back to where she was standing and said, "You want to put your name to this?" She said "No," but he said in an undertone, "It is nothing but a joke," and she signed it.

She said that only one paper was written and it said: "I hereby agree to sell," but the "I" had been changed to "We". However, she said she read what she signed and was then asked, "When you read 'We hereby agree to sell to W. O. Lucy,' what did you interpret that to mean, that particular phrase?" She said she thought that was a cash sale that night; but she also said that when she read that part about "title satisfactory to buyer" she understood that if the title was good Lucy would pay $50,000 but if the title was bad he would have a right to reject it, and that that was her understanding at the time she signed her name.

On examination by her own counsel she said that her husband laid this piece of paper down after it was signed; that Lucy said to let him see it, took it, folded it and put it in his wallet, then said to Zehmer, "Let me give you $5.00," but Zehmer said, "No, this is liquor talking. I don't want to sell the farm, I have told you that I want my son to have it. This is all a joke." Lucy then said at least twice, "Zehmer, you have sold your farm," wheeled around and started for the door. He paused at the door and said, "I will bring you $50,000.00 tomorrow. * * * No, tomorrow is Sunday. I will bring it to you Monday." She said you could tell definitely that he was drinking and she said to her husband, "You should have taken him home," but he said, "Well, I am just about as bad off as he is."

The waitress referred to by Mrs. Zehmer testified that when Lucy first came in "he was mouthy." When Zehmer came in they were laughing and joking and she thought they took a drink or two. She was sweeping and cleaning up for next day. She said she heard Lucy tell Zehmer, "I will give you so much for the farm," and Zehmer said, "You haven't got that much." Lucy answered, "Oh, yes, I will give you that much." Then "they jotted down something on paper * * * and Mr. Lucy reached over and took it, said let me see it." He looked at it, put it in his pocket and in about a minute he left. She was asked whether she saw Lucy offer Zehmer any money and replied, "He had five dollars laying up there, they didn't take it." She said Zehmer told Lucy he didn't want his money "because he didn't have enough money to pay for his property, and wasn't going to sell his farm." Both of them appeared to be drinking right much, she said.

She repeated on cross-examination that she was busy and paying no attention to what was going on. She was some distance away and did not see either of them sign the paper. She was asked whether she saw Zehmer put the agreement down on the table in front of Lucy, and her answer was this: "Time he got through writing whatever it was on the paper, Mr. Lucy reached over and said, 'Let's see it.' He took it and put it in his pocket," before showing it to Mrs. Zehmer. Her version was that Lucy kept raising his offer until it got to $50,000.

The defendants insist that the evidence was ample to support their contention that the writing sought to be enforced was prepared as a bluff or dare to force Lucy to admit that he did not have $50,000; that the whole matter was a joke; that the writing was not delivered to Lucy and no binding contract was ever made between the parties.

It is an unusual, if not bizarre, defense. When made to the writing admittedly prepared by one of the defendants and signed by both, clear evidence is required to sustain it.

In his testimony Zehmer claimed that he "was high as a Georgia pine," and that the transaction "was just a bunch of two doggoned drunks bluffing to see who could talk the biggest and say the most." That claim is inconsistent with his attempt to testify in great detail as to what was said and what was done. It is contradicted by other evidence as to the condition of both parties, and rendered of no weight by the testimony of his wife that when Lucy left the restaurant she suggested that Zehmer drive him home. The record is convincing that Zehmer was not intoxicated to the extent of being unable to comprehend the nature and consequences of the instrument he executed, and hence that instrument is not to be invalidated on that ground. * * * It was in fact conceded by defendants' counsel in oral argument that under the evidence Zehmer was not too drunk to make a valid contract.

The evidence is convincing also that Zehmer wrote two agreements, the first one beginning "I hereby agree to sell." Zehmer first said he could not remember about that, then that "I don't think I wrote but one out." Mrs. Zehmer said that what he wrote was "I hereby agree," but that the "I" was changed to "We" after that night. The agreement that was written and signed is in the record and indicates no such change. * * *

The appearance of the contract, the fact that it was under discussion for forty minutes or more before it was signed; Lucy's objection to the first draft because it was written in the singular, and he wanted Mrs. Zehmer to sign it also; the rewriting to meet that objection and the signing by Mrs Zehmer; the discussion of what was to be included in the sale, the provision for the examination of the title, the completeness of the instrument that was executed, the taking possession of it by Lucy with no request or suggestion by either of the defendants that he give it back, are facts which furnish persuasive evidence that the execution of the contract was a serious business transaction rather than a casual, jesting matter as defendants now contend.

* * *

If it be assumed, contrary to what we think the evidence shows, that Zehmer was jesting about selling his farm to Lucy and that the transaction was intended by him to be a joke, nevertheless the evidence shows that Lucy did not so understand it but considered it to be a serious business transaction and the contract to be binding on the Zehmers as well as on himself. The very next day he arranged with his brother to put up half the money and take a half interest in the land. The day after that he employed an attorney to examine the title. The next night, Tuesday, he was back at Zehmer's place and there Zehmer told him for the first time, Lucy said, that he wasn't going to sell and he told Zehmer, "You know you sold that place fair and square." After receiving the report from his attorney that the title was good he wrote to Zehmer that he was ready to close the deal.

Not only did Lucy actually believe, but the evidence shows he was warranted in believing, that the contract represented a serious business transaction and a good faith sale and purchase of the farm.

In the field of contracts, as generally elsewhere, "We must look to the outward expression of a person as manifesting his intention rather than to his secret and unexpressed intention. 'The law imputes to a person an intention corresponding to the reasonable meaning of his words and acts.' " *First Nat. Bank v. Roanoke Oil Co.*, 169 Va. 99, 114, 192 S.E. 764, 770.

At no time prior to the execution of the contract had Zehmer indicated to Lucy by word or act that he was not in earnest about selling the farm. They had argued about it and discussed its terms, as Zehmer admitted, for a long time. Lucy testified that if there was any jesting it was about paying $50,000 that night. The contract and the evidence show that he was not expected to pay the money that night. Zehmer said that after the writing was signed he laid it down on the counter in front of Lucy. Lucy said Zehmer handed it to him. In any event there had been what appeared to be a good faith offer and a good faith acceptance, followed by the execution and apparent delivery of a written contract. Both said that Lucy put the writing in his pocket and then offered Zehmer $5 to seal the bargain. Not until then, even under the defendants' evidence, was anything said or done to indicate that the matter was a joke. Both of the Zehmers testified that when Zehmer asked his wife to sign he whispered that it was a joke so Lucy wouldn't hear and that it was not intended that he should hear.

The mental assent of the parties is not requisite for the formation of a contract. If the words or other acts of one of the parties have but one reasonable meaning, his undisclosed intention is immaterial except when an unreasonable meaning which he attaches to his manifestations is known to the other party. Restatement of the Law of Contracts, Vol. I, § 71, p. 74.

"* * * The law, therefore, judges of an agreement between two persons exclusively from those expressions of their intentions which are communicated between them. * * *" Clark on Contracts, 4 ed., § 3, p. 4.

An agreement or mutual assent is of course essential to a valid contract but the law imputes to a person an intention corresponding to the reasonable meaning of his words and acts. If his words and acts, judged by a reasonable standard, manifest an intention to agree, it is immaterial what may be the real but unexpressed state of his mind. * * *

So a person cannot set up that he was merely jesting when his conduct and words would warrant a reasonable person in believing that he intended a real agreement. * * *

Whether the writing signed by the defendants and now sought to be enforced by the complainants was the result of a serious offer by Lucy and a serious acceptance by the defendants, or was a serious offer by Lucy and an acceptance in secret jest by the defendants, in either event it constituted a binding contract of sale between the parties.

Defendants contend further, however, that even though a contract was made, equity should decline to enforce it under the circumstances. These circumstances have been set forth in detail above. They disclose some drinking by the two parties but not to an extent that they were unable to understand fully what they were doing. There was no fraud, no misrepresentation, no sharp practice and no dealing between unequal parties. The farm had been bought for $11,000 and was assessed for taxation at $6,300. The purchase price was $50,000. Zehmer admitted that it was a good price. There is in fact present in this case none of the grounds usually urged against specific performance.

* * *

The complainants are entitled to have specific performance of the contracts sued on. The decree appealed from is therefore reversed and the cause is remanded for the entry of a proper decree requiring the defendants to perform the contract in accordance with the prayer of the bill.

Reversed and remanded.

QUESTIONS AND NOTES

1. Questions about the facts of this case

   1.1. Did Mr. Zehmer really intend to sell the farm to Lucy or was he joshing? How about Mrs. Zehmer? Does it matter?

   1.2. Did Lucy believe that his neighbor was joking? Does it matter?

1.3. Remember Zehmer's contention that he was "high as a Georgia pine"? Did the court think that either Lucy or Zehmer was intoxicated? Should that matter? Can you enter into a legally binding contract when you're drunk? This is a question of "capacity" to contract, a topic we take up in Chapter 4.

1.4. Remember the court's mentioning that the next day Lucy hired an attorney to examine title and arranging with his brother for financing? Are these important facts? If these are not important facts, why did Justice Buchanan mention them? Do you think Justice Buchanan is related to Pat Buchanan? How about Edgar Buchanan?

2. Questions about the law

2.1. Does the court in *Lucy* take an objective or subjective approach to contract formation? What is the difference between the two?

2.2. How would the case have been decided if Lucy believed that Zehmer was joking?

2.3. Of what relevance was Zehmer's refusal to accept the $5 that Lucy offered after the "guest check" had been signed? Was acceptance of the payment necessary to seal the deal? If the rationale for the objective theory is to protect the reasonable expectation of parties, for how long was Lucy reasonable in his belief (i.e., expectation) that Zehmer intended to be bound? Should it make a difference at what stage the offeror tells the offeree he's not serious? Is there a "magic moment" that "will last forever; forever til the end of time"* for determining mutual assent, and that what happens after that moment is irrelevant to determining whether there is an agreement?

2.4. Even accepting the court's explanation in *Lucy* for how the existence of contractual assent is to be ascertained by the courts when there is a dispute between the parties, is it clear that a reasonable person in Lucy's position would have understood from Zehmer's outward manifestations an intent to sell the farm for $50,000? Is it appropriate to look only at the words used? If not, what other factors were relevant in *Lucy* that were arguably overlooked by the Virginia Supreme Court. Even if the Supreme Court correctly concluded that the trial court had applied the wrong legal standard for determining intention to be bound, was it appropriate for the Supreme Court, as a matter of law, to decide that Lucy "wins"; i.e., that Lucy was entitled to judgment for specific performance?

* "This Magic Moment" http://www.lynchnet.com/lh/magic.html Regardless of whether "This Magic Moment" is helpful to you in your efforts to make sense of contracts, Epstein claims that it was helpful to him in his efforts to "make out" in the '60's. We don't know whether Epstein is referring to the 1960s or his sixties.

2.5. Can you now articulate the legal standard for ascertaining mutual assent? Can you define "offer," "acceptance," "specific performance," or "remand"? If not, don't worry, it's still early in the semester, so just keep reading (perhaps more carefully and with Black's Law Dictionary by your side)!

3. Notes

3.1. In ascertaining the existence of a binding contract, the courts examine and give legal effect to the outward manifestation of the parties, regardless of what either party may have privately or secretly intended. The question then is not what the offeror may have actually meant by what she said, but the reasonable impression created in the mind of the offeree by the words used and the conduct engaged in by the offeror. This is known as the *objective theory* of contract formation.

Consider this statement from an opinion by Judge Richard Posner of the United States Court of Appeals for the Seventh Circuit: "The premise—that a 'meeting of the minds' is required for a binding contract is strained. Most contract disputes arise because the parties did not foresee and provide for some contingency that has not materialized—so there was no meeting of the minds on the matter at issue—yet such disputes are treated as disputes over contractual meaning. * * * So a literal meeting of the minds is not required for an enforceable contract, which is fortunate, since courts are not renowned as mind readers." *Colfax Envelope Corp. v. Local No. 458–3M*, 20 F.3d 750, 752 (7th Cir. 1994). Judge Posner is really smart and writes a lot of opinions, law review articles, and books—stuff that is not always easy to understand. If a literal meeting of the minds is not required to establish a contract, what is required? A figurative meeting of the minds? Is Judge Posner's dictum in *Colfax* consistent with the objective theory of contract formation?

3.2. "The objective theory of contracts provides that mutual assent to a contract is determined by reference to external acts and manifestations, not by evidence of subjective, internal intention. Stated more simply, contract formation depends on what is communicated, not merely what is thought." Wayne Barnes, *The Objective Theory of Contracts*, 76 U. CINN. L. REV. 1119–20, (2008).

The notion that the law of contracts is not concerned with the parties' undisclosed intent and ideas is traditionally regarded as a relatively new concept. Throughout most of the nineteenth century, courts viewed contractual liability as arising from the conscious, *subjective* agreement on the same undertaking. Hence the origins of the term *meeting of the minds*. *See* LAWRENCE FRIEDMAN, CONTRACT LAW IN AMERICA 87 (1965) (suggesting that the shift from subjective to objective theory of contract formation was a response to the law's concern around the turn of the last century with reducing business risk and enhancing the predictability of market transactions); *but see* Joseph M. Perillo, *The Origins of Objective Theory of Contract Formation and Interpretation,* 69 FORDHAM L. REV. 427, 428–30 (2000) (arguing that objective approaches predominated in the common law of contracts from "time immemorial"). Subjective theory would certainly be consistent with the nineteenth century's general emphasis on free will and individualism. The objective theory of mutual assent obviously places a higher priority on one party's right to rely on the reasonable expectations created by an apparent agreement of the other, a priority perceived as also assuring the need in the marketplace for certainty and predictability.

Although not without its critics, objective theory ultimately triumphed, thanks, in large measure, to the support of its greatest advocate, Professor Samuel Williston, Reporter for the first *Restatement of Contracts.* Objective theory also found its way into the Second Restatement. *See Restatement (Second) of Contracts* § 24.

It is important to recognize that the objective theory of assent has two components, only one of which is purely objective: (1) would a reasonable person in the position of the promisee understand from the promisor's words and conduct an intent to be bound; and (2) did the promisee in fact so believe? Recall Justice Buchanan's statement: "Not only did Lucy actually believe, but the evidence shows he was warranted in believing, that the contract represented a serious business transaction and a good faith sale and purchase of the farm."

3.3. In a frequently-quoted passage from his opinion in *Hotchkiss v. National City Bank of New York*, 200 F. 287, 293 (S.D.N.Y. 1911) the distinguished jurist Learned Hand wrote:

> A contract has, strictly speaking, nothing to do with the personal, or individual, intent of the parties. A contract is an obligation attached by the mere force of law to certain acts of the parties, which ordinarily accompany and represent a known intent. If, however, it were proved by twenty bishops that either party when he used the words intended something else than the usual meaning which the law imposes on them, he would still be held [liable]. * * *

Is this view consistent with *Lucy*? Thirty-five years after *Hotchkiss* was decided, Judge Jerome Frank, actually concurring in an opinion written by then Second Circuit

Judge Hand, criticized the "objectivists" as having gone too far. He complained:

> The objectivists transferred from the field of torts that stubborn anti-subjectivist, the 'reasonable-man'; so that, in part at least, advocacy of the 'objective' standard in contracts appears to have represented a desire for legal symmetry, legal uniformity, a desire seemingly prompted by aesthetic impulses. * * * At any rate, the sponsors of complete 'objectivity' in contracts largely won out in the wider generalization of the Restatement of Contracts and in some judicial opinions.

Ricketts v. Pennsylvania R. Co., 153 F.2d 757, 761 (2d Cir. 1946).

3.4. If contract law is distinguished from tort law as being consent rather than fault-based, think about whether Judge Frank makes a fair point. And, in light of Judge Frank's statement, think about the "aesthetic impulses" that accounted for Professor Williston's wholesale adoption of objective theory in the first *Restatement of Contracts*.

4. **You Be the Lawyer!**

If you had represented Mr. Zehmer at trial, what facts would you have emphasized? If you represented Lucy, what facts would you have emphasized? In either case, would you recommend that your client show up for trial "high as a Georgia pine"?

QUESTIONS BEFORE THE CASE

1. The court spends a lot of time in this case talking about *Lucy*, in which, of course, the court concluded that Mr. Zehmer had made an offer even if he didn't intend to do so. How does the court in *Mason* distinguish *Lucy*?
2. What do we mean when we say a case is "distinguishable"?

KOLODZIEJ V. MASON

United States Court of Appeals, Eleventh Circuit
774 F.3d 736 (2014)

WILSON, CIRCUIT JUDGE:

This case involves a law student's efforts to form a contract by accepting a "million-dollar challenge" that a lawyer extended on nationa television while representing a client accused of murder. Since we find tha the challenge did not give rise to an enforceable unilateral contract,* we hold that the district court properly entered summary judgment for the lawyer and his law firm, * * *.

I.

The current dispute * * * arose from comments Mason made while representing criminal defendant Nelson Serrano, who stood accused of murdering his former business partner as well as the son, daughter, and son-in-law of a third business partner. During Serrano's highly publicized capital murder trial, Mason participated in an interview with NBC News in which he focused on the seeming implausibility of the prosecution's theory of the case. Indeed, his client ostensibly had an alibi—on the day of the murders, Serrano claimed to be on a business trip in an entirely different state, several hundred miles away from the scene of the crimes in central Florida. Hotel surveillance video confirmed that Serrano was at a La Quinta Inn (La Quinta) in Atlanta, Georgia, several hours before and after the murders occurred in Bartow, Florida.

However, the prosecution maintained that Serrano committed the murders in an approximately ten-hour span between the times that he was seen on the security camera. According to the prosecution, after being recorded by the hotel security camera in the early afternoon, Serrano slipped out of the hotel and, traveling under several aliases, flew from Atlanta to Orlando, where he rented a car, drove to Bartow, Florida, and committed the murders. From there, Serrano allegedly drove to the Tampa International Airport, flew back to Atlanta, and drove from the Atlanta International Airport to the La Quinta, to make an appearance on the hotel's security footage once again that evening.

Mason argued that it was impossible for his client to have committed the murders in accordance with this timeline; for instance, for the last leg of the journey, Serrano would have had to get off a flight in Atlanta's busy airport, travel to the La Quinta several miles away, and arrive in that hotel lobby in only twenty-eight minutes. After extensively describing the delays that would take place to render that twenty-eight-minute timeline even more unlikely,[1] Mason stated, "I challenge anybody to show me, and guess what? Did they bring in any evidence to say that somebody made that

* [An offer for a unilateral contract is one formed by performance of a requested act rather than by a return promise. We will return to the distinction between unilateral and bilateral contracts later in this chapter. Eds.]

[1] For example, Mason noted that, "in Atlanta, depending on which concourse you're landing in, you're going to have to wait to get off the airplane. . . . You got people boxed in—the lady with the kids in the carriage. Or people getting down their bags. Or the fat one can't get down the aisle. I mean, whatever the story is, you've got delays in getting off the airplane. . . . Then you have to go from whatever gate you are, . . . to catch the subway train to the terminal. Wait for that. Wait while it stops in the meantime. People getting on and off. Get to that. Go up again, the escalators. Get to where you're in the terminal, out the terminal to ground transportation. And from there to be on the videotape in 28 minutes."

route, did so? State's burden of proof. If they can do it, I'll challenge 'em. I'll pay them a million dollars if they can do it."

NBC did not broadcast Mason's original interview during Serrano's trial. At the conclusion of the trial, the jury returned a guilty verdict in Serrano's case. Thereafter, in December 2006, NBC featured an edited version of Mason's interview in a national broadcast of its "Dateline" television program. The edited version removed much of the surrounding commentary, including Mason's references to the State's burden of proof and Mason's statement aired as, "I challenge anybody to show me—I'll pay them a million dollars if they can do it."

Enter Kolodziej, then a law student at the South Texas College of Law, who had been following the Serrano case. Kolodziej saw the edited version of Mason's interview and understood the statement as a serious challenge, open to anyone, to "make it off the plane and back to the hotel within [twenty-eight] minutes"—that is, in the prosecution's timeline—in return for one million dollars.

Kolodziej subsequently ordered and studied the transcript of the edited interview, interpreting it as an offer to form a unilateral contract—an offer he decided to accept by performing the challenge. In December 2007, Kolodziej recorded himself retracing Serrano's alleged route, traveling from a flight at the Atlanta airport to what he believed was the former location of the now-defunct La Quinta within twenty-eight minutes. Kolodziej then sent Mason a copy of the recording of his journey and a letter stating that Kolodziej had performed the challenge and requested payment. Mason responded with a letter in which he refused payment and denied that he made a serious offer in the interview. Kolodziej again demanded payment, and Mason again refused.

Considering Mason's refusal to pay a breach of contract, Kolodziej sued Mason and Mason's law firm, J. Cheney Mason, P.A., in the United States District Court for the Southern District of Texas. Although the court dismissed the case for lack of personal jurisdiction, it was then that Kolodziej discovered the existence of Mason's unedited interview with NBC and learned that Dateline had independently edited the interview before it aired. Kolodziej subsequently filed suit in the United States District Court for the Northern District of Georgia. That suit was transferred to the Middle District of Florida, where Mason moved for summary judgment.

The district court granted summary judgment on two grounds: first, Kolodziej was unaware of the unedited Mason interview at the time he attempted to perform the challenge, and thus he could not accept an offer he did not know existed; second, the challenge in the unedited interview was unambiguously directed to the prosecution only, and thus Kolodziej could not accept an offer not open to him. The district court declined to address the arguments that Mason's challenge was not a serious offer and that, in any event, Kolodziej did not adequately perform the challenge. This appeal ensued.

* * *

III.

"To prove the existence of a contract, a plaintiff must plead: (1) offer; (2) acceptance; (3) consideration; and (4) sufficient specification of the essential terms." *Vega v. T-Mobile USA, Inc.,* 564 F.3d 1256, 1272 (11th Cir.2009) (citing *St. Joe Corp. v. McIver,* 875 So.2d 375, 381 (Fla.2004)). An oral contract is subject to all basic requirements of contract law, *St. Joe Corp.,* 875 So.2d at 381, and mutual assent is a prerequisite for the formation of any contract, * * *.

Mutual assent is not necessarily an independent "element" unto itself; rather, we evaluate the existence of assent by analyzing the parties' agreement process in terms of offer and acceptance. A valid contract—premised on the parties' requisite willingness to contract—may be "manifested through written or spoken words, or inferred in whole or in part from the parties' conduct." *L & H Constr. Co. v. Circle Redmont, Inc.,* 55 So.3d 630, 634 (Fla.Dist.Ct.App.2011) (internal quotation marks omitted). We use "an objective test . . . to determine whether a contract is enforceable." *See Robbie v. City of Miami,* 469 So.2d 1384, 1385 (Fla.1985); * * *.

IV.

We do not find that Mason's statements were such that a reasonable, objective person would have understood them to be an invitation to contract, regardless of whether we look to the unedited interview or the edited television broadcast seen by Kolodziej. Neither the content of Mason's statements, nor the circumstances in which he made them, nor the conduct of the parties reflects the assent necessary to establish an actionable offer—which is, of course, essential to the creation of a contract.

As a threshold matter, the "spoken words" of Mason's purported challenge do not indicate a willingness to enter into a contract. Even removed from its surrounding context, the edited sentence that Kolodziej claims creates Mason's obligation to pay (that is, "I challenge anybody to show me—I'll pay them a million dollars if they can do it") appears colloquial. The exaggerated amount of "a million dollars"—the common choice of movie villains and schoolyard wagerers alike—indicates that this was hyperbole. As the district court noted, "courts have viewed such indicia of jest or hyperbole as providing a reason for an individual to doubt that an 'offer' was serious." *See Kolodziej v. Mason,* 996 F.Supp.2d 1237, 1252 (M.D.Fla.2014) (discussing, in dicta, a laughter-eliciting joke made by Mason's co-counsel during the interview). Thus, the very content of

Mason's spoken words "would have given any reasonable person pause, considering all of the attendant circumstances in this case." *See id.*

Those attendant circumstances are further notable when we place Mason's statements in context. As Judge Learned Hand once noted, "the circumstances in which the words are used is always relevant and usually indispensable." *N.Y. Trust Co. v. Island Oil & Transp. Corp.,* 34 F.2d 655, 656 (2d Cir.1929). Here, Mason made the comments in the course of representing a criminal defendant accused of quadruple homicide and did so during an interview solely related to that representation. Such circumstances would lead a reasonable person to question whether the requisite assent and actionable offer giving rise to contractual liability existed. Certainly, Mason's statements—made as a defense attorney in response to the prosecution's theory against his client—were far more likely to be a descriptive illustration of what that attorney saw as serious holes in the prosecution's theory instead of a serious offer to enter into a contract.

Nor can a valid contract be "inferred in whole or in part from the parties' conduct" in this case. By way of comparison, consider *Lucy v. Zehmer,* 196 Va. 493, 84 S.E.2d 516 (1954), the classic case describing and applying what we now know as the objective standard of assent. That court held that statements allegedly made "in jest" *could* result in an offer binding the parties to a contract, since "the law imputes to a person an intention corresponding to the reasonable meaning of his words and acts." *Id.* at 522. Therefore, "a person cannot set up that he was merely jesting when his conduct and words would warrant a reasonable person in believing that he intended a real agreement." *Id.*

In so holding, the *Lucy* court considered that the offeror wrote, prepared, and executed a writing for sale; the parties engaged in extensive, serious discussion prior to preparing the writing; the offeror prepared a second written agreement, having changed the content of the writing in response to the offeree's request; the offeror had his wife separately sign the writing; and the offeror allowed the offeree to leave with the signed writing without ever indicating that it was in jest. *Id.* at 519–22. Given that these "words and acts, judged by a reasonable standard, manifest[ed] an intention to agree," the offeror's "unexpressed state of . . . mind" was immaterial. *Id.* at 522. Under the objective standard of assent, the *Lucy* court found that the parties had formed a contract.

Applying the objective standard here leads us to the real million-dollar question: "What did the party say and do?" Here, it is what both parties did not say and did not do that clearly distinguishes this case from those cases where an enforceable contract was formed. Mason did not engage in any discussion regarding his statements to NBC with Kolodziej, and, prior to Kolodziej demanding payment, there was no contact or communication between the parties.[6] Mason neither confirmed that he made an offer nor asserted that the offer was serious. Mason did not have the payment set aside in escrow; nor had he ever declared that he had money set aside in case someone proved him wrong.[9] Mason had not made his career out of the contention that the prosecution's case was implausible;[10] nor did he make the statements in a commercial context for the "obvious purpose of advertising or promoting [his] goods or business." He did not create or promote the video that included his statement, nor did he increase the amount at issue. He did not, nor did the show include, any information to contact Mason about the challenge.[13] Simply put, Mason's conduct lacks any indicia of assent to contract.

In fact, none of Mason's surrounding commentary—either in the unedited original interview or in the edited television broadcast—gave the slightest indication that his statement was anything other than a figure of speech. In the course of representing his client, Mason merely used a rhetorical expression to raise questions as to the prosecution's case. We could just as easily substitute a comparable idiom such as "I'll eat my hat" or "I'll be a monkey's uncle" into Mason's interview in the place of "I'll pay them a million dollars," and the outcome would be the same. We would not be inclined to make him either consume his headwear or assume a simian relationship were he to be proven wrong; nor will we make him pay one million dollars here.[15]

* * *

In further illustration of the lack of assent to contract in this case, we question whether even Kolodziej's conduct—his "acceptance"—manifested assent to any perceived offer. Under the objective standard of assent, we

[6] *Cf. Lucy,* 84 S.E.2d at 520–21 (describing the parties' extensive discussion prior to and during the creation of the contract).

[9] *Cf. James v. Turilli,* 473 S.W.2d 757, 761 (Mo.Ct.App.1971). In *James,* Turilli stated before a nationwide television audience that Jesse James didn't die in 1882 and that Turilli "would pay Ten Thousand Dollars ($10,000.00) to anyone . . . who could prove [him] wrong." *Id.* at 759 (internal quotation marks omitted). In finding that this constituted an offer, the court noted that, in addition to other evidence, Turilli had previously said that he had a "certified check of ten thousand dollars" to be collected upon proof that Jesse James had actually died in 1882. *Id.* at 761.

[10] In *Newman,* a "self-styled 'tax rebel,' " who "made a career and substantial profits out of his tax protest activities" and "promoted his books by appearing on over five hundred radio and television programs," 778 F.2d at 461–62, made a valid, time-limited offer when, in a live television appearance, he stated, "If anybody calls this show . . . and cites any section of this Code that says an individual is required to file a tax return, I will pay them $100,000," *id.* at 462 (internal quotation marks omitted); * * *.

[15] However, unenforceable is not quite the same as "unlitigable," since some people might still take such a challenge literally. For example, Donald Trump recently sued Bill Maher for breach of contract after Maher stated on national television that he would offer five million dollars to Trump, donatable to the charity of Trump's choice, if Trump proved that he was not the spawn of an orangutan. *See* Compl., *Trump v. Maher,* No. BC499537 (Cal. Sup. Ct. filed Feb. 4, 2013), *available at* http://pmcdeadline2.files.wordpress.com/2013/02/trump-maher_130205003242.pdf. Trump claimed to accept this offer by providing a copy of his birth certificate as proof of his non-orangutan origin, filing suit when Maher did not respond to his demand for payment. Trump later voluntarily dismissed the suit.

do not look into the subjective minds of the parties; the law imputes an intention that corresponds with the reasonable meaning of a party's words and acts. *See Lucy,* 84 S.E.2d at 522. We thus find it troublesome that, in all this time—ordering the transcript, studying it, purchasing tickets, recording himself making the trip—Kolodziej never made any effort to contact Mason to confirm the existence of an offer, to ensure any such offer was still valid after Serrano's conviction, or to address the details and terms of the challenge. However, we will not attribute bad intent when inexperience may suffice. Kolodziej may have learned in his contracts class that acceptance by performance results in an immediate, binding contract and that notice may not be necessary, but he apparently did not consider the absolute necessity of first having a specific, definite offer and the basic requirement of mutual assent. We simply are driven to ask, as Mason did in his response letter: "Why did you not just call?" Perhaps a jurist's interpretation of an old aphorism provides the answer: "If, as Alexander Pope wrote, 'a little learning is a dangerous thing,' then a little learning in law is particularly perilous."[17]

V.

Finally, summary judgment was procedurally appropriate in this case. Mason's spoken words, the circumstances in which those words were said, and the parties' conduct are all undisputed, and we find "no genuine issue as to whether the parties' conduct implied a contractual understanding." * * *

No reasonable person and no reasonable juror would think, absent any other indicia of seriousness, that Mason manifested willingness to enter into a contract in either the unedited interview or the edited broadcast relied upon by Kolodziej. Accordingly, Kolodziej cannot establish the basic requirements for contract formation. With no assent, there is no actionable offer; with no offer, there is no enforceable contract. Thus, Kolodziej's breach-of-contract claim was appropriately dismissed on summary judgment.[18]

VI.

Just as people are free to contract, they are also free *from* contract, and we find it neither prudent nor permissible to impose contractual liability for offhand remarks or grandstanding. * * * Having considered the content of Mason's statements, the context in which they were made, and the conduct of the parties, we do not find it reasonable to conclude that Mason assented to enter into a contract with anyone for one million dollars.

---

[17] Chief Judge Gilbert in *Ginn v. Farley,* 43 Md.App. 229, 403 A.2d 858, 859 (1979) (quoting Alexander Pope, *An Essay on Criticism,* Part II, line 15 (n.p. 1711)).

[18] Because we find that Mason's statements in these circumstances do not constitute an enforceable contractual offer, regardless of which version of the statements is considered, we need not address Kolodziej's additional arguments with regard to the district court's reasoning.

We affirm the district court's judgment in favor of Mason and J. Cheney Mason, P.A.

QUESTIONS

1. Questions about the facts of this case

   1.1. What would you say were the most important facts that caused the court to conclude that a reasonable person would not infer that Mr. Mason was seriously willing to pay one million dollars to anyone who could make the trip from Hartsfield International to the La Quinta within 28 minutes?

   1.2. If Mr. Kolodziej had ordered and studied the whole transcript of the interview before recording his actions, might the outcome have been different? Why or why not?

   1.3. Should the court have really referred to the ultimate issue in the case as the "million-dollar question"? Do you think Mr. Kolodziej thought that was funny when he read it?

   1.4. Is Donald Trump really the spawn of an orangutan? If not, why did he drop his lawsuit against Bill Maher?

2. Questions about the law

   2.1. Is *Mason* consistent with objective theory?

   2.2. The court of appeals affirms the district court's grant of summary judgment, but did the court of appeals agree with the lower court's reasoning? If not, what was the difference?

   2.3. What does the court mean by the statement that people are free *from* contract just as they are free to contract?

   2.4. Did it matter to the court that Mr. Mason's statement was not in writing, unlike Mr. Zehmer's? Should it have?

3. **You Be the Lawyer!**

   Should you try to be a lawyer while you're still in law school? Should you try to represent yourself even after you become a member of the bar? In this case, Mr. Kolodziej was represented by a real lawyer, David George of Baker Wotring LLP, in Houston. The firm's website indicates that Mr. George was an honors graduate of Baylor Law School and is an experienced and successful litigator. How much do you suppose he got paid for this case? As the lawyer for Mr. Kolodziej, would you have recommended an appeal to the U.S. Eleventh Circuit Court of Appeals? Would you have recommended that Mr. Kolodziej bring the suit to begin with once Mr. Mason turned down his demand for the money?

PROBLEM

After reading some of the hypotheticals used by Markell in the 4th edition of their Contracts casebook, Ponoroff accused Markell of defamation of character and threatened to sue. Markell denied the allegation but offered, in complete settlement of Ponoroff's claim, to transfer to Ponoroff one-half of all of his royalties from the casebook for the next year. Ponoroff replied that this was acceptable, and the parties proceeded to discuss the arrangements, which would include instruction to West to split Markell's contractual royalties between Markell and Ponoroff for the next year—beginning on January 1. At the conclusion of these discussions, Markell said, "Then we have a deal?" and Ponoroff responded "Yes, I will write up our agreement and send it to you." Ponoroff proceeded to prepare such a writing containing the terms of the deal as agreed, signed it, and sent it to Markell for his signature. On receipt, Markell refused to sign and, in fact, burned the written agreement while cursing Ponoroff. Can Ponoroff enforce a claim against Markell for half of next year's royalties? *See Restatement (Second) of Contracts* § 27. How, if at all, would it change your answer or your analysis if the parties had been negotiating over Ponoroff's purchase of Markell's house rather than the settlement of Ponoroff's defamation claim? *See* cmt. c to § 27. *See also Continental Laboratories v. Scott Paper Co.,* 759 F.Supp. 538 (S.D. Iowa 1990), *aff'd,* 938 F.2d 184 (8th Cir. 1991) (applying the cited *Restatement* provision).

Are the courts' expressions in the last two cases about how objective theory works consistent? How about the courts' application of that standard? Who should decide what a reasonable person in the position of the promisee would infer from the words and actions of the offeror? Who decided in these two cases? Judges, that's who! Markell was a judge! Does that make him a "reasonable person" by definition?* How do *you* now understand objective theory to work in determining mutual assent? Can you think of a better test? Is objective theory consistent with the court's statement in *Mason* that people have a right to "freedom from contract"? Are you having fun yet? Are you at least having more fun than in Torts class?

NOTE ON THE INTENTION TO BE LEGALLY BOUND

Did you notice that in the first three cases none of the defendants made any reference in their alleged contracts to an *intention* to assume a legally

* Maybe, but Epstein and Ponoroff have their doubts and so will you when get to the parts of the book that Markell prepared!

binding obligation? And yet, the decisions seem unconcerned with this point in analyzing whether a contract may have been formed. This is because, ordinarily, such an express manifestation of intent to be bound is not required in order for a promise to bind the promisor; rather, it is inferred from the very act of making the promise. However, should an express manifestation of intention *not* to assume a legal obligation affect the enforceability of a promise? Can you justify a distinction under objective theory? Often, in sophisticated business transactions, such as corporate mergers and asset acquisitions, the deal will entail several individual points of agreement that cannot be arrived at simultaneously, but which, together, may be critical to the willingness of one or both of the parties to proceed with the transaction. Assume you represent one of these parties. Once agreement in principle has been reached on some but less than all of the deal points, how would you propose to protect your client's interests? We will consider this question in greater detail in Section 5.E of this chapter.

As we saw in *Lucy* and *Mason*, the law does not require, as a condition of enforceability, that a promise be accompanied by an express statement of the promisor acknowledging her intention to be legally bound by her promise. Just the opposite is generally true, however, in the context of promises made in a social or familial setting. Why is this the case?

Suppose one of your new classmates invites you out to dinner, "Dutch treat," promising an evening of good food and good fellowship, but then reneges. Do you have a valid claim for breach of promise? If not, why not? If so, what are your damages? Does your answer (or perhaps your inability to fashion a satisfactory answer) to the last question begin to reveal some of the reasons for the presumption against the enforceability of social and familial contracts? Would it change your answer if your new classmate had said: "I intend this to be a legally enforceable promise? If not, what is it about this relationship as a matter of policy, as distinguished say from an arms-length promise to sell particular goods, that makes the promise unenforceable?

Notwithstanding the law's bias against treating promises among family members as enforceable obligations, in recent years, courts have begun to enforce promises between non-married cohabitants even in the absence of an express statement of the promisor's intent that the promise should be regarded as creating a legally enforceable obligation. For example, in the famous case of *Marvin v. Marvin*, 18 Cal.3d 660, 134 Cal.Rptr. 815, 557 P.2d 106 (1976), the court enforced an oral promise made by actor Lee Marvin (of *Cat Ballou* and *The Dirty Dozen* fame) to his cohabitant of seven years, Michelle Marvin, that they would share equally any property acquired during the course of their relationship. Can you distinguish these cases from other kinds of social and domestic promises where there is a general presumption of non-enforceability unless the parties manifest an express intention that legal consequences should attach to a breach of promise?

Professor Melanie Leslie has argued that the traditional distinction drawn in contract law between "self-interested" market-activity and "altruistic" family relations is misguided. *See* Leslie, *Enforcing Family Promises: Reliance, Reciprocity, and Relational Contract,* 77 N.C. L. REV. 551 (1999). She maintains that while personal considerations frequently prevent parties in family and personal situations from casting their understandings in bargain terms, "the ability to make gratuitous transfers, and, more importantly, to promise to make such transfers, is a tool that the donor uses to obtain desired intangible 'goods' and 'services' for which there is no comparable market substitute." *Id.* at 568–69. If this is so, should the law's bias against enforcing family promises be reconsidered? Are there other considerations, beyond intention, that make enforcement problematic?

PROBLEMS ON MUTUAL ASSENT

1. Ponoroff offers to sell his car to Epstein for $20,000, but Ponoroff actually misspoke. He meant to say $22,000. Before Ponoroff could correct the error, Epstein promptly accepted. Who bears the risk of Ponoroff's error? What if Epstein was aware that Ponoroff had misspoken when Ponoroff offered the car for $20,000? Would it make a difference if Ponoroff had instead erroneously first said he would sell Epstein the car for $2,000? What additional facts would you like to know before giving an answer?

2. Markell had a written employment contract with Epstein's Construction Co. which expired on December 15. Before the agreement expired, Markell had tried without success to arrange a meeting with the president of the company, Epstein, to discuss renewal of his contract. Two days before Christmas, at the height of Epstein's busy season, Markell finally met with Epstein and advised him that unless satisfactory arrangements for a new one-year contract were worked out he would have no choice but to quit on the spot and seek another job. Epstein replied: "Go ahead, you're all right; get your men out and don't let that worry you." Markell assumed this meant that his contract was renewed for another year and, therefore, did not seek alternative employment. However, on March 1 of the next year, Epstein advised Markell that Markell's position was being terminated and that, in two weeks, he would be let go by the company. Markell sued for breach of contract claiming that a contract for an additional year was created during the course of the conversation on the previous December 23. At trial, Epstein testified that he had no recollection of ever making the "you're all right" statement and that, in any event, he was in a hurry during this conversation and had no intention at that point to renew the contract. Instead, his intent was to defer the issue until after the busy season. The trial judge instructed the jury that in order to return a verdict for Markell "you must find not only that the conversation occurred as Markell claimed, but that both parties intended by that conversation to contract with each other for Markell's employment for an additional year on the same terms as his prior agreement." The jury returned a verdict for Epstein. Markell has now appealed, claiming that

the trial court erred by giving the jury this instruction. You are a law clerk to the court of appeals judge who has been assigned to write the opinion on appeal. The judge has asked you to advise her as to how she should rule in this case and why. What will you tell her?

---

2. OFFER

We observed in Section 1 that the courts employ objective theory in deciding whether or not the parties assented to be bound. An objective manifestation of assent can occur in numerous ways. As a practical matter, in most instances, assent occurs simply by mutual concurrence and understanding of the parties. For example, two people are negotiating and at some point in these negotiations one says to the other, "Do we have a deal"? The other responds, "Yes, we have a deal." It is not necessary to determine who made the "offer" and, in fact, it may not even be possible to identify who made the "offer." *See* Shawn J. Bayern, *Offer and Acceptance in Modern Contract Law: A Needless Concept,* 103 CAL. L. REV. 67 (2015). Professor Bayern points out that most modern contracts are actually formed without an identifiable "offer" and "acceptance."

In first year Contracts classes, however, the method generally used to illustrate mutual assent is the more formalized, two-step process consisting of an *offer* and an *acceptance*. And, so, it becomes necessary to determine who made the "offer," and, in order to do so, to learn exactly what the heck an "offer" is in the first place.

As you have perhaps already figured out, an offer is the manifestation of assent by the "offeror" that essentially says to the offeree, "I commit to a deal on these terms. You now have the power to seal the deal with your assent to these terms." Look (hopefully, again) at what the *Restatement (Second) of Contracts* § 24 says about an "offer":

> An offer is the manifestation of willingness to enter into a bargain, so made as to justify another person in understanding that his assent to that bargain is invited and will conclude it.

Consider the *Restatement's* statement about offers as you read the cases in this section.

QUESTION BEFORE THE CASE

As you read this decision, ask yourself what is the proper legal characterization of each communication in the case; *e.g.*, was this letter an offer, an acceptance, or even something else entirely?

LONERGAN V. SCOLNICK

Court of Appeal of California
129 Cal.App.2d 179, 276 P.2d 8 (1954)

BARNARD, J.

The complaint alleged that on April 15, 1952, the parties entered into a contract whereby the defendant agreed to sell, and plaintiff agreed to buy a 40-acre tract of land for $2,500; that this was a fair, just and reasonable value of the property; that on April 28, 1952, the defendant repudiated the contract and refused to deliver a deed; that on April 28, 1952, the property was worth $6,081; and that plaintiff has been damaged in the amount of $3,581. The answer denied that any contract had been entered into, or that anything was due to the plaintiff.

By stipulation, the issue of whether or not a contract was entered into between the parties was first tried, reserving the other issues for a further trial if that became necessary. The issue as to the existence of a contract was submitted upon an agreed statement, including certain letters between the parties, without the introduction of other evidence.

The stipulated facts are as follows: During March, 1952, the defendant placed an ad in a Los Angeles paper reading, so far as material here, "Joshua Tree vic. 40 acres, * * * need cash, will sacrifice." In response to an inquiry resulting from this ad the defendant, who lived in New York, wrote a letter to the plaintiff dated March 26, briefly describing the property, giving directions as to how to get there, stating that his rock-bottom price was $2,500 cash, and further stating that "This is a form letter." On April 7, the plaintiff wrote a letter to the defendant saying that he was not sure he had found the property, asking for its legal description, asking whether the land was all level or whether it included certain jutting rock hills, and suggesting a certain bank as escrow agent "should I desire to purchase the land." On April 8, the defendant wrote to the plaintiff saying "From your description you have found the property"; that this bank "is O.K. for escrow agent"; that the land was fairly level; giving the legal description; and then saying, "If you are really interested, you will have to decide fast, as I expect to have a buyer in the next week or so." On April 12, the defendant sold the property to a third party for $2,500. The plaintiff received defendant's letter of April 8 on April 14. On April 15 he wrote to the defendant thanking him for his letter "confirming that I was on the right land," stating that he would immediately proceed to have the escrow opened and would deposit $2,500 therein "in conformity with your offer," and asking the defendant to forward a deed with his instructions to the escrow agent. On April 17, 1952, the plaintiff started an escrow and placed in the hands of the escrow agent $100, agreeing to furnish an additional $2,400 at an unspecified time, with the provision that if the escrow was not closed by May 15, 1952, it should be completed as soon thereafter as possible unless a written demand for a return of the money or instruments was made by either party after that date. It was further stipulated that the plaintiff was ready and willing at all times to deposit the $2,400.

The matter was submitted on June 11, 1953. On July 10, 1953, the judge filed a memorandum opinion stating that it was his opinion that the letter of April 8, 1952, when considered with the previous correspondence, constituted an offer of sale which offer was, however, qualified and conditioned upon prompt acceptance by the plaintiff; that in spite of the condition thus imposed, the plaintiff delayed more than a week before notifying the defendant of his acceptance; and that since the plaintiff was aware of the necessity of promptly communicating his acceptance to the defendant his delay was not the prompt action required by the terms of the offer. Findings of fact were filed on October 2, 1953, finding that each and all of the statements in the agreed statement are true, and that all allegations to the contrary in the complaint are untrue. As conclusions of law, it was found that the plaintiff and defendant did not enter into a contract as alleged in the complaint or otherwise, and that the defendant is entitled to judgment against the plaintiff. Judgment was entered accordingly, from which the plaintiff has appealed.

The appellant contends that the judgment is contrary to the evidence and to the law since the facts, as found, do not support the conclusions of law upon which the judgment is based. It is argued that there is no conflict in the evidence, and this court is not bound by the trial court's construction of the written instruments involved; that the evidence conclusively shows that an offer was made to the plaintiff by the defendant, which offer was accepted by the mailing of plaintiff's letter of April 15; that upon receipt of defendant's letter of April 8 the plaintiff had a reasonable time within which to accept the offer that had been made; that by his letter of April 15 and his starting of an escrow the plaintiff accepted said offer; and that the agreed statement of facts establishes that a valid contract was entered into between the parties. In his briefs the appellant assumes that an offer was made by the defendant, and confined his argument to contending that the evidence shows that he accepted that offer within a reasonable time.

There can be no contract unless the minds of the parties have met and mutually agreed upon some specific thing. This is usually evidenced by one party making an offer which is accepted by the other party. Section 25 of the Restatement of the Law on Contracts reads:

"If from a promise, or manifestation of intention, or from the circumstances existing at the time, the person to whom the promise or manifestation is addressed knows or has reason to know that the person making it does not intend it as an expression of his fixed purpose until he has given a further expression of assent, he has not made an offer."

The language used in *Niles v. Hancock*, 140 Cal. 157 [73 P. 840], "It is also clear from the correspondence that it was the intention of the defendant that the negotiations between him and the plaintiff were purely preliminary," is applicable here. The correspondence here indicates an intention on the part of the defendant to find out whether the plaintiff was interested, rather than an intention to make a definite offer to the plaintiff. The language used by the defendant in his letters of March 26 and April 8 rather clearly discloses that they were not intended as an expression of fixed purpose to make a definite offer, and was sufficient to advise the plaintiff that some further expression of assent on the part of the defendant was necessary.

The advertisement in the paper was a mere request for an offer. The letter of March 26 contains no definite offer, and clearly states that it is a form letter. It merely gives further particulars, in clarification of the advertisement, and tells the plaintiff how to locate the property if he was interested in looking into the matter. The letter of April 8 added nothing in the way of a definite offer. It merely answered some questions asked by the plaintiff, and stated that if the plaintiff was really interested he would have to act fast. The statement that he expected to have a buyer in the next week or so indicated that the defendant intended to sell to the first-comer, and was reserving the right to do so. From this statement, alone, the plaintiff knew or should have known that he was not being given time in which to accept an offer that was being made, but that some further assent on the part of the defendant was required. Under the language used the plaintiff was not being given a right to act within a reasonable time after receiving the letter; he was plainly told that the defendant intended to sell to another, if possible, and warned that he would have to act fast if he was interested in buying the land.

Regardless of any opinion previously expressed, the court found that no contract had been entered into between these parties, and we are in accord with the court's conclusion on that controlling issue. The court's construction of the letters involved was a reasonable one, and we think the most reasonable one, even if it be assumed that another construction was possible.

The judgment is affirmed.

QUESTIONS

1. Questions about the facts of this case

   1.1. What is the specific communication that the plaintiff points to as the defendant's offer to which the plaintiff contends his April 15 communication accepted?

1.2. Remember that on April 17 the plaintiff started an escrow and placed $100 in the hands of the escrow agent. Was that fact significant to either the trial court or the court of appeals? [By the way, just what is an "escrow" anyway?]

2. Questions about the law

2.1. The court of appeals affirms the judgment of the trial court in *Lonergan*. Nevertheless, did the two courts take a different legal journey in reaching the same destination?

2.2. If the plaintiff's letter of April 15 was not an acceptance, what was it?

2.3. Quoting from the appellate court opinion in *Lonergan:* "There can be no contract unless the minds of the parties have met and mutually agreed upon some specific thing." Immediately after making that statement, the court went on to quote the following from Section 25 of the first *Restatement of Contracts*:

> A manifestation of willingness to enter into a bargain is not an offer if the person to whom it is addressed knows or has reason to know that the person making it does not intend to conclude a bargain until he has made a further manifestation of assent.

Notice the *Restatement's* (and, in a sense, the court of appeals') phrase "reason to know." Do we know whether the plaintiff actually knew that the defendant was not making an offer with the April 8th letter? Do we know whether the plaintiff had "reason to know"?

3. **You Be the Lawyer!**

If, upon receiving the Scolnick's letter of April 8 on April 14, Lonergan had called you before sending his reply, how you would you have counseled him to proceed in order to assure that he would be able to enforce an agreement with Scolnick to purchase the property?

QUESTIONS BEFORE THE CASE

1. Can you to articulate the difference between a price quote and an offer?
2. Are the two mutually exclusive?

J.D. FIELDS & COMPANY, INC. v. UNITED STATES STEEL INTERNATIONAL, INC.

United States Court of Appeals, Fifth Circuit*
426 Fed.Appx. 271 (2011)

Opinion

AYCOCK, DISTRICT JUDGE:

J.D. Fields & Company, Inc. appeals the district court's grant of summary judgment in favor of United States Steel International. The district court held that two separate price quotations sent from United States Steel International could not be construed as offers as a matter of law. * * *

Background

United States Steel International ("USSI") sells and markets steel products manufactured at domestic steel mills for international sale. J.D. Fields is a steel-product distributor, serving as a conduit between manufacturers and end-users. On at least thirty occasions from 2003 through 2008, J.D. Fields entered into contracts with USSI to purchase steel products. USSI produced copied documents pertaining to its prior transactions with J.D. Fields. These documents appear to show that, on most occasions, USSI and J.D. Fields followed a general course of dealing. This course of dealing appears to be as follows: (1) J.D. Fields requested a price quotation from USSI, either orally or via email; (2) USSI sent J.D. Fields a price quotation; (3) J.D. Fields sent USSI a purchase order; (4) USSI sent J.D. Fields an order acknowledgment; and (5) USSI shipped the product and sent J.D. Fields an invoice. J.D. Fields contests this general course of dealing, stating that USSI had an "inconsistent pattern of delivering its acknowledgments."

The current dispute arises out of two specific transactions stemming from a series of emails. In both transactions, it is undisputed that while USSI sent J.D. Fields a price quotation and J.D. Fields responded with a purchase order, USSI never transmitted an order acknowledgment. USSI did, however, correspond with J.D. Fields several times regarding the orders. J.D. Fields contends that the series of emails created two separate binding contracts. Specifically, J.D. Fields asserts that USSI's price quotations constituted "offers," which J.D. Fields accepted by submitting purchase orders.

* "Fed.Appx." stands for Federal Appendix which contains judicial opinions of the U.S. courts of appeals that have not been expressly selected for publication. Sometimes referred to as "unpublished opinions," these decisions are of limited precedential value. They can, however, be instructional for law students (Eds.).

A. First Alleged Contract: Purchase Order 45850

On February 6, 2008, Guillermo Moll, a J.D. Fields representative, sent an email to Kris Blackman, a USSI representative, requesting "price and delivery options" for 800 feet of a type of seamless carbon steel pipe. After a short email exchange between the parties specifying the destination of the product, Blackman responded by email on the same day providing Moll with a price quote. Blackman's email stated as follows:

> I can offer:
>
> 800 FT–16″ OD x 0.844″ WT (SCH80) $2133/mt ($132.30/ft)
>
> Subject to heat lot accumulation 100 tons
>
> Net 30 days
>
> Quote valid for 14 days
>
> Delivery: Rolling end of March

Moll then, on the same day, requested a modification in the steel specifications, asking Blackman if USSI could "roll it to API 5L–X56/60 PSL–2" since the customer had sent Moll a new note. Blackman responded with a new price quote of "$2205/mt ($136.74/ft)."

Five days later, on February 11, 2008, Moll faxed Blackman Purchase Order ("P.O.") 45850 for 880 feet at a unit price of $136.74 per foot. It is entirely undisputed that 880 feet of the specified type of pipe requires approximately 60 tons of steel. It is also undisputed that "[s]ubject to heat lot accumulation 100 tons" means that the steel mill will only roll the steel in a batch of at least 100 tons.

On February 14, 2008, Moll emailed Blackman regarding this order, stating "Please advise when is the expected rolling for the subject PO." Blackman responded the same day as follows:

> The mill has gotten back with me . . . this material is subject to heat lot of 100 tons and has to be rolled. This material is subject to roll at the mill the first part of April. Please let me know if we can proceed with the order of 100 tons and if so I will need a revised PO.

It is undisputed that Moll never sent a revised purchase order. It is also undisputed that USSI never remitted an order acknowledgment regarding P.O. 45850.

On March 26, 2008, another email exchange took place between the parties regarding P.O. 45850. Moll initially contacted Blackman stating:

> Per our conversation of last Wednesday pertaining the subject purchase order, could you please provide us with an update on the heat-lot accumulation and where this order stands, including the

> increase? Also, please send to us an order confirmation form [sic] the mill.

Blackman responded the same day as follows:

> I have ran [sic] my traps and have not found any other order to piggy back on, so that means 100 tons minimum and I can not [sic] deliver this until August 08 and is subject to price increase. Let me know how you would like to proceed.

Moll then responded:

> Thank you for your reply; unfortunately, we cannot keep our overseas customers waiting indefinitely, we have to give them a more accurate answer or we risk loosing [sic] them. Therefore, we are looking into increasing our order to the point you have the minimum 100 tons; have you received any other orders for this size? Please advise when we can have the material rolled considering that we will reach the 100 tons.

As the district court noted, Moll alleged in his deposition testimony that he also discussed this order with Blackman on the phone and stated that, "if need be, we will go up to 100 tons." However, Moll never sent a revised purchase order for an order of 100 tons or greater.

On April 24, 2008, Moll sent another email to Tom Verellen, Blackman's supervisor at USSI, requesting a status update and order acknowledgment regarding purchase orders 45850 and 46110. * * *

Verellen responded that Blackman would respond to the email when he returned to town the following week. Blackman's follow-up email to Moll, sent on May 30, 2008, stated:

> I will attempt to address the issues below. As I stated in our last phone conversation about 4–5 weeks ago concerning these PO's, we were in the middle of a price increase and not taking orders at that time. Both of these PO's fell into these categories.
>
> We still are currently not taking orders because 1 our mills are full and 2 we have consumed all of our tons for export. I apologize for the inconvenience or misunderstanding but I recall stating in our conversation on the phone that these orders were never excepted [sic] nor acknowledged therefore, we do not have these orders in our system and do not have the material available at this time.

Moll responded:

> The fact that these Purchase orders were sent to U.S. Steel in early February and early March, did not put them in the same group of our conversation of 4 to 5 weeks ago and my follow-up emails. What really worries me, is that we commited [sic] to

> customers based on U.S. Steel's word of profunction [sic] for June 2008 and proceeded to send you purchase orders and increase our order to meet minimums, as well; now we will have to tell them that their orders were never accepted?

Blackman in turn responded that, after checking his records, he confirmed that USSI was indeed not taking orders in February and March. Blackman stated that USSI could not accept the orders, as there was no material available to offer. Moll responded that Blackman's previous emails "pointed towards [USSI's] acceptance" of the orders. To this, Blackman responded that the "fact of the matter is these orders were never acknowledged." Blackman further concluded that he had "given [ ] valid information why these orders were not accepted," and that USSI would "not be accepting orders from J.D. Fields from this point forward."

B. Second Alleged Contract: Purchase Order 46110

On March 5, 2008, Moll emailed Blackman stating that he had "another inquiry for [him]" regarding two types of seamless pipe. Moll requested Blackman provide him with a quote on the two types of pipe to be delivered FOB Port of Houston:

> Please quote the following materials from a LATAM request: 3260 ft 16″ x . 500 wall, SMLS, API5LX52 PSL2, 40 ft max., NACE MRO 175 certified 2890 ft 12″ x .500 wall, SMLS, API5LX52 PSL2, 40 ft max., NACE MRO 175 certified

Blackman responded to this email on March 13, 2008:

> We can offer
>
> $2000/nt for the 12″
>
> $2040/nt for the 16″
>
> June or sooner
>
> FCA Houston
>
> Net 30 days
>
> Valid for 14 days

On March 18, 2008, Moll faxed Blackman P.O. 46110, ordering 3,260 feet of a specified sixteen-inch pipe at $2,040 per net ton ($84.507 per foot) and 2,890 feet of a specified twelve-inch pipe at $2,000 per net ton ($136.740 per foot). It is entirely unclear what happened to P.O. 46110 after Moll faxed it to USSI. In his deposition testimony, Blackman stated that the order may have "fallen through the cracks," and thus was never processed at USSI.

* * *

Discussion

A. Contract Formation

The first issue on appeal is whether the district court properly granted summary judgment on J.D. Fields' breach of contract claims when it concluded that USSI's price quotations could not reasonably be construed as offers as a matter of law. Because this case is before the Court on diversity jurisdiction, state law supplies the applicable substantive authority. *Erie R.R. Co. v. Tompkins,* 304 U.S. 64, 78–79, 58 S.Ct. 817, 82 L.Ed. 1188 (1938). " 'When parties enter into a contract for the sale of goods, the Uniform Commercial Code ("UCC") controls the conduct of the parties.' " *Coburn Supply Co., Inc. v. Kohler Co.,* 342 F.3d 372, 375 (5th Cir.2003) (quoting *Glenn Thurman, Inc. v. Moore Constr., Inc.,* 942 S.W.2d 768, 771 (Tex.App.1997)). There is no dispute that Article 2 of the UCC governs this transaction, as the contracts at issue concern the sale of steel. * * * Where the UCC applies, it displaces all common law rules of law regarding breach of contract and substitutes instead those rules of law and procedures set forth in the UCC. However, common law principles of law and equity continue to supplement its provisions. *Crest Ridge Constr. Group, Inc. v. Newcourt Inc.,* 78 F.3d 146, 152 (5th Cir.1996).

In Texas, "the essential elements of a breach of contract claim are: (1) the existence of a valid contract; (2) performance or tendered performance by the plaintiff; (3) breach of the contract by the defendant, and (4) damages sustained by the plaintiff as a result of the breach." *Mullins v. TestAmerica, Inc.,* 564 F.3d 386, 418 (5th Cir.2009). The central dispute in this action revolves around the first element: whether the parties ever formed a valid contract as to Purchase Order 45850 and Purchase Order 46110. "Contract formation [ ] hinge[s] on the existence of an acceptable offer. The UCC, however, provides no guidance as to what an 'offer' is." Although the UCC does not define the term "offer," we have held that "[a]n offer is an act that leads the offeree reasonably to believe that assent (i.e., acceptance) will conclude the deal." *Axelson, Inc. v. McEvoy-Willis,* 7 F.3d 1230, 1232 (5th Cir.1993).

A contract for the sale of goods may be made in any manner sufficient to show agreement, including conduct by both parties which recognizes the existence of such a contract [U.C.C. § 2–204(1)]. Generally, a price quotation, such as one appearing in a brochure or on a flyer, is not considered an offer; rather, it is typically viewed as an invitation to offer. Despite this general rule, a price quotation, if detailed enough, can constitute an offer capable of acceptance. "However, to do so, it must reasonably appear from the price quote that assent to the quote is all that is needed to ripen the offer into a contract." *Crest Ridge,* 78 F.3d at 152 (Benavides, J., concurring) (citations omitted).

Contract formation is a question of fact under Texas law. Summary judgment, however, is proper if "there is no genuine dispute as to any material fact and the movant is entitled to judgment as a matter of law." FED. R. CIV. P. 56(A). All fact questions must be viewed in the light most favorable to the nonmovant.

Purchase Order 45850

The first emailed price quotation was sent from USSI to J.D. Fields on February 6, 2008. The price quotation contained the following: (i) a specified price per ton, (ii) specified payment term, (iii) a general delivery time, (iv) a validity period ("valid for 14 days"), (v) specified rolling/manufacturing time frame, (vi) product specification, (vii) the quantity (800 feet), and (viii) that the price quote was subject to heat lot accumulation of 100 tons. The price quote did not contain the specific shipping location, the mode of shipping, or the legal terms and conditions. Five days after receiving this price quote, J.D. Fields faxed USSI Purchase Order 45850.

Purchase Order 45850 contained a different quantity than the initial inquiry. That is, the purchase order requested 880 feet, whereas the price quote was for 800 feet. Importantly, neither a quantity of 800 feet nor 880 feet was enough to meet the 100-ton minimum expressly required by USSI. J.D. Fields, while conceding that its quantity specifications failed to meet this 100-ton minimum, asserts that it told USSI it would increase its order. On March 26, 2008, J.D. Fields' representative, Guillermo Moll, emailed USSI representative, Kris Blackman, stating that J.D. Fields was "looking into increasing [the] order to . . . the minimum 100 tons." Similarly, Moll alleged in his deposition testimony that he also discussed this order with Blackman on the phone and stated that, "if need be, we will go up to 100 tons."

The exchange between Moll and Blackman at most establishes that J.D. Fields was considering—or "looking into"—increasing its order to reach the 100-ton minimum. There is no evidence that J.D. Fields in fact did increase its order or that the parties ever reached an agreement as to a quantity term meeting the 100-ton minimum. The quote contained a 14-day validity period. By the time the March 2008 exchange between Moll and Blackman occurred, the validity period for the price quote had long lapsed. Further, USSI representative Blackman repeatedly informed Moll that it would need a revised purchase order. J.D. Fields concedes that it never submitted such a revised order. As such, the district court did not err in finding that it was unreasonable as a matter of law for J.D. Fields to believe that the price quotation was an offer. Thus, we affirm the grant of summary judgment as to Purchase Order 45850.

Purchase Order 46110

Purchase Order 46110 falls on different footing than Purchase Order 45850. While the general rule is that a price quote is not an offer, we have held that a price quote, if detailed enough, can constitute an offer capable of acceptance. *See, e.g., Axelson,* 7 F.3d at 1232–33. In *Tubelite, Inc. v. Risica & Sons, Inc.,* 819 S.W.2d 801, 803 (Tex.1991), the Texas Supreme Court found a price quotation sufficiently detailed to constitute an offer under the Texas UCC when the quote stated it was valid for 60 days, was signed by Tubelite's authorized agent, and did not limit acceptance to a specified manner. Further, in affirming the lower court in *Delta Brands v. Wysong & Miles Company,* we found that the characteristics of the price quote at issue "compel[ed] the conclusion that it qualifi[ed] as a firm offer under the Texas UCC and Texas precedent." 203 F.3d 828, 1999 WL 1240802, at *1; *see also Axelson,* 7 F.3d at 1233 (noting that a price quote containing material terms could be construed as an offer capable of acceptance by the buyer). * * *

Here, the price quotation preceding Purchase Order 46110 was considerably detailed. It was also only transmitted to J.D. Fields. *See* RESTATEMENT (SECOND) OF CONTRACTS § 26, cmt c (stating that a "relevant factor" for "determining whether an offer is made" is the "number of persons to whom a communication is addressed"). The quote contained the following information: (i) a specified price, (ii) delivery time, (iii) a validity period ("valid for 14 days"), (iv) specified rolling/manufacturing time frame, (v) product specification, (vi) a reference to the quantity listed in J.D. Fields' email, and (vii) a delivery location. Further, unlike some of the previous price quotations sent to J.D. Fields from USSI, this particular price quote was devoid of any language which would condition the formation of a contract on some further step, such as approval by the mill, corporate headquarters, or subject to prior sell. *See Crest Ridge,* 78 F.3d at 152 (Benavides, J., concurring) ("The inclusion of [a] condition [can] preclude[ ] [a] price quote from operating as an offer."). Specifically, J.D. Fields provided evidence that previous emailed price quotes were explicitly conditioned on "mill and steel availability" or were "subject to prior sale." Moll testified via sworn affidavit that it was his understanding that when a quote from USSI gave a validity period without further condition on mill approval, it meant that the representative presenting the quote had already checked with the mill regarding the availability of the steel needed to meet the request. * * * J.D. Fields transmitted Purchase Order 46110 five days after receiving USSI's price quote, and the purchase order mirrored the terms contained in the price quotation.

While the district court's conclusions regarding industry custom and course of dealing in this case are relevant to the issue of reasonableness, the UCC never informs that industry custom and course of dealing are alone determinative of the issue of contract *formation. See, e.g., Crest*

Ridge, 78 F.3d at 152 (Benavides, J., concurring) ("Industry custom can fill in missing terms of a contract or determine the meaning of an agreement"); *Audio Visual Assocs., Inc. v. Sharp Elecs. Corp.,* 210 F.3d 254 260 (4th Cir.2000) (noting that the UCC "does not suggest that course of dealing may in and of itself provide the basis for a contract. Rather, it supplies a mode of interpretation for construing *existing* contracts.") (emphasis in original). As such, industry custom and course of dealing do not compel the conclusion that a price quotation cannot be construed as an offer as a matter of law.

Contract formation is a question of fact under Texas law and, here, the price quotation was detailed, transmitted only to J.D. Fields, void of any conditional language, sent in direct response to an inquiry from J.D. Fields' representative, did not limit acceptance to a specified manner, and contained a validity period. Viewing the evidence in the light most favorable to the nonmovant, there are questions of material fact present as to whether J.D. Fields could reasonably construe the price quote relating to Purchase Order 46110 as an offer. At the summary judgment stage, we may not weigh or decide factual disputes or make credibility determinations. Although we find that summary judgment was not appropriate, we express no view on the ultimate merits of J.D. Fields' breach of contract claim. Accordingly, the grant of summary judgment as to Purchase Order 46110 is reversed and remanded for further proceedings as the district court may deem appropriate.

* * *

QUESTIONS AND NOTES

1. Questions about the facts of this case

   1.1. What were the facts that distinguished the circumstances surrounding Purchase Order 45880 from the circumstances surrounding Purchase Order 46110 in terms of the legal question of contract formation?

   1.2. Is it the case that U.S. Steel's fax of March 13, 2008, which resulted in Purchase Order 46110, was not a price quote?

2. Questions about the law

   2.1. Does Article 2 follow objective theory in terms of determining when a communication constitutes an offer?

   2.2. Why didn't the drafters of Article 2 define the term "offer"? Do you think maybe they just forgot? Where do we look to determine the meaning of a term that is not defined in the UCC? How does the answer to this question make the Uniform Commercial *Code* different from a civil code? How the heck are you supposed to know the answer to that question? We guess you could Google it, yes?

2.3. Why did the district court in *J.D. Fields* find that both purchase orders could not as a matter of law be construed as offers?

2.4. According to the court of appeals, what is the relevance of industry practices and course of dealing in contract formation?

3. Notes

3.1. In *Nebraska Seed Co. v. Harsh*, 98 Neb. 89, 152 N.W. 310 (1915), the defendant sent a letter to plaintiff in which he stated he had about 1,800 bushels of millet seed, of which he was mailing plaintiff a sample. He further stated: "I want $2.25 per cwt. for this seed f.o.b. Lowell." Upon receipt of the letter the plaintiff replied in part: "Sample and letter received. Accept your offer." The defendant refused to deliver and the plaintiff brought suit for such non-delivery. The court ruled that the defendant's letter was not an offer but was an invitation for offers, quoting in part:

> If a proposal is nothing more than an invitation to the person to whom it is made to make an offer to the proposer, it is not such an offer as can be turned into an agreement by acceptance. Proposals of this kind, although made to definite persons and not to the public generally, are merely invitations to trade; they go no further than what occurs when one asks another what he will give or take for certain goods. Such inquiries may lead to bargains, but do not make them. They ask for offers which the proposer has a right to accept or reject as he pleases.

Id. at 91, 152 N.W. at 311. Some decisions suggest that the reason for the general rule that a price quote is not an offer is that the price quote lacks sufficient words of commitment, such as "agree" or "offer." *See Courteen Seed v. Abraham,* 129 Or. 427, 275 P. 684 (1929). Is that a sufficient explanation? How would the court in *J.D. Fields* answer that question? Identify the interests of the merchant who makes the quote and those of the prospective buyer who reads it, and see if that helps to sharpen the focus.

3.2. Should it make a difference whether the quote is in response to a particular inquiry? How important are the contextual circumstances in which the price quote is made? What other problems do you see with treating a price quotation as an offer? What if the quote is not made to the buyer but to the public at large? Does that help or hinder the argument for making the case that the price quote is an offer? Perhaps the next case will shed some light for you on this last question.

4. **You Be the Lawyer!**

   How would might you modified Blackmun's communication of March 13, 2008, so that USSI would not be locked into those terms should Fields fire back an acceptance? Now, that was actually easy, but what are the business considerations that need to be taken into account in deciding if those changes should be made? Who will make that decision?

NOTE ON U.C.C. ARTICLE 2

Because *J.D. Fields* involved a transaction in goods, Article 2 of the Uniform Commercial Code applies. Section 2–204 is the Article 2 provision that addresses the formation of a contract. It is plain to see from that section that the U.C.C. takes a fairly liberal approach to contract formation, recognizing, as noted in the *J.D. Fields* opinion, that any manner of assent as sufficient to show agreement of the parties. In turn, U.C.C. § 1–201(3) defines the term *agreement* broadly to mean the parties *bargain in fact,* derived not only from what was spoken between them but also "from other circumstances, including course of dealing or usage of trade or course of performance."

The inclusion of all three of those concepts as part of the agreement of the parties in fact is consistent with the Code's general philosophy of bringing the law into line with prevailing commercial reality and expectation. Judge Posner put it this way: "The Uniform Commercial Code, its draftsmen mindful of the haste and sloppiness, and disregard for lawyerly niceties, that characterize commercial dealing, tolerates a good deal of incompleteness and even contradiction in offer and acceptance." *Architectural Metal Systems v. Consolidated Systems*, 58 F.3d 1227, 1230 (7th Cir. 1995). The test for an offer, according to Judge Posner, is whether it induces a reasonable belief in the recipient that his acceptance is all that is necessary to seal the deal. Thus, the statement "I would like to buy your hamster" is not intended to empower the recipient of that solicitation to reply: "My price is $1 million. We have a contract." *Id.* at 1229.

Article 2's incorporation of course of dealing, usage of trade, and course of performance into the parties' bargain-in-fact means that if a party to a commercial transaction does *not* want a particular prior course of dealing or trade usage to become part of a new contract she must affirmatively say so in the new agreement. In a manner of speaking, this reverses the usual presumption that the terms of the contract consist only of those matters which the parties deliberately chose to *include*. Does this violate the principle of freedom of contract or *freedom from contract*? How did course of dealing and usage of trade evidence influence the court in *J.D. Fields*? Moreover, the definitions of "agreement" and "contract" in, respectively, § 1–201(b)(3) & (12) make clear that the object is to ferret out as precisely as possible what the parties actually agreed to, whether discovered in the words they used or inferred from other circumstances.

QUESTIONS BEFORE THE CASE

1. As you read this case, can you articulate the distinction between an advertisement and an offer?
2. Are the two mutually exclusive?

KEARNEY V. EQUILON ENTERPRISES, LLC

U. S. District Court for the District of Oregon
65 F.Supp.3d 1033 (2014)

OPINION & ORDER

HERNANDEZ, DISTRICT JUDGE:

Plaintiffs bring a proposed class action with a nationwide breach of contract claim, and substantially similar state subclass claims based on state unlawful trade practice statutes. Defendant moves to dismiss for failure to state a claim. I deny Defendant's motion regarding Plaintiffs' nationwide breach of contract claim. * * *

BACKGROUND

At the heart of Plaintiffs' claims is an advertisement allegedly displayed by Defendant at Shell-brand service stations. Plaintiffs allege the advertisement looked like this:

This advertisement was part of Defendant's "Ski Free" promotion. Under this promotion, after individuals purchased ten gallons of fuel and requested a voucher for a free lift ticket, they received a voucher with their purchase receipt. This voucher could not be exchanged directly for a free lift ticket, but rather was a "two for one" coupon that allowed the individual to obtain a free lift ticket only after purchasing a lift ticket at full price at a participating ski resort. Moreover, the voucher contained various other restrictions.

Plaintiffs assert that Defendant's advertisement created a contract, the terms of which entitled Plaintiffs to a free ski resort lift ticket in exchange for buying ten gallons of gas at a participating Shell station. Plaintiffs argue Defendant breached the terms of the contract, and also violated state unlawful trade practices, when Defendant failed to provide a voucher that could be directly exchanged for a free lift ticket at a participating resort, but instead provided a "two for one" voucher that required the purchase of a second lift ticket in order to receive a "free" lift ticket.

STANDARDS

A motion to dismiss for failure to state a claim under Federal Rule of Civil Procedure 12(b)(6) may be granted only when there is no cognizable legal theory to support the claim, or when the complaint lacks sufficient factual allegations to state a facially plausible claim for relief. In evaluating the sufficiency of a complaint's factual allegations, the court must accept all material facts alleged in the complaint as true and construe them in the light most favorable to the plaintiff. * * *

DISCUSSION

I. Breach of Contract

Defendant contends that any offer proposed by the "Ski Free" advertisement lacks specificity, and since "[a] contract requires a clear and unequivocal acceptance of a certain and definite offer" the advertisement cannot constitute an offer. Defendant argues that without necessary details—and the specificity these details would convey—there can be no offer, no acceptance, and no meeting of the minds, all of which are necessary for a contract to exist.

Overall, "[t]he general rule is that an advertisement does not constitute an offer." *Leonard v. Pepsico, Inc.,* 88 F.Supp.2d 116, 122 (S.D.N.Y.1999), *aff'd,* 210 F.3d 88 (2d Cir.2000); *see also Sateriale v. R.J. Reynolds Tobacco Co.,* 697 F.3d 777, 785 (9th Cir.2012). This is because "advertisements are understood to be mere requests to consider and examine and negotiate; and no one can reasonably regard them as otherwise unless the circumstances are exceptional and the words used are very plain and clear." Additionally, advertisements do not generally constitute offers due to the incompleteness of terms. Restatement (Second) of Contracts § 33 cmt. c.

However, there are exceptions to this general rule. For instance, if an advertisement is "clear, definite, and explicit, and leaves nothing open for negotiation," then the advertisement "constitutes an offer, acceptance of which will complete the contract." *Lefkowitz v. Great Minneapolis Surplus Store,* 251 Minn. 188, 86 N.W.2d 689, 691 (1957). Additionally, there is another exception to the general rule for "an offer of a reward." *Arthur Linton Corbin et al., Corbin on Contracts* § 2.4 (2012).

A. Sateriale v. R.J. Reynolds Tobacco Co.

The Ninth Circuit recently addressed when an advertisement may constitute an offer in *Sateriale,* 697 F.3d 777. *Sateriale* concerned a customer rewards program operated by R.J. Reynolds Tobacco Company that encouraged the purchase of Camel cigarettes by providing "C-Notes" along with the cigarettes. *Id.* at 782. These "C-Notes" could later be redeemed for merchandise after participants enrolled in the customer rewards program and redeemed their certificates for goods featured in a catalog. *Id.* at 783. After customers had been amassing "C-Notes" for years, R.J. Reynolds announced that it was ending the customer rewards program, and that participants had approximately six months to redeem their "C-Notes" before the program's termination. *Id.* However, when the plaintiffs attempted to redeem their "C-Notes" before the termination of the rewards program, R.J. Reynolds did not allow them to do so. *Id.* at 784. In response, the plaintiffs filed a lawsuit alleging breach of contract, promissory estoppel, and violations of two California consumer protection laws. *Id.* The district court granted defendant's motion to dismiss.

On appeal, the *Sateriale* court found that "[t]he determination of whether a particular communication constitutes an operative offer, rather than an inoperative step in the preliminary negotiation of a contract, depends upon all the surrounding circumstances." *Sateriale,* 697 F.3d at 784 (internal quotation marks omitted). Furthermore, the court explained that "the pertinent inquiry is whether the individual to whom the communication was made had reason to believe that it was intended as an offer." *Id.*

* * *

B. Whether the "Ski Free" Advertisement is an Offer in a Unilateral Contract Capable of Acceptance Through Performance

Again, the common law's general rule is that "[a]dvertisements of goods by display, sign, handbill, newspaper, radio or television are not ordinarily intended or understood as offers to sell." *Sateriale,* 697 F.3d at 785. However, there is "an exception for offers of a reward, including offers of a reward for the redemption of coupons." *Id.* at 786. This is because the common law rule "arose to address a specific problem—the potential for over—acceptance." *Id.* at 787. The ultimate question is—based on "the totality of the circumstances" surrounding the advertisement—"whether the advertiser, in clear and positive terms, promised to render performance in exchange for something requested by the advertiser, and whether the recipient of the advertisement reasonably might have concluded that by acting in accordance with the request a contract would be formed." *Id.* at 787–88.

* * * [I]n *Sateriale,* the court noted that failing to reasonably hold advertisers to what appeared to be a clearly understood offer is

"inconsistent with the reasonable expectations of consumers and [can] lead to haphazard results." *Sateriale,* 697 F.3d at 786 (citations omitted). Accordingly, the Ninth Circuit found that there was, "no question . . . that plaintiffs—in their complaint, as well as in the district court and on appeal—have consistently alleged acceptance by performance, which is the essence of a unilateral contract." *Id.* at 788 n. 4. In this case, Plaintiffs similarly allege that they "accepted Defendant's offer when they purchased ten or more gallons of fuel, and requested a Voucher for a free lift ticket."

Construing the alleged facts in the light most favorable to Plaintiffs, the *only* advertisement the consumer saw was the sign stating, "buy 10 gallons of fuel, get a voucher for a free lift ticket!". Based on this allegation, Defendant, in clear and positive terms, promised to render performance in exchange for the purchase of ten gallons of fuel. Namely, if one purchases ten gallons of fuel at a Shell Station participating in the "Ski Free" promotion, then the purchaser is rewarded with a voucher for a free lift ticket. Additionally, Plaintiff, as the recipient of the advertisement, "reasonably might have concluded that by acting in accordance with the request a contract would be formed." *Sateriale,* 697 F.3d at 787. The clear offer in the advertisement established a unilateral contract, and Plaintiffs accepted the offer through performance by purchasing ten gallons of fuel at a Shell station participating in the "Ski Free" promotion.

I emphasize the fact that my ruling is based on the allegations contained in the Amended Complaint. "Whether the plaintiffs' allegations are true has not been decided," but to deny Plaintiffs' claim at this stage of the pleadings would be premature. *Id.* at 783. Such a fact-based determination is more appropriately made at the summary judgment stage. Therefore, Defendant's motion to dismiss for failure to state a claim with regard to the national class breach of contract claim, based on the premise that the advertisement cannot constitute an offer, is denied.

* * *

IT IS SO ORDERED.

QUESTIONS, NOTES, AND CONNECTIONS

1. Questions about the facts of this case

    1.1. What were the factors that led the court to believe that the defendant's public communications constituted an offer?

    1.2. What exactly was the substance of the offer that the court found had been made by the defendant?

2. Questions about the law

2.1. Why did the defendant in *Kearney* emphasize how many of the terms of the program were either not spelled out or left undefined?

2.2. Why is it the "general rule" that "an advertisement does not constitute an offer"? *See Restatement (Second) of Contracts* § 26, cmt. B. What, if anything, does your understanding of objective theory suggest to you about this issue?

2.3. If Epstein places an ad in his local newspaper offering to pay a reward to anyone who returns his lost ferret, Chico, and Ponoroff returns Chico the next day, is Ponoroff entitled to the reward? Consider the case described in the following article by Bruce Golding in the *New York Post* on-line:

> Jurors taught a big-talking hip-hop artist a lesson about broken promises yesterday when they ordered him to pay the $1 million reward he had offered for the return of his stolen laptop.
>
> Cheapskate performer and producer Ryan Leslie must fork over the Benjamins to auto-repair-shop owner Armin Augstein, who found the computer while walking his dog and turned it over to German cops in November 2010.
>
> In a YouTube video, Leslie had promised a $1 million reward to whoever found the missing laptop and an external hard drive. But when Augstein produced the goods, Leslie went from big-money mogul to double-talking skinflint.
>
> * * *
>
> "I'm very happy [Augstein stated] . . . that the American judicial system, which is so totally different from ours, functioned so well with a jury that are not professionals and are laymen," he said in German through one his lawyers, Steven Thal.
>
> * * *
>
> "No one forced him to make an offer of so much money for a finder's fee," Augstein said. "It seems like he believes that that which he promised, he doesn't have to live up to."
>
> * * *
>
> Leslie testified Tuesday that his offer was contingent upon his ability to retrieve several unreleased multitrack songs stored on the hard drive, which he said couldn't be accessed after he got it back.
>
> But Judge Harold Baer Jr. yesterday told jurors that because Leslie disposed of the hard drive by returning it to

> the manufacturer after Augstein claimed the reward, they could assume that the data was there when Augstein handed it over.
>
> * * *
>
> Last night, Leslie seemed to accept the verdict, tweeting. "Ain't no way to get around ups & downs.' Jury of my peers rules for the plaintiff."
>
> * * *
>
> Augstein, who testified that learning about Leslie's reward offer felt like winning the lottery, said yesterday that while he was eager to collect on his windfall, he wasn't about to start spending the dough.
>
> "As we say here in Germany, we can only eat the chicken after it's been plucked," he said.

http://www.nypost.com/p/news/local/manhattan/rap_slap_kvST BaoDlN18eNtiOLK72L (Posted: 1:48 AM, November 29, 2012. Last Updated: 9:09 AM, November 29, 2012). *See also Augstein v. Leslie,* 2012 WL 4928914 (S.D.N.Y. 2012).

2.4. Were there other considerations, beyond application of objective theory at work in the Ninth Circuit's decision in *Sateriale* (and perhaps in this case as well) that may have influenced the courts' decisions in both cases to find an offer originating in a public advertisement? Would we ask that if we didn't think there were? No.

3. Notes

3.1. In the famous case of *Lefkowitz v. Great Minneapolis Surplus Store, Inc.*, 251 Minn. 188, 86 N.W.2d 689 (1957) (cited by the court in *Kearney*), the defendant placed advertisements in a local newspaper on *two* consecutive weeks, each time offering certain expensive items of apparel for one dollar each *"First Come, First Served."* On *both* occasions, the plaintiff was the first to show-up and indicated a readiness to pay the dollar, but the defendant refused to sell the merchandise to him, citing the "house rule" that the offer was intended for women only. The court ruled that "because the ads in question were "clear, definite, and left nothing open for negotiation," an offer had been made which the plaintiff accepted when he successfully managed to be the first person to appear at the defendant's store and tendered the stated purchase price. The court quickly dispatched of the defendant's further argument that the offer had been modified by the "house rule" since the ad itself contained no such restriction. Was the court's holding in *Lefkowitz* concerning the undisclosed house rule consistent with objective theory? Even if so, could you draw a distinction between the first and second transactions based on the existence of this rule?

3.2. The court in *Kearney* also cites Judge Wood's opinion *Leonard v. Pepsi Co.* In that case, the plaintiff, John Leonard, claimed that Pepsi had made an offer when, as part of a promotional campaign, it ran a television commercial in which, among other prizes, Pepsi featured a Marine Harrier Fighter Jet that the commercial indicated could be acquired by redeeming 7 million Pepsi Points. You can see the commercial here. https://www.youtube.com/watch?v=ZdackF2H7Qc. Although Mr. Leonard amazingly did accumulate the necessary Pepsi Points and wanted the jet, Pepsi declined. The company advised Mr. Leonard that, unlike the other items (such as sun glasses, a leather jacket, a mountain bike, etc.) that could be redeemed for Pepsi Points, the jet had been included in the commercial to create a humorous and entertaining ad; that is, it was a joke—just like Mr. Zehmer's offer. In her opinion, later adopted on appeal by the U.S. Second Circuit Court of Appeal, Judge Leonard granted summary judgment in favor of Pepsi, concluding that the case was distinguishable from *Lefkowitz* in two respects: (1) the definiteness of the terms of the offer and who could accept, and (2) the presence of language of limitation—"first come, first served"—in *Lefkowitz.*

Based on the decision in *Leonard*, how would you have expected the same court—the U.S. District Court for the Southern District of New York—to rule in a class action lawsuit filed against Red Bull for breach of its public "promise" that "Red Bull Gives You Wings"? *See* http://www.businessinsider.com/red-bull-settles-false-advertising-lawsuit-for-13-million-2014-10.

3.3. If *Leonard* is distinguishable from *Lefkowitz*, what do you think about the following situation from http://news.yahoo.com/blogs/sideshow/macys-necklace-mistake-1500-47-170235677.html?.tsrc=appleww:

> Posted on March 29, 2013 at 5:17 PM
>
> DALLAS—Macy's mailed an advertisement across the country this month with a major pricing mistake, which listed a $1,500 necklace on sale for $47. It wasn't just a typo in the ad, customers actually purchased them for that price and bought all the inventory at the Macy's in Collin Creek Mall, according to Robert Bernard.
>
> He tried to purchase two of them.
>
> "It says 'Super Buy!,'" Bernard added holding up the 44-page advertisement Macy's mailed to him.

Bernard said he thought it was quite a deal and he was shopping for an anniversary gift for his wife.

The necklace is listed as a sterling silver and 14-karat gold. Macy's said it is regularly priced at $1,500. But the mailer listed it on sale for $47.

Bernard suspected it might not be true. But when he got to the Macy's at Collin Creek Mall people were actually paying that price for the expensive necklace. In fact, a customer in front of him brought every one of them the store had in stock, he said.

The clerk offered to sell Bernard two of necklaces for $47 and have them shipped to his home. Total Savings was $1,400, his receipt reads.

But a couple days later, Macy's left him a voicemail.

"This item has the wrong price for $47," a Macy's call center employee said in Bernard's voicemail. "The correct price is $479 dollars and because of that pricing error, your order has been canceled and I apologize."

Most upsetting, Bernard says, Macy's never offered him anything else for the money he spent but said it would process a refund for him.

"I'm very, very bothered by it because I don't want anybody else to feel the way I feel," Bernard added.

Friday afternoon, Macy's apologized for the error but didn't explain how it happened.

"When the mistake was caught, signage did go up in the fine jewelry department and on store doors alerting customers that a mistake had been made," wrote Beth Charlton, Macy's spokeswoman in an e-mail to News 8. "For those customers who bought the necklace at the $47 price, they were fortunate. For the gentleman you spoke with, he was not so fortunate. We are sincerely sorry he was disappointed and unable to buy the necklace at the $47 price for his wife."

3.4. As opposed to a general public advertisement, what about the display of an item with a price—as in a store window (even though no one window shops any more unless you include virtual window shopping). In *Fisher v. Bell,* 3 All E.R. 731 (Queen's Bench Div. 1960), the defendant displayed a "flick knife" (switchblade) in his shop window with a sign reading "Ejector-knife—4s." At the time, English statutes prohibiting offering switchblades for sale and the defendant was prosecuted and convicted for violating that law. On appeal, the issue was whether the "exhibition of that knife in the window with a ticket constituted an offer for sale. . . ."? In his opinion Lord Parker stated that most lay people would be inclined to say that it is "nonsense" to say that, under these circumstances, the shop owner was not offering the knife for sale. He went on, however, to hold that "It is clear that, according to the ordinary law of contract, the display of an article with a price on it in a shop window is merely an invitation to treat." Thus, the defendant's conviction was overturned. Is it that "clear" to you that this was not an offer?

3.5. Because of the general rule that advertisements are not offers, contract law doctrine and remedies often proved of little help to consumers who were "taken in" by a false or misleading ad. Recognizing the need for additional protection, Section 5 of the Federal Trade Commission Act proscribes certain "deceptive" trade practices, including the notorious "bait and switch" advertising. 16 C.F.R. § 238. The bait and switch was used by unscrupulous merchants to lure customers into their stores with "promises" of deals too good to be true. When the consumer showed to take advantage of the deals, they would be told that the advertised merchandise (the bait) was no longer available, and then be steered into a higher priced product (the switch). However, because the Federal Trade Commission Act provides for only administrative remedies, such as cease and desist orders, many states have promulgated their own false or deceptive advertising laws that permit for a monetary recovery, including attorney's fees, by aggrieved consumers.

For example, Georgia's Fair Business Practice Act, OCGA § 10–1–390 *et seq.* provides a private right of action in favor of any person who suffers an injury or damages as a result of consumer practices in violation of the Act. In *Agnew v. Great Atlantic & Pacific Tea Co.,* 232 Ga.App. 708, 502 S.E.2d 735 (1998). Gary Agnew, a lawyer, saw a large sign in front of a grocery store which read: *"Nobody's Gonna Beat Us Now. Buy One Get One Free. 1=2 Sale. All This Week. Single Purchases Will be Charged Regular Retail Price, Second Item Free."* The sign contained no additional limitations. Agnew entered the store, selected two bags of sugar, two boxes of Rice-A-Roni, and two boxes of crackers. The cashier rang up his purchases but no discount appeared. When Agnew inquired about the promotional sale he was told it only applied to certain items, not including those he had selected. Agnew paid full price for his purchases, but then filed a complaint under the Georgia Fair Business Practice Act against the grocery store claiming that the sign caused him injury when he paid full price for the six items. The court concluded that because he purchased the items with knowledge that the sign did not mean what it said, his deliberate choice, and not the misleading sign, was the proximate cause of his injury. Therefore, the court sustained the trial court's dismissal of his claim. Would Agnew have been better off suing for breach of contract? How would you analyze such a claim?

3.6. We've noted that an offer involves some *manifestation* by the offeror of a willingness to be bound upon assent by the offeree. But does that assent have to be expressed in either spoken or written words? The answer is clearly not.

What must be *manifested* is assent, but this manifestation of assent can be found (or *implied*) from conduct. Courts sometimes use the phrase "express contracts" to describe contracts based solely on words, and "implied-in-fact contracts" to describe contracts based at least in part on conduct. There is no legal difference between the two. Both are contracts in the strict sense of the word.

Thus, if you are passing a hot dog vendor who holds out a sandwich that you take and consume, it should be fairly clear that there is an obligation to pay for it. While purely implied-in-fact contracts may be somewhat rare, many, if not most, contracts are partially express and partially implied-in-fact.

For example, when a lawyer expressly agrees to handle a new client's case, there is an implied understanding that the client will pay for those services even if nothing is said about fees (although we hasten to add that we personally think that it is always advisable to have an express agreement concerning fees; the point being, however, that it often doesn't happen that way). However, in situations involving family members or parties who otherwise have an intimate relationship, courts have generally been reluctant to find the existence of a binding obligation to pay for the services. Should it matter, insofar as contractual liability is concerned, whether the client is a stranger or the lawyer's spouse? How about the lawyer's father-in-law? Try to couch your answer in terms of objective theory.

4. **You Be the Lawyer!**

If Equilon Enterprises had come to you to help with the design of the "Ski Free" program, what would you have suggested be done differently in structuring the program compared to the structure of the program as described in the case?

5. Connections

What do the cases in this section, all dealing with when a communication rises to the level of an offer; *i.e.,* place the power of acceptance on the offeree, have in common? How do they relate to the cases in the last section dealing with the method courts use to determine mutual assent? Suppose Ponoroff sends a letter addressed to both Epstein and Markell stating, "I'm selling my autographed Dirty Harry DVD collection for $100." If Markell calls Ponoroff the next day and says, "I accept" has a contract been formed?

Is it possible for a contract to come into existence without a specific, identifiable "offer" being made? Consider the problem that follows.

PROBLEM ON IMPLIED-IN-FACT CONTRACT

In October, 2017, Mongo Markell applied for admission to the Last Choice State Law School ("LCLS") and was accepted for the class of 2021, entering in fall of 2018. At the time of his application and his enrollment, the catalogues for LCLS stated that, in addition to tuition, each student would be charged a Professional Development Fee (the "PDF"). The catalogue went on to state that: "The PDF is one component of the total fee for JD students. For students entering in 2018 the PDF is $4,000 per year, and it will remain at the same level for the three years of the J.D. program." In other words, any increase would be applied to new students only. LCLS's catalogues also contained general language in numerous places to the effect that fees and policies were subject to change and that "LCLS reserves the right to add, amend, delete or otherwise modify its policies. This includes, but is not limited to, modifications of its degree programs, courses of study, the academic calendar, and its fees, tuition, or other charges."

On July 23, 2019, LCLS's Board of Trustees voted to increase the PDF by 20% for continuing as well as newly enrolling students for the forthcoming year. Mongo complained to his uncle, a former federal judge in Nevada, pointing out that based on what he learned in contract law, LVS could not increase the PDF for members of his class. Mongo's uncle was sympathetic, but pointed out to him that there was no formal contract and that the university's promulgated guidelines could only constitute a contractual obligation if the parties had expressly agreed that the guidelines would govern their relationship. Because there was no formal contract, Mongo's uncle told him he thought he was out of luck.

Outraged, Mongo replied, "I bet you wouldn't be taking this position if you were using some of the royalty money you get from your Contracts casebook to help me pay for law school instead of making me take out student loans for the full cost of my education." He went on, stating, "by the act of matriculation, together with payment of the required charges, I believe a contract was formed between LCLS and me, which included the express promise not to raise the PDF, and I'm not going to let those flabby-assed administrators get away with this." True to his word, Mongo, along with a number of his classmates, filed suit against LCLS. How should the court rule on this claim? *See Kashmiri v. Regents of the University of California,* 156 Cal.App.4th 809, 67 Cal.Rptr.3d 635 (2007).

---

3. DESTROYING THE OFFER

Even though we cannot point you to a case that you have read so far that explicitly says this, we know (and so expect you to know) that an offer, once communicated by the offeror to the offeree, creates in the offeree the *power of acceptance*. We expect you to know from Game of Thrones that a Dragon lives forever (we know it from Peter, Paul, and Mary's 1963 recording of "Puff the Magic Dragon" (http://www.youtube.com/watch?v=3OiOlnoyljk), which we expect you to know about since Ben Stiller sang a part of the song while driving with Robert De Niro in the flick *Meet the Parents*. Ok, but that's a dragon; how long does an offer live for? Can it be killed? What does it take to kill an offer? Kryptonite?

Actually, there are four ways to "kill" or, more delicately put, to terminate an offer: rejection, revocation, lapse, and death or incompetence of the offeror. We examine each in this section.

[Throughout this section on termination of offer we must assume that the offeree has not exercised the power of acceptance. Once acceptance occurs (something we have not yet examined but will soon), there is no more offer to terminate. Instead, at that point the offer has been subsumed into the contract. Kind of like a caterpillar becoming a butterfly.]

A. REJECTION

Contract law, like life, is rich with rejection. If you can't handle rejection, we suggest you skip this subsection—and maybe law school.

The first way (at least in the order of our treatment of them) in which an unaccepted offer may be terminated is rejection by the offeree. This occurs, for example, when Markell offers to sell his Kinky Friedman CD collection to Epstein for $500, and Epstein replies, "Hell no!" That is a rejection. The offer is terminated; dead.

What do you think is the basis for this rule?

Suppose Epstein comes to his senses and quickly calls Markell back and says, "I don't know what I was thinking, I accept your offer, I'd love to buy your Kinky CDs for the price you quoted." If Markell says "no," can Epstein sue and recover? Hell no! Epstein already rejected, at which point the offer was terminated. Dead. Dead forever. Not even in the deepest, most Fundamentalist, most Republican parts of the South, is there any such thing as a "born again offer."

In the example above, Epstein initially told Markell that he wasn't interested. In other words, Markell made an offer and Epstein said, in a less polite fashion, "no thanks." This is what we call an "express" rejection.

Like ice cream or jello, however, rejections come in more than one flavor. In Section 5(E) below we will take up the topic that we have termed "imperfect acceptances." When we do, you'll be introduced to another form of rejection; namely, "implied" rejections.

For example, when the offeree, rather than turning down the offer, makes a "counteroffer," he is rejecting the offer. If Epstein replies to Markell's offer above by saying, "I'll buy your Kinky collection for $450," he is indirectly rejecting the offer.

For now, we suggest only that you appreciate that an offer, once rejected, whether expressly or impliedly, is terminated; dead as a doornail. So, in a sense, the making of an offer not only creates the power of acceptance in the offeree, it also creates in the offeree the power to destroy the offer through rejection.

B. REVOCATION

1. Direct Revocation

The offeror also has the power to destroy the offer, but the offeror's power is not called "rejection." Rather, the term used to describe the offeror's termination of her offer is "revocation." The offeror's right to revoke (take back) her offer derives from the fact that, until acceptance, the offeror retains full control and mastery over her offer including the right to modify or terminate the offer.

Suppose Markell offers to sell to Epstein his entire collection of Kinky Friedman CDs for $500. Epstein may well be very excited and eager to accept. If, however, before Epstein is able to communicate his acceptance to Markell, Markell calls Epstein and says, "I changed my mind. I don't want to sell my Kinky collection to you," the offer is gone—terminated; killed; or, more technically put, revoked. There's nothing for Epstein to accept.

This squares with objective theory because Epstein would no longer be reasonable in assuming that his assent will seal the deal once Markell has taken the offer off the table. This is a direct revocation. If Epstein nevertheless tells Markell, "No, wait, I'll buy your Kinky Friedman collection for $500," what is the proper legal characterization of that communication? Suppose after Markell pulls the offer, a stunned and deeply disappointed Epstein says, "No, please don't change your mind, I'll pay $750." Is there a contract? Why or why not, and if not, where do the parties stand?

---

2. Indirect Revocation

A direct revocation is easy to identify and understand. It is an affirmative statement by the offeror to the offeree expressly withdrawing the offer. What other kind of communication is sufficient to revoke an offer, who may it come from, and when is it effective? These are some of the questions that are addressed in the next case.

We should let you know that this case will expose you for the first time to the doctrine of consideration—although at a sufficiently low dosage so as not to pose any hazard to your health. We also know that we (and you) haven't yet considered consideration and, in fact, will not formally do so until the next chapter. However, in order to understand this case, as well as some other aspects of contract formation that come up in Section 4 *infra*, you need to know a little about—have a little exposure to—consideration. So consider our consideration of consideration in this chapter as just an appetizer and we'll bring on the main course later. We hope you're hungry.

QUESTIONS BEFORE THE CASE

1. As you read the case, ask yourself whether the holding is consistent with objective theory?
2. Irrespective of how you answer the first question, ask yourself whether the result makes common sense?

DICKINSON V. DODDS

Court of Appeal, Chancery Division
2 Ch. Div. 463 (1876)

On Wednesday, the 10th of June, 1874, the Defendant John Dodds signed and delivered to the Plaintiff, George Dickinson, a memorandum, of which the material part was as follows:

> I hereby agree to sell to Mr. George Dickinson the whole of the dwelling-houses, garden ground, stabling, and outbuildings thereto belonging, situate at Croft, belonging to me, for the sum of £800. As witness my hand this tenth day of June, 1874.
>
> £800 /signed/ John Dodds
>
> P.S.—This offer to be left open until Friday, 9 o'clock, A.M. J.D. (the twelfth), 12th June 1874.
>
> /signed/ J. Dodds

The bill alleged that Dodds understood and intended that the Plaintiff should have until Friday 9 a.m. within which to determine whether he would or would not purchase, and that he should absolutely have until that time the refusal of the property at the price of £800, and that the Plaintiff in fact determined to accept the offer on the morning of Thursday, the 11th of June, but did not at once signify his acceptance to Dodds, believing that he had the power to accept it until 9 a.m. on the Friday.

In the afternoon of the Thursday the Plaintiff was informed by a Mr. Berry that Dodds had been offering or agreeing to sell the property to Thomas Allan, the other Defendant. Thereupon the Plaintiff, at about half-past seven in the evening, went to the house of Mrs. Burgess, the mother-in-law of Dodds, where he was then staying, and left with her a formal acceptance in writing of the offer to sell the property. According to the evidence of Mrs. Burgess this document never in fact reached Dodds, she having forgotten to give it to him.

On the following (Friday) morning, at about seven o'clock, Berry, who was acting as agent for Dickinson, found Dodds at the Darlington railway station, and handed to him a duplicate of the acceptance by Dickinson, and explained to Dodds its purport. He replied that it was too late, as he had sold the property. A few minutes later Dickinson himself found Dodds entering a railway carriage, and handed him another duplicate of the notice of acceptance, but Dodds declined to receive it, saying, "You are too late. I have sold the property."

It appeared that on the day before, Thursday, the 11th of June, Dodds had signed a formal contract for the sale of the property to the Defendant Allan for £800, and had received from him a deposit of £40.

The bill in this suit prayed that the Defendant Dodds might be decreed specifically to perform the contract of the 10th of June, 1874; that he might be restrained from conveying the property to Allan; that Allan might be restrained from taking any such conveyance; that, if any such conveyance had been or should be made, Allan might be declared a trustee of the property for, and might be directed to convey the property to, the Plaintiff; and for damages.

The cause came on for hearing before Vice-Chancellor Bacon on the 25th of January, 1876.

[Vice Chancellor Bacon declared that Allan had no interest in the property and entered a decree of specific performance in favor of Dickinson, from which Dodds and Allan appealed]

JAMES, L.J., after referring to the document of the 10th of June, 1874 continued:—

The document, though beginning "I hereby agree to sell," was nothing but an offer, and was only intended to be an offer, for the Plaintiff himself tells us that he required time to consider whether he would enter into an agreement or not. Unless both parties had then agreed there was no concluded agreement then made; it was in effect and substance only an offer to sell. * * * There was no consideration given for the undertaking or promise, to whatever extent it may be considered binding, to keep the property unsold until 9 o'clock on Friday morning; but apparently Dickinson was of opinion, and probably Dodds was of the same opinion, that he (Dodds) was bound by that promise, and could not in any way withdraw from it, or retract it, until 9 o'clock on Friday morning, and this probably explains a good deal of what afterwards took place. But it is clear settled law, on one of the clearest principles of law, that this promise, being a mere *nudum pactum*, was not binding, and that at any moment before a complete acceptance by Dickinson of the offer, Dodds was as free as Dickinson himself. Well, that being the state of things, it is said that the only mode in which Dodds could assert that freedom was by actually and distinctly saying to Dickinson, "Now I withdraw my offer." It appears to me that there is neither principle nor authority for the proposition that there must be an express and actual withdrawal of the offer, or what is called a retraction. It must, to constitute a contract, appear that the two minds were at one, at the same moment of time, that is, that there was an offer continuing up to the time of the acceptance. If there was not such a continuing offer, then the acceptance comes to nothing. Of course it may well be that the one man is bound in some way or other to let the other man know that his mind with regard to the offer has been changed; but in this case, beyond all question, the Plaintiff knew that Dodds was no longer minded to sell the property to him as plainly and clearly as if Dodds had told him in so many words, "I withdraw the offer." This is evident from the Plaintiff's own statements in the bill.

* * *

It is to my mind quite clear that before there was any attempt at acceptance by the Plaintiff, he was perfectly well aware that Dodds had changed his mind, and that he had in fact agreed to sell the property to Allan. It is impossible, therefore, to say there was ever that existence of the same mind between the two parties which is essential in point of law to the making of an agreement. I am of opinion, therefore, that the Plaintiff has failed to prove that there was any binding contract between Dodds and himself.

MELLISH, L.J.:

I am of the same opinion. * * * He [Dodds] was not in point of law bound to hold the offer over until 9 o'clock on Friday morning. He was not so bound either in law or in equity. Well, that being so, when on the next day he made an agreement with Allan to sell the property to him, I am not aware of any ground on which it can be said that that contract with Allan was not as good and binding a contract as ever was made. Assuming Allan to have known (there is some dispute about it, and Allan does not admit that he knew of it, but I will assume that he did) that Dodds had made the offer to Dickinson, and had given him till Friday morning at 9 o'clock to accept it, still in point of law that could not prevent Allan from making a more favorable offer than Dickinson, and entering at once into a binding agreement with Dodds.

Then Dickinson is informed by Berry that the property has been sold by Dodds to Allan. Berry does not tell us from whom he heard it, but he says that he did hear it, that he knew it, and that he informed Dickinson of it. Now, stopping there, the question which arises is this—If an offer has been made for the sale of property, and before that offer is accepted, the person who has made the offer enters into a binding agreement to sell the property to somebody else, and the person to whom the offer was first made receives notice in some way that property has been sold to another person, can he after that make a binding contact by the acceptance of the offer? I am of opinion that he cannot. The law may be right or wrong in saying that a person who has given to another a certain time within which to accept an offer is not bound by his promise to give that time; but, if he is not bound by that promise, and may still sell the property to some one else, and if it be the law that, in order to make a contract, the two minds must be in agreement at some one time, that is, at the time of the acceptance, how is it possible that when the person to whom the offer has been made knows that the person who made the offer has sold the property to someone else, and that, in fact, he has not remained in the same mind to sell it to him, he can be at liberty to accept the offer and thereby make a binding contract? It seems to me that would be simply absurd. * * * If the rule of law is that a mere offer to sell property, which can be withdrawn at any time, and which is made dependent on the acceptance of the person to whom it is made, is a mere *nudum pactum*, how is it possible that the person to whom the offer has been made can by acceptance make a binding contract after he knows that the person who has made the offer has sold the property to some one else? * * * I am clearly of opinion that * * * once the person to whom the offer was made knows that the property has been sold to some one else, it is too late for him to accept the offer, and on that ground I am clearly of opinion that there is no binding contact for the sale of this property by Dodds to Dickinson, and even if there had been, it seems to me that the sale of the property to Allan was first in point of time. However, it is not necessary to consider, if there had been two binding contracts, which of them would be entitled to priority in equity, because there is no binding contact between Dodds and Dickinson.

QUESTIONS, NOTE, AND CONNECTIONS

1. Questions about the facts of this case

   1.1. If you'll excuse the expression, Dodds dodged the bullet in this case because of the court's holding that the offer was revoked once Dickinson learned through Berry that Dodds was no longer of a mind to sell the property to him. How much did Dickinson really know, however, about the dealings between Dodds and Allan?

   1.2. The court obviously considered Berry to be a reliable messenger. Why was that fact important to the court? Do you agree with the court's judgment?

2. Questions about the law

   2.1. Suppose Berry was mistaken in what he told Dickinson. Is the offer still revoked? What if Berry was not just mistaken, but deliberately lying to Dickinson? Does that change the analysis?

   2.2. Suppose that even though Dodds entered into an agreement with Allan for the sale of the property, Dickinson did not learn of this fact, directly or indirectly, until after he had accepted the offer. This is the problem that Lord Judge Mellish says at the end of his concurring opinion that the court does not have to address. If, however, the court were faced with those circumstances, would a contract have been formed with Allan? Would a contract also be formed between Dickinson and Dodds? Is it possible to have *two* contracts for the same property? If so, and both purchasers sue for specific performance, who gets the property? What does the other party get? Is there any way in which a person in Dickinson's position can protect himself against an intervening contract buyer? In this scenario, how would you have advised Dodds to proceed once he decided that he might be interested in selling the property to Allan?

   2.3. Suppose the facts in *Dickinson* had been different so that Dodds learned from a reliable source on the afternoon of Thursday, June 11, that Dickinson was not interested in buying his property and, in fact, was actively negotiating with someone else for the purchase of another parcel of land. Would the offer then be terminated by indirect rejection? But suppose that information was inaccurate and, before 9 a.m. on Friday, Dickinson accepts. Would Dodds be obligated to sell? Would there be an "indirect" rejection?

3. Note

   In a case where an offer is made by a public advertisement, does the offeror retain the power to revoke the offer? If so, how is it done? Does the offeror have to personally contact everyone that might have read the advertisement? *See Shuey v. United States*, 92 U.S. 73 (1875), involving an attempt to collect a reward that had been offered for the apprehension of John H. Surratt, an alleged accomplice of John Wilkes Booth in the murder of President Lincoln.

4. **You Be the Lawyer!**

   The court states that although Dodds promised that his offer would be held open until Friday morning, this promise was unenforceable *even though* both parties probably believed that Dodds was bound by that promise. We will take up the subject of when offers will be regarded as irrevocable in the next section of this chapter. For the time being, accepting the court's statement of the law as true, what steps would you have taken to ensure that this promise to hold the offer open would be enforced?

5. Connections

   Think back to the cases in the last section about what constitutes an offer. Ok, now that you've refreshed your recollection, ask yourself, "Self, what is it about what turns a communication into an offer that justified the court's conclusion in *Dickinson* that Dodd's offer died when Berry told Dickinson on Thursday, June 11, that Dodds was knoodling with Allan?"

C. LAPSE

With the subsection entitled "Rejection," we considered the possibility of termination of an offer because of actions by the offeree. And with the subsection entitled "Revocation," we considered the possibility of termination of an offer because of the actions of the offeror. Now, with this subsection entitled "Lapse," we consider the possibility of termination of an offer because of *inaction.*

QUESTIONS BEFORE THE CASE

1. Can you identify the contract at issue in this case?
2. What exactly is the rule in this case as to when an offer for an unstated or indefinite period lapses?

MINNESOTA LINSEED OIL CO. V. COLLIER WHITE LEAD CO.

Circuit Court, District of Minnesota
17 F. Cas. 447 (1876)

* * * The plaintiff seeks to recover the sum of $2,151.50, with interest from September 20, 1875—a balance claimed to be due for oil sold to the defendant. The defendant, in its answer, alleges that on August 3d, 1875, a contract was entered into between the parties, whereby the plaintiff agreed to sell and deliver to the defendant, at the city of St. Louis, during the said month of August, twelve thousand four hundred and fifty (12,450) gallons of linseed oil for the price of fifty-eight (58) cents per gallon, and that the plaintiff has neglected and refused to deliver the oil according to the contract; that the market value of oil after August 3d and during the month was not less than seventy (70) cents per gallon, and therefore claims a set-off or counter-claim to plaintiff's cause of action. The reply of the plaintiff denies that any contract was entered into between it and defendant.

* * * The contract is alleged to have been made by telegraph.

The plaintiff sent the following dispatch to the defendant: *"Minneapolis, July 29, 1875. To Alex. Easton, Secretary Collier White Lead Company, St. Louis, Missouri: Account of sales not enclosed in yours of 27th. Please wire us best offer for round lot named by you—one hundred barrels shipped. Minnesota Linseed Oil Company."*

The following answer was received: *"St. Louis, Mo., July 30, 1875. To the Minnesota Linseed Oil Company: Three hundred barrels fifty-five cents here, thirty days, no commission, August delivery. Answer. Collier Company."*

The following reply was returned: *"Minneapolis, July 31, 1875. Will accept fifty-eight cents (58c), on terms named in your telegram. Minnesota Linseed Oil Company."*

This dispatch was transmitted Saturday, July 31, 1875, at 9:15 p.m., and was not delivered to the defendant in St. Louis, until Monday morning, August 2, between eight and nine o'clock.

On Tuesday, August 3, at 8:53 a.m., the following dispatch was deposited for transmission in the telegraph office: *"St. Louis, Mo., August 3, 1875. To Minnesota Linseed Oil Company, Minneapolis: Offer accepted—ship three hundred barrels as soon as possible. Collier Company."*

The following telegrams passed between the parties after the last one was deposited in the office at St. Louis: *"Minneapolis, August 3, 1875. To Collier Company, St. Louis: We must withdraw our offer wired July 31st. Minnesota Linseed Oil Company."*

Answered: *"St. Louis, August 3, 1875. Minnesota Linseed Oil Company: Sale effected before your request to withdraw was received. When will you ship? Collier Company."*

It appeared that the market was very much unsettled, and that the price of oil was subject to sudden fluctuations during the month previous and at the time of this negotiation, varying from day to day, and ranging between fifty-five and seventy-five cents per gallon. It is urged by the defendant that the dispatch of Tuesday, August 3d, 1875, accepting the offer of the plaintiff transmitted July 31st, and delivered Monday morning, August 2d, concluded a contract for the sale of the twelve thousand four hundred and fifty gallons of oil. The plaintiff, on the contrary, claims, 1st, that the dispatch accepting the proposition made July 31st, was not received until after the offer had been withdrawn; 2d, that the acceptance of the offer was not in due time; that the delay was unreasonable, and therefore no contract was completed.

NELSON, DISTRICT JUDGE.

It is well settled by the authorities in this country, and sustained by the later English decisions, that there is no difference in the rules governing the negotiation of contracts by correspondence through the post-office and by telegraph, and a contract is concluded when an acceptance of a proposition is deposited in the telegraph office for transmission. * * *

The reason for this rule is well stated in Adams v. Lindsell, 1 Barn. & Ald. 681. The negotiation in that case was by post. The court said: 'That if a bargain could not be closed by letter before the answer was received, no contract could be completed through the medium of the post-office; that if the one party was not bound by his offer when it was accepted (that is, at the time the letter of acceptance is deposited in the mail), then the other party ought not to be bound until after they had received a notification that the answer had been received and assented to, and that so it might go on ad infinitum.' * * * In the case at bar the delivery of the message at the telegraph office signified the acceptance of the offer. If any contract was entered into, the meeting of minds was at 8:53 of the clock, on Tuesday morning, August 3d, and the subsequent dispatches are out of the case. * * *

This rule is not strenuously dissented from on the argument, and it is substantially admitted that the acceptance of an offer by letter or by telegraph completes the contract, when such acceptance is put in the proper and usual way of being communicated by the agency employed to carry it; and that when an offer is made by telegraph, an acceptance by telegraph takes effect when the dispatch containing the acceptance is deposited for transmission in the telegraph office, and not when it is received by the other party. Conceding this, there remains only one question to decide, which will determine the issues: Was the acceptance of defendant deposited in the telegraph office Tuesday, August 3d, within a reasonable time, so as to consummate a contract binding upon the plaintiff?

It is undoubtedly the rule that when a proposition is made under the circumstances in this case, an acceptance concludes the contract if the offer is still open, and the mutual consent necessary to convert the offer of one party into a binding contract by the acceptance of the other is established, if such acceptance is within a reasonable time after the offer was received.

The better opinion is, that what is, or is not, a reasonable time, must depend upon the circumstances attending the negotiation, and the character of the subject matter of the contract, and in no better way can the intention of the parties be determined. If the negotiation is in respect to an article stable in price, there is not so much reason for an immediate acceptance of the offer, and the same rule would not apply as in a case where the negotiation related to an article subject to sudden and great fluctuations in the market.

The rule in regard to the length of the time an offer shall continue, and when an acceptance completes the contract, is laid down in Parsons on Contracts (volume 1, p. 482). He says: "It may be said that whether the offer be made for a time certain or not, the intention or understanding of the parties is to govern. * * * If no definite time is stated, then the inquiry as to a reasonable time resolves itself into an inquiry as to what time it is rational to suppose the parties contemplated; and the law will decide this to be that time which as rational men they ought to have understood each other to have had in mind." Applying this rule, it seems clear that the intention of the plaintiff, in making the offer by telegraph, to sell an article which fluctuates so much in price, must have been upon the understanding that the acceptance, if at all, should be immediate, and as soon after the receipt of the offer as would give a fair opportunity for consideration. The delay here was too long, and manifestly unjust to the plaintiff, for it afforded the defendant an opportunity to take advantage of a change in the market, and accept or refuse the offer as would best subserve its interests.

Judgment will be entered in favor of the plaintiff for the amount claimed. The counter-claim is denied. Judgment accordingly.

QUESTIONS AND NOTES

1. Questions about the facts of this case

   1.1. Why is the party who is alleged to have breached the contract the *plaintiff* in this action instead of the defendant?

   1.2. Can you identify the key fact that, in the court's estimation, made the August 3 transmission untimely as an acceptance?

2. Questions about the law

   2.1. If a prompt acceptance was critical to the plaintiff in this case, why didn't plaintiff's telegram say so? Was it proper for the court to read a time limitation into the offer that the plaintiff had neglected to include of its own accord?

   2.2. Can you justify the court's decision under objective theory?

   2.3. The parties seemed to be in agreement in *Minnesota Linseed Oil* that if the offer were still open, a contract would have been completed when the defendant's August 3 telegraph was deposited for transmission. Is this rule consistent with objective theory? If you're confused, you ought to be, but keep the faith because we return to the issue of when an acceptance is effective in Section 5 of this chapter. For purposes of this case, however, it didn't matter when the acceptance would have been effective—transmission or receipt—because of the court's conclusion that the offer *lapsed* prior to either of those events.

3. Notes

   3.1. *Minnesota Linseed Oil* suggests that an offer for an unstated period lapses after a *reasonable* time. If Epstein approaches Markell and offers him employment for a specific wage and Markell does not respond during that conversation but instead sends notice of acceptance the next day, is there a contract between Epstein and Markell? *See Akers v. J.B. Sedberry, Inc.*, 39 Tenn.App. 633, 286 S.W.2d 617 (1955). If not, what is the proper legal characterization of Markell's notice of "acceptance"? *Compare Restatement (Second) of Contracts* § 70, *with* Art. 21(2), *United Nations Convention on Contracts for the International Sale of Goods* and Article 2.9(1), *UNIDROIT Principles of International Commercial Contracts* (both providing that a late acceptance may be effective as an acceptance if the offeror gives notice to that effect without undue delay). Does it change your answer if, during the conversation, Markell replies, "Alright, I accept, but you really should pay me more"? See *Brangier v. Rosenthal,* 337 F.2d 952 (9th Cir. 1964), involving a so-called "grumbling acceptance."

   3.2. As illustrated by *Dickinson v. Dodds, supra*, an offer for a stated period of time ("will give you eight days to accept") remains open, unless earlier revoked, for the time stated in the offer. But when does that time period begin to run when there is a delay between the date the offer is made and the date it is received? *See Caldwell v. Cline*, 109 W.Va. 553, 156 S.E. 55 (1930). Which party is in the best position to avoid the ambiguity? Should that affect the determination? If so, and you are drafting an offer for a client intended to be good for eight days, how will you express this intention?

4. **You Be the Lawyer!**

You represent Collier White Lead. Your client wants to appeal this decision to the Supreme Court of the United States. What will you tell your client about the prospects for reversal on appeal?

D. DEATH (OR INCAPACITY) OF THE OFFEROR (OR OFFEREE)

Obviously, if the offeree dies after an offer is made to her but before she accepts the offer, she cannot still accept the offer. She is dead. And so the offer also is dead. But what about if the offeror dies before her offer is accepted? Well, under objective theory, one might reasonably assume that the offer remains good until such time as the offeree is notified of or becomes aware of the death. In that situation, the resulting contract could be enforced against the offeror's estate but, if estate could not perform the contract without the continued existence of the offeror, it would have a defense. That's what you'd reasonably assume, but you'd be wrong. Not wrong about objective theory, but wrong about the rule on death of the offeror. Say what?? Yep, read the next case.

QUESTIONS BEFORE THE CASE

1. As you read the case, ask yourself whether the holding is consistent with objective theory?
2. Irrespective of how you answer the first question, ask yourself whether the result makes common sense?

PAINE V. PACIFIC MUT. LIFE INS. CO.

Circuit Court of Appeals, Eighth Circuit
51 F. 689 (1892)

Statement by SANBORN, CIRCUIT JUDGE:

This was an appeal from a decree of the circuit court for the district of Nebraska, dismissing the bill of appellant to enforce specific performance of a contract which the bill alleged the appellee made with Forrest L. Kendall on May 29, 1890, to insure his life for $10,000, and to recover of the appellee for his death that amount, less a few dollars of unpaid premium. The answer denied that such a contract was made, and the court below, after hearing the cause on the pleadings and proofs, dismissed the bill. From the pleadings and proofs the following facts appear:

The complainant was the administrator of the estate of Forrest L. Kendall, and the defendant was a corporation organized under the laws of California, and authorized to insure lives in the state of Nebraska. Its home office and principal place of business was in San Francisco, Cal. One Limback was the agent of the defendant at Grand Island, in Nebraska, to solicit applications and collect premiums, but without authority to make, or to agree to make, contracts of insurance for the defendant. On May 29, 1890, he solicited and obtained from Kendall his application to the defendant, in writing and print, for a policy of insurance on his life. This application was signed by Kendall, and contained the following stipulations:

'Do you understand and agree that only the officers of the home office have authority to determine whether or not a policy shall issue on any application, and that they act only on the statements and representations in the application, and that no statements, representations, or information made or given by or to the person soliciting or taking this application for a policy, or to any other person, shall be binding on the company, or in any manner affect its rights, unless such statements, representations, or information be reduced to writing, and presented to the officers of the company at the home office in this application? Yes. * * * And it is agreed that there shall be no contract of insurance until a policy shall have been issued and delivered by the said company, and the first premium thereon paid, while the person proposed for insurance is living and in the same condition of health described in this application; and that, if said policy be issued, the declarations, agreements, and warranties herein contained shall constitute a part of the contract, and the contract of insurance, when made, shall be held and construed at all times and places to have been made in the city of San Francisco, in the state of California; * * * policy to be dated the first day of June, 1890. (All policies of the company are issued as of the first day of each month.) * * * It is agreed that the foregoing statements and answers, as well as all others made or to be made to the company's medical examiner or soliciting agent, are warranted to be true, and are offered to the company as a consideration of the contract, which shall not take effect until the first premium shall have been paid during the life and good health of the person herein proposed for insurance.'

When he obtained the application, the agent, Limback, agreed to take $10 of the first quarterly premium in trade at Kendall's store, and after Kendall's death he did get from that store, on this account, a box of cigars. Kendall agreed to pay the balance of this premium, $59.90, when the policy was delivered. The application was forwarded to the home office. On June 3, 1890, Kendall was drowned. On June 6, 1890, the application first reached the defendant's home office, and on June 7, 1890, it was examined and approved by its medical director, in ignorance of Kendall's death. On June 9, 1890, defendant learned of his death, and refused to issue a policy. On June 30, 1890, complainant tendered $59.90 to Limback in payment of the first quarterly premium, but he refused to receive it, and offered to pay $10 to complainant, which he refused to accept. This suit was then brought.

Opinion

* * *

The material facts in this case are undisputed, and the evidence calls for no comment. There is neither doubt nor difficulty as to the rules of law applicable to these facts. To discuss them would be futile, for they are not debatable; they are founded in reason, settled by long lines of decisions, and conclusively demonstrate that there could have been no contract by this defendant, under the facts of this case, to insure the life of the decedent. Ample reason for this conclusion will appear from the bare statement of some of these rules. As no policy was issued, and the custom of insurance companies is to issue a policy when a contract of life insurance is made, the presumption is that on May 29, 1890, when the application was signed, there were negotiations, but no contract, and no purpose to contract otherwise than by a policy made and delivered upon simultaneous payment of premium.

The provisions of the application that the decedent understood and agreed that only the officers of the home office of the defendant company had authority to determine whether or not a policy should issue on any application, that he agreed that there should be no contract of insurance until a policy should have been issued and delivered by the company, and the first premium thereon paid, * * * make conclusive this legal presumption, and establish the fact that by the transaction of May 29, 1890, and the delivery of the application to the local agent of the company, the decedent merely made a proposal to become insured by the defendant company, which could not become a contract until it was accepted by the officers of the defendant at the home office in San Francisco.

* * * That the application provided that the date of the policy should be June 1, 1890, when it also provided that all policies should be dated the first of some month, is immaterial, in view of the fact that the decedent twice expressly stipulated in this application that the contract of insurance should not take effect until the first premium was paid and the policy delivered during the life and good health of the applicant. That the local agent agreed to take, or did take, $10 of the first premium of $69.90 in trade from decedent's store in no way modified or affected the positive and clearly expressed terms of this proposal relative to the time when, and the conditions upon which, the contract should take effect.

* * * The death of Kendall on June 3, 1890, before the application had reached defendant's home office, revoked his offer to become insured by the

defendant company, which was contained in this application, and rendered the making of the proposed contract of insurance impossible. An offer is revoked by the death of the proposer, or by the death of the party to whom the offer is made before acceptance. 'The continuance of an offer is in the nature of its constant repetition, which necessarily requires some one capable of making a repetition. Obviously, this can no more be done by a dead man than a contract can in the first instance be made by a dead man.' Pratt v. Trustees, 93 Ill. 475, 479; Dickinson v. Dodds, L.R. 2 Ch.Div. 463, 475; Phipps v. Jones, 20 Pa.St. 260, 264; Wallace v. Townsend, 43 Ohio St. 537, 3 N.E.Rep. 601.

Conceding that the defendant could and did determine to accept the application on June 7, 1890, one day after its receipt and four days after the death of Kendall, still such acceptance and the contract, if so made, were void, because the life that was the subject-matter of the contract was not then in existence. * * * Parties make no contract where the thing which they supposed to exist, and the existence of which was indispensable to the making of their contract, had no existence. Franklin v. Long, 7 Gill.& J. 407, 419; * * *

There is no view of the facts or the law under which it can be found that there was a contract between the decedent and the defendant company in this case, and the decree below is affirmed, with costs.

QUESTIONS AND NOTE

1. Questions about the facts of this case

   1.1. Why do you suppose that only $10 (in the form of a box of cigars) of the first premium was paid? Does it matter?

   1.2. Suppose Kendall was in a vegetative state as a result of his swimming accident of June 6, but did not die. Would the offer then have remained good?

2. Questions about the law

   2.1. Does it matter that when defendant decided to issue the policy on June 7 it was ignorant of the fact that Kendall had drowned the previous day?

   2.2. Would it have made any difference to the court if the application had not contained the language delaying the effectiveness of the policy until approved at the home office?

   2.3. Would it have made any difference if Mr. Kendall didn't drown until after June 7?

   2.4. What is the proper legal characterization of the application once dispatched to the company?

2.5. Does Mr. Limback have to give back the cigars?

3. Note

Ok, we know what you're thinking: *Paine* is an old case; older even than Epstein, and its holding is just some ancient legal history. But you'd be wrong again. Section 48 of the *Restatement (Second) of Contracts* provides: "An offeree's power of acceptance terminates when the offeree or offeror dies or is deprived of legal capacity to enter into the proposed contract." Here's how one somewhat more contemporary decision justified the rule:

> In the making of a contract there must be two minds, at least, concurring at the moment of its completion. But this cannot occur if there be but one of the contracting parties in existence. Hence, the death of a party who had the right of revocation or withdrawal of an offer to contract renders the completion impossible and terminates the negotiations or proceedings at the very point where they were when he died. So, an acceptance by the optionee or the other party subsequent to that event is ineffectual to close the bargain. Therefore, the death of a party while a contract is being made, even though only a single act remains to be done, renders the completion of the contract impossible. * * * *New Headley Tobacco Warehouse Co. v. Gentry's Ex'r,* 307 Ky. 857, 212 S.W.2d 325 (Ky Ct. App. 1948).

"Two minds"? Is this court out of its mind? Is the above statement consistent with the objective theory? Is the Restatement consistent with the objective theory?

Restatement (Second) of Contracts § 48 has been criticized on the ground that, under the modern view of the formation of contracts, it is not the actual meeting of the minds of the contracting parties that is the determining factor, but rather the apparent state of mind of the parties embodied in an expression of mutual consent. Thus, the acceptance by an offeree of an offer, which is apparently still open, should result in an enforceable contract notwithstanding the prior death of the offeror unknown to the offeree. Although the rule that the death of the offeror terminates the offer regardless of notice to the offeree is retained in the *Restatement (Second) of Contracts*, comment (a) to § 48 suggests that it is without much support. Why do you think the drafters retained the rule?

4. **You Be the Lawyer!**

If you represented Mr. Paine in this action, what arguments, other than the ones described in the opinion, would you have raised? What advice would you have given to Mr. Kendall on May 29?

Even if the "termination by death" rule didn't raise conceptual problems, do you have problems with its application? Try the following problems:

PROBLEMS

Case #1. Markell offers Epstein a ten-year lease on one of the many pieces of commercial real estate he owns in Chicago, and at which Epstein plans to open a branch of his wonderful restaurant, Tex's Knedlicki. Before accepting Markell's offer, Epstein wants to be sure that he can obtain the necessary financing from Friendly Finance. Upon being assured about the financing a couple of days later, he plans to accept. Before doing so, however, he reads in the newspaper that Markell choked on chorizo-stuffed dates while eating at Avec and died. Is it too late for Epstein to accept Markell's offer?

Case #2. Same facts as #1 above, but Epstein does not read of Markell's earlier death until after he has sent Markell both an e-mail and a letter communicating his acceptance. Can Epstein enforce the lease agreement against Markell's estate?

Case #3. Same facts as #2, except Markell does not die until six months after Epstein's acceptance. Can Epstein enforce the lease against Markell's estate?

Case #4. Same facts as #2, except that Epstein had not only arranged for financing, but entered into long-term contracts for the delivery of 200 cases of ribs and other foodstuffs to the new restaurant. Does that change your answer?

NOTE ON TERMINATION BY SUPERVENING INCAPACITY

At common law, the offeror's supervening mental incapacity, as established by an adjudication of incompetence or appointment of a guardian, has the same effect on the offeree's power of acceptance as the offeror's death. Professor Arthur Corbin, never a fan to begin with of the rule that the death of the offeror automatically terminates the offeree's power of acceptance, opined that the case for terminating an offer on the subsequent insanity of the offeror without the knowledge of the offeree is "even more doubtful than the rule as to the offeror's death." 1 CORBIN, CONTRACTS § 54, at 231.

Why do you suppose Corbin felt that way? Bear in mind that we are speaking of incapacity occurring *after* the offer has been made, and, of course, before it is accepted.

Mental incompetence at the time the offer is made raises a different issue, namely *capacity* to contract, a subject we take up in the next chapter. As you will see, such a contract is voidable at the instance of the mentally incompetent party.

That means that if Epstein offers to sell his Lexus to Ponoroff for $100 before he loses his mind, the issue of whether Ponoroff can enforce his deal will turn on whether Epstein's dementia occurs before or after Ponoroff accepts the offer, regardless of what Ponoroff knows about Epstein's condition at the time he accepts. On the other hand, if Epstein was already around the bend at the time the offer was made, he (or his guardian) can avoid the contract. Is that logical or does Professor Corbin's position make more sense to you?

---

4. PRESERVING THE OFFER

Sometimes, even though an offer is attractive to the offeree, the offeree may not be ready to commit to the deal. For example, the offeree may need time to be sure he can arrange necessary financing or order his other affairs (locate customers, suppliers, etc.) in a manner that ensures that the proposed contract will be a beneficial one. If the offeree simply accepts the offer now, he assumes the risk if the contingencies creating the uncertainty do not occur. On the other hand, if he doesn't accept now, he runs the risk that the offer may be withdrawn or that some other event may occur that terminates the offer.

The logical course of action, therefore, is to request the offeror's agreement to hold the offer open—make it irrevocable—for a specified period of time. If the offeror agrees, in effect, a separate, ancillary promise has been made under the terms of which the offeror surrenders his right to revoke the offer for the principal contract for the agreed period of time. But what has the offeror received in return? If the offeror receives nothing in return, can this ancillary promise be enforced? Obviously, in *Dickinson v. Dodds* the court answered that question in the negative *unless* the ancillary promise is supported by a separate consideration. The cases and materials collected in this section address the issue of when a promise of irrevocability may become binding on the offeror and also examine the consequences of irrevocability as they relate not only to revocation by the offeror, but also to other circumstances that ordinarily terminate an offer.

QUESTIONS BEFORE THE CASE

1. Can you count how many option contracts are involved in this case?
2. What do each of these option contracts have in common? How, if at all, do they differ?

BEALL V. BEALL

Court of Special Appeals of Maryland
45 Md.App. 489, 413 A.2d 1365 (1980),
rev'd on other grounds, 291 Md. 224, 434 A.2d 1015 (1981)

MOORE, J.

This appeal concerns an alleged option agreement and a suit by Carlton G. Beall for the specific performance thereof. The Circuit Court for Prince George's County (Melbourne, J.) found the agreement unsupported by consideration and dismissed plaintiff's bill of complaint pursuant to Maryland Rule 535. From that order, he appeals to this Court.

I

In 1968, the plaintiff, Carlton G. Beall, purchased a farm in Prince George's County from Pearl Beall. At that time, the property was farmed by Pearl's son, Calvin Beall. The record discloses that Carlton, the plaintiff, and Calvin were second cousins. Calvin was married to Cecelia M. Beall, the defendant herein. Carlton agreed that Calvin could continue to farm the property if he would pay the annual property taxes. Calvin and Cecelia owned and resided on a parcel of about one-half acre that was bordered on three sides by the farm bought by the plaintiff; and it is that parcel that is the subject of this dispute.

On the day that plaintiff contracted to buy Pearl's farm, he obtained a three-year option to purchase Calvin's and Cecelia's parcel for $28,000.00. The option recited a consideration of $100.00 which was paid by check. In 1971, the parties executed a new option, for five years, but on the same terms and reciting an additional $100.00 consideration.

This 1971 option was never exercised by the plaintiff, but prior to its expiration the following language was appended at the bottom of the page:

> "As of October 6, 1975, we, Calvin E. Beall and Cecelia M. Beall, agree to continue this option agreement three more years—Feb. 1, 1976 to Feb. 1, 1979.
>
> /s/ Calvin E. Beall
>
> /s/ Cecelia M. Beall."

It is this purported extension that forms the basis for plaintiff's bill of complaint seeking specific performance of the agreement. Calvin died in August 1977, and Cecelia now holds the fee simple title by right of survivorship. In letters dated May 24, 1978 and September 14, 1978, the plaintiff advised Cecelia that he was electing to exercise the option. He scheduled settlement for October 5, 1978. As the chancellor found:

> "It is undisputed in this case that Mr. Carlton Beall did eventually hire attorneys to search the title, set a settlement date, attend the

settlement, and was ready, willing and able to perform the contract."

Cecelia refused to attend settlement, and this suit for specific performance ensued.

At trial, after plaintiff presented his evidence, Cecelia moved to dismiss the bill of complaint. The chancellor granted the motion because she felt that the option agreements were not supported by consideration in that "no benefit * * * flowed to Cecelia Beall." In addition, as to the 1975 alleged option, the chancellor ruled:

> "[T]here is no consideration recited in that extension or purported extension of the original option contract. And the one extension that had occurred in the interim, even then would also fail because there is no consideration stated in the extension. It is clear that consideration must pass for the extension each time, in some form of consideration. None is stated within the written four lines."

On appeal, the plaintiff contends that the chancellor erred in dismissing the bill of complaint and in excluding certain testimony relative to oral transactions with Calvin, the deceased husband of the defendant.

II

Under Maryland law it is clear that "an option is not a mere offer to sell, which can be withdrawn by the optionor at any time before acceptance, but a binding agreement if supported by consideration." *Blondell v. Turover*, 195 Md. 251, 256, 72 A.2d 697, 699 (1950). In other words, an option is an agreement to keep an offer open that requires consideration to give it its irrevocable character. * * * Once the option is exercised by the optionee a binding contract is created that may be enforced through a decree commanding specific performance. * * * It is apparent, then, that an option must be supported by consideration in order to be irrevocable for the period provided in the option.

When, however, the consideration allegedly supporting an option fails or is nonexistent, the option is no longer irrevocable but rather it becomes "a mere offer to sell, which can be withdrawn by the optionor at any time before acceptance. * * *" *Blondell v. Turover, supra*, 195 Md. at 256, 72 A.2d at 699. The failure of consideration destroys the irrevocability of the option; it nonetheless retains its essential characteristic as an offer to buy or sell for the period stated in the option or until revoked. It has been recognized that equity will enforce a resulting contract despite lack of consideration for the option:

> "While the rule that equity will enforce a contract consummated by the acceptance of an option within the time and upon the terms of the option is often stated in such a way as to suggest or imply the necessity of consideration for the option, all that is meant in

> most cases is that a consideration is necessary to prevent the defendant from asserting his withdrawal of the option before its acceptance by the plaintiff and before the expiration of the time fixed in the option within which acceptance could be made."

71 Am. Jur. 2d, Specific Performance § 143 (1973) (footnotes omitted). See 1A Corbin on Contracts § 263 (1963). See generally *Kahn v. General Development Corp.*, 40 Del. Ch. 83, 92, 174 A.2d 307, 312 (1961) (failure of consideration "destroyed the irrevocability of the option"). * * *

Assuming, arguendo, that the 1975 option was unsupported by consideration, it remained as an offer to sell the parcel for $28,000. The offer was open until February 1, 1979, but it was revocable at any time by action of Calvin and Cecelia Beall. As stated in the case of *Holifield v. Veterans' Farm & Home Board*, 218 Miss. 446, 450, 67 So. 2d 456, 457 (1953):

> "It is well settled that an option is not binding as a contract where there is no consideration, unless it is accepted within the time limit and before the offer is withdrawn. Since there was no consideration paid by the Veterans' Farm and Home Board and Mauldin for the option, it could have been revoked by the Holifields at any time before the Veterans' Farm and Home Board and Mauldin notified them that they intended to buy the land; *but since the offer was accepted within the time limit and before withdrawal, the contract became binding upon all parties as it was thereafter supported by the consideration of the mutual promises.*" (Emphasis added.)

This statement is generally in accord with the Maryland cases, *supra.*

The chancellor should, therefore, have determined whether or not there was a valid, unrevoked offer to sell the property in dispute and whether or not there was a proper acceptance of that offer sufficient to create a contract specifically enforceable in equity.[1] These issues of offer and acceptance primarily involve factual determinations that initially must be evaluated by the chancellor. As an appellate court, we are limited to a review of the chancellor's findings under the "clearly erroneous" standard. Md. Rule 1086. But our review is dependent upon the existence of factual findings on the issues material to the case. Such findings were not made below.

It was error for the chancellor to dismiss plaintiff's bill of complaint at the close of his case. A new trial, in accordance with this opinion, is necessitated.

---

1 We express no opinion concerning the validity of the chancellor's finding that there was no consideration for the option.

Order reversed; cause remanded for a new trial in accordance with this opinion; costs to abide the final result.

QUESTIONS, NOTES, AND CONNECTIONS

1. Questions about the facts of this case

   1.1. In 1975, when the option was extended for an additional three years, what was each side bargaining for?

   1.2. What was the mistake that Carlton made in 1975? According to the court, when did Carlton's option to purchase the Calvin/Cecelia property expire?

2. Questions about the law

   2.1. Why does the law impose a requirement that the promise of irrevocability be supported by a separate consideration? Would the outcome in *Beall* have been different if, in 1971, the extension of the option had been for eight years instead of five even though the consideration remained $100?

   2.2. What would the result have been if the 1971 extension had been for eight years, but in year six, and before Carlton exercised the option, Cecelia joined Calvin in the great beyond? Does an option, if enforceable, survive the death of the optionor? Suppose the option had been for eight years, but in year five Carlton told Cecelia that he had decided not to exercise the option. If Carlton changes his mind, can he still enforce the option, or was it terminated by his prior rejection? *See Restatement (Second) of Contracts* § 37. If your answer is "yes," what if Cecelia, having taken Carlton at his word, has already entered into a contract to sell the property to someone else? Is Cecelia just SOL (that's a technical legal term meaning up the creek without a paddle) or is there some other way in which Cecelia might avoid liability under the option?

3. Notes

   3.1. You will note in the citation following the caption of the case a reference to "reversed on other grounds." Well, here's, as Paul Harvey used to say, "the rest of the story."* The Maryland Court of Appeals ordered reinstatement of the decision of the trial court on the basis that the offer to sell in 1975 was revocable since it was not supported by consideration, and was revoked by Calvin's death in 1977. The majority opinion based this conclusion on the

---

* Paul Harvey was Epstein's generation's Rush Limbaugh, albeit kinder and thinner. *Cf.* Alan Smith, *Rush Limbaugh is not Paul Harvey,* Baton Rouge Advocate, March 7, 2009; WLNR 4451001.

particular fashion in which Calvin and Cecelia held title—tenancy by the entirety—stating that continuation of an offer to sell by tenants by the entireties depends on the continuous assent of both tenants, which was no longer viable after the death of one tenant. In a perhaps better reasoned dissenting opinion, Judge Smith noted, "Given the fact that the wife in this instance was a party to the offer and that the entire title is now vested in her by operation of law [upon Calvin's death], I see no logical reason for holding that she is not bound by *her* offer."

3.2. Apropos of almost nothing, other than as a reminder that these cases do involve real people, here is a blurb from Carlton's obituary in 1987:

> Carlton G. Beall, 69, former postmaster of Washington, chief U.S. marshal for the District of Columbia and sheriff of Prince George's County, died of heart and kidney ailments July 20 at Georgetown University Hospital.
>
> A supporter of the Republican Party all his life, Mr. Beall was an unsuccessful candidate for the GOP nomination for governor of Maryland in 1978, and made an unsuccessful bid for Prince George's County executive when that office was created in 1971. Since he retired from the Postal Service in 1976, he had been a real estate developer and investor in Prince George's County.
>
> http://www.highbeam.com/doc/1P2-1333999.html

The timeframes correspond nicely with the case. The parties entered into the option extensions in 1971 and 1975—times that were very busy for Carlton Beall, thus perhaps accounting for his failure to provide for consideration on the latter occasion. His attempt to exercise the option in 1978 coincides with the time after he left public service and became a real estate investor and developer in Prince Georges County.

3.3. Option contracts can take a variety of different forms, such as an offer with an ancillary contract not to revoke (*"I offer to sell you my land for $50,000 and, in consideration of $50, I agree not to revoke this offer for 30 days"*) or a contract with a condition (*"In consideration of $50, I agree to sell you my land if, within 30 days, you pay me $50,000"*). In either case, it comes down to pretty much the same thing. For some separate consideration, the offeror is bound for a period of time pending a decision by the offeree.

3.4. As a general rule, in civil law systems, the mere statement of irrevocability will be enforced. Indeed, both the *United Nations Convention on Contracts for the International Sale of Goods*, § 16(2)(a), and the *UNIDROIT Principles of International*

Commercial Contracts, Principle 2.4(2)(a), effectively provide that an offer cannot be revoked if it states that it is irrevocable, whether by providing a fixed time for acceptance or otherwise. You might wonder why the rule is different in common law jurisdictions. Your answer lies in the common law's general requirement of consideration as a condition for enforcement of promises, a topic that we examine in depth in the next chapter. The next case, however, considers what it takes to satisfy this requirement of consideration in the context of an option contract.

4. **You Be the Lawyer!**

   If you represent Carlton on remand, what evidence will you seek to put forward? How about if you represent Cecelia?

5. Connections

   How is this case different, if at all, from *Dickinson v. Dodds*? What does your answer to that question tell you about the relationship between the rules on terminating and preserving the offer? Consider again the rule on termination by death. Would it matter if an offer expressly stated: "This offer shall survive my death and be binding upon my heirs and successors"?

QUESTION BEFORE THE CASE

Is an option contract not supported by consideration void or voidable?

BOARD OF CONTROL OF EASTERN MICHIGAN UNIVERSITY V. BURGESS

Court of Appeals of Michigan
45 Mich.App. 183, 206 N.W.2d 256 (1973)

Opinion by: BURNS.

On February 15, 1966, defendant signed a document which purported to grant to plaintiff a 60-day option to purchase defendant's home. That document, which was drafted by plaintiff's agent, acknowledged receipt by defendant of "One and no/100 ($1.00) Dollar and other valuable consideration". Plaintiff concedes that neither the one dollar nor any other consideration was ever paid or even tendered to defendant. On April 14, 1966, plaintiff delivered to defendant written notice of its intention to exercise the option. On the closing date defendant rejected plaintiff's tender of the purchase price. Thereupon, plaintiff commenced this action for specific performance.

At trial defendant claimed that the purported option was void for want of consideration [and] that any underlying offer by defendant had been revoked prior to acceptance by plaintiff. * * * The trial judge * * * held that defendant's acknowledgment of receipt of consideration bars any subsequent contention to the contrary. Accordingly, the trial judge entered judgment for plaintiff.

Defendant appeals. She claims that acknowledgment of receipt of consideration does not bar the defense of failure of consideration. * * *

Options for the purchase of land, if based on valid consideration, are contracts which may be specifically enforced. * * * Conversely, that which purports to be an option, but which is not based on valid consideration, is not a contract and will not be enforced. * * * One dollar is valid consideration for an option to purchase land, provided the dollar is paid or at least tendered. * * * In the instant case defendant received no consideration for the purported option of February 15, 1966.

A written acknowledgment of receipt of consideration merely creates a rebuttable presumption that consideration has, in fact, passed. [Nothing] * * * bars the presentation of evidence to contradict any such acknowledgment. * * *

It is our opinion that the document signed by defendant on February 15, 1966, is not an enforceable option, and that defendant is not barred from so asserting.

The trial court premised its holding to the contrary on *Lawrence v. McCalmont*, 43 U.S. (2 How) 426, 452; 11 L Ed 326, 336 (1844). That case is significantly distinguishable from the instant case. Mr. Justice Story held that "[t]he guarantor acknowledged the receipt of one dollar, and is now estopped to deny it." However, in reliance upon the guaranty substantial credit had been extended to the guarantor's sons. The guarantor had received everything she bargained for, save one dollar. * * * In the instant case defendant claims that she never received any of the consideration promised her.

That which purports to be an option for the purchase of land, but which is not based on valid consideration, is a simple offer to sell the same land. * * * An option is a contract collateral to an offer to sell whereby the offer is made irrevocable for a specified period. * * * Ordinarily, an offer is revocable at the will of the offeror. Accordingly, a failure of consideration affects only the collateral contract to keep the offer open, not the underlying offer.

A simple offer may be revoked for any reason or for no reason by the offeror at any time prior to its acceptance by the offeree. * * * Thus, the question in this case becomes, "Did defendant effectively revoke her offer to sell before plaintiff accepted that offer?"

* * *

Defendant testified that within hours of signing the purported option she telephoned plaintiff's agent and informed him that she would not abide by the option unless the purchase price was increased. Defendant also testified that when plaintiff's agent delivered to her on April 14, 1966, plaintiff's notice of its intention to exercise the purported option, she told him that "the option was off".

Plaintiff's agent testified that defendant did not communicate to him any dissatisfaction until sometime in July, 1966.

If defendant is telling the truth, she effectively revoked her offer several weeks before plaintiff accepted that offer, and no contract of sale was created. If plaintiff's agent is telling the truth, defendant's offer was still open when plaintiff accepted that offer, and an enforceable contract was created. The trial judge thought it unnecessary to resolve this particular dispute. In light of our holding the dispute must be resolved.

An appellate court cannot assess the credibility of witnesses. We have neither seen nor heard them testify. * * * Accordingly, we remand this case to the trial court for additional findings of fact based on the record already before the court.

* * *

QUESTIONS, NOTE, AND CONNECTIONS

1. Questions about the facts of this case

    1.1. Why didn't the university just pay the dollar?

    1.2. What was the "other valuable consideration"?

    1.3. Who drafted the February 15, 1966 document? Was that a factor in the case? Should it have been?

    1.4. On February 15, 1966, do you think that the defendant believed that the university had a non-revocable 60-day option to purchase her property? What do you think the university believed?

2. Questions about the law

    2.1. How did the reasoning of the trial court and the court of appeals differ?

    2.2. How is the Michigan Court of Appeals' decision in *Board of Control* distinguishable from the U.S. Supreme Court's holding in *Lawrence v. McCalmont*, the case on which the trial court relied?

2.3. Is the holding in *Board of Control* consistent with *Beall*?

2.4. Just what is a "rebuttable presumption"?

3. Note

Not all courts agree with *Board of Control* insofar as the effect of a recital of consideration is concerned. Some courts, for example, treat the recital as a binding acknowledgement of payment. *See Real Estate Co. v. Rudolph*, 301 Pa. 502, 153 A. 438 (1930). The *Restatement (Second) of Contracts* adopts a somewhat different approach in § 87(1)(a). Take a look at that provision now. How would *Board of Control* have been decided if the court of appeals had applied that rule? As a general proposition, most lay people like it when the law conforms to their own intuitive, common sense judgment of what the law ought to be. Which rule—*Board of Control* or *Restatement (Second)* § 87(1)(a)—more closely conforms to what the true intentions of the parties probably are in these cases where the contract recites a consideration?

4. **You Be the Lawyer!**

Assume you represent the University (not a great client, by the way, since universities always want fee discounts). Anyway, after this decision has been rendered, what steps will you take in deciding how to approach the hearing on remand? And why?

5. Connections

Is the traditional standard governing when an irrevocable offer will be enforced consistent with the rules discussed in the last section concerning destruction of the offer? Why should the enforceability of an option contract turn on whether something of value has passed from the optionee to the optionor? Or does it? What is required to make an option enforceable?

The classical view that a mere promise to hold an offer open for a stated period of time is not itself enforceable is carried forward in the *Restatement (Second) of Contracts* § 25, which provides that: *"An option contract is a promise which meets the requirements for the formation of a contract and limits the promisor's power to revoke an offer."* Of course, the central "requirement for the formation of a contract" is the existence of payment or some other form of consideration given in exchange for the promise of irrevocability, separate and apart from the consideration supporting the underlying offer.*

* At common law, a promise not to revoke would also be enforceable if given under seal. Most states no longer attribute any legal significance to the use of a seal—although the seal is still pretty popular, we understand, at Sea World.

Thus, today, a typical option contract might take the following form: "In return for payment of $100, A hereby grants B the right through January 5, 2002, to purchase his property for $100,000." The consideration for the promise of irrevocability in this example is the $100, while the consideration for the property, if B elects before the expiry of the option to accept, is $100,000.

The brief remaining materials in this section consider whether there are any other circumstances in our legal system where a promise of irrevocability will be enforced despite the absence of consideration. By now you have surely learned in law school that there are few rules without exception, so it will come as no surprise to you to learn that such circumstances do indeed exist.

NOTE ON FIRM OFFERS

Consistent with its philosophy of conforming the governing principles of commercial law with the norms and expectations of the marketplace, the U.C.C. creates an exception to the rule set forth in *Beall* that an offer, even though stated to be irrevocable, may be still revoked unless supported by consideration. The exception is in § 2–205 for so-called "firm offers."

§ 2–205. Firm Offers.

An offer by a merchant to buy or sell goods in a signed writing which by its terms gives assurance that it will be held open is not revocable, for lack of consideration, during the time stated or if no time is stated for a reasonable time, but in no event may such period of irrevocability exceed three months; but any such term of assurance on a form supplied by the offeree must be separately signed by the offeror.

PROBLEMS ON FIRM OFFERS

Markell, the owner of a chain of high-end wine and spirituous liquors stores, runs an internet ad at the beginning of May offering a case of 750 ml bottles of Finlandia Vodka for only $200. The ad states that the deal will remain open until the end of the month. Thinking this is a great deal on Finlandia, and tired of drinking cheap Seagram's Vodka, on May 20, Ponoroff goes to one of Markell's stores, where he sees the Finlandia case, but with a price of $280 per case. Upon inquiring about the special deal, the manager tells Ponoroff that Markell decided to withdrew that offer about a week ago.

1. Can Ponoroff successfully claim entitlement to the price in the ad?

2. How, if at all, would it change your answer if Markell ran a marijuana store in Colorado Springs, but had 40 cases of the Finlandia Vodka shipped back to his store during a recent vacation to Helsinki?

The theory behind U.C.C. § 2–205, as stated in the Official Comments, is that when a merchant makes such a promise he understands and intends for it to be binding, and such offers are so understood in the marketplace. Thus, the provision gives effect to this deliberate intention and reasonable expectation. The requirements that the promise be signed and in writing ensures the seriousness of the merchant's promise to effectively create an option contract. A similar form of statutory option contract, applicable to merchants in the non-sale of goods context, can be found in § 5–1109 of the New York General Obligations Law. However, in either case, it is important to bear in mind that there cannot be an enforceable *firm offer* until there is an *offer*, ascertained in the usual way. *See Coastal Aviation, Inc. v. Commander Aircraft Co.*, 937 F.Supp. 1051 (S.D.N.Y. 1996) (holding that the defendant's statement concerning its intent to hold a particular area open for the plaintiff in connection with a proposed exclusive dealership arrangement did not evince an intent to be bound by a promise to do so and, hence, could not be enforced as a "firm offer" within the meaning of U.C.C. § 2–205).

PROBLEM ON RIGHT OF FIRST REFUSAL

Epstein owned two four-acre parcels of land on which he grew marijuana that he sold for medicinal use in California. Markell, deciding that this looked like a pretty lucrative business, offered to purchase one of the two parcels for $100,000. As part of the final contract for purchase and sale, Epstein granted Markell a three-year "right of first refusal" in the event of any proposed sale of the second parcel by Epstein. A year later, Epstein solicited an offer from Ponoroff to purchase the second parcel for $125,000. Upon learning of this offer, Markell promptly notified Epstein that he was exercising his first refusal right and that he would send a certified check for $125,000 to Epstein the next day in payment for the other parcel. Epstein turned down Ponoroff's offer and returned Markell's check, claiming that he was going to retain the property.

Incensed, Markell has brought an action against Epstein for specific performance on the basis that he timely exercised his right of first refusal and that Epstein breached this contract both by (1) soliciting Ponoroff's offer, and (2) returning Markell's check. What result in Markell's suit and why?

NOTE ON OPTION CONTRACTS AND RELIANCE

So far, our examination of irrevocability can be boiled down to the following set of rules: All offers are revocable, even when they're stated to be irrevocable (or open for a specified period of time), *unless* the promise of irrevocability is supported by independent consideration (including perhaps the mere recital of consideration) or made enforceable by statute. Are there any other circumstances where an offer will be deemed irrevocable?

Suppose Epstein offers Markell, a recent law school graduate with significant student loans, a job as an associate at Epstein's highly successful law firm in Richmond. Epstein tells Markell, "this offer is good for one week." At the time, Markell is working for another firm, which although not as prestigious or lucrative as Epstein's, still pays a decent wage. Flush with excitement over the offer, the next day Markell calls his current boss and tells him, in no uncertain terms, to take this job and shove it. Thereupon he calls Epstein to accept the offer, but before Markell can say anything, Epstein says: "Sorry pal, but I must revoke my offer." Markell responds: "You can't do that, I just quit my other job as you had to know I would; this is unfair"! Epstein's rejoinder is short and sweet: "Look, Ace, maybe you should have paid a little more attention in Contracts. My offer could be revoked at any time before acceptance regardless of how long I said it would be good for; if you wanted an option you should have paid for one." Under the traditional rules of contract law does Markell have any recourse? How about under *Restatement (Second) of Contracts* § 87(2)? Does it change your answer at all if Epstein's offer had not been for a stated period of time; *i.e.*, one week? We will return to § 87(2) in the next chapter when we examine "promissory estoppel." For now, however, we shift our attention from "offer" to "acceptance."

---

5. MODES AND METHODS OF ACCEPTANCE

In Section 2 we saw that an offer, so long as it remains open, confers on the offeree the power of acceptance. The acceptance is the other piece of the mutual assent puzzle. But how does an offeree exercise this power of acceptance? What constitutes an acceptance and when is it effective? These are some of the questions we examine in this section.

Restatement (Second) of Contracts § 50(1) provides that *"Acceptance of an offer is a manifestation of assent to the terms thereof made by the offeree in a manner invited or required by the offer."* Is that definition consistent with the objective theory of contract formation? Bear that definition in mind as you consider the next two cases dealing with who controls the permitted form of acceptance.

A. OFFEROR'S CONTROL OVER THE MANNER OF ACCEPTANCE

The plaintiff in the next case is a bank acting in its capacity as a trustee of a trust. A trust is a common law invention whose original purpose was to avoid taxes—in 14th and 15th Century England! Whether from utility or sheer cussedness, trusts survive to this day. Most trusts involve large sums of money entrusted to banks and other moneyed interests to administer for others. In these cases, a trust consists of property (often called the "*res*" from the Latin for "thing") transferred to the trusted individual (the "trustee") who has legal title to the property but holds it for the use or benefit of another (the "beneficiary"). All things considered, it is good to be the beneficiary of a trust. In fact, if we were trust beneficiaries we might not have written this book.

In the next case, however, the common law origins of tax and regulatory avoidance play a role. In Illinois and some other states, land or other real property is often held in a "land trust" in which the legal title holder is the trustee. That trustee holds title for the benefit of the beneficiary. So far, so good; the format is just like regular trusts. But why would the beneficiary not just take title directly? The twist here is that Illinois common law considers beneficial interests in land trusts as *personal* property and not as *real* property, even if the trust *res* is dirt. Thus, in Illinois, those who hold property in a land trust are not listed in the public record as owners. Also, they can transfer their interests quickly without the inherited formality that usually attends a real estate transfer.

Such arrangements, however, involve risk to the bank/trustees. They are on the title, and are in a position to make mistakes. As a consequence, they charge a fee for their services, and they also very carefully specify in the contract creating the trust what they need to do and what they do not need to do. This care usually permeates the formation process, because the bank/trustee certainly doesn't want to sign documents indicating it will buy property if the beneficiary suddenly has a change of heart and refuses to put up the funds to buy the land.* Keep this background in mind when reading the next case.

QUESTIONS BEFORE THE CASE

1. Is the law governing "acceptance" consistent with the law governing "offer'? How so?

---

* For those curious about Illinois land trusts, see Eric T. Freyfogle, *Land Trusts and the Decline of Mortgage Law*, 1988 U. ILL. L. REV. 67. This is Markell's footnote. Neither Epstein nor Ponoroff has ever had a student, in any of the 20 law schools at which they have taught, who was the least bit curious about Illinois land trusts.

2. Who is the offeror in this case?

LA SALLE NATIONAL BANK V. VEGA

Appellate Court of Illinois, Second District
167 Ill.App.3d 154, 117 Ill.Dec. 778, 520 N.E.2d 1129 (1988)

LINDBERG, J.

* * *

Plaintiff's first amended complaint alleged the existence of a contract for the sale of real estate between it and Mel [Vega] and sought specific performance of the alleged contract and damages from defendants for willfully and intentionally breaching it. Borg was permitted to intervene and filed a counterclaim naming plaintiff and defendants as counterdefendants. As finally amended, the counterclaim sought specific performance of a different contract for sale of the same real estate to Borg; a judgment declaring the alleged contract between Mel and plaintiff void and holding it for naught; and, if the alleged contract with plaintiff was "held to be a valid and enforceable contract," damages from defendants for fraud for failure to disclose the contract with plaintiff to Borg.

Borg moved for partial summary judgment * * * requesting a determination by the court that the alleged contract between plaintiff and Mel was unenforceable because it was not "signed in accordance with its terms and provisions" and because plaintiff abandoned it. The trial court granted partial summary judgment on the basis of the first ground argued by Borg.

In its verified first amended complaint, plaintiff alleged, inter alia:

> "The Defendant, MEL VEGA, on March 12, 1985, in his own behalf and in behalf of all the owners of record, entered into a Real Estate Sale Contract (herein 'Contract') with the Plaintiff, a true and correct copy of said Contract is attached hereto and incorporated herein as Exhibit A."

Exhibit A is a document, drafted by counsel for plaintiff, entitled "Real Estate Sale Contract." On the first page of this document appears the date March 12, 1985, and the statement that "Attached Rider is part of this Contract." One of the Rider's provisions states:

> "This contract has been executed and presented by an authorized agent for the purchaser, the beneficiaries of the La Salle National Bank, under Trust No. 109529, as Trustee aforesaid for the benefit of the Trust only and not personally. Upon execution of this contract by the Seller, this contract shall be presented to the trust for full execution. Upon the trust's execution, this contract

> will then be in full force and a copy of a fully executed contract along with evidence of the earnest money deposit will be delivered back to Seller."

The document was signed by Bernard Ruekberg as the purchaser's purchasing agent and by Mel Vega (on March 19, 1985, according to the date by his signature on the Rider) as the seller but not by the trustee for the purchaser.

* * *

The trial court held that there was no genuine issue of material fact that no contract was formed because the offer was made by Mel, the offer could only be accepted by execution of the document at issue by the trust, and the document was not executed by the trust. Plaintiff argues that the trial court erred because there were genuine issues of material fact regarding whether the document was ever executed by the trust and whether execution of the document by the trust was necessary to the formation of a contract. Plaintiff is incorrect on both of these points.

[The court first rejected the argument that there was a genuine issue of material fact concerning whether the document was executed by the trust, noting that the exhibit attached to the plaintiff's complaint, which was alleged to be a "true and correct copy" of the written instrument on which the claim of plaintiff was founded, did not show execution by the trust. Therefore, the plaintiff had effectively admitted that the document was never executed by the trust]

* * *

Whether a contract was formed without execution of the document by the trust may now be considered. This requires first an analysis of the events which occurred with respect to the document in terms of offer and acceptance.

The pertinent provision of the document stated:

> "This contract has been executed and presented by an authorized agent for the purchaser, the beneficiaries of the La Salle National Bank, under Trust No. 109529, as Trustee aforesaid for the benefit of the Trust only and not personally. Upon execution of this contract by the Seller, this contract shall be presented to the trust for full execution. Upon the trust's execution, this contract will then be in full force and a copy of a fully executed contract along with evidence of the earnest money deposit will be delivered back to Seller."

Thus, a specific order of events was contemplated, after which the contract would be in full force. Ruekberg (the purchasing agent) was to execute the document and present it to Mel (the seller). Then Mel was to execute it.

After Mel executed it, the document was to be presented to the trust for execution. Finally, "upon the trust's execution," the contract would be in full force.

An offer is an act on the part of one person giving another person the legal power of creating the obligation called a contract. * * * Where "the so-called offer is not intended to give the so-called offeree the power to make a contract there is no offer." * * * From the provisions contained in the document at bar, particularly the language quoted, it is apparent that there was to be no contract (i.e., the "contract" was not to be in full force) until it was executed by the trust. Thus, Ruekberg's presentation of the document he had executed to Mel was not an offer because it did not give Mel the power to make a contract by accepting it. On the other hand, when Mel executed the document and gave it back to Ruekberg he made an offer which could be accepted by execution of the document by the trust.

An offeror has complete control over an offer and may condition acceptance to the terms of the offer. * * * The language of an offer may moreover govern the mode of acceptance required, and where an offer requires a written acceptance, no other modes may be used. * * * In the case at bar, the document at issue stated clearly that the contract would be in full force upon the trust's execution. This indicates that the only mode by which Mel's offer could be accepted was execution of the document by the trust. The trust not having executed the document, there was no acceptance of the offer, and so there was no contract. * * *

Affirmed.

QUESTIONS BEFORE THE CASE

1. What does it take for a purported acceptance to be effective?
2. What's the court's explanation for why the plaintiff may not recover its attorney's fees in this case? Do you agree?

EVER-TITE ROOFING CORP. V. GREEN

Court of Appeal of Louisiana
83 So.2d 449 (1955)

AYERS, J.

This is an action for damages allegedly sustained by plaintiff as the result of the breach by the defendants of a written contract for the re-roofing of defendants' residence. Defendants denied that their written proposal or offer was ever accepted by plaintiff in the manner stipulated therein for its acceptance, and hence contended no contract was ever entered into. The trial court sustained defendants' defense and rejected plaintiff's demands and dismissed its suit at its costs. From the judgment thus rendered and signed, plaintiff appealed.

Defendants executed and signed an instrument June 10, 1953, for the purpose of obtaining the services of plaintiff in re-roofing their residence situated in Webster Parish, Louisiana. The document set out in detail the work to be done and the price therefor to be paid in monthly installments. This instrument was likewise signed by plaintiff's sale representative, who, however, was without authority to accept the contract for and on behalf of the plaintiff. This alleged contract contained these provisions:

> "This agreement shall become binding only upon written acceptance hereof, by the principal or authorized officer of the Contractor, *or upon commencing performance of the work.* This contract is Not Subject to Cancellation. * * *" (Emphasis supplied.)

Inasmuch as this work was to be performed entirely on credit, it was necessary for plaintiff to obtain credit reports and approval from the lending institution which was to finance said contract. With this procedure defendants were more or less familiar and knew their credit rating would have to be checked and a report made. On receipt of the proposed contract in plaintiff's office on the day following its execution, plaintiff requested a credit report, which was made after investigation and which was received in due course and submitted by plaintiff to the lending agency. Additional information was requested by this institution, which was likewise in due course transmitted to the institution, which then gave its approval.

The day immediately following this approval, which was either June 18 or 19, 1953, plaintiff engaged its workmen and two trucks, loaded the trucks with the necessary roofing materials and proceeded from Shreveport to defendants' residence for the purpose of doing the work and performing the services allegedly contracted for the defendants. Upon their arrival at defendants' residence, the workmen found others in the performance of the work which plaintiff had contracted to do. Defendants notified plaintiff's workmen that the work had been contracted to other parties two days before and forbade them to do the work.

Formal acceptance of the contract was not made under the signature and approval of an agent of plaintiff. It was, however, the intention of plaintiff to accept the contract by commencing the work, which was one of the ways provided for in the instrument for its acceptance, as will be shown by reference to the extract from the contract quoted hereinabove. Prior to this time, however, defendants had determined on a course of abrogating the agreement and engaged other workmen without notice thereof to plaintiff.

The basis of the judgment appealed was that defendants had timely notified plaintiff before 'commencing performance of work'. The trial court held that notice to plaintiff's workmen upon their arrival with the materials that defendants did not desire them to commence the actual work was sufficient and timely to signify their intention to withdraw from the contract. With this conclusion we find ourselves unable to agree.

Defendants' attempt to justify their delay in thus notifying plaintiff for the reason they did not know where or how to contact plaintiff is without merit. The contract itself, a copy of which was left with them, conspicuously displayed plaintiff's name, address and telephone number. Be that as it may, defendants at no time, from June 10, 1953, until plaintiff's workmen arrived for the purpose of commencing the work, notified or attempted to notify plaintiff of their intention to abrogate, terminate or cancel the contract.

Defendants evidently knew this work was to be processed through plaintiff's Shreveport office. The record discloses no unreasonable delay on plaintiff's part in receiving, processing or accepting the contract or in commencing the work contracted to be done. No time limit was specified in the contract within which it was to be accepted or within which the work was to be begun. It was nevertheless understood between the parties that some delay would ensue before the acceptance of the contract and the commencement of the work, due to the necessity of compliance with the requirements relative to financing the job through a lending agency. The evidence as referred to hereinabove shows that plaintiff proceeded with due diligence.

The general rule of law is that an offer proposed may be withdrawn before its acceptance and that no obligation is incurred thereby. This is, however, not without exceptions. For instance, Restatement of the Law of Contracts stated:

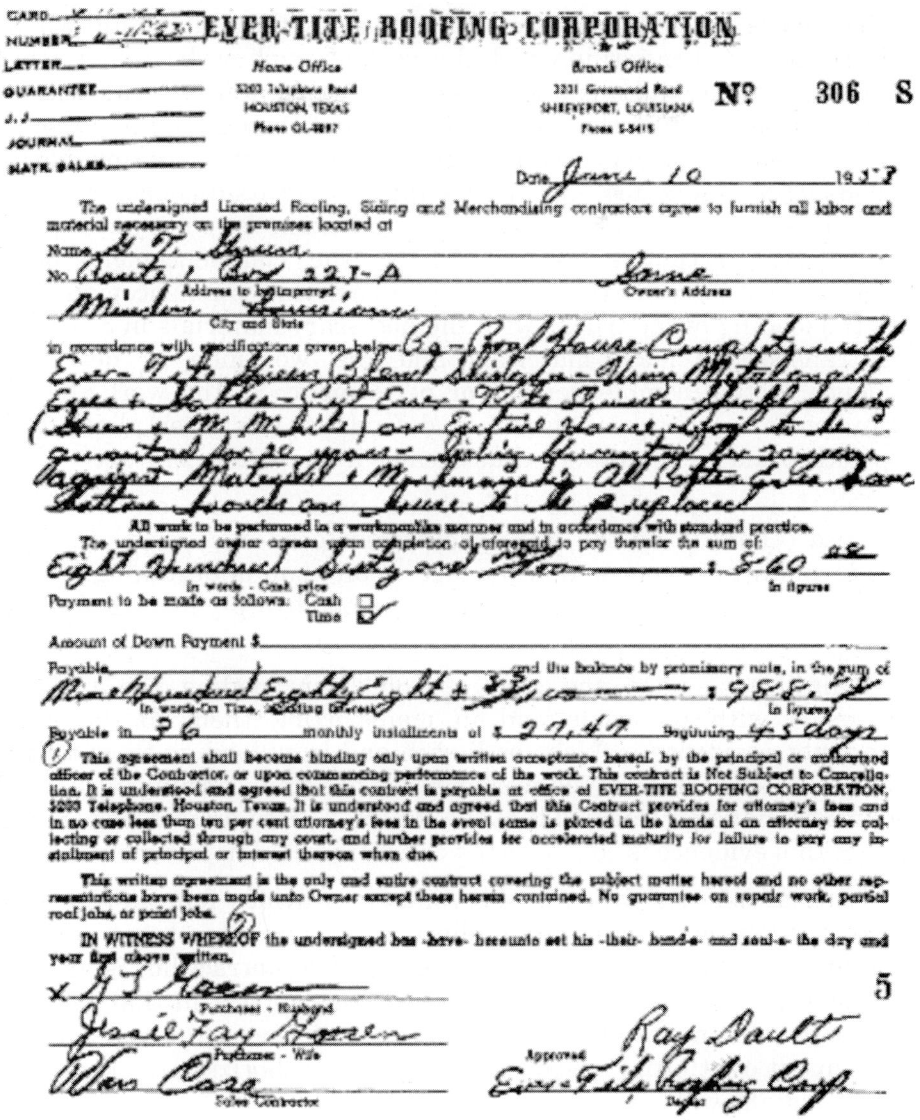

EVER-TITE ROOFING CORPORATION

CARD

NUMBER

LETTER

GUARANTEE

J. J.

JOURNAL

MATR. SALES

Home Office
5203 Telephone Road
HOUSTON, TEXAS
Phone OL-8897

Branch Office
3231 Greenwood Road
SHREVEPORT, LOUISIANA
Phone 5-5415

Nº 306 S

Date June 10 1957

The undersigned Licensed Roofing, Siding and Merchandising contractors agree to furnish all labor and material necessary on the premises located at

Name G. T. Green

No. Route 1 Box 227-A — Same

Address to be improved — Owner's Address

Minden, Louisiana

City and State

in accordance with specifications given below:

All work to be performed in a workmanlike manner and in accordance with standard practice.

The undersigned owner agrees upon completion of aforesaid to pay therefor the sum of:

Eight Hundred Sixty and no/100 — $ 860.00

In words - Cash price — In figures

Payment to be made as follows: Cash ☐ Time ☑

Amount of Down Payment $

Payable ________ and the balance by promissory note, in the sum of

Nine Hundred Eighty Eight & 35/100 — $ 988.35

In words-On Time, including interest — In figures

Payable in 36 monthly installments of $ 27.47 Beginning 45 days

(1) This agreement shall become binding only upon written acceptance hereof, by the principal or authorized officer of the Contractor, or upon commencing performance of the work. This contract is Not Subject to Cancellation. It is understood and agreed that this contract is payable at office of EVER-TITE ROOFING CORPORATION, 5203 Telephone, Houston, Texas. It is understood and agreed that this Contract provides for attorney's fees and in no case less than ten per cent attorney's fees in the event same is placed in the hands of an attorney for collecting or collected through any court, and further provides for accelerated maturity for failure to pay any installment of principal or interest thereon when due.

This written agreement is the only and entire contract covering the subject matter hereof and no other representations have been made unto Owner except these herein contained. No guarantee on repair work, partial roof jobs, or paint jobs. (2)

IN WITNESS WHEREOF the undersigned has -have- hereunto set his -their- hand-s- and seal-s- the day and year first above written.

x G. T. Green
Purchaser - Husband

Jessie Fay Green
Purchaser - Wife

Sales Contractor

Approved Ray Dault
Ever-Tite Roofing Corp.
Buyer

5

Ever-Tite Contract

"(1) The power to create a contract by acceptance of an offer terminates at the time specified in the offer, or, if no time is specified, at the end of a reasonable time.

'What is a reasonable time is a question of fact depending on the nature of the contract proposed, the usages of business and other circumstances of the case which the offeree at the time of his acceptance either knows or has reason to know."

* * *

Therefore, since the contract did not specify the time within which it was to be accepted or within which the work was to have been commenced, a reasonable time must be allowed therefor in accordance with the facts and circumstances and the evident intention of the parties. A reasonable time is contemplated where no time is expressed. What is a reasonable time depends more or less upon the circumstances surrounding each particular case. The delays to process defendants' application were not unusual. The contract was accepted by plaintiff by the commencement of the performance of the work contracted to be done. This commencement began with the loading of the trucks with the necessary materials in Shreveport and transporting such materials and the workmen to defendants' residence. Actual commencement or performance of the work therefore began before any notice of dissent by defendants was given plaintiff. The proposition and its acceptance thus became a completed contract.

By their aforesaid acts defendants breached the contract. They employed others to do the work contracted to be done by plaintiff and forbade plaintiff's workmen to engage upon that undertaking. By this breach defendants are legally bound to respond to plaintiff in damages. * * *

Plaintiff expended the sum of $85.37 in loading the trucks in Shreveport with materials and in transporting them to the site of defendants' residence in Webster Parish and in unloading them on their return, and for wages for the workmen for the time consumed. Plaintiff's Shreveport manager testified that the expected profit on this job was $226. None of this evidence is controverted or contradicted in any manner.

True, as plaintiff alleges, the contract provides for attorney's fees where an attorney is employed to collect under the contract, but this is not an action on the contract or to collect under the contract but is an action for damages for a breach of the contract. The contract in that respect is silent with reference to attorney's fees. In the absence of an agreement for the payment of attorney's fees or of some law authorizing the same, such fees are not allowed.

For the reasons assigned, the judgment appealed is annulled, avoided, reversed and set aside and there is now judgment in favor of plaintiff, Ever-Tite Roofing Corporation, against the defendants, G. T. Green and Mrs. Jessie Fay Green, for the full sum of $311.37, with 5 per cent per annum interest thereon from judicial demand until paid, and for all costs.

Reversed and rendered.

NOTE ON REQUIRED FORM OF ACCEPTANCE

The following statements in *La Salle National Bank*, *"An offeror has complete control over an offer and may condition acceptance to the terms of the offer. * * * The language of an offer may moreover govern the mode of acceptance required, and, where an offer requires a written acceptance, no other mode may be used"* reflect the principle that we encountered earlier; namely, that the offeror is "king." Not only does this principle explain why revocation will terminate an offer, but, as illustrated by *La Salle* and *Ever-Tite*, it also explains why if an offer prescribes the time, place, and/or manner of assent, the purported acceptance—the manifestation of intent to be bound—in order to be effective *must* comply without variation to the terms of the offer. This notion is, of course, consistent with the core policy of freedom of and *from* contract. The offeror has the unfettered right to determine the terms on which she is willing to deal, such that, if the offer requires as a condition to acceptance that the offeree place a paper bag over his head, dance in circles, and squawk like a chicken, then nothing less than what is bargained for will be sufficient to constitute a valid acceptance of the offer.

Sometimes, however, this rule, which is obviously intended to protect the offeror from liability other than on her terms, will end up frustrating the offeror. Consider again *La Salle National Bank.* Obviously, Mel intended to sell the property to the bank and certainly the bank wanted the property (why else did it sue?). We are often reminded in the caselaw that contract law is about "effectuating the intention of the parties." And yet, Mel was able to escape liability because, by the bank's own requirement, the proposal could not ripen into a contract until the document had been fully executed by an authorized trust officer of the bank. We think this raises some interesting questions, the answers to which may have a bearing on your advice to a client engaged in contract negotiations and how you draft a proposed agreement for that client.

QUESTIONS ABOUT *LA SALLE* AND *EVER-TITE*

1. According to the courts' decisions, who were the offerors in *La Salle National Bank* and *Ever-Tite*? Who drafted the instruments on which the assertion of contractual liability was based? Did that have a bearing on the outcome in either case? Should it have? Is it the *offeror* who controls the terms of the offer or is it more accurate to say that it is the terms of the *offer* that control the deal?

2. In *La Salle National Bank,* how important was "full execution" to the bank? Who was that provision intended to protect? Suppose it was just a formality? If so, under the guise of protecting the offeror (the king), have we not assisted the offeree in walking on the deal?

3. Why didn't La Salle National Bank simply have an officer in its trust department execute the Real Estate Sale Contract before the bank filed its complaint against Mel?

4. Returning to *Ever-Tite*, what does the following statement from the Ever-Tite form mean: "written acceptance, hereof, by the principal * * *"? What does the following statement from the *Ever-Tite* opinion mean: "Formal acceptance of the contract was not made under the signature and approval of an agent of the plaintiff"?

5. Suppose that the day before Ever-Tite planned to do the job, the Greens had called and said they were no longer interested. Would there have been a contract? Would it have mattered if, at the time they called, the Greens were aware that their credit had checked out? How could Ever-Tite have protected itself?

6. In *Ever-Tite*, the trial court had concluded that the work did not "commence" until the Ever-Tite workers arrived at the site. Is this a less reasonable construction of the language in the instrument than the appellate court's construction that the work commenced with the loading of the trucks? Even if so, was that a judgment that was appropriate to make on appeal? Accepting, *arguendo*, the trial court's construction of when the work commenced, did that justify the trial court's conclusion that there was no contract? How did the Greens *manifest* their intention to revoke? Does this square with the objective theory of contract formation?

7. Suppose that, after the Greens' credit report had been received, the Vice President of the Ever-Tite Roofing Co. had scribbled at the bottom of the instrument executed by the Greens on June 10 the notation "OK, June 13, 1953, Chester Ponoroff, Vice Pres."? *See International Filter Co. v. Conroe Gin, Ice, & Light Co.*, 277 S.W. 631 (1925).

8. **You Be the Lawyer!**

   If the Ever-Tite Roofing Company retains you after this case has been decided in order to review its "Contract" form, what suggestions will you make? Or, is the form ok as it is? After all, Ever-Tite won the case, right?

9. What happens when the offer does not stipulate the required manner or method of acceptance? Consider the next case and the material that follows.

INTRODUCTION TO *DAVIS V. JACOBY*

The next case uses the terminology *unilateral contract* and *bilateral contract*. The latter refers to a contract that is wholly executory; *i.e.*, unperformed obligations exist on the part of both parties. Thus, a bilateral contract will typically involve a promise made in exchange for another promise. A unilateral contract refers to a contract that is only executory on the part of the offeror. That is to say, the offeree's full performance is also the acceptance that gives rise to a binding contract. You encountered the concept of unilateral contract earlier in connection with some of the cases relating to advertisements as offers. That is, the plaintiffs would argue that the ad was an offer that they accepted by performing whatever was requested, such as purchasing ten gallons of gasoline.

Davis v. Jacoby reflects the attitude of the common law and the first *Restatement of Contracts*, an attitude consistent with the view of offeror as king, that every offer had to be regarded as an offer for a "unilateral" or a "bilateral" contract, and, as we'll see, this, in turn, affected the manner in which the offer could be accepted; *i.e.*, by performance or return promise.

These terms—unilateral and bilateral contract—are not to be found anywhere in either the *Restatement (Second) of Contracts* or Article 2 of the U.C.C. Nonetheless, this distinction between offers for so-called unilateral and bilateral contracts still shows up from time-to-time in the caselaw. Thus, it is important to understand the differences between the two and their implications in determining whether the parties have made a deal.

The perspective of the drafters of the *Restatement* and the U.C.C. was to make the law less formal and less inflexible. That being the case, the sentiment was that use of the terminology "unilateral" and "bilateral" tended to promote unnecessary rigidity into the law of contract formation. The thinking was that in most instances the offeror is indifferent as to what manner of assent, promise or performance, is necessary to accept the offer. She only cares that there be assent. If that's so, than strict adherence to the rigid distinction between unilateral and bilateral offers creates a risk that real contractual intent might actually be defeated because of the failure of the acceptance to comport with the form of the offer. In our judgment, this is almost what happens in *Davis v. Jacoby*. See what you think.

QUESTION BEFORE THE CASE

In determining whether an offer is seeking a performance or a return promise, how much sense does it make to focus on the *intent* of the promisor?

DAVIS V. JACOBY

Supreme Court of California
1 Cal.2d 370, 34 P.2d 1026 (1934)

PER CURIAM.

Plaintiffs appeal from a judgment refusing to grant specific performance of an alleged contract to make a will. The facts are not in dispute and are as follows:

The plaintiff Caro M. Davis was the niece of Blanche Whitehead who was married to Rupert Whitehead. Prior to her marriage in 1913 to her coplaintiff Frank M. Davis, Caro lived for a considerable time at the home of the Whiteheads, in Piedmont, California. The Whiteheads were childless and extremely fond of Caro. The record is replete with uncontradicted testimony of the close and loving relationship that existed between Caro and her aunt and uncle. During the period that Caro lived with the Whiteheads she was treated as and often referred to by the Whiteheads as their daughter. In 1913, when Caro was married to Frank Davis the marriage was arranged at the Whitehead home and a reception held there. After the marriage Mr. and Mrs. Davis went to Mr. Davis' home in Canada, where they have resided ever since. During the period 1913 to 1931 Caro made many visits to the Whiteheads, several of them being of long duration. The Whiteheads visited Mr. and Mrs. Davis in Canada on several occasions. After the marriage and continuing down to 1931 the closest and most friendly relationship at all times existed between these two families. They corresponded frequently, the record being replete with letters showing the loving relationship.

By the year 1930 Mrs. Whitehead had become seriously ill. She had suffered several strokes and her mind was failing. Early in 1931 Mr. Whitehead had her removed to a private hospital. The doctors in attendance had informed him that she might die at any time or she might linger for many months. Mr. Whitehead had suffered severe financial reverses. He had had several sieges of sickness and was in poor health. The record shows that during the early part of 1931 he was desperately in need of assistance with his wife, and in his business affairs, and that he did not trust his friends in Piedmont. On March 18, 1931, he wrote to Mrs. Davis telling her of Mrs. Whitehead's condition and added that Mrs. Whitehead was very wistful. "Today I endeavored to find out what she wanted. I finally asked her if she wanted to see you. She burst out crying and we had great difficulty in getting her to stop. Evidently, that is what is on her mind. It is a very difficult matter to decide. If you come it will mean that you will have to leave again, and then things may be serious. I am going to see the doctor, and get his candid opinion and will then write you again. * * * Since writing the above, I have seen the doctor, and he thinks it will help considerably if you come." * * * On March 24, 1931, Mr. Davis, at the request of his wife, telegraphed to Mr. Whitehead as follows: "Your letter received. Sorry to hear Blanche not so well. Hope you are feeling better yourself. If you wish Caro to go to you can arrange for her to leave in about two weeks. Please wire me if you think it advisable for her to go." On March 30, 1931, Mr. Whitehead wrote a long letter to Mr. Davis, in which he explained in detail the condition of Mrs. Whitehead's health and also referred to his own health. He pointed out that he had lost a considerable portion of his cash assets but still owned considerable realty, that he needed someone to help him with his wife and some friend he could trust to help him with his business affairs and suggested that perhaps Mr. Davis might come to California. He then pointed out that all his property was community property; that under his will all the property was to go to Mrs. Whitehead; that he believed that under Mrs. Whitehead's will practically everything was to go to Caro. Mr. Whitehead again wrote to Mr. Davis under date of April 9, 1931, pointing out how badly he needed someone he could trust to assist him, and giving it as his belief that if properly handled he could still save about $150,000. He then stated: "Having you [Mr. Davis] here to depend on and to help me regain my mind and courage would be a big thing." Three days later, on April 12, 1931, Mr. Whitehead again wrote, addressing his letter to "Dear Frank and Caro", and in this letter made the definite offer, which offer it is claimed was accepted and is the basis of this action. In this letter he first pointed out that Blanche, his wife, was in a private hospital and that "she cannot last much longer * * * my affairs are not as bad as I supposed at first. Cutting everything down I figure 150,000 can be saved from the wreck." He then enumerated the values placed upon his various properties and then continued "my trouble was caused by my friends taking advantage of my illness and my position to skin me.

"Now if Frank could come out here and be with me, and look after my affairs, we could easily save the balance I mentioned, provided I dont get into another panic and do some more foolish things.

"The next attack will be my end, I am 65 and my health has been bad for years, so, the Drs. dont give me much longer to live. So if you can come, Caro will inherit everything and you will make our lives happier and see Blanche is provided for to the end.

"My eyesight has gone back on me, I cant read only for a few lines at a time. I am at the house alone with Stanley [the chauffeur] who does everything for me and is a fine fellow. Now, what I want is some one who will take charge of my affairs and see I dont lose any more. Frank can do it, if he will and cut out the booze.

"Will you let me hear from you as soon as possible, I know it will be a sacrifice but times are still bad and likely to be, so by settling down you can help me and Blanche and gain in the end. If I had you here my mind would get better and my courage return, and we could work things out."

This letter was received by Mr. Davis at his office in Windsor, Canada, about 9:30 A. M. April 14, 1931. After reading the letter to Mrs. Davis over the telephone, and after getting her belief that they must go to California, Mr. Davis immediately wrote Mr. Whitehead a letter, which, after reading it to his wife, he sent by air mail. This letter was lost, but there is no doubt that it was sent by Davis and received by Whitehead, in fact the trial court expressly so found. Mr. Davis testified in substance as to the contents of this letter. After acknowledging receipt of the letter of April 12, 1931, Mr. Davis unequivocally stated that he and Mrs. Davis accepted the proposition of Mr. Whitehead and both would leave Windsor to go to him on April 25th. This letter of acceptance also contained the information that the reason they could not leave prior to April 25th was that Mr. Davis had to appear in court on April 22d as one of the executors of his mother's estate. The testimony is uncontradicted and ample to support the trial court's finding that this letter was sent by Davis and received by Whitehead. In fact under date of April 15, 1931, Mr. Whitehead again wrote to Mr. Davis and stated "Your letter by air mail received this a. m. Now, I am wondering if I have put you to unnecessary trouble and expense, if you are making any money dont leave it, as things are bad here. * * * You know your business and I dont and I am half crazy in the bargain, but I dont want to hurt you or Caro.

"Then on the other hand if I could get some one to trust and keep me straight I can save a good deal, about what I told you in my former letter."

This letter was received by Mr. Davis on April 17, 1931, and the same day Mr. Davis telegraphed to Mr. Whitehead "Cheer up—we will soon be there, we will wire you from the train."

Between April 14, 1931, the date the letter of acceptance was sent by Mr. Davis, and April 22d, Mr. Davis was engaged in closing out his business affairs, and Mrs. Davis in closing up their home and in making other arrangements to leave. On April 22, 1931, Mr. Whitehead committed suicide. Mr. and Mrs. Davis were immediately notified and they at once came to California. From almost the moment of her arrival Mrs. Davis devoted herself to the care and comfort of her aunt, and gave her aunt constant attention and care until Mrs. Whitehead's death on May 30, 1931. * * *

After the death of Mrs. Whitehead, for the first time it was discovered that the information contained in Mr. Whitehead's letter of March 30, 1931, in reference to the contents of his and Mrs. Whitehead's wills was incorrect. By a duly witnessed will dated February 28, 1931, Mr. Whitehead, after making several specific bequests, had bequeathed all of the balance of his estate to his wife for life, and upon her death to respondents Geoff Doubble and Rupert Ross Whitehead, his nephews. Neither appellant was mentioned in his will. * * *

After the discovery of the manner in which the property had been devised was made, this action was commenced upon the theory that Rupert Whitehead had assumed a contractual obligation to make a will whereby "Caro Davis would inherit everything"; that he had failed to do so; that plaintiffs had fully performed their part of the contract; * * *.

It should also be added that the evidence shows that as a result of Frank Davis leaving his business in Canada he forfeited not only all insurance business he might have written if he had remained, but also forfeited all renewal commissions earned on past business. According to his testimony this loss was over $8,000.

The trial court found that the relationship between Mr. and Mrs. Davis and the Whiteheads was substantially as above recounted and that the other facts above stated were true; * * *.

The theory of the trial court and of respondents on this appeal is that the letter of April 12th was an offer to contract, but that such offer could only be accepted by performance and could not be accepted by a promise to perform, and that said offer was revoked by the death of Mr. Whitehead before performance. In other words, it is contended that the offer was an offer to enter into a unilateral contract, and that the purported acceptance of April 14th was of no legal effect.

The distinction between unilateral and bilateral contracts is well settled in the law. It is well stated in section 12 of the American Institute's Restatement of the Law of Contracts as follows:

> "A unilateral contract is one in which no promisor receives a promise as consideration for his promise. A bilateral contract is one in which there are mutual promises between two parties to the contract; each party being both a promisor and a promisee."

This definition is in accord with the law of California. (*Chrisman v. Southern Cal. Edison Co.*, 83 Cal. App. 249[, 256 Pac. 618].)

In the case of unilateral contracts no notice of acceptance by performance is required. Section 1584 of the Civil Code provides, "Performance of the conditions of a proposal, * * * is an acceptance of the proposal." * * *

Although the legal distinction between unilateral and bilateral contracts is thus well settled, the difficulty in any particular case is to determine whether the particular offer is one to enter into a bilateral or unilateral contract. Some cases are quite clear cut. Thus an offer to sell which is accepted is clearly a bilateral contract, while an offer of a reward is a clear-cut offer of a unilateral contract which cannot be accepted by a promise to perform, but only by performance. * * * Between these two extremes is a vague field where the particular contract may be unilateral or bilateral depending upon the intent of the offerer and the facts and circumstances of each case. The offer to contract involved in this case falls within this category. By the provisions of the Restatement of the Law of Contracts it is expressly provided that there is a presumption that the offer is to enter into a bilateral contract. Section 31 provides:

> "In case of doubt it is presumed that an offer invites the formation of a bilateral contract by an acceptance amounting in effect to a promise by the offeree to perform what the offer requests, rather than the formation of one or more unilateral contracts by actual performance on the part of the offeree."

Professor Williston in his Treatise on Contracts, volume 1, section 60, also takes the position that a presumption in favor of bilateral contracts exists.

In the comment following section 31 of the Restatement the reason for such presumption is stated as follows:

> "It is not always easy to determine whether an offerer requests an act or a promise to do the act. As a bilateral contract immediately and fully protects both parties, the interpretation is favored that a bilateral contract is proposed."

While the California cases have never expressly held that a presumption in favor of bilateral contracts exists, the cases clearly indicate a tendency to treat offers as offers of bilateral rather than of unilateral contracts. * * *

Keeping these principles in mind we are of the opinion that the offer of April 12th was an offer to enter into a bilateral as distinguished from a unilateral contract. Respondents argue that Mr. Whitehead had the right as offerer to designate his offer as either unilateral or bilateral. That is undoubtedly the law. It is then argued that from all the facts and circumstances it must be implied that what Whitehead wanted was performance and not a mere promise to perform. We think this is a non sequitur, in fact the surrounding circumstances lead to just the opposite conclusion. These parties were not dealing at arm's length. Not only were they related, but a very close and intimate friendship existed between them. The record indisputably demonstrates that Mr. Whitehead had confidence in Mr. and Mrs. Davis, in fact that he had lost all confidence in everyone else. The record amply shows that by an accumulation of occurrences Mr. Whitehead had become desperate, and that what he wanted was the promise of appellants that he could look to them for assistance. He knew from his past relationship with appellants that if they gave their promise to perform he could rely upon them. The correspondence between them indicates how desperately he desired this assurance. Under these circumstances he wrote his offer of April 12th, above quoted, in which he stated, after disclosing his desperate mental and physical condition, and after setting forth the terms of his offer: "Will you let me hear from you as soon as possible—I know it will be a sacrifice but times are still bad and likely to be, so by settling down you can help me and Blanche and gain in the end." By thus specifically requesting an immediate reply Whitehead expressly indicated the nature of the acceptance desired by him—namely, appellants' promise that they would come to California and do the things requested by him. This promise was immediately sent by appellants upon receipt of the offer, and was received by Whitehead. It is elementary that when an offer has indicated the mode and means of acceptance, an acceptance in accordance with that mode or means is binding on the offerer.

* * *

For the foregoing reasons we are of the opinion that the offer of April 12, 1931, was an offer to enter into a bilateral contract which was accepted by the letter of April 14, 1931. * * *

For the foregoing reasons the judgment appealed from is reversed.

QUESTIONS, NOTES, AND CONNECTIONS

1. Questions about the facts of this case

   1.1. Did Rupert Whitehead make an offer to Frank and Caro Davis? If so, what was it?

   1.2. Did that offer invite or require acceptance in any particular manner?

   1.3. Did Rupert Whitehead ever revoke that offer? What is the importance of the April 14th letter? Of the February 28th will? Of Rupert's will "maturing"?

   1.4. Who was Jacoby?

2. Questions about the law

   2.1. How did Frank and Caro accept? Can every offer be accepted by a mere promise? How would *Restatement (Second)* § 32 answer that question? *See* Note 3.2 below.

   2.2. What if the letter of March 30th had said, "Caro and you can accept this offer to inherit everything only by moving to California"? What is the difference between that hypothetical language and the language of the April 12th letter—"So if you can come, Caro will inherit everything"?

   2.3. What do you think Mr. Whitehead was *really* bargaining for, the Davis' promise or their performance? Do you think he even thought about it in those terms? If not, should important legal consequences—such as when an acceptance is effective and whether notice of acceptance is required—turn on the distinction between offers for unilateral and bilateral contracts?

3. Notes

3.1. We will deal more directly with the question of what a party to an agreement was bargaining for when we deal with consideration in Chapter 3. Examination of "incapacity" is deferred until Chapter 4. Professor Monroe Freedman suggests that the lawyers for Davis and Jacoby also decided to defer consideration of incapacity:

> [T]he adversary system will occasionally fail to bring out facts or arguments that might be highly relevant to the court's decision. One illustration is *Davis v. Jacoby*, where the contest was between parties claiming under a will and parties claiming under a contract to make a different will. A material fact was that the testator/contractor was very likely incompetent during the period of time when both instruments were executed. Accordingly, neither party appears to have argued the legal relevance of the testator/contractor's mental condition, one side because they did not want to impeach the will, the other side because they did not want to impeach the contract."

Monroe H. Freedman, *Arguing the Law in the Adversary System*, 16 GA. L. REV. 833, 838 (1982).

3.2. We have seen that the traditional common law view, incorporated into the first *Restatement,* was to use the terms "unilateral contract" and "bilateral contract," and to treat the offeror's designation as to the manner of acceptance as mandatory. Under the first *Restatement*, an offer was either an offer that could only be accepted by performance or one that could only be accepted by a return promise to perform. Sort of binary, if you get our drift.

In contrast to its predecessor, the approach of the *Restatement (Second)* is to presume that the offeror is more flexible (or indifferent) as to the manner of acceptance. That is to say, the *Restatement (Second)* does not use the bilateral/unilateral contract terminology anywhere in the document.

More specifically, § 50(1) provides that *"[a]cceptance of an offer is a manifestation of assent to the terms thereof made by the offeree in a manner invited or required by the offer."* This provision recognizes the principle that the offeror can dictate the permissible manner of assent. However, § 30(2) creates a presumption that, *"unless otherwise indicated by the language or circumstances,"* an offer will be treated as inviting acceptance in any manner that is reasonable under the circumstances. Section

32 then continues that, *"[i]n the case of doubt an offer is interpreted as inviting the offeree to accept either by promising to perform what the offeror requests or by rendering the performance as the offeree chooses."*

3.3. The above provisions of the *Restatement (Second)* are consistent with the general approach taken by the U.C.C. concerning acceptance. Specifically, § 2–206(1)(a) provides that "[u]nless otherwise unambiguously indicated by the language or circumstances an offer to make a contract shall be construed as inviting acceptance in any manner and by any medium reasonable in the circumstances."

Both the U.C.C. and the *Restatement (Second)* reflect a belief that, in the vast majority of cases, the offeror is indifferent to the manner in which assent is expressed. Is that a fair assumption? In *Packgen v. Berry Plastics Corp.,* 973 F.Supp.2d 48 (D. Maine 2013), the court put it as follows:

> The commentary to section 2–206 notes that "[a]ny reasonable manner of acceptance is intended to be regarded as available unless the offeror has made quite clear that it will not be acceptable." 11 M.R.S.A. § 2–206, cmt. 1. Further, the UCC's understanding of acceptance embraces
>
> > [t]he common law idea that the offeror is the master of the offer. However, it reflects an underlying assumption that the offeror is often indifferent as to what words or non-verbal conduct will create an acceptance . . . [c]onsequently, a buyer's offer for the current shipment of goods may be accepted not only by shipment or promise to ship, but also by commencement of performance, as, for example, the preparation of the goods for shipment.

Corbin on Contracts § 3.8 (2013).

Would application of the U.C.C. or *Restatement (Second)* approach have changed the outcome in *Davis v. Jacoby*? How about the analysis?

4. **You Be the Lawyer!**

Let's suppose you represent Geoff Dubble and Rupert Ross Whitehead, Mr. Whitehead's nephews. Your clients want to know if the result of this decision alters Mr. Whitehead's will, which left the bulk of his estate to them. What do you tell them? Do you have some good news and some bad news for your clients?

5. Connections

   How do the rules on modes and manner of acceptance, as illustrated in the last several cases cohere* with the rules on what constitutes an offer? What policy objectives do you see as intending to be served by these rules? How well are those objectives actually served by either or both the traditional and more contemporary iterations** of these rules? Why have modern courts, and the *Restatement (Second)* eliminated the sharp distinction between offers for unilateral and bilateral contracts? Does that development mean the distinction is no longer important? Read on.

B. EFFECTIVENESS OF PROMISSORY ACCEPTANCE

INTRODUCTION TO *HENDRICKS*

Davis v. Jacoby illustrates that a promise can be effective as an acceptance, at least under most circumstances. The next two cases raise two different questions relating to the *point in time* at which a promise as an acceptance is effective. In the first case, *Hendricks*, we see an attempt to accept and an attempt to revoke an offer. Accordingly, the time at which each becomes effective is going to be critical in determining whether or not there is mutual assent.

QUESTIONS BEFORE THE CASE

1. Does the court construe Mr. Behee's offer as an offer for a unilateral contract or an offer for a bilateral contract?
2. Do the sellers sign the agreement before or after the buyer withdraws his offer and how is that relevant?

---

* "Cohere" is a word that Ponoroff recently learned and insisted on using. It is, apparently, the verb form of the noun "coherent" and means "to be logically and aesthetically consistent" or "to be united in principles, relationship, or interest." Epstein and Markell think he might just have said that, but, again, he insisted. * * *

** Yes, we know, there he goes again (Epstein & Markell).

HENDRICKS V. BEHEE

Court of Appeals of Missouri, Southern District
786 S.W.2d 610 (1990)

FLANIGAN, J.

Plaintiff Steve L. Hendricks, d/b/a Hendricks Abstract & Title Co., instituted this interpleader action, * * * against defendants Eugene Behee, Artice Smith, and Pearl Smith. Plaintiff was the escrowee of $5,000 which had been paid by defendant Behee as a deposit accompanying Behee's offer to purchase real estate owned by defendants Artice and Pearl Smith, husband and wife, in Stockton, Missouri. A dispute between Behee and the Smiths as to whether their dealings resulted in a binding contract prompted the interpleader action. Behee filed a crossclaim against the Smiths.

After a nonjury trial, the trial court awarded plaintiff $997.50 to be paid out of the $5,000 deposit. None of the parties challenges that award. The trial court awarded the balance of $4,002.50 to defendant Behee. Defendants [Smiths] appeal.

In essence the Smiths contend that the dealings between them and Behee ripened into a contract and entitled the Smiths to the balance of $4,002.50, and that the trial court erred in ruling otherwise.

After Behee, as prospective buyer, and the Smiths, as prospective sellers, had engaged in unproductive negotiations, Behee, on March 2, 1987, made a written offer of $42,500 for the real estate and $250 for a dinner bell and flower pots. On March 3 that offer was mailed to the Smiths, who lived in Mississippi, by their real estate agent. There were two real estate agents involved. The trial court found that both were the agents of the Smiths, and that finding has not been disputed by the Smiths in this appeal. For simplicity, the two agents will be considered in this opinion as one agent who acted on behalf of the Smiths.

On March 4 the Smiths signed the proposed agreement in Mississippi. Before Behee was notified that the Smiths had accepted the offer, Behee withdrew the offer by notifying the real estate agent of the withdrawal. That paramount fact is conceded by this statement in the Smiths' brief: "On either March 5, 6 or 7, 1987, Behee contacted [the Smiths' real estate agent] and advised her that he desired to withdraw his offer to purchase the real estate. Prior to this communication, Behee had received no notice that his offer had been accepted by the Smiths."

* * *

An uncommunicated intention to accept an offer is not an acceptance. * * * When an offer calls for a promise, as distinguished from an act, on the part of the offeree, notice of acceptance is always essential. * * * A mere private act of the offeree does not constitute an acceptance. * * *

Communication of acceptance of a contract to an agent of the offeree is not sufficient and does not bind the offeror. * * *

Unless the offer is supported by consideration, * * * an offeror may withdraw his offer at any time "before acceptance and communication of that fact to him." * * * To be effective, revocation of an offer must be communicated to the offeree before he has accepted. * * *

Notice to the agent, within the scope of the agent's authority, is notice to the principal, and the agent's knowledge is binding on the principal. * * *

Before Behee was notified that the Smiths had accepted his offer, Behee notified the agent of the Smiths that Behee was withdrawing the offer. The notice to the agent, being within the scope of her authority, was binding upon the Smiths. Behee's offer was not supported by consideration and his withdrawal of it was proper. * * *

The judgment is affirmed.

QUESTIONS

1. Questions about the facts of this case

    1.1. What did Mr. Behee indicate to the Smiths concerning the permissible or required manner of acceptance?

    1.2. The court notes that the real estate agents involved in the deal were both agents of the Smiths. Why is that fact important? How would the analysis change if one or both of the agents were agent(s) for Behee?

2. Questions about the law

    2.1. The final sentence of the opinion, before the disposition, states, "Behee's offer was not supported by consideration and his withdrawal of it was proper." What do you suppose the court means by that?

    2.2. Does the holding in *Hendricks* suggest that in *Ever-Tite Roofing, supra,* even if an authorized representative of the Ever-Tite corporation had actually signed the Green's offer as soon as their credit checked out, there still would have been no contract until notice of the signature had been given to the Greens? Why not? By the same token, how could the loading of the truck in *Ever-Tite* have constituted acceptance by commencement of performance if the Greens were not aware that the trucks were being loaded?

    2.3. Is the holding in *Hendricks* consistent with *Restatement (Second) of Contracts* § 50(3)'s language that, **"Acceptance by a**

promise requires that the offeree complete every act essential to the making of the promise"?

3. **You Be the Lawyer!**

How would you, as their lawyer, have advised the Smiths to proceed once they decided to accept Behee's offer?

INTRODUCTION TO *ADAMS V. LINDSELL*

When, under the terms of the offer, acceptance by return promise is permitted or required, an issue arises if the parties are not face-to-face. *Hendricks* suggests that an uncommunicated intention to accept an offer is not an acceptance; that notice of acceptance is always an essential aspect of a promissory acceptance. Is this consistent with objective theory? In *Hendricks*, there is no indication that the Smiths made any attempt to communicate their acceptance to Behee before Behee withdrew his offer. What about, however, if the offeree does send an acceptance? Unless the parties are face-to-face, inevitably there will be some length of time between the moment the acceptance is actually sent and the moment it is received. If the mail is involved, this could be a matter of days, or, as we all know, even longer. The period of transmission will be much shorter of course if the offeree uses FedEx or another overnight courier, but, even then, there will be some time—a gap—between the offeree's sending and the offeror's receiving the acceptance. Thus, the question arises whether during this period of transmission a contract exists or whether the offeror is still sovereign until the acceptance is actually received. Based on objective theory of contract formation, what would you predict? Of course, you would say that the acceptance is not effective until received by the offeror. However, you may recall that in *Minnesota Linseed Oil Co. v. Collier White Lead Co.*, *supra*, at p. 100, the court suggested that a different rule pertains in these circumstances, citing the next case, *Adams v. Lindsell*. Now we get to see what that case was all about.

Before we do, however, we need to make a disclosure. We admit all three of us are old, although Markell and Ponoroff wish to point out that Epstein is the oldest of the three by far. But that's not the disclosure. Despite our advanced years, we are keenly aware that in a commercial economy increasingly dominated by electronic transactions the rule of *Adams v. Lindsell* is fast becoming something of a relic: a vestigial remnant of an earlier era. Indeed, just to show you how with it we are, we have a section coming up on "electronic acceptances." Nevertheless, we think it is still important to consider *Adams v. Lindsell* and the legal proposition it has come to stand for. We believe this is so for three reasons. First, folks still do business from time to time by mail or other non-electronic means, and letters still get lost in the mail. Second, the rule in *Adams v. Lindsell* provides law professors with an irresistible opportunity to probe both the logic and the limits of the objective theory of contract formation. Finally, three years from now, when you prepare to take a bar exam, you will hear Epstein lecturing about the "mailbox rule" and you should have some vague recollection as to what he is talking about.

QUESTIONS BEFORE THE CASE

1. Identify the rationale that the court offers in support of the mailbox rule?
2. Does that rationale make sense (hint: "no")? Can you formulate a better justification for the mailbox rule?

ADAMS V. LINDSELL

Court of King's Bench
106 Eng. Rep. 250 (1818)

Action for non-delivery of wool according to agreement. At the trial at the last Lent Assizes for the county of Worcester, before Burrough J. it appeared that the defendants who were dealers in wool, at St. Ives, in the county of Huntingdon, had, on Tuesday the 2d of September 1817, written the following letter to the plaintiffs, who were woolen manufacturers residing in Bromsgrove, Worcestershire. "We now offer you eight hundred tods of wether fleeces, of a good fair quality of our country wool, at 35s. 6d. per tod, to be delivered at Leicester, and to be paid for by two months' bill in two months, and to be weighed up by your agent within fourteen days, receiving your answer in course of post."

This letter was misdirected by the defendants, to Bromsgrove, Leicestershire, in consequence of which it was not received by the plaintiffs in Worcestershire till 7 p.m. on Friday, September 5th. On that evening the plaintiffs wrote an answer, agreeing to accept the wool on the terms proposed. The course of the post between St. Ives and Bromsgrove is through London, and consequently this answer was not received by the defendants till Tuesday, September 9th. On Monday September 8th, the defendants not having, as they expected, received an answer on Sunday September 7th, (which in case their letter had not been misdirected, would have been in the usual course of the post,) sold the wool in question to another person. Under these circumstances, the learned Judge held, that the delay having been occasioned by the neglect of the defendants, the jury must take it, that the answer did come back in due course of post; and that then the defendants were liable for the loss that had been sustained; and the plaintiffs accordingly recovered the verdict.

Jervis having in Easter term obtained a rule nisi for a new trial, on the ground that there was no binding contract between the parties.

Dauncey, Puller, and Richardson, showed cause. They contended, that at the moment of the acceptance of the offer of the defendants by the plaintiffs, the former became bound. And that was on the Friday evening, when there had been no change of circumstances. They were then stopped by the Court, who called upon Jervis and Campbell in support of the rule. They relied on *Payne v Cave* [3 T.R. 148], and more particularly on *Cooke v. Oxley* [Ibid. 653]. In that case, Oxley, who had proposed to sell goods to Cooke, and given him a certain time at his request, to determine whether he would buy them or not, was held not liable to the performance of the contract, even though Cooke, within the specified time, had determined to buy them, and given Oxley notice to that effect. So here the defendants who have proposed by letter to sell this wool are not to be held liable, even though it be now admitted that the answer did come back in due course of post. Till the plaintiffs' answer was actually received, there could be no binding contract between the parties; and before then, the defendants had retracted their offer, by selling the wool to other persons. But—

The Court said, that if that were so, no contract could ever be completed by the post. For if the defendants were not bound by their offer when accepted by the plaintiffs till the answer was received, then the plaintiffs ought not to be bound till after they had received notification that the defendants had received their answer and assented to it. And so it might go on ad infinitum. The defendants must be considered in law as making, during every instant of the time their letter was travelling, the same identical offer to the plaintiffs; and then the contract is completed by the acceptance of it by the latter. Then as to the delay in notifying the acceptance, that arises entirely from the mistake of the defendants, and it therefore must be taken as against them, that the plaintiffs answer was received in course of post.

Rule discharged.

QUESTIONS AND NOTE

1. Questions about the facts of this case

   1.1. *Adams* is celebrated for establishing the so-called "mailbox rule," which holds that an acceptance is effective on *dispatch* rather than *receipt*. This rule continues to the present day. *See Restatement (Second) of Contracts* § 63. Along with automatic termination of an offer on death or disability of the offeror, the dispatch rule represents perhaps the most glaring exception to the objective theory of contract formation. However, the dispatch rule is only operative under certain circumstances. What was the critical fact in *Adams* that convinced the court to employ this rule?

1.2. In *Adams*, the court invoked the mailbox rule to protect the plaintiffs since the misdirection of the offer letter was the fault of the defendants. However, review the facts closely. Did the court need to resort to the mailbox rule in order to find for the plaintiffs? Also, is it clear that the plaintiffs were entitled to protection? Shouldn't the plaintiffs have been aware that by September 8 the defendants might no longer be interested in selling the fleeces to them? If so, did they still have the power of acceptance?

1.3. Just how much was at stake in this case? According to Markell, who seems to have this proclivity to traveling to places where there are sheep (Ponoroff doesn't go to any place that does not have Michigan State Law alumni, and, Epstein, bless his heart, is of course too old to travel), a "tod" is equivalent to 28 pounds, so the contract involved 22,400 pounds of "wether fleeces" (fleeces from castrated male sheep). At 35S. 6d. per tod, or roughly $15.00, we're talking about $12,000 worth of wool, not an inconsiderable sum in 1818.

1.4. By the way, are you as impressed as we are with the speed of the early nineteenth century English post?

2. Questions about the law

2.1. If the offeror is truly sovereign and, as such, entitled to dictate the terms on which she is willing to deal, is there some way in which the offeror can protect herself against the mailbox rule; against having legal consequences established based on uncommunicated intent?

2.2. Who is the superior bearer of the risk that a communication will be lost or delayed during transit? Does your answer to this question suggest a more principled justification for the rule than the one offered by the court in *Adams*? *See* A. CORBIN, CONTRACTS § 78 (1950).

2.3. Under the rationale of *Adams,* if an offer is made by FedEx, and the acceptance by return post, does the mailbox rule apply? How about the other way around?

2.4. As the pace of technology has made communications between parties almost instantaneous even when those parties are at a distance from one another, e.g., facsimile transmissions and e-mail, does the rationale for the mailbox rule break down? How so? *Cf. Restatement (Second) of Contracts* § 64, cmt. a ("*Where the parties are in each other's presence, the offeree can accept without being in doubt as to whether the offeror has attempted to revoke his offer or whether the offeror has received the acceptance.*")

3. Note

What role would you anticipate that the "dispatch rule" will or should play in the legal rules governing so-called "electronic contracts"; that is, contracts formed by means of computer transmissions or over the Internet and stored solely in the form of an electronic record? There is an emerging body of statutory law being developed to deal with electronic contracts. This includes the federal Electronic Signature in Global and National Commerce (E-Sign) Act and the Uniform Electronic Transactions Act, both designed to give legal effect to electronic signatures.

For the most part, the law has treated electronic contracts as tending to raise issues of *form* (*e.g.*, when is an electronic signature effective) rather than involving new substantive rules. Therefore, we discuss electronic contracting again in Part F of this Section, as well as in Chapter 3 as part of our study of the Statute of Frauds.

4. **You Be the Lawyer!**

If you are advising the person who purchased the wool on September 8, does this decision affect your client's rights against the defendants?

PROBLEMS CONCERNING APPLICATION OF THE "MAILBOX RULE"

1. Assume that, on November 26, Ponoroff executes a contract for the purchase and sale of certain real property and mails it to Markell for acceptance. On receipt of the agreement, Markell executes it and sends it, by return mail, to Ponoroff's attorney. Subsequently, Markell changes his mind and calls Ponoroff's attorney to inform her that he is not interested in selling and that she should ignore the agreement when it shows up. The next day, the signed agreement arrives at Ponoroff's attorney's office. What should the attorney advise Ponoroff in terms of whether or not he has a binding contract to buy the property? Would it affect your advice if Markell failed to inform the attorney during their telephone conversation that he had already signed and mailed back the agreement? In that case, suppose, after being informed of the telephone call by his attorney, Ponoroff goes out and enters into a contract to purchase another parcel of property. Thereafter, the signed agreement arrives in Ponoroff's attorney's office and Markell brings an action for specific performance. Is there a contract between Ponoroff and Markell? If so, does Ponoroff have a defense to liability?

2. Assume the same facts as stated at the beginning of Problem 1 above, except that, instead of mailing the agreement to Ponoroff's attorney, Markell mails it to his own lawyer with instructions to deliver to it Ponoroff. Can Markell still change his mind? If so, up to what point in time?

Why didn't the mailbox rule protect the sellers in *Hendricks v. Behee*, *supra*?

3. Suppose that, on Day 1, Epstein sends Markell an offer by mail. The offer does not contain any specification relating to manner of acceptance. On Day 2, Epstein changes his mind and mails a revocation of the offer. On Day 3, Markell receives the offer and immediately mails an acceptance. On Day 5 the revocation arrives, and on Day 6 the acceptance arrives.
   (a) Has a contract been formed? If so, when?
   (b) Does it change your answer if, on Day 2, right after dropping his letter in the mail, Epstein clutches his chest and dies right there at the mailbox?
   (c) How about if Epstein dies on Day 3? Is there anything else you want to know?
   (d) How does it affect your answer if, before Epstein dies on Day 3, Markell mails a rejection and then changes his mind and mails an acceptance? *See Restatement (Second) of Contracts* § 40.
   (e) Assume the same facts as part (d), except that Epstein doesn't die at all. In analyzing whether a contract is formed, does it matter which communication arrives first?
4. Now assume that, on February 1, Epstein sends Markell an offer by mail agreeing that, in return for $100, he will grant Markell a 60-day option (to expire on April 2) to purchase Epstein's house for $150,000. Markell promptly pays the $100. There are no further communications between the parties until, on March 29, Markell sends a letter to Epstein notifying him that he is exercising the option. The letter reaches Epstein on April 3, whereupon Epstein calls Markell and tells him that it's "too late," and he has already arranged to sell the property to Ponoroff for $155,000. Does Markell have a claim against Epstein? *See Restatement (Second)* § 63(b) & cmt. f. How about against Ponoroff?

C. EFFECTIVENESS OF ACCEPTANCE BY PERFORMANCE

Subject to the mailbox rule, we've seen that an acceptance in the form of a return promise is not effective until communicated to the offeror. However, recall that *"[U]nless otherwise indicated by the language or the circumstances, an offer [is treated as inviting] acceptance in any manner and by any medium reasonable in the circumstances." Restatement (Second) of Contracts* § 30(2). Thus, in most cases, acceptance may occur by performance as well as by promise. If the offeree accepts by performance, when is the acceptance effective? Is it when the act is begun; when it is completed; or when the offeror receives notice that the act has been completed? The next two cases and the material that follow address these questions and the answers may just surprise you.

QUESTIONS BEFORE THE CASE

1. According to the court in this case, why should the rule on notice to the offeror be different when acceptance is by performance rather than promise?
2. Do you think the rule should be different?

CARLILL V. CARBOLIC SMOKE BALL CO.

Court of Appeal
1 Q.B. 256 (1893)

[The defendant, a London-based company, ran an advertisement promising to pay a 100£ "reward" to anyone who contracted the flu after inhaling the company's smoke ball three times daily for a two-week period in accordance with the printed directions. The ad noted that, in a gesture of its sincerity, the company had deposited 1,000£ pounds with a local bank. This action was brought by Lilli Carlill who, after seeing the ad, purchased a smoke ball and used it as directed for a period of two months whereupon she contracted influenza.]

LINDLEY, L.J. [The Lord Justice stated the facts, and proceeded:]

Smoke Ball Contract

I will begin by referring to two points which were raised in the Court below. I refer to them simply for the purpose of dismissing them. First, it is said no action will lie upon this contract because it is a policy. You have only to look at the advertisement to dismiss that suggestion. Then it was said that it is a bet. Hawkins, J., came to the conclusion that nobody ever dreamt of a bet, and that the transaction had nothing whatever in common with a bet. I so entirely agree with him that I pass over this contention also as not worth serious attention.

Then, what is left? The first observation I will make is that we are not dealing with any inference of fact. We are dealing with an express promise to pay 100£ in certain events. Read the advertisement how you will, and twist it about as you will, here is a distinct promise expressed in language which is perfectly unmistakable—"100£ reward will be paid by the Carbolic Smoke Ball Company to any person who contracts the influenza after having used the ball three times daily for two weeks according to the printed directions supplied with each ball."

We must first consider whether this was intended to be a promise at all, or whether it was a mere puff which meant nothing. Was it a mere puff? My answer to that question is No, and I base my answer upon this passage:

"1000£ is deposited with the Alliance Bank, showing our sincerity in the matter." Now, for what was that money deposited or that statement made except to negative the suggestion that this was a mere puff and meant nothing at all? The deposit is called in aid by the advertiser as proof of his sincerity in the matter—that is, the sincerity of his promise to pay this 100£ in the event which he has specified. I say this for the purpose of giving point to the observation that we are not inferring a promise; there is the promise, as plain as words can make it.

Then it is contended that it is not binding. In the first place, it is said that it is not made with anybody in particular. Now that point is common to the words of this advertisement and to the words of all other advertisements offering rewards. They are offers to anybody who performs the conditions named in the advertisement, and anybody who does perform the condition accepts the offer. In point of law this advertisement is an offer to pay 100£ to anybody who will perform these conditions, and the performance of the conditions is the acceptance of the offer. * * *

But then it is said, "Supposing that the performance of the conditions is an acceptance of the offer, that acceptance ought to have been notified." Unquestionably, as a general proposition, when an offer is made, it is necessary in order to make a binding contract, not only that it should be accepted, but that the acceptance should be notified. But is that so in cases of this kind? I apprehend that they are an exception to that rule, or, if not an exception, they are open to the observation that the notification of the acceptance need not precede the performance. This offer is a continuing offer. It was never revoked, and if notice of acceptance is required—which I doubt very much, for I rather think the true view is that which was expressed and explained by Lord Blackburn in the case of *Brogden v. Metropolitan By Co.*—if notice of acceptance is required, the person who makes the offer gets the notice of acceptance contemporaneously with his notice of the performance of the condition. If he gets notice of the acceptance before his offer is revoked, that in principle is all you want. I, however, think that the true view, in a case of this kind, is that the person who makes the offer shows by his language and from the nature of the transaction that he does not expect and does not require notice of the acceptance apart from notice of the performance.

We, therefore, find here all the elements which are necessary to form a binding contract enforceable in point of law, subject to two observations. First of all it is said that this advertisement is so vague that you cannot really construe it as a promise—that the vagueness of the languages shows that a legal promise was never intended or contemplated. The language is vague and uncertain in some respects, and particularly in this, that the 100£ is to be paid to any person who contracts the increasing epidemic after having used the balls three times daily for two weeks. It is said, When are they to be used? According to the language of the advertisement no time is fixed, and, construing the offer most strongly against the person who has made it, one might infer that any time was meant. I do not think that was meant, and to hold the contrary would be pushing too far the doctrine of taking language most strongly against the person using it. I do not think that business people or reasonable people would understand the words as meaning that if you took a smoke ball and used it three times daily for two weeks you were to be guaranteed against influenza for the rest of your life, and I think it would be pushing the language of the advertisement too far to construe it as meaning that. But if it does not mean that, what does it mean? It is for the defendants to show what it does mean; and it strikes me that there are two, and possibly three reasonable constructions to be put on this advertisement, any one of which will answer the purpose of the plaintiff. Possibly it may be limited to persons catching the "increasing epidemic" (that is, the then prevailing epidemic), or any colds or diseases caused by taking cold, during the prevalence of the increasing epidemic. That is one suggestion; but it does not commend itself to me. Another suggested meaning is that you are warranted free from catching this epidemic, or colds or other diseases caused by taking cold, whilst you are using this remedy after using it for two weeks. If that is the meaning, the plaintiff is right, for she used the remedy for two weeks and went on using it till she got the epidemic. Another meaning, and the one which I rather prefer, is that the reward is offered to any person who contracts the epidemic or other disease within a reasonable time after having used the smoke ball. Then it is asked, What is a reasonable time? It has been suggested that there is no standard of reasonableness; that it depends upon the reasonable time for a germ to develop! I do not feel pressed by that. It strikes me that a reasonable time may be ascertained in a business sense and in a sense satisfactory to a lawyer, in this way; find out from a chemist what the ingredients are; find out from a skilled physician how long the effect of such ingredients on the system could be reasonable expected to endure so as to protect a person from an epidemic or cold, and in that way you will get a standard to be laid before a jury, or a judge without a jury, by which they might exercise their judgement as to what a reasonable time would be. It strikes me, I confess, that the true construction of this advertisement is that 100£ will be paid to anybody who uses this smoke ball three times daily for two weeks according to the printed directions, and who gets the influenza or cold or other diseases caused by taking cold within a reasonable time after so using it; and if that is the true construction, it is enough for the plaintiff.

* * *

It appears to me, therefore, that the defendants must perform their promise, and, if they have been so unwary as to expose themselves to a great many actions, so much the worse for them.

QUESTIONS AND NOTES

1. Questions about the facts of this case

   1.1. The court dismissed "as not worth serious consideration" the argument that the advertisement was a bet. Did the Carbolic Smoke Ball Company really think inhalation of its smoke ball would prevent the flu or was it betting that most users would not contract the flu anyway?

   1.2. What's the difference between a promise and a "puff"? Does that difference depend on what you're "puffing"? [Ok, ignore that last question!]

   1.3. The court in *Carlill* describes the Carbolic's Smoke Ball Company's advertisement as offering a *reward.* Is this a fair analogy? How does Carbolic's advertisement differ from an offer of "$100 for anyone who returns my lost gerbil, Bruce"? More on this advertisement/reward distinction below.

   1.4. The court rejected the Carbolic Smoke Ball Company's argument that the offer was too vague to enforce on the basis that the promise was to give the reward to anyone contracting influenza within a *reasonable* time after using the smoke ball for two weeks as directed. Some lay people might suggest that this is an equally vague standard but, as you probably already know from your Torts class, for whatever reasons, lawyers are perfectly content with the "reasonable" answer. So just how long is a reasonable time?

2. Questions about the law

   2.1. Can this rule be reconciled with objective theory? Is there anything the offeror can do to alter this rule?

   2.2. *See Restatement (Second) of Contracts* § 54. Are the *Restatement* rules regarding notice of acceptance by performance consistent with the holding in *Carlill*? If not, how do they differ?

   2.3. In distinguishing the situation in *Carlill* from the typical advertisement case, Lord Justice Lindley construed the advertisement as offering a *reward* and noted that "advertisements offering rewards * * * are offers to anybody who performs the conditions named in the advertisement, and anybody who performs the condition accepts the offer." John Leonard tried to make the same argument in *Leonard v. Pepsi Co., supra*, but, in a portion of the opinion we edited out, Judge Wood rejected the argument noting that: "In the present case [unlike *Carlill*], the Harrier Jet commercial did not direct that anyone who appeared at Pepsi headquarters with 7,000,000

Pepsi Points on the Fourth of July would receive a Harrier Jet. Instead, the commercial urged consumers to accumulate Pepsi Points and to refer to the Catalog to determine how they could redeem their Pepsi Points. The commercial sought a reciprocal promise, expressed through acceptance of, and compliance with, the terms of the Order Form * * * Because the alleged offer in this case was, at most, an advertisement to receive offers rather than an offer of reward, plaintiff cannot show that there was an offer made in the circumstances of this case." Do you agree that *Carlill* and *Leonard* are distinguishable on this basis? How about *Carlill* and *Sateriale v. R.J. Reynolds, supra?*

2.4. Suppose you were able to get your hands on a Carbolic smoke ball today and snort (er, we mean inhale) it three times daily for two weeks and then, within a reasonable time thereafter, develop the flu. Could you collect the reward?

3. Notes

3.1. Assume another customer, Mortimer Markell (great, great grandfather of guess who) purchased a Carbolic smoke ball with no knowledge of the company's advertisement. After using the ball as directed for two weeks, Mortimer also contracted the flu. While at the doctor's office, he ran into Lilli Carlill and, upon striking up a conversation, the two discovered the similarity of their circumstances. Carlill told Mortimer that she planned to sue the Carbolic Smoke Ball Co., and he decided he would as well. Should Mortimer also prevail in his suit? *See Broadnax v. Ledbetter*, 100 Tex. 375, 99 S.W. 1111 (1907). Would it change your answer if Mortimer learned of the advertisement *after* he purchased the smoke ball but *before* he finished the two-week regime? *See Restatement (Second) of Contracts* § 51. How about if the offer had been made in a personal letter from the Smoke Ball Company to Ms. Carlill which Mortimer happened to see and, thereupon, went out and purchased a smoke ball, used it properly for two weeks, and then caught the flu? Can he collect?

3.2. Under traditional analysis, an offeree must know of the offer before there can be mutual assent. Is this rule consistent with objective theory? Should it apply in a reward case? If Epstein offered a $100 reward for the return of his lost gerbil, Bruce, and Ponoroff does not learn of the reward until after he's found and returned the gerbil, should Epstein be able to refuse payment of the $100? Hasn't Epstein gotten what he bargained for, regardless of what Ponoroff knew or didn't know? *See Glover v. Jewish War Veterans*, 68 A.2d 233 (D.C.Mun.App. 1949). What is the situation if, upon reading of the reward, Ponoroff calls Epstein and says, "I accept, I am now off to look for Bruce the gerbil"? If Ponoroff doesn't find the gerbil, is he liable to Epstein?

How about if he gets distracted by a wealthy Michigan State College of Law alumna and never even goes out to look for Bruce the gerbil?

3.3. According to Clive Coleman, host of the program, *The Cases That Changed Our World*, on BBC Radio, Mrs. Carlill died on March 10, 1942, at the age of 96. Clearly, her considerable age contributed to her death, but, on her death certificate, there was only one cause stated: influenza!

4. **You Be the Lawyer!**

If approached, how would you recommend to the Carbolic Smoke Ball Co. that it change its advertisement concerning the reward for contracting the flu? Or do you suggest that perhaps no change is necessary?

In *Carlill,* the offeree had fully performed what was requested by the offer, and the court found that the offeror was bound, notice notwithstanding. Suppose, however, the offeree has only begun performance when the offeror changes his mind and revokes the offer. Is the revocation too late? Is there a contract? If not, are both parties free to walk away without any further liability? Assume that Markell offers Epstein $1,000 to paint Markell's house. Right after Epstein starts painting, Ponoroff tells Markell that he will paint the house for only $600. Can Markell still revoke his offer to Epstein? Or, if Kate Hudson offers Epstein a job as a co-star in her next movie, can Epstein stop painting Markell's house without liability? Does the next case, involving a revocation of an offer to pay commission to a real estate agent, help you answer any of these questions? (Or do you just wish we'd stop asking so many questions!)

QUESTIONS BEFORE THE CASE

1. What interest is the court protecting in this case?
2. Why is it necessary to protect this interest?

MARCHIONDO V. SCHECK

Supreme Court of New Mexico
78 N.M. 440, 432 P.2d 405 (1967)

WOOD, JUDGE.

The issue is whether the offeror had a right to revoke his offer to enter a unilateral contract.

Defendant, in writing, offered to sell real estate to a specified prospective buyer and agreed to pay a percentage of the sales price as a commission to the broker. The offer fixed a six-day time limit for acceptance. Defendant, in writing, revoked the offer. The revocation was received by the broker on the morning of the sixth day. Later that day, the broker obtained the offeree's acceptance.

Plaintiff, the broker, claiming breach of contract, sued defendant for the commission stated in the offer. On the above facts, the trial court dismissed the complaint.

We are not concerned with the revocation of the offer as between the offeror and the prospective purchaser. With certain exceptions, the right of a broker to the agreed compensation, or damages measured thereby, is not defeated by the refusal of the principal to complete or consummate a transaction. * * *

Plaintiff's appeal concerns the revocation of his agency. As to that revocation, the issue between the offeror and his agent is not whether defendant had the power to revoke; rather, it is whether he had the right to revoke. * * *

When defendant made his offer to pay a commission upon sale of the property, he offered to enter a unilateral contract; the offer was for an act to be performed, a sale. * * *

Many courts hold that the principal has the right to revoke the broker's agency at any time before the broker has actually procured a purchaser. * * * The reason given is that until there is performance, the offeror has not received that contemplated by his offer, and there is no contract. Further, the offeror may never receive the requested performance because the offeree is not obligated to perform. Until the offeror receives the requested performance, no consideration has passed from the offeree to the offeror. Thus, until the performance is received, the offeror may withdraw the offer. * * *

Defendant asserts that the trial court was correct in applying this rule. However, plaintiff contends that the rule is not applicable where there has been part performance of the offer.

Hutchinson v. Dobson-Bainbridge Realty Co., [31 Tenn. App. 490 (1946)], states:

> "A greater number of courts, however, hold that part performance of the consideration may make such an offer irrevocable and that where the offeree or broker manifests his assent to the offer by entering upon performance and spending time and money in his efforts to perform, then the offer becomes irrevocable during the time stated and binding upon the principal according to its terms. * * *"

Defendant contends that the decisions giving effect to a part performance are distinguishable. He asserts that in these cases the offer was of an exclusive right to sell or of an exclusive agency. Because neither factor is present here, he asserts that the "part performance" decisions are not applicable.

Many of the decisions do seem to emphasize the exclusive aspects of the offer. * * *

Defendant's offer did not specifically state that it was exclusive. * * * [However,] [i]t is not the exclusiveness of the offer that deprives the offeror of the right to revoke. It is the action taken by the offeree which deprives the offeror of that right. Until there is action by the offeree—a partial performance pursuant to the offer—the offeror may revoke even if his offer is of an exclusive agency or an exclusive right to sell. * * *

Once partial performance is begun pursuant to the offer made, a contract results. This contract has been termed a contract with conditions or an option contract. This terminology is illustrated as follows:

> "If an offer for a unilateral contract is made, and part of the consideration requested in the offer is given or tendered by the offeree in response thereto, the offeror is bound by a contract, the duty of immediate performance of which is conditional on the full consideration being given or tendered within the time stated in the offer, or, if no time is stated therein, within a reasonable time." Restatement of Contracts, § 45 (1932).

Restatement (Second) of Contracts, § 45, Tent. Draft No. 1, (approved 1964, Tent. Draft No. 2, p. vii) states:

> "(1) Where an offer invites an offeree to accept by rendering a performance and does not invite a promissory acceptance, an option contract is created when the offeree begins the invited performance or tenders part of it.
>
> "(2) The offeror's duty of performance under any option contract so created is conditional on completion or tender of the invited performance in accordance with the terms of the offer."

Restatement (Second) of Contracts, § 45, Tent. Draft No. 1, comment (g), says:

> "This Section frequently applies to agency arrangements, particularly offers made to real estate brokers. * * *"

See Restatement (Second) of Agency § 446, comment (b).

The reason for finding such a contract is stated in *Hutchinson v. Dobson-Bainbridge Realty Co., supra*, as follows:

> "This rule avoids hardship to the offeree, and yet does not hold the offeror beyond the terms of his promise. It is true by such terms he was to be bound only if the requested act was done; but this implies that he will let it be done, that he will keep his offer open till the offeree who has begun can finish doing it. At least this is so where the doing of it will necessarily require time and expense. In such a case it is but just to hold that the offeree's part performance furnishes the 'acceptance' and the 'consideration' for a binding subsidiary promise not to revoke the offer, or turns the offer into a presently binding contract conditional upon the offeree's full performance."

We hold that part performance by the offeree of an offer of a unilateral contract results in a contract with a condition. The condition is full performance by the offeree. Here, if plaintiff-offeree partially performed prior to receipt of defendant's revocation, such a contract was formed. Thereafter, upon performance being completed by plaintiff, upon defendant's failure to recognize the contract, liability for breach of contract would arise. Thus, defendant's right to revoke his offer depends upon whether plaintiff had partially performed before he received defendant's revocation. * * *

What constitutes partial performance will vary from case to case since what can be done toward performance is limited by what is authorized to be done. Whether plaintiff partially performed is a question of fact to be determined by the trial court.

The trial court denied plaintiff's requested finding concerning his partial performance. It did so on the theory that partial performance was not material. In this the trial court erred.

Because of the failure to find on the issue of partial performance, the case must be remanded to the trial court. * * *

The cause is remanded for findings on the issue of plaintiff's partial performance of the offer prior to its revocation, and for further proceedings consistent with this opinion and the findings so made.

It is so ordered.

QUESTIONS

1. Questions about the facts of this case

   1.1. Did the defendant make one offer or two offers?

   1.2. How, if at all, did the plaintiff perform?

   1.3. Did the specified prospective buyer agree to buy the real property? Was that important?

   1.4. Did the specified prospective buyer agree to buy the real property before the plaintiff received the defendant's revocation? Was that important?

2. Questions about the law

   2.1. What does the court mean by the statement that, "part performance by the offeree of a unilateral contract results in a condition. The condition is full performance by the offeree"?

   2.2. Is there any language that the defendant could have added to its offer to the plaintiff that would have eliminated the possibility of this litigation?

   2.3. The New Mexico Supreme Court looked to what eventually became *Restatement (Second) of Contracts* § 45. Take a look at that section yourself. How can a real estate agent prove that she "begins the invited performance"? How can the real estate agent deal with the "performance/preparation" distinction of *comment f* to § 45 which provides: "What is begun or tendered must be part of the actual performance invited in order to preclude revocation under this Section. Beginning preparations, though they may be essential in carrying out the contract or accepting the offer is not enough"?

   2.4. Assuming, on remand, the trial court does find that the plaintiff partially performed before the defendant's attempted revocation, is there consideration for holding the defendant's offer irrevocable? If not, what is the basis for finding an enforceable option contract?

3. **You Be the Lawyer!**

   Assume you represent an owner who plans to list her property for sale with a broker. Your client tells you that it is important to her to preserve her ability to change her mind about her decision to sell and, if she does so, she does not want to risk being liable for a commission. How will you approach the crafting of the listing agreement in order to accomplish you client's aims?

PROBLEMS ON ACCEPTANCE BY PROMISE, PERFORMANCE, AND PART PERFORMANCE

Consider how the following hypotheticals would be resolved both under classical principles of contract law and under the *Restatement (Second) of Contracts*:

1. Markell says to Ponoroff, "I'll pay you $20 if you wash and wax my car." Ponoroff says, "I accept." Has a contract been formed? If Ponoroff fails to wash and wax Markell's car is Ponoroff in breach? How about if Ponoroff says nothing in response, but begins washing Markell's car? Is there a contract? *See Restatement (Second)* §§ 50(2) & 62.

2. Suppose Markell's offer is phrased, "I'll pay you $20 if you wash and wax my car, and this offer can be accepted only by your doing the job, not by merely promising to do the job." Ponoroff replies, "I accept." Is either party bound at this point? How about if Ponoroff goes out and buys some rags and a can of wax to do the job? What about when he actually begins the job? Suppose Ponoroff is nearly finished, having put in over two hours on the job under a hot sun, when Markell walks up to him and says, "I revoke my offer." Is the revocation effective? If not, what must Ponoroff do in order to prevail in a suit for breach of contract? *See Restatement (Second)* § 45. If Markell does not revoke, and instead Ponoroff abandons the job without finishing, can Markell sue Ponoroff for breach?

3. Now suppose Markell's offer is phrased, "I'll pay you $20 if you will agree to wash and wax my car this weekend, but I want your promise." Ponoroff replies, "I accept." Is either party bound at this point? Suppose Ponoroff says nothing, but that weekend he shows up and begins working on Markell's car. Has a contract been formed? Suppose, just prior to Ponoroff's completing the job, Markell shows up and says, "I revoke my offer." Will Ponoroff prevail if he sues Markell for breach? How about if Markell says nothing until after Ponoroff has completed the job and then Markell revokes? *See Restatement (Second)* § 50(3).

4. Finally, suppose Markell makes the offer, "I'll pay you $20 to wash and wax my car," and then promptly heads off to Monaco to try to win enough money so that he can take a year off from teaching Contracts. Ponoroff locates Markell's car and gives it a first class wash and wax. Two weeks later, Markell, who has lost all his money, e-mails Ponoroff from Monaco to tell him that he is withdrawing his offer. Ponoroff fires back a reply, "Too late, dude, I did the job two weeks ago. Did you forget *Carlill*? You owe me the money." Markell responds with the following message: "Spare me the 19th century case law from merry old England, Bud, go read § 54(2) of the *Restatement (Second) of Contracts*." Was there a contract here? Can Ponoroff recover his $20 fee if he sues?

D. ACCEPTANCE BY SILENCE OR INACTION

QUESTION BEFORE THE CASE

What is the relationship between circumstances where silence is considered an acceptance and circumstances involving an implied-in-fact contract?

LAREDO NATIONAL BANK V. GORDON

United States Court of Appeals, Fifth Circuit
61 F.2d 906 (1932)

BRYAN, CIRCUIT JUDGE.

This is an action at law by an attorney Bernard Gordon, against his client, Laredo National Bank, to recover $12,500 as a fee agreed upon in the settlement of a suit which the attorney had brought for the bank against Abraham Rosenblum, Aaron Rosenblum, and the Abe Rosenblum Corporation. The suit against the Rosenblums was to recover $144,000 which it was alleged they and one Joseph Rosenblum had fraudulently procured from the bank by means of drafts to which were attached fictitious delivery orders falsely purporting to cover actual carload shipments of produce. Gordon brought the suit upon an agreement that he was to receive a contingent fee of 25 percent of the amount recovered. While the suit was pending, the bank and its local attorney entered into negotiations with the Rosenblums for a compromise settlement. During the continuance of those negotiations, and on March 4, 1930, the bank wired Gordon that, acting upon his suggestion, it would refuse to accept a proposition of settlement which the Rosenblums had made, but added "in case there should be a counter proposition from them which we may consider acceptable advise what are your minimum fees." On the same day Gordon replied by wire that he felt confident his fee could be adjusted reasonably in the light of prior arrangements and subsequent developments, but that he would welcome the bank's suggestion in regard to his fee. On March 10 the bank wired Gordon, stating that its proposition had not been accepted, but that "we must know immediately what will be your fees in the event we accept settlement offered us. Answer quick"; and Gordon replied, "Answering today's telegram twelve thousand five hundred dollars." Nothing further was said about fees pending negotiations for settlement, which continued until June 16, 1930, when the bank received in settlement of its claim against the Rosenblums about $50,000 in cash, securities of the estimated value of $94,000, and a note of Joseph Rosenblum for $66,000. On June 29 the local attorney for the bank, who lived at Laredo, Tex., addressed a letter to Gordon who lived in New York, advising that a settlement had been effected, directing dismissal of the suit which Gordon had brought in New

York and which was still pending, and stating that the bank's president "will write you direct and take up the matter of your fee and its payment." On July 3, 1930, the bank's president wrote Gordon that the bank would pay a reasonable fee, but that the amount mentioned in his telegram of March 10 was beyond reason. Gordon testified that before he received this last-mentioned letter he had already dismissed the suit against the Rosenblums, in compliance with the directions of the bank's local attorney. At the close of the evidence in this case, both sides moved for a directed verdict; whereupon the trial court charged the jury to render a verdict in favor of Gordon for $12,500 with interest. After this charge was given, the bank undertook to withdraw its motion, and requested the court to submit to the jury the question whether it had accepted Gordon's offer contained in his telegram of March 10 to take $12,500 in settlement of his fee.

It is argued that the bank never became bound to pay the $12,500 fee, because it never replied to or accepted Gordon's offer to take that amount in settlement for his services. It is true that, generally speaking, an offeree has a right to make no reply to offers, and hence that his silence is not to be construed as an acceptance. But, where the relation between the parties is such that the offeror is justified in expecting a reply, or the offeree is under a duty to reply, the latter's silence will be regarded as acceptance. Under such circumstances, "one who keeps silent, knowing that his silence will be misinterpreted, should not be allowed to deny the natural interpretation of his conduct," etc. It was upon the bank's insistence that Gordon agreed to accept the fee he named in his telegram, in order that the bank might go ahead with its compromise settlement. It was not until after a settlement had been made, the suit against the Rosenblums had been dismissed, and Gordon had lost all opportunity of earning a larger contingent fee, that the bank made any objection or expressed any dissatisfaction with the amount of the fee Gordon had agreed to accept in the event of a compromise settlement. Its silence amounted to conduct which misled its attorney to his detriment, for the bank could not have failed to know that Gordon was acting in the belief that the fee which he had agreed to accept would be paid without question. Under the circumstances, the bank's silence was equivalent to its acceptance of and assent to Gordon's offer to forego his contingent fee and receive instead the lump sum payment which he named.

* * *

It is true, of course, that an attorney ought not to take advantage of his client, or be permitted to drive a hard bargain. But the evidence shows that Gordon thought a better settlement could be made with the Rosenblums, did not suggest giving up the trial of the case, was reluctant to accept the bank's suggestion of a compromise and its taking the case out of his hands, and expressed himself as perfectly willing to let the question of his fee be postponed until the case in which he was employed was disposed of. It was only when the bank insisted upon making its own settlement that he agreed to accept a fee which was less than he would have been entitled to receive if he had been paid the contingent fee originally agreed upon. So far as this record shows, his conduct was above reproach. The duty of fair dealing applies to the client as well as to the attorney. The record before us leaves no room for reasonable doubt that Gordon was justly entitled to the verdict which the court directed the jury to render in his favor.

The judgment is affirmed.

QUESTIONS, NOTES, AND CONNECTIONS

1. Questions about the facts of this case

   1.1. Is it just us, or did the Laredo National Bank get a pretty good settlement on its $144,000 case against the Rosenblums?

   1.2. The court states that Gordon thought a better settlement could be obtained and that it was only after the settlement had been arranged and he lost the opportunity for a larger contingency fee that the bank made any objection. But could Gordon really hold up a settlement that his client wanted because of the prospect of earning a larger fee?

2. Questions about the law

   2.1. What is the basis for the general rule that silence or inaction does not constitute an acceptance?

   2.2. Please read *Restatement (Second) of Contracts* § 69; it reflects the general rule that ordinarily acceptance cannot be based on silence or inaction. Note that there are three exceptions. Which exception would have applied in *Gordon*?

   2.3. Who are the exceptions in § 69 intended to benefit, the offeror or the offeree? Are these exceptions consistent with objective theory?

3. Notes

   3.1. Assume Broker represents a party looking to purchase new warehouse space. Broker is aware of what may be suitable space and shows it to his client, who expresses some interest. Thereupon, Broker sends Owner, with whom Broker has never dealt before, a letter stating that "if you are successful in selling this property to my client, I shall be entitled to a 5% commission at closing." Owner acknowledged receipt of the letter and began negotiations with Broker's client that ultimately culminated in a sale. When Broker demanded his 5% commission, Owner responded that there was no agreement regarding payment of such a commission and, therefore, there is no liability for the commission. Broker claims that if Owner disagreed with Broker's request for the commission, Owner had a duty to let Broker know that she objected to the terms of Broker's letter. Assess the validity of these arguments.

3.2. In the leading case of *Austin v. Burge,* 156 Mo.App. 286, 137 S.W. 618 (1911), the defendant's subscription for a newspaper expired, but the publisher continued to have it sent to him, even though the defendant ordered the paper stopped. When the publisher sued for the subscription price, the defendant argued that there was no contract. The court disagreed, observing that because the defendant had continued accepting and reading the paper, even after his order to stop delivery, the defendant had accepted the publisher's offer for the price of the paper. In light of this case, what should you do when a merchant continues to send you unordered goods through the mail? Does this open the door to abusive marketing practices? Are the rules of contract law adequate to address the abuse? If not, what should be done? *See United States v. Random Stationers, Inc.,* 1984 U.S. Dist. LEXIS 24709 (S.D. Fla. 1984) (applying a federal statute, 39 U.S.C. § 3009, adopted as part of the Postal Reorganization Act of 1970, making it an unfair trade practice in violation of § 5 of the Federal Trade Commission Act to bill a recipient for unsolicited merchandise and permitting such merchandise to be retained by the recipient as a gift).

4. **You Be the Lawyer!**

In fact, you're going to be a lawyer in a few years. So, if you were undertaking representation of a new client in a case like this, how would you draft the fee agreement to avoid the problem that Gordon got himself into of having to sue his own client to collect his fee?

5. Connections

So, an offer can be accepted by promise, performance, partial performance, and even silence or inaction. In each situation, the corresponding rule on the effectiveness of a purported acceptance is slightly different. Can you articulate the differences? Do these different rules make sense to you? Are they all consistent with the objective theory of contract formation? Are they consistent with one another? If Ponoroff tells Epstein, I offer to purchase your share of next year's royalties from MADD for $250,000,* and will assume this is acceptable to you unless I hear otherwise by Noon on next

* Incidentally, based on past experience, the offer in this hypothetical is probably an attractive one from the perspective of the offeree (eds.).

Tuesday," what are the different ways in which Epstein might accept this offer, and, in each case, when would the acceptance be effective?

E. IMPERFECT ACCEPTANCES

Earlier, we saw that one way in which an offer can be destroyed is express rejection by the offeree. For example, Ponoroff offers to buy Epstein's car for $100 and Epstein replies, "No way dude." At that point the offer is dead and cannot be resuscitated unless Ponoroff chooses to do so.

But, if Ponoroff offers to buy Epstein's car for $100 and Epstein replies, "I want $120," nobody would seriously regard Epstein's reply as an acceptance. However, neither has he unequivocally rejected the offer, as in the first example. Instead, that reply would be treated as a *counteroffer*, which is simultaneously an *implied* rejection of the original offer and a new offer over which Ponoroff now has the power of acceptance.

So if Ponoroff offers to buy Epstein's car for $100 and Epstein responds "I want $120," and Ponoroff says: "Okay. I agree to pay $120," then there is a contract for the sale of the car for $120.

But remember that a counteroffer is also an implied rejection. And, an implied rejection is still a rejection. Still terminates—kills—the offer. So assume Ponoroff offers to buy Epstein's car for $100 and Epstein responds "I want $120." If Ponoroff says "No," and Epstein replies, "Ok, I'll take $100," there is *no* contract. Epstein is trying to accept a terminated offer—an offer he killed by his implied rejection—and, well, you just can't do that.

A counteroffer—"No, I won't pay X but I will pay Y"—is described not only as an implied rejection, but also as kind of imperfect acceptance. An imperfect acceptance can also take the form of an acceptance with a condition. For example, Ponoroff offers to buy Epstein's car for $100 and Epstein responds, "I'll accept your offer to buy my car for $100, but my acceptance is conditioned on any later disputes about the quality of the car being submitted to arbitration by Markell." No contract, just a new offer. Such a conditional acceptance is treated just like a counteroffer. Epstein's response is simultaneously an implied rejection of Ponoroff's offer and a new offer to Ponoroff.

Counteroffers and conditional acceptances are not the only forms of implied rejection; not the only forms of imperfect acceptances. Under common law, a third form of imperfect acceptance is a response that merely adds a new or different term, but does not condition acceptance on the new term. For example, Ponoroff offers to buy Epstein's car for $100 and Epstein responds, "I'll accept your offer to buy my car for $100 and I propose that any later disputes about the quality of the car be submitted to arbitration by Markell."

Do you see any meaningful distinction between the hypotheticals in the preceding two paragraphs? Would the court in the next case distinguish between the two? As you read the next case, also consider what the implications of an imperfect acceptance are as they relate to both the existence of an agreement and the status of the original offer.

QUESTIONS BEFORE THE CASE

1. What is the rationale for the mirror-image rule applied in this case?
2. Does this rule effectuate the intent of the parties regarding contract formation in this case? Generally?

GRESSER V. HOTZLER

Court of Appeals of Minnesota
604 N.W.2d 379 (2000)

LANSING, JUDGE.

Michael Gresser sued Calvin and Cheryl Hotzler for specific performance of a purchase agreement for commercial real estate and, alternatively, for breach of contract. On the Hotzlers' motion for partial summary judgment on Gresser's specific-performance claim, the district court held that the purchase agreement was invalid and entered final judgment against Gresser pursuant to Minn. R. Civ. P. 54.02, dismissing both the specific-performance and breach-of-contract claims. Gresser appeals from the judgment.

FACTS

The property in dispute includes five acres of land and a building that formerly housed the Stagecoach Theatre in Shakopee. In early 1998, Michael Gresser, a real estate investor, began negotiating with landowners Calvin and Cheryl Hotzler to purchase the property. In July, Gresser submitted to the Hotzlers an unsigned, proposed purchase agreement that, among other items, required the Hotzlers to deliver a recertified survey on August 10, 1998, and provided for closing on September 1, 1998. The Hotzlers changed several terms, initialed the changes, signed the purchase agreement, and returned it to Gresser's attorney on August 4, 1998.

On August 10, 1998, Gresser initialed the Hotzlers' changes and signed the purchase agreement. Gresser, however, made two additional changes. He changed the survey delivery date to September 10, 1998, and the closing date to October 15, 1998. Gresser initialed both date changes. Gresser made these changes on the advice of his attorney, who had talked to the Hotzlers' realtor. The attorney and the realtor agreed that, because of the time that had elapsed, the original survey and closing dates had become impractical. The attorney knew that the realtor had not consulted the Hotzlers about the changes, and both Gresser and his attorney knew that the realtor did not have the power to bind the Hotzlers.

Gresser's attorney returned the signed purchase agreement to the realtor on August 12, 1998, along with $2,000 earnest money. Gresser and his attorney expected that the Hotzlers would initial the date changes and return the purchase agreement to them. The realtor delivered the purchase agreement to Calvin Hotzler on August 12, 1998, but testified that he did not indicate whether Gresser had signed the counteroffer. Calvin Hotzler assumed the parties had a deal, but he did not read the purchase agreement. Instead, he placed it on the kitchen counter to await the return of Cheryl Hotzler, who was out of town. Later that day, Calvin Hotzler showed Gresser the property and introduced him to tenants as the buyer.

On the afternoon of August 12, 1998, the realtor received another offer for the property, which he forwarded to the Hotzlers. Calvin Hotzler placed this document on the kitchen counter as well. On August 13, the Hotzlers reviewed both documents, decided to accept the new offer, and signed that purchase agreement.

ISSUES

I. Given the undisputed facts in the record, did the district court err by concluding that the purchase agreement between the Hotzlers and Gresser was not legally binding?

II. Did the district court err by refusing to apply equitable estoppel?

ANALYSIS

On appeal from summary judgment, the reviewing court determines whether any genuine issues of material fact exist and whether the district court erred in its application of the law. Whether a contract exists is generally an issue for the factfinder. But when "the record taken as a whole could not lead a rational trier of fact to find for the nonmoving party," summary judgment is proper.

I.

Whether a contract is formed is judged by the objective conduct of the parties and not their subjective intent. Minnesota has followed the "mirror image rule" in analyzing acceptance of offers. Under that rule, "an acceptance must be coextensive with the offer and may not introduce additional terms or conditions." *Podany v. Erickson,* 235 Minn. 36, 39, 49

N.W.2d 193, 194 (1951). When the offer is positively accepted, however, a requested or suggested modification does not prevent contract formation, regardless of whether the modification is accepted. *Podany,* 235 Minn. at 39, 49 N.W.2d at 194; * * *. *See also Restatement (2d) of Contracts* § 61 (1981).

Gresser first argues the district court erred by making findings on disputed facts material to whether the parties formed a contract. We disagree. The district court's function on a summary judgment motion is to determine whether genuine factual issues exist. In making this determination, the court may consider whether reasonable persons could draw only one inference from the evidence. In this case, after reviewing the evidence, the district court listed the facts it found to be uncontroverted. The district court did not exceed the scope of its function on a summary judgment motion in so doing. * * * Even if the court engaged in unwarranted factfinding, however, its error is harmless because its legal conclusion is premised on undisputed facts.

Gresser primarily argues that his changes to the purchase agreement are within the modification exception to the mirror-image rule because he unconditionally accepted the Hotzlers' counteroffer and merely suggested the date changes. According to Gresser, he accepted unconditionally because he would have been willing to comply with the original dates, the realtor encouraged Gresser to make the changes, and Calvin Hotzler introduced Gresser as the owner of the property on August 12.

Viewed objectively, these facts do not demonstrate that Gresser positively accepted the purchase agreement. First, Gresser's uncommunicated subjective intent is not relevant, and, second, these facts do not suggest that the Hotzlers knew or should have known that Gresser offered the change in dates only as a suggestion. To the contrary, the undisputed facts regarding absence of any express communication, the method of initialing the changes, and the prior course of dealings between the parties indicate that the changes were part of the series of counteroffers.

Minnesota has applied the modification exception sparingly and only to those cases in which objective manifestations of acceptance existed separately from the suggestions for modifications. *See Podany,* 235 Minn. at 38, 49 N.W.2d at 195 (offeree's written acceptance clearly stated it had elected to exercise option to purchase property); * * *. Gresser proposed his changes on the face of the purchase agreement and provided no objective indication that his acceptance was not conditioned on them.

Gresser alternatively argues that his changes to the purchase agreement did not preclude contract formation because the changes were immaterial. The mirror-image rule historically has been strictly construed to forbid even minor variations between offer and acceptance. Many modern courts have relaxed the rule, holding that only an acceptance that differs *materially* from the terms of the original offer prevents contract formation.

The corollary to this modern rule is that an immaterial variation in the acceptance does not impede contract formation. For instance, several courts have held that, under this exception, variations implied in the offer do not interfere with the completed contract.

The Minnesota Supreme Court used the language of the immateriality exception in *Markmann v. H.A. Bruntjen Co.,* 249 Minn. 281, 286, 81 N.W.2d 858, 862 (Minn.1957). In *Markmann,* the court held that "an acceptance which differs substantially and materially from the terms of the original offer does not give rise to a completed contract." *Id.* The *Markmann* court did not, however, find an immaterial variation or make clear that it was diverging from its former strict construction of the mirror-image rule. *Id.* (citing *Minar v. Skoog,* 235 Minn. 262, 265, 50 N.W.2d 300, 302 (1951) (holding acceptance must comply *exactly* with terms of the offer)). The Hotzlers argue that Minnesota caselaw has retained the strict mirror-image rule for real estate contracts, while tempering the rule in its application to other types of contracts. Although we note that the Supreme Court and this court have more often applied the strict-construction standard in cases involving real estate, caselaw provides no explicit distinction. *Compare Minar,* 235 Minn. at 265, 50 N.W.2d at 302 (applying strict-construction standard to acceptance of option to purchase real estate), *and Rose v. Guerdon Indus., Inc.,* 374 N.W.2d 282, 284 (Minn.App.1985) (applying strict construction to acceptance of offer to sell real estate), *with Markmann,* 249 Minn. at 286, 81 N.W.2d at 862 (using material-difference standard to analyze contract for sale of product distribution rights). It is, however, unnecessary to define the scope of an immateriality exception unless the changes to the purchase agreement are immaterial.

"Authority on what constitutes a material variation is meager." *Northwest Television Club,* 634 P.2d at 841. Black's Law Dictionary defines "material alteration" as "a change in a legal instrument sufficient to alter the instrument's legal meaning or effect." *Black's Law Dictionary,* 78 (7th ed.1999). Similarly, the Florida Court of Appeals found the addition of "and/or assignees" did not constitute a material variation because it did not "change the legal effect of the contract." *Kitsos v. Stanford,* 291 So.2d 632, 634 (Fla.Dist.Ct.App.1974). We agree that the focus should be on the legal operation of the contract. Thus, only minor changes that do not substantially alter the performance obligations of the parties may be immaterial.

Under this principle, the date changes Gresser made are material. The changes directly affect Gresser's performance obligations under the contract, postponing his duty to perform by almost six weeks. The law of contracts is not advanced by allowing a contracting party to manipulate the finality of an obligation by rejecting an insubstantial change, but few terms are more important to sellers of real estate than the date on which they will receive the purchase money. The purchase agreement's inclusion of a time-is-of-the-essence clause further evidences the materiality of the performance date. As a matter of law, the exception to the mirror-image rule for immaterial variations does not apply to the changes Gresser made to the purchase agreement.

In retrospect, Gresser may have been very willing to expressly note that the changed dates were proposals rather than conditions or to retain the earlier closing date rather than risk the loss of the property. But contract formation proceeds on an objective basis and courts should not reconstruct, much less call back, the written word. The high volume of real estate transactions in Minnesota reinforces the importance of identifying and preserving a bright line in the formation of purchase agreements.

II.

The district court rejected Gresser's argument that the Hotzlers should be equitably estopped from denying the validity of the purchase agreement. * * *

Equitable estoppel arises when "one by his acts or representations, or by his silence when he ought to speak, intentionally or through culpable negligence, induces another to believe certain facts to exist, and such other rightfully acts on the belief so induced in such a matter that if the former is permitted to deny the existence of the facts it will prejudice the latter." *Transamerica Ins. Group v. Paul,* 267 N.W.2d 180, 183 (Minn.1978). The first element necessary to establish estoppel is a misrepresentation. *Id.* Gresser does not allege the Hotzlers made misrepresentations directly, but contends that the realtor's statements that the changes would not affect the deal are attributable to the Hotzlers under agency theories.

The general rule is that real estate agents have no implied authority to contract on behalf of their principals. *La Plant v. Loveland,* 142 Minn. 89, 92, 170 N.W. 920, 921 (Minn.1919). And apparent authority must be founded on the principal's actions "since no agent by his own act can create evidence of authority." *West Concord Conservation Club, Inc. v. Chilson,* 306 N.W.2d 893, 897 (Minn.1981); *see also Hagedorn v. Aid Ass'n for Lutherans,* 297 Minn. 253, 258, 211 N.W.2d 154, 158 (1973). Gresser has not identified any conduct or statements by the Hotzlers that would support a variance from the general rule on implied authority or a finding of apparent authority.

* * *

Gresser's equitable estoppel claim also fails on the essential element of reasonable reliance. *See Transamerica,* 267 N.W.2d at 183 (listing reasonable reliance as element of equitable estoppel). Both Gresser and his attorney admit that they knew real estate agents are not authorized to contract on behalf of their principals. And Gresser's attorney also knew that the realtor had not contacted the Hotzlers before making the assurances. On these facts, any reliance on the realtor's assurances was unreasonable as a matter of law. *See West Concord Conservation Club,* 306 N.W.2d at 897 (to invoke estoppel doctrine, "truth must have been unknown" to party when he acted).

DECISION

Because the date changes to the purchase agreement precluded contract formation as a matter of law, and because Gresser failed to assert facts sufficient to support an equitable estoppel claim, the district court properly granted summary judgment to the Hotzlers.

Affirmed.

QUESTIONS AND NOTES

1. Questions about the facts of this case

   1.1. Did Calvin Hotzler believe the parties had a deal on August 12 when he showed Gresser the property? Was that relevant to the court? Should it have been?

   1.2. How important to the Hotzlers were Gresser's two changes in dates? Were the two changes the reason that the Hotzlers decided to accept the other offer for the property?

   1.3. How important was it to Gresser that the dates for survey delivery and closing be moved back? Was that relevant to the court? Should it have been?

2. Questions about the law

   2.1. In the note before *Gresser*, we considered counteroffers and conditional acceptances. Does the *Gresser* case involve either a counteroffer or a conditional acceptance? What is the difference, if any, between a response to an offer that triggers the conditional acceptance rule and a response to an offer that triggers the common law mirror image rule?

   2.2. In Section 3.A., *supra*, we noted that when an offeree *expressly* rejects an offer, the offer is terminated and may not be revived unless the offeror elects to renew it. In this case, by signing and returning on August 12 the proposed purchase agreement that the Hotzlers had submitted on August 4, the court suggests that the offeree, Gresser, has *implicitly* rejected the offer. What is the legal effect of an implied rejection? As of August 12, who had the power of acceptance according to the court?

2.3. What is the scope of the "modification exception" to the mirror-image rule to which the court refers and how is its applicability determined?

2.4. What is the scope of the "immateriality exception" to the mirror-image rule in Minnesota? Who determines "materiality"?

2.5. What is the effect of a counteroffer when the original offer is an irrevocable offer? Suppose on February 1, in exchange for $100, Markell granted Epstein a 60-day option to acquire certain real property owned by Markell for $150,000. Epstein pays the $100 at the time the option is granted. On March 1, Epstein calls Markell and offers to give him $145,000 for the property. Markell refuses. Ten days later Epstein contacts Markell to tell him that he has decided to exercise the option and buy the property for $150,000. Markell, however, citing *Gresser,* contends that it is too late. Does Epstein have a claim for breach against Markell? *See Restatement (Second) of Contracts* § 37. How, if at all, does it affect your answer if, in the March 1 conversation, Epstein also tells Markell that he was simply not interested in the property at the $150,000 price?

3. Notes

3.1. *Gresser* introduces the common law "mirror image" rule, which derives from the first principle that the offeror is sovereign. Specifically, that the offeror is not to be required to deal other than on the terms she specified in her offer. Thus, the mirror image rule holds that an acceptance must be a total assent on the terms of the offer. Any variation, request or condition in the acceptance, a so-called "imperfect acceptance," renders it ineffective to form a contract.

What if the reason that the purported acceptance varies or adds to the terms of the offer is that the offeree simply makes a mistake in fashioning her reply, which she is quick to rectify upon having it pointed out to her?

In *Minneapolis & St. Louis Railway Co. v. Columbus Rolling-Mill Co.*, 119 U.S. 149 (1886), the defendant offered iron rails at $54 per gross ton for quantities of between 2,000 and 5,000 tons. The plaintiff responded by ordering 1,200 tons at the quoted price. When the defendant replied that it was impossible to book the order at that price because it was below the minimum quantity, the plaintiff entered an order for 2,000 tons, but the defendant refused to deliver, denying the existence of a contract. What result on plaintiff's claim for breach?

3.2. *Restatement (Second) of Contracts* §§ 59–61 attempt to draw a distinction between a truly conditional acceptance, which operates as a counteroffer, and an acceptance with suggestions or inquiries, which is still sufficient to form a contract. Is this a break with the common law mirror image rule? Does Minnesota seem to apply the *Restatement* rules? How do these rules relate to the two exceptions to the mirror-image rule that, according to the Gresser court, are recognized to a limited extent in Minnesota? Read those Restatement sections again (or for the first time) and decide whether there is mutual assent in either of these situations. Epstein says to Ponoroff, "I'll sell you my car for $3,000 cash," and Ponoroff replies, "I accept; I'll write you a check?" How about if Ponoroff replies, "I accept, but would a check be ok? Does it change your answers at all if the offer doesn't specify "cash"?"

4. **You Be the Lawyer!**

How would you have counseled Gresser to craft the two changes to the purchase agreement that were made on August 10?

Just like the rule that the *manner* of acceptance must abide by the terms of the offer (recall *La Salle National Bank v. Vega*, *supra*, at 123), the mirror image rule (or what the court in *Gresser* refers to as the "strict" mirror-image rule), which focuses on the *substance* of the acceptance, can work some harsh and unexpectedly restrictive results, both with respect to the aim of protecting the interests of the offeror and in enforcing an arrangement with respect to which the parties indeed intended to be bound. For example, in *Gresser*, after receiving the signed purchase agreement back from Gresser, an argument can be made that Mr. Hotzler considered that the parties had a deal, viewing the changes in dates as either unimportant or details that could be worked out later. However, upon receiving what was a more attractive third-party offer, the Hotzlers changed their minds. Because of the operation of the mirror image rule, they were able to claim no contract existed with Gresser and, effectively, walk on a deal even though there truly had been an agreement reached by the parties on all of the essential terms of the transaction.

The problems of a strict mirror image rule are compounded in an era when so much business is done on the basis of an exchange of standard printed forms between buyer and seller containing lots of detailed and technical language, typically prepared by the parties' lawyers, which neither party may be reading very carefully or capable of understanding. Under the mirror image rule, any divergence in the fine print of these forms prevents formation of a contract on the documents. Nevertheless, if the parties have commenced performance before a dispute occurs or a problem arises, clearly there is a contract of some type, but what are its terms if we can't rely on the documents?

To address both this question and the problem of the offeree being able to use the mirror image rule manipulatively either to renege on a deal or to covertly add new terms to the deal, the drafters of the U.C.C. came up with § 2–207 applicable in contracts involving the sale of goods. It goes far beyond the reach of the Restatement (second)'s rules.

Section 2–207 has been very controversial and subjected to considerable criticism as flawed in its design and unnecessarily cumbersome in its application. As you read the next three cases, see if you agree with those critics.

---

§ 2–207. Additional Terms in Acceptance or Confirmation.

(1) A definite and seasonable expression of acceptance or a written confirmation which is sent within a reasonable time operates as an acceptance even though it states terms additional to or different from those offered or agreed upon, unless acceptance is expressly made conditional on assent to the additional or different terms.

(2) The additional terms are to be construed as proposals for addition to the contract. Between merchants such terms become part of the contract unless:

(a) the offer expressly limits acceptance to the terms of the offer;

(b) they materially alter it; or

(c) notification of objection to them has already been given or is given within a reasonable time after notice of them is received.

(3) Conduct by both parties which recognizes the existence of a contract is sufficient to establish a contract for sale although the writings of the parties do not otherwise establish a contract. In such case the terms of the particular contract consist of those terms on which the writings of the parties agree, together with any supplementary terms incorporated under any other provisions of this Act.

QUESTIONS BEFORE THE CASE

1. How would this case have been decided under the common law mirror image rule? Does U.C.C. § 2–207 change the result?
2. Can you identify the "mistake," according to the court of appeals, made by the trial court that results in reversal and remand?

DORTON V. COLLINS & AIKMAN CORPORATION

United States Court of Appeals, Sixth Circuit
453 F.2d 1161 (1972)

CELEBREZZE, CIRCUIT JUDGE.

This is an appeal from the District Court's denial of Defendant-Appellant's motion for a stay pending arbitration, pursuant to Section 3 of the United States Arbitration Act of 1925, 9 U.S.C. § 3. The suit arose after a series of over 55 transactions during 1968, 1969, and 1970 in which Plaintiffs-Appellees [hereinafter The Carpet Mart], carpet retailers in Kingsport, Tennessee, purchased carpets from Defendant-Appellant [hereinafter Collins & Aikman], incorporated under the laws of the State of Delaware, with its principal place of business in New York, New York, and owner of a carpet manufacturing plant [formerly the Painter Carpet Mills, Inc.] located in Dalton, Georgia. The Carpet Mart originally brought this action in a Tennessee state trial court, seeking compensatory and punitive damages in the amount of $450,000 from Collins & Aikman for the latter's alleged fraud, deceit, and misrepresentation in the sale of what were supposedly carpets manufactured from 100% Kodel polyester fiber. The Carpet Mart maintains that in May, 1970, in response to a customer complaint, it learned that not all of the carpets were manufactured from 100% Kodel polyester fiber but rather some were composed of a cheaper and inferior carpet fiber. After the cause was removed to the District Court on the basis of diversity of citizenship, Collins & Aikman moved for a stay pending arbitration, asserting that The Carpet Mart was bound to an arbitration agreement which appeared on the reverse side of Collins & Aikman's printed sales acknowledgment forms. Holding that there existed no binding arbitration agreement between the parties, the District Court denied the stay. For the reasons set forth below, we remand the case to the District Court for further findings.

* * *

The primary question before us on appeal is whether the District Court, in denying Collins & Aikman's motion for a stay pending arbitration, erred in holding that The Carpet Mart was not bound by the arbitration agreement appearing on the back of Collins & Aikman's acknowledgment forms. In reviewing the District Court's determination, we must look closely at the procedures which were followed in the sales transactions which gave rise to the present dispute over the arbitration agreement.

In each of the more than 55 transactions, one of the partners in The Carpet Mart, or, on some occasions, Collins & Aikman's visiting salesman, telephoned Collins & Aikman's order department in Dalton, Georgia, and ordered certain quantities of carpets listed in Collins & Aikman's catalogue. There is some dispute as to what, if any, agreements were reached through the telephone calls and through the visits by Collins & Aikman's salesman. After each oral order was placed, the price, if any, quoted by the buyer was checked against Collins & Aikman's price list, and the credit department was consulted to determine if The Carpet Mart had paid for all previous shipments. After it was found that everything was in order, Collins & Aikman's order department typed the information concerning the particular order on one of its printed acknowledgment forms. Each acknowledgment form bore one of three legends: "Acknowledgment," "Customer Acknowledgment," or "Sales Contract." The following provision was printed on the face of the forms bearing the "Acknowledgment" legend:

> "The acceptance of your order is subject to all of the terms and conditions on the face and reverse side hereof, including arbitration, all of which are accepted by buyer; it supersedes buyer's order form, if any. It shall become a contract either (a) when signed and delivered by buyer to seller and accepted in writing by seller, or (b) at Seller's option, when buyer shall have given to seller specification of assortments, delivery dates, shipping instructions, or instructions to bill and hold as to all or any part of the merchandise herein described, or when buyer has received delivery of the whole or any part thereof, or when buyer has otherwise assented to the terms and conditions hereof."

Similarly, on the face of the forms bearing the "Customer Acknowledgment" or "Sales Contract" legends the following provision appeared:

> "This order is given subject to all of the terms and conditions on the face and reverse side hereof, including the provisions for arbitration and the exclusion of warranties, all of which are accepted by Buyer, supersede Buyer's order form, if any, and constitute the entire contract between Buyer and Seller. This order shall become a contract as to the entire quantity specified either (a) when signed and delivered by Buyer to Seller and accepted in writing by Seller or (b) when Buyer has received and retained this order for ten days without objection, or (c) when Buyer has accepted delivery of any part of the merchandise specified herein or has furnished to Seller specifications or assortments, delivery dates, shipping instructions, or instructions to bill and hold, or when Buyer has otherwise indicated acceptance of the terms hereof."

The small print on the reverse side of the forms provided, among other things, that all claims arising out of the contract would be submitted to arbitration in New York City. Each acknowledgment form was signed by an employee of Collins & Aikman's order department and mailed to The Carpet Mart on the day the telephone order was received or, at the latest, on the following day. The carpets were thereafter shipped to The Carpet Mart, with the interval between the mailing of the acknowledgment form and shipment of the carpets varying from a brief interval to a period of several weeks or months. Absent a delay in the mails, however, The Carpet Mart always received the acknowledgment forms prior to receiving the carpets. In all cases The Carpet Mart took delivery of and paid for the carpets without objecting to any terms contained in the acknowledgment form.

In holding that no binding arbitration agreement was created between the parties through the transactions above, the District Court relied on * * * [UCC § 2–207], * * *.

The District Court found that Subsection 2–207(3) controlled the instant case, quoting the following passage from 1 W. Hawkland, A Transactional Guide to the Uniform Commercial Code § 1.090303, at 19–20 (1964):

> "If the seller * * * ships the goods and the buyer accepts them, a contract is formed under subsection (3). The terms of this contract are those on which the purchase order and acknowledgment agree, and the additional terms needed for a contract are to be found throughout the U.C.C. * * * [T]he U.C.C. does not impose an arbitration term on the parties where their contract is silent on the matter. Hence, a conflict between an arbitration and an [*sic*] no-arbitration clause would result in the no arbitration clause becoming effective."

Under this authority alone the District Court concluded that the arbitration clause on the back of Collins & Aikman's sales acknowledgment had not become a binding term in the 50-odd transactions with The Carpet Mart.

In reviewing this determination by the District Court, we are aware of the problems which courts have had in interpreting Section 2–207. This section of the UCC has been described as a "murky bit of prose," Southwest Engineering Co. v. Martin Tractor Co., 205 Kan. 684, 694, 473 P.2d 18, 25 (1970), as "not too happily drafted," Roto-Lith Ltd. v. F. P. Bartlett & Co., 297 F.2d 497, 500 (1st Cir. 1962), and as "one of the most important, subtle, and difficult in the entire Code, and well it may be said that the product as it finally reads is not altogether satisfactory." Duesenberg & King, Sales and Bulk Transfers under the Uniform Commercial Code, (Vol. 3, Bender's Uniform Commercial Code Service) § 3.03, at 3–12 (1969). Despite the lack of clarity in its language, Section 2–207 manifests definite objectives which are significant in the present case.

As Official Comment No. 1 indicates, UCC § 2–207 was intended to apply to two situations:

> "The one is where an agreement has been reached either orally or by informal correspondence between the parties and is followed by one or both of the parties sending formal acknowledgments or memoranda embodying the terms so far as agreed upon and adding terms not discussed. The other situation is one in which a wire or letter expressed and intended as the closing or confirmation of an agreement adds further minor suggestions or proposals such as 'ship by Tuesday,' 'rush,' 'ship draft against bill of lading inspection allowed,' or the like." * * *

Although Comment No. 1 is itself somewhat ambiguous, it is clear that Section 2–207, and specifically Subsection 2–207(1), was intended to alter the "ribbon matching" or "mirror" rule of common law, under which the terms of an acceptance or confirmation were required to be identical to the terms of the offer or oral agreement, respectively. * * * Under the common law, an acceptance or a confirmation which contained terms additional to or different from those of the offer or oral agreement constituted a rejection of the offer or agreement and thus became a counter-offer. The terms of the counter-offer were said to have been accepted by the original offeror when he proceeded to perform under the contract without objecting to the counter-offer. Thus, a buyer was deemed to have accepted the seller's counter-offer if he took receipt of the goods and paid for them without objection.

Under Section 2–207 the result is different. This section of the Code recognizes that in current commercial transactions, the terms of the offer and those of the acceptance will seldom be identical. Rather, under the current "battle of the forms," each party typically has a printed form drafted by his attorney and containing as many terms as could be envisioned to favor that party in his sales transactions. Whereas under common law the disparity between the fineprint terms in the parties' forms would have prevented the consummation of a contract when these forms are exchanged, Section 2–207 recognizes that in many, but not all, cases the parties do not impart such significance to the terms on the printed forms. * * *. Subsection 2–207(1) therefore provides that "[a] definite and seasonable expression of acceptance or a written confirmation * * * operates as an acceptance even though it states terms additional to or different from those offered or agreed upon, unless acceptance is expressly made conditional on assent to the additional or different terms." Thus, under Subsection (1), a contract is recognized notwithstanding the fact that an acceptance or confirmation contains terms additional to or different from those of the offer or prior agreement, provided that the offeree's intent to accept the offer is definitely expressed, see Sections 2–204 and 2–206, and provided that the offeree's acceptance is not expressly conditioned on the offeror's assent to the additional or different terms. When a contract is recognized under Subsection (1), the additional terms are treated as "proposals for addition to the contract" under Subsection (2), which contains special provisions under which such additional terms are deemed to have been accepted when the transaction is between merchants. Conversely, when no contract is recognized under Subsection 2–207(1)—either because no definite expression of acceptance exists or, more specifically, because the offeree's acceptance is expressly conditioned on the offeror's assent to the additional or different terms—the entire transaction aborts at this point. If, however, the subsequent conduct of the parties—particularly, performance by both parties under what they apparently believe to be a contract—recognizes the existence of a contract, under Subsection 2–207(3) such conduct by both parties is sufficient to establish a contract, notwithstanding the fact that no contract would have been recognized on the basis of their writings alone. Subsection 2–207(3) further provides how the terms of contracts recognized thereunder shall be determined.

With the above analysis and purposes of Section 2–207 in mind, we turn to their application in the present case. We initially observe that the affidavits and the acknowledgment forms themselves raise the question of whether Collins & Aikman's forms constituted acceptances or confirmations under Section 2–207. The language of some of the acknowledgment forms ("The acceptance of your order is subject to * * *") and the affidavit of Mr. William T. Hester, Collins & Aikman's marketing operations manager, suggest that the forms were the only acceptances issued in response to The Carpet Mart's oral offers. However, in his affidavit Mr. J. A. Castle, a partner in The Carpet Mart, asserted that when he personally called Collins & Aikman to order carpets, someone from the latter's order department would agree to sell the requested carpets, or, alternatively, when Collins & Aikman's visiting salesman took the order, he would agree to the sale, on some occasions after he had used The Carpet Mart's telephone to call Collins & Aikman's order department. Absent the District Court's determination of whether Collins & Aikman's acknowledgment forms were acceptances or, alternatively, confirmations of prior oral agreements, we will consider the application of section 2–207 to both situations for the guidance of the District Court on remand.

Viewing Collins & Aikman's acknowledgment forms as acceptances under Subsection 2–207(1), we are initially faced with the question of whether the arbitration provision in Collins & Aikman's acknowledgment forms were in fact "additional to or different from" the terms of The Carpet Mart's oral offers. In the typical case under Section 2–207, there exist both a written purchase order and a written acknowledgment, and this determination can be readily made by comparing the two forms. In the present case, where the only written forms were Collins & Aikman's sales acknowledgments, we believe that such a comparison must be made between the oral offers and the written acceptances. Although the District Court apparently assumed that The Carpet Mart's oral orders did not include in their terms the arbitration provision which appeared in Collins & Aikman's acknowledgment forms, we believe that a specific finding on this point will be required on remand.

Assuming, for purposes of analysis, that the arbitration provision was an addition to the terms of The Carpet Mart's oral offers, we must next determine whether or not Collins & Aikman's acceptances were "expressly made conditional on assent to the additional * * * terms" therein, within the proviso of Subsection 2–207(1). As set forth in full above, the provision appearing on the face of Collins & Aikman's acknowledgment forms stated that the acceptances (or orders) were "subject to all of the terms and conditions on the face and reverse side hereof, including arbitration, all of which are accepted by buyer." The provision on the "Acknowledgment" forms further stated that Collins & Aikman's terms would become the basis of the contract between the parties * * *.

Although Collins & Aikman's use of the words "subject to" suggests that the acceptances were conditional to some extent, we do not believe the acceptances were "expressly made conditional on [the buyer's] assent to the additional or different terms," as specifically required under the Subsection 2–207(1) proviso. In order to fall within this proviso, it is not enough that an acceptance is expressly conditional on additional or different terms; rather, an acceptance must be expressly conditional on the offeror's assent to those terms. Viewing the Subsection (1) proviso within the context of the rest of that Subsection and within the policies of Section 2–207 itself, we believe that it was intended to apply only to an acceptance which clearly reveals that the offeree is unwilling to proceed with the transaction unless he is assured of the offeror's assent to the additional or different terms therein. * * * That the acceptance is predicated on the offeror's assent must be "directly and distinctly stated or expressed rather than implied or left to inference." * * *

* * *

To recognize Collins & Aikman's acceptances as "expressly conditional on [the buyer's] assent to the additional * * * terms" therein, within the proviso of Subsection 2–207(1), would thus require us to ignore the specific language of that provision. Such an interpretation is not justified in view of the fact that Subsection 2–207(1) is clearly designed to give legal recognition to many contracts where the variance between the offer and acceptance would have precluded such recognition at common law.

Because Collins & Aikman's acceptances were not expressly conditional on the buyer's assent to the additional terms within the proviso of Subsection 2–207(1), a contract is recognized under Subsection (1), and the additional terms are treated as "proposals" for addition to the contract under Subsection 2–207(2). Since both Collins & Aikman and The Carpet Mart are clearly "merchants" as that term is defined in Subsection 2–104(1), the arbitration provision will be deemed to have been accepted by The Carpet Mart under Subsection 2–207(2) unless it materially altered the terms of The Carpet Mart's oral offers. * * * [UCC § 2–207(2)(b)]. We believe that the question of whether the arbitration provision materially altered the oral offer under Subsection 2–207(2)(b) is one which can be resolved only by the District Court on further findings of fact in the present case. If the arbitration provision did in fact materially alter The Carpet Mart's offer, it could not become a part of the contract "unless expressly agreed to" by The Carpet Mart. * * * [UCC § 2–207], Official Comment No. 3.

We therefore conclude that if on remand the District Court finds that Collins & Aikman's acknowledgments were in fact acceptances and that the arbitration provision was additional to the terms of The Carpet Mart's oral orders, contracts will be recognized under Subsection 2–207(1). The arbitration clause will then be viewed as a "proposal" under Subsection 2–207(2) which will be deemed to have been accepted by The Carpet Mart unless it materially altered the oral offers.

If the District Court finds that Collins & Aikman's acknowledgment forms were not acceptances but rather were confirmations of prior oral agreements between the parties, an application of Section 2–207 similar to that above will be required. Subsection 2–207(1) will require an initial determination of whether the arbitration provision in the confirmations was "additional to or different from" the terms orally agreed upon. Assuming that the District Court finds that the arbitration provision was not a term of the oral agreements between the parties, the arbitration clause will be treated as a "proposal" for addition to the contract under Subsection 2–207(2), as was the case when Collins & Aikman's acknowledgments were viewed as acceptances above. The provision for arbitration will be deemed to have been accepted by The Carpet Mart unless the District Court finds that it materially altered the prior oral agreements, in which case The Carpet Mart could not become bound thereby absent an express agreement to that effect.

* * *

For the reasons set forth above, the case is remanded to the District Court for further findings consistent with this opinion.

QUESTIONS AND NOTES

1. Questions about the facts of this case

   1.1. U.C.C. § 2–207 is often called the "battle of the forms" provision. Did *Dorton* involve a battle of *forms*?

   1.2. In *Dorton*, when were the contracts for the purchase of carpeting formed? Were these contracts oral or written? When did the district court think the contracts were formed?

   1.3. Why did The Carpet Mart accept and pay for the carpet shipments if it objected to the arbitration provisions contained in the acknowledgements, which were admittedly received prior to delivery of each shipment?

2. Questions about the law

   2.1. In the classic battle of the forms scenario, the buyer's standard form purchase order and the seller's standard form acknowledgement don't match, but the goods are nevertheless shipped by the seller and accepted by the buyer. Section 2–207 was designed to eliminate the unearned "last-shot" advantage that the offeree/seller would enjoy under the common law mirror image rule; *i.e.*, acknowledgment is a counteroffer which buyer accepts by paying for the goods. Did § 2–207 accomplish this objective in *Dorton*?

   2.2. If some of the contracts were formed during the telephone conversations between The Carpet Mart and Collins & Aikman, does the court's opinion suggest that § 2–207 can be used to alter the terms of an existing agreement? If so, is this a proper interpretation of the statute? *See* U.C.C. § 2–207, Official Comment 1. As lawyer for the buyer, what steps could you take to prevent this possibility?

   2.3. In *Dorton*, the court found that Collins & Aikman's acceptances were *not* expressly conditional on The Carpet Mart's assent to the additional terms. Thus, a contract was deemed to exist under § 2–207(1) and the only issue is, what were its terms under § 2–207(2)? If the acceptances had been made expressly conditional on the offeror's assent to such additional terms, could The Carpet Mart's acceptance of and payment for the goods be recognized as assent?

   2.4. Ultimately, what difference would it make under § 2–207 if, on remand, the district court determined that the Collins & Aikman acknowledgements were confirmations of prior oral agreements rather than acceptances?

   2.5. How did the district court and the Sixth Circuit's § 2–207 analyses in *Dorton* differ? Did it affect the result? Under the district court's analysis, was there a contract? If so, was arbitration a term of the contract? Was "100% Kodel polyester" a term of the contract?

3. Notes

3.1. Section 2–207(1) makes an "imperfect acceptance" effective as an acceptance rather than as a counteroffer, provided that it constitutes a "definite and seasonable expression of acceptance" but one which is not the mirror image of the offer because it contains terms additional to or different from those specified in the offer. There are, however, a couple of points about the scope of § 2–207 that you need to be aware of.

First, § 2–207(1) does not create a contract in every instance where there are additional or different terms. Remember the hypothetical we started this section with? Ponoroff offered to buy Epstein's car for $100 and Epstein replied that he wanted $120. Would that reply operate as an acceptance under § 2–207(1)? Certainly not, as there was no "seasonable expression of acceptance." Therefore, § 2–207(1) does not apply.

Second, even when the reply would otherwise operate as an acceptance under § 2–207(1), the offeree can prevent the application of § 2–207(1) by expressly making his assent conditional on the offeror's assent to the additional or different terms contained in the reply. This is because of the proviso in the last part of § 2–207(1).

In *Dorton,* however, the court stated, "In order to fall within this proviso, it is not enough that an acceptance is expressly conditional on additional or different terms; rather, an acceptance must be expressly conditional on the offeror's assent to those terms." What does that mean? Do you agree with that interpretation of the language of the statute? How would you draft a conditional acceptance that would satisfy the court in *Dorton*? Assuming you are able to do so, what is the effect of the conditional acceptance?

3.2. Note that § 2–207(1) deals with "additional or different terms," but § 2–207(2) only deals with "additional terms." Assume in *Dorton* that The Carpet Mart's offers to purchase the carpet had been in the form of written purchase orders containing an explicit provision to the effect that any disputes arising between the parties would be resolved by arbitration. Assume further that the acknowledgment forms from Collins & Aikman contained an express provision to the effect that disputes will *not* be resolved by arbitration. When a disagreement concerning the quality of the carpet breaks out, how should the court go about determining whether there is an obligation to submit the matter to binding arbitration? Based on the caselaw thus far, there are at least three possibilities for dealing with "different" terms. Can you figure out what they are? *See Northrop Corp. v. Litronic Industries,* 29 F.3d 1173 (7th Cir. 1994).

4. **You Be the Lawyer!**

   How would you advise Carpet Mart to change its practices relative to ordering carpets in the future so as to preclude with certainty any possibility of an additional term sneaking in and becoming part of the contract?

QUESTIONS BEFORE THE CASE

1. How, for purposes relevant to § 2–207, does the seller's acknowledgement form in this case differ from the acknowledgement form in *Dorton*?
2. *Dorton* suggested that the term "conditional" has a specialized meaning for § 2–207 purposes. This case suggests the same is true for the term "assent." Can you articulate the difference between the conventional understanding of "assent" and the meaning attributed to "assent" by the court in this case?

DIAMOND FRUIT GROWERS, INC. V. KRACK CORPORATION

United States Court of Appeals, Ninth Circuit
794 F.2d 1440 (1986)

WIGGENS, CIRCUIT JUDGE:

Metal-Matic, Inc. (Metal-Matic) appeals from judgment entered after a jury verdict in favor of Krack Corporation (Krack) on Krack's third-party complaint against Metal-Matic. Metal-Matic also appeals from the district court's denial of its motion for judgment n.o.v. * * *

FACTS AND PROCEEDINGS BELOW

Krack is a manufacturer of cooling units that contain steel tubing it purchases from outside suppliers. Metal-Matic is one of Krack's tubing suppliers. At the time this dispute arose, Metal-Matic had been supplying tubing to Krack for about ten years. The parties followed the same course of dealing during the entire ten years. At the beginning of each year, Krack sent a blanket purchase order to Metal-Matic stating how much tubing Krack would need for the year. Then, throughout the year as Krack needed tubing, it sent release purchase orders to Metal-Matic requesting that tubing be shipped. Metal-Matic responded to Krack's release purchase orders by sending Krack an acknowledgment form and then shipping the tubing.

Metal-Matic's acknowledgment form disclaimed all liability for consequential damages and limited Metal-Matic's liability for defects in the tubing to refund of the purchase price or replacement or repair of the tubing. As one would expect, these terms were not contained in Krack's purchase order. The following statement was printed on Metal-Matic's form: "Metal-Matic, Inc.'s acceptance of purchaser's offer or its offer to purchaser is hereby expressly made conditional to purchaser's acceptance of the terms and provisions of the acknowledgment form." This statement and the disclaimer of liability were on the back of the acknowledgment form. However, printed at the bottom of the front of the form in bold-face capitals was the following statement: "SEE REVERSE SIDE FOR TERMS AND CONDITIONS OF SALE."

* * *

In February 1981, Krack sold one of its cooling units to Diamond Fruit Growers, Inc. (Diamond) in Oregon, and in September 1981, Diamond installed the unit in a controlled-atmosphere warehouse. In January 1982, the unit began leaking ammonia from a cooling coil made of steel tubing.

After Diamond discovered that ammonia was leaking into the warehouse, Joseph Smith, the engineer who had been responsible for building Diamond's controlled-atmosphere warehouses, was called in to find the source of the leak. Smith testified that he found a pinhole leak in the cooling coil of the Krack cooling unit. Smith inspected the coil while it was still inside the unit. He last inspected the coil on April 23, 1982. The coil then sat in a hall at Diamond's warehouse until May, 1984, when John Myers inspected the coil for Metal-Matic.

Myers cut the defective tubing out of the unit and took it to his office. At his office, he did more cutting on the tubing. After Myers inspected the tubing, it was also inspected by Bruce Wong for Diamond and Paul Irish for Krack.

Diamond sued Krack to recover the loss in value of fruit that it was forced to remove from the storage room as a result of the leak. Krack in turn brought a third-party complaint against Metal-Matic * * * seeking contribution or indemnity in the event it was held liable to Diamond. At the close of the evidence, both Metal-Matic * * * moved for a directed verdict on the third party complaint. The court * * * denied Metal-Matic's motion.

The jury returned a verdict in favor of Diamond against Krack. It then found that Krack was entitled to contribution from Metal-Matic for thirty percent of Diamond's damages. Metal-Matic moved for judgment n.o.v. The court denied that motion and entered judgment on the jury verdict.

Metal-Matic raises two grounds for reversal. First, Metal-Matic contends that as part of its contract with Krack, it disclaimed all liability for consequential damages and specifically limited its liability for defects in the tubing to refund of the purchase price or replacement or repair of the tubing. Second, Metal-Matic asserts that the evidence does not support a finding that it manufactured the tubing in which the leak developed or that it caused the leak. We address each of these contentions in turn.

* * *

DISCUSSION

A. *Metal-Matic's Disclaimer of Liability for Consequential Damages*

If the contract between Metal-Matic and Krack contains Metal-Matic's disclaimer of liability, Metal-Matic is not liable to indemnify Krack for part of Diamond's damages. Therefore, the principal issue before us on this appeal is whether Metal-Matic's disclaimer of liability became part of the contract between these parties.

Relying on Uniform Commercial Code (U.C.C.) § 2–207, Krack argues that Metal-Matic's disclaimer did not become part of the contract. Metal-Matic, on the other hand, argues that section 2–207 is inapplicable to this case because the parties discussed the disclaimer, and Krack assented to it.

Krack is correct in its assertion that section 2–207 applies to this case. One intended application of section 2–207 is to commercial transactions in which the parties exchange printed purchase order and acknowledgment forms. *See* U.C.C. § 2–207 comment 1. The drafters of the U.C.C. recognized that "[b]ecause the [purchase order and acknowledgment] forms are oriented to the thinking of the respective drafting parties, the terms contained in them often do not correspond." *Id.* Section 2–207 is an attempt to provide rules of contract formation in such cases. In this case, Krack and Metal-Matic exchanged purchase order and acknowledgment forms that contained different or additional terms. This, then, is a typical section 2–207 situation. The fact that the parties discussed the terms of their contract after they exchanged their forms does not put this case outside section 2–207. Section 2–207 provides rules of contract formation in cases such as this one in which the parties exchange forms but do not agree on all the terms of their contract.

A brief summary of section 2–207 is necessary to an understanding of its application to this case. Section 2–207 changes the common law's mirror-image rule for transactions that fall within article 2 of the U.C.C. At common law, an acceptance that varies the terms of the offer is a counteroffer and operates as a rejection of the original offer. *See Idaho Power Co. v. Westinghouse Electric Corp.*, 596 F.2d 924, 926 (9th Cir.1979). If the offeror goes ahead with the contract after receiving the counteroffer, his performance is an acceptance of the terms of the counteroffer. * * *

Generally, section 2–207(1) "converts a common law counteroffer into an acceptance even though it states additional or different terms." *Idaho Power,* 596 F.2d at 926; *see* U.C.C. § 2–207(1). The only requirement under section 2–207(1) is that the responding form contain a definite and seasonable expression of acceptance. The terms of the responding form that correspond to the offer constitute the contract. Under section 2–207(2), the additional terms of the responding form become proposals for additions to the contract. Between merchants the additional terms become part of the contract unless the offer is specifically limited to its terms, the offeror objects to the additional terms, or the additional terms materially alter the terms of the offer. U.C.C. § 2–207(2).

However, section 2–207(1) is subject to a proviso. If a definite and seasonable expression of acceptance expressly conditions acceptance on the offeror's assent to additional or different terms contained therein, the parties' differing forms do not result in a contract unless the offeror assents to the additional terms. If the offeror assents, the parties have a contract and the additional terms are a part of that contract. If, however, the offeror does not assent, but the parties proceed with the transaction as if they have a contract, their performance results in formation of a contract. U.C.C. § 2–207(3). In that case, the terms of the contract are those on which the parties' forms agree plus any terms supplied by the U.C.C. * * *

In this case, Metal-Matic expressly conditioned its acceptance on Krack's assent to the additional terms contained in Metal-Matic's acknowledgment form. That form tracks the language of the section 2–207(1) proviso, stating that "Metal-Matic, Inc.'s acceptance . . . is hereby *expressly made conditional* to purchaser's acceptance of the terms and provisions of the acknowledgment form." (emphasis added). Therefore, we must determine whether Krack assented to Metal-Matic's limitation of liability term.

* * * Metal-Matic contends that Krack assented to the limitation of liability term when it continued to accept and pay for tubing after Metal-Matic insisted that the contract contain its terms.

To address Metal-Matic's argument, we must determine what constitutes assent to additional or different terms for purposes of section 2–207(1). The parties have not directed us to any cases that analyze this question and our research has revealed none. We therefore look to the language and structure of section 2–207 and to the purposes behind that section to determine the correct standard.

One of the principles underlying section 2–207 is neutrality. If possible, the section should be interpreted so as to give neither party to a contract an advantage simply because it happened to send the first or in some cases the last form. *See* J. White & R. Summers, § 1–2 at 26–27. Section 2–207 accomplishes this result in part by doing away with the common law's "last shot" rule. At common law, the offeree/counterofferor gets all of its terms simply because it fired the last shot in the exchange of forms. Section 2–207(3) does away with this result by giving neither party the terms it attempted to impose unilaterally on the other. Instead, all of the terms on which the parties' forms do not agree drop out, and the U.C.C. supplies the missing terms.

Generally, this result is fair because both parties are responsible for the ambiguity in their contract. The parties could have negotiated a contract and agreed on its terms, but for whatever reason, they failed to do so. Therefore, neither party should get its terms. However, as White and Summers point out, resort to section 2–207(3) will often work to the disadvantage of the seller because he will "wish to undertake less responsibility for the quality of his goods than the Code imposes or else wish to limit his damages liability more narrowly than would the Code." J. White & R. Summers, § 1–2 at 34. Nevertheless, White and Summers recommend that section 2–207(3) be applied in such cases. We agree. Application of section 2–207(3) is more equitable than giving one party its terms simply because it sent the last form. Further, the terms imposed by the code are presumably equitable and consistent with public policy because they are statutorily imposed.

With these general principles in mind, we turn now to Metal-Matic's argument that Krack assented to the disclaimer when it continued to accept and pay for tubing once Metal-Matic indicated that it was willing to sell tubing only if its warranty and liability terms were part of the contract. Metal-Matic's argument is appealing. Sound policy supports permitting a seller to control the terms on which it will sell its products, especially in a case in which the seller has indicated both in writing and orally that those are the only terms on which it is willing to sell the product. Nevertheless, we reject Metal-Matic's argument because we find that these considerations are outweighed by the public policy reflected by Oregon's enactment of the U.C.C.

If we were to accept Metal-Matic's argument, we would reinstate to some extent the common law's last shot rule. To illustrate, assume that the parties in this case had sent the same forms but in the reverse order and that Krack's form contained terms stating that Metal-Matic is liable for all consequential damages and conditioning acceptance on Metal-Matic's assent to Krack's terms. Assume also that Metal-Matic objected to Krack's terms but Krack refused to change them and that the parties continued with their transaction anyway. If we applied Metal-Matic's argument in that case, we would find that Krack's term was part of the contract because Metal-Matic continued to ship tubing to Krack after Krack reaffirmed that it would purchase tubing only if Metal-Matic were fully liable for consequential damages. Thus, the result would turn on which party sent the last form, and would therefore be inconsistent with section 2–207's purpose of doing away with the last shot rule.

That result is avoided by requiring a specific and unequivocal expression of assent on the part of the offeror when the offeree conditions its acceptance on assent to additional or different terms. If the offeror does not give specific and unequivocal assent but the parties act as if they have a contract, the provisions of section 2–207(3) apply to fill in the terms of the contract. Application of section 2–207(3) is appropriate in that situation because by going ahead with the transaction without resolving their dispute, both parties are responsible for introducing ambiguity into the contract. Further, in a case such as this one, requiring the seller to assume more liability than it intends is not altogether inappropriate. The seller is most responsible for the ambiguity because it inserts a term in its form that requires assent to additional terms and then does not enforce that requirement. If the seller truely [*sic*] does not want to be bound unless the buyer assents to its terms, it can protect itself by not shipping until it obtains that assent.

We hold that because Krack's conduct did not indicate unequivocally that Krack intended to assent to Metal-Matic's terms, that conduct did not amount to the assent contemplated by section 2–207(1).

* * *

B. *Sufficiency of the Evidence*

[The court concluded that there was sufficient evidence to support the jury's verdict that the leak was caused by Metal-Matic's tubing.]

AFFIRMED.

QUESTIONS AND NOTE

1. Questions about the facts of this case

   1.1. How does the language of the acknowledgements in *Krack* differ from the language of the acknowledgements in *Dorton* concerning whether the acceptance is conditional, and why is that important?

   1.2. Should it have mattered that Metal-Matic and Krack had been doing business for about ten years before this dispute arose?

2. Questions about the law

   2.1. Why was the court not persuaded by Metal-Matic's argument that Krack had assented to Metal-Matic's additional terms by accepting and paying for the tubing? What are the "public policy considerations" that the court believed outweighed that argument?

2.2. What do you think would have been an indication of Krack's assent sufficient to satisfy the court in this case?

3. Note

In *Krack,* the court observed that application of § 2–207(3) typically works to the disadvantage of the seller. To begin to see why this is so, note that many § 2–207 cases involve disputes over warranties. The U.C.C. Article 2 warranty scheme is a topic we take up in much greater depth in Chapter 5. For now, it is sufficient to understand a few things about Article 2's approach to warranties. In particular, § 2–314 provides that in every contract for the sale of goods in which the seller is a merchant (i.e., someone in the business of selling goods of that kind) there is an implied warranty of *merchantability.* The implied warranty of merchantability is an assurance that the goods are fit for the ordinary purposes for which such goods are used. Thus, if Epstein were to buy a lawnmower from Sears that didn't cut grass very well, there would probably be a breach of this warranty. However, if Epstein, having grown up in the South where it doesn't snow much, naively purchased a lawn mower to blow snow off of his driveway, there would be no breach of the implied warranty of merchantability even though the lawnmower didn't do a very good job on clearing the driveway. Finally, you need to be aware that § 2–316 allows the seller to exclude any and all warranties from the contract of sale by making an effective *disclaimer* of warranties. Ok, with this brief summary in mind, consider the following:

Ponoroff sends a purchase order for widgets that says nothing about warranties. Markell responds with an acknowledgment that matches all of the terms of the purchase order with respect to price, quantity, shipment terms, etc., but also contains a provision that says: *"Markell hereby disclaims all warranties with respect to these widgets, including the warranty of merchantability. This acknowledgment, if issued in response to an offer, shall only constitute an acceptance of such offer subject to the express condition that Buyer assent to any terms herein which vary, add to, or conflict with such offer."* Ponoroff never assents to the disclaimer, but when the goods are shipped Ponoroff accepts and pays for them. Later, it turns out that the widgets are defective. Ponoroff sues for breach of the implied warranty of merchantability. Markell moves to dismiss, pointing to the disclaimer in the acknowledgment form. How would this case be decided under the mirror image rule? How does § 2–207 change the result?

4. **You Be the Lawyer!**

Metal-Matic is very frustrated by the outcome in this case and has fired its former counsel and hired you. In your first meeting with the president of the company, he points out that Metal-Matic could not have been clearer in its acknowledgment and asks, "Just what the "heck" [he doesn't actually say "heck"; we're paraphrasing here] do we have to do to be sure the terms in our form will be part of the deal with those Krack-heads" [he really does say that!]?

INTRODUCTION TO *KLOCEK*

It's a simple story—the plaintiff in the next case bought a computer from Gateway over the phone, paying for the computer with a credit card. The plaintiff is unhappy with the computer's performance and sues Gateway for breach of contract and breach of warranty. In response to the complaint, Gateway argues that the "Standard Terms and Conditions Agreement" that was in the box in which the computer was shipped prevented the plaintiff from bringing the lawsuit. The parts of that Agreement relevant to the cases were:

> "This document contains Gateway Standard Terms and Conditions. By keeping your Gateway computer system beyond five (5) days after the date of delivery, you accept these Terms and Conditions."
>
> "Any dispute or controversy arising out of or relating to this Agreement or its interpretation shall be settled exclusively and finally by arbitration. The arbitration shall be conducted in accordance with the Rules of Conciliation and Arbitration of the International Chamber of Commerce. The arbitration shall be conducted in Chicago, Illinois, U.S.A. before a sole arbitrator. Any award rendered in any such arbitration proceeding shall be final and binding on each of the parties, and judgment may be entered thereon in a court of competent jurisdiction."

QUESTION BEFORE THE CASE

Is the court in this case saying that a vendor's "delayed" terms can never become part of the contract without the assent of the purchaser?

KLOCEK V. GATEWAY, INC.

United States District Court for the District of Kansas
104 F. Supp. 2d 1332, order vacated for lack of jurisdiction, 2000 WL 1372886 (D.Kan.), *aff'd*, 2001 WL 1568346 (D.Kan.)

MEMORANDUM AND ORDER

VRATIL, DISTRICT JUDGE.

William S. Klocek brings suit against Gateway, Inc. * * * on claims arising from purchases of a Gateway computer * * *. This matter comes before the Court on the Motion to Dismiss which Gateway filed November 22, 1999 * * * For reasons stated below, the Court overrules Gateway's motion to dismiss. * * *

A. Gateway's Motion to Dismiss

Plaintiff brings * * * claims against Gateway, alleging that it induced him * * * to purchase [a] computer and special support package by making false promises of technical support. Individually, plaintiff also claims breach of contract and breach of warranty, in that Gateway breached certain warranties that its computer would be compatible with standard peripherals and standard internet services.

Gateway asserts that plaintiff must arbitrate his claims under Gateway's Standard Terms and Conditions Agreement ("Standard Terms"). Whenever it sells a computer, Gateway includes a copy of the Standard Terms in the box which contains the computer battery power cables and instruction manuals. * * *

When deciding whether the parties have agreed to arbitrate, the Court applies ordinary state law principles that govern the formation of contracts. * * * The existence of an arbitration agreement "is simply a matter of contract between the parties; [arbitration] is a way to resolve those disputes-but only those disputes—that the parties have agreed to submit to arbitration." * * * If the parties dispute making an arbitration agreement, a jury trial on the existence of an agreement is warranted if the record reveals genuine issues of material fact regarding the parties' agreement.

* * *

[The court at this point engaged in a discussion of which state law to apply: Missouri, where the plaintiff lived, or Kansas, where plaintiff claimed he purchased the computer at a Gateway store. Ultimately, the court concluded that it did not matter because the issue was one of first impression in both jurisdictions.]

Regardless whether plaintiff purchased the computer in person or placed an order and received shipment of the computer, the parties agree that plaintiff paid for and received a computer from Gateway. This conduct clearly demonstrates a contract for the sale of a computer * * *. Thus the issue is whether the contract of sale includes the Standard Terms as part of the agreement.

State courts in Kansas and Missouri apparently have not decided whether terms received with a product become part of the parties' agreement. Authority from other courts is split. *Compare Step-Saver* [*Data Sys., Inc. v. Wyse Tech.*], 939 F.2d 91 (printed terms on computer software package not part of agreement); *Arizona Retail Sys., Inc. v. Software Link, Inc.*, 831 F. Supp. 759 (D. Ariz. 1993) (license agreement shipped with computer software not part of agreement); and *U.S. Surgical Corp. v. Orris, Inc.*, 5 F. Supp. 2d 1201 (D. Kan. 1998) (single use restriction on product package not binding agreement); *with Hill v. Gateway 2000, Inc.*, 105 F.3d 1147 (7th Cir.), cert. denied, 522 U.S. 808 (1997) (arbitration provision shipped with computer binding on buyer); *ProCD, Inc. v. Zeidenberg*, 86 F.3d 1447 (7th Cir. 1996) (shrinkwrap license binding on buyer);[6] and *M.A. Mortenson Co., Inc. v. Timberline Software Corp.*, 140 Wn.2d 568, 998 P.2d 305 (Wash. 2000) (following *Hill* and *ProCD* on license agreement supplied with software).[7] It appears that at least in part, the cases turn on whether the court finds that the parties formed their contract *before* or *after* the vendor communicated its terms to the purchaser. *Compare Step-Saver*, 939 F.2d at 98 (parties' conduct in shipping, receiving and paying for product demonstrates existence of contract; box top license constitutes proposal for additional terms under § 2–207 which requires express agreement by purchaser); *Arizona Retail*, 831 F. Supp. at 765 (vendor entered into contract by agreeing to ship goods, or at latest by shipping goods to buyer; license agreement constitutes proposal to modify agreement under § 2–209 which requires express assent by buyer); and *Orris*, 5 F. Supp. 2d at 1206 (sales contract concluded when vendor received consumer orders; single-use language on product's label was proposed modification under § 2–209 which requires express assent by purchaser); *with ProCD*, 86 F.3d at 1452 (under § 2–204 vendor, as master of offer, may propose limitations on kind of conduct that constitutes acceptance; § 2–207 does not apply in case with only one form); *Hill*, 105 F.3d at 1148–49 (same); and *Mortenson*, 998 P.2d at 311–314 (where vendor and purchaser utilized license agreement in

---

6 The term "shrinkwrap license" gets its name from retail software packages that are covered in plastic or cellophane "shrinkwrap" and contain licenses that purport to become effective as soon as the customer tears the wrapping from the package. * * *

7 The *Mortenson* court also found support for its holding in the proposed Uniform Computer Information Transactions Act ("UCITA") (formerly known as proposed UCC Article 2B) (text located at www.law.upenn.edu/library/ulc/ucita/UCITA99.htm), which the National Conference of Commissioners on Uniform State Laws approved and recommended for enactment by the states in July 1999. *See Mortenson*, 998 P.2d at 310 n.6, 313 n.10. The proposed UCITA, however, would not apply to the Court's analysis in this case. The UCITA applies to computer information transactions, which are defined as agreements "to create, modify, transfer, or license computer information or informational rights in computer information." UCITA, §§ 102(11) and 103. In transactions involving the sale of computers, such as our case, the UCITA applies only to the computer programs and copies, not to the sale of the computer itself. *See* UCITA § 103(c)(2).

prior course of dealing, shrinkwrap license agreement constituted issue of contract formation under § 2–204, not contract alteration under § 2–207).

Gateway urges the Court to follow the Seventh Circuit decision in *Hill*. That case involved the shipment of a Gateway computer with terms similar to the Standard Terms in this case, except that Gateway gave the customer 30 days—instead of 5 days—to return the computer. In enforcing the arbitration clause, the Seventh Circuit relied on its decision in *ProCD*, where it enforced a software license which was contained inside a product box. In *ProCD*, the Seventh Circuit noted that the exchange of money frequently precedes the communication of detailed terms in a commercial transaction. Citing UCC § 2–204, the court reasoned that by including the license with the software, the vendor proposed a contract that the buyer could accept by using the software after having an opportunity to read the license.[8] *ProCD*, 86 F.3d at 1452. Specifically, the court stated:

> A vendor, as master of the offer, may invite acceptance by conduct, and may propose limitations on the kind of conduct that constitutes acceptance. A buyer may accept by performing the acts the vendor proposes to treat as acceptance.

The *Hill* court followed the *ProCD* analysis, noting that "practical considerations support allowing vendors to enclose the full legal terms with their products." *Hill*, 105 F.3d at 1149.[9]

The Court is not persuaded that Kansas or Missouri courts would follow the Seventh Circuit reasoning in *Hill* and *ProCD*. In each case the Seventh Circuit concluded without support that UCC § 2–207 was irrelevant because the cases involved only one written form. *See ProCD*, 86

---

[8] Section 2–204 provides: "A contract for sale of goods may be made in any manner sufficient to show agreement, including conduct by both parties which recognizes the existence of such contract." [U.C.C. § 2–204].

[9] Legal commentators have criticized the reasoning of the Seventh Circuit in this regard. *See, e.g.*, Jean R. Sternlight, Gateway Widens Doorway to Imposing Unfair Binding Arbitration on Consumers, Fla. Bar J., Nov. 1997, at 8, 10–12 (outcome in Gateway is questionable on federal statutory, common law and constitutional grounds and as a matter of contract law and is unwise as a matter of policy because it unreasonably shifts to consumers search cost of ascertaining existence of arbitration clause and return cost to avoid such clause); Thomas J. McCarthy et al., Survey: Uniform Commercial Code, 53 Bus. Law. 1461, 1465–66 (Seventh Circuit finding that UCC § 2–207 did not apply is inconsistent with official comment); Batya Goodman, Honey, I Shrink-Wrapped the Consumer: the Shrinkwrap Agreement as an Adhesion Contract, 21 Cardozo L. Rev. 319, 344–352 (Seventh Circuit failed to consider principles of adhesion contracts); Jeremy Senderowicz, Consumer Arbitration and Freedom of Contract: A Proposal to Facilitate Consumers' Informed Consent to Arbitration Clauses in Form Contracts, 32 Colum. J.L. & Soc. Probs. 275, 296–299 (judiciary (in multiple decisions, including Hill) has ignored issue of consumer consent to an arbitration clause). Nonetheless, several courts have followed the Seventh Circuit decisions in *Hill* and *ProCD*. *See, e.g.*, *Mortenson*, 2000 WL 550845 (license agreement supplied with software); Rinaldi v. Iomega Corp., 1999 Del. Super. LEXIS 563, 1999 WL 1442014, Case No. 98C–09–064–RRC (Del. Sept. 3, 1999) (warranty disclaimer included inside computer Zip drive packaging); Westendorf v. Gateway 2000, Inc., 2000 Del. Ch. LEXIS 54, 2000 WL 307369, Case No. 16913 (Del. Ch. March 16, 2000) (arbitration provision shipped with computer); Brower v. Gateway 2000, Inc., 246 A.D.2d 246, 676 N.Y.S.2d 569 (N.Y. App. Div. 1998) (same); Levy v. Gateway 2000, Inc., 1997 WL 823611, 33 U.C.C. Rep. Serv. 2d (Callaghan) 1060 (N.Y. Sup. Ct. August 12, 1997) (same).

F.3d at 1452 (citing no authority); *Hill*, 105 F.3d at 1150 (citing *ProCD*). This conclusion is not supported by the statute or by Kansas or Missouri law. Disputes under § 2–207 often arise in the context of a "battle of forms," * * * but nothing in its language precludes application in a case which involves only one form. The statute provides:

> Additional terms in acceptance or confirmation.
>
> (1) A definite and seasonable expression of acceptance or a written confirmation which is sent within a reasonable time operates as an acceptance even though it states terms additional to or different from those offered or agreed upon, unless acceptance is expressly made conditional on assent to the additional or different terms.
>
> (2) The additional terms are to be construed as proposals for addition to the contract [if the contract is not between merchants]. * * *

[U.C.C. § 2–207.] By its terms, § 2–207 applies to an acceptance or written confirmation. It states nothing which requires another form before the provision becomes effective. In fact, the official comment to the section specifically provides that §§ 2–207(1) and (2) apply "where an agreement has been reached orally * * * and is followed by one or both of the parties sending formal memoranda embodying the terms so far agreed and adding terms not discussed." Official Comment 1 of UCC § 2–207. Kansas and Missouri courts have followed this analysis. *See Southwest Engineering Co. v. Martin Tractor Co.*, 205 Kan. 684, 695, 473 P.2d 18, 26 (1970) (stating in dicta that § 2–207 applies where open offer is accepted by expression of acceptance in writing or where oral agreement is later confirmed in writing); *Central Bag Co. v. W. Scott and Co.*, 647 S.W.2d 828, 830 (Mo. App. 1983) (§§ 2–207(1) and (2) govern cases where one or both parties send written confirmation after oral contract). Thus, the Court concludes that Kansas and Missouri courts would apply § 2–207 to the facts in this case. * * *

In addition, the Seventh Circuit provided no explanation for its conclusion that "the vendor is the master of the offer." *See ProCD*, 86 F.3d at 1452 (citing nothing in support of proposition); *Hill*, 105 F.3d at 1149 (citing *ProCD*). In typical consumer transactions, the purchaser is the offeror, and the vendor is the offeree. *See Brown Mach., Div. of John Brown, Inc. v. Hercules, Inc.*, 770 S.W.2d 416, 419 (Mo. App. 1989) (as general rule orders are considered offers to purchase); *Rich Prods. Corp. v. Kemutec Inc.*, 66 F. Supp. 2d 937, 956 (E.D. Wis. 1999) (generally price quotation is invitation to make offer and purchase order is offer). While it is possible for the vendor to be the offeror, see *Brown Machine*, 770 S.W.2d at 419 (price quote can amount to offer if it reasonably appears from quote that assent to quote is all that is needed to ripen offer into contract), Gateway provides no factual evidence which would support such a finding in this case. The Court therefore assumes for purposes of the motion to dismiss that plaintiff offered to purchase the computer (either in person or through catalog order) and that Gateway accepted plaintiff's offer (either by completing the sales transaction in person or by agreeing to ship and/or shipping the computer to plaintiff).[11]

Under § 2–207, the Standard Terms constitute either an expression of acceptance or written confirmation. As an expression of acceptance, the Standard Terms would constitute a counter-offer only if Gateway expressly made its acceptance conditional on plaintiff's assent to the additional or different terms. [U.C.C. § 2–207(1).] "The conditional nature of the acceptance must be clearly expressed in a manner sufficient to notify the offeror that the offeree is unwilling to proceed with the transaction unless the additional or different terms are included in the contract." *Brown Machine*, 770 S.W.2d at 420.[12] Gateway provides no evidence that at the time of the sales transaction, it informed plaintiff that the transaction was conditioned on plaintiff's acceptance of the Standard Terms. Moreover, the mere fact that Gateway shipped the goods with the terms attached did not communicate to plaintiff any unwillingness to proceed without plaintiff's agreement to the Standard Terms. *See, e.g., Arizona Retail,* 831 F. Supp. at 765 (conditional acceptance analysis rarely appropriate where contract formed by performance but goods arrive with conditions attached); *Leighton Indus., Inc. v. Callier Steel Pipe & Tube, Inc.*, 1991 WL 18413, *6,

---

[11] UCC § 2–206(b) provides that "an order or other offer to buy goods for prompt or current shipment shall be construed as inviting acceptance either by a prompt promise to ship or by the prompt or current shipment * * *" The official comment states that "either shipment or a prompt promise to ship is made a proper means of acceptance of an offer looking to current shipment." UCC § 2–206, Official Comment 2.

[12] Courts are split on the standard for a conditional acceptance under § 2–207. *See Daitom* [*v. Pennwalt Corp.*], 741 F.2d 1569, 1576 (finding that Pennsylvania would most likely adopt "better" view that offeree must explicitly communicate unwillingness to proceed with transaction unless additional terms in response are accepted by offeror). On one extreme of the spectrum, courts hold that the offeree's response stating a materially different term solely to the disadvantage of the offeror constitutes a conditional acceptance. *See Daitom*, 741 F.2d at 1569 (citing *Roto-Lith. Ltd v. F.P. Bartlett & Co.*, 297 F.2d 497 (1st Cir. 1962)). At the other end of the spectrum courts hold that the conditional nature of the acceptance should be so clearly expressed in a manner sufficient to notify the offeror that the offeree is unwilling to proceed without the additional or different terms. *See Daitom*, 741 F.2d at 1569 (citing *Dorton v. Collins & Aikman Corp.*, 453 F.2d 1161 (6th Cir. 1972)). The middle approach requires that the response predicate acceptance on clarification, addition or modification. *See Daitom*, 741 F.2d at 1569 (citing *Construction Aggregates Corp. v. Hewitt-Robins, Inc.*, 404 F.2d 505 (7th Cir. 1968)). The First Circuit has since overruled its decision in *Roto-Lith, see Ionics, Inc. v. Elmwood Sensors, Inc.*, 110 F.3d 184, and the Court finds that neither Kansas nor Missouri would apply the standard set forth therein. *See Boese-Hilburn Co. v. Dean Machinery Co.*, 616 S.W.2d 520, (Mo. App. 1981) (rejecting *Roto-Lith* standard); *Owens-Corning Fiberglas Corp. v. Sonic Dev. Corp.*, 546 F. Supp. 533, 538 (D. Kan. 1982) (acceptance is not counteroffer under Kansas law unless it is made conditional on assent to additional or different terms (citing *Roto-Lith* as comparison)); *Daitom*, 741 F.2d at 1569 (finding that *Dorton* is "better" view). Because Gateway does not satisfy the standard for conditional acceptance under either of the remaining standards (*Dorton* or *Construction Aggregates*), the Court does not decide which of the remaining two standards would apply in Kansas and/or Missouri.

Case No. 89–C–8235 (N.D.Ill. Feb. 6, 1991) (applying Missouri law) (preprinted forms insufficient to notify offeror of conditional nature of acceptance, particularly where form arrives after delivery of goods).

Because plaintiff is not a merchant, additional or different terms contained in the Standard Terms did not become part of the parties' agreement unless plaintiff expressly agreed to them. *See* [U.C.C. § 2–207] Comment 2 (if either party is not a merchant, additional terms are proposals for addition to the contract that do not become part of the contract unless the original offeror expressly agrees). Gateway argues that plaintiff demonstrated acceptance of the arbitration provision by keeping the computer more than five days after the date of delivery. Although the Standard Terms purport to work that result, Gateway has not presented evidence that plaintiff expressly agreed to those Standard Terms. Gateway states only that it enclosed the Standard Terms inside the computer box for plaintiff to read afterwards. It provides no evidence that it informed plaintiff of the five-day review-and-return period as a condition of the sales transaction, or that the parties contemplated additional terms to the agreement.[14] * * * The Court finds that the act of keeping the computer past five days was not sufficient to demonstrate that plaintiff expressly agreed to the Standard Terms. *Accord Brown Machine*, 770 S.W.2d at 421 (express assent cannot be presumed by silence or mere failure to object). Thus, because Gateway has not provided evidence sufficient to support a finding under Kansas or Missouri law that plaintiff agreed to the arbitration provision contained in Gateway's Standard Terms, the Court overrules Gateway's motion to dismiss.

* * *

IT IS THEREFORE ORDERED that the Motion to Dismiss * * * which defendant Gateway filed November 22, 1999 be and hereby is OVERRULED. * * *

QUESTIONS AND NOTES

1. Questions about the facts of this case

    1.1. Does it matter how Mr. Klocek bought his computer? Whether by mail order, by phone order, or at a physical "Gateway Country" store?

    1.2. What *Klocek* fact was most important to Judge Vratil?

---

[14] The Court is mindful of the practical considerations which are involved in commercial transactions, but it is not unreasonable for a vendor to clearly communicate to a buyer—at the time of sale—either the complete terms of the sale or the fact that the vendor will propose additional terms as a condition of sale, if that be the case.

1.3. From the court's description of the facts, do we know why the Mr. Klocek did not want to settle his dispute with Gateway by arbitration in Chicago under the International Chamber of Commerce Rules?*

2. Questions about the law

2.1. What is the benefit that Gateway hopes to attain by having disputes resolved by arbitration rather than through conventional civil litigation? *See* the discussion in Note 3.2 below. *Cf. DIRECTV v. Imburgia*, 577 U.S. ___, 136 S.Ct. 463 (2015) (applying preemption analysis to strike a state law that prohibited contracts from excluding class action arbitration)?

2.2. Under § 2–207(1), does it matter who is the offeror and who is the offeree?

2.3. In footnote 12 of the case, the court describes the split in the caselaw on what constitutes a "conditional acceptance" for purposes of § 2–207(1). *Dorton*, of course, is cited for the strict view on this question, while other courts take a much more expansive view of when an acceptance should be regarded as conditional. Given the purposes of and policies behind § 2–207, which view do you think has the better of it?

3. Notes

3.1. One might have expected that Gateway would take the district court's decision refusing to dismiss Klocek's complaint and compel arbitration up to the Tenth Circuit. As it happened, Gateway had a better idea. Shortly after this opinion was rendered, Gateway filed a motion to dismiss for lack of subject matter jurisdiction alleging that plaintiff had not satisfied his burden of establishing the requisite amount in controversy to invoke the court's diversity jurisdiction. Klocek conceded the point and the case was dismissed. *See* 2000 WL 1372886 (D. Kan. 2000). Left lingering is the precedential value of this decision in light of the subsequent dismissal. Because the court in the order of dismissal did not vacate its earlier opinion, we think *Klocek*

---

* Here is an excerpt from a similar case, *Brower v. Gateway 2000, Inc.*, 246 A.D.2d 246, 676 N.Y.S.2d 569 (1998), discussed further in Note 3.1 below, that perhaps sheds a little light on this question.

> In support of their arguments, appellants submitted a copy of the ICC's Rules of Conciliation and Arbitration and contended that the cost of ICC arbitration was prohibitive, particularly given the amount of the typical consumer claim involved. For example, a claim of less than $50,000 required advance fees of $4,000 (more than the cost of most Gateway products), of which the $2000 registration fee was nonrefundable even if the consumer prevailed at the arbitration. Consumers would also incur travel expenses disproportionate to the damages sought, which appellants' counsel estimated would not exceed $1,000 per customer in this action, as well as bear the cost of Gateway's legal fees if the consumer did not prevail at the arbitration; in this respect, the ICC rules follow the "loser pays" rule used in England. Also, although Chicago was designated as the site of the actual arbitration, all correspondence must be sent to ICC headquarters in France.

continues to have some persuasive force as a source of law and, of course, the subsequent dismissal does not in any way lessen its instructional value, which is important because in our view, this court got it right—even if it ended up not really counting.

3.2. In *AT&T Mobility LLC v. Concepcion*, 563 U.S. 333 (2011), the Supreme Court upheld the enforceability of class action waivers in arbitration agreements. Specifically, the Court found that the public policy favoring arbitration reflected in the Federal Arbitration Act preempted a state law invalidating class waivers. The Supreme Court has insisted on enforcing arbitration agreements according to their terms even in those situations where the cost of individually pursuing a federal statutory claim in arbitration will *exceed* the potential recovery, and notwithstanding the fact that the arbitration agreement may have the practical effect of denying an aggrieved party's effective vindication of his or her federal rights. Absent fraud or duress in the formation of the agreement, or other such grounds as exist at law or in equity for the revocation of any contract, the Court has instructed the lower courts to enforce class action waivers.

3.3. The approach of the *U.N. Convention on Contracts for the International Sales of Goods* to the "battle of the forms" problem is contained in Article 19, which provides:

(1) A reply to an offer which purports to be an acceptance but contains additions, limitations or other modifications is a rejection of the offer and constitutes a counter-offer.

(2) However, a reply to an offer which purports to be an acceptance but contains additional or different terms which do not materially alter the terms of the offer constitutes an acceptance unless the offeror, without undue delay, objects orally to the discrepancy or dispatches a notice to that effect. If he does not so object, the terms of the contract are the terms of the offer with the modifications contained in the acceptance.

(3) Additional or different terms relating, among other things, to the price, payment, quality, or quantity of the goods, place and time of delivery, extent of one party's liability to the other or the settlement of disputes are considered to alter the terms of the offer materially.

How would *Dorton* and *Klocek* have been decided under this provision?

3.4. As if you weren't having enough headaches with § 2–207, Epstein insists we reprint his 2–207 song parody here. It's titled "2–207 " 'KNOWS' OF VIRGINIA" and it's sort of sung to the tune of *Yellow Rose of* Texas, which you can pick up here if you're not familiar with it: *http://www.lsjunction.com/midi/songs.htm)*

There's a UCC provision that you will have to do

It's two-two oh seven of the original Article 2

You have to read the language with precision and with care

And tell me what the statute says and not just what is fair

If just the words of the offer in the acceptance you don't see

Then under mirror image, a contract cannot be

Now if it is a sale of goods, no mirror to apply

Instead it is UCC two-two oh seven you must apply

It's the most confusing section, but stuff you got to know

If language of condition, from 1 to 3 you'll go

But if without conditions—and more than "subject to"—

Then it's a sub one contract, and sub two that you then do

And do only two's first sentence, unless they're both in "bus"

So merely a proposal is what the new term is

Now if both of them are merchants, to the 2d sentence go

And whether it's material, is what you need to know

In finding a sub 3 contract, conduct is the key

There is no counter offer in the words of the offeree

Unlike under mirror image, the response can never be

The basis for new terms on which the two do not agree

Now you understand it, no more worries, no more woe

If two-two oh seven is the question, to Epstein's song y'll go

And while his in-class singing was painful to be heard

Stand now and clap for Epstein, or you're a dirty little turd.

4. **You Be the Lawyer!**

   (a) If you were Gateway's counsel, what would you tell Gateway's sales division that it should do to ensure that future purchasers of Gateway computers would be bound to arbitrate their disputes against the company?

   (b) Your friend Bill calls. He wants your help with his New York landlord who won't let him keep his dog in the apartment. Bill rented the apartment by telephone outside a bar in Cancun. Bill paid for the first month's rent and the security deposit by credit card. The landlord told Bill that when he arrived, he would give Bill a copy of the apartment rules and regulations. The rules and regulations which Bill received (but did not read) clearly provides "no dogs." What do you tell Bill? Is *Klocek* relevant to this situation?

NOTE ON "ROLLING CONTRACTS"

You may have noticed the references in *Klocek* to two earlier decisions from the United States Court of Appeals for the Seventh Circuit, *ProCD, Inc. v. Zeidenberg* and *Hill v. Gateway 2000, Inc.*, both opinions authored by Judge Frank Easterbrook, and in both cases the court found that the buyer became bound by the vendor's delayed terms once the buyer retained the product beyond the period provided for return. Obviously, Judge Easterbrook has a very different take on *when* the contract is formed in these "terms in the box" or delayed term cases. As for the argument that the arbitration provision in *Hill* was not part of the parties' contract under § 2–207, Judge Easterbrook held that 2–207 was "irrelevant to the analysis" because there "was only one form." Really???*

Transactions of the sort illustrated by *Klocek* and *Hill* are typical of what have come to be termed "rolling contracts." They are problematic because, as we have seen, classical contract law principles were developed based on the traditional on the model of "assent" where all of the terms of the deal come together at more or less the same time. However, this model, which works fine when the transaction involves two neighboring farmers negotiating over the price of a chicken, does not reflect the reality of many modern day deals where the seller does not (and, practically speaking, cannot) present all the terms of the deal to the customer, or obtain the customer's assent to those terms, before the shipment and delivery of the product. What does this suggest to you about the classic "offer" and "acceptance" model for determining contract formation?

Hill, in particular, has been a very controversial case that has been criticized by many law professors. For example, Professor James J. White** describes the shrinkwrap contract in cases like *ProCD* and *Hill* as an "autistic contract":

> Parties to modern form contracts sometimes interact with one another in the same way a parent of an autistic child interacts with

---

* Here's what one commentator had to say about Judge Easterbrook's take on § 2–207: "Even more troublesome is the superficial notion that UCC § 2–207 applies only when there are two conflicting forms, which ignores the UCC's application where a single confirmation containing variant terms follows an oral contract for the sale of goods." John E. Murray, Jr., *Contract Theory and the Rise of Neoformalism*, 71 FORDHAM L. REV. 869, 905 n. 193 (2002).

** Why should you care what Jim White, a short, old, bald guy who teaches at another law school, thinks about the *Hill* decision? By the way, White is even older than Epstein. We disagree as to whether White is shorter or balder than Ponoroff, but there is no question that he is thinner than Markell.

> that child. When a licensor offers a software license with the assertion that it will infer acceptance of all the license terms if the licensee removes the power cord from its plastic wrapper, the licensor is drawing an inference from the licensee's behavior just as doubtful as the inference a hopeful parent draws from an autistic child's apparently knowing response to the parent's statement.

James J. White, *Autistic Contracts*, 45 WAYNE L. REV. 1693 (2000).

Hill and *Klocek* are hardly the only reported decisions on shrinkwrap agreements and "terms in the box." *See* footnote 9 in *Klocek*. In *Brower v. Gateway 2000, Inc.,* 246 A.D.2d 246, 676 N.Y.S.2d 569 (1998), involving facts similar to *Hill* and *Klocek*, the court concluded that although a contract had been formed that included the "in-the-box" arbitration provision, the contract was not enforceable on the ground that the arbitration provision was unconscionable due to the unduly burdensome procedure and cost for the individual consumer.* Obviously, the outcome in *Klocek* as to the ultimate enforceability of the delayed term is much more consistent with the outcome in *Brower* than the outcome in *Hill*. Nevertheless, the approaches taken in *Klocek* and *Brower* to reach that outcome are quite different.

Lest you think we're picking on Gateway, in *Defontes v. Dell Computers Corp.,* 52 UCC Rep. Serv.2d 795 (R.I. Super. 2004), the court found Dell's shrinkware arbitration agreement to be unenforceable because 1) the plaintiffs did not "assent" to the provision, and 2) the language of the contract was so one-sided that the provision was unenforceable as an illusory promise; i.e., that it bound the customer but not Dell.

Cases like *Defontes* send the message that all delayed terms are "rough" on consumers. This may not necessarily be the case. Observing that, "Pay now, terms later, or rolling, contracts are an increasingly important form of commercial contracting," Professor Marotta-Wurgler recently performed an empirical study to "inform the debate about whether rolling contracts impose harsher terms on buyers." She collected and analyzed the terms of several hundred EULAs [end-user licensing agreements] for software packages sold online, involving wide variation in the degree of pre-purchase accessibility of these EULAs. She postulated that "[t]he wide variation in the degree of pre-purchase accessibility of these EULAs enables me to give a fairly rigorous answer to whether rolling contracts offer worse terms to buyers, at least in this particular market setting." Her conclusion was perhaps a bit of a surprise:

> "I find that the terms included in rolling contracts are not systematically more pro-seller than those included in contracts disclosed before purchase. In fact, contrary to fears often associated with rolling contracts, I find that contracts displayed pre-purchase are actually slightly more pro-seller than rolling contracts"

* Unconscionability was also argued, you will recall, in *R.R. v. M.H*, our very first case. We will study unconscionability, as a reason not to enforce a deal, further in Chapter 4.

Florencia Marotta-Wurgler, *Are "Pay Now, Terms Later" Contracts Worse for Buyers? Evidence From Software Licensing Agreements*, 38 J. LEGAL STUDIES 309, 341 (2009).

It is also true that the *Klocek* approach may not always be good for consumers, since it implies that the contract is formed when the vendor accepts payment, thereby possibly meaning that the consumer could lose the return privilege. Moreover, the *Klocek* approach does not necessarily mean that vendors can never bind buyers by the terms in the box. In fact, in footnote 14 of the case, the court provides vendors with guidance as to exactly how they should proceed and implying that the issue is really one of "knowing consent." For example, in *Lima v. Gateway, Inc.,* 886 F.Supp.2d 1170 (C.D. Cal. 2012), Gateway sought to compel arbitration of the plaintiff's dispute regarding a monitor the plaintiff had ordered from Gateway over the phone. When the monitor arrived, the box contained a "One Year Limited Warranty Agreement" and a "Standard Terms of Sale Agreement." Per company policy, the plaintiff was told by the Gateway sales representative when he ordered the monitor that it would be subject to the Warranty Agreement (with a 15 day return period), a copy of which would be included in the shipment. The representative did not mention the Standard Terms Agreement. The court concluded that the plaintiff had assented to the Warranty Agreement, but, applying § 2–207, not the Standard Terms, agreement. Ultimately, however, even though the arbitration provision was contained in the Warranty Agreement, the court denied Gateway's motion on the ground that the arbitration provision was unconscionable.

F. ELECTRONIC ACCEPTANCES

Increasingly, commerce is occurring over the internet or through other forms of electronic communication where the deal is consummated between computers and without the benefit of human interaction, written signatures, or physical agreements. Needless to say, these transactions put traditional contract law rules and assumptions (which developed in a very different world) to the test. However, conventional contract law principles nonetheless pertain and are by no means unhelpful, though many questions remain unanswered.

The threshold issue of whether wholly electronic contracts are even valid has now been settled by both Federal and State legislation. Specifically, the Uniform Electronic Transactions Act (1999), which has now been adopted in every state, and the Electronic Signatures in Global and National Commerce Act (so-called "E-Sign"), both enable electronic commerce by validating and effectuating electronic records and signatures.

Neither of these laws, however, displaces the common law of contracts, and, thus, neither addresses the substantive questions of what are the terms of an electronic contract and at what point in time does the contract come into existence? The latter issue—"pay now-terms later" is the same one we just encountered in connection with *Klocek* and our discussion of rolling contracts, even though most of those transactions occurred by phone. Of course, as we all know, it is just as easy to buy a computer online as it is to order by telephone; indeed, perhaps even easier.

One early case in this area that, while far from the final word, was very instructive is *Specht v. Netscape Communications Corp.,* 306 F.3d 17 (2d Cir. 2002). In somewhat simplified form, the issue for the court in *Specht* was whether consumers assented to the terms of an agreement when they downloaded software from an Internet website. In that case, the terms of the licensing agreement were available by a hyperlink at the bottom of the page, below the download button. Therefore, it was possible for the plaintiffs to download the software without scrolling down the webpage and seeing the link. Therefore, the plaintiffs, who clicked the download button without having their attention drawn to the whole license agreement (if you could imagine ever doing that!) contended that they downloaded the software without knowing the terms that Netscape insisted applied to the transaction, or without reading those terms.

Netscape, in turn, argued that failing to read a contract is no defense to the contract and that parties are nevertheless bound by its terms, including an arbitration of disputes provision. While acknowledging this general principle, the court nevertheless found that the downloading of software did not constitute an acceptance of Netscape's terms because there was no reasonably conspicuous notice and because a reasonable internet user would not expect to submit to an arbitration clause upon installing a free download. In explanation, the court stated:

> [T]his principle of knowing consent applies with particular force to provisions for arbitration. Clarity and conspicuousness of arbitration terms are important in securing informed assent. If a party wishes to bind in writing another to an agreement to arbitrate future disputes, such purpose should be accomplished in a way that each party to the arrangement will fully and clearly comprehend that the agreement to arbitrate exists and binds the parties thereto.

Id. at 30.

In specific response to the argument that a party that fails to read a contract does so at her peril, the court stated: "An exception to this general rule exists when the writing does not appear to be a contract and the terms are not called to the attention of the recipient. In such a case, no contract is formed with respect to the undisclosed term."

Is *Specht* in direct conflict with the holdings in cases like *Hill* and *ProCD,* which have enforced delayed term arbitration agreements, or can they be distinguished? Would it have made a difference if the consumer had to "accept" the license before downloading? That is, if they had to click "I accept"? This is what's termed a clickwrap agreement. What does it take for a clickwrap terms to be enforceable?

Also as electronic commerce continues to expand, new ways of reaching agreement and signifying assent electronically, have evolved in addition to clickwrap agreements. Some of these, and the standards governing enforceability, are addressed in the next case.

QUESTIONS BEFORE THE CASE

1. What are the differences among the various types of online consumer contracts identified by the court in this case?
2. Which of these types of online contracts is "fairest" (of them all) and which is least fair to consumers?

BERKSON V. GOGO LLC

United States District Court, E.D. New York
97 F.Supp.3d 359 (2015)

JACK B. WEINSTEIN, SENIOR DISTRICT JUDGE:

I. INTRODUCTION

There is a huge percentage of the United States population using the internet for purchases. *See infra* Part IV. In many instances, these consumers are accepting important contracts of adhesion when they order a product or service through a computer. With convenience has come much widened opportunities for consumer fraud and overreaching by merchants, as claimed in the present case. The instant putative class action involves purchase of internet service connection ("Wi-Fi") on air flights.

Plaintiffs Adam Berkson and Kerry Welsh sue Gogo LLC and Gogo Inc. (collectively, "Gogo," "the company," or "defendants"). Alleged is that defendants improperly increased their sales and profits by misleading customers into purchasing a service that charged a customer's credit card, on an automatically-renewing continuing monthly basis, without adequate notice or consent. The graphics and text on defendants' website, it is argued, led internet consumers during the proposed class period—between February 2008 and December 2012—to believe that they were only buying a one-month subscription when they signed up for in-flight Wi-Fi through Gogo. Gogo's position is that the terms plaintiffs consented to not only clearly provided for automatic renewal, but that they included mandatory arbitration and waiver of venue protection.

* * *

Before the court are defendants' three motions: (1) to transfer venue; (2) to compel arbitration; and (3) to dismiss for lack of standing.

The motions to transfer venue and compel arbitration are premised on the company's "terms of use," which defendants argue plaintiffs assented to online when they subscribed to Gogo's in-flight Wi-Fi. Plaintiff alleges that these terms and conditions were "hidden" and never seen, or agreed to, by them. Hidden provisions in an electronic contract of adhesion do not bind the parties; they cannot dictate venue or compel arbitration.

The central factual-legal question in the case is: were plaintiffs given effective notice of the need to make inquiry ("inquiry notice") of the "terms of use," in what can be characterized as Gogo's electronic contract of adhesion? The question is answered in the negative, compelling denial of defendants' motions on venue and arbitration.

Plaintiffs' standing depends on whether they suffered concrete and particularized injury on the dates their credit cards were billed for allegedly unauthorized charges. That Berkson was reimbursed by his credit card company when defendants refused to do so does not defeat his standing. Nor has Welsh's standing been negated because, when put on notice of the class action lawsuit, Gogo directly sent him—not his attorney—a settlement offer in the form of a full refund. Defendants' motion to dismiss for lack of standing is denied.

The case raises three policy questions:

First, how should courts deal with hybrid versions of "browsewrap" and "clickwrap" electronic contracts of adhesion (referred to in this memorandum as "sign-in-wraps") that do not provide internet users with a compelling reason to examine terms favoring defendants?[1]

* * *

It is concluded that the average internet user would not have been informed, in the circumstances present in this case, that he was binding himself to a sign-in-wrap. The sign-in-wrap used in this case does not support the venue and arbitration clauses relied upon by defendants. It was open to defendants to show special circumstances indicating that the plaintiffs were aware, or should have been aware, of such clauses because of their special knowledge, but they have not done so.

Applied is a four-part test to analyze the validity of electronic contracts of adhesion generally. This approach casts significant doubt on the validity

---

1 The terms "browsewrap," "clickwrap," "scrollwrap," and "sign-in-wrap" are defined *infra,* Part V.B.3. "The single common characteristic [of all 'wrap' contracts] is that the adhering party does not have to use a pen." Nancy S. Kim, *Wrap Contracts: Foundations and Ramifications* 3 (2013).

of those sign-in-wrap and clickwrap agreements that fail to adequately present material terms to internet users.

* * *

II. PROCEDURAL HISTORY

On February 25, 2014, Berkson filed a class action complaint in the United States District Court for the Eastern District of New York. On behalf of a New York sub-class, he alleged violation of New York General Business Law section 349, and, on behalf of a nationwide class, he alleged breach of the implied covenant of good faith and fair dealing, and violation of various consumer protection statutes. A fourth cause of action on behalf of the nationwide class, unjust enrichment, was alleged in the alternative. On the same day, a motion for class certification was filed.

On April 4, 2014, defendants filed a motion to compel arbitration or transfer the action to the Northern District of Illinois, or, alternatively, to dismiss the action for lack of jurisdiction or failure to state a claim.

Three weeks later, on April 24, 2014, plaintiff Berkson, joined by plaintiff Welsh, filed an amended class action complaint adding three new causes of action for purported violations of several California statutes.

On May 12, 2014, defendants filed a motion to compel arbitration or transfer the amended action to the Northern District of Illinois, or, alternatively, to dismiss the amended complaint for lack of jurisdiction or failure to state a claim.

* * *

III. FACTS

A. Defendant Gogo

Gogo provides passengers with Wi-Fi access on many domestic airlines. Thirty-eight percent of domestic flights in the United States, 8,700 flights, offer Wi-Fi. * * *

B. Monthly Service Charge

At all times relevant to this action, Gogo's website advertised the cost of a monthly Wi-Fi subscription and the cost of a single day pass. Monthly access cost approximately $40, and a day pass cost approximately $10.

It is alleged that, when potential customers registered for the monthly service, no notice was given about a recurring monthly charge. * * *

Plaintiffs claim that they each purchased Wi-Fi from Gogo in reliance on representations they saw on the company's website. This information, they argue, led them to believe that, when they signed up for the service, they were only agreeing to a one-month subscription. Gogo, it is alleged, obtained no signature or affirmative authorization to charge plaintiffs for recurring fees if they failed to cancel the service by phone. Nor did Gogo, it is claimed, send any communication to plaintiffs on a monthly basis, as is customary, to notify them of continuing new charges if the service was not cancelled by the subscriber.

After the month-long period from the date of original sign-up ended, Gogo continued to bill each of plaintiffs' credit cards monthly. Only when the charges were recognized by plaintiffs was the unwanted service cancelled.

* * *

IV. ASSESSING ATTRIBUTES OF THE "AVERAGE INTERNET USER"

In the absence of expert reports comparing the average North American internet user's understanding of websites' "terms of use" to that of the plaintiffs in this suit, the court consulted available empirical and academic sociological studies. It did this to formulate an acceptable understanding of the knowledge reasonably attributable to today's "average internet user" regarding electronic contracts of adhesion to obtain Wi-Fi connections on North American air flights. Social science research in the form of consumer surveys have been used in American courts for decades.

A. Studies

[The court concluded that these studies were inadequate to assess the attributes of the average internet user's understanding of websites' "terms of use."] * * *

B. Anecdotal Evidence

Anecdotal evidence suggests that even those individuals with heightened expertise, who would be knowledgeable about the ramifications of internet contracts of adhesion, do not read the terms. *See, e.g.,* Debra Cassens Weiss, *Chief Justice Roberts Admits He Doesn't Read the Computer Fine Print,* ABA Journal (Oct. 20, 2010) ("Answering a student question, Roberts admitted he doesn't usually read the computer jargon that is a condition of accessing websites."), *available at* http://www.abajournal.com/news/article/chief_justice_roberts_admits_he_doesnt_read_the_computer_fine_print (last visited Apr. 6, 2015).

Comedian John Oliver, on his June 8, 2014 Home Box Office show, "Last Week Tonight with John Oliver," highlighted the underlying problem regarding electronic contracts of adhesion as follows: "If Apple put the entire text of *Mein Kampf* in their user agreement, you'd still click agree." *See* Caroline Moss, "John Oliver Hilariously Explains the Dire Importance of Net Neutrality in a Way That Makes Sense," Business Insider (June 8,

2014), *available at* http://www.businessinsider.com/john–oliver–explains–net–neutrality–2014–6 (last visited Apr. 6, 2015).

C. The Reasonable Communicativeness Test

The ability to formulate a reliable description of how the average internet user would have interacted with the "terms of use" in this case is limited. Available are the outdated fundamentals associated with the "reasonable communicativeness test" adopted by courts in the 1950s and 1960s. They were then reflecting on how to assess the validity and enforceability of contracts produced through vending machines, and their bearing on the doctrine of inquiry notice. Their conclusions were:

> (1) The burden is on the offeror to impress upon the offeree the importance of the binding contract being entered into by the latter; and
>
> (2) The duty is on the offeror to explain the relevance of the critical terms governing the offeree's substantive rights contained in the contract.

* * *

It is not unreasonable to assume that there is a difference between paper and electronic contracting. Based on assumptions about internet consumers, they require clearer notice than do traditional retail buyers. In the absence of contrary proof, it can be assumed that the burden should be on the offeror to impress upon the offeree—*i.e.,* the average internet user—the importance of the details of the binding contract being entered into.

The burden should include the duty to explain the relevance of the critical terms governing the offeree's substantive rights contained in the contract. *See generally* Nancy S. Kim, *Wrap Contracts: Foundations and Ramifications* 211 (2013) ("Courts justify wrap contracts by claiming that the nondrafting party manifested consent, but their construction of what constitutes manifestation of consent has wandered too far from the truth."); *see also Specht [v. Netscape],* 306 F.3d [17] at 31–32, 35 [2d. Cir. 2002] ("We are not persuaded that a reasonably prudent offeree in these circumstances would have known of the existence of [the company's] terms. Plaintiffs were responding to an offer [on the internet] that did not carry an immediately visible notice of the existence of license terms or require unambiguous manifestation of assent to those terms. . . . We conclude that in circumstances such as these . . . a reference to the existence of [ ] terms on a submerged screen is not sufficient to place consumers on inquiry or constructive notice of those terms. . . . Reasonably conspicuous notice of the existence of contract terms and unambiguous manifestation of assent to those terms by consumers are essential if electronic bargaining is to have integrity and credibility.").

The offeror has thought through the problems with the aid of lawyers and other experts and is a "repeat player." *See* Marc Galanter, *Why the "Haves" Come out Ahead: Speculations on the Limits of Legal Change,* 9 L. & Soc'y Rev. 95, 97–104 (1974) (arguing that litigants who are "repeat players" as opposed to "one-shotters" shape the development of the law by playing for favorable rules—settling cases likely to produce adverse precedent and litigating cases likely to produce rules that promote their interests). The consumer is usually a transient user, a "myopic" "one-shotter" experiencing "behavioral lock-in." * * *

V. CONTRACT FORMATION AND ASSENT

A substantial number of court opinions in recent years assume the validity of provisions contained in online contracts of adhesion. The starting point of analysis must be the method through which an electronic contract of adhesion is formed. The inquiry does not begin, as defendants argue, with the content of the provisions themselves.

A. Legal Research and Scholarship

Sometimes forgotten in the Internet Age—where contracts of adhesion are often the rule for online consumers—is the essential element of contract formation: mutual manifestation of assent. *See* Mark A. Lemley, *Terms of Use,* 91 Minn. L. Rev. 459, 459–60 (2006) (noting how courts are moving away from the principle that affirmative evidence of agreement is necessary to find a contract binding); * * *.

Fading into the background are the "battle of the forms" debates of the late twentieth century, challenging the use of "boilerplate" contract terms by powerful corporations. * * *

1. "Informed Minority" Hypothesis

Lauded by many law and economic experts is the "informed minority" hypothesis, which presumes that, in competitive markets, "a minority of term-conscious buyers is sufficient to discipline sellers from using unfavorable boilerplate terms." * * *.

Recent empirical studies analyzing the internet browsing behavior of consumers cast significant doubt on the applicability of the "informed minority" assumption to online shoppers. * * *

2. American Bar Association Working Group

The Electronic Contracting Working Group of the ABA suggested that a user should only be considered to have "validly and reliably" assented to the terms of an electronic agreement if the following four conditions are met:

(1) The user is provided with adequate notice of the existence of the proposed terms.

(2) The user has a meaningful opportunity to review the terms.

(3) The user is provided with adequate notice that taking a specified action manifests assent to the terms.

(4) The user takes the action specified in the latter notice.

Over a decade has passed since these recommendations were made. "Unfortunately, many courts have not followed [them] and have instead [ ] swapped the signpost for the information, disregarding that notice requires both attracting user attention *and* providing at least some of the relevant information." Kim, *Wrap Contracts*, at 132.

3. Traditional Contract Doctrine and the Internet Age

Consumers spent over $300 billion in online purchases in 2014. * * * The studies conducted to date and their implications reinforce the need to reconsider principles underlying contract law, developed in an age of paper and orality.

* * *

Experts in commercial practice have recommended as best practices for businesses that they ensure internet users have a realistic opportunity to read the "terms of use" on a business's website. *See, e.g.,* Allison S. Brehm and Cathy D. Lee, "*Click Here to Accept the Terms of Service,*" 31-WTR Comm. Law. 4, 6–7 (2015). Designing a website so that the user must scroll through the "terms of use" *and* click "accept" in order to complete an internet transaction is one such good practice. *Id.* at 6.

For ease of reference, and to create a necessary distinction from clickwrap agreements, the instant memorandum refers to such contracts as "scrollwraps." * * *

B. Law

* * *

2. Common Law Contracting

a. Acceptance

"Mutual manifestation of assent" is the "touchstone" of a binding contract. *Specht,* 306 F.3d at 29 (citations omitted) (applying New York and Utah law in denying enforcement of arbitration clause where software user was not given sufficient notice of terms of agreement). A "transaction," even if created online, "in order to be a contract, requires a manifestation of agreement between the parties" as to its terms. *Id.* at 28 (citations omitted).

Where the terms of the contract are offered by one party to another, unequivocal acceptance of the terms by the receiving party is required. "As a general principle, at common law[,] an acceptance [of a contract], in order to be effective, must be positive and unambiguous." 2 Williston on Contracts § 6:10 (4th ed.).

b. Adhesion Contracts

In the modern commercial world, there are reasons to allow parties to contract without the consideration or negotiation of every term. *Schnabel,* 697 F.3d at 124 (holding that where purported assent to a contract is largely passive, the contract-formation question will often turn on whether a reasonably prudent offeree would be on notice of the terms at issue). A contract on a printed standardized form that is offered on a take-it or leave-it basis—usually by a merchant that monopolizes a particular market, or whose bargaining power significantly outweighs that of the consumer—is a contract of adhesion. Such a contract exists where a party of superior bargaining strength, *e.g.,* a vendor, provides a subscribing party only with the opportunity to adhere to the contract or forfeit use, ownership or access to the vendor's services and goods. But, the assumption is that the parties have a reasonable opportunity to examine terms before adhering. * * *

Often overlooked in our electronic age is the principle undergirding the validity of contracts of adhesion—knowledge by parties of terms. * * *

Valid contracts of adhesion typically meet seven conditions:

(1) The document whose legal validity is at issue is a printed form that contains many terms and clearly purports to be a contract.

(2) The form has been drafted by, or on behalf of, one party to the transaction.

(3) The drafting party participates in numerous transactions of the type represented by the form and enters into these transactions as a matter of routine.

(4) The form is presented to the adhering party with the representation that, except perhaps for a few identified items (such as the price term), the drafting party will enter into the transaction only on the terms contained in the document. This representation may be explicit or may be implicit in the situation, but it is understood by the adherent.

(5) After the parties have dickered over whatever terms are open to bargaining, the document is signed by the adherent.

(6) The adhering party enters into few transactions of the type represented by the form—few, at least, in comparison with the drafting party.

(7) The principal obligation of the adhering party in the transaction considered as a whole is the payment of money.

Todd D. Rakoff, *Contracts of Adhesion: An Essay in Reconstruction,* 96 Harv. L.Rev. 1173, 1177 (1983).

Terms in contracts of adhesion are subject to a reasonableness standard. *See Carnival Cruise Lines, Inc. v. Shute,* 499 U.S. 585, 595, 111 S.Ct. 1522, 113 L.Ed.2d 622 (1991) ("forum-selection clauses contained in form . . . contracts are subject to judicial scrutiny for fundamental fairness"). * * *

e. Notice

Where the assent to terms of a contract is "largely passive," as is often the case with electronic contracts of adhesion, "the contract-formation question will often turn on whether a reasonably prudent offeree would be on [inquiry] notice of the term[s] at issue." *Schnabel [v. Triegiant Corp.],* 697 F.3d [110] at 120, 126–27 (2d Cir. 2012) (holding that under contract law of Connecticut or California, consumers were not put on inquiry notice of arbitration provision for online discounts program through transmission of terms by e-mail after initial enrollment and did not assent to arbitration clause by failing to cancel their memberships after expiration of free-trial period). * * *

Where there is no actual notice of contractual terms, "an offeree is still bound by the provision[s] if he or she is on *inquiry* notice of the term[s] and assents to [them] through the conduct that a reasonable person would understand to constitute assent." *Schnabel,* 697 F.3d at 120 (emphasis in original). "Inquiry notice is actual notice of circumstances sufficient to put a prudent man upon inquiry." *Specht,* 306 F.3d at 30 n. 14 (internal quotation marks and citation omitted); * * *.

The Court of Appeals for the Second Circuit observed:

> While "it is true that a party cannot avoid the terms of a contract on the ground that he or she failed to read it before signing, an exception to this general rule exists when the writing does not appear to be a contract and the terms are not called to the attention of the recipient. In such a case no contract is formed with respect to the undisclosed term[s]."

Hirsch v. Citibank, N.A., 542 Fed.Appx. 35, 37 (2d Cir. 2013). * * *

3. Electronic Adhesion Contracts

Before assessing the validity and enforceability of the contracts in the instant action by applying common law principles of contract formation and assent, it is necessary to turn to case law regarding electronic contracts of adhesion. Four general types of online consumer contracts exist: (a) browsewrap; (b) clickwrap; (c) scrollwrap; and (d) sign-in-wrap.

As used in this memorandum, the following brief definitions apply: *Browsewrap* exists where the online host dictates that assent is given merely by using the site. *Clickwrap* refers to the assent process by which a user must click "I agree," but not necessarily view the contract to which she is assenting. *Scrollwrap* requires users to physically scroll through an internet agreement and click on a separate "I agree" button in order to assent to the terms and conditions of the host website. *Sign-in-wrap* couples assent to the terms of a website with signing up for use of the site's services; it is the form used by Gogo in the instant case.

a. Browsewrap

"Browsewraps can take various forms but basically the website will contain a notice that—by merely using the services of, obtaining information from, or initiating applications within the website—the user is agreeing to and is bound by the site's terms of service." *United States v. Drew,* 259 F.R.D. 449, 462 n. 22 (C.D.Cal.2009). Because of the passive nature of acceptance in browsewrap agreements, courts closely examine the factual circumstances surrounding a consumer's use. "Despite their ubiquity, browsewrap agreements are still relatively new to courts." *Be In, Inc. v. Google Inc.,* No. 12–CV–03373, 2013 WL 5568706, at *7 (N.D.Cal. Oct. 9, 2013). For an internet browsewrap contract to be binding, consumers must have reasonable notice of a company's "terms of use" and exhibit "unambiguous assent" to those terms. *Specht,* 306 F.3d at 35; *see also Be In,* 2013 WL 5568706, at *6–8 (collecting cases).

At issue in *Specht* was an arbitration clause contained in license terms on a website. *Specht,* 306 F.3d at 20. It was allegedly accepted when plaintiffs downloaded a plug-in (*i.e.,* software that supplements or enhances the capabilities of an existing program) from the site. *Id.* at 23. When plaintiffs downloaded free software from the site by the click of a button, they could not initially see a reference to license terms. *Id.* The sole reference to terms could have been seen by plaintiffs only if they had scrolled down to the bottom of the screen before commencing a download. *Id.*

Defendants moved to compel arbitration and stay court proceedings. The motion was denied by the district court. *Id.* at 25. Applying California law, the Court of Appeals for the Second Circuit affirmed, finding that plaintiffs were not put on sufficient notice of terms. *Id.* at 32. It noted that "there is no reason to assume that viewers will scroll down to subsequent screens simply because screens are there." *Id.*

* * *

Following the ruling in *Specht,* courts generally have enforced browsewrap terms only against knowledgeable accessors, such as corporations, not against individuals. *See, e.g., Register,* 356 F.3d at 403 (applying California law in finding that defendant using automated programs to repeatedly access competitor's website was put on notice of "terms of use" that were sent to defendant each time after it accessed the website's data); * * *.

b. Clickwrap

Clickwrap agreements necessitate an active role by the user of a website. Courts, in general, find them enforceable. * * *

Courts of Appeals, while accepting the general definition of what constitutes a clickwrap agreement, have yet to rule on their presumptive validity. The term "clickwrap" only appears in seven reported Courts of Appeals decisions, none of which decide the *per se* enforceability of these agreements. * * *

By contrast, almost "[e]very [lower] court to consider the issue has found 'clickwrap' licenses, in which an online user clicks 'I agree' to standard form terms, enforceable." *Lemley,* 91 Minn. L.Rev. at 459 (citations omitted). * * *

c. Scrollwrap

There is a crucial distinction between online agreements that a user must view because of the nature of the website's construction and design—*i.e.,* scrollwraps—and those that merely require a user to click an "I agree" box that appears next to a hyperlink containing "terms of use"—*i.e.,* clickwraps. * * *

Some court decisions that use the term "clickwrap" are in fact dealing with "scrollwrap" agreements where an internet consumer had a realistic opportunity to review and scroll through the electronic agreement. * * * *Bar-Ayal v. Time Warner Cable Inc.,* No. 03–CV–9905, 2006 WL 2990032, at *9–10 (S.D.N.Y. Oct. 16, 2006) (finding acceptance where scrolling though thirty-eight screens of text was required—essentially the entire agreement); * * *.

Reference to scrollwrap agreements as clickwraps is misleading. *Cf.* Juliet M. Moringiello and William L. Reynolds, *From Lord Coke to Internet Privacy: The Past, Present, and Future of the Law of Electronic Contracting,* 72 Md. L.Rev. 452, 466 (2013) ("In the world of electronic contracts . . . clickwrap is a meaningless term. Click-to-agree transactions come in many flavors. Sometimes the click is at the end of the terms so that a reader must at least scroll through to reach the 'I agree' icon, while [at] other times the click is next to a hyperlink that leads to the terms, either in one click or in several. Whether the terms are classified as clickwrap says little about whether the offeree had notice of them.").

d. Sign-in-wrap

A questionable form of internet contracting has been used in recent years—sign-in-wraps. These internet consumer contracts do not require the user to click on a box showing acceptance of the "terms of use" in order to continue. Rather, the website is designed so that a user is notified of the existence and applicability of the site's "terms of use" when proceeding through the website's sign-in or login process. Courts of Appeals have yet to rule on the validity and enforceability of the terms of such contracts.

* * *

Fteja v. Facebook, Inc. supported enforceability of sign-in-wraps. *Fteja v. Facebook, Inc.,* 841 F.Supp.2d 829 (S.D.N.Y.2012) (applying both New York and California law). In the *Fteja* case, the plaintiff claimed emotional distress and reputational damage when defendant Facebook disabled his account on its social networking service. *Id.* at 831. * * *

The court deemed this internet consumer contract construction a hybrid of browsewrap and clickwrap. *Id.* at 838. It noted:

> Facebook's Terms of Use are somewhat like a browsewrap agreement in that the terms are only visible via a hyperlink, but also somewhat like a clickwrap agreement in that the user must do something else—click "Sign Up"—to assent to the hyperlinked terms. Yet, unlike some clickwrap agreements, the user can click to assent whether or not the user has been presented with the terms.

Id. Analogizing terms found through a hyperlink to terms found on the back of the ticket in *Carnival Cruise,* the court held in *Fteja* that the plaintiff was bound by the forum selection clause: * * *

Lower courts upholding sign-in-wrap arrangements, such as the one presented in *Fteja,* have done so under three circumstances. They emphasized notice and an effective opportunity to access terms and conditions.

First, where the hyperlinked "terms and conditions" is next to the only button that will allow the user to continue use of the website. * * *

Second, where the user "signed up" to the website with a clickwrap agreement and was presented with hyperlinks to the "terms of use" on subsequent visits. * * *

Third, where notice of the hyperlinked "terms and conditions" is present on multiple successive webpages of the site. * * *

e. General Principles

The following general principles regarding the validity and enforceability of internet agreements emerge from an analysis of the cases:

First, "terms of use" will not be enforced where there is no evidence that the website user had notice of the agreement; "the validity of the [internet] agreement turns on whether the website puts a *reasonably prudent user* on inquiry notice of the terms of the contract." *Nguyen [v.*

Barnes & Noble, Inc.], 763 F.3d [1171] at 1177 (9th Cir. 2014) (emphasis added) (collecting cases).

Second, "terms of use" will be enforced when a user is encouraged by the design and content of the website and the agreement's webpage to examine the terms clearly available through hyperlinkage. *See, e.g., Ticketmaster Corp. [v. Tickets.com, Inc.],* 2003 WL 21406289, at *2 [C.D. Cal. 2003] (noting that the warning on website that further use binds a user to the "terms of use" "could not be missed"); * * *.

Third, "terms of use" will not be enforced where the link to a website's terms is buried at the bottom of a webpage or tucked away in obscure corners of the website where users are unlikely to see it. *See, e.g., Specht,* 306 F.3d at 23 (refusing to enforce "terms of use" that "would have become visible to plaintiffs only if they had scrolled down to the next screen"); * * *.

4. Assessing Validity and Enforceability of Electronic Adhesion Contracts

Analyzing established common law contract formation doctrine, alongside the general contract principles and cases regarding inquiry notice and the validity and enforceability of internet agreements, the following four-part inquiry in analyzing sign-in-wraps, and electronic contracts of adhesion generally, is required:

> (1) Aside from clicking the equivalent of sign-in (*e.g.,* log-in, buy-now, purchase, etc.), is there substantial evidence from the website that the user was aware that she was binding herself to more than an offer of services or goods in exchange for money? If not, the "terms of use," such as those dealing with venue and arbitration, should not be enforced against the purchaser.
>
> (2) Did the design and content of the website, including the homepage, make the "terms of use" (*i.e.,* the contract details) readily and obviously available to the user? If not, the "terms of use," such as those dealing with venue and arbitration, should not be enforced against the purchaser.
>
> (3) Was the importance of the details of the contract obscured or minimized by the physical manifestation of assent expected of a consumer seeking to purchase or subscribe to a service or product? If yes, then the "terms of use," such as those dealing with venue and arbitration, should not be enforced against the purchaser.
>
> (4) Did the merchant clearly draw the consumer's attention to material terms that would alter what a reasonable consumer would understand to be her default rights when initiating an online consumer transaction from the consumer's state of residence: The right to (a) not have a payment source charged without notice (*i.e.,* automatic payment renewal); (b) bring a civil

consumer protection action under the law of her state of residence and in the courts in her state of residence; and (c) participate in a class or collective action? If not, then (a), (b), or (c) should not be enforced against the consumer.

It is desirable to have hard-edged rules of adhesion that apply no matter what the consumer's background. Such rules reduce substantial litigation costs. But, until useful consumer studies demonstrate that average consumers using the computer understand what contract terms are being accepted when a purchase is made, preemptive rules in favor of vendors who do not forcefully draw purchasers' attention to terms disadvantageous to them should be rejected. The burden of showing agreement to details of a contract on a website's contract of adhesion is on the vendors. It is the vendor who designs the website and puts into it terms favoring itself.

Proof of special know-how based on the background of the potential buyer or adequate warning of adverse terms by the design of the agreement page or pages should be required before adverse terms, such as compelled arbitration or forced venue, are enforced.

C. Application of Law to Facts

1. Plaintiff Welsh

The evidence presented to date does not demonstrate that Welsh agreed to Gogo's "Terms of Use." * * *.

2. Plaintiff Berkson

The sign-in-wrap at issue in Berkson's case most closely resembles the online contract discussed in *Fteja.* But *Fteja,* and lower court cases that follow its lead, mischaracterize important Supreme Court and Court of Appeals precedent regarding contracts and the reasonable person standard that must be applied to inquiry notice of, and manifestation of assent to, the terms in a contract of adhesion. The offeror must show that a reasonable person in the position of the consumer would have known about what he was assenting to. *See supra* V.B.2.b & e.

There are significant differences between a hyperlink available near a sign-in button, which is never subsequently mailed in hardcopy or softcopy to a consumer, as is the case here, and a hardcopy cruise ticket saying in all caps, "SUBJECT TO CONDITIONS OF CONTRACT ON LAST PAGES IMPORTANT! PLEASE READ CONTRACT ON LAST PAGES 1, 2, 3." *Carnival Cruise,* 499 U.S. at 587, 111 S.Ct. 1522.

First, the hyperlink presented to Berkson was not related to an in-person transaction. This is not a contract of adhesion situation where a cashier "cannot be expected to read legal documents to customers before ringing up sales." *Hill,* 105 F.3d at 1149.

Second, Gogo did not have a practice of emailing or mailing the contents of the "terms of use" to its customers. Berkson never had a hardcopy in his possession to refer to. *See supra* Part III.B.

Third, Gogo did not make an effort to draw Berkson's attention to its "terms of use." The hardcopy ticket in *Carnival Cruise* announced its terms by (1) using the word "contract" twice; (2) addressing the reader in all caps; (3) indicating where to find the contract; and (4) inserting the word "important" and the phrase "please read." The "terms of use" presented to Berkson, aside from assuming the consumer's knowledge of the significance of a hyperlink, had none of the precautions taken by Carnival Cruise Lines Inc. *See Carnival Cruise,* 499 U.S. at 587, 111 S.Ct. 1522; *see supra* Part III.D.

The contract scenario in *Carnival Cruise* should not be analogized to electronic websites' contracts of adhesion. It is inapposite. Crucially, respondents in *Carnival Cruise* "conceded that they were given notice of the forum provision." *Carnival Cruise,* 499 U.S. at 595, 111 S.Ct. 1522. This is not true in the instant case.

Applying the proposed framework for analyzing sign-in-wrap agreements to Berkson, it is necessary to decide whether sufficient evidence has been proffered by defendants demonstrating that Berkson knew he was binding himself to more than a one-time offer of service in exchange for money. The evidence to date indicates that he was unaware.

* * *

Defendants' motions to transfer Berkson's claims to Illinois or, alternatively, compel arbitration are denied. As in Welsh's case, motions to dismiss may be renewed after discovery is completed.

3. Generally

Unlike the basic internet contract for a sale and payment, arbitration and forum selection clauses materially alter the substantive default rights of a consumer. They are not enforceable against ordinary consumers who are unlikely to be aware of them. *See supra* Part V.B.2. Where the seller "has reason to believe that the [buyer] manifesting assent would not do so if [he knew] that the writing contained a particular term, the term is not part of the agreement." Restatement (Second) of Contract § 212(3); *cf. Mastrobuono [v. Shearson],* 514 U.S. [52] at 63 [1995], 115 S.Ct. 1212 ("As a practical matter, it seems unlikely that petitioners . . . had any idea that by signing a standard-form agreement to arbitrate disputes they might be giving up an important substantive right. In the face of such doubt, we are unwilling to impute this intent to petitioners.").

Neither Berkson nor Welsh can, at this stage of the litigation, be considered to have knowingly bound themselves to the purported terms of an agreement adverse to them. They are not precluded from asserting the putative class claims alleged in the amended complaint.

VIII. CONCLUSION

Berkson and Welsh have standing.

Transfer of venue and compelling arbitration are denied.

* * *

SO ORDERED.

QUESTIONS AND NOTES

1. Questions about the facts of this case

 1.1. What are the differences between clickwrap, scrollwrap, browserwrap, and sign-in-wrap agreements? All of these terms dervice from the original term "shrinkwrap," which was first used by the court in *ProCD, Inc. v. Zeidenberg*, 86 F.3d 1447 (7th Cir. 1996) in describing terms inside a shrinkwrapped box of software, which of course the customer would not see until the box was purchased. Yes, software used to come in boxes!

 1.2. How common are auto-renewing services, such as was employed by Gogo, where your credit card gets billed unless you affirmatively take steps to terminate the service? Has it ever happened to you? Be honest.

 1.3. Why would Apple want to put the entire text of *Mein Kampf* in its agreement? Is a contract of adhesion one that sticks to you when you pick it up? Can you even believe your wasting your precious time reading these dumb questions?

 1.4. Do you agree with the court in *Gogo* that internet users require "clearer notice than do traditional retail buyers"? Why or why not?

2. Questions about the law

 2.1. The court says that the "starting point of analysis must be the method through which an electronic contract of adhesion is formed. The inquiry does not begin, as defendants argue, with the content of the provisions themselves." Do you agree with the court? Why did Gogo argue that ther focus should be on the provisions themselves?

 2.2. Are contracts of adhesion violative of public policy? Should they be illegal?

 2.3. Recently, one of us noticed on CNN.com that a little red banner has popped up on the home page with the message: "Our Terms of Service and Privacy Policy have changed. By using this site, you agree to the Privacy Policy and the Terms of Service." Both the Terms of Service and Privacy Policy are hyperlinked so that they can be viewed. Why did CNN do this? Is it a good practice? Epstein mentioned that some different kind of things have been popping up on the websites he frequents, but we decided not to discuss those here.

2.4. What is the distinction between notice of a website's terms of use and the opportunity to read those terms, on the one hand, and the substance of those terms, on the other?

2.5. The court says that browserwrap agreements are usually only enforceable against "knowledgeable accssessors," but that clickwrap agreements are usually found to be enforceable. Into which of these camps do sign-in-wrap agreements fall?

3. Notes

3.1. With the recognition of electronic contracts by the E-Sign Act and the Uniform Electronic Transactions Act, two new terms entered the vocabulary of contract law. Specifically, the term "record" was adopted to refer to "information that is inscribed on a tangible medium and is retrievanble in perceivable form," and the term "electronic record" has been adopted to refer to any record created, used, or stored in a medium other than paper." *See Uniform Electronic Transactions Act,* §§ 10 and 6.

3.2. *Tompkins v. 23andMe, Inc.,* 2014 WL 2903752 (N.D. Cal. June 25, 2014), involved enforcement of an arbitration clause in the genetic testing company's terms and conditions. Interestingly, the website did not require buyers of the test to assent in any way to those terms and conditions prior to purchasing a test, but, in order to access their results after the purchase, they did have to click through the 23&Me terms and conditions. Not surprisingly, the court held that there was no acceptance of these terms and conditions at purchase, even though there was a reference on the site that buyers "accept" the company's terms of service by actually using the service. A bit more surprisingly, however, because buyers could not access their test results until after clicking a link that they "accepted" the company's terms of service, the court concluded that acceptance did occur at that point—*after* the contract had been formed!

4. **You Be the Lawyer!**

If Gogo retained you to provide legal advice concerning the redesign of its website pages for creating a new account and signing into that account once created, what would you recommend?

One final issue of interest in these cases is what law governs when the transaction involves the license of computer software? Although clearly not a "good," within the meaning of Article 2 (at least when not delivered by means of a tangible media), some courts nonetheless apply the U.C.C. by analogy. The *Specht* court ultimately applied common law. To some extent software licenses exist in a legislative void. NCCUSL has tried to fill that void, but without much success. In the 1990's lawmakers began to draft a new Article 2B (licenses) for the U.C.C., which would have complemented Article 2 (sales) and Article 2A (leases). After a few years the effort was abandoned and in 1999 those lawmakers instead promulgated an independent body of law for software licenses, which is known as the Uniform Computer Information Transactions Act ("UCITA"). However, UCITA has only been adopted in two states, Maryland and Virginia, and seems to be something of a legislative dead letter.

Recognizing the host of legal questions surrounding software contracts, in 2009 the American Law Institute promulgated PRINCIPLES OF THE LAW OF SOFTWARE CONTRACTS that, based on the caselaw, purports to suggest "best practices, [but] without unduly hindering the law's adaptability to future developments." In terms of end-user license agreements for software downloaded from the internet, the PRINCIPLES focus on: (a) notice and accessible terms, (b) user indication of assent to the terms, and (c) the ability to store and reproduce the terms as key factors bearing on enforceability. These factors, while offering general guidance at most, do seem to reflect the general direction being taken in the case law in relation to these issues.

NOTE ON SMART CONTRACTS

Smart contracts are self-executing contracts with the terms of the contract between buyer and seller directly written into lines of code. They rely on blockchain technology, which ensures integrity and trust between strangers by making it almost *impossible* to cheat. Smart contracts are intended to permit you to exchange money, property, shares, or anything of value in a transparent, conflict-reduced way while avoiding the services of an intermediary.

Blockchain is a vast, global distributed ledger or database running on millions of devices and open to anyone, where not just information but anything of value—money, titles, deeds, music, art, scientific discoveries, intellectual property—can be moved and securely stored. A smart contract based on blockchain might work like this: Ponoroff wishes to let a beach house from Epstein for the summer. He might do this by going through the blockchain established for this purpose and pay using a cryptocurrency, like Bitcoin. A virtual contract now exists between Ponoroff and Epstein. Ponoroff gets a receipt for his payment and, when the lease term is to commence, he receives a digital entry key from Epstein. If the key is not delivered when due, the blockchain releases a refund to Ponoroff. Epstein would presumably send the key through the blockchain prior to the rental date, but the function does not release the money to Epstein or the key to Ponoroff until the date for possession arrives. The code that facilitates the transaction cannot be interfered by either party without the other being alerted instantly. Thus, in addition to reducing transaction costs, smart contracts are secure.

Still, things can always go wrong, and when they do, in the absence of a specific regulatory structure, a smart contract is still a contract. This means that contract law will have to supply the answer, however ill-suited it may be to doing so.

---

6. DEFICIENT AGREEMENTS: INSUFFICIENT, INADEQUATE, AND POSTPONED TERMS

INTRODUCTION

So far in this Chapter we have been focused on various dimensions of the issue of when an agreement is formed; *i.e.*, up to what point in time is either party free to walk from the "deal" without liability?

In this final section of the Chapter we consider a related problem or series of problems; namely, what happens when: 1) the parties both believe they have assented to a deal, but each of them has attached a materially different meaning or understanding to their outward manifestations of assent, or 2) the parties have reached some agreement on the proposed exchange, but have not: (i) agreed on all terms, or (ii) expressed their agreement in an indefinite manner, or (iii) deliberately left some terms for future agreement.

Now, in any of these situations, when, if ever, should the law permit one party to withdraw without consequence? In other words, should the law provide that there can be no contract unless the parties have attached the same meaning to all material terms, can be no contract until there is clear and complete agreement on all terms? Or, in the former situation, should the law choose one meaning over the other, and, in the latter case, should we allow the parties to conclude a deal without clear and complete agreement if that's what they intend? If the court does enforce the deal, how does it go about the task of fashioning an appropriate remedy in light of either the misunderstanding or the lack of clarity? What if the parties "agree to agree" on a particular term and do not? Is there a pre-contractual duty to negotiate in good faith? These and others are some of the questions we address in this final section.

In Part A, we will consider the issues surrounding misunderstood terms and indefiniteness. Then, in Part B, we will examine how courts deal with situations where either the parties have made a deal but intentionally decided to defer agreement on a particular term or terms, or have reached agreement on some but less than all of the terms on which the deal hinges. After that, everyone gets 20 minutes of recess to decompress!

A. PROBLEMS OF MISUNDERSTOOD, INCOMPLETE, AND INDEFINITE TERMS

INTRODUCTION TO MUTUAL MISUNDERSTANDING OF A CONTRACT TERM—*RAFFLES*

The next case illustrates the problem known as "mutual misunderstanding." One party is contending that even though the parties thought they had a deal, there never was a deal because they later discovered that their respective understandings of what a contract term meant were fundamentally different. In essence, the argument is that there can be no mutual assent if the parties have assented to different things; i.e., there are mutual misunderstandings.

The questions you should be asking yourself as you read *Raffles* are: 1) under what facts should such different understandings of a key term of the deal preclude a finding that a contract was formed; 2) are those facts present in this case; and 3) which of the parties should end up in cases of this sort bearing the risk of different understandings?

QUESTIONS BEFORE THE CASE

1. Is the term "Peerless" objectively ambiguous?
2. How does mutual misunderstanding differ from cases involving "mutual mistake"?

RAFFLES V. WICHELHAUS

Court of Exchequer
2 H. & C. 906, 159 Eng. Rep. 375 (1864)

Declaration. For that it was agreed between the plaintiff and the defendants, to wit, at Liverpool, that the plaintiff should sell to the defendants, and the defendants buy of the plaintiff, certain goods, to wit, 125 bales of Surat cotton, guaranteed middling fair merchant's Dhollarah, to arrive tex "Peerless" from Bombay; and that the cotton should be taken from the quay, and that the defendants would pay the plaintiff for the same at a certain rate, to wit, at the rate of 17¼ d. per pound, within a certain time then agreed upon after the arrival of said goods in England.

Averments: that the said goods did arrive by the said ship from Bombay in England, to wit, at Liverpool, and the plaintiff was then and there ready and willing and offered to deliver the said goods to the defendants, & c. Breach: that the defendants refused to accept the said goods or pay the plaintiff for them.

Plea. That the said ship mentioned in the said agreement was meant and intended by the defendants to be the ship called the "Peerless," which sailed from Bombay, to wit, in October; and that the plaintiff was not ready and willing, and did not offer to deliver to the defendants any bales of cotton which arrived by the last-mentioned ship, but instead thereof was only ready and willing, and offered to deliver to the defendants 125 bales of Surat cotton which arrived by another and different ship, which was also called the "Peerless," and which sailed from Bombay, to wit, in December.

Demurrer, and joinder therein.

Milward, in support of the demurrer. The contract was for the sale of a number of bales of cotton of a particular description, which the plaintiff was ready to deliver. It is immaterial by what ship the cotton was to arrive, so that it was a ship called the "Peerless." The words "to arrive ex 'Peerless,' " only mean that if the vessel is lost on the voyage, the contract is to be at an end. [Pollock, C.B. It would be a question for the jury whether both parties meant the same ship called the "Peerless."] That would be so if the contract was for the sale of a ship called the "Peerless"; but it is for the sale of cotton on board a ship of that name. [Pollack, C.B. The defendant only bought that cotton which was to arrive by a particular ship. It may as well be said, that if there is a contract for the purchase of certain goods in warehouse A., that is satisfied by the delivery of goods of the same description in warehouse B.] In that case there would be goods in both warehouses; here it does not appear that the plaintiff had any goods on board the other "Peerless." [Martin, B. It is imposing on the defendant a contract different from that which he entered into. Pollack, C.B. It is like a contract for the purchase of wine coming from a particular estate in France or Spain, where there are two estates of that name.] The defendant has no right to contradict by parol evidence a written contract good upon the face of it. He does not impute misrepresentation or fraud, but only says that he fancied the ship was a different one. Intention is of no avail, unless stated at the time of the contract. [Pollock, C.B. One vessel sailed in October and the other in December.] The time of sailing is no part of the contract.

Mellish (Cohen with him), in support of the plea. There is nothing on the face of the contract to shew that any particular ship called the "Peerless" was meant; but the moment it appears that two ships called the "Peerless" were about to sail from Bombay there is a latent ambiguity, and parol evidence may be given for the purpose of shewing that the defendant meant one "Peerless," and the plaintiff another. That being so, there was no consensus ad idem, and therefore no binding contract. He was then stopped by the Court.

PER CURIAM. There must be judgment for the defendants.

Judgment for the defendants.

QUESTIONS

1. Questions about the facts of this case

 1.1. Who sets out the facts of the case? Who were Milward and Mellish?

 1.2. Why did it matter what the parties privately may have intended when they made reference to the ship *Peerless*? And while we're at it, why did it even matter what vessel the cotton was being shipped by? Wasn't the important thing that the plaintiff delivered the proper quantity of the agreed-upon commodity to the defendant? Why then did the parties even specify the ship on which the cotton would be carried? Was it to establish the time of delivery or to protect the seller if the ship went down? Does that make a difference?

 1.3. Why do you suppose that the defendant refused to accept the cotton that arrived on the December *Peerless*? Do you (especially those of you who were history majors) understand why the dates were important? Did the court understand that? Did it care? Presumably, the October *Peerless* arrived in London some weeks or even months before the December *Peerless* and yet there is no indication that defendant raised any inquiry as to why his cotton was not on the October ship.

 1.4. Did the court's decision benefit one party over the other?

2. Questions about the law

 2.1. Is *Raffles* consistent with objective theory? In discussing *Raffles,* Justice Holmes said, "The true ground of the decision was not that each party meant a different thing from the other, as has been implied in the explanation that has been mentioned, but that each said a different thing." O.W. HOLMES, THE COMMON LAW 242 [1881] (Howe ed. 1963). Do you agree with that analysis? Here's what Professor Gilmore had to say about it: "The magician who could 'objectify' *Raffles v. Wichelhaus* * * * could, the need arising, objectify anything. But why bother?" GRANT GILMORE, THE DEATH OF CONTRACT 41 (1974).

 2.2. Did the *Raffles* court go pretty "light" on Mellish compared to Milward? What else might you have asked if you sat on the bench in this case before you were convinced that there was no contract?

2.3. Read *Restatement (Second) of Contracts* § 20, which deals with the effects of misunderstanding. Is *Restatement (Second) of Contracts* § 20(1) essentially a codification of the Court of Exchequer's decision in *Raffles*? If not, how does it differ and would its application have changed the result in *Raffles*?

2.4. Notice the five illustrations at the end of *Restatement (Second) of Contracts* § 20. Four of the five use "ex steamer Peerless." Can you illustrate *Restatement (Second) of Contracts* § 20(1) without using the term "Peerless"?

3. **You Be the Lawyer!**

If you had represented the seller (plaintiff) in this case, what points would you have stressed in your argument to the court?

PROBLEM ON MUTUAL MISUNDERSTANDING OF A CONTRACT TERM

Epstein has two prized hunting dogs, a black lab and a beagle. Because he was so fond of the name, Epstein named both dogs Goober. Ponoroff has been negotiating with Epstein to purchase one of the dogs, as Epstein has become desperate for money after losing his job due to the commission of certain acts of moral turpitude. After much haggling, Epstein says, "Ok, I'll sell Goober to you for $1,000." Epstein has in mind the beagle when he makes this offer. Ponoroff promptly replies, "I accept." When Epstein shows up at Ponoroff's house with the beagle and demands his $1,000, Ponoroff refuses to pay, demanding that Epstein turn over the lab "as agreed." Ponoroff knows that Epstein is uncommonly, and perhaps even unnaturally, attached to the black lab and would never part with him for any price. Consult § 20 of *Restatement (Second) of Contracts* and answer the following questions.

- Is there a contract here, and, if so, for which dog?
- How, if at all, does it change your answer if Ponoroff had no reason to know of Epstein's unusual attachment to the lab?
- How, if at all, does it change your answer if the facts were different in that Epstein deliberately showed up with the beagle, a less valuable dog, knowing that Ponoroff meant the lab when Ponoroff agreed to pay the $1,000 price for "Goober," and Ponoroff assumed that was what Epstein meant as well?
- Suppose in the last question, Ponoroff was aware of what Epstein was up to, but still accepted, intending to assert a claim for the lab?

INTRODUCTION TO INDEFINITE AND INCOMPLETE TERMS—*VARNEY*

In *Raffles,* (1) the parties both agreed to term "ex Peerless"; (2) the court held that there was no contract; and (3) we suggested that you look at *Restatement (Second)* § 20. In the next case, *Varney*, (1) the parties agree to the term "fair share of the profits"; and (2) we suggest that you look at *Restatement (Second)* § 33. As you read the next case, think about how *Raffles* and *Varney* are similar and how they differ. When will you discuss *Raffles* on your final exam, and when will you discuss *Varney*?

Analytically, *indefiniteness* can be viewed as a *defense* to liability rather than as an aspect of contract formation. However, it is equally appropriate to conceptualize the requirement of definiteness as an aspect of the bargaining process that must be satisfied, no less than mutual assent, in order for a contract to arise. The purpose of contract enforcement is, as we shall see in Chapter 6, to protect the promisee's *expectation* in the event of breach; that is, to put the non-breaching party in as good a position as performance would have. If the parties have not expressed their agreement with sufficient clarity or completeness to permit the court to fashion an appropriate remedy, than an essential component of contract formation is missing.

As a practical matter, it is impossible for the parties' agreement to speak to every aspect of their relationship. Unquestionably, the requirement of definiteness means something less than specific agreement down to the finest minutiae. The question that forms the basis of contention in the next two cases is when the parties have intended to make a contract but have failed to express their mutual obligations with perfect clarity, how far should the court go in resolving ambiguities and supplying missing terms in order to provide a remedy for nonperformance?

QUESTIONS BEFORE THE CASE

1. What is the reason why the law requires a certain level of definiteness?
2. When a court refuses to enforce an agreement based on indefiniteness, who "wins"? Is that fair?

VARNEY V. DITMARS

Court of Appeals of New York
217 N.Y. 223, 111 N.E. 822 (1916)

CHASE, J.

This is an action brought for an alleged wrongful discharge of an employee. The defendant is an architect employing engineers, draftsmen and other assistants. The plaintiff is an architect and draftsman. In October, 1910, he applied to the defendant for employment and when asked what wages he wanted, replied that he would start for $40 per week. He was employed at $35 per week. A short time thereafter he informed the defendant that he had another position offered to him and the defendant said that if he would remain with him and help him through the work in his office he thought he could offer him a better future than anybody else. He continued in the employ of the defendant and became acquainted with a designer in the office and said designer and the plaintiff from time to time prior to the 1st of February, 1911, talked with the defendant about the work in his office. On that day by arrangement the two remained with the defendant after the regular office hours and the defendant said: "I am going to give you $5 more a week; if you boys will go on and continue the way you have been and get me out of this trouble and get these jobs started that were in the office three years, on the first of next January I will close my books and give you a fair share of my profits. That was the result of the conversation. That was all of that conversation." The plaintiff was given charge of the drafting. Thereafter suggestions were made by the plaintiff and said designer about discharging many of the defendant's employees and employing new men and such suggestions were carried out and the two worked in the defendant's office over time and many Sundays and holidays. At least one piece of work that the defendant said had been in his office for three years was completed. The plaintiff on his cross-examination told the story of the employment of himself and said designer as follows: 'And he says at that time 'I am going to give you $5 more a week starting this week.' This was about Thursday. He says 'You boys go on and continue the work you are doing and the first of January next year I will close my books and give you a fair share of my profits.' Those were his exact words."

Thereafter the plaintiff was paid $40 a week. On November 6, 1911, the night before the general election in this state, the defendant requested that all of his employees that could do so, should work on election day. The plaintiff told the defendant that he wanted to remain at home to attend an election in the village where he lived. About four o'clock in the afternoon of election day he was taken ill and remained at his house ill until a time that as nearly as can be stated from the evidence was subsequent to December 1, 1911. On Saturday, November 11, the defendant caused to be delivered to the plaintiff a letter in which he said:

"I am sending you herewith your pay for one day's work of seven hours, performed on Monday, the 6th inst. On Monday night, I made it my special duty to inform you that the office would be open all day Election Day and that I expected you and all the men to report for work. Much to my surprise and indignation, on Tuesday you made no appearance and all the men remained away, in obedience of your instructions to them of the previous evening. An act of this kind I consider one of extreme disloyalty and insubordination and I therefore am obliged to dispense with your services."

After the plaintiff had recovered from his illness and was able to do so he went to the defendant's office (the date does not appear) and told him that he was ready, willing and able to continue his services under the agreement. The defendant denied that he had any agreement with him and refused to permit him to continue in his service. Thereafter and prior to January 1, 1912, the plaintiff received for special work about $50.

The plaintiff seeks to recover in this action for services from November 7, 1911, to December 31, 1911, inclusive, at $40 per week and for a fair and reasonable percentage of the net profits of the defendant's business from February 1, 1911, to January 1, 1912, and demands judgment for $1,680.

At the trial he was the only witness sworn as to the alleged contract and at the close of his case the complaint was dismissed.

The statement alleged to have been made by the defendant about giving the plaintiff and said designer a fair share of his profits is vague, indefinite and uncertain and the amount cannot be computed from anything that was said by the parties or by reference to any document, paper or other transaction. The minds of the parties never met upon any particular share of the defendant's profits to be given the employees or upon any plan by which such share could be computed or determined. The contract so far as it related to the special promise or inducement was never consummated. It was left subject to the will of the defendant or for further negotiation. It is urged that the defendant by the use of the word "fair" in referring to a share of his profits, was as certain and definite as people are in the purchase and sale of a chattel when the price is not expressly agreed upon, and that if the agreement in question is declared to be too indefinite and uncertain to be enforced a similar conclusion must be reached in every case where a chattel is sold without expressly fixing the price therefor.

The question whether the words "fair" and "reasonable" have a definite and enforceable meaning when used in business transactions is dependent upon the intention of the parties in the use of such words and upon the subject-matter to which they refer. In cases of merchandising and in the purchase and sale of chattels the parties may use the words "fair and reasonable value" as synonymous with "market value." A promise to pay the fair market value of goods may be inferred from what is expressly agreed by the parties. The fair, reasonable or market value of goods can be shown by direct testimony of those competent to give such testimony. The competency to speak grows out of experience and knowledge. The testimony of such witnesses does not rest upon conjecture. The opinion of this court in *United Press v. N. Y. Press Co.* (164 N. Y. 406) was not intended to assert that a contract of sale is unenforceable unless the price is expressly mentioned and determined.

In the case of a contract for the sale of goods or for hire without a fixed price or consideration being named it will be presumed that a reasonable price or consideration is intended and the person who enters into such a contract for goods or service is liable therefor as on an implied contract. Such contracts are common, and when there is nothing therein to limit or prevent an implication as to the price, they are, so far as the terms of the contract are concerned, binding obligations.

The contract in question, so far as it relates to a share of the defendant's profits, is not only uncertain but it is necessarily affected by so many other facts that are in themselves indefinite and uncertain that the intention of the parties is pure conjecture. A fair share of the defendant's profits may be any amount from a nominal sum to a material part according to the particular views of the person whose guess is considered. Such an executory contract must rest for performance upon the honor and good faith of the parties making it. The courts cannot aid parties in such a case when they are unable or unwilling to agree upon the terms of their own proposed contract.

It is elementary in the law that, for the validity of a contract, the promise, or the agreement, of the parties to it must be certain and explicit and that their full intention may be ascertained to a reasonable degree of certainty. Their agreement must be neither vague nor indefinite, and, if thus defective, parol proof cannot be resorted to. * * *

The courts in this state, in reliance upon and approval of the rule as stated in the *United Press* case, have decided many cases involving the same rule. Thus, in *Mackintosh v. Thompson,* (58 App. Div. 25), and again in *Mackintosh v. Kimball,* (101 App. Div. 494), the plaintiff sought to recover compensation in addition to a stated salary which he had received and which additional amount rested upon a claim by him that while he was employed by the defendants he informed them that he intended to leave their employ unless he was given an increase in salary, and that one of the defendants said to him that they would make it worth his while if he would stay on, and would increase his salary, and that his idea was to give him an interest in the profits on certain buildings that they were then erecting. The plaintiff further alleges that he asked what would be the amount of the increase and was told, "You can depend upon me; I will see that you get a satisfactory amount." The court held that the arrangement was too indefinite to form the basis of any obligation on the part of the defendants.

In *Bluemner v. Garvin,* (120 App. Div. 29), the plaintiff and defendant were architects, and the plaintiff alleged that he drew plans for a public building in accordance with a contract held by the defendant and pursuant to a special agreement that if the plans were accepted the defendant would give him a fair share of the commissions to be received by him. The court held that a good cause of action was stated on quantum meruit, but that the contract was too vague and indefinite to be enforced.

* * *

The rule stated from the *United Press* case does not prevent a recovery upon quantum meruit in case one party to an alleged contract has performed in reliance upon the terms thereof, vague, indefinite and uncertain though they are. In such case the law will presume a promise to pay the reasonable value of the services. Judge Gray, who wrote the opinion in the *United Press* case, said therein: "I entertain no doubt that, where work has been done, or articles have been furnished, a recovery may be based upon quantum meruit, or quantum valebat; but, where a contract is of an executory character and requires performance over a future period of time, as here, and it is silent as to the price which is to be paid to the plaintiff during its term, I do not think that it possesses binding force. As the parties had omitted to make the price a subject of covenant, in the nature of things, it would have to be the subject of future agreement, or stipulation." (p. 412.)

* * *

So, in this case, while I do not think that the plaintiff can recover anything as extra work, yet if the work actually performed as stated was worth more than $40 per week, he having performed until November 7, 1910, could, on a proper complaint, recover its value less the amount received.

* * *

The plaintiff claims that he at least should have been allowed to go to the jury on the question as to whether he was entitled to recover at the rate of $40 per week from November 7, 1911, to December 31, 1911, inclusive. He did not perform any services for the defendant from November 6 until some time after December 1st, by reason of his illness. He has not shown just when he offered to return. It appears that between the time when he offered to return and January 1st he received $50 for other services.

The amount that the plaintiff could recover, therefore, if any, based upon the agreement to pay $40 per week would be very small, and he did not present to the court facts from which it could be computed. His employment by the defendant was conditional upon his continuing the way he had been working, getting the defendant out of his trouble and getting certain unenumerated jobs that were in the office three years, started. There was nothing in the contract specifying the length of service except as stated. It was not an unqualified agreement to continue the plaintiff in his service until the first of January, and it does not appear whether or not the special conditions upon which the contract was made had been performed. Even apart from the question whether the plaintiff's absence from the defendant's office by reason of his illness would permit the defendant to refuse to take him back into his employ, I do not think that on the testimony as it appears before us it was error to refuse to leave to the jury the question whether the plaintiff was entitled to recover anything at the rate of $40 per week.

The judgment should be affirmed, with costs.

CARDOZO, J. (dissenting).

I do not think it is true that a promise to pay an employee a fair share of the profits in addition to his salary is always and of necessity too vague to be enforced * * *. The promise must, of course, appear to have been made with contractual intent * * *. But if that intent is present, it cannot be said from the mere form of the promise that the estimate of the reward is inherently impossible. The data essential to measurement may be lacking in the particular instance, and yet they may conceivably be supplied. It is possible, for example, that in some occupations an employee would be able to prove a percentage regulated by custom. The difficulty in this case is not so much in the contract as in the evidence. Even if the data required for computation might conceivably have been supplied, the plaintiff did not supply them. He would not have supplied them if all the evidence which he offered, and which the court excluded, had been received. He has not failed because the nature of the contract is such that damages are of necessity incapable of proof. He has failed because he did not prove them.

There is nothing inconsistent with this view in *United Press v. N.Y. Press Co.,* (164 N.Y. 406). The case is often cited as authority for the proposition that an agreement to buy merchandise at a fair and reasonable price is so indefinite that an action may not be maintained for its breach in so far as it is still executory. Nothing of the kind was decided, or with reason could have been. What the court did was to construe a particular agreement, and to hold that the parties intended to reserve the price for future adjustment. If instead of reserving the price for future adjustment, they had manifested an intent on the one hand to pay and on the other to accept a fair price, the case is far from holding that a jury could not determine what such a price would be and assess the damages accordingly. Such an intent, moreover, might be manifested not only through express words, but also through reasonable implication. It was because there was neither an express statement nor a reasonable implication of such an intent that the court held the agreement void to the extent that it had not been executed.

On the ground that the plaintiff failed to supply the data essential to computation, I concur in the conclusion that profits were not to be included as an element of damage. I do not concur, however, in the conclusion that he failed to make out a case of damage to the extent of his loss of salary. The amount may be small, but none the less it belongs to him. The hiring was not at will * * *. The plain implication was that it should continue until the end of the year when the books were to be closed. The evidence would permit the jury to find that the plaintiff was discharged without cause, and he is entitled to damages measured by his salary for the unexpired term.

The judgment should be reversed and a new trial granted, with costs to abide the event.

QUESTIONS

1. Questions about the facts of this case

 1.1. What did the defendant intend when he told plaintiff and the designer that if they would continue the work they had been doing he would give them "a fair share of my profits"? What did the plaintiff understand when the defendant told him and the designer that he would give them "a fair share of my profits"? Were the answers to these questions important to the court? How did the court determine that, "The minds of the parties never met upon any particular share of the defendant's profits to be given the employees"? Why was that important to the court?

 1.2. According to Justice Chase, what was the time duration of the plaintiff's employment contract? According to Justice Cardozo? Was the time duration of the plaintiff's employment contract relevant to the resolution of the plaintiff's contract claim? To the resolution of the plaintiff's quantum meruit claim? By the way, what is "quantum meruit"?

2. Questions about the law

 2.1. The majority opinion in *Varney* represents the traditional common law attitude toward issues of definiteness. What is the concern that accounts for this attitude? What is Justice Cardozo's take and how does it differ from the approach adopted by the majority?

 2.2. The majority opinion seems concerned that the determination of a "fair share of profits" is inherently more speculative than the determination of a "fair" or "reasonable" price for goods. Do you agree? Does Justice Cardozo agree? What kind of evidence would you try to produce to prove the dollar amount of "fair share of the profits" if given the opportunity?

3. **You Be the Lawyer!**

   How would you have advised Varney on February 1, 1911 (assuming you were alive then, even though we all know that none of us was alive then . . . except for Epstein)?

QUESTION BEFORE THE CASE

When the judge or jury "fills in" an indefinite or incomplete term in an agreement, is this supplied term determined based on the intent of the parties or is it based on something else?

COMMUNITY DESIGN CORPORATION V. ANTONELL

District Court of Appeal of Florida
459 So.2d 343 (1984)

NESBITT, JUDGE.

Community Design Corporation (CDC) appeals a final judgment against it in a contract case and the award of attorney's fees and costs. * * * We affirm in all respects.

Joseph Antonell was hired by CDC to work as an architectural draftsman on the Brickell Key project. He worked on a weekly basis at $10.00 per hour, with time and one-half for overtime.

Sometime in the fall of 1980, Charles Cheezum, the then-president of CDC, promised a bonus to any employee still working at Christmastime of 1980, if the drawings were complete by that time.[1] The amount each employee was to receive was apparently to be determined by the recommendation of Shirley Wooster, CDC's vice president. Wooster, Antonell's supervisor, promised a one-week paid vacation if the drawings were completed on time. After these promises were made, Antonell worked overtime in an effort to complete the drawings by the specified date.

On December 24, 1980, with Antonell still in CDC's employ, the draftsmen's drawings were collected and blueprints were made. After Christmas, and through much of 1981, changes were made to the drawings, some of which were necessitated by a February 23, 1981 contract which required CDC to coordinate the drawings of various subcontractors. Final

---

[1] The amount of the bonus was disputed, but was clearly between $20,000 and $35,000. The degree of completion required was also disputed.

acceptance of the drawings for construction purposes occurred by March of 1982.

When Antonell received neither the bonus nor the paid vacation, he sued to recover both. The jury found for him on both claims, finding for CDC on a third claim for a promised raise.

CDC [argues] * * * that the contract is too indefinite and uncertain to be enforced because there was no agreement as to the amount of the bonus, the degree of completion required and the division among the employees. We disagree.

Courts are reluctant to hold contracts unenforceable on grounds of uncertainty, especially where, as here, one party has received the benefit of the other's performance. When the existence of a contract is clear, the jury may properly determine the exact terms of an oral contract, which often depend on the credibility of the witnesses. While the exact amount of the bonus[2] and the degree of completion required[3] were disputed, there was sufficient evidence for the jury to find an oral contract between the parties with terms which support the award in this case.

CDC asserts that there was no agreement as to exactly how much each employee would receive. While this is true, it is necessarily so because the bonus was to be divided among those still employed at Christmastime and in amounts recommended by Ms. Wooster. Once the drawings were completed, CDC's contractual duty to act in good faith in recommending a bonus for those who qualified arose. It was Wooster's failure to recommend a bonus, and CDC's subsequent failure to pay one, which constituted the breach.[4] It was appropriate for the jury to resolve the compensation question, and the amount awarded is reasonable based on Antonell's efforts in completing the drawings.

* * *

Accordingly, the judgment is, in all respects, affirmed.

---

2 The parties acknowledge that a particular amount was offered, which distinguishes this case from those in which the amount is indefinite or left for future agreement. *See, e.g., Drake v. Block,* 247 Iowa 517, 74 N.W.2d 577 (1956); *Varney v. Ditmars,* 217 N.Y. 223, 111 N.E. 822 (1916).

3 While there were many changes made to the drawings after the initial blueprinting, there was evidence both that such changes are normal in the industry and that many were required by a February, 1981 contract which called for coordination of the architectural drawings with the electrical and mechanical drawings. Therefore, the jury could have found that the completion contemplated was the initial blueprinting and that the changes made were either those common in the industry, those required by a subsequent contract, or both.

4 We are in no way suggesting that employers are not free to establish bonus plans like that in *Parrish v. General Motors Corp.,* 137 So.2d 255 (Fla. 2d DCA 1962). There, the bonus plan gave the employer, in writing, the discretion to award, or choose not to award, a bonus. Such a writing clearly establishes the employer's intention and does not give rise to a contractual bonus right. Here, the contract is oral and the evidence is reasonably susceptible to the conclusion that once the drawings were complete the duty to recommend and pay a bonus arose. To find otherwise would allow CDC to induce extra efforts from its employees by oral promises and then hide behind a cloak of vagueness resulting from conflicting testimony.

QUESTIONS, NOTES, AND CONNECTIONS

1. Questions about the facts of this case

   1.1. What was the bonus promise in *Antonell* and how did it differ from the promise in *Varney*? Did the court in *Antonell* think the two promises were qualitatively different? Do you?

   1.2. Why didn't Ms. Wooster make a recommendation about Antonell's bonus amount? If she had, would this court have enforced that recommendation?

2. Questions about the law

   2.1. How important was the fact that the Community Design Corp. had received the benefit of Antonell's performance?

   2.2. The *Antonell* court says that while the amount of the bonus was not fixed, this is "necessarily so" because it was not known how many employees would still be employed at Christmastime. Does this provide a principled basis for distinguishing the case from *Varney?*

   2.3. What role does "good faith" play in the court's analysis? Can the obligation of good faith overcome problems of indefiniteness?

   2.4. *Restatement (Second)* § 33(2) suggests that the court may imply a missing term when there is a "reasonable basis" for doing so. Does this refer to a reasonable basis for assuming that the parties *intended* that the court would fill in the omitted or ambiguous item, or just an objectively reasonable basis for supplying or construing that missing or vague term?

   2.5. How would the *Varney* court have decided this case? How about Justice Cardozo?

3. Notes

   3.1. While *Antonell* and *Restatement (Second) of Contracts* § 33(2) reflect the contemporary attitude of increasing tolerance of indefiniteness, even today some courts still take the definiteness requirement quite seriously. In *Goldstick v. ICM Realty,* 788 F.2d 456, 461 (7th Cir. 1986), for example, Judge Posner, in insisting that the parties must express their agreement with sufficient definiteness to guide the court in determining what they intended, observed: "The parties have a competitive advantage over the court in deciding on what terms a voluntary transaction is value-maximizing; that is the premise of a free enterprise system." Do you agree? Is the concern over inadvertent, judicially-created market inefficiencies sufficient to justify depriving a party of his "fair share of the profits"?

3.2. There is no shortage of litigation over the validity of contracts based on the alleged indefiniteness of terms. If found, does indefiniteness render the contract unenforceable or should the court, as Justice Cardozo suggested in his *Varney* dissent, consider each contested term contextually?

3.3. Should the reason why the parties failed to address some aspect of their relationship with definiteness affect the court's willingness to supply the missing or ambiguous term? For instance, would it make a difference to you if the parties left an item open because they were unable to reach agreement? How about if they left the item open because of the inability to accurately forecast at the time of contracting what the needs of the parties were likely to be over the life of a contract?

3.4. The shift in attitude and approach from the majority opinion in *Varney* to the decision in *Antonell* is reflective of a more generalized shift in contract law from strict rules to much more flexible standards, such as those set out in *Restatement (Second)* § 33(2) and in U.C.C. § 2–204(3), discussed below in the Note of U.C.C. Gap Fillers. There are many reasons for this shift from "rules to standards," but most notably among them, insofar as the requirement of definiteness is concerned, is the increasing complexity of modern transactions. The traditional theory of mutual assent evolved in an era when simple, one-shot transactions were the norm. As contractual relationships increasingly began to involve multiple performances over an extended period of time, new approaches had to be devised to accommodate the disputes that would inevitably arise in the course of performance and could not possibly have been anticipated by the parties in advance. As discussed in the Note below on long-term agreements and relational contracts, one of the first contract law scholars to examine the impact of long-term relational contracts on traditional doctrine was Professor Ian Macneil. *See* Macneil, *The Many Faces of Contracts,* 47 S. CAL. L. REV. 691 (1974).

4. **You Be the Lawyer!**

Does the decision in this case suggest to you some steps you might have urged CDC to take back in the fall of 1980 in order to avoid liability for the promised bonus?

5. Connections

Conceptually, what are the differences between cases involving "indefiniteness," like *Varney* and *Antonell*, and cases dealing with "mutual misunderstanding," like *Raffles*? Are both kinds of cases different as well from the other cases you have read in this chapter on contract formation? Are these cases really about contract formation at all? If not, what are they doing in this chapter titled, "Has Your Client Made a Deal"? Did your favorite authors mess up (again)?

NOTE ON LONG-TERM AGREEMENTS AND RELATIONAL CONTRACTS

The basic principles of contract law, including the requirement of definiteness, evolved in simpler economic times. In those simpler economic times, most contractual relations tended to involve discrete, "one-shot" transactions of short duration and limited interpersonal dealings between the parties. Understandably, many of the basic rules of contract law were developed to accommodate this type of transaction.

Now, however, contractual dealings are increasingly characterized by long-term, on-going relations between the contracting parties involving a complex series of performances over time. Of necessity, circumstances will change over the course of this relationship and, because it is impossible to anticipate all of these changes at the inception of the relationship, adjustments inevitably will have to be made by the parties during the course of performance. In a series of articles and an important book, Professor Ian R. Macneil has challenged many of the assumptions upon which both classical and contemporary principles of contract law are based as still misguidedly wedded to the traditional conception of contracts involving discrete transactions rather than long-term *relational* dealings between the parties. *See* MACNEIL, THE NEW SOCIAL CONTRACT (1980). Professor Macneil's work has important implications for the contract formation process, including the traditional demand of classical contract law that all material terms be agreed to at the moment of contracting. He suggests that while this may be possible in the typical one-shot deal, it is unrealistic in the long-term relational contract and is at odds with the needs of the parties to work collaboratively, rather than purely out of self-interest, during the course of their relationship. Ideally, the relational contract will serve more as a private constitution for the parties—setting forth the general standards that will govern their relationship—than an ordinary contract—setting forth in specific detail the terms of performance. In Professor Macneil's view, this should not make the contract any less enforceable in the eyes of the law.

While this is not the place to discuss the full impact of Professor Macneil's work, recognition of the relational character of many modern contracts does help provide perspective on the definiteness requirement and the impracticability of requiring complete projection of the transaction into the future through promises as a condition of meeting the law's demand for certainty. Indeed, while not necessarily reflected in the black-letter rules of contract law, the reality of contract litigation is that the character of the contract and the needs of the parties ultimately affect the degree of indefiniteness that the courts may be willing to allow. This tolerance suggests that the drafter of the long-term contract may be able to preserve some measure of flexibility for the parties in fashioning the agreement without running a serious risk that the agreement will later be declared to be too indefinite to enforce.

NOTE ON U.C.C. GAP FILLERS

The Uniform Commercial Code takes a very liberal attitude toward the definiteness requirement once it is established that the parties intended to be bound. Section 2–204 makes clear that the fact that one or more terms of a contract are left open does not render the contract too indefinite as long as the court concludes that (i) the parties intended to make a contract and (ii) there is a reasonable basis for affording an appropriate remedy.

This break with the traditional disinclination of common law judges to "make" a contract for the parties is consistent with the general philosophy of the drafters of the U.C.C. to bring the law into line with prevailing commercial practices and expectation. In many business contexts it is desirable, and sometimes even necessary, for the parties to be less than entirely clear in specifying one of the essential terms of the transaction. This can occur for a variety of reasons, ranging from uncertainty about future events to, in the case of agreements involving a series of performances over a lengthy period of time, an inability at the time of contracting to foresee every eventuality. For instance, in connection with the purchase and sale of a particular commodity subject to rapid price fluctuations, neither party may wish today to take the risk of an adverse move in the market. Nevertheless, if it is clear that they intend to be bound to one another at prevailing market prices at the time or times for performance, the thinking of the drafters was that this intention should not be frustrated merely because the parties left the price term open or tied it to an external standard. Similarly, if the parties clearly manifested an intention to be bound and expressed all of the other critical terms of their agreement but for, due to oversight, the place where delivery should occur, a contract for the sale of goods will not fail for indefiniteness.

The Code deals with these "open terms" in two ways. First, as discussed earlier, § 1–201(b)(3) defines "Agreement" as the parties' bargain-in-fact as ascertained not only from the language used but implied from "other circumstances including course of dealing or usage of trade or course of performance as provided in this Act." We will take up each of these concepts in Chapter 4 when we consider "What are the Terms of the Deal"? Second, the U.C.C. contains numerous "gap filling" provisions in Article 2. These provisions operate as "default rules" that supply the governing rule as to various aspects of the agreement if the parties, though intending to be bound, have failed to address the particular term.

Be sure that you understand this phrase "default rules." It is a phrase that your professor will use and expect you to use. And, when you graduate, it is a term that older lawyers will use in an effort to intimidate you.

"Default rule" does not mean that someone is in default. A default rule is a rule that applies where the parties have *not* otherwise agreed. Thus, if the parties to a contract governed by Article 2 fail to specify the time for shipment or delivery, the default rules in §§ 2–308 and 2–309(1) provide the missing term. Similarly, even if the parties omit the price term but otherwise intend to conclude a contract, default rule § 2–305(1) applies and "the price is a reasonable price at the time of delivery."

The one term in a sale of goods contract that cannot be supplied by a default rule is quantity; *e.g.,* how many bushels of grits. This is because unlike price, time for shipment, time for delivery, etc., it is impossible to determine a reasonable quantity.

In theory, default rules are designed to reflect what the parties *would have* agreed to had they spoken to the issue. In reality, they will sometimes hit their mark and sometimes miss. Moreover, we do not necessarily mean what *these* parties would have agreed to, since they failed to tell us what they wanted, but rather what reasonable persons in the position of these parties would have agreed to assuming that they were bargaining from relatively equal positions of strength. Some commentators have urged that perhaps it would be better in some instances if the default rule was not one that the parties would likely have agreed to had they spoken to the issue. Instead, it has been suggested that if the default rule is an unattractive one—one that neither party would presumably want—then there is more incentive for the parties to express their preference by negotiating more complete agreements. *See* Ian Ayres & Robert Gertner, *Filling Gaps in Incomplete Contracts: An Economics Theory of Default Rules,* 99 YALE L.J. 87 (1989) (distinguishing between "tailored" and "penalty" default rules and urging that in the interests of minimizing the costs of contracting "efficiency-minded courts and legislatures" should move "beyond the received wisdom that default rules should simply be what the majority of contracting parties would have wanted").

While Article 2 has no default rule to apply where the parties have not agreed on quantity, the parties nonetheless can agree on quantity without using actual numbers. Take a look at the *Black's Law Dictionary* of "outputs" and "requirements" contracts. § 2–306.

If Epstein agrees to buy all of the Viagra he needs from Jim Meyers Pharmacy, this is a requirements contract, and it is valid (enforceable) even though there is no specific quantity stated. If Ponoroff agrees to purchase all of the Mesquite Beer produced by the Mesquite microbrewery, this is an outputs contract and is valid despite the absence of a specific numerical quantity. Why?

B. PROBLEMS OF POSTPONED AGREEMENT

Sometimes during the course of their negotiations, parties will leave a key term of their deal open or vague not because they have failed to reach agreement, but because, although they consider themselves bound, they have deliberately decided to defer agreement on a particular term or aspect of their deal until a later time. This is most often because neither party wishes to make a future commitment until more facts are known or more information is available.

We call such arrangements "agreements to agree." If the parties later reach agreement on the open term everything is copasetic. When, however, the parties fail to come to agreement on that open term, the issue for the courts is whether the agreement as struck is too indefinite to enforce or whether the court should supply the missing term in order to save the deal. The next two cases reveal the approaches taken by courts in this situation.

QUESTIONS BEFORE THE CASE

1. Why would the parties deliberately leave a gap in their agreement?
2. If the court were to order enforcement of an agreement where a term had been left for later negotiation, would that deprive the parties of their freedom *not* to contract?

WALKER V. KEITH

Court of Appeals of Kentucky
382 S.W.2d 198 (1964)

CLAY, COMMISSIONER.

In this declaratory judgment proceeding the plaintiff appellee sought an adjudication that he had effectively exercised an option to extend a lease, and a further determination of the amount of rent to be paid. The relief prayed was granted by the Chancellor. The principal issue is whether the option provision in the lease fixed the rent with sufficient certainty to constitute an enforceable contract between the parties.

In July 1951 appellants, the lessors, leased a small lot to appellee, the lessee, for a 10-year term at a rent of $100 per month. The lessee was given an option to extend the lease for an additional 10-year term, under the same terms and conditions except as to rental. The renewal option provided:

> "rental will be fixed in such amount as shall actually be agreed upon by the lessors and the lessee with the monthly rental fixed

on the comparative basis of rental values as of the date of the renewal with rental values at this time reflected by the comparative business conditions of the two periods."

The lessee gave the proper notice to renew but the parties were unable to agree upon the rent. Preliminary court proceedings finally culminated in this lawsuit. Based upon the verdict of an advisory jury, the Chancellor fixed the new rent at $125 per month.

The question before us is whether the quoted provision is so indefinite and uncertain that the parties cannot be held to have agreed upon this essential rental term of the lease. There have been many cases from other jurisdictions passing on somewhat similar lease provisions and the decisions are in hopeless conflict. We have no authoritative Kentucky decision.

At the outset two observations may be made. One is that rental in the ordinary lease is a very uncomplicated item. It involves the number of dollars the lessee will pay. It, or a method of ascertaining it, can be so easily fixed with certainty. From the standpoint of stability in business transactions, it should be so fixed.

Secondly, as an original proposition, uncomplicated by subtle rules of law, the provision we have quoted, on its face, is ambiguous and indefinite. The language used is equivocal. It neither fixes the rent nor furnishes a positive key to its establishment. The terminology is not only confusing but inherently unworkable as a formula.

The above observations should resolve the issue. Unfortunately it is not that simple. Many courts have become intrigued with the possible import of similar language and have interpolated into it a binding obligation. The lease renewal option has been treated as something different from an ordinary contract. The law has become woefully complicated. For this reason we consider it necessary and proper to examine this question in depth.

The following basic principles of law are generally accepted:

"It is a necessary requirement in the nature of things that an agreement in order to be binding must be sufficiently definite to enable a court to give it an exact meaning." Williston on Contracts (3rd Ed.) Vol. 1, section 37 (page 107).

"Like other contracts or agreements for a lease, the provision for a renewal must be certain in order to render it binding and enforceable. Indefiniteness, vagueness, and uncertainty in the terms of such a provision will render it void unless the parties, by their subsequent conduct or acts supplement the covenant and thus remove an alleged uncertainty. The certainty that is required is such as will enable a court to determine what has been agreed upon." 32 Am.Jur., Landlord and Tenant, section 958 (page 806).

"The terms of an extension or renewal, under an option therefor in a lease, may be left for future determination by a prescribed method, as by future arbitration or appraisal; but merely leaving the terms for future ascertainment, without providing a method for their determination, renders the agreement unenforceable for uncertainty." 51 C.J.S. Landlord and Tenant 56b (2), page 597. * * *

The degree of certainty is the controlling consideration. An example of an appropriate method by which a non-fixed rental could be determined appears in *Jackson v. Pepper Gasoline Co.,* 280 Ky. 226, 133 S.W.2d 91, 126 A.L.R. 1370. The lessee, who operated an automobile service station, agreed to pay "an amount equal to one cent per gallon of gasoline delivered to said station". Observing that the parties had created a definite objective standard by which the rent could with certainty be computed, the court upheld the lease as against the contention that it was lacking in mutuality. * * *

On the face of the rent provision, the parties had not agreed upon a rent figure. They left the amount to future determination. If they had agreed upon a specific method of making the determination, such as by computation, the application of a formula, or the decision of an arbitrator, they could be said to have agreed upon whatever rent figure emerged from utilization of the method. This was not done.

It will be observed the rent provision expresses two ideas. The first is that the parties agree to agree. The second is that the future agreement will be based on a comparative adjustment in the light of "business conditions". We will examine separately these two concepts and then consider them as a whole.

The lease purports to fix the rent at such an amount as shall "actually be agreed upon." It should be obvious that an agreement to agree cannot constitute a binding contract. Williston on Contracts (3rd Ed.) Vol. 1, section 45 (page 149) * * *

As said in Williston on Contracts (3rd Ed.) Vol. 1, section 45 (page 149):

"Although a promise may be sufficiently definite when it contains an option given to the promisor, yet if an essential element is reserved for the future agreement of both parties, the promise gives rise to no legal obligation until such future agreement. Since either party, by the very terms of the agreement, may refuse to agree to anything the other party will agree to, it is impossible for the law to fix any obligation to such a promise."

We accept this because it is both sensible and basic to the enforcement of a written contract. We applied it in *Johnson v. Lowery, Ky.*, 270 S.W.2d 943, page 946, wherein we said:

> "To be enforceable and valid, a contract to enter into a future covenant must specify all material and essential terms and leave nothing to be agreed upon as a result of future negotiations."

This proposition is not universally accepted as it pertains to renewal options in a lease. We have examined the reasons set forth in those opinions and do not find them convincing. The view is taken that the renewal option is for the benefit of the lessee; that the parties intended something; and that the lessee should not be deprived of his right to enforce his contract. This reasoning seems to overlook the fact that a party must have an enforceable contract before he has a right to enforce it. We wonder if these courts would enforce an original lease in which the rent was not fixed, but agreed to be agreed upon.

Surely there are some limits to what equity can or should undertake to compel parties in their private affairs to do what the court thinks they should have done. * * * In any event, we are not persuaded that renewal options in leases are of such an exceptional character as to justify emasculation of one of the basic rules of contract law. An agreement to agree simply does not fix an enforceable obligation.

As noted, however, the language of the renewal option incorporated a secondary stipulation. Reference was made to "comparative business conditions" which were to play some part in adjusting the new rental. It is contended this provides the necessary certainty, and we will examine a leading case which lends support to the argument.

In *Edwards v. Tobin,* 132 Or. 38, 284 P. 562, 68 A.L.R. 152, the court upheld and enforced a lease agreement which provided that the rent should be "determined" at the time of renewal, "said rental to be a *reasonable rental* under the then existing conditions". (Our emphasis) Significance was attached to the last quoted language, the court reasoning that since the parties had agreed upon a reasonable rent, the court would hold the parties to the agreement by fixing it.

All rents tend to be reasonable. When parties are trying to reach an agreement, however, their ideas or claims of reasonableness may widely differ. In addition, they have a right to bargain. They cannot be said to be in agreement about what is a reasonable rent until they specify a figure or an exact method of determining it. The term "reasonable rent" is itself indefinite and uncertain. Would an original lease for a "reasonable rent" be enforceable by either party? The very purpose of a rental stipulation is to remove this item from an abstract area.

It is true courts often must imply such terms in a contract as "reasonable time" or "reasonable price". This is done when the parties fail to deal with such matters in an otherwise enforceable contract. Here the parties were undertaking to fix the terms rather than leave them to implication. Our problem is not what the law would imply if the contract did not purport to cover the subject matter, but whether the parties, in removing this material term from the field of implication, have fixed their mutual obligations.

We are seeking what the agreement actually was. When dealing with such a specific item as rent, to be payable in dollars, the area of possible agreement is quite limited. If the parties did not agree upon such an unequivocal item or upon a definite method of ascertaining it, then there is a clear case of nonagreement. The court, in fixing an obligation under a non-agreement, is not enforcing the contract but is binding the parties to something they were patently unable to agree to when writing the contract.

The opinion in the *Tobin* case, which purportedly was justifying the enforcement of a contractual obligation between the lessor and lessee, shows on its face the court was doing something entirely different. This question was posed in the opinion: "What logical reason is there for equity to refuse to act when the parties themselves *fail to agree* on the rental?" (Our emphasis) The obvious logical answer is that even equity cannot enforce as a contract a nonagreement. No distortion of words can hide the fact that when the court admits the parties "fail to agree," then the contract it enforces is one it makes for the parties.

* * *

We have examined the *Tobin* case at length because it exemplifies lines of reasoning adopted by some courts to dredge certainty from uncertainty. Other courts balk at the process. The majority of cases, passing upon the question of whether a renewal option providing that the future rent shall be dependent upon or proportionate to the valuation of the property at the time of renewal, hold that such provision is not sufficiently certain to constitute an enforceable agreement. * * * The valuation of property and the ascertainment of "comparative business conditions," which we have under consideration, involve similar uncertainties.

* * *

We do not think our problem can be solved by determining which is the "majority" rule and which is the "minority" rule. We are inclined, however, to adhere to a sound basic principle of contract law unless there are impelling reasons to depart from it, particularly so when the practical problems involved in such departure are so manifest. Let us briefly examine those practical problems.

What the law requires is an adequate key to a mutual agreement. If "comparative business conditions" afforded sufficient certainty, we might possibly surmount the obstacle of the unenforceable agreement to agree. This term, however is very broad indeed. Did the parties have in mind local conditions, national conditions, or conditions affecting the lessee's particular business?

* * *

We realize that litigation is oft times inevitable and courts should not shrink from the solution of difficult problems. On the other hand, courts should not expend their powers to establish contract rights which the parties, with an opportunity to do so, have failed to define. As said in *Morrison v. Rossignol,* 5 Cal. 64, quoted in 30 A.L.R. at page 579:

> "A court of equity is always chary of its power to decree specific performance, and will withhold the exercise of its jurisdiction in that respect, unless there is such a degree of certainty in the terms of the contract as will enable it at one view to do complete equity."

That cannot be done in this case.

Stipulations such as the one before us have been the source of interminable litigation. Courts are called upon not to enforce an agreement or to determine what the agreement was, but to write their own concept of what would constitute a proper one. Why this paternalistic task should be undertaken is difficult to understand when the parties could so easily provide any number of workable methods by which rents could be adjusted. As a practical matter, courts sometimes must assert their right not to be imposed upon. This thought was thus summed up in *Slayter v. Pasley, Or.*, 264 P.2d 444, page 449:

> "We should be hesitant about completing an apparently legally incomplete agreement made between persons sui juris enjoying freedom of contract and dealing at arms' length by arbitrarily interpolating into it our concept of the parties' intent merely to validate what would otherwise be an invalid instrument, lest we inadvertently commit them to an ostensible agreement which, in fact, is contrary to the deliberate design of all of them. It is a dangerous doctrine when examined in the light of reason. Judicial paternalism of this character should be as obnoxious to courts as is legislation by judicial fiat. Both import a quality of jural ego and superiority not consonant with long-accepted ideas of legistic propriety under a democratic form of government. If, however, we follow the urgings of the lessee in the instant matter, we will thereby establish a precedent which will open the door to repeated opportunities to do that which, in principle, courts should not do and, in any event, are not adequately equipped to do."

We think the basic principle of contract law that requires substantial certainty as to the material terms upon which the minds of the parties have met is a sound one and should be adhered to. A renewal option stands on the same footing as any other contract right. Rent is a material term of a lease. If the parties do not fix it with reasonable certainty, it is not the business of courts to do so.

The renewal provision before us was fatally defective in failing to specify either an agreed rental or an agreed method by which it could be fixed with certainty. Because of the lack of agreement, the lessee's option right was illusory. The Chancellor erred in undertaking to enforce it.

The judgment is reversed.

QUESTIONS

1. Questions about the facts of this case

   1.1. Why didn't the parties simply fix the rent for the option period in their original lease agreement?

   1.2. The reported decision in *Walker* does not indicate why the parties were unable to reach agreement upon the rent for the option period. Suppose it was because the lessor insisted on an outrageously high figure relative to market value or the lessee demanded an equally outrageous number on the low side. Would those facts have been relevant to the court? Do you think the reason why the parties were unable to reach agreement should matter to a court in deciding whether to imply a "reasonable rate" of rent?

2. Questions about the law

   2.1. If, as the court of appeals suggests, the determination of rental value is such an uncomplicated affair, why did it set aside the Chancellor's determination of $125 per month?

   2.2. As the court seems to recognize, the effect of its decision in *Walker* is to leave the lessee without the right to enforce the option. Do you think that's what the parties contemplated when the renewal option was negotiated, that the lessee would have an option enforceable only at the pleasure of the lessor?

3. **You Be the Lawyer!**

   The court in *Walker* indicates that the parties did not in their original agreement specify an objective method or standard for determining rent in the option period. Do you agree with this conclusion? How would you redraft the renewal option provision so as to satisfy the court of appeals?

QUESTIONS BEFORE THE CASE

1. Why do lease renewal agreements present particularly compelling cases for enforcement of a postponed term?
2. In filling in the postponed term is the court effectuating the intent of the parties or is something else going on? Are you getting a little sick of that question?

MOOLENAAR V. CO-BUILD COMPANIES, INC.

District Court of the Virgin Islands
354 F.Supp. 980 (1973)

WARREN H. YOUNG, DISTRICT JUDGE.

This case involves the proper construction of the renewal clause in a lease. Briefly stated, two issues are presented. First, is a valid and specifically enforceable renewal option created by a clause which leaves the rent for this period to be determined by subsequent agreement between the parties? And secondly, if the clause is valid but the parties are unable to agree on the rent, how is this rental figure to be determined? Here I must decide whether the court must look to fair market value at the time when the option is exercised, or whether the court may take a lower figure if it is shown that the parties contemplated that the land would be put to less than its most remunerative use. For the reasons given below, I hold that such a renewal clause contains an implicit term that the new rent shall be fixed at its "reasonable" or "fair market" value. The clause is thus specific enough to be valid and enforceable. I further hold that parol evidence is admissible to explain this implicit term, and to show that the parties intended the rent to be set at the fair market value of the land as if it were subject to certain use restrictions.

The facts of this case are not in dispute. In October of 1967, plaintiff Moolenaar, a sheep and goat farmer, leased 150 acres of land from one Aurea Correa. His leasehold was to run for a period of five years with an option to renew for an additional five. Moolenaar was to pay $375 per month during the initial term, but the rent for the renewal period "shall be renegotiated."[1] Moolenaar took possession under this lease and expanded his sheep and goat farm onto the demised premises. Before the time came

---

[1] The renewal clause provides in full as follows:

4. OPTION OF RENEWAL: Provided that Tenant shall not be declared in default at any time during the term hereof, the Tenant shall be entitled to an option to extend the term of this lease for an additional period of FIVE (5) YEARS upon the same terms and conditions except that the rental shall be renegotiated.

to exercise the renewal option, however, Mrs. Correa sold the land to real estate speculators who in turn sold it to West Indies Enterprises, the predecessor corporation to the defendant Co-Build Companies, Inc. ("Co-Build"). The new owners nonetheless took subject to Moolenaar's rights under the pre-existing and duly recorded lease. At this point I should mention that the testimony disclosed, and I so find, that the representatives of Co-Build negotiating the purchase of the land had actual knowledge of the lease and its renewal clause. They discussed its validity or purported lack of validity with their counsel and accepted title insurance with an exception taken by the title insurer to the rights of the tenant in possession, including the lease renewal clause.

In April of 1972, some six months before the first five year term expired, Moolenaar informed Co-Build of his intention to exercise the renewal option. Co-Build expressed its willingness to extend the lease at a "renegotiated" rent of $17,000 per month. Co-Build justified this figure by the high price it had paid for the land, and by its unquestionably great value if put to industrial use. Such a rent, however, is obviously beyond the resources of the less profitable goat husbandry business. Moolenaar therefore proposed a considerably lower figure and indicated his desire to meet for direct negotiations. All such offers were declined. Upon Co-Build's refusal to recede from its initial position, Moolenaar filed the present action for a declaratory judgment setting out the rights of the parties under the lease.

I

The threshold question is, of course, whether Moolenaar possesses a renewal option at all. A number of jurisdictions would hold that he does not, reasoning that a clause which neglects to stipulate the rent is void for uncertainty and indefiniteness. * * * The better view, however, would hold that such a clause intends renewal at a "reasonable" rent, and would find that market conditions are ascertainable with sufficient certainty to make the clause specifically enforceable. A number of policy considerations support this result. First, it will probably effectuate the intent of the parties better than would striking out the clause altogether. A document should be construed where possible to give effect to every term, on the theory that the signatories inserted each for a reason and if one party had agreed to the clause only in the secret belief that it would prove unenforceable, he should be discouraged from such paths. Secondly, a renewal option has a more sympathetic claim to enforcement than do most vague contractual terms, since valuable consideration will often have already been paid for it. The option of renewal is one factor inducing the tenant to enter into the lease, or to pay as high a rent as he did during the initial period. To this extent the landlord benefited from the tenant's reliance on the clause, and so the tenant has a stronger claim to receive the reciprocal benefit of the option. * * *

It then remains to be determined only whether this resolution is within the powers of the Court. In the absence of an applicable statute, the Restatement of Contracts has been designated as positive law in this jurisdiction. Section 32 of the Restatement provides that a contract is valid if it is "so definite in its terms" that the "performances to be rendered by each party are reasonably certain." Under this standard the renewal clause would appear sufficiently definite to be binding. * * *

Even if it were thought that the Restatement is ambiguous or silent on the precise issue *sub judice*, Moolenaar would still recover. In that case we must make our determination under the common law "as generally understood" in courts of other jurisdictions. The rule which I have followed here is admittedly the minority view. * * * But for the reasons which I gave in an earlier opinion, I think it is appropriate to give greater weight to recent decisions rather than weighing the authorities on a strictly numerical basis. * * * Briefly, the common law is in a state of perpetual evolution and recent decisions will more accurately reflect the current understanding on an issue. For the issue at hand the minority view is nonetheless a widely followed one * * * and has been gaining adherents at a rate which indicates that the common law is moving in that direction. * * * And while, of course, not controlling here, the U.C.C. provisions on the Sale of Goods also illustrate the approach of the modern law, with its emphasis on reasonable commercial dealings and its rejection of technical requirements. [U.C.C. § 2–305] provides as follows:

> (1) The parties if they so intend can conclude a contract for sale even though the price is not settled. In such a case the price is a reasonable price at the time for delivery if
>
> (a) nothing is said as to price; or
>
> (b) the price is left to be agreed by the parties and they fail to agree. * * *"

The comments to this section are also informative, and state in part as follows:

> This article rejects in these instances the formula that "an agreement to agree is unenforceable" * * * and rejects also defeating such agreements on the grounds of "indefiniteness." Instead this Article recognizes the dominant intention of the parties to have the deal continue to be binding upon both.

For all the above reasons, I hold that the renewal clause is valid and enforceable.

II

Given that the clause is enforceable, there remains the question of what rent Moolenaar should pay during the additional five years. As a general rule the "reasonable rent" will be established at its "fair market value," which is to say, at the highest rent which a responsible bidder is apt to offer. This in turn suggests that the leasehold should be valued at its "highest and best use," for a lessee using the land in the most intensive and remunerative way possible will be able to outbid a person who would use it less efficiently. From this Co-Build asks us to conclude that the rent should be many times higher than it had been, since the 150 acres are now zoned 1–2 and may be subdivided for light industry.

Nonetheless, I believe that Moolenaar is entitled to have the rent established at its fair value for the land as used for agricultural or animal husbandry purposes only. I conclude that this will most accurately reflect the intent of the original signatories to the lease. From the testimony presented at trial, I find that Mrs. Correa intended that Moolenaar be able to use the land for the purpose of raising sheep and goats during the renewal period, and that the rent be set at a fair value for this purpose. It is true that under this arrangement she will lose the possibility of a higher rent if circumstances changed to make a more profitable use practicable. But one purpose of a long-term lease, or of a renewal clause, is precisely to insulate the parties from such changes in circumstances. In any event, I further find that Mrs. Correa was aware of such possibilities but determined that she was willing to see the land remain in an agricultural state for ten years, and so accepted a rent low enough to make this possible.

Co-Build then took title to the land subject to the provisions of the lease as outlined above. In other circumstances, a new owner who has purchased land subject to a lease might defeat the lower agricultural-use rental by arguing lack of notice. The lease states that the land may be used for any legal purpose, and from that a purchaser might reasonably conclude that the rent is to be set according to the "highest and best" such purpose. Nothing in the document indicates the contrary, and a bona fide purchaser charged with constructive notice of the recorded lease ordinarily should not be bound by additional parol understandings which would depart from the basic presumption of fair market valuation.

I believe, however, that Co-Build is fairly chargeable with actual notice of the circumstances here. At the time the company acquired the property in 1970, it was zoned R-10. This classification permitted agricultural use or residential in quarter-acre lots. The latter use is obviously impractical where, as here, the land can be held only for an additional five-year term. Thus, it was evident that the landlord and tenant had contemplated continuous agricultural or animal husbandry use. When Co-Build bought the land, it could well have deduced the nature of the underlying understanding in the lease agreement which encumbered the land. It was to this agreement that the company succeeded when it acquired the land. A subsequent change in the zoning laws should not be permitted to defeat that understanding. I find that the "renegotiation" clause was intended to deal only with fluctuations in real estate values and was not intended to permit a response to the major contingency of rezoning. In any event, the clause had a built-in "red flag" to put Co-Build on a duty of inquiry, since execution of the lease under the old zoning law would at least have left the intentions of the parties unclear. This duty would not have been burdensome; those who participated in the drafting of the original lease were available on St. Croix and in San Juan.

Since the parties have been unable to agree on a fair rental value for agricultural purposes, that figure will now be determined by the Court. The testimony at trial indicated that the present rental of $375 per month is, if anything, somewhat high for grazing use. Nonetheless I must take this figure as a freely bargained one, and hence fair. I also feel that I should make a rough adjustment for intervening inflation. A round figure of $400 per month would seem appropriate in the circumstances. Therefore, from the expert testimony given by Mr. Roebuck who has been engaged for many years in St. Croix in the sheep and goat husbandry business, and from the expert testimony of Mr. Hamilton who made an appraisal of the land on a rather novel but nonetheless convincing basis, I find that a reasonable rental would be $400 per month. With all due respect to Mr. Gaztambide, a most learned, respected and highly professional real property appraiser in Puerto Rico and the Virgin Islands, I must reject his appraisal but only for the reason that it was determined on the basis of the land's highest and most productive use—which, for the reasons explained herein—cannot be used in arriving at the reasonable rental for the use contemplated by the original parties to the lease agreement.

* * *

A declaratory judgment will be entered in accordance with this Opinion.

DECLARATORY JUDGMENT

For the reasons set forth in the Memorandum Opinion above, it is hereby adjudged and declared as follows:

1. The renewal clause is valid and enforceable.
2. The clause contemplates a rent for the additional term at a reasonable rate, as calculated by the value of the land for agricultural and animal husbandry purposes.
3. The fair rental in this case is $400 per month, retroactive to the end of the original five-year term.

QUESTIONS AND NOTES

1. Questions about the facts of this case

   1.1. Review the renewal option provisions in both *Walker* and *Moolenaar*. Which provision provided a greater insight into the intention of the parties concerning rent for the option term?

   1.2. Of what significance was the fact in *Moolenaar* that Co-Build refused to meet for direct negotiations?

   1.3. Other than its "roundness," on what factual basis does the court conclude that $400 per month constituted a reasonable rent?

2. Questions about the law

   2.1. In *Walker,* the court dismissed the lessee's equities in the renewal option stating that the lessee is not deprived of the right to enforce the option provision if there is no enforceable contract to begin with. How does the *Moolenaar* court's analysis of the issue differ?

   2.2. Does Co-Build have any claim against the prior owners of the property based on the fact that it will be precluded for five years from putting the land to its highest and best use? Does the answer to that question have any bearing on Moolenaar's right to have rent determined based on the value of the land used for agricultural and animal husbandry, rather than industrial, purposes?

   2.3. Would the case have been decided differently if, after further negotiations, Co-Build had agreed to $1,000 per month in rent during the option term? How about $500 per month? In other words, does the lessee have a claim any time there's a failure to agree?

3. Notes

   3.1. The basis for the traditional reluctance to enforce agreements to agree, even when the parties have manifested an intent to be immediately bound, has been that since there is no assurance that the parties themselves would have reached agreement on the postponed term, the court has no basis for supplying the omitted term in order to enforce the contract. Thus, the courts tended to distinguish cases where the parties simply *neglected* to include a material term—implying a reasonable term—from cases where the parties acknowledged a conscious awareness of the term and deliberately chose to defer agreement. Nevertheless, doubtless influenced by the liberal attitude taken in the Uniform Commercial Code toward enforcing incomplete agreements, decisions like *Moolenaar* represent the trend of modern authority. *Restatement (Second) of Contracts* § 33, illus. 11 offers the following example.

A promises B to construct a building according to stated plans and specification, and B promises to pay A $30,000 therefor. It is also provided that the character of the window fasteners shall be subject to further agreement of the parties. Unless a contrary intention is manifested, the indefiniteness of the agreement with reference to this matter will not prevent the formation of a contract.

3.2. If a particular agreement is too indefinite at its inception to enforce, may that initial indefiniteness as to material terms subsequently be cured by construing those indefinite terms with reference to the parties' performance up to the point that the dispute arises? *See Blackhawk Heating & Plumbing Co. v. Data Lease Financial Corp.*, 302 So.2d 404 (Fla. 1974).

3.3. Obviously, careful drafting of the agreement at the onset can eliminate most of the issues relating to indefiniteness. This is true even when the parties deliberately decide to leave a term open because neither wants to take the risk of adverse market fluctuations or the parties otherwise desire to defer agreement on a particular term until a later time.

In either case, the keys are to indicate clearly somewhere in the writing the parties' intention to be bound and then to point the court toward a mechanism for supplying the missing term. For instance, if the price term is deliberately left open, it behooves the drafter to set forth in the agreement the parties' intention that the price should be set by "fair market value" or some other measurable external standard as of a date certain.

Sometimes, however, particular terms of an agreement will not be addressed because the parties have not really reached agreement on an important issue and perhaps don't want to address it for fear of having the whole deal fall apart over it. If the lawyer who is commissioned to document the deal makes a point of pressing the matter she is likely to receive a chilly reception from her client. On the other hand, if she drafts the agreement without addressing this important term there is a risk that it will not be enforceable, a result also likely to make for an unhappy client. How would you handle this dilemma if you were that lawyer?

3.4. Recall from the Note on U.C.C. gap fillers that particular problems arise when the omitted term relates to quantity. Nevertheless, sometimes a buyer will want to be assured of a specific source of supply and will even be willing to commit to a fixed price, but does not yet know what its needs are and does not wish to be obligated to exclusivity or to purchase more than it needs or to have a commitment for less than is required. Because, unlike the price term, it is virtually impossible for a court to determine what is a *reasonable* quantity, how would you address this problem as a drafting matter from your buyer/client's perspective? Can similar issues arise from the seller's side?

4. **You Be the Lawyer!**

After losing this case, Co-Build's senior vice president, Cruella De Ville, contacts you. She's quite angry about the decision, and tells you, "given what we paid for this land, we can't afford to wait five years before converting it to industrial use; we need some help." What do you recommend to Ms. De Ville?

We have now seen that if the parties intend to be bound, the courts will endeavor to enforce that intention even if the parties' expression of that agreement is unclear or incomplete. The key is that there must be an intent to be bound to something; *i.e.*, mutual assent. Until that point, of course, the traditional view is that either party is free to break off negotiations without fear of being in breach of contract. In the business world, no less than in the flea market, fervent negotiations sometimes lead nowhere and the parties go off in search of other opportunities. Inevitably, time and money are spent during the course of these negotiations in the hope that they will lead to the consummation of a mutually advantageous bargain. If these hopes are not ultimately realized, ordinarily each party absorbs its own out-of-pocket expenses, recognizing them simply as the costs of doing business.

In certain circumstances, however, these costs can be substantial and one party may feel that the other *ought* to be held accountable for these costs—but on what basis?

Common law courts, steeped in the traditional approach to contractual liability, were reluctant to establish an intermediate point after the commencement of negotiations but before the conclusion of the final agreement at which liability might attach. But the traditional "contract/no contract" distinction was a product of a simpler time and simpler transactions. Sophisticated modern business transactions, such as corporate mergers and acquisitions, require multiple points of agreement that must be reached before the deal is final, and because of the number and complexity of issues to be resolved, the agreement tends to come together in stages or pieces over time. These transactions are "heavily lawyered," and at some stage in the process the lawyers will memorialize the points of agreement reached so far, and the matters still subject to negotiation, in a document typically called an "agreement in principle" or "letter of intent." Professor Farnsworth described additional purposes for the letter of intent as follows:

> Usually the parties expect that a record of the understandings that they have reached at a particular stage will facilitate further negotiations. Such a record may prevent misunderstandings, suggest formulas for reaching further agreements, and provide a basis for drafting a definitive text. The parties may also anticipate that it will inform others of the progress of the negotiations. It may be of interest to employees or shareholders of the negotiating parties and to third parties such as prospective lenders and investors. At least one party may hope that it will enhance its position in future negotiations. Thus it may make it harder for the other party to withdraw concessions, especially if they have been made known to prospective lenders and investors, and more disadvantageous for the other party to allow the negotiations to fail, especially if the prospect of success has been made public.

E. Allan Farnsworth, *Precontractual Liability and Preliminary Agreements: Fair Dealing and Failed Negotiations*, 87 COLUM. L. REV. 217, 257–58 (1987).

Because, unlike in the "agreement to agree" cases, neither of the parties is ready at the letter of intent stage to commit to the transaction *in toto*, the letter of intent will also almost always contain a standard "not legally binding" clause indicating that the writing is not intended as a legal agreement or that the understandings expressed in the letter shall not be binding pending, among other things, regulatory approvals, execution of definitive documentation, or further agreement on matters as yet unresolved.

Under the *Restatement (Second) of Contracts* § 21, express manifestations of the parties that their legal relations are not to be affected are generally accorded deference by the courts. In some cases, however, a court may be persuaded that the letter, though denominated "non-binding," nevertheless evidenced the parties' intention to make a binding agreement. *See Borg-Warner Corp. v. Anchor Coupling,* 16 Ill.2d 234, 156 N.E.2d 513 (1958). A less extreme view is to regard the letter of intent as imposing a duty to negotiate in good faith independent of the underlying transaction. Under this view, while neither party is yet bound to the principal transaction, neither may walk away from negotiations without having made every reasonable effort to conclude the deal.

If one party breaches such "contract to bargain," how should the other party's damages be measured? If the parties do not express an undertaking to engage in further good faith negotiations, how far should the court go in implying one? Are there alternative legal theories that a disappointed suitor might pursue when the other party breaks off negotiations before a final agreement can be concluded? One court's answers to some of these questions can be found in the next case.

QUESTIONS BEFORE THE CASE

1. Under what circumstances should a court enforce a preliminary agreement?
2. Even if the preliminary agreement itself is not enforced, under what circumstances should a court consider imposing liability when the final agreement is never concluded?

BUDGET MARKETING, INC. V. CENTRONICS CORPORATION

United States Court of Appeals, Eighth Circuit
927 F.2d 421 (1991), *appeal after remand*, 979 F.2d 1333 (1992)

GIBSON, CIRCUIT JUDGE.

Budget Marketing, Inc. (BMI) and Charles A. Eagle appeal from an order of summary judgment denying their claims against Centronics Corporation for: (1) breach of implied duty to negotiate in good faith; (2) promissory estoppel; and (3) negligent misrepresentation. This suit arises out of the breakdown in negotiations for the purchase of BMI by Centronics. The district court also entered summary judgment against Centronics on its counterclaim of negligent misrepresentation. Both parties appeal. We affirm in part, but reverse on BMI's and Eagle's claim of promissory estoppel and remand for further consideration of this issue.

BMI is a Des Moines-based firm that markets and services magazine subscription agreements. Eagle is the president and principal shareholder of BMI. Centronics is a Delaware corporation based in New Hampshire.

In April 1987, BMI and Centronics executed a letter of intent outlining the basic terms of a proposed acquisition of BMI by Centronics. The letter stated that: (1) initial consideration would be $10 million; (2) additional consideration of up to $7 million would be contingent upon BMI meeting certain cash flow objectives over a 36-month period; (3) Centronics would provide additional capital during the 36-month "earn out" period, but BMI was responsible for cash needs until closing; and (4) BMI was responsible for dealing with any outstanding Federal Trade Commission or Federal Reserve complaints. The letter of intent also stated that completion of the merger depended on four express conditions: (1) satisfactory completion of an accounting, legal, and business review of BMI by Centronics; (2) purchase by BMI of "key man" life insurance coverage for Eagle; (3) avoidance by Centronics of a "significant cash outlay" for taxes because of BMI's planned change in accounting methods; and (4) execution of a definitive and legally binding agreement between BMI and Centronics.

The letter of intent provided that the transaction was subject to approval by the boards of directors of both corporations and by the BMI shareholders. It also contained a specific disclaimer: "This letter shall not be construed as a binding agreement on the part of BMI or Centronics." The letter set a target date for a definitive agreement of May 31, 1987.

Between January and May 1987, Centronics' officials carefully evaluated BMI. On May 21, the parties executed an addendum to the letter of intent that included changes favorable to Centronics. The Centronics' board approved the addendum on May 26, 1987. The addendum changed the target date for the definitive documents to June 30, 1987.

Other steps leading to the proposed merger followed: Centronics' public relations firm issued a press release about the letter of intent, the directors of BMI's parent company and the BMI shareholders approved the proposed merger, and Centronics received all documents necessary to complete the legal, business, and accounting review of BMI.

At the same time, Centronics began considering the acquisition of companies larger than BMI, and, in June 1987, made a formal proposal to acquire the assets of Ecko Group, Inc., for $127 million. In August, Centronics sent its draft of the final agreement to BMI.

Meanwhile, BMI and Eagle began taking the steps necessary to meet the conditions imposed by the letter of intent. Eagle borrowed $750,000 for BMI's use that he personally secured. BMI opened additional branch offices and expanded existing branch operations. BMI also purchased "key man" life insurance coverage for Eagle. Throughout the summer and fall of 1987, Eagle kept Centronics informed of BMI's expansion efforts and the other developments.

During this time, Centronics did not disclose that it might not complete the deal. In August, a Centronics representative confirmed a planned closing date no later than September 30 during a conversation with an official of Norwest Bank, BMI's lender. In mid-September, a Centronics executive participated in a meeting with BMI representatives, an investment banker from R.G. Dickinson, and representatives of Norwest Bank regarding post-closing financing for BMI. All of those present at the meeting proceeded on the assumption that the deal would close, and the Centronics representative said nothing to the contrary. In October, a Centronics representative discussed with a BMI official a necessary SEC filing that would have to be completed after closing. Also in October, Centronics' president and chief executive officer, Robert Stein, told Philip Boesel, an investment banker with R.G. Dickinson who had been involved with the planned merger, that Centronics was ready to move toward closing the deal with BMI.

In November 1987, Centronics abruptly halted preparations for the merger. After evaluating proposed federal tax legislation, Stein sent a letter to Eagle stating that in spite of Centronics' "good faith efforts," conditions beyond its control made the deal "no longer feasible." The letter stated that the merger would lead to a cash outlay for taxes because of BMI's change in accounting methods, thereby triggering one of the negative conditions of the letter of intent.

On appeal, BMI challenges Centronics' stated reason for terminating negotiations as mere "pretext"[3] because the proposed tax legislation did not apply to the proposed merger and the change of accounting methods would not in fact have resulted in Centronics having to make a cash outlay for taxes.

Eagle and BMI brought this action against Centronics, alleging that together they had invested "hundreds of thousands of dollars" to meet the cash flow requirements of the letter of intent. Eagle and BMI originally filed suit in an Iowa district court, but Centronics removed the case to federal court. Centronics filed a counterclaim alleging negligent misrepresentation concerning an FTC investigation of BMI and BMI's financial prospects.

The district court granted Centronics' motion for summary judgment, concluding that: (1) Centronics breached no agreement to acquire BMI: (2) the letter of intent disclaimed a duty to negotiate in good faith; (3) Centronics made no agreement or promise that was sufficiently definite to support recovery under promissory estoppel; and (4) Centronics owed BMI and Eagle no duty to supply the information upon which the negligent misrepresentation claim was based. * * * The court also granted BMI's motion for summary judgment on Centronics' counterclaim. Both parties appeal.

* * *

I.

BMI concedes that the letter of intent did not constitute a binding agreement to merge, but it contends that the letter did establish a duty on the part of both parties to negotiate in good faith. Breach of that duty, it argues, entitles BMI to reliance damages. Specifically, BMI points to language in the letter setting a target date for executing a definitive agreement and stating that the definitive agreement "will contain mutually agreed terms." BMI further points to the extensive efforts devoted by both parties to bring the merger to fruition during the months preceding and following the execution of the letter as confirming the existence of a good faith duty.

Centronics counters by arguing that the specific language in the letter stating that it "shall not be construed as a binding agreement on the part

[3] BMI alleges that the October 1987 stock market "crash" caused Centronics to be interested in other, more lucrative acquisition opportunities.

of BMI or Centronics" means that no binding agreement to negotiate in good faith existed between the parties.

The district court found that the language of the letter of intent "plainly disclaimed any such [implied] duty." * * *

BMI relies primarily on three cases, Teachers Insurance & Annuity Association v. Tribune Company, 670 F. Supp. 491 (S.D.N.Y. 1987); Channel Home Centers v. Grossman, 795 F.2d 291 (3d Cir. 1986); Itek Corp. v. Chicago Aerial Industries, Inc., 248 A.2d 625 (Del. 1968), arguing that the overall language of the letter, coupled with the parties' conduct, gave rise to an implied duty to negotiate in good faith. The facts of these three cases are plainly distinguishable from the facts before us now.

In *Teachers Insurance & Annuity Association*, the parties had signed a financing commitment letter that, far from disclaiming an intent to be bound, stated that the parties had entered a " 'binding agreement.' " 670 F. Supp. at 491. The court concluded that " 'the intention to create mutually binding contractual obligations is stated with unmistakable clarity. * * *' " *Id.* at 499.

Such an intent is not present here. The letter of intent between BMI and Centronics clearly stated that it should not be construed as a binding agreement "except for the confidentiality obligations set forth in paragraphs 11 and 12." The fact that the parties expressly designated the confidentiality obligations as the sole exception to the general disclaimer lends further support to our conclusion that no binding agreement to negotiate in good faith can be implied from the overall language of the letter. In *Teachers Insurance & Annuity Association*, the court observed that it must determine the intent of the parties "at the time of their entry into the understanding," 670 F. Supp. at 499, and that a party not wanting to be bound by a preliminary letter can "very easily protect itself by not accepting language that indicates a 'firm commitment' or 'binding agreement.' " *Id.* With these observations in mind, we conclude that the parties here evinced no intent to be bound at the time they signed the letter; the letter clearly disclaims that it is a binding agreement.

Similarly, in *Channel Home Centers*, the Third Circuit found that a detailed letter of intent, signed by a property owner and a prospective tenant, gave rise to a duty to negotiate in good faith because the parties intended their promise to be binding. 795 F.2d at 299–300. The court concluded that the agreement contained "an unequivocal promise by [the landlord] to withdraw the store from the rental market and to negotiate the proposed leasing transaction with [the prospective tenant] to completion." *Id.* at 299. No such binding promises are contained in the letter signed by BMI and Centronics. Moreover, *Channel Home Centers* does not suggest that such promises can be implied in the presence of express language disclaiming an intent to be bound.

Finally, *Itek* is equally unpersuasive. The *Itek* court, applying Illinois law, concluded that a jury could find that the parties entered a binding agreement to negotiate in good faith. 248 A.2d at 629. The court relied in part on language in the letter of intent stating that although the parties would have " 'no further obligation' " to each other if they failed to reach ultimate agreement, they would " 'make every reasonable effort' " to agree upon and execute a final contract. *Id.* at 627. The letter signed by BMI and Centronics did not contain similar language. To the contrary, the letter expressly stated that the parties were not bound.

The language of the letter of intent signed by BMI and Centronics is clear, and its interpretation is therefore a matter of law for the court. * * * *Chariton Feed and Grain, Inc. v. Harder,* 369 N.W.2d 777, 785 (Iowa 1985).

Our conclusion that the letter of intent is not binding and did not give rise to an implied agreement to negotiate in good faith is consistent with Iowa authorities. See *Chariton,* 369 N.W.2d at 785 ("in construction of written contracts, the cardinal principle is that the intent of the parties must control; and except in cases of ambiguity, this is determined by what the contract itself says") * * *.

Courts are reluctant to find implied covenants. * * * They "must arise from the language used or be indispensable to effecting the intention of the parties." [*Pathology Consultants v. Gratton,* 343 N.W.2d 428, 434 (Iowa 1984).] While the court may find an implied term on a point not covered by the express terms of the agreement, "there can be no implied contract on a point fully covered by an express contract and in direct conflict therewith." *Snater v. Walters,* 250 Iowa 1189, 98 N.W.2d 302, 307 (1959). Because the facts here fail to meet the Iowa test for an implied contract and because finding an implied duty would contradict the express disclaimer of the letter of intent, we conclude that the parties did not bind themselves to an obligation to negotiate in good faith, and that the district court did not err in so holding.

* * *

For the reasons stated above, we affirm in part the district court's order and remand for further consideration of BMI's promissory estoppel claim.

QUESTIONS, NOTES, AND CONNECTIONS

1. Questions about the facts of this case

   1.1. What was the purpose of the letter of intent between BMI and Centronics?

1.2. What did BMI and Centronics expressly agree to in the letter of intent?

1.3. The court distinguished all three cases that BMI invoked to support its contention that the letter of intent established a duty on each party to negotiate in good faith. What were the critical factual distinctions between those cases and the case at hand? Were those differences enough to justify the difference in outcome?

1.4. Did we make a mistake by including this case in the book? Is this really a "contracts" case at all?

2. Questions about the law

2.1. Assuming that a court concludes that a binding duty to negotiate in good faith does arise out of a letter of intent, what exactly does that mean? Is it bad faith if one party terminates negotiation for no apparent reason? How about if that party receives a better offer from a third party, or if the reason is that the first party won't yield to that party's demands?

2.2. Does the duty to negotiate in good faith include a duty to accept all reasonable terms? In stressing that a precontractual duty to negotiate in good faith does not encompass an automatic duty to approve the final deal, consider the following observation from the Seventh Circuit:

> In a business transaction both sides presumably try to get the best of the deal. This is the essence of bargaining and the free market. And in the context of this case, no legal rule bounds the run of business interest. No particular demand in negotiations could be termed dishonest, even if it seemed outrageous to the other party. The proper recourse is to walk away from the bargaining table, not to sue for "bad faith" in negotiations.

A/S Apothekernes Laboratorium v. I.M.C. Chemical, 873 F.2d 155, 159 (7th Cir. 1989).

2.3. In its summary of the facts giving rise to this lawsuit, the court discusses several events occurring *after* the letter of intent was signed. Should the parties' post-signing conduct be relevant to the determination of whether a duty to negotiate in good faith arose out of the letter? In its analysis of the legal issue, did the court give sufficient weight to that conduct?

2.4. How do the pre-contract formation liability cases like *Budget Marketing* differ from the "agreement to agree" cases that we examined in Section 6 of this chapter? Ponoroff argues that in the later cases the parties have manifested an intention to be bound at the time of the initial agreement and the only issue is whether the court may imply a reasonable term if the parties fail to subsequently agree or whether the agreement is fatally indefinite from the inception. In cases like *Budget Marketing*, there is clearly no intention to be bound to the terms of the deal in principle, but the question remains whether the parties' negotiations have proceeded to the point where liability may be imposed if one party breaks off negotiations in bad faith. Epstein believes that Ponoroff is splitting hairs (notwithstanding his limited supply of that commodity) and the analytic distinction between the two types of cases is just not all that sharp. Markell thinks Ponoroff and Epstein need to get a life. What do you think?

3. Notes

3.1. The clearer the letter of intent is with respect to whether or not it is intending to impose any precontractual obligations on the parties to negotiate in good faith, the more likely it is that this expressed intent will be enforced, although, as *Budget Marketing* suggests, other theories may be available where one party "misbehaves." If a letter of intent is ambiguous, however, the issue of whether a cause of action may lie for breach of the duty to negotiate in good faith must be ascertained from the specificity of the language used by the parties as well as all of the surrounding circumstances.

For example, in *Schwanbeck v. Federal Mogul Corp.*, 31 Mass.App.Ct. 390, 578 N.E.2d 789 (1991), one corporation was negotiating to acquire the assets of another corporation. The parties reached the stage where they had their lawyers draft a letter of intent. The letter contained one provision stating that, "this letter is not intended to create, nor do you or we presently have any binding legal obligation whatsoever in any way relating to such sale and purchase * * *" and a later provision stating that, "it is our intention, and, we understand, your intention immediately to proceed in good faith in the negotiation of * * * a binding definitive agreement." In determining whether the selling corporation had breached its duty of good faith when it arranged a sale of the assets to a third party before attempting to conclude a deal with the first buyer, the court of appeals commented: "To the degree this cordial language [speaking of the second provision] smoothed the hard edge of the 'this is not yet a binding deal' language that had preceded it, the letter soon (on the second page) reverts to a 'keep-your-hands-on-your-wallet' tone." Thus, the court concluded, "even if given legal effect to some extent, we are of opinion that, in the context of a proposed business acquisition, as to which the parties have agreed not to be bound by their preliminary agreement, and the seller has reserved the right to deal with other buyers, the obligation to proceed in good faith means something less than unremitting efforts to get to 'yes,' with the players at all times playing their cards face up." *Id.* at 795. On further appeal, the Supreme Judicial Court of Massachusetts concurred with the result in the court of appeal, but decided "it is not necessary to determine what constitutes an obligation to negotiate in good faith or whether [the selling corporation] breached any such obligation, because we conclude that the parties did not bind themselves contractually to any such obligation." 412 Mass. 703, 592 N.E.2d 1289, 1291 (1992).

3.2. Perhaps the most famous case involving precontractual liability was not a contracts case at all, but a tort case. In 1983, Pennzoil, seeking to acquire control of its substantial oil reserves, negotiated with Getty Oil and its major shareholder for the purchase of 57% of that company's stock at $110 per share. Although awaiting documentation of the transaction, the parties entered into a letter of intent. Subsequently, Texaco offered $128 per share for all of the stock of Getty Oil, which was promptly accepted by Getty Oil's major shareholder. Pennzoil then sued Texaco for the common law tort of inducement of breach of contract. Obviously, central to recovery under this theory was the requirement that the court find a binding obligation under the letter of intent. It did. *Texaco, Inc. v. Pennzoil Co.*, 729 S.W.2d 768 (Tex. App. 1987), *cert. denied*, 485 U.S. 994 (1988). The result was entry of a judgment against Texaco and in favor of Pennzoil for $7.53 *billion* with an additional $1 billion in punitive damages thrown in for good measure. As a result of this judgment, Texaco eventually had to file for reorganization under the federal Bankruptcy Code. Clearly this case serves as a warning to the corporate lawyers negotiating and drafting these sorts of "gentlemen's agreements," and boards of directors properly seeking the best price for the company's shareholders, that the mere fact that *final* documents have not yet been prepared and signed may not prevent the assignment of liability if the circumstances point to the manifestation of assent by the parties.

3.3. A more recent case involving precontract liability was decided by the California Court of Appeals in 2002. *Copeland v. Baskin Robbins U.S.A.*, 96 Cal.App.4th 1251, 117 Cal.Rptr.2d 875. Copeland purchased one of Baskin Robbins's ice cream manufacturing plants under an agreement that provided for a separate "co-packing" agreement under which Baskin Robbins would purchase a significant portion of Copeland's output from the plant for a three-year period. Baskin Robbins ended negotiations regarding the co-packing agreement and Copeland sued. The trial court granted Baskin Robbins summary judgment finding no agreement for the purchase of the plant's ice cream. The court of appeals, noting that when Baskin Robbins refused to continue negotiating the terms of the co-packing agreement, "many millions of dollars in anticipated profits melted away like so much banana ripple ice cream on a hot summer day," came to a different conclusion. Distinguishing the situation from an unenforceable mere "agreement to agree," the court held that a party can commit itself to negotiate in good faith and that a cause of action may lie for the breach of such agreement. In explaining the policy rationale for its decision, the court noted:

> Gone are the days when our ancestors sat around a fire and bargained for the exchange of stone axes. Today the stakes are much higher and negotiations more complex. Deals are rarely made in a single negotiating session. Rather, they are the product of a gradual process in which agreements are reached piecemeal on a variety of issues. * * * For these reasons, the parties should have some assurance that their investments in time and money and effort will not be wiped out by the other party's footdragging or change of heart * * *

Ultimately, however, because Copeland was unable to establish its damages, the court of appeals affirmed the summary judgment in favor of Baskin Robbins. A classic pyrrhic victory for Copeland, but an important precedent.

4. **You Be the Lawyer!**

If you had represented BMI in these negotiations with Centronics, how could you have drafted the letter of intent so as to prevent Centronics from simply "changing its mind," but without making the letter of intent a binding agreement?

5. Connections

In an article written probably before most of you were born, Professor Charles Knapp (a co-author of a "competing" Contracts casebook who is even older than Epstein) examined several cases where the parties had either: (1) left one or more terms to future agreement (agreements to agree), or (2) had reached agreement on most essential terms, but delayed final agreement pending additional negotiation as to certain unresolved details. He ultimately concluded that in either situation, where the parties concededly considered themselves committed to one another to some extent, neither should be able to walk away from the deal except for a good and sufficient reason. Charles L. Knapp, *Enforcing the Contract to Bargain,*44 N.Y.U. L. REV. 673 (1969). By contrast, in a more recent analysis, Professors Alan Schwartz and Robert Scott argued that while the courts in these cases can play an important facilitative role by protecting a promisee's reliance when the promisor "strategically delays investment and thus breaches an *ex ante* agreement to pursue a profitable deal," imposing a further duty on the parties to "negotiate in good faith" over the remaining terms is not necessary. Alan Schwartz & Robert E. Scott, *Precontractual Liability and Preliminary Agreements*, 120 HARV. L. REV. 661, 704–05 (2007). What do you think?

Well, now that you know whether your client has made a deal, assuming she has, it's time to find out whether it's a deal that the law will enforce. Are you ready for Chapter 3? Good, because that's where we're going right after recess.

CHAPTER 3

WHAT IS "CONSIDERATION" AND WHY IS IT STILL AN IMPORTANT PART OF CONTRACT LAW (OR IS CONSIDERATION STILL AN IMPORTANT PART OF CONTRACT LAW?)

■ ■ ■

Consider the following exchange of emails between Pamela Siege Chandler [PSC] of West Academic Publishing and Ponoroff (she likes him best) after completing work on the fifth edition of this book:

> PSC: "I am so pleased by your work on the fifth edition. You deserve a reward. Something nice. A hairpiece? A Leading Man hairpiece? Wouldn't a brown, Leading Man 9333 hair piece https://www.bestwigoutlet.com/product/rex-mens-toupee-by-leading-man.html be a wonderful reward?"
>
> Ponoroff: "I agree. A hairpiece would be a wonderful reward."
>
> PSC: "It's a deal. I will order it right away."

Later Ms. Chandler changes her mind. Is this a deal that the law will enforce?

Recall that in Chapter 2 we learned how to deal with disputes over whether there was an agreement. Here there is no dispute over whether there was an *agreement*: Ms. Chandler and Ponoroff had agreed that he would get a hairpiece.

And, recall that at the beginning of Chapter 1, we learned that there are two key elements to the existence of a *contract*:

#1. A promise or set of promises.

#2. Enforcement.

From element #1 (and common sense*), we see that it is the promise or promises that make up the agreement that the law enforces, not the

* Common sense. You and one of your study buddies agree that this is the best law school casebook ever. Later, when you read some of the stuff in the book that Markell wrote, you change your mind. No obligation for the law to enforce. An agreement, but no promise.

"agreement." Second, from element #2 (but not necessarily common sense*) we see that not all promises are legally enforceable. What we will see from this Chapter is that, under these facts, Ms. Chandler's promise of a hairpiece for Ponoroff is not a legally enforceable promise because there was no "consideration."

We have already seen the term "consideration" in various cases that we have read in Chapter 2. In this Chapter [and *Restatement (Second) of Contracts* §§ 17 and 71] we will see that:

(1) a promise will be legally enforceable only if there is consideration or a consideration substitute;

(2) consideration for a promise is either some performance or forbearance, or promise of performance or forbearance bargained for by the promisor.

Even before reading any more of the consideration material in this Chapter, it should now be obvious to you that there was no "consideration" for Ms. Chandler's promise—she did not ask for (*i.e.*, bargain for) Ponoroff to do anything, forbear from doing anything, promise to do anything or promise to forbear from doing anything. And, it should be equally obvious to you even before reading the consideration material in this Chapter, that there is no issue as to consideration in *R.R. v. M.H.* or *Lucy v. Zehmer* or other cases that we have read.

Regrettably, what we cannot make obvious is (1) why contract law requires consideration or a consideration substitute and (2) why you are required to learn about consideration. The answers to these questions are not obvious to us. To borrow from Brandt, "Well dude, we just don't know."**

---

1. BARGAIN AND THE LEGAL CONCEPT OF CONSIDERATION

The contracts scholar Patrick Atiyah provides the following introduction to consideration:

> The 'doctrine' of consideration is generally seen by lawyers as a set of rules which limits the freedom of individuals to make binding legal promises. Only those promises which are supported by a legal consideration are legally binding; other promises are not binding, even if the promisor *intends* to bind himself by his

---

* *Cf.* "[N]o legal system makes all promises enforceable. The legal enforcement of promises is costly, and the conception of the sanctity of promises says little about which promises justify this cost of enforcement." E. ALLAN FARNSWORTH, CHANGING YOUR MIND: THE LAW OF REGRETTED DECISIONS 37 (1998).

** Cf http://www.getyarn.io/yarn-clip/68227e38-759f-4196-ac4b-b1132d575f3d

> promise. Thus to many lawyers, the central function of the doctrine of consideration is to prevent people from making gratuitous promises because the typical gratuitous promise is made without any consideration as lawyers understand that term. On this view, the purpose of the law of consideration is to distinguish between gratuitous and non-gratuitous promises. This may, indeed, be one of the chief purposes of the doctrine of consideration, but it is doubtful if it is the only purpose, and certainly, this has not traditionally been the only purpose of this doctrine in its very long history. * * *
>
> The [consideration] doctrine is in a sense a *limitation* on the free power of individuals to bind themselves as they wish. It is, therefore, a paternalistic device. If a promise or a contract is declared not binding even where there has been a clear promise, on the ground of absence of consideration, the law is in effect saying that it is better that individuals should not bind themselves unless they receive some benefit in return * * *

P. S. ATIYAH, AN INTRODUCTION TO THE LAW OF CONTRACT, 118, 120–21 (5th ed. 1995).

The history of consideration goes back to 13th century England, to a time when the enforceability of an agreement was limited by the common law system of pleading. A case had to fit within a specific form of pleading or writ.

One such early common law writ, covenant, was largely limited to writings with a seal. Today, in England and most states, the absence or existence of a seal does not affect the enforceability of an agreement.

Assumpsit developed as the primary common law writ for the enforcement of agreements without seals. Assumpsit had a series of requirements that came to be described as "consideration."

Courts and lawyers no longer use the writ of assumpsit, but they continue to use the term "consideration." While courts consistently use the term "consideration," the term is not used consistently, and it is not a real issue in many real world problems or cases. In other words,

1. courts, lawyers, and law professors (especially law professors) regularly mention "consideration"; BUT
2. there is not a single, universally accepted definition of consideration; AND
3. it is unusual for an agreement to be unenforceable because of a lack of consideration.

A. CONSIDERATION: "BARGAINED FOR"

First, *Restatement (Second) of Contracts* § 71 defines consideration as follows:

§ 71 Requirement of Exchange; Types of Exchange

(1) To constitute consideration, a performance or a return promise must be bargained for.

(2) A performance or return promise is bargained for if it is sought by the promisor in exchange for his promise and is given by the promisee in exchange for that promise.

(3) The performance may consist of:

(a) an act other than a promise, or

(b) a forbearance, or

(c) the creation, modification, or destruction of a legal relation.

(4) The performance or return promise may be given to the promisor or to some other person. It may be given by the promisee or by some other person.

In sum, the *Restatement (Second) of Contracts* in § 71(1) defines consideration as a bargained for promise or performance, and § 71(3) explains "performance."

Even though § 71(2) purports to explain "bargained for," it is necessary to read *Restatement (Second) of Contracts* § 81 excerpted below to understand the "bargained for" requirement:

§ 81 Consideration as Motive or Inducing Cause

(1) The fact that what is bargained for does not of itself induce the making of a promise does not prevent it from being consideration for the promise.

Comment:

a. "Bargained for." Consideration requires that a performance or return promise be "bargained for" in exchange for a promise; this means that the promisor must manifest an intention to induce the performance or return promise and to be induced by it and that the promisee must manifest an intention to induce the making of the promise and to be induced by it. * * *

b. Immateriality of motive or cause. * * *, it is immaterial that the promisor's desire for the consideration is incidental to other objectives and even that the other party knows this to be so.

Please apply the Restatement's definition of consideration in the following problems.

PROBLEMS

1. RR and MH enter into a traditional surrogacy agreement that provides that RR will pay MH $10,000 and RH will have initial custody of their child. RR pays MM the $10,000, MH now refuses to relinquish custody of their child to RR. Is RR's payment of the $10,000 consideration for MH's promise of initial custody?
2. L leases an apartment to T. The lease is due to expire next month, L promises T that it will extend the lease for another year and not increase the rent. T then paints the apartment. Does T's painting the apartment belonging to L qualify as consideration for L's promise to extend the lease for another year at the same rental rate?
3. S Corporation (S) and B Incorporated (B) agree that S will sell a machine to B and B will pay S $300,000 when the machine is delivered Before S delivers the machine, B learns that T will sell B a comparable machine for $200,000. Does B have a winning argument that its agreement with S is not enforceable because of the absence of consideration?

Some states have enacted statutes defining consideration. For example, the North Dakota Code contains the following definition of "good consideration":

9–05–01 Good consideration defined.

Any benefit conferred or agreed to be conferred upon the promisor by any other person to which the promisor is not entitled lawfully, or any prejudice suffered or agreed to be suffered by such person, other than such as he, at the time of consent, is lawfully bound to suffer as an inducement to the promisor, is a good consideration for a promise.

The North Dakota statutorily defines "good consideration." There is not a North Dakota statute that defines "bad consideration." There is, however, a reported North Dakota case that badly explains how this definition of "good consideration" should be applied.

QUESTIONS BEFORE THE CASE

1. In this case, who is the "promisor" as that term is used in the North Dakota statute?

2. What is the "benefit conferred" on that promisor"?

REED V. UNIVERSITY OF NORTH DAKOTA* AND THE NORTH DAKOTA ASSOCIATION FOR THE DISABLED, INC.

Supreme Court of North Dakota
589 N.W.2d 880 (1999)

[The plaintiff, Jace Reed, was a student at the University of North Dakota (UND) on a hockey scholarship. As part of UND's preseason conditioning program, Reed ran in a ten-kilometer race sponsored by the North Dakota Association for the Disabled (NDAD). As a result of the race, Reed himself became "disabled," suffering extensive damage to his kidneys and liver as a result of dehydration. More specifically, Reed required one kidney and two liver transplants.

Reed sued NDAD on a tort theory, alleging that NDAD negligently failed to provide adequate medical services and water at the race site. NDAD defended on a contract theory, alleging that the race registration form that Reed signed was a contract releasing NDAD from any liability. The trial court granted NDAD's motion for summary judgment. Reed appealed.]

MARING, JUSTICE.

Jace Reed appealed a summary judgment dismissing his * * * claims against the North Dakota Association for the Disabled (NDAD). We hold * * * a valid release exonerates NDAD from liability for its alleged negligence * * * We affirm.

* * *

A

Reed contends a release in a race registration form signed by him does not bar his negligence claim against NDAD. Before the race, Reed signed a registration form which provided, in part:

> I am entering this event at my own risk and assume all responsibility for injuries I may incur as a direct or indirect result of my participation. For myself and my heirs, I agree not to hold the participating sponsors and their directors, employees, and/or agents responsible for any claims. I also give permission for the free use of my name and/or picture in a broadcast, telecast, or other account of this event.

---

* Reed's suit against the University of North Dakota was dismissed on the ground of "sovereign immunity," a concept that you have discussed, will discuss or should discuss in torts. Eds.

According to Reed, UND coaches presented the registration form to him before the race, and he had to sign it to run the race, which was a mandatory part of the UND hockey team's preseason conditioning program.

Reed asserts the release is not enforceable, because it was not supported by consideration. Consideration may be any benefit conferred or detriment suffered. See N.D.C.C. § 9–05–01. The forbearance of a legal right is a legal detriment which constitutes good consideration. The existence of consideration is a question of law.

As part of their preseason conditioning program, the UND hockey players were allowed to run on the same course during NDAD's road race. When the hockey players, including Reed, signed the registration form, they agreed not to hold the participating sponsors responsible for any claims arising from their participation in the event and NDAD agreed to let them run on the course during NDAD's road race. Reed's surrender of a legal right in exchange for NDAD allowing him to run the course during the race constitutes consideration for the release. *See Malecha v. St. Croix Valley Skydiving Club,* 392 N.W.2d 727, 731 (Minn. App. 1986) (holding payment of fee and surrender of right to sue for negligence in exchange for skydiving training course constitutes valid consideration for release).

* * *

V

We affirm the summary judgment dismissing Reed's complaint against NDAD. * * *

QUESTIONS

1. Questions about the facts of this case

   1.1. Who is contending that his promise is not legally enforceable?

   1.2. Did that promisor ask for something in return for that promise, i.e., did the promisor bargain for something in return?

   1.3. Did the person seeking to enforce the promise confer some bargained for benefit on that promisor?

2. Questions about the law

   2.1. Compare the North Dakota statute with *Restatement (Second) of Contracts* § 71. Does the *Restatement (Second)* use the words "benefit" and "prejudice"? Will a "bargained for" "performance" or "return promise" always be a "benefit" to the promisor or "prejudice" to the promisee?

2.2. Should the enforceability of the release that Reed signed be decided by the contract law concept of consideration?

3. **You Be the Lawyer!**

If you had been the law clerk writing the first draft of the opinion for Justice Maring would you have included the sentence "The forbearance of a legal right is a legal detriment which constitutes good consideration" in the opinion?

Most disputes are settled without a legal proceeding. But, sometimes, after the settlement, there is a legal proceeding challenging the enforceability of the settlement agreement. The next case involves such a challenge based, in part, on an alleged lack of consideration to "William" for his promises in the settlement agreement.

QUESTIONS BEFORE THE CASE

1. Can a promise be consideration?
2. Did the "Confidential Settlement Agreement and General Release" contain a promise by Marcella?
3. Does William contend that Marcella's promise is not consideration?
4. Does the court conclude Marcella's promise was not consideration?

MCCORMICK V. DRESDALE

United States District Court, D. Rhode Island
2010 WL 1740853 (2010)

WILLIAM E. SMITH, DISTRICT JUDGE.

Briefly stated by way of introduction, Plaintiff William McCormick (hereinafter "William") was a freshman student on a full scholarship at Brown University ("Brown") when, he alleges, Defendant Marcella Dresdale, then a fellow Brown freshman, falsely accused him of misconduct, including rape. The accusation, however, was not made to law enforcement authorities, but rather to college administrators. The accusation fairly quickly resulted in William's "withdrawal" from Brown and the corresponding loss of his full scholarship. William filed suit, joined by his parents, Mr. and Mrs. McCormick ("the parents"), against Brown University, a number of Brown's agents (collectively the "Brown Defendants"), and the Dresdales. The Dresdales filed a motion to dismiss, pursuant to Rule 12(b)(6), for failure to state a clam upon which relief could be granted, asserting the affirmative defense of release and waiver. . . . The Dresdales attached to their motion a copy of the "Confidential Settlement Agreement and General Release" signed by William, which purports to release all legal claims he and his parents may have held against the Dresdales arising out of this incident

Where Defendants are seeking to dismiss Plaintiffs' claims on the basis of a settlement agreement, the burden is on the Defendants to prove that there is a valid agreement which bars the claims, such that "the facts establishing the defense [are] clear 'on the face of the plaintiff's pleadings.' " In opposition to the Dresdales' motion, Plaintiffs argue that the Agreement is invalid for lack of valid consideration. . . .

The Court now denies the Dresdales' motion to dismiss, as the Dresdales have not met their burden to demonstrate that on the face of the pleadings (and taking all of the averments in the First Amended Complaint as true) the Agreement is supported by valid consideration. In particular, Plaintiffs clearly allege that the claims forgone by the Dresdales, in consideration for William's release of the same, were false and made in bad faith. Accepting this as true, Defendants cannot prevail at this juncture.

Confidential Settlement Agreement and General Release

The First Circuit has said that it is the responsibility of the district court to "discern whether or not a valid and binding settlement had been reached, and if so, to enforce it." *Mathewson Corp. v. Allied Marine Indus., Inc.,* 827 F.2d 850, 853 (1st Cir.1987). Indeed, "[w]here the parties, acting in good faith, settle a controversy, the courts will enforce the compromise without regard to what the result might have been had the parties chosen to litigate." *Id.* The Agreement between William and Marcella provides in ¶ 2.1 that:

> As consideration for the mutual promises contained herein, Dresdale hereby releases and forever discharges McCormick from any and all claims, demands, damages, remedies, contracts (express or implied) and causes of action, whether known or unknown, asserted or unasserted, fixed or contingent, which Dresdale ever had, now has or in the future may or could have, including but not limited to, any allegations of misconduct while at Brown University, against McCormick arising out of or relating to any matter up to the date of the execution of this Agreement. . . .
>
> And in ¶ 2.2 it provides that:
>
> As consideration for the promises contained herein, McCormick hereby releases and forever discharges Dresdale from any and all claims, demands, damages, remedies, contracts (express or implied) and causes of action of any kind or nature whatsoever,

> whether known or unknown, asserted or unasserted, fixed or contingent which McCormick ever had, now has or in the future may or could have, against Dresdale, including but in no way limited to an action for defamation.

In the Agreement, William further promises that he will voluntarily withdraw as a student from Brown, he will never attend any another school that Marcella attends, he will not come within one thousand (1000) feet of Marcella, he will not enter the City of Providence so long as Marcella is a student at Brown, and he will undergo neurological testing, psychological counseling, and successfully complete a course of instruction on sensitivity to women. The Agreement also contains mutual promises to maintain the Agreement's confidentiality, as well as a Non-Disparagement clause.

In order to determine whether the Agreement is supported by adequate consideration the Court must first delve into the claims that Marcella and William agreed to mutually release. Plaintiffs argue that Marcella's good faith belief regarding the validity of her claims is front and center in this analysis and it is a question that in many ways represents the eye of the storm in this case. Described generally in the Agreement as "allegations of misconduct while at Brown University," the First Amended Complaint indicates that Marcella's claims could range from harassment to stalking to rape.

It is hornbook law that "[a] fundamental requisite to a contract that can be enforced by a court is an exchange of legal consideration by the parties." *Ross-Simons of Warwick, Inc. v. Baccarat, Inc.,* 182 F.R.D. 386, 397 (D.R.I.1998) This may take the form of a benefit conferred on another or a detriment suffered voluntarily.

In Rhode Island, the forbearance of a legal right may also qualify as valid consideration "for a settlement agreement if the claim is 'premised on an honest belief in its justness.'" *Id.*). Indeed, "the weight of authority holds that although forbearance from suit on a known invalid claim is insufficient consideration for a promise, forbearance from suit on a claim of doubtful validity is sufficient consideration for a promise if there is a sincere belief in the validity of the claim." 3 Richard A. Lord, *Williston on Contracts* § 7:47 Forbearance or promise of forbearance—Forbearance to litigate or promise to forbear—Doubtful claims (4th ed.2008).

Thus, while good faith is a necessary prerequisite, a clear win is not. Indeed, "[i]f a claim is known by the claimant to have no foundation, it is clear that the forbearance to prosecute the claim is not sufficient consideration." *Sweeney v. Sweeney Inv. Co.,* 90 P.2d 716, 719 (Wash.1939); *See Restatement (Second) of Contracts* § 74 "Settlement of Claims" (1981) ("[f]orbearance to assert or the surrender of a claim or defense which proves to be invalid is not consideration unless . . . the forbearing or surrendering party believes that the claim or defense may be fairly determined to be valid"). Even a "doubtful claim" that is likely to be defeated on the merits may qualify as adequate consideration to support an agreement. The claim, however, "must not be absurd in fact, from the standpoint of a reasonable person in the position of the claimant. [Moreover] the preference of the Restatement Second is to enforce the compromise if the claimant held a subjective good-faith belief in the claim's validity." 3 *Williston on Contracts* § 7:47.

After careful consideration, the Court concludes that the validity of the release cannot be established upon the face of the pleadings. Here, Plaintiffs allege that Marcella Dresdale conjured false and exaggerated allegations of misconduct, including rape, against William, thereafter entering into a settlement agreement promising not to bring those very claims that she knew were false. Assuming, as is mandated upon a motion to dismiss, that her allegations against William were false and therefore, not "premised on an honest belief in its justness[,]" it cannot be shown on the face of the pleadings that there was valid consideration for the Agreement.

It must be emphasized, however, that the Court is not holding that the Agreement is invalid; rather, at this juncture where the Court must accept the facts alleged by Plaintiffs, dismissal would be improper. Marcella's good faith and the truth of the statement that "William had not raped [Marcella]" are not issues amenable to resolution upon a motion to dismiss. (Pls.' First Am. Compl. ¶ 79.) Unfortunately for the Dresdales, these thorny factual questions dovetail with whether the Agreement is a viable defense, supported by adequate consideration.

Conclusion

For the foregoing reasons, the Court concludes that the validity of the Agreement cannot be established on the face of the pleadings. Therefore, the Dresdales' motion to dismiss is DENIED.

QUESTIONS AND NOTES

1. Questions about the facts of this case

    1.1. Do we know who is suing whom for what?

    1.2. What is the relevance of the "Confidential Settlement Agreement and Release" ["Agreement"] to this law suit?

    1.3. Do we know why William entered into this Agreement?

1.4. Do you think that the Dresdales were represented by an attorney in negotiating the Agreement? [Mr. Dresdale* was the Co-founder and Managing Director of Fenway Partners—a multi-billion-dollar private equity fund.] Do you think William was represented by an attorney in negotiating the Agreement? [Remember, William was attending Brown on a full scholarship.]

2. Questions about the law

2.1. Is *McCormick* consistent with *Restatement (Second) of Contracts* § 74?

Settlement of Claims

(1) Forbearance to assert or the surrender of a claim or defense which proves to be invalid is not consideration unless

(a) the claim or defense is, in fact, doubtful because of uncertainty as to the facts or the law, or

(b) the forbearing or surrendering party believes that the claim or defense may be fairly determined to be valid.

2.2. In this case, who will have the burden of proof with respect to consideration? What sort of evidence might be relevant in determining the absence or existence of consideration in this case?

2.3. Should the validity of this settlement agreement be governed by the doctrine of consideration?

2.4. Isn't a plea bargain entered into between prosecutors and criminal defendants a form of settlement agreement? Should the enforceability of a plea agreement depend upon the contract law doctrine of consideration? In Santobello v. New York, 404 U.S. 257, 262 (1971), the court analyzed plea bargains in terms suggesting traditional contract law, and ruled, "when a plea rests in any significant degree on a promise or agreement of the prosecutor, so that it can be said to be part of the inducement or consideration, such promise must be fulfilled." Do you agree with the ruling? With the court's use of the contract law concept of consideration to reach such a ruling?

3. Notes

3.1. Subsequently, the McCormicks dismissed their suit. According to a lawyer for the Dresdales, "The McCormicks and the Dresdales have resolved all of the disputes between them which are the subject of the lawsuit to their mutual satisfaction. The McCormicks and the Dresdales have agreed to not make any

* As best we can tell, no relation to Milburn Drysdale of the Beverly Hillbillies. https://www.facebook.com/pages/Milburn-Drysdale/108171925882481?nr Different spelling. Perhaps another example of life imitating "art."

further statements or comments on the matter." http://www.businessweek.com/news/2011-12-21/suit-dropped-against-brown-university-over-rape-accusation.html People other than the McCormicks and Dresdales, however, have freely commented on the matter. E.g., Ryan Fleming, *A University's Shame: How Brown Betrayed One of its Students*, THE BROWN SPECTATOR, May 26, 2014, http://brown-spectator.com/2012/05/a-universitys-shame-how-brown-betrayed-one-of-its-students/

3.2. Model Rule of Professional Conduct 3.1 commands that, "[a] lawyer shall not bring or defend a proceeding, or assert or controvert an issue therein unless there is a basis in law and fact for doing so that is not frivolous."

4. **You Be the Lawyer!**

If you had been the lawyer for the Dresdales, what would you have done differently?

B. CONSIDERATION AND FAMILY AGREEMENTS

Recall that Professor Atiyah suggested that one purpose of consideration is to distinguish between gratuitous and non-gratuitous promises. Many, if not most, gratuitous promises are made between members of the same family. The next two cases, *Kirksey v. Kirksey* and *Hamer v. Sidway*, use the concept of consideration to determine whether an intra-family promise is gratuitous and so unenforceable.

QUESTIONS BEFORE THE CASE

1. Do we need to know the reason that the defendant Isaac made the promise of "a place to raise your family" to the plaintiff Antillico?
2. Do we need to know the reason that the defendant changed his mind two years later?

KIRKSEY V. KIRKSEY

Supreme Court of Alabama
8 Ala. 131 (1845)

ASSUMPSIT by the defendant, against the plaintiff in error. The question is presented in this Court, upon a case agreed, which shows the following facts:

The plaintiff was the wife of defendant's brother, but had for some time been a widow, and had several children. In 1840, the plaintiff resided on public land, under a contract of lease, she had held over, and was comfortably settled, and would have attempted to secure the land she lived on. The defendant resided in Talladega county, some sixty, or seventy miles off. On the 10th October, 1840, he wrote to her the following letter:

> "Dear sister Antillico—Much to my mortification, I heard, that brother Henry was dead, and one of his children. I know that your situation is one of grief, and difficulty. You had a bad chance before, but a great deal worse now. I should like to come and see you, but cannot with convenience at present. * * * I do not know whether you have a preference on the place you live on, or not. If you had, I would advise you to obtain your preference, and sell the land and quit the country, as I understand it is very unhealthy, and I know society is very bad. If you will come down and see me, I will let you have a place to raise your family, and I have more open land than I can tend; and on the account of your situation, and that of your family, I feel like I want you and the children to do well."

Within a month or two after the receipt of this letter, the plaintiff abandoned her possession, without disposing of it, and removed with her family, to the residence of the defendant, who put her in comfortable houses, and gave her land to cultivate for two years, at the end of which time he notified her to remove, and put her in a house, not comfortable, in the woods, which he afterwards required her to leave.

A verdict being found for the plaintiff, for two hundred dollars, the above facts were agreed, and if they will sustain the action, the judgment is to be affirmed, otherwise it is to be reversed.

ORMOND, J.

The inclination of my mind, is, that the loss and inconvenience, which the plaintiff sustained in breaking up, and moving to the defendant's, a distance of sixty miles, is a sufficient consideration to support the promise, to furnish her with a house, and land to cultivate, until she could raise her family. My brothers, however think, that the promise on the part of the defendant, was a mere gratuity, and that an action will not lie for its breach. The judgment of the Court below must therefore be reversed, pursuant to the agreement of the parties.

QUESTIONS AND NOTES

1. Questions about the law

   1.1. Did Judge Ormond believe that there was "sufficient consideration" to make the defendant's promise legally enforceable Is Judge Ormond's one paragraph opinion, in essence, a dissenting opinion?

   1.2. How would this case have been decided under the *Restatement (Second) of Contracts'* definition of consideration?

2. Notes

   2.1. Judge Ormond's cryptic opinion does not answer the questions: (i) why is a promise not enforceable because it is a "mere gratuity"; and (ii) how can a court (and, more importantly, a law student) determine whether a promise is supported by consideration or a "mere gratuity." Does the following excerpt from *Maughs v. Porter*, 157 Va. 415, 418, 161 S.E. 242, 243 (Ct. App. 1931), better answer these questions?

   A gift is a contract without a consideration, and, to be valid, must be executed. A valid gift is, therefore, a contract executed. It is to be executed by the actual delivery by the donor to the donee, or someone for him, of the thing given, or by delivery of the means of obtaining the subject of the gift, without further act of the donor to enable the donee to reduce it to his own possession. "The intention to give must be accompanied by a delivery, and the delivery must be made with an intention to give." Otherwise, there is only an intention or promise to give, which, being gratuitous, would be a mere nullity. Delivery of possession of the thing given or of the means of obtaining it so as to make the disposal of it irrevocable is indispensable to a valid gift.

   Clearly then, the plaintiff, under the facts shown here, cannot recover unless defendant is bound by a promise which is supported by a consideration sufficient to support the action. It is often quite difficult to determine in such cases whether or not there is such a consideration. 1 *Williston on Contracts*, thus illustrates the difficulty: "If a benevolent man says to a tramp: 'If you go around the corner to the clothing shop there, you may purchase an overcoat on my credit,' no reasonable person would understand that the short walk was requested as the consideration for the promise, but that in the event of the tramp going to the shop the promisor would make him a gift. Yet the walk to the shop is in its nature capable of being consideration. It is a legal detriment to the tramp to make the walk, and the only reason why the walk is not consideration is because on a reasonable construction it must be held that the walk was not requested as the price of the promise, but was merely a condition of a gratuitous promise. It is often difficult to determine whether words of condition in a promise indicate a request for consideration or state a mere condition in a gratuitous promise. An aid, though not a conclusive test, in determining which construction of the promise is more reasonable is an inquiry whether the happening of the condition will be a benefit to the promisor. If so, it is a fair inference that the happening was requested as a consideration. On the other hand, if, as in the case of the tramp stated above, the happening of the condition will be not only of no benefit to the promisor but is obviously merely for the purpose of enabling the promisee to receive a gift, the happening of the event on which the promise is conditional, though brought about by the promisee in reliance on the promise, will not properly be construed as consideration. In case of doubt where the promisee has incurred a detriment on the faith of the promise, courts will naturally be loath to regard the promise as a mere gratuity and the detriment incurred as merely a condition. But in some cases, it is so clear that a conditional gift was intended that even though the promisee has incurred detriment, the promise has been held unenforceable."

2.2. Professor Williston included *Kirksey* in his casebook on contracts and concluded that the result in the case was unjust.* Do you believe that the facts of *Kirksey* are different from the facts of Williston's tramp hypothetical, discussed in note 2.1 above?

2.3. "In the first few weeks of contracts class, we study *Kirksey v. Kirksey,* an 1845 Alabama case in which the defendant made the following statement to his sister-in-law: 'Poor Henry and one of the kids are dead. If I were you, I'd get control of the land, sell it, and move over here to Talladega. If you come, I will let you have a place to raise the family, and I have more land than I can tend.'

"Was this a contract or merely a gratuitous promise with a condition, like 'if you stop by on Saturday, we'll go get ice cream cones?' The Alabama Supreme Court held that it was not a contract. A student approached me after class and was troubled by the fact that his intuition about the result was inconsistent with the court's ruling. In essence, the student was asking, 'How did I get it wrong?'

"The drive for coherence reflects the fact that scholars and students still aspire to the philosophers' aspirational 'view from nowhere,' in which the objective observer studies cases in which the parties are fighting after the fact over the consequences of their actions in the before the fact setting. But it is not a view from nowhere. . . . Even an impartial judge must make a

* *See* Carol Weisbrod, *An Uncertain Trumpet: A Gloss on Kirksey v. Kirksey*, 32 CONN. L. REV. 1699, 1701 (2000).

seemingly irreducible subjective judgment in order to . . . apply what appear to be the parties' objective manifestations of agreement to the dispute under adjudication." Jeffrey M. Lipshaw, *Metaphors, Models and Meaning in Contract*, 116 PENN ST. L. REV. 987, 1031 (2012).

3. **You Be the Lawyer!**

If you were the trial attorney for Antilico, and Isaac testified, what questions would you ask him?

QUESTIONS BEFORE THE CASE

1. What was the consideration in *Hamer*?
2. Why did the defendant argue the nephew "was not harmed but benefitted"?

HAMER V. SIDWAY

Court of Appeals of New York
124 N.Y. 538, 27 N.E. 256 (1891)

[The facts of this case are somewhat confusing in that none of the parties to the agreement was named either "Hamer" or "Sidway." Both were named "William Story." The older William was the uncle and the promisor to the younger William who was (obviously) the nephew and the promisee.

The trial court found that the promise was legally enforceable; the intermediate appellate court reversed, and then this court reversed the intermediate appellate court and reinstated the decision of the trial court. The intermediate appellate court* provided the following information about the promise:

The testimony introduced by the plaintiff was to the effect that in March, 1869, when the testator and William E. Story were attending the golden wedding anniversary of the father of the testator, he said to William: "Willie, I am going to make you a proposition." William told him he would like to hear it. That the testator then said: "If you will not drink any liquor, will not smoke, will not play cards or billiards until you are 21, I will give you $5,000 that day. Of course, if you want to play for fun, that I don't consider playing cards." William said he would endeavor to carry it out; that he would do it. When William became 21 years of age he wrote the testator the following letter: "Dear Uncle: I am twenty-one years old to-day,

---

* 11 N.Y. Supp 182 (N.Y. Supreme Court, 4th Dept. 1890). Eds.

and I am now my own boss, and I believe, according to agreement, that there is due me five thousand dollars. I have lived up to the contract to the letter in every sense of the word." The testator's reply to this letter, so far as material to the questions involved in this case, was as follows: "Buffalo, February 26, 1875. W. E. Story, Jr.—Dear Nephew: Your letter of the 31st ult. came to hand all right, saying you had lived up to the promise made me several years ago. I have no doubt but what you have, for which you shall have $5,000, as I promised you. I had the money in the bank the day you were twenty-one years old that I intended for you, and you shall have the money certain. Now, Willie, I do not intend to interfere with this money in any way until I think you are capable of taking care of it, and the sooner that time comes the better it will please me. I would hate very much to have you start out in some adventure that you thought all right, and lose this money in one year. The first five thousand dollars I got together cost me a heap of hard work. * * * Willie, you are twenty-one, and you have many a thing to learn yet. This money you have earned much easier than I did, besides acquiring good habits at the same time, and you are quite welcome to the money. Hope you will make good use of it. I was ten long years getting this together after I was your age. Now, hoping this will be satisfactory, I stop. * * * P.S. You can consider this money on interest."

Uncle William then died before paying nephew William; the executor of Uncle William's estate refused to pay the promised $5,000 to nephew William and this law suit was filed.]

* * *

PARKER, J.

The question which provoked the most discussion by counsel on this appeal, and which lies at the foundation of plaintiff's asserted right of recovery, is whether by virtue of a contract defendant's testator, William E. Story, became indebted to his nephew, William E. Story, 2d, on his twenty-first birthday in the sum of $5,000. The trial court found as a fact that "on the 20th day of March, 1869, * * * William E. Story agreed to and with William E. Story, 2d, that if he would refrain from drinking liquor using tobacco, swearing, and playing cards or billiards for money until should become twenty-one years of age, then he, the said William E. Story, would at that time pay him, the said William E. Story, 2d, the sum of $5,000 for such refraining, to which the said William E. Story, 2d, agreed," and that he "in all things fully performed his part of said agreement." The defendant contends that the contract was without consideration to support it, and therefore invalid. He asserts that the promisee, by refraining from the use of liquor and tobacco, was not harmed, but benefitted; that which he did was best for him to do, independently of his uncle's promise,—and insists that it follows that, unless the promisor was benefitted, the contract was without consideration,—a contention which, if well founded, would seem to leave open for controversy in many cases whether that which the promisee did or omitted to do was in fact of such benefit to him as to leave no consideration to support the enforcement of the promisor's agreement. Such a rule could not be tolerated, and is without foundation in the law. The exchequer chamber in 1875 defined "consideration" as follows: "A valuable consideration, in the sense of the law, may consist either in some right, interest, profit, or benefit accruing to the one party, or some forbearance, detriment, loss, or responsibility given, suffered, or undertaken by the other." Courts "will not ask whether the thing which forms the consideration does in fact benefit the promisee or a third party, or is of any substantial value to any one. It is enough that something is promised, done, forborne, or suffered by the party to whom the promise is made as consideration for the promise made to him." Anson, Cont. 63. "In general a waiver of any legal right at the request of another party is a sufficient consideration for a promise." Pars. Cont. "Any damage, or suspension, or forbearance of a right will be sufficient to sustain a promise." 2 Kent, Comm. (12th Ed.) Pollock in his work on Contracts, (page 166,) after citing the definition given by the exchequer chamber, already quoted, says: "The second branch of this judicial description is really the most important one. 'Consideration' means not so much that one party is profiting as that the other abandons some legal right in the present, or limits his legal freedom of action in the future, as an inducement for the promise of the first." Now, applying this rule to the facts before us, the promisee used tobacco, occasionally drank liquor, and he had a legal right to do so. That right he abandoned for a period of years upon the strength of the promise of the testator that for such forbearance he would give him $5,000. We need not speculate on the effort which may have been required to give up the use of those stimulants. It is sufficient that he restricted his lawful freedom of action within certain prescribed limits upon the faith of his uncle's agreement, and now, having fully performed the conditions imposed, it is of no moment whether such performance actually proved a benefit to the promisor, and the court will not inquire into it; but, were it a proper subject of inquiry, we see nothing in this record that would permit a determination that the uncle was not benefitted in a legal sense.

The order appealed from should be reversed, and the judgment of the special term affirmed, with costs payable out of the estate. All concur.

QUESTIONS AND NOTES

1. Questions about the facts of this case

   1.1. Did Sidway, the executor for the estate of William E. Story, contend that Mr. Story did not promise to pay his nephew $5,000 if he refrained from drinking, using tobacco, swearing, and playing cards or billiards for money?

1.2. Did Sidway contend that the nephew did not so refrain?

2. Questions about the law

2.1. The *Hamer* opinion quotes from an 1875 Exchequer Chamber definition of consideration. Apply the definition to the facts of the *Hamer* case. Was there a "benefit accruing to the one party"? Was there a "forbearance, detriment, loss or responsibility given, suffered or undertaken by the other"?

2.2. Would *Hamer* have been decided differently under the North Dakota statutory definition of "good consideration"? Under *Restatement (Second) of Contracts* § 71?

2.3. Would *Hamer* have been decided differently if Uncle William's promise had not been made until after Nephew William turned 21 and Uncle William's promise was "Since you did not drink any liquor or smoke or play cards or billiards for money until you reached the age of 21, I will give you $5,000 at your birthday party next week"?

2.4. Would *Hamer* have been decided differently if (i) the original conversation between Uncle William and Nephew William had simply been "Willie, you are a fine lad? I will give you $5,000 when you are 21" and (ii) Willie then decided on his own to show his uncle what a fine lad he really was by not drinking liquor, playing cards or billiards, or smoking until he was 21?

2.5. Would *Hamer* have been decided differently if Uncle William had been really rich and promised $500,000 instead of $5,000?

3. Notes

3.1. A later New York Court of Appeals decision, *Weiner v. McGraw-Hill, Inc.*, 57 N.Y.2d 458, 457 N.Y.S.2d 193, 443 N.E.2d 441 (Ct. App. 1982) describes *Hamer* as the "seminal" case on consideration. *Hamer* appears as a principal case in virtually every contracts casebook. *Hamer,* with variations, can be used to illustrate such basic consideration concepts as:

- legal detriment different from actual detriment;
- no inquiry into adequacy of amount of consideration;
- bargained for requirement.

3.2. Professor Melvin Eisenberg argues that the world of contracts and the world of donative promises are two different worlds:

> To begin with, the world of contract is a market world, largely driven by relatively impersonal considerations and focused on commodities and prices. The impersonal organs

> of the state are an appropriate means to enforce promises made in such a world. In contrast, much of the world of gift is driven by affective considerations like love, affection, friendship, gratitude, and comradeship. That world would be impoverished if it were to be collapsed into the world of contract. * * *
>
> Similarly, making simple, affective donative promises enforceable would have the effect of commodifying the gift relationship. Under an enforceability regime, it could never be clear to the promisee, or even to the promisor, whether a donative promise that was made in a spirit of love, friendship, affection, or the like, was also performed for those reasons, or instead was performed to discharge a legal obligation or avoid a lawsuit. Accordingly, gifts made pursuant to simple, affective donative promises would be seriously impoverished, because at the point of the transfer, the promisor's motives would invariably be mixed.
>
> It can now be seen that the principle that simple donative promises are unenforceable does not show that the law fails to value donative promises. Just the opposite is true. The principle that simple donative promises are unenforceable is justified not because simple donative promises are less important than bargain promises, but because they are more important.

Melvin Aron Eisenberg, *The World of Contract and the World of Gift*, 85 CAL. L. REV. 821, 846 (1997).

4. **You Be the Lawyer!**

If you had been the law clerk for Judge Parker would you have suggested that he use paragraphs in writing opinions? If you were a law professor giving students suggestions about how to do well on their first year exams, would you suggest that they use paragraphs in answering exam questions—short paragraphs, with short sentences?

Kirksey v. Kirksey, *Hamer v. Sidway*, involve "personal" agreements between two individuals. Most cases in which consideration is an issue involve "personal" agreements between two individuals. It is very, very, very unusual for agreements involving two businesses to be unenforceable because of no consideration.

C. CONSIDERATION: ONE PROMISE AS CONSIDERATION FOR ANOTHER PROMISE

1. Promise as Consideration

In *Reed*, the consideration took the form of performance: NDAD allowed the promisor, Reed, to run in the race in exchange for his promise not to sue. In *Hamer*, the consideration took the form of forbearance by the promisee: the nephew Willie refrained from drinking, etc. until he reached the age of 21.

Recall that one promise can be consideration for another promise. Most business transactions involve an exchange of promises to do something (or not do something) in the future. Consider the following problem involving a common business transaction."

Faber SPCA (F) contracts with Blutarsky Building Contractors (B) for the construction of a new animal shelter. B promises to complete the building by April 5. F promises to pay $400,000 within 30 days after completion of the building. B never even starts on the building. F hires Stratton Construction Company (S) which builds the building at a cost of $500,000. Can F recover from B for breach of contract? What was the consideration for B's promise? Since F did not yet pay B, what is the detriment to the promisee F or the benefit to promisor B?

Under *Restatement (Second) of Contracts* §§ 71 and 75, a promise can serve as consideration for another promise. Thus, F's promise to pay was consideration for B's promise to build. Comment a to section 75 "explains": "The promise is enforced by fact of bargain, without more."

"Without more"? "Without more," is hardly an explanation for why F's promise to pay was consideration for B's promise to build. Since F did not yet pay B, what is the detriment to F or the benefit of to B? Perhaps a better explanation is that a promise is consideration because a promise is consideration. F's promise to pay B is consideration for B's promise to build because B's promise to build is consideration for F's promise to pay and so each promise creates an enforceable obligation which is a detriment.

---

2. Illusory Promise

Sometimes people use words of promise without really promising anything. As comment e to *Restatement of Contracts (Second) section 77* states: "Words of promise which by their terms make performance entirely optional with the 'promisor' * * * do not constitute a promise. Although such words are often referred to as forming an illusory promise, they do not fall within the present definition of promise."

The Restatement provides this example of "words of promise which by their terms make performance entirely optional: "2. A promises B to act as B's agent for three years from a future date on certain terms; B agrees that A may so act, but reserves the power to terminate the agreement at any time. B's agreement is not consideration since it involves no promise by him."

Is the following problem distinguishable from the Restatement section 77 example?

PROBLEM

Lyle is working as a manager at Los Pollos Hermanos under an employment at will agreement that he entered into before beginning work at Los Pollos.. Employment at will means that Lyle's employer can terminate Lyle at any time for no reason at all. The Lyle/Los Pollos Hermanos employment agreement includes Lyle's promise that he will be not work as a manager for any Albuquerque fast food restaurant for three months after his Los Pollos Hermanos employment ends. After working at Los Pollos Hermanos for almost a year, Lyle has received a job offer from Chirping Chicken to manage its Albuquerque restraurants. Is Lyle's promise not to compete* legally enforceable by Los Pollos Hermanos?

QUESTIONS BEFORE THE CASE

1. Was it important to the Court that the Defendant Groupon promised to arbitrate?
2. Was the reason that the Plaintiff agreed to arbitrate important to the Court?

KEENA V. GROUPON

U.S. District Court, Western District of North Carolina
192 F.Supp.3d 630 (2016)

GRAHAM C. MULLEN, UNITED STATES DISTRICT JUDGE.

THIS MATTER is before the Court on Defendant Groupon Inc.'s Motion to Compel Arbitration or in the Alternative Dismiss * * *.

Defendant is a web-based company that partners with retail businesses and offers the businesses' products and services for a discounted price if purchased from Defendant's website. On February 1, 2015, Plaintiff

* We will more completely consider covenants not to compete in the materials on unconscionability.

purchased a voucher for massage services through Defendant's website to be rendered by the company Mutatio Wellness. However, Plaintiff was unable to contact Mutatio Wellness to schedule the massage. Plaintiff requested a refund from Defendant, and Defendant refunded Plaintiff's purchase by crediting her account with "Groupon Bucks," which can only be used to make purchases on Defendant's website.

Before purchasing the massage voucher through Defendant's website, Plaintiff acknowledged and accepted Defendant's Terms of Use, including its arbitration provision, on two separate occasions. First, in order to make purchases on Groupon, Plaintiff was required to create an account. She entered her name, email address, and password, and agreed to Defendant's Terms of Use by clicking a box immediately next to the words "I agree to the Terms of Use and Privacy Statement." The words "Terms of Use" appeared as a prominent blue hyperlink that linked to the full version of Defendant's Terms of Use. Second, when Plaintiff purchased the massage voucher, she was required to click a button that said "Complete Order" in order to complete the purchase. Directly above the "Complete Order" button was a sentence stating: "[b]y clicking 'Complete Order' I accept the current Terms and Conditions and Privacy Policy." The words "Terms and Conditions" were again a blue hyperlink that linked to Defendant's Terms of Use.

The version of Defendant's Terms of Use that was in effect in 2015 was an eight page agreement that included an arbitration provision on the seventh page. The arbitration provision was bolded and listed under a blue heading entitled "Dispute Resolution provision stated:

> **Except as specifically stated herein, any dispute or claim between you and Groupon arising out of, or relating in any way to, the Terms of Use, the Site or your use of the Site, or any Products, Merchant Offerings or services offered or distributed through the Site ("Disputes") shall be resolved exclusively by final, binding arbitration . . . By virtue of this Agreement (defined below), you and Groupon are each giving up the right to go to court and have a Dispute heard by a judge or jury. . . .**

(*Id.*) (emphasis in original). The provision established that Illinois law, the Federal Arbitration Act, and the American Arbitration Association rules would govern any disputes. (*Id.*) It also guaranteed that Defendant would reimburse arbitration fees up to $10,000 for non-frivolous disputes, and that Defendant would not seek attorney fees or arbitration costs for non-frivolous disputes. (*Id.*) Additionally, the arbitration agreement contained a class action waiver, under which the parties agreed that all disputes would be arbitrated on an individual basis. (*Id.*)

Plaintiff filed this suit on October 29, 2015, alleging breach of contract, breach of the covenant of good faith and fair dealing, fraud and deceit, unjust enrichment, unfair and deceptive trade practices, fraudulent inducement, and negligence. On April 8, 2016, Defendant filed a Motion to Compel Arbitration or in the Alternative to Dismiss Pursuant to Rule 12(b)(6).

The plaintiff argues the arbitration clause is unenforceable because it is illusory. An illusory promise "appears to be a promise, but on closer examination reveals that the promisor has not promised to do anything," such that it does not provide sufficient consideration to establish a contract. *W.E. Erickson Const., Inc. v. Chicago Title Ins. Co.*, 266 Ill.App.3d 905, 204 Ill.Dec. 431, 641 N.E.2d 861, 864 (1994). Plaintiff alleges that the arbitration provision is illusory because "although the verbiage used in the arbitration agreement appears as though it relates to both parties, in actuality, it only relates to one." Plaintiff points to the language in the arbitration agreement that states "we each agree that disputes shall be arbitrated only on an individual basis".

Plaintiff argues that although this provision appears on its face to benefit both parties, it in fact only benefits Defendant because there is no situation where Defendant would initiate a class action against Plaintiff. Further, the Terms of Use state that "either party" can bring a dispute in court for intellectual property claims or claims based on Section 7 (prohibited user conduct). However, Plaintiff argues that only consumers can violate the intellectual property and consumer conduct provisions, so that allowing either party to bring suits on these violations is illusory because Defendant will actually be able to do so.

Plaintiff's argument fails because Defendant did provide consideration for the arbitration provisions, even if the obligations required of Plaintiff and Defendant are not equivalent. A contract is valid and not illusory if there is consideration for the contract, even if the obligations of the parties are not mutual. * * * Under the arbitration provision in the Terms of Use, Defendant gave up the ability to bring claims other than intellectual property and consumer conduct violations in court just as Plaintiff did. (Doc. No. 30, Exhibit B at 7 ("you and Groupon are each giving up the right to go to court and have a Dispute heard by a judge or jury")). Thus, Defendant did provide consideration for the arbitration provisions, even if the Terms of Use affords Defendant more opportunities to bring intellectual property or consumer conduct claims in court than Plaintiff. * * *

Plaintiff makes no valid arguments that the Terms of Use or arbitration provision are illusory. * * * The Court finds that the arbitration provision in the Terms of Use binds the parties to settle their current dispute through arbitration.

QUESTIONS AND NOTE

1. Questions about the facts

   1.1. Do we know the cost of the massage voucher? Is that relevant? Is the purchase of the massage voucher the contract in this case?

   1.2. Does the contract in this case contain more than one promise?

2. Question about the law

   2.1. If a contracting party makes more than one promise in a contract, is it necessary for there to be separate consideration for each promise?

   2.2. What if the Defendant's Terms of Use provided "These Terms of Use may be modified in whole or in part by Groupon from time to time, without notice"?

3. Note

   Recall that the *Keena* opinion tells us "A contract is valid and not illusory if there is consideration for the contract, even if the obligations of the parties are not mutual" What about the phrase "mutuality of obligation?" Great phrase. The kind of combination of words that sounds like "law." The words "mutuality of obligation" just sort of flow together. Kind of like "heartbreak of psoriasis" http://www.psorsite.com/heartbreak.html. The Maine Supreme Court in *Zamore v. Whitten*, 395 A.2d 435, 443 n.3 (Me. 1978) questions whether the phrase "mutuality of obligation" is helpful.

   > The phrase "mutuality of obligation" has caused much confusion to courts and commentators over the years. Professor Corbin criticizes the expression for its tendency to connote a need for obligations equivalent in terms of detriment and value. In fact, mutuality embodies a particularized application of the consideration doctrine in the context of formation of a bilateral contract. In a bilateral contract, one promise is good consideration for another.

4. **You Be the Lawyer!**

   Your firm represents the Plaintiff, and you are responsible for drafting interrogatories. If the court grants discovery as to whether the arbitration provision is enforceable, what questions would you ask the Defendant Groupon?

D. CONSIDERATION AND CONTRACT MODIFICATION

The next two cases illustrate that consideration questions sometimes arise in agreements to modify business contracts. Especially employment contracts.

QUESTIONS BEFORE THE CASE

1. Would the court have reached a different result if the agreement to increase the fixed salary had been in writing?
2. Would the court have reached a different result if the court had concluded that the nets were defective?

ALASKA PACKERS' ASS'N V. DOMENICO

Circuit Court of Appeals, Ninth Circuit
117 F. 99 (1902)

ROSS, CIRCUIT JUDGE:

[This is a case involving the enforceability of an employer's written agreement to modify an employment agreement by increasing employees' minimum salary. The employer contends that this modification agreement is not enforceable because of lack of consideration. More specifically, the employer, Alaska Packers ("appellant"), owned a salmon packing factory in Alaska. The employees ("libelants"*) were California sailors and fishermen who contracted to work for appellant in Alaska during the salmon season for $50 per sailor or fisherman plus two cents for each red salmon he caught. The libelants arrived in Alaska in April; in late May, the libelants stopped worked and demanded an increase in salary. It was impossible for the appellant to find any replacement workers in Alaska or bring replacement workers from California in time to take full advantage of the short salmon season. The appellant agreed in writing to increase the libelants' fixed salary from $50 to $100. The libelants returned to work. After the catch was in and the libelants returned to California, appellant refused to pay more than the amount originally promised. Libelants sued to enforce the agreement modifying the employment contract.]

* * *

On the trial in the court below, the libelants undertook to show that the fishing nets provided by the respondent were defective, and that it was on that account that they demanded increased wages. On that point, the evidence was substantially conflicting, and the finding of the court was against the libelants the court saying:

> The contention of libelants that the nets provided them were rotten and unserviceable is not sustained by the evidence. The defendants' interest required that libelants should be provided

* A libelant is the admiralty counterpart to a plaintiff. Eds.

> with every facility necessary to their success as fishermen, for on such success depended the profits defendant would be able to realize that season from its packing plant, and the large capital invested therein. In view of this self-evident fact, it is highly improbable that the defendant gave libelants rotten and unserviceable nets with which to fish. It follows from this finding that libelants were not justified in refusing performance of their original contract.'

The evidence being sharply conflicting in respect to these facts, the conclusions of the court, who heard and saw the witnesses, will not be disturbed.

* * * From the foregoing statement of the case, it will have been seen that the libelants agreed in writing, for certain stated compensation, to render their services to the appellant in remote waters where the season for conducting fishing operations is extremely short, and in which enterprise the appellant had a large amount of money invested; and, after having entered upon the discharge of their contract, and at a time when it was impossible for the appellant to secure other men in their places, the libelants, without any valid cause, absolutely refused to continue the services they were under contract to perform unless the appellant would consent to pay them more money. Consent to such a demand, under such circumstances, if given, was, in our opinion, without consideration, for the reason that it was based solely upon the libelants' agreement to render the exact services, and none other, that they were already under contract to render.

* * * The circumstances of the present case bring it, we think, directly within the sound and just observations of the supreme court of Minnesota in the case of King v. Railway Co., 61 Minn. 482, 63 N.W. 1105:

> No astute reasoning can change the plain fact that the party who refuses to perform, and thereby coerces a promise from the other party to the contract to pay him an increased compensation for doing that which he is legally bound to do, takes an unjustifiable advantage of the necessities of the other party. Surely it would be a travesty on justice to hold that the party so making the promise for extra pay was estopped from asserting that the promise was without consideration. A party cannot lay the foundation of an estoppel by his own wrong, where the promise is simply a repetition of a subsisting legal promise. There can be no consideration for the promise of the other party, and there is no warrant for inferring that the parties have voluntarily rescinded or modified their contract. The promise cannot be legally enforced, although the other party has completed his contract in reliance upon it.

In Lingenfelder v. Brewing Co., 103 Mo. 578, 15 S.W. 844, the court, in holding void a contract by which the owner of a building agreed to pay its architect an additional sum because of his refusal to otherwise proceed with the contract, said:

> It is urged upon us by respondents that this was a new contract. New in what? Jungenfeld was bound by his contract to design and supervise this building. Under the new promise, he was not to do anything more or anything different. What benefit was to accrue to Wainwright? He was to receive the same service from Jungenfeld under the new, that Jungenfeld was bound to tender under the original, contract. What loss, trouble, or inconvenience could result to Jungenfeld that he had not already assumed? No amount of metaphysical reasoning can change the plain fact that Jungenfeld took advantage of Wainwright's necessities, and extorted the promise of five per cent. on the refrigerator plant as the condition of his complying with his contract already entered into. Nor had he even the flimsy pretext that Wainwright had violated any of the conditions of the contract on his part. Jungenfeld himself put it upon the simple proposition that 'if he, as an architect, put up the brewery, and another company put up the refrigerating machinery, it would be a detriment to the Empire Refrigerating Company,' of which Jungenfeld was president. To permit plaintiff to recover under such circumstances would be to offer a premium upon bad faith, and invite men to violate their most sacred contracts that they may profit by their own wrong. That a promise to pay a man for doing that which he is already under contract to do is without consideration is conceded by respondents. The rule has been so long imbedded in the common law and decisions of the highest courts of the various states that nothing but the most cogent reasons ought to shake it. (Citing a long list of authorities.) But it is 'carrying coals to Newcastle' to add authorities on a proposition so universally accepted, and so inherently just and right in itself. The learned counsel for respondents do not controvert the general proposition. Their contention is, and the circuit court agreed with them, that, when Jungenfeld declined to go further on his contract, the defendant then had the right to sue for damages, and not having elected to sue Jungenfeld, but having acceded to his demand for the additional compensation defendant cannot now be heard to say his promise is without consideration. While it is true Jungenfeld became liable in damages for the obvious breach of his contract, we do not think it follows that defendant is estopped from showing its promise was made without consideration. * * * What we hold is that, when a party merely does what he has already obligated himself to do, he cannot demand an additional

compensation therefor; and although, by taking advantage of the necessities of his adversary, he obtains a promise for more, the law will regard it as nudum pactum, and will not lend its process to aid in the wrong.

* * *

It results from the views above expressed that the judgment must be reversed, and the cause remanded, with directions to the court below to enter judgment for the respondent, with costs. It is so ordered.

QUESTIONS AND NOTES

1. Questions about the facts of this case

   1.1. Did the libelants argue that there was consideration for appellant's promise to pay more? If so, what?

   1.2. Do you think that it is "highly improbable" that appellant gave libelants "rotten and unserviceable nets"? Is what you think happened helpful to your understanding the "law" in this case?

2. Questions about the law

   2.1. Consider the following hypothetical based on *Alaska Packers* posed by Professor David Snyder in an article critical of the case: "Say the seamen in Alaska stopped work and said to the boss 'We want our wages doubled. In return, we'll spread the word back in San Fran that you are a great employer.' The boss, with no other labor for thousands of miles, is just as stuck as in the actual *Alaska Packers* case, and he agrees to the sailors' proposal." David V. Snyder, *The Law of Contract and the Concept of Change: Public and Private Attempts to Regulate Modification, Waiver and Estoppel*, 1999 WISC. L. REV. 607, 614. How would Professor Snyder's hypothetical be decided under the Restatement (Second) definition of consideration?

   2.2. Should the legal right of the workers to $100 instead of $50 be determined by the contract law concept of consideration?

   2.3 Do you agree with the following defense of the result in *Alaska Packers:* "Law and economics, however, provides a mechanism for understanding why the court's decision in *Alaska Packers* makes sense (leaving aside the hoary fiction of the pre-existing duty rule). . . . Why do we treat the bargain struck in San Francisco as the "real" bargain as opposed to the bargain on the boat in Alaska? Because in San Francisco, there is a competitive labor market. In Alaska there is not. And why can the fishermen succeed in getting a higher price for their work in Alaska? Because of the exigencies of time and the ability of the fishermen essentially to hold hostage the company's investment in the salmon cannery. The company needs them to work in order to get enough fish to recover its capital investment in the construction and operation of the salmon cannery. What is driving the fishermen's actions in *Alaska Packers* is rent-seeking behavior where the fishermen are expending real resources (the opportunity cost of remaining idle and the canning factory remaining idle) that are designed to expropriate the company's investment in the cannery to raise their wages. By not working, they can essentially destroy the value of the cannery by there being no fish. . . . [W]e do not want to encourage people to invest real resources in what is primarily rent-seeking activity designed just to extract a larger distributional share rather than an efficiency gain by the fishermen essentially trying to capture some of the value of the cannery itself. So again, the transaction costs are high—but here the transaction costs are high because of the threat of strategic behavior by the fishermen. Once more it appears that law and economics gives us both the positive and normative explanations—wherever possible, we want parties to bargain in situations with competitive markets, such as on the dock in San Francisco rather than on the boat in Alaska. So here, rather than essentially creating a forced transaction, we are nullifying a freely-bargained transaction." Todd Zywicki, *Libertarianism, Law and Economics and the Common Law*, 16 CHAPMAN L.REV. 309, 320–21 (2013). Does law and economics give you a "positive and normative explanation" of *Alaska Packers*?

3. Notes

3.1. Professor Craswell has given a musical explanation of *Alaska Packers*, http://www.youtube.com/watch?v=pKtZ6DTB8Qc&list=PL36131D32992573A4

3.2. Professor Debora L. Threedy has explored the historical and social background of the *Alaska Packers* case and concludes: "I confess from my first reading of the case I was skeptical about the reality of the traditional reading, doubting that Alaska Packers was ever at the mercy of the fishermen. Everything that I have since learned about the case has only deepened my skepticism." Debora L. Threedy, *A Fish Story: Alaska Packers' Association v. Domenico*, 2000 UTAH L. REV. 185, 197, n. 78.

4. **You Be the Lawyer!**

If you were the attorney for the libelants, how would you "under[take] to show that the fishing nets provided by the respondents were defective"?

Notwithstanding Professor Threedy's skepticism about what really happened, courts continue to cite and even rely on *Alaska Packers*. In the next case, the Rhode Island Supreme Court describes *Alaska Packers* as the "classic example of the 'hold-up game."

QUESTIONS BEFORE THE CASE

1. Do we know whether Maher requested the additional payments?
2. Do we know what Maher would have done if he had not received the additional payments?

ANGEL V. MURRAY

Supreme Court of Rhode Island
113 R.I. 482, 322 A.2d 630 (1974)

ROBERTS, C.J.

This is a civil action brought by Alfred L. Angel and others against John E. Murray, Jr., Director of Finance of the City of Newport, the city of Newport, and James L. Maher, alleging that Maher had illegally been paid the sum of $20,000 by the Director of Finance and praying that the defendant Maher be ordered to repay the city such sum. The case was heard by a justice of the Superior Court, sitting without a jury, who entered a judgment ordering Maher to repay the sum of $20,000 to the city of Newport. Maher is now before this court prosecuting an appeal.

The record discloses that Maher has provided the city of Newport with a refuse-collection service under a series of five-year contracts beginning in 1946. On March 12, 1964, Maher and the city entered into another such contract for a period of five years commencing on July 1, 1964, and terminating on June 30, 1969. The contract provided, among other things, that Maher would receive $137,000 per year in return for collecting and removing all combustible and noncombustible waste materials generated within the city.

In June of 1967 Maher requested an additional $10,000 per year from the city council because there had been a substantial increase in the cost of collection due to an unexpected and unanticipated increase of 400 new dwelling units. Maher's testimony, which is uncontradicted, indicates the 1964 contract had been predicated on the fact that since 1946 there had been an average increase of 20 to 25 new dwelling units per year. After a public meeting of the city council where Maher explained in detail the reasons for his request and was questioned by members of the city council, the city council agreed to pay him an additional $10,000 for the year ending on June 30, 1968. Maher made a similar request again in June of 1968 for the same reasons, and the city council again agreed to pay an additional $10,000 for the year ending on June 30, 1969.

The trial justice found * * * that Maher was not entitled to extra compensation because the original contract already required him to collect all refuse generated within the city and, therefore, included the 400 additional units. The trial justice further found that these 400 additional units were within the contemplation of the parties when they entered into the contract. It appears that he based this portion of the decision upon the rule that Maher had a preexisting duty to collect the refuse generated by the 400 additional units, and thus there was no consideration for the two additional payments.

* * *

As previously stated, the city council made two $10,000 payments. The first was made in June of 1967 for the year beginning on July 1, 1967, and ending on June 30, 1968. Thus, by the time this action was commenced in October of 1968, the modification was completely executed. That is, the money had been paid by the city council, and Maher had collected all of the refuse. * * *

It is generally held that a modification of a contract is itself a contract, which is unenforceable unless supported by consideration. In *Rose v. Daniels,* 8 R. I. 381 (1866), this court held that an agreement by a debtor with a creditor to discharge a debt for a sum of money less than the amount due is unenforceable because it was not supported by consideration.

Rose is a perfect example of the preexisting duty rule. Under this rule an agreement modifying a contract is not supported by consideration if one of the parties to the agreement does or promises to do something that he is legally obligated to do or refrains or promises to refrain from doing something he is not legally privileged to do. In *Rose* there was no consideration for the new agreement because the debtor was already legally obligated to repay the full amount of the debt.

* * *

The primary purpose of the preexisting duty rule is to prevent what has been referred to as the "hold-up game." A classic example of the "hold-up game" is found in *Alaska Packers' Ass'n v. Domenico,* 117 F. 99 (9th Cir. 1902). There 21 seamen entered into a written contract with Domenico to sail from San Francisco to Pyramid Harbor, Alaska. They were to work as sailors and fishermen out of Pyramid Harbor during the fishing season of 1900. The contract specified that each man would be paid $50 plus two cents for each red salmon he caught. Subsequent to their arrival at Pyramid Harbor, the men stopped work and demanded an additional $50. They threatened to return to San Francisco if Domenico did not agree to their demand. Since it was impossible for Domenico to find other men, he agreed to pay the men an additional $50. After they returned to San Francisco, Domenico refused to pay the men an additional $50. The court found that the subsequent agreement to pay the men an additional $50 was not supported by consideration because the men had a preexisting duty to work on the ship under the original contract, and thus the subsequent agreement was unenforceable.

Another example of the "hold-up game" is found in the area of construction contracts. Frequently, a contractor will refuse to complete work under an unprofitable contract unless he is awarded additional compensation. The courts have generally held that a subsequent agreement to award additional compensation is unenforceable if the contractor is only performing work which would have been required of him under the original contract.

These examples clearly illustrate that the courts will not enforce an agreement that has been procured by coercion or duress and will hold the parties to their original contract regardless of whether it is profitable or unprofitable. However, the courts have been reluctant to apply the preexisting duty rule when a party to a contract encounters unanticipated difficulties and the other party, not influenced by coercion or duress, voluntarily agrees to pay additional compensation for work already required to be performed under the contract.

* * *

Although the preexisting duty rule has served a useful purpose insofar as it deters parties from using coercion and duress to obtain additional compensation, it has been widely criticized as a general rule of law. With regard to the preexisting duty rule, one legal scholar has stated: "There has been a growing doubt as to the soundness of this doctrine as a matter of social policy. * * * In certain classes of cases, this doubt has influenced courts to refuse to apply the rule, or to ignore it, in their actual decisions. Like other legal rules, this rule is in process of growth and change, the process being more active here than in most instances. The result of this is that a court should no longer accept this rule as fully established. It should never use it as the major premise of a decision, at least without giving careful thought to the circumstances of the particular case, to the moral deserts of the parties, and to the social feelings and interests that are involved. It is certain that the rule, stated in general and all-inclusive terms, is no longer so well-settled that a court must apply it though the heavens fall." 1A *Corbin*, [Contracts] § 171 [(1963)]. * * *

The modern trend appears to recognize the necessity that courts should enforce agreements modifying contracts when unexpected or unanticipated difficulties arise during the course of the performance of a contract, even though there is no consideration for the modification, as long as the parties agree voluntarily.

Under the Uniform Commercial Code, § 2–209(1), which has been adopted by 49 states, "[an] agreement modifying a contract [for the sale of goods] needs no consideration to be binding." Although at first blush this section appears to validate modifications obtained by coercion and duress, the comments to this section indicate that a modification under this section must meet the test of good faith imposed by the Code, and a modification obtained by extortion without a legitimate commercial reason is unenforceable.

The modern trend away from a rigid application of the preexisting duty rule is reflected by § 89D(a) of the American Law Institute's Restatement Second of the Law of Contracts, which provides: "A promise modifying a duty under a contract not fully performed on either side is binding (a) if the modification is fair and equitable in view of circumstances not anticipated by the parties when the contract was made. * * *"

We believe that § 89D(a) is the proper rule of law and find it applicable to the facts of this case. It not only prohibits modifications obtained by coercion, duress, or extortion but also fulfills society's expectation that agreements entered into voluntarily will be enforced by the courts. Section 89D(a), of course, does not compel a modification of an unprofitable or unfair contract; it only enforces a modification if the parties voluntarily agree and if (1) the promise modifying the original contract was made before the contract was fully performed on either side, (2) the underlying circumstances which prompted the modification were unanticipated by the parties, and (3) the modification is fair and equitable.

* * *

The evidence, which is uncontradicted, reveals that in June of 1968 Maher requested the city council to pay him an additional $10,000 for the year beginning on July 1, 1968, and ending on June 30, 1969. This request was made at a public meeting of the city council, where Maher explained in detail his reasons for making the request. Thereafter, the city council voted to authorize the Mayor to sign an amendment to the 1954 contract which provided that Maher would receive an additional $10,000 per year for the duration of the contract. Under such circumstances we have no doubt that the city voluntarily agreed to modify the 1964 contract.

Having determined the voluntariness of this agreement, we turn our attention to the three criteria delineated above. First, the modification was made in June of 1968 at a time when the five-year contract which was made in 1964 had not been fully performed by either party. Second, although the 1964 contract provided that Maher collect all refuse generated within the city, it appears this contract was premised on Maher's past experience that the number of refuse-generating units would increase at a rate of 20 to 25 per year. Furthermore, the evidence is uncontradicted that the 1967–1968 increase of 400 units "went beyond any previous expectation." Clearly, the circumstances which prompted the city council to modify the 1964 contract were unanticipated. Third, although the evidence does not indicate what proportion of the total this increase comprised, the evidence does indicate that it was a "substantial" increase. In light of this, we cannot say that the council's agreement to pay Maher the $10,000 increase was not fair and equitable in the circumstances. . . .

The judgment appealed from is reversed, and the cause is remanded to the Superior Court for entry of judgment for the defendants.

QUESTIONS AND NOTE

1. Questions about the facts of this case

   1.1. Why did the city agree to make the additional payments to Maher? Is that relevant to the court's decision?

   1.2. Under the 1964 contract, was Maher legally obligated to collect refuse from the 400 additional units? Should that be relevant to the court's decision?

   1.3. Under the 1964 contract, would the city be legally obligated to pay Maher the $137,000 contract amount even though there was a decrease of 800 housing units instead of the 400 unit increase?

2. Questions about the law

   2.1. The *Murray* decision discusses the *Alaska Packers* case and the preexisting duty rule. What was the holding in *Alaska Packers*? Did the court in *Alaska Packers* mention the preexisting duty rule? What is the preexisting duty rule? Is the *Murray* holding consistent with the preexisting duty rule?

   2.2. Is the *Murray* holding consistent with the holding in *Alaska Packers*? Would the court that decided *Murray* have decided *Alaska Packers* differently? Would the court that decided *Alaska Packers* have decided *Murray* differently?

   2.3. The *Murray* case involves a question about the enforceability of a modification to a contract. (Didn't the *Hooters* case and the *Alaska Packers* case also involve a contract modification?) Should courts treat the question of whether a contract modification is legally enforceable differently from the question of whether a "new" agreement is legally enforceable?

   2.4. *Murray* holding: A later decision of the Rhode Island Supreme Court, *Fondedile, S.A. v. C.E. Maguire, Inc.*, 610 A.2d 87, 92 (1992), cites the *Murray* decision for the following proposition:

"parties to a contract can mutually assent to modify the contract if the modification does not violate the law or public policy and the modification is supported by adequate consideration." Is that an accurate summary of the *Murray* holding?

2.5. *Murray* reasoning: The court in *Murray* cites to and relies on the provisions in § 89 of the *Restatement (Second) of Contracts*. *Restatement (Second)* § 89(a) now states "A promise modifying a duty under a contract not fully performed on either side is binding (a) if the modification is fair and equitable in view of the circumstances not anticipated by the parties when the contract was made." Is the Rhode Island Supreme Court obligated to follow the statements in the *Restatement*?

2.6. More *Murray* reasoning: Note that the court in *Murray* discusses § 2–209 of the Uniform Commercial Code. Is the Rhode Island Supreme Court obligated to follow the sections of the Uniform Commercial Code? Does the *Murray* case involve a sale of goods? If not, why does the court consider § 2–209 of the Uniform Commercial Code?

2.7. Modification of contracts for sale of goods: How does § 2–209 of the Uniform Commercial Code differ from *Restatement (Second)* § 89(a)? Apply § 2–209 to the following sale of goods problem: Ponoroff contracts to deliver one hundred pounds of Michigan apples to Markell for $400. Ponoroff, who is relatively new to Michigan, then discovers that picking and packaging apples is much harder than he expected. He explains this to Markell and asks Markell to modify the contract by reducing the quantity from one hundred pounds to fifty pounds without reducing the price. Markell agrees. Markell later changes his mind. Is the modification agreement legally enforceable?

2.8. Modification of debt contracts: D owes C $3,200. The debt is due right now and undisputed. D and C agree that if D pays C $2,000, then C will release the rest of the debt. D pays C $2,000. Is the release agreement legally enforceable? Should it be?

3. Note

Professor Robert Hillman is critical of the pre-existing duty rule and *Restatement (Second) of Contracts* § 89(a):

> The approach of the *Restatement (Second) of Contracts* to modification enforceability suffers from a lack of clarity and fails to reflect the goals of contract-modification law. The weaknesses of the approach stem both from adherence to the preexisting-duty doctrine—a doctrine which, most commentators agree, has outlived its usefulness—and from failure to apply the doctrine of economic duress directly to the modification problem.

> The *Restatement (Second)* approach suffers from lack of clarity because of the difficulties of defining "unanticipated circumstances" and the broadness of the "fair and equitable," "honesty" and "justice requires" terminology. In addition, in light of the goals of contract modification law, the approach wrongly bars the enforcement of voluntary modification in the absence of consideration, "unanticipated circumstances," or material reliance (unless the promisee reasonably or honestly believes in a defense to performance). The approach is also potentially harmful because the occurrence of "unanticipated circumstances" does not ensure the voluntariness of a modification and because the "fair and equitable" and "pretense of a bargain" language may be insufficient to direct courts to the issue of economic duress.
>
> Proper application of each of the sections of the Restatement Second examined here (sections 73, 74, 89(a), and 89(c)) ultimately requires reference to the issues of duress. Accordingly, to cut through the morass of technical and unclear rules of the past, the duress doctrine should be applied to the problem of contract modification directly. Duress is a superior vehicle for analyzing the voluntariness of a modification because it requires inquiry into all of the factual elements that are probative of the issue. Undoubtedly, courts will face difficult decisions in weighing the various factors involved in the duress inquiry. Nevertheless, even if terms such as "unanticipated circumstances" were capable of clear definition and increased predictability of results, use of such tests would come at the expense of the appropriate broader inquiry—the voluntariness of modifications.

Robert A. Hillman, *Contract Modification Under the Restatement (Second) of Contracts*, 67 CORNELL L. REV. 680, 702–703 (1982).

4. **You Be the Lawyer!**

Assume that you are Maher's attorney and, immediately after the trial court entered its $20,000 judgment, the plaintiff had offered to settle for $10,000. Would you have recommended to Maher that he accept that settlement offer?

The pre-existing duty rule is the end of our consideration of the contract law doctrine of consideration. What are the ends served by the contract law doctrine of consideration? Numerous law review articles question whether consideration serve any ends. Our favorite article advocating the end of consideration, is James D. Gordon, III, *A Dialogue About the Doctrine of Consideration*, 75 CORNELL L. REV. 987 (1990), a wonderful article which begins by comparing consideration to Elvis:

"Consideration is to contract law as Elvis is to rock and roll—the King. Revisionists have questioned Elvis' greatness. They have wrestled with one disturbing issue: if Elvis is so great, how come he is buried in his own back yard—like a hamster."

Should courts and legislatures consider ending use of the doctrine of consideration? In 1925, the National Conference of Commissioners on Uniform State Laws approved the Uniform Written Obligations Act. Section One of that Act reads: "A written release or promise hereafter made and signed by the person releasing or promising shall not be invalid or unenforceable for lack of consideration, if the writing also contains an express statement in any form of language that the signer intends to be legally bound." Only Pennsylvania and Utah adopted the act, and Utah repealed it. Why didn't other states adopt the Uniform Written Obligations Act?

---

2. PROMISE TO PAY FOR SOMETHING THAT HAPPENED BEFORE THE PROMISE: MORAL OBLIGATIONS

Even though courts and the legislatures have not yet heeded the call of Professor Gordon and others to abolish consideration as a legal requirement for the enforcement of agreements and promises, courts and legislatures have developed concepts that are alternatives to or substitutes for consideration.

Recall that consideration is bargained for: "To constitute consideration, a performance or a return promise must be bargained for." *Restatement (Second) of Contracts* § 71(1). You can't bargain for someone to do something that she has already done—stuff that happened before a promise can't be "bargained for"; it can't be consideration. Or, as the *Restatement* more elegantly puts it: " 'Past consideration' is inconsistent with the meaning of consideration stated in section 71." *Restatement (Second) of Contracts* § 86, Comment a.

Assume, for example, that Ms. Chandler's promise [from the beginning of this chapter] to buy a Leading Man hair piece for Ponoroff was motivated not by his fine work on the fourth edition of MADD, but rather on the fact that several months earlier Ponoroff wrote a letter to the President of West Academic Publishing praising Ms. Chandler as a superior employee and an exemplary representative of the company. As a direct result, Ms. Chandler got a nice big fat raise. Grateful beyond words, she makes the call to Ponoroff promising him to deliver the hair piece next month—and also to take him to Sansu in East Lansing for an expensive Japanese dinner. Again, however, Ms. Chandler later changes her mind. Ponoroff (having once been a real lawyer) decides to sue, and Ms. Chandler contends that her promise should not be enforced because Ponoroff's letter, which was written and sent before her promises about the hair piece and dinner at Sansu were made, cannot be consideration for those promises. Should the court enforce Ms. Chandler's promises nevertheless? Would the courts that decided the next two cases have enforced those promises?

QUESTION BEFORE THE CASE

Was the promise in this case was a serious one by which the defendant fully intended to be bound?

HARRINGTON V. TAYLOR

Supreme Court of North Carolina
225 N.C. 690, 36 S.E.2d 227 (1945)

PER CURIUM.

The plaintiff in this case sought to recover of the defendant upon a promise made by him under the following peculiar circumstances:

The defendant had assaulted his wife, who took refuge in plaintiff's house. The next day the defendant gained access to the house and began another assault upon his wife. The defendant's wife knocked him down with an axe, and was on the point of cutting his head open or decapitating him while he was laying on the floor, and the plaintiff intervened, caught the axe as it was descending, and the blow intended for defendant fell upon her hand, mutilating it badly, but saving defendant's life.

Subsequently, defendant orally promised to pay the plaintiff her damages; but, after paying a small sum, failed to pay anything more. So, substantially, states the complaint.

The defendant demurred to the complaint as not stating a cause of action, and the demurrer was sustained. Plaintiff appealed.

The question presented is whether there was a consideration recognized by our law as sufficient to support the promise. The Court is of the opinion that however much the defendant should be impelled by common gratitude to alleviate the plaintiff's misfortune, a humanitarian act of this kind, voluntarily performed, is not such consideration as would entitle her to recover at law.

The judgment sustaining the demurrer is

Affirmed.

QUESTIONS BEFORE THE CASE

1. Do you feel that the court thinks that Seth Wyman's promise is one that should be performed?
2. Consider as you read the case how satisfying you find the court's explanation as to why the promise is not enforceable? Should Parker, C.J. have ruled that Seth Wyman's promise to pay Mills for the costs that Mills incurred in taking care of Seth's son was legally enforceable? Could Parker, C.J. have so ruled? Would Judge Judy, T.V. J, have so ruled?

MILLS V. WYMAN

Supreme Judicial Court of Massachusetts
20 Mass. (3 Pick.) 207 (1825)

This was an action of assumpsit brought to recover a compensation for the board, nursing, etc. of Levi Wyman, son of the defendant, from the 5th to the 20th of February 1821. The plaintiff then lived in Hartford, in Connecticut; the defendant, as Shrewsbury, in this county. Levi Wyman, at the time when the services were rendered, was about 25 years of age, and had long ceased to be a member of his father's family. He was on his return from a voyage at sea, and being suddenly taken sick at Hartford, and being poor and in distress, was relieved by the plaintiff in the manner and to the extent above stated. On the 24th of February, after all the expenses had been incurred, the defendant wrote a letter to the plaintiff, promising to pay him such expenses. There was no consideration for this promise, except what grew out of the relation which subsisted between Levi Wyman and the defendant, and Howe J., before whom the cause was tried in the Court of Common Pleas, thinking this not sufficient to support the action, directed a nonsuit. To this direction the plaintiff filed exceptions.

PARKER, CHIEF JUSTICE.

General rules of law established for the protection and security of honest and fair-minded men, who may inconsiderably make promises without any equivalent, will sometimes screen men of a different character from engagements which they are bound in *foro conscientiae* to perform. This is a defect inherent in all human systems of legislation. The rule that a mere verbal promise, without any consideration, cannot be enforced by action, is universal in its application, and cannot be departed from to suit particular cases in which a refusal to perform such a promise may be disgraceful.

The promise declared on in this case appears to have been made without any legal consideration. The kindness and services toward the sick son of the defendant were not bestowed at his request. The son was in no respect under the care of the defendant. He was twenty-five years old, and had long left his father's family. On his return from a foreign country he fell sick among strangers, and the plaintiff acted the part of the good Samaritan, giving him shelter and comfort until he died. The defendant, his father, on being informed of this event, influenced by transient feeling of gratitude, promises in writing to pay the plaintiff for the expenses he had incurred.* But he has determined to break this promise, and is willing to have his case appear on record as a strong example of particular injustice sometimes necessarily resulting from the operation of general rules.

It is said a moral obligation is sufficient consideration to support an express promise; and some authorities lay down the rule thus broadly; but upon examination of the case we are satisfied that the universality of the rule cannot be supported, and that there must have been some pre-existing obligation, which has become inoperative by positive law, to form a basis for an effective promise. The cases of debts barred by the statute of limitations, of debts incurred by infants, of debts of bankrupts, are generally put for illustration of the rule. Express promises founded on such pre-existing equitable obligations may be enforced; there is a good consideration for them; they merely remove an impediment created by law to the recovery of debts honestly due, but which public policy protects the debtors from being compelled to pay. In all these cases there was originally a quid pro quo; and according to the principle of natural justice the party receiving ought to pay; but the legislature has said he shall not be coerced; then comes the promise to pay the debt that is barred, the promise of the man to pay the debt of the infant, of the discharged bankrupt to restore to his creditor what by the law he has lost. In all these cases there is a moral obligation founded upon an antecedent valuable consideration. These promises therefore have a sound legal basis. They are not promises to pay something for nothing; not naked pacts; but the voluntary revival or creation of obligation which before existed in natural law, but which had been dispensed with, not for the benefit of the party obliged solely, but

* The letter is not reproduced in the opinion. Through some nice detective work, Dr. Watson found the letter and reproduced it in his article on *Mills v. Wyman*:

> Dear Sir:
>
> I received a line from you relating to my Son Levi's sickness and requesting me to come up and see him, but as the going is very bad I cannot come up at the present, but I wish you to take all possible care of him and if you cannot have him at your house I wish you to remove him to some convenient place and if he cannot satisfy you for it I will.
>
> I want that you should write me again immediately how he does and greatly oblige your most obedient servant
>
> Seth Wyman Feb 24th 1821.

Geoffrey R. Watson, *In the Tribunal of Conscience: Mills v. Wyman Reconsidered*, 71 TUL. L. REV. 1749, 1758 (1997). Eds.

principally for the public convenience. If moral obligation, in its fullest sense, is a good substratum for an express promise, it is not easy to perceive why it is not equally good to support an implied promise. What a man ought to do, generally he ought to be made to do, whether he promise or refuse. But the law of society has left most of such obligations to the *interior* forum, as the tribunal of conscience has been aptly called. Is there not a moral obligation upon every son who has become affluent by means of the education and advantages bestowed upon him by his father, to relieve that father from pecuniary embarrassment, to promote his comfort, and happiness, and even to share with him his riches, if thereby he will be made happy? And yet such a son may, with impunity, leave such a father in any degree of penury above that which will expose the community in which he dwells, to the danger of being obliged to preserve him from absolute want. Is not a wealthy father under strong moral obligation to advance the interest of an obedient, well disposed son, to furnish him with the means of acquiring and maintaining a becoming rank in life, to rescue him from the horrors of debt incurred by misfortune? Yet the law will uphold him in any degree of parsimony, short of that which would reduce his son to the necessity of seeking public charity.

Without doubt there are great interests of society which justify withholding the coercive arm of the law from these duties of imperfect obligation, as they are called; imperfect, not because they are less binding upon the conscience than those which are called perfect, but because the wisdom of the social law does not impose sanctions upon them.

A deliberate promise in writing, made freely and without any mistake, one which may lead the party to whom it is made into contracts and expenses, cannot be broken without a violation of moral duty. But if there was nothing paid or promised for it, the law, perhaps wisely, leaves the execution of it to the conscience of him who makes it. It is only when the party making the promise gains something, or he to whom it is made loses something, that the law gives the promise validity. And in the case of a promise of an adult to pay the debt of the infant, of the debtor discharged by the statute of limitations or bankruptcy, the principle is preserved by looking back to the origin of the transaction, where an equivalent is to be found. An exact equivalent is not required by the law; for there being a consideration, the parties are left to estimate its value; though here the courts of equity will step in to relieve from gross inadequacy between the consideration and the promise.

These principles are deduced from the general current of decided cases upon the subject, as well as from the known maxims of the common law. The general position, that moral obligation is a sufficient consideration for an express promise, is to be limited in its application to cases where at some time or other a good or valuable consideration has existed.

* * *

For the foregoing reasons, we are all of the opinion that the nonsuit directed by the Court of Common Pleas was right, and that judgment be entered thereon for the costs of the defendant.

QUESTIONS AND NOTES

1. Questions about the facts of this case

   1.1. Who is suing whom for what?

   1.2. Why did the plaintiff Mills take care of Levi Wyman? Was he a doctor? Was he expecting to be paid?

   1.3. Why didn't Mills sue Levi Wyman's estate? Why did Mills sue Seth Wyman, Levi's father?

   1.4. Did Mills continue to take care of Levi Wyman after receiving the letter from the defendant? Is that important to the court's decision?

2. Questions about the law

   2.1. Did Chief Justice Parker conclude that Seth Wyman was morally obligated to pay the plaintiff for taking care of his son? What is the basis for any such moral obligation?

   2.2. Is there a pre-existing duty issue in this case? Why not?

3. Notes

   3.1. Here's one writer's view of *Mills*:

> Many lawyers remember great common-law cases more for their facts than their reasoning. Ask a lawyer about the holding of *Mills v. Wyman* and you probably get a blank look. Ask if the lawyer remembers the case about father promising to pay the Good Samaritan for caring for the sick son, and you may get a smile of recognition. * * * Everyone remembers the facts; no one remembers the holding.
>
> For *Mills*, perhaps that is the way it should be. The rule in the case is eminently forgettable: it is as incoherent as it is inefficient. It will be a dead letter in another hundred years. But the facts of the case are memorable. Indeed, the story told by Justice Parker—Seth's hasty promise in a fleeting moment of gratitude, the death of Levi Wyman, Seth's willingness to stand up in court and be counted as a scoundrel—is more compelling than the story told by the surviving documents, in which Seth makes no promise, Levi does not die, and Seth deserves to win. For the law teacher,

> the reported facts stand as a morality play for lawyers and as a reminder of the limits of the profession. The mythical facts of Mills are an important part of our legal culture.

Geoffrey R. Watson, *In the Tribunal of Conscience:* Mills v. Wyman *Reconsidered*, 71 TUL. L. REV. 1749, 1806 (1997).

3.2. Lord Mansfield, Lord Chief Justice from 1756 to 1788 of the King's Bench, and a giant figure in the development of the commercial law in England, authored several opinions advancing the view that the moral obligation associated with any *written* agreement ought to serve as a sufficient basis to make that agreement enforceable. *See, e.g., Hawkes v. Saunders*, 1 Cowper 289, 98 Eng. Rep. 1091 (K.B. 1782). He regarded the existence of the writing as a suitable substitute for the evidentiary and cautionary functions purportedly served by the doctrine of consideration or, in early time, the seal. However, by Mansfield's time, the requirement of consideration was too deeply embedded in the common law to be uprooted, although it was not until 1840 that moral obligation alone was eliminated in England as satisfying the requirement of a good consideration for a promise. *See Eastwood v. Kenyon, 11 Ad. & E. 438, 113 Eng. Rep. 482.* As the decisions in *Harrington* and *Mills* illustrate, courts in this country were also skeptical of accepting moral obligation as a sufficient basis for enforcement of a promise. In *Manwill v. Oyler*, 11 Utah 2d 433, 361 P.2d 177, 178 (1961), the Utah Supreme Court expressed the generally-held sentiment that "if a mere moral, as distinguished from a legal, obligation were recognized as a valid consideration for a contract, that would practically erode to the vanishing point the necessity for finding a consideration" in the first place. Clearly, Chief Justice Parker in *Mills* was bothered by the defendant's abnegation of his promise, indicating his apparent disbelief that Wyman was "willing to have his case appear on record." How much of a deterrent do you suppose this form of shaming is likely to be in the case of persons already inclined to avoid their promises because of the technical absence of consideration?

3.3. The court in *Mills* makes reference to three circumstances in which the law has long recognized exceptions to the rule that past consideration is not good consideration: (1) a promise reviving a previously legally enforceable obligation now barred by an applicable limitations period, (2) a promise to pay an obligation rendered discharged by insolvency, and (3) a promise to pay an obligation incurred by an infant. The enforceability of the first type of promise—reviving an earlier enforceable obligation—is now recognized in *Restatement (Second) of Contracts* § 82, although many states also require a writing as a condition to the enforceability of such promises. *See, e.g.,*

Manwill v. Oyler, supra. As for the second type of promise, Section 83 of *Restatement (Second) of Contracts* provides that an express promise to pay all or part of a debt discharged in bankruptcy is binding. Since 1978, however, the matter has been preempted by the federal Bankruptcy Code, which expressly makes promises to repay a discharged debt unenforceable. On the other hand, agreements (called "reaffirmations") by a bankruptcy debtor to reinstate personal liability for debts that would otherwise be subject to the discharge may, subject to certain stringent conditions, be binding provided that they are entered into and approved by the court *prior* to the entry of the discharge in bankruptcy. *See Bankruptcy Code* §§ 524(c) & (d). In addition, purely *voluntary* repayment of discharged debts is permitted under the bankruptcy law. *See Bankruptcy Code* § 524(f). Finally, as to the third type of promise, modern courts continue to recognize that a minor with the power to avoid by disaffirmance his contractual obligations may, upon reaching the age of majority and without the requirement of new consideration, make a new enforceable undertaking to perform his duties under the contract. *See generally Restatement (Second) of Contracts* § 85.

3.4. While moral obligation and past consideration as bases for enforcing a promise have always presented some problems for the common law, the civil law has long recognized the concept of "natural obligation," making for an easier time of it. A natural obligation exists when there is a moral, but not judicially enforceable, duty to render performance where "the law implies a particular moral duty to render a performance." La. Civ. Code Ann. art. 1760. *See* Thomas v. Bryant, 639 So.2d 378 (La. Ct. App. 1994), enforcing the promise of a father to pay for the medical expenses of his adult son.

4. **You Be the Lawyer!**

In light of *Harrington v. Taylor,* would you have advised Mr. Mills to bring this lawsuit? Are you going to have a problem getting paid? Read on.

NOTE ON UNJUST ENRICHMENT AND RESTITUTION

Now it seems that justice and equity might have been better served had the plaintiffs in *Harrington* and *Mills* been permitted to recover. They were unable to do so because, even though each plaintiff conferred a benefit on the respective defendants, there was no contemporaneous exchange of promise and consideration. A similar situation arises when, unlike in *Harrington* and *Mills*, there is no subsequent promise to pay for the benefit conferred. In other words, suppose Ponoroff and Epstein own adjoining properties. Ponoroff decides he wants to have a swimming pool and hot tub installed on his property, but mistakenly makes plans to locate the pool and spa on land that is actually part of Epstein's lot. From the get-go, Epstein sees what's going on but says nothing. Rather, he waits for the work to be completed and, then, the first time Ponoroff shows up in his speedo and clogs (now there's an image), Epstein pops up, survey in hand, and says "beat it, you're trespassing."

Now clearly Epstein has been benefitted by Ponoroff's actions and Epstein knew about it all along, but he never declined that benefit, or notified Ponoroff, before the benefit was fully conferred on him. However, Epstein did not, by either his words or conduct, *promise* to pay for the benefit. So Ponoroff has no claim for breach of an actual or implied-in-fact contract. Is Ponoroff just up the creek without the proverbial paddle—as is usually the case? Maybe not. The law recognizes another theory of liability known as unjust enrichment. Now we have an entire chapter later devoted to unjust enrich and restitution; that deals with what is termed implied-in-law or quasi-contract. We raise the subject now, however, for two reasons: (1) because most professors don't have time to actually get to Chapter 8, and (2) because there is a relationship between those materials and the materials in this section based on enforcement of promises made in return for an antecedent benefit.*

We will discuss that relationship in greater depth in the "Connections" section following the next case. For now, however, we want to summarize the elements of a claim based on quasi-contract. Specifically, if a party can prove that he conferred a benefit on another, without intending to act gratuitously, and under circumstances where it would be inequitable for the other party to retain the benefit without providing compensation therefor, then the first party should be entitled to *restitution* for the value of the benefit conferred. So if we go back to our hypothetical, we see Ponoroff might be able to recover the value by which he improved Epstein's property, even though there was no promise from Epstein.

Now what's the difference between the unjust enrichment scenario, like our hypothetical, and *Harrington* and *Mills*? Answer: there is a *real* promise in those cases, it's just that the promise is not enforceable because the promise was not supported by good consideration. Ok, now ask yourself, "self, could the plaintiff in either *Harrington* or *Mills* have recovered on a quasi-contract theory"? If you answered "no," we agree. Now ask yourself, "self, how did I get to the right answer"? Perhaps it was just a good guess; after all, it was a 50/50 shot of being right. On the other hand, if you focused on whether the plaintiff in each of those cases had an expectation of compensation or was acting gratuitously, well, now you're getting somewhere.

So let's read another case involving a promise made in return for a prior benefit conferred that comes out differently than *Harrington* and *Mills* and then return to the connection between this section and the materials in

* Damn, could Ponoroff just say "prior"? Oh no, he has to say "antecedent." Sheesh (Epstein and Markell).

Chapter 8. In the interests of full disclosure, Epstein and Markell believe Ponoroff has just confused you for no good reason, but Ponoroff believes there is a method to his madness; or is that a madness to his method? Never mind, just keep reading.

QUESTIONS BEFORE THE *WEBB* CASES

1. Do the holdings of the Alabama Court of Appeals and Supreme Court open the Pandora's Box that the court in *Mills v. Wyman* was concerned about?
2. If not, what are the limiting principles and are they adequate?

WEBB V. MCGOWIN

Court of Appeals of Alabama
27 Ala.App. 82, 168 So. 196 (1935)

BRICKEN, PRESIDING JUDGE.

This action is in assumpsit. The complaint as originally filed was amended. The demurrers to the complaint as amended were sustained, and because of this adverse ruling by the court the plaintiff took a non-suit, and the assignment of errors on this appeal are predicated upon said action or ruling of the court.

A fair statement of the case presenting the questions for decision is set out in appellant's brief, which we adopt.

> "On the 3d day of August, 1925, appellant while in the employ of the W. T. Smith Lumber Company, a corporation, and acting within the scope of his employment, was engaged in clearing the upper floor of mill No. 2 of the company. While so engaged he was in the act of dropping a pine block from the upper floor of the mill to the ground below; this being the usual and ordinary way of clearing the floor, and it being the duty of the plaintiff in the course of his employment to so drop it. The block weighed about 75 pounds.
>
> "As appellant was in the act of dropping the block to the ground below, he was on the edge of the upper floor of the mill. As he started to turn the block loose so that it would drop to the ground, he saw J. Greeley McGowin, testator of the defendants, on the ground below and directly under where the block would have fallen had appellant turned it loose. Had he turned it loose it would have struck McGowin with such force as to have caused him serious bodily harm or death. Appellant could have remained safely on the upper floor of the mill by turning the block loose and

allowing it to drop, but had he done this the block would have fallen on McGowin and cause him serious injuries or death. The only safe and reasonable way to prevent this was for appellant to hold to the block and divert its direction in falling from the place where McGowin was standing and the only safe way to divert it so as to prevent its coming into contact with McGowin was for appellant to fall with it to the ground below. Appellant did this, and by holding to the block and falling with it to the ground below, he diverted the course of its fall in such way that McGowin was not injured. In thus preventing the injuries to McGowin appellant himself received serious bodily injuries, resulting in his right leg being broken, the heel of his right foot torn off and his right arm broken. He was badly crippled for life and rendered unable to do physical or mental labor.

"On September 1, 1925, in consideration of appellant having prevented him from sustaining death or serious bodily harm and in consideration of the injuries appellant had received, McGowin agreed with him to care for and maintain him for the remainder of appellant's life at the rate of $15 every two weeks from the time he sustained his injuries to and during the remainder of appellant's life; it being agreed that McGowin would pay this sum to appellant for his maintenance. Under the agreement McGowin paid or caused to be paid to appellant the sum so agreed on up until McGowin's death on January 1, 1934. After his death the payments were continued to and including January 27, 1934, at which time they were discontinued. Thereupon plaintiff brought suit to recover the unpaid installments accruing up to the time of the bringing of the suit.

"The material averments of the different counts of the original complaint and the amended complaint are predicated upon the foregoing statement of facts."

In other words, the complaint as amended averred in substance: (1) That on August 3, 1925, appellant saved J. Greeley McGowin, appellee's testator, from death or grievous bodily harm; (2) that in doing so appellant sustained bodily injury crippling him for life; (3) that in consideration of the services rendered and the injuries received by appellant, McGowin agreed to care for him the remainder of appellant's life, the amount to be paid being $15 every two weeks; (4) that McGowin complied with this agreement until he died on January 1, 1934, and the payments were kept up to January 27, 1934, after which they were discontinued.

The action was for the unpaid installments accruing after January 27, 1934, to the time of the suit.

The principal grounds of demurrer to the original and amended complaint are: (1) It states no cause of action; (2) its averments show the contract was without consideration; (3) it fails to allege that McGowin had, at or before the services were rendered, agreed to pay appellant for them; (4) the contract declared on is void under the statute of frauds.

1. The averments of the complaint show that appellant saved McGowin from death or grievous bodily harm. This was a material benefit to him of infinitely more value than any financial aid he could have received. Receiving this benefit, McGowin became morally bound to compensate appellant for the services rendered. Recognizing his moral obligation, he expressly agreed to pay appellant as alleged in the complaint and complied with this agreement up to the time of his death; a period of more than 8 years.

Had McGowin been accidentally poisoned and a physician, without his knowledge or request, had administered an antidote, thus saving his life, a subsequent promise by McGowin to pay the physician would have been valid. Likewise, McGowin's agreement as disclosed by the complaint to compensate appellant for saving him from death or grievous bodily injury is valid and enforceable.

Where the promisee cares for, improves, and preserves the property of the promisor, though done without his request, it is sufficient consideration for the promisor's subsequent agreement to pay for the service, because of the material benefit received. * * *

In *Boothe v. Fitzpatrick,* 36 Vt. 681, the court held that a promise by defendant to pay for the past keeping of a bull which had escaped from defendant's premises and been cared for by plaintiff was valid, although there was no previous request, because the subsequent promise obviated that objection; it being equivalent to a previous request. On the same principle, had the promisee saved the promisor's life or his body from grievous harm, his subsequent promise to pay for the services rendered would have been valid. Such service would have been far more material than caring for his bull. Any holding that saving a man from death or grievous bodily harm is not a material benefit sufficient to uphold a subsequent promise to pay for the service, necessarily rests on the assumption that saving life and preservation of the body from harm have only a sentimental value. The converse of this is true. Life and preservation of the body have material, pecuniary values, measurable in dollars and cents. Because of this, physicians practice their profession charging for services rendered in saving life and curing the body of its ills, and surgeons perform operations. The same is true as to the law of negligence, authorizing the assessment of damages in personal injury cases based upon the extent of the injuries, earnings, and life expectancies of those injured.

In the business of life insurance, the value of a man's life is measured in dollars and cents according to his expectancy, the soundness of his body, and his ability to pay premiums. The same is true as to health and accident insurance.

It follows that if, as alleged in the complaint, appellant saved J. Greeley McGowin from death or grievous bodily harm, and McGowin subsequently agreed to pay him for the service rendered, it became a valid and enforceable contract.

2. It is well settled that a moral obligation is a sufficient consideration to support a subsequent promise to pay where the promisor has received a material benefit, although there was no original duty or liability resting on the promisor. * * * In the case of *State ex rel. Bayer v. Funk, supra,* [105 Or. 134, 199 P. 592] the court held that a moral obligation is a sufficient consideration to support an executory promise where the promisor has received an actual pecuniary or material benefit for which he subsequently expressly promised to pay.

The case at bar is clearly distinguishable from that class of cases where the consideration is a mere moral obligation or conscientious duty unconnected with receipt by promisor of benefits of a material or pecuniary nature. * * * Here the promisor received a material benefit constituting a valid consideration for his promise.

3. Some authorities hold that, for a moral obligation to support a subsequent promise to pay, there must have existed a prior legal or equitable obligation, which for some reason had become unenforceable, but for which the promisor was still morally bound. This rule, however, is subject to qualification in those cases where the promisor, having received a material benefit from the promisee, is morally bound to compensate him for the services rendered and in consideration of this obligation promises to pay. In such cases the subsequent promise to pay is an affirmance or ratification of the services rendered carrying with it the presumption that a previous request for the service was made. * * *

Under the decisions above cited, McGowin's express promise to pay appellant for the services rendered was an affirmance or ratification of what appellant had done raising the presumption that the services had been rendered at McGowin's request.

4. The averments of the complaint show that in saving McGowin from death or grievous bodily harm, appellant was crippled for life. This was part of the consideration of the contract declared on. McGowin was benefited. Appellant was injured. Benefit to the promisor or injury to the promisee is a sufficient legal consideration for the promisor's agreement to pay. * * *

5. Under the averments of the complaint the services rendered by appellant were not gratuitous. The agreement of McGowin to pay and the acceptance of payment by appellant conclusively shows the contrary.

6. The contract declared on was not void under the statute of frauds.

* * *

From what has been said, we are of the opinion that the court below erred in the ruling complained of; that is to say, in sustaining the demurrer, and for this error the case is reversed and remanded.

SAMFORD, JUDGE (Concurring)

The questions involved in this case are not free from doubt, and perhaps the strict letter of the rule, as stated by judges, though not always in accord, would bar a recovery by plaintiff, but following the principle announced by Chief Justice Marshall in *Hoffman v. Porter, Fed.Cas. No. 6,577,* 2 Brock. 156, 159, where he says, "I do not think that law ought to be separated from justice, where it is at most doubtful," I concur in the conclusions reached by the court.

WEBB V. MCGOWIN

Supreme Court of Alabama
232 Ala. 374, 168 So. 199 (1936)

FOSTER, J.

We do not in all cases in which we deny a petition for certiorari to the Court of Appeals approve the reasoning and principles declared in the opinion, even though no opinion is rendered by us. But when the opinion of the Court of Appeals asserts important principles or their application to new situations, and it may be uncertain whether this court agrees with it in all respects, we think it advisable to be specific in that respect when the certiorari is denied. We think such a situation here exists.

Neither this court nor the Court of Appeals has had before it questions similar to those here presented.

The opinion of the Court of Appeals here under consideration recognized and applies the distinction between a supposed moral obligation of the promisor, based upon some refined sense of ethical duty, without material benefit to him, and one in which such a benefit did in fact occur. We agree with that court that if the benefit be material and substantial, and was to the person of the promisor rather than to his estate, it is within the class of material benefits which he has the privilege of recognizing and compensating either by an executed payment or an executory promise to pay. The cases are cited in that opinion. The reason is emphasized when the compensation is not only for the benefits which the promisor received, but also for the injuries either to the property or person of the promisee by reason of the service rendered.

Writ denied.

QUESTIONS, NOTES, AND CONNECTIONS

1. Questions about the facts of this case

   1.1. Was there a written promise in *Webb*?

   1.2. Why was plaintiff paid $15 every two weeks until January 27, 1934? Why did the payments stop on January 27, 1934?

   1.3. Can the facts of *Webb* be distinguished from the facts of *Mills*? Which, if any, of the factual differences explain the different legal result?

   1.4. Recall that in *Webb*, the Alabama Court of Appeals reproduced the statement of facts from the appellant/plaintiff's brief. What were the grounds for the defendant's demurrers that were sustained by the trial court?

2. Questions about the law

   2.1. Did the Court of Appeals in *Webb* hold that there was an agreement to pay plaintiff $15 every two weeks? That there was consideration for such a promise?

   2.2. Would a court applying any of our definitions of consideration hold that such a promise was enforceable because of consideration?

   2.3. Both the Alabama Court of Appeals decision and the Alabama Supreme Court decision mention "material benefit." The Reporter to *Restatement (Second) of Contracts* described section 86, set out below, as a "material benefit rule":*

   > ***§ 86. Promise for Benefit Received***
   >
   > *(1) A promise made in recognition of a benefit previously received by the promisor from the promisee is binding to the extent necessary to prevent injustice.*
   >
   > *(2) A promise is not binding under Subsection (1):*
   >
   > *(a) if the promisee conferred the benefit as a gift or for other reasons the promisor has not been unjustly enriched; or*

---

* Robert Braucher, *Freedom of Contract and the Second Restatement*, 78 YALE L.J. 598, 615 (1969).

> *(b) to the extent that its value is disproportionate to the benefit.*

How would *Webb* be decided by a court applying this *Restatement* provision? How would *Mills* be decided by a court applying this *Restatement* provision? Is there a difference between *Webb* and *Mills* in terms of the circumstances under which the services were rendered? If so, does this help you reconcile the decisions? Can you reconcile *Webb* and *Harrington* on the same basis?

3. Notes

3.1. Professor Charles Fried, described the Alabama Court of Appeals decision in *Webb* as "a process of reasoning too strained to repeat." CHARLES FRIED, CONTRACT AS PROMISE 33 (1981). Do you agree?

3.2. In his widely-celebrated book, THE DEATH OF CONTRACT, written in 1974, Professor Grant Gilmore, pointing to the general direction being taken in the *Restatement (Second) of Contracts,* concluded, "we might say that what is happening is that 'contract' is being reabsorbed into the mainstream of 'tort.' " *Id.* at 95. As one of the primary illustrations of this trend, Professor Gilmore pointed to allowing enforcement of a promise made in recognition of a past benefit. He noted: "The principal thing is that *Restatement (Second)* gives overt recognition to an important principle whose existence *Restatement (First)* ignored and, by implication denied. By the time we get to Restatement (Third) it may well be that § 89A* will have flowered like Jack's bean-stalk in the same way that § 90 did between *Restatement (First)* and *Restatement (Second).*" *Id.* at 76.

3.3. Twenty-one years later, Professor Kastely offered the following evaluation of this prediction:

> This prediction has not proved true. Very few reported decisions since 1974 have even mentioned Section 86, and most of those references have been made only in passing, often in reference to contract actions barred by the statute of limitations. I have found only four reported decisions involving Section 86; in two, the courts found that Section 86 would not support enforcement of the promise. Moreover, the two cases holding that Section 86 might support enforcement of the promise involve situations that fit a traditional quasi-contract model**—one involved service rendered by a broker and another care provided by a sister. These cases do not represent movement toward the idea

* Section 89A, to which Professor Gilmore refers, became § 86 in the final draft of the *Restatement (Second).* Eds.

** We take up the subject of "quasi contract" in Chapter 7. Eds.

> that "to prevent unjust enrichment, any benefit received by a defendant must be paid for unless it was clearly meant as a gift" as Gilmore suggested.
>
> Following some initial expansion, many courts have domesticated the doctrines of promissory estoppel and promise for benefit received, making them compatible with classical contract theory, or at least much less of a threat to it. Most current versions of these doctrines offer little threat to the idea that no one should be liable for anything, at least not anything that she or he has not explicitly agreed to do. It seems that the pressures of contract ideology are so strong that, over time, they have reshaped the rebellious versions of these doctrines, fitting them into line with contract ideology.

Amy H. Kastely, *Cogs or Cyborgs, Blasphemy and Irony in Contract Theories*, 90 NW. U. L. REV. 132, 138–39 (1995).

3.4. Think back to the purposes for the requirement of a bargained-for consideration, as discussed in earlier sections of this chapter, as the basic ingredient necessary for an agreement to be legally enforceable. How are those purposes served by enforcement of a promise made in recognition of a benefit previously conferred? How are they done violence? Do you think moral obligation alone should provide a sufficient basis for enforcement?

In the eighteenth century, long after the doctrine of consideration had been firmly rooted in English law, Lord Chief Justice Mansfield attempted to introduce the proposition that any moral obligation arising from a promise should be sufficient to make non-performance of that promise actionable. Eager to break down the barriers between law and equity, and to apply equitable principles in the operation of the common law, Lord Mansfield opined that consideration had only evidentiary value and was not essential to the validity of a contract. But the tradition of the common law was too strong even for Lord Mansfield, whose opinion was overruled by the House of Lords, which reasserted that need for consideration in all contracts.

What role did moral obligation play in *Wells v. McGowin*? Ask yourself the same question with respect to the cases that follow in the next subsection dealing with another recognized "consideration substitute," reliance.

4. **You Be the Lawyer!**

If you represented Mr. McGowin's estate back in January of 1934, would you (and be honest now) have recommended that the payments to Webb be discontinued?

5. Connections

Could Webb have recovered from McGowin's estate on a quasi-contract claim? Certainly, McGowin had been enriched by Webb's actions, and it does seem unjust that he not have to provide compensation for the injuries suffered by Webb in saving his life. However, as in *Harrington* and *Mills*, the benefit was conferred gratuitously. That is to say, Webb did not act with an expectation of compensation. On the other hand, all three of those cases have something that the standard implied-in-law contract case does not; namely, a real, honest-to-god, genuine promise. It is this fact that seems to turn the tide in favor of enforcement despite the technical absence of consideration and the gratuitous nature of the act that later prompts the promise. In fact, § 86 of the *Restatement (Second)*, quoted above and which endorses the holding in *Webb*, creates an exception in subsection 2(a) to recovery based on prior benefit conferred where the "the promisee conferred the benefit as a gift or for other reasons the promisor has not been unjustly enriched." We noted that McGowin was almost surely unjustly enriched, but was the benefit conferred by Webb as a gift? Is there a difference between an act being a gift and an act being gratuitious?

---

3. RELIANCE AND THE LEGAL CONCEPT OF PROMISSORY ESTOPPEL

A. OVERVIEW

Recall Ms. Chandler and her promise to Ponoroff of a Leading Man 9333 hair piece? When she changed her mind, her promise was not legally enforceable because there was no consideration.

What if, after Ms. Chandler's promise, Ponoroff, in reliance on that promise, contracts to have an expensive portrait of himself done, in the new hair piece of course, by the famous portrait artist Daisy Rembrandt. Or suppose Ponoroff has had his bathroom remodeled with a separate dust-free, climate-controlled chamber in which he planned to keep the hair piece at night while he slept. Should Ms. Chandler's promise of the hair piece now be legally enforceable?

Classical contract law was primarily concerned with protecting the promisee's expectation interest in an exchange transaction. The requirement of consideration, as we have seen, ensures that promises that are part of a bargained-for exchange will be enforceable. By the same token, mere reliance on a promise that was not part of an economic exchange was not cognizable in the eyes of the law; hence, the adage that gift promises are not enforceable. Nonetheless, there are circumstances where leaving a party who detrimentally changed her position in reliance on a promise without a remedy of any sort was perceived as unduly harsh. Accordingly, one of the most important developments in contract law over the course of the twentieth century was the evolution of the principle that, in an appropriate case, unbargained-for reliance may provide a suitable basis for enforcing a promise, even in a non-exchange transaction. This evolution culminated in the *Restatement (Second) of Contracts*' revision of § 90, which now provides:

> *(1) A promise which the promisor should reasonably expect to induce action or forbearance on the part of the promisee or a third person and which does induce such action or forbearance is binding if injustice can be avoided only by enforcement of the promise. The remedy granted for breach may be limited as justice requires.*

Compare this formulation with § 90 of the first *Restatement of Contracts*

> *A promise which the promisor should reasonably expect to induce action or forbearance of a definite and substantial character on the part of the promisee and which does induce such action or forbearance is binding if injustice can be avoided only by enforcement of the promise.*

Section 90 has been described as "perhaps the most radical and expansive development of this century in the law of promissory liability." *See* Charles L. Knapp, *Reliance in the Revised* Restatement: *The Proliferation of Promissory Estoppel*, 81 COLUM. L. REV. 52, 52 (1981). Reliance, or more properly, compensation for harm suffered as a consequence of reliance on a promise, plays a central role in the *Restatement (Second)*. Section 90 offers a mechanism whereby a purely gratuitous promise might be enforced. In fact, one might not unfairly regard reliance as a substitute for consideration in cases to which § 90 applies. And, as we'll see, many courts regard promissory estoppel as providing a wholly new theory of liability. Thus, § 90 has vastly expanded the potential scope of contractual responsibility to the point, at least according to one commentator, that it has "swallowed up the bargain principle" embodied in the doctrine of consideration. GRANT GILMORE, THE DEATH OF CONTRACT 77 (1974).

From where did this seemingly revolutionary doctrine arise? Professor Williston is generally given credit for coining the term "promissory estoppel" in the first edition of his famous Contracts treatise originally published in 1920. 1 WILLISTON ON CONTRACTS § 139 (1st ed. 1920). Not surprisingly, Williston was instrumental in the incorporation of the doctrine of promissory estoppel into the first *Restatement of Contracts* in the form of § 90, quoted above. In Anglo-American jurisprudence, however, the roots of the doctrine go back to at least the nineteenth century, although, as we see in our first case, the courts were not always sure as to the category of the law to which the doctrine belonged.

B. HISTORICAL DEVELOPMENT

QUESTION BEFORE THE CASE

Do you think there was a bargain in this case? If so, what was it?

RICKETTS V. SCOTHORN

Supreme Court of Nebraska
57 Neb. 51, 77 N.W. 365 (1898)

SULLIVAN, J.

In the district court of Lancaster county the plaintiff, Katie Scothorn, recovered judgment against the defendant, Andrew D. Ricketts, as executor of the last will and testament of John C. Ricketts, deceased. The action was based upon a promissory note, of which the following is a copy:

> "May the first, 1891. I promise to pay to Katie Scothorn on demand, $2,000, to be at 6 per cent. per annum. J. C. Ricketts."

In the petition the plaintiff alleges that the consideration for the execution of the note was that she should surrender her employment as bookkeeper for Mayer Bros., and cease to work for a living. She also alleges that the note was given to induce her to abandon her occupation, and that, relying on it, and on the annual interest, as a means of support, she gave up the employment in which she was then engaged. These allegations of the petition are denied by the administrator. The material facts are undisputed. They are as follows: John C. Ricketts, the maker of the note, was the grandfather of the plaintiff. Early in May—presumably on the day the note bears date—he called on her at the store where she was working. What transpired between them is thus described by Mr. Flodene, one of the plaintiff's witnesses:

> "A. Well, the old gentleman came in there one morning about nine o'clock, probably a little before or a little after, but early in the morning, and he unbuttoned his vest, and took out a piece of paper in the shape of a note; that is the way it looked to me; and he says to Miss Scothorn, 'I have fixed out something that you have not got to work any more.' He says, none of my grandchildren work, and you don't have to.
>
> Q. Where was she?

A. She took the piece of paper and kissed him, and kissed the old gentleman, and commenced to cry."

It seems Miss Scothorn immediately notified her employer of her intention to quit work, and that she did soon after abandon her occupation. The mother of the plaintiff was a witness, and testified that she had a conversation with her father, Mr. Ricketts, shortly after the note was executed, in which he informed her that he had given the note to the plaintiff to enable her to quit work; that none of his grandchildren worked, and he did not think she ought to. For something more than a year the plaintiff was without an occupation, but in September, 1892, with the consent of her grandfather, and by his assistance, she secured a position as bookkeeper with Messrs. Funke & Ogden. On June 8, 1894, Mr. Ricketts died. He had paid one year's interest on the note, and a short time before his death expressed regret that he had not been able to pay the balance. In the summer or fall of 1892 he stated to his daughter, Mrs. Scothorn, that if he could sell his farm in Ohio he would pay the note out of the proceeds. He at no time repudiated the obligation. We quite agree with counsel for the defendant that upon this evidence there was nothing to submit to the jury, and that a verdict should have been directed peremptorily for one of the parties. The testimony of Flodene and Mrs. Scothorn, taken together, conclusively establishes the fact that the note was not given in consideration of the plaintiff pursuing, or agreeing to pursue, any particular line of conduct. There was no promise on the part of the plaintiff to do, or refrain from doing, anything. Her right to the money promised in the note was not made to depend upon an abandonment of her employment with Mayer Bros., and future abstention from like service. Mr. Ricketts made no condition, requirement, or request. He exacted no quid pro quo. He gave the note as a gratuity, and looked for nothing in return. So far as the evidence discloses, it was his purpose to place the plaintiff in a position of independence, where she could work or remain idle, as she might choose. The abandonment of Miss Scothorn of her position as bookkeeper was altogether voluntary. It was not an act done in fulfillment of any contract obligation assumed when she accepted the note. The instrument in suit, being given without any valuable consideration, was nothing more than a promise to make a gift in the future of the sum of money therein named. Ordinarily, such promises are not enforceable, even when put in the form of a promissory note. * * * But it has often been held that an action on a note given to a church, college, or other like institution, upon the faith of which money has been expended or obligations incurred, could not be successfully defended on the ground of a want of consideration. * * * In this class of cases the note in suit is nearly always spoken of as a gift or donation, but the decision is generally put on the ground that the expenditure of money or assumption of liability by the donee on the faith of the promise constitutes a valuable and sufficient consideration. It seems to us that the true reason is the preclusion of the defendant, under the doctrine of estoppel, to deny the consideration. Such seems to be the view of the matter taken by the supreme court of Iowa in the case of *Simpson Centenary College v. Tuttle,* 71 Iowa, 596, 33 N. W. 74, where Rothrock, J., speaking for the court, said:

> Where a note, however, is based on a promise to give for the support of the objects referred to, it may still be open to this defense [want of consideration], unless it shall appear that the donee has, prior to any revocation, entered into engagements, or made expenditures based on such promise, so that he must suffer loss or injury if the note is not paid. This is based on the equitable principle that, after allowing the donee to incur obligations on the faith that the note would be paid, the donor would be estopped from pleading want of consideration.

And in the case of *Reimensnyder v. Gans,* 110 Pa. St. 17, 2 Atl. 425, which was an action on a note given as a donation to a charitable object, the court said: "The fact is that, as we may see from the case of *Ryerss v. Trustees,* 33 Pa. St. 114, a contract of the kind here involved is enforceable rather by way of estoppel than on the ground of consideration in the original undertaking." It has been held that a note given in expectation of the payee performing certain services, but without any contract binding him to serve, will not support an action. *Hulse v. Hulse,* 84 E. C. L. 709. But when the payee changes his position to his disadvantage in reliance on the promise, a right of action does arise. * * *

Under the circumstances of this case, is there an equitable estoppel which ought to preclude the defendant from alleging that the note in controversy is lacking in one of the essential elements of a valid contract? We think there is. An estoppel in pais is defined to be "a right arising from acts, admissions, or conduct which have induced a change of position in accordance with the real or apparent intention of the party against whom they are alleged." Mr. Pomeroy has formulated the following definition: "Equitable estoppel is the effect of the voluntary conduct of a party whereby he is absolutely precluded, both at law and in equity, from asserting rights which might, perhaps, have otherwise existed, either of property, of contract, or of remedy, as against another person who in good faith relied upon such conduct, and has been led thereby to change his position for the worse, and who on his part acquires some corresponding right, either of property, of contract, or of remedy." 2 Pom. Eq. Jur. 804. According to the undisputed proof, as shown by the record before us, the plaintiff was a working girl, holding a position in which she earned a salary of $10 per week. Her grandfather, desiring to put her in a position of independence, gave her the note, accompanying it with the remark that his other grandchildren did not work, and that she would not be obliged to work any longer. In effect, he suggested that she might abandon her employment, and rely in the future upon the bounty which he promised. He doubtless desired that she should give up her occupation, but, whether he did or not, it is entirely certain that he contemplated such action on her part as a reasonable and probable consequence of his gift. Having intentionally influenced the plaintiff to alter her position for the worse on the faith of the note being paid when due, it would be grossly inequitable to permit the maker, or his executor, to resist payment on the ground that the promise was given without consideration. The petition charges the elements of an equitable estoppel, and the evidence conclusively establishes them. If errors intervened at the trial, they could not have been prejudicial. A verdict for the defendant would be unwarranted. The judgment is right, and is affirmed.

QUESTIONS AND NOTES

1. Questions about the facts of this case

   1.1. Why did Katie's grandfather offer to pay her the $2,000? Did he want her to quit her job?

   1.2. Did Katie quit her job? Do we know whether grandfather's offer was the reason that she quit?

2. Questions about the law

   2.1. Equitable estoppel (estoppel *in pais*) is a doctrine that prohibits one party from asserting the truth of a matter previously misrepresented by that party. The elements of equitable estoppel are "conduct by one party which leads another party, in reliance thereon, to adopt a course of action resulting in detriment or damage if the first party is permitted to repudiate his conduct." *United American Life Insurance Co. v. Zions First National Bank,* 641 P.2d 158 (Utah 1982). In this case, Katie's grandfather's estate was estopped to deny the existence of consideration for the promise to pay her $2,000. But did John Ricketts ever misrepresent that there was consideration for his promise? What's going on here? Is this a proper application of the doctrine of equitable estoppel? If not, why do you suppose the court invoked the doctrine?

   2.2. Why wasn't Katie's quitting her job consideration for the promise? Is there any less of a bargain here in terms of benefit to the promisor or detriment to the promisee than in *Hamer v. Sidway, supra*?

   2.3. Would Katie have been better off if the court accepted the argument made in the original petition that John Ricketts' execution of the note met the traditional requirements for enforcement, *i.e.*, that it was supported by consideration?

2.4. Suppose Katie had taken her old job back a week after her grandfather's promise. Would she have been in breach? Even if not, would she have been entitled to recover the whole $2,000? How would the case come out under *Restatement (Second) of Contracts* § 90? What are the similarities between the first and second *Restatements*' versions of § 90? What are the differences?

3. Notes

3.1. Until fairly recently, enforcement of non-bargain promises based on reliance was limited to certain categories of cases that existed outside of or on the periphery of the marketplace and where the equities favoring enforcement were unusually compelling. Most notable among these was the willingness of courts to enforce gratuitous promises made to charitable organizations. Sometimes courts would do this by stretching the doctrine of consideration. For example, in *Allegheny College v. National Chautauqua County Bank,* 246 N.Y. 369, 159 N.E. 173 (1927), Justice Cardozo concluded that the donor's desire for posthumous remembrance, coupled with the college's agreement to set up a memorial fund in her name, constituted good consideration to support the donor's pledge to have her estate pay the college $5,000 thirty days after her death. Other courts took a more direct approach to enforcing donative promises by invoking an estoppel in situations where the donee could demonstrate detrimental reliance on the promise. *See, e.g.*, *Gittings v. Mayhew*, 6 Md. 113 (1854).

3.2. Students (and sometimes courts) are often confused by the distinction between a promissory and an equitable estoppel. While doctrinally distinct, the two can sometimes overlap. Consider the following scenario: Suppose Ponoroff signs a promissory note promising to pay Epstein $24,000 in 48 equal monthly installments of $500 each together with interest. The note expressly provides that payments are due on the first of each month and, in the event of non-payment, Epstein shall have the right to declare the entire debt due and owing in full (*i.e.*, an "acceleration" clause). For the first 18 months, Ponoroff makes all the required payments, but always pays between the 5th and the 10th of the month. Epstein says nothing about this. However, when Epstein fails to receive the 19th monthly payment on the first of the month Epstein immediately declares a default. Even though Ponoroff promptly tenders the past due monthly installment, Epstein brings suit for breach of contract seeking recovery of the entire outstanding balance of the note. In Ponoroff's defense (usually something nobody is much interested in, but then this is a hypothetical), can you successfully raise a defense based on estoppel? Is that an equitable or a promissory estoppel? Are there any other defenses you can think of? What if the contract rate of interest was 6% and the market rate of interest had risen over 18 months to 11%?

4. **You Be the Lawyer!**

   How could Mr. Ricketts, if he had chosen to do so, written the promissory note so as to avoid liability for *either* breach of contract or under promissory estoppel?

C. CONTEMPORARY APPLICATIONS OF THE DOCTRINE

QUESTIONS BEFORE THE CASE

1. According to this decision, what are the elements of a claim based on promissory estoppel?
2. According to this decision, what is the purpose for the doctrine of promissory estoppel?

WEITZ COMPANY, LLC V. HANDS, INC.

Supreme Court of Nebraska
294 Neb. 215 (2016)

CONNOLLY, J.

I. SUMMARY

The Weitz Company, LLC (Weitz), a general contractor, received an invitation to bid on a planned nursing facility. Hands, Inc., doing business as H & S Plumbing and Heating (H & S), submitted a bid to Weitz for the plumbing work, as well as the heating, ventilation, and air conditioning (HVAC) parts of the job. Weitz' bid to the project owner incorporated the amount of H & S' bid. After the owner awarded the project to Weitz, H & S refused to honor its bid. Weitz completed the project with different subcontractors at greater expense.

At trial, Weitz sought to enforce H &S' bid under promissory estoppel. The court determined that Weitz reasonably and foreseeably relied on H & S' bid, and it therefore estopped H & S from reneging. The court measured Weitz' damages as the difference between H & S' bid and the amount Weitz paid to substitute subcontractors. H & S appeals. We affirm the judgment and the amount of damages.

II. BACKGROUND

1. WEITZ IS INVITED TO BID

In 2011, the Evangelical Lutheran Good Samaritan Society (Good Samaritan) invited four "prequalified General Contractors," including Weitz, to bid on a proposed nursing facility in Beatrice, Nebraska. Good Samaritan chose the four prequalified general contractors based on "prior relationships" recommendations from its architect and its own research.

Good Samaritan is a "big player" in the retirement living market. Weitz is a "dominant contractor" in the same market. Alan Kennedy, a Weitz executive, said that Weitz had sought to build a relationship with Good Samaritan that would lead to "negotiated work," meaning that Good Samaritan would work with Weitz without inviting other general contractors to bid. Kennedy testified that negotiated work is "one of the best places to be as a contractor." When Good Samaritan invited Weitz to bid on the Beatrice project, Weitz knew of another potential project with Good Samaritan in Sarpy County, Nebraska.

Good Samaritan's "Invitation to Bid" stated that it would not consider bids received after 2 p.m. on August 30, 2011 (bid day). The invitation incorporated certain "Instructions to Bidders," which provided that Good Samaritan and its architect could object to a general contractor's proposed subcontractors. The invitation stated that "[n]o bids may be withdrawn for a period of 60 days after opening of bids." If a general contractor refused to enter into a contract, the instructions provided to bidders state that the general contractor would forfeit its bid security as liquidated damages. A bid security is a bond that "assures the owner that [it] can rely upon the *bids." But Good Samaritan did not ask for bid securities, because it prequalified the general contractors.

2. BID-DAY MADNESS

Before bid day, Weitz assigned "lead person[s]" to the different categories of work on the project, referred to as "tickets." The ticket leaders reviewed the project specifications and created a "scope checklist" that described the work for each ticket. Weitz prepared scope checklists because subcontractors sometimes excluded certain work from their bid.

On bid day, Weitz assembled its people in a conference room to collect and organize the hundreds of bids from subcontractors. Ticket leaders called out the bids after comparing them with the scope checklist. Weitz then added the numbers to a "bid day spreadsheet."

Subcontractors in the mechanical, engineering, and plumbing fields typically submit their bids within 15 minutes of the deadline. As a result, Weitz is often "at the wire turning in [its] number to an owner." Brian Mahlendorf, a project executive for Weitz, oversaw Weitz' bid for the Good

Samaritan project. Mahlendorf said that Weitz received H & S' bid "less than 15 minutes or so" before the 2 p.m. deadline.

Kennedy, who had been involved in "well over a hundred bids," testified that it was "customary for general contractors to rely on bids submitted by subcontractors" and that subcontractors submit bids because they want the job. Mahlendorf, who had more than 20 years of experience in the construction industry, testified that it was customary for Weitz to rely on subcontractors' bids, that subcontractors knew that Weitz relied on their bids, and that subcontractors submitted bids because they wanted to procure work. Mahlendorf said it was "very rare" for a subcontractor to refuse to honor its bid.

3. H & S SUBMITS A BID TO WEITZ

On bid day, H & S sent Weitz a bid for the plumbing and HVAC parts of the project. H & S' base bid was $2,430,600. For alternate duct and radiant heating work, H & S quoted $39,108 and $52,500, respectively. * * *

Kennedy and Mahlendorf testified that the market for construction services was weak in 2011. Subcontractors were "aggressively seeking work" and making low bids to "keep their people busy." Kennedy said that subcontractors' bids had "ranges that you hadn't traditionally seen in the marketplace." A difference of 15 percent between the lowest and second-lowest bids was not uncommon.

4. WEITZ SUBMITS ITS BID TO GOOD SAMARITAN

* * *

On bid day, Weitz sent Good Samaritan a base bid of $9.2 million. Kennedy and Mahlendorf testified that Weitz' base bid of $9.2 million included H & S' $2,430,600 bid. Weitz promised Good Samaritan that it would execute a contract for its base bid if offered the project within 60 days. Weitz' bid to Good Samaritan included a list of "Major Sub-Contractors." For the plumbing subcontractor, Weitz wrote "HEP or H & S." For the HVAC subcontractor, Weitz wrote "Falcon or H & S."

* * *

5. GOOD SAMARITAN AWARDS THE PROJECT TO WEITZ

On September 1, 2011, Weitz received "early indications" that Good Samaritan would select its bid. Weitz received "[f]inal notification" on September 2. Mahlendorf called H & S on September 6 and told the head of H & S' engineering department that Weitz had won the bidding and had "carried the H & S number." He said that he told H & S that "we used [its] number in our bid, and we were prepared to enter into a contract with [H & S] and move forward."

* * *

Weitz signed a contract with Good Samaritan for the base bid of $9.2 million plus six additional areas of work not included in the base bid. The opening paragraph of the contract states that it was "made and entered" on, and has an "Effective Date" of, September 7, 2011. But "Date: 9–19–11" appears below the signature of Good Samaritan's representatives.

* * *

6. H & S RENEGES ON ITS BID

Hugh Sieck, Jr., H & S' owner and chief executive officer, was fishing in Alaska on bid day. Sieck testified that he told his team of estimators before he left for Alaska not to send a bid to Weitz. He had "bitter feelings" for Weitz because it had a "history of bid shopping," meaning that Weitz would "get a bid, . . . look at it, and [it] will go to another contractor to get a lower number." Sieck said every general contractor "bid shops," but he thought Weitz did more than most.

John Sampson, who worked for one of the other prequalified general contractors, called Sieck on bid day and suggested that Sieck review H & S' bid. Sampson noticed a "considerable difference" between H & S' bid and the other subcontractors' bids, although he did not say what the difference was or whether the scope of the subcontractors' bids differed. Asked what might prompt him to confirm a bid with a subcontractor, Sampson said a difference of 10 or 15 percent between bids might be enough "if I had to pull a number out of the air," but "when it gets 20 or 30 percent then you really start getting concerned."

According to Sieck, he ordered a member of H & S' estimating team to "[p]ull your bid" after Sieck spoke with Sampson. But when Sieck returned to H & S' offices on September 6, 2011, he learned that his employees had, contrary to orders, submitted a bid to Weitz and had failed to withdraw the bid. He "surmised" that H & S' bid contained errors, so he "told [his] team to go out and find a mistake."

Lloyd Ness, the person responsible for preparing the plumbing and piping parts of H & S' bid, said that Sieck was upset after bid day because H & S "left too much money on the table." Ness testified that H & S' estimating team reviewed its bid after Sieck returned but concluded there "was not a hair out of place." So, according to Ness, Sieck told him to "lie to Weitz and tell Weitz that we forgot travel time and we missed showers." Ness refused to lie and resigned because of the incident. Sieck denied asking Ness to lie. Another member of H & S' estimating team, Thomas Santillan, Jr., said that Sieck did not ask him to lie.

Sieck personally took a hand in looking for a mistake and ultimately landed on a miscalculation involving shower units. He told Santillan to inform Weitz of H & S' " 'belief of the mistake.' "

On September 8, 2011, Santillan sent an e-mail with a letter attachment to Mahlendorf stating that H & S had found two errors after "thoroughly reviewing" its bid: (1) a miscalculation of the cost of shower installation and (2) the omission of travel time from the cost of labor. The collective magnitude of the claimed errors exceeded $250,000.

Santillan later took another look at H & S' bid and concluded that the original calculation of the cost for shower installation was, in fact, correct. But Santillan maintained that H & S had underbid travel costs. And Santillan said that H & S eventually unearthed "numerous mistakes" in its bid. Specifically, "the material was just not accurate," "the dollar amount did not appear to be accurate," and "there wasn't enough material."

Mahlendorf came to H & S' offices for a meeting on September 9, 2011. According to Sieck, Mahlendorf mentioned, " 'I've got to get to Beatrice because I haven't got all my shopping done.' " Sieck understood Mahlendorf's statement to mean that "as per usual, they are out shopping the bids."

But Mahlendorf said that Sieck's recollection did not "comport with [Mahlendorf's] memory." Asked if Weitz would ever "carry one number but you continue negotiating and replace it with a different bidder," Mahlendorf said he was "sure that has happened for some reason or another." But he said that Weitz did not intend to shop H & S' bid. H & S' bid was "comprehensive," and Weitz was "willing to take it as is."

Weitz and H & S could not come to terms. The magnitude of H & S' error kept growing and eventually ballooned to more than $430,000. In October 2011, Weitz informed H & S that it would use other subcontractors.

7. WEITZ HONORS ITS BID TO GOOD SAMARITAN

Weitz did not try to withdraw its bid from Good Samaritan because of its dispute with H & S. Instead, it completed the project with other plumbing and HVAC subcontractors. Kennedy and Mahlendorf testified that the bidding documents prohibited Weitz from withdrawing or modifying its bid for 60 days. And the contract between Weitz and Good Samaritan was "already in progress" by the time Weitz learned that H & S would not honor its bid.

Business reasons also prevented Weitz from abandoning the project. Kennedy testified that the "integrity of our bids" was particularly important if the owner selected Weitz as a prequalified general contractor. Mahlendorf explained that backing out would have harmed Weitz' reputation in its industry:

> On a project like this where the architect and owner have preselected general contractors, if we wouldn't honor our bid, we would be at risk for future work from the design firm that did it and in addition to the owner group. From a business standpoint,

> we do a lot of [business with] senior living [clients], and it would be detrimental if we were starting to be excluded from senior living clients like the Good Samaritan Society.

Withdrawal would have also lowered Weitz' standing with Good Samaritan's architect, with which Weitz had an "ongoing business relationship."

8. WEITZ MEASURES ITS LOSSES

After H & S made it clear that it would not stand by its bid, Weitz asked for bids from other subcontractors. Weitz selected the subcontractors Falcon and "MMC" for the plumbing and HVAC portions of the project because their bids had the "lowest cost complete scope that we could obtain." The amount Weitz paid Falcon and MMC under their subcontracts was $1,187,900 and $1,626,800, respectively. * * *

To calculate Weitz' damages, Mahlendorf added Falcon's and MMC's subcontract prices for the sum of $2,814,700. From that sum, Mahlendorf subtracted H & S' base bid of $2,430,600 and its bids of $39,108 and $52,500 on optional work which Good Samaritan ultimately asked Weitz to perform. The difference is $292,492.

9. PROCEDURAL HISTORY

Weitz pleaded two causes of action in its complaint against H & S. First, Weitz alleged that H & S breached a contract formed by Weitz' acceptance of H & S' bid. Second, Weitz argued that promissory estoppel bound H & S to its bid because Weitz reasonably and foreseeably relied on the bid.

* * *

After a bench trial, the court determined that the parties had not formed a contract. But it enforced H & S' bid under promissory estoppel. The court awarded Weitz damages of $292,492.

III. ASSIGNMENTS OF ERROR

H & S assigns, restated, that the court erred by (1) entering a judgment for Weitz on its promissory estoppel claim, (2) "awarding breach of contract damages instead of reliance damages for promissory estoppel," * * *

V. ANALYSIS

1. PROMISSORY ESTOPPEL

H & S argues that the court should not have enforced its bid under promissory estoppel. Courts often use promissory estoppel to hold a subcontractor to its bid until the general contractor has had a reasonable length of time to accept the bid after receiving the prime contract. The leading case is *Drennan v. Star Paving Co.*[5] There, the California Supreme Court held that because the general contractor was bound by its bid, fairness required that the general contractor have an opportunity to accept the subcontractor's bid after receiving the prime contract. *Drennan* has had a "very broad following."

In Nebraska, a claim of promissory estoppel requires a plaintiff to show: (1) a promise that the promisor should have reasonably expected to induce the plaintiff's action or forbearance, (2) the promise did in fact induce the plaintiff's action or forbearance, and (3) injustice can only be avoided by enforcing the promise. The promise need not be definite enough to support a unilateral contract, but it must be definite enough to show that the plaintiff's reliance on it was reasonable and foreseeable. Here, we start our review of the court's judgment by asking if H & S' bid was a promise on which it should have foreseen reliance.

(a) H & S' Bid Was a Promise on Which Reliance Was Foreseeable

H & S' bid was a promise to perform the work described in the bid. H & S said it was "bidding the Plumbing, Hydronic Piping, & HVAC portion" of the Good Samaritan project and specifically listed the work that it was willing to perform. H & S asked for the general contractors' "consideration" and hoped to "be of service" to them.

And H & S should have foreseen that Weitz would rely on its bid. Kennedy and Mahlendorf testified that subcontractors generally expect (and hope) that general contractors will rely on their bids. Usages of trade are strong evidence of the foreseeability of reliance. Furthermore, Weitz received H & S' bid about 15 minutes before the 2 p.m. deadline. Evidence that a promisee had little time to act on the promise shows that the promisee's reliance was foreseeable. And, as noted, H & S expressly asked Weitz to consider its bid. Having determined that H & S should have expected Weitz to rely on its bid, our next question is whether Weitz in fact relied on the bid and, if so, whether its reliance was reasonable.

(b) Weitz Reasonably Relied on H & S' Bid

Weitz relied on H & S' bid by including the base amount of H & S' bid in Weitz' own bid to Good Samaritan. Mahlendorf testified that he slotted H & S' bid into the plumbing and HVAC tickets, which is reflected in the bid-day spreadsheet. Although Weitz disjunctively listed the major subcontractors in its bid to Good Samaritan, the evidence shows that Weitz actually relied on H & S' bid. Both Kennedy and Mahlendorf testified that Weitz' $9.2 million base bid incorporated H & S' base bid of $2,430,600.

We further conclude that Weitz' reliance on H & S' bid was reasonable. The evidence shows that general contractors customarily rely on

---

[5] *Drennan v. Star Paving Co.*, 51 Cal.2d 409, 333 P.2d 757 (1958).

subcontractors' bids. Mahlendorf testified that it was "very rare" for a subcontractor to refuse to honor its bid. In particular, Weitz had worked with H & S 10 or 15 times before without incident. Weitz' reliance was also reasonable because it had only 15 minutes to review H & S' bid. Weitz could not independently verify every item in H & S' bid in a quarter of an hour. How could competitive bidding function at all if general contractors *did not* rely on subcontractors' bids?

H & S marshals a number of arguments why Weitz did not reasonably rely on its bid, which we consolidate into five that merit discussion. First, H & S argues that the bidding documents "absolutely precluded any reliance." Specifically, H & S emphasizes that Good Samaritan had the right to veto subcontractors.

But the bare fact that Good Samaritan could have, in theory, rejected H & S' bid did not make Weitz' reliance on H & S' bid unreasonable. Good Samaritan did not object to any of Weitz' subcontractors. Mahlendorf testified that despite an owner's reservation of the right to veto subcontractors, owners generally do not exercise that right "[i]n the real world." If the chance that Good Samaritan would nix H & S were significant, Weitz' reliance on H & S' bid might not have been reasonable. But the record lacks this evidence.

We similarly reject H & S' second argument, which is that Weitz' reliance was unreasonable because Weitz "did not require any quotation be kept open for any period of time as a precondition to its consideration." General contractors customarily rely on subcontractors' bids, as discussed above, and the record lacks any evidence that prudent general contractors turn away bids that do not have such a provision. We cannot find any authority that conditions promissory estoppel, as a matter of law, on a demand by the general contractor that subcontractors insert such clauses into their bids. * * *

H & S' third argument is that Weitz did not reasonably rely on its bid because it could have pulled out of the project without any consequences. H & S notes that, although the invitation to bid required Weitz to hold its bid open for 60 days, Good Samaritan did not ask for a bid security. Furthermore, Weitz knew that H & S had cold feet before Weitz and Good Samaritan formally signed a contract.

But H & S could not expect Weitz to abandon the project because H & S decided its bid was too low. Weitz promised Good Samaritan that it would hold its bid open for 60 days, and breaking that promise would have sullied Weitz' reputation. In particular, Good Samaritan might have been reluctant to work with Weitz again. Losing Good Samaritan's business would have been a significant loss to Weitz because Weitz and Good Samaritan are both active in the retirement living market. Pulling out of the project would also have jeopardized Weitz' preexisting relationship with the project architect. Good Samaritan selected the prequalified general contractors based, in part, on the architect's recommendations. Weitz did not have to tell Good Samaritan that, as things turned out, it would not build the facility because of a squabble with a plumbing and HVAC subcontractor.

The fourth reason why, according to H & S, Weitz did not reasonably rely on its bid is that Weitz "attempted to accept quotations on materially different terms." H & S argues, restated, that Weitz did not rely on its subcontractors' bids, because it later asked subcontractors to sign a subcontract that did not mirror the terms of the subcontractors' bids. H & S backed out before Weitz could send it a subcontract. But H & S suggests that Weitz would have sent it a subcontract similar to the one that Weitz sent to its other subcontractors and that this hypothetical subcontract would have been materially different from H & S' bid.

A general contractor can reasonably rely on a subcontractor's bid even if the general contractor and subcontractor contemplate signing a formal subcontract with additional standard terms after the bidding process ends. But a general contractor cannot demand that a subcontractor agree to unusual and onerous terms while still holding the subcontractor to its original bid. For example, in *Hawkins Constr. Co. v. Reiman Corp.*,[19] a general contractor demanded that a subcontractor agree to multiple "nonstandard additional conditions which could be considered onerous." After the subcontractor refused to accept the terms, the general contractor tried to enforce the subcontractor's bid under promissory estoppel. We held that the general contractor's reliance was not reasonable because it could not assume that the subcontractor would acquiesce to onerous nonstandard terms.

But differences between a subcontractor's bid and the subcontract do not matter if they are an "afterthought" raised by a subcontractor that wants to avoid its promise for other reasons. Here, H & S reneged because its bid was too low, and it did so before Weitz sent it a subcontract. So, H & S' dispute with the terms of the subcontract is even less than an afterthought: It is imaginary. Plus, Sieck testified that Weitz had always accepted H & S' revisions to the subcontract.

Finally, we reach H & S' fifth argument as to why Weitz did not reasonably rely on its bid: It was so low that Weitz was on notice that H & S had made mistakes. Differences between the scope of H & S' bid and the scopes of the other bids make a dollar-for-dollar comparison difficult, but H & S asserts that its bid was "considerably lower" than the those of its rivals.

---

[19] *Hawkins Constr. Co. v. Reiman Corp.*, 245 Neb. 131, 136, 511 N.W.2d 113, 117 (1994).

We conclude that H & S' bid was not so low that Weitz' reliance on it was unreasonable. If a bid is so low that a mistake should be apparent, a general contractor cannot reasonably rely on the bid. But H & S' bid was higher than what Weitz had budgeted based on historical data. Furthermore, the market for construction services was weak in 2011 and subcontractors were bidding aggressively. Kennedy and Mahlendorf testified that bids during this period could be unusually low compared to years in which the market was more robust. H & S sent its bid to all four of the prequalified general contractors. Two of the general contractors, including Weitz, chose H & S without first checking to see if H & S had made a mistake.

So, H & S' bid was a promise on which reliance was foreseeable and Weitz reasonably relied on the bid. One question remains: Did the court have to enforce H & S' bid to prevent injustice?

(c) Enforcement of H & S' Bid Was Necessary to Prevent Injustice

We conclude that the court could avoid injustice only by enforcing H & S' bid. As discussed above, many courts have recognized the unfairness of allowing a subcontractor to renege after the general contractor has relied on the subcontractor's bid in the general contractor's own successful bid to the owner. H & S argues that it is not fair to enforce its bid, because it made mistakes. But Weitz should not have to bear the cost of H & S' errors: "As between the subcontractor who made the bid and the general contractor who reasonably relied on it, the loss resulting from the mistake should fall on the party who caused it."[23]

H & S argues that we should not enforce its bid, because Weitz engaged in the "unethical practice of bid shopping." A general contractor bid shops by taking the lowest subcontractor's bid to other subcontractors and asking them to undercut it. Courts are reluctant to use promissory estoppel if the general contractor bid shopped, either because bid shopping shows that the general contractor did not rely on the bid, or because injustice no longer requires enforcement of the bid, or both.

But the record does not show that Weitz shopped H & S' bid. Sieck testified that he had "bitter feelings" about an earlier project in which Weitz bid shopped. That project, however, involved a bidding process different from the competitive process used by Good Samaritan. The only direct evidence that Weitz bid shopped during the Beatrice project is Sieck's testimony about Mahlendorf's aside about "shopping" in Beatrice. Mahlendorf did not remember making that statement. He testified that Weitz had no intent to shop H & S' bid. In a credibility battle, Mahlendorf

[23] See *Powers Constr. Co., Inc. v. Salem Carpets, Inc.*, 283 S.C. 302, 322 S.E.2d 30 (1984).

has the better of the admittedly bitter Sieck, who candidly testified about "toying with" his memory of the communications between H & S and Weitz.

In conclusion, H & S' bid was a promise on which reliance was foreseeable. Weitz actually and reasonably relied on the bid. And justice required the court to enforce H & S' bid. So the court did not err by entering a judgment for Weitz on its promissory estoppel claim.

2. DAMAGES

H & S does not agree with the amount of damages. It argues that the court erred by "awarding benefit of the bargain/contract damages rather than reliance damages." * * *

No single measure of damages applies in every promissory estoppel case. The commentary to the Restatement (Second) of Contracts explains that the ultimate standard for enforcing the promise—the prevention of injustice—also guides the measurement of damages. The damages that the promisor ought to pay are those that justice requires. In some cases, justice requires only reliance damages.

* * *

In the construction bidding context, courts have "consistently and uniformly" measured the general contractor's damages as the difference between the reneging subcontractor's bid and the amount the general contractor paid to replacement subcontractors. Here, the court measured Weitz' damages in a consistent manner. It is "plain that justice required this measure of damages."

* * *

VI. CONCLUSION

We affirm the judgment for Weitz on its promissory estoppel claim. H & S' bid was a promise, and it should have foreseen that Weitz, as was usual in the construction industry, might rely on the bid. Weitz reasonably relied on the bid by incorporating it in Weitz' own bid to the project owner. And the court could avoid injustice only by enforcing H & S' bid. * * *

AFFIRMED.

QUESTIONS, NOTES, AND CONNECTIONS

1. Questions about the facts of this case

   1.1. Why didn't The Weitz Company accept H & S's bid after deciding to include it in Weitz's bid sent to Good Samaritan?

1.2. What is it about the nature of the construction industry that makes it the subject of so many important promissory estoppel cases?

2. Questions about the law

2.1. Why did the trial court conclude that there was no recovery for breach of contract? Could you make an argument supporting a breach of contract recovery?

2.2. Why did H & S argue that Weitz engaged in the "unethical practice of bid shopping"? Is bid shopping unethical?

2.3. Under what standard does an appellate court review the trial court's findings on the elements of promissory estoppel?

2.4. What was all that chatter about "reliance" damages vs. "benefit of the bargain" damages?

3. Notes

3.1. In the *Drennan* case, mentioned in *Weitz,* Justice Traynor first employed the doctrine of promissory estoppel to find that the subcontractor could not revoke its bid once it had been relied upon by the general contractor. However, this was really an *expansion* of the doctrine of promissory estoppel since the bid involved an offer for an *exchange* transaction and not a gift promise. Thus, in *Drennan*, the court used promissory estoppel (or detrimental reliance) to *imply* a promise of irrevocability where none actually existed, as well as to *enforce* that promise despite the absence of consideration. Section 87(2) of *Restatement (Second) of Contracts* follows *Drennan.*

3.2. Recognizing the one-sided nature of the option contract created by *Drennan*, and the potential for bid-shopping by the general contractor that it creates, in 1963 the California legislature adopted a statute that: 1) requires the general contractor in any public project to list the identities of its subcontractors in its bid, and then, 2) proscribes the substitution by the general contractor of any subcontractor listed in the original bid, except upon a showing of exceptional circumstances such as the subcontractor's insolvency or refusal to do the work. Cal. Gov't Code §§ 4100–4108 (Subletting and Subcontractors Fair Practices Act). Does such an approach, which has been followed in other states, level the playing field for general and subcontractors?

3.3. In *Barnhart v. CMC Fabricators, Inc.*, 211 Cal.App.4th 230, 149 Cal.Rptr.3d 440 (2012), the court was faced with a situation where a subcontractor's bid contained a reciprocal attorney's fees provision; meaning that in the event of dispute, the prevailing party would be entitled to recover its legal fees. After the general contractor was awarded the primary contract, it attempted to accept the bid, but the subcontractor refused to perform. At trial, the court concluded that, while there was no basis for a breach of contract claim, the general contractor was entitled to recover based on promissory estoppel. The subcontractor, who had prevailed on the breach of contract claim, sought to recover its attorney's fees, totaling over $150,000, based on the provision in the bid. The trial court denied the subcontractor's motion for an award of attorney's fees, and the subcontractor appealed. The court of appeal reversed the trial court holding that: "[A] plaintiff who prevails on a promissory estoppel claim but recovers nothing on a breach of contract claim * * * in the same action is not 'the party prevailing on the contract' entitled to recover under the attorney fees clause in the alleged contract. Instead, the defendant who defeats the breach of contract claim * * * but loses on the promissory estoppel claim is 'the party prevailing on the contract' entitled to recover under the attorney fees clause in the alleged contract." Do you agree?

3.4. It is has been noted that, although the doctrine of promissory estoppel in the United States derived from certain English common law concepts, there is still no unified theory of promissory estoppel in English contract law today. *See* Joel M. Ngugi, *Promissory Estoppel: The Life History of and Ideal Legal Transplant,* 41 U. RICH. L. REV. 425 (2007). Promissory estoppel is a creature of the common law, ordinarily thought to be unknown to the civil law. *See* David V. Snyder, *Comparative Law in Action: Promissory Estoppel, The Civil Law, and the Mixed Jurisdiction,* 15 ARIZ. J. INT'L & COMP. LAW 695, 704 (1998) (pointing out that the flexibility of the civil law doctrine of cause, compared to the stringencies of bargained-for consideration, has arguably lessened the need for promissory estoppel in the civil law).

4. **You Be the Lawyer!**

If you represent a subcontractor that wishes to preserve its ability to withdraw a bid made to a prime contractor prior to acceptance, how will you accomplish that for your client? How about if you represent a general contractor who wants to be sure it can hold its sub to their bids without having to rely on promissory estoppel?

5. Connections

Drennan and *Restatement (Second) of Contracts* § 87(2), which we first encountered back in Section 4 of Chapter 2, demonstrate that courts will sometimes use a promissory estoppel theory as a basis for barring an offeror from revoking an offer on which the offeree has relied. Can you identify other areas where reliance has been invoked by courts as the basis for development of a new rule other than unbargained for reliance as a substitute for consideration?

Ricketts v. Scothorn illustrates the evolution of equitable estoppel into an affirmative basis for imposing promissory liability without consideration. As it originally emerged, the doctrine of promissory estoppel was generally relegated to circumstances outside the commercial arena. That is to say, promissory estoppel was limited to a few distinct types of cases that did not involve a commercial exchange or bargain, such as family gift promises and charitable subscriptions. In time, however, the doctrine began to make in-roads into garden variety business transactions, although its application has neither been consistent nor without controversy.

Some courts have taken the position that the doctrine of promissory estoppel should be limited to enforcing gratuitous *promises*, and, therefore, applies only in cases like *Ricketts* where enforcement of the promise would otherwise be denied because of the absence of consideration. The trend, however, in recent years has been in the other direction; that is, to recognizing promissory estoppel as independent theory of liability on which recovery may be had in a wide variety of situations, even though a cause of action for breach of contract would fail for a reason *other than* a failure of consideration. *Weitz* is an example of that.

Other common circumstances where courts have been willing to entertain promissory estoppel claims in the bargain context include agreements that are too vague or indefinite to be enforced under traditional bargain theory. For example, in *Blinn v. Beatrice Community Hosp. & Health Ctr.,* 708 N.W.2d. 235 (Neb. 2006), the court noted that promissory estoppel does not require that the promise giving rise to the cause of action must meet all of the requirements of an offer that would ripen into a contract if accepted by the promisee; that instead of requiring reasonable definiteness, promissory estoppel requires only that the reliance be reasonable and foreseeable. Similarly, oral promises to a homeowner made by a mortgage holder to obtain casualty insurance on the property subject to the mortgage have been held enforceable under the basis of promissory estoppel. *See Charleswell v. Chase Manhattan Bank, N.A.,* 308 F.Supp.2d 545 (D.V.I. 2004); *Restatement (Second) of Contracts* § 90, cmt. e, illus. 13.

In addition, *Restatement (Second) of Contracts* § 139(1) tracks the promissory estoppel section almost verbatim, except that it makes a promise "enforceable notwithstanding the Statute of Frauds" instead of "binding notwithstanding. . . ," the terminology used in § 90(1).

QUESTIONS BEFORE THE CASE

1. According to Judge Posner, what is the purpose for the doctrine of promissory estoppel?

2. Is this case about nonreasonable reliance on a promise or reasonable reliance on a nonpromise?

GARWOOD PACKAGING, INC. V. ALLEN & COMPANY, INC.

United States Court of Appeals, Seventh Circuit
378 F.3d 698, reh'g & reh'g en banc denied (2004)

POSNER, CIRCUIT JUDGE.

This is a diversity suit, governed by Indiana law, in which substantial damages are sought on the basis of promissory estoppel. The suit pits Garwood Packaging, Inc., which created a packaging system designed to increase the shelf life of fresh meat, and its two principals, Garwood and McNamara, against Allen & Company (an investment company) and a vice-president of Allen named Martin. We shall refer to the plaintiffs collectively as "GPI" and the defendants collectively as "Allen." The district court granted summary judgment in favor of Allen and dismissed the suit.

* * *

GPI had flopped in marketing its food-packaging system and by 1993 had run up debts of $3 million and was broke. It engaged Martin to help find investors. After an initial search turned up nothing, Martin told GPI that Allen (Martin's employer, remember) would consider investing $2 million of its own money in GPI if another investor could be found who would make a comparable investment. The presence of the other investor would reduce the risk to Allen not only by augmenting GPI's assets but also by validating Allen's judgment that GPI might be salvageable, because it would show that someone else was also willing to bet a substantial sum of money on GPI's salvation. To further reduce its risk Allen decided to off-load half its projected $2 million investment on other investors.

Martin located a company named Hobart Corporation that was prepared to manufacture $2 million worth of GPI packaging machines in return for equity in the company. Negotiations with Hobart proved arduous, however. There were two sticking points: the amount of equity that Hobart would receive and the obtaining of releases from GPI's creditors. Hobart may have been concerned that unless the creditors released GPI the company would fail and Hobart wouldn't be able to sell the packaging systems that it manufactured. Or it may have feared that the creditors would assert liens in the systems. All that is clear is that Hobart insisted on releases. They were also important to the other investors whom Allen wanted to bring into the deal, the ones who would contribute half of Allen's offered $2 million.

Martin told Garwood and McNamara (GPI's principals) that he would see that the deal went through "come hell or high water." Eventually, however, Allen decided not to invest, the deal collapsed, and GPI was forced to declare bankruptcy. The reason for Allen's change of heart was that the investors who it thought had agreed to put up half of "Allen's" $2 million had gotten cold feet. When Allen withdrew from the deal, no contract had been signed and no agreement had been reached on how much stock either Allen or Hobart would receive in exchange for their contributions to GPI. Nor had releases been obtained from the creditors.

GPI's principal claim on appeal, and the only one we need to discuss (the others fall with it), is that Martin's unequivocal promise to see the deal through to completion bound Allen by the doctrine of promissory estoppel, which makes a promise that induces reasonable reliance legally enforceable. * * * If noncontractual promises were never enforced, reliance on their being enforceable would never be reasonable, so let us consider why the law might want to allow people to rely on promises that do not create actual contracts and whether the answer can help GPI.

The simplest answer to the "why" question is that the doctrine merely allows reliance to be substituted for consideration as the basis for making a promise enforceable. * * * On this view promissory estoppel is really just a doctrine of contract law. The most persuasive reason for the requirement of consideration in the law of contracts is that in a system in which oral contracts are enforceable—and by juries, to boot—the requirement provides some evidence that there really *was* a promise that was intended to be relied on as a real commitment. * * * Actual reliance, in the sense of a costly change of position that cannot be recouped if the reliance turns out to have been misplaced, is substitute evidence that there may well have been such a promise. * * * The inference is especially plausible in a commercial setting, because most businesspeople would be reluctant to incur costs in reliance on a promise that they believed the promisor didn't consider himself legally bound to perform.

In other words, reasonable reliance is seen as nearly as good a reason for thinking there really was a promise as bargained-for reliance is. In many such cases, it is true, no promise was intended, or intended to be legally enforceable; in those cases the application of the doctrine penalizes the defendant for inducing the plaintiff to incur costs of reliance. The penalty is withheld if the reliance was unreasonable; for then the plaintiff's wound was self-inflicted—he should have known better than to rely.

A relevant though puzzling difference between breach of contract and promissory estoppel as grounds for legal relief is that while the promise relied on to trigger an estoppel must be definite in the sense of being clearly a promise and not just a statement of intentions, its terms need not be as clear as a contractual promise would have to be in order to be enforceable. * * * Indiana may go furthest in this direction: "Even though there were insufficient terms for the enforcement of an express oral contract, and unfulfilled pre-existing conditions prohibiting recovery for breach of a written contract . . . , we are not precluded from finding a promise under these circumstances. Indeed, it is precisely under such circumstances, where a promise is made but which is not enforceable as a 'contract,' that the doctrine of promissory estoppel is recognized." *First National Bank of Logansport v. Logan Mfg. Co., supra*, 577 N.E.2d [949], 955 [1991].

The reason for this difference between breach of contract and promissory estoppel is unclear. A stab at an explanation is found in *Rosnick v. Dinsmore*, 235 Neb. 738, 457 N.W.2d 793, 800 (1990), where the court said that "promissory estoppel only provides for damages as justice requires and does not attempt to provide the plaintiff damages based upon the benefit of the bargain." * * * The only problem with this explanation is that its premise is mistaken; if the promise giving rise to an estoppel is clear, the plaintiff will usually be awarded its value, which would be the equivalent of the expectation measure of damages in an ordinary breach of contract case. *Goldstick v. ICM Realty*, 788 F.2d 456, 463–64 (7th Cir.1986); *Restatement, supra,* § 90 comment d. The rationale in both cases is that the benefit of the contract to the promisee is a good proxy for the opportunities that he forewent in making the contract. * * *

But even though the court is "not precluded from finding a promise" by its vagueness, the vaguer the alleged promise the less likely it is to be found to *be* a promise. *Mays v. Trump Indiana, Inc.*, 255 F.3d 351, 358–59 (7th Cir.2001) (Indiana law); *All-Tech Telecom, Inc. v. Amway Corp.*, 174 F.3d 862, 868–69 (7th Cir.1999); *Restatement, supra,* § 33(3) and comment f. And if it is *really* vague, the promisee would be imprudent to rely on it—he wouldn't know whether reliance was worthwhile. The broader principle, which the requirement that the promise be definite and at least minimally clear instantiates, is that the promisee's reliance must be reasonable; if it is not, then not only is he the gratuitous author of his own disappointment, but probably there wasn't really a promise, or at least a promise intended or likely to induce reliance. The "promise" would have been in the nature of a hope or possibly a prediction rather than a commitment to do something within the "promisor's" power to do ("I promise it will rain tomorrow"); and the "promisee" would, if sensible, understand this. He would rely or not as he chose but he would know that he would have to bear the cost of any disappointment.

We note, returning to the facts of this case, that there was costly reliance by GPI, which forewent other opportunities for salvation, and by Garwood and McNamara, who moved from Indiana to Ohio to be near Hobart's plant where they expected their food-packaging system to be manufactured, and who forgave their personal loans to GPI and incurred other costs as well. The reliance was on statements by Martin, of which "come hell or high water" was the high water mark but is by no means an isolated example. If GPI's evidence is credited, as it must be in the procedural posture of the case, Martin repeatedly confirmed to GPI that the deal would go through, that Allen's commitment to invest $2 million was unconditional, that the funding would be forthcoming, and so on; and these statements induced the plaintiffs to incur costs they would otherwise not have done.

But were these real promises, and likely to be understood as such? Those are two different questions. A person may say something that he intends as merely a prediction, or as a signal of his hopes or intentions, but that is reasonably understood as a promise, and if so, as we know (this is the penal or deterrent function of promissory estoppel), he is bound. * * * But what is a reasonable, and indeed actual, understanding will often depend on the knowledge that the promisee brings to the table. McNamara, with whom Martin primarily dealt, is a former investment banker, not a rube. He knew that in putting together a deal to salvage a failing company there is many a slip 'twixt cup and lips. Unless blinded by optimism or desperation he *had* to know that Martin could not mean *literally* that the deal would go through "come hell or high water," since if Satan or a tsunami obliterated Ohio that would kill the deal. Even if Allen had dug into its pockets for the full $2 million after the investors who it had hoped would put up half the amount defected, the deal might well not have gone through because of Hobart's demands and because of the creditors. GPI acknowledges that the Internal Revenue Service, one of its largest creditors, wouldn't give a release until paid in full. Some of GPI's other creditors also intended to fight rather than to accept a pittance in exchange for a release. Nothing is more common than for a deal to rescue a failing company to fall apart because all the creditors' consent to the deal cannot be obtained—that is one of the reasons for bankruptcy law. Again these were things of which McNamara was perfectly aware.

The problem, thus, is not that Martin's promises were indefinite, which they were not if GPI's evidence is credited, but that they could not have been reasonably understood by the persons to whom they were addressed (mainly McNamara, the financial partner in GPI) to *be* promises rather than expressions of optimism and determination. * * * To move to Ohio, to forgive personal loans, to forgo other searches for possible investors, and so forth were in the nature of gambles on the part of GPI and its principals. They may have been reasonable gambles, in the sense that the prospects for a successful salvage operation were good enough that taking immediate, even if irrevocable, steps to facilitate and take advantage of the expected happy outcome was prudent. But we often reasonably rely on things that are not promises. A farmer plants his crops in the spring in reasonable reliance that spring will be followed by summer rather than by winter. There can be reasonable reliance on statements as well as on the regularities of nature, but if the statements are not reasonably understood as legally enforceable promises there can be no action for promissory estoppel.

Suppose McNamara thought that there was a 50 percent chance that the deal would go through and believed that reliance on that prospect would cost him $100,000, but also believed that by relying he could expect either to increase the likelihood that the deal would go through or to make more money if it did by being able to start production sooner and that in either event the expected benefit of reliance would exceed $100,000. Then his reliance would be reasonable even if not induced by enforceable promises. The numbers are arbitrary but the example apt. GPI and its principals relied, and may have relied reasonably, but they didn't rely on Martin's "promises" because those were not promises reasonably understood as such by so financially sophisticated a businessman as McNamara. * * * So we see now that the essence of the doctrine of promissory estoppel is not that the plaintiff have reasonably relied on the defendant's promise, but that he have reasonably relied on its *being* a promise in the sense of a legal commitment, and not a mere prediction or aspiration or bit of puffery.

One last point. Ordinarily the question whether a plaintiff reasonably understood a statement to be a promise is a question of fact and so cannot be resolved in summary judgment proceedings. But if it is clear that the question can be answered in only one way, there is no occasion to submit the question to a jury. * * * This, we believe, is such a case.

AFFIRMED.

QUESTIONS AND NOTE

1. Questions about the facts of this case

   1.1. Could the facts of the case as pled establish a cause of action for breach of contract? Why or why not?

   1.2. How was McNamara's background relevant in the case?

   1.3. Since they are "different questions," what's the difference between a real promise and one "not likely to be understood as such"?

2. Question about the law

   2.1. According to the court, did GPI reasonably rely on statements made by the defendants?

2.2. What is the relevance, according to the court, of the vagueness of a promise in relation to promissory estoppel? Can a promise that's too vague to enforce in a breach of contract action form the basis of a claim for promissory estoppel? If so, isn't promissory estoppel more than just a "substitute for consideration"?

2.3. According to Judge Posner, in assessing the reasonableness of reliance, do we look to the promisee or the promisor? How about under § 90 of the *Restatement (Second)*?

2.4. There's some noise here again about whether damages for a claim based on promissory estoppel are measure by the "benefit of the bargain" or some lesser sum. What's that about? *Hint*: more discussion about that in Subsection D below.

3. Note

In *Growers v. Pilgrim's Pride Corp. (In re Pilgrim's Pride Corp.)*, 706 F.3d 636 (5th Cir. 2013), Pilgrim's Pride Corporation began operating a chicken processing plant in Clinton, Arkansas,* following its acquisition of ConAgra Poultry Company in 2003. Pilgrim's Pride contracted with various chicken farmers to supply the company with poultry. As part of this arrangement, the farmers built and maintained chicken houses on their land at a cost of approximately $150,000 per house. Pursuant to the farmers' contracts, which all contained similar terms, the agreements were to continue on a "flock to flock basis" and either party could terminate the contract without cause between flocks. The contracts also stipulated that Pilgrim's Pride could terminate the agreements at any time for "cause or economic necessity."

Due to a downturn in the poultry industry, Pilgrim's Pride shut down its Clinton plant and terminated the contracts with the farmers in 2008. Pilgrim's Pride then filed for Chapter 11 protection. A group of more than 100 chicken farmers whose contracts were terminated (the "Clinton Growers") then got plucky and brought promissory estoppel claims against Pilgrim's Pride when the company filed for bankruptcy protection. The Clinton Growers alleged that Pilgrim's Pride had made oral promises of a long-term relationship in order to induce the farmers into investing in the chicken houses. Among the alleged oral promises, Pilgrim's Pride assured the farmers it "was here for the long haul," that the farmers would "more than cover the costs of building and raising the chickens" if they upgraded the chicken houses, and that the farmers would continue to receive chickens as long as they met the contract specifications.

Applying Arkansas state law, the U.S. Fifth Circuit affirmed the dismissal of the Clinton Growers' claims on the basis that promissory

* Clinton is named for DeWitt Clinton, the New York governor who built the Erie Canal and was also a U.S. Senator not the other "Clinton" from Arkansas.

estoppel applies only when "the elements of a contract cannot be shown." In other words, promissory estoppel is applicable only in the absence of an otherwise enforceable contract. Thus, a party alleging promissory estoppel can succeed only by showing that the written contract does not cover the subject matter underlying the promissory estoppel claim. In this case, the circuit court agreed with the lower courts that the alleged oral promises and the written contracts covered the same subject matter, specifically the duration of the agreements.

4. **You Be the Lawyer!**

The court acknowledges substantial reliance on GPI, but allows no recovery. How could GPI have assured itself of recouping those reliance costs if the deal with Martin and Hobart did not go through?

NOTE ON PROMISSORY ESTOPPEL AND PROMISES TO MAKE LOAN MODIFICATIONS

The mortgage crisis and meltdown of the residential real estate market beginning in 2008 prompted numerous cases where a frustrated homeowner invoked, among other theories, promissory estoppel to enforce an alleged promise by the mortgage lender to modify the terms of a delinquent home loan. Most of these claims met with little success in the courts. For instance, in *Johnson v. HSBC Bank,* 2012 WL 3966323 (E.D. Mich.), the plaintiff claimed that the defendant-bank orally promised her that if she made a certain number of additional full payments on her loan she would be granted a loan modification. She alleged she made those payments in reliance on the promise, but was never granted the promised modification. The bank filed a motion for summary judgment, and the federal magistrate judge recommended it be granted on the basis of an applicable state law precluding any action to enforce a promise or commitment of a financial institution unless in writing and signed by an authorized representative of the institution. Likewise, a number of cases have concluded that a lender's indication of a willingness to negotiate over a loan modification was not sufficient to constitute a clear and unambiguous promise sufficient to support a claim predicated on promissory estoppel. *E.g., Sherman v. Litton Loan Servicing, L.P.*, 796 F.Supp. 753, 766 (E.D. Va. 2011).

By contrast, in *Tedder v. Deutsche Bank Nat'l Trust Co.*, 863 F.Supp.2d 1020 (D. Haw. 2012), the plaintiff alleged that she had relied to her detriment on the defendant's promise not to continue foreclosure proceedings. The defendant sought dismissal on summary judgment, but the court concluded that the allegations of the complaint, if proven, could support recovery on the basis of a promissory estoppel claim. Promises made under the Home Affordable Modification Program, implemented by the U.S. Department of the Treasury in 2009, have been a frequent source of challenge on the ground of both breach of contract and promissory estoppel, with plaintiffs achieving modest success, at best. *See, e.g.*, *Miller v. Chase Home Finance, LLC,* 677 F.3d 1113 (11th Cir. 2011).

In *Aceves v. U.S. Bank Nat'l Assoc.,* 192 Cal.App.4th 218, 120 Cal.Rptr.3d 507 (2011), the court concluded that the plaintiff had stated a cause of action for promissory estoppel where the bank holding the plaintiff homeowner's mortgage agreed to work with the plaintiff on a mortgage reinstatement and loan modification if she no longer pursued relief in bankruptcy court. *Aceves,* 120 Cal.Rptr.3d at 514–18. Similarly, in *Dixon v. Wells Fargo Bank,* 798 F.Supp.2d 336 (D. Mass. 2011), the U.S. district court concluded that the plaintiff homeowners could maintain a cause of action for promissory estoppel where the gravamen of their complaint was that the bank holding their mortgage "promised to engage in negotiations to modify their loan, provided that they took certain 'steps necessary to enter into a mortgage modification.' " *Dixon,* 798 F.Supp.2d at 340. If you're interested in reading more (yeah, we realize how that sounds, but . . .), the lengthy and quite scholarly *Dixon* opinion contains a full discussion of the law, the cases, and the policies.

NOTE ON PROMISSORY ESTOPPEL IN EMPLOYMENT AND RETIREMENT AGREEMENTS

Promissory estoppel theory is frequently invoked in connection with employment contracts as a mechanism to convert what is otherwise an "at will" employment. For example, in *Blinn v. Beatrice Community Hospital and Health Center, Inc.,* 708 N.W.2d 235 (Neb. 2006) (first mentioned above in the material preceding the *G* case), Blinn, a hospital administrator, received an offer from another facility. Beatrice, Blinn's current employer assured him that they wanted him to stay and he could do so until he retired. Seven months later Blinn was asked to resign by Beatrice, and he brought suit. After dismissal on summary judgment, the Nebraska Supreme Court concluded that while the facts did not make out a claim for breach of contract, there was a genuine issue of material fact on Blinn's promissory estoppel claim as to which he was entitled to a trial on the merits.

Several cases have dealt with the promise to pay a lifetime annuity or other benefit on retirement. Generally, where the pension promise is determined to have induced an early retirement, enforcement may be had under § 90 of the *Restatement (Second) of Contracts. See, e.g., Feinberg v. Pfeiffer Co.,* 322 S.W.2d 163 (Mo. App. 1959). By contrast, in *Pitts v. McGraw-Edison Co.,* 329 F.2d 412 (6th Cir. 1964), the employee was informed that he had been retired at the same time that the promise was made to pay a pension. Finding that there was no promise made to Pitts on which he acted to his detriment—that he had not given up anything to which he was legally entitled—the court denied recovery under promissory estoppel.

Some cases fall in-between. In *Katz v. Danny Dare, Inc.,* 610 S.W.2d 121 (Mo. App. 1980), the plaintiff, I.G. Katz, was offered a pension of $13,000 per year, whereupon he retired. Several years later, the company reduced the promised monthly payment and Katz sued. Katz claimed he would not have retired but for the pension, while the company testified that had Katz not retired, he would have been terminated. The trial court found for the company on the basis that Katz had not given up anything in reliance on the promise since he could have been discharged at any time. The court of appeals reversed, holding that because Katz voluntarily elected to retire after being promised the annual pension payment, a right to recovery under promissory estoppel was established. Here's what one law professor had to say about the case:

> The *Danny Dare* decision is one that I teach in my class, and it causes no small level of consternation because of the court's distinction between a legal entitlement to employment (which the plaintiff did not have) and an interest in relying on a promise that the promisor may not have been obligated to make (the defendant really could have fired the plaintiff anytime he wanted to). Students catch on to this kind of reasoning and conclude, * * * that what we really have is judicial acrobatics to achieve a desired result.

Craig L. Jackson, *Traditional Contract Theory: Old and New Attacks and Old and New Defenses*, 33 NEW ENG. L. REV. 365, 422 (1998).

Why did the trial court in *Danny Dare* think the fact that Katz faced being fired if he did not accept retirement (with the promise of the pension) made the case distinguishable from *Feinberg v. Pfeiffer*, the case on which the court of appeals placed considerable reliance? Are the cases distinguishable or is the promise in *Danny Dare* actually more like the promise in *Pitts* than in *Feinberg*?

In *Langer v. Superior Steel,* 105 Pa.Super. 579, 161 A. 571 (1932), the president of the defendant/employer sent a letter to the plaintiff, Langer, upon his retirement promising "a pension of $100 per month as long as you live and preserve your present attitude of loyalty to the company and its officers and are not employed in any competitive occupation." After four years, the company ceased the payments and Langer sued. The company defended on the basis that the letter was a gratuitous promise and, as such, unenforceable. The court, however, concluded that there was a sufficient consideration because the company had received a benefit in Langer's not seeking employment with a competitor. Do you think the promise in *Langer* was any less gratuitous than the one in *Danny Dare*? Could you make an argument, based on *Langer*, that Danny Dare's promise was enforceable under traditional bargain theory?

Mr. Katz's victory over Danny Dare may have been even more impressive than he realized. Professor Robert Hillman published the results of an empirical study he conducted of promissory estoppel cases in the employment context decided during the period from 1994 through 1996. Surprisingly, he found that the employees succeeded *less than five percent* of the time. *See* Robert A. Hillman, *The Unfulfilled Promise of Promissory Estoppel in the Employment Setting*, 31 RUTGERS L. J. 1 (1999). In part, Professor Hillman attributed this low rate of success to an increasing judicial preference for written contracts supported by traditional bargained-for consideration. Indeed, like the rumors of Mark Twain's death, it is possible that Grant Gilmore's fear that promissory estoppel might "swallow up" the bargain principle in contract enforcement was vastly exaggerated!

Historically, enforcement of private employer-sponsored pension plans was handled under state common law theories of breach of contract and promissory estoppel. Much of the litigation over private employer pension promises was abated by the enactment in 1974 of the Employee Retirement Income Security Act (ERISA). ERISA, which was adopted to strengthen and improve pension and welfare security payments for plan participants, establishes a statutory enforcement mechanism that preempts state law. However, the common law contract theories remain viable as to plans that are unfunded or otherwise exempt from ERISA. *See also Schonholz v. Long Island Jewish Medical Center*, 87 F.3d 72 (2d Cir. 1996) (holding that promissory estoppel theory might be applied even in an ERISA case under extraordinary circumstances). The resolution granting Katz's pension likely was not covered by ERISA because it was not a company "plan," but rather a one-time obligation incurred to a single employee.

PROBLEM ON PROMISSORY ESTOPPEL

Let's assume that, in his third year of law school, Epstein accepts a job offer upon graduation from Cornbath, Swine & Moorg, a highly prestigious Wall Street firm with a reputation for paying the highest new associate salaries in the country. Secure in his decision, Epstein turns down other interviews with firms paying well, but not as well as old CS & M. After graduation, Epstein packs up his belongings and moves to New York to begin studying for the bar and working for CS & M. The day before he is to begin work, he receives a call at home from the hiring partner who informs Epstein that CS & M has a policy of only employing new associates who graduated in the top 5% of their law school class. Because, in his last semester of law school, Epstein dropped just below the top 5%, the partner tells him that the firm has filled his slot by hiring someone else. Enraged, Epstein responds by reminding the partner that he had a contract with the firm. The partner replies by telling him, "Ah, but that's where you're wrong. Because this was an employment at will, either party could terminate at any time. This bilateral power of termination means neither of us was committed to performance to the other. Therefore, these mutual so-called promises were illusory and could not give rise to a contract in fact. Perhaps if you studied a little harder, Dave, you would have known that, as well as graduated in the top 5%." Feeling betrayed, lamenting the money he spent to move to New York, and thinking about the other attractive interviews he passed up, Epstein decides to sue. Assuming the partner is right that, under applicable law, no contract arose between Epstein and CS & M, can Epstein successfully bring an action under the theory of promissory estoppel? If so, what damages should he seek?

NOTE ON PROMISSORY ESTOPPEL AND PRE-CONTRACT NEGOTIATIONS

In recent decades, and without any great consistency, courts have occasionally shown a willingness to extend liability under promissory estoppel to situations involving either pre-contract formation negotiations or where one party makes a specific promise in order to entice the other party to enter into negotiations and then the first party breaks the promise for no apparent reason. Commonly, these cases have involved negotiations over franchise agreements, although *Dixon v. Wells Fargo Bank, supra,* represents a more contemporary application in a non-franchise context. Typically, in many of the earlier cases, the franchisor will have offered assurance that a franchise would be forthcoming, and, in reliance on that "promise," the prospective franchisee would have made substantial expenditures in order to meet the conditions for receiving the franchise. When the franchisor refuses to go through with the deal, and the negotiations had never ripened into an enforceable agreement, authority exists for the disappointed franchisee to at least recover its expenses in preparing to do business, under promissory estoppel theory. *See, e.g., Midwest Energy, Inc. v. Orion Food Systems, Inc.,* 14 S.W.3d 154 (2000).

In perhaps the most far-reaching application of the doctrine of promissory estoppel to police conduct occurring in the stage of pre-contract negotiations, the Wisconsin Supreme Court, in *Hoffman v. Red Owl Stores, Inc.*, 26 Wis.2d 683, 133 N.W.2d 267 (1965), held that assurances made by a grocery store franchisor to a prospective franchisee concerning the award of a store at a new location could form the basis for recovery of out-of-pocket expenses incurred by the promisee in anticipation of the contract, even though the negotiations of the parties never ripened into a contractually enforceable promise. In justifying its holding, the court stated: "We deem it would be a mistake to regard an action grounded on promissory estoppel as the equivalent of a breach of contract action. As Dean Boyer points out, it is desirable that fluidity in the application of the concept be maintained."

The *Restatement (Second) of Contracts* appears to approve of the holding in *Red Owl. See* § 90 cmt. d, illus 10. Nevertheless, the decision represents a significant expansion of the doctrine of promissory estoppel as a basis for enforcing gift promises inducing reliance since there was no actual offer or "promise" in *Red Owl.* In other words, negotiations had not advanced to the point where there was a sufficiently clear and definite agreement that might have supported an action for breach of contract. Instead, recovery of reliance expenditures was based solely on positive assurances made by the franchisor during the course of negotiations that ultimately failed to reach fruition. Failed negotiations are, of course, a fact of life in business. Thus, something else was going on in *Red Owl.* What do you suppose it was? Does it have anything to do with the fact that the court in *Dixon v. Wells Fargo Bank* cited *Red Owl*? Also, go back to Chapter 2 and review *Budget Marketing, Inc. v. Centronics Corp.*

Does that offer any hints? Sometimes we begin to wonder whether this class is about contracts or torts. Maybe you're wondering the same thing.

In a 2007 law review article (before the housing market meltdown we hasten to add) very critical of *Red Owl,* here's what the authors had to say:

> The conventional wisdom among contemporary scholars is that courts will sometimes impose liability for reliance investments undertaken before any agreement between the parties. * * * Commentators identify as grounds for such enforcement the existence of unjust enrichment, misrepresentations made during negotiation, a specific promise made and relied upon during the negotiation process, and a "general obligation arising out of the negotiations themselves." * * * But even a casual survey of contemporary case law casts significant doubt on the accuracy of this conventional view. Courts actually make some form of agreement a necessary condition to a promisee's recovery. For courts, the real issues are when an agreement will be found and how the nature of the agreement will determine the type of damages a promisee can recover.
>
> Much of the confusion can be traced to the frequently taught case of Hoffman v. Red Owl Stores, Inc.
>
> * * *
>
> There is scant support in the law of contracts for this legal analysis. To the contrary, the Restatement of Contracts has only one definition of a promise, and that definition applies equally to a promise that is the product of a bargained-for exchange and a promise for which enforcement is sought on the grounds of induced reliance. Thus, if Hoffman stands for the proposition that a commitment can be binding under a theory of promissory estoppel even though it lacks the clarity and certainty required of a bargained-for promise, the case is wrong as a matter of doctrine. More importantly, it is an outlier: the case has not been followed in its own or other jurisdictions. Alan Schwartz & Robert Scott, Contractual *Liability and Preliminary Agreements*, 120 HARV. L. REV. 661, 668 (2007).

D. REMEDIAL CONSIDERATIONS

Some commentators have urged that the remedy in promissory estoppel cases should be limited to *reliance* damages—the amount necessary to put the promisee back in the position she would have been had the promise not been made. In fact, however, many decisions support the view that a court should award standard *expectation* or *benefit of the bargain* damages in the event a claim based on promissory estoppel is sustained. That is the approach, you'll recall, that the court took in *Weitz.*

Expectation damages are measured by the amount necessary to put the promisee in as good of a position as performance would have.

We will return to the subject of expectation and reliance damages in Chapter 7 dealing with how the law enforces a deal. For now, bear in mind that section 90 simply says: "The remedy for breach may be limited as justice requires." Does that help? So you find "justice" and say: "what do you require in this case, justice"? Not much help, which is why remedies so often come up as an issue in promissory estoppel cases.

E. THE DIMINISHING IMPORTANCE OF RELIANCE?

Oddly, even though the doctrine of promissory estoppel developed in the context of charitable subscription cases, proving reliance in the form of action or forbearance is often most difficult for the promisee in those cases. If you pledge $100 to your alma mater and then stiff the school, how can the institution show that it was *induced* by your pledge to take a particular course of action that it would not otherwise have taken? Chances are, it can't. Thus, courts typically engaged in various fictions to find detrimental reliance when none existed in fact. The drafters of the *Restatement (Second)* took a more straightforward approach by adding subsection (2) to § 90. It provides that in the case of charitable subscriptions enforcement may be had under subsection (1) of § 90 *without proof* of reliance. Does that mean your school can go after you for that pledge? Maybe "yes" and maybe "no." Not a very helpful answer, we appreciate, but just because the *Restatement* says it's so don't mean it is so—so to speak.

QUESTIONS BEFORE THE CASE

1. What do you suppose is the public interest that supports treating charitable subscriptions differently (and more leniently) than other kinds of promises? Why do you think the the court in this case was not swayed by that public interest?

2. Do you think Rabbi Halbfinger would have made a good law school Dean?

CONGREGATION KADIMAH TORAS-MOSHE V. DELEO

Supreme Judicial Court of Massachusetts
405 Mass. 305 (1989)

LIACOS, CHIEF JUSTICE.

Congregation Kadimah Toras-Moshe (Congregation), an Orthodox Jewish synagogue, commenced this action in the Superior Court to compel the administrator of an estate (estate) to fulfil the oral promise of the decedent to give the Congregation $25,000. The Superior Court transferred the case to the Boston Municipal Court, which rendered summary judgment for the estate. The case was then transferred back to the Superior Court, which also rendered summary judgment for the estate and dismissed the Congregation's complaint. We granted the Congregation's application for direct appellate review. We now affirm.

The facts are not contested. The decedent suffered a prolonged illness, throughout which he was visited by the Congregation's spiritual leader, Rabbi Abraham Halbfinger. During four or five of these visits, and in the presence of witnesses, the decedent made an oral promise to give the Congregation $25,000. The Congregation planned to use the $25,000 to transform a storage room in the synagogue into a library named after the decedent. The oral promise was never reduced to writing. The decedent died intestate in September, 1985. He had no children, but was survived by his wife.

The Congregation asserts that the decedent's oral promise is an enforceable contract under our case law, because the promise is allegedly supported either by consideration and bargain, or by reliance. * * * We disagree.

The Superior Court judge determined that "[t]his was an oral gratuitous pledge, with no indication as to how the money should be used, or what [the Congregation] was required to do if anything in return for this promise." There was no legal benefit to the promisor nor detriment to the promisee, and thus no consideration. Furthermore, there is no evidence in the record that the Congregation's plans to name a library after the decedent induced him to make or to renew his promise.

As to the lack of reliance, the judge stated that the Congregation's "allocation of $25,000 in its budget[,] for the purpose of renovating a storage room, is insufficient to find reliance or an enforceable obligation." We agree. The inclusion of the promised $25,000 in the budget, by itself, merely reduced to writing the Congregation's expectation that it would have additional funds. A hope or expectation, even though well founded, is not equivalent to either legal detriment or reliance.

The Congregation cites several of our cases in which charitable subscriptions were enforced. These cases are distinguishable because they involved written, as distinguished from oral, promises and also involved substantial consideration or reliance. See, e.g., *Trustees of Amherst Academy v. Cowls,* 6 Pick. 427, 434 (1828) (subscribers to written agreement could not withdraw "after the execution or during the progress of the work which they themselves set in motion"); *Trustees of Farmington Academy v. Allen,* 14 Mass. 172, 176 (1817) (trustees justifiably "proceed[ed] to incur expense, on the faith of the defendant's subscription"). Conversely, in the case of *Cottage St. Methodist Episcopal Church v. Kendall,* 121 Mass. 528 1877), we refused to enforce a promise in favor of a charity where there was no showing of any consideration or reliance.

The Congregation asks us to abandon the requirement of consideration or reliance in the case of charitable subscriptions. The Congregation cites the Restatement (Second) of Contracts § 90 (1981), which provides, in subsection (2): "A charitable subscription . . . is binding under Subsection (1) without proof that the promise induced action or forbearance." Subsection (1), as modified in pertinent part by subsection (2), provides: "A promise which the promisor should reasonably expect to induce action or forbearance on the part of the promisee or a third person . . . is binding if injustice can be avoided only by enforcement of the promise. . . ."

Assuming without deciding that this court would apply § 90, we are of the opinion that in this case there is no injustice in declining to enforce the decedent's promise. Although § 90 dispenses with the absolute requirement of consideration or reliance, the official comments illustrate that these are relevant considerations. Restatement (Second) of Contracts, *supra* at § 90 comment f. The promise to the Congregation is entirely unsupported by consideration or reliance. Furthermore, it is an oral promise sought to be enforced against an estate. To enforce such a promise would be against public policy.

Judgment affirmed.

QUESTIONS AND NOTE

1. Questions about the facts of this case

   1.1. Could you have made a little better reliance-based argument than inclusion of the pledged amount in the Congregation's budget? What additional facts, had they existed, would have made a more compelling case for enforcement based on reliance?

   1.2. Was the court concerned that because the alleged promise was oral perhaps it had not really been made?

2. Questions about the law

   2.1. Given the *Restatement (Second's)* elimination in subsection (2) of section 90 of the reliance requirement for charitable subscriptions, why didn't the court enforce the decedent's promise in this case? Did the court decide it wasn't prepared to adopt subsection (2), or is the holding that, even if subsection (2) does apply, the promise is still unenforceable? In either case, the result is non-enforcement, so what's the difference?

   2.2. What public policy is violated by enforcement of an oral promise against an estate?

3. Note

Reliance remains a necessary element of promissory estoppel under § 90 in the commercial context. But what kind of showing is required? Must the reliance result in some form of measurable economic loss? In *Vastoler v. American Can Co.,* 700 F.2d 916 (3d Cir. 1983), the plaintiff brought suit against his former employer to enforce a promise to the effect that his years of service on behalf of the company occurring prior to his promotion would count for purposes of calculating his pension benefits at retirement. The plaintiff's acceptance of the promotion was conditioned on receiving this credit, so when, at retirement, the employer did not count the years of past service, the plaintiff sued on a promissory estoppel theory alleging the promise induced him to accept the promotion. The trial court granted the employer's summary judgment motion on the basis that the plaintiff had not been disadvantaged by accepting a promotion. The court of appeals reversed and remanded the case for trial, noting that the district court's reasoning contained the following flaw:

> The second error in the district court's reasoning involves an even more fundamental deficiency. It failed to consider the human dynamics and anxieties inherent in supervisory positions. All jobs are not the same, and work involves more than one's "daily bread" and the weekly paycheck. Certain jobs have higher levels of stress and anxiety. Often, increased responsibilities torture the mind as well as the body. The different levels of stress associated with different jobs explains why some qualified people do not want to be President of Fortune 500 corporations, nominee for the Presidency of the United States, or foreman of their plants. Some privates do not want the decision-making burdens of majors and generals. Following Justice Frankfurter's admonition that "this Court should not be ignorant as judges of what we know as men [or women]," *Watts v. Indiana,* 338 U.S. 49, 52, 69 S.Ct. 1347, 1349, 93 L.Ed. 1801 (1949), we find that the trial judge erred in failing to recognize that absorption of the stress and anxiety inherent in supervisory

positions could be one of the factors that constitutes detrimental reliance.

700 F.2d at 919.

Do you think this is the kind of detrimental reliance the drafters of the *Restatement (Second)* had in mind? Reliance, of course, is very much a tort-based concept. If proof of reliance is becoming less central to recovery under promissory estoppel, how does that bear on the issue we discussed in Subsection 4, *supra*, concerning the decision to award expectation or reliance damages in promissory estoppel cases?

4. **You Be the Lawyer!**

   a. This time you get to represent yourself, so watch out! Let's assume that shortly before graduating from law school, as part of a class gift effort, you sign a pledge promising your school ten percent of your income over the next five years as a charitable contribution. Six months following graduation you receive a notice as to what the monthly payments are going to be on your student loans; as it turns out, they are going to be nearly seventy-five percent of your current monthly salary. Can you get yourself out of your pledge to your school?

   b. Suppose you call and make a $10 pledge to Jerry's Kids on Labor Day but fail to follow-up with the money. Can the Muscular Dystrophy Association sue you and recover? What if your donation was made in an uncontrollable surge of emotion after watching a particularly poignant segment of the telethon, but you cannot really afford to pay the amount you pledged?

CHAPTER 4

IS THE AGREEMENT UNENFORCEABLE BECAUSE OF THE FLAWS IN THE AGREEMENT PROCESS OR PROBLEMS WITH THE LANGUAGE OF THE AGREEMENT?

■ ■ ■

This Chapter surveys legal grounds for *not* enforcing an agreement based on either the provisions in the agreement or the agreement process. For example, in the first case in the book, *R.R. v. M.H.*, the agreement was unenforceable because of provisions in the agreement. The court found that an agreement for R.R.'s custody of the baby was unenforceable as against public policy because the agreement provided for payment to M.H. In the very next case we considered, *Lucy v. Zehmer*, there was an issue of agreement process: whether the Zehmers were drunk. It was important that the court determined that the Zehmers were not intoxicated because a person who is intoxicated lacks capacity to contract

Public policy and lack of capacity are only two of the legal grounds for not enforcing an agreement because of either problems with the language of the agreement or the agreement process. Those are two of the easier grounds to understand.

With the possible exception of the Statute of Frauds, the particulars of, and the policy basis for, the various legal grounds for not enforcing an agreement are obvious. So, let's get the Statute of Frauds out of the way, and then we can do the easy stuff.

---

1. CONTRACT LAW REASONS FOR *NOT* ENFORCING AGREEMENTS: STATUTES OF FRAUD

Because of the Statute of Frauds, *some* agreements are not enforceable unless there is objective proof that the agreement was made. This relatively simple sentence raises five not always simple questions that lawyers and law students need to be able to answer.

1) What is a Statute of Frauds?

2) What are the reasons for a Statute of Frauds?

3) Which agreements are covered by a Statute of Frauds, *i.e.*, "within" the Statute of Frauds?

4) How is the Statute of Frauds' requirement of objective proof of the agreement met, *i.e.*, "satisfied"?

5) What are the legal consequences of failure to satisfy the Statute of Frauds?*

First, what is a Statute of Frauds? The first Statute of Frauds was enacted in England in 1677: "An Act for Prevention of Frauds and Perjuries." It required that certain kinds of agreements must be in writing to be legally enforceable. It remained the law in England until 1954 when most of its provisions were repealed.

While the Statute of Frauds has been virtually eliminated from the law of contracts in England, it remains an important (albeit unpopular with judges) part of the law of contracts in the United States. States have enacted one or more statutes of frauds providing that certain kinds of agreements are not legally enforceable unless set out in a signed writing.

Second, what are the reasons for a Statute of Frauds? The title of the first Statute of Frauds sets out the purpose of the Statute of Frauds: "Prevention of Frauds or Perjuries." As the note preceding § 110 of the *Restatement (Second) of Contracts* explains: "In general, the primary purpose of the Statute of Frauds is assumed to be evidentiary, to provide reliable evidence of the existence and terms of the contract, and the classes of contracts covered seem for the most part to have been selected because of importance or complexity."

Third, what kinds of agreements are covered by the Statute of Frauds? Again, Statutes of Frauds vary from state to state. Section 110 of the *Restatement (Second) of Contracts* sets out the kinds of agreements generally covered by a state's Statute of Frauds.

§ 110 Classes of Contracts Covered

(1) The following classes of contracts are subject to a statute, commonly called the Statute of Frauds, forbidding enforcement unless there is a written memorandum or an applicable exception;

(a) a contract of an executor or administrator to answer for a duty of his decedent (the executor-administrator provision);

* There is a sixth "basic question" about the "statute of frauds": Should it be capitalized? While the Restatement capitalizes the Statute of Frauds, Black's Law Dictionary does not. *See* BLACK'S LAW DICTIONARY 1636 (10th ed. 2014). Reported cases do both, sometimes on the same page. *See Bank of Tex. v. Gaubert*, 286 S.W.3d 546, 553 (Tex. App-Dallas 2009, pet. dism'd w.o.j.).

(b) a contract to answer for the duty of another (the suretyship provision);

(c) a contract made upon consideration of marriage (the marriage provision);

d) a contract for the sale of an interest in land (the land contract provision);

(e) a contract that is not to be performed within one year from the making thereof (the one-year provision).

(2) The following classes of contracts, which were traditionally subject to the Statute of Frauds, are now governed by Statute of Frauds provisions of the Uniform Commercial Code:

(a) a contract for the sale of goods for the price of $500 or more (Uniform Commercial Code § 2–201). * * *

* * *

The following three cases illustrate three kinds of contracts that are commonly within a state's Statute of Frauds: (1) land transfer agreements, (2) agreements to buy or sell goods for $500 or more, and (3) agreements that cannot be performed within one year from the date the agreement was made. Additionally, the cases are helpful in answering question 4—how are the requirements of a Statute of Frauds satisfied, and question 5—what are the consequences of failure to satisfy the Statute of Frauds.

In the first of the cases, *Radke v. Brenon*, the court considers whether a typed letter offering to sell land was sufficient to comply with the Minnesota Statute of Frauds governing land transfers. You will find it helpful to read the relevant Minnesota statute, before reading the case.

Minn. St. 513.05 provides: "Every contract for the leasing for a longer period of than one year or for the sale of any lands, or any interest in lands, shall be void unless the contract, or some note or memorandum thereof, expressing the consideration, is in writing and subscribed by the party by whom the lease or sale is to be made, or by his lawful agent thereunto authorized in writing; and no such contract, when made by an agent, shall be entitled to record unless the authority of such agent be also recorded."

QUESTIONS BEFORE THE CASE

1. Who was the "party by whom the . . . sale is to be made" in this case?
2. Is there a "contract or some note or memorandum thereof" signed by "the party by whom the . . . sale is to be made"?

RADKE V. BRENON

Supreme Court of Minnesota
271 Minn. 35, 134 N.W.2d 887 (1965)

ROGOSHESKE, JUSTICE.

Defendants appeal from a judgment of the district court decreeing specific performance of a contract for the sale of real estate.

The judgment was entered upon findings made after trial that "subsequent to the Defendant acquiring" the property in question they "did offer to sell the property to the Plaintiff for the sum of Two Hundred Sixty-two ($262.00) Dollars, which offer the Plaintiff did accept"; and that "at all times relevant, the Plaintiff has been ready, willing and able to complete the agreement for the sale of Defendants' property but the Defendants have refused to do so." The court concluded that defendants "have wrongfully and improperly failed and refused" to deliver a deed of the property to plaintiff.

Resolving the conflicts in the evidence in plaintiff's favor, as we must, these appear to be the facts. Plaintiff and defendants are neighbors owning adjoining lots in Wakefield Park addition in Ramsey County. At the times each acquired ownership, their lots and eight neighboring lots did not extend to the west shoreline of Wakefield Lake, located nearby. The strip of land between the shoreline of the lake and the east boundary of the platted lots was owned by Dr. Gulden * * * until December 1, 1959, when defendants acquired ownership of the entire strip. Preston Brenon, hereinafter referred to as defendant, was a licensed real estate agent. Following his purchase, he had the property surveyed, and on June 28, 1960, he sent an identical letter to plaintiff and the eight other neighbors offering to sell them the irregular parcels that separated their lots from the lake. In the letter he explained that since he was interested only in that part of the strip adjoining his property, he had no desire to retain the remainder. He stated he had "no desire to make any profit on this transaction if everyone owning adjoining property is willing to buy their portion" and divide the cost "equally among all 10 including (him)self." He itemized the total cost at $2,120 and offered to sell each lot for $212 on any terms agreeable. This letter was not signed by defendant but his name was typewritten thereon, he having authorized this and considered such to be tantamount to his signature. Previous to the receipt of this letter, plaintiff and defendant had discussed the latter's intent of acquiring the property for the neighborhood on at least two occasions. About [two] weeks after plaintiff received this offer, he orally accepted it. Sometime later, plaintiff learned from a neighbor that two neighbors declined to purchase, and thus the divided cost of each lot was increased to $262. * * * It is clear that plaintiff accepted defendant's offer on May 7, at which time plaintiff knew of the price increase. Defendant testified:

'Q. * * * And did he agree to buy that time?

'A. At that time he did.'

On August 14, plaintiff delivered to his attorney a check for $262 payable to defendants for the purpose of completing the sale. On August 16, plaintiff's attorney wrote defendant informing him that he held the check for payment of the sale price to be delivered on receipt of a deed. Sometime after August 16, plaintiff received a letter from defendant dated August 16 informing him that the offer to sell was revoked.

The question is whether these facts establish a valid and enforceable contract for the sale of land. Defendants contend they do not.

As admitted by defendant, an oral contract to sell the land was made, and the trial court was clearly justified in so finding. There being no formal, integrated, written contract, however, the problem is whether the oral contract is unenforceable because it comes within Minn. St. 513.05 of the statute of frauds. Briefly, that provision decrees void any contract for the sale of lands unless the contract or some memorandum of the contract is in writing. The precise issue in this case is whether, under the circumstances, the letter written by defendant offering the land to plaintiff is a memorandum sufficient to satisfy the requirements of the statute.

The statute expresses a public policy of preventing the enforcement by means of fraud and perjury of contracts that were never in fact made. To inhibit perversion of this policy by those who would deny an oral contract actually made, the statute itself permits enforcement of an oral contract if there exists a note or memorandum as evidence of the contract. To the courts, then, is left promotion of the policy of the statute, either by denying enforcement urged by defrauders or by granting enforcement against wrongful repudiators. As an aid in this objective, the statute itself lists some requisites of a memorandum and this court has added others, so that we have some indication of what content a memorandum normally must have in order to be sufficient evidence of the contract.

The statute requires that the writing express the consideration and that it be subscribed by the party by whom the sale is to be made or by his lawful agent authorized in writing. This court has stated that the memorandum is sufficient when, in addition to the above requirements, it states expressly or by necessary implication the parties to the contract, the lands involved, and the general terms and conditions upon which the sale will be made.

These latter elements are clearly present in the letter written by defendant. Plaintiff's name is included in the inside address heading the letter, and Brenon's name is typewritten at the bottom. The land to be sold is positively delineated. The letter offers "their portion" to "everyone owning adjoining property," and the survey map accompanying the letter depicts each tract. Considering the conversation both before the after the letter was sent, it is inconceivable that the parties could be uncertain concerning the land to be sold. As to other terms of the contract, such as manner of payment, Brenon merely held himself ready "to work out any kind of terms" with the purchasers.

The elements expressly required by statute are not so obvious. First, the consideration of $212 stated in the letter is not the same as the $262 tendered in accord with the oral understanding. Despite this discrepancy, we think that the letter sufficiently expresses the consideration because the $212 represented an equal share of the cost divided by all ten interested parties. As Brenon said in the letter, "I feel the only fair way to share the cost is to divide equally among all 10 including myself." There is no dispute that the price was changed from that stated in the letter when two property owners declined to buy. The consideration then was simply a mathematical computation according to the formula specified in the letter. We do not believe this variation in the dollar amount renders the letter's expression of the consideration insufficient, especially since plaintiff paid more under the admitted agreement than he would have paid according to the letter.

The necessity of a subscription presents the final problem. A "subscription" is the same as a "signing," and it is clear that Brenon's typewritten name, which according to his testimony was typed with the intent that it be tantamount to a written signature, is a sufficient subscription. A problem here is that his wife, who owned the property with him in joint tenancy, apparently neither signed the letter nor authorized him in writing to sell her share. But this deficiency was at no time claimed or asserted before the trial court or in defendants' brief to this court. It was suggested for the first time upon oral argument. If it is a fact, it was not a part of the theory upon which the case was tried and submitted. We must therefore adhere to our well-settled rule that an unlitigated issue may not be asserted for the first time on appeal.

We by no means intend to hold that Brenon's letter would be a sufficient memorandum in every case. We will overlook technical requirements only if proof of the oral contract is clear and uncontradicted as in this case where defendant admitted that a contract had been made. But those technical requirements are only aids to discern where the truth lies in a given case, and we will not blindly apply those technicalities if they lead to a conclusion repugnant to common sense. As Professor Williston has said:

> "In brief, the Statute 'was intended to guard against the perils of perjury and error in the spoken word.' Therefore, if after a consideration of the surrounding circumstances, the pertinent

facts and all the evidence in a particular case, the court concludes that enforcement of the agreement will not subject the defendant to fraudulent claims, the purpose of the Statute will best be served by holding the note or memorandum sufficient even though it be ambiguous or incomplete."

Most persuasive is defendant's admission during trial that a contract was in fact made between plaintiff and himself. Although we have followed the majority rule that admission of the contract does not preclude assertion of the statute of frauds, an admission that a contract was made certainly cannot be ignored when all other evidence submitted supports the same conclusion. Even though it may be argued that the formal requirements contemplated by the statute are lacking, when all the evidence is taken into account we are of the opinion that the letter should be held a sufficient memorandum in this case. The policy of the statute of frauds would be perverted if the admitted contract were not enforced. The judgment of the trial court is therefore affirmed.

QUESTIONS, NOTES, AND CONNECTIONS

1. Questions about the facts of this case

   1.1. Which party raised the Statute of Frauds issue?

   1.2. Was the letter from the defendant to the plaintiff a contract or an offer?

   1.3. Did the defendant sign the letter?

   1.4. Was there a writing signed by the plaintiff in which he agreed to buy the land?

   1.5. Did the defendant contend that he did not offer to sell the land? Did the defendant argue that the plaintiff did not accept his offer?

2. Questions about the law

   2.1. What was the reason for the court's statement: "We by no means hold that Brenon's letter would be a sufficient memorandum in every case"?

   2.2. Why was the defendant's admission of an agreement "most persuasive"? Would the court have reached the same result if defendant's June 28 offer to sell was in an e-mail message? In a voice mail message left on plaintiff's answering machine? In some states, statutes of fraud have been revised to answer these questions.

   2.3. Assume that the buyer Radke, not the seller Brenon, changed his mind about the deal and Brenon was suing Radke for $262 for breach of contract. Would the agreement be enforceable against Radke?

3. Notes

3.1. The Minnesota Statute of Frauds seems to contemplate a single writing: "the contract, some note or memorandum thereof." Such language is typical of Statutes of Fraud. Nonetheless, courts generally conclude that several writings can be pieced together to satisfy the Statute of Frauds, even though any one of the writings taken alone would not have been sufficient.

3.2. Federal and state statutes answer the question how do electronic contracts satisfy the "writing" requirement of a Statute of Frauds. Some version of the Uniform Electronic Trasnsactions Act (UETA) has been adopted in virtually every state. UETA section 7(b) and (c) set out below provide that the electronic equivalent of a signed writing satisfies a Statute of Frauds:

UETA SECTION 7. LEGAL RECOGNITION OF ELECTRONIC RECORDS, ELECTRONIC SIGNATURES, AND ELECTRONIC CONTRACTS.

(c) If a law requires a record to be in writing, an electronic record satisfies the law.

(d) If a law requires a signature, an electronic signature satisfies the law.

4. **You Be the Lawyer!**

Your client, YC, has told you that they agreed to sell Redacre to B but that they never signed a written contract. When YC refuses to convey Redacre, B sues YC for specific performance. Can you ethically assert a Statute of Frauds defense? Is it unethical not to assert a Statute of Frauds defense?

5. Connections

Before going forward to the next case on satisfying the Statute of Frauds without a writing under the Uniform Commercial Code, go back to a case on the sale of real estate that we considered earlier. How would *Lucy v. Zehmer*, page 44, have been decided if: (i) the farm was in Minnesota, and (ii) the Zehmers had asserted a Statute of Frauds defense?

The requirements for satisfying a Statute of Frauds vary from state to state, and from statute to statute within a state. Compare the requirements of the Minnesota Statute of Frauds with respect to real estate transfers in the *Radke* case with the requirements of the Uniform Commercial Code's Statute of Frauds for sales of goods for $500 or more set out below. Note the differences in: (i) what the writing must provide; (ii) who must sign the writing and (iii) the significance of an admission that there was an agreement,

2–201 Formal Requirements; Statute of Frauds

(1) Except as otherwise provided in this section a contract for the sale of goods for the price of $500 or more is not enforceable by way of action or defense unless there is some writing sufficient to indicate that a contract for sale has been made between the parties and signed by the party against whom enforcement is sought or by his authorized agent or broker. A writing is not insufficient because it omits or incorrectly states a term agreed upon but the contract is not enforceable under this paragraph beyond the quantity of goods shown in such writing.

(2) Between merchants if within a reasonable time a writing in confirmation of the contract and sufficient against the sender is received and the party receiving it has reason to know its contents, it satisfies the requirements of subsection (1) against such party unless written notice of objection to its contents is given within 10 days after it is received.

(3) A contract which does not satisfy the requirements of subsection (1) but which is valid in other respects is enforceable

(a) if the goods are to be specially manufactured for the buyer and are not suitable for sale to others in the ordinary course of the seller's business and the seller, before notice of repudiation is received and under circumstances which reasonably indicate that the goods are for the buyer, has made either a substantial beginning of their manufacture or commitments for their procurement; or

(b) if the party against whom enforcement is sought admits in his pleading, testimony or otherwise in court that a contract for sale was made, but the contract is not enforceable under this provision beyond the quantity of goods admitted; or

(c) with respect to goods for which payment has been made and accepted or which have been received and accepted (Sec. 2–606).

Reconsider the phrase in section 2–201(1): "signed by the party against whom enforcement is sought." Who is the "party against whom enforcement is sought"? Is that person always the seller?

How is section 2–201(2) different from section 2–201(1)? Is it the writing alone that satisfies the requirements of section 2–201(2)?

While a writing, or writings is the most common method of satisfying the Statute of Frauds, note the alternate ways of satisfying the Statute of Frauds set out in section 2–201(3). The next case deals with the "judicial admission" alternative set out in 2–201(3)(b).

QUESTIONS BEFORE THE CASE

1. Did the party against whom enforcement is sought "admits in his pleading, testimony or otherwise in court that a contract for sale was made."?

2. What is the "interesting question concerning the statute of frauds" raised in this case?

DF ACTIVITIES CORPORATION V. BROWN

United States Court of Appeals, Seventh Circuit
851 F.2d 920 (1988)

POSNER, CIRCUIT JUDGE.

This appeal in a diversity breach of contract case raises an interesting question concerning the statute of frauds, in the context of a dispute over a chair of more than ordinary value. The plaintiff, DF Activities Corporation (owner of the Domino's pizza chain), is controlled by a passionate enthusiast for the work of Frank Lloyd Wright. The defendant, Dorothy [*sic*] Brown, a resident of Lake Forest (a suburb of Chicago) lived for many years in a house designed by Frank Lloyd Wright—the Willits House—and became the owner of a chair that Wright had designed, the Willits Chair. This is a stark, high-backed, uncomfortable-looking chair of distinguished design that DF wanted to add to its art collection. In September and October 1986, Sarah-Ann Briggs, DF's art director, negotiated with Dorothy Brown to buy the Willits Chair. DF contends—and Mrs. Brown denies—that she agreed in a phone conversation with Briggs on November 26 to sell the chair to DF for $60,000, payable in two equal installments, the first due on December 31 and the second on March 26. On December 3 Briggs wrote Brown a letter confirming the agreement, followed shortly by a check for $30,000.* Two weeks later Brown returned the letter and the check with the following handwritten note at the bottom

* The letter stated:

Dear Mrs. Brown:

This letter is to confirm our agreement to purchase from you the high back dining chair from the Ward W. Willits Residence (Highland Park, Illinois, 1901) for $60,000. As agreed to down payment of $30,000 is to be paid in December 1986 and the remaining $30,000 within 90 days. On completion of payment I will contact you to make transportation arrangements for the chair to Domino's Farms.

Domino's Pizza will carry insurance on the chair. Also, we would like to illustrate the chair in future publications. Do you have a transparency we could use?

Sincerely,

Sara-Ann B. Briggs

Director, Archives & Galleries

Eds.

of the letter: "Since I did not hear from you until December and I spoke with you the middle of November, I have made other arrangements for the chair. It is no longer available for sale to you." Sometime later Brown sold the chair for $198,000, precipitating this suit for the difference between the price at which the chair was sold and the contract price of $60,000. Brown moved under Fed. R. Civ. P. 12(b)(6) to dismiss the suit as barred by the statute of frauds in the Uniform Commercial Code. See UCC § 2–201. * * * Attached to the motion was Brown's affidavit that she had never agreed to sell the chair to DF or its representative, Briggs.* The affidavit also denied any recollection of a conversation with Briggs on November 26, and was accompanied by both a letter from Brown to Briggs dated September 20 withdrawing an offer to sell the chair and a letter from Briggs to Brown dated October 29 withdrawing DF's offer to buy the chair.

The district judge granted the motion to dismiss and dismissed the suit. DF appeals, contending that although a contract for a sale of goods at a price of $500 or more is subject to the statute of frauds, the (alleged) oral contract made on November 26 may be within the statutory exception for cases where "the party against whom enforcement is sought admits in his pleading, testimony or otherwise in court that a contract for sale was made." UCC § 2–201(3)(b). * * *

---

* AFFIDAVIT OF DOROTHEA F. BROWN

I, Dorothea F. Brown, having been first duly deposed and sworn to all states as follows:

i. My name is Dorothea F. Brown and I reside at 671 Beverly Place, Lake Forest, Illinois.

ii. I am the defendant in the above-captioned case.

iii. On August 19, 1986, I drafted a letter to Domino's Pizza Incorporated regarding my Frank Lloyd Wright chair, which is the subject matter of this suit.

iv. In response to my letter, Helen M. McNulty drafted her August 26, 1986 correspondence. (exhibit A)

v. For a short while thereafter, I negotiated with Sarah Briggs of Domino's Pizza relative to a possible sale of my chair to Domino Farms.

vi. I terminated my negotiation with the Plaintiff, herein with my correspondence dated September 20, 1986. (exhibit B)

vii. On October 29, 1986, the agent working on behalf of Domino's Farms drafted her letter to terminate further negotiation with respect to the chair, (exhibit C)

viii. Thereafter, I was contacted by a person who represented that she was Sarah Briggs and in a November 6, 1986 phone conversation, she further discussed the matter with me, but I did not agree to sell my chair to them.

ix. To the best of my recollection, I had no conversation with Sarah Ann Briggs on November 26, 1986.

x. I did not accept any offer from Domino's Farms or Sarah Briggs for their purchase of my chair.

xi. I did not sign any agreement to sell my chair to DF Activities, Sarah Briggs, or Domino's Farms nor was any person or entity authorized to enter into any alleged agreement in my behalf.

xii. I have not accepted any payment whatsoever from Domino's Farms or Sarah Briggs with respect to this matter.

Further deponent saith not.

Eds.

At first glance DF's case may seem quite hopeless. Far from admitting in her pleading, testimony, or otherwise in court that a contract for sale was made, Mrs. Brown denied under oath that a contract had been made. DF argues, however, that if it could depose her, maybe she would admit in her deposition that the affidavit was in error, that she had talked to Briggs on November 26, and that they had agreed to the sale of the chair on the terms contained in Briggs' letter of confirmation to her.

There is remarkably little authority on the precise question raised by this appeal—whether a sworn denial ends the case or the plaintiff may press on, and insist on discovery. In fact we have found no authority at the appellate level, state or federal. Many cases hold, it is true, that the defendant in a suit on an oral contract apparently made unenforceable by the statute of frauds cannot block discovery aimed at extracting an admission that the contract was made, simply by moving to dismiss the suit on the basis of the statute of frauds or by denying in the answer to the complaint that a contract had been made. There is also contrary authority. * * * We need not take sides on the conflict. When there is a bare motion to dismiss, or an answer, with no evidentiary materials, the possibility remains a live one that, if asked under oath whether a contract had been made, the defendant would admit it had been. The only way to test the proposition is for the plaintiff to take the defendant's deposition, or, if there is no discovery, to call the defendant as an adverse witness at trial. But where as in this case the defendant swears in an affidavit that there was no contract, we see no point in keeping the lawsuit alive. Of course the defendant may blurt out an admission in a deposition, but this is hardly likely, especially since by doing so he may be admitting to having perjured himself in his affidavit. Stranger things have happened, but remote possibilities do not warrant subjecting the parties and the judiciary to proceedings almost certain to be futile. * * *

[A]ffidavits in litigation are prepared by lawyers, and merely signed by affiants. Yet to allow an affiant to be deposed by opposing counsel would be to invite the unedifying form of discovery in which the examining lawyer tries to put words in the witness's mouth and construe them as admissions.

The history of the judicial-admission exception to the statute of frauds reinforces our conclusion. The exception began with common-sense recognition that if the defendant admitted in a pleading that he had made a contract with the plaintiff, the purpose of the statute of frauds—protection against fraudulent or otherwise false contractual claims—was fullfilled. (The situation would be quite otherwise, of course, with an oral admission, for a plaintiff willing to testify falsely to the existence of a contract would be equally willing to testify falsely to the defendant's having admitted the existence of the contract.) Toward the end of the eighteenth century the courts began to reject the exception, fearing that it was an invitation to the defendant to perjure himself. Later the pendulum swung again, and the exception is now firmly established. The concern with perjury that caused the courts in the middle period to reject the exception supports the position taken by Mrs. Brown in this case. She has sworn under oath that she did not agree to sell the Willits Chair to DF. DF wants an opportunity to depose her in the hope that she can be induced to change her testimony. But if she changes her testimony this will be virtually an admission that she perjured herself in her affidavit (for it is hardly likely that her denial was based simply on a faulty recollection). She is not likely to do this. What is possible is that her testimony will be sufficiently ambiguous to enable DF to argue that there should be still further factual investigation—perhaps a full-fledged trial at which Mrs. Brown will be questioned again about the existence of the contract.

With such possibilities for protraction, the statute of frauds becomes a defense of meager value. And yet it seems to us as it did to the framers of the Uniform Commercial Code that the statute of frauds serves an important purpose in a system such as ours that does not require that all contracts be in writing in order to be enforceable and that allows juries of lay persons to decide commercial cases. The methods of judicial factfinding do not distinguish unerringly between true and false testimony, and are in any event very expansive. People deserve some protection against the risks and costs of being hauled into court and accused of owing money on the basis of an unacknowledged promise. And being deposed is scarcely less unpleasant than being cross-examined—indeed, often it is more unpleasant, because the examining lawyer is not inhibited by the presence of a judge or jury who might resent hectoring tactics. The transcripts of depositions are often very ugly documents.

* * * [O]nce the defendant has denied the contract under oath, the safety valve of section 2–201(3)(b) is closed. The chance that at a deposition the defendant might be badgered into withdrawing his denial is too remote to justify prolonging an effort to enforce an oral contract in the teeth of the statute of frauds. If Dorothy [*sic*] Brown did agree on November 27 to sell the chair to DF at a bargain price, it behooved Briggs to get Brown's signature on the dotted line, posthaste.

Affirmed.

FLAUM, CIRCUIT JUDGE, dissenting.

Because I disagree with the majority's holding that additional discovery is prohibited whenever a defendant raises a statute of frauds defense and submits a sworn denial that he or she formed an oral contract with the plaintiff, I respectfully dissent. Neither would I hold, however, that a plaintiff is automatically entitled to additional discovery in the face of a defendant's sworn denial that an agreement was reached. Rather, in my view district courts should have the authority to exercise their discretion to determine the limits of permissible discovery in these cases.

This flexibility is particularly important where, as here, the defendant's affidavit does not contain a conclusive denial of contract formation. * * *

QUESTIONS AND NOTE

1. Questions about the facts of this case

   1.1. Why didn't the defendant want to sell the chair to the plaintiff for $60,000?

   1.2. Who is the person "against whom enforcement is sought"? Is there an agreement signed by that person as required by § 2–201(1)?

   1.3. Is there a writing signed by that person that was important to the court's application of § 2–201(3)?

2. Questions about the law

   2.1. Writing: Why didn't the December 3rd letter satisfy § 2–201(2)? Would the letter have satisfied § 2–201(2) if the defendant was a merchant?

   2.2. Part performance: Why didn't the $30,000 payment satisfy the Statute of Frauds? *See* § 2–201(3)(c).

3. Note

   Common law judicial admission exception: Notwithstanding the obiter dictum in *DF Activities* that the "judicial admissions exception is firmly established," cases not governed by U.C.C. § 2–201(3) are divided as to whether an oral judicial admission satisfies the Statute of Frauds. Remember the dictum in the *Radke* case.

4. **You Be the Lawyer!**

   As the attorney making the oral argument at the Eighth Circuit for DF Activities, how would you respond to the following question from Judge Posner: "Why shouldn't Mrs. Brown's affidavit in which she swore under oath that she did not agree to sell the Willits Chair to DF be determinative"?

The final Statute of Frauds case involves an employment agreement. The Hawaiian Statute of Frauds set out below is representative of Statute of Frauds' provisions affecting employment agreements:

HRS § 656–1 Certain contracts, when actionable.

No action shall be brought and maintained in any of the following cases: * * *

(5) Upon any agreement that is not to be performed within one year from the making thereof; unless the promise, contract, or agreement, upon which the action is brought, or some memorandum or note thereof, is in writing, and is signed by the party to be charged therewith, or by some person thereunto by the party in writing lawfully authorized.

QUESTIONS BEFORE THE CASE

1. Why does McIntosh contend that the employment agreement was for a one-year term and not employment at will?
2. Does the Hawaiian statute require a one-year employment agreement be in writing in order to be legally enforceable?
3. Does the Hawaiian statute mention "part performance" or "reliance"?

MCINTOSH V. MURPHY

Supreme Court of Hawai'i
52 Haw. 29, 469 P.2d 177 (1970)

LEVINSON, JUSTICE.

This case involves an oral employment contract which allegedly violates the provision of the Statute of Frauds requiring "any agreement that is not to be performed within one year from the making thereof" to be in writing in order to be enforceable. HRS § 656–1(5). In this action the plaintiff-employee Dick McIntosh seeks to recover damages from his employer, George Murphy and Murphy Motors, Ltd., for the breach of an alleged one-year oral employment contract.

While the facts are in sharp conflict, it appears that defendant George Murphy was in southern California during March, 1964 interviewing prospective management personnel for his Chevrolet-Oldsmobile dealerships in Hawaii. He interviewed the plaintiff twice during that time. The position of sales manager for one of the dealerships was fully discussed but no contract was entered into. In April, 1964 the plaintiff received a call from the general manager of Murphy Motors informing him of possible employment within thirty days if he was still available. The plaintiff indicated his continued interest and informed the manager that he would be available. Later in April, the plaintiff sent Murphy a telegram to the effect that he would arrive in Honolulu on Sunday, April 26, 1964. Murphy then telephoned McIntosh on Saturday, April 25, 1964, to notify him that the job of assistant sales manager was open and work would begin on the following Monday, April 27, 1964. At that time McIntosh expressed surprise at the change in job title from sales manager to assistant sales manager but reconfirmed the fact that he was arriving in Honolulu the next day, Sunday. McIntosh arrived on Sunday, April 26, 1964, and began work on the following day, Monday, April 27, 1964.

As a consequence of his decision to work for Murphy, McIntosh moved some of his belongings from the mainland to Hawaii, sold other possessions, leased an apartment in Honolulu and obviously forwent any other employment opportunities. In short, the plaintiff did all those things which were incidental to changing one's residence permanently from Los Angeles to Honolulu, a distance of approximately 2,200 miles. McIntosh continued working for Murphy until July 16, 1964, approximately two and one-half months, at which time he was discharged on the grounds that he was unable to close deals with prospective customers and could not train the salesmen.

At the conclusion of the trial, the defense moved for a directed verdict arguing that the oral employment agreement was in violation of the Statute of Frauds, there being no written memorandum or note thereof. The trial court ruled that as a matter of law the contract did not come within the Statute, reasoning that Murphy bargained for acceptance by the actual commencement of performance by McIntosh, so that McIntosh was not bound by a contract until he came to work on Monday, April 27, 1964. Therefore, assuming that the contract was for a year's employment, it was performable within a year exactly to the day and no writing was required for it to be enforceable. Alternatively, the court ruled that if the agreement was made final by the telephone call between the parties on Saturday, April 25, 1964, then that part of the weekend which remained would not be counted in calculating the year, thus taking the contract out of the Statute of Frauds. With commendable candor the trial judge gave as the motivating force for the decision his desire to avoid a mechanical and unjust application of the Statute.[1]

The case went to the jury on the following questions: (1) whether the contract was for a year's duration or was performable on a trial basis, thus making it terminable at the will of either party; (2) whether the plaintiff was discharged for just cause; and (3) if he was not discharged for just cause, what damages were due the plaintiff. The jury returned a verdict for the plaintiff in the sum of $12,103.40. The defendants appeal to this court on four principal grounds, three of which we find to be without merit. The remaining ground of appeal is whether the plaintiff can maintain an action on the alleged oral employment contract in light of the prohibition of the

[1] THE COURT: You make the law look ridiculous, because one day is Sunday and the man does not work on Sunday; the other day is Saturday; he is up in Fresno. He can't work down there. And he is down here Sunday night and shows up for work on Monday. To me that is a contract within a year. I don't want to make the law look ridiculous, Mr. Clause, because it is one day after, one day too much, and that one day is a Sunday, and a non-working day.

Statute of Frauds making unenforceable an oral contract that is not to be performed within one year.

I. TIME OF ACCEPTANCE OF THE EMPLOYMENT AGREEMENT

The defendants contend that the trial court erred in refusing to give an instruction to the jury that if the employment agreement was made more than one day before the plaintiff began performance, there could be no recovery by the plaintiff. The reason given was that a contract not to be performed within one year from its making is unenforceable if not in writing.

The defendants are correct in their argument that the time of acceptance of an offer is a question of fact for the jury to decide. But the trial court alternatively decided that even if the offer was accepted on the Saturday prior to the commencement of performance, the intervening Sunday and part of Saturday would not be counted in computing the year for the purposes of the Statute of Frauds. The judge stated that Sunday was a non-working day and only a fraction of Saturday was left which he would not count. In any event, there is no need to discuss the relative merits of either ruling since we base our decision in this case on the doctrine of equitable estoppel which was properly briefed and argued by both parties before this court, although not presented to the trial court.

II. ENFORCEMENT BY VIRTUE OF ACTION IN RELIANCE ON THE ORAL CONTRACT

In determining whether a rule of law can be fashioned and applied to a situation where an oral contract admittedly violates a strict interpretation of the Statute of Frauds, it is necessary to review the Statute itself together with its historical and modern functions. The Statute of Frauds, which requires that certain contracts be in writing in order to be legally enforceable, had its inception in the days of Charles II of England. Hawaii's version of the Statute is . . . substantially the same as the original English Statute of Frauds.

The first English Statute was enacted almost 300 years ago to prevent "many fraudulent practices, which are commonly endeavored to be upheld by perjury and subornation of perjury." Certainly, there were compelling reasons in those days for such a law. At the time of enactment in England, the jury system was quite unreliable, rules of evidence were few, and the complaining party was disqualified as a witness so he could neither testify on direct-examination nor, more importantly, be cross-examined. The aforementioned structural and evidentiary limitations on our system of justice no longer exist.

Retention of the Statute today has nevertheless been justified on at least three grounds: (1) the Statute still serves an evidentiary function thereby lessening the danger of perjured testimony (the original rationale); (2) the requirement of a writing has a cautionary effect which causes reflection by the parties on the importance of the agreement; and (3) the writing is an easy way to distinguish enforceable contracts from those which are not, thus channeling certain transactions into written form.

In spite of whatever utility the Statute of Frauds may still have, its applicability has been drastically limited by judicial construction over the years in order to mitigate the harshness of a mechanical application. Furthermore, learned writers continue to disparage the Statute regarding it as "a statute for promoting fraud" and a "legal anachronism."

Another method of judicial circumvention of the Statute of Frauds has grown out of the exercise of the equity powers of the courts. Such judicially imposed limitations or exceptions involved the traditional dispensing power of the equity courts to mitigate the "harsh" rule of law. When courts have enforced an oral contract in spite of the Statute, they have utilized the legal labels of "part performance" or "equitable estoppel" in granting relief. Both doctrines are said to be based on the concept of estoppel, which operates to avoid unconscionable injury.

Part performance has long been recognized in Hawaii as an equitable doctrine justifying the enforcement of an oral agreement for the conveyance of an interest in land where there has been substantial reliance by the party seeking to enforce the contract. Other courts have enforced oral contracts (including employment contracts) which failed to satisfy the section of the Statute making unenforceable an agreement not to be performed within a year of its making. This has occurred where the conduct of the parties gave rise to an estoppel to assert the Statute.

It is appropriate for modern courts to cast aside the raiments of conceptualism which cloak the true policies underlying the reasoning behind the many decisions enforcing contracts that violate the Statute of Frauds. There is certainly no need to resort to legal rubrics or meticulous legal formulas when better explanations are available.

In seeking to frame a workable test which is flexible enough to cover diverse factual situations and also provide some reviewable standards, we find very persuasive section [139] of the Second Restatement of Contracts. That section specifically covers those situations where there has been reliance on an oral contract which falls within the Statute of Frauds. Section [139] states:

> (1) A promise which the promisor should reasonably expect to induce action or forbearance on the part of the promisee or a third person and which does induce the action or forbearance is enforceable notwithstanding the Statute of Frauds if injustice can be avoided only by enforcement of the promise. The remedy granted for breach is to be limited as justice requires.

(2) In determining whether injustice can be avoided only by enforcement of the promise, the following circumstances are significant: (a) the availability and adequacy of other remedies, particularly cancellation and restitution; (b) the definite and substantial character of the action or forbearance in relation to the remedy sought; (c) the extent to which the action or forbearance corroborates evidence of the making and terms of the promise, or the making and terms are otherwise established by clear and convincing evidence; (d) the reasonableness of the action or forbearance; (e) the extent to which the action or forbearance was forseeable by the promisor.

We think that the approach taken in the Restatement is the proper method of giving the trial court the necessary latitude to relieve a party of the hardships of the Statute of Frauds. This is to be preferred over having the trial court bend over backwards to take the contract out of the Statute of Frauds. In the present case the trial court admitted just this inclination and forthrightly followed it.

There is no dispute that the action of the plaintiff in moving 2200 miles from Los Angeles to Hawaii was foreseeable by the defendant. In fact, it was required to perform his duties. Injustice can only be avoided by the enforcement of the contract and the granting of money damages. No other remedy is adequate. The plaintiff found himself residing in Hawaii without a job.

It is also clear that a contract of some kind did exist. The plaintiff performed the contract for two and one-half months receiving $3,484.60 for his services. The exact length of the contract, whether terminable at will as urged by the defendant, or for a year from the time when the plaintiff started working, was up to the jury to decide.

In sum, the trial court might have found that enforcement of the contract was warranted by virtue of the plaintiff's reliance on the defendant's promise. Naturally, each case turns on its own facts. Certainly there is considerable discretion for a court to implement the true policy behind the Statute of Frauds, which is to prevent fraud or any other type of unconscionable injury. We therefore affirm the judgment of the trial court on the ground that the plaintiff's reliance was such that injustice could only be avoided by enforcement of the contract.

Affirmed.

ABE, JUSTICE (dissenting).

The majority of the court has affirmed the judgment of the trial court; however, I respectfully dissent.

I believe this court is begging the issue by its holding because to reach that conclusion, this court is ruling that the defendant agreed to hire the plaintiff under a one-year employment contract. The defendant has denied that the plaintiff was hired for a period of one year and has introduced into evidence testimony of witnesses that all hiring by the defendant in the past has been on a trial basis. The defendant also testified that he had hired the plaintiff on a trial basis.

Here on one hand the plaintiff claimed that he had a one-year employment contract; on the other hand, the defendant claimed that the plaintiff had not been hired for one year but on a trial basis for so long as his services were satisfactory. I believe the Statute of Frauds was enacted to avoid the consequences this court is forcing upon the defendant. In my opinion, the legislature enacted the Statute of Frauds to negate claims such as has been made by the plaintiff in this case. But this court holds that because the plaintiff in reliance of the one-year employment contract (alleged to have been entered into by the plaintiff, but denied by the defendant) has changed his position, "injustice could only be avoided by enforcement of the contract." Where is the sense of justice?

Now assuming that the defendant had agreed to hire the plaintiff under a one-year employment contract and the contract came within the Statute of Frauds, I cannot agree, as intimated by this court, that we should circumvent the Statute of Frauds by the exercise of the equity powers of courts. As to statutory law, the sole function of the judiciary is to interpret the statute and the judiciary should not usurp legislative power and enter into the legislative field. Thus, if the Statute of Frauds is too harsh as intimated by this court, and it brings about undue hardship, it is for the legislature to amend or repeal the statute and not for this court to legislate.

QUESTIONS, NOTE, AND CONNECTIONS

1. Questions about the facts of this case

   1.1. Did the defendant admit that he agreed to employ the plaintiff for one year?

   1.2. Was there part performance by the plaintiff in this case? Was there reliance? Are the part performance facts the same as the reliance facts?

2. Questions about the law

   2.1. Not to be performed within one year from the making thereof

      (a) The plaintiff alleged that there was a one-year oral employment contract. Can a one-year employment contract "be performed within one year from the making thereof"? Is that relevant in this case?

(b) Epstein hires you to work as his research assistant on the Corpus Juris Thirdundum project—an update and complete rewriting of Corpus Juris Secondum, a treatise for lawyers with more than 160 volumes. Epstein and you orally agree that you will be paid $60,000 a year until the treatise is complete. Is the contract "not to be performed within one year from the making"?

(c) Most people work as employees at will. Is an employment at will agreement within the Statute of Frauds?

2.2. *McIntosh* and the language of the Statute of Frauds: What language in the Hawaii Statute of Frauds supports the holding in this case?

2.3. *McIntosh* and the purpose of the Statute of Frauds: The Hawaii Supreme Court reminds us that the purpose of the original Statute of Frauds was to prevent "many fraudulent practices, which are commonly endeavored to be upheld by perjury and subornation of perjury." Is the holding in this case consistent with this original purpose?

3. Note

Judge Richard Posner is critical of the use of promissory estoppel "to get around" the Statute of Frauds, particularly in employment cases:

> Employment at will (i.e., without a contract of employment) remains the dominant type of employment relationship in this country, and would be seriously undermined if employees could use the doctrine of promissory estoppel to make alleged oral contracts of employment enforceable. Reliance is easily, perhaps too easily, shown in the employment setting. Agreeing to work for a particular employer, thereby giving up alternative opportunities for employment, can easily be described as reliance on the employer's alleged oral promises concerning the terms of employment. Maybe the cases that erode it in the area of promissory estoppel exaggerate the ability of courts to distinguish true oral promises from fabricated promises and language misunderstood as promissory. Maybe they overlook the simple logical point that the promisee should know the promise is unenforceable because of the statute of frauds and therefore shouldn't rely on it. But for what it is worth the logic of such cases is that the element of reliance that is required to make a promise enforceable on grounds of estoppel takes the place of a writing in giving adequate assurance that the promise has not been fabricated, or misunderstood without fault on the part of the promisor. The "promisee" takes a great risk if he gives up something in purported reliance on a nonexistent promise, merely to bolster his claim that there was a promise.

Goldstick v. ICM Realty, 788 F.2d 456, 465 (7th Cir. 1986). Do you agree with Judge Posner? Would Justice Abe of the Hawaii Supreme Court agree?

4. **You Be the Lawyer!**

   Assume that you are the attorney for the plaintiff and that after the $12,103.40 jury verdict for the plaintiff, the defendant offered to settle for $5,000. Would you have recommended to the plaintiff that he accept the settlement offer?

5. Connections

   5.1. Connection between part performance and *Restatement (Second)* § 130: Recall that (1) under section 2–201(3), part performance can satisfy the Statute of Frauds in agreements involving the sale of goods, and (2) the *McIntosh* case mentions (and your property professor will discuss) part performance satisfying the Statute of Frauds in real estate transfer deals. Recall also that the plaintiff worked for the defendant for two and one-half months. According to *Restatement (Second) of Contracts* § 130, comment e: "Part performance not amounting to full performance on one side does not in general take a contract out of the one-year provision." Why?

   5.2. Connection between *Restatement (Second)* § 139 and *Restatement (Second)* § 90: How are *Restatement (Second)* § 139 and *Restatement (Second)* § 90 similar? How are *Restatement (Second)* § 139 and *Restatement (Second)* § 90 different? Did the defendant in the *McIntosh* case argue that its promise was unenforceable because of no consideration?

Consider some of the ruminations of Professor John Kidwell on teaching the Statute of Frauds:

> [A] requirement that a contract be in writing is functionally very like the requirement of a seal. Such a requirement is attractive for the same reasons that the seal requirement is attractive. If everyone knew and followed the forms there would be less conflict, and justice would be speedy and certain. Social order would be enhanced. But we don't care just about social order. We care also about individual justice. And we know that not all people know the rules, and even when they do they might find reasons not to follow them. If we enforce the formal requirement in these cases, we sacrifice individual justice in favor of social order, which always at least makes us pause. And sometimes we yield to the urge to make an exception and soften the formal rule. I then suggest that it can be argued that every formal rule is under

> relentless pressure from our desire for individual justice. * * * We always are tempted to make exceptions to rules that depend on form because we always care, to some extent, about the injustice, which results when we enforce the formal requirement. Thus, formal requirements tend to decay. Not always, and not perhaps as dramatically as in the case of the seal, but often. Writing requirements, notice requirements, filing requirements, statutes of limitations—all invite exceptions.

John Kidwell, *Ruminations on Teaching the Statute of Frauds*, 44 ST. LOUIS U. L.J. 1427, 1432 (2000).

---

2. CONTRACT LAW REASONS FOR *NOT* ENFORCING AGREEMENTS: FRAUD, FRAUDULENT OR MATERIAL MISREPRESENTATIONS AND NONDISCLOSURE

The contract law of misrepresentation is similar to the tort law of fraud and misrepresentation. Misrepresentation can be the basis for either a tort action or a contract action. The tort action is generally a suit for actual (and possibly punitive damages) for deceit or fraud or misrepresentation. And, the contract action is generally a suit for rescission to make an agreement unenforceable.

Restatement (Second) of Contracts § 164.

§ 164. When A Misrepresentation Makes A Contract Voidable

> (1) If a party's manifestation of assent is induced by either a fraudulent or a material misrepresentation by the other party upon which the recipient is justified in relying, the contract is voidable by the recipient.

Largely common sense stuff.

Assume, for example, that Markell and Ponoroff agree to do a contracts book with Epstein. Should Markell and Ponroff be able to get out of their agreement with Epstein because he told them that he had a masters degree in law from the Harvard Law School, when in reality his LL.M. degree was a Litvak Latkes Macher degree from the Havud Low Shul? What if Epstein honestly believes that he went to Harvard (at his age, he gets confused a lot)? What if Markell and Ponoroff could have easily checked on whether Epstein graduated from Harvard?

The next case, *Halpert v. Rosenthal*, involves equally easy facts—a defendant buyer arguing that a court should not enforce an agreement to buy the plaintiff's house because of the plaintiff's misrepresentation as to termites.

QUESTIONS BEFORE THE CASE

1. Did the defendant agree to buy the plaintiff's house?
2. What is the misrepresentation?
3. What is "the issue of first impression in this state"?

HALPERT V. ROSENTHAL

Supreme Court of Rhode Island
107 R.I. 406, 267 A.2d 730 (1970)

KELLEHER, J.

This is a civil action wherein the plaintiff vendor seeks damages for the breach by the defendant vendee of a contract for the sale of real estate. The defendant filed a counter-claim in which he sought the return of his deposit. A jury trial was held in the Superior Court. The jury found for the defendant and judgment followed. The case is before us on the plaintiff's appeal.

On February 21, 1967, the parties hereto entered into a real estate agreement whereby plaintiff agreed to convey a one-family house located in Providence on the southeasterly corner of Wayland and Upton Avenues to defendant for the sum of $54,000. The defendant paid a deposit of $2,000 to plaintiff. The agreement provided for the delivery of the deed and the payment of the balance of the purchase price by June 30, 1967.

On May 17, 1967, a termite inspection was made of the premises, and it was discovered that the house was inhabited by termites. The defendant then notified plaintiff that, because of the termite infestation, he was not going to purchase the property. The defendant did not appear for the title closing which plaintiff had scheduled for June 30, 1967.

The plaintiff immediately commenced this suit. Her complaint prayed for specific performance or monetary damages. When the case came on for trial, the property had been sold to another buyer for the sum of $35,000. The plaintiff then sought to recover from defendant the $19,000 difference between the selling price called for in the sales agreement and the actual selling price. The defendant in his answer alleged that plaintiff and her agent had, during the preagreement negotiation, intentionally misrepresented the house as being free of termites. The defendant's counterclaim sought the return of the $2,000 deposit.

At the conclusion of the presentation of all the evidence, plaintiff made a motion for a directed verdict on the issue of the alleged fraudulent misrepresentations. The trial justice reserved decision on the motion and submitted the case to the jury. After the jury's verdict, he denied the motion.

This case is unique in that plaintiff made no motion for a new trial. Her appeal is based for the most part on the trial court's refusal to direct a verdict in her favor on the counterclaim. She has also alleged that the trial justice erred in certain portions of his charge to the jury and in failing to adopt some 15 requests to charge submitted by plaintiff.

The absence of a motion for a new trial narrows the scope of an inquiry on appeal. Instead of being concerned with the credibility of witnesses or the weight of the evidence as we would be were we reviewing the usual motion for a new trial, we apply the standards applicable to a motion for a directed verdict. In doing so, it is our duty to consider all of the evidence and reasonable inferences deducible therefrom in the light most favorable to defendant.

Since we consider only the evidence favorable to defendant, we shall set forth defendant's version of three different occasions in 1967 when the alleged misrepresentations relative to absence of any termites were made.

1. In early February, defendant and his wife inspected the Halpert home. They asked the agent about termites and he told them that there was no termite problem and that he had never experienced any termite problem with any of the houses he sold in the East Side section of Providence.

2. Later on in February, defendant, his wife, his sister-in-law and his brother-in-law met plaintiff. The brother-in-law inquired about the presence of termites; plaintiff said that there were no termites in the house.

3. When defendant was about to sign the purchase and sales agreement, he asked plaintiff's real estate agent whether it might not be advisable if the home be inspected for termites before the agreement was signed. The agent told defendant that such a step was unnecessary because there were no termite problems in the house.

* * *

In contending that she was entitled to a directed verdict, plaintiff contends that to sustain the charge of fraudulent misrepresentation, some evidence had to be produced showing that either she or her agent knew at the time they said there were no termites in the house, that such a statement was untrue. Since the representations made to defendant were made in good faith, she argues that, as a matter of law, defendant could not prevail on his counterclaim.

The defendant concedes that there was no evidence which shows that plaintiff or her agent knowingly made false statements as to the existence of the termites but he maintains that an innocent misrepresentation of a material fact is grounds for rescission of a contract where, as here, a party relies to his detriment on the misrepresentation.

We affirm the denial of the motion for a directed verdict.

The plaintiff, when she made her motion for a directed verdict, stated that her motion was restricted to the issue of "fraud." The word "fraud" is a generic term which embraces a great variety of actionable wrongs. It is a word of many meanings and defies any one all-inclusive definition. Fraud may become important either for the purpose of giving the defrauded person the right to sue for damages in an action for deceit or to enable him to rescind the contract. In this jurisdiction a party who has been induced by fraud to enter into a contract may pursue either one of two remedies. He may elect to rescind the contract to recover what he has paid under it, or he may affirm the contract and sue for damages in an action for deceit.

The distinction between a claim for damages for intentional deceit and a claim for rescission is well defined. Deceit is a tort action, and it requires some degree of culpability on the misrepresenter's part. An individual who sues in an action of deceit based on fraud has the burden of proving that the defendant in making the statements knew they were false and intended to deceive him. On the other hand, a suit to rescind an agreement induced by fraud sounds in contract. It is this latter aspect of fraud that we are concerned with in this case, and the pivotal issue before us is whether an innocent misrepresentation of a material fact warrants the granting of a claim for rescission. We believe that it does.

When he denied plaintiff's motion, the trial justice indicated that a false, though innocent, misrepresentation of a fact made as though of one's knowledge may be the basis for the rescission of a contract. While this issue is one of first impression in this state, it is clear that the trial judge's action finds support in the overwhelming weight of decisional and textual authority which has established the rule that where one induces another to enter into a contract by means of a material misrepresentation, the latter may rescind the contract. It does not matter if the representation was "innocent" or fraudulent.

In 12 Williston, *supra*, § 1500 at 400–01, Professor Jaeger states:

> It is not necessary, in order that a contract may be rescinded for fraud or misrepresentation, that the party making the misrepresentation should have known that it was false. Innocent misrepresentation is sufficient, for though the representation may have been made innocently, it would be unjust and inequitable to permit a person who has made false representations, even

innocently, to retain the fruits of a bargain induced by such representations.

This statement of law is in accord with Restatement of Contracts, § 476 at 908 which states: "Where a party is induced to enter into a transaction with another party that he was under no duty to enter into by means of the latter's fraud or material misrepresentation, the transaction is voidable as against the latter. * * *" Misrepresentation is defined as "* * * any manifestation by words or other conduct by one person to another that, under the circumstances, amounts to an assertion not in accordance with the facts." Restatement of Contracts, § 470

The comment following this section explains that a misrepresentation may be innocent, negligent or known to be false. A misrepresentation becomes material when it becomes likely to affect the conduct of a reasonable man with reference to a transaction with another person. Restatement of Contracts, § 470 (2) at 891. * * *

A misrepresentation, even though innocently made, may be actionable, if made and relied on as a positive statement of fact. The question to be resolved in determining whether a wrong committed as the result of an innocent misrepresentation may be rectified is succinctly stated in 12 Williston, *supra*, § 1510 at 462 as follows:

> "When a defendant has induced another to act by representations false in fact although not dishonestly made, and damage has directly resulted from the action taken, who should bear the loss?"

The question we submit is rhetorical. The answer is obvious. Simple justice demands that the speaker be held responsible. Accordingly, we hold that here defendant vendee could maintain his counterclaim.

* * *

Before leaving this phase of plaintiff's appeal, we think it appropriate that we allude to the tendency of many courts to equate an innocent misrepresentation with some species of fraud. Usually the word "fraud" connotes a conscious dishonest conduct on the part of the misrepresenter. Fraud, however, is not present if the speaker actually believes that what he states as the truth is the truth. We believe that it would be better if an innocent misrepresentation was not described as some specie of fraud. Unqualified statements imply certainty. Reliance is more likely to be placed on a positive statement of fact than a mere expression of opinion or a qualified statement. The speaker who uses the unqualified statement does so at his peril. The risk of falsity is his. If he is to be liable for what he states, the liability is imposed because he is to be held strictly accountable for his words. Responsibility for an innocent misrepresentation should be recognized for what it is—an example of absolute liability rather than as many courts have said, an example of constructive fraud.

* * *

The appeal of the plaintiff is denied and dismissed, and the case is remanded to the Superior Court for entry of judgment thereon.

Motion for reargument denied.

QUESTIONS AND NOTE

1. Questions about the facts of this case

   1.1. Who is suing whom for what?

   1.2. Which of the various statements by the plaintiff seller or the plaintiff seller's agent was most favorable to the defendant buyer's position?

   1.3. Did the seller or the seller's agent know that there were termites in the house? Was that important to the court? Should it be important?

2. Questions about the law

   2.1. Would the case have been decided differently if the court had applied *Restatement (Second) of Contracts* § 164(1), which provides:

   > If a party's manifestation of assent is induced by either a fraudulent or a material misrepresentation by the other party upon which the recipient is justified in relying, the contract is voidable by the recipient.

   2.2. Would the case have been decided differently if the seller and the seller's agent had simply and truthfully said "we have not seen any termites" or "I do not believe that there are any termites in the house"?

   2.3. This case uses the terms "deceit," "fraud," and "misrepresentation." How do these terms differ? Which is involved in this case?

   2.4. In negotiating to buy Epstein's 1973 Cadillac, Ponoroff tells Epstein that "$400 is my best offer—it is as much as I am willing to pay for the car." Being an extremely trusting sort of person, Epstein believes Ponoroff and agrees to sell him the car for $400. Shortly thereafter, Epstein learns from Markell that Ponoroff had said that he was willing to pay as much as $1,600 for the car. Can Epstein argue a fraud, deceit, or misrepresentation defense to the enforcement of his agreement to sell the car to Ponoroff based on Ponoroff's statement to him?

3. Note

   The facts in *Halpert* (and the facts in the various examples in *Restatement (Second) of Contracts* § 164) involve a statement or representation that is not a part of the contract language. It is of course possible to include representations in the contract language. For example, in a typical business acquisition agreement, the seller will make representations about the conditions of the business and the agreement will provide that the buyer can walk away from the deal if any of the "representations" are instead "misrepresentations."

4. **You Be the Lawyer!**

   If you had been the plaintiff's attorney, would you have filed a motion for a new trial?

Halpert shows the legal consequences of a misstatement that was arguably innocent. In the next two cases, we consider the legal consequences of a "non-statement" that was arguably not so innocent.

QUESTIONS BEFORE THE CASE

1. Did the plantiff buyer ask about termites?
2. Did the defendant seller do anything to make it more difficult for the plaintiff buyer to learn about whether the house had termites?

SWINTON V. WHITINSVILLE SAVINGS BANK

Supreme Judicial Court of Massachusetts
311 Mass. 677, 42 N.E.2d 808 (1942)

[Plaintiff-appellant Swinton sued defendant-appellee Whitinsville Savings Bank to recover damages for defendant's alleged fraudulent concealment in the sale of a house to plaintiff. Plaintiff appeals an order by the court below which sustained the defendant's demurrer to plaintiff's declaration.]

QUA, J.

The declaration alleges that on or about September 12, 1938, the defendant sold the plaintiff a house in Newton to be occupied by the plaintiff and his family as a dwelling; that at the time of the sale the house "was infested with termites, an insect that is most dangerous and destructive to buildings"; that the defendant knew the house was so infested; that the plaintiff could not readily observe this condition upon inspection; that, "knowing the internal destruction that these insects were creating in said house," the defendant falsely and fraudulently concealed from the plaintiff its true condition; that the plaintiff at the time of his purchase had no knowledge of the termites, exercised due care thereafter, and learned of them about August 30, 1940; and that, because of the destruction that was being done and the dangerous condition that was being created by the termites, the plaintiff was put to great expense for repairs and for the installation of termite control in order to prevent the loss and destruction of said house.

There is no allegation of any false statement or representation, or of the uttering of a half truth which may be tantamount to a falsehood. There is no intimation that the defendant by any means prevented the plaintiff from acquiring information as to the condition of the house. There is nothing to show any fiduciary relation between the parties, or that the plaintiff stood in a position of confidence toward or dependence upon the defendant. So far as appears the parties made a business deal at arm's length. The charge is concealment and nothing more; and it is concealment in the simple sense of mere failure to reveal, with nothing to show any peculiar duty to speak. The characterization of the concealment as false and fraudulent of course adds nothing in the absence of further allegations of fact.

If this defendant is liable on this declaration every seller is liable who fails to disclose any nonapparent defect known to him in the subject of the sale which materially reduces its value and which the buyer fails to discover. Similarly it would seem that every buyer would be liable who fails to disclose any nonapparent virtue known to him in the subject of the purchase which materially enhances its value and of which the seller is ignorant. The law has not yet, we believe, reached the point of imposing upon the frailties of human nature a standard so idealistic as this. That the particular case here stated by the plaintiff possesses a certain appeal to the moral sense is scarcely to be denied. Probably the reason is to be found in the facts that the infestation of buildings by termites has not been common in Massachusetts and constitutes a concealed risk against which buyers are off their guard. But the law cannot provide special rules for termites and can hardly attempt to determine liability according to the varying probabilities of the existence and discovery of different possible defects in the subjects of trade. * * *

The order sustaining the demurrer is affirmed, and judgment is to be entered for the defendant.

So ordered.

QUESTIONS AND NOTE

1. Questions about the facts of this case

   1.1. Did the defendant know that the house was infested with termites?

   1.2. Did the defendant make any representation to the plaintiff about termites?

2. Questions about the law

   2.1. The court points out that "there is nothing to show any fiduciary relationship between the parties." What is the point of that statement?

   2.2. Later the court states, "The charge is concealment and nothing more; and it is concealment in the simple sense of mere failure to reveal." Is nondisclosure, i.e., mere failure to reveal, the same thing as concealment?

3. Note

   Most states now have statutes governing home sale contracts that require that the seller disclose known defects and problems including any history of insect infestation.

4. **You Be the Lawyer!**

   As attorney for the plaintiff, what is your strongest argument? Is that argument strong enough to recommend an appeal after the trial court sustained the defendant's demurrer?

The next case involves another home sale contract. This time the home is in New Jersey, not Massachusetts. And, the New Jersey Supreme Court seems to suggest that in New Jersey the "sense of justice or fair dealing" is greater than that in Massachusetts.

QUESTIONS BEFORE THE CASE

1. The buyer's attorney alleged that "every time that they inspected this house prior to this time every light in the place was illuminated," Was that allegation important to the trial court?
2. Was that allegation important to the Supreme Court of New Jersey?

WEINTRAUB V. KROBATSCH

Supreme Court of New Jersey
64 N.J. 445, 317 A.2d 68 (1974)

JACOBS, J.

* * *

Mrs. Weintraub owned and occupied a six-year-old English-town home which she placed in the hands of a real estate broker (The Serafin Agency, Inc.) for sale. The Krobatsches were interested in purchasing the home, examined it while it was illuminated and found it suitable. On June 30, 1971 Mrs. Weintraub, as seller, and the Krobatsches, as purchasers, entered into a contract for the sale of the property for $42,500. The contract provided that the purchasers had inspected the property and were fully satisfied with its physical condition, that no representations had been made and that no responsibility was assumed by the seller as to the present or future condition of the premises. A deposit of $4,250 was sent by the purchasers to the broker to be held in escrow pending the closing of the transaction. The purchasers requested that the seller have the house fumigated and that was done. A fire after the signing of the contract caused damage but the purchasers indicated readiness that there be adjustment at closing.

During the evening of August 25, 1971, prior to closing, the purchasers entered the house, then unoccupied, and as they turned the lights on they were, as described in their petition for certification, "astonished to see roaches literally running in all directions, up the walls, drapes, etc." On the following day their attorney wrote a letter to Mrs. Weintraub, care of her New York law firm, advising that on the previous day "it was discovered that the house is infested with vermin despite the fact that an exterminator has only recently serviced the house" and asserting that "the presence of vermin in such great quantities, particularly after the exterminator was done, rendered the house as unfit for human habitation at this time and therefore, the contract is rescinded." On September 2, 1971 an exterminator wrote to Mr. Krobatsch advising that he had examined the premises and that "cockroaches were found to have infested the entire house." He said he could eliminate them for a relatively modest charge by two treatments with a twenty-one day interval but that it would be necessary to remove the carpeting "to properly treat all the infested areas."

Mrs. Weintraub rejected the rescission by the purchasers and filed an action in the Law Division joining them and the broker as defendants. Though she originally sought specific performance she later confined her claim to damages in the sum of $4,250, representing the deposit held in escrow by the broker. * * * There were opposing motions for summary judgment by the purchasers and Mrs. Weintraub. * * * At the argument on the motions it was evident that the purchasers were claiming fraudulent concealment or nondisclosure by the seller as the basis for their rescission. Thus at one point their attorney said: "Your honor, I would point out, and it is in my clients' affidavit, every time that they inspected this house prior to this time every light in the place was illuminated. Now, these insects are nocturnal by nature and that is not a point I think I have to prove through someone. I think Webster's dictionary is sufficient. By keeping the lights on it keeps them out of sight*. These sellers had to know they had this problem. You could not live in a house this infested without knowing about it."

The Law Division denied the motion by the purchasers for summary judgment but granted Mrs. Weintraub's motion and directed that the purchasers pay her the sum of $4,250. * * * On appeal, the Appellate Division sustained the summary judgment in Mrs. Weintraub's favor. * * *

Before us the purchasers contend that they were entitled to a trial on the issue of whether there was fraudulent concealment or nondisclosure entitling them to rescind; if there was then clearly they were under no liability to either the seller or the broker and would be entitled to the return of their deposit held by the broker in escrow.

Mrs. Weintraub asserts that she was unaware of the infestation and the Krobatsches acknowledge that, if that was so, then there was no fraudulent concealment or nondisclosure on her part and their claim must fall. But the purchasers allege that she was in fact aware of the infestation and at this stage of the proceedings we must assume that to be true. She contends, however, that even if she were fully aware she would have been under no duty to speak and that consequently no complaint by the purchasers may legally be grounded on her silence. She relies primarily on cases such as *Swinton v. Whitinsville Sav. Bank*, 311 Mass. 677, 42 N.E. 2d 808, 141 A.L.R. 965 (1942). * * * *Swinton* is pertinent but, as Dean Prosser has noted, it is one of a line of "singularly unappetizing cases" which are surely out of tune with our times.

In *Swinton* the plaintiff purchased a house from the defendant and after he occupied it he found it to be infested with termites. The defendant had made no verbal or written representations but the plaintiff, asserting that the defendant knew of the termites and was under a duty to speak, filed a complaint for damages grounded on fraudulent concealment. The Supreme Judicial Court of Massachusetts sustained a demurrer to the complaint and entered judgment for the defendant. In the course of its opinion the court acknowledged that "the plaintiff possesses a certain appeal to the moral sense" but concluded that the law has not "reached the point of imposing upon the frailties of human nature a standard so idealistic as this." 42 N.E. 2d at 808–809. That was written several decades ago and we are far from certain that it represents views held by the current

---

* [Cf. https://www.youtube.com/watch?v=z4qUEoVfBKQ.]

members of the Massachusetts court. In any event we are certain that it does not represent our sense of justice or fair dealing and it has understandably been rejected in persuasive opinions elsewhere. *See Obde v. Schlemeyer,* 56 Wash. 2d 449, 353 P. 2d 672 (1960).

In *Obde v. Schlemeyer,* 353 P. 2d 672, the defendants sold an apartment house to the plaintiffs. The house was termite infested but that fact was not disclosed by the sellers to the purchasers who later sued for damages alleging fraudulent concealment. The sellers contended that they were under no obligation whatever to speak out and they relied heavily on the decision of the Massachusetts court in *Swinton* (311 Mass. 677, 42 N.E. 2d 808, 141 A.L.R. 965). The Supreme Court of Washington flatly rejected their contention, holding that though the parties had dealt at arms length the sellers were under "a duty to inform the plaintiffs of the termite condition" of which they were fully aware. In the course of its opinion the court quoted approvingly from Dean Keeton's article in 15 Tex. L. Rev. 1. There the author first expressed his thought that when Lord Cairns suggested in *Peek v. Gurney*, L.R. 6 H.L. 377 (1873), that there was no duty to disclose facts, no matter how "morally censurable" (at 403), he was expressing nineteenth century law as shaped by an individualistic philosophy based on freedom of contracts and unconcerned with morals. He then made the following comments which fairly embody a currently acceptable principle on which the holding in *Obde* may be said to be grounded:

> In the present stage of the law, the decisions show a drawing away from this idea, and there can be seen an attempt by many courts to reach a just result in so far as possible, but yet maintaining the degree of certainty which the law must have. The statement may often be found that if either party to a contract of sale conceals or suppresses a material fact which he is in good faith bound to disclose then his silence is fraudulent.
>
> The attitude of the courts toward nondisclosure is undergoing a change and contrary to Lord Cairns' famous remark it would seem that the object of the law in these cases should be to impose on parties to the transaction a duty to speak whenever justice, equity, and fair dealing demand it. This statement is made only with reference to instances where the party to be charged is an actor in the transaction. This duty to speak does not result from an implied representation by silence, but exists because a refusal to speak constitutes unfair conduct.

15 Tex. L. Rev. at 31.

* * *

The purchasers here were entitled to withstand the seller's motion for summary judgment. They should have been permitted to proceed with their efforts to establish by testimony that they were equitably entitled to rescind because the house was extensively infested in the manner described by them, the seller was well aware of the infestation, and the seller deliberately concealed or failed to disclose the condition because of the likelihood that it would defeat the transaction. The seller may of course defend factually as well as legally and since the matter is primarily equitable in nature the factual as well as legal disputes will be for the trial judge alone.

If the trial judge finds such deliberate concealment or nondisclosure of the latent infestation not observable by the purchasers on their inspection, he will still be called upon to determine whether, in the light of the full presentation before him, the concealment or nondisclosure was of such significant nature as to justify rescission. Minor conditions which ordinary sellers and purchasers would reasonably disregard as of little or no materiality in the transaction would clearly not call for judicial intervention. While the described condition may not have been quite as major as in the termite cases which were concerned with structural impairments, to the purchasers here it apparently was of such magnitude and was so repulsive as to cause them to rescind immediately though they had earlier indicated readiness that there be adjustment at closing for damage resulting from a fire which occurred after the contract was signed. We are not prepared at his time to say that on their showing they acted either unreasonably or without equitable justification.

Our courts have come a long way since the days when the judicial emphasis was on formal rules and ancient precedents rather than on modern concepts of justice and fair dealing. While admittedly our law has progressed more slowly in the real property field than in other fields, there have been notable stirrings even there. * * * [W]e are satisfied that current principles grounded on justice and fair dealing, embraced throughout this opinion, clearly call for a full trial below; to that end the judgment entered in the Appellate Division is:

Reversed and remanded.

QUESTIONS

1. Questions about the facts of this case

   1.1. Did the contract mention cockroaches?

   1.2. Did either the seller or the buyer mention cockroaches before the contract was signed?

   1.3. Did the defendant seller do anything to make it more difficult for the plaintiff buyer to learn whether the house had roaches?

2. Questions about the law

   2.1. What is the new New Jersey test for determining when an agreement will not be enforced because of a non-disclosure?

   2.2. The New Jersey court quotes a Washington court's quote from a law review article by Dean Keeton which (to quote yet again) advocates:

   > "The attitude of the courts toward non-disclosure is undergoing a change and contrary to Lord Cairns' famous remark it would seem that the object of the law in these cases should be to impose on parties to the transaction *a duty to speak whenever justice, equity, and fair dealing demand it*." (emphasis added).

   What does the italicized language mean? Is the Dean Keeton in this case just as "illusive" as the Dean Keaton in *The Usual Suspects*? To defend "Epstein's dean*," the *Restatement (Second) of Contracts* uses similar language:

   § 161 When Non-Disclosure Is Equivalent to an Assertion

   A person's non-disclosure of a fact known to him is equivalent to an assertion that the fact does not exist in the following cases only:

   > (b) where he knows that disclosure of the fact would correct a mistake of the other party as to a basic assumption on which that party is making the contract and if non-disclosure of the fact amounts to a failure to act in good faith and in accordance with reasonable standards of fair dealing.

   2.3. *Weintraub* involved a consumer transaction. Should nondisclosure be a basis for rescission of commercial transactions? B Corp. contracts to buy S Food Processing, Inc. After entering into the contract but before closing on the contract, B Corp. learns that S Food Processing, Inc. had health department licensing problems that it failed to disclose. Should B Corp. be able to rescind the contract?

3. **You Be the Lawyer!**

   As the attorney arguing before the New Jersey Supreme Court on behalf of the Krobatsches, how would you answer the question: Can *Swinton* be distinguished from this case?

---

* W. Page Keeton was one of the University of Texas Law School's "early deans" http://tarlton.law.utexas.edu/early-deans. He was dean way back when Epstein would walk miles through the snow to attend his Monday through Saturday classes (or so he remembers.)

3. CONTRACT LAW REASONS FOR *NOT* ENFORCING AGREEMENTS: DEFENDANT'S LACK OF CAPACITY

Some agreements are unenforceable against a person because of who he is. Assume for example that Bruce, a three-year-old child who is a big fan of Tinky-Winky, *http://en.wikipedia.org/wiki/Tinky_Winky#Characters,* signs a "contract" to purchase a purple Porsche for $100,000.* Should the agreement be legally enforceable?

What if Bruce, the buyer of the $100,000 purple Porsche, is a fifty-three-year-old** law professor who is a big fan of the Northwestern Wildcats? Should that agreement to pay $100,000 for a purple Porsche be legally enforceable against Bruce?

In the "Bruce hypotheticals," was there a "meeting of the minds"? Did the Bruces have the capacity to contract?

Common law and then statutes have long recognized categories of individuals who do not have the capacity to contract. At one time, the law of capacity to contract considered a person's sex, color, and even occupation. The present law of capacity in most states resembles

Restatement (Second) of Contracts § 12 Capacity to Contract

(1) No one can be bound by contract who has not legal capacity to incur at least voidable contractual duties. . . .

(2) A natural person who manifests assent to a transaction has full legal capacity to incur contractual duties thereby unless he is

(a) under guardianship, or

(b) an infant, or

(c) mentally ill or defective, or

(d) intoxicated.

Historically, an "infant" or minor was anyone under the age of 21. Today, in most states, the "age of majority" is 18.

PROBLEMS

1. While David was intoxicated, David contracted with Larry to paint David's house for $1,000, a very low price considering the size of David's

---

* Cf Thumbs Up, Irish Times, October 2, 2006, 2006 WLNR 17011112 ("A three-year-old English boy bought a pink convertible car for £9,000 (€13,292) on eBay last week but before he had time to drive it (or at least play in it), his mean mammy cancelled the sale. Jack Neal apparently logged on to his mother's PC and used the "buy it now" option on eBay to complete the purchase. "Jack's a whiz on the PC and just pressed all the right buttons," Rachel Neal said. The seller of the second-hand car, a dealer from Worcestershire, England, agreed not to force the sale through.")

** Unchanged from an earlier edition.

house. At the time of the contract, Larry was not intoxicated and not knowledgeable about paint costs. Now knowledgeable about paint costs, Larry refuses to perform. Can David recover from Larry for breach of contract?

2. Your firm represents Jive Records, Inc. which wants to sign Gooberhead, an 11-year-old bluegrass rapper, to a recording contract. What do you advise?

4. CONTRACT LAW REASONS FOR *NOT* ENFORCING AGREEMENTS: DURESS AND UNDUE INFLUENCE

A. DURESS

In the previous section on capacity, the defense to enforceability of an agreement was based on who happened to make the agreement. In these materials on duress and undue influence, like the materials on misrepresentation and nondisclosure, the defense to enforceability of an agreement is based primarily on how the agreement happened.

Obviously, if Epstein agrees to write a book with Markell and Ponoroff only because they have guns pointed at his head, that agreement should not be legally enforceable. Physical duress.

Duress by physical compulsion is too easy. The facts are easy; the law is easy. Duress by physical compulsion is not going to be on your Contracts exam this year; it is not going to be on your bar exam in three years.

The contract law defense of duress has been extended to economic duress. Economic duress is harder than duress by physical compulsion. The facts are harder, the law is harder.

Many if not most contracts involve some element of economic pressure. Epstein agrees to do bar review lectures for BARBRI for minimum wage because he needs the money for drugs (the drugs that an old person needs).

And, economic pressure is not limited to employment contracts or other contracts involving individuals. "Walmart has a long and contentious history with its suppliers—using its thousands of brick-and-mortar stores and millions of shoppers as leverage to pressure them to cut prices."*

When should such economic pressure constitute economic duress, i.e., when should agreements not be legally enforceable because of economic pressure? Here is the *Restatement (Second) of Contracts* answer.

---

* 2017 WLNR 18900272.

§ 175 When Duress by Threat Makes a Contract Voidable

(1) If a party's manifestation of assent is induced by an improper threat by the other party that leaves the victim no reasonable alternative, the contract is voidable by the victim. * * *

§ 176 When a Threat Is Improper

(1) A threat is improper if

(d) the threat is a breach of the duty of good faith and fair dealing under a contract with the recipient.

(2) A threat is improper if the resulting exchange is not on fair terms, and

(a) the threatened act would harm the recipient and would not significantly benefit the party making the threat,

Professor Meredith Miller begins her law review article about the next case with the statement: "*Austin Instrument, Inc. v. Loral Corp.* is a favorite among Contracts casebooks because the New York Court of Appeals held that it was a "classic" example of economic duress."* Before reading Professor Miller's article or the next case, consider

---

QUESTIONS BEFORE THE CASE

1. What is the "improper threat" by Austin Instrument?
2. Why did Austin's "improper threat" leave Loral with "no reasonable alternative"?

AUSTIN INSTRUMENT, INC. V. LORAL CORPORATION

Court of Appeals of New York
29 N.Y.2d 124, 324 N.Y.S.2d 22, 272 N.E.2d 533 (1971)

FULD, C.J.

The defendant, Loral Corporation, seeks to recover payment for goods delivered under a contract which it had with plaintiff Austin Instrument, Inc., on the ground that the evidence establishes, as a matter of law, that it was forced to agree to an increase in price on the items in question under circumstances amounting to economic duress.

In July of 1965, Loral was awarded a $6,000,000 contract by the Navy for the production of radar sets. The contract contained a schedule of

---

* Meredith R. Miller, *Revisiting Austin v Loral: A Study in Economic Modification and Framing*, 2 HASTINGS BUS. L.J. 357 (2006).

deliveries, a liquidated damages clause applying to late deliveries and a cancellation clause in case of default by Loral. The latter thereupon solicited bids for some 40 precision gear components needed to produce the radar sets, and awarded Austin a subcontract to supply 23 such parts. That party commenced delivery in early 1966.

In May, 1966, Loral was awarded a second Navy contract for the production of more radar sets and again went about soliciting bids. Austin bid on all 40 gear components but, on July 15, a representative from Loral informed Austin's president, Mr. Krauss, that his company would be awarded the subcontract only for those items on which it was low bidder. The Austin officer refused to accept an order for less than all 40 of the gear parts and on the next day he told Loral that Austin would cease deliveries of the parts due under the existing subcontract unless Loral consented to substantial increases in the prices provided for by that agreement—both retroactively for parts already delivered and prospectively on those not yet shipped—and placed with Austin the order for all 40 parts needed under Loral's second Navy contract. Shortly thereafter, Austin did, indeed, stop delivery. After contacting 10 manufacturers of precision gears and finding none who could produce the parts in time to meet its commitments to the Navy, Loral acceded to Austin's demands; in a letter dated July 22, Loral wrote to Austin that:

> We have feverishly surveyed other sources of supply and find that because of the prevailing military exigencies, were they to start from scratch as would have to be the case, they could not even remotely begin to deliver on time to meet the delivery requirements established by the Government. * * * Accordingly, we are left with no choice or alternative but to meet your conditions.

Loral thereupon consented to the price increases insisted upon by Austin under the first subcontract and the latter was awarded a second subcontract making it the supplier of all 40 gear parts for Loral's second contract with the Navy. Although Austin was granted until September to resume deliveries, Loral did, in fact, receive parts in August and was able to produce the radar sets in time to meet its commitments to the Navy on both contracts. After Austin's last delivery under the second subcontract in July, 1967, Loral notified it of its intention to seek recovery of the price increases.

On September 15, 1967, Austin instituted this action against Loral to recover an amount in excess of $17,750 which was still due on the second subcontract. On the same day, Loral commenced an action against Austin claiming damages of some $22,250—the aggregate of the price increases under the first subcontract—on the ground of economic duress. The two actions were consolidated and, following a trial, Austin was awarded the sum it requested and Loral's complaint against Austin was dismissed on the ground that it was not shown that "it could not have obtained the items in question from other sources in time to meet its commitment to the Navy under the first contract." A closely divided Appellate Division affirmed. * * *

The applicable law is clear and, indeed, is not disputed by the parties. A contract is voidable on the ground of duress when it is established that the party making the claim was forced to agree to it by means of a wrongful threat precluding the exercise of his free will. The existence of economic duress or business compulsion is demonstrated by proof that "immediate possession of needful goods is threatened" or, more particularly, in cases such as the one before us, by proof that one party to a contract has threatened to breach the agreement by withholding goods unless the other party agrees to some further demand. However, a mere threat by one party to breach the contract by not delivering the required items, though wrongful, does not in itself constitute economic duress. It must also appear that the threatened party could not obtain the goods from another source of supply and that the ordinary remedy of an action for breach of contract would not be adequate.

We find without any support in the record the conclusion reached by the courts below that Loral failed to establish that it was the victim of economic duress. On the contrary, the evidence makes out a classic case, as a matter of law, of such duress.

It is manifest that Austin's threat—to stop deliveries unless the prices were increased—deprived Loral of its free will. As bearing on this, Loral's relationship with the Government is most significant. As mentioned above, its contract called for staggered monthly deliveries of the radar sets, with clauses calling for liquidated damages and possible cancellation on default. Because of its production schedule, Loral was, in July, 1966, concerned with meeting its delivery requirements in September, October and November, and it was for the sets to be delivered in those months that the withheld gears were needed. Loral had to plan ahead, and the substantial liquidated damages for which it would be liable, plus the threat of default, were genuine possibilities. Moreover, Loral did a substantial portion of its business with the Government, and it feared that a failure to deliver as agreed upon would jeopardize its chances for future contracts. * * * It was perfectly reasonable for Loral, or any other party similarly placed, to consider itself in an emergency, duress situation.

* * *

Loral, as indicated above, also had the burden of demonstrating that it could not obtain the parts elsewhere within a reasonable time, and there can be no doubt that it met this burden. The 10 manufacturers whom Loral contacted comprised its entire list of "approved vendors" for precision gears, and none was able to commence delivery soon enough. As Loral was producing a highly sophisticated item of military machinery requiring parts made to the strictest engineering standards, it would be unreasonable to hold that Loral should have gone to other vendors, with whom it was either unfamiliar or dissatisfied, to procure the needed parts. * * *

It is hardly necessary to add that Loral's normal legal remedy of accepting Austin's breach of the contract and then suing for damages would have been inadequate under the circumstances, as Loral would still have had to obtain the gears elsewhere with all the concomitant consequences mentioned above. In other words, Loral actually had no choice, when the prices were raised by Austin, except to take the gears at the "coerced" prices and then sue to get the excess back. * * *

In sum, the record before us demonstrates that Loral agreed to the price increases in consequence of the economic duress employed by Austin. Accordingly, the matter should be remanded to the trial court for a computation of its damages.

The order appealed from should be modified, with costs, by reversing so much thereof as affirms the dismissal of defendant Loral Corporation's claim and, except as so modified, affirmed.

* * *

QUESTIONS

1. Questions about the facts of this case

    1.1. Who is suing whom for what?

    1.2. Did Loral agree to Austin's demand for price increases?

    1.3. Do you think that Loral's July 22d letter was written, or at least reviewed, by a lawyer? By a lawyer familiar with the concept of excuse by reason of economic duress?

    1.4. Why did Austin ask for price increases? According to the statement of facts in the Appellate Division opinion:

    > Austin claimed that it was losing a substantial sum on the existing job; that it could not afford to do this; and that the prices being paid to it were only a fraction of what it was entitled to. Parenthetically, we note that it is well known that in this time of continual rising of material and manufacturing costs, renegotiation of contract prices does sometimes occur in business and commercial dealings.

316 N.Y.S. 2d 530. Is that relevant? Was it relevant to the New York Court of Appeals?

2. Question about the law

   2.1. Is this case consistent with the *Restatement (Second) of Contracts*?

   2.2. Is the contract in this case a sale of goods? If so, why didn't the court discuss the Uniform Commercial Code? More specifically, why didn't the court discuss Official Comment 2 to section 2–209 ("modifications made thereunder must meet the test of good faith imposed by this Act. . . . [T]he extortion of a 'modification' without legitimate commercial reasons is ineffective as a violation of the duty of good faith.")?

3. **You Be the Lawyer!**

   As attorney for Austin, what would you have recommended Austin do after receiving Loral's letter dated July 22?

Recently, two experienced trial lawyers labeled economic duress a "poor excuse for nonperformance":

> "To avoid the breach of contract and the consequences of such breach, the breaching party sometimes tries to justify its nonperformance by invoking economic duress as a defense to the claim of breach of contract. While economic duress can be pled in an effort to avoid the requirements of any contract, it is most often invoked in efforts to avoid the effects of arbitration agreements, loan and loan modification agreements, releases and employment agreements. Over the course of the defense's existence in Alabama, economic duress has been frequently invoked but only rarely found to be available as an excuse for non-performance."*

B. UNDUE INFLUENCE

According to the note in the *Restatement (Second) of Contracts,* introducing the sections on duress and undue influence: "Undue influence involves unfair persuasion, a milder form of pressure than duress." The next case considers "undue influence."

---

* George M. Walker & Robert S. Walker, *Economic Duress: A Poor Excuse for Non-Performance*, 74 ALA. LAW. 386 (2013). Courts' denying relief for economic duress is not just an Alabama "thingee." In published state cases from 1996 through 2003, contractual duress was discussed in eighty-eight opinions but the court decided in favor of duress in only nine of those cases. See Grace M. Giesel, *A Realistic Proposal for the Contract Duress Doctrine*, 107 W. VA. L. REV. 443, 463 (2005).

QUESTIONS BEFORE THE CASE

1. There are two Odorizzi/Bloomfield School District contracts: (i) an employment contract for the 1964–65 school year, and (ii) the June resignation. Which is involved in this litigation?
2. Was it important to the California appellate court that the two people who came to Odorizzi's apartment to talk about his resigning were his superintendent and his principal?

ODORIZZI V. BLOOMFIELD SCHOOL DISTRICT

Court of Appeal of California, Second Appellate District
246 Cal.App.2d 123, 54 Cal.Rptr. 533 (1966)

FLEMING, J.

Appeal from a judgment dismissing plaintiff's amended complaint on demurrer.

Plaintiff Donald Odorizzi was employed during 1964 as an elementary school teacher by defendant Bloomfield School District and was under contract with the district to continue to teach school the following year as a permanent employee. On June 10 he was arrested on criminal charges of homosexual activity, and on June 11 he signed and delivered to his superiors his written resignation as a teacher, a resignation which the district accepted on June 13. In July the criminal charges against Odorizzi were dismissed under Penal Code, section 995, and in September he sought to resume his employment with the district. On the district's refusal to reinstate him he filed suit for declaratory and other relief. Odorizzi's amended complaint asserts his resignation was invalid because obtained through duress, fraud, mistake, and undue influence and given at a time when he lacked capacity to make a valid contract. Specifically, Odorizzi declares he was under such severe mental and emotional strain at the time he signed his resignation, having just completed the process of arrest, questioning by the police, booking, and release on bail, and having gone for 40 hours without sleep, that he was incapable of rational thought or action. While he was in this condition and unable to think clearly, the superintendent of the district and the principal of his school came to his apartment. They said they were trying to help him and had his best interests at heart, that he should take their advice and immediately resign his position with the district, that there was no time to consult an attorney, that if he did not resign immediately the district would suspend and dismiss him from his position and publicize the proceedings, his "aforedescribed arrest" and cause him "to suffer extreme embarrassment and humiliation"; but that if he resigned at once the incident would not be publicized and would not jeopardize his chances of securing employment as a teacher elsewhere. Odorizzi pleads that because of his faith and confidence in their representations they were able to substitute their will and judgment in place of his own and thus obtain his signature to his purported resignation. A demurrer to his amended complaint was sustained without leave to amend.

By his complaint plaintiff in effect seeks to rescind his resignation pursuant to Civil Code, section 1689,* on the ground that his consent had not been real or free * * *, but had been obtained through duress, menace, fraud, undue influence, or mistake. * * * In our view the facts in the amended complaint are insufficient to state a cause of action for duress, menace, fraud, or mistake, but they do set out sufficient elements to justify rescission of a consent because of undue influence. We summarize our conclusions on each of these points.

1. No duress or menace has been pleaded. Duress consists in unlawful confinement of another's person, or relatives, or property, which causes him to consent to a transaction through fear. Duress is often used interchangeably with menace, but in California menace is technically a threat of duress or a threat of injury to the person, property, or character of another. We agree with respondent's contention that neither duress nor menace was involved in this case, because the action or threat in duress or menace must be unlawful, and a threat to take legal action is not unlawful unless the party making the threat knows the falsity of his claim. The amended complaint shows in substance that the school representative announced their intention to initiate suspension and dismissal proceedings under Education Code, section 13403,** 13408, * * * et seq. at a time when the filing of such proceedings was not only their legal right but their positive duty as school officials. (Ed.Code, § 13409***). * * *

* § 1689. "(b) A party to a contract may rescind the contract in the following cases: (1) If the consent of the party rescinding, or of any party jointly contracting with him, was given by mistake, or obtained through duress, menace, fraud, or undue influence, exercised by or with the connivance of the party as to whom he rescinds, or of any other party to the contract jointly interested with such party." Eds.

** § 134.03. "Grounds for dismissal of permanent employee. No permanent employee shall be dismissed except for one or more of the following causes: (a) Immoral or unprofessional conduct. * * * (k) Knowing membership by the employee in the Communist Party." Eds.

*** § 13409. "Compulsory leave of absence on charge of sex offenses and narcotics offenses; effect on salary of acquittal. Whenever any certificated employee of a school district is charged with the commission of any sex offense as defined in Section 12912 by complaint, information or indictment filed in a court of competent jurisdiction, the governing board of the school district shall immediately place the employee upon compulsory leave of absence for a period of time extending for not more than 10 days after the date of the entry of the judgement in the proceedings. The governing board of the school district may extend the compulsory leave of absence of the employee beyond such period by giving notice to the employee within 10 days after the entry of judgment in the proceedings that the employee will be dismissed at the expiration of 30 days from the date of service of the notice, unless the employee demands a hearing as provided in Sections 13313, 13327 and 13338, and Sections 13403 to 13441, inclusive." Eds.

2. Nor do we find a cause of action for fraud, either actual or constructive.

* * *

3. As to mistake, the amended complaint fails to disclose any facts which would suggest that consent had been obtained through a mistake of fact or of law. * * *

4. However, the pleading does set out a claim that plaintiff's consent to the transaction had been obtained through the use of undue influence.

Undue influence, in the sense we are concerned with here, is a shorthand legal phrase used to describe persuasion which tends to be coercive in nature, persuasion which overcomes the will without convincing the judgment. The hallmark of such persuasion is high pressure, a pressure which works on mental, moral, or emotional weakness to such an extent that it approaches the boundaries of coercion. In this sense, undue influence has been called overpersuasion. Misrepresentations of law or fact are not essential to the charge, for a person's will may be overborne without misrepresentation. By statutory definition undue influence includes "taking an unfair advantage of another's weakness of mind, or * * * taking a grossly oppressive and unfair advantage of another's necessities or distress." While most reported cases of undue influence involve persons who bear a confidential relationship to one another, a confidential or authoritative relationship between the parties need not be present when the undue influence involves unfair advantage taken of another's weakness or distress.

We paraphrase the summary of undue influence given the jury by Sir James P. Wilde in *Hall v. Hall*, L.R. 1, P. & D. 481, 482 (1868): To make a good contract a man must be a free agent. Pressure of whatever sort which overpowers the will without convincing the judgment is a species of restraint under which no valid contract can be made. Importunity or threats, if carried to the degree in which the free play of a man's will is overborne, constitute undue influence, although no force is used or threatened. A party may be led but not driven, and his acts must be the offspring of his own volition and not the record of someone else's.

In essence undue influence involves the use of excessive pressure to persuade one vulnerable to such pressure, pressure applied by a dominant subject to a servient object. In combination, the elements of undue susceptibility in the servient person and excessive pressure by the dominating person make the latter's influence undue, for it results in the apparent will of the servient person being in fact the will of the dominant person.

Undue susceptibility may consist of total weakness of mind which leaves a person entirely without understanding; or, a lesser weakness which destroys the capacity of a person to make a contract even though he is not totally incapacitated; or, the first element in our equation, a still lesser weakness which provides sufficient grounds to rescind a contract for undue influence. Such lesser weakness need not be longlasting nor wholly incapacitating, but may be merely a lack of full vigor due to age, physical condition, emotional anguish, or a combination of such factors. The reported cases have usually involved elderly, sick, senile persons alleged to have executed wills or deeds under pressure. In some of its aspects this lesser weakness could perhaps be called weakness of spirit. But whatever name we give it, this first element of undue influence resolves itself into a lessened capacity of the object to make a free contract.

In the present case plaintiff has pleaded that such weakness at the time he signed his resignation prevented him from freely and competently applying his judgment to the problem before him. Plaintiff declares he was under severe mental and emotional strain at the time because he had just completed the process of arrest, questioning, booking, and release on bail and had been without sleep for forty hours. It is possible that exhaustion and emotional turmoil may wholly incapacitate a person from exercising his judgment. As an abstract question of pleading, plaintiff has pleaded that possibility and sufficient allegations to state a case for rescission.

Undue influence in its second aspect involves an application of excessive strength by a dominant subject against a servient object. Judicial consideration of this second element in undue influence has been relatively rare, for there are few cases denying persons who persuade but do not misrepresent the benefit of their bargain. Yet logically, the same legal consequences should apply to the results of excessive strength as to the results of undue weakness. Whether from weakness on one side, or strength on the other, or a combination of the two, undue influence occurs whenever there results "that kind of influence or supremacy of one mind over another by which that other is prevented from acting according to his own wish or judgment, and whereby the will of the person is overborne and he is induced to do or forbear to do an act which he would not do, or would do, if left to act freely." *Webb v. Saunders*, 79 Cal. App. 2d 863, 871. Undue influence involves a type of mismatch which our statute calls unfair advantage. Whether a person of subnormal capacities has been subjected to ordinary force or a person of normal capacities subjected to extraordinary force, the match is equally out of balance. If will has been overcome against judgment, consent may be rescinded.

The difficulty, of course, lies in determining when the forces of persuasion have overflowed their normal banks and become oppressive flood waters. There are second thoughts to every bargain, and hindsight is still better than foresight. Undue influence cannot be used as a pretext to avoid bad bargains or escape from bargains which refuse to come up to expectations. A woman who buys a dress on impulse, which on critical inspection by her best friend turns out to be less fashionable than she had thought, is not legally entitled to set aside the sale on the ground that the saleswoman used all her wiles to close the sale. A man who buys a tract of desert land in the expectation that it is in the immediate path of the city's growth and will become another Palm Springs, an expectation cultivated in glowing terms by the seller, cannot rescind his bargain when things turn out differently. If we are temporarily persuaded against our better judgment to do something about which we later have second thoughts, we must abide the consequences of the risks inherent in managing our own affairs.

However, overpersuasion is generally accompanied by certain characteristics which tend to create a pattern. The pattern usually involves several of the following elements: (1) discussion of the transaction at an unusual or inappropriate time, (2) consummation of the transaction in an unusual place, (3) insistent demand that the business be finished at once, (4) extreme emphasis on untoward consequences of delay, (5) the use of multiple persuaders by the dominant side against a single servient party, (6) absence of third-party advisers to the servient party, (7) statements that there is no time to consult financial advisers or attorneys. If a number of these elements are simultaneously present, the persuasion may be characterized as excessive. * * *

The difference between legitimate persuasion and excessive pressure * * * rests to a considerable extent in the manner in which the parties go about their business. For example, if a day or two after Odorizzi's release on bail the superintendent of the school district had called him into his office during business hours and directed his attention to those provisions of the Education Code compelling his leave of absence and authorizing his suspension on the filing of written charges, had told him that the district contemplated filing written charges against him, had pointed out the alternative of resignation available to him, had informed him he was free to consult counsel or any adviser he wished and to consider the matter overnight and return with his decision the next day, it is extremely unlikely that any complaint about the use of excessive pressure could ever have been made against the school district.

But, according to the allegations of the complaint, this is not the way it happened, and if it had happened that way, plaintiff would never have resigned. Rather, the representatives of the school board undertook to achieve their objective by overpersuasion and imposition to secure plaintiff's signature but not his consent to his resignation through a high-pressure carrot-and-stick technique—under which they assured plaintiff they were trying to assist him, he should rely on their advice, there wasn't time to consult an attorney, if he didn't resign at once the school district would suspend and dismiss him from his position and publicize the proceedings, but if he did resign the incident wouldn't jeopardize his chances of securing a teaching post elsewhere.

Plaintiff has thus pleaded both subjective and objective elements entering the undue influence equation and stated sufficient facts to put in issue the question whether his free will had been overborne by defendant's agents at a time when he was unable to function in a normal manner. It was sufficient to pose "* * * the ultimate question * * * whether a free and competent judgment was merely influenced, or whether a mind was so dominated as to prevent the exercise of an independent judgment." (*Williston on Contracts*, § 1625 [rev. ed.]; Rest., Contracts, § 497, com. c.) The question cannot be resolved by an analysis of pleading but requires a finding of fact.

We express no opinion on the merits of plaintiff's case, or the propriety of his continuing to teach school, or the timeliness of his rescission. We do hold that his pleading, liberally construed, states a cause of action for rescission of a transaction to which his apparent consent had been obtained through the use of undue influence.

The judgment is reversed.

QUESTIONS AND NOTE

1. Questions about the facts of this case

   1.1. What is Odorizzi's "best fact", i.e., the fact that provides the strongest support for his undue influence claim?

   1.2. Do we know the grounds for dismissal in the employment contract? Is that relevant? Do we know the grounds for dismissal in the California Education Code? Is that relevant?

2. Questions about the law

   2.1. The appellate court holds "the facts in the amended complaint are insufficient to state a cause of action for duress * * * but they do set out sufficient elements to justify rescission of a consent because of undue influence." What alleged facts justify rescission because of undue influence? What additional facts are needed for duress?

   2.2. The *Odorizzi* case identifies two elements of undue influence. The two elements of undue influence are: (i) the susceptibility of the weaker party, and (ii) the overpersuasion of the stronger party. Which of these two elements is more important?

   2.3. The *Odorizzi* opinion then lists seven elements of the second element "overpersuasion." Which of the seven elements of overpersuasion were alleged by the plaintiff?

3. Note

   As Professor Jeffrey Harrison points out, "*Odorizzi* itself has rarely been cited outside of California."*

4. **You Be the Lawyer!**

   The court states "his pleading, liberally construed, states a cause of action for rescission." If, in 1964, you had been Odorizzi's attorney, what relief would you have requested?

---

5. CONTRACT LAW REASONS FOR *NOT* ENFORCING AGREEMENTS: ILLEGALITY AND PUBLIC POLICY

A. ILLEGALITY

It is easy to think of agreements that are illegal and understand why an agreement's illegal subject matter makes the agreement unenforceable by either party. For example, Markell hires Ray Donovan to kill Epstein. That agreement would be unenforceable by either Markell or Donovan. It is against the law to kill someone—even a contracts professor.

The law in question does not have to be a criminal law. We all know and understand that a court will not enforce an agreement to pay interest in excess of the rate set in the usury laws or an agreement to combine businesses that violates the antitrust laws.

A more common illegality problem is the enforceability of an agreement by someone who has failed to comply with a licensing statute. Consider the following illustrative problem.

PROBLEM

Assume that Michigan has statutes that provide (1) "No natural person shall engage in doing the work of a plumber unless he possesses a license or renewal thereof issued by the Michigan Plumbing Board" and (2) "Whoever violates the provisions of this Chapter shall be fined not less than five hundred dollars nor more than five thousand dollars, or imprisoned for not more than ninety days or both."

Ponoroff enters into an agreement with Epstein, who is not a licensed plumber, to pay Epstein $200 to install a urinal in his office. Epstein does the agreed work. Ponoroff refuses to pay. Should Epstein be able to enforce the

* Jeffrey Harrison, *Defects in Consent and Dividing the Benefit of the Bargain: Recent Developments*, 53 LOUISVILLE L. REV. 193 fn 212 (2015).

agreement even though Epstein acted in violation of the state licensing statute? (Board regulations describe the work of a plumber as including the installation of plumbing fixtures.) How would you answer the problem? How would the *Restatement (Second)* answer the problem?

> **§ 181 Effect of Failure to Comply with Licensing or Similar Requirement**
>
> If a party is prohibited from doing an act because of his failure to comply with a licensing, registration or similar requirement, a promise in consideration of his doing that act or of his promise to do it is unenforceable on grounds of public policy if:
>
> (a) the requirement has a regulatory purpose, and
>
> (b) the interest in the enforcement of the promise is clearly outweighed by the public policy *behind the requirement.*

(Emphasis added).

B. PUBLIC POLICY

The defense of public policy is not limited to agreements that directly or even indirectly violate a legislative enactment. *Restatement (Second) of Contracts* § 178 provides:

> A promise or other term of an agreement is unenforceable on grounds of public policy if legislation provides that it is unenforceable or the interest in its enforcement is clearly outweighed in the circumstances by a public policy against the enforcement of such terms.

Who decides whether there is a "public policy against the enforcement"? What are the relative roles of legislatures and courts?

The most complicated and controversial cases considering a public policy defense to enforceability of an agreement are cases affecting family relationships such as palimony agreements or surrogacy contracts. Attorneys, judges, and professors continue to discuss not only the legal issues, but also the gender, moral, political, and religious issues raised by these contracts. *R.R. v. M.H.*, the first case in the book is illustrative.

Arguments that a contract is unenforceable because of public policy also regularly arise in connection with "exculpatory contracts." We saw an exculpatory contract in the *Reed* case, supra at 276. You see exculpatory contracts every time you participate in The Burning Man Festival, every time you park your car in a parking garage. And, you will see an exculpatory contract in the next case.

QUESTIONS BEFORE THE CASE

1. Do you understand the excerpt from the "Waiver, Defense, Indemnity, and Hold Harmless Agreement, and Release of Liability" contract in the opinion?
2. What is the public policy that the "Waiver, Defense, Indemnity, and Hold Harmless Agreement, and Release of Liability" contract violates?

HANKS V. POWDER RIDGE RESTAURANT CORP.

Supreme Court of Connecticut
276 Conn. 314, 885 A.2d 734 (2005)

SULLIVAN, C.J.

This appeal arises out of a complaint filed by the plaintiff, Gregory D. Hanks, against the defendants, Powder Ridge Restaurant Corporation and White Water Mountain Resorts of Connecticut, Inc., doing business as Powder Ridge Ski Resort, seeking compensatory damages for injuries the plaintiff sustained while snowtubing at the defendants' facility. The trial court rendered summary judgment in favor of the defendants, ... We reverse the judgment of the trial court.

The record reveals the following factual and procedural history. The defendants operate a facility in Middlefield, known as Powder Ridge, at which the public, in exchange for a fee, is invited to ski, snowboard and snowtube. * * * [I]n order to snowtube at Powder Ridge, patrons were required to sign a "Waiver, Defense, Indemnity and Hold Harmless Agreement, and Release of Liability" (agreement). The plaintiff read and signed the agreement * * * While snowtubing, the plaintiff's right foot became caught between his snowtube and the man-made bank of the snowtubing run, resulting in serious injuries that required multiple surgeries to repair. Thereafter, the plaintiff filed the present negligence action against the defendants. * * * [T]he . . . defendants moved for summary judgment, claiming that the agreement barred the plaintiff's negligence claim as a matter of law. The trial court agreed and rendered summary judgment in favor of the defendants. Specifically, the trial court determined . . . that the plaintiff, by signing the agreement, unambiguously had released the defendants from liability for their allegedly negligent conduct. * * *

The agreement at issue in the present case provides in relevant part:

"I understand that there are inherent risks involved in snowtubing, including the risk of serious * physical injury or death and I fully assume all risks associated with [s]nowtubing, even if due to the NEGLIGENCE of [the defendants] * * * including but not limited to: variations in the snow conditions; steepness and terrain; the presence of ice, moguls, bare spots and objects beneath the snowtubing surface such as rocks, debris and tree stumps; collisions with objects both on and off the snowtubing chutes such as hay bales, trees, rocks, snowmaking equipment, barriers, lift cables and equipment, lift towers, lift attendants, employees, volunteers, other patrons and spectators or their property; equipment or lift condition or failure; lack of safety devices or inadequate safety devices; lack of warnings or inadequate warnings; lack of instructions or inadequate instructions; use of any lift; and the like. * * * I * * * agree I will defend, indemnify and hold harmless [the defendants] * * * from any and all claims, suits or demands by anyone arising from my use of the Powder Ridge snowtubing facilities and equipment including claims of NEGLIGENCE on the part of [the defendants]. * * * I * * * hereby release, and agree that I will not sue [the defendants] * * * for money damages for personal injury or property damage sustained by me while using the snowtubing facilities and equipment even if due to the NEGLIGENCE of [the defendants]. * * *" (Emphasis in original.)

We conclude that the agreement expressly and unambiguously purports to release the defendants from prospective liability for negligence. The agreement expressly provides that the snowtuber "fully assume[s] all risks associated with [s]nowtubing, even if due to the NEGLIGENCE" of the defendants. (Emphasis in original.) Moreover, the agreement refers to the negligence of the defendants three times and uses capital letters to emphasize the term "negligence." Accordingly, we conclude that an ordinary person of reasonable intelligence would understand that, by signing the agreement, he or she was releasing the defendants from liability for their future negligence. * * *

II

We next address the issue * * * whether the enforcement of a well drafted exculpatory agreement purporting to release a snowtube operator from prospective liability for personal injuries sustained as a result of the operator's negligent conduct violates public policy. We conclude that it does and, accordingly, reverse the judgment of the trial court.

Although it is well established "that parties are free to contract for whatever terms on which they may agree"; it is equally well established "that contracts that violate public policy are enforceable." * * * "[T]he question [of] whether a contract is against public policy is [a] question of law dependent on the circumstances of the particular case, over which an appellate court has unlimited review."

As previously noted, "[t]he law does not favor contract provisions which relieve a person from his own negligence. * * *" This is because exculpatory provisions undermine the policy considerations governing our tort system. Although this court previously has not addressed the enforceability of a release of liability for future negligence, the issue has been addressed by many of our sister states. * * *

Having reviewed the various methods for determining whether exculpatory agreements violate public policy, we conclude, * * * that "[n]o definition of the concept of public interest can be contained within the four corners of a formula." * * * The ultimate determination of what constitutes the public interest must be made considering the totality of the circumstances of any given case against the backdrop of current societal expectations." * * *

We now turn to the merits of the plaintiff's claim. The defendants are in the business of providing snowtubing services to the public generally, regardless of prior snowtubing experience, with the minimal restriction that only persons at least six years old or forty-four inches tall are eligible to participate. Given the virtually unrestricted access of the public to Powder Ridge, a reasonable person would presume that the defendants were offering a recreational activity that the whole family could enjoy safely. Indeed, this presumption is borne out by the plaintiff' own testimony. Specifically, the plaintiff testified that he "trusted that [the defendants] would, within their good conscience, operate a safe ride."

The societal expectation that family oriented recreational activities will be reasonably safe is even more important where, as in the present matter, patrons are under the care and control of the recreational operator as a result of an economic transaction. The plaintiff, in exchange for a fee, was permitted access to the defendants' snowtubing runs and was provided with snowtubing gear. As a result of this transaction, the plaintiff was under the care and control of the defendants and, thus, was subject to the risk of the defendants' carelessness. Specifically, the defendants designed and maintained the snowtubing run and, therefore, controlled the steepness of the incline, the condition of the snow and the method of slowing down or stopping patrons. Further, the defendants provided the plaintiff with the requisite snowtubing supplies and, therefore, controlled the size and quality of the snowtube as well as the provision of any necessary protective gear. Accordingly, the plaintiff voluntarily relinquished control to the defendants with the reasonable expectation of an exciting, but reasonably safe, snowtubing experience.

Moreover, the plaintiff lacked the knowledge, experience and authority to discern whether, much less ensure that, the defendants' snowtubing runs were maintained in a reasonably safe condition. As the Vermont Supreme Court observed, in the context of the sport of skiing, it is consistent with public policy "to place responsibility for maintenance of the land on those who own or control it, with the ultimate goal of keeping accidents to the minimum level. [T]he defendants, not recreational skiers, have the expertise and opportunity to foresee and control hazards, and to guard against the negligence of their agents and employees. They alone can properly maintain and inspect their premises, and train their employees in risk management. They alone can insure against risks and effectively spread the costs of insurance among their thousands of customers. Skiers, on the other hand, are not in a position to discover and correct risks of harm, and they cannot insure against the ski area's negligence.

Further, the agreement at issue was a standardized adhesion contract offered to the plaintiff on a "take it or leave it" basis. The "most salient feature [of adhesion contracts] is that they are not subject to the normal bargaining processes of ordinary contracts. * * * Not only was the plaintiff unable to negotiate the terms of the agreement, but the defendants also did not offer him the option of procuring protection against negligence at an additional reasonable cost. See *Restatement (Third), Torts, Apportionment of Liability § 2,* comment (e), p. 21 (2000) (factor relevant to enforcement of contractual limit on liability is "whether the party seeking exculpation was willing to provide greater protection against tortious conduct for a reasonable, additional fee"). Moreover, the defendants did not inform prospective snowtubers prior to their arrival at Powder Ridge that they would have to waive important common-law rights as a condition of participation. Thus, the plaintiff, who traveled to Powder Ridge in anticipation of snowtubing that day, was faced with the dilemma of either signing the defendants' proffered waiver of prospective liability or forgoing completely the opportunity to snowtube at Powder Ridge. Under the present factual circumstances, it would ignore reality to conclude that the plaintiff wielded the same bargaining power as the defendants. * * *

For the foregoing reasons, we conclude that the agreement in the present matter affects the public interest adversely and, therefore, is unenforceable because it violates public policy.[12] Accordingly, the trial court improperly rendered summary judgment in favor of the defendants.

The defendants and the dissent point out that our conclusion represents the "distinct minority view" and is inconsistent with the majority of sister state authority upholding exculpatory agreements in similar recreational settings. We acknowledge that most states uphold

[12] We clarify that our conclusion does not extend to the risks inherent in the activity of snowtubing. . . . As we have explained, inherent risks are those risks that are innate to the activity, "are beyond the control of the [recreational] area operator and cannot be minimized by the operator's exercise of reasonable care." For example, risks inherent in the sport of skiing include, but are not limited to, the risk of collision with another skier or a tree outside the confines of the slope. * * *

adhesion contracts releasing recreational operators from prospective liability for personal injuries caused by their own negligent conduct. Put simply, we disagree with these decisions for the reasons already explained in this opinion. * * * The judgment is reversed and the case is remanded for further proceedings according to law.

In this opinion KATZ, VERTEFEUILLE and ZARELLA, JS., concurred.

NORCOTT, J., with whom BORDEN and PALMER, JS., join, dissenting.

QUESTIONS

1. Questions about the facts of this case

   1.1. The court describes the agreement as a "well drafted exculpatory agreement." Do you think that the agreement was drafted by a lawyer? If so, do you think that the lawyer told the defendant that the exculpatory agreement might be "unenforceable because it violates public policy"?

   1.2. Do you think that the defendant had liability insurance? If so, why did the defendant also have a release agreement?

2. Questions about the law

   2.1. In *R.R. v. M.H.*, the court looked to adoption legislation to determine public policy on surrogacy parenting contracts. Did the court in *Hanks v. Powder Ridge Restaurant Corp.* look to legislation to determine public policy on exculpatory clauses?

   2.2. What is an exculpatory clause? Are all exculpatory clauses unenforceable against public policy?

3. **You Be the Lawyer!**

   Defendants retain you to revise their "Waiver, Defense, Indemnity and Hold Harmless Agreement, and Release of Liability" agreement. What changes do you recommend?

Covenants not to compete are fairly common in the business world. For example, a buyer of a tavern might want some assurances that their seller is not going to open a competing tavern in the same neighborhood. Or, an employer might want assurances that a key employee will not later work for a competitor.

And law suits challenging the enforceability of covenants not to compete on public policy grounds are fairly common in the "legal" world. The holding of a particular case depends in the main on facts relating to the business need for a protective agreement and the reasonableness of the protective agreement.

The opinions on public policy challenges to covenants not to compete regularly discuss the public policies of: (i) freedom of contract, (ii) freedom to compete, and (iii) employee mobility. The next case, involving a covenant not to compete agreement among doctors, discusses an additional "public policy" as the basis for not enforcing the agreement.

QUESTIONS BEFORE THE CASE

1. Why did Doctor Farber and the other doctors in the Valley Medical Specialists professional corporation enter into employment contracts with covenants not to compete?
2. Does the court balance the competing interests of Valley Medical Specialists and Doctor Farber?

VALLEY MEDICAL SPECIALISTS V. FARBER

Supreme Court of Arizona
194 Ariz. 363, 982 P.2d 1277 (1999)

FELDMAN, J.

We granted review to determine whether the restrictive covenant between Dr. Steven Farber and Valley Medical Specialists is enforceable. We hold that it is not. Public policy concerns in this case outweigh Valley Medical's protectable interests in enforcing the agreement. We thus vacate the court of appeals' opinion, affirm the trial court's judgment, and remand to the court of appeals to resolve any remaining issues. * * *

FACTS AND PROCEDURAL HISTORY

In 1985, Valley Medical Specialists ("VMS"), a professional corporation, hired Steven S. Farber, D.O., an internist and pulmonologist who, among other things, treated AIDS and HIV-positive patients and performed brachytherapy—a procedure that radiates the inside of the lung in lung cancer patients. Brachytherapy can only be performed at certain hospitals that have the necessary equipment. A few years after joining VMS, Dr. Farber became a shareholder and subsequently a minority officer and director. In 1991, the three directors, including Dr. Farber, entered into new stock and employment agreements. The employment agreement contained a restrictive covenant, the scope of which was amended over time.

In 1994, Dr. Farber left VMS and began practicing within the area defined by the restrictive covenant, which at that time read as follows:

> The parties recognize that the duties to be rendered under the terms of this Agreement by the Employee are special, unique and of an extraordinary character. The Employee, in consideration of the compensation to be paid to him pursuant to the terms of this Agreement, expressly agrees to the following restrictive covenants:
>
> (a) The Employee shall not, directly or indirectly:
>
> (i) Request any present or future patients of the Employer to curtail or cancel their professional affiliation with the Employer;
>
> (ii) Either separately, jointly, or in association with others, establish, engage in, or become interested in, as an employee, owner, partner, shareholder or otherwise, or furnish any information to, work for, or assist in any manner, anyone competing with, or who may compete with the Employer in the practice of medicine.
>
> * * *
>
> (iv) Either separately, jointly or in association with others provide medical care or medical assistance for any person or persons who were patients or [*sic*] Employer during the period that Employee was in the hire of Employer.
>
> * * *
>
> (d) The restrictive covenants set forth herein shall continue during the term of this Agreement and for a period of three (3) years after the date of termination, for any reason, of this Agreement. The restrictive covenants set forth herein shall be binding upon the Employee in that geographical area encompassed within the boundaries measured by a five (5) mile radius of any office maintained or utilized by Employer at the time of execution of the Agreement or at any time thereafter.
>
> (e) The Employee agrees that a violation on his part of any covenant set forth in this Paragraph 17 will cause such damage to the Employer as will be irreparable and for that reason, that Employee further agrees that the Employer shall be entitled, as a matter of right, and upon notice as provided in Paragraph 20 hereof, to an injunction from any court of competent jurisdiction, restraining any further violation of said covenants by Employee, his corporation, employees, partners or agents. Such right to injunctive remedies shall be

> in addition to and cumulative with any other rights and remedies the Employer may have pursuant to this Agreement or law, including, specifically with regard to the covenants set forth in subparagraph 17(a) above, the recovery of liquidated damages equal to forty percent (40%) of the gross receipts received for medical services provided by the Employee, or any employee, associate, partner, or corporation of the Employee during the term of this Agreement and for a period of three (3) years after the date of termination, for any reason, of this Agreement. The Employee expressly acknowledges and agrees that the covenants and agreement contained in this Paragraph 17 are minimum and reasonable in scope and are necessary to protect the legitimate interest of the Employer and its goodwill.

VMS filed a complaint against Dr. Farber seeking (1) preliminary and permanent injunctions enjoining Dr. Farber from violating the restrictive covenant, (2) liquidated damages for breach of the employment agreement, and (3) damages for breach of fiduciary duty, conversion of patient files and confidential information, and intentional interference with contractual and/or business relations.

Following six days of testimony and argument, the trial court denied VMS's request for a preliminary injunction, finding that the restrictive covenant violated public policy or, alternatively, was unenforceable because it was too broad. Specifically, the court found that: any covenant over six months would be unreasonable; the five-mile radius from each of the three VMS offices was unreasonable because it covered a total of 235 square miles; and the restriction was unreasonable because it did not provide an exception for emergency medical aid and was not limited to pulmonology.

The court of appeals reversed, concluding that a modified covenant was reasonable. The court noted that there were eight hospitals outside the restricted area where Dr. Farber could practice. Although the covenant made no exceptions for emergency medicine, the court held that the severability clause permitted the trial court to modify the covenant so Dr. Farber could provide emergency services within the restricted area. Moreover, VMS was allowed to stipulate that Dr. Farber could perform brachytherapy and treat AIDS and HIV patients within the restricted area, again even though the covenant contained no such exceptions.

The court of appeals found the restriction, when so modified, reasonable as to time and place. Although non-emergency patients might be required to travel further to see Dr. Farber, they could continue to see him if they were willing to drive that far. Three years was reasonable because the record contained testimony that it might take Dr. Farber's replacement three to five years to develop his pulmonary practice referral sources to the level they were when Dr. Farber resigned.

The court found that the restrictive covenant did not violate public policy, believing that courts must not unnecessarily restrict the freedom of contract. Moreover, the record was void of any evidence that the availability of pulmonologists in the restricted area would be inadequate without Dr. Farber.

History of restrictive covenants

A brief reference to basic principles is appropriate. Historically, covenants not to compete were viewed as restraints of trade and were invalid at common law. Eventually, ancillary restraints, such as those incident to employment or partnership agreements, were enforced under the rule of reason. To be enforced, the restriction must do more than simply prohibit fair competition by the employee. In other words, a covenant not to compete is invalid unless it protects some legitimate interest beyond the employer's desire to protect itself from competition.

It is true that in this case, unlike typical employer-employee agreements, Dr. Farber may not have been at a bargaining disadvantage, which is one of the reasons such restrictive covenants are strictly construed. Unequal bargaining power may be a factor to consider when examining the hardship on the departing employee. But in cases involving the professions, public policy concerns may outweigh any protectable interest the remaining firm members may have. Thus, this case does not turn on the hardship to Dr. Farber.

The doctor-patient relationship is special and entitled to unique protection. It cannot be easily or accurately compared to relationships in the commercial context. In light of the great public policy interest involved in covenants not to compete between physicians, each agreement will be strictly construed for reasonableness.

Reasonableness of covenant

Reasonableness is a fact-intensive inquiry that depends on the totality of the circumstances. A restriction is unreasonable and thus will not be enforced: (1) if the restraint is greater than necessary to protect the employer's legitimate interest; or (2) if that interest is outweighed by the hardship to the employee and the likely injury to the public. Thus, in the present case, the reasonableness inquiry requires us to examine the interests of the employer, employee, patients, and public in general. Balancing these competing interests is no easy task and no exact formula can be used.

VMS's protectable interest

VMS contends, and the court of appeals agreed, that it has a protectable interest in its patients and referral sources. In the commercial context, it is clear that employers have a legitimate interest in retaining their customer base. In the medical context, however, the personal relationship between doctor and patient as well as the patient's freedom to see a particular doctor, affects the extent of the employer's interest.

Even in the commercial context, the employer's interest in its customer base is balanced with the employee's right to the customers. Where the employee took an active role and brought customers with him or her to the job, courts are more reluctant to enforce restrictive covenants. Dr. Farber was a pulmonologist. He did not learn his skills from VMS.

Scope of the restrictive covenant

The restriction cannot be greater than necessary to protect VMS's legitimate interests. A restraint's scope is defined by its duration and geographic area. The frequency of contact between doctors and their patients affects the permissible length of the restraint. The idea is to give the employer a reasonable amount of time to overcome the former employee's loss, usually by hiring a replacement and giving that replacement time to establish a working relationship.

In this case, the trial judge found that the three-year period was an unreasonable duration because all of the experts agree that the practice of pulmonology entails treating patients with chronic conditions which require more hospital care than office care and which requires regular contact with the treating physician at least once within each six-month period so that any provision over six months is onerous and unnecessary to protect VMS's economic interests where virtually all of Dr. Farber's VMS patients had an opportunity by late 1994 or early 1995 (Farber left September 12, 1994) to decide which pulmonologist * * * they would consult for their ongoing treatment[.]

On this record, we cannot say this factual finding was clearly erroneous. The three-year duration is unreasonable.

The activity prohibited by the restraint also defines the covenant's scope. The restraint must be limited to the particular specialty of the present employment. On its face, the restriction here is not limited to internal medicine or even pulmonology. It precludes any type of practice, even in fields that do not compete with VMS. Thus, we agree with the trial judge that this restriction is too broad. * * *

Public policy

The court of appeals held that the restrictive covenant does not violate public policy, pointing out that the record contains nothing to suggest there will be a lack of pulmonologists in the restricted area if Dr. Farber is precluded from practicing there. Even if we assume other pulmonologists will be available to cover Dr. Farber's patients, we disagree with this view. It ignores the significant interests of individual patients within the restricted area. * * * A court must evaluate the extent to which enforcing the covenant would foreclose patients from seeing the departing physician if they desire to do so.

Concluding that patients' right to see the doctor of their choice is entitled to substantial protection, VMS's protectable interests here are comparatively minimal. The geographic scope of this covenant encompasses approximately 235 square miles, making it very difficult for Dr. Farber's existing patients to continue treatment with him if they so desire. After six days of testimony, the trial judge concluded that this restrictive covenant was unreasonably broad and against public policy. Specifically, the judge found:

> (1) the three year duration was unreasonable because pulmonology patients typically require contact with the treating physician once every six months. Thus, a restriction over six months is unnecessary to protect VMS's economic interests. Patients would have had opportunity within approximately six months to decide which doctor to see for continuing treatment;
>
> (2) the five mile radius was unreasonable because with the three offices, the restriction covered more than 235 square miles;
>
> (3) the restriction was unreasonable because it did not expressly provide for an exception for emergency medical treatment;
>
> (4) the restriction was overly broad because it is not limited to pulmonology;
>
> (5) the covenant violates public policy because of the sensitive and personal nature of the doctor-patient relationship.

Given the facts and the principles discussed, that finding is well supported factually and legally.

Severance—the blue pencil rule

This contract contains a severance clause. The court of appeals accepted a stipulation by VMS that the restriction would not prohibit Dr. Farber from treating HIV-positive and AIDS patients or from performing brachytherapy. On its face, however, the restriction is broader than that, restricting him from providing "medical care or medical assistance for any person or persons who were patients or [*sic*] Employer during the period that Employee was in the hire of Employer." Arizona courts will "blue pencil" restrictive covenants, eliminating grammatically severable, unreasonable provisions. Here, however, the modifications go further than cutting grammatically severable portions. The court of appeals, in essence, rewrote the agreement in an attempt to make it enforceable. This goes too far. "Where the severability of the agreement is not evident from the contract itself, the court cannot create a new agreement for the parties to uphold the contract."

Even the blue pencil rule has its critics. For every agreement that makes its way to court, many more do not. Thus, the words of the covenant have an in terrorem effect on departing employees. Employers may therefore create ominous covenants, knowing that if the words are challenged, courts will modify the agreement to make it enforceable. *Id.* Although we will tolerate ignoring severable portions of a covenant to make it more reasonable, we will not permit courts to add terms or rewrite provisions.

* * *

CONCLUSION

We hold that the restrictive covenant between Dr. Farber and VMS cannot be enforced. Valley Medical Specialists' interest in enforcing the restriction is outweighed by the likely injury to patients and the public in general. In so holding, we need not reach the question of the hardship imposed on Dr. Farber. The public policy implications here are enough to invalidate this particular agreement. We stop short of holding that restrictive covenants between physicians will never be enforced, but caution that such restrictions will be strictly construed. The burden is on the party wishing to enforce the covenant to demonstrate that the restraint is no greater than necessary to protect the employer's legitimate interest, and that such interest is not outweighed by the hardship to the employee and the likely injury to the public. Here VMS has not met that burden. The restriction fails because its public policy' implications outweigh the legitimate interests of VMS.

* * *

QUESTIONS AND NOTE

1. Questions about the facts of this case

    1.1. Was there any evidence that there is a shortage of pulmonologists in the Valley of the Sun? Is that relevant?

    1.2. Were Dr. Farber's former patients the plaintiffs in this case? The defendants?

1.3. Was the "restrictive covenant" the entire contract between Dr. Farber and Valley Medical Specialists? Did the Arizona Supreme Court hold that the entire contract was unenforceable?

2. Questions about the law

2.1. Reconsider the first three sentences of the opinion: "We granted review to determine whether the restrictive covenant between Dr. Steven Farber and Valley Medical Specialists is enforceable. We hold that it is not. Public policy concerns in this case outweigh Valley Medical's protectable interests in enforcing this agreement." What are the "public policy concerns"? What are Valley Medical's "protectable interests"?

2.2. A is an accountant. Her employment agreement with Valley Accountancy Specialists, Inc., includes a covenant not to compete similar in scope to the covenant not to compete in *Valley Medical Specialists*. A has now decided that she would like to leave Valley Accountancy Specialists, Inc. and start her own accounting practice. Would this court find her covenant not to compete unenforceable because of public policy?

2.3. Would the court have had the same public policy concerns and issued the same ruling if the covenant not to compete had been limited (i) to pulmonology, (ii) to one year, and (iii) to three miles from Valley Medical's principal office?

2.4. In discussing the contrary ruling of the court of appeals, the opinion mentions a "severability clause"—"the severability clause permitted the trial court to modify the covenant so Dr. Farber could provide emergency service within the restricted area." What is a severability clause? How is a severability clause connected to the blue pencil rule discussed later in the opinion?

3. Note

"The law governing non-competition agreements is a mess. There is wide state-to-state variation in the treatment of non-compete provisions. Some states routinely enforce "reasonable" non-competition agreements while other states refuse to enforce virtually all such provisions. Many others are somewhere in the middle: scrutinizing non-competition agreements more closely than other contracts but allowing enforcement of many. Some states have statutes governing the enforceability of non-competes, whereas others have left the question of enforceability to common-law development. These differences are substantial and result in significantly different legal rights and obligations among the states. Notably, however, not a single state takes a pure private ordering approach; the extra scrutiny given to these agreements reflects the philosophical and public policy tensions that inhere in attempts to impose post-employment restrictions on employees. . . . [T]his Article advocates for wholesale reform. Employee non-competes should be unenforceable, and the states should adopt a rule to that effect" Viva R. Moffat, *Making Non-Competes Unenforceable,* 54 ARIZ. L.REV.939, 943, 984 (2012)

4. **You Be the Lawyer!**

   Assume that after the Arizona Supreme Court decision, VMS and Farber settle. Under the settlement agreement, VMS makes a $400,000 payment to Dr. Farber, and he agrees to comply with the terms of the covenant not to compete. Thereafter, a group of Dr. Farber's former patients meet with you to discuss your representing them in a lawsuit to invalidate the settlement agreement as against public policy. What advice do you give them?

---

6. CONTRACT LAW REASONS FOR *NOT* ENFORCING AN AGREEMENT: UNCONSCIONABILITY

In studying duress and undue influence, misrepresentation, and non-disclosure, we have seen courts refuse to enforce agreements because of problems in the bargaining procedures. And, in studying illegality and public policy, we have seen courts refuse to enforce agreements because of problems with the substance of the bargain.

Unconscionability, in a sense, is a combination of all that. Unconscionability looks to both the bargaining process and the terms of the bargain.

Scholars trace the concept of unconscionability back to Roman law and find traces of an unconscionability doctrine in basic equity maxims such as "clean hands." The modern American law of unconscionability has its roots in section 2–302 of the Uniform Commercial Code.

§ 2–302. Unconscionable Contract or Clause.

(1) If the court as a matter of law finds the contract or any clause of the contract to have been unconscionable at the time it was made the court may refuse to enforce the contract, or it may enforce the remainder of the contract without the unconscionable clause, or it may so limit the application of any unconscionable clause as to avoid any unconscionable result. * * *

OFFICIAL COMMENT

1. This section is intended to allow the court to pass directly on the unconscionability of the contract or particular clause therein and to make a conclusion of law as to its unconscionability. * * * The principle

is one of the prevention of oppression and unfair surprise and not of disturbance of allocation of risks because of superior bargaining power.

The most "famous" case on unconscionability, *Williams v. Walker-Thomas Furniture Co.*, involves sale of goods contracts entered into before the enactment of the Uniform Commercial Code. The United States Court of Appeals for the District of Columbia concluded that unconscionability is not only a part of the Uniform Commercial Code but also a part of the common law, and so remanded the case for findings as to whether the contracts were unconscionable.

A recent law review article reproduced the language of the Walker-Thomas contracts from the transcript.

READ CONTRACT BEFORE SIGNING

This Deed Witnesseth that upon and subject to the terms and conditions hereinafter stated, I __________ have this day hired of and from THE WALKER-THOMAS FURNITURE COMPANY, (a partnership) having an office at Nos. 1027–1031 Seventh Street, Northwest, in the City of Washington, District of Columbia, certain property of the description and value as follows, viz:

____

____

____

____

____

Total value _____ Dollars. The terms and conditions aforesaid which I hereby agree to perform and abide by are as follows, viz: Said hiring is only for my own personal use of said property at my home No. _____ Street _____ in said City of Washington, where, at my said home, said property may be seen at all times by the agents of said Company, and I shall not without the consent of said Company in writing and subject to the conditions of such consent, cause or permit any of said property to be removed therefrom or placed in storage, nor shall I without such consent in writing transfer any of my rights hereunder; nor shall I mortgage, rent, pawn, dispose of or sell said property or any part thereof; nor shall I do anything whereby the rights of said Company hereunder or its title to, or my actual possession of, said property or any part thereof, shall or might be in anywise endangered, impaired or lost. For such use I shall pay to said Company now the sum of _____ dollars cash, and hereafter I shall pay, without any demand therefor, to said Company at its store, or at such other place or places in said City as said Company shall hereafter in writing direct _____ dollars on the ___ day of each ___ until all said payments actually and promptly made shall in the aggregate equal the total value aforesaid; and thereupon the said Company, upon the surrender to said Company of the receipts given for all such payments, shall transfer to me at my own expense by bill of sale the title to said property, but until such transfer such title shall remain in said Company, and I shall not have or claim the same, provided, that before such transfer of title, in case of default by me hereunder, I shall also fully reimburse said Company for all its expenses reasonably incurred in any efforts it may make to recover and maintain possession of said property hereunder. For every such payment the Company shall give me a written receipt, which shall be my only evidence of such payment, and I shall never claim any benefit of any payment of which such evidence shall have been lost or destroyed. Upon my failure to make any of said payments at the time or place aforesaid, although there shall have been no legal or formal demand therefor, or in case of failure on my part to take such care of any of said property as is required of a bailee for hire, or my failure to perform or abide by any of the terms and conditions of this agreement the said Company, by its agents, or the United States Marshal in and for the District of Columbia, or his deputies at the instance of said Company, may enter my said home or any place where any of said property may be found or where said Company may have reasonable cause to believe the same to be, and take actual possession of such property and remove the same therefrom either with or without legal process, and without previous demand therefor, and in such case I hereby waive and relinquish to, and forever discharge the said Company of and from all payments previously made hereunder, and I hereby release and discharge the said Company and its agents and the said United States Marshal and his deputies of and from any and all damages caused by such entry or by such taking or removal and of and from all claims which I may ever have by reason of any such payments, entry, taking, or removal. If I am now indebted to the Company on any prior leases, bills or accounts, it is agreed that the amount of each periodical installment payment to be made by me to the Company under this present lease shall be inclusive of and not in addition to the amount of each installment payment to be made by me under such prior leases, bills or accounts; and all payments now and hereafter made by me shall be credited pro rata on all outstanding leases, bills and accounts due the Company by me at the time each such payment is made. No indulgence to me by said Company as to time, amount, or place of payment or otherwise hereunder shall be construed to be a waiver by said Company of any of its rights or any of my duties hereunder, and no clause or stipulation of this agreement shall be deemed rescinded as against said Company unless such rescission is in writing and signed by the said Company. The word "Company" wherever it appears in this deed includes and shall be construed to mean The Walker Thomas Furniture Company aforesaid and its successors and assigns and each of them. This agreement is made subject to the approval of said Company, such approval to be evidenced only by the delivery to me of said property, and at any time before such delivery the said Company may, if it so elect, refuse to deliver said property to me, which refusal shall operate as a cancellation of this deed, and any rights which I may have or might have had hereunder shall immediately cease and determine. I also agree to pay attorney's fees of no less than $10 resulting from my breach of this lease in case a judgment for the deficiency in balance is awarded against me or possession of articles listed above is awarded to said Company. And hereunto I bind myself, my heirs, executors, administrators and assigns forever.

WITNESS my hand and seal this ___ day of ___ 19 __

Husband

____

Wife

____

NO DEPOSITS REFUNDED	FREE STORAGE FOR CUSTOMERS	NO GOODS EXCHANGED*

Did you read the contract? Did you read the top line "READ CONTRACT BEFORE SIGNING"? Well, at least read the case.

QUESTIONS BEFORE THE CASE

1. By 1962, had the plaintiff paid for the items she purchased from the defendant in 1957?
2. Does the United States Court of Appeals for the District of Columbia rule that it is unconscionable to sell a $514 stereo to mothers on public assistance with seven children?

---

* Anne Fleming, *The Rise and Fall of Unconscionability as the "Law of the Poor,"* 102 GEO. L.J. 1383, 1439–41 (2014).

WILLIAMS V. WALKER-THOMAS FURNITURE COMPANY

Court of Appeals, District of Columbia
198 A.2d 914 (1964)

QUINN, ASSOCIATE JUDGE.

Appellant, a person of limited education separated from her husband, is maintaining herself and her seven children by means of public assistance. During the period 1957–1962 she had a continuous course of dealings with appellee from which she purchased many household articles on the installment plan. These included sheets, curtains, rugs, chairs, a chest of drawers, beds, mattresses, a washing machine, and a stereo set. In 1963 appellee filed a complaint in replevin for possession of all the items purchased by appellant, alleging that her payments were in default and that it retained title to the goods according to the sales contracts. By the writ of replevin appellee obtained a bed, chest of drawers, washing machine, and the stereo set. After hearing testimony and examining the contracts, the trial court entered judgment for appellee.

Appellant's principal contentions on appeal are (1) there was a lack of meeting of the minds, and (2) the contracts were against public policy.

Appellant signed fourteen contracts in all. They were approximately six inches in length and each contained a long paragraph in extremely fine print. One of the sentences in this paragraph provided that payments, after the first purchase, were to be prorated on all purchases then outstanding. Mathematically, this had the effect of keeping a balance due on all items until the time balance was completely eliminated. It meant that title to the first purchase, remained in appellee until the fourteenth purchase, made some five years later, was fully paid.

At trial appellant testified that she understood the agreements to mean that when payments on the running account were sufficient to balance the amount due on an individual item, the item became hers. She testified that most of the purchases were made at her home; that the contracts were signed in blank; that she did not read the instruments; and that she was not provided with a copy. She admitted, however, that she did not ask anyone to read or explain the contracts to her.

We have stated that "one who refrains from reading a contract and in conscious ignorance of its terms voluntarily assents thereto will not be relieved from his bad bargain." "One who signs a contract has a duty to read it and is obligated according to its terms." "It is as much the duty of a person who cannot read the language in which a contract is written to have someone read it to him before he signs it, as it is the duty of one who can read to peruse it himself before signing it."

A careful review of the record shows that appellant's assent was not obtained "by fraud or even misrepresentation falling short of fraud." This is not a case of mutual misunderstanding but a unilateral mistake. Under these circumstances, appellant's first contention is without merit.

Appellant's second argument presents a more serious question. The record reveals that prior to the last purchase appellant had reduced the balance in her account to $164. The last purchase, a stereo set, raised the balance due to $678. Significantly, at the time of this and the preceding purchases, appellee was aware of appellant's financial position. The reverse side of the stereo contract listed the name of appellant's social worker and her $218 monthly stipend from the government. Nevertheless, with full knowledge that appellant had to feed, clothe and support both herself and seven children on this amount, appellee sold her a $514 stereo set.

We cannot condemn too strongly appellee's conduct. It raises serious questions of sharp practice and irresponsible business dealings. A review of the legislation in the District of Columbia affecting retail sales and the pertinent decisions of the highest court in this jurisdiction disclose, however, no ground upon which this court can declare the contracts in question contrary to public policy. We think Congress should consider corrective legislation to protect the public from such exploitive contracts as were utilized in the case at bar.

Affirmed.

WILLIAMS V. WALKER-THOMAS FURNITURE COMPANY

U.S. Court of Appeals, District of Columbia Circuit
350 F.2d 445 (1965)

J. SKELLY WRIGHT, CIRCUIT JUDGE.

* * *

We do not agree that the court lacked the power to refuse enforcement to contracts found to be unconscionable. In other jurisdictions, it has been held as a matter of common law that unconscionable contracts are not enforceable. While no decision of this court so holding has been found, the notion that an unconscionable bargain should not be given full enforcement is by no means novel. In *Scott v. United States*, 79 U.S. (12 Wall.) 443, 445, 20 L.Ed. 438 (1870), the Supreme Court stated:

> "* * * If a contract be unreasonable and unconscionable, but not void for fraud, a court of law will give to the party who sues for its breach damages, not according to its letter, but only such as he is equitably entitled to. * * *"

Since we have never adopted or rejected such a rule, the question here presented is actually one of first impression.

Congress has recently enacted the Uniform Commercial Code, which specifically provides that the court may refuse to enforce a contract which it finds to be unconscionable at the time it was made. The enactment of this section, which occurred subsequent to the contracts here in suit, does not mean that the common law of the District of Columbia was otherwise at the time of enactment, nor does it preclude the court from adopting a similar rule in the exercise of its powers to develop the common law for the District of Columbia. In fact, in view of the absence of prior authority on the point, we consider the congressional adoption of § 2–302 persuasive authority for following the rationale of the cases from which the section is explicitly derived. Accordingly, we hold that where the element of unconscionability is present at the time a contract is made, the contract should not be enforced.

Unconscionability has generally been recognized to include an absence of meaningful choice on the part of one of the parties together with contract terms which are unreasonably favorable to the other party. Whether a meaningful choice is present in a particular case can only be determined by consideration of all the circumstances surrounding the transaction. In many cases the meaningfulness of the choice is negated by a gross inequality of bargaining power. The manner in which the contract was entered is also relevant to this consideration. Did each party to the contract, considering his obvious education or lack of it, have a reasonable opportunity to understand the terms of the contract, or were the important terms hidden in a maze of fine print and minimized by deceptive sales practices? Ordinarily, one who signs an agreement without full knowledge of its terms might be held to assume the risk that he has entered a one-sided bargain. But when a party of little bargaining power, and hence little real choice, signs a commercially unreasonable contract with little or no knowledge of its terms, it is hardly likely that his consent, or even an objective manifestation of his consent, was ever given to all the terms. In such a case the usual rule that the terms of the agreement are not to be questioned should be abandoned and the court should consider whether the terms of the contract are so unfair that enforcement should be withheld.

In determining reasonableness or fairness, the primary concern must be with the terms of the contract considered in light of the circumstances existing when the contract was made. The test is not simple, nor can it be mechanically applied. The terms are to be considered "in the light of the general commercial background and the commercial needs of the particular trade or case." Corbin suggests the test as being whether the terms are "so extreme as to appear unconscionable according to the mores and business practices of the time and place." We think this formulation correctly states the test to be applied in those cases where no meaningful choice was exercised upon entering the contract.

Because the trial court and the appellate court did not feel that enforcement could be refused, no findings were made on the possible unconscionability of the contracts in these cases. Since the record is not sufficient for our deciding the issue as a matter of law, the cases must be remanded to the trial court for further proceedings.

So ordered.

DANAHER, CIRCUIT JUDGE (dissenting):

The District of Columbia Court of Appeals obviously was as unhappy about the situation here presented as any of us can possibly be. Its opinion in the *Williams* case, quoted in the majority text, concludes: "We think Congress should consider corrective legislation to protect the public from such exploitive contracts as were utilized in the case at bar."

My view is thus summed up by an able court which made no finding that there had actually been sharp practice. Rather the appellant seems to have known precisely where she stood.

There are many aspects of public policy here involved. What is a luxury to some may seem an outright necessity to others. Is public oversight to be required of the expenditures of relief funds? A washing machine, e.g., in the hands of a relief client might become a fruitful source of income. Many relief clients may well need credit, and certain business establishments will take long chances on the sale of items, expecting their pricing policies will afford a degree of protection commensurate with the risk. * * *

I mention such matters only to emphasize the desirability of a cautious approach to any such problem, particularly since the law for so long has allowed parties such great latitude in making their own contracts. I dare say there must annually be thousands upon thousands of installment credit transactions in this jurisdiction, and one can only speculate as to the effect the decision in these cases will have.

I join the District of Columbia Court of Appeals in its disposition of the issues.

QUESTIONS AND NOTE

1. Questions about the facts of the case
   - 1.1. Who is suing whom for what?
   - 1.2. Was there a written agreement?
   - 1.3. Did the Walker-Thomas Furniture Company do anything that was illegal, i.e., that was expressly prohibited by D.C. law?

2. Questions about the law

2.1. In the first *Williams* opinion, the intermediate appellate court focused on the contention that the "contracts were against public policy" and concluded that there was "no ground upon which this court can declare the contracts in question contrary to public policy." The appeal of that decision resulted in a remand for further proceedings on unconscionability. What are the differences between Williams' public policy argument and Williams' unconscionability argument?

2.2. Is unconscionability federal statutory law? State statutory law? Common law?

2.3. What was unconscionable about the agreement between Ms. Williams and the Walker-Thomas store? What did Judge Wright decide?

2.4. How would Judge Wright have decided this case if all agreements contained the following warning in bold print: "**BE SURE AND READ THIS, IF YOU ARE LATE ON ANY PAYMENT FOR WHAT YOU JUST BOUGHT, WE WILL BE ABLE TO TAKE BACK FROM YOU EVERYTHING WE HAVE EVER SOLD TO YOU. EVERYTHING.**"

3. Note

According to Professor David Slawson, "The theoretical underpinnings of unconscionability * * * are not simple, and to some extent they are self-contradictory. They require one to accept the legitimacy of contracts to which one party did not give meaningful consent but to deny their legitimacy to the extent that they operate unfairly." W. DAVID SLAWSON, BINDING PROMISES, 144 (1996).

4. **You Be the Lawyer!**

4.1. On remand, what evidence would you try to introduce if you represented Ms. Williams? Would it be helpful to show her education and economic situation? Would it be helpful to show why she purchased a $514 stereo? Would it be helpful to show that repossessed "sheets, curtains, rugs" have almost no resale value to Walker-Thomas? Would it be helpful to show that other merchants in the area used similar contracts?

4.2. On remand, what evidence would you try to find and introduce if you represented Walker-Thomas? Would it be helpful to show that other merchants in the area used similar contracts? Would it be helpful to show that consumer goods lose value so rapidly that the amount owed for consumer goods is generally greater than any resale value? Would it be helpful to show that D.C. law restricted Walker-Thomas to the recovery of the debt owed by Ms. Williams and its collection costs?

Many of the recent reported cases on unconscionability since *Walker-Thomas* have involved challenges to clauses requiring arbitration in employment contracts and contracts for the sale of goods or services to consumers.

At the very beginning of the book, Ponoroff reviewed legal and policy issues in commercial arbitration. Even though you are not as old as Epstein who forgets damn near everything he reads, we don't expect you to remember Ponoroff's boring text at the beginning of the book.

And, that's okay. There are obviously different concerns about the enforceability of a mandatory arbitration provision in a commercial contract negotiated by the lawyers of Apple Corp and the lawyers for Beats Music and Beats Electronic* as part of a three billion dollar deal and the enforceability of the arbitration provision in the ITunes contract entered into by Apple Corp and Kyle Broflovski.**

Recall Judge Wright's language in *Williams v. Walker-Thomas*: "Unconscionability has generally been recognized to include an absence of meaningful choice on the part of one of the parties together with contract terms which are unreasonably favorable to the other party." Wouldn't you like your chances of arguing "absence of meaningful choice" with Kyle as your client more than with Beats as your client? (Of course, you would like your chances of getting your attorney's fees paid with Beats as your client.)

Regardless of whether Kyle is your client or Beats is your client, the unconscionability of a mandatory arbitration provision in a consumer contract or a commercial contract requires consideration not only of UCC section 2–302 but also section 2 of the Federal Arbitration Act (FAA).

The FAA was enacted to limit courts' ability to invalidate arbitration clauses. FAA section 2 provides "A written provision in . . . a contract evidencing a transaction involving commerce to settle by arbitration a controversy . . . shall be valid, irrevocable, and enforceable, save upon such grounds as exist at law or in equity for the revocation of any contract."

Since unconscionability is a ground for the "revocation of any contract", it would seem that FAA would not affect unconscionability challenges to arbitration clauses. But then a divided Supreme Court "decided" *AT & T Mobility v. Concepcion*, 131 S.Ct. 1740 (2011).

Concepcion involved a cellular telephone service contract that mandated arbitration and prohibited class wide arbitration. The California

---

* Cf. https://www.apple.com/pr/library/2014/05/28Apple-to-Acquire-Beats-Music-Beats-Electronics.html.

** Cf. https://www.youtube.com/watch?v=WberQSoM6Rs.

Supreme Court in the *Discover Bank** case had deemed unconscionable class arbitration waivers in consumer adhesion contracts where damages are likely small. The question in *Concepion* was whether the FAA preempted California's *Discover Bank* rule. A 5–4 majority opinion answered the question: "Because it "stands as an obstacle to the accomplishment and execution of the full purposes and objectives of Congress, California's *Discover Bank* rule is preempted by the FAA."

The *Concepcion* decision was not based on the language of the FAA. Instead, the Court looked to the FAA's "purposes and objectives." The majority opinion concludes that a state law rule that mandates class action procedures in arbitration makes the arbitration process slower and more formal and thus is a barrier to purposes and objectives of the FAA.

Justice Scalia's majority opinion in *Concepcion* acknowledges by way of dictum that unconscionability is one of the "grounds . . . for a revocation of any contract" under FAA section 2. Thus, notwithstanding the *Concepcion* decision, a court *can* rule that a mandatory arbitration provision is unconscionable and is unenforceable.

It is, however, unclear as to what weight a court will give the *Concepcion* case in so ruling. As Professor David Horton more eloquently stated, "*Concepcion* has sown confusion about the degree to which judges remain free to find arbitration clauses unconscionable**."

QUESTIONS BEFORE THE CASE

1. Is this a sale of goods case?
2. What is the difference between procedural unconscionability and substantive unconscionability?

VERNON V. QWEST COMMUNICATIONS INTERNATIONAL, INC.

United States District Court, Colorado
925 F.Supp.2d 1185 (2013)

ORDER

R. BROOKE JACKSON, DISTRICT JUDGE.

This matter comes before the Court on plaintiffs' objection to an order issued by United States Magistrate Judge Craig B. Shaffer granting

* Discover Bank v. Superior Court, 113 P.3d 1100 (Cal. 2005).

** David Horton, Federal Arbitration Act: Preemption, Purposivism, and Public Policy, 101Geo.L.J. 1217,1244 (2013).

defendants' renewed motion to compel arbitration and staying this matter pending further proceedings. For the reasons set forth herein, the Court denies the plaintiffs' objection and affirms the magistrate judge's recommendation.

Facts

The plaintiffs are former customers of Qwest who signed up for its "Price for Life" program which was a minimum two-year contract under which subscribers were guaranteed a discounted rate for as long as they maintained their service without change.. Subscribers who terminated the program within the first two years were charged a $200 early cancellation fee. . . .

The Price for Life program was subject to a set of terms and conditions set forth in a Subscriber Agreement. Paragraph 17 of the Subscriber Agreement, captioned "Dispute Resolution and Arbitration," contains two provisions of particular importance to the present case. First, any dispute or claim arising out of or relating to the services provided by Qwest must be resolved in arbitration or in small claims court. Second, the subscriber waived his or her right to pursue any claims on a class or consolidate basis or in a representative capacity. . . .

Plaintiffs brought this ***action . . .*** in 2008 purporting to represent a multi-state class of similarly situated consumers who were, in their view, subjected to an invalid $200 early termination fee. . . . Defendants filed a . . . motion to compel arbitration]. . . . The motion to compel arbitration was later stayed pending the United States Supreme Court's decision in *AT & T Mobility, LLC v. Concepcion*, . . . The Supreme Court issued its decision in that case on April 27, 2011. Defendants then filed a renewed motion to compel arbitration. . . .

Plaintiffs contend that the arbitration agreement is not enforceable for two reasons: it is illusory and, it is unconscionable. [We have omitted the court's discussion of whether the promise to arbitrate is illusory; we considered that issue earlier in our consideration of consideration]. . . .

In Colorado, for a contract to be unconscionable, it must be both substantively and procedurally unconscionable. The Colorado Supreme Court listed seven factors that are relevant in determining whether a contract is unconscionable: (1) a standardized agreement executed by parties of unequal bargaining power; (2) lack of opportunity to read or become familiar with the document before signing it; (3) use of fine print in the portion of the contract containing the provision; (4) absence of evidence that the provision was commercially reasonable; (5) the terms of the contract; (6) the relationship of the parties, including factors of assent, unfair surprise, and notice; and (7) all the circumstances surrounding the formation of the contract.

The first, second, third, sixth, and seventh factors relate to procedural unconscionability. Looking at the first factor, the arbitration agreement at issue was a standardized agreement between parties with unequal bargaining power. However, this factor by itself is not enough for a finding of procedural unconscionability. *See also Concepcion,* 131 S.Ct. at 1750 ("the times in which consumer contracts were anything other than adhesive are long past"). The second and third factors concern whether there was an opportunity to read and become familiar with the document before signing it and whether the arbitration provision was hidden in the equivalent of "fine print." . . . The sixth factor requires analysis of the relationship between the parties including issues of assent, notice and unfair surprise. . . . [T]he plaintiffs had notice of the arbitration agreement, it was reasonably conspicuous, and the plaintiffs gave their unambiguous consent. The seventh factor is a catchall that allows for consideration of all of the factors surrounding formation of the contract. I have not identified any circumstances in the formation of this contract that made the arbitration clause procedurally unconscionable.

Plaintiffs also argue that the arbitration agreement is substantively unconscionable. The plaintiffs point out that the terms of the Subscriber Agreement are much less consumer-friendly than those examined by the Supreme Court in *Concepcion.* I agree, but I do not agree that they rise to the level of substantive unconscionability. Under the terms of the Subscriber Agreement the plaintiffs were required to pay half of the arbitrators' fees up to $125 for claims not exceeding $10,000. Plaintiffs argue that this cost would deter consumers from filing suit. That might be true. However, a filing fee is not unique to arbitration. A filing fee is also required in state and federal court, even in small claims court, and $125 is not exorbitant. Moreover, whether the potential recovery is limited to $200 or less (the Subscriber Agreement purports to limit damages to the monthly and usage charges paid by the subscriber during the month preceding the event giving rise to the claim), as plaintiffs fear, or could be supplemented by statutory damages, as defendants argue, is a matter for the arbitrator to address. In any event, the Court acknowledged in *Concepcion* its ruling could make it such that small dollar claims would slip through the cracks. However, "States cannot require a procedure that is inconsistent with the FAA, even if it is desirable for unrelated reasons." *Id.* at 1753. Neither can this Court. . . .

This action is stayed pending arbitration or, in the discretion of the Court of Appeals, pending an immediate appeal pursuant to 28 U.S.C. § 1292(b).

QUESTIONS AND NOTE

1. Questions about the facts of this case

    1.1. Do we have any facts that indicate how much an individual plaintiff can recover if successful? Do we have any facts that indicate how many hours plaintiffs' lawyers have worked on this litigation and who will be paying them?

    1.2. What do we know about the plaintiffs? Do we know more about Ms. Williams in *Williams v. Walker-Thomas Furniture Co*, than we know about the plaintiffs in this case? Is that important?

2. Questions about the law

    2.1. Procedural/substantive unconscionability: The *Vernon* opinion uses the terms "procedural unconscionability' and "substantive unconscionability." So do many reported decisions on unconscionability. Does UCC section 2–302 use the phrase "procedural unconscionability" or the phrase "substantive unconscionability"?

    2.2. Adhesive: Note the court's quote from the Supreme Court's *Concepcion* opinion: "the times in which consumer contracts were anything other than adhesive are long past". What does this statement mean? While neither the U.C.C. nor the *Restatement (Second) of Contracts* uses the term "adhesion contracts," the term "adhesion contracts" is widely used in cases and adhesion contracts are widely used in the "real world." Have any of the cases we have previously considered in this book involved "adhesion contracts"?

3. Note

    "The American Arbitration Association—the leading non-profit provider of arbitration—adjudicates fewer than 1,500 consumer cases annually. In contrast, the online marketplace eBay alone internally handles 60 million disputes each year between buyers and sellers. Comcast's customer service department has over a million customer touch points *each day*. The main institutional actor in the private consumer legal system is not the arbitration tribunal, but the consumer-facing corporation. Although legal scholars have written thousands of pages about arbitration in recent years, they have largely ignored businesses' internal processes for resolving consumer disputes." Rory Van Loo, *The Corporation as a Courthouse*," 35 YALE J. REG. 547, 548–9 (2016).

4. **You Be the Lawyer!**

    As the lawyer for Qwest, what other actions would you have recommended Qwest take to minimize the possibility of a successful unconscionability challenge to the arbitration provisions?

7. CONTRACT LAW REASONS FOR *NOT* ENFORCING AGREEMENTS: MISTAKEN FACTUAL ASSUMPTIONS AND OTHER KINDS OF MISTAKES

A. MISTAKEN FACTUAL ASSUMPTIONS

All agreements are based on various factual assumptions. Sometimes, these assumptions can be found in the terms of the agreement, and the terms of the agreement sometimes spell out whether a party can cancel the agreement if such an express factual assumption turns out to be erroneous.

It is unlikely, however, that even the most comprehensive commercial agreement sets out all of the factual assumptions of the parties. And, agreements prepared by the parties themselves are likely to omit many if not most factual assumptions. This part of the book focuses on such unstated factual assumptions that are erroneous, i.e., mistakes.

Back when Epstein was a "baby professor" in the "Southern Part of Heaven", Chapel Hill*, all contracts casebooks used *Sherwood v. Walker*, 66 Mich. 568, 33 N.W. 919 (1887), as the first case on mistaken factual assumptions.** *Sherwood* involved a contract to sell a cow with the wonderful name of Rose 2d of Aberlone. The sale price was only $80 because according the facts as found by the majority of the judges on the Michigan Supreme Court, "both parties supposed that this cow was barren and would not breed and she was sold by the pound for an insignificant sum, as compared with her real value as a breeder."

It turned out that Rose was not barren—at worst, she was slightly shy. Indeed, before the buyer took possession of Rose, the sellers learned that Rose was "with calf and therefore of great value, and undertook to rescind the sale . . . The question arises whether they had a right to do so [because of the mistaken unstated factual assumption]."

In answering that the sellers had a right to rescind, *Sherwood* emphasized that the (1) mistake was mutual and (2) the "mistake went to the whole substance of the agreement." As the Michigan Supreme Court "explained": "The mistake was not of the mere quality of the animal but

* Cf William Meade Prince, The Southern Part of Heaven (1950).

** One of the reasons 1970's contracts casebooks included *Sherwood* case is that a famous law professor, Brainerd Currie, wrote a lengthy poem in rhymed verse about the case that was published originally in the Harvard Law School student newspaper in 1954, and then republished in the Green Bag more than 50 years later. See Brainerd Currie, *Rose of Aberlone*, 1 GREEN BAG 2d 445 (1998). Today, Professor Craswell's YouTube video http://www.youtube.com/watch?v=pjjRBAQ7ET8&list=PL36131D32992573A4 is an even stronger argument for including *Sherwood* in our book—an argument that two of your three authors did not find persuasive.

went to the very nature of the thing. A barren cow is substantially a different creature than a breeding cow."

Ninety-five years after *Sherwood v. Walker*, the Michigan Supreme Court, in *Lenawee County Board of Health v. Messerly*, 417 Mich. 17, 331 N.W.2d 203 (1982), described the test in *Sherwood* as "inexact and confusing," stated that *Sherwood* should be "limited to [its] facts," and adopted the rule stated in the *Restatement (Second) of Contracts*:

> We think that the better-reasoned approach is a case-by-case analysis whereby rescission is indicated when the mistaken belief relates to a basic assumption of the parties upon which the contract is made, and which materially affects the agreed performance of the parties. [*Restatement (Second) of Contracts* § 152.] * * * Rescission is not available, however, to relieve a party who has assumed the risk of loss, in connection with a mistake. [*Restatement (Second) of Contracts* §§ 152, 154.]

More recently, the Michigan Supreme Court cited to *Sherwood v. Walker,* approvingly, *Briggs Tax Service, LLC v. Detroit Public Schools,* 485 Mich. 69 780 N.W.2d 753, 758–9 (2010) ("seminal case"). And, in 2013, a Connecticut court not only cited to but relied on *Sherwood* (although the court referred to Rose as "Old Bess"): "In contrast to 'Old Bess,' the supposed mistake at issue involves the condition of the trailer, not the nature of the trailer."*

Sherwood v, Walker and the cases in this section raise three core problems for courts and lawyers:

First, there is the problem of proof. How can a lawyer prove what their client was thinking about but did not say when they entered into the agreement? In *Sherwood v Walker*, for example, the dissenting judge (whose name happened to be "Sherwood") accepted the buyer's (whose name happened to be Sherwood) version of the facts which was that the buyer was not mistaken about Rose, that the buyer "thought she could be made to breed."

Second, there is the problem of policy. Why should courts excuse a person from doing what she agreed to do because of a mistaken, unstated factual assumption? Is the concern conceptual—mistake somehow prevents mutual assent, *i.e.*, no meeting of the minds? Is the concern ethical—it is somehow unfair for one party to benefit from mistaken, factual assumptions? Is the concern economic—the law should reward efficient bargaining behavior, whatever that is?

Third, there is the related problem of "rules." Once the courts have decided what the relevant policy consideration(s) is (are), what rule with

* Environmental Services, Inc. v. Hill Forest Products, Inc., 2013 WL 1408629 (Conn. Super. 2013)

respect to relief for unstated factual assumptions advances that policy? Should it matter whether the mistake relates to "quality" or "nature"? Whether the mistake is a mistake of judgment or a clerical error? Whether the mistake relates to facts or law? Whether both parties have made the same mistake?

Here are the *Restatement (Second) of Contracts*'s rules on relief for mutual mistaken factual assumptions:

§ 152 When Mistake of Both Parties Makes a Contract Voidable

(1) Where a mistake of both parties at the time a contract was made as to a basic assumption on which the contract was made has a material effect on the agreed exchange of performances, the contract is voidable by the adversely affected party unless he bears the risk of the mistake under the rule stated in § 154.

* * *

§ 154 When a Party Bears the Risk of a Mistake

A party bears the risk of a mistake when

(a) the risk is allocated to him by agreement of the parties, or

(b) he is aware, at the time the contract is made, that he has only limited knowledge with respect to the facts to which the mistake relates but treats his limited knowledge as sufficient, or

(c) the risk is allocated to him by the court on the ground that it is reasonable in the circumstances to do so.

The next case applies these Restatement rules.

QUESTIONS BEFORE THE CASE

1. Did both the Estate and Rice contend that they were both mistaken? Did the court find that they were both mistaken?
2. Was the mistake in this case "made as to a basic assumption on which the contract was made"?

ESTATE OF NELSON V. RICE

Court of Appeals of Arizona
198 Ariz. 563, 12 P.3d 238 (2000)

ESPINOSA, CHIEF JUDGE.

Plaintiff/appellant the Estate of Martha Nelson, through its copersonal representatives Edward Franz and Kenneth Newman, appeals from a summary judgment in favor of defendants/appellees Carl and Anne Rice in the Estate's action seeking rescission or reformation of the sale of two paintings to the Rices. The Estate argues that these remedies are required because the sale was based upon a mutual mistake. The Estate also contends that enforcing the sale "contract" would be unconscionable. We affirm.

Facts and Procedural History

After Martha Nelson died in February 1996, Newman and Franz, the copersonal representatives of her estate, employed Judith McKenzie-Larson to appraise the Estate's personal property in preparation for an estate sale. McKenzie-Larson told them that she did not appraise fine art and that, if she saw any, they would need to hire an additional appraiser. McKenzie-Larson did not report finding any fine art, and relying on her silence and her appraisal, Newman and Franz priced and sold the Estate's personal property.

Responding to a newspaper advertisement, Carl Rice attended the public estate sale and paid the asking price of $60 for two oil paintings. Although Carl had bought and sold some art, he was not an educated purchaser, had never made more than $55 on any single piece, and had bought many pieces that had "turned out to be frauds, forgeries or * * * to have been [created] by less popular artists." He assumed the paintings were not originals given their price and the fact that the Estate was managed by professionals, but was attracted to the subject matter of one of the paintings and the frame of the other. At home, he compared the signatures on the paintings to those in a book of artists' signatures, noticing they "appeared to be similar" to that of Martin Johnson Heade. As they had done in the past, the Rices sent pictures of the paintings to Christie's in New York, hoping they might be Heade's work. Christie's authenticated the paintings, Magnolia Blossoms on Blue Velvet and Cherokee Roses, as paintings by Heade and offered to sell them on consignment. Christie's subsequently sold the paintings at auction for $1,072,000. After subtracting the buyer's premium and the commission, the Rices realized $911,780 from the sale.

Newman and Franz learned about the sale in February 1997 and thereafter sued McKenzie-Larson on behalf of the Estate, believing she was entirely responsible for the Estate's loss. The following November, they settled the lawsuit because McKenzie-Larson had no assets with which to pay damages. During 1997, the Rices paid income taxes of $337,000 on the profit from the sale of the paintings, purchased a home, created a family trust, and spent some of the funds on living expenses.

The Estate sued the Rices in late January 1998, alleging the sale contract should be rescinded or reformed on grounds of mutual mistake and unconscionability. In its subsequent motion for summary judgment, the Estate argued the parties were not aware the transaction had involved fine art, believing instead that the items exchanged were "relatively valueless, wall decorations." In their opposition and cross-motion, the Rices argued the Estate bore the risk of mistake, the doctrine of laches precluded reformation of the contract, and unconscionability was not a basis for rescission. The trial court concluded that, although the parties had been mistaken about the value of the paintings, the Estate bore the risk of that mistake. The court ruled the contract was not unconscionable, finding the parties had not negotiated Carl's paying the prices the Estate had set. Accordingly, the court denied the Estate's motion for summary judgment and granted the Rices' cross-motion. The Estate's motion for new trial was denied, and this appeal followed. * * *

The Estate first argues that it established a mutual mistake sufficient to permit the reformation or rescission of the sale of the paintings to the Rices.[1] A party seeking to rescind a contract on the basis of mutual mistake must show by clear and convincing evidence that the agreement should be set aside. A contract may be rescinded on the ground of a mutual mistake as to a " 'basic assumption on which both parties made the contract.' " Renner v. Kehl, 150 Ariz. 94, 97, 722 P.2d 262, 265 (1986), quoting *Restatement (Second) of Contracts* § 152 cmt. b (1979). Furthermore, the parties' mutual mistake must have had " 'such a material effect on the agreed exchange of performances as to upset the very bases of the contract.' " Id., quoting Restatement § 152 cmt. a. However, the mistake must not be one on which the party seeking relief bears the risk under the rules stated in § 154(b) of the Restatement.

In concluding that the Estate was not entitled to rescind the sale, the trial court found that, although a mistake had existed as to the value of the paintings, the Estate bore the risk of that mistake under § 154(b) of the Restatement, citing the example in comment a. Section 154(b) states that a party bears the risk of mistake when "he is aware, at the time the contract is made, that he has only limited knowledge with respect to the facts to which the mistake relates but treats his limited knowledge as sufficient." In explaining that provision, the Washington Supreme Court stated, "In

[1] Reformation is not an available remedy under these facts. It is a remedy to correct a written instrument that fails to express the terms agreed upon by the parties and "is not intended to enforce the terms of an agreement the parties never made."

such a situation there is no mistake. Instead, there is an awareness of uncertainty or conscious ignorance of the future."

The Estate contends neither party bore the risk of mistake, arguing that § 154 and comment a are not applicable to these facts. In the example in comment a, the risk of mistake is allocated to the seller when the buyer discovers valuable mineral deposits on property priced and purchased as farmland. Even were we to accept the Estate's argument that this example is not analogous, comment c clearly applies here and states:

Conscious ignorance. Even though the mistaken party did not agree to bear the risk, he may have been aware when he made the contract that his knowledge with respect to the facts to which the mistake relates was limited. If he was not only so aware that his knowledge was limited but undertook to perform in the face of that awareness, he bears the risk of the mistake. It is sometimes said in such a situation that, in a sense, there was not mistake but "conscious ignorance."

Through its personal representatives, the Estate hired two appraisers, McKenzie-Larson and an Indian art expert, to evaluate the Estate's collection of Indian art and artifacts. McKenzie-Larson specifically told Newman that she did not appraise fine art. In his deposition, Newman testified that he had not been concerned that McKenzie-Larson had no expertise in fine art, believing the Estate contained nothing of "significant value" except the house and the Indian art collection. Despite the knowledge that the Estate contained framed art other than the Indian art, and that McKenzie-Larson was not qualified to appraise fine art, the personal representatives relied on her to notify them of any fine art or whether a fine arts appraiser was needed. Because McKenzie-Larson did not say they needed an additional appraiser, Newman and Franz did not hire anyone qualified to appraise fine art. By relying on the opinion of someone who was admittedly unqualified to appraise fine art to determine its existence, the personal representatives consciously ignored the possibility that the Estate's assets might include fine art, thus assuming that risk. See Klas v. Van Wagoner, 829 P.2d 135, 141 n. 8 (Utah App.1992) (real estate buyers not entitled to rescind sale contract because they bore risk of mistake as to property's value; by hiring architects, decorators, and electricians to examine realty, but failing to have it appraised, purchasers executed sale contract knowing they "had only 'limited knowledge' with respect to the value of the home"). Accordingly, the trial court correctly found that the Estate bore the risk of mistake as to the paintings' value.[2]

The Estate asserts that the facts here are similar to those in Renner, in which real estate buyers sued to rescind a contract for acreage upon which they wished to commercially grow jojoba after discovering the water

[2] In view of our conclusion that the Estate bore the risk of any mistake in the paintings' value, we need not address the remainder of its mutual mistake arguments.

supply was inadequate for that purpose. The Arizona Supreme court concluded that the buyers could rescind the contract based upon mutual mistake because both the buyers and the sellers had believed there was an adequate water supply, a basic assumption underlying formation of the contract. The parties' failure to thoroughly investigate the water supply did not preclude rescission when "the risk of mistake was not allocated among the parties." 150 Ariz. at 97 n. 2, 722 P.2d at 265 n. 2. The Estate's reliance on Renner is unavailing because, as stated above, the Estate bore the risk of mistake based on its own conscious ignorance.

Furthermore, under Restatement § 154(c), the court may allocate the risk of mistake to one party "on the ground that it is reasonable in the circumstances to do so." In making this determination, "the court will consider the purposes of the parties and will have recourse to its own general knowledge of human behavior in bargain transactions." Restatement § 154 cmt. d. Here, the Estate had had ample opportunity to discover what it was selling and failed to do so; instead, it ignored the possibility that the paintings were valuable and attempted to take action only after learning of their worth as a result of the efforts of the Rices. Under these circumstances, the Estate was a victim of its own folly and it was reasonable for the court to allocate to it the burden of its mistake. * * *

The Estate also argues that enforcement of the "contract" to sell the paintings is unconscionable. The determination of a contract's unconscionability is for the trial court as a matter of law. We review that ruling de novo. * * * 'Unconscionability includes both procedural unconscionability, i.e., something wrong in the bargaining process, and substantive unconscionability, i.e., the contract terms per se.' * * *"

[T]the Estate contends this is a case of substantive unconscionability, which concerns the actual terms of the contract and the relative fairness of the parties' obligations. Indicia of substantive unconscionability include one-sided terms that oppress or unfairly surprise an innocent party, an overall imbalance in the obligations and rights imposed by the bargain, and significant cost-price disparity. Maxwell. Unconscionability is determined as of the time the parties entered into the contract.

In refusing to rescind the sale on the basis of unconscionability, the trial court stated that, "[w]hile the results of the transaction may seem unconscionable to the [Estate] in hindsight, the terms of the contract certainly were not." We agree. The transaction involved no negotiation, the Estate dictated the terms of the contract by naming a price for each painting, and Carl paid the asking prices. " 'Courts should not assume an overly paternalistic attitude toward the parties to a contract by relieving one or another of them of the consequences of what is at worst a bad bargain * * * and in declaring the [contract] at issue here unconscionable, we would be doing exactly that.'

Affirmed.

QUESTIONS AND NOTE

1. Questions about the facts

   1.1. Is it relevant that Judith McKenzie-Larson "was not qualified to appraise fine art"?

   1.2. Is it relevant that the Estate settled with Judith McKenzie-Larson because she had no assets?

2. Questions about law

   2.1. How would the court have decided this case if Judith McKenzie-Larson was qualified to appraise fine art and had made a mistake?

   2.2. How would the court that decided *Sherwood v. Walker* decide this case?

   2.3. Recall that the Michigan Supreme Court rejected the test *in Sherwood v. Walker* as "inexact and confusing" and adopted the rules in the *Restatement (Second) of Contracts*? Is the Restatement less "inexact and confusing" than *Sherwood v. Walker*?

3. Note

   According to Professors Gideon Parchomovosky, Peter Siegelman and Steve Thel, *Sherwood v. Walke*r is a "classic windfall problem . . . Who should get the additional value from the cow's unexpected fertility? . . . We propose that as a matter of both efficiency and fairness, the value should have been split between the parties. Ex ante, the likelihood of the cow being fertile was very low and thus did not justify a contractual provision for this contingency. This in turn implies that there was no principled reason to favor either party and many reasons to share the windfall on fairness grounds." Gideon Parchomovsky, Peter Siegelman, Steve Thiel, *Of Equal Wrongs and Half Rights*, 82 NYU L.REV. 738, 740–41 (2007).

4. **You Be the Lawyer!**

   Note that the phrase "As they [the Rices] had done in the past" in the third paragraph of the opinion. If you were the Rices' attorney, would you have mentioned in your pleadings that the Rices had previously bought and sold art and had previously sent pictures of paintings they had purchased to Christie's?

In *Sherwood* and *Estate of Nelson*, the courts considered the argument that a mutual mistake should be a defense to enforcement of an agreement. Unilateral mistake occurs when only one party to the agreement has an erroneous assumption concerning an important factual aspect of the deal that makes the deal far less favorable to them than they had assumed.

The following excerpt from the Restatement (Second) of Contracts section 153 provides a somewhat different rule for relief for unilateral mistaken and an explanation for its different rule for unilateral mistake than its rule for mutual mistake:

§ 153 When Mistake of One Party Makes a Contract Voidable

Where a mistake of one party at the time a contract was made as to a basic assumption on which he made the contract has a material effect on the agreed exchange of performances that is adverse to him, the contract is voidable by him if he does not bear the risk of the mistake under the rule stated in § 154, and

(a) the effect of the mistake is such that enforcement of the contract would be unconscionable, or

(b) the other party had reason to know of the mistake or his fault caused the mistake.

Comment:

a. *Rationale.* Courts have traditionally been reluctant to allow a party to avoid a contract on the ground of mistake, even as to a basic assumption, if the mistake was not shared by the other party. Nevertheless, relief has been granted where the other party actually knew (see §§ 160, 161) or had reason to know of the mistake at the time the contract was made or where his fault caused the mistake. There has, in addition, been a growing willingness to allow avoidance where the consequences of the mistake are so grave that enforcement of the contract would be unconscionable."

The next case involves a situation "where the consequences of the mistake are so grave that the enforcement of the contract would be unconscionable but the contract is nonetheless held to be enforceable.

QUESTIONS BEFORE THE CASE

1. What was Jean Simes' mistake?
2. Was the mistake in this case "made as to a basic assumption on which the contract was made"?

GRENALL V. UNITED OF OMAHA LIFE INSURANCE COMPANY

Court of Appeals of California, First District
165 Cal.App.4th 188, 80 Cal.Rptr.3d 609 (2008)

[Jean M. Simes (Simes) died of cancer less than four months after purchasing an annuity that provided for monthly benefit payments as long as she lived. On October 2, 2001, Simes paid a single premium of $321,131. United then issued a policy for a single premium immediate annuity, effective the date of Simes' application. On January 25, 2002, after receiving three benefit payments, Simes was diagnosed with ovarian cancer. She died less than a week later on January 30, 2002.

The administrators of her estate (the Estate), sued to rescind the annuity, alleging a mistake of fact, namely, that Simes was unaware at the time of the contract that she was terminally ill. The trial court granted summary judgment in favor of the issuing company, defendant United of Omaha Life Insurance Company (United). The Estate appealed. United filed a motion for sanctions with its respondent's brief.]

STEIN, J.:

The facts on which the Estate relied below purport to show the following: (1) Simes did not know at the time of her application and during the statutory rescission period that she had terminal ovarian cancer that would result in her death four months later; (2) Simes's illness affected her ability to make decisions; and (3) Simes did not receive a copy of the annuity policy until mid-November 2001. The sole issue argued by the Estate on appeal is whether these facts provide a legal basis for rescission of the life annuity contract based on a mistake of fact. We hold, as a matter of law, that they do not, for the following reasons.

California law permits rescission of a contract when a party's consent is given by mistake. On this basis, the Estate asserts a right to rescind the annuity policy, alleging that Simes would not have entered the contract but for a mistake of fact, specifically, the terminal illness she did not know she had. A mistake of fact may consist of a "[b]elief in the present existence of a thing material to the contract, which does not exist." (Civ. Code, § 1577.) The alleged mistake therefore may be characterized as Simes's erroneous belief at the time of the contract that she was in good health and had a reasonable life expectancy.

A mistake of this nature does not support a claim for rescission. The Estate asserts a unilateral mistake and offers no evidence that United had reason to know of or caused the mistake. Accordingly, to prevail at trial, the Estate would have been required to prove the following: (1) Simes was mistaken regarding a basic assumption upon which she made the contract; (2) the mistake materially affected the agreed exchange of performances in a way that was adverse to Simes; (3) Simes did not bear the risk of the mistake; and (4) the effect of the mistake was such that enforcement of the contract would be unconscionable. The facts on which the Estate relies demonstrate that it cannot establish the third of these elements.

We conclude, based on the nature of the contract and the alleged mistake, that Simes bore the risk of the mistake, as a matter of law. A contracting party bears the risk of a mistake when the agreement so provides or when the party is aware of having only limited knowledge of the facts relating to the mistake but treats this limited knowledge as sufficient. Additionally, the court may allocate the risk to a party because it is reasonable under the circumstances to do so. The contract in this case does not expressly assign the risk of the alleged mistake. Nonetheless, parties who contract for "life contingent" benefits necessarily do so based on limited knowledge of the very facts about which Simes was mistaken. We cannot fix the length of our lives or even the state of our health with certainty, and the parties knew that their expectations in this regard were at best an educated guess.

The allocation of this risk to Simes is reasonable because such risks are an inherent part of life annuity contracts, which reflect, at their essence, a longevity wager measured by average life expectancy. (See Rest.2d Contracts, § 154, illus. 3: reasonable allocation of risk that annuitant has incurable disease and will live no more than a year.) Annuitants who survive the average life expectancy receive benefits beyond the premium; those who die earlier do not recoup their investments. Both risks are contemplated by the parties and, indeed, are an integral part of their bargain.

* * *

Our sister states recognize that allocation of the risk to the annuitant in these circumstances is not only reasonable but a practical necessity. * * * In light of these authorities, we hold that Simes bore the risk of the alleged mistake regarding her health and life expectancy at the time of the annuity contract. Because the Estate cannot establish an essential element of its rescission claim, summary judgment is proper. Accordingly, we need not discuss the other elements of this claim or decide the additional grounds for affirmance urged by United in its respondent's brief and its related motion to dismiss.

Finally, although we reject the Estate's arguments, because there is no California authority directly on point, we do not find them so wholly devoid of merit as to warrant the imposition of sanctions.

QUESTIONS

1. Question about the facts

 1.1. What was the Jean Simes Estate's "best" fact?

 1.2. Do we know whether Jean Simes was examined by her physican immediately prior to her purchasing the annuity? Is that relevant to this litigation?

 1.3. Did we know whether United knew, at the time of contract, that Simes was terminally ill? Was that relevant?

2. Question about the law

 2.1. Why didn't the California court rule for the Estate on the ground that the "effect of the mistake is such that enforcement of the contract would be unconscionable"?

 2.2. Mutual mistake and unilateral mistake: Why is *Grenall* a "unilateral mistake" case and *Estate of Nelson* a "mutual mistake" case? Would the holding of *Estate of Nelson* have been different if the court had treated the facts as unilateral mistake and applied *Restatement (Second) Contracts* section 153?

 2.3. Unilateral mistake and unconscionability: How is the law of unilateral mistake similar to and different from the law of unconscionability? The California Supreme Court provides this possible, partial answer:

> The standards of unconscionability warranting rescission for mistake are similar to those for unconscionability * * * An unconscionable contract ordinarily involves both a procedural and a substantive element: (1) oppression or surprise due to unequal bargaining power, and (2) overly harsh or one-sided results) Nevertheless, " 'a sliding scale is invoked which disregards the regularity of the procedural process of the contract formation, that creates the terms, in proportion to the greater harshness or unreasonableness of the substantive terms themselves.' [Citations.]" (Ibid.) For example, the Restatement Second of Contracts states that "[i]nadequacy of consideration does not of itself invalidate a bargain, but gross disparity in the values exchanged may be an important factor in a determination that a contract is

unconscionable and may be sufficient ground, without more, for denying specific performance." (*Rest.2d Contracts, § 208*, com. c, p. 108.) In ascertaining whether rescission is warranted for a unilateral mistake of fact, substantive unconscionability often will constitute the determinative factor, because the oppression and surprise ordinarily results from the mistake—not from inequality in bargaining power. Accordingly, even though defendant is not the weaker party to the contract and its mistake did not result from unequal bargaining power, defendant was surprised by the mistake, and in these circumstances overly harsh or one-sided results are sufficient to establish unconscionability entitling defendant to rescission. Donovan v. RRL Corp, 27 P.3d 702, 723 (2001).

3. **You Be the Lawyer!**

If you had been the attorney for the Estate would have filed this Law suit? Would you have appealed the trial court's summary judgment decision?*

B. OTHER KINDS OF MISTAKES

Both *Estate of Nelson* and *Grenall v. United of Omaha Life Insurance Co*, involved mistaken assumption of existing facts. Contracting parties can make other kinds of mistakes such as computational blunders and clerical errors. Should computational blunders and clerical errors be treated the same as mistaken assumptions of existing facts?

Professor Chirelstein's answer is ""[I]t is plain that contract law needs a rule or principle that affords relief in cases involving clerical errors, arithmetical blunders, misidentifications of persons or property and the like. The rule, itself, however, needs to confined to cases of just that sort. . . ." MARVIN CHIRELSTEIN CONCEPTS AND CASE ANALYSIS IN THE LAW OF CONTRACTS 177 (7th ed 2013).

The next case provides questions, instead of a "plain" answer.

---

* It is not as if the Estate attorneys were classmates of Jimmy McGill at University of American Samoa Law School. One of the Estate's attorneys is a graduate of the University of Chicago Law School (albeit before "our" Epstein and even the famous Epstein taught there).

QUESTIONS BEFORE THE CASE

1. Who do you think *should* win? Should the court order Starboard to sell DePrince the diamond with a market price of $4,850,000 for $235,000, the contract price?
2. Who do you think will win after the Court of Appeal's remand?

DEPRINCE V. STARBOARD CRUISE SERVICES, INC.

District Court of Appeal of Florida
163 So.3d 586 (Ct App. Fla. 2015)

ROTHENBERG, J.

Thomas DePrince ("DePrince") appeals the trial court's order granting summary judgment in favor of Starboard Cruise Services, Inc. ("Starboard") on DePrince's claims against Starboard for breach of contract, specific performance, and conversion. Because we find that disputed issues of material fact remain to be resolved on all three counts of DePrince's complaint, we reverse and remand for further proceedings.

Historical Hollywood starlet Mae West once said, "I never worry about diets. The only carrots that interest me are the number of carats in a diamond." Thus, it appears quite likely that Ms. West would have been interested in the diamond in this case: a twenty carat diamond that Starboard offered to DePrince for a very low sum. As it turns out, the "too good to be true" price of the diamond was just that, and the price conveyed to DePrince was a mistake. Now DePrince wants his twenty carat diamond; Starboard wants out of its sales contract; and Starboard's supplier, who allegedly misquoted the price of the diamond upon which Starboard and DePrince relied, has not even been added as a party to the lawsuit. In short, this is truly a gem of a case.

FACTUAL BACKGROUND

DePrince embarked on a cruise from Miami in February 2013. During that cruise, DePrince visited an onboard jewelry shop that is wholly owned and operated by Starboard. When DePrince expressed some interest in a large loose diamond and specified to the sales manager of the store, Mihai Rusan ("Rusan"), that the stone should be between 15 and 20 carats, Rusan, who had never dealt with a diamond of such magnitude, sent an email inquiry to Starboard's corporate office in Miami ("the Miami Office").

Starboard maintains a consignment agreement with a supplier, Sophia Fiori ("Fiori"), that allows Starboard to obtain gemstones and jewelry for sale in its onboard stores. The consignment agreement between Starboard and Fiori specifies, in relevant part:

3. Title to the Consigned Merchandise shall at all times remain with Consignor until the time of its sale to customers of Consignee, whereupon the Consigned Merchandise shall be deemed to have been purchased from Consignor by Consignee.[3]

Upon receiving the email inquiry from Rusan, the Miami Office relayed the information to Fiori to determine whether Fiori could fill such an order should DePrince decide to purchase a diamond. Fiori responded to the Miami Office via email, informing Starboard that there were two diamonds of that size available. Fiori's email described the diamonds precisely as follows:

1. **EMERALD CUT 20.64 carats D VVS2 GIA VG Price $235,000**
2. **EMERALD CUT 20.73 carats E VVS2 GIA EX EX FNT Price $245,000**

The Miami Office relayed this information to Rusan via email exactly as Fiori had typed it. Rusan notified DePrince of the availability of the size of the diamond he was interested in purchasing and the pricing information contained in the email, telling him that the purchase prices for the diamonds were $235,000 and $245,000 respectively.

DePrince told Rusan that he was interested, but that he would like to take some time to think about the purchase. That night, DePrince spoke with his life partner, Vernon Crawford, a certified gemologist who was on the cruise with DePrince, and also DePrince's sister, Carolyn DePrince, who holds the highest available degree in gemology. Both advised DePrince against making the purchase, telling him that the sale price was too good to be true and that the price for a diamond that large should be at least $2 million.

DePrince, however, ignored their advice and opted to complete the transaction. DePrince returned to Starboard's onboard jewelry store and placed a special mail purchase order for the 20.64 carat diamond the next day. Rusan prepared and signed a one-page sales agreement that listed the total price for the diamond at $235,000 plus a $25 shipping charge. DePrince made an initial down payment of $125,000 on the spot and paid the balance ($110,025) the next day. * * *

Soon after the sale was completed, Starboard learned that Fiori's $235,000 price quote in the email was the **per carat** price for the diamond rather than the **total price** for the diamond ($4,850,400), and thus, Starboard had inadvertently contracted to sell the diamond to DePrince for less than 1/20th of the diamond's actual value. Five days after the sales agreement was executed, Starboard contacted DePrince via telephone to

[3] "Consigned Merchandise" refers to the jewelry items ordered by Starboard; the "Consignor" refers to Fiori; and the "Consignee" refers to Starboard.

explain the situation, stating that the price on the sales agreement was "seriously in error" due to the mix-up in the email. Starboard offered discounted future cruise rates to DePrince to compensate him for the inconvenience, but DePrince demanded that the sale be completed as specified in the sales agreement. Starboard unilaterally reversed the charges on DePrince's credit card to refund him all the money he had paid and then repudiated the sales agreement, informing DePrince that it would not be shipping the diamond as they had originally agreed. * * *

Thereafter, DePrince filed a complaint against Starboard alleging counts for specific performance, breach of contract, and conversion. * * *

Starboard moved for summary judgment on the ground that there had clearly been a unilateral mistake in the pricing, and, after hearing argument on that issue, the trial court granted summary judgment against DePrince on all his claims. * * *

This appeal followed.

ANALYSIS

* * *

We do not agree with the trial court that there are no genuine issues of material fact such that Starboard is entitled to judgment as a matter of law on any of these claims. Thus, Starboard was not entitled to summary judgment. * * *

This Court has held that in order to rescind an otherwise-valid contract based on a unilateral mistake, the party seeking to avoid the contract must show:

> (1) [T]he mistake was induced by the party seeking to benefit from the mistake, (2) there is no negligence or want of due care on the part of the party seeking a return to the status quo, (3) denial of release from the agreement would be inequitable, and (4) the position of the opposing party has not so changed that granting the relief would be unjust.

Examining the facts as alleged and supported by DePrince, Starboard did not conclusively demonstrate either of the first two prongs of this analysis.

First, Starboard presented no evidence that DePrince induced it into making the pricing mistake. The primary focus of Starboard's argument, both at the summary judgment hearing and in its brief, was that DePrince must have known of the mistake in pricing due to his background as a former antiques and jewelry dealer and the advice he received from his gemologist partner and his sister. DePrince, however, denied that he knew there had been a pricing mistake in his affidavit, which is sufficient at the summary judgment phase of the proceedings to create a genuine issue of material fact. More importantly, we note that even if DePrince had known that the price he was quoted to purchase the diamond was in error, knowledge of an error is markedly different than inducement of that error. Because Starboard presented no evidence that the pricing mistake was induced by DePrince, the trial court clearly erred by granting summary judgment in Starboard's favor under the four-prong test.

Second, there is a factual dispute regarding the second prong of the unilateral mistake standard: that the party seeking to avoid the contract (Starboard) was not inexcusably negligent or failed to act with due care. DePrince avers in both his complaint and affidavit that Starboard did **not** act with due care when it sold him the diamond. Starboard claims it simply provided DePrince with the quote provided to it by Fiori, and that it did not act negligently. Thus, whether Starboard made a reasonable and understandable mistake or acted negligently in its handling of the sale is a disputed issue of fact, and, because questions involving reasonableness and negligence determinations are highly factual inquiries upon which reasonable people could disagree, they are rarely appropriately resolved on summary judgment. This case is no exception.

* * *

Florida's new jury instruction, which was adopted in June 2013, *In re Standard Jury Instructions—Contract and Bus. Cases,* 116 So.3d 284, 324 (Fla.2013), pertaining to unilateral mistake states the test in yet another substantially different way:

> To establish [the defense of unilateral mistake], (defendant) must prove all of the following:
>
> 1. (Defendant) was mistaken about (insert description of mistake) at the time the parties made the contract;
>
> 2. [The effect of the mistake is such that enforcement of the contract would be unconscionable]
>
> [or]
>
> [(Claimant) had reason to know of the mistake or [he][she][it] caused the mistake.]
>
> and
>
> 3. (Defendant) did not bear the risk of mistake. A party bears the risk of a mistake when
>
> [the parties' agreement assigned the risk to [him][her][it]]
>
> [or]
>
> [[he][she][it] was aware, at the time the contract was made, that [he][she] [it] had only limited knowledge about the facts relating to the mistake but decided to proceed with the contract].

Fla. Std. Jury Instr. (Civ.) 416.26 (first alteration added).

This instruction is nearly identical to the formulation of the unilateral mistake defense found in the Restatement (Second) of Contracts. *See* Restatement (Second) of Contracts §§ 153, 154 (1979). However, this particular three-prong test has not been adopted or cited by any Florida decision to date.

"Standard jury instructions are not binding precedent," although they can be quite persuasive and instructive "[i]n the absence of a definitive case." *BellSouth Telecomm., Inc. v. Meeks*, 863 So.2d 287, 292 (Fla.2003). In this instance, however, because there are definitive cases in this jurisdiction, we are bound by those cases. And in those cases, this Court clearly applied the four-prong test.

Even if jury instruction 416.26 was the law in Florida, Starboard should not have prevailed on its summary judgment motion. That is because even if DePrince had been aware of the mistake and enforcement of the contract would be unconscionable—either or both of which would satisfy the second prong of the analysis—the third prong requires that the party seeking to assert the unilateral mistake defense show that it did not bear the risk of the mistake. Fla. Std. Jury Instr. (Civ.) 416.26. A party can be found to bear the risk of its mistake if the contract expressly assigns that risk to the party or if that party is aware at the time of the contract's formation that it had only limited knowledge about the facts relating to the mistake but decided to proceed with the contract anyway. The contract in this case does not assign the risk to either party, and factual questions certainly remain as to whether Starboard should have known at the time it formed the contract that it had insufficient information to facilitate such an expensive transaction. Indeed, Rusan himself stated in his deposition that he had never dealt with a diamond this large. Because this factual question remains, summary judgment would also have been inappropriate under the new jury instruction.

* * *

We also note that, for some inexplicable reason, Fiori has not been made a party to this suit. It is difficult to imagine how DePrince's and Starboard's rights and obligations can be completely established and redressed without Fiori's involvement, particularly if specific performance is found to be a proper remedy. Importantly, both parties in their briefs have at times suggested that Fiori is the party who was actually negligent by way of its price quote, which omitted a "per carat" designation. Fiori can undoubtedly shed light on who, if anyone, should shoulder the blame of the price mistake, as well as explain industry standards and its pattern of dealings with Starboard.

We therefore conclude that while some may claim that diamonds are forever, the same cannot be said of the trial court's summary judgment order.

Reversed and remanded.

QUESTIONS

1. Questions about the facts of the case

   1.1. Was there a mistaken factual assumption in this case?

   1.2. Was the mistake in this case a mutual mistake or a unilateral mistake?

   1.3. Did DePrince know about the mistake?

2. Questions about the law

   2.1. In determining whether to rescind a contract because of mistake, do Florida courts apply the same four-prong test to all kinds of mistakes? To all kinds of unilateral mistakes?

   2.2. How does the Florida four-prong test differ from *Restatement (Second) of Contracts* section 153?

   2.3. How does *Restatement (Second) of Contracts* section 153 which was summarized in the *DePrince* case and reproduced on page 451 differ from *Restatement (Second) of Contracts* section 155 which is reproduced below:

   § 155 When Mistake of Both Parties as to Written Expression Justifies Reformation

   Where a writing that evidences or embodies an agreement in whole or in part fails to express the agreement because of a mistake of both parties as to the contents or effect of the writing, the court may at the request of a party reform the writing to express the agreement, except to the extent that rights of third parties such as good faith purchasers for value will be unfairly affected.

   Comment:

   a. *Scope.* The province of reformation is to make a writing express the agreement that the parties intended it should. Under the rule stated in this Section, reformation is available when the parties, having reached an agreement and having then attempted to reduce it to writing, fail to express it correctly in the writing.

   2.4. Is the following statement from Professor Corbin's treatise helpful to DePrince: "Suppose * * * a bidding contractor makes an offer to supply specified goods or to do specified work for a definitely named price, and that he was caused to name this price by an antecedent error of computation. If, before acceptance, the offeree knows, or has reason to know, that a material error has been made, he is seldom mean enough to accept; and if he does accept, the courts have no difficulty in throwing him out. He is not permitted 'to snap up' such an offer and profit thereby. If, without knowledge of the mistake and before any revocation, he has accepted the offer, it is natural for him to feel a sense of disappointment at not getting a good bargain, when the offeror insists on withdrawal; but a just and reasonable man will not insist upon profiting by the other's mistake. There are now many decisions to the effect that if the error was a substantial one and notice is given before the other party has made such a change of position that he cannot be put substantially in status quo, the bargain is voidable and rescission will be decreed."

3 ARTHUR LINTON CORBIN, CORBIN ON CONTRACTS § 609, at 680–82 (1960).

2.5. Unilateral mistake and nondisclosure: If B is making an agreement with A and B realizes that A is making a mistake, does B have a duty to disclose the mistake to A? How is a fact pattern involving a known unilateral mistake different from a fact pattern involving nondisclosure?

Professor Michael Borden discusses these questions in a law review article: "This paper will examine some theoretical aspects of contractual non-disclosure and the related doctrine of unilateral mistake. These two legal rubrics are conceptually similar; each is concerned with the degree to which parties must communicate their understandings about the nature of the contract into which they are about to enter. If one party fails to reveal enough information, the other party may enter into the agreement under a misunderstanding and consequently may attempt to avoid contractual liability on the basis of mistake or on a theory of nondisclosure. The law of contracts clearly attaches a great deal of importance to ensuring that contracting parties have a mutual understanding about their agreement—a meeting of the minds—for that is the cornerstone of mutual assent. Indeed, one of the foundational theoretical goals of contract doctrine is to establish rules of law that will induce parties to reveal information that will reduce the cost of contracting and minimize the negative effects of breach." Michael J. Borden, *Mistake and Nondisclosure in a Model of Two-Sided Informational Inputs*, 73 MO. L. REV. 667 (2007).

3. **You Be the Lawyer!**

You are representing Starboard. After the District Court of Appeals issues its opinion reversing and remanding, your client asks you whether it should settle and, if so, on what terms.

CHAPTER 5

WHAT ARE THE TERMS OF THE DEAL?

■ ■ ■

Up to this point, this book has focused on whether there is a contract. From here on, we assume, for the most part, that a contract exists.

In this chapter, we focus on the content of the contract. More specifically to the questions of (1) what are the terms of the contract, and (2) what do those contract terms require from the parties.

Lawyers deal with these questions much more frequently than they deal with questions of whether there was a contract. For the deal lawyer, her daily focus is the task of drafting language that a future court or jury will construe in the way her client intended. For the trial lawyer, the parallel focus is devising strategies that will lead to a present court or a jury to accept her client's position with respect to the terms of a contract drafted long ago by another lawyer. To accomplish either of these goals, the deft lawyer will know and understand how courts will approach and answer the two questions set forth above.

---

1. WHERE DO TERMS COME FROM?

As stated on page 12, there is a tendency to confuse the written paper signed by the parties with the contract that binds them. It is an easy mistake to make; everyone calls the signed paper "the contract." But that paper is, at best, only *evidence* of the contract. That is, the contract is represented by that paper; it is *not* that paper. Otherwise, if you tore the paper up (or spilled coffee on it) you would also tear up or water down the parties' obligations. While that may be the case with some types of obligations (such as checks or other negotiable instruments), that is not the case with regular, everyday contracts.

So what is a contract? To go back again to the beginning of this book, according to the *Restatement (Second) of Contracts*, it is "a promise or set of promises for the breach of which the law gives a remedy, or the performance of which the law in some way recognizes as a duty." *Restatement (Second) of Contracts* § 1.

How do courts go about determining "the promises, or set of promises," and the terms that affect those promises?

As recognized in *Mellon Bank v. Aetna Business Credit, Inc.*, 619 F.2d 1009 (3d Cir. 1980):

> In construing a contract, a court's paramount consideration is the intent of the parties . . . . It would be helpful if judges were psychics who could delve into the parties' minds to ascertain their or, oiginal intent. However, courts neither claim nor possess psychic power.

Where to start? An obvious place is the terms that the parties themselves used. But to quote Peggy Lee (she's from Epstein's generation, so don't freak if you don't know who she is), "is that all there is"?

Of course not. This section tries to collect all the sources typically consulted to supply or refine contractual terms. In this effort, we look at:

1. The words actually used by the parties, and what those words typically mean;

2. Words, practices, or meanings which are implied in contracts due to the context in which the contract was formed or performed, such as trade usage, course of performance, and course of dealing;

3. Words, practices, or meanings which courts imply in contracts to fill in gaps typically left open or to achieve certain public policies; and

4. Words, practices, or meanings that statutory law implies or inserts in contracts as a matter of public policy or common sense.

Not surprisingly, these four divisions correspond to the four subsections (A, B, C and D) of this Section 1. That's so easy, even Markell can follow it!

A. PARTY-SUPPLIED TERMS: IS THAT ALL THERE IS?

Bereft of psychic powers, where do judges find the promises collectively recognized as the contract? There are many sources. The most important, however, is the words the parties used to express their agreement, be they written words or spoken words. As noted in *Mellon Bank:*

> The strongest external sign of agreement between contracting parties is the words they use in their written contract. Thus, the sanctity of the written words of the contract is embedded in the law of contract interpretation. As it has been variously put:

> (A) court will make no inference or give any construction to the terms of a written contract that may be in conflict with the clearly expressed language of the written agreement . . .
>
> and
>
> A court is not authorized to construe a contract in such a way as to modify the plain meaning of its words, under the guise of interpretation.
>
> and
>
> When a written contract is clear and unequivocal, its meaning must be determined by its contents alone.

Mellon Bank, 619 F.2d at 1009–10.

This passage makes it sound as if interpretation of contracts looks solely to the parties' words. But this view has long been rejected, dismissed as assuming we exist in:

> that lawyer's Paradise where all words have a fixed, precisely ascertained meaning; where men may express their purposes, not only with accuracy, but with fulness; and where, if the writer has been careful, a lawyer, having a document referred to him, may sit in his chair, inspect the text, and answer all questions without raising his eyes.

JAMES BRADLEY THAYER, PRELIMINARY TREATISE ON EVIDENCE AT THE COMMON LAW 428–29 (1898).

We don't live in that Paradise. If we did, this Chapter would be a lot shorter—and maybe Epstein could get through it without nodding off.

But even if we need more than what the parties have uttered, words are where we start. In this course, how a word is used, and what a contract's terms require, frame whether a party to a contract is a complying angel or a breacher who should burn in hell.

B. CONTEXT-SUPPLIED TERMS: COURSE OF PERFORMANCE, COURSE OF DEALING, AND USAGE OF TRADE

In addition to the words the parties chose, all major restatments or reorderings of contract law incorporate context in the rules used to determine the meaning of contracts. This includes the U.C.C., the

Restatement, the international *Convention on the Sale of Goods* (*CISG*),* and the *UNIDROIT Principles of International Commercial Contracts*.**

1. The U.C.C. and Section 1–303

The U.C.C. recognizes that the context in which a contract is made can influence how the parties intended their words to be understood. In particular, Section 1–303 set out below explains the term "usage of trade" as well as the terms "course of performance" and "course of dealing."

§ 1–303. Course of Performance, Course of Dealing, and Usage of Trade.

(a) A "course of performance" is a sequence of conduct between the parties to a particular transaction that exists if:

(1) the agreement of the parties with respect to the transaction involves repeated occasions for performance by a party; and

(2) the other party, with knowledge of the nature of the performance and opportunity for objection to it, accepts the performance or acquiesces in it without objection.

(b) A "course of dealing" is a sequence of conduct concerning previous transactions between the parties to a particular transaction that is fairly to be regarded as establishing a common basis of understanding for interpreting their expressions and other conduct.

(c) A "usage of trade" is any practice or method of dealing having such regularity of observance in a place, vocation, or trade as to justify an expectation that it will be observed with respect to the transaction in question. The existence and scope of such a usage must be proved as facts. If it is established that such a usage is embodied in a trade code or similar record, the interpretation of the record is a question of law.

(d) A course of performance or course of dealing between the parties, or usage of trade in the vocation, or trade in which they are

* *CISG*? What is the *CISG*? It is an international convention drafted by UNCITRAL, the trade arm of the United Nations. It is also the law of the United States. The United States Senate ratified the *CISG* in 1986, and the United States deposited its instrument of ratification at the United Nations Headquarters in New York on December 11, 1986. *See* Preface to Convention, reprinted at 15 U.S.C. App. 52 (1997). The Convention entered into force between the United States and the other States on January 1, 1988. We'll look some more at the *CISG* in Section 2.D. below.

** *UNIDROIT*? What is *UNIDROIT*? It is the *Institut International Pour L'unification Du Droit Privé* (International Institute for the Unification of Private Law). It is a Rome-based, intergovernmental organization, devoted to the harmonization of private international law. UNIDROIT dates from 1926, and is one of the last remaining organizations linked to the ill-fated League of Nations formed after World War I. The United States joined UNIDROIT in 1964.

Its principles of international commercial contracts law were first published in 1994. A second, enlarged edition was published in 2004, and an even larger third edition was published in 2010.

engaged or of which they are, or should be, aware is relevant in ascertaining the meaning of the parties' agreement, may give particular meaning to specific terms of the agreement, and may supplement or qualify the terms of the agreement. * * *

(e) Except as otherwise provided in subsection (f), the express terms of an agreement and any applicable course of performance, course of dealing, or usage of trade must be construed whenever reasonable as consistent with each other. If such a construction is unreasonable: (1) express terms prevail over course of performance, course of dealing, and usage of trade; (2) course of performance prevails over course of dealing and usage of trade; and (3) course of dealing prevails over usage of trade. * * *

---

2. The *Restatement* and Other Summaries of Contract Law

The *Restatement (Second) of Contracts* gets in on this classification as well. Section 222(1) states that "A usage of trade is a usage having such regularity of observance in a place, vocation, or trade as to justify an expectation that it will be observed with respect to a particular agreement. It may include a system of rules regularly observed even though particular rules are changed from time to time." The *Restatement* also covers course of performance and course of dealing in Sections 221 and 223, respectively.

The *CISG* also makes references to such practices, as shown below:

Article 9, Convention on the International Sale of Goods

(1) The parties are bound by any usages to which they have agreed and by any practices which they have established between themselves.

(2) The parties are considered, unless otherwise agreed, to have impliedly made applicable to their contract or its formation a usage of which the parties knew, or ought to have known, and which in international trade is widely known to, and regularly observed by, parties to contracts of the type involved in the particular trade concerned.

The *UNIDROIT Principles of International Commercial Contracts*, also recognize context. They state that the "contractual obligations of the parties may be express or implied" (Article 5.1.1), and that implied obligations "stem from: (a) the nature and purpose of the contract; (b) practices established between the parties and usages; (c) good faith and fair dealing; (d) reasonableness." (Article 5.1.2).

PROBLEMS ON TRADE USAGE AND COURSE OF DEALING

1. Under the U.C.C., what is the difference between a course of dealing and a course of performance? Can you ever have a course of performance in a contract to sell just one item (such as a car)?
2. Under either the U.C.C., the *Restatement*, or the *CISG*,* do you have to be a merchant to be bound by a usage of trade? If not, how do you protect yourself as a novice when buying something for which there is a recognized market and recognized practices of trade?
3. Note that under the U.C.C. and the *Restatement*, a usage of trade may arise with respect to a "place, vocation, or trade." What is the difference among these three items? Does the *CISG* have a similar broad application?
4. You go to a bakery and order a "baker's dozen" of donuts (Markell's favorite). You get twelve donuts. Do you have an action for breach?
5. You want to do some carpentry. The guy at Home Depot says you need "two by fours" to build what you want. He sells you 20 of them. When you measure them, however, they are not two inches by four inches; rather they are 1½ inches by 3½ inches. Do you have an action for breach?

Note that Section 1–303(e) of the U.C.C. tries to prioritize conflicts as among course of performance, course of dealing, trade usage and express terms. Is this a satisfactory ordering?

C. COURT-SUPPLIED TERMS

Clients are often not tidy in their contracting. They bring their lawyers documents that the lawyers themselves would never draft. Even though the parties have acted as though there was a complete contract, a later reading reveals gaps and holes. How do courts fill these (or do they)?

---

1. Terms Implied by Courts to Effectuate Assumed Intent

What happens if the parties' written agreement lacks something legally necessary? The stage is now set for Cardozo's answer.

---

* The *CISG* does not apply to sales of goods bought for personal, family or household use, Article 2(a), but the U.C.C. does not have a similar limitation. So for this problem, assume that you are an entrepreneur seeking to buy goods for your business.

QUESTIONS BEFORE THE CASE

1. What duties do the words of the written contract impose upon Wood? Upon Lucy?
2. What do you think was the motivation for Wood and Lucy to enter into the contract in the first place?

WOOD V. LUCY, LADY DUFF-GORDON

Court of Appeals of New York
222 N.Y. 88, 118 N.E. 214 (1917)

CARDOZO, J.:

The defendant styles herself "a creator of fashions." Her favor helps a sale. Manufacturers of dresses, millinery and like articles are glad to pay for a certificate of her approval. The things which she designs, fabrics, parasols and what not, have a new value in the public mind when issued in her name. She employed the plaintiff to help her to turn this vogue into money. He was to have the exclusive right, subject always to her approval, to place her indorsements on the designs of others. He was also to have the exclusive right to place her own designs on sale, or to license others to market them. In return, she was to have one-half of "all profits and revenues" derived from any contracts he might make. The exclusive right was to last at least one year from April 1, 1915, and thereafter from year to year unless terminated by notice of ninety days. The plaintiff says that he kept the contract on his part, and that the defendant broke it. She placed her indorsement on fabrics, dresses and millinery without his knowledge, and withheld the profits. He sues her for the damages, and the case comes here on demurrer.

The agreement of employment is signed by both parties. It has a wealth of recitals. The defendant insists, however, that it lacks the elements of a contract. She says that the plaintiff does not bind himself to anything. It is true that he does not promise in so many words that he will use reasonable efforts to place the defendant's indorsements and market her designs. We think, however, that such a promise is fairly to be implied. The law has outgrown its primitive stage of formalism when the precise word was the sovereign talisman, and every slip was fatal. It takes a broader view to-day. A promise may be lacking, and yet the whole writing may be "instinct with an obligation," imperfectly expressed. * * * If that is so, there is a contract.

The implication of a promise here finds support in many circumstances. The defendant gave an *exclusive* privilege. She was to have no right for at least a year to place her own indorsements or market her own designs except through the agency of the plaintiff. The acceptance of the exclusive agency was an assumption of its duties. * * * We are not to suppose that one party was to be placed at the mercy of the other. * * * Many other terms of the agreement point the same way. We are told at the outset by way of recital that "the said Otis F. Wood possesses a business organization adapted to the placing of such indorsements as the said Lucy, Lady Duff-Gordon has approved." The implication is that the plaintiff's business organization will be used for the purpose for which it is adapted. But the terms of the defendant's compensation are even more significant. Her sole compensation for the grant of an exclusive agency is to be one-half of all the profits resulting from the plaintiff's efforts. Unless he gave his efforts, she could never get anything. Without an implied promise, the transaction cannot have such business "efficacy as both parties must have intended that at all events it should have" (Bowen, L. J., in *The Moorcock*, 14 P. D. 64, 68). But the contract does not stop there. The plaintiff goes on to promise that he will account monthly for all moneys received by him, and that he will take out all such patents and copyrights and trademarks as may in his judgment be necessary to protect the rights and articles affected by the agreement. It is true, of course, as the Appellate Division has said, that if he was under no duty to try to market designs or to place certificates of indorsement, his promise to account for profits or take out copyrights would be valueless. But in determining the intention of the parties, the promise *has* a value. It helps to enforce the conclusion that the plaintiff *had* some duties. His promise to pay the defendant one-half of the profits and revenues resulting from the exclusive agency and to render accounts monthly, was a promise to use reasonable efforts to bring profits and revenues into existence. For this conclusion, the authorities are ample * * *.

The judgment of the Appellate Division should be reversed, and the order of the Special Term affirmed, with costs in the Appellate Division and in this court.

QUESTIONS AND NOTE

1. Questions about the facts of this case

   1.1. Why do you think the contract lacked any express obligation on the part of Wood to market the designs?

   1.2. Note that Wood brought this lawsuit. Why do you think Lady Duff-Gordon gave her endorsement to others without Wood's knowledge? Didn't she know that Wood would find out?

2. Questions about the law

   2.1. What is Lucy's argument as to why she was entitled to break her promise without liability to Wood?

2.2. Assume that Lady Duff-Gordon had not made another deal, and the case is instead Lady Duff-Gordon suing Wood for breach of contract because Wood hadn't done a darn thing to market Lucy's fashions. What result?

3. Note

In *Wood v. Lucy*, Cardozo states: "The law has outgrown its primitive stage of formalism when the precise word was the sovereign talisman, and every slip was fatal. It takes a broader view to-day." This is a hallmark of Cardozo: catchy language describing a common situation. But think about what it says. Is it true? Think back to our earlier materials about the required level of definiteness for a communication to be an offer. Have your views changed since then?

4. **You Be the Lawyer!**

Wood comes to you to draft his next employment contract. Draft a one-line clause to be inserted in his contract that would avoid the type of litigation he was embroiled in with Lucy, Lady Duff-Gordon.

Lady Duff-Gordon had a curious career, as indicated by the following excerpt:*

DANIEL WM. FESSLER, *TEACHING NOTES FOR FESSLER & LOISEAUX'S CONTRACTS: MORALITY, ECONOMICS AND THE MARKETPLACE*

47–48 (1982)

For some reason I have become fascinated by Lady Duff-Gordon and over the years have collected a good deal of trivia concerning her exploits. The most famous affair involving Lady Duff grew out of her status as a passenger on the Titanic.** It seems that she was traveling with her husband, Sir Cosmo Duff-Gordon, and her maid. In the midst of history's greatest marine disaster, Lady Duff, Sir Cosmo, the maid and two other passengers managed to appropriate a life boat with a capacity of 34. They were accompanied by seven members of the crew! As they were rowed to safety amidst the heroism and the death of the men who volunteered to remain on board Lady Duff is said to have declared to her maid: "Oh look,

---

* For those who can't get enough of Lady Duff-Gordon, or who just want to see a picture of her, you can go to *Encyclopedia Titanica: First Class Passenger: Lady Duff-Gordon (Lucy Christiana Sutherland)* (http://www.encyclopedia-titanica.org/titanic-survivor/lady-duff-gordon.html). Eds.

** For the sharp-eyed, Lady Duff-Gordon is introduced to Leonardo DeCaprio's character in the movie, *Titanic*, in the scene in which Leonardo bluffs his way into the first-class dining room. Eds.

there goes my beautiful dressing gown." Later an Admiralty Court was to examine formal charges that Sir Cosmo had bribed members of the crew. It was established that Sir Cosmo had given £5 checks to the members of the crew on the life boat and had objected when one of the crew suggested that they go back in the attempt to pick up people who were in the sea and crying for help. Notwithstanding, the court acquitted Sir Cosmo of the charge of bribery. This acquittal shocked the press, perhaps because—or in spite of—Lady Duff's appearance in the court as a witness. In a special dispatch to the New York Times on May 21, 1912, we find the following description of a dramatic figure: "[She was] dressed entirely in black except for a white lace collar." Harold Spencer reported that her second day on the stand gave quite a different impression from that of the first:

> * * * she is a fair creation, daintily chiseled, graceful in movement, arresting in speech. Her voice is tuned to the siren's note, her little face is pale and plaintive, and her whole being is braced to the edge of victory over her accusers. The white aigrette of Friday last, erect and challenging, had given place to the sweep of a large black picture hat, shading her eyes to the left and drooping with hint of tears over the right shoulder. A collar of exquisite lace ripples down from the shapely neck to the waist, very white and vivid against the black dress.

My colleague, Jack Ayer, supplied some further information respecting her business activities:

> It was big. When she died in 1935 at the age of 72, the New York Times described her as a 'pioneer in bringing freedom and grace back to women's dress after the Victorian era'. She was a Canadian, daughter of one Douglas Sutherland, sister of Elinor Glyn, the sexy novelist, widow of one James S. Wallace. She married Sir Cosmo in 1900; but before that she had undertaken the dressmaking business which later spanned the hemispheres. At her peak, she operated in London, Paris, Chicago and New York. Her name became synonymous with glamour and high style. Among her injunctions:
>
>> A girl should never dress so that the dress subjects her personality.
>>
>> One should never make 'sex appeal' on the street. Wear black by all means.
>>
>> One should never wear skirts so short as to allow a bit of leg above the top of the boots.
>
> Her eye for fashion apparently did not translate into business sense. She went bankrupt in New York in 1922, and in London in 1924. At a bankruptcy inquiry in London, an examiner asked:

"Can you give me some particulars on your shareholders?" To which she replied: "It is all Greek to me. I don't know what a share is."

Her success as a glamour girl seems to have been coupled with something of a sullen contempt for society at large. Her New York troubles began with an accusation that she engaged in conspiracy to defraud customs laws. In 1919, she gained notoriety of a small sort by answering a creditor's inquiry for non-payment of a $1,500 breach of contract judgment (not Woods!) in person. She wore a pearl necklace with an estimated worth of $5,000, and testified that she drew $365 per week from her firm, Lucille, Inc., and another $100 per week from International Features Services. What did she do for the $100? "Nothing" she replied. Her examiner asked if she ever bought Liberty Bonds. She replied: "Why should I buy any? This country means nothing to me. I have nothing but trouble over here. It is an awful country." She did add: "I believe I have one that my maid bought for me."

The plaintiff, Otis Wood, is almost as interesting. He was the son of Fernando Wood, the first Mayor of New York elected by the Tammany Hall machine.

Fernando Wood was a member of Congress during the Civil War and was a supporter of slavery. More relevant to this case, Fernando Wood played an important role in the appointment of Albert Cardozo, Benjamin Cardozo's father, to the New York Supreme Court and Albert Cardozo's later resignation from the bench after being confronted with impeachment for a ruling in favor of Fernando Wood in a fraud case.

More relevant still, before contracting with Lady Duff Gordon, Otis Wood had entered into an exclusive promotion agreement with Rose O'Neil, the inventor of the Kewpie Doll. That contract contained an explicit best efforts clause. *See generally* Victor Goldberg, FRAMING CONTRACT LAW: AN ECONOMIC PERSPECTIVE 43–73 (2006).

---

2. Terms Implied by Courts to Further Public Policy—The Implied Duty of Good Faith and Fair Dealing

In *Lucy,* Judge Cardozo's justification for implying terms was supplying what the parties surely forgot. In the cases in this part of the book, courts imply terms and conditions in contracts not because the parties forgot them, but either: (1) to achieve substantial justice, whatever that may ultimately mean; or (2) to supply terms that the parties would have agreed to had they thought about the matter at all.

When assessing either of these types of terms, ask yourself whether the implication of such terms is based on pure public policy—that is, whether they represent society's collective judgment as to what ought to be in every contract. Also ask yourself to what extent such implication is based on rough empiricism—that is, do they represent society's collective judgment as to what parties in similar transactions would usually insert if they thought about it?*

Early on in our studies, and as recently as the last case, we encountered assertions that contract law, or at least the enforcement of contracts, is infused and imbued with notions of good faith. The next few cases examine that concept in several different contexts.

QUESTIONS BEFORE THE CASE

1. What is the harm that Stokes and Felzien have suffered? Why won't DISH just give them a monetary rebate?
2. What does it mean to say that "all contracts are subject to an implied duty of good faith and fair dealing." Why "implied"? Why doesn't the law just require everyone to act in good faith all the time?

STOKES V. DISH NETWORK, L.L.C.

838 F.3d 948 (8th Cir. 2016)

LOKEN, CIRCUIT JUDGE.

DISH Network, L.L.C. ("DISH"), is a Colorado corporation that sells satellite television access packages nationwide. DISH's "carriage" agreement with Turner Network Sales, Inc., expired on October 21, 2014, and was not renewed until November 20, 2014. DISH's carriage agreement with FOX News Network L.L.C. expired on December 21, 2014, and was not renewed until January 15, 2015. DISH subscribers who had selected programming packages that included popular Turner and FOX News channels did not have access to those channels during these interruptions. Though DISH continued to provide hundreds of other channels, it did not provide complaining subscribers any form of monetary relief for the Turner and FOX News interruptions.

Neil Stokes and Craig Felzien, DISH subscribers since 2008 and 2000, respectively, commenced this action on behalf of themselves and a putative nationwide class of DISH subscribers (collectively, "Plaintiffs") seeking

* You also might ask yourself if you (or the judges deciding these cases) are in the best position to make that empirical call.

monetary relief for the Turner and FOX News services interruptions. Applying Colorado law, as the DISH Subscription Agreements expressly provide, the district court denied DISH's motion to dismiss Plaintiffs' claims for breach of contract and breach of the covenant of good faith and fair dealing. The court certified two questions for immediate interlocutory appeal under 28 U.S.C. § 1292(b). We granted a timely request to appeal the certified questions * * *

I. Relevant Contract Terms.

Plaintiffs subscribed to specific DISH access packages, paying in advance. They received Subscription Agreements after DISH installed satellite equipment in their homes, comprised of a Digital Home Advantage Plan Agreement ("Plan Agreement") and a Residential Customer Agreement ("RCA"). The certified questions on appeal turn on the following contract provisions. The Plan Agreement provides in relevant part:

> BY SIGNING BELOW YOU ACKNOWLEDGE AND AGREE THAT YOU HAVE RECEIVED, READ, UNDERSTAND, AND AGREE TO BE BOUND BY ALL OF THE TERMS AND CONDITIONS OF THIS AGREEMENT, INCLUDING . . . THE RESIDENTIAL CUSTOMER AGREEMENT . . . AND THAT THE FOLLOWING TERMS WERE DISCLOSED TO YOU PRIOR TO LEASE:
>
> . . .
>
> WE RESERVE THE RIGHT TO CHANGE PRICES, PACKAGES, AND PROGRAMMING AT ANY TIME, INCLUDING WITHOUT LIMITATION, DURING ANY TERM AGREEMENT PERIOD TO WHICH YOU HAVE AGREED.

The RCA provides in relevant part:

> 1. THE DISH NETWORK SERVICE
>
> . . .
>
> I. <u>Changes in Services Offered</u>. We may add, delete, rearrange and/or change any and all programming, programming packages and other Services that we offer, as well as the prices and fees related to such programming, programming packages and Services, at any time, including . . . during any term commitment period to which you have agreed. If a change affects you, we will notify you of such change and its effective date. In the event that we delete, rearrange or change any programming, programming packages or other Services, we have no obligation to replace or supplement such programming, programming packages or other Services. You are not entitled to any refund

because of deletion, rearrangement or change of any programming, programming packages or other Services.

7. LIMITATION OF OUR LIABILITY

A. INTERRUPTIONS AND DELAYS. NEITHER WE NOR OUR THIRD-PARTY BILLING AGENTS . . . WILL BE LIABLE FOR ANY INTERRUPTION IN ANY SERVICE OR FOR ANY DELAY OR FAILURE TO PERFORM, INCLUDING WITHOUT LIMITATION: IF SUCH INTERRUPTION, DELAY OR FAILURE TO PERFORM ARISES IN CONNECTION WITH THE TERMINATION OR SUSPENSION OF DISH NETWORK'S ACCESS TO ALL OR ANY PORTION OF SERVICES; THE RELOCATION OF ALL OR ANY PORTION OF THE SERVICES TO DIFFERENT SATELLITE(S); A CHANGE IN THE FEATURES AVAILABLE WITH YOUR EQUIPMENT; ANY SOFTWARE OR OTHER DOWNLOADS INITIATED BY US; OR ANY ACTS OF GOD, FIRES, EARTHQUAKES, FLOODS, POWER OR TECHNICAL FAILURE, SATELLITE OR UPLINK FAILURE, ACTS OF ANY GOVERNMENTAL BODY OR ANY OTHER CAUSE BEYOND OUR REASONABLE CONTROL.

II. The First Certified Question.

1. Under Colorado law, is the Subscription Agreement between Stokes and DISH, which is comprised of both a Digital Home Advantage Plan Agreement and a Residential Customer Agreement, illusory?

In our view, this issue is a classic red herring.[2] The phrase "illusory promise" means "words in promissory form that promise nothing." 2 Corbin on Contracts § 5.28, at 142 (rev. ed. 1995). In most cases, the purported contract fails for lack of consideration because, "[w]here the apparent assurance of performance is illusory, it is not consideration for a return promise." Restatement (Second) of Contracts § 77 cmt. a. . . .

In this case, the district court concluded that, if the Subscription Agreements provided "that DISH cannot be held liable for any interruption or delay of any or all programs for any period of time . . . such an interpretation would of course render the contract illusory." We disagree. An illusory contract is unenforceable from its inception. Here, the Subscription Agreement between Stokes and DISH had been in effect for years when the Turner and FOX News service interruptions occurred. Both parties had provided substantial performance of their respective contractual promises, and DISH continued to provide many uninterrupted channels to its subscribers. Under Colorado law, a contract is not illusory for lack of consideration where a party with seemingly unlimited discretion

[2] Defined in Webster's Third New International Dictionary as "a diversion intended to distract attention from the real issue."

in performing has at least partially performed and thereby "incurred a sufficient detriment to provide consideration." O'Hara Grp. Denver, Ltd. v. Marcor Housing Sys., Inc., 197 Colo. 530, 595 P.2d 679, 683–84 (1979); see United Press Int'l, Inc. v. Sentinel Publ'g Co., 166 Colo. 47, 441 P.2d 316, 318–19 (1968). The answer to the first certified question is no.

III. The Second Certified Question.

2. Under Colorado Law, if the Subscription Agreement between Stokes and DISH, which is comprised of both a Digital Home Advantage Plan Agreement and a Residential Customer Agreement, is not illusory, may, in light of the express terms of the Subscription Agreement, the duty of good faith and fair dealing be applied to require DISH to provide any monetary relief when it deletes or changes programming for which subscribers have already paid?

Under Colorado law, all contracts are subject to an implied duty of good faith and fair dealing, as DISH concedes on appeal. The Plan Agreement, and Section 1.I. of the RCA, entitled "Changes in Services Offered," granted DISH discretion to change "programming, programming packages and other Services that we offer, as well as the prices and fees related to such . . . Services, at any time." Under Colorado law (as elsewhere), the "implied duty of good faith and fair dealing 'requires that a party vested with contractual discretion exercise that discretion reasonably.' " Bloom v. Nat'l Collegiate Ass'n, 93 P.3d 621, 624 (Colo. App. 2004). As the Colorado Supreme Court has explained:

> The good faith performance doctrine is generally used to effectuate the intentions of the parties or to honor their reasonable expectations. Good faith performance of a contract involves faithfulness to an agreed common purpose and consistency with the justified expectations of the other party. . . . [A]dherence to this principle promotes the central policy underlying contract law, that of construing contracts so as to effectuate the parties' intentions.
>
> The duty of good faith and fair dealing applies when one party has discretionary authority to determine certain terms of the contract, such as quantity, price, or time. The covenant may be relied upon only when the manner of performance under a specific contract term allows for discretion on the part of either party. However, it will not contradict terms or conditions for which a party has bargained.

Amoco Oil Co. v. Ervin, 908 P.2d 493, 498 (Colo. 1995) (quotations omitted).

The duty of good faith and fair dealing "will not contradict terms or conditions for which a party has bargained." Id. The duty "does not obligate a party . . . to assume obligations that vary or contradict the contract's express provisions, nor does it permit a party to inject substantive terms into the contract." ADT Sec. Servs., Inc. v. Premier Home Prot., Inc., 181 P.3d 288, 293 (Colo. App. 2007). Rather, "the doctrine of good faith performance is a means of finding within a contract an implied obligation not to engage in the particular form of conduct which, in the case at hand, constitutes 'bad faith.' " Tymshare, Inc. v. Covell, 727 F.2d 1145, 1152 (D.C. Cir. 1984). The covenant is not about establishing new, independent rights or duties; it is about "securing to the parties the sort of good faith performance that . . . they reasonably thought they were securing at the time they entered the bargain." Flood v. ClearOne Commc'ns, Inc., 618 F.3d 1110, 1122 (10th Cir. 2010); see Tymshare, 727 F.2d at 1153–54.

Count II of Plaintiffs' First Amended Complaint pleaded a claim for breach of the covenant of good faith and fair dealing. But Plaintiffs did not allege that DISH interrupted their access to Turner and FOX News channels in bad faith. They instead alleged that DISH breached its duty of good faith and fair dealing "by unfairly charging and collecting monies . . . for satellite television programming that DISH did not provide . . . without providing a credit or other monetary relief . . . for the failure to provide the programming." Consistent with the contractual claims as pleaded, the district court in denying DISH's motion to dismiss concluded that "[t]he operative question is whether it was reasonable for DISH to stop providing Turner and FOX News Programming, keep the payments it would have been paying previously to the providers for those channels, and provide no recompense to its customers."

DISH argues that the covenant of good faith and fair dealing, while applicable to its Subscription Agreement, cannot support Plaintiffs' claim for monetary relief for the two programming interruptions, because the Subscription Agreement expressly provides that customers are not entitled to monetary relief for interruptions and performance delays resulting from the loss of DISH's access to the programming services it provides. We agree, and therefore answer this second question in the negative. The covenant "will not contradict terms or conditions for which a party has bargained." *Amoco*, 908 P.2d at 498. Therefore, DISH's duty to exercise its discretion to change programming in good faith cannot be the legal basis for a claim to monetary relief that is precluded by unambiguous terms of the Subscription Agreement. In applying the covenant to specific contractual relationships, courts must "take care to ensure that we don't use the covenant as another means for substituting a different deal from the one the parties contemplated." *Flood*, 618 F.3d at 1121. The Supreme Court of Colorado has repeatedly recognized this principle. "It is axiomatic that in construing a document courts should not rewrite the provisions of an unambiguous document, but must enforce an unambiguous contract in accordance with the plain and ordinary meaning of its terms." USI Props. E., Inc. v. Simpson, 938 P.2d 168, 173 (Colo. 1997). * * *

We conclude that the district court's interpretation of Section 1.I. and Section 7.A. of the RCA improperly converted the covenant of good faith and fair dealing into an additional contract term. It allowed Plaintiffs to recover monetary relief for Services interruptions, a remedy that is unambiguously precluded by the express terms of the parties' contractual bargain. Accordingly, the answer to the * * * certified question is no. As pleaded, Plaintiffs' claims for class-wide monetary relief in this case and in the related case of Padberg v. DISH Network LLC failed to state a claim upon which relief can be granted. Our jurisdiction over this interlocutory appeal extends no further.

The order of the district court dated July 15, 2015 is reversed and the case is remanded for further proceedings not inconsistent with this opinion.

QUESTIONS

1. Questions about the facts of this case

   1.1. Why do you think there was an interruption in providing Turner and Fox network programming?

   1.2. The contract stated that DISH could "add, delete, rearrange and/or change any and all programming, programming packages and other Services that we offer, as well as the prices and fees related to such programming, programming packages and Services, at any time, including . . . during any term commitment period to which you have agreed." So why did the plaintiffs complain?

   1.3. Don't the plaintiffs have a point? Doesn't this opinion mean that your cable provider can cut off your favorite network and still collect the same monthly charge from you? No wonder cable is dying.

2. Questions about the law

   2.1. The court says that the implied "covenant is not about establishing new, independent rights or duties; it is about 'securing to the parties the sort of good faith performance that . . . they reasonably thought they were securing at the time they entered the bargain.'" If that is the case, what is the difference between breaching the implied covenant of good faith and fair dealing and breaching other substantive provisions of the contract?

   2.2. Just what is a "covenant" anyway? How is it different from a promise or any other term of the contract?

   2.3. Review question: If DISH has so much contractual discretion as to what to show, when to show it, and how much to charge, why isn't this contract illusory? Did the court answer the first certified question correctly?

3. **You Be the Lawyer!**

   Stokes and Felzien have just moved to Colorado, and bring to you the preprinted contract that DISH has given them for service. They tell you that they are on a budget, and need to know for sure that they will get Free Speech TV, https://www.freespeech.org/, which DISH currently carries, without price changes for at least a year. What do you tell them?

QUESTIONS BEFORE THE CASE

1. What actions taken by Warner Bros. executives in the next case breached the express terms of the contract signed by both parties?
2. How would you explain the possible violation of the implied covenant of good faith and fair dealing in this case to a friend of yours who is not in law school or a lawyer (you do have such friends, right?)

LOCKE v. WARNER BROS., INC.

Court of Appeals of California, Second District
57 Cal. App. 4th 354, 66 Cal. Rptr. 2d 921 (1997)

KLEIN, P. J.

Plaintiffs and appellants Sondra Locke (Locke) and Caritas Films, a California corporation (Caritas) (sometimes collectively referred to as Locke) appeal a judgment following a grant of summary judgment in favor of defendant and respondent Warner Bros., Inc. (Warner). * * *

We conclude triable issues are present with respect to whether Warner breached its development deal with Locke by categorically refusing to work with her. * * * The judgment therefore is reversed. * * *

FACTUAL AND PROCEDURAL BACKGROUND

1. *Locke's dispute with Eastwood.*

In 1975, Locke came to Warner to appear with Clint Eastwood in *The Outlaw Josey Wales* (Warner Bros. 1976). During the filming of the movie, Locke and Eastwood began a personal and romantic relationship. For the next dozen years, they lived in Eastwood's Los Angeles and Northern California homes. Locke also appeared in a number of Eastwood's films. In 1986, Locke made her directorial debut in *Ratboy* (Warner Bros. 1986).

In 1988, the relationship deteriorated, and in 1989 Eastwood terminated it. Locke then brought suit against Eastwood, alleging numerous causes of action. That action was resolved by a November 21, 1990, settlement agreement and mutual general release. Under said agreement, Eastwood agreed to pay Locke additional compensation in the sum of $450,000 "on account of past employment and Locke's contentions" and to convey certain real property to her.

2. Locke's development deal with Warner.

According to Locke, Eastwood secured a development deal for Locke with Warner in exchange for Locke's dropping her case against him. Contemporaneously with the Locke/Eastwood settlement agreement, Locke entered into a written agreement with Warner, dated November 27, 1990. It is the Locke/Warner agreement which is the subject of the instant controversy.

The Locke/Warner agreement had two basic components. The first element states Locke would receive $250,000 per year for three years for a "non-exclusive first look deal." It required Locke to submit to Warner any picture she was interested in developing before submitting it to any other studio. Warner then had 30 days either to approve or reject a submission.

The second element of the contract was a $750,000 "pay or play" directing deal. The provision is called "pay or play" because it gives the studio a choice: It can either "play" the director by using the director's services, or pay the director his or her fee.

Unbeknownst to Locke at the time, Eastwood had agreed to reimburse Warner for the cost of her contract if she did not succeed in getting projects produced and developed. Early in the second year of the three-year contract, Warner charged $975,000 to an Eastwood film, *Unforgiven* (Warner Bros. 1992).

Warner paid Locke the guaranteed compensation of $1.5 million under the agreement. In accordance with the agreement, Warner also provided Locke with an office on the studio lot and an administrative assistant. However, Warner did not develop any of Locke's proposed projects or hire her to direct any films. Locke contends the development deal was a sham, that Warner never intended to make any films with her, and that Warner's sole motivation in entering into the agreement was to assist Eastwood in settling his litigation with Locke.

3. Locke's action against Warner.

On March 10, 1994, Locke filed suit against Warner, alleging four causes of action.

* * *

The second cause of action alleged that Warner breached the contract by refusing to consider Locke's proposed projects and thereby deprived her of the benefit of the bargain of the Warner/Locke agreement.

* * *

4. Warner's motion for summary judgment and opposition thereto.

On January 6, 1995, Warner filed a motion for summary judgment. Warner contended it did not breach its contract with Locke because it did consider all the projects she presented, and the studio's decision not to put any of those projects into active development or "hand" Locke a script which it already owned was not a breach of any express or implied contractual duty. Warner asserted the odds are slim a producer can get a project into development and even slimmer a director will be hired to direct a film. During the term of Locke's deal, Warner had similar deals with numerous other producers and directors, who fared no better than Locke.

* * *

In opposing summary judgment, Locke contended Warner breached the agreement in that it had no intention of accepting any project regardless of its merits. Locke also asserted Warner committed fraud by entering into the agreement without any intention of approving any project with Locke or allowing Locke to direct another film.

Locke's opposition papers cited the deposition testimony of Joseph Terry, who recounted a conversation he had with Bob Brassel, a Warner executive, regarding Locke's projects. Terry had stated to Brassel: " 'Well, Bob, this woman has a deal on the lot. She's a director that you want to work with. You have a deal with her. * * * I've got five here that she's interested in.' [¶] And then I would get nothing. [¶] * * * [¶] I was told [by Brassel], 'Joe, we're not going to work with her,' and then, 'That's Clint's deal.' And that's something I just completely did not understand."

Similarly, the declaration of Mary Wellnitz stated: She worked with Locke to set up projects at Warner, without success. Shortly after she began her association with Locke, Wellnitz submitted a script to Lance Young, who at the time was a senior vice-president of production at Warner. After discussing the script, Young told Wellnitz, "Mary, I want you to know that I think Sondra is a wonderful woman and very talented, but, if you think I can go down the hall and tell Bob Daly that I have a movie I want to make with her he would tell me to forget it. They are not going to make a movie with her here."

5. Trial court's ruling.

On February 17, 1995, the trial court granted summary judgment in favor of Warner. Thereafter, the trial court signed an extensive order granting summary judgment. The order stated:

> Under the contract, Warner had no obligation either to put into development any of the projects submitted to the studio for its consideration, or to 'hand off' to Locke any scripts for her to direct that it previously had acquired from someone else. The implied covenant of good faith and fair dealing cannot be imposed to create a contract different from the one the parties negotiated for themselves. Warner had the option to pass on each project Locke submitted. Warner was not required to have a 'good faith' or 'fair' basis for declining to exercise its right to develop her material. Such a requirement would be improper and unworkable. A judge or jury cannot and should not substitute its judgment for a film studio's when the studio is making the creative decision of whether to develop or produce a proposed motion picture. Such highly subjective artistic and business decisions are not proper subjects for judicial review. Moreover, Warner had legitimate commercial and artistic reasons for declining to develop the projects Locke submitted.

* * *

Locke filed a timely notice of appeal from the judgment.

CONTENTIONS

Locke contends: The trial court erred by granting Warner's motion for summary judgment based on its conclusion there were no disputed issues of material fact; the trial court erred in weighing the evidence, resolving doubts against Locke, the nonmoving party, and adopting only those inferences favorable to Warner where the evidence supported contrary inferences; and the trial court committed reversible error first by failing to make any findings or evidentiary rulings and then by adopting Warner's defective ruling.

DISCUSSION

* * *

2. A triable issue exists as to whether Warner breached its contract with Locke by failing to evaluate Locke's proposals on their merits.

As indicated, the second cause of action alleged Warner breached the contract by "refusing to consider the projects prepared by [Locke] and depriving [Locke] of the benefit of the bargain of the Warner-Locke agreement."

In granting summary judgment on this claim, the trial court ruled "[a] judge or jury cannot and should not substitute its own judgment for a film studio's when the studio is making the creative decision of whether to develop or produce a proposed motion picture. Such highly-subjective artistic and business decisions are not proper subjects for judicial review."

The trial court's ruling missed the mark by failing to distinguish between Warner's right to make a subjective creative decision, which is not reviewable for reasonableness, and the requirement the dissatisfaction be bona fide or genuine.

a. General principles.

" '[W]here a contract confers on one party a discretionary power affecting the rights of the other, a duty is imposed to exercise that discretion in good faith and in accordance with fair dealing.' [Citations.]" * * * It is settled that in " 'every contract there is an implied covenant that neither party shall do anything which will have the effect of destroying or injuring the right of the other party to receive the fruits of the contract. * * *

Therefore, when it is a condition of an obligor's duty that he or she be subjectively satisfied with respect to the obligee's performance, the subjective standard of *honest satisfaction* is applicable. * * * "Where the contract involves matters of fancy, taste or judgment, the promisor is the sole judge of his satisfaction. If he asserts *in good faith* that he is not satisfied, there can be no inquiry into the reasonableness of his attitude. Traditional examples are employment contracts * * * and agreements to paint a portrait, write a literary or scientific article, or produce a play or vaudeville act. [Citations.]" * * * In such cases, "the promisor's determination that he is not satisfied, *when made in good faith*, has been held to be a defense to an action on the contract. [Citations.]" * * *

Therefore, the trial court erred in deferring entirely to what it characterized as Warner's "creative decision" in the handling of the development deal. If Warner acted in bad faith by categorically rejecting Locke's work and refusing to work with her, irrespective of the merits of her proposals, such conduct is not beyond the reach of the law.

b. Locke presented evidence from which a trier of fact reasonably could infer Warner breached the agreement by refusing to consider her proposals in good faith.

Merely because Warner paid Locke the guaranteed compensation under the agreement does not establish Warner fulfilled its contractual obligation. As pointed out by Locke, the value in the subject development deal was not merely the guaranteed payments under the agreement, but also the opportunity to direct and produce films and earn additional sums, and most importantly, the opportunity to promote and enhance a career.

Unquestionably, Warner was entitled to reject Locke's work based on its subjective judgment, and its creative decision in that regard is not subject to being second-guessed by a court. However, bearing in mind the requirement that subjective dissatisfaction must be an honestly held dissatisfaction, the evidence raises a triable issue as to whether Warner breached its agreement with Locke by not considering her proposals on their merits. * * *

The above evidence raises a triable issue of material fact as to whether Warner breached its contract with Locke by categorically refusing to work with her, irrespective of the merits of her proposals. While Warner was entitled to reject Locke's proposals based on its subjective dissatisfaction, the evidence calls into question whether Warner had an honest or good faith dissatisfaction with Locke's proposals, or whether it merely went through the motions of purporting to "consider" her projects.

c. No merit to Warner's contention Locke seeks to rewrite the instant agreement to limit Warner's discretionary power.

Warner argues that while the implied covenant of good faith and fair dealing is implied in all contracts, it is limited to assuring compliance with the express terms of the contract and cannot be extended to create obligations not contemplated in the contract. * * *

This principle is illustrated in *Carma Developers (Cal.), Inc. v. Marathon Development California, Inc.* (1992) 2 Cal. 4th 342, 351–352 [6 Cal. Rptr. 2d 467, 826 P.2d 710], wherein the parties entered into a lease agreement which stated that if the tenant procured a potential sublessee and asked the landlord for consent to sublease, the landlord had the right to terminate the lease, enter into negotiations with the prospective sublessee, and appropriate for itself all profits from the new arrangement. *Carma* recognized "[t]he covenant of good faith finds particular application in situations where one party is invested with a discretionary power affecting the rights of another." (*Id.*, at p. 372.) The court expressed the view that "[s]uch power must be exercised in good faith." (*Ibid.*) At the same time, *Carma* upheld the right of the landlord under the express terms of the lease to freely exercise its discretion to terminate the lease in order to claim for itself—and deprive the tenant of—the appreciated rental value of the premises. (*Id.*, at p. 376.)

In this regard, *Carma* stated: "We are aware of no reported case in which a court has held the covenant of good faith may be read to prohibit a party from doing that which is expressly permitted by an agreement. On the contrary, as a general matter, implied terms should never be read to vary express terms. [Citations.] 'The general rule [regarding the covenant of good faith] is plainly subject to the exception that the parties may, by express provisions of the contract, grant the right to engage in the very acts and conduct which would otherwise have been forbidden by an implied covenant of good faith and fair dealing. * * * [¶] This is in accord with the general principle that, in interpreting a contract "an implication * * * should not be made when the contrary is indicated in clear and express words." 3 Corbin, Contracts, § 564, p. 298 (1960). * * * [¶] *As to acts and conduct authorized by the express provisions of the contract*, no covenant of good faith and fair dealing can be implied which forbids such acts and conduct. And if defendants were given the right to do what they did by the express provisions of the contract there can be no breach.' [Citation.]" * * *

In *Third Story Music, Inc. v. Waits* (1995) 41 Cal. App. 4th 798, 801 [48 Cal. Rptr. 2d 747], the issue presented was "whether a promise to market music, or to refrain from doing so, at the election of the promisor is subject to the implied covenant of good faith and fair dealing where substantial consideration has been paid by the promisor."

In that case, Warner Communications obtained from Third Story Music (TSM) the worldwide right to manufacture, sell, distribute and advertise the musical output of singer/songwriter Tom Waits. * * * The agreement also specifically stated that Warner Communications " 'may at our election refrain from any or all of the foregoing.' " * * * TSM sued Warner Communications for contract damages based on breach of the implied covenant of good faith and fair dealing, claiming Warner Communications had impeded TSM's receiving the benefit of the agreement. * * * Warner Communications demurred to the complaint, alleging the clause in the agreement permitting it to " 'at [its] election refrain' from doing anything to profitably exploit the music is controlling and precludes application of any implied covenant." * * * The demurrer was sustained on those grounds. * * *

The reviewing court affirmed, holding the implied covenant was unavailing to the plaintiff. * * * Because the agreement *expressly* provided Warner Communications had the right to *refrain* from marketing the Waits recordings, the implied covenant of good faith and fair dealing did not limit the discretion given to Warner Communications in that regard. * * *

Warner's reliance herein on *Third Story Music, Inc.*, is misplaced. The Locke/Warner agreement did not give Warner the express right to refrain from working with Locke. Rather, the agreement gave Warner *discretion* with respect to developing Locke's projects. The implied covenant of good faith and fair dealing obligated Warner to exercise that discretion honestly and in good faith.

In sum, the Warner/Locke agreement contained an implied covenant of good faith and fair dealing, that neither party would frustrate the other party's right to receive the benefits of the contract. * * * Whether Warner violated the implied covenant and breached the contract by categorically refusing to work with Locke is a question for the trier of fact.

* * *

DISPOSITION

The judgment is reversed * * * Locke to recover costs on appeal.

QUESTIONS AND NOTES

1. Questions about the facts of this case

   1.1. Was the contract term Ms. Locke claimed Warner Bros. violated an express term of the contract? If not, how do the parties know what the term requires of them in their efforts to perform as promised?

   1.2. Did Ms. Locke not receive the compensation she was promised under the contract with Warner? If she did, what remedy does she want?

   1.3. Of what relevance is Clint Eastwood's relationship with Ms. Locke and his business dealings with Warner?

2. Questions about the law

   2.1. Based on the last two cases can you succinctly state the implied term of good faith that courts insert into every contract?

   2.2. Section 205 of the *Restatement (Second) of Contracts* states:

   > Every contract imposes upon each party a duty of good faith and fair dealing in its performance and its enforcement.

   Comment *d* adds:

   > Subterfuges and evasions violate the obligation of good faith in performance even though the actor believes his conduct to be justified. But the obligation goes further: bad faith may be overt or may consist of inaction, and fair dealing may require more than honesty. A complete catalogue of types of bad faith is impossible, but the following types are among those which have been recognized in judicial decisions: evasion of the spirit of the bargain, lack of diligence and slacking off, willful rendering of imperfect performance, abuse of a power to specify terms, and interference with or failure to cooperate in the other party's performance.

   The Uniform Commercial Code also imposes such a duty:

   > Every contract or duty within [the Uniform Commercial Code] imposes an obligation of good faith in its performance and enforcement.

   U.C.C. § 1–304.

In turn, the U.C.C. defines good faith by stating that "good faith" means:

> honesty in fact and the observance of reasonable commercial standards of fair dealing.

U.C.C. § 1–201(b)(20).

Is California law, as set forth in *Locke*, consistent with these statements, or is it aberrational?

2.3. Would it be a valid defense on remand if Warner Bros. asserted that each idea that Ms. Locke pitched was silly or non-commercial?

2.4. What if Warner Bros. had given serious consideration to Ms. Locke's first 10 projects, but had found them all wanting and then just internally decided not to consider any more projects? What if its refusal came after only one project?

2.5. What if Warner Bros. had wanted to have complete and total discretion to "pay or play," even if they were being capricious (imagine them rolling dice or playing darts with movie names). If the contract gave them that level of discretion, what could go wrong?

3. Notes

3.1. *Hey, That's Hollywood.* According to the *Los Angeles Times*, here's how the suit was resolved on remand:

Actress' Settlement Ends Long Legal Saga

LOS ANGELES TIMES, Part B, May 27, 1999, at 2.

> They said she'd never work in this town again, but all is forgiven between Sondra Locke and Warner Bros.
>
> The actress is going back to work for the studio under terms of a legal settlement. The agreement came at the start of a trial on her lawsuit accusing Warner Bros. of harming her career by going along with a sham movie directing deal allegedly engineered by Locke's former lover and co-star, Clint Eastwood.
>
> The last-minute settlement gives Locke a new lease on her career behind the camera, said her attorney, Neil Papiano.
>
> The lawyer acknowledged that at times the three hours of settlement talks Monday more closely resembled a Hollywood pitch session as Locke discussed projects that caught her interest.
>
> Asked how it felt to be back in business with a studio that a few years ago had rejected all her ideas, a beaming Locke quipped, "Hey, that's Hollywood."

The settlement came as jury selection was about to begin in a case that had been dismissed by a Los Angeles judge, then reinstated by a state appeals court.

The lawyers would not discuss the financial terms. But as he left the Burbank courthouse, Papiano said the agreement reaches beyond money considerations to create writing and directing opportunities for Locke, who had been all but blacklisted by the major studios for a decade.

"It involves a business arrangement beneficial to Ms. Locke," Papiano said. "She's going to be paid for her services—we believe handsomely."

Locke said, "This is my best day in a long, long time." She said she felt vindicated as a professional.

"We're happy too," said Warner Bros. attorney Robert Schwartz, who declined to discuss the matter further.

The case was the second installment in Locke's legal fight to regain her professional viability after the acrimonious split with Eastwood, a popular box office draw and Academy Award-winning director.

The lanky, laconic star settled with Locke for an undisclosed sum of money 2½ years ago, just as a jury was about to return a verdict in her favor. Testimony during that trial showed that he had paid $1.5 million under the table to subsidize her development deal with Warner Bros.

Eastwood acknowledged on the witness stand that he never told Locke about his role in subsidizing her development deal, struck as partial settlement of her palimony case against him.

Locke testified at the previous trial that she would never accept such a deal because it gave Eastwood too much control and sent a signal that she wasn't to be taken seriously.

Indeed, she pitched more than 30 ideas to the studio over three years, and none was accepted.

Monday's settlement finally lays to rest a long legal saga that began when Eastwood packed up Locke's belongings and changed the locks to their Brentwood home after the New Year's holiday in 1989.

Discovered in Nashville, Tenn., during a national talent search, Locke won a Golden Globe and an Academy Award nomination for her first film, "The Heart Is a Lonely Hunter."

> She was in her 20s when she became romantically involved with Eastwood, and soon was his constant companion and co-star, even sharing billing with Clyde the orangutan in his "Every Which Way" films. The couple split after spending 14 years together.

According to IMDB.com, after the settlement in 1999, Ms. Locke never directed anything, and only appeared once in a movie, and that was in 2000.

http://www.imdb.com/name/nm0516800/?ref_=fn_al_nm_1

3.2. All readers of this note will no doubt recall the joys of the SAT and LSAT exams. Did you ever wonder what would happen if, after getting 170 on the LSAT, you then got a letter from the Educational Testing Service questioning your performance, and refusing to forward your score to the schools of your choice? If you did wonder, you might well ask what contract law has to do with any answer.

That's where *Dalton v. Educational Testing Service*, 87 N.Y.2d 384, 663 N.E.2d 289, 639 N.Y.S.2d 977 (1995) would come in. In that case, Brian Dalton took the SAT test twice, improving his score by 410 points on the second try. After finding what it thought was different handwriting on each test, the test administrator, Educational Testing Service (ETS) canceled Dalton's second score. It believed it could do this because Dalton had signed a form agreement upon registering for the test allowing ETS to take such an action if it found any unexplained discrepancies.

But the form, held to be a contract by the New York Court of Appeals, also obligated ETS to "notif[y] the test taker of the reasons for questioning the score" and offer the test-taker the * * * five options: (1) the opportunity to provide additional information, (2) confirmation of the score by taking a free retest, (3) authorization for ETS to cancel the score and refund all fees, (4) third-party review by any institution receiving the test score or (5) arbitration.

Dalton took the first option and supplied ETS with additional information (he had been ill during the first exam, and other tests indicated that his second score was a better indicator of his abilities). ETS promptly ignored this information, since they did not deem it relevant to whether Dalton had used a "ringer" in the second test.

This refusal, the court said, was a breach of the duty of good faith inherent in all contracts. "Where * * * ETS refuses to exercise its discretion * * * by declining even to consider relevant material submitted by the test-taker, the legal question is whether this refusal breached an express or implied term of the contract. * * * Here, the courts below agreed that ETS did not consider the relevant information furnished by Dalton. By doing so, ETS failed to comply in good faith with its own test security procedures, thereby breaching its contract with Dalton."

So Dalton won the battle. Did he win the war and obtain an order forcing ETS to release his scores? No. "Dalton is entitled to relief that comports with ETS' contractual promise—good-faith consideration of the material he submitted to ETS. We cannot agree with Dalton's assumption that ETS will merely rubber-stamp its prior determination without good-faith attention to his documentation and that reconsideration by ETS will be an empty exercise. Our conclusion that the contract affords Dalton a meaningful remedy rests also on the provision in the Procedures for Questioned Scores [contained in the contract] allowing Dalton to utilize one or more of the remaining four options in combination with renewed consideration by the Board of Review. Those options—including third-party review by any institution receiving the test score as well as arbitration—remain available should ETS determine that the information submitted fails to resolve its concerns about the validity of the [second test] score."

Based on *Dalton*, how satisfying is it to prevail on a claim that someone did not consider information in good faith before making a decision related to a contract?

4. **You Be the Lawyer!**

Warner Sisters, a movie studio, calls you up and tells you the following: they have a situation in which they have a "pay or play" director contract with Epstein that is very similar to the one Sondra Locke had with Warner Bros. They tell you that the contract was a mistake; Epstein couldn't direct his way out of a wet paper bag. But Epstein is litigious, and they know that if they don't produce one of his gas-bag disasters, he'll sue them like Locke sued Warner. What strategies can you suggest to minimize the changes that Epstein will sue, and maximize their probability of winning if he does?

PROBLEM ON GOOD FAITH

Vista, a large public company specializing in outdoor recreation, bought Jimmy Styks, a stand-up paddleboard company, from Reeves and Wilkens. The purchase price was $40 million at closing (when Jimmy Styks' assets transferred to Vista), with up to $40 million extra to be paid to Reeves and Wilkens during the next three years depending on how the paddleboard business performed during that period. In deal lingo, this $40 million component is called an "earnout."

In the Jimmy Styks acquisition, Vista agreed to pay an earnout to Reeves and Wilkens if Jimmy Styks met certain profit goals during each of the three years following the acquisition. The aggregate amount of earnout payments was set at $40 million, and was payable in stages if Jimmy Styks met annual profit goals. On this schedule, the contract set the first year earnout payment for Reeves and Wilkens at $10 million if Jimmy Styks' 2016 gross profits equaled or exceeded $12 million.

During the first year after the acquisition, issues arose. Although Vista hired Reeves and Wilkens to aid in the transition, all agreed that Vista generally did a poor job integrating Jimmy Styks into Vista's larger corporate structure. Reeves and Wilkens didn't help; they repeatedly took combative stances with Vista's management in profanity-laden emails. Regardless, as the end of the first year approached, it became clear that Jimmy Stykes would not earn the profits that would trigger the $10 million earnout payment.

Undeterred by bad results, Reeves and Wilkens developed a plan to "buy" the earnout. Near the end of the earnout period, Reeves, as an officer of Vista, placed an order on behalf of (and billable to) Vista for one million stickers for an aggregate price of $60,000, to be rush delivered to Jimmy Styks' California office. Jimmy Styks had a practice of giving stickers to purchasers of its paddleboards, but one million paddleboards was far beyond what Jimmy Styks could ever hope to sell in a year.

Upon learning that the stickers were ready, Reeves then emailed Wilkens stating: "Haha, this is real dude! 60k worth of stickers!!! We are going to go down in the history books . . ." Wilkens responded, "How much for the beer fridge? Is this all of them?"

On June 22, 2016, seven business days prior to the end of the 2016 earnout period, Reeves and Wilkens, acting for themselves, attempted to purchase approximately 900,000 stickers from Jimmy Styks for about $4.45 a sticker, resulting in a total purchase price of about $4 million. The profit on this sale (calculated at $4 million less $60,000) would have been sufficient to meet the 2016 earnout target set in the acquisition contract, resulting in a payment to Reeves and Wilkens of $10 million.

Vista, however, learned of this maneuver after the stickers were bought, but before the buyback for $4 million. It canceled the sale of the stickers to Reeves and Wilkens, fired Reeves and Wilkens, and refused to pay the $10 million earnout. Reeves and Wilkens sue; Vista counterclaims. What would you do? *See Vista Outdoor Inc. v. Reeves Family Tr.*, 234 F. Supp. 3d 558 (S.D.N.Y. 2017), *reconsideration denied*, No. 16 Civ. 5766, 2017 WL 1094568 (S.D.N.Y. Mar. 10, 2017), *appeal docketed*, No. 17–1059 (2d Cir., April 12, 2017).

D. LEGISLATURE-SUPPLIED TERMS

Courts are not alone in implying terms into contracts. Legislatures write provisions that are to be a part of every contract made within their jurisdiction. We have seen this in the Uniform Commercial Code with good faith (§ 1–304).

More often though, legislation adds terms to fill gaps—default terms that apply when the parties have not otherwise agreed Consider the following examples from Article 2 of the Uniform Commercial Code.

§ 2–305. Open Price Term.

(1) The parties if they so intend may conclude a contract for sale even though the price is not settled. In such a case the price is a reasonable price at the time for delivery if:

(a) nothing is said as to price;

(b) the price is left to be agreed by the parties and they fail to agree; or

(c) the price is to be fixed in terms of some agreed market or other standard as set or recorded by a third person or agency and it is not so set or recorded. * * *

§ 2–308. Absence of Specified Place for Delivery.

Unless otherwise agreed:

(a) the place for delivery of goods is the seller's place of business or if none, the seller's residence; but

(b) in a contract for sale of identified goods that to the knowledge of the parties at the time of contracting are in some other place, that place is the place for their delivery. * * *

§ 2–309. Absence of Specific Time Provisions. * * *

(1) The time for shipment or delivery or any other action under a contract if not provided in this Article or agreed upon shall be a reasonable time. * * *

There are other legislature-supplied terms, and important ones. When merchants sell goods, the U.C.C. implies terms regarding the quality and suitability of the goods sold. These are referred to as warranties of merchantability and suitability for a particular purpose. We study them in detail in Section 4 below, starting at page 581.

CONNECTIONS

We have discussed the U.C.C. gap fillers before. We first encountered them in Chapter 2 in connection with incomplete agreements. That's the same place where we encountered a related U.C.C. provision; namely, § 2–306 dealing with outputs and requirements contracts. Section 2–306's imposition of "good faith" limitation to insulate outputs and requirements contracts from vulnerability on grounds of both indefiniteness and lack of mutuality. *See* Official Comment 2 to § 2–306.

Now consider the U.C.C. gap fillers, or implied terms, in connection with the following problems.

PROBLEMS ON TERMS IMPLIED BY THE U.C.C.

1. Epstein and Markell meet and agree that Markell will sell, and Epstein will buy, Markell's 1965 Cadillac convertible, painted fire engine red, for $50,000. No delivery date is specified.

   Two months later, after calling Markell several times and getting no response, Epstein sues Markell for breach of contract. Issues of damages aside, who will prevail?

2. Markell and Ponoroff see each other at a Star Trek convention in Wawautosa, Wisconsin, and Markell agrees that he will purchase, and Ponoroff agrees he will sell, Ponoroff's prize pair of plastic Vulcan ears.

   Two weeks later, Markell shows up on Ponoroff's doorstep, flashes a crisp $100 bill at Ponoroff, and demands the ears. Ponoroff yawns and slams the door in Markell's face.

   Markell sues for breach. Issues of damages aside, who will prevail?

3. Ponoroff places an order for a Galaxy 950 computer over the telephone with Galaxy Computers, Inc. The price agreed upon is $999, but no delivery date is discussed. The next day, Galaxy sends a confirming invoice stating the computer will arrive in three weeks, and indicating a price of $1,099. There is no explanation for the increase.

   When the computer arrives in three weeks as indicated, Ponoroff refuses delivery, stating that it is late. Issues of damages aside, what result if Galaxy sues Ponoroff for breach?

4. Epstein sells asphalt; Ponoroff uses it to pave roads. Ponoroff and Epstein have a contract under which Epstein agrees to sell Ponoroff all of Ponoroff's requirements of asphalt for a period of five years, with the price to be the "posted price" at Tucson for Grade A asphalt. Epstein gets a bigger contract to supply asphalt, and doesn't want to supply Ponoroff's puny needs anymore. When Ponoroff orders some asphalt he needs for a

job, Epstein tells him that they have no contract, because there is no agreement on price. What result?

---

2. PAROL EVIDENCE: WHAT IF THE PARTIES DISAGREE ABOUT WHETHER CERTAIN WORDS ARE EVEN PART OF THE CONTRACT?

When there is a final written version of the deal, contract law affords a great deal of deference to that final writing. The court's determining that there is final written version of the deal triggers a body of law with the misleading name, "parol evidence rule."* We will use this "parol evidence rule" to answer questions similar to (but more difficult than) the following:

1. S and B enter into a written contract providing that each week in 2018, S will deliver 100 chickens to B, and B will pay S $3 for each chicken delivered. B later initiates litigation to reform the contract contending that S told her before the contract was entered into that S would deliver as many chickens as B wants for $3 a chicken. Should the court grant S's motion to dismiss B's suit on the ground that the terms in the written contract should be conclusive and exclusive?

2. S and B enter into a written contract providing that each week in 2018, S will deliver 100 chickens to B, and B will pay S $3 for each chicken delivered. The written contract is silent as to how the chickens are to be wrapped. B later sues to reform the contract contending that S told her before the contract was entered into that S would deliver the chickens wrapped for freezing. Should the court grant S's motion to dismiss B's suit on the ground the contract terms are limited to the terms in the written contract?

3. Same facts as 2 except that the written contract provides: "This is the complete and final agreement between the parties and supersedes any previous understandings and agreements between the parties, written or oral."

The parol evidence rule is a rule of venerable heritage, as illustrated by the following explanation of its purpose, written by Chief Justice Popham almost four hundred years ago, but still relevant today:

* It is not parol*e* evidence with an ending "e." It is simply "parol" evidence. "Parole" comes from Old French for "promise"; someone on "parole" promises not to engage in certain behavior. "Parol," in contrast, comes from Norman French and means "oral" or "outside of the contract."

Don't confuse the two on the final. It ticks off discriminating contracts professors.

> It would be inconvenient that matters in writing made by advice and on consideration, and which finally import the certain truth of the agreement of the parties should be controlled by averment of the parties to be proved by the uncertain testimony of slippery memory. And it would be dangerous to purchasers and farmers, and all others in such cases, if such averments against matter in writing should be admitted.

The Countess of Rutland's Case, 5 Co. 26a, 77 Eng. Rep. 89 (K.B. 1604).

Regardless of this salutary purpose, the effect of the parol evidence rule is to exclude evidence you or I might think relevant to the interpretation of a contract. It is also full of (some might say riddled with) exceptions and shadings. Before stating the rule, however, it is wise to keep in mind the following statement about the rule by Professor James Thayer, as true now as it was when it was written over one hundred years ago: "Few things are darker than this, or fuller of subtle difficulties." JAMES B. THAYER, A PRELIMINARY TREATISE ON EVIDENCE AT THE COMMON LAW 390 (1898).

A. COMMON LAW

For starters, the name "parol evidence rule" is a misnomer. As we will see, there is more than one rule, and it is not limited to parol statements. Moreover, it is not even a rule of evidence. As comment *a* to Section 213 of the *Restatement (Second) of Contracts* states:

> [T]he parol evidence rule * * * is not a rule of evidence but a rule of substantive law. Nor is it a rule of interpretation; it defines the subject matter of interpretation. It renders inoperative prior written agreements as well as prior oral agreements. Where writings relating to the same subject matter are assented to as parts of one transaction, both form part of the integrated agreement. Where an agreement is partly oral and partly written, the writing is at most a partially integrated agreement.

So what is this substantive rule of law? As with most rules in this course, there is no definitive statement of the parol evidence rule—it is a rule of common law origin, which means that it must be derived from cases applying it. For purposes of our study, however, we can start with the *Restatement (Second)*, as it provides a workable statement of the general rule:

§ 213 Effect of Integrated Agreement on Prior Agreements (Parol Evidence Rule)

(1) A binding integrated agreement discharges prior agreements to the extent that it is inconsistent with them.

(2) A binding completely integrated agreement discharges prior agreements to the extent that they are within its scope.

To understand this text, let's start with an examination of some of the consequences of discharging prior agreements.

QUESTIONS BEFORE THE CASE

1. Why is the time of formation critical to the court's holding?
2. What is the effect of the parol evidence rule on Ahmeds' efforts to terminate their relationship with their realtor?

BLONDELL V. AHMED

Court of Appeals of North Carolina
786 S.E.2d 405 (2016), aff'd, 804 S.E.2d 183 (N.C. 2017) (mem.)

DILLON, JUDGE.

Plaintiff Colleen Blondell ("Agent") brought this action to collect a real estate commission she claims is due under a listing agreement ("Listing Agreement") that her real estate firm entered into with Defendants Shakil and Shabana Ahmed ("Sellers") to sell Sellers' home. Agent appeals from the trial court's order granting the Sellers' motion for summary judgment. Because we believe that there is a genuine issue of fact as to whether Sellers breached their duty of good faith and fair dealing when they negotiated for the termination of the Listing Agreement, we reverse and remand for further proceedings consistent with this opinion.

I. Background

Agent is a real estate broker licensed by the North Carolina Real Estate Commission. She works as an agent with the firm Kiegiel, LLC d/b/a Keystone Properties ("Keystone Properties"). Sellers owned a home in Wake County. A timeline of events necessary for understanding the issues on appeal is as follows:

A. Parties Enter Into Listing Agreement; Agent Procures Offer

In March 2013, Sellers and Keystone Properties entered into the Listing Agreement. The parties used the "Exclusive Right to Sell Listing Agreement" form produced by the North Carolina Association of

REALTORS®, Inc. Pursuant to the Agreement, the listing would be for a period of one year (expiring in March 2014).

On 3 April 2013, Agent showed Sellers' home to Michael and Susan Fekete ("Buyers"). On 6 April 2013, Buyers made an offer which Agent presented to Sellers. Sellers promptly rejected the offer. Over the course of the next few weeks, Agent had a number of communications with both Sellers and Buyers regarding the Sellers' home.

B. Parties Enter Termination Agreement; Sellers Sell Home To Buyers

On 22 April 2013, the Sellers informed Agent that they no longer wished to list their home for sale and of their desire to terminate the Listing Agreement. Accordingly, Agent prepared the Termination Agreement using another form provided by the Association of REALTORS® (entitled "Termination of Agency Agreement and Release," hereinafter "Termination Agreement"). This Termination Agreement essentially provided that the parties would no longer be bound by the Listing Agreement. Further, the Termination Agreement provided that it would become "effective on the date that it has been signed by ***both*** the Parties." (Emphasis added.)

That same evening (22 April), Agent e-mailed Sellers, attaching the Termination Agreement *unsigned.* The next day (23 April), Sellers executed the Termination Agreement and e-mailed it back to Agent.

Sometime thereafter, but prior to 2 May 2013—without the knowledge of Agent—Buyers and Sellers met to discuss a possible transaction. On 2 May 2013, Sellers and Buyers tentatively agreed to a purchase price for the home. On 9 May 2013, Buyers presented a written offer to Sellers based on their verbal understanding.

Prior to executing Buyers' offer, Sellers contacted Agent about the status of the Termination Agreement (which Sellers had signed and returned on 23 April). During this communication, Sellers did not disclose to Agent that they had a written offer from Buyers that they intended to sign.

On 10 May 2013, Agent executed the Termination Agreement on behalf of Keystone Properties and e-mailed a copy to Sellers.

On 11 May 2013, Sellers executed the contract to sell their home to Buyers. The transaction closed in late June 2013, unbeknownst to Agent.

Agent commenced this action against Sellers contending that, pursuant to the Listing Agreement, Sellers became obligated to pay Keystone Properties a real estate commission when Sellers sold their home to Buyers. Sellers answered, alleging that no commission was due because the Listing Agreement had been terminated in the Termination

Agreement. After a hearing, the trial court entered summary judgment in favor of Sellers. Agent timely appealed.

II. Analysis

The parties agree that the Listing Agreement would entitle Keystone Properties to a real estate commission in the absence of an effective termination agreement. Specifically, the Listing Agreement obligated Sellers to pay a commission if their home sold within the Agreement's one-year term.

The Termination Agreement, however, unambiguously states that Sellers were released from any obligation they may otherwise have under the Listing Agreement. Specifically, the Termination Agreement states:

> 2. **Termination of Agreement.** The Parties agree that all rights and obligations arising on account of the [Listing] Agreement are hereby terminated, and hereby release each other from their respective obligations under the Agreement.
>
> 3. **Release from Liability.** The Parties further release and forever discharge each other and their respective successors in interest from any and all claims, demands, rights and causes of action of whatsoever kind and nature arising from the [Listing] Agreement and the agency relationship existing between them.

Accordingly, if the Termination Agreement is enforceable, Sellers would be entitled to summary judgment in this case.

Agent argues that Sellers should not be allowed to benefit from the Termination Agreement. Specifically, Agent contends that Sellers breached their duty of good faith and fair dealing when Sellers negotiated for the termination of the Listing Agreement without disclosing to Agent or Keystone Properties that Sellers were negotiating directly with Buyers.

It is axiomatic that Sellers owed a duty of good faith and fair dealing to Keystone Properties during the term of the Listing Agreement and during the negotiation of the termination of that Agreement. Indeed, our Supreme Court has recently reiterated the long standing principle that there is implied in every contract a covenant of good faith and fair dealing. *Arnesen v. Rivers Edge Golf Club,* 368 N.C. 440, 450–451, 781 S.E.2d 1, 9 (2015); *see also Great Am. Ins. Co. v. C.G. Tate Constr. Co.,* 303 N.C. 387, 399, 279 S.E.2d 769, 776 (1981) (recognizing "the common law principle that implicit in every contract is the obligation of each party to act in good faith"). Also, our Court has consistently held that "[i]t is a basic principle of contract law that a party who enters into an enforceable contract is required to act in good faith and to make reasonable efforts to perform his obligations under the agreement." *Weyerhaeuser Co. v. Godwin Bldg. Supply Co.,* 40 N.C.App. 743, 746, 253 S.E.2d 625, 627 (1979).

The parties dispute when the Listing Agreement was actually terminated. Sellers contend that the Listing Agreement terminated on 23 April when Sellers executed the Termination Agreement. Sellers point to the language in Agent's 22 April e-mail (attaching the Termination Agreement *unsigned*) in which Agent stated:

> Attached you will find the Termination Agreement for the listing of your home. Please sign the form and return it to me at your earliest convenience thereby severing any obligation we have with one another.

Sellers contend that the e-mail constituted an offer that was accepted when they signed the agreement on 23 April. However, based on the Parol Evidence Rule, which has been adopted by our Supreme Court, we cannot consider this e-mail language because it contradicts the unambiguous language contained in the Termination Agreement. *See Root v. Allstate Ins. Co.,* 272 N.C. 580, 587, 158 S.E.2d 829, 835 (1968) (recognizing the general rule that "when a written instrument is introduced into evidence, its terms may not be contradicted by parol or extrinsic evidence, and it is presumed that all prior negotiations are merged into the written instrument") The Termination Agreement unambiguously stated that "[t]his Agreement shall be effective on the date it has been signed by *both the Parties.*"

Our Court has recognized that the Parol Evidence Rule is a rule of substantive law which "prohibits the consideration of evidence as to anything which happened prior to or simultaneously with the making of a contract which would vary the terms of the agreement." *Harrell v. First Union Nat. Bank,* 76 N.C.App. 666, 667, 334 S.E.2d 109, 110 (1985). In *Harrell,* the plaintiff signed a "Letter of Consent" with a bank that provided that certain common stock he owned could be used as collateral for advances to his son-in-law in the future. *Id.* At the time of signing, however, the plaintiff told the loan officer (defendant) that he did not want any advances to be made to his son-in-law unless he approved the advances, though the "Letter of Consent" did not require that he approve advances. The loan officer replied, "That's right." *Id.* Subsequently, several advances were made to the son-in-law secured by the plaintiff's stock without the plaintiff's approval, and the loan officer sold the stock when the loans were not paid. The plaintiff filed an action for the wrongful sale of his stock, and this Court affirmed the trial court's directed verdict in favor of the bank, holding that the Parol Evidence Rule barred the Court from considering the communication made contemporaneously with the signing of the contract. *Id.* at 667, 334 S.E.2d at 110–11.

Here, there is nothing within the four corners of the Termination Agreement that obfuscates or contradicts the term that it would not be effective until signed by *both* parties. Just as this Court did not consider a conversation that the plaintiff had with a loan officer in *Harrell* directly contradicting a term in the contract, we cannot consider the language in Agent's 22 April e-mail. The Termination Agreement is unambiguous. *See Thompson v. First Citizens Bank & Trust Co.,* 151 N.C.App. 704, 709, 567 S.E.2d 184, 188 (2002) ("Generally, the parol evidence rule prohibits the admission of evidence to contradict or add to the terms of a clear and unambiguous contract."). Accordingly, we hold that the Listing Agreement was not terminated nor did the obligations thereunder cease until the Termination Agreement was executed by Agent (on behalf of Keystone Properties) on 10 May. That is, Sellers' execution of the Termination Agreement was an *offer* to terminate the Listing Agreement, which was not accepted until the Termination Agreement was executed by Agent.

Having concluded that the Listing Agreement was still in full effect until 10 May, we conclude that there is evidence which creates a genuine issue of material fact whether Sellers breached their duty of good faith and fair dealing under that Agreement. Specifically, prior to 10 May, before Sellers' offer to terminate the Listing Agreement was accepted by Agent and while Sellers still owed a duty of good faith and fair dealing toward Agent under the Listing Agreement: (1) Agent presented an offer from Buyers to Sellers, which would involve the paying of a commission to Agent under the Listing Agreement; (2) Sellers rejected the offer and then informed Agent that they no longer wanted to list their house for sale; (3) Sellers made an offer to Agent to terminate the Listing Agreement; (4) Sellers began negotiating directly with Buyers; (5) Sellers received a written offer in hand from Buyers that they were prepared to sign and which would not involve the paying of any real estate commission; (6) with Buyers' offer in hand, Sellers contacted Agent and asked her to accept their offer to terminate the Listing Agreement; (7) Sellers made the request to Agent without disclosing to Agent that they were about to accept Buyers' offer; and (8) Sellers signed Buyers' offer almost immediately after receiving the fully executed Termination Agreement from Agent. Clearly, a jury could determine that Sellers breached their duty of good faith and fair dealing by failing to disclose to Agent the pending offer when they asked Agent to accept their offer to terminate the Listing Agreement.

* * *

Reversed and Remanded.

JUDGE ZACHARY concurs.

JUDGE BRYANT dissents by separate opinion [which is omitted].

QUESTIONS

1. Questions about the facts of this case

   1.1. Did the Ahmeds check with the Agent before signing with the Feketes? Would you like to know the content of any such conversation?

   1.2. Does it matter that the Agent did not immediately sign the Termination Agreement? Do we know why the Agent waited? Should that matter?

2. Questions about the law

   2.1. Under the court's reasoning, who was the offeror on the Termination Agreement? Should that matter?

   2.2. Would it help the Ahmeds if they could interpose a defense of mistake to the Termination Agreement? Could they?

   2.3. Do the Ahmeds have any counterclaims or counter-actions for the Agent's breach of the implied covenant of good faith and fair dealing for her actions in handling the Termination Agreement?

3. **You Be the Lawyer!**

   You represent the Ahmeds. When the Feketes contact the Ahmeds after the Ahmeds' initial rejection, what should you advise the Ahmeds before they do anything with respect to that offer?

What happens under the parol evidence rule if the parties have signed writings but those writings are not complete expressions of their agreement; that is, what if the agreement is not fully integrated? Read on.

QUESTIONS BEFORE THE CASE

1. How many sources of contractual obligations are there between Barker and Price?

2. What would be the legal consequence if the court applied the parol evidence rule to the term related to the model year of the van?

BARKER V. PRICE

Court of Appeals of Indiana
48 N.E.3d 367 (2015)

NAJAM, JUDGE.

Statement of the Case

John Barker and Specialty Limos, LLC (collectively, "Barker") appeal the trial court's entry of summary judgment for Jason Price. Barker raises a single issue for our review, which we restate as whether the trial court erred when it interpreted the parties' contract. We affirm in part, reverse in part, and remand for further proceedings.

Facts and Procedural History

In 2014, Barker contacted Price about a van Price had advertised for sale. The advertisement described the van as a 1994 Ford E-350. The advertisement promised a "clean" certificate of title but did not indicate a sale price.

Barker and Price agreed to meet, and, on April 9, Barker inspected the van. Following Barker's inspection, he orally agreed to purchase the van from Price for $15,000. The parties then agreed in writing that Barker would make an immediate $2,000 deposit and Price would provide Barker "title by 4/14/14 or deposit will be refunded in full" ("the deposit agreement"). *Id.* at 15. The deposit agreement described the van as a Ford E-350 but did not specify the model year.

Sometime prior to April 14, 2014, Price provided Barker with a certificate of title for the van. The certificate indicated that the owner of the van was a third party. On the reverse side of the certificate, the owner appeared to have assigned her interest as a "seller," although the place for the purchaser's name was blank. *Id.* at 17. The certificate also described the van as a 1993 model rather than a 1994 model. Barker refused to accept the certificate of title and demanded a refund of his $2,000. Price, in turn, refused to refund the deposit.

Barker filed a small claim against Price for breach of contract .... After a hearing, the trial court entered summary judgment for Price. In relevant part, the trial court concluded that the year of the van was not a term material to the deposit agreement because that "agreement makes no reference to the year of the vehicle"; that Barker had accepted the van when he inspected it and paid the deposit; and that the certificate of title that Price tendered satisfied his obligation under the deposit agreement. This appeal ensued.

Discussion and Decision

Overview

* * *

This appeal requires the interpretation of a contract. Interpretation and construction of contract provisions are questions of law. *John M. Abbott, LLC v. Lake City Bank,* 14 N.E.3d 53, 56 (Ind.Ct.App.2014). * * * We review the contract as a whole, attempting to ascertain the parties' intent and making every attempt to construe the contract's language "so as not to render any words, phrases, or terms ineffective or meaningless." *Four Seasons Mfg., Inc. v. 1001 Coliseum, LLC,* 870 N.E.2d 494, 501 (Ind.Ct.App.2007).

Generally, Indiana's courts apply the "four corners rule" to determine the parties' intent in entering into a written contract. *Brill v. Regents Comm'ns, Inc.,* 12 N.E.3d 299, 309 (Ind.Ct.App.2014), *trans. denied.* That is, if the contract unambiguously demonstrates the parties' intent, we will simply apply the contract as written and, generally, "parol or extrinsic evidence is inadmissible to expand, vary, or explain the instrument. . . ." *Id.* (quotations omitted). However, the prohibition against the use of parol evidence "is by no means absolute." *Id.* (quotations omitted). And "where the existence . . . of a contract or the terms thereof is the point in issue, and the evidence is conflicting or admits of more than one inference, it is for the [trier of fact] to determine whether a contract in fact exists." *City of Indianapolis v. Twin Lakes Enter., Inc.,* 568 N.E.2d 1073, 1079 (Ind.Ct.App.1991), *trans. denied.*

Here, Barker asserts that the entry of summary judgment for Price is erroneous for two reasons. First, he asserts that the model year of the van was a term material to his agreement to purchase it, and Price failed to present a certificate of title for a 1994 van. Second, he asserts that the certificate of title was in the name of a third party and, therefore, that Price did not satisfy his obligation to deliver title as provided under the deposit agreement. We address each argument in turn.

Whether the Model Year of the Van was a Material Contract Term

We first consider Barker's argument that the certificate of title presented by Price did not comply with the deposit agreement because the certificate showed a different model year for the van than the year specified in the advertisement. This issue turns on the scope of the deposit agreement, which is the only writing between the parties regarding sale of the van. The deposit agreement simply states that, in exchange for a $2,000 deposit, Price "will have title by 4/14/14" for a "Ford E-350 Van." Because the deposit agreement does not specify the model year of the vehicle, Price asserts that the year must not have been a material term. As Price puts it, "the advertisement merged into the [deposit agreement]." We must agree with Barker that there is a genuine issue of material fact regarding whether the model year of the vehicle was a term material to the parties' agreement.

We begin with a basic point: the deposit agreement does not contain the entire agreement between the parties. As our supreme court has explained:

> An integrated agreement is a writing constituting the final expression of one or more terms of the parties' agreement. Restatement (Second) of Contracts § 209 (1981). The question of whether an agreement is an integration is one of fact[ ] that[,] unlike other questions of fact, is decided by the judge as a question preliminary to application of the parol evidence rule. *Id.* In determining whether a writing is integrated, the judge should examine the writing itself to see whether it appears complete on its face and should also consider any other relevant evidence. *Id.*

Sees v. Bank One, Ind., N.A., 839 N.E.2d 154, 162 n. 7 (Ind.2005).

The deposit agreement is not the entire agreement in that it omits at least one essential term, namely, the sale price for the van. And it does not contain an integration clause. Thus, we cannot agree with Price's contention that the advertisement or any other prior negotiations "merged" into the deposit agreement. *See, e.g., I.C.C. Protective Coatings, Inc. v. A.E. Staley Mfg. Co.,* 695 N.E.2d 1030, 1035–36 (Ind.Ct.App.1998), *trans. denied.* To the contrary, it is apparent that the deposit agreement was only part of a larger agreement between the parties and that part of the agreement was not reduced to writing.

Likewise, we are not persuaded by Price's argument that the deposit agreement speaks for itself when it omitted the model year from the vehicle's description. Price contends, in effect, that he could have produced a certificate of title for a Ford E-350 van manufactured in any year without affecting his deal with Barker. When the entire agreement between the parties is taken into account, we cannot say as a matter of law that the model year was not a material term. Indeed, in most automobile sales, the model year is a material term. Both new and used vehicles are typically offered for sale and sold based, in part, on the model year. And there is usually a correlation between the model year and the sale price.

As the deposit agreement did not contain the entire agreement, it is necessary for the trier of fact to consider parol evidence. That is, the parol evidence rule, which operates to exclude "contemporaneous oral statements that contradict the terms of an integrated written agreement," does not apply here because there is no integrated written agreement. *See,* 839 N.E.2d at 162; *cf. Krieg v. Hieber,* 802 N.E.2d 938, 943–44 (Ind.Ct.App.2004) (noting that, even when the parol evidence rule does apply, there are numerous exceptions, such as using extrinsic evidence to show a mistake in the formation of a contract or "to apply the terms of a contract to its subject matter").

Accordingly, whether the parties here considered the model year of the vehicle to be a term material to their agreement must be resolved by considering evidence extrinsic to the deposit agreement, including the original advertisement. The advertisement demonstrates that Price offered a 1994 vehicle, and the evidence suggests that Barker agreed to purchase the vehicle advertised. Thus, we must conclude that whether the year of the vehicle was a term material to the parties' agreement is a question of fact that must be resolved by considering all the evidence, not merely a question of law based only on an interpretation of the deposit agreement. *See id.*

Thus, we affirm in part, reverse in part, and remand for further proceedings.

QUESTIONS

1. Questions about the facts of this case

   1.1. In 2014, what was the the difference between a 1993 and a 1994 van?

   1.2. When the court states that "whether the year of the vehicle was a term material to the parties' agreement is a question of fact that must be resolved by considering all the evidence," what evidence does it mean?

2. Questions about the law

   2.1. Barker inspected the vehicle. Why doesn't that make the advertisement irrelevant?

   2.2. Would there be a different result if the title raised no questions as to ownership or model year, but was delivered on April 30 (and Price refuses to refund Barker's deposit)?

3. **You Be the Lawyer!**

   You represent Price. He tells you that his contract with Barker is not unusual; deals are often struck on minimal terms. He wants you, however, to give him a form with no more than three blanks for future use. What would it say?

B. UNIFORM COMMERCIAL CODE

According to *Barker*, one key to the applicability of the parol evidence rule is whether the document is complete, or, in legal lingo, "integrated."

The Uniform Commercial Code has its own version of the parol evidence rule, which is reprinted below.

§ 2–202. Final Expression in a Record: Parol or Extrinsic Evidence.

(1) Terms with respect to which the confirmatory records of the parties agree or which are otherwise set forth in a record intended by the parties as a final expression of their agreement with respect to such terms as are included therein may not be contradicted by evidence of any prior agreement or of a contemporaneous oral agreement but may be supplemented by evidence of:

(a) course of performance, course of dealing, or usage of trade (Section 1–303); and

(b) consistent additional terms unless the court finds the record to have been intended also as a complete and exclusive statement of the terms of the agreement.

(2) Terms in a record may be explained by evidence of course of performance, course of dealing, or usage of trade without a preliminary determination by the court that the language used is ambiguous.

Does this language change the common law parol evidence rule? Note that nowhere in this section is the term "integrated" used. Nevertheless, does it appear that the U.C.C. also has an "integration" concept?

QUESTIONS BEFORE THE CASE

1. What are the essential differences (if any) between the parol evidence rule at common law and the parol evidence rule under the U.C.C.?
2. What exceptions to the parol evidence rule does the court apply or mention in its analysis?

POSEY V. FORD MOTOR CREDIT CO.

Court of Appeals of Idaho
141 Idaho 477, 111 P.3d 162 (2005)

Opinion

LANSING, JUDGE.

Gregory R. Posey sued Ford Motor Credit Company (Ford) for breach of contract * * * in connection with the lease of a truck. The district court granted summary judgment to Ford based, in part, on the common law parol evidence rule. Posey appeals. Because we conclude that the district court did not apply the governing statutory parol evidence rule, we vacate the summary judgment and remand for further proceedings.

I.

BACKGROUND

According to the allegations of Posey's verified complaint, in mid-January 2000, he signed a contract to lease a new Ford truck from a dealership in Caldwell. The lease agreement called for 48 monthly payments of $635.43, with an option to purchase the truck for $9,514.00 at the end of the lease term. Posey alleges that about three days later a Ford representative informed Posey of errors in the agreement regarding the lease term and the identity of the lease holder. The Ford representative said that the lease term should have been 36 months instead of 48, and asked that Posey sign a new lease agreement reflecting the correct term of months. On January 24, Posey and the dealership, as lessor, executed a new lease agreement. The lease was a pre-printed form with blanks into which entries were typed. The blank at line 7(n) for "lease term in months" was not filled in, but at two other places on the form, the lease clearly called for 48 monthly payments of $612.72 per month. The lease also provided that Posey would have the option to purchase the vehicle for $10,873.60 at the end of the lease. The space on the form for identification of the lease "holder" was also left empty. Posey signed this lease, allegedly without noticing that it again provided for a 48-month term.

On January 31, 2000, a letter concerning the January 24, 2000 lease was sent to Posey from the Ford office in Murray, Utah. It stated in part:

> On reviewing the lease agreement, we noticed and corrected the following error(s).
>
> The holder on your lease agreement should show; FORD MOTOR CREDIT CO.
>
> Line n of your lease agreement should show a term of 36 months.
>
> No further action is required from you. Keep this notice as your record of the change(s) made.

Posey asserts that he relied upon alleged oral representations by the dealership representatives that the January 24 lease was for a 36-month term and asserts that this understanding was confirmed by the January 31 letter. Posey alleges that as a consequence of the oral representations and the letter, he understood that he would have the option to purchase the vehicle for $10,873.60 after making 36 monthly payments of $612.72. Posey made 36 monthly payments and then tried to exercise his option to purchase the truck for $10,873.60, but Ford refused.

Posey initiated this action, alleging breach of contract * * *. Both parties moved for summary judgment. As the basis for its motion, Ford argued that the January 24 written lease was complete and unambiguous, that it set forth a 48-month lease and that the parol evidence rule therefore precluded Posey from presenting evidence of any inconsistent agreement. The parol evidence rule, Ford argued, precluded introduction of not only alleged oral representations made by dealership representatives before the January 24 lease was signed, but also Ford's own January 31 letter. Ford also argued that Posey could not claim that the letter modified the lease because any alleged modification was not supported by consideration.

In support of its motion and in opposition to Posey's, Ford submitted an affidavit of Frank Griffith, the Central Operations Manager for Ford at Ford's Colorado Springs Service Center. * * * The affidavit averred, among other things, that Ford's letter of January 31 to Posey was in error in stating that the blank on "line n" should show a lease term of 36 months. The district court struck that statement from Griffith's affidavit but refused to strike the balance of the affidavit and attached documents.

The district court granted Ford's summary judgment motion, concluding that the January 24 lease unambiguously stated the lease term to be 48 months, that the January 31 letter did not alter or modify the terms of the lease * * *.

Posey appeals, arguing that the district court erred in granting summary judgment for Ford on the contract claim because Ford's subsequent letter clarifies and completes the January 24 written lease, resulting in internal ambiguity as to whether the parties intended the lease term to be 36 or 48 months and, thus, a material issue of fact remains. * * *

II.

ANALYSIS

A. Breach of Contract Claim

1. Parol evidence rule

Before both the district court and this Court on appeal, the parties have presented their arguments concerning the parol evidence rule based solely upon the common law. That common law rule has been stated thusly: "If a written contract is complete upon its face and unambiguous, no fraud or mistake being alleged, extrinsic evidence of prior or contemporaneous negotiations or conversations is not admissible to contradict, vary, alter, add to, or detract from the terms of the contract." [Citations] Our Supreme Court recently reiterated in *Howard* that under the common law rule, the presence of a merger clause in a written contract conclusively establishes that the agreement is integrated and therefore subject to the parol evidence rule. In the present case, although the district court did not expressly reference the parol evidence rule in its written decision, it is apparent that the court applied the common law rule in granting summary judgment to Ford after concluding that the January 24 lease agreement "is unambiguous as a matter of law."

The analysis of the parties and the district court was flawed, however, because the common law rule is not applicable here. Rather, the lease transaction was subject to Chapter 12 of the Uniform Commercial Code (UCC), I.C. § 28–12–101, et seq., which governs leases and includes a specific parol evidence provision. The controlling statute, I.C. § 28–12–202, states:

> Terms with respect to which the confirmatory memoranda of the parties agree or which are otherwise set forth in a writing intended by the parties as a final expression of their agreement with respect to such terms as are included therein may not be contradicted by evidence of any prior agreement or of a contemporaneous oral agreement but may be explained or supplemented:
>
> (a) By course of dealing or usage of trade or by course of performance; and
>
> (b) By evidence of consistent additional terms unless the court finds the writing to have been intended also as a complete and exclusive statement of the terms of the agreement.

This UCC parol evidence provision was intended to liberalize the common law rule and to abolish any presumption that a writing is a total integration. Anderson & Nafziger v. G.T. Newcomb, Inc., 100 Idaho 175, 180, 595 P.2d 709, 714 (1979).[1]

Where a written lease exists, it is apparent from the language of section 28–12–202 that the initial inquiry is not whether the writing is "complete upon its face and unambiguous" as under the common law.[2] Instead, the initial question is the intent of the parties—whether the writing was intended by the parties to be a "final expression of their agreement with respect to such terms as are included therein" and whether the writing was intended to be a "complete and exclusive statement of [all] the terms of the agreement." See Anderson, 100 Idaho at 180, 595 P.2d at 714; and Hoff Co., Inc. v. Danner, 121 Idaho 39, 43, 822 P.2d 558, 562 (Ct.App.1991). In addressing the identical parol evidence statute governing sales, I.C. § 28–2–202, in Hoff, we observed:

---

[1] In *Anderson*, the Idaho Supreme Court was referring to the parol evidence rule found in Chapter 2 of the UCC on sales, I.C. § 28–2–202, rather than § 28–12–202 governing leases. However, the language of the two statutes is identical, and we therefore view decisions interpreting and applying I.C. § 28–2–202 to be equally applicable to I.C. § 28–12–202.

[2] The official comment to section 2–202 of the UCC (I.C. § 28–2–202) states that the statute "definitely rejects" any requirement that, as a condition precedent to the admissibility of parol evidence, the court must determine that the language of the written agreement is ambiguous.

> [A] writing may inaccurately state the intentions of the parties, and its language will not create an agreement that previously did not exist. Moreover, the trial court's task is to give effect to agreements in accordance with the parties' intentions, even when the forms employed suggest otherwise. Whether the parties intended the writing as the final expression of their agreement, and whether the additional terms sought to be proved are contradictory, are questions for the court.

Hoff, 121 Idaho at 43–44, 822 P.2d at 562–63 (citations omitted).

In making the required factual findings under section 28–12–202, a trial court should go beyond the "four corners" of the written agreement and consider not only the language of the agreement but all extrinsic evidence relevant to the parties' intent. *Anderson*, 100 Idaho at 180, 595 P.2d at 714. The *Anderson* Court noted that the application of the statutory standards does not deprive a merger or integration clause of all effect but does limit the conclusiveness of such language. *Id.* "The terms of the writing still have superior probative value but are tempered by the trial court's ability to consider extrinsic evidence of the parties' intentions." *Id.*

This process, in which factual findings are made by a judge to determine whether certain evidence will be excluded from a jury's consideration, is a marked exception to the general rule that issues of fact are left for determination by the jury and that factual issues may not be resolved on summary judgment. [Citations] As explained by a leading treatise:

> [T]he division of functions between judge and jury in administering the rule can "give preference" to written evidence over oral evidence of contract terms. So, too, can allocations of burden of proof. Section 2–202 does not state very clearly what the division of functions is supposed to be. But the way the rule is worded, the trial is certainly not to be a free-wheeling affair in which the parties may introduce before the jury all evidence of terms, including the writing, with the jury then to decide on terms. Rather, it is plain from the rule and from prior history of similar rules that some of the evidence is to be heard initially only by the judge and that the judge may invoke the rule to keep this evidence from the jury. The evidence that is in this way subject to exclusion will usually be oral evidence. Indeed, before a judge can invoke a parol evidence rule at all, the judge must first admit a writing into evidence before the jury. If the judge thereafter excludes oral evidence of terms on the basis of the parol evidence rule, the judge gives preference to the writing already in evidence by prohibiting the jury from considering the oral evidence.

> But when can the judge invoke 2–202 to exclude oral evidence of terms? First, the judge may exclude the evidence on finding that the parties intended the writing to be a complete and exclusive statement of the terms of the agreement (unless it be evidence of course of dealing, usage of trade, or course of performance introduced only to explain or supplement the writing). Code and comments both state that the question of completeness and exclusivity is for the judge. Second, the judge may exclude evidence extrinsic to terms set forth in the writing if he or she decides that the writing is a final written expression as to these terms and that the other evidence contradicts these terms. The Code does not say that this question is for the judge, but if "completeness and exclusivity" is for the judge, then whether a writing is a final written expression to the terms it does include would be for the judge, for the greater ordinarily includes the lesser. The issue of contradictoriness is also generally for the judge. Third, in passing on any parol evidence rule objection, the judge may decide that the proffered evidence of terms extrinsic to the writing is not credible, and he or she may exclude it on that ground alone.

JAMES J. WHITE & ROBERT S. SUMMERS, UNIFORM COMMERCIAL CODE, § 2–9, at 86–87 (4th ed.1995).

The factual findings required of the court by I.C. § 28–12–202 were not made by the district court in the present case because only the common law parol evidence rule was argued by the parties and considered by the court. Making such findings is the province of the district court and is not a matter for initial determination by this Court on appeal. See Anderson, 100 Idaho at 179–80, 595 P.2d at 713–14 (where the trial court had made no findings, as required under I.C. § 28–2–202, regarding whether an order form was intended as a fully integrated agreement, the case was remanded to the trial court for that determination). It follows that remand for appropriate findings is necessary here.

For guidance on remand we briefly address an additional point concerning the parol evidence rule. Posey has argued for application of the common law exception to the parol evidence rule that allows the use of extrinsic evidence when a party alleges that, by reason of mistake, the written instrument does not memorialize the true agreement of the parties. See Belk v. Martin, 136 Idaho 652, 657–58, 39 P.3d 592, 597–98 (2001) and Bailey v. Ewing, 105 Idaho 636, 640–41, 671 P.2d 1099, 1103–04 (Ct.App.1983). Idaho Code § 28–1–103 specifies that "unless displaced by the particular provisions of [the UCC], the principles of law and equity, including . . . mistake . . . [shall] supplement its provisions." *See also* WHITE & SUMMERS, § 2–11 at 103. The common law mistake doctrine is not inconsistent with I.C. § 28–12–202 and therefore may be applied to transactions that are governed by the statute. The mistake exception makes extrinsic evidence admissible to show that by reason of either mutual mistake or one party's unilateral mistake which is known to the other party, the written agreement does not express the parties' true intent. *Belk*, 136 Idaho at 657–58, 39 P.3d at 597–98. A mistake is an unintentional act or omission arising from ignorance, surprise, or misplaced confidence. Bailey, 105 Idaho at 639–41, 671 P.2d at 1102–04. Posey's assertion of the mistake exception, if reiterated on remand, must be addressed by the district court.

2. Modification

In addition to arguing that the January 31 letter from Ford to Posey is inadmissible under the parol evidence rule, Ford asserts that, in relying upon the letter, Posey seeks to enforce a modification of the lease without consideration. Ford relies upon the common law rule that the modification of the contract must be supported by valid consideration. See, e.g., Brand S Corp. v. King, 102 Idaho 731, 733, 639 P.2d 429, 431 (1981). This argument is without merit for two reasons. First, Posey is not contending that there was a subsequent agreement to modify the January 24 lease but, rather, that the parties' intent was always to have a 36-month term, as expressed in the January 31 letter. Second, the common law rule requiring consideration for contract modification, like the common law parol evidence rule, has been superseded by the UCC. The statute that governs in this case, I.C. § 28–12–208(1) [as well as U.C.C. § 2–209(1)], provides that "[a]n agreement modifying a lease contract needs no consideration to be binding."

* * *

III.

CONCLUSION

For the reasons explained above, the summary judgment dismissing Posey's claims for breach of lease * * * is vacated and the case is remanded for further proceedings consistent with this opinion. Costs to appellant.

CHIEF JUDGE PERRY and JUDGE GUTIERREZ concur.

QUESTIONS AND NOTE

1. Questions about the facts of this case

    1.1. How many times did Ford attempt to change the agreement?

    1.2. How long was the term of the lease that Posey actually signed? Why shouldn't Posey be held to that term?

2. Questions about the law

   2.1. Would either the common law or the U.C.C. parol evidence rule have barred introduction of the January 31 letter Ford sent Posey? Why or why not?

   2.2. If you represented Posey, and the court rejected your argument that the January 24 agreement was for 36 months, what would your arguments be that the January 31 letter modified the agreement? That is, if the court is correct (and it is) that no consideration is necessary for contract modification, where is the offer; where is the acceptance?

3. **You Be the Lawyer (and sneaky review question)!**

   On remand, if you represented Posey, what evidence would you marshal and present to establish a mistake? By the way, how does a mistake defense assist Posey in obtaining the truck after 36 months for the stated option price?

4. Note

   Wait a minute. Didn't the last case (*Barker*) involve the sale of a van? Isn't a van a "moveable"? Shouldn't the Indiana court have applied the U.C.C. to decide that case? Would it have made any difference?

C. EXCEPTIONS AND SCOPE OF PAROL EVIDENCE RULE

As we have seen above, there are exceptions to the parol evidence rule, essentially making understanding the "subtle difficulties" mentioned by James Thayer above more important than the ability to state the rule itself. Start first with a subtlety present in *Posey*. Although technically not an exception, the rule does not apply to evidence relating to terms discussed or agreed to *after* the execution of the agreement. Under the *Restatement*, the rule applies only to acts to "discharge[ ] *prior* agreements." *Restatement (Second) of Contracts* § 213(1) (emphasis added). This is a sensible result; if the rule acted prospectively, it would effectively eliminate any possibility of amendment or individual waiver of provisions of an integrated agreement. Contracts are typically not that static or rigid.

There are, however, other exceptions to the parol evidence rule.

QUESTIONS BEFORE THE CASE

1. How many agreements exist under Weiss's theory of the case? Under Smulders'?

2. If there is more than one agreement between two parties, how close does the subject matter of each agreement have to be to the other agreements before the parol evidence rule applies in any litigation between the parties?

WEISS V. SMULDERS

Supreme Court of Connecticut.
313 Conn. 227, 96 A.3d 1175 (2014)

PALMER, ZARELLA, EVELEIGH, MCDONALD and BEACH, JS.

Opinion

MCDONALD, J.

These appeals arise out of a dispute between two specialty food businesses regarding the scope of their obligations under a distribution agreement and the legal effect of oral promises regarding the formation of a joint venture between the businesses. The plaintiffs, Randall Weiss and his company, Gourmet and Specialty Food Works, LLC (Food Works), commenced this action against the defendants, Michael D. Smulders and his company, Garden of Light Natural Food Markets, Inc. (Garden of Light), seeking to recover money damages for, inter alia, breach of an oral contract and promissory estoppel for failing to form the joint venture. The defendants filed counterclaims asserting, inter alia, that the plaintiffs had breached the parties' written contract by failing to pay for goods purchased. Following a bench trial, the court rendered judgment for the plaintiffs on their promissory estoppel claim against Smulders, but awarded limited damages on the ground that the plaintiffs had not proved the value of their share of the new venture to a reasonable certainty, and rendered judgment for the defendants on their breach of contract counterclaim. The plaintiffs and the defendants filed separate appeals from the judgment. * * * We affirm the judgment of the trial court in all respects.

The trial court reasonably could have found the following facts. Smulders and Weiss had their first business interaction in 2001. At that time, Smulders was the president and sole shareholder of Garden of Light, a company that owned and operated two natural foods grocery stores in Avon and Glastonbury and a bakery that produced natural granola products sold in those stores. Weiss was the owner and operator of Aegean International, an olive oil and balsamic vinegar distribution and marketing company. The business relationship between the two men began when Weiss approached Smulders about selling his olive oil in Garden of Light's Glastonbury store. Smulders agreed, and due to successful sales, Smulders continued to purchase olive oil from Weiss.

In the late spring or early summer of 2003, while Weiss was visiting the Garden of Light grocery store, Smulders asked Weiss if he thought that Garden of Light's granola could be packaged for wholesale distribution. At that time, the granola products were being sold only in the two Garden of Light grocery stores, and were packed in a plastic bag bearing a plain black and white "scale" label. Weiss responded that, if properly packaged, the product potentially could do well. Smulders acknowledged that he did not have any wholesale marketing experience. He further indicated to Weiss that he would need Weiss' assistance in this area and that he had approached Weiss because of Weiss' olive oil marketing campaign. As a result of this conversation, the interest of both parties was piqued, and they had numerous subsequent conversations in the late spring or early summer of 2003, in which they agreed to work to distribute the granola products.

In or around August, 2003, the parties discussed working together as two separate companies to produce and distribute the granola products. Smulders also indicated that they would merge their companies to form a new enterprise if that relationship proved successful. Shortly thereafter, Weiss formed Food Works to distribute Garden of Light's granola products. In December, 2003, Garden of Light and Food Works executed a written "Master Distributorship Agreement" (distribution agreement), the purpose of which was to designate Food Works the exclusive distributor of granola products produced by Garden of Light. The distribution agreement expressly acknowledged that the parties had entered into discussions with respect to the formation of a new company. Subsequent to the execution of the distribution agreement and until approximately the time their relationship ended in 2006, Smulders made repeated representations to Weiss that he would spin off his bakery business from Garden of Light, merge it with Food Works, and that he and Weiss would be equal partners in the new company, which they referred to as "NEWCO."

In the period that followed the execution of the distribution agreement, Weiss wound down his olive oil business to focus primarily on the granola products business, expending many hours on marketing and research. Weiss also paid a brand manager $14,000 to promote that business. At some point during this period, Weiss and Smulders began labeling the granola products with the trade name Bakery on Main. While Food Works purchased and distributed Garden of Light's granola products, Weiss and Smulders continued to maintain their separate companies.

In September, 2006, Smulders sent an e-mail to Weiss, informing Weiss that he would not merge companies. At the same time, Smulders sent a letter to Weiss, asserting that Food Works was not in compliance with the distribution agreement because it had failed to compensate Garden of Light for products that had been purchased for distribution. As required by the distribution agreement, Smulders, acting on behalf of Garden of Light, gave Food Works thirty days to cure the breach.

Thereafter, Garden of Light continued to fulfill Food Works' orders, as it was bound to do under the distribution agreement, and Food Works' debt continued to accumulate. After Food Works failed to make full payment within the thirty day period, Garden of Light formally terminated the distribution agreement.

The record reveals the following procedural history. The plaintiffs commenced this action against the defendants, alleging in the operative complaint: breach of oral contract and promissory estoppel as to Smulders; breach of written contract as to Garden of Light; * * * [the] defendants asserted various special defenses and two counterclaims against the plaintiffs, alleging breach of contract and fraudulent misrepresentation.

After the close of evidence, * * * the court found in favor of the defendants on all of the plaintiffs' claims except promissory estoppel. With respect to that claim, the court found that the plaintiffs had met their burden of establishing that Smulders made promises regarding an eventual merger of their two companies and that Weiss acted in reliance on those promises to his detriment. With respect to the defendants' counterclaims, the court found that the defendants had met their burden of establishing that the plaintiffs breached the distribution agreement by failing to compensate Garden of Light for products that the plaintiffs had purchased for distribution * * *.

With respect to damages, the court awarded the defendants $110,463.50 in principal and interest for the plaintiffs' breach of the distribution agreement. As to the plaintiffs' damages for promissory estoppel, the court found that they were entitled to be compensated as if the companies had merged as promised and for costs expended on the venture that never came to be. With respect to the latter, the court found that Weiss was entitled to one half of the $14,000 that he had paid to the brand manager to promote the granola products, as he would have benefited from one half of those services as a partner in NEWCO. The court also found that Weiss was entitled to the value of a 50 percent share of NEWCO, but that neither party had offered sufficient evidence to demonstrate the value of NEWCO.*

I

All of the parties raise claims challenging the trial court's judgment with respect to the plaintiffs' promissory estoppel claim—the defendants on the merits and the plaintiffs on damages. The defendants contend that * * * the court improperly allowed the plaintiffs to recover on this claim because it contradicted the fully integrated distribution agreement. * * *

---

* [And without acceptable and certain evidence of damages, you don't get any. See the note at the end of the case. Eds.]

B

We next turn to the defendants' claim that the plaintiffs cannot recover on their promissory estoppel claim because it contradicts the fully integrated distribution agreement. Specifically, the defendants point to a merger clause in the distribution agreement, and to language therein indicating that any agreement regarding the formation of a new business must be evidenced in writing. As such, the defendants argue that the trial court violated the parol evidence rule by allowing the plaintiffs to prevail on their promissory estoppel claim. In response, the plaintiffs argue * * * that the defendants' claim fails on the merits because the subject matter of Smulders' promise to merge companies did not come within the scope of the distribution agreement. We conclude * * * that the trial court properly admitted evidence in support of the plaintiffs' promissory estoppel claim because Smulders' promise did not vary or contradict the subject matter of the distribution agreement.

"[T]he parol evidence rule is not an exclusionary rule of evidence . . . but a rule of substantive contract law . . . to which we afford plenary review." (Internal quotation marks omitted.) *Alstom Power, Inc. v. Balcke-Durr, Inc.,* 269 Conn. 599, 609, 849 A.2d 804 (2004); *Ravenswood Construction, LLC v. F.L. Merritt, Inc.,* 105 Conn.App. 7, 14, 936 A.2d 679 (2007). "The rule is premised upon the idea that when the parties have deliberately put their engagements into writing, in such terms as import a legal obligation, without any uncertainty as to the object or extent of such engagement, it is conclusively presumed, that the whole engagement of the parties, and the extent and manner of their understanding, was reduced to writing. After this, to permit oral testimony, or prior or contemporaneous conversations, or circumstances, or usages . . . in order to learn what was intended, or to contradict what is written, would be dangerous and unjust in the extreme." (Internal quotation marks omitted.) *Schilberg Integrated Metals Corp. v. Continental Casualty Co.,* 263 Conn. 245, 277, 819 A.2d 773 (2003). "Ordinarily, a merger clause provision indicates that the subject agreement is completely integrated, and parol evidence is precluded from altering or interpreting the agreement. *Tempo Shain Corp. v. Bertek, Inc.,* 120 F.3d 16, 21 (2d Cir.1997)." (Internal quotation marks omitted.) *Western Dermatology Consultants, P.C. v. VitalWorks, Inc.,* 146 Conn.App. 169, 191, 78 A.3d 167 (2013).

"The parol evidence rule does not of itself, therefore, forbid the presentation of parol evidence, that is, evidence outside the four corners of the contract concerning matters governed by an integrated contract, but forbids only the use of such evidence to vary or contradict the terms of such a contract. Parol evidence offered solely to vary or contradict the written terms of an integrated contract is, therefore, legally irrelevant. When offered for that purpose, it is inadmissible not because it is parol evidence, but because it is irrelevant. By implication, such evidence may still be admissible if relevant . . . to prove [inter alia] a collateral oral agreement which does not vary the terms of the writing. . . ." (Internal quotation marks omitted.) *Schilberg Integrated Metals Corp. v. Continental Casualty Co.,* supra, 263 Conn. at 277, 819 A.2d 773; see also *Tallmadge Bros., Inc. v. Iroquois Gas Transmission System, L.P.,* 252 Conn. 479, 503 n. 14, 746 A.2d 1277 (2000) (proof of integrated agreement does not bar proof of collateral oral agreement that does not vary terms of writing); 2 Restatement (Second), Contracts § 213(2), p. 129 (1981) ("[a] binding completely integrated agreement discharges prior agreements to the extent that they are within its scope").

With these principles in mind, we turn to the language contained in the distribution agreement. The preface to the distribution agreement sets forth several recital provisions, including the following: "This Master Distribution Agreement . . . is made and entered into . . . with reference to the following facts . . .

> "2. The parties have entered into discussions with respect to the formation of a new company, joint venture or other similar arrangement which would replace the business arrangement detailed in this [a]greement;
>
> "3. Unless and until the above-described arrangement has been finalized and evidenced by written agreement(s), [Garden of Light] wishes to appoint [Food Works] as its exclusive distributor for the sale of Products under the Marks to Dealers in the Territory (as such terms are hereinafter defined). . . ."

Following the recitations, the distribution agreement then provides: "THEREFORE, [Garden of Light] and [Food Works] hereby agree as follows. . . ." The distribution agreement then prescribes substantive terms of the agreement, including, among others, the grant of a distributorship to Food Works, Food Works' general obligations, Garden of Light's general obligations, prices and terms of payment, the duration of the agreement, and termination. One such term is a merger clause, which provides in relevant part: "This [a]greement contains all of the terms and conditions agreed upon by the parties hereto *with reference to the subject matter hereof.* No other agreements, oral or otherwise, shall be deemed to exist or to bind either of the parties hereto, and all prior agreements and understandings are superseded hereby. . . ." (Emphasis added.)

We conclude that, even if the distribution agreement is fully integrated, the defendants' claim fails because an examination of the distribution agreement clearly indicates that the evidence admitted at trial to prove that Smulders promised Weiss that they would merge companies to form NEWCO is collateral to the subject matter of the distribution agreement. The subject matter of the distribution agreement is Food Works' purchase and distribution of Garden of Light's products, not the formation of NEWCO. Cf. *Perricone v. Perricone,* 292 Conn. 187, 196, 972 A.2d 666 (2009) (holding confidentiality agreement collateral to separation agreement because "relevant subject matter of the separation agreement was the *division of property* between the parties, while the subject matter of the confidentiality agreement was the *disclosure of information* concerning the parties' property and the parties themselves" [emphasis in original]); *Shelton Yacht & Cabana Club, Inc. v. Suto,* 150 Conn. 251, 257, 259–60, 188 A.2d 493 (1963) (holding that although written and unwritten contracts related to advertising and promotion of defendant's clubs, unwritten contracts are collateral to written contracts because written contracts concern promise to advertise, promote, and sell memberships to defendant's clubs, while unwritten contracts concerned expenses paid and incurred by plaintiffs in promoting clubs, therefore exceeding scope of written contracts). All of the substantive rights and obligations under the distribution agreement pertain to that distribution agreement. There is no provision in the distribution agreement addressing the parameters under which NEWCO would be created or the parties' obligations upon the creation of NEWCO. Indeed, the trial court's finding that the distribution agreement merely pertained to the distribution relationship is wholly consistent with the title of the agreement—"Master Distributorship Agreement"—and the obligations imposed thereunder.

The only reference to the future formation of the new company is in the recital provisions. The related language in the recital on which the defendants rely that addresses the new venture being "finalized and evidenced by written agreement(s)," however, appears to conflict with substantive provisions of the distribution agreement. Specifically, the recital indicates that Food Works will continue as distributor unless and until a new company or joint venture has been finalized. The substantive provision pertaining to the duration of the contract states that the agreement is to last for three years from the date of execution "[u]nless sooner terminated in accordance with the provisions of [a]rticle 9 [Termination]." Article 9 enumerates specific grounds on which either party may terminate the agreement, none of which includes the formation of NEWCO or any other joint venture. Any conflict between the recital provisions and the substantive terms of the distribution agreement is resolved by the fact that the subject matter of the distribution agreement is the distribution relationship between the parties. As such, the substantive provisions regarding the duration and termination of that matter necessarily would control over what is evidently a collateral matter. See *McKinnon v. Baker,* 220 Neb. 314, 317, 370 N.W.2d 492 (1985) (noting well settled principle that "[i]f both the recitals and the operative part are clear, but they are inconsistent with each other, the operative part must control" [internal quotation marks omitted]); see also *Jamison v. Franklin Life Ins. Co.,* 60 Ariz. 308, 317, 136 P.2d 265 (1943) (same); *Williams v. Barkley,* 165 N.Y. 48, 57, 58 N.E. 765 (1900) (same). In light of these considerations, it is apparent that the formation of NEWCO was collateral to the subject matter of the distribution agreement. Therefore, the trial court properly admitted evidence to prove Smulders' promises to Weiss because such evidence did not vary the terms of the writing contained in the distribution agreement. * * *

The judgment is affirmed.

QUESTIONS AND NOTE

1. Questions about the facts of this case

   1.1. What is a merger or integration clause? What was the merger (or integration) clause in this case?

   1.2. Do we know why the business combination did not occur? Is that relevant?

   1.3. How different was the distribution agreement from the agreement to possibly combine or merge the two business operations? Can you state a general rule distinguishing the two? Does the court?

2. Questions about the law

   2.1. What is the legal effect of a merger clause? What was the effect of the merger clause in this case?

   2.2. What if the price of goods sold by Smulder and Garden of Light to Food Works differered depending on whether the Garden of Light and Food Works combined operations? For example, would it have made a difference if the distribution agreement had said: "Granola shall be $1 a pound if there is a business combination as referred to in the recitals; $2 a pound if there is no business combination."?

   2.3 If the parol evidence rule is a rule of substantive law, what is this court's rule of evidence law that excludes parol evidence of prior or contemporaneous discussions or negotiations between the parties?

3. **You Be the Lawyer!**

   Having read this case, what terms would you add or subtract in the distribution agreement had you represented Smulder? Weiss?

4. Note

   Weiss and Food Works won on promissory estoppel liability, but received no damages because they could not prove their injury due to the failure to combine. We deleted the discussion of that point, because you'll study the issue—certainty of damages—when you study remedies in Chapter 7.

Any other exceptions? What, for example, can you do when buying a car or a house if the seller tells you that "I've never had to repair" the car or the house—but doesn't put that in the contract. When you find out that the seller spent a ton of money in repairs, and those repairs relate to problems you are having, can you bring up the Seller's statement when you sue to get out of the contract if the the contract has a merger or integration clause? Next case.

QUESTIONS BEFORE THE CASE

1. If the parol evidence rule applied in this case, what evidence would be omitted? Would it be evidence of the terms or other provisions of the contract?
2. Is the interposition of fraud being used here as a basis for the recovery of damages, or as a basis for negating the existence of an otherwise valid contract?

POEPPEL V. LESTER

Supreme Court of South Dakota
827 N.W.2d 580 (2013)

WILBUR, JUSTICE.

In 2008, Rob Poeppel brought suit against Luke Lester for breach of contract for Lester's failure to purchase Poeppel's voting interest in Coldwell Banker Lewis-Kirkeby-Hall Real Estate, Inc. (CBLKH). Following Lester's stipulation as to breach, a court trial was held on the issue of damages. The court awarded damages to Poeppel in the amount of $250,000 plus prejudgment interest and costs.

FACTS AND PROCEDURAL BACKGROUND

Poeppel was the owner of a 25% (100 no-par shares) voting interest in CBLKH. In March 2008, Lester, an independent contractor and broker associate at CBLKH, approached Poeppel about purchasing Poeppel's 25% voting interest in the company. Also during this time, Mel Dreyer, another broker associate of the company, approached Diana Hooper, another owner of a 25% voting interest in CBLKH, about Dreyer purchasing Hooper's 25% voting interest.

On March 28, 2008, Poeppel and Lester entered into a contract for the sale of the shares. The parties agreed that Poeppel would sell Lester one hundred shares (25%) of no-par CBLKH voting stock for $500,000. The contract signed by the parties was a form that Lester received from Dreyer. Dreyer had used the form during his negotiations with Hooper. Lester then made changes to the contract and presented it to Poeppel for signature. Paragraph five of the contract entitled "Access to Information" provides:

> The parties acknowledge that Seller has provided to Buyer certain financial information with respect to the Shares and that Buyer has formed his own opinion as to the value of the Shares being purchased hereunder. Notwithstanding the foregoing, prior to Closing, Seller shall, or shall cause the Company to, provide to Buyer and to Buyer's counsel, accountants, or other representatives full access throughout the period prior to Closing to all of the Company's properties, books, contracts, commitments, and records, and shall furnish to Buyer during such period all information concerning the Company's affairs as the Buyer may reasonably request. SELLER MAKES NO WARRANTY OF THE INCOME PRODUCING ABILITY OF THE SHARES OR THE PROFITABILITY OF THE COMPANY. BUYER RECOGNIZES THAT THE VALUE OF THE SHARES IS DEPENDENT IN PART UPON BUYER'S SKILL AND ABILITY.

Additionally, paragraph seven, section c, "Warranties of Buyer," provides: "That all documents and records requested by Buyer have been delivered or made available to Buyer, and Buyer's investment decision is based upon Buyer's own investigation and analysis and not the representations or inducements of Seller or Seller's agents."

The closing date on the contract was set for May 15, 2008. Lester failed to attend the closing and did not pay $500,000 for Poeppel's shares. Additionally, Lester notified Poeppel in a letter dated May 22, 2008, that he was unable to secure financing with the right structure for the purchase of the stock.

After continued negotiations between the parties failed, Poeppel brought suit for breach of contract against Lester in September 2008. In his answer, Lester raised the defense that his consent to enter into the contract was obtained by fraud. Lester alleged that Poeppel failed to give him important financial information regarding the company; made a false claim about the income producing ability of the shares of stock; and told Lester that the company held an exclusive franchise with Coldwell Banker.

Poeppel moved for summary judgment on three separate occasions alleging that the contract was unambiguous as to Lester's receipt of CBLKH's financial information. Each motion was denied.

A trial was scheduled for November 2–3, 2011. On the day before trial, the trial court concluded that the terms of the contract were unambiguous and that parol evidence as to financial documents was inadmissible. The court also granted Poeppel's motions in limine to exclude evidence relating to CBLKH's financial information and to exclude statements made by Poeppel to Lester concerning income that was generated by the stock and the exclusive franchise agreement. Following these rulings, Lester stipulated to the breach of contract.

The issue of damages was tried in a court trial on November 3, 2011. The trial court entered judgment against Lester for $250,000 plus prejudgment interests and costs. * * *

ANALYSIS

Whether the trial court erred in concluding that the contract was unambiguous and in granting Poeppel's motions in limine.

The trial court concluded that the language of the contract is clear and unambiguous and that it would "stay with the language of the contract." Based on this conclusion, the trial court also granted Poeppel's motion in limine to prohibit Lester from introducing parol evidence that Poeppel had represented to Lester: (1) that Lester could not receive financial documents until after he signed the contract; (2) that the stocks Lester sought to purchase would generate approximately $115,000; and (3) that the company had an exclusive franchise arrangement with Coldwell Banker.

" 'Contract interpretation is a question of law' reviewed de novo." [Citations] " 'When interpreting a contract, this Court looks to the language that the parties used in the contract to determine their intention.' " [Citations] " 'In order to ascertain the terms and conditions of a contract, we examine the contract as a whole and give words their plain and ordinary meaning.' " [Citations] " 'When the words of a contract are clear and explicit and lead to no absurd consequences, the search for the parties' common intent is at an end.' " [Citations].

The express language of the contract, when read as a whole, is clear and unambiguous. By signing the contract that he presented to Poeppel, Lester represented that he received financial documents from Poeppel and that Lester formed his own opinion as to the value of the shares.

However, even though the contract was unambiguous, Lester should have been allowed to present his defense to a jury that he was fraudulently induced to sign the stock purchase agreement through several misrepresentations made by Poeppel. The trial court erred as a matter of law by barring this evidence under the parol evidence rule.

South Dakota's parol evidence rule provides: "The execution of a contract in writing, whether the law requires it to be written or not, supersedes all the oral negotiations or stipulations concerning its matter which preceded or accompanied the execution of the instrument." SDCL 53–8–5. This rule " 'is in no sense a rule of evidence, but a rule of substantive law.' " *Auto-Owners Ins. Co. v. Hansen Housing, Inc.*, 2000 S.D. 13, ¶ 14, 604 N.W.2d 504, 510 (quoting 9 John Wigmore, Evidence § 2400 at 4 (Chadbourn rev. ed. 1981)). * * * In excluding Lester's fraud evidence, the trial court ruled, as a matter of law, that the parol evidence rule precluded any extrinsic evidence. Yet the parol evidence rule does not apply in cases of fraud in the inducement.

1. *Fraud in the Inducement*

Fraud as an inducement to enter a contract is a question of fact for the jury. "Actual fraud is always a question of fact." SDCL 53–4–5. And parol or extrinsic evidence is admissible to prove fraud. "It is generally agreed that the parol evidence rule does not bar extrinsic evidence to show fraud as a ground for rescission. . . ." E. Allen Farnsworth, Contracts § 7.4 at 429 (4th ed. 2004). The parol evidence rule is simply not applicable when fraud has been employed as enticement to enter a contract. So universal is this principle that Professor Farnsworth writes, "[T]here is very little that the parties can do in their agreement to prevent the use of extrinsic evidence to attack the written agreement on" grounds of fraud. *Id.* at 430. Additionally, "evidence of misrepresentation is admissible even if the agreement is completely integrated, . . . [even] in the face of the usual merger clause. . . ." *Id.* Likewise, the Restatement provides:

> Agreements and negotiations prior to or contemporaneous with the adoption of a writing are admissible in evidence to establish
>
> * * *
>
> (d) illegality, fraud, duress, mistake, lack of consideration, or other invalidating cause. . . .

RESTATEMENT (SECOND) OF CONTRACTS § 214(d) (1981).

In South Dakota, this principle has been in place since early statehood. "Great latitude . . . has been allowed in the admission of parol evidence to prevent fraud or injustice." *D.M. Osborne & Co. v. Stringham,* 1 S.D. 406, 47 N.W. 408, 409 (1890); *see M.E. Smith & Co. v. Kimble,* 31 S.D. 18, 139 N.W. 348 (1913). No matter how clear and unambiguous a contract might be, parol evidence may be offered to show that the contract is invalid because of fraud in its inducement. *See Engels v. Ranger Bar, Inc.,* 2000 S.D. 1, ¶ 15, 604 N.W.2d 241, 245; *Holmes v. Couturier,* 452 N.W.2d 135, 137 (S.D.1990); *Sabbagh v. Prof'l & Bus. Men's Life Ins. Co.,* 79 S.D. 615, 116 N.W.2d 513 (1962). Were it not so, contracting parties could insulate themselves from their own fraud.

A substantial majority of jurisdictions follow the traditional, majority view that the parol evidence rule is inapplicable in cases of fraudulent inducement. As one California court explained, " 'A party to a contract who has been guilty of fraud in its inducement cannot absolve himself from the effects of his fraud by any stipulation in the contract, either that no representations have been made, or that any right which might be grounded upon them is waived.' " *Ron Greenspan Volkswagen, Inc. v. Ford Motor Land Dev. Corp.*, 32 Cal.App.4th 985, 38 Cal.Rptr.2d 783, 788 n. 7 (1995) (additional citation omitted). Many other courts have held similarly. Promoting honesty in contractual relations forms part of the rationale: "We continue to believe that parties to contracts, whether experienced in business or not, should deal with each other honestly, and that a party should not be permitted to engage in fraud to induce the contract." *McEvoy Travel Bureau, Inc. v. Norton Co.*, 408 Mass. 704, 563 N.E.2d 188, 194 (1990). Likewise, the RESTATEMENT (SECOND) OF CONTRACTS declares that "[a] term unreasonably exempting a party from the legal consequences of a misrepresentation is unenforceable on grounds of public policy." RESTATEMENT (SECOND) OF CONTRACTS § 196 (1981).

South Dakota cases fall squarely within the traditional, majority rule. In *Holmes,* we rejected the argument that a specific contract disclaimer precluded extrinsic evidence of fraud, quoting with approval the following: "Fraud will vitiate any contract, regardless of the fact that the contract contains a provision to the effect that . . . the party who claims the fraud entered into the contract with knowledge of the condition of the subject matter of the contract and agrees to accept the same 'as is.' " 452 N.W.2d at 137 (additional citation and quotations marks omitted). Again, in *Engels,* we examined a contract disclaimer, much like the one presented here. It provided: "It is agreed and understood by and between the parties hereto that this agreement is based upon the purchaser[']s personal inspection and investigation of the property involved and the ledgers and books of the Sellers and not upon any representations or warranties of the Seller other than set out herein." 2000 S.D. 1, ¶ 7, 604 N.W.2d at 243. We held that the defendant was not allowed to use the disclaimer clause in the "purchase agreement or the contract for deed to shield itself from liability for fraud." *Id.* ¶ 15. * * *

To establish fraud, Lester must prove that Poeppel committed any of the following acts:

> (1) The suggestion as a fact of that which is not true by one who does not believe it to be true; (2) The positive assertion, in a manner not warranted by the information of the person making it, of that which is not true, though he believe it to be true; (3) The suppression of that which is true by one having knowledge or belief of the fact; (4) A promise made without any intention of performing it; or (5) Any other act fitted to deceive.

SDCL 53–4–5. If fraud is established, the contract can be rescinded, regardless of whether it is unambiguous.

Here, Lester alleged that Poeppel falsely represented to him that Lester would receive the company's financial information at the close of the contract (when in fact he never received it), that the stocks Lester sought to purchase would generate approximately $115,000 (when in fact an accounting firm's report in Poeppel's possession concluded the value was 50% less), and that the company had an exclusive franchise arrangement with Coldwell Banker. Accepting the truth of Lester's assertions, Poeppel misrepresented the value of his stock and the status of the franchise arrangement, with a promise that Lester would see the company's financial status at the contract execution, which facts and representations Poeppel used to fraudulently induce Lester to enter into the contract. Poeppel disputes Lester's allegations. Thus, these disputes form genuine issues of material fact on the fraud question and are suitable for a jury. * * *

CONCLUSION

The trial court correctly concluded that the contract was clear and unambiguous as to Lester's receipt of financial documents. However, even though the contract is unambiguous, Lester should have been allowed to present evidence to a jury that he was fraudulently induced to sign the stock purchase agreement. The trial court erred as a matter of law by barring Lester's fraudulent inducement evidence under the parol evidence rule. Because of our ruling on this issue, we need not address the other issues raised. We reverse and remand for trial.

QUESTIONS AND NOTES

1. Questions about the facts of this case
    - 1.1. What is being bought and sold here?
    - 1.2. What evidence does Lester wish to introduce?
    - 1.3. How does the evidence Lester wants to introduce add or supplement the terms of the contract between Lester and Poeppel?
2. Questions about the law
    - 2.1. Is justifiable reliance an element of fraud according to this court?
    - 2.2. Does the court address Lester's reliance and whether it was justifiable?
    - 2.3. If Poeppel gave the financial information to Lester one week after the closing of the contract, would that change the result? What if Lester planned to change franchises from Coldwell Banker to Collier Real Estate?
3. Notes
    - 3.1. Some courts construe the fraud exception narrowly by excluding parol evidence if the asserted misrepresentation is directly at variance with the writing. As one court recently stated the rule: " 'Where prior fraudulent representations are alleged, the parol evidence rule bars such representations where the written

agreement: (1) contains terms which directly deal with the subject matter of the alleged oral representation; and (2) represents the entire contract between the parties.' " *Vino 100, LLC v. Smoke on the Water, LLC*, 864 F. Supp. 2d 269, 280 (E.D. Pa. 2012) (quoting *Atl. Pier Assocs., LLC v. Boardkan Rest. Partners*, 647 F. Supp. 2d 474, 489 (E.D. Pa. 2009). *See also Road & Highway Builders v. N. Nev. Rebar*, 284 P.3d 377, 380–81 (Nev. 2012). Are these cases consistent with *Poeppel*?

3.2 To test your understanding, assume that a fully integrated agreement has a clause that states: "There are no promises related to this agreement that are not contained in this writing," and one party seeks to show that there was fraud in the creation of the contract through a misrepresentation. For example, assume that you are presented with a preprinted form and the person asking you to sign "summarizes" the contents (if you've ever rented a car, think about what the person at the counter says to move you along), but gets her summarization wrong, and in a material way. Courts adhering to this rule stated in Note 4.1 would not allow the introduction of testimony of the incorrect summary. Can that be right?

3.3. Recent decisions, however, have relaxed this rule to allow parol evidence to show whether there was fraud or some other affirmative defense, regardless of an integration clause. In so doing, they have often relied on the necessity of the party alleging fraud to plead and prove it under the principles set forth in Rule 9 of the Federal Rules of Civil Procedure. *See, e.g., Judson Atkinson Candies, Inc. v. Kenray Associates, Inc.*, 719 F.3d 635 (7th Cir. 2013); *Riverisland Cold Storage, Inc. v. Fresno-Madera Prod. Credit Ass'n*, 55 Cal. 4th 1169, 151 Cal. Rptr. 3d 93, 291 P. 3d 316 (2013); *Cronkelton v. Guaranteed Constr. Servs.*, 988 N.E.2d 656, 659–60 (Ohio App. 2013).

3.4. A fine, but important, distinction is drawn in *Italian Cowboy Partners, Ltd. v. Prudential Ins. Co.*, 341 S.W.3d 323 (Tex. S. Ct. 2011). There, the issue was not whether evidence of fraud could be introduced—the court held that it could—but whether the parties could rely on provisions of the contract indicating that the party alleging fraud could not rely on any statements or representations of the party alleged to have committed the fraud. In summarizing the general rule, the court stated: "In other words, fraudulent inducement is almost always grounds to set aside a contract despite a merger clause, but in certain circumstances, it may be possible for a contract's terms to preclude a claim for fraudulent inducement by a clear and specific disclaimer-of-reliance clause." *Id.* at 332.

So adept lawyers can lose the battle but win the war. Evidence of fraud may be introduced, but so may evidence—the contract's own terms!—that the party claiming fraud did not rely on it.

4. **You Be the Lawyer!**

You represent Poeppel. Lester is able to wriggle out of the deal on remand. How would you redraft the integration clause to prevent the same thing from happening again? Could you?

PROBLEMS ON PAROL EVIDENCE

Try to synthesize your understanding thus far with the following problems based on the facts set out below:

> Ponoroff and Epstein are negotiating for the purchase of a cow. They reach an agreement on a purchase price of $600, after several back and forth negotiations over the price involving other terms such as delivery date, veterinarian inspections, and the like. At the end of negotiations, Ponoroff and Epstein sign the following document:
>
> > Ponoroff agrees to sell to Epstein, and Epstein agrees to buy, for $600, Ponoroff's cow known as Bossie without any veterinarian's certificate. Payment to be by cashier's check.

1. One week after the signing, Epstein shows up at Ponoroff's barn and tries to give Ponoroff a cashier's check for $600. Ponoroff tells Epstein to leave, as he is too late. When Epstein sues Ponoroff for breach, can Epstein introduce evidence of discussions between them that tends to indicate that Ponoroff and Epstein had a side agreement to deliver the cow on the date Epstein showed up?

2. If Epstein shows up with a personal check instead of a cashier's check, and Ponoroff refuses to accept it, may Epstein defend Ponoroff's lawsuit by offering evidence that, prior to signing the document, Ponoroff had indicated that a personal check from Epstein would be acceptable? (Assume that Ponoroff had uttered that statement without any fraudulent intent—but would it matter if he had?)

3. Does the result in Problem 2 above change if Epstein's evidence is that instead of before the signing, Ponoroff's assent to a personal check occurred *after* the signing?

4. Same facts as in Problem 1, except now the written agreement has an additional clause that states:

   > This agreement, though short, contains all of the agreements of the parties on this subject, and is intended as a complete and final expression of all of the terms the parties deem relevant to this transaction.

5. Same facts as in Problem 4, except assume that, after signing, Epstein asked Ponoroff to hold the document "in escrow" until Epstein checked the cost of obtaining a cashier's check. When he found that the bank would charge him $25 for the check, Epstein asked Ponoroff to reduce the price to $575. Ponoroff said no. Later, Ponoroff sues Epstein for nonpayment of the $600. When Epstein tries to introduce evidence of their understanding about holding the agreement, Ponoroff asserts that, in light of the integration clause, Epstein is barred from doing so by the parol evidence rule. Who's right?

6. Same facts as in Problem 4, except that when Epstein appears, he demands a veterinarian's certificate attesting to the health of Bossie. Ponoroff points to the contractual term negating such a duty, but Epstein claims that such a certificate is customary in the cattle industry. In litigation over the point, it turns out that neither Epstein nor Ponoroff (both experienced cattle merchants) have ever heard of a cattle transaction in which a veterinarian's certificate was not a precondition to payment.

D. A WORLD WITHOUT PAROL EVIDENCE—THE CONVENTION ON THE INTERNATIONAL SALE OF GOODS

Before we leave direct consideration of the parol evidence rule, it is helpful to step back and wonder about its value. Would Western civilization as we know it collapse if the parol evidence rule were not part of our jurisprudence? Although the tone of some opinions might assume that outcome, the issue arose in *MCC-Marble Ceramic Center, Inc. v. Ceramica Nuova D'Agostino, S.p.A.*, 144 F.3d 1384 (11th Cir. 1998).

There, an American named Monzon, as representative of MCC-Marble Ceramic Center, went to Italy to buy ceramic tiles. Speaking no Italian, he attended an Italian trade show, apparently liked what he saw, and signed a preprinted document to buy ceramic tiles. This document was written completely in Italian, and had a clause on its reverse side that limited Monzon's remedies if the Italian company breached. When Monzon sued the Italian company later, he maintained that he wasn't bound by terms on the reverse side of the document because of a contrary remedy provided by something called the *Convention on the International Sale of Goods* ("CISG"), and because he said the Italians, notwithstanding the written document, had orally agreed to the CISG remedy instead of what was provided on the preprinted form.

CISG? What is the CISG? It is an international convention drafted by UNCITRAL, the trade arm of the United Nations. It is also the law of the United States. See the description all the way back at page 27.

Article 1(1) of the CISG states in relevant part:

> This Convention applies to contracts of sale of goods between parties whose places of business are in different States: [¶] (a) When the States are Contracting States. * * *

CISG, art. 1.

When the CISG does apply, its Article 8 has a slightly different approach to determining contractual intent than does the U.C.C. As the court stated at page 1387:

> Contrary to what is familiar practice in United States courts, the CISG appears to permit a substantial inquiry into the parties' subjective intent, even if the parties did not engage in any objectively ascertainable means of registering this intent. Article 8(1) of the CISG instructs courts to interpret the "statements * * * and other conduct of a party * * * according to his intent" as long as the other party "knew or could not have been unaware" of that intent. The plain language of the Convention, therefore, requires an inquiry into a party's subjective intent as long as the other party to the contract was aware of that intent.

MCC-Marble Ceramic Center explores this variance from United States' law in footnote 8 on page 1387 of the opinion:

> In the United States, the legislatures, courts, and the legal academy have voiced a preference for relying on objective manifestations of the parties' intentions. For example, Article Two of the Uniform Commercial Code, which most states have enacted in some form or another to govern contracts for the sale of goods, is replete with references to standards of commercial reasonableness. *See e.g.*, U.C.C. § 2–206 (referring to reasonable means of accepting an offer); *see also Lucy v. Zehmer*, 196 Va. 493, 503, 84 S.E.2d 516, 522 (1954) ("Whether the writing signed * * * was the result of a serious offer * * * and a serious acceptance * * *, or was a serious offer * * * and an acceptance in secret jest * * *, in either event it constituted a binding contract of sale between the parties."). Justice Holmes expressed the philosophy behind this focus on the objective in forceful terms: "The law has nothing to do with the actual state of the parties' minds. In contract, as elsewhere, it must go by externals, and judge parties by their conduct." Oliver W. Holmes, *The Common Law* 242 (Howe ed. 1963) quoted in John O. Honnold, Uniform Law for International Sales under the 1980 United Nations Convention § 107 at 164 (2nd ed. 1991) (hereinafter Honnold, Uniform Law).

Why did all this matter? Because Monzon claimed he had a different understanding than the Italians as to the effect of the preprinted document. Were Monzon's case governed by the U.C.C., we know he would be out of luck; he would be attempting to supplement an integrated term of the agreement with a pre-formation subjective understanding.

But Monzon won! Given the different approach represented by Article 8 of the CISG, the court held that Monzon should be able to argue that the subjective intent of both parties was different that the objective text of the agreement.

As *MCC-Marble Ceramic Center* indicates, the CISG is yet another source of law that must be consulted in this era of increasing globalization. Lazy lawyers, however, are assisted by Article 6 of the CISG, which states:

> The parties may exclude the application of this Convention or, subject to Article 12 [related to writing requirements], derogate from or vary the effect of any of its provisions.

So if Monzon had gone to Italy with a stamp (provided by his lawyers) that said (in English): "United States law governs this contract," and had stamped it on the Italian's form, would the result have changed? What more would you need to know to answer this question?

How about if the stamp had said: "This contract is to be governed by the Uniform Commercial Code as in force in Florida, USA, on the date of this contract"?

Think about the traditional justifications for the parol evidence rule. Does Article 8 of the CISG portend that international transactions will be more litigation-prone in the future?

---

3. USING EXTRINSIC OR OTHER PAROL EVIDENCE TO DISCOVER THE MEANING OF THE TERMS USED IN THE WRITTEN CONTRACT

Words are a lawyer's stock-in-trade—especially for a deal lawyer. He has to make the words of the deal work for his client. But words can be loosely or carelessly used—or used to intentional confuse. As Lewis Carroll wrote in THROUGH THE LOOKING GLASS:

> "When I use a word," Humpty Dumpty said, in rather a scornful tone, "it means just what I choose it to mean—neither more nor less." "The question is," said Alice, "whether you can make words mean so many different things." "The question is," said Humpty Dumpty, "which is to be master—that's all."*

* Lewis Carroll (born as Charles L. Dodgson), THROUGH THE LOOKING-GLASS, chapter 6, p. 205 (1934). The book was first published in 1872.

A. THE PROBLEM: CONTRACTS AND WORDS

When reading contracts, sometimes it is difficult to determine "which is to be master." When time comes for performance, the dispute that arises isn't over what words were used (the primary province of the parol evidence rule), but over the meaning of those words actually used.

This brings us to another putative exception to the parol evidence rule. Parol evidence may be admitted to interpret the agreement's terms in order to establish "the meaning of the writing, whether or not it is integrated." *Restatement (Second) of Contracts* § 214(c).

If unchecked, however, this could be the loophole that swallows the parol evidence rule. As Oliver Wendell Holmes stated:

> [Y]ou cannot prove a mere private convention between the two parties to give language a different meaning from its common one. It would open too great risks if evidence were admissible to show that when they said five hundred feet they agreed it should mean one hundred inches, or that Bunker Hill Monument should signify the Old South Church.

Goode v. Riley, 153 Mass. 585, 586, 28 N.E. 228 (1891).

Accordingly, we need to know not only (1) how courts use parol and other extrinsic evidence to find the meaning of the words in the written contract, but also (2) when it is appropriate for courts to look to parol and other extrinsic evidence to interpret the meaning of the words in the written contract. The next case, a classic, shows the tangles that can come from failing to anticipate that a word as common as "chicken" might be the basis for disagreement.

QUESTIONS BEFORE THE CASE

1. In Judge Friendly's view, just what does the plaintiff in the following case have to prove to win?
2. How many sources other than the contract itself did the parties proffer to persuade Judge Friendly that their interpretation of the word "chicken" was the interpretation that the parties intended when they entered into the contract?

FRIGALIMENT IMPORTING CO., LTD. V. B.N.S. INT'L SALES CORP.

U.S. District Court, Southern District of New York
190 F.Supp. 116 (1960)

FRIENDLY, J.:

OPINION:

The issue is, what is chicken? Plaintiff says 'chicken' means a young chicken, suitable for broiling and frying. Defendant says 'chicken' means any bird of that genus that meets contract specifications on weight and quality, including what it calls 'stewing chicken' and plaintiff pejoratively terms 'fowl'. Dictionaries give both meanings, as well as some others not relevant here. To support its [sic. The word "meaning" should probably be inserted here. Eds.], plaintiff sends a number of volleys over the net; defendant essays to return them and adds a few serves of its own. Assuming that both parties were acting in good faith, the case nicely illustrates Holmes' remark 'that the making of a contract depends not on the agreement of two minds in one intention, but on the agreement of two sets of external signs—not on the parties' having meant the same thing but on their having said the same thing.' The Path of the Law, in Collected Legal Papers, p. 178. I have concluded that plaintiff has not sustained its burden of persuasion that the contract used 'chicken' in the narrower sense.

The action is for breach of the warranty that goods sold shall correspond to the description, New York Personal Property Law, McKinney's Consol. Laws, c. 41, § 95. Two contracts are in suit. In the first, dated May 2, 1957, defendant, a New York sales corporation, confirmed the sale to plaintiff, a Swiss corporation, of

> 'US Fresh Frozen Chicken, Grade A, Government Inspected, Eviscerated 2½–3 lbs. and 1½–2 lbs. each all chicken individually wrapped in cryovac, packed in secured fiber cartons or wooden boxes, suitable for export
>
> 75,000 lbs. 2½–3 lbs. * * * @ $33.00
>
> 25,000 lbs. 1½–2 lbs. * * * @ $36.50
>
> per 100 lbs. FAS New York
>
> scheduled May 10, 1957 pursuant to instructions from Penson & Co., New York.'

The second contract, also dated May 2, 1957, was identical save that only 50,000 lbs. of the heavier 'chicken' were called for, the price of the smaller birds was $37 per 100 lbs., and shipment was scheduled for May 30. The initial shipment under the first contract was short but the balance was shipped on May 17. When the initial shipment arrived in Switzerland, plaintiff found, on May 28, that the 2½–3 lbs. birds were not young chicken suitable for broiling and frying but stewing chicken or 'fowl'; indeed, many of the cartons and bags plainly so indicated. Protests ensued. Nevertheless, shipment under the second contract was made on May 29, the 2½–3 lbs. birds again being stewing chicken. Defendant stopped the transportation of these at Rotterdam.

This action followed. Plaintiff says that, notwithstanding that its acceptance was in Switzerland, New York law controls under the principle of Rubin v. Irving Trust Co., 1953, 305 N.Y. 288, 305, 113 N.E.2d 424, 431; defendant does not dispute this, and relies on New York decisions. I shall follow the apparent agreement of the parties as to the applicable law.

Since the word 'chicken' standing alone is ambiguous, I turn first to see whether the contract itself offers any aid to its interpretation. Plaintiff says the 1½–2 lbs. birds necessarily had to be young chicken since the older birds do not come in that size, hence the 2½–3 lbs. birds must likewise be young. This is unpersuasive—a contract for 'apples' of two different sizes could be filled with different kinds of apples even though only one species came in both sizes. Defendant notes that the contract called not simply for chicken but for 'US Fresh Frozen Chicken, Grade A, Government Inspected.' It says the contract thereby incorporated by reference the Department of Agriculture's regulations, which favor its interpretation; I shall return to this after reviewing plaintiff's other contentions.

The first hinges on an exchange of cablegrams which preceded execution of the formal contracts. The negotiations leading up to the contracts were conducted in New York between defendant's secretary, Ernest R. Bauer, and a Mr. Stovicek, who was in New York for the Czechoslovak government at the World Trade Fair. A few days after meeting Bauer at the fair, Stovicek telephoned and inquired whether defendant would be interested in exporting poultry to Switzerland. Bauer then met with Stovicek, who showed him a cable from plaintiff dated April 26, 1957, announcing that they 'are buyer' of 25,000 lbs. of chicken 2½–3 lbs. weight, Cryovac packed, grade A Government inspected, at a price up to 33 cents per pound, for shipment on May 10, to be confirmed by the following morning, and were interested in further offerings. After testing the market for price, Bauer accepted, and Stovicek sent a confirmation that evening. Plaintiff stresses that, although these and subsequent cables between plaintiff and defendant, which laid the basis for the additional quantities under the first and for all of the second contract, were predominantly in German, they used the English word 'chicken'; it claims this was done because it understood 'chicken' meant young chicken whereas the German word, 'Huhn,' included both 'Brathuhn' (broilers) and 'Suppenhuhn' (stewing chicken), and that defendant, whose officers were thoroughly conversant with German, should have realized this. Whatever force this argument might otherwise have is largely drained away by Bauer's testimony that he asked Stovicek what kind of chickens were wanted, received the answer 'any kind of chickens,' and then, in German, asked whether the cable meant 'Huhn' and received an affirmative response. Plaintiff attacks this as contrary to what Bauer testified on his deposition in March, 1959, and also on the ground that Stovicek had no authority to interpret the meaning of the cable. The first contention would be persuasive if sustained by the record, since Bauer was free at the trial from the threat of contradiction by Stovicek as he was not at the time of the deposition; however, review of the deposition does not convince me of the claimed inconsistency. As to the second contention, it may well be that Stovicek lacked authority to commit plaintiff for prices or delivery dates other than those specified in the cable; but plaintiff cannot at the same time rely on its cable to Stovicek as its dictionary to the meaning of the contract and repudiate the interpretation given the dictionary by the man in whose hands it was put. * * * Plaintiff's reliance on the fact that the contract forms contain the words 'through the intermediary of: ______', with the blank not filled, as negating agency, is wholly unpersuasive; the purpose of this clause was to permit filling in the name of an intermediary to whom a commission would be payable, not to blot out what had been the fact.

Plaintiff's next contention is that there was a definite trade usage that 'chicken' meant 'young chicken.' Defendant showed that it was only beginning in the poultry trade in 1957, thereby bringing itself within the principle that 'when one of the parties is not a member of the trade or other circle, his acceptance of the standard must be made to appear' by proving either that he had actual knowledge of the usage or that the usage is 'so generally known in the community that his actual individual knowledge of it may be inferred.' * * * Here there was no proof of actual knowledge of the alleged usage; indeed, it is quite plain that defendant's belief was to the contrary. In order to meet the alternative requirement, the law of New York demands a showing that 'the usage is of so long continuance, so well established, so notorious, so universal and so reasonable in itself, as that the presumption is violent that the parties contracted with reference to it, and made it a part of their agreement.' * * *

Plaintiff endeavored to establish such a usage by the testimony of three witnesses and certain other evidence. Strasser, resident buyer in New York for a large chain of Swiss cooperatives, testified that 'on chicken I would definitely understand a broiler.' However, the force of this testimony was considerably weakened by the fact that in his own transactions the witness, a careful businessman, protected himself by using 'broiler' when that was what he wanted and 'fowl' when he wished older birds. Indeed, there are some indications, dating back to a remark of Lord Mansfield, Edie v. East India Co., 2 Burr. 1216, 1222 (1761), that no credit should be given 'witnesses to usage, who could not adduce instances in verification.' * * * While Wigmore thinks this goes too far, a witness' consistent failure to rely on the alleged usage deprives his opinion testimony of much of its effect. Niesielowski, an officer of one of the companies that had furnished the stewing chicken to defendant, testified that 'chicken' meant 'the male species of the poultry industry. That could be a broiler, a fryer or a roaster', but not a stewing chicken; however, he also testified that upon receiving defendant's inquiry for 'chickens', he asked whether the desire was for 'fowl or frying chickens' and, in fact, supplied fowl, although taking the precaution of asking defendant, a day or two after plaintiff's acceptance of the contracts in suit, to change its confirmation of its order from 'chickens,' as defendant had originally prepared it, to 'stewing chickens.' Dates, an employee of Urner-Barry Company, which publishes a daily market report on the poultry trade, gave it as his view that the trade meaning of 'chicken' was 'broilers and fryers.' In addition to this opinion testimony, plaintiff relied on the fact that the Urner-Barry service, the Journal of Commerce, and Weinberg Bros. & Co. of Chicago, a large supplier of poultry, published quotations in a manner which, in one way or another, distinguish between 'chicken,' comprising broilers, fryers and certain other categories, and 'fowl,' which, Bauer acknowledged, included stewing chickens. This material would be impressive if there were nothing to the contrary. However, there was, as will now be seen.

Defendant's witness Weininger, who operates a chicken eviscerating plant in New Jersey, testified 'Chicken is everything except a goose, a duck, and a turkey. Everything is a chicken, but then you have to say, you have to specify which category you want or that you are talking about.' Its witness Fox said that in the trade 'chicken' would encompass all the various classifications. Sadina, who conducts a food inspection service, testified that he would consider any bird coming within the classes of 'chicken' in the Department of Agriculture's regulations to be a chicken. The specifications approved by the General Services Administration include fowl as well as broilers and fryers under the classification 'chickens.' Statistics of the Institute of American Poultry Industries use the phrases 'Young chickens' and 'Mature chickens,' under the general heading 'Total chickens' and the Department of Agriculture's daily and weekly price reports avoid use of the word 'chicken' without specification.

Defendant advances several other points which it claims affirmatively support its construction. Primary among these is the regulation of the Department of Agriculture, 7 C.F.R. § 70.300–70.370, entitled, 'Grading and Inspection of Poultry and Edible Products Thereof.' and in particular 70.301 which recited:

Chickens. The following are the various classes of chickens:

(a) Broiler or fryer * * *

(b) Roaster * * *

(c) Capon * * *

(d) Stag * * *

(e) Hen or stewing chicken or fowl * * *

(f) Cock or old rooster * * *

Defendant argues, as previously noted, that the contract incorporated these regulations by reference. Plaintiff answers that the contract provision related simply to grade and Government inspection and did not incorporate the Government definition of 'chicken,' and also that the definition in the Regulations is ignored in the trade. However, the latter contention was contradicted by Weininger and Sadina; and there is force in defendant's argument that the contract made the regulations a dictionary, particularly since the reference to Government grading was already in plaintiff's initial cable to Stovicek.

Defendant makes a further argument based on the impossibility of its obtaining broilers and fryers at the 33 cents price offered by plaintiff for the 2½–3 lbs. birds. There is no substantial dispute that, in late April, 1957, the price for 2½–3 lbs. broilers was between 35 and 37 cents per pound, and that when defendant entered into the contracts, it was well aware of this and intended to fill them by supplying fowl in these weights. It claims that plaintiff must likewise have known the market since plaintiff had reserved shipping space on April 23, three days before plaintiff's cable to Stovicek, or, at least, that Stovicek was chargeable with such knowledge. It is scarcely an answer to say, as plaintiff does in its brief, that the 33 cents price offered by the 2½–3 lbs. 'chickens' was closer to the prevailing 35 cents price for broilers than to the 30 cents at which defendant procured fowl. Plaintiff must have expected defendant to make some profit—certainly it could not have expected defendant deliberately to incur a loss.

Finally, defendant relies on conduct by the plaintiff after the first shipment had been received. On May 28 plaintiff sent two cables complaining that the larger birds in the first shipment constituted 'fowl.' Defendant answered with a cable refusing to recognize plaintiff's objection and announcing 'We have today ready for shipment 50,000 lbs. chicken 2½–3 lbs. 25,000 lbs. broilers 1½–2 lbs.,' these being the goods procured for shipment under the second contract, and asked immediate answer 'whether we are to ship this merchandise to you and whether you will accept the merchandise.' After several other cable exchanges, plaintiff replied on May 29 'Confirm again that merchandise is to be shipped since resold by us if not enough pursuant to contract chickens are shipped the missing quantity is to be shipped within ten days stop we resold to our customers pursuant to your contract chickens grade A you have to deliver us said merchandise we again state that we shall make you fully responsible for all resulting costs.'[2] Defendant argues that if plaintiff was sincere in thinking it was entitled to young chickens, plaintiff would not have allowed the shipment under the second contract to go forward, since the distinction between broilers and chickens drawn in defendant's cablegram must have made it clear that the larger birds would not be broilers. However, plaintiff answers that the cables show plaintiff was insisting on delivery of young chickens and that defendant shipped old ones at its peril. Defendant's point would be highly relevant on another disputed issue—whether if liability were established, the measure of damages should be the difference in market value of broilers and stewing chicken in New York or the larger difference in Europe, but I cannot give it weight on the issue of interpretation. Defendant points out also that plaintiff proceeded to deliver some of the larger birds in Europe, describing them as 'poulets'; defendant argues that it was only when plaintiff's customers complained about this that plaintiff developed the idea that 'chicken' meant 'young chicken.' There is little force in this in view of plaintiff's immediate and consistent protests.

When all the evidence is reviewed, it is clear that defendant believed it could comply with the contracts by delivering stewing chicken in the 2½–3 lbs. size. Defendant's subjective intent would not be significant if this did not coincide with an objective meaning of 'chicken.' Here it did coincide with one of the dictionary meanings, with the definition in the Department of Agriculture Regulations to which the contract made at least oblique reference, with at least some usage in the trade, with the realities of the market, and with what plaintiff's spokesman had said. Plaintiff asserts it to be equally plain that plaintiff's own subjective intent was to obtain broilers and fryers; the only evidence against this is the material as to market prices and this may not have been sufficiently brought home. In any event it is unnecessary to determine that issue. For plaintiff has the burden of showing that 'chicken' was used in the narrower rather than in the broader sense, and this it has not sustained.

This opinion constitutes the Court's findings of fact and conclusions of law. Judgment shall be entered dismissing the complaint with costs.

QUESTIONS, NOTES, AND CONNECTION

1. Questions about the facts of this case

   1.1. What was Frigaliment suing for? Put another way, why does Frigaliment think BNS breached the contract?

---

[2] These cables were in German; 'chicken', 'broilers' and, on some occasions, 'fowl,' were in English.

1.2. This is a trick question: Does the court hold that BNS did not breach the contract?

1.3. Given the result and the Court's reason for its ruling, and the likely cost of procuring all the various experts and testimony about the meaning of chicken, what more could Frigaliment's lawyers done to persuade the Court that its definition of chicken was the intended one?

2. Questions about the law

2.1. According to Judge Friendly, the "word 'chicken' standing alone is ambiguous." Do you agree? Was this finding of ambiguity important? Reconsider that question after considering the remaining cases in this chapter.

2.2. Did Judge Friendly consider parol evidence in interpreting the word "chicken"? Did Judge Friendly even consider the parol evidence rule?

2.3. Change the facts somewhat. Instead of stopping the shipment at Rotterdam, and suing BNS for breach, assume that Frigaliment had accepted the second shipment of chickens, but paid BNS an amount equal to the contract price less its damages. If BNS was thereby forced to sue Frigaliment for the difference, does BNS win on the facts as alleged and proved at trial?

2.4. Change the facts even more. BNS shipped alligator. When sued by Frigaliment for breach of contract, BNS argues that the contract term "chicken" includes alligator because alligator tastes like chicken? See http://www.evergladesadventure.com/blog/what-does-alligator-tail-taste-like/. Would Judge Friendly decide this case differently?

3. Notes

3.1. *Frigaliment* was decided before the Uniform Commercial Code or the *Convention on the International Sale of Goods* were in effect. The types of evidence adduced in *Frigaliment* would today come under the heading of "usage of trade" and would be admissible under section 2–202(a) to explain the term "chicken."

3.2. Judge Henry Friendly was one of the best federal judges in our nation's history. He not only wrote well-crafted opinions, but also contributed to the legal literature with numerous law review articles on many subjects. As noted by Judge Richard Posner:

> He was the greatest federal appellate judge of his time—in analytic power, memory, and application perhaps of any time. His opinions have exhibited greater staying power than that of any of his contemporaries on the federal courts of appeals. In addition, his extrajudicial scholarship has

been extraordinarily influential, more so, perhaps, than any judge's since Cardozo.

Richard Posner, *In Memoriam: Henry J. Friendly*, 99 HARV. L. REV. 1724, 1724 (1986).

Before appointment to the federal Second Circuit Court of Appeals, Judge Friendly had been a successful business practitioner in New York City. As recalled by one of the attorneys involved in *Frigaliment*, "Judge Friendly [who had been appointed from practice directly to the Second Circuit without any trial experience] felt that he needed trial court experience in order to be able to perform his function as an appellate court judge and requested a case to be assigned to him as a trial judge. The *Frigaliment* case was assigned." One wonders if the parties knew then what lay in store for the reported opinion, which is a staple in all major contracts casebooks.

4. **You Be the Lawyer!**

You are a lawyer for a sales company liked BNS. You don't know chicken, or beef, or pork, or even tofu. How would you educate yourself so that you could draft an unambiguous contract that would be immune to litigation of the type BNS went through? Put another way, how do you know or find out what you don't know? (And would you charge your client for that education?)

5. Connection

Think back to *Raffles v. Wichelhaus* and the cases regarding mistake in formation. Why doesn't the court rule that since neither party had the same conception of chicken, then no contract was formed? *See Restatement (Second) of Contracts* § 20. A year after issuing the *Frigaliment* decision, Judge Friendly acknowledged that the case might better have been decided on other grounds. *Dadourian Exp. Corp. v. United States*, 291 F.2d 178, 187 n.4 (2d Cir. 1961).

B. AMBIGUITY: WHEN DOES IT EXIST?

Judge Friendly's *Frigaliment* opinion helps us identify the tools a court uses in interpreting a contract term the court has found to be ambiguous. *Frigaliment* does not, however, help us answer the following questions: (1) can a court use these interpretative tools *only if* the contract term is ambiguous? If so, (2) how does a court determine whether a term is ambiguous?

In the next case, the question involves whether words used at one time can encompass actions or developments that occur later on. Is such a situation one in which ambiguity is created?

QUESTIONS BEFORE THE CASE

1. What is the contract that the court is interpreting?
2. What is the ambiguity?

IN RE KOHN

Supreme Court, Appellate Division, Second Department, New York
144 A.D.3d 684, 39 N.Y.S.3d 825 (2016)

L. PRISCILLA HALL, J.P., LEONARD B. AUSTIN, ROBERT J. MILLER, and JOSEPH J. MALTESE, JJ.

Opinion

* * *

After the death of Daniel N. Kohn (hereinafter the decedent) in December 2009, Joel M. Hockett (hereinafter the executor), as the executor of the decedent's estate, petitioned * * * against Barbara Lutz, also known as Barbara Kohn, who is the decedent's surviving spouse (hereinafter the wife), to recover certain property on behalf of the decedent's estate. In her answer, the wife asserted a counterclaim for a decree declaring that pursuant to a prenuptial agreement dated November 10, 2006, she was entitled to a payment upon the decedent's death in the amount of $3,500,000, reduced by the amount of four mortgages and one-half of the value of the funds in joint accounts identified in the prenuptial agreement. Subsequently, the wife moved for summary judgment on her counterclaim, and the executor cross-moved, inter alia, for summary judgment dismissing the counterclaim. The executor contended that the prenuptial agreement provided for a payment to the wife upon the decedent's death in the amount of $3,500,000, reduced by the amounts of the four mortgages and the entire value of the funds in the joint accounts. In support of his interpretation of the prenuptial agreement, the executor submitted with his cross motion, among other things, a transcript of his deposition testimony, a transcript of the wife's deposition testimony, an affirmation of the decedent's former attorney, and letters from the decedent's former attorney to the wife's former attorney.

In an order dated June 30, 2014, the Surrogate's Court, among other things, granted the wife's motion and denied that branch of the executor's cross motion which was for summary judgment dismissing the counterclaim. The court found that the disputed clause in the prenuptial agreement required that the payment to the wife be reduced by the amount of the mortgages and only one-half of the value of the joint accounts. Thereafter, the executor moved for leave to renew his opposition to the wife's motion and his cross motion. In support of that motion, the executor submitted extrinsic evidence not previously available, namely, a transcript of the testimony of the wife's former attorney taken at a deposition held subsequent to the original motion practice. In the order appealed and cross-appealed from, dated June 30, 2015, the court, upon renewal, adhered to those portions of its original determination. Moreover, the court, among other things, granted that branch of the executor's motion which was for leave to amend his reply to the counterclaim to assert an affirmative defense based on mutual mistake. The executor appeals and the wife cross-appeals.

" 'Where a prenuptial agreement is clear and unambiguous on its face, the intent of the parties is gleaned from the four corners of the writing as a whole with a practical interpretation of the language employed so that the parties' reasonable expectations are met' " [Citations] "Extrinsic and parol evidence of the parties' intent may not be admitted to create ambiguity in a contract that is unambiguous on its face, but such evidence may be considered where a contract is determined to be ambiguous." [Citations]

Here, the decedent agreed in the prenuptial agreement that, upon his death, the wife shall receive liquid assets in the amount of $3,500,000, "reduced by the amounts of four (4) mortgages . . . and any accounts that pass to [the wife] by operation of law." The executor argues that the plain meaning of this provision unambiguously establishes that the payment to the wife must be reduced by the entire value of the funds in the joint accounts. The wife, as the surviving joint owner, was "entitled to the entire funds in those accounts" upon the decedent's death (*Matter of Pollard,* 254 A.D.2d 292, 678 N.Y.S.2d 126; *see Matter of Bricker v. Krimer,* 13 N.Y.2d 22, 27, 241 N.Y.S.2d 413, 191 N.E.2d 795). In support of her motion, the wife contended that only one-half of the value of the funds in the joint accounts must be deducted from the $3,500,000 payment pursuant to the prenuptial agreement, since she received "an immediate one-half interest in the joint property" when the decedent opened the accounts (*Matter of Covert,* 97 N.Y.2d 68, 75, 735 N.Y.S.2d 879, 761 N.E.2d 571; *see Matter of Kleinberg v. Heller,* 38 N.Y.2d 836, 841, 382 N.Y.S.2d 49, 345 N.E.2d 592; *Matter of Granwell,* 20 N.Y.2d 91, 95, 281 N.Y.S.2d 783, 228 N.E.2d 779; *Rosenzweig v. Friedland,* 84 A.D.3d 921, 923, 924 N.Y.S.2d 99). Thus, she already owned a one-half interest in the joint accounts prior to the decedent's death, and only the decedent's one-half interest in the joint accounts passed to her upon his death (*see Matter of Covert,* 97 N.Y.2d at 75, 735 N.Y.S.2d 879, 761 N.E.2d 571).

Since both parties advanced reasonable interpretations of the disputed provision, the Surrogate's Court, upon renewal, should have considered the new evidence submitted by the executor, which, together with the evidence previously submitted by the executor on his cross motion, established, prima facie, that the parties intended for the $3,500,000 payment to the wife to be reduced by the amounts of the mortgages and the value of the entire funds in the joint accounts. [Citations] In opposition to the executor's prima facie showing, the wife failed to raise a triable issue of fact.

Accordingly, the Surrogate's Court, upon renewal, should have vacated its determination in the prior order, and thereupon denied the wife's motion for summary judgment on her counterclaim, and granted that branch of the executor's cross motion which was for summary judgment dismissing the counterclaim and, in effect, declaring that the prenuptial agreement entitled the wife to a payment in the amount of $3,500,000 reduced by the amounts of the subject mortgages and the full value of the funds in the joint accounts. * * *

Since this is, in part, a declaratory judgment action, the matter must be remitted to the Surrogate's Court, Suffolk County, for the entry of a decree declaring that the prenuptial agreement entitled the wife to a payment in the amount of $3,500,000 reduced by the value of the four mortgages and the full value of the funds in the joint accounts that were identified in the prenuptial agreement (*see Lanza v. Wagner,* 11 N.Y.2d 317, 334, 229 N.Y.S.2d 380, 183 N.E.2d 670).

QUESTIONS

1. Questions about the facts of this case

   1.1. Who won? The wife or the executor? After remand, will the trial court be authorized to conduct any further evidentiary hearings?

   1.2. Are there any facts in dispute in this case?

2. Questions about the law

   2.1. How important was it that "[i]n opposition to the executor's prima facie showing, the wife failed to raise a triable issue of fact"?

   2.2. What definition or standard of ambiguity does the court use, or seem to use?

   2.3. What is the difference in ambiguity in this case from the ambiguity that Judge Friendly found in *Frigaliament*?

The four corners rule seems simple on its face. Look at the contract, and determine ambiguity. Is it really that simple?

QUESTIONS BEFORE THE CASE

1. What is the contract that the court is interpreting?
2. What is the ambiguity?

GASSNER V. RAYNOR MFG. CO.

Appellate Court of Illinois, Second District
409 Ill.App.3d 995, 948 N.E.2d 315, 350 Ill.Dec. 246 (2011)

OPINION

PRESIDING JUSTICE JORGENSEN delivered the judgment of the court, with opinion.

On May 30, 2000, plaintiff-appellant and cross-appellee, Gunther Gassner, sustained a work-related back injury and, following surgery for the injury, a staphylococcal (staph) infection originating in his back area. On May 1, 2002, in settlement thereof, the Industrial Commission (Commission) approved a "settlement contract" between Gassner and his employer, defendant-appellee and cross-appellant, Raynor Manufacturing Company (RMC). The settlement contract contained an "open medical provision," the scope of which is at the center of the instant appeal. In that provision, despite Gassner's general release, RMC agreed to pay for certain approved treatment for a year following the Commission's approval of the settlement contract. After the approval, the staph infection spread to Gassner's heart, and Gassner incurred approximately $190,000 in medical expenses for treatment to his heart. Gassner thought that the open medical provision covered the expenses related to the staph infection surrounding his heart (provided he could prove that it was the *same* staph infection that began in his back), but RMC disagreed. * * *

[In the lawsuit over this dispute, RMC] moved for summary judgment, and the trial court granted the motion. * * * For the reasons that follow, we affirm the trial court's denial of RMC's motion to dismiss, we reverse the trial court's grant of summary judgment to RMC, and we remand the cause.

I. BACKGROUND

On May 30, 2000, Gassner fell down the stairs while at work for RMC. As a result, Gassner suffered a herniated disk at L4–L5, which required a fusion that was performed on February 25, 2002. Following the surgery, Gassner developed a deep staph infection at the site of the surgical incision.

He was treated with oral and intravenous antibiotics. Gassner and RMC subsequently entered into an agreement entitled "Illinois Industrial Commission Settlement Contract Lump Sum Petition and Order" (settlement contract). The settlement contract stated in pertinent part:

> [RMC] offers and [Gassner] accepts the sum of $47,500 [less attorney fees and expenses], subject to approval by the Industrial Commission, in full settlement of all claims, known or unknown, including all claims for specific loss, temporary total compensation[,] * * * resulting from said alleged accident of 5/30/00 and any other accident, injury, or aggravation of a pre-existing condition arising out of and in the course of [Gassner's] employment with [RMC] to the date he signed this contract, involving alleged disability to any portion of [Gassner's] anatomy. * * * *Notwithstanding anything to the contrary contained herein, as additional consideration, [RMC] agrees to pay reasonable and necessary medical expenses for treatment to the low back causally related to the alleged injury of 5/30/00 for a period of one year after the date of approval of this settlement contract, but not thereafter.*" (Emphasis added to the controversial "open medical provision.")

* * *

A few months later, in September 2002, Gassner began to experience chest pain, shortness of breath, and fever. By late October 2002, doctors diagnosed Gassner with septic pericardis near his heart, and Gassner underwent multiple surgeries as a result of the infection. Between May 1, 2002, and May 1, 2003, Gassner incurred $190,000 in medical expenses for treatment of his heart infection. Dr. Jeffrey Coe examined Gassner, and Dr. Coe provided the opinion that Gassner's heart infection was caused by the *same* bacteria responsible for Gassner's low back infection.

[Gassner ultimately sued RMC. RMC sought summary judgment, contending that the contract was a release that did not cover Gassner's treatment. The court ruled for RMC.]

* * *

2. Contract-Interpretation Issue

The parties dispute the scope of the open medical provision [the italicized portion above, eds.], which is contained within the general release. A release is a contract and, therefore, is governed by contract law. *Janowiak v. Tiesi,* 402 Ill.App.3d 997, 1014, 342 Ill.Dec. 442, 932 N.E.2d 569 (2010). General words in the release are restrained by specific recitals contained in the document. *Id.* Releases are strictly construed against the benefitting party and must be written with great particularity. *Id.* Additionally, an oft-cited principle in release cases is that "[t]he intention of the parties controls the scope and effect of the release, and this intent is discerned from the release's express language as well as the circumstances surrounding the agreement." *Id.* (quoting *Fuller Family Holdings, LLC v. Northern Trust Co.,* 371 Ill.App.3d 605, 614, 309 Ill.Dec. 111, 863 N.E.2d 743 (2007)).

Courts have used two approaches in discerning the intent of the parties in typical contract-interpretation cases: the four corners rule and the provisional admission approach. The traditional, four corners rule of contract interpretation states:

> "An agreement, when reduced to writing, must be presumed to speak to the intention of the parties who signed it. It speaks for itself, and the intention with which it was executed must be determined from the language used. It is not to be changed by extrinsic evidence." (Internal quotation marks omitted.) * * *

In applying the four corners rule, a court initially looks to the language of the contract alone. *Id.* at 462, 236 Ill.Dec. 8, 706 N.E.2d 882. If the language of an agreement is facially unambiguous, then it is interpreted as a matter of law, *without* resort to parol (or extrinsic) evidence. *Id.* If, however, a facial ambiguity is present, then parol evidence may be admitted to aid the trier of fact in resolving the ambiguity. *Id.* at 462–63, 236 Ill.Dec. 8, 706 N.E.2d 882. Whether an ambiguity is present is a matter of law, subject to *de novo* review. *Installco, Inc. v. Whiting Corp.,* 336 Ill.App.3d 776, 783, 271 Ill.Dec. 94, 784 N.E.2d 312 (2002).

The provisional admission approach, also known as the extrinsic ambiguity approach, can be summed up as follows:

> "Under the provisional admission approach, although the language of [the] contract is facially unambiguous, a party may still proffer parol evidence to the trial judge for the purpose of showing that an ambiguity exists which can be found only by looking beyond the clear language of the contract. [Citation.] Under this method, an extrinsic ambiguity exists 'when someone who knows the context of the contract would know if the contract means something other than what it seems to mean.' [Citation.] * * * [I]f, after 'provisionally' reviewing the parol evidence, the trial judge finds that an 'extrinsic ambiguity' is present, then the parol evidence is admitted to aid the trier of fact in resolving the ambiguity." *Air Safety,* 185 Ill.2d at 463, 236 Ill.Dec. 8, 706 N.E.2d 882.

The theory behind the provisional admission approach is that it corrects for flaws inherent in a strict application of the four corners rule. According to advocates of the provisional admission approach, the four corners rule is flawed because "it assumes precision in language that cannot exist and requires the judge to determine the true intent of the parties in a transaction that is removed from time and circumstances." *Id.* at 465, 236 Ill.Dec. 8, 706 N.E.2d 882. The provisional admission approach allows for the consideration of negotiations leading up to the agreement so that parties' use of particular words and phrases may be better understood. *Arrington v. Walter E. Heller International Corp.,* 30 Ill.App.3d 631, 637, 333 N.E.2d 50 (1975). Therefore, the provisional admission approach is more similar to the oft-quoted principle in release cases, that "[t]he intention of the parties controls the scope and effect of the release, and this intent is discerned from the release's express language as well as the circumstances surrounding the agreement." (Internal quotation marks omitted.) *Janowiak,* 402 Ill.App.3d at 1014, 342 Ill.Dec. 442, 932 N.E.2d 569.

In any case, under both the four corners rule and the provisional admission approach, the first step is to determine whether an ambiguity exists. An ambiguity exists where there is doubt as to the true sense or meaning of the words themselves or an indefiniteness in the words' expression, resulting in a difficulty in the application of the words under the circumstances of the dispute that the contract is supposed to govern. *Central Illinois Light Co. v. Home Insurance Co.,* 213 Ill.2d 141, 153, 290 Ill.Dec. 155, 821 N.E.2d 206 (2004); 18 Christine Gimeno *et al.,* Ill. L. & Prac. Evidence § 290 (2011) (using the "difficulty in application" definition) (citing *Martindell v. Lake Shore National Bank,* 15 Ill.2d 272, 280–81, 154 N.E.2d 683 (1958) (finding ambiguous the phrase " '*[d]ebentures paid and discharged by the new corporation shall not thereafter be available for purchase by the Buyer under [the] option*' " (emphasis added) because, if one considers the primary relationship between the parties to be that of lender and borrower, the option granted by the agreement seems to be an unconditionally revocable offer, but, in the context of the case, if one considers the primary relationship between the parties to be that of buyer and seller, then the option was not revocable at the seller's whim and only those debentures paid and discharged in the normal course of business would no longer be available for purchase by the buyer)). Additionally, when dealing with a settlement contract involving a work injury that would be covered under the Act, a court construes the contract strongly against the drafter, *and the risk of ambiguity and lack of clarity is on the drafting party. Johnson v. State,* 55 Ill.Ct.Cl. 410, 412, 2002 WL 32705311 (2002) (dealing specifically with such a settlement contract); see also *Dowd & Dowd, Ltd. v. Gleason,* 181 Ill.2d 460, 479, 230 Ill.Dec. 229, 693 N.E.2d 358 (1998) (ambiguity in the contract must be resolved against the drafter of the disputed provision).

With this background, we proceed to determine whether the disputed language in the contract is ambiguous so as to require the introduction of parol evidence and preclude summary judgment. The disputed language reads:

> "Notwithstanding anything to the contrary contained herein, as additional consideration, [RMC] agrees to pay reasonable and necessary medical expenses for treatment to the low back causally related to the alleged injury of 5/30/00 for a period of one year after the date of approval of this settlement contract, but not thereafter."

In particular, the parties dispute whether the phrase "treatment to the low back" creates a facial ambiguity. Black's Law Dictionary defines the word "treatment" as "[a] broad term covering all the steps taken to effect a cure of an injury or disease; including examination and diagnosis as well as application of remedies." Black's Law Dictionary 1502 (6th ed.1990). Dorland's Medical Dictionary defines "treatment" as "the management and care of a patient for the purpose of combating disease or disorder." Dorland's Medical Dictionary 1388 (26th ed.1981).

Gassner's primary argument is that the plain language of the open medical provision includes treatment for the *heart* staph infection, provided that he can establish that the heart staph infection was the same infection that originated in his low back and was causally related to the initial injury. That would, of course, be an issue for trial. Thus, Gassner requests that this court remand the cause for a determination of whether the staph infection surrounding his heart was the same infection that originated in his low back and was causally related to his initial injury. Alternatively, Gassner contends that the terms of the open medical provision are, at the very least, ambiguous, requiring a remand for a determination of the parties' intent regarding the scope and extent of the open medical provision. Gassner notes that RMC was well aware of the staph infection, then localized near the site of the surgical incision, when the parties entered into the open medical provision, and he posits that the open medical provision was an acknowledgment of and agreement to pay for Gassner's then-unresolved health issue (the staph infection) for the next year only.

RMC, on the other hand, argues that the plain language of the open medical provision includes treatment administered to or directed at healing the low back *only,* regardless of whether a condition originating in the low back spreads to other parts of the body. At oral argument, RMC set forth that it was aware that Gassner had a staph infection when the parties entered into the settlement contract, and it noted that it (RMC) had paid for treatment of Gassner's staph infection *up to that point.* However, it was RMC's position that the term "treatment to the low back" *unambiguously* excluded treatment of the staph infection and released RMC from any further duty to pay for such treatment. In other words, RMC posited that the purpose of the open medical provision was to limit its obligation to paying for treatment to the low back (in the muscular-skeletal, chiropractic sense), so long as it was causally related to the initial injury, for a term of one year.

RMC's preferred reading of the open medical provision, *i.e.,* that it was not obligated to pay for treatment of the staph infection even while it remained localized in the low back, is not obvious from the language of the provision. To the contrary, absent any parol evidence, we read the term "treatment to the low back" to include treatment for a staph infection manifesting in the low back—the open medical provision does not specify the *type* of low-back medical condition (muscular-skeletal injury or infectious illness) and requires only that the low-back condition be causally related to the initial injury. RMC, as the drafter of the settlement contract, should have set forth the terms of the release with a greater degree of clarity. If it meant to exclude treatment for the staph infection, it should have so stated.

Once one considers the obligation to pay for treatment as including an *infection* manifesting in the low back, it becomes difficult to define the limits of the obligation. Assuming that the facts later show that the infection in the heart was the *same* infection as that originating in the back, is RMC obligated to pay for treatment aimed at the *infection* or merely for treatment aimed at the resulting *damage*? The former interpretation is more consistent with the term "treatment," *i.e.,* a broad term covering all steps to effect a cure, while the latter more readily lends itself to literal compliance with the open medical provision's reference to the "low back."

The fact that the health issue for which coverage is disputed is an *infection,* as opposed to a more discrete injury such as a broken arm, creates the greatest difficulty in applying the terms of the open medical provision. By way of counter-example, if, within the year following the approval of the settlement contract, the initial injury caused Gassner to have a spasm that in turn caused him to fall and break his arm, treatment for his arm would not be covered under the open medical provision. Even though the broken arm would arguably be causally related to the initial injury, it would not be covered because its treatment could in no way be construed as treatment to the low back. In contrast, treatment of an *infection* originating in the low back, once bloodborne, is not so easily localized. The infection was not treated at the site of origin but, rather, was treated by intravenous and oral antibiotics. If Gassner is able to establish before a trier of fact that the infection surrounding his heart was the *same* infection as the one that originated in his low back, then, in order to "treat" the infection that originated in the low back, *i.e.,* in order to "effect a cure of the [condition]," it would seem that one would have had to treat the entire infection, however it may have manifested, evolved, or spread.

In sum, even under a four corners approach, the contract is ambiguous. The open medical provision does not, as a matter of law, exclude treatment for Gassner's staph infection. Summary judgment was therefore inappropriate. Should Gassner continue to pursue his claim in the trial court, we allow for the introduction of (reliable) parol evidence to determine the intent of the parties in entering into the release and in creating the open medical provision. Whether the parties created the open medical provision to include or exclude treatment of the staph infection is a question of fact to be decided in the trial court, as is the question of whether the staph infection that damaged Gassner's heart is the *same* infection that originated in his low back as a result of the low back surgery that corrected the initial work injury.

III. CONCLUSION

For the aforementioned reasons, we affirm the trial court's denial of RMC's motion to dismiss, we reverse the trial court's grant of RMC's motion for summary judgment, and we remand the cause.

Affirmed in part and reversed in part; cause remanded.

JUSTICES MCLAREN and BURKE concurred in the judgment and opinion.

QUESTIONS AND NOTES

1. Questions about the facts of this case

   1.1. The court rattles off a location of "L4–L5" for the herniated disk. Where is that? Does it matter?

   1.2. Just exactly what words of the contract did the court think were ambiguous? What evidence did Gassner seek to introduce to show this ambiguity?

   1.3. The court states that "we read the term 'treatment to the low back' to include treatment for a staph infection manifesting in the low back." Do you agree that interpretation is the best interpretation of this language? Why or why not?

2. Questions about the law

   2.1. Does the court limit its holding in this case to contracts which release claims between the parties to the contract? Or does it have a more universal application?

   2.2. What is the difference between a facial ambiguity and an ambiguity which only is seen after the context of the agreement is shown?

   2.3. How does this court's standard of when a contractual term is ambiguous compare with the standard applied in *Kohn*?

3. Notes

3.1. There are many variations on the definition of ambiguity sufficient to allow the introduction of evidence outside the contract. Many courts use the following:

> "[C]ontract language is ambiguous if it is capable of more than one meaning when viewed objectively by a reasonably intelligent person who has examined the context of the entire integrated agreement and who is cognizant of the customs, practices, usages and terminology as generally understood in the particular trade or business."

Random House, Inc. v. Rosetta Books LLC, 150 F. Supp. 2d 613, 618 (S.D.N.Y. 2001), aff'd, 283 F.3d 490 (2d Cir. 2002) (quoting Sayers v. Rochester Tel. Corp. Supplemental Mgmt. Pension Plan, 7 F.3d 1091, 1095 (2d Cir. 1993)). See also Constellation Power Source, Inc. v. Select Energy, Inc., 467 F. Supp. 2d 187, 204 (D. Conn. 2006).

How does the language in *Random House* differ from what the court in *Gassner* used?

3.2. Perhaps the most notorious uses of the provisional admission standard are found in California. As explained recently,

> Where the meaning of the words used in a contract is disputed, the trial court must provisionally receive any proffered extrinsic evidence which is relevant to show whether the contract is reasonably susceptible of a particular meaning. . . Indeed, it is reversible error for a trial court to refuse to consider such extrinsic evidence on the basis of the trial court's own conclusion that the language of the contract appears to be clear and unambiguous on its face. Even if a contract appears unambiguous on its face, a latent ambiguity may be exposed by extrinsic evidence which reveals more than one possible meaning to which the language of the contract is yet reasonably susceptible.

Wolf v. Superior Court, 114 Cal. App. 4th 1343, 1350–51, 8 Cal. Rptr. 3d 649, 655–56 (2004).

4. **You Be the Lawyer!**

The insurer who lost gives you the above opinion, and asks you to redraft their standard open medical provision, and to draft notes for its use by the many attorneys the insurance company employes throughout the United States. What terms would you include?

Gassner and California courts seem to take a sensible—but expansive—view of what courts will consider when construing what a contract requires the parties to do. Maybe that's appropriate given its factual setting. When all is said and done, however, certainty of obligation and reduction of litigation may not be served by such an expansive rule.

In the next case, a federal judge applies similar state law, but in a widely different factual setting. The judge, Alex Kozinski of the Ninth Circuit Court of Appeals, is applying California law. And he doesn't like it.* When reading this opinion, keep in mind that Judge Kozinski and Judge Ideman (the trial court judge) both had the same texts relating to California law at their disposal, but came to diametrically opposite views. Has Judge Kozinski overplayed his hand? Or was Judge Ideman just trying to clear his trial docket?

TRIDENT CENTER V. CONNECTICUT GENERAL LIFE INS. CO.

U.S. Court of Appeals, Ninth Circuit
847 F.2d 564 (1988)

KOZINSKI, CIRCUIT JUDGE:

The parties to this transaction are, by any standard, highly sophisticated business people: Plaintiff is a partnership consisting of an insurance company and two of Los Angeles' largest and most prestigious law firms; defendant is another insurance company. Dealing at arm's length and from positions of roughly equal bargaining strength, they negotiated a commercial loan amounting to more than $56 million. The contract documents are lengthy and detailed; they squarely address the precise issue that is the subject of this dispute; to all who read English, they appear to resolve the issue fully and conclusively.

Plaintiff nevertheless argues here, as it did below, that it is entitled to introduce extrinsic evidence that the contract means something other than what it says. This case therefore presents the question whether parties in California can ever draft a contract that is proof [*sic*] to parol evidence. Somewhat surprisingly, the answer is no.

Facts

The facts are rather simple. Sometime in 1983 Security First Life Insurance Company and the law firms of Mitchell, Silberberg & Knupp and

---

* He may not like it, but he has to apply California law. Federal law requires application of state law when the parties have invoked the federal court's diversity jurisdiction; that is, when both parties are citizens of different states. Thus, federal judges, who have no ability to extend or limit California law, must determine it and apply it (or some estimate of what it is in case of a lacuna) as it stands.

Manatt, Phelps, Rothenberg & Tunney formed a limited partnership for the purpose of constructing an office building complex on Olympic Boulevard in West Los Angeles. The partnership, Trident Center, the plaintiff herein, sought and obtained financing for the project from defendant, Connecticut General Life Insurance Company. The loan documents provide for a loan of $56,500,000 at 12¼ percent interest for a term of 15 years, secured by a deed of trust on the project. The promissory note provides that "maker shall not have the right to prepay the principal amount hereof in whole or in part" for the first 12 years. Note at 6. In years 13–15, the loan may be prepaid, subject to a sliding prepayment fee. The note also provides that in case of a default during years 1–12, Connecticut General has the option of accelerating the note and adding a 10 percent prepayment fee.

Everything was copacetic for a few years until interest rates began to drop. The 12¼ percent rate that had seemed reasonable in 1983 compared unfavorably with 1987 market rates and Trident started looking for ways of refinancing the loan to take advantage of the lower rates. Connecticut General was unwilling to oblige, insisting that the loan could not be prepaid for the first 12 years of its life, that is, until January 1996.

Trident then brought suit in state court seeking a declaration that it was entitled to prepay the loan now, subject only to a 10 percent prepayment fee. Connecticut General promptly removed to federal court and brought a motion to dismiss, claiming that the loan documents clearly and unambiguously precluded prepayment during the first 12 years. The district court agreed and dismissed Trident's complaint. The court also "*sua sponte*, sanction[ed] the plaintiff for the filing of a frivolous lawsuit.". * * * Trident appeals both aspects of the district court's ruling.

Discussion

I

Trident makes two arguments as to why the district court's ruling is wrong. First, it contends that the language of the contract is ambiguous and proffers a construction that it believes supports its position. Second, Trident argues that, under California law, even seemingly unambiguous contracts are subject to modification by parol or extrinsic evidence. Trident faults the district court for denying it the opportunity to present evidence that the contract language did not accurately reflect the parties' intentions.

A. The Contract

As noted earlier, the promissory note provides that Trident "shall not have the right to prepay the principal amount hereof in whole or in part before January 1996." Note at 6. It is difficult to imagine language that more clearly or unambiguously expresses the idea that Trident may not unilaterally prepay the loan during its first 12 years. Trident, however, argues that there is an ambiguity because another clause of the note provides that "in the event of a prepayment resulting from a default hereunder or the Deed of Trust prior to January 10, 1996 the prepayment fee will be ten percent (10%)." Note at 6–7. Trident interprets this clause as giving it the option of prepaying the loan if only it is willing to incur the prepayment fee.

We reject Trident's argument out of hand. In the first place, its proffered interpretation would result in a contradiction between two clauses of the contract; the default clause would swallow up the clause prohibiting Trident from prepaying during the first 12 years of the contract. The normal rule of construction, of course, is that courts must interpret contracts, if possible, so as to avoid internal conflict. * * *

In any event, the clause on which Trident relies is not on its face reasonably susceptible to Trident's proffered interpretation. Whether to accelerate repayment of the loan in the event of default is entirely Connecticut General's decision. The contract makes this clear at several points. *See* Note at 4 ("in each such event [of default], the entire principal indebtedness, or so much thereof as may remain unpaid at the time, shall, *at the option of Holder*, become due and payable immediately" (emphasis added)); *id.* at 7 ("in the event Holder exercises its *option to accelerate* the maturity hereof * * *" (emphasis added)); Deed of Trust para. 2.01, at 25 ("in each such event [of default], Beneficiary *may* declare all sums secured hereby immediately due and payable * * *" (emphasis added)). Even if Connecticut General decides to declare a default and accelerate, it "may rescind any notice of breach or default." *Id.* para. 2.02, at 26. Finally, Connecticut General has the option of doing nothing at all: "Beneficiary reserves the right at its sole option to waive noncompliance by Trustor with any of the conditions or covenants to be performed by Trustor hereunder." *Id.* para. 3.02, at 29.

Once again, it is difficult to imagine language that could more clearly assign to Connecticut General the exclusive right to decide whether to declare a default, whether and when to accelerate, and whether, having chosen to take advantage of any of its remedies, to rescind the process before its completion.

Trident nevertheless argues that it is entitled to precipitate a default and insist on acceleration by tendering the balance due on the note plus the 10 percent prepayment fee.[1] The contract language, cited above, leaves

[1] Trident's position is that the prepayment fee must either be a fee imposed as part of an "alternative method of performance" or "a liquidated damages provision specifying the amount of damages payable by Trident in the event that it defaults by prepaying the * * * loan." Appellant's Reply Brief at 12–13. Trident contends that if the prepayment fee is instead read as a provision for liquidated damages triggered by any default whatsoever, it would be invalid as a penalty because it would not be a reasonable estimate of the likely injury to Connecticut General resulting from most types of default: "If, for example, Trident were to default on the payment of a single

no room for this construction. It is true, of course, that Trident is free to stop making payments, which may then cause Connecticut General to declare a default and accelerate. But that is not to say that Connecticut General would be required to so respond. The contract quite clearly gives Connecticut General other options: It may choose to waive the default, or to take advantage of some other remedy such as the right to collect "all the income, rents, royalties, revenue, issues, profits, and proceeds of the Property." Deed of Trust para. 1.18, at 22. By interpreting the contract as Trident suggests, we would ignore those provisions giving Connecticut General, not Trident, the exclusive right to decide how, when and whether the contract will be terminated upon default during the first 12 years.

In effect, Trident is attempting to obtain judicial sterilization of its intended default. But defaults are messy things; they are supposed to be. Once the maker of a note secured by a deed of trust defaults, its credit rating may deteriorate; attempts at favorable refinancing may be thwarted by the need to meet the trustee's sale schedule; its cash flow may be impaired if the beneficiary takes advantage of the assignment of rents remedy; default provisions in its loan agreements with other lenders may be triggered. Fear of these repercussions is strong medicine that keeps debtors from shirking their obligations when interest rates go down and they become disenchanted with their loans.[4] That Trident is willing to suffer the cost and delay of a lawsuit, rather than simply defaulting, shows far better than anything we might say that these provisions are having their intended effect. We decline Trident's invitation to truncate the lender's remedies and deprive Connecticut General of its bargained-for protection.

B. Extrinsic Evidence

Trident argues in the alternative that, even if the language of the contract appears to be unambiguous, the deal the parties actually struck is in fact quite different. It wishes to offer extrinsic evidence that the parties had agreed Trident could prepay at any time within the first 12 years by tendering the full amount plus a 10 percent prepayment fee. As discussed

---

installment, a fee of 10% of the outstanding balance of the loan would not qualify as a valid liquidated damages payment." *Id.* at 8.

California law is unsettled on this point and it may be that Connecticut General could not enforce the 10 percent fee in the event of certain defaults by Trident. *See generally* 1 H. Miller & M. Starr, *Current Law of California Real Estate* § 3:71 n.12 (Supp. 1987). But the contract assigns to Connecticut General alone the right to decide whether and under what circumstances to seek the prepayment fee. Connecticut General may well attempt to enforce the fee only in circumstances where it is valid. What the contract clearly does not provide is what Trident suggests. If the parties had wanted to give Trident the option of prepaying with a 10 percent fee, they certainly could have done so expressly.

4 This provides a symmetry with the situation where interest rates go up and it is the lender who is stuck with a loan it would prefer to turn over at market rates. In an economy where interest rates fluctuate, it is all but certain that one side or the other will be dissatisfied with a long-term loan at some time. Mutuality calls for enforcing the contract as written no matter whose ox is being gored.

above, this is an interpretation to which the contract, as written, is not reasonably susceptible. Under traditional contract principles, extrinsic evidence is inadmissible to interpret, vary or add to the terms of an unambiguous integrated written instrument. * * *

Trident points out, however, that California does not follow the traditional rule. Two decades ago the California Supreme Court in *Pacific Gas & Electric Co. v. G. W. Thomas Drayage & Rigging Co.*, 69 Cal. 2d 33, 442 P.2d 641, 69 Cal. Rptr. 561 (1968), turned its back on the notion that a contract can ever have a plain meaning discernible by a court without resort to extrinsic evidence. The court reasoned that contractual obligations flow not from the words of the contract, but from the intention of the parties. "Accordingly," the court stated, "the exclusion of relevant, extrinsic, evidence to explain the meaning of a written instrument could be justified only if it were feasible to determine the meaning the parties gave to the words from the instrument alone." 69 Cal. 2d at 38, 442 P.2d 641. This, the California Supreme Court concluded, is impossible: "If words had absolute and constant referents, it might be possible to discover contractual intention in the words themselves and in the manner in which they were arranged. Words, however, do not have absolute and constant referents." *Id.* In the same vein, the court noted that "the exclusion of testimony that might contradict the linguistic background of the judge reflects a judicial belief in the possibility of perfect verbal expression. This belief is a remnant of a primitive faith in the inherent potency and inherent meaning of words." *Id.* at 37 (citation and footnotes omitted).[5]

Under *Pacific Gas*, it matters not how clearly a contract is written, nor how completely it is integrated, nor how carefully it is negotiated, nor how squarely it addresses the issue before the court: the contract cannot be rendered impervious to attack by parol evidence. If one side is willing to claim that the parties intended one thing but the agreement provides for another, the court must consider extrinsic evidence of possible ambiguity. If that evidence raises the specter of ambiguity where there was none before, the contract language is displaced and the intention of the parties must be divined from self-serving testimony offered by partisan witnesses whose recollection is hazy from passage of time and colored by their conflicting interests. * * * We question whether this approach is more likely to divulge the original intention of the parties than reliance on the seemingly clear words they agreed upon at the time. * * *

Pacific Gas casts a long shadow of uncertainty over all transactions negotiated and executed under the law of California. As this case

[5] In an unusual footnote, the court compared the belief in the immutable meaning of words with " 'the elaborate system of taboo and verbal prohibitions in primitive groups * * * [such as] the Swedish peasant custom of curing sick cattle smitten by witchcraft, by making them swallow a page torn out of the psalter and put in dough. * * *' " *Id.* n.2 (quoting Ullman, *The Principles of Semantics* 43 (1963)).

illustrates, even when the transaction is very sizeable, even if it involves only sophisticated parties, even if it was negotiated with the aid of counsel, even if it results in contract language that is devoid of ambiguity, costly and protracted litigation cannot be avoided if one party has a strong enough motive for challenging the contract. While this rule creates much business for lawyers and an occasional windfall to some clients, it leads only to frustration and delay for most litigants and clogs already overburdened courts.

It also chips away at the foundation of our legal system. By giving credence to the idea that words are inadequate to express concepts, *Pacific Gas* undermines the basic principle that language provides a meaningful constraint on public and private conduct. If we are unwilling to say that parties, dealing face to face, can come up with language that binds them, how can we send anyone to jail for violating statutes consisting of mere words lacking "absolute and constant referents"? How can courts ever enforce decrees, not written in language understandable to all, but encoded in a dialect reflecting only the "linguistic background of the judge"? Can lower courts ever be faulted for failing to carry out the mandate of higher courts when "perfect verbal expression" is impossible? Are all attempts to develop the law in a reasoned and principled fashion doomed to failure as "remnant[s] of a primitive faith in the inherent potency and inherent meaning of words"?

Be that as it may. While we have our doubts about the wisdom of *Pacific Gas*, we have no difficulty understanding its meaning, even without extrinsic evidence to guide us. As we read the rule in California, we must reverse and remand to the district court in order to give plaintiff an opportunity to present extrinsic evidence as to the intention of the parties in drafting the contract.[6] It may not be a wise rule we are applying, but it is a rule that binds us. *Erie R.R. Co. v. Tompkins*, 304 U.S. 64, 78, 82 L. Ed. 1188, 58 S. Ct. 817 (1938).

II

In imposing sanctions on plaintiff, the district court stated:

> Pursuant to Fed. R. Civ. P. 11, the Court, *sua sponte*, sanctions the plaintiff for the filing of a frivolous lawsuit. The Court concludes that the language in the note and deed of trust is plain and clear. No reasonable person, much less firms of able attorneys, could possibly misunderstand this crystal-clear language. Therefore, this action was brought in bad faith.

---

[6] Nothing we say should be construed as foreclosing Connecticut General from moving for summary judgment after completion of discovery; given the unambiguous language of the contract itself, such a motion would succeed unless Trident were to come forward with extrinsic evidence sufficient to render the contract reasonably susceptible to Trident's alternate interpretation, thereby creating a genuine issue of fact resolvable only at trial.

Order of Dismissal at 3. Having reversed the district court on its substantive ruling, we must, of course, also reverse it as to the award of sanctions. While we share the district judge's impatience with this litigation, we would suggest that his irritation may have been misdirected. It is difficult to blame plaintiff and its lawyers for bringing this lawsuit. With this much money at stake, they would have been foolish not to pursue all remedies available to them under the applicable law. At fault, it seems to us, are not the parties and their lawyers but the legal system that encourages this kind of lawsuit. By holding that language has no objective meaning, and that contracts mean only what courts ultimately say they do, *Pacific Gas* invites precisely this type of lawsuit.[9] With the benefit of 20 years of hindsight, the California Supreme Court may wish to revisit the issue. If it does so, we commend to it the facts of this case as a paradigmatic example of why the traditional rule, based on centuries of experience, reflects the far wiser approach.

Conclusion

The judgment of the district court is REVERSED. The case is REMANDED for reinstatement of the complaint and further proceedings in accordance with this opinion. The parties shall bear their own costs on appeal.

QUESTIONS, NOTE, AND CONNECTIONS

1. Questions about the facts of this case

   1.1. Why do the law firms wish to prepay the loan? Where are they likely to get the money to make the payment?

   1.2. Do the law firms contend that the provisions regarding inability to prepay the loan for the first twelve years of the loan are ambiguous? How do the law firms interpret these provisions?

   1.3. What possible extrinsic evidence could the law firms offer to support their position? And if the evidence supports what the law firms are contending—a unilateral prepayment right—what answer do the law firms have as to why that wasn't spelled out more clearly in the contract?

2. Questions about the law

   2.1. Do you agree with the following statement by the court? Why or why not?

---

[9] This is not to say, of course, that all lawsuits seeking to challenge the interpretation of facially unambiguous contracts are necessarily immune from imposition of sanctions. Even under *Pacific Gas*, a party urging an interpretation lacking any objectively reasonable basis in fact might well be subject to sanctions for bringing a frivolous lawsuit.

Under *Pacific Gas*, it matters not how clearly a contract is written, nor how completely it is integrated, nor how carefully it is negotiated, nor how squarely it addresses the issue before the court: the contract cannot be rendered impervious to attack by parol evidence.

2.2. Trident's second argument was that "under California law, even seemingly unambiguous contracts are subject to modification by parol or extrinsic evidence." Does either this case (or what you can discern from this case) or *Pacific Gas* so hold?

2.3. Is California law consistent with either *Kohn* or *Gassner*? How would Judge Kozinski, if freed from the restraining influence of state law, decide *Gassner*? *Kohn*? If Judge Kozinski were the trial court judge in *Trident*, how would he rule on remand?

2.4. Did you read the footnotes? Footnote 6? Is footnote 6 important? We of course think it is—that is why we included it in the book. The Ninth Circuit also thinks footnote 6 is important; in *A. Kemp Fisheries, Inc. v. Castle & Cooke, Inc., Bumble Bee Seafoods Division*, 852 F.2d 493, 497 n.2 (9th Cir. 1988), the Ninth Circuit explained: "The broad language in *Trident* suggests that under California law courts must always admit extrinsic evidence to determine the meaning of disputed contract language. *Trident* held only that courts may not dismiss on the pleadings when one party contends that extrinsic evidence renders the contract ambiguous. The case must proceed beyond the pleadings so that the court may consider the evidence. If, after considering the evidence, the court determines that the contract is not susceptible to the interpretation advanced, the parol evidence rule operates to exclude the evidence. The court may then decide the case on a motion for summary judgment. See *Trident* at 570 n.6."

3. Note

Is the California method as wasteful as *Trident* suggests? Lessons can be learned from *Wolf v. Walt Disney Pictures & Television*, 162 Cal. App. 4th 1107, 1116, 76 Cal. Rptr. 3d 585, 593–94 (2008), which saw the creator of *Who Framed Roger Rabbit* pitted again Walt Disney Pictures & Television. The two had entered into a license agreement allowing Disney use Wolf's book as the basis for a movie (which was wildly successful).*

In return, Wolf was to receive 5% of the "gross receipts" related to the movie and to merchandise related to the movie or to the movie's characters. The contract did not, however, define "gross receipts." An issue arose when Disney entered into deals with others in which it

* Epstein loves Jessica Rabbit's line from the movie: "I'm not bad; I'm just drawn that way." He recalls it often when reflecting on his contributions to this casebook.

licensed the images in the movie for non-cash consideration. Wolf claimed that "gross receipts" was ambiguous, and included the value of what Disney received in these deals; Disney disagreed.

Initially, the California courts ruled for Wolf. In an opinion quoted after *Glassner* above, they held it reversible error to not consider whatever evidence Wolf wanted to introduce to show the value of whatever Disney received for licensing his work was "gross receipts," regardless of whether Disney received cash for it or not. *Wolf v. Superior Court*, 114 Cal. App. 4th 1343, 1350–51, 8 Cal. Rptr. 3d 649, 655–56 (2004).

So the court sent the matter back to the trial court, which held a jury trial. As reported in the appeal from the jury verdict, "[t]he jury concluded the term 'gross receipts' meant monetary consideration or nonmonetary consideration only 'if and when it was turned into monies' by Disney. It rejected Cry Wolf's contention 'gross receipts' included the value of nonmonetary benefits Disney received in connection with its promotional agreements with third parties." *Wolf v. Walt Disney Pictures & Television*, 162 Cal. App. 4th 1107, 1116, 76 Cal. Rptr. 3d 585, 593–94 (2008).

Note that it took another four years for this result to be reached. Try to imagine how much the lawyers for each side likely charged their clients during that time (which would include the cost of a jury trial). If you think a stricter standard for ambiguity would have prevented this expense, you start to see Judge Kosinski's point.*

4. **You Be the Lawyer!**

Part II of *Trident* talks about sanctions. Read it again (and the last note). You represent a client who had a valid contract with Vlad, the main clause of which stated: "Vlad agrees to take all funds received and put them in a bank." Your client gave Vlad $100, which he promptly buried in a river bank. Vlad answers the complaint asserting that his interpretation is the correct construction of the contract term. Now, your client not only wants his $100 back, but he wants sanctions for the silly construction Vlad put on the contract. For his part, Vlad will testify that he thought "river bank" was what was meant, although there is no earthly reason why he would think that.

Can you obtain sanctions under Part II of *Trident*?

---

* Or maybe not. Wolf did have a legitimate dispute. As noted in a press reporting of the results of the trial: "A jury determined that Disney had underreported its gross receipts by more than $1.9 million, and awarded Wolf 5 percent of those profits, or about $98,000. It added another $80,000 in royalties from Roger Rabbit-based records, tapes and CDs, and $216,000 in royalties that Disney acknowledged having withheld." *Court Remands Tiff Over Roger Rabbit Royalties*, Courthouse News Service, https://www.courthousenews.com/court-remands-tiff-over-roger-rabbit-royalties/ (May 13, 2008).

5. Connections

Remember in *Frigaliment*, the reasonableness of the litigants' contract interpretation was important to Judge Friendly: "Defendant's subjective intent would not be significant if this did not coincide with an objective meaning of 'chicken.' " Does Judge Kozinski think that the reasonableness of the litigants' contract interpretation was important to Judge Traynor?

C. THE USE OF RULES, MAXIMS AND EXTRINSIC EVIDENCE TO CONSTRUE CONTRACT LANGUAGE

Once ambiguity exists, counsel for the parties can introduce extrinsic evidence to show what the parties meant by the words they used. Sometimes, as in the cases above, the extrinsic evidence can take the form of testimony of the parties who negotiated the contract.

Other times, however, the extrinsic evidence may be guides or manuals on style, or guides prepared by experts. In In re Envirodyne Industries, Inc., 29 F.3d 301, 305 (7th Cir. 1994), Chief Judge Posner had this to say about such extrinsic aids to interpretation:

> If the written contract is clear without extrinsic evidence, then such evidence could have no office other than to contradict the writing, and is therefore excluded. The object in excluding such evidence is to prevent parties from trying to slip out of their clearly stated, explicitly assumed contractual obligations through self-serving testimony or documents—which, though self-serving, might impress a jury—purporting to show that the parties didn't mean what they said in the written contract. Contractual obligations would be too uncertain if such evidence were allowed. But dictionaries, treatises, articles, and other published materials created by strangers to the dispute, like evidence of trade usage, which is also admissible because it is also evidence created by strangers rather than by a party trying to slip out of a contractual bind, do not present a similar danger of manufactured doubts and are therefore entirely appropriate for use in contract cases as interpretive aids. Appropriate, and sometimes indispensable. It would be passing odd to forbid people to look up words in dictionaries, or to consult explanatory commentaries that, like trade usage, are in the nature of specialized dictionaries.

Contract law has also developed common law rules for interpretation in doubtful cases. The *Restatement (Second) of Contracts* lists the following:

§ 203 Standards of Preference in Interpretation

In the interpretation of a promise or agreement or a term thereof, the following standards of preference are generally applicable:

(a) an interpretation which gives a reasonable, lawful, and effective meaning to all the terms is preferred to an interpretation which leaves a part unreasonable, unlawful, or of no effect;

(b) express terms are given greater weight than course of performance, course of dealing, and usage of trade, course of performance is given greater weight than course of dealing or usage of trade, and course of dealing is given greater weight than usage of trade;

(c) specific terms and exact terms are given greater weight than general language;

(d) separately negotiated or added terms are given greater weight than standardized terms or other terms not separately negotiated.

In addition, the *Restatement* adopts a rebuttable presumption that may trouble those who think that they should draft everything on behalf of their clients:

§ 206 Interpretation Against the Draftsman

In choosing among the reasonable meanings of a promise or agreement or a term thereof, that meaning is generally preferred which operates against the party who supplies the words or from whom a writing otherwise proceeds.

Finally, over 50 years ago, Professor Edwin Patterson set forth ten general maxims of interpretation, some of which are in Latin. An edited version of those ten maxims appears below.

EDWIN W. PATTERSON, *THE INTERPRETATION AND CONSTRUCTION OF CONTRACTS*

64 COLUM. L. REV. 833, 852–54 (1964)

In this brief treatment we can only quote a list of standard maxims, which may not be complete. The ones most often phrased in Latin are given first.

1. *Noscitur a sociis*. The meaning of a word in a series is affected by others in the same series; or, a word may be affected by its immediate context. The example for the next maxim may be taken to illustrate this one.

2. *Ejusdem generis.* A general term joined with a specific one will be deemed to include only things that are like (of the same genus as) the specific one. This one if applied usually leads to a restrictive interpretation. *E.g.*, S contracts to sell R his farm together with the "cattle, hogs, and other animals." This would probably not include S's favorite house-dog, but might include a few sheep that S was raising for the market.

3. *Expressio unius exclusio alterius.* If one or more specific items are listed, without any more general or inclusive terms, other items although similar in kind are excluded. *E.g.*, S contracts to sell R his farm together with "the cattle and hogs on the farm." This language would be interpreted to exclude the sheep and S's favorite house-dog.

4. *Ut magis valeat quam pereat.* By this maxim, an interpretation that makes the contract valid is preferred to one that makes it invalid.

5. *Omnia praesumuntur contra proferentem.* This maxim states that if a written contract contains a word or phrase which is capable of two reasonable meanings, one of which favors one party and the other of which favors the other, that interpretation will be preferred which is less favorable to the one by whom the contract was drafted. This maxim favors the party of lesser bargaining power, who has little or no opportunity to choose the terms of the contract, and perforce accepts one drawn by the stronger party. * * * [T]he maxim is commonly invoked in cases that do not reveal any disparity of bargaining power between the parties.

6. *Interpret contract as a whole.* A writing or writings that form part of the same transaction should be interpreted together as a whole, that is, every term should be interpreted as a part of the whole and not as if isolated from it. This maxim expresses the contextual theory of meaning, which is, perhaps, a truism.

7. *"Purpose of the parties."* "The principal apparent purpose of the parties is given great weight in determining the meaning to be given to manifestations of intention or to any part thereof." This maxim must be used with caution. In fact, the two parties to a (bargain) contract necessarily have different purposes, and if these are apparent, then the court can construe a principal or common purpose from the two as a guide to the interpretation of language or the filling of gaps. Thus a contract to sell, buy, and export scrap copper was construed to make the buyer's obtaining of an export license

a condition of the seller's promise to deliver. However, if the purposes of the parties are obscure the court may well fall back upon "plain meaning."

8. *Specific provision is exception to a general one.* If two provisions of a contract are inconsistent with each other and if one is "general" enough to include the specific situation to which the other is confined, the specific provision will be deemed to qualify the more general one, that is, to state an exception to it. A lease of a truck-trailer provided that the lessee should be absolutely liable for loss or damage to the vehicle, yet another clause stated that no party's liability should be increased by this contract. It was held that the former was more specific and therefore controlled the general provision, hence the lessee was liable. A careful draftsman would have stated the former as an exception to the latter, and the court in effect does it for him.

9. *Handwritten or typed provisions control printed provisions.* Where a written contract contains both printed provisions and handwritten or typed provisions, and the two are inconsistent, the handwritten or typed provisions are preferred. This maxim is based on the inference that the language inserted by handwriting or by typewriter for this particular contract is a more recent and more reliable expression of their intentions than is the language of a printed form. While this maxim is used in interpreting insurance contracts and other contracts of adhesion, it is also applicable to all contracts drawn up on a printed form.

10. *Public interest preferred.* If a public interest is affected by a contract, that interpretation or construction is preferred which favors the public interest. The proper scope of application of this rule seems doubtful. It may have some appropriate uses in construing contracts between private parties. However, as applied to government contracts it would, if applied, be used to save the taxpayers' money as against those contracting with the government. But this is not, it is believed, a standard of interpretation or construction uniformly applied to government contracts.

PROBLEMS ON CONSTRUCTION OF CONTRACTS

1. During World War II, various oil companies entered into contracts with the federal government to produce aviation fuel, a necessary ingredient for the war effort. One known by-product of that production, however, was

an acidic and toxic waste that the companies dumped at a site known as the "McColl site." Many years later, under a statute known as the Comprehensive Environmental Response, Compensation, and Liability Act of 1978, 42 U.S.C. § 9601, et seq. ("CERCLA"), the U.S. Government and the State of California undertook a substantial effort to clean up the McColl Site. It wound up costing more than $92 million.

The contracts signed during World War II, however, contained identical clauses that obligated the United States, as buyer of the aviation fuel, to

> pay in addition to the prices as established [in the price provisions of the contract], any new or additional taxes, fees, or charges, other than income, excess profits, or corporate franchise taxes, which Seller may be required by any municipal, state, or federal law in the United States, or any foreign country to pay by reason of the production, manufacture, sale or delivery of the commodities delivered hereunder.

The oil companies contend that the $92 million liability under CERCLA is a "charge" as contemplated by the original purchase contract. Who has to pay the $92 million?

2. James wants to buy a sailboat at Sears. He seeks to use his Sears credit card to complete the purchase. On the credit card slip to be signed, right above where his signature is to be placed, are the words "By signing this, the Cardholder agrees to grant to Sears a security interest in the goods purchased hereby, as set forth in more detail in the most recent Cardholder agreement between Sears and the undersigned."

   a. James has no idea what a "security interest" is, but he signs anyway. He finds out what a security interest is when he doesn't pay his credit card bill, and Sears sends some of its workers over to "repossess" the sailboat, which they accomplish by sailing the boat away without any fuss. Assume for now (and you'll confirm this later in your Article 9 course) that Sears could do this only if they had been contractually granted a "security interest." Based on your reading so far, have they been? What maxims or rules would help you here?

   b. Now assume that James sees the language above his signature, and then crosses it out before signing. The clerk at the register makes no complaint, and lets James drive off with his new boat. If James doesn't pay, can Sears repossess the boat? What maxims or rules would help you here?

3. A contract to sell land states that the buyer is reserving all rights to "all coal and other minerals." Who gets the subsurface oil and gas? *See McCormick v. Union Pac. R.R. Co.*, 983 P.2d 84 (Colo. Ct. App. 1998).

4. Fred is a book collector. He advertises the following on eBay:

   > For sale: One first edition Trollope, *circa* 1860. Signed by author. Excellent condition.

   Lucinda enters the auction, ultimately entering the highest bid of $500. When she receives the book, she notices that it is written and signed by Thomas Adolphus Trollope, the brother of Anthony Trollope. Thomas wrote travel books; Anthony was more in the literary vein. Both she and Fred believe they have a contract. Questions of mistake aside, what are the best arguments you can muster using the maxims that Lucinda should have received an Anthony Trollope book?

D. SPECIAL INTERPRETIVE RULES FOR CONTRACTS OF ADHESION

How often have you wanted to rent a car or obtain some other good or service, and were then presented with a pre-printed form to sign (and no opportunity to negotiate anything)? Are these types of contracts just as valid as fully-negotiated, specially-prepared custom contracts? Are they subject to the same interpretive rules? The next two cases examine this issue.

QUESTIONS BEFORE THE CASE

1. What did the Meyers subjectively know when they formed the contract with State Farm?
2. Based on what they knew or didn't know, what was the Meyers' theory of the case; that is, based on the admitted facts, what legal theories did they put forward to win their case?

MEYER V. STATE FARM FIRE & CAS. CO.

Court of Special Appeals of Maryland
85 Md.App. 83, 582 A.2d 275 (1990)

OPINION:

For over 100 years, it has been common—indeed standard—for fire insurance policies to contain a clause requiring disputes concerning the amount of a covered loss suffered by the insured to be resolved through an appraisal process. Such a clause is at issue here. It provides, in relevant part, that, if the company and the insured are unable to agree on the amount of loss, either one can demand that the amount be determined by appraisal. Upon such a demand, each party is obliged to select an appraiser; the two appraisers so selected then "select a competent, impartial umpire." If the two appointed appraisers agree on an amount, that amount "shall be the amount of loss." If they are unable to agree, they submit their differences to the umpire. Written agreement signed by any two of the three then will constitute the amount of loss. The policy further provides that "[n]o action shall be brought unless there has been compliance with the policy provisions."

Appellants purchased a policy of fire insurance containing that clause from appellee. A fire occurred at their home, but, unfortunately, they and the company were unable to agree on the amount of loss. Although it is not entirely clear from the Agreed Statement of the Case that constitutes the record in this appeal, it appears that the company, at some point, sought to invoke the appraisal process. Appellants instead filed suit for damages in the Circuit Court for Wicomico County, contending that the appraisal provisions were invalid. The basis of their claim was that [among other things,] because the policy was a contract of adhesion and because they were actually unaware that it contained the appraisal provision, there was no effective waiver of their Constitutional right.

The company moved to dismiss the action. Though conceding the factual averments of appellants' complaint for purpose of the motion, it contended that the dispute resolution clause was not invalid and that, by omitting to allege compliance with it, appellants had failed to state a claim upon which relief could be granted. The court found merit in that defense and dismissed the action. Hence, this expedited appeal. * * *

* * *

[W]e are not dealing here with a statute mandating this form of dispute resolution. It is a contractual provision. The issue is whether appellants can escape its effect because the policy was a contract of adhesion and, as they were allegedly (and for purposes of this case concededly) unaware that such a provision was in the policy, they did not knowingly, voluntarily, and intelligently waive their right to try the issue of the amount of their loss before a jury. In urging their position, we think that the appellants give too expansive a meaning to both the requirements for waiving their right to a judicial resolution of the controversy and the effect of a contract of adhesion.

A contract of adhesion has been defined as one "that is drafted unilaterally by the dominant party and then presented on a 'take-it-or-leave-it' basis to the weaker party who has no real opportunity to bargain about its terms." *Restatement (Second) of Conflict of Laws* § 187, Comment b. The comment goes on to note that such contracts "are usually prepared in printed form, and frequently at least some of their provisions are in extremely small print." It is generally recognized that insurance policies qualify as contracts of adhesion, and so we shall assume that the policy at issue here is such a contract.

The fact that a contract is one of adhesion does not mean that either it or any of its terms are invalid or unenforceable. A court will, to be sure, look at the contract and its terms with some special care. As in most cases, it will refuse to enforce terms that it finds unconscionable and will construe ambiguities against the draftsman; but it will not simply excise or ignore terms merely because, in the given case, they may operate to the perceived detriment of the weaker party. *See*, in general, *Restatement (Second) of Contracts* § 211, Comment c; also *Corbin on Contracts* §§ 559, 1376.

There is no asserted ambiguity in the appraisal provision; indeed, in *Aetna Cas. & Sur., supra*, 293 Md. at 420, 445 A.2d 14, the Court declared such a provision "plain and unambiguous." Nor do we see anything unconscionable about it. The appraisal process has generally been regarded by the courts as a fair method of resolving disputes over the amount of loss. As Appleman notes, rather than being stricken down as unconscionable, appraisal provisions are usually *upheld* on grounds of public policy "since they tend to fair dealing and the prevention of litigation." J. Appleman, *Insurance Law and Practice* § 3921. Moreover, although certainly standard language in the policy, the appraisal provision at issue here is by no means "buried" or enunciated in the proverbial "fine print." It is worded in plain, colloquial English as part of the stated Conditions of the policy and, except for headings, is in the same size and type print as the other provisions of the policy.

It is true, of course, that a waiver of basic Constitutional rights is not ordinarily valid unless it is knowing and voluntary. * * * It is also true that where such a waiver is founded upon a provision in a contract of adhesion, the court will, as noted above, be especially careful to protect against an unconscionable result. * * *

These precepts, however, must be weighed against the equally well-established view that favors and enforces agreements to arbitrate disputes, including disputes over insured losses. An agreement to arbitrate either future or existing disputes involves more than just the waiver of a right to jury trial, although that is certainly implicit in such an agreement. It constitutes an election to use an alternative dispute resolution mechanism that the law not only recognizes but encourages. If appellants' position were correct, the whole foundation of the Federal and uniform arbitration acts could be placed in jeopardy. Arbitration clauses are standard not only in insurance contracts but in construction contracts, employment agreements, and a variety of other contracts that may, in some instances, be regarded as being of adhesion. If the "weaker" party to such contracts were able to escape the duty to arbitrate on the premise that he was unaware of the arbitration clause and therefore had not validly waived his Federal or State Constitutional right to a jury trial, the viability of this favored method of dispute resolution would be significantly circumscribed.

We recognize that if the insertion of an arbitration clause in a contract is induced by *fraud*, the clause will not be enforced. * * * But that is not the case here. On the record before us, we hold that the appraisal clause is not invalid and that the procedure required by it must be used in good faith.

Judgment Affirmed; Appellants to Pay the Costs.

QUESTIONS

1. Questions about the facts of this case

   1.1. Did the insurance company refuse to pay anything on the policy?

   1.2. Why did Meyer pay money to State Farm if she had never read the contract under which State Farm provided her fire insurance?

2. Questions about the law

   2.1. In Maryland, are parties always bound to contract language in adhesion contracts they don't read or understand? What exceptions would this court recognize?

   2.2. Would it have made any difference to this court if the practice contained in the adhesion contract had not been "standard," that is, if the insurance company defendant had language different from all other insurance companies?

3. **You Be the Lawyer!**

   If Meyer had come to your office before she paid her money to State Farm, and had showed you the form the insurance company gave her, what kind of advice do you think you could give that would be practical? What are her options at this point? Would it make any difference if the form of the policy had been approved by the relevant state insurance commissioner?

QUESTIONS BEFORE THE CASE

1. The contract for this case is reprinted at the end of the case. Read it (it's short) before you read the main case. Are the terms understandable?

2. Is the issue of what Broemmer knew or should have known an issue of fact or of law? Does that matter?

BROEMMER V. ABORTION SERVICES OF PHOENIX, LTD.

Supreme Court of Arizona
173 Ariz. 148, 840 P.2d 1013 (1992)

MOELLER, VICE CHIEF JUSTICE.

STATEMENT OF THE CASE

Melinda Kay Broemmer (plaintiff) asks this court to review a court of appeals opinion that held that an "Agreement to Arbitrate" which she signed prior to undergoing a clinical abortion is an enforceable, albeit an adhesive, contract. *Broemmer v. Otto,* 169 Ariz. 543, 821 P.2d 204 (1991). * * * Because we hold the agreement to arbitrate is unenforceable as against plaintiff, we reverse the trial court and vacate in part the court of appeals opinion. * * *

FACTS AND PROCEDURAL HISTORY

In December 1986, plaintiff, an Iowa resident, was 21 years old, unmarried, and 16 or 17 weeks pregnant. She was a high school graduate earning less than $100.00 a week and had no medical benefits. The father-to-be insisted that plaintiff have an abortion, but her parents advised against it. Plaintiff's uncontested affidavit describes the time as one of considerable confusion and emotional and physical turmoil for her.

Plaintiff's mother contacted Abortion Services of Phoenix and made an appointment for her daughter for December 29, 1986. During their visit to the clinic that day, plaintiff and her mother expected, but did not receive, information and counselling on alternatives to abortion and the nature of the operation. When plaintiff and her mother arrived at the clinic, plaintiff was escorted into an adjoining room and asked to complete three forms, one of which is the agreement to arbitrate at issue in this case. The agreement to arbitrate included language that "any dispute aris[ing] between the Parties as a result of the fees and/or services" would be settled by binding arbitration and that "any arbitrators appointed by the AAA [American Arbitration Association] shall be licensed medical doctors who specialize in obstetrics/gynecology." The two other documents plaintiff completed at the same time were a 2-page consent-to-operate form and a questionnaire asking for a detailed medical history. Plaintiff completed all three forms in less than 5 minutes and returned them to the front desk. Clinic staff made no attempt to explain the agreement to plaintiff before or after she signed, and did not provide plaintiff with copies of the forms.

After plaintiff returned the forms to the front desk, she was taken into an examination room where pre-operation procedures were performed. She was then instructed to return at 7:00 a.m. the next morning for the termination procedure. Plaintiff returned the following day and Doctor Otto performed the abortion. As a result of the procedure, plaintiff suffered a punctured uterus that required medical treatment.

Plaintiff filed a malpractice complaint in June 1988, approximately 1½ years after the medical procedure. By the time litigation commenced, plaintiff could recall completing and signing the medical history and consent-to-operate forms, but could not recall signing the agreement to arbitrate. Defendants moved to dismiss, contending that the trial court lacked subject matter jurisdiction because arbitration was required. In opposition, plaintiff submitted affidavits that remain uncontroverted. The trial court considered the affidavits, apparently treated the motion to dismiss as one for summary judgment, and granted summary judgment to the defendants. * * *

On appeal, the court of appeals held that although the contract was one of adhesion, it was nevertheless enforceable because it did not fall outside plaintiff's reasonable expectations and was not unconscionable. Following the court of appeals opinion, the parties stipulated to dismiss the Ottos from the lawsuit and from this appeal. We granted plaintiff's petition for review. * * *

DISCUSSION

I. The Contract is One of Adhesion

* * *

An adhesion contract is typically a standardized form "offered to consumers of goods and services on essentially a 'take it or leave it' basis without affording the consumer a realistic opportunity to bargain and under such conditions that the consumer cannot obtain the desired product or services except by acquiescing in the form contract." *Wheeler v. St. Joseph Hosp.*, 63 Cal.App.3d 345, 356, 133 Cal.Rptr. 775, 783 (1976) (citations omitted) * * * The *Wheeler* court further stated that "[t]he distinctive feature of a contract of adhesion is that the weaker party has no realistic choice as to its terms." 63 Cal.App.3d at 356, 133 Cal.Rptr. at 783 (citations omitted). Likewise, in *Contractual Problems in the Enforcement of Agreements to Arbitrate Medical Malpractice,* 58 Va.L.Rev. 947, 988 (1972), Professor Stanley Henderson recognized "the essence of an adhesion contract is that bargaining position and leverage enable one party 'to select and control risks assumed under the contract.'" (quoting Friedrich Kessler, *Contracts of Adhesion-Some Thoughts About Freedom of Contract,* 43 Colum.L.Rev. 629 (1943)).

The printed form agreement signed by plaintiff in this case possesses all the characteristics of a contract of adhesion. The form is a standardized contract offered to plaintiff on a "take it or leave it" basis. In addition to removing from the courts any potential dispute concerning fees or services, the drafter inserted additional terms potentially advantageous to itself requiring that any arbitrator appointed by the American Arbitration Association be a licensed medical doctor specializing in obstetrics/gynecology. The contract was not negotiated but was, instead, prepared by defendant and presented to plaintiff as a condition of treatment. Staff at the clinic neither explained its terms to plaintiff nor indicated that she was free to refuse to sign the form; they merely represented to plaintiff that she had to complete the three forms. The conditions under which the clinic offered plaintiff the services were on a "take it or leave it" basis, and the terms of service were not negotiable. Applying general contract law to the undisputed facts, the court of appeals correctly held that the contract was one of adhesion.

II. Reasonable Expectations

Our conclusion that the contract was one of adhesion is not, of itself, determinative of its enforceability. "[A] contract of adhesion is fully enforceable according to its terms [citations omitted] unless certain other factors are present which, under established legal rules-legislative or judicial-operate to render it otherwise." *Graham v. Scissor-Tail, Inc.,* 28 Cal.3d 807, 171 Cal.Rptr. 604, 611, 623 P.2d 165, 172 (1981) (footnotes omitted). To determine whether this contract of adhesion is enforceable, we look to two factors: the reasonable expectations of the adhering party and whether the contract is unconscionable. As the court stated in *Graham:*

> Generally speaking, there are two judicially imposed limitations on the enforcement of adhesion contracts or provisions thereof. The first is that such a contract or provision which does not fall within the reasonable expectations of the weaker or "adhering" party will not be enforced against him. [citations omitted] The second-a principle of equity applicable to all contracts generally-is that a contract or provision, even if consistent with the reasonable expectations of the parties, will be denied enforcement if, considered in its context, it is unduly oppressive or "unconscionable."

171 Cal.Rptr. at 612, 623 P.2d at 172–73 (citations omitted).

* * *

Clearly, the issues of knowing consent and reasonable expectations are closely related and intertwined. In *Darner Motor Sales, Inc. v. Universal Underwriters Ins. Co.,* 140 Ariz. 383, 682 P.2d 388 (1984), this court used the *Restatement (Second) of Contracts* § 211 (Standardized Agreements), as a guide to analyzing, among other things, contracts that contain non-negotiated terms. The comment to subsection (3), quoted with approval in *Darner,* states in part:

> Although customers typically adhere to standardized agreements and are bound by them without even appearing to know the standard terms in detail, they are not bound to unknown terms which are beyond the range of reasonable expectation.

See 140 Ariz. at 391, 682 P.2d at 396.

The Restatement focuses our attention on whether it was beyond plaintiff's reasonable expectations to expect to arbitrate her medical malpractice claims, which includes waiving her right to a jury trial, as part of the filling out of the three forms under the facts and circumstances of this case. Clearly, there was no conspicuous or explicit waiver of the fundamental right to a jury trial or any evidence that such rights were knowingly, voluntarily and intelligently waived. The only evidence presented compels a finding that waiver of such fundamental rights was beyond the reasonable expectations of plaintiff. Moreover, as Professor Henderson writes, "[i]n attempting to effectuate reasonable expectations consistent with a standardized medical contract, a court will find less reason to regard the bargaining process as suspect if there are no terms unreasonably favorable to the stronger party." Henderson, *supra,* at 995. In this case failure to explain to plaintiff that the agreement required all potential disputes, including malpractice disputes, to be heard only by an arbitrator who was a licensed obstetrician/gynecologist requires us to view the "bargaining" process with suspicion. It would be unreasonable to enforce such a critical term against plaintiff when it is not a negotiated term and defendant failed to explain it to her or call her attention to it.

Plaintiff was under a great deal of emotional stress, had only a high school education, was not experienced in commercial matters, and is still not sure "what arbitration is." Given the circumstances under which the agreement was signed and the nature of the terms included therein, our reading of * * * *Darner,* the Restatement and the affidavits in this case compel us to conclude that the contract fell outside plaintiff's reasonable expectations and is, therefore, unenforceable. Because of this holding, it is unnecessary for us to determine whether the contract is also unconscionable. * * *

DISPOSITION

Those portions of the opinion of the court of appeals inconsistent with this opinion are vacated. The judgment of the trial court is reversed and this case is remanded for further proceedings consistent with this opinion. * * *

FELDMAN, C.J., and CORCORAN and ZLAKET, JJ., concur.

MARTONE, JUSTICE, dissenting.

The court's conclusion that the agreement to arbitrate was outside the plaintiff's reasonable expectations is without basis in law or fact. I fear today's decision reflects a preference for litigation over alternative dispute resolution that I had thought was behind us. I would affirm the court of appeals.

We begin with the undisputed facts that the court ignores. Appendix "A" to this dissent is the agreement to arbitrate. At the top it states in bold capital letters "PLEASE READ THIS CONTRACT CAREFULLY AS IT EFFECTS [*sic*] YOUR LEGAL RIGHTS." Directly under that in all capital letters are the words "AGREEMENT TO ARBITRATE." The recitals indicate that "the Parties deem it to be in their respective best interest to settle any such dispute as expeditiously and economically as possible." The parties agreed that disputes over services provided would be settled by arbitration in accordance with the rules of the American Arbitration Association. They further agreed that the arbitrators appointed by the American Arbitration Association would be licensed medical doctors who specialize in obstetrics/gynecology. Plaintiff, an adult, signed the document. * * *

The court seizes upon the doctrine of reasonable expectations to revoke this contract. But there is nothing in this record that would warrant a finding that an agreement to arbitrate a malpractice claim was not within the reasonable expectations of the parties. On this record, the exact opposite is likely to be true. For all we know, both sides in this case might wish to avoid litigation like the plague and seek the more harmonious waters of alternative dispute resolution. Nor is there anything in this record that would suggest that arbitration is bad. Where is the harm? In the end, today's decision reflects a preference in favor of litigation that is not shared by the courts of other states and the courts of the United States.

* * *

Darner and the *Restatement* [do not] support for this court's conclusion. *Darner* held that an adhesive contract term that is "contrary to the negotiated agreement made by the parties," 140 Ariz. at 387, 682 P.2d at 392, will not be enforced because it collides with expectations that "have been induced by the making of a promise." 140 Ariz. at 390, 682 P.2d at 395 (quoting 1 Corbin, *Contracts* § 1 at 2 (1963)). The defendant here did not promise the plaintiff that malpractice claims could be litigated. Thus, the agreement to arbitrate is not contrary to any negotiated deal. * * *

Under *Restatement (Second) of Contracts* § 211(3), standardized agreements are enforceable except where a party has reason to believe that the other party would not manifest assent if he knew that the writing contained a particular term. Comment f to § 211 tells us:

> Such a belief or assumption may be shown by the prior negotiations or inferred from the circumstances. Reason to believe may be inferred from the fact that the term is bizarre or oppressive, from the fact that it eviscerates the non-standard terms explicitly agreed to, or from the fact that it eliminates the dominant purpose of the transaction. The inference is reinforced if the adhering party never had an opportunity to read the term, or if it is illegible or otherwise hidden from view.

Plainly, there are no facts in this case to support any of these factors. There were no prior negotiations that were contrary to arbitration. An agreement to arbitrate is hardly bizarre or oppressive. * * * Arbitration does not eviscerate any agreed terms. Nor does it eliminate the dominant purpose of the transaction. The plaintiff here had an opportunity to read the document, the document was legible and was hardly hidden from plaintiff's view. This arbitration agreement was in bold capital letters. Thus, the reasonable expectations standard of the *Restatement (Second) of Contracts* § 211 does not support this court's conclusion.

There is another reason why § 211(3) fails to support the court's conclusion. The *Restatement (Second) of Contracts* chapter 8 describes the whole range of unenforceable contracts. Its introductory note states:

> A particularly important change has been effected by statutes relating to arbitration, which have now been enacted in so many jurisdictions that it seems likely that even in the remaining states, there has been a change in the former judicial attitude of hostility toward agreements to arbitrate future disputes. . . . Such agreements are now widely used and serve the public interest by saving court time. *The rules stated in this Chapter do not preclude their enforcement even in the absence of legislation.*

Restatement (Second) of Contracts ch. 8, intro. note at 4 (emphasis added). It is difficult to reconcile the court's reliance on the *Restatement* in light of this.

* * *

Today's decision sends a mixed message. In light of all of these developments, how can it be that an agreement to arbitrate "fell outside plaintiff's reasonable expectations?" The court's answer * * * merely confuses the concept of a contract of adhesion with the doctrine of reasonable expectations. * * * I dissent.

F. / : READ THIS CONTRACT C...I 'LLY
A. IT EFFECTS YOUR LEGAL RIGHTS

AGREEMENT TO ARBITRATE DEC 2 9 1986

THIS AGREEMENT is made and entered into at Phoenix, Arizona this ________ day of ________, 198__, by and between Robert H. Tamis, M.D., Abortion Services of Phoenix, referred to hereinafter as Doctor, its agents, servants and employees, and ________________ referred to hereinafter as Patient. (Doctor and Patient hereinafter sometimes collectively referred to as Parties).

WITNESSETH:

WHEREAS, Doctor will be performing certain services on behalf of Patient; and

WHEREAS, the Parties hereto recognize that a dispute could develop regarding the fees and or services rendered by Doctor; and

WHEREAS, the Parties deem it to be in their respective best interest to settle any such dispute as expeditiously and economically as possible.

NOW, THEREFORE, in accordance with the provisions herein set forth, and other good and valuable consideration the sufficiency of which is hereby acknowledged, the Parties agree as follows.

1. In the event any dispute arises between the Parties as a result of the fees and/or services provided by Doctor the Parties hereto mutually agree that any such dispute shall be settled by binding arbitration in the City of Phoenix in accordance with the rules then prevailing of the American Arbitration Association (AAA). The Parties further agree that any arbitrators appointed by the AAA shall be licensed medical doctors who specialize in obstetrics/gynecology.

2. This Agreement shall be binding not only upon the parties hereto, but also as appropriate their respective heirs, devisees, personal representatives, guardians or any person deriving any claim through or on behalf of them.

It is understood by the Patient that he or she is not required to use the aforesaid Doctor and that there are numerous other physicians in Phoenix, Arizona who are qualified to provide the same services as aforesaid Doctor.

IN WITNESS WHEREOF, the Parties hereto have executed this Agreement the Day and year first above written.

Doctor

By ________________
Authorized Agent

Patient

By ________________
Patient

____
Patient's Spouse (If available)

The above parties appeared and signed this document before me on ________ day of ________, 198__. In witness thereof I set my seal. ________________

QUESTIONS AND NOTE

1. Questions about the facts of this case

   1.1. Why do you think the dissent appended a copy of the contract?

1.2. Is the court saying that Ms. Broemmer relied in any way on her reasonable expectations regarding the "Agreement to Arbitrate"? Does reliance have any role here?

2. Questions about the law

2.1. So, in Arizona can any consumer simply state that they didn't know what the contract meant and avoid unpleasant clauses such as arbitration clauses?

2.2. Can you apply *Broemmer* to an individually-negotiated contract, such as one to buy a particular tract of land? Would it matter if the contract were documented through the use of a standardized form?

2.3. After *Broemmer*, what evidence would a consumer introduce to establish his or her reasonable expectations? What evidence could the other party introduce?

2.4. Could you apply *Broemmer* to a business setting? If one of the parties was a sole proprietor with an idea but no business experience?

3. Note

Section 211(3) of the *Restatement (Second) of Contracts* has not had a uniform following. Indeed, it has even not garnered a majority of states. *See* James J. White, *Form Contracts Under Revised Article 2*, 75 Wash. U. L. Q. 315, 324–25 (1997). Why do you think courts have been hesitant to adopt it? And why did the *Restatement* "restate" it in the way it did?

4. **You Be the Lawyer!**

You represent Verizone, a seller of cellular telephone service. Your business contact wants you to draft a form contract that will bind consumers to a $350 "early termination fee" if they attempt to cancel any service contract within two years after signing up. He's heard about *Broemmer*—"some socialist crap from Arizona." But he wants to sell in Arizona—there are lots of old people there who want cell service; the problem is, however, that they will switch in a minute to another carrier if they think it is cheaper unless there is some significant disincentive to do so. "$350 ought to keep them," he says.

What types of provisions would you suggest to include in the form contract? What type of instructions should you draft for Verizone's sales force when selling their service?

4. WARRANTIES AND THE U.C.C.

A. INTRODUCTION

As we have seen, contract liability is promise-based. An alternative theory of obligation that may or may not be based on agreement of the parties is "warranty" liability. At its most basic level, a warranty is, in essence, an allocation of risk. That is to say, a party who makes a warranty accepts the risk of the untruth of the subject matter of that warranty. For instance, a seller of a business might warrant to the buyer that the assets of the company are free and clear of liens and encumbrances. If it should later turn out that some third party, perhaps a creditor or even the IRS, does have a claim against the assets of the business, then the seller must make it good to the buyer by satisfying the amount of the third party's claim. It makes no difference whether the seller-warrantor was aware of the claim, whether he intended to mislead the buyer, or even whether the buyer relied on the warranty in agreeing to buy the business. Unlike an action for fraud, which requires proof of bad intent, breach of warranty is a "strict liability" kind of offense.

The law recognizes several kinds of warranties concerning the nature or quality of one party's performance to the other. For instance, you may have learned in your property law class that many states recognize an implied "warrant of habitability" with respect to residential leases. If the premises are not habitable, the tenant has a defense to liability under the lease. Our focus in this section is on the statutory warranty scheme contained in Article 2 of the U.C.C. relating to contracts for the sale of goods. While you will probably receive more in-depth instruction on warranty theory in your upper-level commercial law courses, we think it is useful to briefly introduce warranty liability here for two reasons. First, it will allow you to contrast warranty liability with traditional contract liability. Second, it will give you an opportunity to engage in close statutory analysis which, as you will see, is very different from caselaw analysis.

The U.C.C. warranties come in two flavors: (1) "express warranties," which are statements made or assurances given by the seller concerning the quality or characteristics of the goods subject to the contract, and (2) "implied warranties," which are assurances concerning the seller's title to the goods and their basic quality. While express warranties arise from overt manifestations from the seller to the buyer, implied warranties are supplied by operation of law. That is to say, implied warranties are deemed to automatically become part of the contract *unless* they are excluded from the contract by affirmative agreement of the parties. Thus, warranties are "in" unless they are consciously taken "out." This is just the opposite from ordinary contract terms which are "out" unless they're deliberately put "in." Confused? Well, the U.C.C.'s warranty scheme is contained in § 2–312 through § 2–316. Review those provisions now before reading on to the next case, but bear in mind that we are only introducing warranty liability in this section. In most law schools, as we mentioned, the subject is treated in much more detail in one of the upper-level commercial law courses.

B. EXPRESS WARRANTIES

We begin our examination of warranty liability by considering express warranties. Unlike the other terms considered in this section, these are not implied terms. However, we think it will help you to understand the U.C.C. implied warranties if you first understand how the U.C.C. handles express warranties.

U.C.C. § 2–313(1) provides that an express warranty may be created by (a) any affirmation of fact or promise that relates to the goods, (b) any description of the goods, or (c) any sample or model. In each case, however, the affirmation, description, or sample must be made part of the *basis of the bargain*. What does that language mean?

---

§ 2–313. Express Warranties by Affirmation, Promise, Description, Sample.

(1) Express warranties by the seller are created as follows:

(a) Any affirmation of fact or promise made by the seller to the buyer which relates to the goods and becomes part of the basis of the bargain creates an express warranty that the goods shall conform to the affirmation or promise.

(b) Any description of the goods which is made part of the basis of the bargain creates an express warranty that the goods shall conform to the description.

(c) Any sample or model which is made part of the basis of the bargain creates an express warranty that the whole of the goods shall conform to the sample or model.

(2) It is not necessary to the creation of an express warranty that the seller use formal words such as "warrant" or "guarantee" or that he have a specific intention to make a warranty, but an affirmation merely of the value of the goods or a statement purporting to be merely the seller's opinion or commendation of the goods does not create a warranty.

QUESTIONS BEFORE THE CASE

1. How is an express warranty different from any other contractual term?
2. How does an express warranty differ from an express misrepresentation?

DAUGHTREY V. ASHE

Supreme Court of Virginia
243 Va. 73, 413 S.E.2d 336 (1992)

WHITING, JUSTICE.

In this dispute between the buyers and the sellers of a diamond bracelet, the principal issues arise under the Uniform Commercial Code—Sales. [Article 2]. Specifically, they are: (1) whether the sellers' appraisal statement of the grade of diamonds on the bracelet is a description of the goods under Code § 8.2–313(1)(b), and therefore an express warranty; and (2) whether such a statement made the description "a part of the bargain" under Code § 8.2–313(1)(b), and therefore an express warranty, when the buyers did not know of the warranty until some time after the purchase price was paid and the bracelet was delivered. * * *

In October 1985, W. Hayes Daughtrey consulted Sidney Ashe (Ashe), a jeweler, about the purchase of a diamond bracelet as a Christmas gift for his wife, Fenton C. Daughtrey. Ashe exhibited, and offered to sell, a diamond bracelet to Daughtrey for $15,000. Although Ashe "knew" and "classified" the bracelet diamonds as v.v.s. grade (v.v.s. is one of the highest ratings in a quality classification system employed by gemologists and jewelers), he merely described the diamonds as "nice" in his conversation with Daughtrey. Ashe told Daughtrey that if he was later dissatisfied with the bracelet, he would refund the purchase price upon its return.

When Daughtrey later telephoned Ashe and told him he would buy the bracelet, Ashe had Adele Ashe, his business associate, complete an appraisal form which he signed. The form contained the following pertinent language:

THE FOLLOWING REPRESENTS OUR ESTIMATE *FOR INSURANCE PURPOSES ONLY, OF THE PRESENT RETAIL REPLACEMENT COST OF IDENTICAL ITEMS*, AND NOT NECESSARILY THE AMOUNTS THAT MIGHT BE OBTAINED IF THE ARTICLES WERE OFFERED FOR SALE.

* * *

DESCRIPTION	APPRAISED VALUE
platinum diamond bracelet, set with 28 brilliant full ct diamonds weighing a total of 10 carats. H color and v.v.s. quality.	$25,000.00

(emphasis added).

When Daughtrey came with his daughter to close the sale, he showed the bracelet to his daughter and then paid Ashe for it. As Ashe was counting the money, Daughtrey handed the bracelet to Adele Ashe, who put it in a box together with the appraisal and delivered the box to Daughtrey. Daughtrey later gave the bracelet to his wife as a Christmas present.

In February 1989, Daughtrey discovered that the diamonds were not of v.v.s. quality when another jeweler looked at the bracelet. Shortly thereafter, Daughtrey complained to Ashe, who refused to replace the bracelet with one mounted with diamonds of v.v.s. quality but offered to refund the purchase price upon return of the bracelet. Because the value of diamonds generally had increased in the meantime, Daughtrey declined Ashe's offer.

On May 8, 1989, Daughtrey and his wife filed this specific performance suit against Sidney Ashe and Adele Ashe t/a Ashe Jewelers (the Ashes) to compel them to replace the bracelet with one mounted with v.v.s. diamonds or pay appropriate damages. After hearing the evidence, the trial court found that the diamonds "were of substantially lesser grade" than v.v.s. Nevertheless, because it concluded that the Daughtreys had not proven that "the appraisal was a term or condition of the sale nor a warranty upon which [they] relied in the purchase of the bracelet," the court denied relief for breach of warranty.* The Daughtreys appeal.

First, we consider whether Ashe's statement of the grade of the diamonds was an express warranty. Code § 2–313 provides in pertinent part:

(1) Express warranties by the seller are created as follows:

---

* In conformity with the court's order, the Ashes refunded the purchase price without interest to the Daughtreys upon their return of the bracelet. However, the refund of the purchase price did not satisfy the Daughtreys' claim for the cost of replacing the bracelet with one with diamonds of v.v.s. quality.

* * *

> (b) any description of the goods which is made part of the basis of the bargain creates an express warranty that the goods shall conform to the description.

The Ashes argue that the statement in the appraisal form is not an express warranty for two reasons.

First, they say the "appraisal on its face stated that it was 'for insurance purposes only.'" However, we think that the balance of the emphasized language in the appraisal form demonstrates that the limiting language relates *only* to the statement of the *appraised value*. Therefore, Ashe's description of the grade of the diamonds should be treated as any other statement he may have made about them.

Second, the Ashes contend that Ashe's statement of the grade of the diamonds is a mere opinion and, thus, cannot qualify as an express warranty under Code § 2–313(2). Code § 2–313(2) provides:

> It is not necessary to the creation of an express warranty that the seller use formal words such as "warrant" or "guarantee" or that he have a specific intention to make a warranty, but an affirmation merely of the value of the goods or a statement purporting to be merely the seller's opinion or commendation of the goods does not create a warranty.

The Ashes rely principally upon a North Carolina case construing the identical code section from the North Carolina Uniform Commercial Code. *Hall v. T.L. Kemp Jewelry, Inc.,* 71 N.C. App. 101, 104, 322 S.E.2d 7, 10 (1984) (jeweler's assurance of value of jewels mere opinion under N.C. Gen. Stat. § 25–2–313, not warranty). However, here, Ashe did more than give a mere opinion of the value of the goods; he specifically described them as diamonds of "H color and v.v.s. quality."

Ashe did not qualify his statement as a mere opinion. And, if one who has superior knowledge makes a statement about the goods sold and does not qualify the statement as his opinion, the statement will be treated as a statement of fact. * * *

Nor does it matter that the opinions of other jewelers varied in minor respects. All of them said, and the trial judge found, that the diamonds were of a grade substantially less than v.v.s.

Clearly, Ashe intended to sell Daughtrey v.v.s. diamonds. He testified that he used only the term "nice" diamonds but "[n]ever mentioned vvs because [Daughtrey] didn't know anything about vvs." Later, Ashe testified that "I know when I sold the bracelet and I classified it as vvs, I knew it was vvs."

Given these considerations, we conclude that Ashe's description of the goods was more than his opinion; rather, he intended it to be a statement of a fact. Therefore, the court erred in holding that the description was not an express warranty under Code § 2–313(2).

Next, the Ashes maintain that because the description of the diamonds as v.v.s. quality was not discussed, Daughtrey could not have relied upon Ashe's warranty and, thus, it cannot be treated as "a part of the basis of the bargain."

In our opinion, the "part of the basis of the bargain" language of Code § 2–313(1)(b) does not establish a buyer's reliance requirement. Instead, this language makes a seller's description of the goods that is not his mere opinion a representation that defines his obligation. * * *

Our construction of [Virginia's version of] § 2–313, containing language identical to § 2–313 of the Uniform Commercial Code, is supported by a consideration of the following pertinent portions of the Official Comment to the Uniform Commercial Code section:

> The present section deals with affirmations of fact by the seller, descriptions of the goods * * * exactly as any other part of a negotiation which ends in a contract is dealt with. No specific intention to make a warranty is necessary if any of these factors is made part of the basis of the bargain. In actual practice affirmations of fact made by the seller about the goods during a bargain are regarded as a part of the description of those goods; hence *no particular reliance* on such statements need be shown in order to weave them into the fabric of the agreement. Rather, any fact which is to take such affirmations, once made, out of the agreement requires clear affirmative proof. The issue normally is one of fact. Official Comment 3 (emphasis added).
>
> In view of the principle that *the whole purpose of the law of warranty is to determine what it is that the seller has in essence agreed to sell*, the policy is adopted of those cases which refuse except in unusual circumstances to recognize a material deletion of the seller's obligation. Thus, a contract is normally a contract for a sale of something describable and described. Official Comment 4 (emphasis added).

Paragraph (1)(b) makes specific some of the principles set forth above when a description of the goods is given by the seller. * * * Official Comment 5.

> The precise time when words of description or affirmation are made * * * is not material. The sole question is whether the language [is] fairly to be regarded as part of the contract. If language is used after the closing of the deal (as when the buyer when taking delivery asks and receives an additional assurance), the warranty becomes a modification, and need not be supported

> by consideration, if it is otherwise reasonable and in order (Section 2–209). Official Comment 7.
>
> Concerning affirmations of value or a seller's opinion or commendation under subsection (2), the basic question remains the same: What statements of the seller have in the circumstances and in objective judgment become part of the basis of the bargain? As indicated above, all of the statements of the seller do so unless good reason is shown to the contrary. The provisions of subsection (2) are included, however, since common experience discloses that some statements or predictions cannot fairly be viewed as entering into the bargain. Official Comment 8 (emphasis added).

We conclude from the language used in Code § 2–313 and the Official Comment thereto that the drafters of the Uniform Commercial Code intended to modify the traditional requirement of buyer reliance on express warranties. Such a requirement was contained in the following pertinent language of the earlier Uniform Sales Act § 12: "[a]ny affirmation of fact or any promise by the seller relating to the goods is an express warranty if the natural tendency of such affirmation or promise is to *induce* the buyer to purchase the goods, and if the buyer purchases the goods *relying thereon*." (Emphasis added.) We note that "induce" and "reliance" appear nowhere in Code § 2–313, as contrasted with the reference to buyer reliance in the subsequent section, Code § 2–315, dealing with an implied warranty of fitness for a particular purpose.

Hence, the seller's representation need only be "a part of the basis of the bargain," as set forth in Code § 2–313(1)(b). The term "bargain" is not defined in the Code, but it is used in the following definition of "agreement" as

> the bargain of the parties in fact as found in their language or by implication from other circumstances. * * * Whether an agreement has legal consequences is determined by the provisions of this act, if applicable; otherwise by the law of contracts as provided in Code § 1–103. (Compare 'Contract'). Code § 1–201(3). The word " 'Contract' means the total legal obligation which results from the parties' agreement as affected by this act and any other applicable rules of law. (Compare 'Agreement')." Code § 1–201(11).

Ashe introduced no evidence of any factor that would take his affirmation of the quality of the diamonds out of the agreement. Therefore, his affirmation was "a part of the basis of the bargain." Accordingly, we hold that the Daughtreys are entitled to recover for their loss of bargain, and that the court erred in ruling to the contrary.

Therefore, we will reverse the judgment of the trial court and remand the case for further proceedings to ascertain the Daughtreys' damages.

Reversed and remanded.

QUESTIONS, NOTES, AND CONNECTIONS

1. Questions about the facts of this case

   1.1. How important to Mr. Daughtrey's purchase of the bracelet was the fact that the diamonds were of v.v.s. quality? Does that matter?

   1.2. Was the representation concerning the grade of the diamonds a contractual term of the sale?

   1.3. Should the fact that the appraisal was for "insurance purposes only" make a difference in determining whether the seller's statement was part of the "basis of the bargain"? Why wasn't it an important factor for the court in this case?

   1.4. Another issue raised by *Daughtrey* is whether the representation concerning the grade of the diamonds was a statement of fact or a "mere opinion." What is the distinction between the two? Would the outcome in the case have been different if the appraisal had not referred to "v.v.s. quality" but it turned out that, unrelated to changes in the market price for diamonds, the bracelet was worth considerably less than $25,000?

2. Questions about the law

   2.1. Under the precursor to Article 2, the Uniform Sales Act, the buyer's reliance on the seller's statement was an essential element for a cause of action based on express warranty. The view in *Daughtrey* that the buyer need not prove that she *relied* on the seller's representation to establish a claim under § 2–313 is widely followed. *See, e.g., CBS Inc. v. Ziff-Davis Publishing Co.,* 75 N.Y.2d 496, 553 N.E.2d 997 (N.Y. 1990) (holding that "basis of the bargain" does not require proof of reliance). Thus, unlike proof of specific contract terms, the buyer does not have to establish that the statement or description was consciously *bargained for*. Does it affect the analysis, however, if the buyer *knows* prior to consummation of the sale that the goods are *not* as represented by the seller? *See generally Galli v. Metz,* 973 F.2d 145, 151 (2d Cir. 1992).

   2.2. The court in *Daughtrey* specifically refers to the seller's *superior knowledge* about the goods. Does this suggest a different outcome if the Daughtreys knew only that the grade of the diamonds was less than v.v.s.? Or does it mean they must have known the actual grade of the diamonds? Whatever level of knowledge is required, should access to that knowledge be sufficient or must the buyer have actual knowledge? What are the practical consequences from a litigation standpoint of having the "basis of the bargain" requirement depend on the buyer's knowledge or access to knowledge? In *Rogath v. Siebenmann,* 129 F.3d 261 (2d Cir. 1997), the court observed that the issue was not whether the buyer believed the truth of the seller's statement, but rather whether he was purchasing the seller's promise. Does that make sense?

2.3. In addition to determining (by virtue of factors such as superior knowledge) which party is best placed to bear the risk if the goods fail to conform to a specific statement or description, are there economic considerations that bear on the issue as well? Are you willing to pay more for goods with a warranty than without? If so, what does that tell you about how broadly the "basis of the bargain" language in § 2–313(1)(a)) should be construed?

2.4. What was Ashe prepared to give the Daughtreys when they found out the diamonds were not v.v.s. grade? What will they likely receive after remand as a result of the court's holding in this case?

3. Notes

3.1. Official Comment 7 to U.C.C. § 2–313, cited by the court in *Daughtrey,* makes clear that a statement or description made after the deal closes does not preclude that statement or description from constituting an express warranty as long as it is part of the basis for the bargain. The post-closing statement is simply considered a *modification* of the original agreement and, of course, under the U.C.C. modifications require no separate consideration. *See* U.C.C. § 2–209. However, if the buyer is completely unaware of the seller's affirmation of fact, arguably that statement did not become part of the basis of the bargain. This possible limitation played a key role in the well-known case of *Cipollone v. Liggett Group,* 893 F.2d 541 (3d Cir. 1990), *aff'd in part, rev'd in part,* 505 U.S. 504 (1992). In that case, the plaintiff brought suit against a cigarette manufacturer for breach of express warranty based on the company's general advertisements relating to its product. The court of appeals rejected the lower court's holding that an express warranty may be created by statements to the public at large *regardless* of whether the buyer heard or could remember hearing or seeing those advertisements. Instead, the court ruled that the "basis of the bargain" limitation requires the buyer to establish that she saw, heard, or was otherwise aware of the statements. Upon making this showing, there is a presumption that the statements did become part of the basis of the bargain. According to the court, however, the seller can rebut this presumption by "clear and affirmative" proof that the buyer *knew* the statements to be untrue, at which point, the plaintiff may still make out a claim by proving *reliance* despite the non-belief. You got all that? Is it any surprise that plaintiffs' lawyers in subsequent tobacco litigation turned their attention from warranty to tort theories of liability? *See also In re Bridgestone/Firestone Inc. Tires Products Liability Litigation*, 205 F.R.D. 503 (S.D. Ind. 2001) (advertising-related warranty claims cannot form the basis of a class action).

Suppose you purchase an appliance which is accompanied by a manual containing certain affirmations of fact about the product, but you're one of those people who never reads the manual. If the appliance doesn't comply with one of those affirmations are you just out of luck? How the heck is anyone going to know whether you read it or not? Also, can merchant-sellers have it both ways? Remember *Hill v. Gateway 2000, Inc.*, *supra* p. 142? If sellers can add the terms they want to the contract by materials included inside of the box, should they also be able to claim that warranties contained in the box were not part of the basis of the bargain?

3.2. What the courts in cases like *Cipollone* and *Bridgestone*, *supra*, have struggled with is warranties (and sometimes remedial promises; *i.e.*, assurances to repair or replace defective products) made to "remote purchasers." This situation arises because, more often than not, the product will pass from the manufacturer to one or more wholesalers and then eventually to a retailer who will sell to the ultimate purchaser. Thus, there is no contract or direct bargain between the manufacturer and the buyer who will actually use or consume the product. Nevertheless, the manufacturer may have made certain factual affirmations or promises packaged with the goods, fully intending that they would pass through the various intermediaries in the distribution chain to the remote purchaser. Likewise, as in *Cipollone*, the manufacturer may make certain promises or assurances regarding the goods in public advertisements designed to induce parties to buy the product from a seller other than the manufacturer.

3.3. All courts recognize that there is some room for sellers to "talk up" their products without subsequently being held accountable under warranty theory. The terminology generally used to refer to these communications is "sales puffery." The next problem provides an opportunity to consider the fact/opinion (puffery) distinction further.

4. **You Be the Lawyer!**

If you had represented the Ashes in this suit, would you have argued that the alleged representation concerning the quality of the diamonds was barred by the parol evidence rule? If you represented the Daughtreys, would you have asserted a claim for intentional misrepresentation rather than breach of warranty? In thinking about this decision, consider, what would be the advantages of a recovery in tort for false representation? What are the advantages of the contract/warranty action?

5. Connections

What is the difference between a claim for breach of contract and a claim for breach of an express warranty? Are "affirmations of fact" promises? Why is "an affirmation merely of the value of the goods" not an express warranty? What does the use of the term "merely" in this context mean?

PROBLEM ON EXPRESS WARRANTY

Markell is in the market for a new car. As it happens, Epstein happens to have the make and model car that Markell is looking for and Epstein is interested in selling. Although Markell never specifically asked, during the course of their discussions over price and other terms, Epstein volunteered that the car was "a sweet runner" and that "you won't have any problems with her; I even had the carburetor rebuilt just last month." Eventually, the two agree on price and close the deal. Markell drives off with the car of his dreams, only to have things turn into a nightmare. Over the course of the next month, the car breaks down several times, and it is anything but a "sweet runner." During one of his visits to the repair shop, Markell's mechanic informs him the carburetor is in bad shape and was never rebuilt. Does Markell have any claims against Epstein based on breach of express warranty? *Compare Crothers v. Cohen,* 384 N.W.2d 562 (Minn. App. 1986) *with Performance Motors, Inc. v. Allen,* 280 N.C. 385, 186 S.E.2d 161 (1972). Are there any other facts you'd like to know before reaching a final conclusion? How, if at all, would it change your analysis if Epstein were a used car dealer and this was one of the cars on Epstein's lot?

C. IMPLIED WARRANTIES GENERALLY

Article 2 contains two *implied* warranties relating to the quality of the goods forming the subject matter of the contract: an implied warranty of merchantability, provided that the seller is a merchant with respect to goods of that kind (§ 2–314), and, under certain circumstances, an implied warranty that the goods are fit for the particular purpose to which the buyer intends to put them (§ 2–315). We will briefly examine both of those warranties here. In addition, you will recall from our discussion in the very beginning of our discussion of warranties in subsection A, *supra*, the U.C.C.

also provides implied warranties relating to the seller's *title* to the goods. Specifically, that the goods are free and clear of any third party claims, including liens, encumbrances, and claims arising by way of infringement or the like. *See* U.C.C. § 2–312. Bear in mind that implied warranties do not depend on anything the seller says or does. Recall as well that, unlike normal contract terms, an implied warranty becomes part of the contract without any affirmative undertaking by the seller. As we will see in subsection F, *infra*, however, a seller can, by taking affirmative steps under the Code, eliminate the warranty from the contract by way of an express disclaimer. First, however, let's look at each of these implied warranties.

2–314. Implied Warranty: Merchantability; Usage of Trade.

(1) Unless excluded or modified (Section 2–316), a warranty that the goods shall be merchantable is implied in a contract for their sale if the seller is a merchant with respect to goods of that kind. Under this section the serving for value of food or drink to be consumed either on the premises or elsewhere is a sale.

(2) Goods to be merchantable must be at least such as

(a) pass without objection in the trade under the contract description; and

(b) in the case of fungible goods, are of fair average quality within the description; and

(c) are fit for the ordinary purposes for which such goods are used; and

(d) run, within the variations permitted by the agreement, of even kind, quality and quantity within each unit and among all units involved; and

(e) are adequately contained, packaged, and labeled as the agreement may require; and

(f) conform to the promise or affirmations of fact made on the container or label if any.

(3) Unless excluded or modified (Section 2–316) other implied warranties may arise from course of dealing or usage of trade.

QUESTIONS BEFORE THE CASE

1. What are the requirements that must be satisfied for goods to be of "merchantable" quality?

2. Is the defendant in this case a "merchant with respect to good of that kind" for purposes of § 2–314?

D. IMPLIED WARRANTY OF MERCHANTABILITY

WEBSTER V. BLUE SHIP TEA ROOM, INC.

Supreme Judicial Court of Massachusetts
347 Mass. 421, 198 N.E.2d 309 (1964)

REARDON, JJ.

This is a case which by its nature evokes earnest study not only of the law but also of the culinary traditions of the Commonwealth which bear so heavily upon its outcome. It is an action to recover damages for personal injuries sustained by reason of a breach of implied warranty of food served by the defendant in its restaurant. An auditor, whose findings of fact were not to be final, found for the plaintiff. On a retrial in the Superior Court before a judge and jury, in which the plaintiff testified, the jury returned a verdict for her. The defendant is here on exceptions to the refusal of the judge (1) to strike certain portions of the auditor's report, (2) to direct a verdict for the defendant, and (3) to allow the defendant's motion for the entry of a verdict in its favor under leave reserved.

The jury could have found the following facts: On Saturday, April 25, 1959, about 1 p.m., the plaintiff, accompanied by her sister and her aunt, entered the Blue Ship Tea Room operated by the defendant. The group was seated at a table and supplied with menus.

This restaurant, which the plaintiff characterized as "quaint," was located in Boston "on the third floor of an old building on T Wharf which overlooks the ocean."

The plaintiff, who had been born and brought up in New England (a fact of some consequence), ordered clam chowder and crabmeat salad. Within a few minutes she received tidings to the effect that "there was no more clam chowder," whereupon she ordered a cup of fish chowder. Presently, there was set before her "a small bowl of fish chowder." She had previously enjoyed a breakfast about 9 a.m. which had given her no difficulty. "The fish chowder contained haddock, potatoes, milk, water and seasoning. The chowder was milky in color and not clear. The haddock and potatoes were in chunks" (also a fact of consequence). "She agitated it a little with the spoon and observed that it was a fairly full bowl. * * * It was hot when she got it, but she did not tip it with her spoon because it was hot * * * but stirred it in an up and under motion. She denied that she did this because she was looking for something, but it was rather because she wanted an even distribution of fish and potatoes." "She started to eat it, alternating between the chowder and crackers which were on the table with * * * [some] rolls. She ate about 3 or 4 spoonfuls then stopped. She looked at the spoonfuls as she was eating. She saw equal parts of liquid, potato and fish as she spooned it into her mouth. She did not see anything unusual about it. After 3 or 4 spoonfuls she was aware that something had lodged in her throat because she couldn't swallow and couldn't clear her throat by gulping and she could feel it." This misadventure led to two esophagoscopies at the Massachusetts General Hospital, in the second of which, on April 27, 1959, a fish bone was found and removed. The sequence of events produced injury to the plaintiff which was not insubstantial.

We must decide whether a fish bone lurking in a fish chowder, about the ingredients of which there is no other complaint, constitutes a breach of implied warranty under applicable provisions of the Uniform Commercial Code,[1] the annotations to which are not helpful on this point. As the judge put it in his charge, "Was the fish chowder fit to be eaten and wholesome? * * * [N]obody is claiming that the fish itself wasn't wholesome. * * * But the bone of contention here—I don't mean that for a pun—but was this fish bone a foreign substance that made the fish chowder unwholesome or not fit to be eaten?"

The plaintiff has vigorously reminded us of the high standards imposed by this court where the sale of food is involved (see *Flynn v. First Natl. Stores Inc.,* 296 Mass. 521, 523) and has made reference to cases involving stones in beans (*Friend v. Childs Dining Hall Co.,* 231 Mass. 65), trichinae in pork (*Holt v. Mann,* 294 Mass. 21, 22), and to certain other cases, here and elsewhere, serving to bolster her contention of breach of warranty.

The defendant asserts that here was a native New Englander eating fish chowder in a "quaint" Boston dining place where she had been before; that "[f]ish chowder, as it is served and enjoyed by New Englanders, is a hearty dish, originally designed to satisfy the appetites of our seamen and fishermen"; that "[t]his court knows well that we are not talking of some insipid broth as is customarily served to convalescents." We are asked to rule in such fashion that no chef is forced "to reduce the pieces of fish in the chowder to minuscule size in an effort to ascertain if they contained any pieces of bone." "In so ruling," we are told (in the defendant's brief), "the court will not only uphold its reputation for legal knowledge and acumen,

---

[1] "(1) Unless excluded or modified by section 2–316, a warranty that the goods shall be merchantable is implied in a contract for their sale if the seller is a merchant with respect to goods of that kind. Under this section the serving for value of food or drink to be consumed either on the premises or elsewhere is a sale. (2) Goods to be merchantable must at least be such as * * * (c) are fit for the ordinary purposes for which such goods are used. * * *" G. L. c. 106, § 2–314.

"* * * (3) (b) [W]hen the buyer before entering into the contract has examined the goods or the sample or model as fully as he desired or has refused to examine the goods there is no implied warranty with regard to defects which an examination ought in the circumstances to have revealed to him. * * *" G. L. c. 106, § 2–316.

but will, as loyal sons of Massachusetts, save our world-renowned fish chowder from degenerating into an insipid broth containing the mere essence of its former stature as a culinary masterpiece." Notwithstanding these passionate entreaties we are bound to examine with detachment the nature of fish chowder and what might happen to it under varying interpretations of the Uniform Commercial Code.

Chowder is an ancient dish preexisting even "the appetites of our seamen and fishermen." It was perhaps the common ancestor of the "more refined cream soups, purees, and bisques." *Berolzheimer, The American Woman's Cook Book* (Publisher's Guild Inc., New York, 1941) p. 176. The word "chowder" comes from the French "chaudiere," meaning a "cauldron" or "pot." "In the fishing villages of Brittany * * * 'faire la chaudiere' means to supply a cauldron in which is cooked a mess of fish and biscuit with some savoury condiments, a hodgepodge contributed by the fishermen themselves, each of whom in return receives his share of the prepared dish. The Breton fishermen probably carried the custom to Newfoundland, long famous for its chowder, whence it has spread to Nova Scotia, New Brunswick, and New England." *A New English Dictionary* (MacMillan and Co., 1893) p. 386. Our literature over the years abounds in references not only to the delights of chowder but also to its manufacture. A namesake of the plaintiff, Daniel Webster, had a recipe for fish chowder which has survived into a number of modern cookbooks[2] and in which the removal of fish bones is not mentioned at all. One old time recipe recited in the New English Dictionary study defines chowder as "A dish made of fresh fish (esp. cod) or clams, stewed with slices of pork or bacon, onions, and biscuit. 'Cider and champagne are sometimes added.' " Hawthorne, in *The House of the Seven Gables* (Allyn and Bacon, Boston, 1957) p. 8, speaks of "[a] codfish of sixty pounds, caught in the bay, [which] had been dissolved into the rich liquid of a chowder." A chowder variant, cod "Muddle," was made in Plymouth in the 1890s by taking "a three or four pound codfish, head added. Season with salt and pepper and boil in just enough water to keep from burning. When cooked, add milk and piece of butter."[3] The recitation of these ancient formulae suffices to indicate that in the construction of chowders in these parts in other years, worries about fish bones played no

---

[2] "Take a cod of ten pounds, well cleaned, leaving on the skin. Cut into pieces one and a half pounds thick, preserving the head whole. Take one and a half pounds of clear, fat salt pork, cut in thin slices. Do the same with twelve potatoes. Take the largest pot you have. Try out the pork first, then take out the pieces of pork, leaving in the drippings. Add to that three parts of water, a layer of fish, so as to cover the bottom of the pot; next a layer of potatoes, then two tablespoons of salt, 1 teaspoon of pepper, then the pork, another layer of fish, and the remainder of the potatoes. Fill the pot with water to cover the ingredients. Put over a good fire. Let the chowder boil twenty-five minutes. When this is done have a quart of boiling milk ready, and ten hard crackers split and dipped in cold water. Add milk and crackers. Let the whole boil five minutes. The chowder is then ready to be first-rate if you have followed the directions. An onion may be added if you like the flavor." "This chowder," he adds, "is suitable for a large fishing party." Wolcott, *The Yankee Cook Book* (Coward-McCann, Inc., New York City, 1939) p. 9.

[3] Atwood, Receipts for Cooking Fish (Avery & Doten, Plymouth, 1896) p. 8.

role whatsoever. This broad outlook on chowders has persisted in more modern cookbooks. "The chowder of today is much the same as the old chowder. * * *" *The American Woman's Cook Book*, supra, p. 176. The all embracing Fannie Farmer states in a portion of her recipe, fish chowder is made with a "fish skinned, but head and tail left on. Cut off head and tail and remove fish from backbone. Cut fish in 2-inch pieces and set aside. Put head, tail, and backbone broken in pieces, in stewpan; add 2 cups cold water and bring slowly to boiling point. * * *" The liquor thus produced from the bones is added to the balance of the chowder. Farmer, *The Boston Cooking School Cook Book* (Little Brown Co., 1937) p. 166.

Thus, we consider a dish which for many long years, if well made, has been made generally as outlined above. It is not too much to say that a person sitting down in New England to consume a good New England fish chowder embarks on a gustatory adventure which may entail the removal of some fish bones from his bowl as he proceeds. We are not inclined to tamper with age old recipes by any amendment reflecting the plaintiff's view of the effect of the Uniform Commercial Code upon them. We are aware of the heavy body of case law involving foreign substances in food, but we sense a strong distinction between them and those relative to unwholesomeness of the food itself, e.g., tainted mackerel (*Smith v. Gerrish,* 256 Mass. 183), and a fish bone in a fish chowder. Certain Massachusetts cooks might cavil at the ingredients contained in the chowder in this case in that it lacked the heartening lift of salt pork. In any event, we consider that the joys of life in New England include the ready availability of fresh fish chowder. We should be prepared to cope with the hazards of fish bones, the occasional presence of which in chowders is, it seems to us, to be anticipated, and which, in the light of a hallowed tradition, do not impair their fitness or merchantability. While we are buoyed up in this conclusion by *Shapiro v. Hotel Statler Corp.,* 132 F. Supp. 891 (S. D. Cal.), in which the bone which afflicted the plaintiff appeared in "Hot Barquette of Seafood Mornay," we know that the United States District Court of Southern California, situated as are we upon a coast, might be expected to share our views. We are most impressed, however, by *Allen v. Grafton,* 170 Ohio St. 249, where in Ohio, the Midwest, in a case where the plaintiff was injured by a piece of oyster shell in an order of friend [*sic*] oysters, Mr. Justice Taft (now Chief Justice) in a majority opinion held that "the possible presence of a piece of oyster shell in or attached to an oyster is so well known to anyone who eats oysters that we can say as a matter of law that one who eats oysters can reasonably anticipate and guard against eating such a piece of shell. * * *" (P. 259.)

Thus, while we sympathize with the plaintiff who has suffered a peculiarly New England injury, the order must be

Exceptions sustained. Judgment for the defendant.

QUESTIONS AND NOTES

1. Questions about the facts of this case

 1.1. Just how important was it to the court's decision in *Webster* that the plaintiff had been born and brought up in New England? Would the result have been different if the plaintiff was from Wyoming visiting Boston on vacation? And while we're at it, did the court conclude the chowder was merchantable because it contained no foreign substances or no *unexpected* foreign substances? If you find yourself intrigued by this question, you might want to take a look at *Green v. American Tobacco Co.,* 304 F.2d 70 (5th Cir. 1962), one of the early cigarette cases, where the court, in denying the claim, noted, "We are not dealing with an obvious, harmful foreign body in a product. * * * They (the cigarettes) are exactly like all others of the particular brand and virtually the same as all other brands on the market."

 1.2. Goods are "merchantable" if they *would pass in the trade* without objection or they are *fit for the ordinary purposes* for which such goods are used. But what does this mean? Obviously, the presence of a large fish bone did not render the chowder in *Webster* unmerchantable, but what if the facts had been that the bone was in a cup of cream of broccoli soup?

2. Questions about the law

 2.1. Should it make a difference in terms of warranty liability if the defect was latent and, therefore, not readily ascertainable to the buyer *or* the seller? In *Willis Mining, Inc. v. Noggle,* 235 Ga.App. 747, 509 S.E.2d 731 (1998), the seller made just that argument with respect to granite blocks to be used by the buyer as gravestone monuments. About 18 months after sale of the blocks, they became discolored and had to be replaced. How would you expect the court to respond? Suppose the defect had been patent, rather than latent, and discoverable to the buyer upon exercise of reasonable diligence; how would that alter your analysis under § 2–314?

 2.2. Note that, unlike the provisions of § 2–313 relating to express warranties, the implied warranty of merchantability applies only if *the seller is a merchant with respect to goods of that kind.* What do you suppose is the reason for this limitation? How do you tell whether a seller is or is not a merchant? *See* U.C.C. § 2–104(1).

 2.3. In *Bayliner Marine Corp. v. Crow,* 257 Va. 121, 509 S.E.2d 499 (1999), the court suggested that the first phrase—would pass without objection in the trade—concerns whether a significant segment of the buying public would object to buying the goods, while the second phrase—fit for the ordinary purpose—concerns whether the goods are capable of performing their ordinary functions. The claim in *Crow* was that a certain fishing boat was unmerchantable because of its inability to reach a maximum speed of 30 miles per hour. How would you resolve that question under each of these tests of merchantability? What kind of evidence would be relevant to your determination? Would a significant segment of the public object to a creamy chowder that might mask the existence of a nasty fish bone? What is the ordinary function of a bowl of chowder?

3. Notes

3.1. Although most of the merchantability cases are litigated under the "fitness for the ordinary purpose" or the "would pass without objection in the trade" standard, to be merchantable for purposes of § 2–314(1) the good must also, among other things, conform with any promises or representations made on the container or label. U.C.C. § 2–314(2)(f). Wouldn't such a promise or representation ordinarily constitute an express warranty? If so, what, if anything, does § 2–314(2)(f) add from the buyer's perspective?

3.2. Article 35(2)(a) of the *U.N. Convention on Contracts for the International Sale of Goods* has its own implied warranty of merchantability that requires that the goods be "fit for the purposes for which goods of the same description would ordinarily be used." How does this language compare with U.C.C. § 2–314(2)(c)?

3.3. Obviously, Justice Reardon, the author of the opinion in *Webster*, had a lot of fun with this case. Some people, however, think the term "judicial humor" is an oxymoron. Here's what Professor William Prosser (of tort law fame) had to say on the subject:

> Judicial humor is a dreadful thing. In the first place, the jokes are usually bad; * * * There seems to be something about the judicial ermine which puts its wearer in the same general class with the radio comedian. He is just not funny. In the second place, the bench is not an appropriate place for levity. The litigant has vital interests at stake. His entire future, or even his life, may be trembling in the balance, and the robed buffoon who makes merry at his expense should be chocked with his own wig.

THE JUDICIAL HUMORIST: A COLLECTION OF JUDICIAL OPINIONS AND OTHER FRIVOLITIES (1952) vii–viii. We suspect Ms. Webster might be inclined to agree with Professor Prosser.

4. **You Be the Lawyer!**

Epstein, a native Texan—but not exactly your typical Texan—goes to a restaurant named Bubba's BBQ while visiting Dallas. One of the appetizers on the menu is breaded and fried "Rocky Mountain Oysters." Epstein, not being familiar with that particular brand of oyster, orders a dozen and consumes them. Later, upon learning that he had not exactly consumed something from the sea, Epstein becomes violently ill and has to be hospitalized for a week. Upon his release, he consults you about representing him in a suit against Bubba's. Will you take the case, bearing in mind it will have to be a contingency fee case since Epstein cannot afford to pay based on an hourly rate?

NOTE ON CAUSATION

Official Comment 13 to § 2–314 states that "it is of course necessary to show not only the existence of the warranty but the fact that the warranty was broken and that the breach was the *proximate cause* of the loss sustained" (emphasis added). In many cases, the trickiest element for the buyer in a claim for breach of the implied warranty of merchantability is establishing a causal link between the breach and the loss for which recovery is sought. And you thought causation issues only came up in torts? Sorry.

In *Reybold Group, Inc. v. Chemprobe Technologies, Inc.*, 721 A.2d 1267 (Del. 1998), the court suggested that proof of causation must "tend to negate other reasonable causes of the injury sustained." Thus, a buyer could presumably show that the defect in the seller's product was the cause in fact of her injury and still not prevail if she was unable to eliminate other intervening or supervening events. How can that be? Consider a buyer who purchases a chainsaw from a hardware store. On assembling the product, the buyer notices that the blade is not seated firmly in the housing. Nevertheless, the buyer fires up the chain saw and proceeds to mangle his arm when the blade comes loose. Was the chain saw unmerchantable? Presumably so; this product would hardly pass muster in the trade. Was the defect in the chainsaw the cause in fact for the buyer's injury? Sure, but for the defect the injury would never have occurred. But was the defect the proximate cause of the buyer's injury? Maybe not. Does it matter whether the instructions contained a warning not to use the chainsaw unless the blade is seated firmly in the housing?

The court in *Reybold* also stated that typically expert testimony is required to prove causation in a claim for breach of the implied warranty of merchantability. Why should this be so? Are there circumstances when the connection between the defect and the injury are so obvious that expert proof would be superfluous? Suppose the housing in which the chainsaw blade was seated was enclosed in a casing and not visible to the naked eye? If the buyer is injured when the blade comes loose is expert testimony really necessary to prove causation between the defect and the loss? And by the way, who are these experts? Do they work for free? Of course not, they're retained and paid for by the parties. Doesn't that tend to color their judgment? How can their testimony be taken seriously? Put another way, what safeguards exist to ensure that the expert will not just give the opinion that the party paying him or her wants? Are these safeguards adequate?

PROBLEMS ON MERCHANTABILITY

1. You may remember a device widely advertised and marketed through TV ads several years ago called the "Clapper." This little device allowed you to turn an appliance on and off by clapping your hands twice; at the time it was a real novelty. Well, it seems Edna Hubbs, an 80-year-old woman suffering from arthritis and osteoporosis, purchased a Clapper. Alas, upon installing the Clapper, she found that her claps were not activating the device. Determined to make it work, Edna thereupon attempted one last, extra hard clap. Lamentably, however, the effort was too much and Edna sustained injuries to her hand and wrist. Edna proceeded to file suit against the manufacturer and the retailer of the device for breach of the warranty of merchantability. How should Edna's case be resolved? Lest you think we're making this up, see *Hubbs v. Joseph Enterprises*, 198 A.D.2d 757, 604 N.Y.S.2d 292 (1993).

2. Bruce Markell, Jr., a first year law student with a rare blood type, received a call from the local Red Cross office telling him that there was a critical shortage of his blood type and asking him to consider donating. The Red Cross official explained that a bloodmobile would be on campus the next week. Being a compassionate soul, Bruce showed up at the bloodmobile and donated a pint of his blood. Afterwards, a nurse insisted that he have a glass of orange juice and some cookies supplied by the Red Cross to help him regain his strength and prevent light-headedness or even fainting. Bruce, never one to pass on freebies, had about six cookies along with his juice. As a goodwill gesture, Briesckes Bakery had donated the cookies to the Red Cross. Later that afternoon, Bruce became violently ill and had to be hospitalized. Tests revealed a form of food poisoning typically associated with bacteria that germinate in processed flour. Bruce is convinced that the cookies were the source of his woes. As a result of his illness, which came toward the end of the semester, Bruce was unable to take his final exams. Therefore, he will now have to spend an extra semester in law school in order to graduate. Bruce has brought a suit against both the Red Cross and Briesckes seeking to recover the additional education costs he will now incur and the wages he has lost by having to delay accepting full-time employment. What result in Bruce's case and why? *See*, *inter alia*, U.C.C. § 2–318.

E. IMPLIED WARRANTY OF FITNESS FOR PARTICULAR PURPOSE

§ 2–315. Implied Warranty: Fitness for Particular Purpose.

Where the seller at the time of contracting has reason to know any particular purpose for which the goods are required and that the buyer is relying on the seller's skill or judgment to select or furnish suitable goods, there is unless excluded or modified under the next section an implied warranty that the goods shall be fit for such purpose.

In many instances a buyer will have purchased goods for a particular purpose or with a particular objective in mind. In some of these cases the goods will not be fit for the particular purpose the buyer had in mind. If the seller affirmed that the goods would serve that purpose, the buyer will have a claim for breach of express warranty. In other situations, the goods will not accomplish the purpose because they are unmerchantable, *i.e.* not fit for the purposes for which such goods are ordinarily used. In still other cases, however, there will be no express warranty concerning the suitability of the goods to the purpose for which they were acquired *and* the failure to satisfy the buyer's purpose will not be attributable to a defect that renders the goods unmerchantable. What recourse does the buyer have in these situations? Sometimes, for example when the buyer was relying on her own judgment about the adequacy of the goods, there will be no recourse. In these cases, the hard lesson learned would be that the buyer should have done a more careful investigation into the suitability of the goods to the purpose for which they were acquired before purchasing. In other circumstances, however, the buyer may have recourse against the seller for breach of the implied warranty of fitness for a particular purpose under U.C.C. § 2–315. Nevertheless, establishing a breach of the fitness warranty when the goods fail to do what the buyer wanted them to do is a little trickier than establishing breach of the merchantability warranty when the goods are simply defective. The next case and the material that follow, are intended to help you to flesh out what the buyer must prove to make out a case under § 2–315.

QUESTIONS BEFORE THE CASE

1. What is the relationship between an implied warranty of merchantability and an implied warranty of fitness for a particular purpose?
2. What are the elements of the implied warranty of fitness?

LEAL V. HOLTVOGT

Court of Appeals of Ohio
123 Ohio App.3d 51, 702 N.E.2d 1246 (1998)

FAIN, J.

* * *

Joseph and Claudia Holtvogt owned and operated Shady Glen Arabians, a horse barn in Miami County, Ohio. They were experienced in Arabian horse training, breeding, boarding, selling, and showing. In 1992, the Leals, novices in the equine industry, decided to begin raising horses. In April, 1993, Ferdinand Leal began visiting Shady Glen Arabians regularly to learn how to ride and handle horses. Before long, a friendship developed between the Holtvogts and Leals, and Ferdinand Leal began spending three to four days each week at the Holtvogts' barn helping Joseph Holtvogt with the horses.

In late 1993, the Leals decided they wanted to start a breeding program by purchasing a stallion to breed with a mare they owned. At first, they were interested in purchasing Procale, a stallion owned by John Bowman. After talking to Mr. Holtvogt about Procale, the Leals decided not to buy him. The Holtvogts then offered the Leals a one-half interest in Mc Que Jabask, an Arabian stallion that the Holtvogts owned. At trial, the Leals testified that before they agreed to invest in Mc Que Jabask, Mr. Holtvogt made a number of statements regarding the stallion, such as: Mc Que Jabask was a national top ten champion in three categories; he was an all-around winning stallion; he earns $20,000.00 per year in stud fees; he is capable of attaining national show titles again; and his foals were selling for $6,000 to $10,000 each [these statements will be referred to hereinafter as "the five contested statements"].

In January, 1994, the Leals and Holtvogts entered into a contract of sale for a one-half interest in Mc Que Jabask for $16,000. The contract also established a partnership agreement, which called for the parties to share equally in the expenses and profits arising from their joint ownership of Mc Que Jabask.

There was expert testimony that prior to January, 1994, Mc Que Jabask had been treated for lameness and was suffering a chronic lameness condition in his right rear and fore fetlocks. Mr. Holtvogt testified that he had taken the stallion for lameness treatments numerous times. He also stated that he did not disclose this information to the Leals.

By July, 1994, the Leals were dissatisfied with the partnership and indicated to the Holtvogts that they wanted either a refund of their money or a remedy for their concerns. In March, 1995, the mortality insurance on

Mc Que Jabask lapsed when neither the Leals nor the Holtvogts paid the insurance premium.

* * *

On January 17, 1996, Mc Que Jabask died from stomach ulcer complications. Since neither party had renewed the stallion's mortality insurance, Mc Que Jabask was uninsured.

In February, 1995, the Leals filed suit against the Holtvogts, who then brought counterclaims against the Leals. The Miami Country Common Pleas Court found that the Holtvogts had negligently misrepresented the stallion's condition and that they had breached an "express warranty on the condition of the horse for the purposes intended" and awarded the Leals $16,000 in compensatory damages. * * *

II

The Holtvogts' Second Assignment of Error is as follows:

> THE TRIAL COURT COMMITTED REVERSIBLE ERROR WHEN IT HELD THAT DEFENDANTS' ACTIONS CONSTITUTED NEGLIGENT MISREPRESENTATION BECAUSE PLAINTIFFS FAILED TO PRESENT ANY FACTUAL EVIDENCE WHATSOEVER WHICH WOULD LEAD A REASONABLE PERSON TO BELIEVE THAT MC QUE JABASK WAS LAME AT THE TIME THE PARTIES ENTERED INTO THE PARTNERSHIP AGREEMENT OR THAT MC QUE JABASK WAS NOT FIT TO BE SHOWN.

* * *

Negligent misrepresentation is defined as follows:

> [One] who, in the course of his business, profession or employment, or in any other transaction in which he has a pecuniary interest, *supplies false information* for the guidance of others in their business transactions, is subject to liability for pecuniary loss caused to them by their justifiable reliance upon the information, if he fails to exercise reasonable care or competence in communicating the information. *Textron Financial Corp. v. Nationwide Mut. Ins. Co. (1996),* 115 Ohio App. 3d 137, 149, 684 N.E.2d 1261, *cert. denied*, 78 Ohio St. 3d 1425, 1425, 676 N.E.2d 531. (Emphasis in original.)

[The court ruled that the concealment of Mc Que Jabask's lameness did not support a claim of negligent misrepresentation since it was not an *affirmative* false statement. However, the court concluded that the record did support the trial court's finding that the Holtvogts negligently misrepresented to the Leals that Mc Que Jabask was fit to be shown, and thus overruled the Holtvogts' second assignment of error.]

III

The Holtvogts' First Assignment of Error is as follows:

> THE TRIAL COURT COMMITTED REVERSIBLE ERROR WHEN IT FOUND THAT DEFENDANTS' ACTIONS CONSTITUTED A BREACH OF AN EXPRESSED WARRANTY BECAUSE THE TRANSACTION BETWEEN THE PARTIES DOES NOT MEET THE DEFINITIONAL REQUIREMENTS UNDER OHIO EXPRESSED WARRANTY LAW; DEFENDANTS' CONDUCT DOES NOT RISE TO THE LEVEL OF AN EXPRESSED WARRANTY; AND THE INTEGRATION CLAUSE IN THE PARTNERSHIP AGREEMENT PRECLUDES THE COURT'S CONSIDERATION OF ANY AND ALL PRIOR ORAL REPRESENTATIONS.

The Holtvogts' argument that there was no breach of an express warranty is three-fold. First, they argue that Ohio's express warranty law is not applicable to their transaction. Second, they argue that their conduct was not sufficient to constitute an express warranty. Third, they argue that there was a clause in the parties' agreement precluding consideration of any oral representations.

We begin with the Holtvogts' argument that Ohio's express warranty law does not apply to the transaction that occurred between the parties. The Holtvogts contend that an express warranty can arise only if there has been a "sale" between the parties and that their transaction with the Leals created a "partnership agreement," not a "sale."

We first address this argument by noting that Ohio warranty law is governed by the Uniform Commercial Code, Sales, R.C. [Article 2]. The scope of [Article 2] is set forth in [§ 2–102], which provides in part that "sections [§§ 2–101 to 2–725], inclusive, of the Revised Code, apply to transactions in goods." Goods are defined as "all things * * * which are moveable at the time of identification to the contract for sale * * * [and] must be both existing and identified before any interest in them can pass." [§ 2–105(1), (2)]. The Arabian stallion, Mc Que Jabask, was moveable, existing, and could be identified at the time of the contract. Thus, he would qualify as a "good" under [§ 2–102].

As for the Holtvogts' contention that the transaction was not a "sale," they correctly argue that a "sale" is defined as "the passing of title from the seller to the buyer for a price." [§ 2–106(1)]. There is no statutory requirement, however, that full title to the good must pass from the buyer to the seller. In fact, [Article 2] explicitly states, in its definition of "goods," "there may be a sale of a part interest in existing identified goods." [§ 2–103(3)]. Thus, although the transaction involved the sale of only a half-interest in Mc Que Jabask, the transaction was within the definitional requirements of [Article 2] and thus is governed by Ohio warranty law. Therefore, the first part of the Holtvogts' argument is not well-taken.

We next address the Holtvogts' argument that their conduct did not amount to an express warranty. The trial court found that "* * * the [Holtvogts] engaged in 'puffing' at the time of the sale of the one-half interest in the horse but did not fraudulently misrepresent a material fact." Although the trial court did not enlighten us as to what part of the Holtvogts' conduct it believed to be "puffing," our review of the record leads us to believe that the trial court was talking about the five contested statements that the Leals claim the Holtvogts made. The Holtvogts contend that the trial court's finding that they engaged in "puffing" is inconsistent with the trial court's conclusion that they gave the Leals an express warranty.

* * *

"Puffing," or merely stating the seller's opinion, cannot amount to an express warranty. * * * The five contested statements were the subject of extensive testimony during the trial. Mr. Holtvogt denied making any of these statements and the Leals repeatedly testified that Mr. Holtvogt did make these statements. The trial court seems to have found the five contested statements to be "puffing." Our review of the record shows that there is credible and competent evidence that these five contested statements were no more than "puffing." The Holtvogts correctly argue that when statements are mere "puffing," they cannot constitute an express warranty.

We cannot sustain this Assignment of Error, however, because we find that the Holtvogts breached an implied warranty of fitness for a particular purpose.

In its entry, the trial court found the following:

> "* * * the information the [Holtvogts] failed to apprise the [Leals] was the lameness of the horse at the time the contract was executed in January 1994.
>
> The [Leals] suffered damages in the amount of $16,000.00 as a result of this negligent misrepresentation.
>
> The *same set of facts* establish a cause of action for breach of express warranty *on the condition of the horse for the purposes intended* * * *" (emphasis added).

In its entry, the trial court did not just say an express warranty was breached, but rather said that an "express warranty on the condition of the horse for the purposes intended" was breached. We conclude that the trial court intended to say that an implied warranty of fitness for a particular purpose was breached. Our conclusion is supported by the trial court's statement that the same set of facts establishes claims for both a breach of express warranty on the condition of the horse for the purposes intended and negligent misrepresentation. We note that the elements of a claim for negligent misrepresentation and breach of an implied warranty of fitness for a particular purpose are quite similar, while the elements of negligent misrepresentation and breach of an express warranty are not similar. Thus, we conclude that the trial court, in its conclusions of law, intended to say that an implied warranty of fitness for a particular purpose was given and breached by the Holtvogts when they failed to disclose Mc Que Jabask's lameness to the Leals.

An implied warranty of fitness for a particular purpose is covered by the Uniform Commercial Code, Sales, [§ 2–315], which provides:

> "Where the seller at the time of contracting has reason to know any particular purpose for which the goods are required and that the buyer is relying on the seller's skill or judgment to select or furnish suitable goods, there is unless excluded or modified under section [2–316] of the Revised Code an implied warranty that the goods shall be fit for such purpose."

Ohio courts have set forth the following test to determine whether an implied warranty of fitness for a particular purpose has been created: (1) the seller must have reason to know of the buyer's particular purpose; (2) the seller must have reason to know that the buyer is relying on the seller's skill or judgment to furnish or select appropriate goods; and (3) the buyer must, in fact, rely upon the seller's skill or judgment. * * *

The first element requires that Mr. Holtvogt knew why the Leals decided to buy an interest in Mc Que Jabask. From our review of the record, we see that Mr. Holtvogt clearly knew that the Leals wanted to buy an interest in the stallion to start a breeding program. Mr. Holtvogt testified:

> "* * * [The Leals] had explained what type of horse they were looking for [and] it seemed to me that [Mc Que] Jabask fit the bill [of] what they were looking for and that's why I mentioned to them, uh, to Ferdinand that there might be a possibility that we would be interested in selling part interest in him.
>
> * * * The things that they were saying, * * * those things were, were present in, in [Mc Que] Jabask. * * *
>
> * * * It just, it made sense that, you know, in the fact that the Leals could breed to [Mc Que] Jabask. * * * Um, we could, uh, with the experience and the reputation that we had we could help market their foals, um, it was, I really felt that it was something that could work."

Thus, evidence of the first element of an implied warranty of fitness for a particular purpose was presented at trial.

The second element requires that Mr. Holtvogt had reason to know that the Leals were relying on his skill and judgment to select or furnish the appropriate goods. Evidence presented at trial shows that Mr. Holtvogt knew, or at least should have known, that the Leals were relying on his judgment when they purchased an interest in the stallion. The relationship between Mr. Holtvogt and Mr. Leal was like that of a teacher and student. Mr. Leal spent a great deal of time at the Holtvogts' barn, helping Mr. Holtvogt with the horses and learning from Mr. Holtvogt. Mr. Holtvogt testified that he was an expert trainer and breeder with Arabian horses, and the evidence shows that he knew Mr. Leal knew very little about horses. Furthermore, the Leals testified that they were interested in purchasing another horse, Procale, but that Mr. Holtvogt steered them away from that horse, saying that horse was not the type of horse that the Leals wanted to buy. Mr. Holtvogt even testified that he mentioned Mc Que Jabask to the Leals because the stallion was the type of horse that they were looking for. Thus, evidence of the second element of an implied warranty of fitness for a particular purpose was presented at trial.

The third element requires that the Leals actually did rely upon Mr. Holtvogt's skill and judgment when they purchased an interest in the stallion. The trial court found that the Leals justifiably relied upon the Holtvogts' representations regarding the stallion. This finding is not against the manifest weight of the evidence. As stated earlier, there was competent and credible evidence presented at trial to support this finding as both Leals were novices in the horse industry and they testified that they trusted Mr. Holtvogt and considered him to be the expert. Thus, evidence of the third element was presented at trial.

Because all three elements were proven at trial, we conclude that an implied warranty of fitness for a particular purpose was given by the Holtvogts to the Leals at the time of the sale. There must be evidence that the warranty was breached if the Leals are to recover. *Delorise Brown, M.D., Inc.*, 86 Ohio App. 3d at 363. "Whether a warranty has failed to fulfill its essential purpose is ordinarily a determination for the factfinder." *Id.*

The trial court found that a warranty was breached by the Holtvogts because the horse was lame. As stated above, competent and credible evidence was presented to support the trial court's finding that Mc Que Jabask suffered from chronic lameness at the time of the sale. At trial, Dixie Gansmiller testified that even though a lame stallion could stand for stud, its lameness would affect her decision whether to breed her mares with it. Thus, we conclude that competent and credible evidence in the record does demonstrate that Mc Que Jabask was not fit for the particular purpose intended by the Leals when they invested in him.

* * *

Judgment accordingly.

QUESTIONS

1. Questions about the facts of this case

   1.1. Presumably, the court came up with the $16,000 in "compensatory damages" based upon the amount the Leals had paid for a one-half interest in Mc Que Jabask. Did that award really give the Leals the "benefit of their bargain"?

   1.2. What was the "purpose" for which the Leals acquired an interest in Mc Que Jabask? Did the horse's lameness make him no longer fit for that purpose?

   1.3. The court describes the relationship between Mr. Holtvogt and Mr. Leal as "like that of teacher and student." Why was that fact important?

2. Questions about the law

   2.1. The court of appeals in *Leal* agreed with the trial court that the "five contested statements" were no more than mere puffing. Do you agree? How do you think the court in *Daughtrey, supra,* at 583, would have characterized those statements? Should evidence relating to those statements have been excluded under the parol evidence rule?

   2.2. The court of appeals also concluded that the failure to disclose Mc Que Jabask's lameness could not support a negligent misrepresentation claim because it was not an *affirmative* false statement. Isn't deliberate concealment of a material fact tantamount to an affirmative misstatement of fact? Why didn't the Leals make a non-disclosure argument along the lines of *Weintraub v. Krobatsch, supra,* at 396?

   2.3. The court of appeals concludes that when the trial court in its entry of judgment stated not just that an express warranty was breached, but that an "express warranty on the condition of the horse for the purposes intended" was breached, it really meant to say that the sellers breached the implied warranty of fitness for a particular purpose. Do you think the trial court really just misspoke? If not, how should the court of appeals have disposed of the case?

   2.4. Obviously, the Leals did not bring a claim for breach of the warranty of merchantability. Why do you suppose their lawyer made that judgment? What would you have done? Is there an upside to including alternative causes of action in a complaint even though you know they may be weak? Is there a downside? How does a court deal with multiple warranties? As for the last question, consider the next case.

3. **You Be the Lawyer!**

If you had represented the Leals in their negotiations for the purchase of a half-interest in Mc Que Jabask and the partnership with the Holtvogts, how would you have protected your clients?

QUESTION BEFORE THE CASE

If the goods conform to an express warranty provided by the seller, can the buyer still recover for breach of an implied warranty?

SINGER COMPANY V. E.I. DU PONT DE NEMOURS AND COMPANY

United States Court of Appeals, Eighth Circuit
579 F.2d 433 (1978)

HANSON, SENIOR DISTRICT JUDGE.

In this diversity contract action, the Singer Company sued to recover losses incurred when the E.I. du Pont de Nemours and Company allegedly breached both an express warranty and an implied warranty of fitness in failing to provide plaintiff with suitable industrial paint for its plant operations at Red Bud, Illinois. The case was submitted to a jury only on the implied warranty theory, and judgment was returned for Singer in the amount of $108,367.00. Defendant was awarded no recovery on either of its two attendant counterclaims. Du Pont unsuccessfully moved for judgments notwithstanding the verdict and for new trial, contending that the trial court improperly instructed the jury and that there was insufficient evidence to support the jury verdicts. Du Pont appeals from those rulings. We affirm.

Singer became interested during late 1972 in obtaining an electrodeposition paint system for its Red Bud, Illinois plant, where until this time the metal, or ware, used in the manufacture of air-conditioners and furnaces had been painted in a spray system. Electrodeposition is a method of painting by which pretreated ware is conveyed through an electrically charged paint tank and the ware, serving as an anode, is coated with paint in an electroplating type of process. After a period of negotiation between representatives from the two parties, Du Pont, in September and October of 1972, was contracted to provide Singer with paint for its approximately 22,000 gallon tank. Three additional companies were contracted to provide other interrelated steps in the overall finishing process, steps such as pretreatment of the ware and conveyance of the ware through the entire system.

From the beginning, in October of 1973, Singer experienced problems with the electrodeposition system. Ware frequently emerged from the paint tank with "blotches" and "streaks." Repainting was necessary. Du Pont, which supervised the installation and starting up of this electrodeposition system, tried unsuccessfully for six months to correct this problem. Finally, in April of 1974, the Du Pont paint was removed from the tank and replaced with paint supplied by the Sherwin-Williams Company. This lawsuit was filed the following year.

The nub of the factual controversy in the trial court was the cause for the blotches and streaks on the painted ware. Du Pont maintained that the problem was with the substrate, pretreated ware; Singer, however, insisted that the paint was at fault. In countering Singer's claim, Du Pont argued that the paint provided to plaintiff met contract specifications until the substrate was altered in February of 1974, at which time Du Pont could no longer be held to have expressly warranted its product. Singer contends that even if the specifications of this express warranty were met, Du Pont had given an implied warranty of fitness for a particular purpose by representing throughout the period in question that its paint would satisfy plaintiff's needs. Over Du Pont's objection, the trial court instructed the jury on implied warranty for a particular purpose. The issue of express warranty was not submitted.

I. The Uniform Commercial Code

While disagreeing on whether the trial court should have instructed as to an implied warranty of fitness for a particular purpose, the parties are properly in accord that the Illinois adoption of the Uniform Commercial Code governs the disposition of this case. * * * There is also no dispute that the "all tests" provision of the contract, which specified such set standards as color and texture that the paint was to satisfy upon pretreated laboratory test panels, was an express warranty pursuant to Section 2–313(1)(b) of the U.C.C. But Singer claims that the contract further preserved an implied warranty of fitness, a warranty that pursuant to Section 2–315 assured plaintiff the paint supplied would satisfactorily cover its substrate. A paragraph in the contract provided:

> None of the provisions or remedies herein are in lieu of any claims for damages Buyer may have at law or equity under the Uniform Commercial Code or otherwise, for the breach of any contracts or warranties with Buyer, which rights are specifically reserved by Buyer.

Du Pont contends that parties who have an express warranty regarding a contracted for item cannot also have an implied warranty of fitness for that same item. The warranty of fitness for a specific purpose is alleged to have been limited by expressly defining it in a set of specifications, and Du Pont claims that to find otherwise would permit Singer to escape the parties' true contractual bargain.

* * *

Pertinent sections of the U.C.C., and the comments pursuant thereto, lend inferential support to Singer's position that the implied warranty of fitness was cumulative to and not excluded by the express warranty. Section 2–316(2), with regard to the exclusion or modification of such warranties, states:

> * * * To exclude or modify any implied warranty of fitness the exclusion must be a writing and *conspicuous*. (Emphasis added.)

Comment 9 to that section provides in part:

> The situation in which the buyer gives precise and complete *specifications to the seller* is not explicitly covered in this section, but this is a frequent circumstance by which the implied warranties may be excluded. The warranty of fitness for a particular purpose would not normally arise since in such a situation there is usually *no reliance on the seller by the buyer*. (Emphasis added.)

See also U.C.C. § 2–315, comment 2. Because the evidence in this case fully indicates that it was not the buyer but the seller who in fact recommended and supplied the paint specifications, and remained in control of the paint tank, it would appear that the trial court did not err in its determination that an implied warranty of fitness was at issue. This is especially so in view of the purported exclusion of this warranty, which could be scarcely termed "conspicuous."

A reading of the U.C.C. to suggest that an express warranty and an implied warranty of fitness are not necessarily mutually exclusive, as Singer has argued, receives support from Code authority.

> The fact that a warranty of fitness for a particular purpose does or does not exist has no bearing on any other warranty or theory of product liability. Conversely, the fact that there may be some other basis for liability of the defendant does not preclude the existence of a warranty for a particular purpose. *Thus the fact that there is a warranty of conformity to sample [an express warranty] does not preclude the existence of a warranty for a particular purpose*. (Emphasis added.) Anderson, Uniform Commercial Code § 2–315:5 (1970).

* * * Relevant case law, in the balance, further indicates that an express warranty would not control under the circumstances of this case.

Cases can be found prior to the adoption of the U.C.C. to support Du Pont's argument of mutual exclusiveness. This Court, without specific adoption of the position, recognized in *Hercules Powder Co. v. Rich,* 3 F.2d 12 (8th Cir. 1924) that there was law to the effect that an implied warranty of fitness could not prevail in the presence of an express warranty on the same item or subject.

An express warranty excludes an implied warranty relating to the same subject or of the same general nature, on the theory that no warranty should be implied where the parties with relation to the very same subject have expressed by words the warranty by which they will be bound. *Id.* at 18.

There was also case law to the contrary. * * * But while there may have once been a split of authority, we fail to find since the general adoption of the above-quoted sections of the U.C.C. any case holding directly in favor of Du Pont's mutual exclusivity agreement. In fact unless the exclusion of the implied warranty of fitness is specifically and conspicuously excluded, courts, often relying upon Section 2–317,[4] have found that such implied and express warranties can be cumulative and co-exist within the same agreement. * * *

Du Pont, in arguing the law upon appeal, relies principally upon two types of cases that have arisen under the U.C.C.: those in which there has been a showing that the buyer, in possession or control of the item, failed to follow the express warranty specifications; and those where an enforceable disclaimer of an implied warranty has been established. With respect to the first type of case, it is clear that the trial court did not confront a situation where a buyer in possession or control of an item failed to follow seller's specifications, used the item in a manner for which it was not intended, lost that for which he had contracted, and then erroneously claimed a breach of an implied warranty for fitness. * * * Here, Du Pont, as the seller, was in control of the disputed item. No one denies that Du Pont was throughout this time in control of Singer's paint tank, directing its operation and determining its contents.

The disclaimer cases are likewise inapplicable. Even without a paragraph in the contract reserving all further warranties under the U.C.C., Du Pont would have difficulty in arguing that an express warranty of the paint effected a disclaimer of any further warranty. It is clear from these cases that disclaimers under the Code are not favored and are limited whenever possible. * * *

Du Pont also argues in general that to permit Singer to assert an implied warranty of fitness would be to allow utilization of the U.C.C. in avoidance of the parties' true bargain. The true bargain, though, is less than apparent from the face of the contract. This was not a situation where

4 Section 2–317 of the U.C.C. provides in part:

Warranties whether express or implied shall be construed as consistent with each other and as cumulative. * * *

a buyer ordered according to specifications and then claimed an implied warranty of fitness when the product failed to measure up to expectations. In this instance, the buyer approached the seller describing the results desired and the seller professed to be able to supply it, thereby inducing a reliance that created the possibility of an implied warranty of fitness. Notwithstanding the express warranty contained within the specifications particularly defining and describing the item to be supplied, there may have been a further warranty that an item with those specifications would accomplish certain results or be adequate for the specified purpose. That is, the accomplishment of the purpose might be viewed as the essence of the contractual undertaking, and not the mere furnishing of the specified item. Nothing within this contract, or in writings or statements subsequent to it, indicate whether the end of the agreement was the specified item or the use for which the item was intended. * * *

Du Pont simply failed to negotiate a contract that clearly delineated and limited allocation of risk. This case would never have arisen had defendant, as a party to and a scrivener of the contract, either inserted a specific disclaimer or demanded that the warranty savings clause be deleted.

Having left the contract ambiguous, the question as to whether use rather than supply of the product was intended to be of the essence, as well as questions regarding buyer's reliance and seller's knowledge of that reliance, are for jury determination. Such were submitted to the jury in this case under the trial court's following instruction.

> Your verdict on the plaintiff's claim must be for the plaintiff if you believe:
>
> First: The defendant sold paint to the plaintiff.
>
> Second: The defendant knew the use for which plaintiff purchased the paint, and
>
> Third: Plaintiff reasonably relied upon defendant's judgment for the suitability of the paint for such use, and,
>
> Fourth: The paint was not suitable for such use, and
>
> Fifth: As a direct result plaintiff was damaged.

Du Pont contends on appeal, as it did below, that the trial court was in error giving an instruction which allowed the jury to determine the construction of the contract. The question regarding the presence of an implied warranty, defendant maintains, constituted a question of law that should have been determined by the trial judge. Moreover, it is claimed that the jury should have been instructed with respect to the express warranty.

The better rule, when there remains an issue of contractual intent, is to submit the issue to the jury unless the evidence is so clear that no reasonable person would determine the issue but one way. * * * Du Pont fails to offer any sustaining reason as to why the construction of an ambiguous contract, which involves the existence or nonexistence of an implied warranty of fitness under the U.C.C., should also not be left to a jury determination. * * * The question of buyer's reliance and seller's knowledge of that reliance is a factual inquiry particularly well-suited for jury deliberation. U.C.C. §§ 2–316, 2–317 * * *

There was no prejudicial error in refusing to instruct the jury with respect to the express warranty. As concluded above, the law is that an implied warranty of fitness is not necessarily excluded by the presence of an express warranty. Thus, satisfaction of the express warranty, a factual issue that could be and was argued to the jury, would not preclude the jury from further consideration of the alleged implied warranty. We note that defendant, in presenting its appeal, did indicate that its primary purpose in requesting the express warranty instruction was to implement this mistaken contention that no implied warranty could be present by the fact that it had been specified and those specifications met. Plaintiff, while not conceding that the express warranty had been satisfied, agreed to go to the jury on the issue of implied warranty alone.

II. Substantial Evidence

Once having determined that the issue of implied warranty was properly submitted to the jury, sufficiency of the evidence becomes the controlling inquiry. We review the evidence to determine whether there was sufficient evidence for the jury to find that Singer reasonably relied upon Du Pont's judgment regarding the suitability of the paint, that Du Pont knew the use for which Singer purchased the paint, and that the paint was not suitable for such use. On appeal, Du Pont does not appear to contest the interrelated issues of buyer's "reliance" and seller's "knowledge." In view of the extensive negotiations prior to the contract, Du Pont's supervision of the installation of the paint tank, and the continuing presence of Du Pont in a supervisory capacity throughout the period in question, defendant's reason for not pursuing these lines of argument is apparent. Du Pont does contend, however, that there is insufficient proof to show that the paint was not suitable for Singer's use and was the cause of the blotches and streaks on the painted ware. It insists that an uneven pretreatment, with resulting un-uniform substrate, was the source of the problem.

[The court proceeded to review the evidence put on by Singer at trial concerning the cause for the blotches and streaks on painted ware. This consisted of expert scientific testimony to the effect that impurities and non-uniformity of elements within the paint tank were the source of the problem as well as evidence that after the Du Pont paint was removed and replaced with a different manufacturer's paint the problem was resolved.]

III. Conclusion

In reviewing the evidence pursuant to the judgment n.o.v. standards, we cannot conclude that Singer failed to offer the necessary evidence to sustain a jury verdict against Du Pont for a breach of an implied warranty of fitness. Clearly, Du Pont, which reviewed the entire finishing system, knew at the time of contracting the particularized use for which plaintiff purchased the paint, and Singer reasonably relied upon Du Pont's judgment that its paint was suitable for the electrodeposition system. Du Pont makes some argument that the change in substrate affected the suitability, but it was an argument not pressed upon appeal. In any event, if defendant did not consider itself bound by warranty to do anything more than furnish a paint of particular specifications, we find it difficult to explain not only why Du Pont supervised the installation of the system, but worked to alleviate the problems during the entire period its paint was in the tank.

Finally, in satisfaction of the last element necessary to an implied warranty of fitness, the evidence was sufficient to show that Du Pont's paint was not suitable for Singer's use. The evidence here presents a close question. Yet giving the "jury verdict the benefit of all reasonable inferences to be drawn from the evidence," this Court, though we might have cast our verdict otherwise, cannot say there was no more than a scintilla of evidence to support the jury verdict. The testimony of Singer employees and [plaintiff's expert] De Vittorio, and such evidence as the unexplained blotches and streaks upon the laboratory test panels, sufficiently takes this case from the undeterminative equipoise for which defendant argues. * * *

With respect to damages, which were reasonably assessed, we find the trial court did not err in denying a judgment n.o.v. on Du Pont's counterclaim for paint sold and delivered or further counterclaim for value of services rendered. Nor did the trial court abuse its discretion in denying defendant's motions for new trial.

The judgment appealed from is affirmed.

QUESTIONS, NOTES, AND CONNECTIONS

1. Questions about the facts of this case

   1.1. What specific facts were most favorable to Singer? What facts tended to support Du Pont's argument?

1.2. What did Du Pont *expressly* warrant? Why do you suppose the issue of express warranty was not submitted to the jury? Why did Du Pont think it was prejudicial error not to submit the issue of express warranty to the jury?

1.3. Of what significance was the fact that the Sherman-Williams paint apparently performed without any of the problems experienced with the Du Pont paint? Why does the court refer to the evidence regarding breach of the fitness warranty as presenting a close call? What other facts would you like to know about the Sherwin-Williams paint?

2. Questions about the law

2.1. The decision in *Singer* is a good example of how a court goes about analyzing issues arising under a statute, but why did the court relegate its discussion of § 2–317 to a footnote? That curiosity aside, note how the court used the specific provisions of Article 2 and the Official Comments to dismantle each of Du Pont's contentions. Sometimes, however, the statute does not address every issue that arises in a case. For example, in *Singer,* Du Pont contended that the issue regarding the presence of a warranty is a question of law for the court and not one of fact for the jury. Article 2 simply does not offer any guidance as to whether the question should be regarded as one of law or fact. What should a court do in that situation? What did the *Singer* court do? *See* U.C.C. § 1–103.

2.2. In deciding that the issue of contractual intent was properly submitted to the jury, was the court saying that the issue of the presence of a fitness warranty was not a question of law?

2.3. According to the court in *Singer,* for there to be a breach of the fitness warranty the buyer must show that the seller *knew* both the buyer's purpose in acquiring the goods and that the buyer was relying on the seller's expertise in selecting suitable goods. Is that consistent with the *Leal* court's view of the elements of an action under § 2–315?

3. Notes

3.1. Article 35(2)(b) of the *U.N. Convention on Contracts for the International Sale of Goods* provides that goods will not be deemed as conforming to the contract unless they "are fit for any particular purpose expressly or impliedly made known to the seller at the time of the conclusion of the contract, except where the circumstances show that the buyer did not rely, or that it was unreasonable for him to rely, on the seller's skill and judgment." How does this provision differ from the comparable U.C.C. warranty? Can you construct a situation where there would be a breach of warranty under domestic law but not under *CISG*?

3.2. As the facts in *Singer* illustrate, sometimes warranties can conflict. Du Pont's argument that its express warranty negated the implied warranty of fitness was directly contradicted by § 2–317(c). However, the exception in that provision for the fitness warranty does not apply to other implied warranties, including an implied warranty of merchantability. Thus, if the two warranties cannot be construed consistently with one another, under the terms of § 2–317(c), the express warranty displaces the merchantability warranty. Is this an invitation to crafty sellers to deprive their buyers of a merchantability warranty with an express warranty that is not as broad? Suppose a seller warrants that her product is free from defects in workmanship and materials for three months. In the middle of the fourth month, the product breaks down because of a serious, latent manufacturing defect. Does the buyer have a valid breach of implied warranty claim? *See Koellmer v. Chrysler Motors Corp.*, 6 Conn.Cir.Ct. 478, 276 A.2d 807 (1970). If so, what does the language in § 2–317(c) mean? If not, hasn't the seller effectively disclaimed the merchantability warranty without going through the required statutory procedure? To answer these questions, perhaps we better also take a look at the Code's provisions relating to warranty disclaimers.

4. **You Be the Lawyer!**

Assume you represent Du Pont. After this case is decided, what changes would you recommend that the company make in supply contracts of this type?

5. Connections

In what manner is the implied warranty of merchantability broader than the implied warranty of fitness for a particular purpose? In what way is it narrower? How does the concept of an "implied warranty" differ from the basic scheme of contract liability? Have you encountered implied warranties in other contexts? What do these implied warranties all have in common?

F. DISCLAIMERS OF WARRANTIES

The court in *Singer* obviously considered it relevant that Du Pont had not followed the regular statutory procedure for excluding an implied warranty of fitness for particular purpose. This implies, of course, that, had Du Pont been more conscientious, it could have disclaimed the warranty. But why should this ever be permitted? As we have discussed, the purpose for warranty theory is to allocate to the seller the risk that the goods do not conform to general or specific expectations. After all, usually the seller, and particularly a professional seller, is in the best position to know whether there is a problem with the goods and, in any event, the seller can pass the risk along via insurance, higher prices, etc. But this is not always the case. Sometimes the seller is in no better position than the buyer to avoid the loss. Moreover, sometimes the buyer is willing to accept the risk, typically because it means a better price. If warranties were absolute, the parties would lose the flexibility to negotiate over this term and the buyer would always pay the higher price. Have you purchased a computer, a television, or perhaps a stereo system lately? Did the cashier offer you an extended warranty? Did you take it? We bet you didn't. Why not?

The U.C.C.'s rules governing effective warranty disclaimers are set forth in U.C.C. § 2–316. Take a look at that statute right now. You'll see that the procedures differ depending on which warranty is at issue and that some warranties are harder to get rid of than others. It should also be apparent that the subject is a technical one. Therefore, an extended discussion of warranty disclaimers, and the related topic of seller efforts to limit liability for breach of warranty, must await the upper-level commercial law courses. However, we think it might be instructional, and perhaps even helpful in your personal life, to examine the basic framework right now.

QUESTIONS BEFORE THE CASE

1. What is the difference between a warranty disclaimer and a limitation on remedies?
2. Do you think this decision would have come out the same if the defendant had been Jeff Lebowski, an unemployed L.A. bowler, instead of a corporation?

OFFICE SUPPLY CO., INC. V. BASIC/FOUR CORPORATION

United States District Court, Eastern District of Wisconsin
538 F.Supp. 776 (1982)

REYNOLDS, CHIEF JUDGE.

This is an action for damages brought pursuant to 28 U.S.C. § 1332. The plaintiff Office Supply Co., Inc. ("Office Supply") is a corporation located in Racine, Wisconsin, which sells office supplies. The defendant Basic/Four Corporation ("Basic/Four") is a California corporation which manufactures and sells computer hardware and software. In 1975, Office

Supply purchased computer hardware and leased computer software from Basic/Four. Office Supply claims that the system was defective and caused it to suffer substantial losses. It seeks compensation for "lost customers, income, good will and executive time and incurred additional hardware and software expense, office form expense, personnel expense and maintenance expense, all to its damage in the sum of $186,000 plus reasonable interest since April, 1975."

* * *

On January 31, 1975, the plaintiff's president, James F. Bruno, signed a contract for the purchase of computer hardware from the defendant and of computer software which was intended to control order processing, inventory control, sales analysis, and accounts receivable. Mr. Bruno mailed the contract to the defendant, and it was accepted by the defendant's assistant treasurer, R. C. Trost, on February 7, 1975. On April 1, 1975, the hardware was installed. In a letter dated May 22, 1975, the defendant advised the plaintiff that the warranty on the hardware would expire on July 1, 1975. The input of data on the software programs took longer to complete, and for a period of time the plaintiff ran parallel operations on the computer and manually as a check on the accuracy of the software applications. In a letter dated October 6, 1975, Mr. Bruno advised Basic/Four:

> "All of the applications anticipated by our company in agreeing to acquire our BASIC/FOUR System are complete and the system appears to be satisfactory. This fulfills your contractual obligation.
>
> "Although the applications programs appear to be operating satisfactorily, some 'defects' might become apparent [*sic*] later. (Defects might comprise misinterpretation of data, mishandling of a keyboarding error, or a confusing operator instruction—but would not include anything beyond the scope of the system design specification.) It is my understanding that you warrant your programs, when used in accordance with Basic/Four operating instructions, to be free from 'defects' for a period of ninety days, and that you will correct such 'defects' promptly when they are brought to your attention." (Exhibit E to defendant's memorandum in support of motion for summary judgment, filed December 15, 1981.)

Basic/Four took the position that its warranty on the software expired on January 6, 1976. As to complaints received after that date from Office Supply, it did continue to work with Office Supply in an effort to correct any claimed defects in the computer system. Office Supply also hired Ted Templeton, an independent programmer with a company called Computer Methods, Inc., who was recommended by Basic/Four, to work on its

Basic/Four system starting some time after Basic/Four advised that the warranty period was over. The record established that Mr. Templeton made some modifications in the Basic/Four software. He also added at least one new program, the ABC program which involved inventory control, to the system. Starting in January 1978, Office Supply also hired a programmer, Marc Jerome, as a fulltime employee. He found what he claims were three major defects in the software system. The record establishes that two of those defects were in programs which Basic/Four did not supply to the plaintiff. The third defect was in the UJ portion of the Basic/Four accounts receivable program, but there is no evidence that the defect arose in the UJ program until after July 1976, which was after the end of the ninety-day period during which Basic/Four continued to warrant its software applications to be free from defects.

The plaintiff's vice president, David Carlson, testified during his deposition that starting at the end of October 1975 and continuing through early 1978, approximately 20% of the customer accounts were out of balance and the Basic/Four system performed up to 78% of expectation for Office Supply. Since February 1978, when Marc Jerome finished correcting the defects in the system, Carlson testified that it has performed up to 100% of expectation. The plaintiff's president, James Bruno, testified that the system only performed up to 50% of expectation prior to 1978, that the accounts receivable first went out of balance on the October 1975 monthly statement printed during the first week of November 1975, that it printed through for the first time in February 1976, but that thereafter the accounts receivable problem continued on an intermittent basis until it was corrected by Marc Jerome in early 1978. Both men testified that there were also problems with the hardware but that those problems were always corrected by Sorbus, a service corporation related to Basic/Four with which Office Supply had a hardware maintenance contract, with only a very few minimal extra charges not covered by the monthly maintenance charges.

On June 17, 1980, Office Supply commenced its action against Basic/Four.

The portion of the Office Supply-Basic/Four contract dealing with the purchase of the hardware is a straightforward document. It describes on the front of the document the computer model and features and the purchase price. Additional terms and conditions of sale are set forth on the reverse. In relevant part it provides on the reverse that it constitutes the entire agreement and understanding between the parties, that it shall be governed by the law of California, and as to warranties and remedies for breach of warranty:

> "3. For ninety (90) days after the Equipment is installed * * * the Seller warrants the Equipment to be free from defects in material, workmanship, and operating failure from ordinary use, and the

> Seller's liability is limited solely to correcting any such defect or failure without charge. * * *"

In italic print paragraph 3 also states:

> "The warranties contained in this Agreement are in lieu of all other warranties, express or implied, including any regarding merchantability or fitness for a particular purpose, arising out of or in connection with any Equipment (or the delivery, use or performance thereof). The Seller will not be liable * * * (b) for loss of profits or other incidental or consequential damages. * * *"

The portion of the contract dealing with the lease of the software is not as clearly drafted. On its first page, which is page 3 of the contract, it states:

> "This Addendum to the Agreement for the Purchase of BASIC/FOUR Equipment, dated as of the 31 day of January 1975, between Basic/Four Corporation and Office Supply Inc. is hereby incorporated therein and made a part thereof."

Page 3 describes the program applications and their price. Additional terms and conditions are set forth on the reverse side. As to warranties and limitation of remedies, paragraph 3 provides:

> "The Seller believes that the programming being furnished hereunder is accurate and reliable and when programming accomplishes the results set forth in the 'Design Specifications,' to be agreed to by the Seller and the Purchaser, such programming will be considered completed."

Paragraph 3 continues in italics:

> "However, the amounts to be paid to the Seller under this Agreement and this Addendum do not include any assumption of risk, and the Seller disclaims any and all liability for incidental or consequential damages arising out of the delivery, use or operation of the programs provided herein.
>
> "If the purchaser, without the written consent of the Seller, makes any modification to the programming or any deviations from the operating instructions or violates the provisions of paragraph 2, all warranties set forth herein cease immediately.
>
> "All warranties set forth herein are in lieu of all other warranties, express or implied, including any regarding merchantability or fitness for a particular purpose, arising out of or in connection with any program (or the delivery, use or performance thereof)."

The contract also contains a fourteen-page description of the program applications.

The parties agree that the contract is a sales contract, that the choice of law provision which it contains is valid, and consequently that the parties' rights and liabilities are governed by the Uniform Commercial Code ("UCC") as adopted in California. They agree about very little else.

The defendant contends in its motion for summary judgment that * * * the warranty disclaimer and damage limitation provisions in the contact are valid and binding and therefore the plaintiff is entitled to no relief, * * * The plaintiff's summary judgment motion consists of a denial of each of those contentions and arguments favoring the application of contrary rules of law at the ultimate trial of this action.

Each of the defendant's contentions, along with the arguments as to the applicable legal principles raised by the plaintiff in opposing defendant's summary judgment motion, is discussed separately below.

* * *

(2) Disclaimer of Warranties

The Office Supply-Basic/Four contract specifically provides that it constitutes the entire agreement and understanding between the parties. That being so, parol evidence is not admissible under California law to vary the terms of the agreement. * * * The language of the contract must be interpreted in an effort to determine the intent of the contracting parties. * * *

If there are no exclusions or modifications in the contract, every sales contract governed by the UCC contains an implied warranty of merchantability and, if the seller has reason to know of a particular purpose for which the goods are required, an implied warranty of fitness for a particular purpose. Section 2315, Cal. Comm. Code [UCC § 2–315]. Express warranties are created if the seller makes an affirmation of fact or promise to the buyer and the affirmation becomes part of the bargain between the parties. Section 2313, Cal. Comm. Code [UCC § 2–313]. Thus, any express warranties must be found in the language of the contract. Implied warranties, in contrast, will be held to exist unless they are specifically excluded.

With regard to the computer hardware, the contract expressly warrants the hardware to be free from defects in material, workmanship, and operating failure from ordinary use for ninety days after installation.

With regard to the computer software, the most reasonable interpretation of the contract is that the same ninety-day warranty of material, workmanship, and operating failure applies, dating from the time when the "programming accomplishes the results set forth in the 'Design Specifications,'" which in this case was on October 6, 1975, when plaintiff's president so advised the defendant.

The plaintiff contends that the language just quoted is a warranty of future performance, and that in fact the programming did not accomplish the desired results until 1978. Courts have been parsimonious in finding warranties of future performance where there is no explicit language in the contract creating such a warranty. *Standard Alliance Industries, Inc. v. Black Clawson Company,* 587 F.2d 813, 820 (6th Cir. 1978). For example, a representation as to the performance ability of an existing product will not be construed as an explicit warranty of future performance ability of the product. *Jones & Laughlin Steel Corporation v. Johns-Manville Sales Corporation,* 626 F.2d 280, 291 (3d Cir. 1980) (interpreting California law). Section 2316(1), Cal. Comm. Code [UCC § 2–316(1)], provides in part:

> "(1) Words or conduct relevant to the creation of an express warranty and words or conduct tending to negate or limit warranty shall be construed wherever reasonable as consistent with each other. * * *"

The first page of the software addendum (page 3 of the contract) provides that it is incorporated within and made a part of the hardware purchase agreement. That agreement contains the ninety-day express warranty provision which, as a result of the incorporation, also applies to the software purchase. In light of the ninety-day express warranty, the most reasonable construction of the software addendum language regarding the results to be accomplished by the programming is that the completion of the programming and installation of all of the bargained-for applications starts the running of the ninety-day warranty period, and not that the applications are warranted to run perfectly once their installation is apparently successfully completed.

The UCC allows contracting parties to exclude or modify all implied warranties. There is no correlative requirement that if implied warranties are excluded, express warranties must be given. Thus it is permissible, for example, to exclude all implied warranties and to provide for a ninety-day express warranty limited to repair or replacement of defective goods. * * *

In order to make an effective waiver of implied warranties, the provisions of § 2316(2), Cal. Comm. Code [UCC § 2–316(2)], must be followed:

> "* * * to exclude or modify the implied warranty of merchantability or any part of it the language must mention merchantability and in case of a writing must be conspicuous, and to exclude or modify any implied warranty of fitness the exclusion must be by a writing and conspicuous. * * *"

There is no dispute that the language contained in the contract was in this case sufficient to waive all implied warranties. The issue is whether the disclaimer was "conspicuous." Section 1201(1), Cal. Comm. Code, [UCC § 1–201(1)] provides:

> "(10) 'Conspicuous.' A term or clause is conspicuous when it is so written that a reasonable person against whom it is to operate ought to have noticed it. A printed heading in capitals (as: NONNEGOTIABLE BILL OF LADING) is conspicuous. Language in the body of a form is 'conspicuous' if it is in larger or other contrasting type or color. But in a telegram any stated term is 'conspicuous.' Whether a term or clause is 'conspicuous' or not is for decision by the court."

Basic/Four points out that it disclaimed the implied warranties not once but twice, and that the disclaimers were written in italicized print, in contrast to the regular print used on the rest of the contract. Nevertheless, the disclaimers are not conspicuous. In *Dorman v. International Harvester Company,* 46 Cal. App. 3d 11, 120 Cal. Rptr. 516 (Cal. App. 1975), the California court of appeals noted that under pre-Code California law, disclaimers of warranty are strictly construed, and, applying the code, it found that an attempted disclaimer written in only slightly contrasting print and without a heading adequate to call the buyer's attention to the disclaimer clause was not effective. That decision controls in this case. The two disclaimers in the Office Supply-Basic/Four contract are on the reverse sides of the first two pages of the contract. They are not positioned close to the buyer's signature line. The contracts are printed on pale green paper and the disclaimers are set forth in print which, although italicized, is only slightly contrasting with the remainder of the contract. There are no headings noting the disclaimers of warranty. Since there is only " 'some slight contrasting set-off' " and there is " 'only a slight contrast with the balance of the instrument,' " *Dorman, supra,* 120 Cal. Rptr. at 522, *quoting Woodruff v. Clark County Farm Bureau Coop. Ass'n,* (Ind. App. 1972), 153 Ind. App. 31, 286 N.E.2d 188, 198, *quoting* in turn *Greenspun v. American Adhesives, Inc.,* 320 F. Supp. 442 (E.D. Pa. 1970), therefore, the disclaimers are not conspicuous.

Discussion of the effectiveness of the disclaimer provisions in the contract does not end with the finding of lack of conspicuousness. In their treatise Uniform Commercial Code § 12–5 at 444 (2d ed. 1980), Messrs. White and Summers note "with apprehension" the growing number of cases which hold that if a buyer is actually aware of a warranty disclaimer, then the disclaimer is effective even if not conspicuous. * * * The Official Comment to UCC § 2–316 states that the section is designed "to protect a buyer from unexpected and unbargained language of disclaimer." Pointing to that language, the Court in *Dorman, supra, at 521–522,* indicated that California will follow the trend:

> "* * * [W]e must rely predominantly on the official comments to sections 2–316 and 1–201, subdivision (1), and to foreign law. The official comment to subdivision (10) of section 1201 states that the 'test [of conspicuousness] is whether attention can reasonably be

> expected to be called to [the disclaimer provision].' * * * We must examine this comment in the light of the official comment to section 2–316, which states: 'This section is designed principally to deal with those frequent clauses in sales contracts which seek to exclude "all warranties, express or implied." It seeks to protect a buyer from unexpected and unbargained language of disclaimer by denying effect to such language when inconsistent with language of express warranty and permitting the exclusion of implied warranties only by conspicuous language or other circumstances which protect the buyer from surprise.' In other words, section 2–316 seeks to protect the buyer from the situation where the salesman's 'pitch,' advertising brochures, or large print in the contract, giveth, and the disclaimer clause—in fine print—taketh away."

The *Dorman* Court also noted that under pre-Code California law as well, a provision disclaiming implied warranties "was ineffectual unless the buyer assented to the provision or was charged with notice of the disclaimer before the bargain was completed." *Id.* at 521.

James Bruno testified during his deposition taken on November 3, 1980, that before he purchased the Basic/Four system, he spent approximately two months comparing it with other systems, and that he drew up a written comparison of the Basic/Four and Qantel systems, including their guarantees. Basic/Four, 90 days; and Qantel had one year." He read the back of the contract before he signed it, when he received the contract from Basic/Four he made out a list of questions to ask Basic/Four before signing and one subject on his list was the ninety-day guarantee, and before he signed he showed the warranty provision in the contract to someone he knew in the data processing filed. He discussed the warranties with Basic/Four before signing and tried to have them modified:

> "Q Did you read the provisions of the warranty?
>
> "A Yes.
>
> "Q And did you discuss those provisions with Basic/Four, or with someone from Basic/Four?
>
> "A Yes.
>
> "Q And what was said to you about those provisions?
>
> "A That that was the condition that I had to accept.
>
> "Q All right. And was that discussion before or after the contract as signed?
>
> "A I would say before.

"Q * * * did you call up Darryl Bannister, for example, and say I want to buy this system but I refuse to agree to the warranty provisions in the contract?

"A Well, I argued with him, but it was to no avail. Nothing."

He also was aware of the warranty limitations before he signed the contract:

"Q Well, were you aware of the provisions of that warranty before you signed the contract?

"A That there were limitations?

"Q That there are limitations to the warranty? Were you aware of that?

"A Certainly.

"Q You were?

"A Yes."

That testimony establishes that the warranty disclaimers were neither unexpected nor unbargained for, and that, consequently, under *Dorman*, they should be enforced.

* * *

ORDER

For the foregoing reasons.

IT IS ORDERED that the plaintiff's motions to compel discovery and for partial summary judgment are denied.

IT IS FURTHER ORDERED that the defendant's motion for summary judgment is granted, and that judgment be entered dismissing this action with prejudice and awarding costs to the defendant.

QUESTIONS, NOTES, AND CONNECTIONS

1. Questions about the facts of this case

    1.1. What exactly did Basic/Four warrant with respect to the performance of its software programs and for how long?

    1.2. What facts did the court consider most important in making its finding that the Basic/Four warranty began to run on October 6, 1975?

    1.3. Were the Basic/Four software applications merchantable? Did that matter to the court?

1.4. The court states at one point in its opinion that "the plaintiff is also an established commercial operation of significant size, and the plaintiff's president testified during his deposition that he is accustomed to engaging in contract negotiation on behalf of Office Supply." To what issue were those factual findings relevant?

2. Questions about the law

2.1. Most courts that have spoken to the issue agree with *Office Supply* that a non-conspicuous warranty disclaimer may be effective where it can be shown that the buyer had actual knowledge of the disclaimer. *See, e.g., Cate v. Dover Corp.*, 790 S.W.2d 559 (Tex. 1990). However, in a separate opinion in *Cate,* Justice Ray offered the following rationale against permitting this exception to the conspicuousness requirement:

> The statute, on its face, provides for no actual knowledge exception. There is no room for judicial crafting of those omitted by the legislature. I would hold that the extent of a buyer's knowledge of a disclaimer is irrelevant to a determination of enforceability under § 2–316(b) of the UCC.

The effect of actual knowledge is subject to debate among leading commentators on commercial law. The purpose of the objective standard of conspicuousness adopted by the court today reflects the view that "The drafters intended rigid adherence to the conspicuousness requirement in order to avoid arguments concerning what the parties said about the warranties at the time of sale." J. WHITE AND R. SUMMERS, Uniform Commercial Code § 12–5 (2d ed. 1980). An absolute rule that an inconspicuous disclaimer is invalid, despite the buyer's actual knowledge, encourages sellers to make their disclaimers conspicuous, thereby reducing the need for courts to evaluate swearing matches as to actual awareness in particular cases. * * * Today's decision condemns our court to a parade of such cases.

Do you agree with this argument? Does it make a difference if the transaction involves a consumer rather than a commercial sale? If actual knowledge is irrelevant, does that also mean that a conspicuous disclaimer is effective regardless of whether the buyer had actual knowledge of it? *See* U.C.C. § 1–201(10). How many buyers seeking to establish a claim for breach of warranty do you think admit that they had knowledge of the disclaimer? No, we're not suggesting anyone would perjure themselves, we just think maybe it's not as big of a problem as some courts seem to have made it out to be.

2.2. We understand why the court applied Article 2 to the sales of the computer hardware, but should Article 2 have been applied to the *lease* of the software? Also, Article 2 applies to "transactions in goods." U.C.C. § 2–102. Is software a "good"?

2.3. In the course of its opinion, the court in *Office Supply* states that, "If there are no exclusions or modifications in the contract, *every* sale contract governed by the U.C.C. contains an implied warranty of merchantability * * *" (emphasis ours). What statute was Judge Reynolds reading? Not one we're acquainted with!

2.4. While the enforceability of disclaimers of implied warranties focuses on the conspicuousness of the language of disclaimer, § 2–316(1) adopts a different standard for attempts to disclaim express warranties. As noted in *Office Supply*, contractual language attempting to negate or limit an express warranty is required to be construed consistently with the language creating the warranty and, if that cannot be done, the negation or limitation is inoperative. In short, it's more difficult for a seller to get rid of an express warranty than an implied warranty. Is this as it should be? Why? Even if you agree with the judgment of the drafters on this point, there is one fly in the ointment. Look closely at the language in § 2–316(1). The negation of words of limitation that are inconsistent with an express warranty is made *subject* to § 2–202, the parol evidence rule for Article 2 contracts. Does this mean that a seller can effectively eliminate an express warranty made during the course of contract negotiations by including an expansive merger or integration clause into the final writing, thereby excluding introduction of the contradictory oral warranty? Technically it would seem so, but courts, not surprisingly, tend to have limited tolerance for that sort of elevation of form over substance. Thus, Professors White and Summers suggest that to be effective the merger clause needs to be: 1) conspicuous, and 2) explicit that it is intended to exclude prior oral assurances made by the seller or its sales staff. *See* J. WHITE & R. SUMMERS, UNIFORM COMMERCIAL CODE, § 12–5, at p. 421 (4th ed. 1995). Is this a satisfactory resolution of the problem?

3. Notes

3.1. Note that in *Office Supply* the court was dealing not only with the effectiveness of Basic/Four's disclaimer under § 2–316, but also the enforceability of Basic/Four's attempt to: (1) limit the remedy (to repair or replace) for breach of the express warranty that was given, and (2) exclude liability for consequential damages. In Article 2, the enforceability of remedy limitations and exclusions is governed by § 2–719. We omitted the portion of the opinion dealing with that provision because we cover limitations on damage remedies in Chapter 6. Suffice it to say for now that the relationship between § 2–719 and § 2–716 is subtle, but important. An effective disclaimer eliminates any cause of action for breach of warranty. A remedy limitation, by contrast, restricts the buyer's access to the remedy provisions of Article 2, or substitutes an entirely different remedy in their place, in the event of a breach. As we said, more on that to come.

3.2. The approach used by Basic/Four in *Office Supply* to include a limited express warranty that at the same time disclaims the broader Code warranties is not uncommon. In effect, the warranty "takes much and gives little." Recognizing that these provisions can be a trap for the unwary or the unsophisticated consumer, in 1975 Congress enacted the Magnuson-Moss Warranty—Federal Trade Commission Improvement Act (15 U.S.C. § 2301 *et seq.*). The Act, which only applies to the sale of goods used primarily for personal, family, and household purposes, is primarily a disclosure statute. This is consistent with the general approach taken in federal consumer protection legislation. Specifically, Magnuson-Moss requires manufacturers that elect to make written warranties do so in a manner that is least likely to mislead or confuse consumers. For example, § 103 of Magnuson-Moss requires sellers to designate their warranties as "full," meeting specified federal minimum standards in § 104, or "limited," not meeting those federal minimum standards. In addition, § 108 of the Act precludes a seller that makes any written warranty to a consumer from simultaneously attempting to disclaim or modify any implied warranty, except as to duration. Congress' hope was that many, if not most, manufacturers would feel competitive pressures to offer consumers full warranties. Alas, this hope has not been realized as will become obvious to you if you start reading the warranties that accompany the products you buy. Nevertheless, Magnuson-Moss, with its restrictions on disclaimers, has enlarged the scope of warranty protection for consumer buyers and, perhaps just as importantly, has provided an effective mechanism for enforcement of warranty obligations by allowing recovery of attorneys' fees by a consumer who is damaged by a seller's failure to comply with any obligation under the Act or under any written or implied warranty. *See* Magnuson-Moss § 110(d)(2).

4. **You Be the Lawyer!**

If you were documenting this transaction, how could you have protected Office Supply against a latent defect in the software, as arose in this case?

5. Connections

The implied warranties of Article 2 are said to be "default terms." What does that mean? Can other terms of a contract be disclaimed? What about express warranties? What does this suggest about the difference between promissory liability and liability based on breach of an implied warranty? Where else, quite recently, have you observed a court addressing the extent to which an implied undertaking can be negated (or limited) by contractual agreement?

CHAPTER 6

PERFORMANCE, CONDITIONS, AND EXCUSE: WHEN DOES SOMEONE WHO MADE AN ENFORCEABLE DEAL NOT HAVE TO DO WHAT SHE AGREED TO DO?

■ ■ ■

To this point, we have looked at how the terms of a contract are selected and included. We've also looked at how courts approach interpreting those terms (and inserting other ones) into the bundle of promises that constitute the contract. If everyone always did what they said they would, we could end this book at this point. But the fact that there are many, many pages to go should lead you to the conclusion that parties often don't do what contracts require them to do.

This chapter looks at the parties' post-formation conduct, and tries to assess the effect of such conduct on their contractual liability. Before we do this, however, we need to be clear on the terms we are using.

1. PERFORMANCE AND BREACH

In any contract dispute, one side alleges that the other hasn't done what they said they would do. In short, they allege breach. What is a "breach"?* Easy.** As stated in the *Restatement*, "[w]hen performance of a duty under a contract is due any non-performance is a breach." *Restatement (Second) of Contracts* § 235(2) (1981). Note that it says "any" non-performance. So provision of any "just-as-good" but non-complying performance is a breach. If the contract calls for Kleenex® tissues, and you provide bargain-brand Target generics, it's a breach even if the Target tissues are softer. And vice-versa.

Contract law thus focuses on the performance due and rendered from each party. It does this by first determining what the terms of the contract (the focus of last chapter), and then by comparing what the terms require with what the party did. The terms set the obligations, and the court compares the parties' action (or inaction) with those obligations. If there is a match, no breach; if there is any variance, breach.

* That's Markell's question. Seems pretty basic to the other co-authors. But then, Markell has never set the world on fire with his quickfire analysis of anything.

** That's the answer Epstein and Ponoroff would give. Markell made us put in the rest.

But sometimes courts use confusing terms to describe the obligations. Promises. Covenants. Warranties. Representations. What do they all mean? And how do they lead to breach?

A. CONTRACTUAL OBLIGATIONS: OF PROMISES, COVENANTS AND WARRANTIES

We saw that Section 1 of the *Restatement* defined a contract as "a promise or a set of promises." These promises often go by different names: courts talk not only of promises, but also of covenants, representations, and warranties.

Is there any difference? Think of these terms as facets of the same stone—they are all variants of the concept of "promise." If a contract contains any of these terms, a party can incur obligations. Here's a rough breakdown of the terms:

- A *promise*, says the *Restatement*, "is a manifestation of intention to act or refrain from acting in a specified way." *Restatement (Second) of Contracts* § 2(1).
- A *covenant* is just a fancier term for promise. So when you talk about the implied "*covenant*" of good faith and fair dealing, you could just as well say the implied "*promise*" of good faith and fair dealing, and not lose any meaning. By the way, in this taxonomy of terms, a *right* is the inverse of a covenant or promise. A right is the benefit of the obligor's promise owed to the opposing party (which is often referred to as the "obligee").
- A *representation* is an assertion of fact, given by one party to induce another party to enter into a contract or take some other action. For example, a contractual term could read "Party A represents that it has all licenses necessary to enter into and perform this contract." In this sense, a representation is an obligation to bear the consequences of the falsity of what is represented; that is, if untrue, a representation is equivalent to a lie.
- A *warranty* is similar to a representation; it is a promise that an assertion of fact is true, supported by an implied promise of indemnity (that is, a promise to compensate the other party) if the assertion turns out to be false.

There are also terms know as conditions, but we'll get to those later.

B. THE STRICT LIABILITY NATURE OF CONTRACT

This chapter examines defenses to breach, often termed "excuse." Before we start listing recognized excuses, we need to eliminate what is *not* an excuse: inability to perform. As stated in the *Restatement*: "Contract liability is strict liability. It is an accepted maxim that *pacta sunt servanda*, contracts are to be kept. The obligor is therefore liable in damages for breach of contract even if he is without fault . . . ." *Restatement (Second) of Contracts,* ch. 11, intro. note (1981).

Treatises and cases echo this point. Professor Farnsworth has stated that "contract law is, in its essential design, a law of strict liability, and the accompanying system of remedies operates without regard to fault." 3 E. Allan Farnsworth, *Farnsworth on Contracts* § 12.8, at 195–96 (3d ed. 2004). Judge Posner concurs: "[L]iability for breach of contract is a form of strict liability, a promisor is in effect a guarantor of performance even if he is unable and not merely unwilling to perform his contractual obligations." *Moran Foods, Inc. v. Mid-Atl. Mkt. Dev. Co., LLC*, 476 F.3d 436, 439 (7th Cir. 2007).

So if your contract calls for delivery by 5:00 p.m., and you can't make it until 5:01 p.m. due to exceptional and unusual traffic, tough. You're in breach. Same result if you find out that the component part you thought you could get for $1 actually costs $10, and you can't assemble the product you agreed to make without taking a loss. If you don't deliver, you're in breach. Again, the *Restatement*:

> When performance is due, however, anything short of full performance is a breach, even if the party who does not fully perform was not at fault and even if the defect in his performance was not substantial. Non-performance of a duty when performance is due is a breach whether the duty is imposed by a promise stated in the agreement or by a term supplied by the court, as in the case of the duty of good faith and fair dealing.

Restatement (Second) of Contracts § 235, cmt. b (1981).

Note the lead in clause to the above quotation—"when performance is due." To quote Robert W. Service, it may be that "a promise made is a debt unpaid," but not all promises are due immediately upon signing the contract. Some are subject to the passage of time. Think of a promise to pay the monthly rent on an apartment; next month's rent is not due today, so non-payment today cannot be a breach.

Recall that this is Contracts, the study of consensual obligations. The parties may very well wish to commit to certain promises only if other things happen. When you buy a car or a house, for example, you will want to ensure that your promise to pay the purchase price is not due until you've got your financing in order. This sequencing of when obligations are due is typically accomplished by conditions, the next subject of our study.

2. CONDITIONS: NOT HAVING TO PERFORM BECAUSE SOMETHING THAT THE CONTRACT EXPRESSLY SAID HAD TO OCCUR DIDN'T

Earlier, when we considered "imperfect acceptances" in Chapter 2, we encountered language of condition in a response to an offer. For example, S offers to sell his house to B for $100,000. B responds that she accepts "on the condition that the house appraises at $100,000." No contract.

That is the effect of language of condition in a response to an offer. Words such as "on condition that," "if," "provided that," or "so long as" in a response to an offer operate as a rejection and counter offer so that there is not yet a contract.

A. EFFECT OF CONDITIONS

These same words of condition have a very different effect when they appear in an enforceable contract, rather than in a response to an offer. For example, suppose that S and B enter into a contract that provides for the sale of S's house to B for $100,000 "on the condition that the house appraises at least $100,000." Such language of condition in a contract does not affect whether there is a contract. It does, however, affect whether there is a legal obligation to perform that contract. If the house does not appraise for at least $100,000 or more, then B does not have to buy the house. Saying the same thing another way, the non-occurrence of an express condition in a contract can provide an excuse to any legal obligation to perform the promises contained in that contract.

The *Restatement (Second) of Contracts* says the same thing in yet a third way:

§ 224. Condition Defined

A condition is an event, not certain to occur, which must occur, unless its nonoccurrence is excused, before performance is due.

Saying the same thing yet one more time: non-occurrence of a condition excuses performance. Indeed, the next section of the *Restatement (Second) of Contracts* says the same thing.

§ 225. Effects of the Non-Occurrence of a Condition

(1) Performance of a duty subject to a condition cannot become due unless the condition occurs or its non-occurrence is excused.

The non-occurrence of a condition is not, however, a breach. Language of condition in a contract, unlike other language in a contract, does not create a new obligation. Instead, contract language of condition modifies or limits obligations created by other language in the contract. In the above example, B cannot sue S because the house did not appraise at $100,000.

The contract language "on the condition that the house appraises for at least $100,000" is not a promise by S that the house will so appraise; it instead modifies B's promise to buy the house.

This distinction can be critical. If a condition is not satisfied, no duty ever arises and thus there is no breach (and no remedy). If a promise or covenant is not satisfied, that is the definition of breach.

Check your understanding of these distinctions in the next two cases.

QUESTIONS BEFORE THE CASE

1. What is the condition in this case? To what duty does that condition relate?
2. In whose favor is the condition? Should that matter?

LUTTINGER V. ROSEN

Supreme Court of Connecticut
164 Conn. 45, 316 A.2d 757 (1972)

LOISELLE, ASSOCIATE JUSTICE.

The plaintiffs contracted to purchase for $85,000 premises in the city of Stamford owned by the defendants and paid a deposit of $8,500. The contract was 'subject to and conditional upon the buyers obtaining first mortgage financing on said premises from a bank or other lending institution in an amount of $45,000 for a term of not less than twenty (20) years and at an interest rate which does not exceed 8 1/2 per cent per annum.' The plaintiffs agreed to use due diligence in attempting to obtain such financing. The parties further agreed that if the plaintiffs were unsuccessful in obtaining financing as provided in the contract, and notified the seller within a specific time, all sums paid on the contract would be refunded and the contract terminated without further obligation of either party.

In applying for a mortgage which would satisfy the contingency clause in the contract, the plaintiffs relied on their attorney who applied at a New Haven lending institution for a $45,000 loan at 8 1/4 percent per annum interest over a period of twenty-five years. The plaintiffs' attorney knew that this lending institution was the only one which at that time would lend as much as $45,000 on a mortgage for a single-family dwelling. A mortgage commitment was obtained for $45,000 with 'interest at the prevailing rate at the time of closing but not less that [*sic*] 8 3/4%.' Since this commitment failed to meet the contract requirement, timely notice was given to the defendants and demand was made for the return of the down payment. The defendants' counsel thereafter offered to make up the difference between the interest rate offered by the bank and the 8 1/2 percent rate provided in the contract for the entire twenty-five years by a funding arrangement, the exact terms of which were not defined. The plaintiffs did not accept this offer and on the defendants' refusal to return the deposit an action was brought. From a judgment rendered in favor of the plaintiffs the defendants have appealed.

The defendants claim that the plaintiffs did not use due diligence in seeking a mortgage within the terms specified in the contract. The unattacked findings by the court establish that the plaintiffs' attorney was fully informed as to the conditions and terms of mortgages being granted by various banks and lending institutions in and out of the area and that the application was made to the only bank which might satisfy the mortgage conditions of the contingency clause at that time. These findings adequately support the court's conclusion that due diligence was used in seeking mortgage financing in accordance with the contract provisions. The defendants assert that notwithstanding the plaintiffs' reliance on their counsel's knowledge of lending practices, applications should have been made to other lending institutions. This claim is not well taken. The law does not require the performance of a futile act.

The remaining assignment of error briefed by the defendants is that the court erred in concluding that the mortgage contingency clause of the contract, a condition precedent, was not met and, therefore, the plaintiffs were entitled to recover their deposit. 'A condition precedent is a fact or event which the parties intend must exist or take place before there is a right to performance. If the condition precedent is not fulfilled the contract is not enforceable. In this case the language of the contract is unambiguous and clearly indicates that the parties intended that the purchase of the defendants' premises be conditioned on the obtaining by the plaintiffs of a mortgage as specified in the contract. From the subordinate facts found the court could reasonably conclude that since the plaintiffs were unable to obtain a $45,000 mortgage at no more than 8 1/2 percent per annum interest 'from a bank or other lending institution' the condition precedent to performance of the contract was not met and the plaintiffs were entitled to the refund of their deposit. Any additional offer by the defendants to fund the difference in interest payments could be rejected by the plaintiffs. There was no error in the court's exclusion of testimony relating to the additional offer since the offer was obviously irrelevant. There is no error.

QUESTIONS AND CONNECTIONS

1. Questions about the facts of this case

   1.1. Who is suing whom for what? What result if the sellers had sued the buyer for breach of contract for not paying the balance of the purchase price?

   1.2. Was the following fact important to the court: "The defendants' counsel thereafter offered to make up the difference between the interest rate offered by the bank and the $8^1/_2$ percent rate provided in the contract for the entire twenty-five years by a funding arrangement"? Should it have been?

   1.3. Do we know whether the buyers bought another house and, if so, whether the rate of interest on financing for that house exceeded 8.5%? Would that information be helpful in deciding this case?

2. Questions about the law

   2.1. B contracts to buy a house from S on the condition that it is appraised at $200,000 or more. The house is only appraised at $190,000. Is B excused from buying the house? Can B sue S for breach of contract?

   2.2. The court states that "If the condition precedent is not fulfilled the contract is not enforceable." Really? Does that mean that it *never* was enforceable?

   2.3. George Kent (GK) contracts with a plumber Jake Young (JY) to replace some pipes in his house. The contract provides in pertinent part, "Payment by GK is conditioned on JY's using Cohoe Pipe and only Cohoe pipe." In doing the work, JY inadvertently uses Reading Pipe, instead of Cohoe Pipe. Even though the manufacturers of Cohoe Pipe concede that Reading Pipe is at least comparable in quality to Cohoe Pipe, GK refuses to pay. JY sues for breach of contract. Is GK's contract obligation to perform excused by the non-occurrence of the condition? Can GK sue JY for breach of contract?

   2.4. Is it important that the contract expressly required the buyers to use due diligence in attempting to obtain financing? What if:

   — there was no such language in the contract, and

   — buyers decided that they did not want the house and made no effort to obtain financing?

   2.5. The court uses the phrase "condition precedent." What does the word "precedent" add? Can there be language of condition in a contract that is a "condition" but not a "condition precedent"? Assume, for example, that Ponoroff contracts with Spartan Rowdy Bar for his students' exclusive use of its patio for $100 an hour "*until the temperature drops below 32 degrees.*" Is the italicized contract language a condition? A condition precedent? Who can sue whom when the East Lansing temperature dips below 32 degrees (which it does, with regularity, in East Lansing)?

3. **You Be the Lawyer!**

If you were the seller's lawyer in *Luttinger*, how could you have changed the conditional language to be more favorable to your client, while still keeping its character as a condition?

4. Connections

Reconsider question 2.3 when we consider *Restatement (Second)* § 229, *infra* at page 685 and again when we consider *Jacob & Youngs v. Kent*, *infra* at page 711.

QUESTIONS BEFORE THE CASE

1. Who was the plaintiff in the original action, and what remedy did it request?
2. What was the express condition in the contract between Tully Construction and Schindler? What is its origin?

SCHINDLER ELEVATOR CORP. V. TULLY CONST. CO., INC.

Supreme Court, Appellate Division, Second Department, New York
139 A.D.3d 930, 30 N.Y.S.3d 707 (2016)

WILLIAM F. MASTRO, J.P., CHERYL E. CHAMBERS, THOMAS A. DICKERSON, and FRANCESCA E. CONNOLLY, JJ.

Opinion

* * *

In 2000, the defendant entered into a contract with the City of New York Department of Sanitation (hereinafter the City) to construct a garage (hereinafter the project). In August 2003, the defendant entered into a subcontract with the plaintiff, pursuant to which the plaintiff was to furnish and install five elevators for the project. Subsequently, in 2010, the plaintiff commenced this action against the defendant to recover damages allegedly incurred as a result of delays in the performance of the work.

After a nonjury trial, the Supreme Court found that the plaintiff was entitled to delay damages in the principal sum of $209,235.36. It rejected the defendant's contention that the plaintiff waived its claim for delay damages by failing to comply with a contractual notice requirement. We reverse. * * *

"Where a construction contract contains 'a condition precedent-type notice provision setting forth the consequences of a failure to strictly comply,' strict compliance will be required" * * * Express conditions precedent "must be literally performed; substantial performance will not suffice," and "[f]ailure to strictly comply with such provisions generally constitutes a waiver of a claim" * * *.

Here, article 11 of the primary contract between the defendant and the City, which is incorporated into the subcontract, contains such a condition-precedent type notice provision. Article 11.1.2 requires a contractor claiming to be sustaining delay damages to submit, "within forty-five (45) Days from the time such damages are first incurred, and every thirty (30) Days thereafter for as long as such damages are incurred, verified statements of the details and amounts of such damages, together with documentary evidence of such damages." Moreover, pursuant to article 11.2, a failure "to strictly comply with the requirements of Article . . . 11.1.2 shall be deemed a conclusive waiver by the Contractor of any and all claims for damages for delay arising from such condition."

The letters and emails relied upon by the Supreme Court and the plaintiff did not strictly comply with the contractual notice requirement, since they did not contain verified statements of the amount of delay damages allegedly sustained by the plaintiff and were unsupported by documentary evidence. * * * Contrary to the plaintiff's contention, the defendant's actual knowledge of the delay and the claims did not relieve the plaintiff of its obligation to serve a proper notice of claim, and the defendant's alleged breach of the subcontract did not excuse the plaintiff from complying with the notice requirements under the circumstances of this case * * *

Accordingly, the Supreme Court should have found that the plaintiff failed to strictly comply with the notice requirement, and dismissed the complaint on that ground.

The plaintiff's remaining contentions have been rendered academic in light of our determination.

QUESTIONS

1. Questions about the facts of this case

   1.1. Did the trial court find that Schindler had been damaged by delay?

1.2. Did the appeals court disagree with the trial court that Schindler had been damaged by delay?

1.3. Did Schindler tell Tully about the delay and inform them of the likely damage?

2. Questions about the law

2.1. What is the basis for the court's reversal of the trial court if the appeals court does not disagree with the trial court's finding of damage?

2.2. Would the outcome be any different if the contract between the parties did not contain article 11.2?

2.3. By the way, what is the difference between an article of the contract, and a section of the contract, and a provision of the contract?

2.4. Is there a difference between the condition in this case and the condition in *Luttinger*, above at page 635? What is it?

3. **You Be the Lawyer!**

You represent Schindler after it has sent the first couple of emails to Tully about the delay, and the damage it was causing. You check the contract, and find, as the court above did, that the emails did not comply with the conditions set forth in the contract. Is there anything you can do at this point?

B. DISTINGUISHING CONDITIONS FROM COVENANTS

As *Luttinger* and *Schindler* illustrate, conditions matter. If an obligation is subject to a condition, and the condition does not occur, the duty connected to that duty does not arise (and thus its nonperformance is not a breach). In the cases above, Rosen didn't have to buy the house; Tully didn't have to pay damages. Note in particular that in neither case did the court say there was no contract—just no particular duty under an admitted contract.

This all sounds fairly cut and dried. But of course, this is law school. Nothing (or damn little) is cut and dried. Consider the following three hypothetical contract provisions:

- Epstein will pay Ponoroff $250 to photograph Epstein's 2017 Mercedes-Maybach S600. Ponoroff will hire Markell to clean it.
- Epstein will pay Ponoroff $250 to photograph Epstein's 2017 Mercedes-Maybach S600, and Ponoroff will hire Markell to clean it first.

- Epstein will pay Ponoroff $250 to photograph Epstein's 2017 Mercedes-Maybach S600, but only if Ponoroff hires Markell to clean it first.

In which of these provisions is Epstein obligated to pay Ponoroff $250 even if Ponoroff does not hire Markell to clean the car before Ponoroff goes shutter happy? Put another way, which of these provisions contains a *covenant* that Ponoroff must hire Markell first, and which of these provisions contains a *condition* that Ponoroff must hire Markell first? And to make it harder, assume that normal people could not tell the difference if the car was cleaned first, and that a professional could tell the difference only 50% of the time.

See if the next case helps you draw these distinctions.

QUESTIONS BEFORE THE CASE

1. What is the consequence in this case of interpreting the disputed language as a covenant, and not a condition?
2. What arguments and interpretive techniques does the court employ to construe the parties' language?

MIND & MOTION UTAH INVESTMENTS LLC v. CELTIC BANK CORP.

Supreme Court of Utah
367 P.3d 994 (2016)

CHIEF JUSTICE DURRANT, opinion of the Court:

Introduction

* * *

In this case, Mind & Motion entered into a real estate purchase contract (REPC) with Celtic Bank to buy a large piece of property the bank had acquired from a developer through foreclosure. Although the county had approved plans to construct condominiums on the land, the developer had not recorded the plats for the first phase of development. Accordingly, the REPC required Celtic Bank to record the plats by a certain date, and it allowed Mind & Motion sole discretion to extend the recording deadline as necessary to allow Celtic Bank enough time to record. It further provided that any extension of the recording deadline automatically extended the deadline to complete the transaction.

After extending the recording deadline once, Mind & Motion declined to extend it a second time and sued Celtic Bank for breach of contract. The district court granted summary judgment in Mind & Motion's favor, concluding that the recording provision was unambiguously a covenant, not a condition. It then awarded Mind & Motion $100,000 in liquidated damages and more than $200,000 in attorney fees, as well as the return of Mind & Motion's $100,000 earnest money deposit. On appeal, Celtic Bank argues that summary judgment was improper because the recording provision is unambiguously a condition. * * *

Background

* * *

Celtic Bank acquired fourteen acres of real estate in Huntsville, Utah, through a foreclosure sale. The prior owner had partially completed four condominium units and received approval to construct more than 160 additional units. But the prior owner had not recorded the plat for the next phase of development, and neither had Celtic Bank after assuming ownership of the property.

Mind & Motion agreed to purchase the property from Celtic Bank in a real estate purchase contract executed May 25, 2010. The REPC described the property as including "[a]pproximately 14 acres with recorded PRUD for 168 units" and stated that Celtic bank was selling the property "AS RECORDED." The agreement required Mind & Motion to deposit $100,000 in earnest money with an escrow agent, which was fully refundable if the property did not pass a buyer's inspection. Mind & Motion could complete its inspections anytime within fifteen days after receiving notice that the property was substantially complete and that Celtic Bank had recorded the plat.

The REPC also provided that Celtic Bank "shall record Phase 1" and "agrees to complete recording of Phase 1" of the development by June 15, 2010. It further provided that Celtic Bank "will accomplish any necessary construction or repairs required to complete recording of Phase 1." But it granted Mind & Motion "the sole discretion" to extend the deadline "as necessary to allow" Celtic Bank to record. If Mind & Motion extended the deadline, "the Evaluations and Inspection Deadline and the Settlement deadline" would be "automatically extended by the same amount of time."

The recording process requires an applicant to obtain approval from a number of different entities. First, the Weber County Planning Commission requires "an applicant to complete a required landscaping or infrastructure improvement prior to any plat recordation or development activity." After the planning commission approves a final plat, the commission submits it to the county surveyor, county health department, and county engineer for signatures. After the county engineer approves the plat, the engineer submits it to the county attorney and the board of county commissioners for their approval. An applicant who jumps through each hoop is entitled to record—county officials do not have discretion to decline an application that complies with the applicable zoning ordinances.

The REPC also contained a "time is of the essence clause," which provided that "[u]nless otherwise explicitly stated in this Contract," performance must be completed "by 5:00 PM Mountain Time" on the applicable deadline. The clause also stated that "[p]erformance dates and times referenced herein shall not be binding upon title companies, lenders, appraisers, and others not parties to this Contract, except as otherwise agreed to in writing by such non-party."

In the event Mind & Motion defaulted, the REPC allowed Celtic Bank to keep the earnest money as liquidated damages. If Celtic Bank defaulted, Mind & Motion would receive back its earnest money and could either sue to specifically enforce the contract or obtain $100,000 in liquidated damages.

The day the parties signed the REPC, the planning commission recommended final approval of recording the phase 1 plat. But several entities still needed to approve various aspects of Celtic Bank's application. None of them approved the plat by the June 15 recording deadline, and Mind & Motion accordingly extended it to July 26.

That date came and went, however, without the application being approved, and rather than extend the deadline a second time, Mind & Motion claimed Celtic Bank had breached the contract and demanded the return of its earnest money as well as the payment of liquidated damages. Celtic Bank refused to pay, so Mind & Motion filed a breach of contract action. The district court granted Mind & Motion partial summary judgment on its breach of contract claim, concluding that the recording provision was unambiguously a covenant, not a condition. It reasoned that because the REPC phrased Celtic Bank's recording obligation in mandatory terms—the bank "shall record Phase 1"—there was no plausible way to read the provision as anything other than a covenant. Celtic Bank appeals. * * *

Analysis

We conclude that the district court correctly granted summary judgment in Mind & Motion's favor. Although Celtic Bank's ability to meet the recording deadline hinged in large part on the approval of county officials, the parties couched the recording obligation in mandatory language while employing explicitly conditional language elsewhere in the REPC to describe other performance obligations. This shows that Celtic Bank and Mind & Motion, both sophisticated parties, knew how to draft a condition when they so desired. Accordingly, it is not plausible to read Celtic Bank's duty to record the phase 1 plat as anything other than a covenant. * * *

A. Covenants and Conditions

The distinction between covenants and conditions is an important one because each imposes qualitatively different kinds of obligations. A covenant is a "promise[ ] between the parties to the contract about their mutual obligations." In essence, covenants are the core bargained-for exchange of an agreement. They create specific legal duties, the violation of which gives rise to remedies for breach of contract.

Conditions are different. "A condition is 'an event, not certain to occur, which must occur . . . before performance under a contract becomes due.' " We have noted three principal differences between conditions and covenants. First, the parties to the contract have no duty to perform until the condition is fulfilled, so the failure of a condition relieves the parties of all of their contractual duties. Second, the parties have no remedy for breach of contract if a condition is not fulfilled, because at that point there is simply no contract to breach.

Third, conditions "typically fall outside the control of the parties to the contract, often requiring some environmental trigger (such as 'weather permitting') or action by a third party (such as 'upon the lender's approval') for the contract to begin." Stated differently, even if one of the parties has some influence over the fulfillment of a condition, "its incidence usually is a matter of fate or of the decision of one or more third parties." Covenants, by contrast, "are almost always within the control of the contracting parties."

To determine whether a contractual obligation is a covenant or a condition, we examine the language of the provision in question and the nature of the agreement itself. In *McArthur v. State Farm Mutual Automobile Insurance Co.,* [2012 UT 22, 274 P.3d 981,] for example, we held that an exhaustion clause in an insurance policy was a condition, not a covenant, for two reasons: (1) its fulfillment was outside the control of the contracting parties, and (2) the parties employed conditional language to characterize the exhaustion requirement in the agreement. The clause provided in part that the insured would have "NO COVERAGE UNTIL" coverage limits on a separate bodily injury insurance policy had been "USED UP." We noted that the "word 'until' exemplifies a word[ ] of condition" and that satisfying the exhaustion condition was "dependent on the actions of a non-contracting third party—the liability insurer." Accordingly, we concluded that exhaustion of the other policy's limits was "the very event, not certain to occur, which must occur . . . before performance under a contract becomes due."

Our analysis in *McArthur* indicates that express terms like "unless," "on condition that," "provided that," and "if," often create conditions. This implies that more mandatory terms, such as "shall," "must," or "agree," will often create covenants. That is not to say that such terms are talismans—

regardless of the precise terms used in the contract, the parties' degree of control over the fulfillment of an obligation remains "a significant indication" of whether the parties intended a performance obligation to be a condition or a covenant. But when parties employ mandatory terms to characterize an obligation whose fulfillment hinges on the action of a third party, this may indicate an express assumption by one party of the risk that the condition will remain unfulfilled.

B. The Recording Obligation Is Unambiguously a Covenant

Having set forth the key distinctions between covenants and conditions, we now discuss whether the district court correctly interpreted the REPC's recording provision as a covenant. When interpreting a contract, our task is to ascertain the parties' intent. And the best indication of the parties' intent is the ordinary meaning of the contract's terms. Accordingly, "[i]f the language within the four corners of the contract is unambiguous, the parties' intentions are determined from the plain meaning of the contractual language, and the contract may be interpreted as a matter of law." A contract is facially ambiguous if its terms are "capable of more than one reasonable interpretation because of uncertain meanings of terms, missing terms, or other facial deficiencies." But terms are not ambiguous "simply because one party seeks to endow them with a different interpretation according to his or her own interests." Rather, the proffered alternative interpretations "must be plausible and reasonable in light of the language used." If the parties' intentions cannot be determined from the face of the contract, "extrinsic evidence must be looked to in order to determine the intentions of the parties."

Applying these principles, we conclude that the REPC is facially unambiguous. While Mind & Motion's preferred reading of the agreement is strongly supported by the REPC's plain terms, Celtic Bank's interpretation finds no such support in the language of the contract. Below, we examine each party's proffered interpretation of the REPC in turn.

1. Mind & Motion's Reading of the REPC Is Strongly Supported by the Language of the Agreement

Mind & Motion urges us to affirm the district court's conclusion that the recording provision is unambiguously a covenant, citing the mandatory language in the agreement. For several reasons, we agree that this reading of the REPC receives strong support from the language of the contract.

First, the recording provision states that Celtic Bank "shall record [the] Phase 1" plat "no later than 90 calendar days from accepted offer." The next paragraph also states that Celtic Bank "agrees to record" the plat. As we have discussed, when interpreting a contract, we generally give each term its plain and ordinary meaning. And here, Black's Law Dictionary defines "shall" as "a duty to," "is required to," or "mandatory." We have also held that the legislature's use of the word "shall" in statutes creates mandatory obligations. And while it is true, as Celtic Bank argues, that "shall" can be directory or express a future expectation, it is "the mandatory sense that drafters typically intend and that courts typically uphold." The word "agree" similarly means to "exchange promises" or "to unite in an engagement to do or not do something." * * *

These mandatory terms contrast sharply with the explicitly conditional language in *McArthur* that we held created a condition. There, as we have discussed, the contract provided that no insurance coverage would be provided "until" other coverage had been exhausted. And we noted that the "word 'until' exemplifies a word[ ] of condition. The recording provision, of course, contains no such language.

Second, not only is the recording obligation phrased in mandatory terms, but the parties used explicitly conditional language in other provisions of the REPC. For instance, paragraph eight provides, "Buyer's obligation to purchase under this Contract *is conditioned* upon Buyer's approval of the content of each of the Seller Disclosures referenced in Section 7 [and] *is conditioned* upon Buyer's approval of the following tests and evaluations." (Emphasis added). This shows that Mind & Motion and Celtic Bank, both sophisticated parties, understood how to consciously identify a condition precedent when they so desired.

Finally, the recording provision also must be satisfied by a specific date. The REPC contains a "time is of the essence clause," stating that "performance under each Section of this Contract which references a date shall absolutely be required by 5:00 PM Mountain Time on the stated date." While it is true that deadlines can be coupled with conditions, the REPC explicitly makes all deadlines "absolute . . . require[ments]."

Standing alone, language of this kind could conceivably be found to be a conditional obligation, depending on a particular contract's operation and surrounding terms. But together, these features of the REPC—mandatory language, a hard deadline for performance, and other provisions that employ conditional language—strongly suggest that the parties intended the recording provision to operate as covenant, not a condition.

We therefore conclude that Mind & Motion's reading of the contract is strongly supported by the language of the agreement. Consequently, in order for the contract to be facially ambiguous, Celtic Bank's alternative reading must also be reasonably supported by the language of the agreement. For a variety of reasons, however, we conclude that it is not.

2. Celtic Bank's Reading of the REPC Receives No Support from the Agreement's Plain Terms

In arguing that the recording provision is a condition, Celtic Bank relies heavily on the fact that the county ultimately controlled the timing of recordation. It argues that "parties may manifest their intent to create a condition 'by clear implication' " and cites *McArthur* for the proposition that conditions generally fall outside the control of the contracting parties, "often requiring some environmental trigger . . . or action by a third party . . . for the contract to begin." And here, Celtic Bank maintains, there is no dispute that it needed approval from the planning commission, engineers, and other county officials before the phase 1 plat could be recorded. So even though Celtic Bank "controlled whether it completed the various . . . lists of tasks that were prerequisite to the county's approval and recordation process," no ordinance required the county to "approve the Phase 1 plat" by the recording deadline. As a result, Celtic Bank argues, "whether the county approved the Phase 1 plat before the deadline was beyond [its] control." Celtic Bank also argues that none of Mind & Motion's performance obligations became due until the phase 1 plat was recorded, which is consistent with one of the touchstones of conditions precedent we outlined in *McArthur*.

We have no quarrel with Celtic Bank's description of the recording process. It seems clear that even if Celtic Bank complied with the county's every demand, the county officials ultimately controlled the *timing* of the recordation—not Celtic Bank. Celtic Bank is also correct that the deadline for performing many of its obligations under the REPC was automatically extended whenever Mind & Motion extended the recording deadline. But we do not agree that these aspects of the agreement are sufficient to override the explicit mandatory language in the REPC.

It is a basic principle of contract law that parties are generally "free to contract according to their desires in whatever terms they can agree upon." This includes assuming risks that third parties or external environmental circumstances will fail to conform to the parties' expectations. And absent language in the contract to the contrary, "[a] party who contracts knowing that governmental permission or license will be required ordinarily assumes the obligation of assuring that permission will be granted."

* * *

Conclusion

We conclude that Celtic Bank's recording obligation outlined in the REPC is unambiguously a covenant. Even though Celtic Bank could not ultimately control when the county issued its final approval to record the phase 1 development, the recording obligation is framed in mandatory language, and the REPC employs explicitly conditional language elsewhere in the agreement. * * * As a final matter, Mind & Motion has requested it be awarded attorney fees and costs incurred on appeal, and the parties have stipulated to such an award. We accordingly remand for the calculation of reasonable fees and costs.

QUESTIONS AND NOTES

1. Questions about the facts of this case

 1.1. What do you think Mind & Motion's business is? Celtic Bank's? Do these lines of business give you pause as to the nature of the provision regarding recording?

 1.2. What do you think the cost of compliance with the term was as compared to the purchase price?

 1.3. Who do you think drafted the purchase agreement? Should that matter?

2. Questions about the law

 2.1. The court indicates that no particular word is a "talisman" when trying to distinguish a covenant from a condition. Is the result in this case consistent with that statement?

 2.2. Celtic Bank argued "that 'shall' can be directory or express a future expectation." Shall we explore what this means? Your professor shall wait expectantly for your answer.

3. Notes

 3.1. The use of "shall" to indicate a duty (or to signify a covenant) has come under much criticism in drafting circles. As Bryan Garner (the present editor of *Black's Law Dictionary,* which you all have used—and you have used it, right?) has said:

> In the ninth edition of *Black's Law Dictionary*, I list five meanings for *shall*:
>
>> **shall**, vb. (bef. 12c)
>>
>> 1. Has a duty to; more broadly, is required to "the requester *shall* send notice" "notice *shall* be sent". This is the mandatory sense that drafters typically intend and that courts typically uphold.
>>
>> 2. Should (as often interpreted by courts) "all claimants *shall* request mediation".
>>
>> 3. May "no person *shall* enter the building without first signing the roster". When a negative word such as *not* or *no* precedes *shall* (as in the example in angled bracket), the word *shall* often means *may*. What is being negated is permission, not a requirement.
>>
>> 4. Will (as a future tense verb) "the corporation *shall* then have a period of 30 days to object".
>>
>> 5. Is entitled to "the secretary *shall* be reimbursed for all expenses".

Only sense 1 is acceptable under strict standards of drafting.

In short, *shall* is a chameleon-hued word.

For teachers of legal drafting, there are two main pedagogical approaches today for teaching lawyers and aspiring lawyers about this word: (1) restrict *shall* to meaning either "has a duty to" or "is required to" (meaning that 40 to 80 percent of the *shalls* in existing forms will be replaced); or (2) eliminate *shall* altogether on grounds that lawyers as a group cannot realistically master the semantic subtleties of the word (meaning that 100 percent of *shalls* get dropped).

* * *

What about contracts? Isn't *must* a bit bossy-sounding in the context of a private agreement? Yes, it is—unless it's a take-it-or-leave-it consumer contract. If it's an ordinary bilateral agreement, *will* is perfectly adequate. "The parties agree as follows," the lead-in says, and then: "Jones will do this. Smith will do that."

The advantage of *will* is that nobody—nobody—misuses this word in any of the myriad ways in which lawyers misuse *shall*. Nobody writes *will* instead of *may* or *should* or *is entitled to*. In American English, *will* is the ordinary verb of promise.

Reflect on how we, as a profession, landed in this semantic snarl of *shalls* in our documents. Here's how I reconstruct it. If you grew up in this country, you grew up without *shall* as part of your working vocabulary. You encountered *shall* in some of your reading, but you never used it. You did well in school and ultimately enrolled in law school, where you were bombarded by *shalls* in statutes and contracts. You intuited that *shall* is "the drafting verb" that makes legal instruments precise.

In fact, it does the opposite. In most legal instruments, *shall* violates the presumption of consistency: Words are presumed to have a consistent meaning in clause after clause, page after page. Which is why *shall* is among the most heavily litigated words in the English language (with hopelessly inconsistent court holdings).

My own practice is to delete *shall* in all legal instruments and to replace it with a clearer word more characteristic of American English: *must, will, is, may* or the phrase *is entitled to*. * * *

Bryan A. Garner, *Shall We Abandon Shall?*, Am. Bar. Ass'n J. (Aug. 1, 2012), *reprinted at* http://www.abajournal.com/magazine/article/shall_we_abandon_shall/.

3.2. In construction cases, much ink has been spilled over so-called "pay when paid," and "pay if paid" clauses. The issue is simple. If an owner of land wants to build something on it, she usually hires a general contractor to take care of the construction. That general contractor, in turn, enters into separate contracts with specialty contractors for things such as the plumbing, the electrical wiring, the heating, venting and air conditioning and the like.

The general then puts a provision in the contract with each subcontractor that says the subcontractor will get paid when the owner pays the general contractor. Something like: "General will pay subcontractor when Owner pays General." Does this provision contain a condition—meaning the subcontractor will *not* get paid if the owner doesn't pay the general contractor? Or does it contain a covenant—meaning the subcontractor gets paid regardless of whether the owner pays the general contractor? In this latter case, the term is construed as a somewhat awkward timing mechanism, meaning the general contractor's obligation to pay the subcontractor arises when the owner would normally be obligated to pay the general contractor.

If construed as a condition, risks are greatly shifted. The subcontractor, who usually only deals with the general contractor and is not even in privity with the owner, would risk forfeiture of its pay for work done for the general contractor, even if there were no question that the subcontractor did not breach. To illustrate the rule disfavoring forfeiture, the *Restatement* offers the following example:

> [U]nder a provision that a duty is to be performed "when" an event occurs, it may be doubtful whether it is to be performed only if that event occurs, in which case the event is a condition, or at such time as it would ordinarily occur, in which case the event is referred to merely to measure the passage of time. In the latter case, if the event does not occur some alternative means will be found to measure the passage of time, and the non-occurrence of the event will not prevent the obligor's duty from becoming one of performance. If the event is a condition, however, the obligee takes the risk that its non-occurrence will discharge the obligor's duty.

Restatement (Second) Contracts, § 227, cmt b.

This comment was analyzed in *Evans, Mechwart, Hambleton & Tilton, Inc. v. Triad Architects, Ltd.*, 196 Ohio App. 3d 784, 794, 965 N.E.2d 1007, 1014–15 (Ct. App. 2011). There, the court stated:

> This example mirrors the situation presented by a typical pay-when-paid provision. A pay-when-paid provision is susceptible to two interpretations; namely, (1) as setting a condition precedent to payment or (2) as fixing the point in time when payment would ordinarily occur. In the face of this ambiguity, courts avoid forfeiture by construing the pay-when-paid provision as a promise to pay and making payment due within a reasonable time. *Brown & Kerr, Inc. v. St. Paul Fire & Marine Ins. Co.* (N.D.Ill.1996), 940 F.Supp. 1245, 1250; *Fed. Ins. Co.* at 739–740 ("[T]he preferred interpretation for the pay-when-paid clause * * * is one that minimizes the risk of forfeiture to [the subcontractor]"). The owner's nonpayment, therefore, does not excuse the contractor from performing as promised under its contract with the subcontractor. In contrast to a pay-when-paid provision, a pay-if-paid provision is, by definition, a clear and unambiguous condition precedent to payment. By signing a contract that contains a pay-if-paid provision, the subcontractor takes the risk that the owner's nonpayment will discharge the contractor's duty to pay the subcontractor.

4. **You Be the Lawyer!**

You are an in-house lawyer for Celtic Bank. The general counsel hands you a copy of the above opinion, and asks you to revise their forms regarding the sale or transfer of property taken at foreclosure. What kind of checklist would you make for yourself in going through the forms? And what type of reaction would you expect from third parties who will be buying the properties to the changes?

---

3. EXCUSE: LEGITIMATE WAYS TO AVOID PERFORMANCE

Thus far, we have seen that any non-performance, or any variance from the performance required, is a breach. We've tempered this a bit by examining how parties use conditions to regulate when a contractual duty arises. But sometimes, things happen after formation that make it unfair or imprudent to require performance. Contract law refers to these actions as "excuses"; that is, even though a party to a contract does not render the performance required, external factors "excuse" that performance, and thus there is no breach, and no remedy or damages.

We look at four categories of excuse in this section.

First is the effect that the parties' post-formation conduct has on their contractual duties. If the parties amend or modify their contractual duties, then the original obligations no longer bind. They have been superseded them by a later agreement. Similarly, if a party chooses to not enforce an obligation due to it, or to give the other party a "pass," basic fairness says that the party giving the pass can't complain later about the non-performance they themselves approved or tolerated. We study this in Subsection A under the names of modification, waiver, and estoppel.

Second is the effect of external factors on the subject of the contract. If there is a contract for the sale of a car once owned by Elvis, and the car is destroyed by an unanticipated meteor shower, the seller will have an excuse to not deliver the car. There may be lesser impediments, such as subsequent passage of legislation or imposition of regulations that increase the cost of performance, but do not prohibit it. We study this in Subsection B under the names of impossibility, impracticability, and frustration of purpose.

Subsection B also looks at other types of external factors, such as when one party tries to prevent or impede the other party's performance (or conditions to their own performance) and those actions are not breaches of express terms of the contract. We'll call this prevention. We will also examine some public policy limitations on contractual strict liability linked to post-formation effects, such as when the non-occurrence of a condition works an unexpected forfeiture on one party, and what courts do when the parties do not specify the order of their performances.

Third, we'll look at the effect of a breach by one side on the obligations of the other. We'll make distinctions here between material breach of contract and substantial performance of duties. We'll still call any non-performance or defective performance a breach, but we will assign different consequences to it depending on whether we categorize the breach as material or partial. We study this in Subsection C under the names of material breach and, for cases governed by the U.C.C., the perfect tender rule.

Finally, we'll look at the effect of actions by one party taken before performance is due that indicate a rejection of contractual duties—if Epstein says "Hell, no, I'm not going to write my part of this book" before his sections are due, what does that statement do to Markell's and Ponoroff's obligations to perform when their obligations are due? (put aside the fact that such a statement would instill a belief in both of them that the book will be delayed but better.) We study this in Subsection D under the name of anticipatory repudiation.

A. EXCUSE: POST-FORMATION MODIFICATION, WAIVER, AND ESTOPPEL

1. Modification

Sometimes parties change their agreement after it is formed. We saw that above in *Alaska Packers* on page 297, and in *Angel v. Murray* on page 302. Here, we explore that question in a little more depth, beyond the requirements of consideration or good faith.

First, as we saw above, the parol evidence rule and the applicable statute of frauds often bear on the analysis. Is the alleged agreement really post-formation (and thus an exception to the parol evidence rule exists)? If not in writing, does the statute of frauds apply? Do both sides have to agree that they are modifying their agreement? Or will conduct alone suffice?

Start first with the following case.

QUESTIONS BEFORE THE CASE

1. What provisions of the original contract does Maxi-Holding wish to have enforced without reference to subsequent conduct?
2. Does the court actually hold that conduct of the parties after formation modified the original contract (hint: this is as much a procedural question as anything else)?

SCHINKEL V. MAXI-HOLDING, INC.

Appeals Court of Massachusetts, Essex
30 Mass. App. Ct. 41, 565 N.E.2d 1219 (1991)

Before ARMSTRONG, BROWN and PERRETTA, JJ.

ARMSTRONG, JUSTICE.

Maxi-Holding, Inc. (Maxi), the amended complaint alleges, is a holding company organized in Massachusetts to hold shares of Eastern Lumber, Inc., and other corporations that are engaged in lumber and hardware businesses. The capital stock of Maxi is owned by Rake Oy, a Finnish corporation, which is controlled by the defendant Cederberg, who lives in Finland. Cederberg either is or acts as the chief executive officer of Maxi. The plaintiff, a Massachusetts resident, had done work as a consultant for Rake Oy and Maxi from the 1970's and in 1985 was asked by Cederberg to devote the majority of his time as a consultant to managing the affairs of

Maxi and its subsidiaries. The parties entered into a contract, or, more technically, a pair of contracts, the first allowing the plaintiff to purchase shares of Maxi (the signatories were Maxi, Rake Oy, and the plaintiff), the other a management services contract between Maxi and the plaintiff (Cederberg signing for Maxi). The plaintiff rendered management services in 1986 but did not purchase shares.

In 1987 the parties entered into a similar pair of contracts. Cederberg signed for Maxi and, presumably, Rake Oy (Cederberg signed once, but both corporate names were typed in) in Helsinki on January 28, 1987. The plaintiff signed in Massachusetts on March 3, 1987. The management services contract was to run for two years with automatic renewals. The share purchase contract contained undertakings by Maxi and Rake Oy to issue class B, preferred, nonvoting shares of Maxi, representing ten percent of the Maxi capital stock, to be sold to the plaintiff for $70,000, half payable when the plaintiff signed, the other half payable forty-five days later. Another clause gave the plaintiff the right to purchase an additional ten percent in the same form (i.e., class B, non-voting, preferred) from six months into the contract until it expired. The price was to be based on appraisal by counsel agreeable to both parties.

The amended complaint alleges that before the agreements were signed the parties discussed and agreed that, because the plaintiff's compensation under the 1986 management services contract would not be known until later in 1987, and because the plaintiff would almost certainly be owed money by Maxi, he could defer payment for the initial issuance of class B shares until the compensation owed for 1986 should be known and then pay the difference between $70,000 and the compensation owed. In accord with this understanding, the plaintiff received, before signing, a communication from one Saraheimo, Rake Oy's director of business development and corporate lawyer, stating that it was not necessary that the plaintiff make the fifty percent up-front payment for the shares "right away," as the payment term was "flexible."

The compensation owed for 1986 became known in July, 1987, the plaintiff alleges, first in rough estimate ($50,000), later precisely ($55,000). When the estimate was known, the plaintiff tendered to Maxi a check for an additional $20,000, which Maxi accepted. When the precise compensation was known, Maxi refunded to the plaintiff $5,000. Despite receiving payment, the defendants have declined to issue the class B shares, have told the plaintiff they intend not to do so, and are planning to sell all the assets of Maxi to one Berg, a Finnish national, in the near future. The result of the proposed sale is that the shares of Maxi have taken on an enhanced value.

Based on these allegations, the plaintiff * * * sought a declaration of the rights of the parties under the 1987 share-purchase contract and an order for specific performance, i.e., for the issuance of the shares to the plaintiff. * * * Maxi filed a motion to dismiss * * * for failure to state a claim on which relief could be granted. Cederberg filed a similar motion. * * * The judge allowed Maxi's motion to dismiss * * * with a cryptic statement of reasons.

* * *

2. *Parol evidence rule.* The judge dismissed [the] count * * * sounding in breach of contract, in reliance on the parol evidence rule. The defendants had argued that Maxi and Rake Oy could have no duty to issue the class B, non-voting shares unless the plaintiff had complied with his obligations under the written contract: namely, to pay Maxi $35,000 on signing the contract and $35,000 forty-five days thereafter. The plaintiff cannot rely (the defendants argue) on an oral agreement allegedly reached before the execution of the written agreement without violating the parol evidence rule.

On the state of the record before the trial court, a conclusion to that effect was premature. In some circumstances an oral agreement modifying the terms of a later-signed written agreement goes directly to the question whether the written document is an integrated statement of the entire agreement of the parties. See *McEvoy Travel Bureau, Inc. v. Norton Co.,* 408 Mass. 704, 712 & n. 7, 563 N.E.2d 188 (1990).[5] A finding that the writing is not an integrated statement of the parties' agreement can open the way for proof of other elements of the agreement. *Antonellis v. Northgate Constr. Corp.,* 362 Mass. 847, 849–851, 291 N.E.2d 626 (1973). This is so despite the fact that courts have been reluctant, as the defendants argue, to allow proof of terms that contradict those of the written agreement, see, e.g., *Carlo Bianchi & Co. v. Builders' Equip. & Supplies Co.,* 347 Mass. 636, 643–644, 199 N.E.2d 519 (1964); *Alexander v. Snell,* 12 Mass.App.Ct. 323, 324–325, 424 N.E.2d 262 (1981), at least in the absence of fraud . . . .

It is open to parties to modify a written agreement by a later agreement not in writing. See *Zlotnick v. McNamara,* 301 Mass. 224, 225–226, 16 N.E.2d 632 (1938). The later agreement may be proved through the conduct of the parties. See *Flynn v. Wallace,* 359 Mass. 711, 715, 270 N.E.2d 919 (1971); *Church of God in Christ, Inc. v. Congregation Kehillath Jacob,* 370 Mass. 828, 832–834, 353 N.E.2d 669 (1976); *First Pa. Mort. Trust v. Dorchester Sav. Bank,* 395 Mass. 614, 625, 481 N.E.2d 1132 (1985).

---

[5] The plaintiff alleges in the amended complaint that the cover note that accompanied the contract (which had been signed by Cederberg in Helsinki and then sent to the plaintiff for signing) assured the plaintiff that he could disregard the payment provision as written in the share-purchase contract. *Compare* McEvoy Travel Bureau, Inc. v. Norton Co., 408 Mass. at 711 & n. 5, 563 N.E.2d 188. A copy of the cover note, signed by Saraheimo, was attached to the amended complaint. There is authority for treating such a cover letter amendment, accepted by the other party, as effecting a modification of the written contract. See 3 Corbin, Contracts § 577, at 391 (1960).

On parallel reasoning, where the parties' conduct after signing the written agreement conforms with a previous oral modification, rather than with the terms of the written agreement, it may reasonably be inferred that the parties have agreed after the signing to be bound by the oral modification of the written contract, ratifying it, in effect, by their conduct. Here the plaintiff alleges that Maxi accepted his payment of $20,000 for the shares of stock after his 1986 compensation was calculated and, indeed, later refunded $5,000 to him after it was determined that his compensation had been undercalculated by that amount. In the face of those allegations, it cannot be said as matter of law that the orally-agreed-to arrangement is unenforceable.

* * *

The judgments are reversed. * * * The plaintiff is to have costs of appeal. The case is remanded for further proceedings consistent herewith.

So ordered.

QUESTIONS AND NOTES

1. Questions about the facts of this case

   1.1. What was being bought and sold? What was the purchase price? What were the terms?

   1.2. Was Schinkel able to pay the purchase price with something other than his own money? If so, what?

   1.3. What pre-formation acts does Schinkel point to that he claims altered the original terms? What post-formation acts does he point to?

2. Questions about the law

   2.1. Under the court's reasoning, is it possible to amend a contract without actually signing a piece of paper (assuming the original contract was memorialized by paper) which refers to the original contract? If so, how?

   2.2. State the terms of the amended contract as alleged by Schinkel? What standard does the court use to evaluate Schinkel's contention that there was a modification to the contract?

   2.3. Does the evidence Schinkel adduces, if true, convince you that he should prevail at trial? Why or why not?

   2.4. [*Sneaky review question*] What exceptions to the parol evidence rule does the court refer to in its analysis?

3. Notes

3.1. *No Oral Modification—Common Law Version.* What if the parties had agreed to a provision that said "No amendments or modifications to this agreement shall be effective unless contained in a writing authorized and signed by both parties." Does that eliminate the risk of oral amendments?

Probably not. You are far enough along in law school now to see the recursive logic at play in the answer. To give effect to the oral modification, the party seeking to introduce an oral revision will simply say that the "no oral amendment" provision was itself amended by a subsequent oral undertaking. Once the "no oral amendment" provision is modified, then any provision can by modified by an oral understanding.

This argument has often won. Judge Benjamin Cardozo, writing for the Court of Appeals of New York, resoundingly rejected a party's attempt to rely on a non-oral modification clause:

> Those who make a contract may unmake it. The clause which forbids a change may be changed like any other. The prohibition of oral waiver may itself be waived. * * * What is excluded by one act is restored by another. * * * Whenever two men contract, no limitation self-imposed can destroy their power to contract again.

Beatty v. Guggenheim Exploration Co., 225 N.Y. 380, 387–88, 122 N.E. 378, 381 (1919).

Judge Oliver Wendell Holmes, in his opinion in *Bartlett v. Stanchfield,* 148 Mass. 394, 395, 19 N.E. 549, 550 (1889), took the same view:

> Attempts of parties to tie up by contract their freedom of dealing with each other are futile. The contract is a fact to be taken into account in interpreting the subsequent conduct of the plaintiff and the defendant, no doubt. But it cannot be assumed, as a matter of law, that the contract governed all that was done until it was renounced in so many words, because the parties had a right to renounce it in any way and by any mode of expression they saw fit. They could substitute a new oral contract by conduct and intimation, as well as by express words.

3.2. *No Oral Modification—U.C.C. Version.* The U.C.C. specifically authorizes no oral modification clause. Section 2–209(2) states that "A signed agreement which excludes modification or rescission except by a signed writing cannot be otherwise modified or rescinded . . . ."

Judge Richard Posner has stated that this section of "[t]he Uniform Commercial Code abrogated the common law rule [regarding oral modifications of no oral modification clauses] for contracts governed by the Code. *Id.*; UCC § 2–209(2)." *Call v. Ameritech Mgmt. Pension Plan*, 475 F.3d 816, 820 (7th Cir. 2007).

But be careful. White & Summers state that "[p]arties should be aware, however, that courts may require 'magic words,' such as 'modification' to be in the clause to be enforceable." 1 James J. White, Robert S. Summers & Robert A. Hillman, *Uniform Commercial Code* 146 n.5 (6th ed. 2012), and cites numerous instances in which courts ignore such clauses, allow waivers of them, and allow parties to raise estoppel against their use. *Id.* at 146–47. (We'll look at waiver and estoppel in the next section.)

4. **You Be the Lawyer!**

   You represent Schinkel after he's just been refunded the $5,000. He asks you if there is anything he should do to ensure that those "fickle Finns" don't back out of their deal. Is there?

---

2. Waiver and Estoppel (and Retraction)

In a sense, if modification or amendment* is found, it is forever (or at least until the next modification or amendment). An amendment restructures the parties' rights under the contract. But what if there is no change in future duties, just some non-response or some leniency fleetingly given? Say, for example, that Ponoroff rents an apartment to Epstein. Epstein normally pays on time, but West is a little late this month with the royalty check, and so Epstein is a little short of funds. Epstein pays, but pays five days late. That's a breach; as set forth above, any variance from the specified performance set forth in the contract is a breach.

Assume, however, that Ponoroff tells Epstein: "Late once, buddy, I'll overlook it. Late twice, and you're toast." Has there been an amendment or modification of the contract? Not really; Epstein was late without getting Ponoroff's advance consent, and Ponoroff just decides, for once in his life, to be a nice guy and let it slide. No real objective manifestation of an agreement; no offer; no acceptance, and likely no consideration.

So does Epstein have to live with the breach hanging over his hang-dog head for the rest of the lease's life? No. Such actions are covered by the concept of waiver (along with its cousin, estoppel), as set forth in the next case.

---

* By the way, we should have asked this earlier: What's the difference between amending a contract and modifying it?

QUESTIONS BEFORE THE CASE

1. What was Kamco's non-performance? How many times did it breach the contract?
2. What were the consequences to On the Right Track of allowing waivers to occur?

KAMCO SUPPLY CORP. V. ON THE RIGHT TRACK, LLC

Supreme Court of New York, Appellate Division, Second Department
149 A.D.3d 275, 49 N.Y.S.3d 721 (2017)

CHAMBERS, J.P.

OPINION & ORDER

This appeal presents a rare opportunity to consider the circumstances under which a party's conduct, in the course of performing what may be described as a relational contract[1] may support an inference that a material right under the contract has been prospectively waived.

I.

. . . . Southeastern Metal, Inc. (hereinafter SEM), and the . . . plaintiff, On the Right Track, LLC (hereinafter OTRT), are, respectively, a licensee and sublicensee of a patented self-locking stud, track, and header partitioning system used in the construction industry and marketed as "Trakloc," which is owned by . . . defendant Trakloc International, LLC (hereinafter TI).

In 2005, OTRT, SEM, and TI entered into two supply distribution agreements (hereinafter the agreements) with the * * * Kamco parties. The agreements required the Kamco parties to purchase a minimum of 15 million linear feet of Trakloc by December 31, 2005. For the calendar year 2006, the agreements required the Kamco parties to purchase an annual

---

1 The term "relational contract" was coined by the late Ian Roderick Macneil to describe the opposite of a discrete transaction (*see generally* Ian R. Macneil, *Relational Contract Theory: Challenges and Queries*, 94 Nw UL Rev 877 [Spring 2000]; Ian R. Macneil, *Relational Contract: What We Do and Do Not Know*, 1985 Wis L Rev 483 [May 1985/June 1985]). A relational contract has also been described as "a contract that involves not merely an exchange, but also a relationship, between the contracting parties" (Melvin A. Eisenberg, *Why There Is No Law of Relational Contracts*, 94 Nw UL Rev 805, 816 [Spring 2000]), as well as a contract that "creates a continuing relationship flexible enough to adapt to changes of circumstance that could not have been fully anticipated when the contract was negotiated" (*United States v. Moreland*, 703 F3d 976, 985 [7th Cir]). With its emphasis on trust, collaboration, reputation, and the ability to adapt in the face of changing circumstances, the relational contract has been extensively studied by economists, sociologists and game theorists, but thus far has generated little interest among lawyers (*see generally* Eisenberg, 94 Nw UL Rev 805).

minimum of 164.4 million linear feet of Trakloc, and, in the course of satisfying that annual minimum purchase requirement, to purchase a minimum of 8 million linear feet of Trakloc in each month of 2006. The agreements also required the Kamco parties to use their "best efforts" to market, sell, and distribute Trakloc within the relevant territory and to increase sales volumes annually.

Each agreement also contained the following no-oral-waiver provision:

> "19.2 Waiver. No waiver of any provision of this Agreement or any rights or obligations of either party hereunder shall be effective, except pursuant to written instrument signed by the party or parties waiving compliance. This waiver shall be effective only in the specific instance and the specific purpose stated."

The agreements were set to expire on December 31, 2006, but would be renewed automatically for additional one-year terms as long as the Kamco parties met the minimum purchase requirements.

It is undisputed that the Kamco parties did not meet their annual minimum purchase requirement for 2005, or any of their monthly minimum purchase requirements for 2006. According to SEM's records, the Kamco parties purchased only 1,565,406 linear feet of Trakloc in 2005, and only 2,064,263 linear feet of Trakloc in 2006—just over 2% of the combined minimum annual purchase requirements for 2005 and 2006. While SEM and OTRT periodically complained to the Kamco parties, mostly orally, about the low sales figures, the Kamco parties placed the blame on a number of problems outside their control, including shipping, logistics, and pricing issues attributable to SEM.

In April or May 2006, Kamco Supply Corp.—the Kamco entity responsible for the New York market—approached OTRT about ending the relationship. By July 2006, the operating member of OTRT conceded that there was no "realistic possibility" that the Kamco parties would be able to meet their annual minimum purchase requirement for 2006. At that point, Kamco Supply Corp. and OTRT agreed that Kamco Supply Corp. would return $47,709.92 worth of Trakloc to SEM.

At no time up to that point, or even during the following several weeks, did anyone at OTRT or SEM ever send the Kamco parties a notice of default regarding their failure to meet the minimum purchase requirements, or a reservation of OTRT's and SEM's rights to seek damages for past breaches or require strict compliance with such requirements going forward. According to SEM's president, no default notice was sent because there was no desire to terminate the agreements with the Kamco parties, as SEM and OTRT still felt that the best chance of success was to press ahead in the hope that sales might eventually improve.

In November 2006, less than two months before the scheduled expiration of the agreements, Kamco Supply Corp. commenced this action against OTRT seeking to recover damages for breach of contract. [In response,] TI, OTRT and SEM [counterclaimed, seeking] to recover substantial damages for the Kamco parties' failure to meet the minimum purchase requirements under the agreements.

At the conclusion of a nonjury trial, the Supreme Court resolved the counterclaims * * * in favor of the Kamco parties and against OTRT and SEM. The court found that the Kamco parties had met their "best efforts" obligation under the agreements, and that finding is not challenged by OTRT and SEM on this appeal. While the court also found that the minimum purchase requirements were binding, and that the Kamco parties had consistently failed to meet them, it concluded, in relevant part, that OTRT and SEM had no right to sue for the breach. Specifically, the court found that the parties' course of performance supported the view that the Kamco parties' persistent and repeated failure to meet minimum purchase requirements was "a non-actionable mutual failure to live up to expectations." As for the no-oral-waiver clause (see section 19.2 of the agreements, quoted in Part I, supra), the court held that it was not dispositive, as "[t]he factual question of whether waiver occurred may be determined by consideration of words or conduct." [OTRT and SEM appealed]

II.

The general principles relating to the law of waiver and estoppel in New York are well known.

"Once a contract is formed, the parties may of course change their agreement by another agreement, by course of performance, or by conduct amounting to a waiver or estoppel" * * * Thus, "[c]ontractual rights may be waived if they are knowingly, voluntarily and intentionally abandoned," and "[s]uch abandonment may be established by affirmative conduct or by failure to act so as to evince an intent not to claim a purported advantage." * * *

As the intentional relinquishment of a known right, a waiver "should not be lightly presumed" * * *. Ordinarily, mere "[n]egligence, oversight or thoughtlessness" does not create a waiver * * *. Similarly, "a party's reluctance to terminate a contract upon a breach and its attempts to encourage the breaching party to adhere to its obligations under the contract do not necessarily constitute a waiver of the innocent party's rights in the future" * * *.

A waiver, however, may be proved by "undisputed acts or language so inconsistent with [the party's] purpose to stand upon his [or her] rights as to leave no opportunity for a reasonable inference to the contrary" * * *.

III.

In the context of relational contracts such as the subject agreements, where there are repeated occasions for performance over the course of months or years, the application of general principles of waiver and estoppel presents special difficulties, particularly when trying to gauge whether a waiver relates only to a contemporaneous or past obligation, or applies prospectively to executory obligations as well. And when no-oral-waiver clauses are thrown into the mix, the analysis becomes even more complex (see generally David V. Snyder, The Law of Contract and the Concept of Change: Public and Private Attempts to Regulate Modification, Waiver, and Estoppel, 1999 Wis L Rev 607 [1999]).

In approaching this question, it is useful to recall that the roots of waiver lie firmly in equity, and are "designed to prevent the waiving party from lulling the other party into a belief that strict compliance with a contractual duty will not be required and then either suing for noncompliance or demanding compliance for the purpose of avoiding the transaction" (13 Richard A. Lord, Williston on Contracts § 39:15 at 621 [4th ed 2013] [footnotes omitted]).

Where, as here, a contract provides, among other things, for the long-term supply of goods, UCC 2–208* and 2–209 also come into play. Those sections read, in relevant part, as follows:

"2–208. Course of Performance or Practical Construction

> "(1) Where the contract for sale involves repeated occasions for performance by either party with knowledge of the nature of the performance and opportunity for objection to it by the other, any course of performance accepted or acquiesced in without objection shall be relevant to determine the meaning of the agreement.
>
> "(2) The express terms of the agreement and any such course of performance . . . shall be construed whenever reasonable as consistent with each other; but when such construction is unreasonable, express terms shall control course of performance
>
> . . .
>
> "(3) Subject to the provisions of the next section on modification and waiver, such course of performance shall be relevant to show a waiver or modification of any term inconsistent with such course of performance."

* [During the time periods relevant here, New York had not yet adopted Revised Article 1. Revised Article 1 moved the course of performance provisions from § 2–208 to § 1–303. Eds.]

> *"2–209. Modification, Rescission*
>
> "(4) Although an attempt at modification or rescission does not satisfy the requirements of subsection (2) or (3) [relating to certain requirements for a signed writing] it can operate as a waiver.
>
> "(5) A party who has made a waiver affecting an executory portion of the contract may retract the waiver by reasonable notification received by the other party that strict performance will be required of any term waived, unless the retraction would be unjust in view of a material change of position in reliance on the waiver."

Under the above provisions, a party may, through its course of performance, waive a term of the contract, either retrospectively (i.e., in connection with a past obligation or condition) or prospectively (i.e., in connection with an executory obligation). If the waiver applies prospectively, it may be retracted upon reasonable notice, unless such retraction would be unjust in view of a material change of position in reliance on the waiver.

* * *

However, in the case of a waiver that is deemed broad enough to apply prospectively to an executory obligation, the effect of such a waiver would arguably be broader than that of a mere election. Whereas an election to continue the performance of a contract despite the occurrence of a material breach would bar the right to terminate the contract based on that breach * * *, it would not preclude an action based on a subsequent breach * * *. By contrast, a prospective waiver of the breached provision would, unless effectively retracted in accordance with UCC 2–209(5), serve to bar an action based on a subsequent breach of that provision * * *.

IV.

Applying the above principles to the facts at hand, we find that the record broadly supports the view that OTRT and SEM, by electing early on to continue the agreements despite the Kamco parties' breach of the 2005 annual minimum purchase requirement, waived their right to terminate the agreements based on that initial breach * * *. Contrary to the Kamco parties' contentions, however, we do not find that such conduct, without more, evinced "a clear manifestation of intent" prospectively to waive any of the 2006 monthly or annual minimum purchase requirements * * *. The same reasoning also applies to the Kamco parties' continued failure, in early 2006, to meet the monthly minimum purchase requirements. Such conduct can reasonably be understood as a waiver of the 2006 monthly minimum purchase requirements as and when such obligations became due, but not as a prospective waiver of executory minimum purchase requirements, including the 2006 annual minimum purchase requirement.

As time went on, however, and OTRT and SEM continued to accept, month after month, and without any formal reservation of rights or notice of default, the Kamco parties' continued failure to meet monthly minimum purchase requirements, the situation eventually reached a tipping point where the conduct of OTRT and SEM became so inconsistent with an intent to enforce the remaining 2006 minimum purchase requirements "as to leave no opportunity for a reasonable inference to the contrary" * * *. At that point, it can fairly be said that a prospective waiver occurred * * *.

We need not decide precisely when that tipping point happened in this case, as it is clear from the record that it occurred well before OTRT and SEM first attempted formally to enforce their rights under the agreements by asserting counterclaims and the third-party action against the Kamco parties in November or December of 2006.

As early as July of 2006, OTRT had already conceded that there was no "realistic possibility" that the Kamco parties would be able to meet their annual minimum purchase requirement for 2006, yet neither OTRT nor SEM made any effort at that time to put the Kamco parties on notice of their default. On the contrary, OTRT even agreed to allow Kamco Supply Corp. to return $47,709.92 worth of Trakloc to SEM—conduct that is so fundamentally at odds with an intent to enforce the 2006 annual minimum purchase requirement that it would be difficult to characterize it as anything other than a prospective waiver of the annual minimum purchase requirement.

Moreover, by the end of 2006, the Kamco parties' cumulative purchases of Trakloc amounted to barely more than 2% of the total minimum purchase requirements for 2005 and 2006, leaving a monumental shortfall of 175,770,331 linear feet. At the same time, SEM had only negligible inventories of Trakloc on hand, and its capacity to produce new product was limited to approximately 12 million to 18 million linear feet per month. Thus, even assuming that the Kamco parties had been willing to comply with the 2006 annual minimum purchase requirement in November 2006, it is unreasonable to believe that OTRT and SEM had the capacity to deliver such a large amount of Trakloc in less than two months' time.

For all of the above reasons, we find that the Supreme Court properly concluded that, by the end of 2006, the affirmative conduct of OTRT and SEM over the previous weeks and months evinced an unmistakable intent to waive the remaining 2006 minimum purchase requirements, including the 2006 annual minimum purchase requirement * * *.

Nor can the assertion of OTRT's and SEM's counterclaims and the third-party action against the Kamco parties be construed as an effective retraction of their earlier waiver. "A waiver, to the extent that it has been executed, cannot be expunged or recalled, but, not being a binding agreement, can, to the extent that it is executory, be withdrawn, provided the party whose performance has been waived is given notice of withdrawal and a reasonable time after notice within which to perform" (Nassau Trust Co. v Montrose Concrete Prods. Corp., 56 NY2d 175, 184, 436 N.E.2d 1265, 451 N.Y.S.2d 663 [citation omitted]; see UCC 2–209[5]). Under the facts presented, it would have been unjust to allow OTRT and SEM to retract their prior waiver within weeks of the deadline to meet the 2006 annual minimum purchase requirement.

Finally, we agree with the Supreme Court that, under the facts presented, the agreements' no-oral-waiver provision (see section 19.2 of the agreements, quoted in part I, supra) does not compel a different result. As explained above, the Kamco parties' persistent and repeated failure to meet minimum purchase requirements, coupled with OTRT's and SEM's continued acceptance of such conduct without any reservation or protest until a few weeks before the expiration of the agreements (by which time it was, of course, too late to insist upon strict compliance with the terms of the agreements), equitably estops OTRT and SEM from invoking the benefit of the no-oral-waiver provision. * * *

The parties' remaining contentions either are without merit or need not be considered in light of our determination.

Accordingly, the order is affirmed.

QUESTIONS AND NOTES

1. Questions about the facts of this case

    1.1. Why did Kamco sue in the first place? Didn't it know it was in breach? Couldn't it anticipate OTRT and SEM's response?

    1.2. Was there an explicit signed waiver by OTRT and SEM? Wasn't that required by section 19.2 of the agreement?

    1.3. Assume, contrary to the facts, that the contract was set to expire 3 years after Kamco's lawsuit and the counterclaims. Any different result?

2. Questions about the law

    2.1. In this court's view, what is the definition of waiver?

    2.2. Why did the court cite to U.C.C. § 2–209? What parts of that statute are helpful in resolving the dispute between the parties?

2.3. In the last paragraph, the court holds that OTRT and SEM were estopped from raising the no-oral-waiver clause. What is the court's definition of estoppel that justifies this holding?

2.4. The court indicates that a waiver can be retracted, in part because it is not really a binding agreement, but only as to "executory" obligations. What are those?

3. Notes

3.1 The court concludes that OTRT was "estopped" to rely on the no-oral-waiver clause. What's the difference between waiver and estoppel? As stated recently by the West Virginia Supreme Court:

> "Waiver is the voluntary surrender of a right; estoppel is the inhibition to assert a right which the law places on one as a consequence of his own conduct which has resulted in injury or detriment to another . . . Waiver depends upon what one himself intends to do; estoppel depends rather upon what he caused his adversary to do." *Northwestern Nat. Life Ins. Co. v. Ward,* 56 Okla. 188, 155 P. 524, 527 (1915). Waiver arises from the voluntary actions of the contract's obligor alone; to create an estoppel, both the obligor and obligee must act. 8 *Corbin on Contracts* at § 40.1. . . .
>
> In summary, on the question of prejudice or detrimental reliance, the distinction between the common law doctrines of estoppel and waiver is simple: estoppel requires proof of prejudice or detrimental reliance; waiver does not. We therefore hold that the common-law doctrine of waiver focuses on the conduct of the party against whom waiver is sought, and requires that party to have intentionally relinquished a known right. A waiver may be express or may be inferred from actions or conduct, but all of the attendant facts, taken together, must amount to an intentional relinquishment of a known right. There is no requirement of prejudice or detrimental reliance by the party asserting waiver.

Parsons v. Halliburton Energy Services, Inc., 237 W.Va. 138, 785 S.E.2d 844 (W.Va. 2016).

In *Parsons*, the issue was whether Halliburton had waived its contractual right to arbitration by delaying its answer to a complaint, and by leading plaintiff to think it would answer. It responded* by moving to dismiss because Parsons had earlier

* The difference between "answer" and "respond" is litigator pettifogging—*answering* a complaint means filing a formal answer, responding to each allegation in the complaint. *Responding* includes answering, but also includes moving to dismiss for grounds unrelated to the allegations in the complaint, such as lack of jurisdiction, no real claim for relief stated or, as in

agreed to arbitrate all disputes. The court found for Halliburton, given the earlier stage of the proceeding. But would the case have been decided differently if the motion to dismiss was made just before a jury was to return its verdict? Just before trial started? Just after a summary judgment motion was filed by the plaintiff? Just after the defendant filed a formal answer to the complaint?

3.2. But although a waiver doesn't require reliance, doesn't a waiver almost always lead to detrimental reliance by the other side? To quote *Corbin on Contracts*:

> Generally, the promisor's waiver of a condition is followed by the promisee's substantial change of position. At the very least, the promisee will be induced by the waiver not to perform the condition, if the condition consists of some act or forbearance of the promisee. Thus, if a promisor's duty to convey is conditional on payment by a stated day, the promisor's waiver of the condition may induce the promisee to cease efforts to raise the money and to forbear to pay on the day. Here we have ample reason for an estoppel, or for the enforcement of a promise because of subsequent reliance.

8 *Corbin on Contracts* § 40.2 (2017). *See also Restatement (Second) of Contracts* § 84, cmt. b (1981) (" 'Waiver' is often inexactly defined as 'the voluntary relinquishment of a known right.' When the waiver is reinforced by reliance, enforcement is often said to rest on 'estoppel.' ").

3.3. Courts disagree on the exact formulation of waiver. In *Altman v. Munns*, 82 N.C.App. 102, 345 S.E.2d 419 (1986), for example, the parties had entered into a marital settlement agreement under which the husband agreed to pay for the college tuition of the couple's then-eight-year-old daughter. When college time came around, dad was not in great financial condition, and the daughter wanted to go to a pricey private college. After some back and forth, mom testified that she "realized Louisburg College [where the couple's daughter wished to go] was more expensive [than state college]. I felt sorry for Bob and therefore I agreed to pay one-half of Lisa's college expenses."

Well, Mom paid, but Dad didn't. Mom sued Dad to be reimbursed for the entire amount of the year's tuition; after all, the marital settlement agreement did not specify any particular type of college. Dad was in breach.

Parsons's case, by asserting that Parson had previously agreed to arbitrate all disputes, and thus the matter does not belong in court.

Dad defended, claiming Mom had waived at least half of his obligation. In assessing this contention, the court said:

> A party may waive the breach of a contractual provision without consideration or estoppel where (i) the waiving party is the non-breaching party; (ii) the breach is not a total repudiation of the contract so that the non-breaching party continues to receive some benefit of the contract; (iii) the innocent party is aware of the breach; and (iv) the innocent party performs or accepts the partial performance of the breaching party.

In this case, Mom paid the whole tuition (and guaranteed some loans). The court held that these affirmative acts, combined with her statements to Dad, constituted a waiver of the right to receive 100% of Dad's obligation; he only had to pay Mom 50%.

But . . . Daughter did not waive anything. She was, as we will see in Chapter 9, a third-party beneficiary of the contract, which entitled to sue her Dad if he didn't pay (and she was liable). As a result, the court let Mom off the hook for 50% of the obligation, but allowed Daughter to sue Dad for the whole amount.

Aside from the rough justice, how does the standard for waiver in *Altman* compare to the standard articulated in *Kamco*?

4. **You Be the Lawyer!**

You represent OTRT and SEM. Kamco's performance is abysmal—they are making only 2% of the required sales. But your business contacts don't want to rock the boat, because they think the market might turn. At the same time, they tell you: "We're protected by the anti-waiver clause, right? We can sue them if this doesn't work out, correct? We want you to reserve all our rights regardless." What's your answer? And if this request comes with two years left on the contract, what actions would you suggest that they take to "reserve their rights"?

PROBLEM: THE CASE OF THE DRUNKEN LAW PROFESSOR

Professor Clark writes brilliant law prose. He's also a drunk. West wants his output, but they want him to write it sober. West and Clark enter into a contract requiring Clark to write a treatise on corporations, for which they will pay Clark $6 a page if he abstains from all liquor while writing. If he doesn't, the pay is $2 per page.

Clark delivers a crackerjack treatise on time and under budget. West sells a ton of copies. The accounting folks at West find out that Clark hit the bottle more than once during the writing of the treatise. The check they write him is for $2 a page only.

Clark thinks the work is good, and sues for $6 a page. What result?

Would it matter if Clark's editor knew he was drinking while he wrote, but did not tell accounting? If the editor took Clark to dinner (something we hope all casebook editors do with their authors—hint, hint, West), and saw Clark sip a bit of sherry before dinner? If he consumed a bottle of wine during dinner, and then left the table at the end saying, "Well, got to go write more of that blasted treatise." Finally, what if Clark goes to his editor and says "I can't write without hitting the sauce. Especially for only $2 a page. You should get another author," and his editor responds, "Don't worry. Keep writing. We'll work something out," and Clark finishes the treatise on time.

It's a real case. *Clark v. West*, 193 N.Y. 349 (1908).

B. EXCUSE: FAILURE TO PERFORM TERMS OR TO SATISFY CONDITIONS BECAUSE OF EXTERNAL FACTORS

We've seen that any non-performance is a breach, even if beyond the control of the breaching party. Does that extend to all possible explanations for non-performance? What if Epstein, geezer that he is, contracts to teach you contracts, and then, to your dismay and to the schadenfreude of his co-authors, he shuffles off his mortal coil. Or, to put it in non-Shakespearian terms, he passes. Kicks the bucket. Is no more. Is pushing up daisies. Is bereft of life. Is like Monty Python's parrot. https://www.youtube.com/watch?v=4vuW6tQ0218.

What then?

---

1. Impossibility

DEATH AND CONTRACTS

What happens when people die after making, but before performing, a contract? Under *Restatement (Second) of Contracts* § 262, death or incapacity of a person "necessary for the performance of a duty" excuses the nonperformance. What does "necessary for the performance of a duty" mean? Consider the following three problems:

(1) Before dying, Epstein had borrowed $30,000 from Markell. Although Epstein signed a contract agreeing to repay the loan, he had not repaid the loan at the time of his death. Markell sues Epstein's estate. Again, should Epstein's nonperformance be excused because of the later unforeseen occurrence? If a person's contractual obligations to pay debts

disappear when he dies, will lenders and vendors extend credit to really old people like Epstein?

(2) Markell contracts with Epstein to paint his house for $10,000. Epstein dies before painting Markell's house. Markell hires Ponoroff who charges Markell $15,000. Markell sues Epstein's estate for breach of contracts. Should Epstein's nonperformance be excused because of the later unforeseen occurrence?

(3) HBO contracts with Owen Wilson to star in a made-for-television movie, "Law School Legend—The David Epstein Story." Wilson dies before the movie is finished. HBO sues Wilson's estate. Should Wilson's nonperformance be excused?

Consider your response after reading the next case.

QUESTIONS BEFORE THE CASE

1. What are the differences between the rationale that excuses an estate's performance of a decedent's contract that was unperformed at her death (explored above) and the rationale in the next case?
2. What does the court presume that the parties presumed when entering into the contract in the first place?

TAYLOR V. CALDWELL

Court of King's Bench
122 Eng. Rep. 309 (1863)

BLACKBURN, J. In this case the plaintiffs and defendants had, on the 27th May, 1861, entered into a contract by which the defendants agreed to let the plaintiffs have the use of The Surrey Gardens and Music Hall on four days then to come, viz., the 17th June, 15th July, 5th August and 19th August, for the purpose of giving a series of four grand concerts, and day and night fetes at the Gardens and Hall on those days respectively; and the plaintiffs agreed to take the Gardens and Hall on those days, and pay £100 for each day.

The parties inaccurately call this a "letting," and the money to be paid a "rent"; but the whole agreement is such as to shew that the defendants were to retain the possession of the Hall and Gardens so that there was to be no demise of them, and that the contract was merely to give the plaintiffs the use of them on those days. Nothing however, in our opinion, depends on this. The agreement then proceeds to set out various stipulations between the parties as to what each was to supply for these concerts and entertainments, and as to the manner in which they should be carried on. The effect of the whole is to shew that the existence of the Music Hall in the Surrey Gardens in a state fit for a concert was essential for the fulfilment of the contract, such entertainment as the parties contemplated in their agreement could not be given without it.

After the making of the agreement, and before the first day on which a concert was to be given, the Hall was destroyed by fire. This destruction, we must take it on the evidence, was without the fault of either party, and was so complete that in consequence the concerts could not be given as intended. And the question we have to decide is whether, under these circumstances, the loss which the plaintiffs have sustained is to fall upon the defendants. The parties when framing their agreement evidently had not present to their minds the possibility of such a disaster, and have made no express stipulation with reference to it, so that the answer to the question must depend upon the general rules of law applicable to such a contract.

There seems no doubt that where there is a positive contract to do a thing, not in itself unlawful, the contractor must perform it or pay damages for not doing it, although in consequence of unforeseen accidents, the performance of his contract has become unexpectedly burdensome or even impossible. * * * But this rule is only applicable when the contract is positive and absolute, and not subject to any condition either express or implied; and there are authorities which, as we think, establish the principle that where, from the nature of the contract, it appears that the parties must from the beginning have known that it could not be fulfilled unless when the time for the fulfilment of the contract arrived some particular specified thing continued to exist, so that, when entering into the contract, they must have contemplated such continuing existence as the foundation of what was to be done; there, in the absence of any express or implied warranty that the thing shall exist, the contract is not to be construed as a positive contract, but as subject to an implied condition that the parties shall be excused in case, before breach, performance becomes impossible from the perishing of the thing without default of the contractor.

There seems little doubt that this implication tends to further the great object of making the legal construction such as to fulfill the intention of those who entered into the contract. For in the course of affairs men in making such contracts in general would, if it were brought to their minds, say that there should be such a condition.

* * *

There is a class of contracts in which a person binds himself to do something which requires to be performed by him in person; and such promises, e.g. promises to marry, or promises to serve for a certain time, are never in practice qualified by an express exception of the death of the party; and therefore in such cases the contract is in terms broken if the promisor dies before fulfilment. Yet it was very early determined that, if the performance is personal, the executors are not liable; Hyde v. The Dean of Windsor (Cro.Eliz. 552, 553). See 2 Wms.Exors. 1560, 5th ed., where a very apt illustration is given. "Thus," says the learned author, "if an author undertakes to compose a work, and dies before completing it, his executors are discharged from this contract: for the undertaking is merely personal in its nature, and, by the intervention of the contractor's death, has become impossible to be performed." For this he cites a dictum of Lord Lyndhurst in Marshall v. Broadhurst (1 Tyr. 348, 349), and a case mentioned by Patteson J. in Wentworth v. Cock (10 A. & E. 42, 45–46). In Hall v. Wright (E.B. & E. 746, 749), Crompton J., in his judgment, puts another case. "Where a contract depends upon personal skill, and the act of God renders it impossible, as, for instance, in the case of a painter employed to paint a picture who is struck blind, it may be that the performance might be excused."

It seems that in those cases the only ground on which the parties or their executors, can be excused from the consequences of the breach of the contract is, that from the nature of the contract there is an implied condition of the continued existence of the life of the contractor, and, perhaps in the case of the painter of his eyesight. In the instances just given, the person, the continued existence of whose life is necessary to the fulfilment of the contract, is himself the contractor, but that does not seem in itself to be necessary to the application of the principle; as is illustrated by the following example. In the ordinary form of an apprentice deed the apprentice binds himself in unqualified terms to "serve until the full end and term of seven years to be fully complete and ended," during which term it is covenanted that the apprentice his master "faithfully shall serve," and the father of the apprentice in equally unqualified terms binds himself for the performance by the apprentice of all and every covenant on his part. It is undeniable that if the apprentice dies within the seven years, the covenant of the father that he shall perform his covenant to serve for seven years is not fulfilled, yet surely it cannot be that an action lie against the father? Yet the only reason why it would not is that he is excused because of the apprentice's death.

These are instances where the implied condition is of the life of a human being, but there are others in which the same implication is made as to the continued existence of a thing. For example, where a contract of sale is made amounting to a bargain and sale, transferring presently the property in specific chattels, which are to be delivered by the vendor at a future day; there, if the chattels, without fault of the vendor, perish in the interval, the purchaser must pay the price and the vendor is excused from performing his contract to deliver, which has thus become impossible.

It may, we think, be safely asserted to be now English law, that in all contracts of loan of chattels or bailments if the performance of the promise of the borrower or bailee to return the things lent or bailed, becomes impossible because it has perished, this impossibility (if not arising upon the fault of the borrower or bailee from some risk which he has taken upon himself) excuses the borrower or bailee from the performance of his promise to redeliver the chattel.

* * *

In none of these cases is the promise in words other than positive, nor is there any express stipulation that the destruction of the person or thing shall excuse the performance; but that excuse is by law implied, because from the nature of the contract it is apparent that the parties contracted on the basis of the continued existence of the particular person or chattel. In the present case, looking at the whole contract, we find that the parties contracted on the basis of the continued existence of the Music Hall at the time when the concerts were to be given; that being essential to their performance.

We think, therefore, that the Music Hall having ceased to exist, without fault of either party, both parties are excused, the plaintiffs from taking the gardens and paying the money, the defendants from performing their promise to give the use of the Hall and Gardens and other things. Consequently the rule must be absolute to enter the verdict for the defendants.

Rule absolute.

QUESTIONS AND NOTE

1. Questions about the facts of this case

    1.1. Was there any contract language that was relevant to the decision?

    1.2. How was the concert hall destroyed? Was that relevant to the decision?

    1.3. Could Caldwell build a new concert hall before June 17? Would that be relevant to the decision?

2. Questions about the law

    2.1. What legal device ("fiction") did the court use to find that both parties are excused from performing?

    2.2. Today, insurance companies sell not only fire insurance that covers the cost of rebuilding but also "business interruption" insurance that covers losses due to any business interruption resulting from the fire. What result in *Taylor v. Caldwell* if Caldwell had bought such a policy?

2.3. Caldwell later contracts with Epstein Construction Co. (ECC) to build a new concert hall. After ECC begins work but before the concert hall construction is complete, lightning strikes again and fire destroys the construction. ECC has other more rewarding construction contracts that it would prefer to do. Does destruction of the concert hall excuse ECC's performance?

3. Note

Professor Nancy Kim provides the following analysis of *Taylor v. Caldwell*:

> The court decided that the continued existence of the music hall was an implied condition of the contract and because the music hall was destroyed, Caldwell's performance was excused. The "implied condition" was a tacit assumption of the parties. The invalidity of the parties' tacit assumption reveals an absence of cognitive intent for both Taylor and Caldwell. Caldwell would not have agreed to rent out the music hall, and Taylor would not have agreed to rent it, if either had known the hall would be destroyed by fire. Furthermore, each party lacked contextual purposive intent to enter into the actual contract because the fire destroyed both parties' ability to perform. In other words, Caldwell never had the intent to enter into an agreement that required him to deliver possession of a non-existent structure, or one that needed to be entirely rebuilt. Similarly, Taylor lacked contextual purposive intent to enter into the contract because he wanted to rent the premises to stage music performances—something he could no longer do after the fire. He lacked contextual purposive intent because an event subsequent to the formation of the contract—the fire—destroyed his reason for renting the premises. The same circumstances—the fire and the subsequent destruction of the music hall—defeated the contractual intent of both parties.

Nancy Kim, *Mistakes, Changed Circumstances and Intent*, 56 U. KAN. L. REV. 473 (2008). Do you agree with Professor Kim's analysis of *Taylor v. Caldwell*?

4. **You Be the Lawyer!**

When counseling your client about risk, how specific do you want to get in allocating and mentioning specific acts? Do you run any risk if you are too specific? Would Taylor be better protected if his contract said: "This contract shall terminate upon destruction of the music hall" rather than "This contract shall terminate upon any fire, flood, ice storm or other natural calamity that may cause the destruction of the music hall"?

What if the cost of performance is rendered practically (but not actually) impossible by unforeseen economic conditions? That's what one party argues in the next case.

QUESTIONS BEFORE THE CASE

1. What was the breach in this case?
2. According to Ruby Tuesday, what was the cause of the breach?
3. Was the breach anticipated by the contract?

ROUTE 6 OUTPARCELS, LLC v. RUBY TUESDAY, INC.

Supreme Court, Appellate Division, Third Department, New York
88 A.D.3d 1224, 931 N.Y.S.2d 436 (2011)

Before: PETERS, J.P., SPAIN, STEIN, MCCARTHY and GARRY, JJ.

SPAIN, J.

Pursuant to a 2006 ground lease agreement, defendant agreed to construct and open a restaurant on plaintiff's real property, located in Pennsylvania, by March 2009, and to pay plaintiff an annual fixed rent in addition to a percentage of the restaurant's gross sales. Although defendant has consistently paid the fixed rent on the property, it did not construct the anticipated restaurant, prompting plaintiff to commence this breach of contract action. Plaintiff successfully moved for partial summary judgment on the issue of liability, and defendant now appeals.

We affirm. Defendant does not dispute that plaintiff has established a prima facie case for breach of contract under Pennsylvania law, but argues that its performance was excused under the agreement's force majeure provision. "In order to use a force majeure clause as an excuse for non-performance, the event alleged as an excuse must have been beyond the party's control and not due to any fault or negligence by the non-performing party" (*Martin v. Pennsylvania, Dept. of Envtl. Resources,* 120 Pa.Cmwlth. 269, 548 A.2d 675, 678 [Pa.Cmwlth.1988]). "Furthermore, the non-performing party has the burden of proof as well as a duty to show what action was taken to perform the contract, regardless of the occurrence of the excuse" (*id.; accord Rohm & Haas Co. v. Crompton Corp.,* 2002 WL 1023435, *2, 2002 Phila Ct. Com. Pl. LEXIS 20, *6–7 [Pa.Com.Pl.2002]).

Here, the agreement's force majeure provision provides: "Except for any payments due [plaintiff] in accordance with this [l]ease, [plaintiff] and/or [defendant] shall be excused for the period of any delay and shall not be deemed in default with respect to the performance of any of the terms, covenants, and conditions of this [l]ease when prevented from so doing by cause or causes beyond the [plaintiff's] and/or [defendant's] control, which shall include, without limitation, all labor disputes, governmental regulations or controls, fire or other casualty, inability to obtain any material, services, acts of God, or any other cause, *whether similar or dissimilar* to the foregoing, not within the control of the [plaintiff] and/or [defendant]" (emphasis added). Defendant argues that the "global economic downturn that took hold in 2008" prevented its performance under the contract and, thus, its nonperformance was excused under the force majeure provision. Specifically, defendant relies on an affidavit of its vice-president and corporate controller, attesting that due to the economic crisis that began in early 2008, defendant experienced a drastic decline of its stock price, forcing defendant to reclassify over $500 million of its long term debt and to determine that complying with the lease provisions requiring construction of a new restaurant "would divert needed funds away from meeting debt obligations and leverage thresholds under its loan covenants." As a result, defendant communicated to plaintiff in March 2008 that it would not construct the store anticipated by the parties' agreement.

We agree with Supreme Court that the economic factors that led defendant to make this decision cannot, as a matter of law, excuse its nonperformance. "[W]hen the parties have themselves defined the contours of force majeure in their agreement, those contours dictate the application, effect, and scope of force majeure" (*Rohm & Haas Co. v. Crompton Corp.,* 2002 WL 1023435, at *3, quoting *R & B Falcon Corp. v. American Exploration Co.,* 154 F.Supp.2d 969, 973 [S.D.Tex.2001]). Here, although the parties did, after identifying particular force majeure events, agree on a fairly broad clause by including the language "any other cause, whether similar or dissimilar to the foregoing," they still expressly limited the contemplated force majeure events to those beyond the control of the nonperforming party. While defendant, of course, had no control over the world economy, the decisions it made with respect to how to cope with the financial downturn—notwithstanding that its options may have been limited—remained within defendant's power and control. Defendant made a calculated choice to allocate funds to the payment of its debts rather than to perform under the subject lease. Economic factors are an inherent part of all sophisticated business transactions and, as such, while not predictable, are never completely unforeseeable; indeed, "financial hardship is not grounds for avoiding performance under a contract" (*Rohm & Haas Co. v. Crompton Corp.,* 2002 WL 1023435, at *5, quoting *Macalloy Corp. v. Metallurg, Inc.,* 284 A.D.2d 227, 227, 728 N.Y.S.2d 14 [2001]; *see Millers Cove Energy Co., Inc. v. Moore,* 62 F.3d 155, 158 [6th Cir.1995] ["Courts and commentators generally refuse to excuse lack of compliance with contractual provisions due to economic hardship, unless such a ground is specifically outlined in the contract"]; *Morgantown Crossing, L.P. v. Manufacturers & Traders Trust Co.,* 2004 WL 2579613, *6 [E.D.Pa.2004]; *Stand Energy Corp. v. Cinergy Servs., Inc.,* 144 Ohio App.3d 410, 416, 760 N.E.2d 453, 457 [2001] ["worsening economic conditions . . . do not qualify as a force majeure"]; *Hanover Petroleum Corp. v. Tenneco Inc.,* 521 So.2d 1234, 1239–1240 [La.App.3d.Cir.1988] ["adverse economic conditions . . . which tend to render performance burdensome and unprofitable do not constitute force majeure"], *writ denied* 526 So.2d 800 [La.1988]).

Further, having decided not to construct the restaurant as early as March 2008, defendant has failed to demonstrate an attempt to perform, despite the alleged excuse, as required by Pennsylvania law (*see Martin v. Pennsylvania, Dept. of Envtl. Resources,* 548 A.2d at 678). Accordingly, we conclude that defendant's performance was not excused under the agreement's force majeure clause and plaintiff was properly granted partial summary judgment.

ORDERED that the order is affirmed, with costs.

PETERS, J.P., STEIN, MCCARTHY and GARRY, JJ., concur.

QUESTIONS AND NOTE

1. Questions about the facts of this case

   1.1. Was it impossible for Ruby Tuesday to construct the restaurant?

   1.2. Does this mean that Ruby Tuesday had control over the 2008 financial economic crisis? If not, then why doesn't that crisis qualify under the express terms of the contract?

2. Questions about the law

   2.1. What is a "force majeure" provision? What does "force majeure" even mean? Why can't the court speak English?

   2.2. Would this case have been decided differently if the contract did not have the force majeure clause?

   2.3. What is the relationship between a force majeure clause and impossibility? If a contract has a force majeure clause, can a party to that contract still invoke impossibility?

3. Note

   Is there flexibility in the crafting of a force majeure clause? Could it be drafted to excuse performance due to economic recession? At least one court has answered in the affirmative. In *In re Old Carco LLC (f/k/a Chrysler LLC)*, 452 B.R. 100, 120–27 (Bankr. S.D.N.Y. 2011), Chrysler Corporation had entered into a tax exemption agreement with a local municipality. The agreement provided that if Chrysler shut down the plan located in the municipality, then the tax exemptions would end. But Paragraph 16(F) of the contract contained this force majeure clause:

> [Old Carco] shall not be considered . . . in default in the performance of its obligations under this agreement as a result of any cause beyond its reasonable control, including but not limited to severe and unusual weather, acts of God, or explosion, riot, acts of civil disobedience or sabotage, change to economic conditions and productivity and technological changes, power failures or shortages, restraint by court order or order of public authority, action or omission by any government agency, labor strikes or other labor disturbances.

When Chrysler shut down the plant due to the 2008 recession, the municipality sought to terminate the tax exemption. Chrysler opposed, citing the above language.

The court agreed with Chrysler. It stated:

> Therefore, the record supports the finding [the at the force majeure clause excuses performance in] that: (a) the Plant closing was caused by a change in economic conditions; and (b) such change in economic conditions was beyond Old Carco's control, Old Carco having demonstrated that it exerted reasonable efforts to remain a viable business, perform its obligations, and retain the Plant. The Court finds that the ability of Old Carco to remain a viable automobile manufacturer once the Financial Crisis struck was not within its reasonable control. Therefore, the Plant closing in June 2010 does not constitute an event of default under paragraph 16(F) of the 2000 Agreement.

452 B.R. at 126–27.

4. **You Be the Lawyer!**

   If you had represented Ruby Tuesday in the negotiations of the contract, could you have inserted language that would have protected you from the consequences of the 2008 recession? Do you think Route 6 Outparcels would have agreed?

The previous cases involved changes in circumstances that affected the defendant's ability to perform. The next case, *Krell v. Henry*, involves a change in circumstances that affects the value of the performance to the plaintiff.

---

2. Impracticability and Frustration of Purpose

QUESTIONS BEFORE THE CASE

1. What the subject matter of the contract?
2. What happened to make the subject matter of the contract unattainable?

KRELL V. HENRY

Court of Appeal
2 K.B. 740 (1903)

Appeal from a decision of Darling, J. The plaintiff, Paul Krell, sued the defendant, C.S. Henry for £50, being the balance of a sum of £75, for which the defendant had agreed to hire a flat at 56A, Pall Mall on the days of June 26 and 27, for the purpose of viewing the processions to be held in connection with the coronation of His Majesty [Edward VII]. The defendant denied his liability, and counterclaimed for the return of the sum of £25, which had been paid as a deposit, on the ground that, the processions not having taken place owing to the serious illness of the King, there had been a total failure of consideration for the contract entered into by him.

The facts [were undisputed]. The plaintiff on leaving the country in March, 1902, left instructions with his solicitor to let his suite of chambers at 56A, Pall Mall on such terms and for such period (not exceeding six months) as he thought proper. On June 17, 1902, the defendant noticed an announcement in the windows of the plaintiff's flat to the effect that windows to view the coronation processions were to be let. The defendant interviewed the housekeeper on the subject, when it was pointed out to him what a good view of the processions could be obtained from the premises, and he eventually agreed with the housekeeper to take the suite for the two days in question for a sum of £75.

On June 20, the defendant wrote the following letter to the plaintiff's solicitor:

> "I am in receipt of yours of the 18th instant, inclosing form of agreement for the suite of chambers on the third floor at 56A, Pall Mall, which I have agreed to take for the two days the 26th and 27th instant, for the sum of £75. For reasons given you I cannot enter into the agreement, but as arranged over the telephone I inclose herewith cheque for £25, as deposit, and will thank you to confirm to me that I shall have the entire use of these rooms during the days (not the nights) of the 26th and 27th instant. You may rely that every care will be taken of the premises and their

contents. On the 24th inst. I will pay the balance, viz., £50, to complete the £75 agreed upon."

On the same day the defendant received the following reply from the plaintiff's solicitor:

"I am in receipt of your letter of to-day's date inclosing cheque for £25 deposit on your agreeing to take Mr. Krell's chambers on the third floor at 56A, Pall Mall for the two days, the 26th and 27th June, and I confirm the agreement that you are to have the entire use of these rooms during the days (but not the nights), the balance, £50, to be paid to me on Tuesday next the 24th instant."

The processions not having taken place [on] June 26 and 27, the defendant declined to pay the balance of £50 alleged to be due from him under the contract in writing of June 20 constituted by the above two letters. Hence the present action. Darling J., on August 11, 1902, held, upon the authority of Taylor v. Caldwell, 3 B. & S. 826, and The Moorcock, (1889) 14 P.D. 64, that there was an implied condition in the contract that the procession should take place, and gave judgment for the defendant on the claim and counter-claim. The plaintiff appealed.

VAUGHAN WILLIAMS, L.J. The real question in this case is the extent of the application in English law of the principle of the Roman law which has been adopted and acted on in many English decisions, and notably in the case of Taylor v. Caldwell, 3 B. & S. 826. That case at least makes it clear that "where, from the nature of the contract, it appears that the parties must from the beginning have known that it could not be fulfilled unless, when the time for the fulfillment of the contract arrived, some particular specified thing continued to exist, so that when entering into the contract they must have contemplated such continued existence as the foundation of what was to be done; there, in the absence of any express or implied warranty that the thing shall exist, the contract is not to be considered a positive contract, but as subject to an implied condition that the parties shall be excused in case, before breach, performance becomes impossible from the perishing of the thing without default of the contractor."

* * *

I do not think that [the principle] is limited to cases in which the event causing the impossibility of performance is the destruction or nonexistence of some thing which is the subject-matter of the contract or of some condition or state of things expressly specified as a condition of it. I think that you first have to ascertain, not necessarily from the terms of the contract, but, if required, from necessary inferences, drawn from surrounding circumstances recognized by both contracting parties, what is the substance of the contract, and then to ask the question whether that substantial contract needs for its foundation the assumption of the existence of a particular state of things. If it does, this will limit the operation of the general words, and in such case, if the contract becomes impossible of performance by reason of the nonexistence of the state of things assumed by both contracting parties as the foundation of the contract, there will be no breach of the contract thus limited.

Now what are the facts of the present case? The contract is contained in [the] two letters of June 20. * * * These letters do not mention the coronation, but speak merely of the taking of Mr. Krell's chambers, or, rather, of the use of them. * * * [T]he plaintiff [had] exhibited on his premises, third floor, 56A, Pall Mall, an announcement to the effect that windows to view the Royal coronation procession were to be let, and [defendant] was induced by that announcement to apply to the housekeeper on the premises, who said that the owner was willing to let the suite of rooms for the purpose of seeing the Royal procession for both days, but not nights, of June 26 and 27. In my judgment the use of the rooms was let and taken for the purpose of seeing the Royal procession. It was not a demise of the rooms, or even an agreement to let and take the rooms. It is a license to use rooms for a particular purpose and none other. And in my judgment the taking place of those processions on the days proclaimed along the proclaimed route, which passed 56A, Pall Mall, was regarded by both contracting parties as the foundation of the contract; and I think that it cannot reasonably be supposed to have been in the contemplation of the contracting parties, when the contract was made, that the coronation would not be held on the proclaimed days, or the processions not take place on those days along the proclaimed route. * * *

It was suggested in the course of the argument that if the occurrence, on the proclaimed days, of the coronation and the procession in this case were the foundation of the contract, and if the general words are thereby limited or qualified, so that in the event of the nonoccurrence of the coronation and procession along the proclaimed route they would discharge both parties from further performance of the contract, it would follow that if a cabman was engaged to take some one to Epsom on Derby Day at a suitable enhanced price for such a journey, say £10, both parties to the contract would be discharged in the contingency of the race at Epsom for some reason becoming impossible; but I do not think this follows, for I do not think that in the cab case the happening of the race would be the foundation of the contract. No doubt the purpose of the engager would be to go to see the Derby, and the price would be proportionately high; but the cab had no special qualifications for the purpose which led to the selection of the cab for this particular occasion. Any other cab would have done as well. Moreover, I think that, under the cab contract, the hirer, even if the race went off, could have said, "Drive me to Epsom; I will pay you the agreed sum; you have nothing to do with the purpose for which I hired the cab," and that if the cabman refused he would have been guilty of a breach of contract, there being nothing to qualify his promise to drive the hirer to Epsom on a particular day. Whereas in the case of the coronation, there is not merely the purpose of the hirer to see the coronation procession, but it is the coronation procession and the relative position of the rooms which is the basis of the contract as much for the lessor as the hirer; and I think that if the King, before the coronation day and after the contract, had died, the hirer could not have insisted on having the rooms on the days named. It could not in the cab case be reasonably said that seeing the Derby race was the foundation of the contract. * * * Whereas in the present case, where the rooms were offered and taken, by reason of their peculiar suitability from the position of the rooms for a view of the coronation procession, surely the view of the coronation procession was the foundation of the contract, which is a very different thing from the purpose of the man who engaged the cab—namely, to see the race—being held to be the foundation of the contract. Each case must be judged by its own circumstances. In each case one must ask oneself first, what, having regard to all the circumstances, was the foundation of the contract? Secondly, was the performance of the contract prevented? Thirdly, was the event which prevented the performance of the contract of such a character that it cannot reasonably be said to have been in the contemplation of the parties at the date of the contract? If all these questions are answered in the affirmative (as I think they should be in this case), I think both parties are discharged from further performance of the contract. I think that the coronation procession was the foundation of this contract, and that the non-happening of it prevented the performance of the contract. * * * The test seems to be whether the event which causes the impossibility was or might have been anticipated and guarded against. It seems difficult to say, in a case where both parties anticipate the happening of an event, which anticipation is the foundation of the contract, that either party must be taken to have anticipated, and ought to have guarded against, the event which prevented the performance of the contract. * * *

I myself am clearly of opinion that in this case, where we have to ask ourselves whether the object of the contract was frustrated by the nonhappening of the coronation and its procession on the days proclaimed, parol evidence is admissible to shew that the subject of the contract was rooms to view the coronation procession, and was so to the knowledge of both parties. When once this is established, I see no difficulty whatever in the case. It is not essential to the application of the principle of Taylor v. Caldwell that the direct subject of the contract should perish or fail to be in existence at the date of performance of the contract. It is sufficient if a state of things or condition expressed in the contract and essential to its performance perishes or fails to be in existence at that time. In the present case the condition which fails and prevents the achievement of that which was, in the contemplation of both parties, the foundation of the contract, is not expressly mentioned either as a condition of the contract or the purpose of it; but I think for the reasons which I have given that the principle of Taylor v. Caldwell ought to be applied. This disposes of the plaintiff's claim for £50 unpaid balance of the price agreed to be paid for the use of the rooms. The defendant at one time set up a cross-claim for the return of the £25 he paid at the date of the contract. As that claim is now withdrawn it is unnecessary to say anything about it. I have only to add that the facts of this case do not bring it within the principle laid down in Stubbs v. Holywell Ry. Co., L.R., 2 Ex. 311, that in the case of contracts falling directly within the rule of Taylor v. Caldwell the subsequent impossibility does not affect rights already acquired, because the defendant had the whole of June 24 to pay the balance, and the public announcement that the coronation and processions would not take place on the proclaimed days was made early on the morning of the 24th, and no cause of action could accrue till the end of that day. * * *

Appeal dismissed.

QUESTIONS AND NOTES

1. Questions about the facts of this case

   1.1. At the time of the contract, why did Henry want to hire the flat (British English for rent an apartment)? Did Krell know Henry's purpose?

   1.2. Why did Henry later decide he did not want the use of the flat, but wanted instead to be excused from performing?

2. Questions about the law

   2.1. Just as *Taylor v. Caldwell* is viewed as the first "impossibility" case even though it never uses the word "impossibility," *Krell* is regarded as the first frustration of purpose case even though it never uses the phrase "frustration of purpose." How is frustration of purpose similar to impossibility and impracticability? How is it different?

   2.2. Does this court read *Taylor* correctly?

   2.3. What makes the Epsom Derby hypothetical in the *Krell* opinion different from the facts in *Krell*?

   2.4. In Charlottesville, Virginia, all the hotels jack up their room rates around graduation time, and require a minimum two-day, non-refundable deposit. Six months before graduation, Ponoroff reserves a room in Charlottesville around graduation since he wants to use the UVA law school dean's graduation speech at the Michigan State University College of Law graduation ceremonies the following week. Ponoroff pays the two-day minimum. The day before graduation, a tornado sweeps through the town, leaving a trail of desolation and some disconsolate students—the school cancels graduation. Can Ponoroff get his money back? What if he was traveling to Charlottesville not to attend graduation, but rather to schmooze with Epstein about how Markell isn't pulling his (considerable) weight in writing this book?

3. Notes

3.1. Frustration and Impossibility Compared

> The doctrine of frustration of purpose is nearly identical to the doctrine of impossibility and has been referred to as its "companion rule." The difference is that with the frustration of purpose doctrine, "performance remains possible but the expected value of the performance to the party seeking to be excused has been destroyed" by the supervening event. The third changed circumstances doctrine, impracticability, has been referred to as a "catch-all" for situations where performance is physically possible but would entail a much higher cost than originally expected. As Richard Posner and Andrew Rosenfield have noted, "[t]here is thus no functional distinction between impossibility and frustration cases on the one hand and impracticability cases on the other." With all three doctrines, the central issue concerns the allocation of risk, independent of fault, of the event giving rise to the claim of impossibility, frustration of purpose, or impracticability. The allocation of risk, however, is not always readily determinable.

Nancy Kim, *Mistakes, Changed Circumstances and Intent*, 56 U. KAN. L. REV. 473 (2008).

3.2. Who gets the £25 that Henry paid? What if Henry had paid the full £75 up front? Some hints come from *Facto v. Pantagis*, 390 N.J. Super. 227, 915 A.2d 59 (2007). The plaintiffs there had rented defendant's hall for a wedding reception from 6:00 to 11:00 on Saturday, August 3, 2002. It was hot and muggy that day, and 45 minutes into the reception, the power went out and could not be restored. New Jersey being New Jersey, a fight broke out when the wedding hall owner stopped serving liquor. The cops were called, and when they came "the batteries operating the emergency lights had begun to run out of power, and the only illumination was provided by candelabras on the tables." The police then evacuated the hall.

But the plaintiffs had paid the full price up front, amounting to over $10,000. They sued to get it back. The court found that the force majeure clause excused the hall's performance, but also that "the power failure that relieved the Pantagis Renaissance of the obligation to furnish plaintiffs with a wedding reception also relieved plaintiffs of the obligation to pay the contract price for the reception. Nevertheless, since the Pantagis Renaissance partially performed the contract by starting the reception before the power failure, it is entitled, under principles of quantum meruit, to recover the value of the services it provided to plaintiffs."

4. **You Be the Lawyer!**

You represent a hotel in Las Vegas. New Years is coming up, and people are beginning to book their New Year's room, especially since there has been a lot of publicity about a massive fireworks show to kick off the new year. Problem is, around New Years in Vegas it can get windy, and if it is too windy, officials will call off the show. Management wants you to draft a clause for the hotel's booking contract that would bind guests to pay the premium rates regardless of whether the fireworks go off or not. Can you do it?

---

3. Avoidance of Forfeiture

We have already seen that avoiding forfeiture is a reason for interpreting language as not imposing a condition. Sometimes, the language can only be interpreted as a condition—e.g., "This is language of condition. We really mean it. Cross our hearts and hope to die."

Even where the contract language can only be interpreted as language of condition, there is authority for excusing that condition to avoid forfeiture. For example, section 229 of the *Restatement (Second) of Contracts* provides:

§ 229. Excuse of a Condition to Avoid Forfeiture

To the extent that the non-occurrence of a condition would cause disproportionate forfeiture, a court may excuse the non-occurrence of that condition unless its occurrence was a material part of the agreed exchange.

The *Restatement (Second) of Contracts* also provides this illustration of excuse of a condition to avoid forfeiture:

Illustrations:

1. A contracts to build a house for B, using pipe of Reading manufacture.

In return, B agrees to pay $75,000 in progress payments, each payment to be made "on condition that no pipe other than that of Reading manufacture has been used." Without A's knowledge, a subcontractor mistakenly uses pipe of Cohoes manufacture which is identical in quality and is distinguishable only by the name of the manufacturer which is stamped on it. The mistake is not discovered until the house is completed, when replacement of the pipe will require destruction of substantial parts of the house. B refuses to pay the unpaid balance of $10,000. A court may conclude that the use of Reading rather than Cohoes pipe is so relatively unimportant to B that the forfeiture that would result from denying A the entire balance would be disproportionate, and may allow recovery by A subject to any claim for damages for A's breach of his duty to use Reading pipe.

The next case provides another illustration.

ACME MARKETS, INC. V. FEDERAL ARMORED EXPRESS, INC.

Superior Court of Pennsylvania
437 Pa. Super. 41, 648 A.2d 1218 (1994)

Opinion by HESTER, J.:

Acme Markets, Inc., appeals from the order entered in the Court of Common Pleas of Montgomery County on December 21, 1993, which granted Federal Armored Express, Inc. ("Federal") summary judgment. For the reasons set forth below, we reverse that order and remand the matter for further proceedings.

The procedural history of this case may be summarized as follows. On November 20, 1990, appellant filed a breach of contract complaint against Federal. In that complaint, appellant alleged that the parties had entered into a contract for armored car service and that the agreement later was amended to provide for the timely reimbursement of service-related losses. In addition, appellant averred that a Federal employee was robbed on May 19, 1990, after accepting possession of one of appellant's cashbags. Finally, appellant asserted that even though it had notified Federal promptly of the $62,544.32 loss, Federal had not made the reimbursement required by the agreement. Consequently, appellant requested, among other things, an award of damages equivalent to the amount of the loss.

On September 26, 1991, following the effectuation of service, appellant filed an answer and new matter. In connection with one of the defenses asserted in that document, Federal relied upon the fifth paragraph of the agreement which provides, "Responsibility of Federal under this contract shall begin when said [cash]bags or packages have been accepted and receipted for by Federal or its authorized employees, and shall terminate upon delivery to consignee or upon return to shipper." See Complaint at exhibit A. Specifically, Federal claimed that it bore no responsibility for the loss since neither it nor any of its employees had accepted the bag or provided the necessary receipt prior to the robbery.

On June 30, 1993, claiming that discovery was complete and that an examination of the record revealed no genuine issue of material fact, appellant moved for summary judgment. Federal responded by filing a cross-motion for summary judgment in which it acknowledged that one of its employees possessed appellant's cashbag at the time of the robbery. In addition, Federal noted that neither party disputed the fact that the employee in question had not provided a receipt for the bag prior to its loss. Consequently, relying upon both the fifth paragraph of the agreement and an affidavit demonstrating that the receipt requirement conformed with the custom of the armored car industry, Federal requested the entrance of judgment in its favor. On December 21, 1993, the trial court concluded that the fifth paragraph constituted a condition precedent to Federal's liability under the agreement. Thus, the court denied appellant's summary judgment motion and granted Federal relief. This timely appeal followed.

* * *

Appellant asserts that the trial court erroneously concluded that the fifth paragraph of the agreement constituted a condition precedent to Federal's liability for the lost bag. Specifically, appellant argues that since the paragraph was not labelled a condition precedent and does not contain other language normally associated with such a condition, "there is no means by which to state with the certainty required by Pennsylvania law that it creates a condition precedent." Appellant's brief at 13. We find appellant's claim devoid of merit.

Initially, we note that a condition precedent may be defined as a condition which must occur before a duty to perform under a contract arises. * * * While the parties to a contract need not utilize any particular words to create a condition precedent, an act or event designated in a contract will not be construed as constituting one unless that clearly appears to have been the parties' intention. * * * In addition, we note that the purpose of any condition set forth in a contract must be determined in accordance with the general rules of contractual interpretation. * * * Those rules may be summarized as follows.

> When construing agreements involving clear and unambiguous terms, this Court need only examine the writing itself to give effect to the parties['] understanding. * * * The court must construe the contract only as written and may not modify the plain meaning of the words under the guise of interpretation. * * * When the terms of a written contract are clear, this Court will not re-write it to give it a construction in conflict with the accepted and plain meaning of the language used. * * * Conversely, when the language is ambiguous and the intention of the parties cannot

> be reasonably ascertained from the language of the writing alone, the parol evidence rule does not apply to the admission of oral testimony to show both the intent of the parties and the circumstances attending the execution of the contract. * * *

Creeks v. Creeks, 422 Pa.Super. 432, 435, 619 A.2d 754, 756 (1993).

In the present case, the contested paragraph indicates that Federal's responsibility under the contract "shall begin when bags or packages have been accepted and receipted for by Federal or its employees. * * *" Complaint at exhibit A. Our reading of this plain language demonstrates that it clearly and unambiguously conditions Federal's performance under the contract upon both the acceptance of bags or packages and the granting of a receipt for them. Thus, it unquestionably delineates a condition precedent involving those requirements.

Since we have found that Federal's liability under the contract was subject to a condition precedent and neither party disputes that the receipt portion of the condition remained unfulfilled at the time of the robbery, we must determine whether satisfaction of that requirement may be excused. Apparently arguing that strict application of the condition would be unfair, appellant asserts that the receipt requirement was immaterial and could only be seen as incidental to the far more significant satisfied requirement of possession and acceptance by Federal's employee of appellant's property. See Appellant's brief at 15.

Restatement (Second) of Contracts § 229 discusses the excuse of a condition to avoid unfairness in connection with its strict enforcement. More specifically, that section relates to the excuse of a condition leading to a forfeiture, a term referring to "the denial of compensation that results when the obligee loses his right to the agreed exchange after he has relied substantially, as by preparation or performance on the expectation of that exchange." *Restatement (Second) of Contracts* § 229, comment b. Section 229 provides, "To the extent that the non-occurrence of a condition would cause disproportionate forfeiture, a court may excuse the non-occurrence of that condition unless its occurrence was a material part of the agreed exchange." *Restatement (Second) of Contracts* § 229. Since Pennsylvania law "abhors forfeitures and penalties and enforces them with the greatest reluctance when a proper case is presented[,]" * * * section 229 is consistent with the law of this Commonwealth. * * * Consequently, we will apply it in the present case.

There can be little doubt that the operation of the condition in question will lead to a forfeiture since the condition's nonoccurrence results in the denial of compensation for the loss of a cashbag possessed by Federal for transportation in accordance with the contract. Thus, the question becomes whether the forfeiture would be disproportionate.

> In determining whether the forfeiture is "disproportionate," [the] court must weigh the extent of the forfeiture by the obligee against the importance to the obligor of the risk from which he sought to be protected and the degree to which that protection will be lost if the nonoccurrence of the condition is excused to the extent required to prevent forfeiture.

Restatement (Second) of Contracts § 229, comment b.

In the present case, appellant obviously entered into the armored car service contract so that it would have a secure method of transporting cash and checks to the bank. Strict application of the condition precedent would result in the loss of appellant's ability to recover from Federal for the theft of the bag entrusted to Federal's care. Moreover, we believe that the receipting requirement was intended to provide Federal with proof that it accepted, at a specific time, a certain number of cashbags for shipment. Thus, in our opinion, the requirement probably was little more than an accounting device designed to track bags picked up in accordance with the agreement. Under such circumstances, the receipt primarily would serve to protect Federal rather than Acme from, among other things, theft by its own employees and disputes regarding the number of bags accepted. Those are two risks not at issue herein.

While we believe that the receipt requirement probably was an accounting device which had little impact upon the situation presently at issue, our examination of the certified record reveals that it is devoid of any evidence demonstrating the requirement's actual purpose. Thus, even though we have speculated on the matter, the record is inadequate to determine whether our speculation is accurate. In view of the inadequate record, we may not conduct the critical weighing analysis required by the Restatement or determine whether fulfillment of the condition may be excused. Indeed, we note that the trial court erroneously believed that its analysis ended upon concluding that a receipt was required to fulfill the condition precedent. Thus, the court did not consider whether the forfeiture would be disproportionate, decide if the receipt requirement constituted a material part of the exchange, or require the parties to provide an adequate record either for resolving those issues or deciding whether summary judgment in favor of Federal would be appropriate. Accordingly, we must reverse the trial court's grant of summary judgment and remand the matter for further proceedings.

On remand, the trial court should conduct an evidentiary hearing to determine the purpose of the receipt requirement and engage in the necessary weighing analysis. In addition, the court should determine whether the contested requirement constituted a material part of the agreement.[6] While this determination rests to a large extent on the analysis of the requirement's purpose, it also involves a consideration of the negotiations of the parties along with all other circumstances relevant to the formation of the contract or to the requirement itself, including the circumstances surrounding the theft.[7]

Order reversed. Case remanded for further proceedings. Jurisdiction relinquished.

QUESTIONS

1. Questions about the facts of this case

   1.1. When did the robbery occur? Was it as the cashbags were being loaded? Is this clear, or even relevant?

   1.2. Do you think Acme thought about the order of performance when it signed the agreement? Should it have?

   1.3. Does the contract between Acme and Federal use the word "condition"? What is the "plain language" that "clearly and unambiguously conditions Federal's performance"?

   1.4. The court also tells us: "There can be little doubt that the operation of the condition in question will lead to a forfeiture." What is the "forfeiture"?

2. Questions about the law

   2.1. You represent Federal on remand. What evidence do you introduce? Whom do you interview to get this evidence?

   2.2. If the court is correct about the nature of the contract in footnote 6, would this case be better decided as a contract of adhesion?

3. **You Be the Lawyer!**

   Can you redraft the armored car contract to avoid this type of dispute in the future? Do you need to know the importance of obtaining the receipt?

---

[6] We note that the form on which the requirement appears is pre-printed and does not contain any alterations. Thus, while not dispositive, our examination of that document suggests that the requirement was not specifically bargained-for.

[7] In light of our determination, we do not address appellant's two remaining claims which relate to whether Federal assumed liability for the bag immediately upon obtaining possession of it and whether satisfaction of the condition precedent may be excused since the failure of the condition resulted from the conduct of Federal's own employee.

4. Prevention

This is how *Willison on Contracts* explains prevention as an excuse of a condition:

> When a promisor prevents, hinders, or renders impossible the occurrence of a condition precedent to its promise to perform, or to the performance of a return promise, the promisor is not relieved of the obligation to perform and may not legally terminate the contract for nonperformance. Furthermore, the promisor may not invoke the other party's nonperformance as a defense when it is sued on the contract. In short, under the doctrine of prevention, when a party to a contract causes the failure of the performance of the obligation due, it cannot in any way take advantage of that failure.

13 *Williston on Contracts* § 39:3 (4th ed. 2017 Supp.). That makes sense. You can't prevent your own liability from arising; that's not what the parties bargained for (and it might be illusory if they did).

Here is an easy example of prevention: Epstein contracts to buy Ponoroff's house on January 15th. The contract provides "Payment or other performance by Epstein is expressly conditioned on Epstein's receiving a loan from a financial institution of at least $1,000,000." Notwithstanding his immense wealth from sales of this book, Epstein is unable to obtain a loan because each time he visits a financial institution, he is wearing his Spider-Man suit, muttering "With great power comes great responsibility." Prevention, right?

Let's be sure that we (you) understand the legal significance of "prevention" of the occurrence of a condition—of elimination of the excuse of non-occurrence of the condition. If Epstein does not perform—does not pay Ponoroff $1,000,000 for his house on January 15th—Ponoroff could recover from Epstein for breach of contract. Epstein has no excuse—his excuse based on non-occurrence of the loan condition has been extinguished because the loan condition itself has been extinguished by Epstein's "prevention."

The next case is a more realistic example of prevention (albeit less memorable and much longer than the Epstein in a Spider-Man suit example).

QUESTIONS BEFORE THE CASE

1. What was the subject matter of the contract?
2. What did SNAP argue regarding whether the condition to its performance had occurred?

COX V. SNAP, INC.

United States Court of Appeals, Fourth Circuit
859 F.3d 304 (4th Cir. 2017)

DIANA GRIBBON MOTZ, CIRCUIT JUDGE:

In this diversity action for breach of contract, SNAP, Inc. appeals from the grant of summary judgment to Curtis Cox. The district court concluded that SNAP breached its contract with Cox by refusing to repurchase stock options the contract granted to him and awarded Cox $637,867.42 in damages, the full value of his options plus interest. On appeal, SNAP argues that the contract itself did not convey options to Cox but merely included an executory promise to issue those options, which SNAP never in fact issued. SNAP also challenges the calculation of damages. For the reasons that follow, we affirm the judgment of the district court.

I.

In 2006, SNAP, a Virginia corporation, sought to expand its business in the field of federal procurement by contracting with Curtis Cox, a Maryland resident and the president of C^2 Technologies, an established government contracting firm. On January 12, 2006, the parties executed a memorandum of understanding in which Cox agreed "to promote and market [SNAP] in exchange for obtaining an equity stake" in the company. For purposes of this appeal, there is no dispute that the memorandum constitutes a binding contract.

Under the terms of this contract, Cox and C^2 Technologies agreed to provide various forms of assistance to SNAP. Among other things, they agreed to use their best efforts to help SNAP obtain specific contracts, to consider SNAP for any potential leads, and to provide SNAP with approximately $240,000 worth of marketing support and assistance.

In return, the contract provides that "[o]n January 12, 2006," the same day the parties executed the contract, SNAP "will issue a non-qualified stock option to Mr. Cox granting him the right to purchase 308 shares, representing five (5%) percent of the total authorized shares of stock of [SNAP]." The contract announces SNAP's intention to execute a stock split, under which Cox's options would increase proportionally. It gives SNAP the right to re-purchase Cox's options at any time after January 1, 2008 and gives Cox the right to require SNAP to repurchase his options—a "put option"—any time after January 1, 2011. The repurchase price is payable to Cox "over a five-year period with interest at the then current prime rate."

Cox attempted to exercise his put option on March 18, 2011 in a letter to SNAP President Navneet Gupta. The parties discussed but never came to a resolution regarding Cox's request. On October 6, 2015, Cox sent Gupta a second letter demanding that SNAP pay him the full value of his options. On October 9, 2015, Gupta replied that "[SNAP] owes you nothing."

A month later, in November 2015, Cox filed suit for breach of contract against SNAP in Virginia state court. SNAP removed the case to the district court for the Eastern District of Virginia. After removal, Cox filed an amended complaint alleging breach of contract for failure to repurchase, breach of contract for failure to issue his options, and quantum meruit.

In August 2016, the parties filed cross-motions for summary judgment. SNAP contended that the contract did not grant Cox any stock options but merely memorialized SNAP's promise to issue the options in the future. As such, issuing the options was a condition precedent to its obligation to repurchase those options from Cox. In support of its interpretation of the contract, SNAP relied on the future-tense language in the contract's key terms, particularly the phrase "*will issue* a non-qualified stock option" in paragraph 1, along with references to the "necessary documentation" SNAP would prepare after the parties executed the contract.

* * * Cox argued that, under the prevention doctrine, SNAP waived any such condition precedent by refusing to issue the stock options.

The district court granted summary judgment to Cox. The court reasoned that the plain language of the contract showed that SNAP issued the stock options to Cox and that the contract did not require any further steps as a condition precedent before those options issued. * * * Applying the contract's formula for calculating the value of Cox's options and the interest owed, the court awarded Cox a total of $637,867.42 in damages. SNAP timely noted this appeal. * * *

II.

We turn first to liability. The parties dispute whether the contract itself conveyed stock options to Cox or merely obligated SNAP to issue those options at some point in the future.

If, as Cox maintains, the contract conveyed stock options to him, SNAP clearly breached the contract by refusing to repurchase them when Cox exercised his put option. For there is no dispute that Cox otherwise exercised his put option in accordance with the terms of the agreement, and SNAP has not preserved any defense for its refusal to repurchase Cox's options.

However, SNAP maintains that the contract did not convey stock options to Cox. Rather, according to SNAP, in the contract it merely *promised* to issue stock options to Cox, and the contract therefore made the issuance of stock options a condition precedent to SNAP's obligation to repurchase those options. SNAP contends that because it never issued those options, it never incurred the obligation to repurchase them from Cox. SNAP maintains that its refusal to issue the stock options was the only conceivable basis for Cox's lawsuit, and the limitations period for this claim expired well before November 2015, when Cox filed his initial complaint in state court. Thus, in SNAP's view, the statute of limitations bars Cox's only potentially meritorious claim.

SNAP has taken a self-defeating position. Even if issuing the stock options was a condition precedent to SNAP's obligation to repurchase, SNAP has excused that condition by breaching its promise to issue the options, and so the prevention doctrine dooms its case. Under the prevention doctrine, "if a promisor prevents or hinders fulfillment of a condition to his performance, the condition may be waived or excused." *Moore Bros. Co. v. Brown & Root, Inc.*, 207 F.3d 717, 725 (4th Cir. 2000) (applying Virginia law); *see also* Restatement (Second) of Contracts § 245 (Am. Law Inst. 1981); Richard A. Lord, Williston on Contracts § 39:7 (4th ed.), Westlaw (database updated May 2017). For the prevention doctrine to apply, Cox need only show that SNAP materially contributed to the non-occurrence of the condition. *See Moore*, 207 F.3d at 725.

Virginia has recognized the prevention doctrine for many decades. In *Parrish v. Wightman*, the Supreme Court of Virginia adopted the following formulation of the rule:

> Where a contract is performable on the occurrence of a future event there is an implied agreement that the promisor will place no obstacle in the way of the happening of such event, *particularly where it is dependent in whole or in part on his own act*; and, where he prevents the fulfillment of a condition precedent or its performance by the adverse party, he cannot rely on such condition to defeat his liability.

184 Va. 86, 34 S.E.2d 229, 232 (1945) (emphasis added) (quoting 17 C.J.S. Contracts § 468 [now § 707]). Under *Parrish*, the relevant inquiry is whether a condition precedent failed to occur "because of any fault upon the part of the [promisor]." *Id.*

SNAP controlled whether the stock options issued, and, even under its own interpretation, it had a contractual obligation to issue those options. By refusing to do so, SNAP plainly forfeited its right to rely on their issuance as an unfulfilled condition precedent to its obligation to repurchase Cox's options. When a condition in a contract fails to occur solely because a party breached one of its other obligations in the very same contract, there is no doubt that the party caused the non-occurrence for the purposes of the prevention doctrine. As the Restatement explains:

> Where a duty of one party is subject to the occurrence of a condition, the additional duty of good faith and fair dealing imposed on him . . . may require some cooperation on his part, either by refraining from conduct that will prevent or hinder the occurrence of that condition *or by taking affirmative steps to cause*

> *its occurrence.... The rule stated in this Section only applies, however, where the lack of cooperation constitutes a breach, either of a duty imposed by the terms of the agreement itself or of a duty imposed by a term supplied by the court.* There is no breach if the risk of such a lack of cooperation was assumed by the other party or if the lack of cooperation is justifiable.

Restatement (Second) of Contracts § 245 cmt. a (Am. Law Inst. 1981) (emphasis added). This comports with the Supreme Court of Virginia's reasoning in *Parrish* that the implied agreement not to impede the occurrence of a condition applies particularly when the occurrence or non-occurrence of the condition depends entirely on the promisor's own conduct. *See Parrish*, 34 S.E.2d at 232.

* * *

SNAP . . . argues that the prevention doctrine applies only when a party affirmatively obstructs a condition from occurring, not when it merely refrains from bringing the condition about. This asserted limitation does not stand up to scrutiny. Indeed, the lone opinion on which SNAP relies is unreported and bears no resemblance to the facts of this case. *Charlie Norfolk Ctr. Assocs., L.P. v. Norfolk Redevelopment & Hous. Auth.*, 285 Fed.Appx. 80 (4th Cir. 2008). And it simply reiterates that "a condition precedent to a contract is excused when the promisor *prevents or hinders* the occurrence of the condition, and the condition would have occurred in the absence of such prevention or hindrance." *Id.* at 84 n.7 (emphasis added). Both the Supreme Court of Virginia and the Restatement have made clear that a promisor prevents or hinders the occurrence of a condition when it wrongfully refuses to cooperate, either by actively interfering with the occurrence of a condition or by withholding cooperation the promisor was obligated to give.

Accordingly, when a party materially contributes to the non-occurrence of a condition precedent by failing to bring that condition about, the condition is excused if the party's inaction is wrongful under the circumstances. Violation of a contractual duty is plainly wrongful for the purposes of the prevention doctrine. *See* Restatement (Second) of Contracts § 245 cmt. a (Am. Law Inst. 1981). Here, even assuming SNAP's reading of the contract is correct, there is no doubt that SNAP had an obligation to bring about the condition it now tries to hide behind. Because it refused to do so with no justification or excuse, the prevention doctrine applies. *See NLRB v. Local 554, Graphic Commc'ns Int'l Union*, 991 F.2d 1302, 1307–08 (7th Cir. 1993) (excusing a condition precedent that an international union approve a collective bargaining agreement because the local union failed to seek such approval).

Thus, even if we read the contract as merely incorporating a promise to issue stock options, SNAP cannot avoid liability to Cox. * * *

IV.

For the foregoing reasons, the judgment of the district court is *AFFIRMED.*

QUESTIONS

1. Questions about the facts of this case

   1.1. What is a stock option? When is a stock option valuable?

   1.2. What was the condition that the court deemed waived?

2. Questions about the law

   2.1. Do you want to listen to the oral argument in this case? https://player.fm/series/oral-arguments-for-the-court-of-appeals-for-the-fourth-circuit/curtis-cox-v-snap-inc. Spoiler alert: it did not go too well for SNAP's counsel.

   2.2. The court states that SNAP's argument is "self-defeating." Is it right?

   2.3. What does the court mean by citing *Restatement* § 245? What does the duty of good faith and fair dealing have to do with this contract?

3. **You Be the Lawyer!**

   You represent SNAP, and the day after the contract in this case was signed, you ask the client whether they issued the stock options. The client just shrugs her shoulders, and says, "You're the lawyer, ace. We know we promised to issue the options, but do we have to do anything more?" Answer her question.

---

5. Non-Occurrence of a Post-Formation Constructive Condition of Exchange

As we have seen, in every bilateral contract there are usually at least two obligations. Each party makes a promise to the other; if Epstein and Ponoroff agree that Epstein will sell Ponoroff his prized collection of road-kill recipes, Epstein has an obligation to transfer the recipes and Ponoroff has the duty to pay for them.

What's the timing of each party's performance? Does Epstein hold his recipes in one hand high in the air over Ponoroff's head (Epstein's taller, at least in physical stature) while extending the palm of his other hand towards Ponoroff to accept the payment? Does Ponoroff adopt a like stature? In short, who has to perform first and take the risk that the other will not honor his promise? And if the contract doesn't specify who does what when, is that an excuse for the non-performance by a party?

If the parties thought about it, conditions would be a nice way to order things. They would seem to be tailor-made for regulating this type of exchange. The contract could say (as do contracts to buy airline tickets, for example), that one party pays (performs) first, and then (and only then) after that performance, does the other side have to perform.

For some reason, many contracts don't specify an order of performance. Shouldn't the common law, à la Cardozo and Lady Lucy, imply such conditions? As we'll see, it finally came around to that point, but it took some time. In the early case of *Nichols v. Raynbred*, Hobart 88, 80 Eng. Rep. 238 (K.B. 1615), for example, the parties had agreed to buy and sell a cow. The plaintiff sued the defendant for the price of cow, some 50 shillings. The defendant defended on the basis that the plaintiff never had alleged delivery of the cow.

Surprisingly, at least to us now, the court ruled for the plaintiff. It saw two independent promises, each supporting the other. As the parties had not provided directions as to who was to do what when, the court was not going to fill the void. Plaintiff won.

The law evolved after *Nichols*. By 1772 (157 years later), the Court of King's Bench, speaking through inestimable Lord Mansfield, switched gears. In *Kingston v. Preston*, 2 Douglas 689, 99 Eng. Rep. 437 (K.B. 1773), a silk seller proposed to sell his business. The buyer agreed to pay the purchase price over time, but also agreed to provide security for his promise to pay. Oh, and part of the deal was that the buyer was going to run the business out of the seller's house. When time came to transfer the stock of the business, the buyer had not obtained adequate security, but, relying on Nichols, contended that there were two, independent promises: the seller's to transfer the goods, and the buyer's to give security. One did not depend on the other. The buyer thus sued as plaintiff to force the transfer of the goods (and the right to do business in the seller's house).

Balderdash, said Lord Mansfield.* "[I]t would be the greatest injustice if the plaintiff should prevail: the essence of the agreement was, that the defendant should not trust to the personal security of the plaintiff, but before he delivered up his stock and business, should have good security for the payment of the money. The giving such security, therefore, must necessarily be a condition precedent."**

* Or whatever 18th Century expletive you choose.

** Another version of the case (there were no official reports back then) uses stronger language:

> It would be the most monstrous case in the world, if the argument on the side of Mr. Buller's client was to prevail. It's of the very essence of the agreement, that the defendant will not trust the personal security [the promise alone] of the plaintiff. A Court of Justice is to say, that by operation of law he shall, against his teeth. He is to let him into his

Thereafter, promises of payment by the buyer and of delivery by the seller came to be dependent upon each other through the use of court-supplied assumptions called constructive conditions of exchange. In the next case, the contract does not supply express conditions regulating who does what when. What does the court do instead?

QUESTIONS BEFORE THE CASE

1. When did Haight technically pay off his debt?
2. What is a "deed of trust"? What does it mean to "reconvey" such a deed?

BRINTON V. HAIGHT

Idaho Court of Appeals
125 Idaho 324, 870 P.2d 677, 25 UCC Rep.Serv.2d 485 (1994)

LANSING, JUDGE.

This is an action brought by respondents James R. Brinton and Patricia J. Brinton to recover on a promissory note and to foreclose a deed of trust which secures the note. The makers of the note, G. W. Haight and W. Dea Haight, appeal the district court's award of attorney fees and costs and of prejudgment interest accrued after the Haights had tendered payment of the full balance owed on the note. We conclude that the tender of full payment, made approximately seven months prior to commencement of this action and twenty-six months before judgment, halted further accrual of interest on the note and precluded the assessment of costs and attorney fees against the Haights. Therefore, we remand for modification of the judgment.

I. BACKGROUND

In 1983 the Haights purchased a parcel of real property from the Brintons. Part of the purchase price was payable in installments under terms of a promissory note in the amount of $64,500. The note was secured by a deed of trust under which Pioneer Title Co., Coeur d'Alene ("Pioneer") was trustee and the Brintons were beneficiaries. By a separate agreement, Pioneer also was designated to act as escrow holder to receive payments on the promissory note and transfer such payments to the Brintons or their assignee.

---

house to squander every thing there, without any thing to rely on but what he has absolutely refused to trust. This payment, therefore, was a precedent condition before the covenant of putting into possession was to be performed on the part of the defendant.

Jones v. Barkley, 2 Douglas 684, 99 Eng. Rep. 434 (K.B. 1781).

About one week prior to November 9, 1990, the Haights telephoned Pioneer and asked the amount of the payoff balance on the note. On Friday, November 9, 1990, at approximately 12:00 p.m. Mr. Haight called Pioneer again, and informed a Pioneer employee that he would be coming in to pay the note that day. Mr. Haight arrived at Pioneer at approximately 4:00 p.m. and, after being informed that the payoff amount was $53,272.80, began to write a personal check for that sum. Pioneer's escrow supervisor informed Mr. Haight that Pioneer would not accept a personal check and required a cashier's check instead. Mr. Haight then left Pioneer's office but returned several minutes later with a cashier's check for the $53,272.80. He delivered the cashier's check to the escrow supervisor and requested delivery of a trustee's reconveyance deed. The escrow supervisor stated that she could not immediately give a reconveyance deed but that it would be ready the following business day. Finding it unsatisfactory to leave the cashier's check without receiving a reconveyance deed that would remove the encumbrance from his property, Mr. Haight then took back the check after it had been in the escrow supervisor's possession for less than ten minutes.

Over the weekend, the Haights examined the escrow statement provided by Pioneer and determined that the quoted payoff balance included both a $20.00 "payoff fee" and a $28.00 "reconveyance charge." The Haights concluded that neither the escrow agreement nor the deed of trust provided that the Haights were responsible for these charges and, therefore, they should not be required to pay them.[1]

On Tuesday, November 13,[2] Mr. Haight delivered a letter to Pioneer regarding these fees and what he considered to have been the course of conduct to that time. In this letter, Mr. Haight asserted that it was the duty of the beneficiary to furnish a deed of reconveyance under Idaho law and, therefore, he was not obligated to pay the $28.00 reconveyance fee. He further believed himself obligated to pay only one-half of any escrow fees. In his letter Mr. Haight offered to pay to Pioneer by personal check $53,233.80 (principal and interest through November 9 plus $11.00 for escrow fees) if Pioneer would agree to reconvey the premises without the payment of the $28.00 fee. The letter also stated that the reconveyance need not be immediate but within the normal business practice of Pioneer and after the personal check cleared the payor bank. Mr. Haight also

---

1 The deed of trust provided:

> Upon written request of Beneficiary stating that all sums secured hereby have been paid, and upon surrender of the Deed and said note to Trustee for cancellation and retention and *upon payment of its fees,* Trustee shall reconvey, without warranty, the property then held hereunder. (emphasis added).

The deed of trust did not specify the amount of the fee that the trustee could charge nor which party was to pay it.

2 Due to the Veterans' Day Holiday, the next business day after November 9, 1990 was Tuesday, November 13.

offered to pay the same amount by cashier's check, conditioned, however, upon simultaneous delivery of a deed of reconveyance. Apparently in response to this letter, an agent of Pioneer called Mr. Haight and discussed the matter. Although it appears that as a result of this conversation Pioneer agreed to waive the $20.00 payoff fee and $3.00 of the reconveyance fee, Pioneer insisted on receiving a $2.00 escrow fee and a $25.00 reconveyance fee before executing a reconveyance.

On November 14, 1990, Pioneer sent a letter to the Haights explaining that the amount due on the note now included additional interest accrued since November 9, 1990, at a rate of $15.639 per day, bringing the balance to $53,318.63. Pioneer advised that when it received a cashier's check for this amount plus any further accrued interest, it would deliver escrowed documents in compliance with the escrow agreement, but that Pioneer would not prepare a reconveyance deed due to the Haights' refusal to pay the reconveyance fee. The letter further stated that Pioneer was resigning as trustee and that appointment of a new trustee would be necessary in order to accomplish any reconveyance. The letter expressed Pioneer's view that it was not responsible to make arrangements to collect the reconveyance fee.

The Haights thereafter made no payments on the note, although they assert they remained at all times ready, willing and able to remit the November 9, 1990, payoff amount. More than six months after Pioneer resigned, the Brintons appointed a successor trustee.

On June 10, 1991, the Brintons filed this action seeking a judgment for the unpaid principal balance of the promissory note plus interest accrued through date of judgment, and also requesting judicial foreclosure of the deed of trust. On January 6, 1993, following a court trial, the district court awarded judgment for the full amount requested by the Brintons. The judgment included interest in the amount of approximately $12,200 that had accrued at the rate of $15.639 per day from the Haights' tender on November 9, 1990, through the date of judgment. The district court also awarded to the Brintons costs and attorney fees totalling approximately $5,000. The Haights have paid the judgment, but also brought this appeal, asserting that the award of interest accrued after November 9, 1990, and the award of costs and attorney fees were improper.

Thus has a $17,000 conflict grown from the inability of the Haights, Pioneer and the Brintons to resolve a disagreement over a $25.00 fee and three days' interest.

The Haights acknowledge that they are liable for the principal and interest accrued through November 9, 1990. However, they maintain that when they offered to pay the full balance on November 9, 1990, they properly tendered the amount due and that such tender stopped the accrual of interest after that date. The Brintons respond that the Haights unreasonably conditioned their tender upon immediate receipt of a deed of reconveyance and that they withdrew the tender when Pioneer could not immediately comply.

The district court, ruling in favor of the Brintons, found that the Haights had placed an unreasonable condition upon their tender and that Pioneer was never placed in effective control of the funds. The court concluded that proper tender was never made and the Haights consequently were not excused from payment of interest accruing after November 9, 1990.

On appeal, our inquiry is three-fold. First, was an adequate tender physically made by the Haights? Second, was the condition imposed by the Haights-contemporaneous delivery of a deed of reconveyance-one upon which they could rightfully condition their tender? And third, if a valid tender was made on November 9, 1990, was it subsequently kept good?

* * *

III. ANALYSIS

A. PHYSICAL TENDER

We begin with recognition that if the Haights made a proper tender of full payment on November 9 and kept the tender good, that tender discharged them from liability for interest accrued thereafter. Under common law, proper tender of the full amount of a debt, including then-accrued interest, terminates the running of contractual interest. *McClellan v. Davis,* 45 Idaho 541, 550, 263 P. 1002, 1005 (1928); *Machold v. Farnan,* 20 Idaho 80, 89, 92, 117 P. 408, 411, 412 (1911); Osborne, Nelson & Whitman, Real Estate Finance Law, § 6.5 at 385–386 (1979). Richard A. Lord, 1 Williston On Contracts § 21–12 (4th ed. 1990).

* * *

Therefore, the threshold issue in this case is whether the Haights made a proper "tender." Our Supreme Court has defined "tender" as:

> [T]he unconditional offer of a debtor to the creditor of the amount of his debt. This means the real amount of the debt as fixed by the law, and the purpose of the law of tender is to enable the debtor to relieve himself of interest and costs and to relieve his property of encumbrance by offering his creditor all that he has any right to claim. This does not mean that the debtor must offer an amount beyond reasonable dispute, but it means the amount due,-actually due.

Dohrman v. Tomlinson, 88 Idaho 313, 318, 399 P.2d 255, 258 (1965) *quoting Kelley v. Clark,* 23 Idaho 1, 12, 129 P. 921, 924 (1912). *See also Wooten v. Dahlquist,* 42 Idaho 121, 127, 244 P. 407, 409 (1926).

In *Pollard Oil Company v. Christensen,* 103 Idaho 110, 645 P.2d 344 (1982), our Supreme Court further explained that the offer to pay must be accompanied by a manifest present ability to pay.

> Tender implies the physical act of offering the money or thing to be tendered, but this cannot rest in implication alone. The law requires an actual, present, physical offer; it is not satisfied by a mere spoken offer to pay, which, although indicative of present possession of the money and intention to produce it, is unaccompanied by any visible manifestation of intention to make the offer good.

Id. at 116, 645 P.2d at 350.

A treatise writer defines tender as "an offer to perform a condition or obligation coupled with the present ability of immediate performance, so that were it not for the refusal of cooperation by the party to whom tender is made, the condition or obligation would be immediately satisfied." Walter H.E. Jaeger, 15 Williston On Contracts § 1808 at 418 (3d ed. 1972).

Here the Haights offered on November 9 to pay the full amount of the debt plus, unbeknownst to the Haights, a sum covering the subsequently disputed reconveyance fee. They demonstrated the present ability and intent to effectuate payment by presenting a cashier's check to Pioneer. Therefore, under the foregoing criteria, the Haights made an adequate physical tender of full satisfaction of the debt on November 9.

B. CONDITION IMPOSED ON THE TENDER

The Haights' tender would be sufficient to preclude further accrual of interest unless the tender was invalidated by the Haights' express condition that the deed of trust be contemporaneously reconveyed. Accordingly, we must next determine how that condition affected the validity of the tender.

Although as a general matter a tender must be unconditioned, a party may attach as a condition that upon which he or she has a right to insist. *Woods v. Dixon,* 193 Or. 681, 240 P.2d 520 (1952); *Jaynes v. Heron,* 46 N.M. 431, 130 P.2d 29, 33–34 (1942); *Lowe v. Harmon,* 167 Or. 128, 115 P.2d 297 (1941). Thus, where the parties' performances under a contract are due simultaneously, a tender may be accompanied by a demand for performance. 5 Walter H.E. Jaeger, Williston On Contracts § 666A (3d Ed. 1961); *Restatement (Second) of Contracts* § 238, cmt. b, § 234 cmt. c, illus. 6 (1979). However, if the condition is improper, the tender is ineffective and the tenderee need not accept. 74 Am.Jur.2d *Tender* § 24 (1974).

In the instant case, the district court found that upon being informed that he could not receive a deed of reconveyance on November 9, 1990, Mr. Haight requested the return of his cashier's check. The only testimony relating to the request for reconveyance by Mr. Haight on November 9,

1990, was that of Mr. Haight himself. He testified that after giving the check to the escrow supervisor, he inquired about a reconveyance and, upon being told that one would not be available because there was no one presently in the office with authority to sign, he stated:

> Well, if you're not prepared to give me my deed, I believe I'm entitled to the deed, and if you're not prepared to give it to me, then I want to take my check back. And when you call and tell me that the deed is ready, I will come down here and I will give you the check in exchange for my deed of reconveyance.

This testimony indicates that the condition imposed by Haight on his tender was one of contemporaneous exchange of the cashier's check for the deed of reconveyance. He did not withdraw the tender upon learning that he would not receive the reconveyance immediately but, rather, made clear that he would release the check as soon as the reconveyance could be delivered in exchange. This intent was confirmed by Mr. Haight's November 13 letter where he stated that he remained ready to deliver payment of principal, interest through November 9, and the undisputed escrow fees in exchange for a reconveyance deed. Therefore, we must determine whether, by conditioning his tender upon simultaneous delivery of a reconveyance deed, Haight caused the tender to be ineffective to terminate the accrual of interest on the debt.

We note first that [under Idaho statutory law] the Haights were indisputably entitled to a deed of reconveyance upon satisfaction of the note secured by the deed of trust. * * * There remains a question as to whether they could rightfully insist upon a *contemporaneous* exchange of their payment and the reconveyance deed, or whether the Haights were required to first make the payment and then wait to receive the deed sometime thereafter.

* * *

This rule that tender of payment may be conditioned upon contemporaneous release of security for the debt is merely an application of the general rule that:

> Where all or part of the performances to be exchanged under an exchange of promises are due simultaneously, it is a condition of each party's duties to render such performance that the other party either render or, with manifested present ability to do so, offer performance of his part of the simultaneous exchange.

Restatement (Second) of Contracts § 238 at 223 (1979); *see also* Lord, 1 Williston On Contracts § 11–21 at 407 (4th ed. 1990). On the subject of concurrent conditions, it is stated in Jaeger, 5 Williston on Contracts § 666A (3d ed. 1961):

> If two persons are bound to give concurrently, one a book and the other the price, neither party will be liable until performance has either been made or tendered by the other. But though the tender may be absolute, it need be only conditional, that is, subject to receiving concurrent performance from the other side.

Accordingly, we conclude that a grantor of a deed of trust may condition a tender of full payment upon the contemporaneous delivery of a deed of reconveyance, and that such condition does not vitiate the tender's effectiveness to terminate the accrual of interest.

The tenderer is not required to relinquish physical possession of the monies tendered without such a contemporaneous return of the collateral. If the law were otherwise, the right to make the tender conditional would be annulled. Therefore, the district court's focus on the fact that Pioneer only had the check in its possession for approximately ten minutes and that Pioneer's internal policy required that payments be posted and numerous procedures followed before reconveyance would occur is incorrect for, absent a reconveyance deed, Mr. Haight was not obligated to release the check to Pioneer at all. * * *

IV. CONCLUSION

A tender of payment sufficient to stop the running of interest was made by the Haights on Friday, November 9, 1990. The condition imposed by the Haights that Pioneer execute a deed of reconveyance simultaneously with delivery of the check did not vitiate the tender. The Haights' subsequent refusal to pay to Pioneer's charges for reconveyance did not act as a withdrawal of the tender made on November 9, 1990.

This case is remanded with instructions to the district court to modify the judgment by deleting the award of prejudgment interest accrued after November 9, 1990, and the award of attorney fees and costs. The judgment as so modified is affirmed. Costs on appeal to appellants.

Walters, C.J., and Perry, J., concur.

QUESTIONS AND NOTE

1. Questions about the facts of this case

    1.1. What is the connection between Pioneer and Haight?

    1.2. When did Haight make the tender? Did he intend to pay the disputed charges with the cashier's check at that time?

    1.3. Why did Haight care about the deed of reconveyance? Of what benefit was that to him?

2. Questions about the law

   2.1. The court's last quotation from *Williston* contains the following sentence: "But though the tender may be absolute, it need be only conditional, that is, subject to receiving concurrent performance from the other side." So you can have a conditional absolute? Does that make any sense?

   2.2. As you might expect, the Uniform Commercial Code has something to say on this subject. Section 2–507(1) of the Uniform Commercial Code states:

   > Tender of delivery is a condition to the buyer's duty to accept the goods and, unless otherwise agreed, to his duty to pay for them.

   Section 2–511(1) of the Uniform Commercial Code states:

   > Unless otherwise agreed tender of payment is a condition to the seller's duty to tender and complete any delivery.

   Does this set up concurrent conditions? See Comment 2 to Section 2–511.

3. Note

Is all performance concurrent? Of course not. When you fly, you always pay first, and fly later. Your performance comes first, and then the airline performs (if you're lucky). Also, this is Contracts, the study of *consensual* obligations. The parties can *always* vary the order of performance in their contract. This was the issue in *Pullman, Comley, Bradley and Reeves v. Tuck-It-Away, Bridgeport, Inc.*, 28 Conn. App. 460, 611 A.2d 435 (1992). There, the parties had entered into a valid contract to buy real property, but the buyer could not get its financing together. After postponing the closing several times, the buyer was facing an immovable closing date without the money to close. If it did not close, it stood to lose a substantial deposit. Just before the closing date, the buyer's attorney found what he thought were defects in title, and based on these alleged defects, the buyer tried to cancel the contract. The benefit of cancellation is that the buyer would get its deposit back. Due to its cancellation, the buyer failed to show up at the scheduled closing. So did the seller.

But the defects turned out to be either non-existent or immaterial. The buyer then pointed out that the seller didn't show up at the closing either, and since the law was that each side's performance was a concurrent condition to the other's performance, the seller's failure to appear meant that the buyer's obligation to pay never matured. The court, however, looked at the contract, and thought differently: "Here, paragraph 4 of the contract provided: "At the closing, *on payment of the purchase price as provided above,* the seller shall deliver and the buyer shall accept, a full covenant Warranty deed * * *" This language indicates that the parties agreed that the performances would not be rendered simultaneously, but rather that [the buyer's] duty to perform would be a condition precedent to [seller's] obligation to tender and convey title." Result? The contract required the buyer to show up first and pay, and since it didn't, it lost the case and its $100,000 deposit. Ouch.

4. **You Be the Lawyer!**

   If you represented Pioneer, what type of clause would you put in the escrow agreement regarding tender of payment to avoid this type of silliness?

EXPRESS VS. CONSTRUCTIVE CONDITIONS

There is an interplay between implied conditions designed to regulate the order of performance such as the court found in *Haight*, and express conditions, which attempt to do the same. That interplay was analyzed in *MXL Indust., Inc. v. Mulder*, 252 Ill.App.3d 18, 623 N.E.2d 369, 191 Ill. Dec.124 (1993). There, a lease had an early termination clause; the tenant could leave early upon the condition that it paid "all sums then due" plus four months' rent. This is the clause:

> (a) The term of this Lease shall be for a period of five (5) years commencing on the 1st day of March, 1987 and ending on the 29th day of February, 1992 (hereinafter referred to as 'the term of this Lease'). Notwithstanding the foregoing provisions of this Subsection 1 (a), at any time after the 29th day of February, 1988, Lessee may terminate this Lease by paying to Lessor all sums then due pursuant to the provisions of this Lease and an additional sum equal to four (4) months' rent specified in Section 2 hereof. If Lessee exercises such right, the term of this Lease shall end on the date on which Lessor receives such payment from Lessor [sic].

The tenant tried to exercise this option on February 28, 1988, by tendering $11,400, the amount of four months' rent (less a credit for a security deposit), and by vacating the premises. The landlord, however, correctly pointed out that one of the obligations of the lease were that, upon vacating the premises, the tenant was to repair certain damage. The parties debated the exact amount of this obligation for two months, and finally agreed it was $2,000. When the tenant sent a check for that amount along with a check for four months' rent, the landlord rejected it, contending that the tenant owed rent for the two months during which the parties negotiated the settlement. The tenant disagreed, and contended that it had met the condition, or at least substantially met the condition, allowing it to terminate early by its February 28 tender. In response, the court said:

> Illinois courts define a condition precedent as one which must be performed either before a contract becomes effective or which is to be performed by one party to an existing contract before the other party is obligated to perform. * * * The satisfaction of a condition is generally subject to the rule of strict compliance. * * * Professor Williston explains, " 'since an express condition * * * depends for its validity on the manifested intention of the parties, it has the same sanctity as the promise itself. Though the court may regret the harshness of such a condition, as it may regret the harshness of a promise, it must, nevertheless, generally enforce the will of the parties.' " * * * A party seeking the benefit of a condition precedent, however, may waive strict compliance by conduct indicating that strict compliance with the provision will not be required. * * *
>
> Distinctly different, although analogous to the concept of a condition, are constructive conditions of exchange. The concept of constructive conditions of exchange was developed by the courts in order to allow the court to supply terms under which a party's duties to perform are conditioned on the performance to be given in return. * * * The purpose of constructive conditions of exchange is to play an integral role in assuring the parties to a bilateral contract that they will actually receive the performance that they have been promised. * * * A common application of the concept occurs when one party seeks to justify its own refusal to perform on the ground that the other party has committed a breach of the contract. In sum, the doctrine serves the salutary purpose of assuring each party to a bilateral contract that it will receive the promised return performance, and it expresses a judicial preference for dependent promises. * * *
>
> Because constructive conditions of exchange invoked the concept that one party's duty to perform was conditioned on the other party's performance, the need arose to ameliorate the rule of strict compliance ordinarily applied to express conditions. As explained by Professor Farnsworth, "the doctrine evolved that if one party's performance is a constructive condition of the other party's duty, only 'substantial performance' is required of the first party before that party can recover under the contract." (E. Farnsworth, Farnsworth on Contracts § 12, at 415 (1990).) Farnsworth further notes, however, that "the flexible requirement of substantial performance stands in sharp contrast to the requirement of strict compliance that protects a party that has taken the precaution of making its duty expressly conditional." (E.

> Farnsworth, Farnsworth on Contracts § 12, at 415 (1990).) Stated differently, the doctrine does not address substantial performance of a condition; rather, it focuses on substantial performance by one party of its obligations arising out of an agreed exchange of performances. * * * Accordingly, an express condition precedent, unless otherwise excused, operates by agreement of the parties to define the satisfaction of a necessary antecedent to a party's performance under the contract and is subject to the rule of strict compliance, unless such compliance is waived. In contrast, constructive or implied conditions of exchange operate to regulate the parties' course of performance and are subject to the rule of substantial performance.

The court found that the clause, being drafted by the parties, required strict compliance, and held that the tenant's $11,400 tender did not effectively terminate the lease. It was thus not only liable for the extra two months' rent, but also for the total amount of contract damages for the rest of the term (since it vacated and treated the lease as terminated, when it in fact was not); an amount claimed to be in excess of $230,000. And that was not all—because the tenant litigated the case and lost, it also wound up paying the landlord's attorneys' fees under the lease's attorneys' fees clause, and those fees were alleged to be in excess of $65,000.

In the above cases, if the parties were unclear about who was to do what when, the courts imposed constructive conditions of exchange. But before the tender in *Haight*, for example, no one was in breach. Would it have made a difference in formulating an excuse for non-performance if one party had already been in breach? Of course. Next section.

C. EXCUSE: WHEN THE OTHER SIDE FAILS TO SUBSTANTIALLY PERFORM UNDER A COMMON LAW CONTRACT (*AKA* "MATERIAL BREACH")

1. The Material Breach Concept

This next category of excuse may seem strange. It is the excuse provided by the other party's material breach of its obligations. Many think that such a result—you don't have to perform if the other party breaches—is so self-evident as to not require much thought.

For starters, we need to distinguish between the situations in which the other party never even starts to perform and situations in which the other party's nonperformance is incomplete or imperfect. Consider the following situations:

(1) Epstein contracts to paint Markell's office white on Saturday for $1,000. Epstein once again does not perform—once again does not do what he contracted to do. Does Markell still have to perform under the contract—still have to pay Epstein—or is Markell excused from performing because of Epstein's nonperformance?

(2) Same facts as (1) except that Epstein paints Markell's office but paints it purple instead of white as required by the contract. Everything is purple: walls, floor, ceiling, windows. Does Markell still have to perform under the contract—still have to pay Epstein—or is Markell excused from performing because of Epstein's improper performance?

(3) Same facts as (1) except that Epstein does paint Markell's office white and does an incredibly fine job except that he fails to paint the back of one of the doors. Markell pays another painter $25 to do that. Does Markell still have to perform under the contract—still have to pay Epstein—or is Markell excused from performing because of Epstein's improper performance?

The common law rule with respect to a party's ability to suspend performance or terminate the contract when the other party breaches is relatively easy to state. Under common law, you are excused from performing because of the other guy's breach only when the other guy's breach is a "material breach." That much is backed up by the following section of the *Restatement*:

§ 237 Effect on Other Party's Duties of a Failure to Render Performance

[I]t is a condition of each party's remaining duties to render performances to be exchanged under an exchange of promises that there be no uncured material failure by the other party to render any such performance due at an earlier time.

Note the legal device used to implement the material breach rule: conditions. Yet again. Under contract law, the duty to tender performance is conditioned upon the other party's not being in "material breach."

Note as well that all we are talking about here is the effect of the breach on requirement that the nonbreaching party perform her duties under the contract. That is only one possible reaction of course. Regardless of whether the breach is material or not, the nonbreaching party can still sue, and recover damages, for any breach, regardless of whether the breach is material or not. Thus the difference. Any breach: sue for damages. Material breach: sue for damages, *and* suspend performance.

The *Restatement* formulates the analytical backdrop for this distinction through the use of the conditions; it conditions a party's continued performance on the *absence* of a material breach by the other party. But the conditions referred to in the *Restatement* provision above are different from express conditions the parties draft. The conditions the *Restatement* refers to are, in a sense, not "real." Instead, the conditions are "constructive." We've seen these "unreal" conditions before, when looking at constructive conditions of exchange. Let's take a little deeper look at the "constructive" part.

Professor Perillo explains "constructive" conditions:

> Constructive conditions are created by courts in order to do justice. * * * In a bilateral contract, the parties often neglect to state the order in which their promises are to be performed. Constructive conditions fill these gaps. * * * The first and simplest rule is that, unless otherwise agreed, a party who is to perform work over an extended period of time must substantially perform before becoming entitled to payment. Performance of the work is a constructive condition precedent to the duty to pay.

Joseph Perillo, *Calamari and Perillo on Contracts* 428–29 (6th ed. 2009).

Check whether you understand what Professor Perillo is saying. Do you see the relationship between express conditions and strict compliance? Between constructive conditions and substantial performance? Between substantial performance and material breach?

2. What Constitutes a Material Breach

All of talk about constructive conditions turns on whether the non-performance was a "material" breach. What's that? Let's start with another classic Cardozo opinion.

QUESTIONS BEFORE THE CASE

1. What was the breach by Jacob & Youngs? When did it occur?
2. Why didn't Jacob & Young's breach of the contract excuse Kent's obligation to pay the full purchase price of the house?

JACOB & YOUNGS, INCORPORATED V. KENT

Court of Appeals of New York
230 N.Y. 239, 129 N.E. 889 (1921)

CARDOZO, J.:

The plaintiff built a country residence for the defendant at a cost of upwards of $77,000, and now sues to recover a balance of $3,483.46, remaining unpaid. The work of construction ceased in June, 1914, and the defendant then began to occupy the dwelling. There was no complaint of defective performance until March, 1915. One of the specifications for the plumbing work provides that "all wrought iron pipe must be well galvanized, lap welded pipe of the grade known as 'standard pipe' of Reading manufacture." The defendant learned in March, 1915, that some of the pipe, instead of being made in Reading, was the product of other factories. The plaintiff was accordingly directed by the architect to do the work anew. The plumbing was then encased within the walls except in a few places where it had to be exposed. Obedience to the order meant more than the substitution of other pipe. It meant the demolition at great expense of substantial parts of the completed structure. The plaintiff left the work untouched, and asked for a certificate that the final payment was due. Refusal of the certificate was followed by this suit.

The evidence sustains a finding that the omission of the prescribed brand of pipe was neither fraudulent nor willful. It was the result of the oversight and inattention of the plaintiff's subcontractor. Reading pipe is distinguished from Cohoes pipe and other brands only by the name of the manufacturer stamped upon it at intervals of between six and seven feet. Even the defendant's architect, though he inspected the pipe upon arrival, failed to notice the discrepancy. The plaintiff tried to show that the brands installed, though made by other manufacturers, were the same in quality, in appearance, in market value and in cost as the brand stated in the contract—that they were, indeed, the same thing, though manufactured in another place. The evidence was excluded, and a verdict directed for the defendant. The Appellate Division reversed, and granted a new trial.

We think the evidence, if admitted, would have supplied some basis for the inference that the defect was insignificant in its relation to the project. The courts never say that one who makes a contract fills the measure of his duty by less than full performance. They do say, however, that an omission, both trivial and innocent, will sometimes be atoned for by allowance of the resulting damage, and will not always be the breach of a condition to be followed by a forfeiture * * *. The distinction is akin to that between dependent and independent promises, or between promises and conditions * * * Some promises are so plainly independent that they can never by fair construction be conditions of one another. * * * Others are so plainly dependent that they must always be conditions. Others, though dependent and thus conditions when there is departure in point of substance, will be viewed as independent and collateral when the departure is insignificant * * * Considerations partly of justice and partly of presumable intention are to tell us whether this or that promise shall be placed in one class or in another. The simple and the uniform will call for different remedies from the multifarious and the intricate. The margin of departure within the range of normal expectation upon a sale of common chattels will vary from the margin to be expected upon a contract for the construction of a mansion or a "skyscraper." There will be harshness sometimes and oppression in the implication of a condition when the thing upon which labor has been expended is incapable of surrender because united to the land, and equity and reason in the implication of a like condition when the subject-matter, if defective, is in shape to be returned. From the conclusion that promises may not be treated as dependent to the extent of their uttermost minutiae without a sacrifice of justice, the progress is a short one to the conclusion that they may not be so treated without a perversion of intention. Intention not otherwise revealed may be presumed to hold in contemplation the reasonable and probable. If something else is in view, it must not be left to implication. There will be no assumption of a purpose to visit venial faults with oppressive retribution.

Those who think more of symmetry and logic in the development of legal rules than of practical adaptation to the attainment of a just result will be troubled by a classification where the lines of division are so wavering and blurred. Something, doubtless, may be said on the score of consistency and certainty in favor of a stricter standard. The courts have balanced such considerations against those of equity and fairness, and found the latter to be the weightier. The decisions in this state commit us to the liberal view, which is making its way, nowadays, in jurisdictions slow to welcome it * * * Where the line is to be drawn between the important and the trivial cannot be settled by a formula. "In the nature of the case precise boundaries are impossible". * * * The same omission may take on one aspect or another according to its setting. Substitution of equivalents may not have the same significance in fields of art on the one side and in those of mere utility on the other. Nowhere will change be tolerated, however, if it is so dominant or pervasive as in any real or substantial measure to frustrate the purpose of the contract. * * * There is no general license to install whatever, in the builder's judgment, may be regarded as "just as good". * * * The question is one of degree, to be answered, if there is doubt, by the triers of the facts * * * and, if the inferences are certain, by the judges of the law. * * * We must weigh the purpose to be served, the desire to be gratified, the excuse for deviation from the letter, the cruelty of enforced adherence. Then only can we tell whether literal fulfilment is to be implied by law as a condition. This is not to say that the parties are not free by apt and certain words to effectuate a purpose that performance of every term shall be a condition of recovery. That question is not here. This is merely to say that the law will be slow to impute the purpose, in the silence of the parties, where the significance of the default is grievously out of proportion to the oppression of the forfeiture. The willful transgressor must accept the penalty of his transgression. * * * For him there is no occasion to mitigate the rigor of implied conditions. The transgressor whose default is unintentional and trivial may hope for mercy if he will offer atonement for his wrong * * *

In the circumstances of this case, we think the measure of the allowance is not the cost of replacement, which would be great, but the difference in value, which would be either nominal or nothing. Some of the exposed sections might perhaps have been replaced at moderate expense. The defendant did not limit his demand to them, but treated the plumbing as a unit to be corrected from cellar to roof. In point of fact, the plaintiff never reached the stage at which evidence of the extent of the allowance became necessary. The trial court had excluded evidence that the defect was unsubstantial, and in view of that ruling there was no occasion for the plaintiff to go farther with an offer of proof. We think, however, that the offer, if it had been made, would not of necessity have been defective because directed to difference in value. It is true that in most cases the cost of replacement is the measure. * * * The owner is entitled to the money which will permit him to complete, unless the cost of completion is grossly and unfairly out of proportion to the good to be attained. When that is true, the measure is the difference in value. Specifications call, let us say, for a foundation built of granite quarried in Vermont. On the completion of the building, the owner learns that through the blunder of a subcontractor part of the foundation has been built of granite of the same quality quarried in New Hampshire. The measure of allowance is not the cost of reconstruction. "There may be missions of that which could not afterwards be supplied exactly as called for by the contract without taking down the building to its foundations, and at the same time the omission may not affect the value of the building for use or otherwise, except so slightly as to be hardly appreciable". * * * The rule that gives a remedy in cases of substantial performance with compensation for defects of trivial or inappreciable importance, has been developed by the courts as an instrument of justice. The measure of the allowance must be shaped to the same end.

The order should be affirmed, and judgment absolute directed in favor of the plaintiff upon the stipulation, with costs in all courts.

MCLAUGHLIN, J. *(dissenting).* I dissent. The plaintiff did not perform its contract. Its failure to do so was either intentional or due to gross neglect which, under the uncontradicted facts, amounted to the same thing, nor did it make any proof of the cost of compliance, where compliance was possible.

Under its contract it obligated itself to use in the plumbing only pipe (between 2,000 and 2,500 feet) made by the Reading Manufacturing Company. The first pipe delivered was about 1,000 feet and the plaintiff's superintendent then called the attention of the foreman of the subcontractor, who was doing the plumbing, to the fact that the specifications annexed to the contract required all pipe used in the plumbing to be of the Reading Manufacturing Company. They then examined it for the purpose of ascertaining whether this delivery was of that manufacture and found it was. Thereafter, as pipe was required in the progress of the work, the foreman of the subcontractor would leave word at its shop that he wanted a specified number of feet of pipe, without in any way indicating of what manufacture. Pipe would thereafter be delivered and installed in the building, without any examination whatever. Indeed, no examination, so far as appears, was made by the plaintiff, the subcontractor, defendant's architect, or any one else, of any of the pipe except the first delivery, until after the building had been completed. Plaintiff's architect then refused to give the certificate of completion, upon which the final payment depended, because all of the pipe used in the plumbing was not of the kind called for by the contract. After such refusal, the subcontractor removed the covering or insulation from about 900 feet of pipe which was exposed in the basement, cellar and attic, and all but 70 feet was found to have been manufactured, not by the Reading Company, but by other manufacturers, some by the Cohoes Rolling Mill Company, some by the National Steel Works, some by the South Chester Tubing Company, and some which bore no manufacturer's mark at all. The balance of the pipe had been so installed in the building that an inspection of it could not be had without demolishing, in part at least, the building itself.

I am of the opinion the trial court was right in directing a verdict for the defendant. The plaintiff agreed that all the pipe used should be of the Reading Manufacturing Company. Only about two-fifths of it, so far as appears, was of that kind. If more were used, then the burden of proving that fact was upon the plaintiff, which it could easily have done, since it knew where the pipe was obtained. The question of substantial performance of a contract of the character of the one under consideration depends in no small degree upon the good faith of the contractor. If the plaintiff had intended to, and had complied with the terms of the contract except as to minor omissions, due to inadvertence, then he might be allowed to recover the contract price, less the amount necessary to fully compensate the defendant for damages caused by such omissions. * * * But that is not this case. It installed between 2,000 and 2,500 feet of pipe, of which only 1,000 feet at most complied with the contract. No explanation was given why pipe called for by the contract was not used, nor was any effort made to show what it would cost to remove the pipe of other manufacturers and install that of the Reading Manufacturing Company. The defendant had a right to contract for what he wanted. He had a right before making payment to get what the contract called for. It is no answer to this suggestion to say that the pipe put in was just as good as that made by the Reading Manufacturing Company, or that the difference in value between such pipe and the pipe made by the Reading Manufacturing Company would be either "nominal or nothing." Defendant contracted for pipe made by the Reading Manufacturing Company. What his reason was for requiring this kind of pipe is of no importance. He wanted that and was entitled to it. It may have been a mere whim on his part, but even so, he had a right to this kind of pipe, regardless of whether some other kind, according to the opinion of the contractor or experts, would have been "just as good, better, or done just as well." He agreed to pay only upon condition that the pipe installed were made by that company and he ought not to be compelled to pay unless that condition be performed. * * * The rule, therefore, of substantial performance, with damages for unsubstantial omissions, has no application. * * *

What was said by this court in *Smith* v. *Brady* * * * is quite applicable here: "I suppose it will be conceded that everyone has a right to build his house, his cottage or his store after such a model and in such style as shall best accord with his notions of utility or be most agreeable to his fancy. The specifications of the contract become the law between the parties until voluntarily changed. If the owner prefers a plain and simple Doric column, and has so provided in the agreement, the contractor has no right to put in its place the more costly and elegant Corinthian. If the owner, having regard to strength and durability, has contracted for walls of specified materials to be laid in a particular manner, or for a given number of joists and beams, the builder has no right to substitute his own judgment or that of others. Having departed from the agreement, if performance has not been waived by the other party, the law will not allow him to allege that he has made as good a building as the one he engaged to erect. He can demand payment only upon and according to the terms of his contract, and if the conditions on which payment is due have not been performed, then the right to demand it does not exist. To hold a different doctrine would be simply to make another contract, and would be giving to parties an encouragement to violate their engagements, which the just policy of the law does not permit." (p. 186.)

I am of the opinion the trial court did not err in ruling on the admission of evidence or in directing a verdict for the defendant.

For the foregoing reasons I think the judgment of the Appellate Division should be reversed and the judgment of the Trial Term affirmed.

QUESTIONS AND NOTES

1. Questions about the facts of this case

   1.1. Do we know why the contract specified pipe of "Reading manufacture"? Should we know? Should that be relevant?

   1.2. Do we know whether the contract contained an express condition? Should that be relevant?

   1.3. As far as you can tell from the opinion, what is the difference between Reading pipe and Cohoes pipe? Is this difference what is driving the lawsuit? If not, what do you think is?

   1.4. Was Jacob & Youngs in breach?

   1.5. Was Jacob & Youngs' breach unintentional?

2. Questions about the law

   2.1. Does either the majority opinion or the dissenting opinion use the term "material breach"? The dissenting opinion refers to "substantial performance." What is the relationship between substantial performance and material breach?

   2.2. Would the result be different if Jacob & Youngs had used neither Reading nor Cohoes but had instead used the vastly inferior Drek paper mache pipe?

   2.3. Would the result have been different if Kent had sued Jacob & Youngs for damages for breach of contract?

3. Notes

   3.1. The requirement of Reading pipe was found in General Condition 225 of the contract. General Condition 22 of the same contract stated:

   > (22) Where any particular brand of manufactured article is specified, it is to be considered as a standard. Contractors desiring to use another shall first make application in writing to the Architect, stating the difference in cost, and obtain their written approval of the change.

   Does examination of this clause make the result reached more or less palatable? *See* Richard Danzig, *The Capability Problem in Contract Law: Further Readings on Well-Known Cases* 111–12 (1978).

   3.2. Almost 75 years after *Jacob & Youngs*, the New York Court of Appeals had the occasion to review part of that opinion. In *Oppenheimer & Co., Inc. v. Oppenheim, Appel, Dixon & Co.*, 86 N.Y.2d 685, 660 N.E.2d 415, 636 N.Y.S.2d 734 (1995), two parties signed a sub-lease of New York office space, but made the effectiveness of the lease expressly conditional on obtaining the landlord's consent to making certain tenant improvements necessary for the sub-leasee's business. In particular, the relevant language required the sub-tenant to obtain:

> 'the Prime Landlord's written notice of confirmation, substantially to the effect that [defendant] is a subtenant of the Premises reasonably acceptable to Prime Landlord.' If such written notice of confirmation were not obtained 'on or before December 30, 1986, then this letter agreement and the Sublease * * * shall be deemed null and void and of no further force and effect and neither party shall have any rights against nor obligations to the other.'

The deadline was mutually extended to February 25, 1987, but still the sub-tenant could not comply. As noted by the court:

> However, plaintiff never delivered the prime landlord's written consent to the proposed tenant work on or before the modified final deadline of February 25, 1987. Rather, plaintiff's attorney telephoned defendant's attorney on February 25 and informed defendant that the prime landlord's consent had been secured. On February 26, defendant, through its attorney, informed plaintiff's attorney that the letter agreement and sublease were invalid for failure to timely deliver the prime landlord's written consent and that it would not agree to an extension of the deadline. The document embodying the prime landlord's written consent was eventually received by plaintiff on March 20, 1987, 23 days after expiration of paragraph 4(c)'s modified final deadline.

Okay, so they had only oral consent, not written consent, by the deadline. That's substantial performance within *Jacob & Youngs*, isn't it?

No. As phrased by the New York Court of Appeals:

> Plaintiff's reliance on the well-known case of *Jacob & Youngs v. Kent*, is misplaced. There, a contractor built a summer residence and the buyer refused to pay the remaining balance of the contract price on the ground that the contractor used a different type of pipe than was specified in the contract. The buyer sought to enforce the contract as written. This would have involved the demolition of large parts of the structure at great expense and loss to the seller. This Court, in an opinion by then-Judge Cardozo, ruled for the contractor on the ground that "an omission, both trivial and innocent, will sometimes be atoned for by allowance of the resulting damage, and will not always be the breach of a condition to be followed by a

forfeiture." But Judge Cardozo was careful to note that the situation would be different in the case of an express condition:

> 'This is not to say that the parties are not free by apt and certain words to effectuate a purpose that performance of every term shall be a condition of recovery. That question is not here. This is merely to say that the law will be slow to impute the purpose, in the silence of the parties, where the significance of the default is grievously out of proportion to the oppression of the forfeiture.'

So there is no lease; just read the "apt and certain" words of the contract. As the New York appeals court concluded in the *Oppenheimer* case: "Freedom of contract prevails in an arm's length transaction between sophisticated parties such as these, and in the absence of countervailing public policy concerns there is no reason to relieve them of the consequences of their bargain. If they are dissatisfied with the consequences of their agreement, 'the time to say so [was] at the bargaining table.' "

3.3. How does *Oppenheimer* differ from *MXL* (you remember that note case, right? See page 706 above).

4. **You Be the Lawyer!**

According to Judge Cardozo, "This is not to say that the parties are not free by apt and certain words to effectuate a purpose that performance of every term shall be a condition of recovery." How would you draft such "apt and certain" words? Does *Oppenheimer & Co.* help?

The next case does not rely on *Jacob & Youngs*—in fact, it does not even mention *Jacob & Youngs*. Should it have?

QUESTIONS BEFORE THE CASE

1. What was the order of performance as specified in the contract? That is, who was supposed to do what when?
2. What was the effect of Cimco's breach on the unperformed obligations of Bartush?

BARTUSH-SCHNITZIUS FOODS CO. V. CIMCO REFRIGERATION, INC.

Supreme Court of Texas
518 S.W.3d 432, 60 Tex. Sup. Ct. J. 861 (2017)

Opinion

PER CURIAM.

This contract dispute involves competing breach claims by a food-product manufacturer, Bartush-Schnitzius Foods Co. (Bartush), and a refrigeration contractor, Cimco Refrigeration, Inc. (Cimco). The jury found that both parties failed to comply with their agreement and assessed damages accordingly, but the trial court rendered judgment solely for Bartush. * * *

In 2010, Bartush planned to expand its line of food products to include seafood dips. Manufacturing the dips required Bartush's production facilities to maintain a constant temperature no higher than thirty-eight degrees—lower than Bartush's existing refrigeration system could sustain. Bartush therefore contracted with Cimco to install a new system. Cimco sent Bartush an offer letter with three quoted options. The offer letter did not reference a particular temperature range. Bartush orally selected the most expensive of the three options, confirming the selection via email. Bartush then began paying Cimco in agreed-upon installments.

After installation, Bartush started to operate the new system at a temperature setting of thirty-five degrees. However, this resulted in ice forming on the fan motors because the system's defrost unit was not designed to support operation at such a low temperature. The ice caused the motors to overheat and fail, leading to higher temperatures that at times climbed into the 50s and 60s. When Bartush discovered the problem, it had already paid Cimco $306,758 on the contract but still owed $113,400. Bartush communicated with Cimco about a repair, but after several weeks without receiving what it considered a workable plan, Bartush withheld further payment and contacted an independent refrigeration engineer. The engineer recommended a warm-glycol defrost unit, and Bartush contracted with Jax Refrigeration, Inc. to install the unit at a cost of $168,079. After the warm-glycol defrost unit was installed, the system was able to maintain the target temperature of thirty-five degrees.

In response to Bartush's nonpayment, Cimco sued Bartush to recover the balance owed on the contract. Bartush counterclaimed for breach of contract, seeking damages for, among other things, the costs associated with the warm-glycol defrost unit. Bartush also alleged that its failure to pay was justified by Cimco's prior material breach. Cimco asserted that the equipment it installed was exactly as described in the accepted purchase order and denied that it had made any guarantee regarding the equipment's capacity to maintain a specific temperature.

The parties' claims were tried to a jury. The jury answered the relevant liability portions of the charge as follows: "YES" to Question 1, which asked whether Bartush failed to comply with the agreement; "YES" to Question 2, which asked whether Cimco failed to comply with the agreement; "CIMCO" to Question 3, which asked who failed to comply with the agreement first; and "NO" to Question 4, which asked whether Bartush's failure to comply was excused. The jury awarded Bartush $168,079 in damages (the cost of installing the warm-glycol defrost unit) * * *. The jury also awarded Cimco $113,400 (the balance due on the contract). * * *

Despite the jury's findings that both parties failed to comply and Bartush's failure to comply was not excused, the trial court stated in its final judgment that "it appears to the Court that the verdict of the jury was for [Bartush] and against [Cimco]," and rendered judgment in Bartush's favor for $168,079 in damages, plus pre- and post-judgment interest, costs, and attorney's fees. The judgment awarded nothing to Cimco, and Cimco appealed.

* * *

We first address Bartush's argument that the trial court properly rendered judgment entirely in its favor because Bartush's failure to comply (i.e., nonpayment) was excused as a matter of law by Cimco's prior material breach. "It is a fundamental principle of contract law that when one party to a contract commits a material breach of that contract, the other party is discharged or excused from further performance." *Mustang Pipeline Co. v. Driver Pipeline Co.*, 134 S.W.3d 195, 196 (Tex. 2004) (citing *Hernandez v. Gulf Grp. Lloyds*, 875 S.W.2d 691, 692 (Tex. 1994)). By contrast, when a party commits a nonmaterial breach, the other party "is not excused from future performance but may sue for the damages caused by the breach." *Levine v. Steve Scharn Custom Homes, Inc.*, 448 S.W.3d 637, 654 (Tex. App.–Houston [1st Dist.] 2014, pet. denied). The latter principle is consistent with settled Texas law regarding the elements of a contract claim. The claim requires a finding of breach, not a finding of material breach. *See, e.g.*, *Mays v. Pierce*, 203 S.W.3d 564, 575 (Tex. App.–Houston [14th Dist.] 2006, pet. denied) ("A breach of contract occurs when a party fails or refuses to do something he has promised to do."). Accordingly, a material breach by Cimco would have excused Bartush from making further contractual payments, while a nonmaterial breach would have simply given rise to a claim for damages.

In this case, as noted, the jury found that both parties failed to comply with the agreement. The jury was instructed that Bartush's failure to comply was excused if Cimco previously "failed to comply with a material obligation of the same agreement," and listed five nonexclusive "circumstances to consider in determining whether a failure to comply is material." Although the jury found that Cimco failed to comply first, it also found that Bartush's breach was not excused. To make the latter finding, the jury must have concluded that Cimco's prior breach was *not* material. * * *

Notwithstanding the jury's implied finding of nonmateriality, Bartush argues that Cimco's failure to provide a refrigeration system capable of maintaining a temperature of thirty-five degrees was a material breach as a matter of law, excusing Bartush from further performance. We disagree. Generally, materiality is an issue "to be determined by the trier of facts." *Hudson v. Wakefield*, 645 S.W.2d 427, 430 (Tex. 1983). * * *

In *Mustang Pipeline*, we outlined several factors enumerated in the Restatement that are "significant in determining whether a failure to perform is material." 134 S.W.3d at 199 (citing Restatement (Second) of Contracts § 241 (Am. Law Inst. 1981)). These factors include:

(a) the extent to which the injured party will be deprived of the benefit which he reasonably expected;

(b) the extent to which the injured party can be adequately compensated for the part of that benefit of which he will be deprived;

(c) the extent to which the party failing to perform or to offer to perform will suffer forfeiture;

(d) the likelihood that the party failing to perform or to offer to perform will cure his failure, taking account of the circumstances including any reasonable assurances;

(e) the extent to which the behavior of the party failing to perform or to offer to perform comports with standards of good faith and fair dealing.

Id. The jury charge in this case listed these factors for the jury's consideration in evaluating whether Cimco's failure to comply was material. The parties presented trial evidence that could have led the jurors to reasonably disagree regarding the application of these factors, including conflicting evidence on the parties' communications regarding temperature requirements. By contrast, in *Mustang* we held that a contractor's failure to meet a deadline in contravention of an express time-is-of-the-essence clause was a material breach as a matter of law. *Id.* at 199–200. No such conclusive evidence of materiality exists in this case. Because reasonable jurors could have disagreed on whether Cimco breached a material obligation, we may not overrule the jury's implied finding on that issue.

Bartush next argues that, even accepting the jury's finding that its failure to comply with the agreement was not excused, [the court of appeals erred when it held that] "Bartush's unexcused and material breach" (failing to pay the balance due) renders irrelevant the jury's finding that Cimco breached first and "precludes Bartush's recovery under the contract." 518 S.W.3d at 62. Bartush contends that the court should have given effect to the jury's damages awards to both parties. We agree.

While a party's nonmaterial breach does not excuse further performance by the other party, neither does the second breach excuse the first. To the contrary, a material breach does not discharge a claim for damages that has already arisen. Restatement (Second) of Contracts § 237 cmt. e (Am. Law Inst. 1981); *see also Allied Capital Partners, LP v. Proceed Tech. Res., Inc.*, 313 S.W.3d 460, 465 (Tex. App.–Dallas 2010, no pet.) (citing the Restatement for the proposition that "a material breach will not discharge an obligation of the non-breaching party that arose before the alleged breach"). In other words, a material breach excuses *future* performance, not *past* performance. * * *

In sum, the jury's findings that Cimco failed to comply with the agreement first and that its failure to comply was not material mean that (1) Bartush remained liable for its subsequent failure to comply, but (2) Bartush's claim for damages caused by Cimco's prior breach remained viable.[5] Cimco had a preexisting duty to perform under the contract, and the jury found that Cimco violated that duty *before* Bartush breached by withholding payment. * * *

[Reversed and remanded in accordance with opinion]

QUESTIONS AND NOTES

1. Questions about the facts

   1.1. What was Cimco's breach?

   1.2. What was Bartush's breach?

   1.3. Was Cimco's breach material? Was Bartush's?

   1.4. Does this dispute leave you a little cold as to why Cimco's breach was not material?

2. Questions about the law

   2.1. Do you agree with the court in its footnote that Bartush's situation was analogous to the builder suing even though they are in breach (albeit an immaterial breach and after having

[5] A similar state of affairs often arises in the context of construction contracts, when a contractor sues for the balance due and owing on the contract and the property owner counterclaims for damages for incomplete or defective performance. *See Vance v. My Apartment Steak House of San Antonio, Inc.*, 677 S.W.2d 480 (Tex. 1984). In such cases, if the contractor has substantially completed performance, *i.e.*, the contractor's breach is not material, then the contractor has a claim for the unpaid balance and the owner has a claim for damages. *See id.* at 481–82; Restatement (Second) of Contracts § 237 cmt. d (Am. Law Inst. 1981).

substantially performed)? Does that remind you of any case we have read recently?

2.2. Would the outcome have been different if the contract has stated specifically that "all refrigeration equipment must cool the premises to 35° for at least the first three years after installation"?

2.3. Reconsider 2.2. What if the contract had said "it shall be a material breach of this contract if, after the refrigeration equipment is installed and operational, the premises fail to be cooled to no more than 35° for at least the first three years after installation"? See Note 4.3 below.

2.4. Why didn't the court look to the U.C.C. for the rules of decision regarding material breach?

3. **You Be the Lawyer!**

If you represented Bartush, and had perfect knowledge of what the court above would do, what would you advise Bartush to do once Cimco had breached?

4. Notes

4.1. If you want to read widely disparate characterizations of this dispute, you can read the trial court decision at *Cimco Refrigeration, Inc. v. Bartush-Schnitzius Foods Co.*, 2014 WL 10020317 (Tex. Dist. Ct., Dec. 1, 2014), and the intermediate appellate opinion at *Cimco Refrigeration, Inc. v. Bartush-Schnitzius Foods Co.*, 518 S.W.3d 57 (Tex. Ct. App. 2015) (reh'g overruled).

By the way, by the time the case had reached the Texas Supreme Court, Bartush had already spent over $215,000 in attorneys' fees. *Bartush-Schnitzius Foods Co. v. Cimco Refrigeration, Inc.*, 518 S.W.3d 432, 435 (Tex. 2017).

4.2. In *Bartush*, the Texas Supreme Court makes a point that a finding of material breach is a finding of fact. This has serious consequences for appeals; findings of fact are given great deference, and generally are overturned only if there is "clear error" or the findings are "clearly erroneous. FED. R. CIV. PRO. 52.

So how do we actually know what the jury found? In *Bartush*, the jury instruction (or "charge" as it is sometimes called) and the jury's answer is available on-line. Here's the text of the instruction on material breach and the jury's response:

QUESTION NO. 4

Was BARTUSH's failure to comply excused?

"Failure to comply" by BARTUSH may be excused if you find that CIMCO previously failed to comply with a material obligation of the same agreement.

A failure to comply must be material. The circumstances to consider in determining whether a failure to comply is material include:

(a) The extent to which the injured party will be deprived of the benefit which it reasonable expected;

(b) The extent to which the injured party can be adequately compensated for the part of that benefit of which it will be deprived;

(c) The extent to which the party failing to perform or to offer to perform will suffer forfeiture;

(d) The likelihood that the party failing to perform or to offer to perform will cure its failure, taking into account the circumstances including any reasonable assurances;

(e) The extent to which the behavior of the party failing to perform or to offer to perform comports with standards of good faith and fair dealing.

Answer "Yes" or "No".

Answer: NO

Charge of the Court, Cimco Refrigeration, Inc. v. Bartush-Schnitzius Foods Co., Cause No. 2011–11002–1, 2014 WL 10023076 (16th Judicial District Ct., Denton County, Sept. 26, 2014).

Where do you think the trial court got parts (a)–(e) of the jury charge? Hint: Take a look at the *Restatement (Second) of Contracts*.

4.3. Remember *Parsons v. Halliburton Energy Services, Inc.*, 237 W.Va. 138, 785 S.E.2d 844 (W.Va. 2016), which we looked at on page 666? Sure you do. It was a case about waiver involving a delay in asserting arbitration after being sued in court. *Parsons* held that a simple delay in answering a complaint was not a waiver of the right to compel arbitration, and forced the plaintiff to arbitrate his claim.

Now consider *Roach v. BM Motoring, LLC*, 228 N.J. 163, 155 A.3d 985 (2017). In that case, several consumers bought used cars from the same car dealer pursuant to the dealer's identical form contract. That contract had the following arbitration clause:

> [t]he arbitration shall be conducted in accordance with the rules of the American Arbitration Association [AAA] before a single arbitrator, who shall be a retired judge or attorney. Dealership shall advance both party's [sic] filing, service, administration, arbitrator, hearing, or other fees, subject to reimbursement by decision of the arbitrator.

The consumers had problems with their cars after the purchase and initiated arbitration in front of the American Arbitration Association. BM, however, took the position that the AAA was not appropriate (they thought it charged too much), and refused to pay the arbitration fees. The AAA dismissed the arbitration after warning BM Motoring that they would not hear future cases involving BM due to its refusal to pay the fee.

So the consumers filed suit in court. And guess what? BM moved to dismiss the lawsuit and sought to compel arbitration. The trial court agreed, but the AAA was having none it; it bounced BM's application for failure to pay the earlier fees, and refused to arbitrate the dispute.

The consumers then took their case to the New Jersey Supreme Court. After finding that the AAA was a permissible forum under the contract (where else, you might ask?), it then turned to the effect of BM's failure to respond to the consumers' earlier arbitration. After examining Section 341 of the *Restatement (Second) of Contracts*, the court stated:

> The benefit expected under an arbitration agreement is the ability to arbitrate claims. A failure to advance required fees that results in the dismissal of the arbitration claim deprives a party of the benefit of the agreement. Therefore, the failure to advance fees "goes to the essence" of the DRA and amounts to a material breach.

If BM was in material breach, then the consumers were excused from complying with the arbitration provision. The court thus excused the consumers' noncompliance (their filing of a lawsuit instead of consenting to an arbitration), and ordered that the matter be litigated in court, and not before an arbitrator.

4.4. The Texas Supreme Court makes reference to the notion that a "time of the essence" clause automatically turns any untimely performance into a material breach. This is broadly in line with other courts in other jurisdictions. *See 11-01 36 Ave. LLC v. Quamar*, 54 Misc. 3d 622, 624–25, 41 N.Y.S.3d 684, 687 (N.Y. Sup. Ct. 2016) ("Where time is of the essence, performance on the specific date is a material element of the contract, and failure to perform on that date constitutes a material breach of the contract.").

But what about the other performance terms of the contract? May a party insist on a provision of the contract that says "Any breach of any obligation due under this contract is a material breach, regardless of whether such breach would be a material breach under common law"?

Maybe. The issue arose in *RW Power Partners, L.P. v. Va. Elec. & Power Co.*, 899 F. Supp. 1490 (E.D. Va. 1995). There, RW had agreed to continuously keep in place a letter of credit, a sort of bank guaranty, for its monetary obligations under the contract. The initial letter of credit expired, and RW was 6 days late in providing a new letter of credit. So there was a gap period in which no letter of credit was present. Although no damage, since the letter of credit was ultimately replaced, the gap was a breach. Virginia Electric, however, elected to terminate the contract the day before the letter of credit's replacement, citing a contract provision that stated that that if RW Power "fail[ed] to perform any of its obligations pursuant to this Agreement, then Virginia Power may cancel this Agreement."

There was apparently no time of the essence clause, and the parties stipulated that Virginia Electric sustained no damage during the gap period between letters of credit.

The court dealt with the dispute as follows:

> [T]his action presents a question of first impression in which this court is required to determine how the Supreme Court of Virginia would resolve the tension between two well-entrenched doctrines of Virginia's contract law: the common law concept of material breach and the ability of parties through explicit contractual language to override such common law principles. The analysis proceeds from the well-established premise so clearly stated in *Neeley v. White,* the leading Virginia decision, and in the most respected treatises, that cancellation is permitted only for a material breach. The related doctrines of cure and forfeiture avoidance are but reflections of the very basic role which the principle of materiality plays in the law of contracts in Virginia and generally. The basic purpose of these correlative principles is to enforce the societal interest that the contracting parties be accorded security for their justified expectations and, at the same time, to preclude abuse of that protection by foreclosing contract cancellation on the basis of an insignificant breach. *Farnsworth on Contracts,* Power to Suspend Performance and Terminate Contract, § 8.15.
>
> So firmly rooted are these concepts that, although the parties may displace them by agreement, the agreement to

do so must clearly admit of but one interpretation: that a breach—whether material or otherwise—may be the basis for termination. In discussing when one party's breach excuses performance by the other, Williston has explained that "in the absence of a *clearly expressed* intention, the consequence that[,] for even permanent default in prior performance of slight importance[,] subsequent performance should be wholly excused cannot be accepted." *Williston on Contracts,* Non-Performance as Excuse for Breach, § 829 (emphasis added). Or, as the Fourth Circuit framed it in *LeRoy Dyal Company, Inc. v. Allen,* 161 F.2d 152 (4th Cir. 1947):

> [I]f a contract calls for a number of performances on both sides, and there is no *clear intention* as to what shall happen if default is made in a prior performance of *slight importance,* it does not follow that subsequent performance by the other party is excused. The decision depends upon the importance and materiality of the prior default, and the materiality of the failure should be determined by ascertaining whether it would be more just to free the injured person or to require him to perform his promise giving him, in either event, a right of action for any damages he may have suffered.

Id. at 155 (emphasis added). Where the breach is not material and the contract does not explicitly state that an immaterial breach will excuse further performance, termination of the contract is improper, and the injured party is limited to damages for the breach. The Supreme Court of Virginia in *Home Creek Smokeless Coal Co. v. Combs,* 132 S.E.2d at 406, has underscored the principle that, unless there is a provision in a contract clearly and expressly allowing forfeiture, the breach of a covenant does not justify cancellation of the entire contract.

Of course, where the contract language makes it clear that the parties have agreed that any breach, material or not, permits cancellation, the courts must give effect to that agreement. Such an agreement, however, may not be lightly inferred nor may the courts, by interpretation, supply that which has not been made explicit.

Here the contract provides only that if RW Power "fails to perform any of its obligations pursuant to this Agreement, then Virginia Power may cancel this Agreement." Thus, the plain language of Article XI does not clearly state that any breach, material or otherwise, permits cancellation.

RW Power Partners, L.P. v. Va. Elec. & Power Co., 899 F. Supp. 1490, 1501–02 (E.D. Va. 1995).

---

3. Exceptions, Exclusions and Nuances to the Material Breach Concept

In addition to the parties' ability to specify explicitly what non-performance is material, there are also various doctrines which soften the hard consequences of material breach. We categorize them loosely as rules related to divisible contracts, rules related to election of remedies, and, our favorite, the perfect tender rule under the U.C.C.

---

a. Divisible Contracts

As *Bartush* illustrates, improperly labeling any old breach a material breach can lead to harsh consequences—Bartush had to pay for a cooler system that didn't meet its needs. There is a tendency on the part of judges, lawyers, law professors and law students to look for ways to avoid or mitigate these types of harsh consequences.

The concept of "divisible" contract is a mitigating doctrine that reduces the harsh consequences in a class of cases. The California Court of Appeals explained the concept of divisible contracts in *Filet Menu, Inc. v. C.C.L. & G., Inc.*, 79 Cal. App.4th 852, 94 Cal. Rptr. 2d 438 (Cal. Ct. App. 2000):

> A "divisible" contract is one "under which the whole performance is divided into two sets of partial performances, each part of each set being the agreed exchange for a corresponding part of the set of performances to be rendered by the other promisor. * * * It is one in which two or more separate partial performances on each side are agreed to be exchanged for partial performances on the other side. The failure to perform one part does not bar recovery for performance of another. The "performance of each division of the service will be impliedly a condition precedent to the recovery of a corresponding portion of the price."
>
> Once a contract is determined to be divisible, various consequences ensue. "If the performances to be exchanged under an exchange of promises can be apportioned into corresponding pairs of part performances so that the parts of each pair are properly regarded as agreed equivalents, *a party's performance of his part of such a pair has the same effect on the other's duties to render performance of the agreed equivalent as it would have if only that pair of performances had been promised.*" (Rest.2d

> Contracts, § 240, italics added.) Comment a to section 240, states: "This Section embodies another mitigating doctrine which reduces the risk of forfeiture in that important class of cases in which it is proper to regard corresponding parts of the performances of each party as agreed equivalents. Its effect is to give a party who has performed one of these parts the right to its agreed equivalent just as if the parties had made a separate contract with regard to that pair of corresponding parts." (Rest.2d Contracts, § 240, com. a.) Thus, if a party has breached one part of a divisible contract, he or she is not precluded from obtaining the consideration that was allocated to that portion of the contract that he or she performed.

79 Cal.App.4th at 860.

Apply this concept of divisible contract from *Filet Menu* and *Restatement (Second) of Contracts* § 240 to the following problems:

PROBLEMS ON DIVISIBLE CONTRACTS

1. Ponoroff entered into four separate contracts to develop four different video games for EA for $1,000 a game. Ponoroff again falls short and only develops one of the games, the game covered by the third of the four contracts. Should Ponoroff be able to recover $1,000 from EA under the third contract?
2. Same facts as problem 1 except that Ponoroff and EA sign one contract that provides for payment of $1,000 at the time each of the four games is delivered, instead of four separate contracts. Again, Ponoroff only develops one of the games. Should Ponoroff be able to recover $1,000 from EA under the contract?
3. Same facts as problem 1 except that Ponoroff and EA sign one contract that provides for the payment of $4,000 at the time the four games are delivered, instead of four separate contracts. Again, Ponoroff only develops one of the four games. Should Ponoroff be able to recover from EA under the contract?

---

b. Election of Remedies

QUESTIONS BEFORE THE CASE

1. Did ESPN breach the contract? Did Baseball? In each case, how?
2. What were Baseball's choices once it knew of ESPN's breaches? What consequences attached to each of these choices?

ESPN, INC. V. OFFICE OF THE COMMISSIONER OF BASEBALL

U.S. District Court, Southern District of New York
76 F. Supp. 2d 383 (1999)

Opinion and Order

SCHEINDLIN, J.

Introduction

This is a contract dispute between ESPN, Inc. ("ESPN"), an all-sports cable television network, and The Office of Major League Baseball ("Baseball"), which acts on behalf of the Major League Baseball clubs. In 1996, the parties entered into a telecasting agreement (the "1996 Agreement") pursuant to which Baseball granted ESPN the right to telecast regular season major league baseball games on its primary cable service. In exchange, ESPN agreed, among other things, to pay Baseball yearly rights fees and to produce baseball game telecasts on Wednesday and Sunday nights during the regular season.

A. Background

The 1996 Agreement includes two provisions that are the primary focus of this litigation. The first is a representation by ESPN that "it has not made nor will it make any contractual or other commitments that conflict with or will prevent full performance [of the 1996 Agreement]." * * * The second provision permits ESPN to preempt up to ten baseball games a season with Baseball's prior written approval, which may not be unreasonably withheld. The preemption provision states:

> With the prior written approval of Baseball, which shall not be unreasonably withheld or delayed, ESPN may * * * preempt any [Baseball game telecast] hereunder, up to a maximum of ten [Baseball game telecasts] per year, for an event of significant viewer interest.

Pursuant to this provision, Baseball may telecast the preempted baseball games on its secondary cable service, ESPN2.

On January 13, 1998, ESPN entered into a telecasting contract with the National Football League ("NFL") whereby ESPN obtained the rights to broadcast regular season NFL games on Sunday nights. On January 30, 1998, ESPN requested Baseball's approval to telecast NFL games in place of baseball games on three Sunday nights in September 1998. Baseball declined to approve ESPN's request. Despite Baseball's disapproval, however, ESPN substituted NFL games for baseball games on the three Sunday nights in question. Baseball refused to allow ESPN to broadcast the preempted baseball games on ESPN2.

This exact series of events repeated itself in January 1999, when ESPN again sought Baseball's approval to replace three baseball games scheduled for Sunday nights in September 1999 with football games. Baseball denied ESPN's preemption request; ESPN preempted the three September 1999 baseball games in favor of football games; and Baseball refused to allow ESPN to broadcast the preempted games on ESPN2.

B. Contentions of the Parties

In April 1999, Baseball terminated the 1996 Agreement contending that ESPN had materially breached the contract. In response, ESPN commenced the instant litigation in which it alleges that Baseball materially breached the contract by (i) unreasonably withholding its approval of ESPN's preemption requests in 1998 and 1999; (ii) precluding ESPN from broadcasting the preempted baseball games on ESPN2; and (iii) improperly terminating the parties' agreement. ESPN seeks damages and declaratory and injunctive relief.

Baseball has asserted counterclaims against ESPN in which it alleges that ESPN materially breached the 1996 Agreement by (i) entering into a "conflicting" contract with the NFL; (ii) preempting Baseball games in 1998 and 1999 without ESPN's prior written approval; and (iii) utilizing highlight footage of baseball games in excess of the amount authorized by the 1996 Agreement. Baseball also seeks damages and declaratory and injunctive relief.

* * *

I. Baseball's Motion * * * to Strike the Affirmative Defense of Election of Remedies or in the Alternative for Summary Judgment

In its Amended Answer to Baseball's counterclaim, ESPN asserts the affirmative defense of "election of remedies." By this motion, Baseball seeks to preclude ESPN from asserting such a defense.

A. Election of Remedies

The doctrine of "election of remedies" provides as follows:

> When a party materially breaches a contract, the non-breaching party must choose between two remedies—[it] can elect to terminate the contract and recover liquidated damages or [it] can continue the contract and recover damages solely for the breach. A party can indicate that [it] has chosen to continue the contract by continuing to perform under the contract or by accepting the performance of the breaching party. Once a party elects to continue the contract, [it] can never thereafter elect to terminate the contract based on that breach, although [it] retains the option of terminating the contract based on other, subsequent breaches.

Bigda v. Fischbach Corp., 898 F.Supp. 1004, 1011–12 (S.D.N.Y. 1995) (citations omitted). * * *

ESPN contends that because Baseball accepted full performance by ESPN for the 1998 and 1999 seasons, it elected to continue the 1996 Agreement and therefore cannot seek termination of the contract based on any alleged breaches by ESPN during those years. According to ESPN, Baseball can only seek damages for ESPN's alleged breaches of the 1996 Agreement.

B. Ability to Terminate for Alleged 1998 Breaches

To the extent Baseball seeks termination based solely on ESPN's 1998 contract with the NFL or its preemption of three baseball games in 1998—assuming that those acts constitute material breaches of the 1996 Agreement—the election of remedies defense bars such relief. That is, with respect to both of the alleged 1998 breaches, Baseball continued to perform and continued to accept performance under the 1996 Agreement for more than a year, and thus it lost its right to terminate for those breaches. * * *

Baseball concedes that it "continued performance of the 1996 Agreement after ESPN's 1998 breach" but claims that its ability to terminate the agreement based on those breaches is preserved by the contract's broadly worded "no waiver" provision. Essentially, Baseball argues that a contractual "no waiver" provision trumps the common law contract principle of election of remedies. Although Baseball's contention is legally without merit, it raises interesting and seldom addressed issues regarding the relationship between the doctrines of waiver and election and thus merits a more detailed analysis.[3]

1. Waiver Versus Election of Remedies

The doctrines of waiver and election of remedies are complementary rather than competing common law contract principles. Under the doctrine of waiver, "a party may, by words or conduct, waive a provision in a contract or eliminate a condition in a contract which was inserted for [its] benefit." * * * Suppose, for example, that under the 1996 Agreement ESPN is obligated to make bi-weekly payments of $100,000 to Baseball. Suppose further that after several months of making the required bi-weekly payments, ESPN begins to tender monthly payments of $100,000 to Baseball. If Baseball accepts and/or fails to object to ESPN's deficient

[3] Baseball also argues that ESPN must demonstrate that it "changed its position to its detriment in reliance on [Baseball's] indication that [it] elected to treat the contract as valid" in order to establish an election of remedies defense. BB MIL at 4. However, the Second Circuit has clearly held that detrimental reliance is not an essential element of an election of remedies defense. * * *

payments, then Baseball has eliminated or "waived" its contractual right to bi-weekly payments of $100,000 under the 1996 Agreement.[4]

In contrast to a waiver of contractual rights, an election is simply a choice among remedies by the party; it is a decision by that party as to how it should proceed in the wake of the breaching party's nonperformance. In other words, "an election is not a waiver of any rights under the contract but rather a choice between two inconsistent remedies for breach of the contract." * * *

Returning to the hypothetical, suppose that Baseball had, in fact, objected when ESPN began to tender monthly rather than bi-weekly payments. Under these facts, Baseball has preserved its contractual right to bi-weekly payments of $100,000, and thus there is no waiver of that provision. However, Baseball must still decide how to proceed in light of ESPN's hypothetical nonperformance. Assuming that ESPN's hypothetical failure to make timely and sufficient payment is a material breach, Baseball has two choices. It can terminate the parties' contract and claim damages for total breach. Or, it can continue the contract and sue for partial breach. The election of remedies simply requires that Baseball choose or "elect" a single course of action. Thus, if Baseball terminates the contract, then it has elected termination, and it cannot continue to perform or expect performance under the contract. If Baseball chooses to continue the contract, then it has elected to continue, and it cannot later decide to terminate based on the same breach. In essence, the election of remedies doctrine is implicated only in the absence of waiver. That is, if a party waives her right to performance under a contract, then she has no remedies to elect because she has waived her ability to enforce the relevant provision. If a party has not waived her right to enforce a provision in the event of breach, then she can elect the appropriate and desired remedy. The key is that once a party has elected a remedy for a particular breach, her choice is binding with respect to that breach.

* * *

The remedy of termination—or, more accurately, the "right" to terminate—is available only where one party has materially breached the contract. A breach is material if it defeats the object of the parties in making the contract and "deprive[s] the injured party of the benefit that it justifiably expected." Farnsworth, Contracts § 8.16 (3d ed.1999). Where a breach is material, the party is justified in refusing to go on, and thus the law provides that party with the right to terminate. And, a party who terminates in response to a material breach presumably does so because it can no longer derive a worthwhile benefit from its contractual relationship.

---

[4] Note that a party's waiver of a contract provision is not absolute. That is, a previously waived provision may be restored " 'by a reasonable notice demanding performance and stating that the contract will be rescinded if the notice is not complied with.' " * * *

On the other hand, where a party with the right to terminate chooses instead to continue, the only inference to be drawn is that the party will derive a worthwhile benefit from its contractual relationship. Therefore, the party's election to continue rather than end the contract essentially moots its legal justification for termination. Once a party recognizes contractual benefits in the wake of a material breach, that particular breach can no longer be considered the antithesis of the contract, and it can no longer serve as the basis for termination. Of course, if a party chooses to continue with the contract and the other party subsequently commits another material breach, the party has the right to terminate based on the new breach. This is the scenario to which I now turn.[7]

C. Termination for Alleged 1999 Breach

Baseball elected to continue the 1996 Agreement despite ESPN's alleged material breaches in 1998. As a result, Baseball can no longer terminate the parties' contract based on those breaches. However, to the extent Baseball seeks termination based upon ESPN's preemption of three baseball games in 1999—assuming arguendo that the 1999 preemptions constitute material breaches of the parties' agreement—the election of remedies doctrine does not bar such relief.

In January 1999, ESPN sought permission to preempt baseball games on three Sunday nights in September 1999. On February 11, Baseball declined to approve the requested preemption. On March 1, ESPN advised Baseball that it would preempt the September games notwithstanding Baseball's denial of its request. In response, on April 21, 1999, Baseball terminated the parties' agreement effective at the end of the Baseball season in October. Baseball's notice of termination stated: "As outlined above, ESPN has materially breached the [1996] Agreement. Therefore, Baseball hereby terminates the Agreement pursuant to Paragraph XX.B. thereof effective immediately following the last game of the 1999 regular season." See 5/21/99 letter from Paul Beeston, President and CEO of Baseball, to various officers of ESPN * * *

It is useful to compare Baseball's actions in connection with the alleged 1998 breaches to its actions in connection with the alleged 1998 breaches. In 1998, Baseball clearly elected to continue its contract with ESPN. Although Baseball informed ESPN that it considered the NFL contract and the 1998 preemptions to be material breaches, * * *, and although it "reserved" its right to terminate, * * *, there is no question that Baseball elected to continue and did continue the agreement throughout 1998 and

[7] For all of the reasons discussed in the preceding section, I reject Baseball's similar argument that the doctrine of election is inapplicable because "in its written correspondence with ESPN on this matter, [Baseball] in addition, reserved specifically all its rights." BB MIL at 6. Regardless of how many times Baseball "reserved its rights" in written correspondence regarding the alleged 1998 breaches, Baseball cannot avoid the fact that once it elected to continue the contract, it lost its ability to terminate based on the 1998 breaches. * * *

into the 1999 season. In 1999, however, Baseball did not merely mention or reserve its right to terminate, it in fact terminated the agreement.

Despite Baseball's purported election to terminate in April 1999, ESPN maintains that Baseball cannot seek termination based on the 1999 preemptions because even while the parties were litigating their claims and counterclaims about the propriety of termination, in which Baseball was insisting that ESPN's actions threatened not just 1998 or 1999 but all five remaining years on the contract, the parties both continued performing under the contract for the full remainder of the 1999 season, with Baseball again receiving from ESPN the full 1999 rights fee of $3.4 million and the national cable telecasting of over 80 of its games.

According to ESPN, "Baseball plainly made a choice. It elected to continue the contract in the face of the claimed breaches and anticipatory breaches as to five years of the contract that it now cites as the basis for termination, and elected to obtain substantial benefits under the contract from ESPN by so doing." In particular, ESPN argues that because Baseball purported to terminate in April 1999 but continued to accept performance under the contract for nearly six more months, it was pursuing two inconsistent courses of action, the very behavior election of remedies disdains.

In response, Baseball asserts that its method of delayed termination was the most reasonable way to sever the parties' contractual relationship. Baseball argues:

> ESPN has cited no cases, nor, we submit, could they, to suggest that Baseball's termination notice was defective because it was not immediately effective at the time the notice was given. Baseball gave ESPN reasonable notice to wind down its relationship with Baseball once Baseball determined that it had no choice but to terminate the 1996 Agreement in view of ESPN's breaches and anticipatory breaches in 1999.

BB Reply at 7. Baseball also states that "the effective date of termination was chosen out of fairness to ESPN and its scheduling arrangements." Id. at 6.

As Baseball notes, there is little guidance regarding whether a party can give present notice of future termination without running afoul of election of remedies. Again, it is helpful to look at the policy underlying that doctrine. To begin, "the doctrine of election permits parties to wait a 'reasonable time' after learning of the alleged breaches before terminating the contract. * * * [H]ow much time is reasonable depends on the nature of the performance to be rendered under the contract." * * * The critical factor is not the passage of time but "whether the non-breaching party has taken an action (or failed to take an action) that indicated to the breaching party that [it] had made an election." * * *

In the instant case, the issue is not whether Baseball rendered or accepted performance during the time between breach and election but whether Baseball rendered or accepted performance during the time between its election of termination and the effective date of that termination.[8] On the one hand, both Baseball and ESPN tendered and accepted dozens of performances during the six months between April and October 1999. Indeed, ESPN telecast approximately eighty baseball games during the 1999 season. However, those individual performances were part of a more global performance. Stated somewhat differently, the 1996 Agreement, in keeping with its subject matter, is seasonal in nature. As a result, it calls for seasonal performance. For example, the baseball games that are ultimately telecast on ESPN are organized and scheduled months in advance. Indeed, under the 1996 Agreement, Baseball must provide ESPN with a regular season schedule of games "no later than August 15th of the calendar year preceding each Baseball season." * * * By the time the baseball season commences each spring, the parties' global performance for that season is already well under way. Games and other programming have been scheduled and those schedules have been published to, and relied upon by, third parties including sponsors, advertisers, the media and the public. Of course, performance continues throughout the summer and fall as baseball games are telecast and payment is made, but it is clearly all part of the same seasonal undertaking.

This difference is critical because it demonstrates that Baseball did not act inconsistently when it terminated effective at the end of the season. Instead, Baseball's method of termination merely mirrored the nature of the 1996 Agreement. At the time Baseball elected to terminate the contract in April 1999, the 1999 season and performance for that season was well underway. Thus, rather than stop the agreement mid-performance at a high cost to both parties and nonparties, Baseball simply notified ESPN that it would render and accept no "new" performance under the contract; it would not go forward with the 2000 season.[9]

---

[8] There is no question that Baseball's April 1999 termination was timely. Pursuant to the doctrine of anticipatory repudiation, Baseball had no duty to "elect its remedies" prior to ESPN's actual breach of the contract in September 1999. Under New York law, where an anticipatory breach has occurred the party may either sue immediately or wait until there has been actual breach:

> When a promisor repudiates a contract, the injured party faces an election of remedies; [it] can treat the repudiation as an anticipatory breach and immediately seek damages for breach of contract, thereby terminating the contractual relation between parties, or [it] can treat the repudiation as an empty threat, wait until the time for performance arrives and exercise [its] remedies for actual breach if a breach does in fact occur at such time.

Silver Air v. Aeronautic Dev. Corp. Ltd., 656 F.Supp. 170, 178 (S.D.N.Y.1987) (internal quotations omitted). Accordingly, Baseball could have waited until ESPN actually preempted the September 1999 baseball games to seek termination of the contract.

[9] This is markedly different than Baseball's response to the alleged 1998 breaches. In 1998, Baseball not only completed performance of the 1998 season, but it started and continued performance for the new 1999 season.

Not only do I find that Baseball's approach did not violate the doctrine of election, I also find that it was eminently reasonable under the circumstances. Had Baseball terminated effective immediately, not only would both parties have suffered enormous hardship, an immeasurable number of third parties including sponsors, advertisers and the public would have been affected. In an industry where so much time and energy is expended in advance preparation, it makes little sense to treat the fruits of those efforts as a wholly separate "performance" for purposes of the election of remedies defense. I suspect that if ESPN were not Baseball's adversary in this litigation, it would appreciate rather than complain of Baseball's considerate approach to termination.

Accordingly, I find as a matter of law that if the 1999 preemptions by themselves or in connection with other alleged breaches constitute a material breach, Baseball has a right to terminate the 1996 Agreement.

* * *

E. Conclusion

As a matter of law, Baseball cannot terminate the 1996 Agreement based on ESPN's 1998 contract with the NFL or its 1998 preemptions of baseball games, regardless of whether those actions constitute material breaches of the 1996 Agreement. However, if the 1999 preemptions constitute a material breach of the parties' agreement then Baseball can terminate the contract.

QUESTIONS AND NOTE

1. Questions about the facts of this case

    1.1. Did ESPN breach? How many times? What were the breaches in 1998? What were the breaches in 1999? Were the breaches "material"?

    1.2. Did Baseball make an election of remedies? How many times? The same election each time?

    1.3. Were there explicit contract provisions governing termination of the contract?

    1.4. What facts lead the court to conclude that the 1999 termination was "eminently reasonable"?

2. Questions about the law

    2.1. What does the court mean by "election of remedies"? What is the relationship between "material breach" and "election of remedies"?

2.2. Can you make a convincing and short distinction between election of remedies and waiver? Did the court?

2.3. Is the court right that Baseball can terminate for reasons other than the ones it states? Recall that Baseball based its termination on the 1998 *and* 1999 breaches by ESPN; the court disallowed termination based on the 1998 breaches.

3. Note

One More Note on "Substantial Performance" (a/k/a "Partial Breach") and "Material Breach" (a/k/a "Total Breach"))

As *ESPN* notes, remedies often turn on whether the breach is "material." To expand upon *ESPN*, there is an essential link between a material breach and how much you can sue for in damages. As stated in section 243(1) of the *Restatement (Second) of Contracts*, "With respect to performances to be exchanged under an exchange of promises, a breach by non-performance gives rise to a claim for damages for total breach only if it discharges the injured party's remaining duties to render such performance. * * *"

What is the difference between a total and partial breach? Again, the *Restatement*:

> *b.* *Total and partial breach distinguished.* Although every breach gives rise to a claim for damages, not every claim for damages is one for damages based on all of the injured party's remaining rights to performance under the contract. Such a claim is said to be one for damages for total breach. * * * If the injured party elects to or is required to await the balance of the other party's performance under the contract, his claim is said instead to be one for damages for partial breach. For example, an injured party who claims damages in addition to specific performance claims damages for partial breach. Rules for determining whether a particular breach gives rise to a claim for damages for partial breach, for total breach, or for either partial or total breach at the election of the injured party are stated in §§ 243 [relating to material breach] and 253 [relating to repudiation].

Restatement (Second) of Contracts § 236, com. b.

Thus, if the breach is material, then the non-breaching party is not only justified in suspending its performance and, if it is sufficiently serious, canceling the contract (thus preventing any executory duties it has from maturing), but it may also then sue for damages measured by the breaching party's failure to perform now, *and* in the future. As indicated above, this is sometimes referred to as suing for "total" breach, and the remedies examined in Chapter 7 will often assume that such a total breach exists (that is, the breacher's conduct constitutes a material breach).

But what if the breach is not material, or as in *ESPN*, there is an argument that the other side "accepted" the material breach and continued performance? There still is a breach, and there still is a remedy in damages—but only for the present breach, not for a cessation of all future obligations. This is often referred to as "partial" breach.

Whether the breach is "material" or "partial," the nonbreaching party to the contract still has a right to a legal remedy. The next chapter addresses the question of what is the appropriate remedy for a breach of contract.

4. **You Be the Lawyer!**

Epstein contracts with Markell to provide ten lessons on case book writing. If Epstein is a no-show for the first tutoring session, advise Markell based upon *ESPN* what to do if Markell wants to be done with Epstein and hire Ponoroff, a cheaper and more energetic tutor than the aged Epstein. Assume that Markell doesn't really want to pursue any remedies against Epstein (being quit of him is sufficient, thank you), but Markell sure doesn't want Epstein suing him for breach.

---

c. *Huge Exclusion: U.C.C. and "Perfect Tender"*

The third nuance regarding material breach comes from the U.C.C. To understand this nuance, recall that "material breach" is a common law concept. In common law contracts such as contracts for land or for services, a breach by one of the parties to the contract excuses the performance of the other party *only* if the breach is a "material breach."

This material breach concept is not, however, a part of the law governing sales of goods. The comparable Article 2 concept is "perfect tender." In sale of goods contracts, any breach by a seller will excuse the buyer from performing.

In reading U.C.C. section 2–601 set out below (with italics we have supplied), consider why section 2–601 is called the "perfect tender rule" and whether section 2–601 supports our statement that, "In sale of goods contracts, any breach by the seller will excuse the buyer from performing."

§ 2–601. Buyer's Rights on Improper Delivery.

Subject to the provisions of this Article on breach in installment contracts (Section 2–612) and unless otherwise agreed under the sections on contractual limitations of remedy (Sections 2–718 and 2–

719), if the goods or the tender of delivery fail *in any respect* to conform to the contract, the buyer may:

(a) reject the whole; or

(b) accept the whole; or

(c) accept any commercial unit or units and reject the rest.

QUESTIONS BEFORE THE CASE

1. Did Panike supply onions that met the size requirements set in the contract?
2. How did Panike breach the contract?

PANIKE & SONS FARMS, INC. V. SMITH

Supreme Court of Idaho
147 Idaho 562, 212 P.3d 992 (2009)

Opinion

BURDICK, JUSTICE.

This action involves a dispute over a pre-season contract between Appellant Panike & Sons Farms, Inc. (Panike) and Respondent Four Rivers Packing Co. (Four Rivers) for the sale of onions. The contract stated that the buyer (Four Rivers) would designate the fields from which the onions would come, and then required that the onions "meet 75% three-inch minimum requirements." Panike contends that the district court erred in finding that Panike breached the contract by failing to deliver onions from the fields specified by Four Rivers. * * * We affirm in part, but remand. * * *

I. FACTUAL AND PROCEDURAL BACKGROUND

Panike is an Oregon based corporation, operated by Greg Panike, that raises crops including onions. Four Rivers is an Idaho corporation organized for the purpose of purchasing onions from area growers, packing, and contracting to resell those onions nationwide. Randy Smith is the general manager of Four Rivers. In January 2006, Panike entered into a contract with Four Rivers for the sale of onions from Panike's 2006 and 2007 onion crops. The contract required Panike to deliver 25,000 hundredweight (cwt) 75% three-inch minimum field run onions to Four Rivers from fields specified by Four Rivers, for the price of $4.75 per cwt. The field selection clause stated the "[b]uyer will specify field(s)."

In mid-August 2006, Mr. Panike contacted Mr. Smith, who owns farmland adjacent to Panike's land in Malheur County, Oregon, to inform him that water leaking from Mr. Smith's ditch was running into Panike's field. During that conversation, Mr. Smith told Mr. Panike that Four Rivers would be designating the fields from which Panike was to deliver the 25,000 cwt of onions. Mr. Panike then informed Mr. Smith that Panike would not deliver onions from those fields, as Mr. Panike believed those onions were a different variety and larger than those specified by the contract. On August 15, 2006, Four Rivers sent a letter to Panike reiterating that it would designate the fields from which the onions were to be delivered. Four Rivers sent another letter to Panike on August 25 designating the fields, with a map attached that illustrated which fields Four Rivers had chosen.

On October 3, 2006, Panike attempted to deliver two truck loads of onions to Four Rivers's packing shed. When Mr. Panike arrived, Janine Smith, part owner of Four Rivers and wife of Mr. Smith, asked Mr. Panike whether the onions were from the specified fields. When he stated they were not, Mrs. Smith rejected the onions. Panike then had the onions inspected by the Idaho Department of Agriculture, which determined the onions were 89% three-inch minimum or larger. * * *

On November 22, 2006, Panike filed suit against Four Rivers in its corporate capacity. Although originally scheduled for a jury trial, the parties stipulated to waive trial before a jury and tried the case before the court on October 29, 2007. Judgment was entered on January 28, 2008 in favor of Four Rivers in the amount of $311,250.00, with attorney fees in the amount of $16,680.00, and costs in the amount of $1,194.79, for a total judgment of $329,124.79. * * *

II. ANALYSIS

* * *

B. Four Rivers properly rejected the onions tendered by Panike.

Panike argues that the onions it attempted to deliver to Four Rivers conformed to the contract in kind, quality, condition, and amount, and therefore Four Rivers wrongfully rejected onions that met or exceeded every essential element of the contract. Four Rivers counters that the contract speaks in terms of minimum quality requirements and specifically allows Four Rivers to designate the fields. In addition, Four Rivers argues that designation of onion fields is a method of dealing regularly observed in the onion trade justifying an expectation that it would be observed with respect to the transaction here.

Where the language of the contract makes the intentions of the parties clear, the interpretation and legal effect of the contract are questions of law over which this Court exercises free review. *Lickley v. Max Herbold, Inc.,*

133 Idaho 209, 211, 984 P.2d 697, 699 (1999). When interpreting a contract provision, we must view the entire agreement as a whole to discern the parties' intentions. *Id.* Here, the language at issue in the contract simply stated: "Buyer will specify field(s). The onions described above must meet 75% three-inch minimum requirements." That language specifically states that Four Rivers would specify the fields from which Panike would tender onions. However, Mr. Panike testified he believed that any designation of fields was to occur when the contract was signed. In contrast, Four Rivers contends that, in accordance with I.C. § 28–1–303(c) and (d), the usage of trade among onion growers allowed for the fields to be designated during the growing season.

Pursuant to I.C. § 28–1–303(c) "usage of trade" is "any practice or method of dealing having such regularity of observance in a place, vocation, or trade as to justify an expectation that it will be observed with respect to the transaction in question. The existence and scope of such a usage must be proved as facts." In addition, I.C. § 28–1–303(d) provides that usage of trade "of which [the parties] are or should be aware is relevant in ascertaining the meaning of the parties' agreement, may give particular meaning to specific terms of the agreement, and may supplement or qualify the terms of the agreement."

The district court found that Four Rivers had "established through the combined testimony of Steve Walker, George Rodriguez, Floyd Johnson, Dennis Ujiiye, and Randy Smith that the designation of fields in mid to late summer is the normal practice in the industry." Mr. Walker testified that his business monitors the fields of the growers it contracts with throughout the season and then requests certain fields: "So generally with our growers we will go out and say, yeah, we'd like to have this field, and they'll say, well, will you take part of this field and part of this field, you know. So there is a little give and take. . . ." Mr. Rodriguez testified that his company usually makes field designations in July, so if a field does not meet requirements the company can designate another field. Mr. Johnson stated that, as manager and vice president of Lynn Josephson Produce, he enters into pre-season contracts with area growers that reserve the right to specify fields, and that the fields are specified at the time of harvest. In contrast, Mr. Ujiiye, as a grower, testified that he did not sign pre-season contracts because he "didn't want the buyer to be able to designate the fields." Finally, Mr. Smith testified that Four Rivers always includes a provision allowing it to specify fields in preseason contracts. Mr. Panike also testified that he was familiar with the designation of fields in the onion business, but his understanding was that such designation was to take place at the time of contracting.

The district court based its determination that designating fields during the growing season was the usage of the onion trade on substantial and competent evidence. Therefore, Four Rivers had a contractual right to designate the fields from which Panike was to tender the onions.

If goods fail in any respect to conform to the terms of the contract, a buyer may reject them. *Keller v. Inland Metals All Weather Conditioning, Inc.,* 139 Idaho 233, 237, 76 P.3d 977, 981 (2003); I.C. § 28–2–601(a). More specifically, I.C. § 28–2–601 states:

> [I]f the goods or the tender of delivery fail in any respect to conform to the contract, the buyer may
>
> (a) reject the whole; or
>
> (b) accept the whole; or
>
> (c) accept any commercial unit or units and reject the rest.

Four Rivers first sought to exercise the field selection provision on August 15, 2006 when it sent a letter to Panike informing Panike that Four Rivers would be designating the fields within the next few days. On August 25, 2006, Four Rivers sent a letter to Panike designating the fields. Panike concedes that it refused to deliver onions from the fields specified by Four Rivers.

We find, based upon the clear language of the contract and usage of trade, that Four Rivers had a right to designate the fields. Therefore, when Panike attempted to deliver onions that were not from the designated fields, Four Rivers rightfully rejected the non-conforming goods.

* * *

III. CONCLUSION

We affirm the district court's determination that Four Rivers's rejection of the onions was proper, but remand for an entry of judgment consistent with this opinion.

QUESTIONS AND NOTE

1. Questions about the facts of this case

    1.1. So, do you know your onions?* Why do you suppose Four Rivers wanted the right to specify the fields from which the onions were to be originated?

    1.2. What did Panike think the provision "[b]uyer will specify field(s)" meant?

---

* Uh, it's a phrase that means something like "to know one's oats, to know one's oil, to know one's apples, to know one's eggs, and even to know one's sweet potatoes." See http://www.worldwidewords.org/qa/qa-kno1.htm.

1.3. What was the relevance of the USDA's certification that 89% of the onions were three inches (or larger) in diameter?

1.4. Why did Four Rivers introduce the testimony of Steve Walker, George Rodriguez, Floyd Johnson, Dennis Ujiiye, and Randy Smith?

1.5. So what does Panike do now? With onions, it is easy to cry . . . .

2. Questions about the law

2.1. Why did Four Rivers introduce trade usage testimony (this is connected to question 1.4 above)?

2.2. Is it relevant that Panike did not know that buyers could specify fields after the purchase contract was signed and before harvest?

2.3. Would the outcome be different if Panike had introduced uncontroverted testimony that custom in the industry was that if onions delivered met the size and quality requirements specified in the contract, parties used field designation provisions as indications of preference, rather than requirements of origin? Why?

3. Note

The perfect tender rule is not as hard-edged as it might first seem. First, as the discussion of trade usage above indicates, the terms used in a contract have to be interpreted in light of relevant trade usage. If I go to buy 2x4 boards, and they don't measure 2 inches by 4 inches, I cannot invoke the perfect tender rule since trade usage is that 2x4 lumber generally only measures 1.5 inches by 3.5 inches.

Second, the perfect tender rule only applies in single-delivery contracts; the introductory provision of section 2–601 states that the perfect tender rule is "*[s]ubject to* the provisions of this Article on breach in installment contracts (Section 2–612)." We'll leave exploration of section 2–612 to an advanced course in Sales, but the key point is that if one party's performance obligations are numerous and spread over time (imagine a year-long contract calling for monthly delivery of 2 cases of apples on the first of every month) any non-performance with respect to an installment will not be subject to the perfect tender rule.

Finally, as we will see in Chapter 7, parties under the U.C.C. (and common law) can agree to certain remedies such as liquidated damages or such as a repair and replace remedy (check out the paperwork that comes with any consumer good you buy). If the contract contains these types of provisions, then Section 2–601 does not apply. Section 2–601 supplies a right to reject "*unless otherwise agreed* under the sections on contractual limitations of remedy (Sections 2–718 and 2–719)." (emphasis supplied).

D. EXCUSE: "ANTICIPATORY REPUDIATION" AS OTHER GUY'S UNAMBIGUOUS INDICATION OF AN UNWILLINGNESS OR INABILITY TO PERFORM

1. Unequivocal Statement as Anticipatory Repudiation

Ponoroff contracts to paint Epstein's house for $5,000. The contract provides that Epstein is to pay Ponoroff within 15 days after Ponoroff finishes work.

Ponoroff is painting his little heart out, more than halfway finished, when Epstein tells him: "Son, you are doing a great job. Best paint work I have ever seen—painting is what you ought to be doing instead of writing a contracts book. Damn shame that I am one of these people who makes a deal and does not do what he agreed to do. I am not going to pay you anything for your work 15 days after you finish or ever."

Do you think Ponoroff is going to keep on painting? Shouldn't Epstein's statement—his anticipatory repudiation—excuse Ponoroff from doing what he agreed to do and give Ponoroff the right to sue Epstein for breach of contract without waiting 15 days?

Easy questions. *Restatement (Second) of Contracts* § 253 answers both questions "yes," using the word "repudiation" which is defined in *Restatement (Second) of Contracts* § 250. Similarly, section 2–610 of the U.C.C. answers both questions "yes," using the term "anticipatory repudiation" in both the title and the Official Comment.

The next case, *Hochster v. De La Tour*, provides a similar answer, without using the term "anticipatory repudiation" or the word "repudiation" (even though *Hochster v. De La Tour* is generally regarded as the germinal case on anticipatory repudiation).

QUESTIONS BEFORE THE CASE

1. What is the sequence of events here?
2. Why did Hochster sue before the start date of his duties with De La Tour?

HOCHSTER V. DE LA TOUR

Court of Queen's Bench
118 Eng. Rep. 922 (1853)

On the trial, before Erle, J., at the London sittings in last Easter Term, it appeared that plaintiff was a courier, who, in April, 1852, was engaged by defendant to accompany him on a tour, to commence on 1st June 1852, on the terms mentioned in the declaration. On the 11th May 1852, defendant wrote to plaintiff that he had changed his mind, and declined his services. He refused to make him any compensation. The action was commenced on 22d May. The plaintiff, between the commencement of the action and the 1st June, obtained an engagement with Lord Ashburton, on equally good terms, but not commencing till 4th July. The defendant's counsel objected that there could be no breach of the contract before the 1st of June. The learned judge was of a contrary opinion, but reserved leave to enter a nonsuit on this objection. The other questions were left to the jury, who found for plaintiff.

Hugh Hill, in the same Term, obtained a rule *nisi* to enter a nonsuit, or arrest the judgment.

* * *

LORD CAMPBELL, C.J., now delivered the judgment of the Court.

On this motion in arrest of judgment, the question arises, Whether, if there be an agreement between A. and B., whereby B. engages to employ A. on and from a future day for a given period of time, to travel with him into a foreign country as a courier, and to start with him in that capacity on that day, A. being to receive a monthly salary during the continuance of such service, B. may, before the day, refuse to perform the agreement and break and renounce it, so as to entitle A. before the day to commence an action against B. to recover damages for breach of the agreement; A. having been ready and willing to perform it, till it was broken and renounced by B. The defendant's counsel very powerfully contended that, if the plaintiff was not contented to dissolve the contract, and to abandon all remedy upon it, he was bound to remain ready and willing to perform it till the day when the actual employment as courier in the service of the defendant was to begin; and that there could be no breach of the agreement, before that day, to give a right of action. But it cannot be laid down as a universal rule that, where by agreement an act is to be done on a future day, no action can be brought for a breach of the agreement till the day for doing the act has arrived. If a man promises to marry a woman on a future day, and before that day marries another woman, he is instantly liable to an action for breach of promise of marriage; Short v. Stone, (8 Q.B. 358). If a man contracts to execute a lease on and from a future day for a certain term, and, before that day, executes a lease to another for the same term, he may be immediately sued for breaking the contract; Ford v: Tiley, (6 B. & C.

325). So, if a man contracts to sell and deliver specific goods on a future day, and before the day he sells and delivers them to another, he is immediately liable to an action at the suit of the person with whom he first contracted to sell and deliver them; Bowdef v. Parsons, (10 East, 359). One reason alleged in support of such an action is, that the defendant has, before the day, rendered it impossible for him to perform the contract at the day; but this does not necessarily follow; for, prior to the day fixed for doing the act, the first wife may have died, a surrender of the lease executed might be obtained, and the defendant might have repurchased the goods so as to be in a situation to sell and deliver them to the plaintiff. Another reason may be, that, where there is a contract to do an act on a future day, there is a relation constituted between the parties in the meantime by the contract, and that they impliedly promise that in the meantime neither will do anything to the prejudice of the other inconsistent with that relation. As an example, a man and woman engaged to marry are affianced to one another during the period between the time of the engagement and the celebration of the marriage. In this very case, of traveller and courier, from the day of the hiring till the day when the employment was to begin, they were engaged to each other; and it seems to be a breach of an implied contract if either of them renounces the engagement. This reasoning seems in accordance with the unanimous decision of the Exchequer Chamber in Edlerton v. Emmens, [6 Com. B. 160], which we have followed in subsequent cases in this Court. The declaration in the present case, in alleging a breach, states a great deal more than a passing intention on the part of the defendant which he may repent of, and could only be proved by evidence that he had utterly renounced the contract, or done some act which rendered it impossible for him to perform it. If the plaintiff has no remedy for breach of the contract unless he treats the contract as in force, and acts upon it down to the 1st June 1852, it follows that, till then, he must enter into no employment which will interfere with his promise "to start with the defendant on such travels on the day and year," and that he must then be properly equipped in all aspects as a courier for a three months' tour on the continent of Europe. But it is surely much more rational, and more for the benefit of both parties, that, after the renunciation of the agreement by the defendant, the plaintiff should be at liberty to consider himself absolved from any future performance of it, retaining his right to sue for any damage he has suffered from the breach of it. Thus, instead of remaining idle and laying out money in preparations which must be useless, he is at liberty to seek service under another employer; which would go in mitigation of the damages to which he would otherwise be for a breach of the contract. It seems strange that the defendant, after renouncing the contract, and absolutely declaring that he will never act under it, should be permitted to object that faith is given to his assertion, and that an opportunity is not left to him of changing his mind. If the plaintiff is barred of any remedy by entering into an engagement inconsistent with starting as a courier with the defendant on the 1st June, he is prejudiced by putting faith in the defendant's assertion: and it would be more consonant with principle, if the defendant were precluded from saying that he had not broken the contract when he declared that he entirely renounced it. Suppose that the defendant, at the time of his renunciation, had embarked on a voyage for Australia, so as to render it physically impossible for him to employ the plaintiff as a courier on the continent of Europe in the months of June, July, and August 1852: according to decided cases, the action might have been brought before the 1st June; but the renunciation may have been founded on other facts, to be given in evidence, which would equally have rendered the defendant's performance of the contract impossible. The man who wrongfully renounces a contract into which he has deliberately entered cannot justly complain if he is immediately sued for a compensation in damages by the man whom he has injured: and it seems reasonable to allow an option to the injured party, either to sue immediately; or to wait till the time when the act was to be done, still holding it as prospectively binding for the exercise of this option, which may be advantageous to the innocent party, and cannot be prejudicial to the wrongdoer. An argument against the action before the 1st of June, is urged from the difficulty of calculating the damages: but this argument is equally strong against an action before the 1st of September, when the three months would expire. In either case, the jury in assessing the damages would be justified in looking to all that had happened, or was likely to happen, to increase or mitigate the loss of the plaintiff down to the day of trial. We do not find any decision contrary to the view we are taking of this case. * * *

If it should be held that, upon a contract to do an act on a future day, a renunciation of the contract by one party dispenses with a condition to be performed in the meantime by the other, there seems no reason for requiring that other to wait till the day arrives before seeking his remedy by action: and the only ground on which the condition can be dispensed with seems to be, that the renunciation may be treated as a breach of the contract.

Upon the whole, we think that the declaration in this case is sufficient. It gives us great satisfaction to reflect that, the question being on the record, our opinion may be reviewed in a Court of Error. In the meantime we must give judgment for the plaintiff.

Judgment for Plaintiff.

QUESTIONS

1. Questions about the facts of this case

   1.1. What was Hochster hired to do? Why couldn't he do it?

   1.2. What were De La Tour's duties under the contract? Had they yet matured when De La Tour indicated that he would not need Hochster's services?

2. Questions about the law

   2.1. What is a "motion to arrest the judgment"? Sheriffs aren't taking involuntary possession of pieces of paper, are they?

   2.2. If De La Tour's obligations under the contract had not yet matured (he didn't yet owe Hochster anything, right?), how can he be held in breach?

3. **You Be the Lawyer!**

   Suppose that, on the day after Hochster files his lawsuit, De La Tour changes his mind again, and tells Hochster that he wants Hochster to work as promised. One small problem, though: Hochster has contracted to travel with Lord Ashburton. So if De La Tour retracts his repudiation, isn't Hochster immediately in breach with either De La Tour or Lord Ashburton?

---

2. Unambiguous Conduct as Anticipatory Repudiation

In the Ponoroff/Epstein house painting story, Epstein's words clearly indicated his intent not to perform. His words were definite and unequivocal. Similarly, in *Hochster v. De La Tour*, De La Tour's words of repudiation were definite and unequivocal.

As the United States Court of Appeals for the Seventh Circuit stated in *Carnes Co. v. Stone Mechanical, Inc.*, 412 F.3d 845, 854 (7th Cir. 2005):

> In order to constitute an anticipatory repudiation of a contract, there must be a definite and unequivocal manifestation of intention on the part of the repudiator that he will not render the promised performance when the time fixed for it in the contract arrives.

Note the Seventh Circuit's use of the term "manifestation of intention." An intent to repudiate can be manifested by conduct as well as words. The *Restatement* provides the following easy example: "On April 1, A contracts to sell, and B to buy land, delivery of the deed and payment of the price to be on July 29. A says nothing to B on May 1, but on that date he contracts to sell the land to C. A's making of the contract with C is a repudiation." Illustration 5 to *Restatement (Second)* § 250.

How unequivocal does the conduct have to be? In *Wholesale Sand & Gravel, Inc. v. Decker*, 630 A.2d 710 (Me. 1993), Decker, a Maine resident, contracted with Wholesale to replace Decker's dirt driveway with a gravel one. The contract was signed on June 12, about the end of winter in Maine. Payment was to be made within 90 days of the date the contract was signed. The court explains what happens next:

> Wholesale began work on the driveway on the weekend after the contract was executed and immediately experienced difficulty because of the wetness of the ground. In fact, Wholesale's bulldozer became stuck in the mud and had to be removed with a backhoe. Wholesale returned to the site the following weekend, when it attempted to stabilize the driveway site by hauling out mud and hauling in gravel. Because the ground was too wet to allow Wholesale to perform the work without substantially exceeding the contract price. Goodenow [Wholesale's president] decided to wait for the ground to dry out before proceeding further.
>
> On July 12, 1989, Decker contacted Goodenow concerning the lack of activity at the site and his urgent need to have the driveway completed. Goodenow responded that he would "get right on it." On July 19, Decker telephoned Goodenow to inquire again about the lack of activity and gave him one week in which to finish the driveway. Again, Goodenow said that he would "get right on it." On July 28, Decker called Goodenow for the purpose of terminating the contract. When Goodenow stated that he would be at the site the next day, Decker decided to give him one more chance. Goodenow, however, did not appear at the site and Decker subsequently terminated the contract.

630 A.2d at 711.

When Decker sues Wholesale for breach, who wins—Decker, because of Wholesale's repudiation through inaction, or Wholesale, because of Decker's termination?

---

3. Retractions of Repudiations

Have you ever said anything, and then wanted to take it back? If you're human, you have. So you might expect that contract law has rules to deal with the contract version of "taking back" what was said; that is, retracting a repudiation.

QUESTIONS BEFORE THE CASE

1. When did Wild Rose's actions repudiate the 2004 contract? What was the effect of any repudiation on Pavone's damages claims?
2. What actions does Pavone rely upon for its claims that the repudiation was retracted?

PAVONE V. KIRKE

Supreme Court of Iowa
807 N.W.2d 828 (2011)

WIGGINS, JUSTICE.

In this appeal, the parties to a contract contend the district court erred when it granted the opposing parties' motion for summary judgment by finding the opposing parties repudiated the contract. * * * The court of appeals affirmed the district court's ruling. We * * * affirm the decision of the court of appeals and the judgment of the district court.

I. Background Facts and Proceedings.

On October 22, 2004, John Pavone and Signature Management Group, L.L.C. (hereinafter collectively referred to as SMG) and Gerald M. Kirke and Wild Rose Entertainment, L.L.C. (hereinafter collectively referred to as Wild Rose) executed a document entitled "Agreement," which, in part, attempted to delineate the parties' relationship with regard to future casino projects in Iowa. Paragraph five of the agreement deals with future management opportunities and provides:

> 5. *Future Casino Development Opportunities.*
>
> A. First Look and Good Faith Negotiation as to Future Casino Development and Management Opportunities.
>
> i. If Wild Rose has the opportunity to develop or operate *any other casino in Iowa,* Wild Rose will use good faith best efforts to involve SMG when the opportunity is first known, *and to negotiate in good faith a Management Agreement* consistent with the terms outlined in Wild Rose's gaming development agreement with the City of Ottumwa, Iowa. It being understood that the award of any management agreement must also be satisfactory to third party community and non-profit organizations. And it being further understood that any casino in the Central Iowa area will likely require the involvement of a management company, other than SMG.

(Emphasis added.)

On May 11, 2005, the Iowa Racing and Gaming Commission (IRGC) awarded Wild Rose a gaming license to develop a casino in Emmetsburg. On May 24 Wild Rose sent a letter to SMG (hereinafter referred to as the "termination letter") allegedly terminating the October agreement and any future relationship between the parties. This letter stated:

> This letter is to formally notify you that the Agreement dated October 22, 2004 (the "Agreement") between Signature Management Group, L.L.C. ("Signature") and Wild Rose Entertainment, L.L.C., terminated pursuant to its terms effective May 11, 2005. Upon receipt of a final invoice from Signature, Wild Rose will pay the agreed consulting fees and expenses through May 11, 2005.
>
> Since the Iowa Racing and Gaming Commission did not award a license to Wild Rose for the Ottumwa project, and the referendums were defeated in Warren, Madison and Dallas counties last November, the contingencies set forth in the Agreement unfortunately were not satisfied.
>
> We thank you for the consulting services Signature provided to Wild Rose and sincerely regret we were unable to realize our respective expectations under the Agreement.

The attorney for Wild Rose, Jim Krambeck, also e-mailed a copy of the termination letter to SMG's attorney, Ryan Ross, that same day. Ross responded via e-mail asking Krambeck, "Does this mean Wild Rose has ended negotiations as to the Management Agreement/Buy-out, or are you still waiting to talk with your client later this week? Please let me know so that I can advise Signature accordingly." Krambeck responded:

> Ryan, As reported in my e-mail message earlier today I will meet with my clients as soon as they are available to discuss their thoughts concerning the future relationship, if any, with John Pavone. Following that meeting I will be in contact with you.
>
> In response to your 12:10 p.m. e-mail, I strongly disagree with your characterization of the facts, the issues & the position of Wild Rose in this matter. A point by point rebuttal is not appropriate at this time, however, to claim that Wild Rose "walked out of the negotiations" is simply not true. The fact is that we thought we were close to an agreement on the Ottumwa project when your client refused to agree after you told me you thought we had a deal & then sought to revisit issues that had been previously resolved. Unfortunately, the parties simply were unable to reach agreement. I am still willing to work on finding common ground but if this dispute is to be resolved, your adversarial & inflammatory e-mail messages will need to be curtailed.

The next day, Ross e-mailed Krambeck stating,

> Jim: Thank you for clarifying that negotiations continue. I will wait to hear back from you after you speak with your clients. Signature remains prepared to continue negotiating the terms of the Management Agreement as required by the October 22, 2004 agreement.

There is no evidence Wild Rose responded to this last e-mail or that any further negotiations occurred. On July 12, 2005, SMG sent a proposed management agreement for the Emmetsburg casino to Wild Rose, requesting that Wild Rose execute the agreement and return it to SMG. There is no evidence Wild Rose responded, and the parties never executed a management agreement for the Emmetsburg casino.

On March 31, 2006, SMG filed a civil action against Wild Rose (hereinafter referred to as the "Emmetsburg action") alleging, in part, Wild Rose breached the management agreement contained in paragraph 3A of the October agreement for the Emmetsburg casino and failed to negotiate in good faith a management agreement for the Emmetsburg casino in violation of paragraph 5A. * * * During the course of the Emmetsburg action, on June 8, 2006, the IRGC awarded Wild Rose a gaming license to develop a casino in Clinton. Wild Rose did not contact or negotiate a management agreement with SMG regarding management of the Clinton casino. On August 15, 2008, SMG filed [suit against Wild Rose regarding Clinton.] SMG alleged Wild Rose breached paragraph 5A of the October agreement by failing to negotiate in good faith with SMG for the management of the Clinton casino. * * * Wild Rose denied the allegations in the petition and asserted a number of affirmative defenses.

Wild Rose filed a motion for summary judgment, arguing the doctrine of claim preclusion barred SMG's current claim as a matter of law. The district court granted Wild Rose's motion for summary judgment, concluding the doctrine of claim preclusion barred SMG's current claim because both actions involved the same agreement and provision, the parties were the same in both actions, and there was ample time for SMG to seek damages relating to the Clinton casino in the Emmetsburg action. Thus, the district court held, "Plaintiffs have split their claim for breach of the agreement; therefore, this case is barred by the doctrine of claim preclusion."

SMG filed a notice of appeal. * * * The court of appeals affirmed the district court's entry of summary judgment in favor of Wild Rose. The court of appeals concluded the termination letter was a definite and unequivocal repudiation of the entire October agreement, which Wild Rose never nullified or retracted.

* * *

III. Discussion and Analysis.

A. *Repudiation.* SMG claims a genuine issue of material fact exists as to whether Wild Rose repudiated the October agreement. It further claims if there is no genuine issue of fact as to repudiation, a genuine issue of fact exists as to whether Wild Rose retracted its repudiation.

1. *Repudiations generally.* The Restatement (Second) of Contracts defines a contractual repudiation as:

> (a) a statement by the obligor to the obligee indicating that the obligor will commit a breach that would of itself give the obligee a claim for damages for total breach under § 243, or
>
> (b) a voluntary affirmative act which renders the obligor unable or apparently unable to perform without such a breach.

Restatement (Second) of Contracts § 250, at 272 (1981). The Restatement further explains that "[i]n order to constitute a repudiation, a party's language must be sufficiently positive to be reasonably interpreted to mean that the party will not or cannot perform." *Id.* § 250 cmt. *b,* at 273.

Iowa law is consistent with section 250 of the Restatement. *See, e.g., Conrad Bros. v. John Deere Ins. Co.,* 640 N.W.2d 231, 241 (Iowa 2001) (recognizing, to constitute a repudiation, "[t]he statement must be sufficiently positive to be reasonably understood . . . that the breach will actually occur" (internal quotation marks omitted)); *Lane v. Crescent Beach Lodge & Resort, Inc.,* 199 N.W.2d 78, 82 (Iowa 1972) ("Anticipatory breach requires a definite and unequivocal repudiation of the contract."). A repudiation is accomplished by words or acts before the time of performance evidencing an intention to refuse to perform in the future. *Lane,* 199 N.W.2d at 82. Moreover, we have recognized a party does not prove a repudiation by simply showing a party's negative attitude, a party's attitude indicating more negotiations are sought, or that a party may finally perform. *Id.*

2. *Repudiation analysis.* SMG argues the termination letter does not amount to a total repudiation of the October agreement because it is ambiguous. In response, Wild Rose argues the termination letter unambiguously communicated Wild Rose's intent not to perform further under the October agreement and, therefore, constituted a total repudiation of the October agreement.

The termination letter definitely and unequivocally declared Wild Rose's belief that the October agreement "terminated pursuant to its terms effective May 11, 2005." Wild Rose then thanked SMG for its consulting services and expressed its regret that the parties' expectations under the October agreement were not realized.

SMG argues the letter is ambiguous because it is unclear whether the termination letter only applies to the counties specifically mentioned in the letter (i.e., Warren, Madison, and Dallas, but not Clinton) or all projects the parties were working on at the time (i.e., including Clinton). However, the termination letter explicitly evinces Wild Rose's intent to terminate the entirety of the October agreement. Moreover, Wild Rose's expression of regret that the parties' expectations under the October agreement were not realized clearly indicates a total repudiation of any obligations it had under the agreement, including any expectations the parties had about any future projects, including Clinton.

SMG also contends the October agreement required 120 days written notice to terminate "pursuant to its terms." Therefore, because the termination letter attempted to terminate the October agreement retroactively, its intended effect is ambiguous. Simply because Wild Rose failed to abide by the termination provisions of the October agreement does not mean the termination letter was not an unequivocal repudiation. Wild Rose correctly notes that "[t]he letter by definition would not have been a 'repudiation' if Wild Rose had invoked the voluntary termination provision and purported to give 120 days notice." The fact that Wild Rose did not give 120 days written notice before terminating the October agreement reinforces that Wild Rose was in breach of the October agreement due to its unequivocal repudiation.

Additionally, SMG argues the termination letter was not an unambiguous repudiation because SMG did not elect to treat it as such. After the termination letter, SMG's attorney appeared to believe negotiations for the Emmetsburg management agreement were to continue pursuant to the October agreement. Moreover, a few months later, SMG sent Wild Rose a proposed management agreement for the Emmetsburg casino to be executed between the parties. However, the record does not contain any evidence that Wild Rose responded to the proposed management agreement or participated in any further negotiations. "The injured party does not change the effect of a repudiation by urging the repudiator to perform in spite of his repudiation or to retract his repudiation." Restatement (Second) of Contracts § 257, at 296. Therefore, SMG's mistaken belief about the effect of the termination letter and its urging of Wild Rose to execute a management agreement pursuant to the October agreement cannot change the effect of Wild Rose's unequivocal repudiation of its obligations under the October agreement.

Finally, SMG knew Wild Rose repudiated the October agreement because it filed suit in the Emmetsburg action to enforce the agreement. There would have been no reason for SMG to file the Emmetsburg action if Wild Rose had not repudiated the October agreement.

Accordingly, we hold the termination letter was sufficiently positive to be reasonably interpreted to mean that Wild Rose intended not to perform any more obligations it may have had under the October agreement. Therefore, as a matter of law, the termination letter constituted a total repudiation of the October agreement. Consequently, there is no genuine issue of material fact that the language of the termination letter met this requirement.

3. *Retraction of the repudiation.* SMG argues, even if there was an unambiguous repudiation of the October agreement, Wild Rose nullified the repudiation by e-mailing SMG after the termination letter and stating that it was "still willing to work on finding common ground." In response, Wild Rose argues this e-mail did not express a willingness by Wild Rose to engage in further negotiations under the October agreement. According to Wild Rose, the statement, "I am still willing to work on finding common ground," merely represented that its attorney would see whether Wild Rose had any interest in dealing with SMG on some other basis in the future, apart from the October agreement.

A repudiation may be retracted "if notification of the retraction comes to the attention of the injured party before he materially changes his position in reliance on the repudiation or indicates to the other party that he considers the repudiation to be final." *Id.* § 256, at 293. However, as noted above, "[an] injured party does change the effect of a repudiation by urging the repudiator to perform in spite of his repudiation or to retract his repudiation." *Id.* § 257, at 296.

Upon receipt of the termination letter, SMG's attorney responded by e-mail urging Wild Rose to continue to negotiate. After receiving the e-mail from SMG urging Wild Rose to continue to negotiate, Wild Rose's attorney replied with a two-paragraph e-mail. The first paragraph responded directly to SMG's request that Wild Rose continue to negotiate a management agreement. This paragraph stated the attorney for Wild Rose would meet with Wild Rose and discuss "the future relationship, if any, with John Pavone." The use of the phrase "if any" is consistent with Wild Rose's prior repudiation. The first paragraph of the e-mail makes it clear that there will not be a future between the parties unless Wild Rose agrees to continue to negotiate.

The second paragraph of the e-mail responds to a 12:10 p.m. email not contained in the record. This paragraph refers to the negotiations prior to the receipt of the letter by Wild Rose repudiating the contract. It contains the statement, "I am still willing to work on finding common ground but if this dispute is to be resolved, your adversarial & inflammatory e-mail messages will need to be curtailed." This sentence does not retract Wild Rose's repudiation. The sentence only indicates that Wild Rose's attorney

will continue to negotiate as long as SMG's attorney curtails the tone of his e-mails.

A further fact indicating Wild Rose did not retract the repudiation is that Wild Rose did not communicate or negotiate further with SMG after the exchange of e-mails on May 24. Even though SMG sent Wild Rose a proposed management agreement for the Emmetsburg casino on July 12, Wild Rose never responded to the proposal. SMG's filing of the Emmetsburg action confirmed SMG knew of Wild Rose's repudiation.

Wild Rose's failure to get back to SMG after the exchange of e-mails on May 24 and its failure to respond to the proposed management agreement showed Wild Rose's clear intent not to retract its repudiation. SMG cannot claim Wild Rose retracted its repudiation by its unilateral acts urging Wild Rose to continue to perform. *Id.* SMG's filing of the Emmetsburg action shows SMG understood Wild Rose repudiated the October agreement.

Therefore, we agree with the district court that there is no genuine issue of material fact as to whether Wild Rose retracted the repudiation.

* * *

IV. Disposition.

We find no genuine issue of material fact exists as to whether Wild Rose repudiated the October agreement. * * * Therefore, we affirm the decision of the court of appeals and the judgment of the district court.

QUESTIONS AND NOTE

1. Questions about the facts of the case

   1.1. Who wanted the original agreement to continue? SMG or Wild Rose?

   1.2. Did SMG file one or two (or more) actions against Wild Rose? What do you think its theory of recovery regarding the Clinton casino was?

   1.3. What facts did SMG adduce to prove that the letter stating the agreement was terminated was not really a repudiation?

2. Questions about the law

   2.1. Why does the court characterize Wild Rose's actions as "repudiation" rather than "breach"? What's the difference?

   2.2. Would the outcome of the case have been different if Wild Rose's attorney, Krambeck, had responded initially by writing "We are unhappy about the course of negotiations, but as you know, we

still wish to work with you in accordance with our prior agreement." Why or why not?

3. **You Be the Lawyer!**

You are in the position of Krambeck, Wild Rose's attorney. After you sent your termination letter and your responsive emails to SMG's attorney, your client calls and says "Hold everything! We just found out some new stuff about Pavone and SMG—we really want to work with them, because we can make millions! Please go make nice with them and make sure we can keep them in our current agreement." What should you do now?

4. Note

The U.C.C. treats retraction of a repudiation separately. Section 2–611 states:

> **§ 2–611. Retraction of Anticipatory Repudiation.**
>
> (1) Until the repudiating party's next performance is due he can retract his repudiation unless the aggrieved party has since the repudiation cancelled or materially changed his position or otherwise indicated that he considers the repudiation final.
>
> (2) Retraction may be by any method which clearly indicates to the aggrieved party that the repudiating party intends to perform, but must include any assurance justifiably demanded under the provisions of this Article (Section 2–609) . . . .

How does this standard compare with that stated in *Pavone*?

And what does paragraph (2) mean by its reference to section 2–609? Read on . . .

---

4. Failure to Give Adequate Assurance of Future Performance as Repudiation (at least under the U.C.C.)

Given the strong requirements in repudiation doctrine for a definite and unambiguous statement, what is a party to a contract to do if the other side is "just making noises" about not performing? In *Pavone*, it would be like Wild Rose saying "We are unhappy with progress" as opposed to flatly terminating the agreement. Is there anything that can be done?

The next case tries to answer this in a common law setting. In doing so, it borrows from the U.C.C. How does the court accomplish its result? How does the U.C.C.?

QUESTIONS BEFORE THE CASE

1. There is a complicated contract here, with different pricing (and different computations of price) during different time periods. Why is the matter so complex?
2. Is there a term of the contract that the court is interpreting? (caution: that's a trick question)

NORCON POWER PARTNERS, L.P. V. NIAGARA MOHAWK POWER CORP.

Court of Appeals of New York
92 N.Y.2d 458, 705 N.E.2d 656, 682 N.Y.S.2d 664 (1998)

BELLACOSA, J.

The doctrine, known as demand for adequate assurance of future performance, is at the heart of a Federal lawsuit that stems from a 1989 contract between Norcon Power Partners, L.P., an independent power producer, and Niagara Mohawk Power Corporation, a public utility provider. Niagara Mohawk undertook to purchase electricity generated at Norcon's Pennsylvania facility. The contract was for 25 years, but the differences emerged during the early years of the arrangement.

The case arrives on this Court's docket by certification of the substantive law question from the United States Court of Appeals for the Second Circuit. Our Court is presented with an open issue that should be settled within the framework of New York's common-law development. We accepted the responsibility to address this question involving New York contract law:

> "Does a party have the right to demand adequate assurance of future performance when reasonable grounds arise to believe that the other party will commit a breach by non-performance of a contract governed by New York law, where the other party is solvent and the contract is not governed by the U.C.C.?" (*Norcon Power Partners v. Niagara Mohawk Power Corp.*, 110 F.3d 6, 9.)

As framed by the particular dispute, we answer the law question in the affirmative with an appreciation of this Court's traditional common-law developmental method, and as proportioned to the precedential sweep of our rulings.

I.

The Second Circuit Court of Appeals describes the three pricing periods, structure and details as follows:

"In the first period, Niagara Mohawk pays Norcon six cents per kilowatt-hour for electricity. In the second and third periods, the price paid by Niagara Mohawk is based on its 'avoided cost.' The avoided cost reflects the cost that Niagara Mohawk would incur to generate electricity itself or purchase it from other sources. In the second period, if the avoided cost falls below a certain floor price (calculated according to a formula), Niagara Mohawk is obligated to pay the floor price. By the same token, if the avoided cost rises above a certain amount (calculated according to a formula), Niagara Mohawk's payments are capped by a ceiling price. An 'adjustment account' tracks the difference between payments actually made by Niagara Mohawk in the second period and what those payments would have been if based solely on Niagara Mohawk's avoided cost.

"In the third period, the price paid by Niagara Mohawk is based on its avoided cost without any ceiling or floor price. Payments made by Niagara Mohawk in the third period are adjusted to account for any balance existing in the adjustment account that operated in the second period. If the adjustment account contains a balance in favor of Niagara Mohawk—that is, the payments actually made by Niagara Mohawk in the second period exceeded what those payments would have been if based solely on Niagara Mohawk's avoided cost—then the rate paid by Niagara Mohawk will be reduced to reflect the credit. If the adjustment account contains a balance in favor of Norcon, Niagara Mohawk must make increased payments to Norcon. If a balance exists in the adjustment account at the end of the third period, the party owing the balance must pay the balance in full within thirty days of the termination of the third period" (*Norcon Power Partners v. Niagara Mohawk Power Corp.*, 110 F.3d 6, 7, supra).

In February 1994, Niagara Mohawk presented Norcon with a letter stating its belief, based on revised avoided cost estimates, that substantial credits in Niagara Mohawk's favor would accrue in the adjustment account during the second pricing period. "[A]nalysis shows that the Cumulative Avoided Cost Account * * * will reach over $610 million by the end of the second period." Anticipating that Norcon would not be able to satisfy the daily escalating credits in the third period, Niagara Mohawk demanded that "Norcon provide adequate assurance to Niagara Mohawk that Norcon will duly perform all of its future repayment obligations."

Norcon promptly sued Niagara Mohawk in the United States District Court, Southern District of New York. It sought a declaration that Niagara Mohawk had no contractual right under New York State law to demand adequate assurance, beyond security provisions negotiated and expressed in the agreement. Norcon also sought a permanent injunction to stop

Niagara Mohawk from anticipatorily terminating the contract based on the reasons described in the demand letter. Niagara Mohawk counterclaimed. It sought a counter declaration that it properly invoked a right to demand adequate assurance of Norcon's future payment performance of the contract.

The District Court granted Norcon's motion for summary judgment. It reasoned that New York common law recognizes the exceptional doctrine of demand for adequate assurance only when a promisor becomes insolvent, and also when the statutory sale of goods provision under UCC 2–609, is involved. Thus, the District Court ruled in Norcon's favor because neither exception applied, in fact or by analogy to the particular dispute (decided sub nom. *Encogen Four Partners v. Niagara Mohawk Power Corp.*, 914 F. Supp. 57).

The Second Circuit Court of Appeals preliminarily agrees (110 F.3d 6, supra) with the District Court that, except in the case of insolvency, no common-law or statutory right to demand adequate assurance exists under New York law which would affect non-UCC contracts, like the instant one. Because of the uncertainty concerning this substantive law question the Second Circuit certified the question to our Court as an aid to its correct application of New York law, and with an eye toward settlement of the important precedential impact on existing and future non-UCC commercial law matters and disputes.

II.

Our analysis should reference a brief review of the evolution of the doctrine of demands for adequate assurance. Its roots spring from the doctrine of anticipatory repudiation (*see*, Garvin, *Adequate Assurance of Performance: Of Risk, Duress, and Cognition*, 69 U. Colo. L. Rev. 71, 77 [1998]). Under that familiar precept, when a party repudiates contractual duties "prior to the time designated for performance and before" all of the consideration has been fulfilled, the "repudiation entitles the nonrepudiating party to claim damages for total breach" * * * A repudiation can be either "a statement by the obligor to the obligee indicating that the obligor will commit a breach that would of itself give the obligee a claim for damages for total breach" or "a voluntary affirmative act which renders the obligor unable or apparently unable to perform without such a breach". * * *

That switch in performance expectation and burden is readily available, applied and justified when a breaching party's words or deeds are unequivocal. Such a discernible line in the sand clears the way for the nonbreaching party to broach some responsive action. When, however, the apparently breaching party's actions are equivocal or less certain, then the nonbreaching party who senses an approaching storm cloud, affecting the contractual performance, is presented with a dilemma, and must weigh hard choices and serious consequences. One commentator has described the forecast options in this way:

"If the promisee regards the apparent repudiation as an anticipatory repudiation, terminates his or her own performance and sues for breach, the promisee is placed in jeopardy of being found to have breached if the court determines that the apparent repudiation was not sufficiently clear and unequivocal to constitute an anticipatory repudiation justifying nonperformance. If, on the other hand, the promisee continues to perform after perceiving an apparent repudiation, and it is subsequently determined that an anticipatory repudiation took place, the promisee may be denied recovery for post-repudiation expenditures because of his or her failure to avoid those expenses as part of a reasonable effort to mitigate damages after the repudiation" * * *.

III.

The Uniform Commercial Code settled on a mechanism for relieving some of this uncertainty. It allows a party to a contract for the sale of goods to demand assurance of future performance from the other party when reasonable grounds for insecurity exist (*see*, UCC 2–609; II Farnsworth, Contracts § 8.23). When adequate assurance is not forthcoming, repudiation is deemed confirmed, and the nonbreaching party is allowed to take reasonable actions as though a repudiation had occurred (see, 4 Anderson, Uniform Commercial Code § 2–609:3 [3rd ed. 1997 rev.]).

UCC 2–609 provides, in relevant part:

> "(1) A contract for sale imposes an obligation on each party that the other's expectation of receiving due performance will not be impaired. When reasonable grounds for insecurity arise with respect to the performance of either party the other may in writing demand adequate assurance of due performance and until he receives such assurance may if commercially reasonable suspend any performance for which he has not already received the agreed return. * * *
>
> "(4) After receipt of a justified demand failure to provide within a reasonable time not exceeding thirty days such assurance of due performance as is adequate under the circumstances of the particular case is a repudiation of the contract."

In theory, this UCC relief valve recognizes that "the essential purpose of a contract between commercial [parties] is actual performance * * * and that a continuing sense of reliance and security that the promised performance will be forthcoming when due, is an important feature of the bargain" (UCC 2–609, Comment 1). In application, section 2–609 successfully implements the laudatory objectives of quieting the doubt a party fearing repudiation may have, mitigating the dilemma flowing from that doubt, and offering the nonbreaching party the opportunity to interpose timely action to deal with the unusual development. * * *

Indeed, UCC 2–609 has been considered so effective in bridging the doctrinal, exceptional and operational gap related to the doctrine of anticipatory breach that some States have imported the complementary regimen of demand for adequate assurance to common-law categories of contract law, using UCC 2–609 as the synapse (*see, e.g., Lo Re v. Tel-Air Communications*, 200 N.J. Super. 59, 490 A.2d 344 [finding support in U.C.C. 2–609 and *Restatement (Second) of Contracts* § 251 for applying doctrine of adequate assurance to contract to purchase radio station]; *Conference Ctr. v. TRC—The Research Corp. of New England*, 189 Conn. 212, 455 A.2d 857 [analogizing to U.C.C. 2–609, as supported by *Restatement (Second) of Contracts* § 251, in context of constructive eviction]).

Commentators have helped nudge this development along. They have noted that the problems redressed by UCC 2–609 are not unique to contracts for sale of goods, regulated under a purely statutory regime. Thus, they have cogently identified the need for the doctrine to be available in exceptional and qualifying common-law contractual settings and disputes because of similar practical, theoretical and salutary objectives (e.g., predictability, definiteness, and stability in commercial dealings and expectations) * * *.

The American Law Institute through its *Restatement (Second) of Contracts* has also recognized and collected the authorities supporting this modern development. Its process and work settled upon this black letter language:

> "(1) Where reasonable grounds arise to believe that the obligor will commit a breach by non-performance that would of itself give the obligee a claim for damages for total breach under § 243, the obligee may demand adequate assurance of due performance and may, if reasonable, suspend any performance for which he has not already received the agreed exchange until he receives such assurance.
>
> "(2) The obligee may treat as a repudiation the obligor's failure to provide within a reasonable time such assurance of due performance as is adequate in the circumstances of the particular case"

(Restatement [Second] of Contracts § 251).

Modeled on UCC 2–609, Restatement § 251 tracks "the principle that the parties to a contract look to actual performance 'and that a continuing sense of reliance and security that the promised performance will be forthcoming when due, is an important feature of the bargain' "

(Restatement [Second] of Contracts § 251, comment a, quoting UCC 2–609, Comment 1). The duty of good faith and fair dealing in the performance of the contract is also reflected in section 251 (*see*, Restatement [Second] of Contracts § 251, comment a).

Some States have adopted Restatement § 251 as their common law of contracts, in varying degrees and classifications. * * *

IV.

New York, up to now, has refrained from expanding the right to demand adequate assurance of performance beyond the Uniform Commercial Code. * * * Hence, the need for this certified question emerged so this Court could provide guidance towards a correct resolution of the Federal lawsuit by settling New York law with a modern pronouncement governing this kind of contract and dispute.

Niagara Mohawk, before our Court through the certified question from the Federal court, urges a comprehensive adaptation of the exceptional demand tool. This wholesale approach has also been advocated by the commentators (*see generally, Dowling, op. cit.; Campbell, op. cit.*). Indeed, it is even reflected in the breadth of the wording of the certified question.

This Court's jurisprudence, however, usually evolves by deciding cases and settling the law more modestly. * * * The twin purposes and functions of this Court's work require significant professional discipline and judicious circumspection.

We conclude, therefore, that it is unnecessary, while fulfilling the important and useful certification role, to promulgate so sweeping a change and proposition in contract law, as has been sought, in one dramatic promulgation. That approach might clash with our customary incremental common-law developmental process, rooted in particular fact patterns and keener wisdom acquired through observations of empirical application of a proportioned, less than absolute, rule in future cases.

It is well to note the axiom that deciding a specific case, even with the precedential comet's tail its rationale illuminates, is very different from enacting a statute of general and universal application. * * *

Experience and patience thus offer a more secure and realistic path to a better and fairer rule, in theory and in practical application. Therefore, this Court chooses to take the traditionally subtler approach, consistent with the proven benefits of the maturation process of the common law, including in the very area of anticipatory repudiation which spawns this relatively newer demand for assurance corollary. * * *

This Court is now persuaded that the policies underlying the UCC 2–609 counterpart should apply with similar cogency for the resolution of this kind of controversy. A useful analogy can be drawn between the contract at issue and a contract for the sale of goods. If the contract here was in all respects the same, except that it was for the sale of oil or some other tangible commodity instead of the sale of electricity, the parties would unquestionably be governed by the demand for adequate assurance of performance factors in UCC 2–609. We are convinced to take this prudent step because it puts commercial parties in these kinds of disputes at relatively arm's length equilibrium in terms of reliability and uniformity of governing legal rubrics. The availability of the doctrine may even provide an incentive and tool for parties to resolve their own differences, perhaps without the necessity of judicial intervention. Open, serious renegotiation of dramatic developments and changes in unusual contractual expectations and qualifying circumstances would occur because of and with an eye to the doctrine's application.

The various authorities, factors and concerns, in sum, prompt the prudence and awareness of the usefulness of recognizing the extension of the doctrine of demand for adequate assurance, as a common-law analogue. It should apply to the type of long-term commercial contract between corporate entities entered into by Norcon and Niagara Mohawk here, which is complex and not reasonably susceptible of all security features being anticipated, bargained for and incorporated in the original contract. Norcon's performance, in terms of reimbursing Niagara Mohawk for credits, is still years away. In the meantime, potential quantifiable damages are accumulating and Niagara Mohawk must weigh the hard choices and serious consequences that the doctrine of demand for adequate assurance is designed to mitigate. This Court needs to go no further in its promulgation of the legal standard as this suffices to declare a dispositive and proportioned answer to the certified question.

Accordingly, the certified question should be answered in the affirmative.

QUESTIONS AND NOTES

1. Questions about the facts of this case

   1.1. Was Norcon in breach of any relevant contract term at any time relevant for this opinion? Was that relevant to the court? Should that have been relevant?

   1.2. What was Niagara Mohawk's concern? Could that concern have been addressed with a contract term when Niagra Mohawk and Norcon were negotiating and drafting a contract?

2. Questions about the law

   2.1. Does the U.C.C. apply in this case? If not, why does the court cite U.C.C. § 2–609?

2.2. It seems as if *Niagara Mohawk* can turn a case of no breach into a case of breach. Why is that? If the day after the contract was signed, and before there was any balance in the Cumulative Avoided Cost Account, Niagara Mohawk had sent the same letter, would the court order the same result?

3. Notes

3.1. Article 72 of the *Convention for the International Sale of Goods*, which has been adopted by the United States, states as follows:

> (1) If prior to the date for performance of the contract it is clear that one of the parties will commit a fundamental breach of contract, the other party may declare the contract avoided.
>
> (2) If time allows, the party intending to declare the contract avoided must give reasonable notice to the other party in order to permit him to provide adequate assurance of his performance.

Is this superior or inferior to the U.C.C. § 2–609? In thinking about this, consider Article 7.3.4 of the *UNIDROIT* principles which states:

A party who reasonably believes that there will be a fundamental nonperformance by the other party may demand adequate assurance of due performance and may meanwhile withhold its own performance. Where this assurance is not provided within a reasonable time the party demanding it may terminate the contract.

3.2. In referring this case to the New York Court of Appeals, the Second Circuit had this to say about the possible effects of U.C.C. § 2–609:

> [S]ome authorities argue that the right to demand adequate assurance may not mitigate many of the problems faced by a party who has substantial concerns about the ability of the other party to perform the contract. A party, and eventually a court, may have to determine what constitutes "reasonable grounds for insecurity" or "adequate" assurance. "Partly as a result of the uncertain application of the concepts involved, section 2–609 sometimes does little more than extend the minuet between the weaseling party and the contractual counterpart and add a couple of new moves." 1 James J. White & Robert S. Summers, Uniform Commercial Code § 6–2 (4th ed. 1995); cf. Mollohan v. Black Rock Contracting, Inc., 160 W.Va. 446, 235 S.E.2d 813, 816 n.1 (W. Va. 1977) (declining to adopt Restatement position "except to the extent that a demand for assurances and failure to give them may be evidence of repudiation to

present to a jury with other evidence to prove * * * positive repudiation and anticipatory breach"). But see 4 Ronald A. Anderson, Anderson on the Uniform Commercial Code § 2–609:6 (3d ed. 1983) ("courts * * * will undoubtedly expand the application of U.C.C. § 2–609 to transactions that do not come within the * * * Code").

Norcon Power Partners, L.P. v. Niagara Mohawk Power Corp., 110 F.3d 6, 8–9 (2d Cir. 1997).

4. **You Be the Lawyer!**

If you represented Norcon, and your client indicated that it wished to respond to the letter sent, how would you respond? What response would satisfy Niagara Mohawk? Just a letter saying, "We intend to perform"?

CHAPTER 7

HOW DOES THE LAW ENFORCE A DEAL?

■ ■ ■

1. THE PROBLEM EXAMINED

So what's a young lawyer to do when a senior lawyer hands her (as happened to one of your casebook authors on his first day as a lawyer) a contract with a scribbled notation "Get our client out of this"? You know from Chapter 4 that some agreements are unenforceable because of problems with the agreement process or the language of the agreement. And you know from Chapter 6 that contract performance is sometimes excused because of something that happens (or does not happen) after the agreement. More important, you know that the cases in Chapters 4 and 6 are outliers. How should you advise a client who wants out of a legally enforceable agreement?

For example, assume that your client Ponoroff has contracted to wash Markell's car for $10 on Monday, and Ponoroff wants out of the contract. No Chapter 4 defenses, no Chapter 6 excuses. What advice should you give Ponoroff?

Is it "bad" to advise the client to breach? Many judges and professors have said "no," with one of the earliest being Oliver Wendell Holmes, Jr. In his classic series of lectures, *The Common Law,* Holmes said this in 1881:

> The only universal consequence of a legally binding promise is, that the law makes the promisor pay damages if the promised event does not come to pass. In every case it leaves him free from interference until the time for fulfillment has gone by, and therefore free to break his contract if he chooses.

Oliver Wendell Holmes, Jr., THE COMMON LAW 236 (Mark DeWolfe Howe ed., 1963).

Holmes said it more forcefully some sixteen years later, in his article *The Path of the Law:*

> Nowhere is the confusion between legal and moral ideas more manifest than in the law of contract. Among other things, here again the so-called primary rights and duties are invested with a mystic significance beyond what can be assigned and explained. The duty to keep a contract at common law means a prediction that you must pay damages if you do not keep it—and nothing

> else. * * * But such a mode of looking at the matter stinks in the nostrils of those who think it advantageous to get as much ethics into the law as they can.

Oliver Wendell Holmes, Jr., *The Path of the Law*, 10 HARV. L. REV. 457, 462 (1897).

So, according to Holmes, there is no moral component to the law of contracts. And many courts have agreed. Here's a similar statement from the Eleventh Circuit Court of Appeals:

> It is not illegal for a party to breach a contract; a contract gives a party two equally viable options (perform or pay compensation), between which it is generally at liberty to choose. A "promise" contained in a contract is not a certification that the promisor will actually perform the specified acts, or presently intends to perform those acts, but is instead a grant of a legal right to the other party to either enjoy performance or receive damages.

United States v. Blankenship, 382 F.3d 1110, 1133 (11th Cir. 2004).

This formulation, however, begs the question. *Should* there be a moral component to the law of contracts? And, if so, should the law enforce that moral component?

Some might say that if we were really serious about people keeping their promises, we would simply put contract breachers in jail. Or we could just brand the breacher's forehead with a scarlet "B." Of course, we don't do any of these things.

You might take this as an indication of a lack of societal interest in having people honor their contracts, but that would be too hasty a conclusion. While punishment of the breaching party might discourage or deter future breaches of other contracts, it does not accomplish "diddly-squat"* for the party who was expecting performance. For that party (sometimes referred to as the "aggrieved party," sometimes referred to as the "non-breaching party," sometimes referred to as the "injured party"), society does provide courts with enforcement mechanisms to allow a chance for redress.

But what form does this redress take? While we don't throw contract breachers in jail, should we make them do what they promised they would do? Put another way, if Markell has a valid contract with Ponoroff to wash Markell's car for $10 on Monday, and Ponoroff hasn't washed it by lunch, what can Markell do? His normal response of yelling expletives and running around in circles won't get the car clean. What if Epstein, opportunist that he is, swoops in and comforts Markell: "Son, you knew Ponoroff's promise wasn't worth a plug nickel. Always disappoints. But I

* Markell assures us that those of you from the Midwest will recognized that this phrase means that nothing will be accomplished by punishment.

can help you get a clean car. One condition though. It'll cost you $15." If Markell succumbs, and pays Epstein his $15, do we assess damages against Ponoroff of $15, the cost of the new car wash? Or something else?

If you said something else, you're on the right track. Just how much, however, is the subject of the next, rather long, section.

---

2. MONEY DAMAGES

If you think back on the cases we've studied this far, most of them award the winning party money damages. That is, the injury is monetized, and the dollar amount of the harm is what the losing party has to pay.

In this section, we examine how courts calculate those damages. First, however, we need to set down some assumptions.

A. THE PRELIMINARIES: MATERIAL BREACH AND CANCELLATION (AND A SMALL COMMENT ON PARTIAL BREACH)

In our examples and in the cases, the parties are suing because the other side committed a *material* breach. As we know from Chapter 6, that means that the complaining party's remaining obligations have been excused under the contract.

In addition, when there is a material breach, the aggrieved party's rights can cancel the contract. As Comment *a* to section 283 of the *Restatement (Second) of Contracts* states, "a 'cancellation' "occurs when either party puts an end to the contract for breach by the other."* Thus, a material breach not only excuses the non-breaching party's unperformed duties, but also allows the non-breaching party to put an end to the contract. At that point, the non-breaching party does not have to accept any purported performance, as the contract is no more and thus there are no more duties. This allows the court to calculate damages without any reference to, or deduction for, the breacher's attempted future performance.

The upshot is that from here on out we'll be discussing monetary remedies for total breach following material breach and cancellation. But don't worry about remedies for non-material, or partial, breaches. As we've said before, any variance from what is provided in the contract is a breach, and as enshrined in the *Restatement (Second) Contracts*, "Every breach gives rise to a claim for damages, and may give rise to other remedies." *Id.* § 236, cmt. a. If a renter is a week late with her rent, that's a breach, even

* The remedy of cancellation also appears in the U.C.C.—the *Restatement* lifted the embedded quotation in the last sentence from section 2–106(4) of the U.C.C. and, as we will see, sections 2–703(f) and 2–711(1) allow the non-breaching party to cancel the contract as one of its remedies.

if the landlord waives the ability to declare a material breach by accepting the late payment. The non-breaching party's choice not to cancel is significant, as stated in *Bay County v. United States*, 112 Fed. Cl. 195, 200 (2013), " 'If the injured party elects to or is required to await the balance of the other party's performance under the contract, his claim is said . . . to be one for damages for partial breach [rather than for a total breach].' " Restatement (Second) of Contracts § 236 cmt. b (1981)."

What then are the damages? For a partial breach related to the late or untimely payment of money, one of the most common partial breaches, the standard remedy is the assessment of interest for the delay. As Comment *a* to section 354 of the *Restatement (Second) of Contracts* states:

> Had the performance been rendered when it was due, the injured party would have been able to make use of it. Interest is a standardized form of compensation to the injured party for the loss of that use, in the absence of agreement to the contrary. It is payable without compounding at the rate, commonly called the "legal rate," fixed by statute for this purpose.

This may not be much; for a monthly rent of $1,500, interest on a week's delay at 10% is only about $2.88. This underlies one reason why we focus on total breach. Damages for partial breach are real, but tend to be small. Why? Recall that if there is a non-material breach, the other side has substantially performed. As a result, the non-breaching party will have received most of the benefits it expected under the contract, and any remaining injury caused by a partial breach will tend to be small in relation to the contract.

So let's get to the big stuff, the damages allocable to total breach.

B. THE GENERAL MEASURE OF CONTRACT DAMAGES FOR TOTAL BREACH: THE "EXPECTATION INTEREST" (RECEIPT OF THE BENEFIT OF THE BARGAIN)

Let's go back to the contract for car washing between Markell and Ponoroff. Ponoroff was to wash Markell's car on Monday for $10, and he didn't. Recall that Markell could get the same car wash from Epstein for $15.

So Ponoroff is a contract breacher. What does Markell get? Money damages. That is, Markell will seek a document from a court (called a judgment) that Ponoroff owes Markell money. If Ponoroff does not pay the amount ordered by the court (and does not appeal), Markell will then be able to take that judgment to a court and ask them to issue another order (typically, something called a writ of execution or a garnishment order) that can be given to the local sheriff, who will seize and sell as much of Ponoroff's property as he can find until Markell is paid the full amount listed in the judgment (with interest).

But what amount will the court insert in its judgment? In short, what amount does the law say will compensate Markell? Should the amount of the award to Markell be $15, the amount Markell will have to pay to Epstein? No. Ponoroff will argue successfully that Markell was already going to spend $10 for his service, thus, giving Markell $15 would be the same as giving Markell a free car wash, which is not what the deal was. An award of $15 overcompensates Markell, something contract law is loathe to do.

1. The General Theories: Expectation Interest, Reliance Interest, and Restitution Interest

What kind of damages will Markell get? As explained in *Crown Coal & Coke Co. v. Powhatan Mid-Vol Coal Sales, L.L.C.*, 929 F.Supp.2d 460 (W.D. Pa. 2013), the hierarchy of money damages is as follows:

> "In general, contract law espouses three distinct, yet equally important, theories of damages to remedy a breach of contract: 'expectation' damages, 'reliance' damages, and 'restitution' damages." . . . Expectation damages are the preferred approach because they place the injured party in the position that would have resulted from receiving the benefit of the bargain. The standard measurement for such damages are recovery of "the losses caused and gains prevented by defendant's breach, to the extent that are in excess of any savings made possible by nonperformance."

The *Restatement* agrees. According to section 345 of the *Restatement (Second) of Contracts*: "the injured party has a right to damages based on his expectation interest. * * *"

What does "expectation interest" mean? How do you measure someone's "expectation interest"? The *Restatement* has an answer to that too. It states that the expectation interest is measured as:

> (a) the loss in value to [the injured party] of the other party's performance caused by its failure or deficiency, plus

(b) any other loss, including incidental* or consequential** loss, caused by the breach, less

(c) any cost or other loss that [the injured party] has avoided by not having to perform.

Restatement (Second) of Contracts § 347 (1981).

We also have an answer to what "expectation interest" means, and our answer is easier to understand. When a person makes a contract, she expects that the other person will not breach. Accordingly, protection of that expectation means damages should put the nonbreaching party in the same dollar position as if the contract had been performed without breach.

If, in our car washing story, damages were based on Markell's expectation interest, what would Markell get for Ponoroff's breach of the car wash contract? $5. Markell was expecting no breach, i.e., Markell was expecting that Ponoroff would wash his car for the contract price of $10. Instead, because of Ponoroff's breach, Markell has to pay $5 more than the contract price. Accordingly, Ponoroff's paying Markell breach of contract damages of $5 protects that expectation—puts Markell in the same economic position he would have been in had the contract been performed without breach.

2. Basic Expectancy Interest Damages: Benefit of the Bargain Through Price or Cost Differential

So how do you calculate the expectancy interest? Let's try some easy damage problems.

---

* Incidental damages are: (1) easy to understand, and (2) generally insignificant in amount (well, except to the extent that attorneys' fees in litigating the claim are "incidental damages." But we have a note on that later on page 810). Comment *c* to section 347 of the *Restatement (Second)* gives the following helpful explanation and example: "Incidental losses include costs incurred in a reasonable effort, whether successful or not, to avoid loss, as where a party pays brokerage fees in arranging or attempting to arrange a substitute transaction. See Illustration 3." That illustration reads:

> 3. A contracts to employ B for $10,000 to supervise the production of A's crop, but breaks his contract by firing B at the beginning of the season. B reasonably spends $200 in fees attempting to find other suitable employment through appropriate agencies. B can recover the $200 incidental loss in addition to any other loss suffered, whether or not he succeeds in finding other employment. Incidental damages are always recoverable.

** Consequential damages are: (1) ***not*** easy to understand, and (2) can be very significant in amount. Moreover, the *Restatement (Second)*'s explanation and examples of consequential damages are not particularly helpful. And, consequential damages are not always recoverable. We will cover consequential damages later in this chapter.

SOME EASY EXPECTATION DAMAGES PROBLEMS

1. P hired D to paint his house for $10,000. D breaches. What are P's expectation damages if D breaches and P is unable to hire another painter for less than $12,000?

2. B contracts to buy a machine from S. As required by the contract, B prepays S the $400,000 as soon as the contract is signed and before the machine is delivered. S breaches and never delivers the machine. What are B's expectation damages if B is unable to buy a comparable machine for less than $430,000?

3. B buys a machine from S for $600,000. The contract provides that the machine will produce 100 widgets an hour. The machine as delivered only produces 60 widgets an hour. If B decides to keep the machine and sue for money damages, what result?

The next case would answer (3) above "As a general rule, the measure of the vendee's damages is the difference between the value of the goods as they would have been if the warranty as to quality had been true, and the actual value at the time of the sale." As you read the next case, think about whether you agree with the court's application of that rule to George Hawkins.

QUESTIONS BEFORE THE CASE

1. What is the contract at issue here? Who promised to do what, and what is the exact nature of the breach?
2. Why does the court treat the pain and suffering damages in the way it does? Don't those follow from the breach?

HAWKINS V. MCGEE

Supreme Court of New Hampshire
84 N.H. 114, 146 A. 641 (1929)

Assumpsit against a surgeon for breach of an alleged warranty of the success of an operation. Trial by jury. [A $3,000] verdict for the plaintiff. The writ also contained a count in negligence upon which a nonsuit was ordered, without exception.

Defendant's motions for a nonsuit and for a directed verdict on the count in assumpsit were denied, and the defendant excepted. During the argument of plaintiff's counsel to the jury, the defendant claimed certain exceptions, and also excepted to the denial of his requests for instructions and to the charge of the court upon the question of damages, as more fully appears in the opinion. The defendant seasonably moved to set aside the verdict upon the grounds that it was (1) contrary to the evidence; (2) against the weight of the evidence; (3) against the weight of the law and evidence; and (4) because the damages awarded by the jury were excessive. The court denied the motion upon the first three grounds, but found that the damages were excessive, and made an order that the verdict be set aside, unless the plaintiff elected to remit all in excess of $500. The plaintiff having refused to remit, the verdict was set aside "as excessive and against the weight of the evidence," and the plaintiff excepted.

BRANCH, J.

The operation in question consisted in the removal of a considerable quantity of scar tissue from the palm of the plaintiff's right hand and the grafting of skin taken from the plaintiff's chest in place thereof. The scar tissue was the result of a severe burn caused by contact with an electric wire, which the plaintiff received about nine years before the time of the transactions here involved. There was evidence to the effect that before the operation was performed the plaintiff and his father went to the defendant's office, and that the defendant, in answer to the question, "How long will the boy be in the hospital?" replied, "Three or four days, not over four; then the boy can go home and it will be just a few days when he will go back to work with a good hand." Clearly this and other testimony to the same effect would not justify a finding that the doctor contracted to complete the hospital treatment in three or four days or that the plaintiff would be able to go back to work within a few days thereafter. The above statements could only be construed as expressions of opinion or predictions as to the probable duration of the treatment and plaintiff's resulting disability, and the fact that these estimates were exceeded would impose no contractual liability upon the defendant. The only substantial basis for the plaintiff's claim is the testimony that the defendant also said before the operation was decided upon, "I will guarantee to make the hand a hundred per cent perfect hand or a hundred per cent good hand." The plaintiff was present when these words were alleged to have been spoken, and, if they are to be taken at their face value, it seems obvious that proof of their utterance would establish the giving of a warranty in accordance with his contention.

The defendant argues, however, that, even if these words were uttered by him, no reasonable man would understand that they were used with the intention of entering "into any contractual relation whatever," and that they could reasonably be understood only "as his expression in strong language that he believed and expected that as a result of the operation he would give the plaintiff a very good hand." It may be conceded, as the defendant contends, that, before the question of the making of a contract should be submitted to a jury, there is a preliminary question of law for the trial court to pass upon, i.e. "whether the words could possibly have the meaning imputed to them by the party who founds his case upon a certain interpretation," but it cannot be held that the trial court decided this question erroneously in the present case. It is unnecessary to determine at this time whether the argument of the defendant, based upon "common knowledge of the uncertainty which attends all surgical operations," and the improbability that a surgeon would ever contract to make a damaged part of the human body "one hundred per cent perfect" would, in the absence of countervailing considerations, be regarded as conclusive, for there were other factors in the present case which tended to support the contention of the plaintiff. There was evidence that the defendant repeatedly solicited from the plaintiff's father the opportunity to perform this operation, and the theory was advanced by plaintiff's counsel in cross examination of defendant that he sought an opportunity to "experiment on skin grafting," in which he had little previous experience. If the jury accepted this part of plaintiff's contention, there would be a reasonable basis for the further conclusion that, if defendant spoke the words attributed to him, he did so with the intention that they should be accepted at their face value, as an inducement for the granting of consent to the operation by the plaintiff and his father, and there was ample evidence that they were so accepted by them. The question of the making of the alleged contract was properly submitted to the jury.

The substance of the charge to the jury on the question of damages appears in the following quotation: "If you find the plaintiff entitled to anything, he is entitled to recover for what pain and suffering he has been made to endure and for what injury he has sustained over and above what injury he had before." To this instruction the defendant seasonably excepted. By it, the jury was permitted to consider two elements of damage: (1) Pain and suffering due to the operation; and (2) positive ill effects of the operation upon the plaintiff's hand. Authority for any specific rule of damages in cases of this kind seems to be lacking, but, when tested by general principle and by analogy, it appears that the foregoing instruction was erroneous.

"By 'damages,' as that term is used in the law of contracts, is intended compensation for a breach, measured in the terms of the contract." Davis v. New England Cotton Yarn Co., 77 N.H. 403, 92 A. 732. The purpose of the law is "to put the plaintiff in as good a position as he would have been in had the defendant kept his contract." 3 Williston Cont. § 1338. The measure of recovery "is based upon what the defendant should have given the plaintiff, not what the plaintiff has given the defendant or otherwise expended." 3 Williston Cont. § 1341 * * *

The present case is closely analogous to one in which a machine is built for a certain purpose and warranted to do certain work. In such cases, the usual rule of damages for breach of warranty in the sale of chattels is applied, and it is held that the measure of damages is the difference between the value of the machine, if it had corresponded with the warranty and its actual value, together with such incidental losses as the parties knew, or ought to have known, would probably result from a failure to comply with its terms. * * *

The rule thus applied is well settled in this state. "As a general rule, the measure of the vendee's damages is the difference between the value of the goods as they would have been if the warranty as to quality had been true, and the actual value at the time of the sale, including gains prevented and losses sustained, and such other damages as could be reasonably anticipated by the parties as likely to be caused by the vendor's failure to keep his agreement, and could not by reasonable care on the part of the vendee have been avoided." Union Bank v. Blanchard, 65 N.H. 21, 18 A. 90; * * * P.L. ch. 166, § 69, subd. 7. We therefore conclude that the true measure of the plaintiff's damage in the present case is the difference between the value to him of a perfect hand or a good hand, such as the jury found the defendant promised him, and the value of his hand in its present condition, including any incidental consequences fairly within the contemplation of the parties when they made their contract. Damages not thus limited, although naturally resulting, are not to be given.

The extent of the plaintiff's suffering does not measure this difference in value. The pain necessarily incident to a serious surgical operation was a part of the contribution which the plaintiff was willing to make to his joint undertaking with the defendant to produce a good hand. It was a legal detriment suffered by him which constituted a part of the consideration given by him for the contract. It represented a part of the price which he was willing to pay for a good hand, but it furnished no test of the value of a good hand or the difference between the value of the hand which the defendant promised and the one which resulted from the operation.

It was also erroneous and misleading to submit to the jury as a separate element of damage any change for the worse in the condition of the plaintiff's hand resulting from the operation, although this error was probably more prejudicial to the plaintiff than to the defendant. Any such ill effect of the operation would be included under the true rule of damages set forth above, but damages might properly be assessed for the defendant's failure to improve the condition of the hand, even if there were no evidence that its condition was made worse as a result of the operation.

It must be assumed that the trial court, in setting aside the verdict, undertook to apply the same rule of damages which he had previously given to the jury, and, since this rule was erroneous, it is unnecessary for us to consider whether there was any evidence to justify his finding that all damages awarded by the jury above $500 were excessive.

* * *

New trial.

QUESTIONS AND NOTES

1. Questions about the facts of this case

   1.1. Do you agree with Professor Charles Kingsfield's summary of the facts of this case? http://www.youtube.com/watch?v=cZJEhlIefxA. Another version can be found here (there was both a movie and a television show; those were the days of Contracts law professor fame. Sigh): http://www.youtube.com/watch?v=qx22TyCge7w.

   1.2. Why was Dr. McGee liable to Hawkins under contract law? What exactly was the promise made by Dr. McGee to Hawkins?

   1.3. Do we know the contract price, that is, how much the Hawkins family paid Dr. McGee? Do we need to know the contract price to determine the measure of damages for breach of contract?

   1.4. Do we know the cost of fixing George Hawkins' hand so that it is "a hundred per cent perfect hand"? Do we know whether George's hand can be fixed so that it is a hundred per cent perfect hand?

   1.5. What additional facts would Hawkins have to establish in order to recover from Dr. McGee under tort?

2. Questions about the law

   2.1. Rule

   a. What is the measure of damages adopted by this court?

   b. Did Mr. Hart correctly answer Professor Kingfield's question: "What damages do you think the doctor should pay?" http://www.youtube.com/watch?v=qx22TyCge7w (The question is asked around 2:20)

   c. Is *Hawkins v. McGee* consistent with *Restatement (Second)* sections 345 and 347? With our more helpful explanation of expectation interest?

   2.2. Remand

   a. On remand, would evidence about the contract price paid by the Hawkins family be relevant? Why?

   b. What about evidence that Hawkins had been apprenticing as a watchmaker, but he lost that position because he no longer had the necessary manual dexterity?

   c. What about evidence that Hawkins' pain and suffering lasted far longer than the usual recovery period for such surgeries?

2.3. Does this court seriously believe that a hand is like a "chattel"? By the way, what is a chattel?

2.4. Comparison of contract damages with tort damages. If Dr. McGee was found to have been negligent, what would the measure of George Hawkins' damages be?

3. Notes

3.1. Subsequent research into the facts of this case indicate that before the new trial Dr. McGee settled the lawsuit for $1,400. We know this because Dr. McGee then sued his insurance carrier to recover that sum and an additional $2,850 in expenses, mostly attorneys' fees. Dr. McGee lost, because the insurance policy only covered liability "in consequence of any malpractice, error, or mistake." *McGee v. United States Fidelity & Guaranty Co.*, 53 F.2d 953 (1st Cir. 1931).

3.2. The same appellate case tells us what the main case does not: the condition of Hawkins' hand. In the words of the appellate court, after three months of hospitalization, "the new tissue grafted upon said hand became matted, unsightly, and so healed and attached to said hand as to practically fill the hand with an unsightly growth, restricting the motion of the plaintiff's hand so that said hand has become useless to the plaintiff. * * *"

3.3. Cases such as this inspire doggerel:

A terrible need for a fee
Brought great grief to Doctor McGee.
And his promises airy
Led a patient unwary
To a hand that no mortal should see.

Douglass G. Boshkoff, *Selected Poems on The Law of Contracts: Raintree County Memorial Library Occasional Paper No. 1*, 66 N.Y.U. L. REV. 1533, 1542 (1991).

3.4. While *Hawkins v. McGee*, a 1929 case, does not use the term "expectation interest," many, more modern, cases do. In an uncommonly influential law review article, Lon L. Fuller & William R. Perdue, Jr., *The Reliance Interest in Contract Damages,* 46 YALE L.J. 52 (1936), Professor Fuller and his student, William Perdue, suggested the use of the term "expectation interest".

> [W]e may seek to give the promisee the value of the expectancy which the promise created. We may in a suit for specific performance actually compel the defendant to render the promised performance to the plaintiff, or, in a suit for damages, we may make the defendant pay the money value of this performance. Here our object is to put

> the plaintiff in as good a position as he would have occupied had the defendant performed his promise The interest protected in this case we may call the expectation interest.

Id. at 53–55.

3.5. The *Restatement (Second) of Contracts* paid Fuller and Perdue the ultimate compliment of adopting their terminology. See *Restatement (Second) of Contracts* § 344 (1981). And, remember, section 347 of the *Restatement (Second) of Contracts* tells us that protection of the expectation interest is the general rule: "the injured party has a right to damages based on his expectation interest * * *".

4. **You Be the Lawyer!**

If you represented Hawkins, what evidence could you adduce as the value of a "100% perfect" hand? After all, that is what was promised, right?

In *Hawkins v. McGee*, expectation damages were based on diminution in the value of the contract performance resulting from the breach of contract—the difference between the value of the hand that was promised and the hand after Dr. McGee's breach of that promise. There was no alternative method of determining expectation damages in *Hawkins v. McGee.* We could not look to the cost of remedying the defects because George's scarred and hairy hand could not be fixed.

Try the following problems to see if you can apply Hawkins to some relatively simple and common fact patterns.

PROBLEMS ON PRICE DIFFERENTIAL

1. Red lists his farm, Redacre, for sale for $1.3 million. Several bidders clamor for the property, and Ace winds up with the winning bid and Red and Ace sign a valid contract for the sale of Redacre at a purchase price of $1.8 million. After the contract is signed, Ace gets buyer's remorse, and refuses to close the deal. Red turns around and offers Redacre to one of the bidders who lost to Ace, and that bidder agrees to buy the property for $1.9 million. What are Red's damages against Ace?

2. What if the bidder buys the property, but the replacement contract is only for $1.5 million?

3. What if no one buys the property for six months, and Red takes it off the market?

4. Change the facts. Now, instead of selling the farm, Red want to build a new barn. He solicits bids from several bidders, and chooses the lowest bidder, Ace, who agrees to build the barn for $250,000. After signing the

contract, Ace realizes he has underbid the project, and tells Red he needs $300,000. Red scoffs, and contracts with the second-lowest bidder to build the project for $275,000. What are Red's damages?

5. What if Ace is half-way through building the barn (and has been paid $125,000), and demands the contract price be increased to $300,000 before he hammers another nail? If Red scoffs again, and has to pay $175,000 to another contractor to finish the barn, what are Red's damages? Read on.

---

3. Expectation Damages as Cost of Repair and Completion

Sometimes, a person can be put in the position they would have been in had there been full performance by awarding differential price awards. Markell is made whole if he pays Epstein $15 to wash his car, and Ponoroff pays him $5. At the end of the day, he'll have a clean car, and his net expenditure will be $10.

But what if Ponoroff starts washing the car, but quits half way through, leaving a soapy mess in Markell's driveway. Epstein may say, "Well, if I can use Ponoroff's stuff, I'll charge $12 for the wash, but add another $5 because I have to clean up Ponoroff's mess before I start." What damages then? Read on.

---

a. Measuring Expectancy Interest by Cost of Completion

QUESTIONS BEFORE THE CASE

1. How does the court formulate the test for establishing that the injured party is put in the position it would have been in had there been no breach?
2. What does Lewin wind up with after remand?

LEWIN V. LEVINE

Supreme Court, Appellate Division, Second Department, New York
146 A.D.3d 768, 44 N.Y.S.3d 540 (2017)

JOHN M. LEVENTHAL, J.P., JEFFREY A. COHEN, ROBERT J. MILLER, and HECTOR D. LASALLE, JJ.

Opinion

In an action, inter alia, to recover damages for breach of contract, the defendants appeal from an order of the Supreme Court, Westchester County (Adler, J.), dated February 5, 2015, which, after a nonjury trial on the issue of damages, in effect, directed the entry of a judgment in favor of the plaintiffs and against them in the principal sum of $300,500.

* * *

The plaintiffs entered into a contract with the defendant Harmon Development Corp. (hereinafter Harmon Development) to renovate their home located in Chappaqua. The defendant Harmon Levine, as president of Harmon Development, executed the contract. The defendant Randy Levine is Harmon Levine's wife.

The plaintiffs alleged that after they made payments of hundreds of thousands of dollars to the defendants under the contract, they became dissatisfied with the work, terminated Harmon Development's employment, and hired others to complete the project and remediate what they alleged to be improper and poor work. The plaintiffs commenced this action alleging causes of action sounding in breach of contract, conversion, and negligence.

In March 2014, the plaintiffs moved for summary judgment on the complaint. In an order dated September 3, 2014, the Supreme Court (Giacomo, J.) granted the motion to the extent of awarding the plaintiffs summary judgment on the issue of liability on their causes of action. The court noted that the plaintiffs sought the sum of $216,399.05 in damages in their complaint, yet in their motion sought the sum of $468,768.78. Thus, the court directed that a trial be conducted on the issue of damages.

A nonjury trial on the issue of damages was held in December 2014. In an order dated February 5, 2015, the Supreme Court (Adler, J.) determined that the plaintiffs were entitled to damages in the principal sum of $300,500, which represented the amount of money paid by the plaintiffs to the defendants pursuant to the contract. The court found that the plaintiffs failed to establish that they made payments to other contractors to remediate the work or to complete the project.

"In reviewing a determination made after a nonjury trial, the power of the Appellate Division is as broad as that of the trial court and it may render the judgment it finds warranted by the facts, taking into account that in a close case the trial judge had the advantage of seeing and hearing the witnesses" * * *.

It is fundamental to the law of damages that one complaining of injury has the burden of proving the extent of the harm suffered, must demonstrate actual damages, and must lay a basis for a reasonable estimate of the extent of the harm * * *.

Here, the Supreme Court erred in awarding damages equal to the monies paid by the plaintiffs to the defendants on the contract. The proper measure of the plaintiffs' damages was the cost of completion of the construction work and the correction of defects in the defendants' work (see

Metropolitan Switch Bd. Mfg. Co., Inc. v. B & G Elec. Contrs., Div. of B & G Indus., Inc., 96 A.D.3d 725, 726, 946 N.Y.S.2d 178; Marino v. Lewis, 17 A.D.3d 325, 325–326, 792 N.Y.S.2d 572; Ferreira v. Saccento, 286 A.D.2d 366, 729 N.Y.S.2d 178; Kaufman v. Le Curt Construction Corp., 196 A.D.2d 577, 578, 601 N.Y.S.2d 186; Lukoff v. Suzzex Downs, 131 A.D.2d 442, 443, 516 N.Y.S.2d 471). Indeed, in their complaint, the plaintiffs stated that their damages on the breach of contract, negligence, and conversion causes of action were the "total sum" of $201,399.05, which was the cost "to repair the premises to the condition that was agreed upon" in the contract, and to "replace the damaged property and stolen property."

At trial, the plaintiffs failed to demonstrate what portion of the $300,500 they paid to the defendants was attributed to (1) work that was never done, and/or (2) defective work. The only testimony regarding these payments was simply the amount of the payments made under the contract. Such proof of payment to the defendants was inadequate to establish the plaintiffs' damages * * *. Accordingly, the trial court's damages award was not warranted by the facts. Since the plaintiffs failed to demonstrate that they sustained actual damages, the complaint must be dismissed.

QUESTIONS

1. Questions about the facts

   1.1. Is there any question that Levine materially breached the contract?

   1.2. Is there any question as to how much money Lewin paid in the aggregate to all contractors?

   1.3. Whose responsibility was it to gather the amounts Lewin spent for purposes of presenting them to the judge?

2. Questions about the law

   2.1. What standard of damages do you think the plaintiff's lawyer thought he or she was supposed to prove? Was that the correct standard?

   2.2. What if Lewin decided to change the plans after dismissing Levine, and the new plans cost more? Does Levine have to pay for that? What if the change in plans was necessary to remediate the poor work that Levine did?

   2.3. Under what circumstances would Levine be responsible for "damaged property and stolen property"? Didn't Levine just sign up to build a house, and not to insure against losses?

3. **You Be the Lawyer!**

   You represent Lewin after this decision comes down. How would you communicate the court's decision to your client? Do you think you should share some of the blame?

---

b. Limitations on Cost of Completion Due to Economic Waste

Sometimes the cost of completion will be simple to calculate. Often, it will not. In addition, the more esoteric and idiosyncratic the request, the more it may cost to finish the job according to the original specifications.

This can be seen from the following hypothetical. Epstein is obsessed with being a "law school legend." David G. Epstein, *A Few Lines*, 55 AM. U.L. REV. 1291, 1291 at n.* (2006). So obsessed that he wants to erect a statue of himself to that effect. In his own front yard. With 24/7 lights, and haunting dubstep music constantly playing from the base (complete with recursive clips of his own voice taken from his bar lectures). And, for personal reasons that must be kept out of a family casebook, he wants the statue to be fluorescent lime green. Ponoroff agrees to build and erect the statue for $50,000, but then backs out after he is half-way through construction. "The guy's nuts," Ponoroff mutters before wandering down the street.

Epstein sues Ponoroff for $40,000, which is what Epstein's expert will testify is the cost of finishing the monstrous memorial. Ponoroff does not contest breach, but has his own expert testimony at the ready to the effect that completion of the statue according to original plans will *decrease* the value of Epstein's house by $100,000. Ponoroff contends he saved Epstein money, and should not pay any damages.

To puzzle through the answer, take a look at the next two cases.

QUESTIONS BEFORE THE CASE

1. Who breached the contract? When did the breach occur?
2. Was the landowner and plaintiff a human or a corporation? Should that matter?

GROVES V. JOHN WUNDER CO.

Supreme Court of Minnesota
205 Minn. 163, 286 N.W. 235 (1939)

STONE, JUSTICE:

Action for breach of contract. Plaintiff got judgment for a little over $15,000. Sorely disappointed by that sum, he appeals.

In August, 1927, S. J. Groves & Sons Company, a corporation (hereinafter mentioned simply as Groves), owned a tract of 24 acres of Minneapolis suburban real estate. It was served or easily could be reached by railroad trackage. It is zoned as heavy industrial property. But for lack of development of the neighborhood its principal value thus far may have been in the deposit of sand and gravel which it carried. The Groves company had a plant on the premises for excavating and screening the gravel. Near by defendant owned and was operating a similar plant.

In August, 1927, Groves and defendant made the involved contract. For the most part it was a lease from Groves, as lessor, to defendant, as lessee; its term seven years. Defendant agreed to remove the sand and gravel and to leave the property "at a uniform grade, substantially the same as the grade now existing at the roadway * * * on said premises, and that in stripping the overburden * * * it will use said overburden for the purpose of maintaining and establishing said grade."

Under the contract defendant got the Groves screening plant. The transfer thereof and the right to remove the sand and gravel made the consideration moving from Groves to defendant, except that defendant incidentally got rid of Groves as a competitor. On defendant's part it paid Groves $105,000. So that from the outset, on Groves' part the contract was executed except for defendant's right to continue using the property for the stated term. (Defendant had a right to renewal which it did not exercise.)

Defendant breached the contract deliberately. It removed from the premises only "the richest and best of the gravel" and wholly failed, according to the findings, "to perform and comply with the terms, conditions, and provisions of said lease * * * with respect to the condition in which the surface of the demised premises was required to be left." Defendant surrendered the premises, not substantially at the grade required by the contract "nor at any uniform grade." Instead, the ground was "broken, rugged, and uneven." Plaintiff sues as assignee and successor in right of Groves.

As the contract was construed below, the finding is that to complete its performance 288,495 cubic yards of overburden would need to be excavated, taken from the premises, and deposited elsewhere. The reasonable cost of doing that was found to be upwards of $60,000. But, if defendant had left the premises at the uniform grade required by the lease, the reasonable value of the property on the determinative date would have been only $12,160. The judgment was for that sum, including interest, thereby nullifying plaintiff's claim that cost of completing the contract rather than difference in value of the land was the measure of damages. The gauge of damage adopted by the decision was the difference between the market value of plaintiff's land in the condition it was when the contract was made and what it would have been if defendant had performed. The one question for us arises upon plaintiff's assertion that he was entitled, not to that difference in value, but to the reasonable cost to him of doing the work called for by the contract which defendant left undone.

Defendant's breach of contract was wilful. There was nothing of good faith about it. Hence, that the decision below handsomely rewards bad faith and deliberate breach of contract is obvious. That is not allowable. Here the rule is well settled * * * that where the contractor wilfully and fraudulently varies from the terms of a construction contract he cannot sue thereon and have the benefit of the equitable doctrine of substantial performance. That is the rule generally.

Jacob & Youngs, Inc. v. Kent, 230 N.Y. 239, 243, 244, 129 N.E. 889, 891, 23 A.L.R. 1429, is typical. It was a case of substantial performance of a building contract. (This case is distinctly the opposite.) Mr. Justice Cardozo, in the course of his opinion, stressed the distinguishing features. "Nowhere," he said, "will change be tolerated, however, if it is so dominant or pervasive as in any real or substantial measure to frustrate the purpose of the contract." Again, "the willful transgressor must accept the penalty of his transgression."

In reckoning damages for breach of a building or construction contract, the law aims to give the disappointed promisee, so far as money will do it, what he was promised. It is so ruled by a long line of decisions in this state, beginning with Carli v. Seymour, Sabin & Co. 26 Minn. 276, 3 N.W. 348, where the contract was for building a road. There was a breach. Plaintiff was held entitled to recover what it would cost to complete the grading as contemplated by the contract.

Never before, so far as our decisions show, has it even been suggested that lack of value in the land furnished to the contractor who had bound himself to improve it any escape from the ordinary consequences of a breach of the contract. * * *

Even in case of substantial performance in good faith, the resulting defects being remediable, it is error to instruct that the measure of damage is "the difference in value between the house as it was and as it would have been if constructed according to contract." The "correct doctrine" is that the cost of remedying the defect is the "proper" measure of damages.

Value of the land (as distinguished from the value of the intended product of the contract, which ordinarily will be equivalent to its reasonable cost) is no proper part of any measure of damages for wilful breach of a building contract. The reason is plain.

The summit from which to reckon damages from trespass to real estate is its actual value at the moment. The owner's only right is to be compensated for the deterioration in value caused by the tort. That is all he has lost. But not so if a contract to improve the same land has been breached by the contractor who refuses to do the work, especially where, as here, he has been paid in advance. The summit from which to reckon damages for that wrong is the hypothetical peak of accomplishment (not value) which would have been reached had the work been done as demanded by the contract.

* * *

Suppose a contractor were suing the owner for breach of a grading contract such as this. Would any element of value, or lack of it, in the land have any relevance in reckoning damages? Of course not. The contractor would be compensated for what he had lost, i.e., his profit. Conversely, in such a case as this, the owner is entitled to compensation for what he has lost, that is, the work or structure which he has been promised, for which he has paid, and of which he has been deprived by the contractor's breach.

To diminish damages recoverable against him in proportion as there is presently small value in the land would favor the faithless contractor. It would also ignore and so defeat plaintiff's right to contract and build for the future. To justify such a course would require more of the prophetic vision than judges possess. This factor is important when the subject matter is trackage property in the margin of such an area of population and industry as that of the Twin Cities.

* * *

The objective of this contract of present importance was the improvement of real estate. That makes irrelevant the rules peculiar to damages to chattels, arising from tort or breach of contract. *Crowley v. Burns Boiler & Mfg. Co.,* 100 Minn. 178, 187, 110 N.W. 969, 973, dealt with a breach of contract for the sale of a steam boiler. The court observed:

> "If the application of a particular rule for measuring damages to given facts results in more than compensation, it is at once apparent that the wrong rule has been adopted."

That is unquestioned law, but for its correct application there must be ascertainment of the loss for which compensation is to be reckoned. In tort, the thing lost is money value, nothing more. But under a construction contract, the thing lost by a breach such as we have here is a physical structure or accomplishment, a promised and paid for alteration in land.

That is the "injury" for which the law gives him compensation. Its only appropriate measure is the cost of performance.

It is suggested that because of little or no value in his land the owner may be unconscionably enriched by such a reckoning. The answer is that there can be no unconscionable enrichment, no advantage upon which the law will frown, when the result is but to give one party to a contract only what the other has promised; particularly where, as here, the delinquent has had full payment for the promised performance.

It is said by the Restatement, Contracts, § 346, Comment b:

> "Sometimes defects in a completed structure cannot be physically remedied without tearing down and rebuilding, at a cost that would be imprudent and unreasonable. The law does not require damages to be measured by a method requiring such economic waste. If no such waste is involved, the cost of remedying the defect is the amount awarded as compensation for failure to render the promised performance."

The "economic waste" declaimed against by the decisions applying that rule has nothing to do with the value in money of the real estate, or even with the product of the contract. The waste avoided is only that which would come from wrecking a physical structure completed, or nearly so, under the contract. The cases applying that rule go no further. Absent such waste, as it is in this case, the rule of the Restatement, Contracts, § 346, is that "the cost of remedying the defect is the amount awarded as compensation for failure to render the promised performance." That means that defendants here are liable to plaintiff for the reasonable cost of doing what defendants promised to do and have wilfully declined to do.

It follows that there must be a new trial. The initial question will be as to the proper construction of the contract. Thus far the case has been considered from the standpoint of the construction adopted by plaintiff and acquiesced in, very likely for strategic reasons, by defendants. The question has not been argued here, so we intimate no opinion concerning it, but we put the question whether the contract required removal from the premises of any overburden. The requirement in that respect was that the overburden should be used for the purpose of "establishing and maintaining" the grade. A uniform slope and grade were doubtless required. But whether, if it could not be accomplished without removal and deposit elsewhere of large amounts of overburden, the contract required as a condition that the grade everywhere should be as low as the one recited as "now existing at the roadway" is a question for initial consideration below.

The judgment must be reversed with a new trial to follow.

So ordered.

QUESTIONS

1. Questions about the facts of this case

   1.1. Which of the following facts were relevant?

   — Defendant paid Groves $105,000

   — "Defendant breached the contract deliberately"

   — Cost of leveling the property would be $60,000

   — Value of the land after leveling would be $12,160

   — "Plaintiff sues as assignee and successor in right of Groves"

   1.2. Are there any other relevant facts?

   1.3. Does it strike you as odd that there a gravel pit zoned for heavy industrial usage could be described as "suburban real estate"?

2. Questions about the law

   2.1. According to the Minnesota Supreme Court, at the trial court, "the gauge of damages * * * was the difference between the market value of plaintiff's land in the condition it was when the contract was made and what it would have been if the defendant had performed." Is that "gauge of damages" consistent with *Hawkins v. McGee*?

   2.2. The court started off by noting that the breach was wilful. So? Are damages increased just because of the mental state of the contract breacher? If not, then why are the intentions of the breacher relevant?

   2.3. Do you think the court would reach a different result if the cost of repair were $1,000,000 (such as is often the case with environmental cleanups of dumping sites), but the value after repair was still only $12,000? Why or why not?

   2.4. Why does the court mention *Jacob & Youngs*, *supra*, at 711. How are the cases similar? How are they different? Is the breaching party in this case the plaintiff or the defendant? Was the breaching party in *Jacob & Youngs* the plaintiff or the defendant? Does that matter?

   2.5. Recall that the court noted that this contract involves the "improvement of real estate." Why does the court then say that rules for damages for breach of contracts relating to chattels are "irrelevant"?

   2.6. Recall the court's discussion of "economic waste." Does the court understand the concept of economic waste? What is the defendant's economic waste argument in this case?

3. **You Be the Lawyer!**

   Is there anything that Groves could have drafting in the contract that would have avoided this result, and ensured that the property was restored to its original state when Wunder left?

QUESTIONS BEFORE THE CASE

1. In this case, who decides whether damages should equal the cost of completion or the diminution in value caused by the breach?
2. What is the point of disagreement between the majority view and the dissent?

PEEVYHOUSE V. GARLAND COAL & MINING CO.

Supreme Court of Oklahoma
382 P.2d 109 (1962)

JACKSON, JUSTICE.

In the trial court, plaintiffs Willie and Lucille Peevyhouse sued the defendant, Garland Coal and Mining Company, for damages for breach of contract. Judgment was for plaintiffs in an amount considerably less than was sued for. Plaintiffs appeal and defendant cross-appeals.

In the briefs on appeal, the parties present their argument and contentions under several propositions; however, they all stem from the basic question of whether the trial court properly instructed the jury on the measure of damages.

Briefly stated, the facts are as follows: plaintiffs owned a farm containing coal deposits, and in November, 1954, leased the premises to defendant for a period of five years for coal mining purposes. A 'strip-mining' operation was contemplated in which the coal would be taken from pits on the surface of the ground, instead of from underground mine shafts. In addition to the usual covenants found in a coal mining lease, defendant specifically agreed to perform certain restorative and remedial work at the end of the lease period. It is unnecessary to set out the details of the work to be done, other than to say that it would involve the moving of many thousands of cubic yards of dirt, at a cost estimated by expert witnesses at about $29,000.00. However, plaintiffs sued for only $25,000.00.

During the trial, it was stipulated that all covenants and agreements in the lease contract had been fully carried out by both parties, except the remedial work mentioned above; defendant conceded that this work had not been done.

Plaintiffs introduced expert testimony as to the amount and nature of the work to be done, and its estimated cost. Over plaintiffs' objections, defendant thereafter introduced expert testimony as to the 'diminution in value' of plaintiffs' farm resulting from the failure of defendant to render performance as agreed in the contract—that is, the difference between the present value of the farm, and what its value would have been if defendant had done what it agreed to do.

At the conclusion of the trial, the court instructed the jury that it must return a verdict for plaintiffs, and left the amount of damages for jury determination. On the measure of damages, the court instructed the jury that it might consider the cost of performance of the work defendant agreed to do, 'together with all of the evidence offered on behalf of either party'.

It thus appears that the jury was at liberty to consider the 'diminution in value' of plaintiffs' farm as well as the cost of 'repair work' in determining the amount of damages.

It returned a verdict for plaintiffs for $5000.00—only a fraction of the 'cost of performance', but more than the total value of the farm even after the remedial work is done.

On appeal, the issue is sharply drawn. Plaintiffs contend that the true measure of damages in this case is what it will cost plaintiffs to obtain performance of the work that was not done because of defendant's default. Defendant argues that the measure of damages is the cost of performance 'limited, however, to the total difference in the market value before and after the work was performed'.

It appears that this precise question has not heretofore been presented to this court. In Ardizonne v. Archer, 72 Okl. 70, 178 P. 263, this court held that the measure of damages for breach of a contract to drill an oil well was the reasonable cost of drilling the well, but here a slightly different factual situation exists. The drilling of an oil well will yield valuable geological information, even if no oil or gas is found, and of course if the well is a producer, the value of the premises increases. In the case before us, it is argued by defendant with some force that the performance of the remedial work defendant agreed to do will add at the most only a few hundred dollars to the value of plaintiffs' farm, and that the damages should be limited to that amount because that is all plaintiffs have lost.

Plaintiffs rely on Groves v. John Wunder Co., 205 Minn. 163, 286 N.W. 235, 123 A.L.R. 502. In that case, the Minnesota court, in a substantially similar situation, adopted the 'cost of performance' rule as-opposed to the 'value' rule. The result was to authorize a jury to give plaintiff damages in the amount of $60,000, where the real estate concerned would have been worth only $12,160, even if the work contracted for had been done.

It may be observed that Groves v. John Wunder Co., supra, is the only case which has come to our attention in which the cost of performance rule has been followed under circumstances where the cost of performance greatly exceeded the diminution in value resulting from the breach of contract. Incidentally, it appears that this case was decided by a plurality rather than a majority of the members of the court.

Defendant relies principally upon Sandy Valley & E. R. Co., v. Hughes, 175 Ky. 320, 194 S.W. 344; Bigham v. Wabash-Pittsburg Terminal Ry. Co., 223 Pa. 106, 72 A. 318; and Sweeney v. Lewis Const. Co., 66 Wash. 490, 119 P. 1108. These were all cases in which, under similar circumstances, the appellate courts followed the 'value' rule instead of the 'cost of performance' rule. Plaintiff points out that in the earliest of these cases (Bigham) the court cites as authority on the measure of damages an earlier Pennsylvania tort case, and that the other two cases follow the first, with no explanation as to why a measure of damages ordinarily followed in cases sounding in tort should be used in contract cases. Nevertheless, it is of some significance that three out of four appellate courts have followed the diminution in value rule under circumstances where, as here, the cost of performance greatly exceeds the diminution in value.

The explanation may be found in the fact that the situations presented are artificial ones. It is highly unlikely that the ordinary property owner would agree to pay $29,000 (or its equivalent) for the construction of 'improvements' upon his property that would increase its value only about ($300) three hundred dollars. The result is that we are called upon to apply principles of law theoretically based upon reason and reality to a situation which is basically unreasonable and unrealistic.

In Groves v. John Wunder Co., supra, in arriving at its conclusions, the Minnesota court apparently considered the contract involved to be analogous to a building and construction contract, and cited authority for the proposition that the cost of performance or completion of the building as contracted is ordinarily the measure of damages in actions for damages for the breach of such a contract. * * *

Even in the case of contracts that are unquestionably building and construction contracts, the authorities are not in agreement as to the factors to be considered in determining whether the cost of performance rule or the value rule should be applied. The American Law Institute's Restatement of the Law, Contracts, Volume 1, Sections 346(1)(a)(i) and (ii) submits the proposition that the cost of performance is the proper measure of damages 'if this is possible and does not involve unreasonable economic waste'; and that the diminution in value caused by the breach is the proper measure 'if construction and completion in accordance with the contract would involve *unreasonable economic waste*'. (Emphasis supplied.) In an explanatory comment immediately following the text, the Restatement makes it clear that the 'economic waste' referred to consists of the destruction of a substantially completed building or other structure. Of course no such destruction is involved in the case now before us.

On the other hand, in McCormick, Damages, Section 168, it is said with regard to building and construction contracts that '* * * in cases where the defect is one that can be repaired or cured without undue expense' the cost of performance is the proper measure of damages, but where '* * * the defect in material or construction is one that cannot be remedied without *an expenditure for reconstruction disproportionate to the end to be attained*' (emphasis supplied) the value rule should be followed. The same idea was expressed in Jacob & Youngs, Inc. v. Kent, 230 N.Y. 239, 129 N.E. 889, 23 A.L.R. 1429, as follows:

'The owner is entitled to the money which will permit him to complete, unless the cost of completion is grossly and unfairly out of proportion to the good to be attained. When that is true, the measure is the difference in value.'

It thus appears that the prime consideration in the Restatement was 'economic waste'; and that the prime consideration in McCormick, Damages, and in Jacob & Youngs, Inc. v. Kent, supra, was the relationship between the expense involved and the 'end to be attained'—in other words, the 'relative economic benefit'.

In view of the unrealistic fact situation in the instant case, and certain Oklahoma statutes to be hereinafter noted, we are of the opinion that the 'relative economic benefit' is a proper consideration here. This is in accord with the recent case of Mann v. Clowser, 190 Va. 887, 59 S.E.2d 78, where, in applying the cost rule, the Virginia court specifically noted that '* * * the defects are remediable from a practical standpoint and the costs *are not grossly disproportionate to the results to be obtained*' (Emphasis supplied).

* * *

We therefore hold that where, in a coal mining lease, lessee agrees to perform certain remedial work on the premises concerned at the end of the lease period, and thereafter the contract is fully performed by both parties except that the remedial work is not done, the measure of damages in an action by lessor against lessee for damages for breach of contract is ordinarily the reasonable cost of performance of the work; however, where the contract provision breached was merely incidental to the main purpose in view, and where the economic benefit which would result to lessor by full performance of the work is grossly disproportionate to the cost of performance, the damages which lessor may recover are limited to the diminution in value resulting to the premises because of the non-performance.

We believe the above holding is in conformity with the intention of the Legislature as expressed in the statutes mentioned, and in harmony with the better-reasoned cases from the other jurisdictions where analogous fact situations have been considered. It should be noted that the rule as stated does not interfere with the property owner's right to 'do what he will with his own' Chamberlain v. Parker, 45 N.Y. 569), or his right, if he chooses, to contract for 'improvements' which will actually have the effect of reducing his property's value. Where such result is in fact contemplated by the parties, and is a main or principal purpose of those contracting, it would seem that the measure of damages for breach would ordinarily be the cost of performance.

The above holding disposes of all of the arguments raised by the parties on appeal.

Under the most liberal view of the evidence herein, the diminution in value resulting to the premises because of non-performance of the remedial work was $300.00. After a careful search of the record, we have found no evidence of a higher figure, and plaintiffs do not argue in their briefs that a greater diminution in value was sustained. It thus appears that the judgment was clearly excessive, and that the amount for which judgment should have been rendered is definitely and satisfactorily shown by the record.

We are asked by each party to modify the judgment in accordance with the respective theories advanced, and it is conceded that we have authority to do so. * * *

We are of the opinion that the judgment of the trial court for plaintiffs should be, and it is hereby, modified and reduced to the sum of $300.00, and as so modified it is affirmed.

WELCH, DAVISON, HALLEY, and JOHNSON, JJ., concur.

WILLIAMS, C. J., BLACKBIRD, V. C. J., and IRWIN AND BERRY, JJ., dissent.

IRWIN, JUSTICE (dissenting). By the specific provisions in the coal mining lease under consideration, the defendant agreed as follows:

> '. . . 7b Lessee agrees to make fills in the pits dug on said premises on the property line in such manner that fences can be placed thereon and access had to opposite sides of the pits.
>
> '7c Lessee agrees to smooth off the top of the spoil banks on the above premises.
>
> '7d Lessee agrees to leave the creek crossing the above premises in such a condition that it will not interfere with the crossings to be made in pits as set out in 7b.

'7f Lessee further agrees to leave no shale or dirt on the high wall of said pits. * * *'

Following the expiration of the lease, plaintiffs made demand upon defendant that it carry out the provisions of the contract and to perform those covenants contained therein.

Defendant admits that it failed to perform its obligations that it agreed and contracted to perform under the lease contract and there is nothing in the record which indicates that defendant could not perform its obligations. Therefore, in my opinion defendant's breach of the contract was wilful and not in good faith.

Although the contract speaks for itself, there were several negotiations between the plaintiffs and defendant before the contract was executed. Defendant admitted in the trial of the action, that plaintiffs insisted that the above provisions be included in the contract and that they would not agree to the coal mining lease unless the above provisions were included.

In consideration for the lease contract, plaintiffs were to receive a certain amount as royalty for the coal produced and marketed and in addition thereto their land was to be restored as provided in the contract.

Defendant received as consideration for the contract, its proportionate share of the coal produced and marketed and in addition thereto, the right to use plaintiffs' land in the furtherance of its mining operations.

The cost for performing the contract in question could have been reasonably approximated when the contract was negotiated and executed and there are no conditions now existing which could not have been reasonably anticipated by the parties. Therefore, defendant had knowledge, when it prevailed upon the plaintiffs to execute the lease, that the cost of performance might be disproportionate to the value or benefits received by plaintiff for the performance.

Defendant has received its benefits under the contract and now urges, in substance, that plaintiffs' measure of damages for its failure to perform should be the economic value of performance to the plaintiffs and not the cost of performance.

If a peculiar set of facts should exist where the above rule should be applied as the proper measure of damages, (and in my judgment those facts do not exist in the instant case) before such rule should be applied, consideration should be given to the benefits received or contracted for by the party who asserts the application of the rule.

Defendant did not have the right to mine plaintiffs' coal or to use plaintiffs' property for its mining operations without the consent of plaintiffs. Defendant had knowledge of the benefits that it would receive under the contract and the approximate cost of performing the contract.

With this knowledge, it must be presumed that defendant thought that it would be to its economic advantage to enter into the contract with plaintiffs and that it would reap benefits from the contract, or it would have not entered into the contract.

Therefore, if the value of the performance of a contract should be considered in determining the measure of damages for breach of a contract, the value of the benefits received under the contract by a party who breaches a contract should also be considered. However, in my judgment, to give consideration to either in the instant action, completely rescinds and holds for naught the solemnity of the contract before us and makes an entirely new contract for the parties.

* * *

In my judgment, we should follow the case of Groves v. John Wunder Company, 205 Minn. 163, 286 N.W. 235, 123 A.L.R. 502, which defendant agrees 'that the fact situation is apparently similar to the one in the case at bar', and where the Supreme Court of Minnesota held:

'The owner's or employer's damages for such a breach (i. e. breach hypothesized in 2d syllabus) are to be measured, not in respect to the value of the land to be improved, but by the reasonable cost of doing that which the contractor promised to do and which he left undone.'

The hypothesized breach referred to states that where the contractor's breach of a contract is wilful, that is, in bad faith, he is not entitled to any benefit of the equitable doctrine of substantial performance.

In the instant action defendant has made no attempt to even substantially perform. The contract in question is not immoral, is not tainted with fraud, and was not entered into through mistake or accident and is not contrary to public policy. It is clear and unambiguous and the parties understood the terms thereof, and the approximate cost of fulfilling the obligations could have been approximately ascertained. There are no conditions existing now which could not have been reasonably anticipated when the contract was negotiated and executed. The defendant could have performed the contract if it desired. It has accepted and reaped the benefits of its contract and now urges that plaintiffs' benefits under the contract be denied. If plaintiffs' benefits are denied, such benefits would inure to the direct benefit of the defendant.

Therefore, in my opinion, the plaintiffs were entitled to specific performance of the contract and since defendant has failed to perform, the proper measure of damages should be the cost of performance. Any other measure of damage would be holding for naught the express provisions of the contract; would be taking from the plaintiffs the benefits of the contract and placing those benefits in defendant which has failed to perform its obligations; would be granting benefits to defendant without a resulting obligation; and would be completely rescinding the solemn obligation of the contract for the benefit of the defendant to the detriment of the plaintiffs by making an entirely new contract for the parties.

I therefore respectfully dissent to the opinion promulgated by a majority of my associates.

QUESTIONS AND NOTES

1. Questions about the facts of this case

   1.1. Can you distinguish the facts of this case from the facts of *Groves?*

   1.2. Is there an allegation of intentional breach here? Does it matter?

   1.3. Does the dissenting opinion disagree with the majority opinion's "briefly stated" facts in the third paragraph of the majority opinion? Does the dissenting opinion believe that the majority states the facts too "briefly"?

   1.4. Would it be helpful to see the Peevyhouse's farm on Google Maps? https://www.google.com/maps/place/Stigler,+OK+74462/@35.17465,-95.142851,346m/data=!3m1!1e3!4m5!3m4!1s0x87b58641e8d6d031:0x995c1e577975bf34!8m2!3d35.253708!4d-95.1230169?hl=en. To see a documentary about the Peevyhouse's farm? Professor Judith Maute had produced such a documentary and provided a complimentary copy to law school libraries.

2. Questions about the law

   2.1. What does the court mean by the statement "In view of the unrealistic fact situation in the instant case * * * we are of the opinion that 'relative economic benefit' is a proper consideration here"? What makes this fact situation "unrealistic"? What is the "relative economic benefit"? What would be the waste in forcing Garland to do what it said it would do?

   2.2. Both *Peevyhouse* and *Groves* cite Judge Cardozo's opinion in *Jacob & Youngs v. Kent, supra,* at 711. Which case is more consistent with the holding in *Jacob & Youngs v. Kent*? Which case is more consistent with the language in *Jacob & Youngs v. Kent*?

   2.3. Which decision—*Groves* or *Peevyhouse*—is more consistent with the protection of expectation approach to contracts damages? Which decision is more consistent with Section 348 of the *Restatement (Second) of Contracts*?

3. Notes

3.1. Great cases, great doggerel:

We picked a fine time to strip mine, Lucille.
It sure looks to me like we got a raw deal.
That smooth city-slicker said we'd all get rich quicker
I should have known it warn't real.
We picked a fine time to strip mine, Lucille.

* * *

We picked a fine time to strip mine, Lucille.
Make no mistake, hon, we got a raw deal,
I never went to law school,
I didn't know the value rule,
I thought sure we'd win our appeal,
The Supreme Court done gyped us, Lucille.

Sung to the tune of "You Picked a Fine Time to Leave Me Lucille," by Kenny Rogers. *See* Judith Maute, *Peevyhouse v. Garland Coal & Mining Co. Revisited: The Ballad of Willie and Lucille*, 89 NW. U. L. REV. 1341, 1345 (1995), for the full text of the tune, and for a fascinating examination of the case.

3.2. The debate over economic waste and damages still rages. In *BLB Aviation South Carolina LLC v, Jet Linx Aviation LLC*, 808 F.3d 389 (8th Cir. 2015), Jet Linx leased a plane from BLB. In the lease, Jet Linx promised that "[a]ll inspections, repairs, modifications, maintenance, and overhaul work . . . will be performed in accordance with the standards set by the Federal Aviation Regulations" and agreed to "maintain log books and records . . . in accordance with the Federal Aviation Regulations." Relations deteriorated between the two parties, and Jet Linx returned the plane. But it did not do so in accordance with the lease. The trial court had found that "Jet Linx had breached . . . by failing to keep proper records and parts tags for maintenance performed by Jet Linx on the airplanes."

Big deal. A bunch of tags and records. Well, important tags and records. BLB sought damages of $171,363.37, based upon its expert's testimony that it would cost that much "to rectify the lack of maintenance records and part tags by redoing the underlying maintenance work." BLB asserted that the work had to be redone, even if it had originally been done properly by Jet Linx, so that BLB would have a plane in verifiable compliance with FAA regulations. After all, that is what the contract required.

This was potentially wasteful, as the court noted, because "[a]lthough Jet Linx failed to provide a complete set of maintenance records and parts tags when it returned the airplanes, the parties do not dispute that Jet Linx provided the underlying maintenance."

BLB insisted that the only way to bring the plane into compliance was a complete redo of the work, this time with proper tags and records. The court disagreed.

> BLB insists that cost of repair is the proper measure of damages and that repairing the damage of missing maintenance records and parts tags necessitates completely redoing the underlying maintenance work. However, the notion of replacing undisputedly good parts with new parts for the sake of obtaining complete maintenance records exemplifies unreasonable economic waste. Undertaking such repairs would be grossly disproportional to the value a new set of records and parts tags would add to the airplanes, particularly when, as Jet Linx shows here, several cheaper alternatives are available.

Id. at 393. As a consequence, the court held that the measure of damages was not the cost of repair or completion, as that would entail economic waste. Rather, the court found "[d]iminution-in-value damages provide the alternative measure, consisting of the " 'difference in value between the thing as represented and its actual value.' " *Id.*

4. **You Be the Lawyer!**

Remember Cardozo's statement that Kent could have changed the result in *Jacob & Youngs v. Kent* by "apt and certain words"? Could the Peevyhouses have changed the result in this case with "apt and certain words" in their contract with Garland? What if the lease had provided "performance of every term shall be a condition of recovery"? What if the lease provided "Regardless of the economic waste that might be involved, Garland hereby promises to restore the land to its original state upon completion of the strip mining" and included a liquidated damages clause of $29,000 upon non-performance of the restoration obligation?

---

4. Expectation Damages for Lost Profits and Opportunities—Consequential or Direct Damages?

Imagine that you find yourself at FedEx, eager to send your first-year resume to a Biglaw firm. A partner there told you that if you get the resume there tomorrow, a summer job is yours—at $4,000 a week! The guy at the FedEx counter tells you that the price for next-day delivery is $60, and $20 for second-day delivery. You gladly pay the $60, telling the clerk that the letter is your key to big wages next summer.

The next day, you wait for the call from Biglaw. It never comes. The day after that the Biglaw partner calls and tells you job is gone—"Had you gotten the resume here when I said, you'd have the job." She then hangs up.

You march down to FedEx to complain. The same clerk yawns at you, and says, "Sorry. Here's $40 for your trouble." You say that it's going to take a lot more than that, and you remind him how important it was to you. He stares at you and says "Hey, you got second-day service, and that costs $20. The difference between the two is $40. That's what we refunded you, so you are in the same position you would have been in had we performed."

You fulminate. You sputter. But do you have larger contract damages?

Sure. As explained in *Schonfeld v. Hilliard*, 218 F.3d 164, 175–76 (2d Cir. 2000):

> In an action for breach of contract, a plaintiff may seek two distinct categories of damages: (1) "general" or "market" damages; and (2) "special" or "consequential" damages. *See* 3 Dan B. Dobbs, *Dobbs Law of Remedies* § 12.2(3) (1993). A plaintiff is seeking general damages when he tries to recover "the value of the very performance promised." *Id.* General damages are sometimes called "market" damages because, when the promised performance is the delivery of goods, such damages are measured by the difference between the contract price and the market value of the goods at the time of the breach. *See id.* at § 12.4.
>
> "Special" or "consequential" damages, on the other hand, seek to compensate a plaintiff for additional losses (other than the value of the promised performance) that are incurred as a result of the defendant's breach. *See id.* at § 12.2(3). The type of consequential damages most often sought is lost operating profits of a business. *See id.* However, lost profits are not the only kind of consequential damages. A defendant's breach of contract may also cause a plaintiff to lose an asset that was in its possession prior to the breach. *See id.* at §§ 12.4(1) and 12.4(4). In some instances, the asset lost is an *income-producing* asset, the fair market value of which may be based, in whole or in part, on a buyer's projections of what income he could derive from the asset in the future.

Recall, again, that this is the study of consensual obligations. Parties can specify what their damages might be (at least to a point). Because consequential damages can be large, and can be related to actions beyond the parties control, contracts often provide that the parties agree that damages awards will not include consequential damages. So, as set forth in the next case, it often matters how you classify the harm.

QUESTIONS BEFORE THE CASE

1. What was Penncro hired to do?
2. What was Sprint's breach?
3. What damages do you think Sprint would agree Penncro should recover because of Sprint's breach?

PENNCRO ASSOCIATES, INC. V. SPRINT SPECTRUM, L.P.

United States Court of Appeals, Tenth Circuit
499 F.3d 1151 (10th Cir. 2007)

Before KELLY, BALDOCK, and GORSUCH, CIRCUIT JUDGES.

Opinion

GORSUCH, CIRCUIT JUDGE.

Sprint Spectrum, L.P., does not dispute that it breached its contract with its former bill collector, Penncro Associates, Inc. Still, it offers [a] reason[ ]* why, in its view, the district court's judgment for Penncro in excess of $17 million should be reversed. * * * Sprint argues that the parties' agreement precludes the sort of damages Penncro seeks. In their contract, the parties agreed to forego "consequential damages," and Sprint urges us to find that the term, as defined by the parties's agreement, includes any and all "lost profits"—whether flowing directly or consequentially from Sprint's breach. Because all of Penncro's claimed damages are lost profits, Sprint argues the district court's judgment is fatally flawed. * * *

We affirm the district court * * *. While parties to a contract may define their terms as they please—a duck may be a goose—we see no evidence that Sprint's and Penncro's definition of the term *consequential* damages was designed to embrace (and thus foreclose the award of) profits lost as a *direct* result of Sprint's breach. * * *

I

Originally, Sprint, a national telecommunications company, handled for itself the not-inconsiderable task of trying to collect from its cell phone customers behind on their monthly bills. Beginning in April 2002, however, it decided to "outsource," contracting first with Penncro and subsequently with two additional vendors to assume the job. Under the terms of the

* [Eds.: Actually, Sprint offered two reasons. We edited out the second reason. The court didn't buy the second reason.]

parties' agreements, customers with overdue Sprint accounts trying to make outgoing calls were automatically routed to centers run by one of the three vendors, based on which one had the shortest estimated wait time. Penncro's employees introduced themselves as Sprint's agents, informed callers that their accounts were past due, and attempted to collect monies owed to Sprint—a service known as first-party inbound collections work.

A

The nature of the parties' agreement was spelled out in four interrelated documents: (1) a Master Services Agreement ("MSA"); (2) a Contract Order; (3) an attachment to the Contract Order ("Attachment A"); and (4) an Addendum to Attachment A.

The MSA contained certain generic terms and conditions Sprint employed with all vendors. It obligated neither party to perform and expressly indicated that the scope and specific terms of the services provided would be governed by contract orders. MSA § 2.2.

The Contract Order was just such a document, involving only Sprint and Penncro, and detailing the particular services, staffing levels, and compensation rates attending to the parties' relationship. Under the terms of the Contract Order, Penncro agreed, among other things, to "maintain staffing levels" sufficient to provide Sprint with "80,625 productive hours" per month. Contract Order § C. A productive hour was defined as time spent by a fully trained Penncro employee handling calls, waiting for calls, training, or waiting due to system downtime. *Id.* § B. This amounted, more or less, to an agreement to maintain approximately 500 full-time call center employees at Sprint's disposal. In exchange, Sprint agreed "to pay for 80,625 productive hours per month" at a rate of $22 per hour (less for training hours, more for overtime hours). *Id.* §§ B, C.3

* * *

B

* * * Penncro endured considerable staffing problems and was for many months unable to retain sufficient employees to provide the number of productive hours required by the parties' contract. The hours Penncro did provide, moreover, were of sufficiently poor quality to rank Penncro last among Sprint's three vendors in several performance-categories for a number of months. Sprint, meanwhile, did not experience the call volume it had anticipated and so never called on Penncro to provide the contracted-for number of productive hours. From the beginning, Sprint and Penncro discussed the actual number of hours that Sprint needed and Penncro could provide, agreeing, for the time being, to have Penncro bill and Sprint pay only for the hours that Penncro actually supplied. * * *

As call volumes and the hours necessary to handle them waned, Sprint gave notice of its intent to terminate Penncro's first-party inbound collections contract by letter dated January 17, 2003. The parties then entered a four-month ramp-down period during which the number of FTEs requested of Penncro was incrementally reduced. The reason Sprint gave for its action was that Penncro was in third place or below in six agreed performance measures for the six months from July 2002 through December 2002—an event entitling Sprint to terminate the parties' relationship for cause under Section D of the Contract Order.

* * *

C

In November 2004, Penncro sued Sprint for breach of the parties' first-party inbound collections contract in federal district court, invoking the court's diversity jurisdiction. Penncro claimed that Sprint was liable for breach of contract as a matter of law because Sprint's stated reason for termination was erroneous: Penncro was not in last place for the full six consecutive months necessary to justify termination under the parties' contract. The district court agreed and entered summary judgment for Penncro on the question of liability.

For its part, Sprint itself chose to pitch its battle primarily on the field of damages and a three-day trial on damages followed, after which the district court issued a detailed 45-page ruling. During trial, Sprint pointed to Section 13 of the MSA, which rules out the award of consequential damages and proceeds to define the term as "includ[ing], but . . . not limited to, lost profits, lost revenues and lost business opportunities." This language, Sprint submitted, prohibited either party from obtaining recovery of any and all lost profits. The district court disagreed, holding that the MSA forbids only "consequential" or "indirect" damages that are "beyond direct economic loss or ordinary loss of bargain damages," thereby doing nothing to rule out of bounds lost profits suffered as a direct consequence of Sprint's breach.

* * *

Based on these holdings, the district court awarded Penncro $17,136,612 in expectation damages: $53,109,386 in lost contractual revenues (lost profits), minus $28,307,302 in costs avoided by not having to perform and $7,665,472 in losses avoided due to the breach. Penncro contested many of these reductions, especially those concerning avoided losses. * * *

Both parties appeal. We turn first to Sprint's appeal * * *.

II

* * *

A

1. Sprint begins its appeal by renewing its argument that Penncro impermissibly seeks lost profits. Section 13 of the MSA forbids the recovery of "consequential damages," specifying that they "include, but are not limited to, lost profits, lost revenues and lost business opportunities." In Sprint's parlance, this means that *any* lost profits are (forbidden) consequential damages. For several reasons, we are persuaded that Sprint's interpretation is foreclosed by the unambiguous language of the MSA.

Section 13's syntax alone propels us in this direction. The parties' language is not unlike a doctor's prescription that "You really should not eat fried foods—and this includes, but is not limited to, meat and potatoes." Ordinary usage and common experience does not suggest that the patient should avoid *all* meat and potatoes, but only those that are parts or components of the initial, larger group of fried foods (say, chicken fried steak and french fries). The dictionary underscores the point. Webster's defines the term "to include" as meaning "to place, list, or rate as a part or component of a whole or of a larger group, class, or aggregate." *Webster's Third New International Dictionary* 1143 (2002). The more general term informs the subsequently listed examples, not the other way around, and so lost profits here refer only to those that are "a part or component" of the larger group or class of consequential damages.

The common legal meaning of the terms involved confirms this reading. Direct damages refer to those which the party lost from the contract itself—in other words, the benefit of the bargain—while consequential damages refer to economic harm beyond the immediate scope of the contract.[5] Lost profits, under appropriate circumstances, can be recoverable as a component of either (and both) direct and consequential damages. Thus, for example, if a services contract is breached and the plaintiff anticipated a profit under the contract, those profits would be recoverable as a component of direct, benefit of the bargain damages. If that same breach had the knock-on effect of causing the plaintiff to close its doors, precluding it from performing other work for which it had contracted and from which it expected to make a profit, those lost profits might be recovered as "consequential" to the breach. All of this is by way of saying that, under the circumstances we face here, a reading of Section 13 informed by the normal legal meaning of its terms suggests that it bars only the recovery of consequential lost profits, not direct lost profits. Section 13 says that no consequential damages are recoverable,

---

[5] *See* Restatement (Second) of Contracts § 347(a) & cmts. a, c (1981); *Black's Law Dictionary* 416–17 (8th ed. 2004); 24 Samuel Williston & Richard A. Lord, *A Treatise on the Law of Contracts* § 64.12 (4th ed. 1993).

"includ[ing]" lost profits; it simply does not speak to direct damages, or to lost profits recoverable under such a theory.

A review of Section 12 of the MSA further strengthens our confidence about the parties' meaning in Section 13. In Section 12, Sprint obligated Penncro to indemnify Spring against "all claims, damages, losses, liabilities, costs, expenses, and reasonable attorney's fees" arising from claims by third parties for work performed by Penncro. MSA § 12.1. By using the phrase "all . . . damages," the parties manifested a clear intent to insulate Sprint from *any* damages, direct or indirect, claimed by third parties. When it came to insulating Sprint from liability to Penncro itself, however, the parties in the very next section precluded recovery only of the class of damages that are "consequential [or] indirect." *Id.* § 13. When a contract uses different language in proximate and similar provisions, we commonly understand the provisions to illuminate one another and assume that the parties' use of different language was intended to convey different meanings. *See Decatur County Feed Yard, Inc.,* 974 P.2d at 574 (before finding ambiguity, court must view contested language in light of the contract as a whole); *cf. Sosa v. Alvarez-Machain,* 542 U.S. 692, 712 n. 9, 124 S.Ct. 2739, 159 L.Ed.2d 718 (2004) ("[W]hen the legislature uses certain language in one part of the statute and different language in another, the court assumes different meanings were intended.") (internal quotation and citation omitted); *Rogers v. Shanahan,* 221 Kan. 221, 565 P.2d 1384, 1386 (1976) (presuming that "the legislature intended a different meaning when it used different language . . . in different parts of a statute").

Finally, our understanding of the parties' chosen language comports with how Kansas courts have interpreted similar terms. In *Brennan v. Kunzle,* 37 Kan.App.2d 365, 154 P.3d 1094, 1112–13 (2007), for example, a mortgage allowed the plaintiffs to recover expenses incurred to enforce the agreement, "including, but not limited to, reasonable attorneys' fees." The court held that this formulation authorized the recovery only of those attorneys' fees incurred in pursuing remedies under the mortgage and simply did not speak, one way or the other, to other attorney's fees, such as those incurred in defending counterclaims. The same logic applies here: Section 13 is all about consequential lost profits and does not tell us anything, one way or the other, about direct lost profits. *Cf. Dikeman v. Nat'l Educators, Inc.,* 81 F.3d 949, 953 (10th Cir.1996) (allowing, in a statute where examples of a general term were listed, that the more general term limits the scope of the examples).[7]

---

[7] *See also Coremetrics, Inc. v. Atomic Park.com, LLC,* 2005 WL 3310093, at *4 (N.D.Cal. Dec.7, 2005) ("Under the plain reading of this [similarly worded] provision, 'loss of profits' is referenced only as a subset or species of indirect damages."); *In re Ardent, Inc.,* 305 B.R. 133, 138–39 & n. 3 (Bankr.D.D.C.2003); *Combustion Sys. Servs. v. Schuykill Energy Resources, Inc.,* 1993 WL 496946, at *2–5 (E.D.Pa. Nov.19, 1993); *Canal Elec. Co. v. Westinghouse Elec. Corp.,* 756 F.Supp. 620, 623 n. 2, 627 (D.Mass.1990).

2. Sprint responds by observing that parties are free to diverge from linguistic and legal norms and to define terms in their contracts as they see fit. This, Sprint contends, is what the parties did here, defining "consequential damages," to encompass *any* lost profits, including those normally thought to derive directly from a party's breach. And, to be sure, parties to a contract are free to define their terms in any manner they wish. Up may be defined as down, right as left, day as night. But, while the parties may depart from the meanings associated with ordinary English and existing law, courts will recognize and give effect to such private definitions only where the parties' intention to deviate from common usage is manifest. *See Corbin on Contracts* § 24.8; Restatement (Second) of Contracts § 202(3)(a). That is, we are reluctant to shed ordinary meanings and presume unusual private ones without some clear indication that the parties wished us to do so. Here, we are directed to no textual indicia that the parties intended such a departure. Neither do we find Sprint's proffered authority of much help to its cause. In many of the cases Sprint cites, lost profits were not, as here, placed in an illustrative list of the sorts of consequential damages excluded; instead, they were singled out as a separate and distinct category of forbidden damages.[8] Sprint's own authority thus illustrates how parties easily can manifest an intent to preclude lost profits of any stripe and highlights how Section 13, by contrast, simply failed to do so.

* * *

We hold that, in keeping with plain meaning and legal norms, where parties to an agreement exclude liability only for consequential damages, profits lost as a direct result of a breach may be recovered. * * * Accordingly, we affirm the district court's judgment to Penncro in the amount of $17,136,612. Sprint's appeal on the award of attorneys' fees is dismissed as moot.

QUESTIONS AND NOTES

1. Questions about the facts

   1.1. Wasn't Penncro's performance terrible? Why are they getting damages?

---

[8] *See Vaulting & Cash Servs. v. Diebold,* 199 F.3d 440 (5th Cir.1999) (unpub.) (lost profits deemed to be separate category of precluded damages, as "consequential" modifies only "damages," not "lost profits"); *Imaging Sys. Intern., Inc. v. Magnetic Resonance Plus, Inc.,* 227 Ga.App. 641, 490 S.E.2d 124, 127 (1997) (lost profits set off from consequential damages by disjunctive "or"); *CompuSpa, Inc. v. IBM,* 228 F.Supp.2d 613, 626 (D.Md.2002) (same).

1.2. Judge (now Justice) Gorsuch says that the damage calculation starts with "$53,109,386 in lost contractual revenues (lost profits) . . . ." Do revenues equal lost profits?

1.3. Okay, Penncro's profit on the contract is categorized as direct damages. What about the money Penncro lost by not being able to enter into other contracts upon which it could have made money? Just exactly what does it mean to "make money" anyway?

1.4. Can a contract really call a duck a goose? How about a chicken? (Recall *Frigaliament* on page 536).

2. Questions about the law

2.1. What was the point of comparing the drafting of the exclusion of consequential damages with the drafting of the indemnity provision?

2.2. So are lost profits the same as consequential damages? As direct damages?

3. Notes

3.1. Note that Penncro claimed it lost revenues of $53,109,386, but the court only awarded it $17,136,612 in expectation damages. What gives? Why not the full $53 million?

That question was answered in *HCA Health Services of Florida, Inc. v. CyberKnife Center of Treasure Coast, LLC*, 204 So.3d 469 (Fla. Ct. App. 2016). There, the issue was similar to the issue litigated in *Penncro*: did a disclaimer of consequential damages preclude the non-breaching party from recovering the profit it would have make on the contract but for the breach? After taking the same position as *Penncro*, however, the court was faced with a problem. The only evidence that the non-breaching party introduced, however, was the amount of payments due under the breached contract. In short, its evidence was only of the lost revenue under the contract.

This was insufficient, said the court.

> In a lost profits case, the proper computation of damages "requires the non-breaching party to deduct from anticipated contract revenue the costs incurred in performing the contractual services." * * * "Typically these include an appropriate allocation of overhead as well as any personnel expenses that would have been incurred." Id. Evidence pertaining to loss of income or gross receipts, without specific evidence concerning expenses, is inadequate to prove lost profits. * * * Here, CyberKnife did not present evidence of its * * * lost profits, but instead merely proved its lost revenue.

This means that you have to show not only the lost gross amount of contract consideration, but also what you would have had to spend on your own performance to earn that contract price. Shades of *Lewin*, at page 782, right?

What do these costs consist of? That concept was explored in *Magnet Resources, Inc. v. Summit MRI, Inc.*, 318 N.J. Super. 275, 294–95, 723 A.2d 976, 986 (1998). The court there stated:

> Administrative expenses and plant overhead, * * * to the extent reasonably allocable to a contract, are deductible from gross revenue to determine lost profits for breach of the contract only if they are costs which have been "saved" because the non-breaching party has been excused from future performance under the contract. Allocable administrative and overhead costs which do not diminish because of the contract cancellation should be considered "saved" only if the services, facilities and materials for which they continue to be incurred are devoted to some other employment which could not have been undertaken if the contract had not been canceled. Cf. N.J.S.A. 12A:2–708(2); U.C.C. § 2–708(2) (providing that in the event of a buyer's breach of contract one measure of damages which may be available to the seller is the amount of his lost profits, "including reasonable overhead") * * *
>
> Some cases take the position that indirect costs-such as rent, salary of office employees, salary of administrative personnel, utilities, and other 'overhead' items-are a part of the cost of production, and deduct them from the contract price to determine the net profit which may be recovered. [citations omitted] To the extent that the breach of contract allows the plaintiff an opportunity to enter into other contracts which now bear the same portion of the indirect costs as were to be borne by the breached contract, these cases are simply an expression of the doctrine of avoidable consequences. [citation omitted] *But the proper application of the doctrine of avoidable consequences leads to the conclusion that the plaintiff is entitled to recover, as part of an award of profits, fixed indirect costs (those that could not be reduced by defendant's breach), but not variable indirect costs (those that could be avoided after the breach).*

Id. at 294–95 & n.7, 723 A.2d at 986 & n.7 (emphasis in the original).

In *Penncro*, the court found that it had to subtract $28,307,302 in costs avoided by not having to perform, as well as $7,665,472 in losses avoided due to the breach (we'll cover losses in the next note). The net effect of these two deductions was the $17 million damage award.

3.2. What about the "losses avoided"? We'll explore that concept somewhat when we talk about limitation on damages below at page 838. But the court upheld the district court's finding that after Sprint had breached, Penncro found other jobs that netted it about $7.6 million.

4. **You Be the Lawyer!**

If you represented Sprint in the negotiations with Penncro, how would you have drafted the provision limiting Penncro's damages so that they could not obtain lost profits? Or could you?

---

5. Incidental Damages

In addition to direct and consequential damages, we've seen that a non-breaching party can obtain incidental damages. These are damages represented by costs necessary to obtain recompense; damages awarded for the cost of obtaining substitute performance.

What about attorneys' fees? Aren't they a cost of obtaining recompense? Hmm.

NOTE ON ATTORNEYS' FEES AS INCIDENTAL DAMAGES, AND A QUESTION

Recall that damages for breach of contract include "incidental" damages. As noted above on page 774, these are usually easy to identify and quantify. But one potential candidate for significant incidental damages is often excluded: attorneys' fees.

Initially, this may seem odd. Attorneys' fees would seem to be a necessary part of running-to-ground a contract breacher, and if not awarded, would seem to make many smaller contract claims uneconomic to prosecute. But other concerns prevail, leading to what is generally referred to as the "American Rule" regarding payment of attorneys' fees. As described by *U.S. Fidelity and Guar. Co. v. Braspetro Oil Services Co.*, 369 F.3d 34, 74 (2d Cir. 2004):

> "Under the American Rule[,] it is well established that attorney[s'] fees 'are not ordinarily recoverable in the absence of a statute or enforceable contract providing therefor.' " Summit Valley Indus., Inc. v. United Bhd. of Carpenters & Joiners, 456 U.S. 717, 721, 102 S.Ct. 2112, 72 L.Ed.2d 511 (1982) . . . "This policy 'provides freer and more equal access to the courts . . . [and] promotes democratic and libertarian principles.' "

The American Rule is the majority rule in the United States. *See Alyeska Pipeline Service Co. v. Wilderness Society*, 421 U.S. 240, 245–47 (1975). It is not, however, followed worldwide. Most common law countries follow what is generally knows as the "English Rule," under which the litigation loser pays the winner's attorneys' fees. Theodore Eisenberg & Geoffrey P. Miller, *The English Versus The American Rule On Attorney Fees: An Empirical Study Of Public Company Contracts,* 98 CORNELL L. REV. 327 (2013). *See also* Theodore Eisenberg, Talia Fisher & Issi Rosen-Zvi, *Attorneys' Fees in A Loser-Pays System*, 162 U. PA. L. REV. 1619, 1619–20 (2014) (studying "loser-pays" system in Israel, where judges have discretion to award fees to the prevailing party, and finding that fees were awarded to prevailing parties in 72.8% of cases. Judges often exercised their discretion to protect losing litigants, especially individuals, from having to pay fees. In tort cases won by individuals against corporate defendants, corporations paid their own fees plus plaintiffs' fees in 99% of the cases; corporate defendants that prevailed in such cases paid their own fees 48% of the time.)

Even in the United States, however, there are significant exceptions. Alaska, for example, has always followed the English Rule, *Edwards v. Alaska Pulp Corp.*, 920 P.2d 751, 755 (Alaska 1996), and some states have adopted it by statute. *See, e.g.,* Tex. Civ. Prac. & Rem. Code § 38.001 ("A person may recover reasonable attorney's fees from an individual or corporation, in addition to the amount of a valid claim and costs, if the claim is for: . . . (8) an oral or written contract."); Ariz. Rev. Stat. § 12–341.01(A) ("In any contested action arising out of a contract, express or implied, the court may award the successful party reasonable attorney fees."). California (as always) has a different take: it makes attorneys' fees reciprocal. If one side has the right to such fees in the contract, that right is automatically extended to the other party. Cal. Civ. Code § 1717(a).

Even when it applies, there are ways around the American Rule. As the excerpt indicates, and as this course is Contracts—the study of consensual obligations—it makes sense that the "parties may agree by contract to permit recovery of attorneys' fees, and a federal court will enforce contractual rights to attorneys' fees if the contract is valid under applicable state law." *U.S. Fidelity and Guar. Co*, 369 F.3d at 74. Indeed, it makes so much sense that Professors Eisenberg and Miller found that in contracts governed by United States' law, public companies opt out of the American Rule approximately 60% of the time. 98 CORNELL L. REV., at 331.

Question: Given that the American Rule allows the parties to provide for attorneys' fees to the prevailing party by contract, when would you *not* want to include such a clause for your client if you are entrusted with the drafting of her contract?

---

6. Money Damages Under the U.C.C.

Recall that *Hawkins v. McGee* is based on a sale of goods damages rule: "the measure of damages is the difference between the value of the machine, if it had corresponded with the warranty and its actual value." That rule is premised on putting the nonbreaching party in the same position as if the contract had been performed without breach. In other words, that rule protects the expectation interest.

Hawkins v. McGee was decided before: (i) the Fuller and Perdue article which suggested the term "expectation interest," (ii) the *Restatement of Contracts,* which adopted the term, and (iii) Article 2 of the Uniform Commercial Code, which now governs sale of goods contracts. Article 2 devotes 25 sections to "Remedies."

In section 2–703, sellers' remedies are catalogued. Section 2–711 does the same for buyers' remedies. These various sections on money damages are consistent with protection of the expectation interest.

Full examination of these sections awaits you in a Sales course. For now, we will look at some basic concepts and problems (and, if your professor is so inclined, a couple of more challenging cases).

---

a. Buyer's Remedies

The U.C.C. helpfully catalogs the remedies available to non-breaching buyers in Section 2–711. That section reads:

§ 2–711. Buyer's Remedies in General; Buyer's Security Interest in Rejected Goods.

(1) Where the seller fails to make delivery or repudiates or the buyer rightfully rejects or justifiably revokes acceptance then with respect to any goods involved, and with respect to the whole if the breach goes to the whole contract (Section 2–612), the buyer may cancel and whether or not he has done so may in addition to recovering so much of the price as has been paid

(a) "cover" and have damages under the next section as to all the goods affected whether or not they have been identified to the contract; or

(b) recover damages for non-delivery as provided in this Article (Section 2–713).

(2) Where the seller fails to deliver or repudiates the buyer may also

(a) if the goods have been identified recover them as provided in this Article (Section 2–502); or

(b) in a proper case obtain specific performance or replevy the goods as provided in this Article (Section 2–716). . . .

BASIC PROBLEMS ON BUYER'S DAMAGES UNDER THE U.C.C.

What are the damages in each of these cases? (Assume good faith, reasonable purchases in each case, and notice).

1. Contract for sale of a machine for $1,000. Seller breaches. Buyer pays $800 for a replacement machine.

2. Same facts as problem 1 except Buyer pays $1,400 for replacement machine. U.C.C. § 2–712.

3. Same facts as problem 1 except Buyer pays $1,400 for a replacement machine at a time at which the range of prices for a similar machine in the market was between $1,100 and $1,400. What if, on the same facts, the Buyer paid for $1,500 for a replacement machine because they had to do so quickly to avoid a factory shutdown? U.C.C. §§ 2–712; 2–713.

4. Same facts as problem 1 except now Buyer does not replace the machine. He establishes that the market price for a replacement machine is $1,400. (Question: How can the buyer who does not replace prove market price?) U.C.C. § 2–713.

5. A harder problem: Same facts as problem 1 except Buyer replaces at $800 through her "connections." She establishes that the market price for a replacement machine is $1,400.

---

b. The Role of Notice of Breach and Buyer's Remedies

Section 2–607(a)(3) of the U.C.C. states:

(3) Where a tender has been accepted

(a) the buyer must within a reasonable time after he discovers or should have discovered any breach notify the seller of breach or be barred from any remedy. . . .

Really? Be "barred from any remedy"? Check out the effect of that language in the next case. Warning: It's a real dog of a case.

QUESTIONS BEFORE THE CASE

1. Does the court ever say that the seller in the following case is not in breach?
2. Why is a dog like a marine biologist?*

GEBBIA V. SCHULDER

New York Supreme Court, Appellate Term
32 Misc.3d 144(A), 939 N.Y.S.2d 740, 75 UCC Rep.Serv.2d 592 (2011)

Present: PESCE, P.J., WESTON and STEINHARDT, JJ.

Appeal from a judgment of the Civil Court of the City of New York, Queens County (Maureen A. Healy, J.), entered December 15, 2009. The judgment, after a nonjury trial, awarded plaintiff the principal sum of $2,500.

ORDERED that the judgment is reversed, without costs, and the action is dismissed.

In this small claims action, plaintiff alleges that defendant, a dog breeder, breached the implied warranty of merchantability when she sold plaintiff a genetically defective dog. Plaintiff seeks to recover the purchase price of the dog and the expenses she incurred for its treatment. Defendant asserts that plaintiff can not recover damages because she never notified defendant that the dog suffered from any condition or that it had died. After a nonjury trial, the Civil Court awarded plaintiff the principal sum of $2,500.

Upon a review of the record, we find that substantial justice was not done between the parties according to the rules and principles of substantive law (CCA 1804, 1807; *see Ross v. Friedman,* 269 A.D.2d 584 [2000]; *Williams v. Roper,* 269 A.D.2d 125, 126 [2000]).

"Dogs have been held to constitute goods' within the meaning of section 2–105 of the Uniform Commercial Code, and defendant, a private breeder, is a merchant' within the meaning of UCC 2–104(1)" (*Appell v. Rodriguez,* 14 Misc.3d 131[A], 2007 N.Y. Slip Op 50051[U], *2 [App Term, 9th & 10th Jud Dists 2007] [internal citations omitted]). A dog purchaser may recover damages pursuant to UCC 2–714 on the theory that a merchant seller breached the implied warranty of merchantability (*see* UCC 2–314; *Saxton v. Pets Warehouse,* 180 Misc.2d 377, 378 [App Term, 9th & 10th Jud Dists 1999]; *Sacco v. Tate,* 175 Misc.2d 901, 902 [App Term, 9th & 10th Jud Dists 1998]). "This remedy," however, is available only "where the buyer notifies

---

* Yes, we know this question doesn't relate to the case. But by now, you should be able to read a short case without two questions beforehand. So we threw in a joke involving dogs, since the next case involves a dog. The answer? One wags a tail and the other tags a whale.

the seller of its breach within a reasonable time after it discovers or should have discovered the nonconformity of the goods" (*M. Slavin & Sons Ltd. v. Glatt Gourmet Cuisine, Inc.*, 23 Misc.3d 18, 21 [App Term, 9th & 10th Jud Dists 2009]; *see Sears, Roebuck & Co. v. Galloway,* 195 A.D.2d 825, 827 [1993]; *see also* UCC 2–714[1]; 2–607[3][a]).

In this case, plaintiff specifically averred that she had never notified defendant that the dog suffered from any condition or that the dog had died. As a result, plaintiff's cause of action for breach of the implied warranty of merchantability must fail (*see M. Slavin & Sons Ltd. v. Glatt Gourmet Cuisine, Inc.,* 23 Misc.3d at 21). Defendant's remaining contentions are without merit.

Accordingly, the judgment is reversed and the action is dismissed.

QUESTIONS

1. Questions about the facts of this case

   1.1. Why does the case not discuss whether the dog was genetically defective as alleged?

   1.2. If the dog had been genetically defective, would there have been a breach of contract?

   1.3. Even if the defendant had received notice that the dog had died, could the defendant have done anything to cure the breach?

   1.4. Do we know the dog's name?

2. Questions about the law

   2.1. What was the fatal defect in plaintiff's complaint? Could you have drafted around that?

   2.2. What is the purpose behind denying recovery, even if there is a breach, just because the aggrieved party didn't give some stupid notice?

   2.3. Wasn't service of the lawsuit notice that there was something wrong with the dog?

3. **You Be the Lawyer!**

   The dog buyer is now in your office. She wants to know if, next time she buys a defective dog, she should put "All notices under UCC § 2–607(3)(a) waived" and thereby avoid a repeat of this fiasco. Can she? *See* U.C.C. §§ 1–202, 1–205 & 1–302.

---

c. *Seller's Remedies*

The U.C.C. helpfully catalogs the remedies available to non-breaching sellers in Section 2–703. That section reads:

§ 2–703. Seller's Remedies in General.

Where the buyer wrongfully rejects or revokes acceptance of goods or fails to make a payment due on or before delivery or repudiates with respect to a part or the whole, then with respect to any goods directly affected and, if the breach is of the whole contract (Section 2–612), then also with respect to the whole undelivered balance, the aggrieved seller may

(a) withhold delivery of such goods;

(b) stop delivery by any bailee as hereafter provided (Section 2–705);

(c) proceed under the next section respecting goods still unidentified to the contract;

(d) resell and recover damages as hereafter provided (Section 2–706);

(e) recover damages for non-acceptance (Section 2–708) or in a proper case the price (Section 2–709);

(f) cancel.

BASIC PROBLEMS ON SELLER'S DAMAGES UNDER THE U.C.C.

Ok, now you've got some exposure to the basic notions behind seller's remedies. See if you can calculate the damages in each of these basic problems on seller's damages. (Assume notice, good faith, and reasonable resales in each problem).

1. Sales contract for $1,000. Seller delivers the goods. Buyer does not pay. U.C.C. § 2–709(1)(a).

2. Sales contract for $1,000. Buyer breaches before Seller delivers the goods. Seller is unable to sell the goods. U.C.C. § 2–709(1)(b).

3. Sales contract for $1,000. Buyer breaches before Seller delivers the goods. Seller is able to sell the goods for $800. U.C.C. § 2–706.

4. Sales contract for $1,000. Buyer breaches before Seller delivers the goods. Seller is able to resell the goods for $1,000. U.C.C. § 2–706. Do you need more information? What if the seller is Epstein and the "goods" are Epstein's one and only 1973 Cadillac and all its accoutrements? What if the seller is Markell Mega-Metro Honda Superstore Inc., Illinois' largest Honda dealer, and the goods is a new, white Honda Accord? U.C.C. § 2–708(2).

---

d. *The Role of Notice of Breach and Seller's Remedies*

QUESTIONS BEFORE THE CASE

1. What is the role of notice from Fuji to Zalmen?
2. Where does the court get the market price of the chips that it uses in its analysis?

FUJI PHOTO FILM USA, INC. V. ZALMEN REISS & ASSOCIATES, INC.

New York Supreme Court, Kings County, New York
31 Misc.3d 1240(A), 930 N.Y.S.2d 174, 74 UCC Rep.Serv.2d 895 (2011)

CAROLYN E. DEMAREST, J.

This case was tried before the court, without a jury, on March 21, 2011. Both parties have now submitted their post-trial briefs and the court makes the following findings of fact and reaches the following conclusions of law based upon the evidence adduced at trial.

Zalmen Reiss & Associates, Inc. (Zalmen) is a wholesale distributor of electronic products which has been purchasing various merchandise from plaintiff Fuji Photo Film USA, Inc. (Fuji) for approximately 20 years. In November, 2007, defendant placed orders for 10,000 one gigabyte XD Picture Memory Cards for use in digital cameras (cards) at an agreed price of $19.49 each, for a total price of $194,900. Subsequent to the shipment of the merchandise, and after defendant had sold approximately 4000 of the cards, defendant discovered that Fuji's competitor, Olympus, was selling this product at a wholesale price less than that charged by Fuji under the terms of the orders at issue and defendant was no longer able to sell the remaining 6000 cards at a profit. Relying upon what it contended was a custom and practice in the industry to provide "price protection" for goods purchased, defendant sought a credit from Fuji for the unsold cards. On or about December 2, 2008, defendant returned the remaining 6000 cards to Fuji. It was not disputed at trial that no authorization had been issued by Fuji for the return of this merchandise as required under the applicable General Terms and Conditions of Sale.

Based upon the lack of authorization for return of the goods which had been sold and delivered a year earlier, Fuji declined to accept return of the 6000 cards and directed the carrier, Roadway, to return them to Zalmen. Zalmen also declined to accept the return and the cards were again returned to Fuji. After several back and forth transfers between Zalmen and Fuji, in light of Roadway's frustration at continuing to incur the expense of repeated shipment without compensation from either party, Fuji agreed to warehouse the shipment at its distribution center on or about January 26, 2009. The shipment was counted and the unauthorized return was "processed" at a discounted price of $4.50 per unit. A credit was issued to Zalmen for $27,994.50. The entire shipment was sold in a single lot to a reseller contacted by Fuji, at what Fuji contends was the market price for such merchandise, although plaintiff's Director of Marketing at the time of the transaction, James Avato, testified that, at the time of the return in 2009, the price charged by Fuji was still $19.49. Defendant Zalmen was not notified of the intent to sell the returned merchandise at the discounted price.

Plaintiff's Exhibit 9 in evidence is the statement of Fuji's Price Protection Policy as of May 27, 2007. It is clear from the document that, as testified by Mr. Avato, the policy is not applicable to price reductions by Fuji's competitors, but relates only to price adjustments in Fuji's own prices. As the evidence is that Fuji did not reduce the price of the subject cards at any time prior to the return of the cards by defendant, the Price Protection Policy is inapplicable to this case, as this court held at the close of the evidence. The only issue remaining open is whether plaintiff's failure to notify defendant of its sale of the returned merchandise at the discounted price precludes recovery of the difference between the original invoiced price and the credit of $27,994.50 given to Zalmen.

Defendant relies upon Uniform Commercial Code (UCC) § 2–706(3) requiring that a seller reselling goods which have been wrongfully rejected or for which acceptance has been wrongfully revoked, at a private sale pursuant to UCC § 2–703(d) [*sic*], must give notice to the buyer of the intent to resell in such manner. It is not disputed that plaintiff Fuji solicited a private buyer for the returned goods and failed to notify defendant of the intent to sell at the discounted price. Testimony by plaintiff's witness Mr. Amato established that, at the time of the return in 2009, Fuji's price for a card was still $19.49, that, although sales had slowed, there was still a "viable" market for the cards, and that Fuji did not sell below that price except for the resale of the defendant's returned shipment. There was no evidence of the allegedly lower price charged by Olympus or any other vendor of such merchandise. Mr. Amato further testified that the returned merchandise was evaluated as "A Stock", that is, not damaged or defective, but of "top quality". Fuji's justification for the severely discounted sale price was that, by returning the goods without authorization after a full year, defendant had abandoned the merchandise. This court rejects such conclusory argument. Clearly, defendant had not abandoned the goods as it had transferred the goods back to the plaintiff's possession in anticipation of receiving a credit, which it did receive.

Fuji contends that defendant purchased what was an unusually large quantity of merchandise that was "in tight supply" at the time in reliance upon a government order that did not perform as expected and sought to return the cards in order to recoup losses that had nothing to do with Fuji's price. It is noted that neither party produced at trial the individuals personally involved in the transaction so that the actual reason for the return was not established, nor was defendant's contention, that Mitchell, Fuji's Sales Director, authorized the return, competently addressed. Defendant's principal, Zalman Reiss, did not dispute Mr. Amato's testimony, but indicated that he had had no direct contact with Fuji about the matter. In any event, there is no doubt that acceptance of the goods purchased in 2007 was wrongfully revoked in 2008.

However, the mandate of UCC § 2–706(3), that notice be provided to a buyer which has wrongfully revoked acceptance prior to effecting a private sale of goods so returned, is unequivocal when seeking to recover damages pursuant to UCC § 2–703(d) [*sic*]. Recovery of the difference between the contract price and the amount recovered upon resale is unavailable to the seller upon failure to comply. * * *

The only alternative is to seek recovery pursuant to UCC § 2–708 for "the difference between the market price at the time and place for tender and the unpaid contract price". UCC § 2–708(1); *B & R Textile,* 1979 WL 30097. The burden, however, is upon the seller under that section to establish the applicable market price so as to demonstrate that the unnoticed private sale resulted in a fair price reflective of the actual value. *See Acuri,* 91 Misc.2d at 835–36; *Karen v. Cane,* 152 Misc.2d 639, 643 [CCCNY, Queens Co, 1991]. Here, the evidence adduced by plaintiff established that the market value of the cards when returned to it in 2009 remained at $19.49 per unit, exactly the contract price. The merchandise at issue was not custom-made or in any manner unique. Fuji sold a product that it maintained in its inventory and marketed from a catalog. Plaintiff's witness testified that the returned items were not damaged and were "A Stock". Presumably, they could have been returned to inventory and sold at Fuji's market price of $19.49, without a loss.

Having failed to give notice to defendant pursuant to UCC § 2–706(3) so as to afford it the opportunity to participate in the private sale or perhaps determine to pay plaintiff's invoice so as to avoid the greater loss to be sustained under the terms of plaintiff's proposed private sale, plaintiff had the burden to prove that its resale to a third party represented a transaction made in good faith and in a commercially reasonable manner (see UCC § 2–706). This plaintiff failed to do. Plaintiff's evidence actually established that the resale of the returned merchandise, significantly below market value, to a single vendor selected by plaintiff, was not conducted in a commercially reasonable manner. Plaintiff has not, therefore, sustained its burden and its complaint must be dismissed.

CONCLUSION

Judgment is awarded to the defendant dismissing the complaint. No costs.

QUESTIONS

1. Questions about the facts of this case
   - 1.1. Who is the plaintiff? Who is the defendant? What relief is the plaintiff seeking?
   - 1.2. What did Fuji do with the cards? What should it have done before it did what it did?
   - 1.3. Did Mr. Amato's testimony help or hurt Fuji?
2. Questions about the law
   - 2.1. If Fuji had notified Zalmen of the sale, and Zalmen did nothing, how would that have affected the result?
   - 2.2. Can you articulate the differences in damage calculation required by U.C.C. §§ 2–706 and 2–708? Why does the court even talk about § 2–708?
3. **You Be the Lawyer!**

   Fuji's sales department calls you just after they finally took back the cards. They want you to give them a one-page outline of what they should do now to maximize their damages. What do you give them?

C. THE RELIANCE INTEREST AS AN ALTERNATIVE MEASURE OF MONEY DAMAGES

Sometimes, the expectation interest cannot be proved or established. Does that mean that the non-breaching party to a contract takes nothing? Of course not. As stated in *Crown Coal & Coke Co. v. Powhatan Mid-Vol Coal Sales, L.L.C.*, 929 F.Supp.2d 460, 471–72 (W.D. Pa. 2013):

> Reliance damages may be pursued where the ability to recover expectation damages "is clouded because of the uncertainty in measuring the loss in value to the aggrieved contracting party." *Restatement (Second) of Contracts* § 349 cmt. a (1981); 5 Arthur L. Corbin, Corbin on Contracts, § 1031, at 188 (1963). Under this approach the law seeks to protect the injured party' reliance interest by placing it in the position it would have occupied had the contract never been made, which usually encompasses the

recovery of actual expenditures incurred in performance or in anticipation thereof.

The *Restatement (Second) of Contracts* and case law also recognize damages based on reliance interest as an alternative.

§ 349. Damages Based On Reliance Interest*

As an alternative to the expectation measure of damages stated in § 347, the injured party has a right to damages based on his reliance interest, including expenditures made in preparation for performance or in performance, less any loss that the party in breach can prove with reasonable certainty the injured party would have suffered had the contract been performed."

You should now be asking yourself two questions. Just in case you are not, we will ask the two questions: "Self, (1) how do you compute damages using the reliance interest as the measure of damages? and (2) when do you compute damages based on the reliance interest instead of damages based on the expectation interest?" Perhaps the next few cases will assist.

---

1. Expectation vs. Reliance Damages Generally

As noted above, expectation damages—damages sufficient to put the non-breaching party in the same position as it would have been in had there been no breach—are the standard. But what if it is difficult to figure out exactly where you would have been had there been no breach—as if you were financing a movie with an untested director? Try the next case.

QUESTIONS BEFORE THE CASE

1. What type of breach is assumed in the following case: material or partial? Put another way, was there substantial performance?
2. Is this a case about whether an acknowledged breach caused damages, or whether the damages alleged were proved with sufficient evidence?

---

* The *Restatement* "borrowed" not only the term "expectation interest" from Fuller and Perdue but also the term "reliance interest." Fuller and Perdue provide the following explanation of "reliance interest": We may award damages to the plaintiff for the purpose of undoing the harm which his reliance on the defendant's promise has caused. Our object is to put him in as good a position as he was in before the promise was made. The interest protected in this case may be called the reliance interest." Lon L. Fuller & William R. Perdue, Jr., *The Reliance Interest in Contract Damages*, 46 YALE L.J. 52, 54 (1937).

MERRY GENTLEMAN, LLC v. GEORGE AND LEONA PRODUCTIONS, INC.

United States Court of Appeals for the Seventh Circuit
799 F.3d 827 (2015)

Before BAUER, ROVNER, and HAMILTON, CIRCUIT JUDGES.

Opinion

HAMILTON, CIRCUIT JUDGE.

Plaintiff Merry Gentleman, LLC produced the motion picture *The Merry Gentleman,* which was released in 2009. Despite some critical acclaim, the film was a commercial flop. Merry Gentleman blames defendant Michael Keaton, the film's lead actor and director, for the bust. It brought this breach of contract action against Keaton and defendant George and Leona Productions, Inc., Keaton's "loan-out company" that he uses for professional contracting,* alleging that Keaton violated his directing contract by (1) failing to prepare the first cut of the film in a timely fashion, (2) submitting a first cut that was incomplete, (3) submitting a revised cut that was not ready for the producers to watch, (4) communicating directly with officials at the Sundance Film Festival and threatening to boycott the festival if they did not accept his director's cut instead of the producers' preferred cut, (5) failing to cooperate with the producers during the post-production process, and (6) failing to promote the film adequately.

If the case were to go to trial, one might expect Keaton to dispute that any of these alleged breaches actually violated the directing contract. After all, Keaton completed the movie. It was accepted at the prestigious Sundance Film Festival. It received critical praise—Roger Ebert, for example, gave it 3.5 stars out of 4 and called it "original, absorbing and curiously moving." And the film's executive producer, Paul Duggan, admitted during his deposition that he was unaware of any director who did more publicity than Keaton did for a movie with a comparable budget.

Keaton moved for summary judgment, however, on the narrow ground that Merry Gentleman had failed to produce sufficient evidence that his alleged breaches of the directing contract caused it damages. For purposes of deciding this appeal, we must therefore assume as the district court did that Keaton in fact breached the contract.

---

* [Eds.: In the movie biz, a loan-out company "loans" its employees (usually actors) to third parties (like movie studios). Here, Keaton was the employee of George and Leona Productions, and George and Leona Productions "loaned" Keaton to Merry Gentleman for purposes of making the film. Merry Gentleman then paid George and Leona Productions an amount equal to what Keaton agreed to be paid for his services related to the movie. It is thought that his results in more favorable tax treatment for that employee. Put another way, some smart tax lawyer figured out that by using a "loan-out" company, Keaton would save money on taxes.

Trivia point: Who are "George and Leona" of George and Leona Productions? If you guessed that those names are the first names of Keaton's parents, you win.]

Illinois law governs the directing contract. Under Illinois law, a "party injured by another's breach or repudiation of a contract usually seeks recovery in the form of damages based on his 'expectation interest,' which involves obtaining the 'benefit of the bargain,' or his 'reliance interest,' which involves reimbursement for loss caused by reliance on a contract." *MC Baldwin Financial Co. v. DiMaggio, Rosario & Veraja, LLC,* 364 Ill.App.3d 6, 300 Ill.Dec. 601, 845 N.E.2d 22, 30 (2006), quoting Restatement (Second) of Contracts § 344 (1981). The district court granted Keaton's motion for summary judgment, concluding that Merry Gentleman had failed to present a genuine issue of material fact on either damages theory.

First, the district court held that Merry Gentleman forfeited the expectation damages theory by not addressing it sufficiently in its response to summary judgment. *Merry Gentleman, LLC v. George & Leona Productions, Inc.,* 76 F.Supp.3d 756, 761 (N.D.Ill.2014). Merry Gentleman does not dispute this conclusion on appeal, so expectation damages are out.

Second, the district court held that Merry Gentleman failed to produce evidence from which a reasonable trier of fact could find that Keaton's alleged breaches caused the damages Merry Gentleman seeks: all $5.5 million it spent producing the movie. *Id.* at 761–66. This holding is the focus of Merry Gentleman's appeal. . . .

Illinois follows the approach of § 349 of the Restatement (Second) of Contracts (1981), which provides that as an alternative to expectation damages, "the injured party has a right to damages based on his reliance interest, including expenditures made in preparation for performance or in performance, less any loss that the party in breach can prove with reasonable certainty the injured party would have suffered had the contract been performed." See, e.g., *Herbert W. Jaeger & Associates v. Slovak American Charitable Ass'n,* 156 Ill.App.3d 106, 107 Ill.Dec. 710, 507 N.E.2d 863, 868 (1987) (discussing § 349). Reliance damages are designed to put the injured party "in as good a position as [the injured party] would have been in had the contract not been made." Restatement (Second) of Contracts § 344; *MC Baldwin Financial,* 300 Ill.Dec. 601, 845 N.E.2d at 30 (discussing § 344); *Designer Direct, Inc. v. DeForest Redevelopment Auth.,* 313 F.3d 1036, 1049 (7th Cir.2002) (same).

Merry Gentleman argues that the district court required too much when it held that Merry Gentleman failed to establish a causal connection between its expenditures on the film and Keaton's alleged breaches. The causation standard is minimal when the injured party seeks reliance damages under § 349, Merry Gentleman contends, and it cleared this low hurdle when it submitted an affidavit from Duggan stating that the production company spent over $5 million in reliance on the directing contract. Once it produced that evidence, Merry Gentleman continues, the burden shifted to Keaton to prove that the production company would have suffered the alleged losses even if Keaton had fully performed. And because Keaton did not submit evidence with his motion for summary judgment showing beyond reasonable dispute that these losses were inevitable, summary judgment against Merry Gentleman was improper. Or so goes the argument.

We agree with Merry Gentleman that a party seeking reliance damages under § 349 has a relatively low bar to clear to establish causation and that once it makes this showing, the burden shifts to the breaching party to prove any reduction in those damages. This causation threshold is low because the injured party is forced to prove a counterfactual: what would have happened if the contract had not been signed in the first place. See *Autotrol Corp. v. Continental Water Systems Corp.*, 918 F.2d 689, 695 (7th Cir.1990). Proving this kind of counterfactual is difficult because the value of performance can be so difficult to establish. That is especially true in cases where the injured party is seeking reliance damages. If damages were easy to calculate, the injured party likely would have sought expectation damages to begin with on a benefit-of-the-bargain theory under § 347. Reliance damages are appropriate precisely because the injured party is at an evidentiary disadvantage. Cf. Restatement (Second) of Contracts § 349, cmt. a (1981) (reliance damages are appropriate where the injured party "cannot prove his profit with reasonable certainty"). That is why courts use the burden-shifting framework of § 349. As Judge Hand explained long ago:

> It is often very hard to learn what the value of the performance would have been; and it is a common expedient, and a just one, in such situations to put the peril of the answer upon that party who by his wrong has made the issue relevant to the rights of the other. On principle therefore the proper solution would seem to be that the promisee may recover his outlay in preparation for the performance, subject to the privilege of the promisor to reduce it by as much as he can show that the promisee would have lost, if the contract had been performed.

L. Albert & Son v. Armstrong Rubber Co., 178 F.2d 182, 189 (2d Cir.1949) (footnote omitted).

The burden does not shift to the breaching party until the injured party first satisfies this threshold showing of causation, however. And just because the causation threshold under § 349 is low does not mean it is not there, as Merry Gentleman seems to suggest. To oppose summary judgment on this point, the injured party must still produce evidence sufficient to permit a reasonable trier of fact to find that the losses claimed were caused by the breach. See *Spitz v. Proven Winners North America, LLC*, 759 F.3d 724, 730 (7th Cir.2014) ("To prevail on a breach of contract claim, a plaintiff must establish the existence of a valid and enforceable contract, plaintiff's performance, defendant's breach of the terms of the contract, and damages *resulting from the breach.*") (emphasis added); *Avery v. State Farm Mutual Auto. Ins. Co.,* 216 Ill.2d 100, 296 Ill.Dec. 448, 835 N.E.2d 801, 832 (2005) ("basic theory of damages for breach of contract" requires plaintiff to prove "an actual loss or measurable damages *resulting from the breach* in order to recover") (emphasis added); see also *Old Stone Corp. v. United States,* 450 F.3d 1360, 1375 (Fed.Cir.2006) ("[R]eliance damages are subject to two pertinent limitations—the damages must have been both proximately caused by the breach, and foreseeable.").

In the typical case where reliance damages are sought, the defendant has simply repudiated the contract and walked away from the deal. This causal link will be straightforward in those cases. As the district court explained, in such cases the non-breaching plaintiff is left "holding the bag after having made its expenditures." *Merry Gentleman,* 76 F.Supp.3d at 763. In those cases, it is appropriate for the injured party to claim as damages all expenditures it made in preparation for performance because the other side failed to perform at all. In such cases, the complete loss of investment will often be the proximate result of the breach.

But in cases like this one, where the breaching party has substantially performed and the alleged breaches have to do with the quality of the final product, the causal link between reliance damages and the breach is not so direct. An injured party cannot reasonably claim that *all* of its expenditures were caused by the other party's breach without some reason to think the breach destroyed the entire value of the breaching party's performance. In this context, the breach does not cause the complete loss of investment.

Take this case, for example. Who can say why a critically praised movie did not make money? Merry Gentleman claims as damages all $5.5 million it spent to produce the movie. If Keaton had somehow prevented completion of the movie, Merry Gentleman might well have been entitled to all expenditures made in preparation for his performance (subject, of course, to the "losing contract" limitation in § 349). But here, Keaton actually made the movie. Merry Gentleman complains that Keaton slowed down the production process and failed to publicize the movie adequately after it was finished. No doubt, these services have economic value and, on a proper showing, Merry Gentleman might have been entitled to recover damages for these shortcomings. (Imagine, for instance, if Keaton's tardiness in submitting the first cut forced Merry Gentleman to pay the film editors for a longer period. Or, to take a more extreme example, imagine if Keaton had publicly criticized the film released to theaters so harshly that no one bought tickets to see it.) But no reasonable trier of fact could find that Merry Gentleman lost its entire investment of $5.5 million because Keaton failed to submit his first cut on time or failed to publicize the movie better. Merry Gentleman entered the directing contract to have Keaton deliver a finished movie, and he delivered one that showed well at Sundance and won some critical praise. The breaches by Keaton that Merry Gentleman alleges cannot reasonably be said to have rendered the investment completely worthless.

The fundamental problem we have been describing is that Merry Gentleman's damages theory is completely insensitive to the importance and severity of Keaton's alleged breaches. This is how Merry Gentleman explained its damages theory in opposing summary judgment:

> Keaton's actions were in breach of his contract, and caused damage to MG LLC in that it was unable to screen and market the film of its choosing (as was its contractual right); in that it endured substantial additional costs; and in that in reliance on its expectation that Keaton would satisfy his contractual obligations, it spent millions of dollars to finance Keaton's temper tantrum, money it never would have expended if it had been aware of Keaton's unwillingness to conform his behavior to his contractual obligations.

That's it. Merry Gentleman did not explain how Keaton's cut differed from "the film of its choosing." Nor did it explain how that difference caused it damage. It did not identify what it meant by "substantial additional costs." And the last claim—that it never would have signed the contract if it had known that Keaton would breach—is something almost any plaintiff can say in a breach-of-contract dispute.

The only evidence Merry Gentleman cited in support of these conclusory assertions were the following facts:

> MG LLC spent over $5 million to produce the film, the vast majority of which was spent after Keaton entered into his directorial contract.
>
> Had MG LLC known that Keaton would fail to meet his contractual obligations as a director, including honoring MG LLC's right to "sole discretion" over "business and creative decisions," it would not have entered into the directorial contract with him, nor would it have expended millions of dollars with Keaton as the director.

Dkt. No. 79 at 24, ¶¶ 121–22 (internal record citations omitted). Again, Merry Gentleman made no effort to establish any causal connection between the particular breaches asserted—the failure to submit a first cut on time, submitting a revised cut that was incomplete, failing to publicize the film better, etc.—and the $5.5 million that Merry Gentleman spent on the production process as a whole.[1]

We agree with the district court that Merry Gentleman, in seeking $5.5 million in reliance damages, "effectively wants to shift the entire cost—and risk—of producing *The Merry Gentleman* to Keaton for his alleged breaches, giving it a windfall and placing it in a *better* position than it would have been in had the contract never been signed." *Merry Gentleman,* 76 F.Supp.3d at 766. Reliance damages are not insurance. Courts "will not 'knowingly put the plaintiff [receiving a reliance recovery] in a better position than he would have occupied had the contract been fully performed.' " *Bausch & Lomb Inc. v. Bressler,* 977 F.2d 720, 729 (2d Cir.1992), quoting L.L. Fuller & William R. Perdue, Jr., *The Reliance Interest in Contract Damages: 1,* 46 Yale L.J. 52, 79 (1936); see also, e.g., *V.S. Int'l, S.A. v. Boyden World Corp.,* 862 F.Supp. 1188, 1198 (S.D.N.Y.1994) (assuming for sake of argument that defendant breached contract but declining to award reliance damages: "Based on plaintiffs continued running of a successful business, any compensation for these initial expenses would not place plaintiffs in the same position as they were prior to the execution of the contract, as reliance damages are intended to do, but would instead constitute a windfall for plaintiffs.").

As noted, we must assume here that Keaton breached the $100,000 contract as alleged, but these alleged breaches did not render his performance completely worthless. He directed the movie, it was accepted by Sundance, and it was released to the public. Reimbursing Merry Gentleman for all $5.5 million it spent, even though it received from Keaton a finished film praised by critics, would put it in a better position than if the contract had not been made. Perhaps Merry Gentleman might have been able to present a genuine issue for trial on a more modest damages theory, but it decided to shoot for the moon and missed. A reasonable trier of fact could not find that Keaton's alleged breaches caused Merry Gentleman to sustain $5.5 million in damages.

The district court's judgment is AFFIRMED.

---

[1] One of the most troubling aspects of Merry Gentleman's theory here is evident from the disparity between the price Merry Gentleman agreed to pay Keaton under the directing contract ($100,000) and the damages Merry Gentleman seeks ($5,500,000). Comment a to § 349 of the Restatement (Second) of Contracts (1981) teaches: "If the injured party's expenditures exceed the contract price, it is clear that at least to the extent of the excess, there would have been a loss. For this reason, recovery for expenditures under the rule stated in this section may not exceed the full contract price." The relevant contract price here would seem to be the price for the contract that was breached, which would be $100,000. Nevertheless, we do not need to depend on that theory to affirm here.

QUESTIONS AND NOTES

1. Questions about the facts

    1.1. What roles did Keaton play in making the movie? Which of those roles were the subject of this lawsuit?

    1.2. Did Merry Gentleman try to recover damages based on their expectation interest? How would you formulate what they would have to prove to recover such damages?

    1.3. The court somewhat cryptically states that Merry Gentleman might have prevailed on "a more modest damages theory, but it decided to shoot for the moon and missed." Read the notes below and see if you can take a stab at formulating a "more modest damages theory."

2. Questions about the law

    2.1. Was Merry Gentleman entitled to expectation damages? Was it entitled to reliance damages? Both? Neither? What, if anything, is the connection between the two?

    2.2. When does it make sense as a non-breaching party to seek reliance instead of expectation damages?

    2.3. Re-read the court's footnote. Does that indicate that even in its wildest dreams, Merry Gentleman could not have recovered more than $100,000? Why would that be the case?

    2.4 What is the difference between reliance damages for breach of contract, and damages based on tort? Don't both types of damages attempt to put the innocent party in the position where they were before the injury?

3. Notes

    3.1. What went on "behind the scenes"? Here are two accounts of the dispute between Keaton and Merry Gentleman:

> The tale told in the lawsuit is that Keaton became director when the screenwriter (Ron Lazzeretti) got ill. Keaton was paid $100,000 to helm the picture and delivered his first cut in August 2007, which was well after the deadline. The producers weren't happy with what Keaton turned in, so they began cutting their own version, which was accepted at the 2008 Sundance Film Festival.
>
> Keaton wasn't happy about this, and he allegedly told the festival's director that he would only attend if his version was screened. A deal was worked out on the precipices of Sundance, and *Merry Gentleman* showed to good reviews. *The Hollywood Reporter* said it was an "impressive directorial debut . . . edgy entertainment." But despite CAA

> handling sales, it couldn't land distribution from its Sundance premiere.
>
> Eventually, the film was released. Keaton gave some odd interviews in support. On ABC's *Good Morning America*, for instance, he couldn't confirm a description of the plot. Ultimately, the $5.5 million flick was a bomb at the box office, and producers filed a lawsuit against Keaton, blaming him for things such as going fly-fishing when he should have been working on the film.

Eriq Gardner, *Michael Keaton's Legal Victory Over 'Merry Gentleman' Affirmed*, http://www.hollywoodreporter.com/thr-esq/michael-keaton-beats-producers-lawsuit-760029 (Dec. 23, 2014).

A slightly different view of the relationship is given by that peerless paragon of punctilious press proceedings, TMZ:

> M.G. [Merry Gentleman] claims Keaton was a total pain in the ass from the moment production began in 2007.
>
> First example—M.G. claims they put time, energy and money into building an editing facility for Keaton in California . . . and once it was set up, Keaton decided to go on a fly-fishing trip to Montana. M.G claims Keaton forced the production company to build another editing facility in MT, so he could work and play at the same time.
>
> Second example—M.G. claims Keaton slacked on the directing duties at first . . . and he knew it . . . because he personally told producers his first cut was a piece of crap.

Michael Keaton: Bad Director, Diva & Grinch . . . Says Lawsuit, http://www.tmz.com/2013/04/11/michael-keaton-terrible-director-diva-grinch-says-lawsuit/

3.2. Failures of new ventures (be they movies, new businesses, or new products) are fertile ground for reliance damages. A good example is *Hollywood Fantasy Corporation v. Gabor*, 151 F.3d 203 (5th Cir. 1998). There, one Saffir, started a new business called "Hollywood Fantasy Corporation" in which people would pay money to spend a week with a celebrity. Saffir's plan was to charge "$7,500 for a week of 'pampering,' instruction on making movies, rehearsals, and a 'starring' role in a short videotaped film with a 'nationally known' television or movie star. Mr. Saffir hoped that 'bloopers' and 'outtakes' from the videotapes would ultimately become the basis for a television series."

Saffir's first try was with Elliot Gould, and lost money. He then entered into a contract with Zsa Zsa Gabor (one of Epstein's favorites). Bad move. The event was to be in San Antonio. Gabor breached by not showing up, and left Saffir holding the bag. The business eventually folded. As the court described Saffir's claim for damages:

> Saffir's testimony that Hollywood Fantasy lost $250,000 in future profits was based on his estimate that Hollywood Fantasy would make a $25,000 profit from each of ten future events. Hollywood Fantasy was a new venture. It had put on one event, in which nine people participated, and in which it had lost money. Two weeks before the San Antonio event, only two people had bought tickets for the event. Hollywood Fantasy had no commitments to, or arrangements for, specific future events. "Profits which are largely speculative, as from an activity dependent on uncertain or changing market conditions, or on chancy business opportunities, * * * or on the success of a new and unproven enterprise, cannot be recovered." * * * "The mere hope for success of an untried enterprise, even when that hope is realistic, is not enough for recovery of lost profits."

So Hollywood Fantasy was to take nothing, even though the celebrity breached? Nope. In describing Hollywood Fantasy's damages, the court stated:

> Although Hollywood Fantasy did not present evidence to base an award of compensatory damages on either lost profits or lost investment, it did present sufficient evidence as to certain out-of-pocket expenses to justify their recovery. Mr. Saffir testified that Hollywood Fantasy incurred the following out-of-pocket expenses for the San Antonio event: (1) $8,500 in printing costs for color brochures and press releases; (2) $12,000 in marketing costs for mailings and advertising; (3) $22,000 in personnel and miscellaneous expenses, including air fares, staff accommodations, script-writing costs, telephone calls, and logo t-shirts; (4) $9,000 in travel expenses for Mr. Saffir and members of the Hollywood Fantasy "staff," including Margo Mayor, Hollywood Fantasy's president; and (5) $6,000 in expenses relating to preparations to film the San Antonio event for a possible television pilot. These expenses total $57,500. * * *

So instead of hundreds of thousands in damages, Hollywood Fantasy had to settle for $57,500—although after reading the footnote in *Merry Gentleman* above, you'd have to even question that.

4. **You Be the Lawyer!**

Impressed with Keaton's directorial debut (and his academy award nomination for best actor in 2015), your client wants to hire Keaton to star and direct in a movie based on Ponoroff's life—working title *How To Soar Like an Eagle When Surrounded by Co-Authors Who Are Turkeys*. But you've heard rumors of the *Merry Gentleman* debacle. To ensure that you get what you pay for, what clauses would you request be in the contract?

---

2. Reliance Damages and Promissory Estoppel

We looked at promissory estoppel and Section 90 of the *Restatement (Second) of Contracts* a while ago (see pages 326 to 358). Recall that the last part of Section 90(1) states that "[t]he remedy granted for breach may be limited as justice requires." What does that mean?

EDWARD YORIO & STEVE THEL, *THE PROMISSORY BASIS OF § 90*

101 YALE L.J. 111, 116–17 (1991)

During the 1926 proceedings of the American Law Institute, a member of the audience asked Professor Samuel Williston, the reporter for the First Restatement of Contracts, about the following hypothetical. Uncle, aware that Nephew is thinking about buying a car, promises to give Nephew $1000. Nephew buys a car for $600. If Uncle reneges on his promise and Nephew sues, what does the Nephew recover, $1000 or $600? Williston responded that Uncle would be liable for $1000, the amount of his promise. Although Williston's response satisfied the immediate questioner, Frederic Coudert, the famous New York lawyer, challenged Williston's answer in an exchange that has since become one of the most quoted passages in American contract law:

> MR. COUDERT: Allow me to trespass once more, Mr. Reporter, by asking this question. Please let me see if I understand it rightly. Would you say, Mr. Reporter, in your case of Johnny and the uncle, the uncle promising the $1000 and Johnny buying the car—say, he goes out and buys the car for $500—that uncle would be liable for $1000 or would he be liable for $500?
>
> MR. WILLISTON: If Johnny had done what he was expected to do, or is acting within the limits of his uncle's expectation, I think the uncle would be liable for $1000; but not otherwise.
>
> MR. COUDERT: In other words, substantial justice would require that uncle should be penalized in the sum of $500.
>
> MR. WILLISTON: Why do you say "penalized"? * * *

> MR. COUDERT: Because substantial justice there would require, it seems to me, that Johnny get his money for his car, but should he get his car and $500 more? I don't see.

Coudert's bewilderment was shared by other members of the audience, who returned repeatedly to the car hypothetical:

> HOMER ALBERS (Massachusetts): I am still not satisfied that Johnny could have the car and $500 both, if he bought a second-hand Buick for $500. * * *
>
> JUDGE PAGE: To get back to Johnny, how is injustice going to be done Johnny if he is not going to get the other $500; how is he going to be done an injustice, if he only paid $500 for the car?

In the face of this assault, Williston stood his ground:

> MR. WILLISTON: Either the promise is binding or it is not. If the promise is binding it has to be enforced as it is made.

How have courts dealt with this issue? Have they awarded expectation damages? Reliance damages? Restitution damages? All of these? None of these? See if the next case helps to answer this question.

QUESTIONS BEFORE THE CASE

1. This is a case in the classic pattern of Owner, General Contractor and Subcontractor. Who fills these roles in this case, and who is suing whom?
2. To what extent did the general contractor rely on the bid of the subcontractor?

DYNALECTRIC CO. OF NEVADA, INC. V. CLARK & SULLIVAN CONSTRUCTORS, INC.

Supreme Court of Nevada
127 Nev. 480, 255 P.3d 286 (2011)

Before DOUGLAS, C.J., CHERRY, SAITTA, GIBBONS, HARDESTY and PARRAGUIRRE, JJ.

Opinion

PER CURIAM:

In this appeal, we address the measure of damages applicable to promissory estoppel claims. We adopt a flexible approach as suggested in the Restatement (Second) of Contracts and apply the same factors that bear on promissory estoppel relief to the remedy afforded by the breach. The determination of the appropriate measure of damages in any given case turns on considerations of what justice requires and the foreseeability and certainty of the particular damages award sought. We further conclude that the presumptive measure of damages for a general contractor that reasonably relies upon a subcontractor's unfulfilled promise is the difference between the nonperforming subcontractor's original bid and the cost of the replacement subcontractor's performance.

FACTS AND PROCEDURAL HISTORY

This appeal arises from a dispute between appellant Dynalectric Company of Nevada, Inc., a subcontractor, and respondent Clark and Sullivan Constructors, Inc. (C&S), a general contractor, concerning a public works project (the Project). The Project involved the expansion of the University Medical Center (UMC) in Las Vegas. In 2004, UMC solicited bids for the Project. C&S, interested in serving as the general contractor for the Project, sought bids from subcontractors. Dynalectric submitted a bid to C&S to perform the electrical work for the Project and repeatedly assured C&S of the accuracy of its bid. C&S incorporated Dynalectric's bid into its bid to UMC for the general contract (Prime Contract). C&S was the low bidder, and UMC awarded it the Prime Contract. C&S notified Dynalectric. Subsequently, Dynalectric repudiated its obligations to C&S and refused to negotiate with C&S. C&S therefore contracted with three replacement subcontractors to complete the electrical work for the Project.

C&S then sued Dynalectric in district court under various theories of liability, including breach of contract, promissory estoppel, and breach of the covenant of good faith and fair dealing. Dynalectric countersued for, among other theories, breach of an implied contract, fraud, and violation of NRS 338.141.

Following a 12-day bench trial, the district court entered a judgment for C&S on its promissory estoppel claim and rejected each of Dynalectric's counterclaims. The district court awarded C&S $2,501,615 in damages, which represents the difference between Dynalectric's bid ($7,808,983) and the amount C&S paid the three replacement contractors to complete the work ($10,310,598). Dynalectric appealed.

DISCUSSION

Dynalectric contends that the district court applied the incorrect measure of damages. Specifically, it asserts that the district court should not have awarded C&S expectation damages. We disagree.

Standard of review

Whether a party is "entitled to a particular measure of damages is a question of law" reviewed de novo. *Toscano v. Greene Music,* 124 Cal.App.4th 685, 21 Cal.Rptr.3d 732, 736 (2004).

Measure of damages for promissory estoppel claims

Broadly speaking, Nevada follows the doctrine of promissory estoppel articulated in the Restatement (Second) of Contracts. *See Vancheri v. GNLV Corp.,* 105 Nev. 417, 421, 777 P.2d 366, 369 (1989).

The Restatement describes promissory estoppel as follows:

> A promise which the promisor should reasonably expect to induce action or forbearance on the part of the promisee or a third person and which does induce such action or forbearance is binding if injustice can be avoided only by enforcement of the promise. The remedy granted for breach may be limited as justice requires.

Restatement (Second) of Contracts § 90(1) (1981).

Comment d elaborates further upon the remedies available for promissory estoppel:

> *A promise binding under this section is a contract, and full-scale enforcement by normal remedies is often appropriate.* But the same factors which bear on whether any relief should be granted also bear on the character and extent of the remedy. In particular, relief may sometimes be limited to restitution or to damages or specific relief measured by the extent of the promisee's reliance rather than by the terms of the promise.

Id. § 90 cmt. d (emphasis added).

Thus, under the Restatement, an award of expectation damages is often an appropriate remedy for promissory estoppel claims. But, in other instances, reliance damages or restitutionary damages may be more suitable.

Following the lead of the Restatement, we hold that the district court may award expectation, reliance, or restitutionary damages for promissory estoppel claims.[7] Although the doctrine of promissory estoppel is conceptually distinct from traditional contract principles, there is no rational reason " 'for distinguishing the two situations in terms of the damages that may be recovered.' " *Toscano,* 21 Cal.Rptr.3d at 737 (quoting *Signal Hill Aviation Co. Inc. v. Stroppe,* 96 Cal.App.3d 627, 158 Cal.Rptr. 178, 185 (1979)). In sum, no single measure of damages will apply to each and every promissory estoppel claim; instead, to determine the appropriate measure of damages for promissory estoppel claims, the district court should consider the measure of damages that justice requires and that comports with the Restatement's general requirements that damages be

---

[7] Additionally, when a damages award would be inadequate, specific performance or injunctive relief may be appropriate remedies. See Restatement (Second) of Contracts § 359 (1981) (noting that specific performance or an injunction may be appropriate when a damages award would be inadequate); *see also Skebba v. Kasch,* 297 Wis.2d 401, 724 N.W.2d 408, 413 (Wis.Ct.App. 2006) (specific performance may be warranted in promissory estoppel claims to prevent injustice).

foreseeable and reasonably certain.[8] *See* Restatement (Second) of Contracts §§ 351, 352 (1981).

Whether the district court used the appropriate measure of damages

We now consider whether the district court used the appropriate measure of damages when it awarded C&S promissory estoppel damages representing the difference between Dynalectric's bid and the amount that the three replacement contractors charged C&S to complete the same work.

Drennan v. Star Paving Company, 51 Cal.2d 409, 333 P.2d 757, 761 (1958), the seminal promissory estoppel case in the subcontract bidding context, illustrates how damages should typically be computed in this situation. In *Drennan,* a general contractor was preparing a bid for a construction project. *Id.* at 758. Before the general contractor submitted its bid, a subcontractor submitted a bid of $7,131.60 to the general contractor to perform the paving portion of the project. *Id.* The general contractor then incorporated the subcontractor's bid into its own bid for the project. *Id.* Shortly thereafter, the subcontractor informed the general contractor that it would not perform the work for the price it had originally quoted in its bid. *Id.* at 758–59. Ultimately, the general contractor obtained a replacement pavement subcontractor to complete the work at a cost of $10,948. 60. *Id.* at 759. The *Drennan* court affirmed the trial court's determination that the general contractor was entitled to $3,817, the difference between the subcontractor's bid and the amount that the general contractor had to pay the replacement subcontractor to complete the work. *Id.* at 759, 761.

In the decades since *Drennan,* courts have consistently and uniformly applied the same measure of damages for promissory estoppel claims arising from a subcontractor's repudiation of its obligations to a general contractor. *See, e.g., John Price Associates, Inc. v. Warner Elec., Inc.,* 723 F.2d 755, 756–57 (10th Cir.1983) (appropriate measure of damages for

---

[8] Most jurisdictions considering this issue hold, as we do today, that a flexible approach to promissory estoppel damages is optimal. *See Walser v. Toyota Motor Sales, U.S.A. Inc.* 43 F.3d 396, 402 (8th Cir. 1994) (promissory estoppel damages were properly limited to reliance damages where lost profits were "far from a certainty"); *Merex A.G. v. Fairchild Weston Systems, Inc.,* 29 F.3d 821, 826 (2d Cir. 1994) ("If successful [on a promissory estoppel claim], the plaintiff is not entitled, as of right, to expectation damages; the court retains the discretion to award relief to avoid 'injustice,' and can mold that relief 'as justice requires.' "); *Chedd-Angier Production v. Omni Publications Int.,* 756 F.2d 930, 937 (1st Cir. 1985) (plaintiff was properly allowed to recover expectation damages on promissory estoppel claim; "whether to charge full contract damages, or something less, is a matter of discretion delegated to the district court"); *Green v. Interstate United Management Serv. Corp.,* 748 F.2d 827, 831 (3d Cir.1984) (recoverable damages on promissory estoppel claim were properly limited to reliance damages given the "manifestly contingent nature" of the promises in question); *Toscano,* 21 Cal.Rptr.3d at 737, 739 (explaining that because promissory estoppel is rooted in equity, trial courts have the power to "fashion remedies in the interests of justice" and award damages that are "proven with reasonable certainty"); *Hunter v. Hayes,* 533 P.2d 952, 954 (Colo.Ct.App. 1975) ("When a plaintiffs recovery is predicated on findings of a promise and detrimental reliance thereon, there is no fixed measure of damages to be applied in every case. Rather, the amount of damages should be tailored to fit the facts of each case and should be only that amount which justice requires.").

general contractor's promissory estoppel claim was the difference between nonperforming electrical subcontractor's bid and the bid of the substituted subcontractor that completed the work); *Preload Technology v. A.B. & J. Const. Co., Inc.*, 696 F.2d 1080, 1091, 1093 (5th Cir.1983) (damages were properly calculated as the difference between the original subcontractor's bid and the replacement subcontractor's bid); *Janke Const. Co., Inc. v. Vulcan Materials Co.* 527 F.2d 772, 780 (7th Cir. 1976) (general contractor was entitled to award representing the difference between subcontractor's quoted prices for certain construction materials and the cost of replacement materials); *Double AA Builders v. Grand State Const.*, 210 Ariz. 503, 114 P.3d 835, 837, 843 (Ariz.Ct.App. 2005) (upholding award consisting of the difference between nonperforming insulation subcontractor's bid and the cost of a replacement subcontractor); *Riley Bros. Constr., Inc. v. Shuck*, 704 N.W.2d 197, 204 (Minn.Ct.App. 2005) (damages were properly computed as the difference between masonry subcontractor's unperformed bid and the amount paid to two replacement subcontractors to complete the work); *Branco Enterprises v. Delta Roofing*, 886 S.W.2d 157, 158, 161 (Mo.Ct.App.1994) (award based upon the difference between roofing subcontractor's bid and the amount a substitute subcontractor charged was necessary to prevent injustice). We see no reason to depart from the well-established measure of damages used in *Drennan*.

Interestingly, despite the consensus that the measure of damages adopted in *Drennan* is appropriate in the type of situation presented here, courts have not definitively labeled this measure "expectation" or "reliance" damages. *See* Edward Yorio & Steve Thel, *The Promissory Basis of Section 90*, 101 Yale L.J. 111, 146 (1991) (noting the ambiguity in the caselaw with respect to classifying this measure of damages). Scholars appear to agree, however, that the *Drennan* measure of damages is, in fact, expectation damages. *See id.* (concluding that this measure represents expectation damages, even if occasionally labeled "reliance damages"); W. David Slawson, *The Role of Reliance in Contract Damages*. 76 Cornell L.Rev. 197, 221–22 (1990) (discussing the near impossibility of proving true reliance damages in the subcontract-bidding context and indicating that the *Drennan* measure of damages represents expectation damages); Charles L. Knapp, *Reliance in the Revised Restatement: The Proliferation of Promissory Estoppel*, 81 Colum. L.Rev. 52, 57 n.35 (1981) (noting the ambiguity in the caselaw on this issue and stating that an award of damages based upon the difference between the nonperforming subcontractor's bid and the amount paid to a replacement subcontractor is "the classic expectation remedy").

As previously noted, Dynalectric's bid was for $7,808,983. C&S was forced to pay $10,310,598 to three replacement subcontractors to complete the work that Dynalectric refused to perform. Thus, the district court awarded C&S $2,501,615, the difference between Dynalectric's bid and the amount C&S paid to the replacement subcontractors. This measure of damages placed C&S in the same position that it would have occupied if Dynalectric had performed as it promised, and thus, it constitutes expectation damages.

It is plain that justice required this measure of damages and that the damages the district court awarded were foreseeable and reasonably certain. As the district court found, Dynalectric made an unequivocal promise by submitting a bid to C&S for the electrical subcontracting of the Project. Dynalectric thereafter repeatedly assured C&S of the accuracy of the bid that it had submitted. The record demonstrates that Dynalectric fully anticipated that C&S would rely on its bid by incorporating it into its own bid for the Prime Contract. The record also shows that Dynalectric is an experienced and sophisticated subcontractor that could readily anticipate that C&S would be forced to use replacement electrical subcontractors at a higher cost to complete the work that it refused to perform. Finally, the damages that the district court awarded were reasonably certain because C&S presented detailed evidence showing that $2,501,615 represented the difference between Dynalectric's original bid and the amount that the three replacement subcontractors charged.

CONCLUSION

The district court correctly determined that C&S was entitled to expectation damages. Justice required using this measure of damages, and the damages that the district court awarded were foreseeable and reasonably certain. Accordingly, we affirm the district court's judgment granting C&S expectation damages.

QUESTIONS

1. Questions about the facts

    1.1. First things first. What was the promise Dynalectric made?

    1.2. Do we know why Dynalectric repudiated its promise? Does it matter with respect to damages that can be awarded under a promissory estoppel theory?

    1.3. The court says that Dynalectric "could readily anticipate that C&S would be forced to use replacement electrical subcontractors at a higher cost to complete the work that it refused to perform." Does that mean that Dynalectric is always the lowest cost bidder? Or does it indicate that Dynalectric, at some point after it submitted its bid, realized that it had made an error and its bid was too low?

2. Questions about the law

 2.1. Why is there no contract between C&S and Dynalectric?

 2.2. Look at 1.3 above. If Dynalectrict knew its bid was too low, shouldn't have C&S known that as well? If so, what elements of promissory estoppel would have been affected?

3. **You Be the Lawyer!**

 You are C&S's lawyer. What difference would it make if, because of Dynalectric's repudiation, C&S could not perform on the Prime Contract, and was then sued by the owner for the increased price charged by the next highest bidder? Would it be entitled to its lost profits on the contract with the owner? An amount equal to the damages won by the owner? Both?

D. LIMITATIONS ON MONEY DAMAGES AWARDS

1. First Limitation on Money Damages: Avoidable Loss and Mitigation

In performing a contractual duty, often a party will have to buy something, or hire someone, to honor the party's promise. If a baker promises a dozen donuts, she will have to buy the flour and sugar, pay the electricity to run the bakery, and likely hire some help. If the buyer of donuts, however, repudiates or otherwise does not satisfy the perfect tender rule before the baker is finished, the baker won't have to buy as much flour and sugar, use as much energy, and may not need as much help.

Expectation damages, however, often assume that the costs incurred by the non-breaching party are stable and invariable. But if the baker can save a few bucks by not buying sugar she doesn't need, the breacher ought not to have to pay damages based on those costs.

In contract lingo, we say these costs are "avoidable," and that any final damage award should be mitigated (or reduced) by the amount of costs anticipated by not incurred.

Another example. Epstein hires Mike Holmes to repair Epstein's basement for $20,000. Epstein repudiates when the work is partly done (no surprise there)—at a time when it would cost Holmes $7,000 more to finish the work. Holmes' damages are reduced by costs, the $7,000, he actually saved.

Now let's think about reducing damages by the costs that the nonbreaching party did not actually save but could have, and should have, saved. What if Holmes continued work after being told unequivocally that

Epstein was breaching? Should Holmes then be able to recover the full $20,000 contract price?

Holmes should not. Holmes, the non-breaching party, cannot simply continue to perform after being told Epstein breaches and then charge Epstein the full contract price. "[T]he plaintiff has no right, by obstinately persisting in the work, to make the penalty upon the defendant greater than it would otherwise have been." *Rockingham County v. Luten Bridge Co.*, 35 F.2d 301, 308 (4th Cir. 1929).

The question of whether Holmes should stop working on Epstein's basement after being told unequivocally that Epstein was breaching is an easy question. The harder question is whether Holmes should accept other work to minimize his loss from Epstein's breach of contract. What if Ponoroff offers Holmes $6,000 to build a closet—a job that Holmes could complete in the time that he would have spent working Epstein's basement? If Holmes does not accept Ponoroff's offer, should that limit the amount of damages that Holmes can recover from Epstein for breach of contract? Is the following statement from *United States Bank Nat. Ass'n v. Ables & Hall Builders*, 696 F.Supp.2d 428 (S.D.N.Y. 2010), helpful in answering this question?

> In a breach of contract action, a plaintiff ordinarily has a duty to mitigate the damages that he incurs. If the plaintiff fails to mitigate his damages, the defendant cannot be charged with them. This duty applies to those damages that the plaintiff could have avoided with reasonable effort and without undue risk, burden, or expense. *See Restatement (Second) of Contracts* § 350(1)). The duty to mitigate damages, also called the doctrine of avoidable consequences, requires only reasonable, practical care and diligence, not extraordinary measures.

Is the statement from *U.S. Bank* helpful to understanding the next case?

QUESTIONS BEFORE THE CASE

1. What was the breach by Twentieth Century-Fox?
2. According to Twentieth Century, what should Parker have done instead of sitting back and expecting to be paid for work she did not intend to do?

PARKER V. TWENTIETH CENTURY-FOX FILM CORP.

Supreme Court of California
3 Cal.3d 176, 89 Cal.Rptr. 737, 474 P.2d 689 (1970)

BURKE, J.:

Defendant Twentieth Century-Fox Film Corporation appeals from a summary judgment granting to plaintiff the recovery of agreed compensation under a written contract for her services as an actress in a motion picture. As will appear, we have concluded that the trial court correctly ruled in plaintiff's favor and that the judgment should be affirmed.

Plaintiff is well known as an actress,* and in the contract between plaintiff and defendant is sometimes referred to as the "Artist." Under the contract, dated August 6, 1965, plaintiff was to play the female lead in defendant's contemplated production of a motion picture entitled "Bloomer Girl." The contract provided that defendant would pay plaintiff a minimum "guaranteed compensation" of $53,571.42 per week for 14 weeks commencing May 23, 1966, for a total of $750,000. Prior to May 1966 defendant decided not to produce the picture and by a letter dated April 4, 1966, it notified plaintiff of that decision and that it would not "comply with our obligations to you under" the written contract.

By the same letter and with the professed purpose "to avoid any damage to you," defendant instead offered to employ plaintiff as the leading actress in another film tentatively entitled "Big Country, Big Man" (hereinafter, "Big Country"). The compensation offered was identical, as were 31 of the 34 numbered provisions or articles of the original contract.[1] Unlike "Bloomer Girl," however, which was to have been a musical production, "Big Country" was a dramatic "western type" movie. "Bloomer Girl" was to have been filmed in California; "Big Country" was to be produced in Australia. Also, certain terms in the proffered contract varied from those of the original.[2] Plaintiff was given one week within which to

---

* [Eds.: The plaintiff is more commonly known as Shirley MacLaine. Who, incidentally, is Warren Beatty's sister. See http://www.imdb.com/name/nm0000511/?ref_=nv_sr_1.]

1 Among the identical provisions was the following found in the last paragraph of Article 2 of the original contract: "We [defendant] shall not be obligated to utilize your [plaintiff's] services in or in connection with the Photoplay hereunder, our sole obligation, subject to the terms and conditions of this Agreement, being to pay you the guaranteed compensation herein provided for."

2 Article 29 of the original contract specified that plaintiff approved the director already chosen for "Bloomer Girl" and that in case he failed to act as director plaintiff was to have approval rights of any substitute director. Article 31 provided that plaintiff was to have the right of approval of the "Bloomer Girl" dance director, and Article 32 gave her the right of approval of the screenplay.

Defendant's letter of April 4 to plaintiff, which contained both defendant's notice of breach of the "Bloomer Girl" contract and offer of the lead in "Big Country," eliminated or impaired each of those rights. It read in part as follows: "The terms and conditions of our offer of employment are identical to those set forth in the 'BLOOMER GIRL' Agreement, Articles 1 through 34 and Exhibit A to the Agreement, except as follows:

accept; she did not and the offer lapsed. Plaintiff then commenced this action seeking recovery of the agreed guaranteed compensation.

The complaint sets forth two causes of action. The first is for money due under the contract; the second, based upon the same allegations as the first, is for damages resulting from defendant's breach of contract. Defendant in its answer admits the existence and validity of the contract, that plaintiff complied with all the conditions, covenants and promises and stood ready to complete the performance, and that defendant breached and "anticipatorily repudiated" the contract. It denies, however, that any money is due to plaintiff either under the contract or as a result of its breach, and pleads as an affirmative defense to both causes of action plaintiff's allegedly deliberate failure to mitigate damages, asserting that she unreasonably refused to accept its offer of the leading role in "Big Country."

Plaintiff moved for summary judgment under Code of Civil Procedure section 437c, the motion was granted, and summary judgment for $750,000 plus interest was entered in plaintiff's favor. This appeal by defendant followed.

The familiar rules are that the matter to be determined by the trial court on a motion for summary judgment is whether facts have been presented which give rise to a triable factual issue. The court may not pass upon the issue itself. Summary judgment is proper only if the affidavits or declarations in support of the moving party would be sufficient to sustain a judgment in his favor and his opponent does not by affidavit show facts sufficient to present a triable issue of fact. The affidavits of the moving party are strictly construed, and doubts as to the propriety of summary judgment should be resolved against granting the motion. Such summary procedure is drastic and should be used with caution so that it does not become a substitute for the open trial method of determining facts. * * *

As stated, defendant's sole defense to this action which resulted from its deliberate breach of contract is that in rejecting defendant's substitute offer of employment plaintiff unreasonably refused to mitigate damages.

"1. Article 31 of said Agreement will not be included in any contract of employment regarding 'BIG COUNTRY, BIG MAN' as it is not a musical and it thus will not need a dance director.

"2. In the 'BLOOMER GIRL' agreement, in Articles 29 and 32, you were given certain director and screenplay approvals and you had preapproved certain matters. Since there simply is insufficient time to negotiate with you regarding your choice of director and regarding the screenplay and since you already expressed an interest in performing the role in 'BIG COUNTRY, BIG MAN,' we must exclude from our offer of employment in 'BIG COUNTRY, BIG MAN' any approval rights as are contained in said Articles 29 and 32; however, we shall consult with you respecting the director to be selected to direct the photoplay and will further consult with you with respect to the screenplay and any revisions or changes therein, provided, however, that if we fail to agree * * * the decision of * * * [defendant] with respect to the selection of a director and to revisions and changes in the said screenplay shall be binding upon the parties to said agreement."

The general rule is that the measure of recovery by a wrongfully discharged employee is the amount of salary agreed upon for the period of service, less the amount which the employer affirmatively proves the employee has earned or with reasonable effort might have earned from other employment. * * *[4] However, before projected earnings from other employment opportunities not sought or accepted by the discharged employee can be applied in mitigation, the employer must show that the other employment was comparable, or substantially similar, to that of which the employee has been deprived; the employee's rejection of or failure to seek other available employment of a different or inferior kind may not be resorted to in order to mitigate damages. * * *

In the present case defendant has raised no issue of reasonableness of efforts by plaintiffs to obtain other employment; the sole issue is whether plaintiff's refusal of defendant's substitute offer of "Big Country" may be used in mitigation. Nor, if the "Big Country" offer was of employment different or inferior when compared with the original "Bloomer Girl" employment, is there an issue as to whether or not plaintiff acted reasonably in refusing the substitute offer. Despite defendant's arguments to the contrary, no case cited or which our research has discovered holds or suggests that reasonableness is an element of a wrongfully discharged employee's option to reject, or fail to seek, different or inferior employment lest the possible earnings therefrom be charged against him in mitigation of damages.

Applying the foregoing rules to the record in the present case, with all intendments in favor of the party opposing the summary judgment motion—here, defendant—it is clear that the trial court correctly ruled that plaintiff's failure to accept defendant's tendered substitute employment could not be applied in mitigation of damages because the offer of the "Big Country" lead was of employment both different and inferior, and that no factual dispute was presented on that issue. The mere circumstance that "Bloomer Girl" was to be a musical review calling upon plaintiff's talents as a dancer as well as an actress, and was to be produced in the City of Los Angeles, whereas "Big Country" was a straight dramatic role in a "Western Type" story taking place in an opal mine in Australia, demonstrates the difference in kind between the two employments; the female lead as a dramatic actress in a western style motion picture can by no stretch of imagination be considered the equivalent of or substantially similar to the lead in a song-and-dance production.

Additionally, the substitute "Big Country" offer proposed to eliminate or impair the director and screenplay approvals accorded to plaintiff under

---

[4] Although it would appear that plaintiff was not discharged by defendant in the customary sense of the term, as she was not permitted by defendant to enter upon performance of the "Bloomer Girl" contract, nevertheless the motion for summary judgment was submitted for decision upon a stipulation by the parties that "plaintiff Parker was discharged."

the original "Bloomer Girl" contract (see fn. 2, *ante*), and thus constituted an offer of inferior employment. No expertise or judicial notice is required in order to hold that the deprivation or infringement of an employee's rights held under an original employment contract converts the available "other employment" relied upon by the employer to mitigate damages, into inferior employment which the employee need not seek or accept * * *

Statements found in affidavits submitted by defendant in opposition to plaintiff's summary judgment motion, to the effect that the "Big County" offer was not of employment different from or inferior to that under the "Bloomer Girl" contract, merely repeat the allegations of defendant's answer to the complaint in this action, constitute only conclusionary assertions with respect to undisputed facts, and do not give rise to a triable factual issue so as to defeat the motion for summary judgment. * * *

In view of the determination that defendant failed to present any facts showing the existence of a factual issue with respect to its sole defense—plaintiff's rejection of its substitute employment offer in mitigation of damages—we need not consider plaintiff's further contention that for various reasons, including the provisions of the original contract set forth in footnote 1, *ante*, plaintiff was excused from attempting to mitigate damages.

The judgment is affirmed.

MCCOMB, J., PETERS, J., TOBRINER, J., KAUS, J., and ROTH, J., concurred.

Dissent: SULLIVAN, ACTING C. J.

The basic question in this case is whether or not plaintiff acted reasonably in rejecting defendant's offer of alternate employment. The answer depends upon whether that offer (starring in "Big Country, Big Man") was an offer of work that was substantially similar to her former employment (starring in "Bloomer Girl") or of work that was of a different or inferior kind. To my mind this is a factual issue, which the trial court should not have determined on a motion for summary judgment. The majority have not only repeated this error but have compounded it by applying the rules governing mitigation of damages in the employer-employee context in a misleading fashion. Accordingly, I respectfully dissent.

The familiar rule requiring a plaintiff in a tort or contract action to mitigate damages embodies notions of fairness and socially responsible behavior which are fundamental to our jurisprudence. Most broadly stated, it precludes the recovery of damages which, through the exercise of due diligence, could have been avoided. Thus, in essence, it is a rule requiring reasonable conduct in commercial affairs. This general principle governs the obligations of an employee after his employer has wrongfully repudiated or terminated the employment contract. Rather than permitting the employee simply to remain idle during the balance of the contract period, the law requires him to make a reasonable effort to secure other employment.[1] He is not obliged, however, to seek or accept any and all types of work which may be available. Only work which is in the same field and which is of the same quality need be accepted.[2]

Over the years the courts have employed various phrases to define the type of employment which the employee, upon his wrongful discharge, is under an obligation to accept. Thus in California alone it has been held that he must accept employment which is "substantially similar" * * * employment "in the same general line of the first employment". * * *

It has never been the law that the mere existence of differences between two jobs in the same field is sufficient, as a matter of law, to excuse an employee wrongfully discharged from one from accepting the other in order to mitigate damages. Such an approach would effectively eliminate any obligation of an employee to attempt to minimize damage arising from a wrongful discharge. The only alternative job offer an employee would be required to accept would be an offer of his former job by his former employer.

Although the majority appear to hold that there was a difference "in kind" between the employment offered plaintiff in "Bloomer Girl" and that offered in "Big Country" * * *, an examination of the opinion makes crystal clear that the majority merely point out differences between the two films (an obvious circumstance) and then apodically [*sic*] assert that these constitute a difference in the kind of employment. The entire rationale of the majority boils down to this; that the "mere circumstances" that "Bloomer Girl" was to be a musical review while "Big Country" was a straight drama "demonstrates the difference in kind" since a female lead in a western is not "the equivalent of or substantially similar to" a lead in a musical. This is merely attempting to prove the proposition by repeating it. It shows that the vehicles for the display of the star's talents are different but it does not prove that her employment as a star in such vehicles is of necessity different in kind and either inferior or superior. * * *

---

[1] The issue is generally discussed in terms of a duty on the part of the employee to minimize loss. The practice is long-established and there is little reason to change despite Judge Cardozo's observation of its subtle inaccuracy. "The servant is free to accept employment or reject it according to his uncensored pleasure. What is meant by the supposed duty is merely this, that if he unreasonably reject, he will not be heard to say that the loss of wages from then on shall be deemed the jural consequence of the earlier discharge. He has broken the chain of causation, and loss resulting to him thereafter is suffered through his own act." (*McClelland v. Climax Hosiery Mills* (1930) 252 N.Y. 347, 359 [169 N.E. 605, 609], concurring opinion.).

[2] This qualification of the rule seems to reflect the simple and humane attitude that it is too severe to demand of a person that he attempt to find and perform work for which he has no training or experience. Many of the older cases hold that one need not accept work in an inferior rank or position nor work which is more menial or arduous. This suggests that the rule may have had its origin in the bourgeois fear of resubmergence in lower economic classes.

Resolving whether or not one job is substantially similar to another or whether, on the other hand, it is of a different or inferior kind, will often (as here) require a critical appraisal of the similarities and differences between them in light of the importance of these differences to the employee. This necessitates a weighing of the evidence, and it is precisely this undertaking which is forbidden on summary judgment. * * *

It is not intuitively obvious, to me at least, that the leading female role in a dramatic motion picture is a radically different endeavor from the leading female role in a musical comedy film

I believe that the judgment should be reversed so that the issue of whether or not the offer of the lead role in "Big Country, Big Man" was of employment comparable to that of the lead role in "Bloomer Girl" may be determined at trial.

Appellant's petition for a rehearing was denied October 28, 1970. Mosk, J., did not participate therein. Sullivan, J., was of the opinion that the petition should be granted.

QUESTIONS AND NOTES

1. Questions about the facts of this case

   1.1. What facts are most favorable to the plaintiff? Most favorable to the defendant?

   1.2. Do the plaintiff and the defendant disagree as to what the facts are? Do the majority and dissent disagree as to what the facts are?

   1.3. Recall from footnote 1 that the contract at issue provided: "We [defendant] shall not be obligated to utilize your [plaintiff's] services in or in connection with the Photoplay hereunder; our sole obligation, subject to the terms and conditions of this Agreement, being to pay you the guaranteed compensation herein provided for." Was this provision relevant to the decision of the Supreme Court of California? Should it have been relevant?

   1.4. Should it be relevant that the contract repeatedly referred to the specific film *Bloomer Girl*, instead of "a Photoplay to be selected at the sole discretion of the defendant"?

2. Questions about the law

   2.1. Recall that the excerpt from *U.S. Bank Nat'l Ass'n* which preceded *Parker* suggests that the non-breaching party to a contract has a duty to mitigate her damages. In *Parker*, do the majority and the dissent differ as to whether there is such a duty to mitigate?

2.2. Is the relevant test a "substantially similar" test or a "not of a different or inferior kind" test? Is there any substantive difference between the two phrases?

2.3. Note the procedural context in this case: the matter comes up after denial of summary judgment. If "the issue of whether or not the offer of the lead role in "Big Country, Big Man" was of employment comparable to that of the lead role in "Bloomer Girl" had been determined at a trial, what evidence would you proffer as attorney for the defendant?

3. Notes

3.1. Subsequent commentary on this case has brought out other facts. "Bloomer Girl" was based on the life of Amelia Jenks Bloomer, a champion for women's rights in the 19th Century. Its literary antecedent, a Broadway musical comedy, had strong strains of what we would identify today as feminism and the promotion of racial justice. Shirley MacLaine had publicly identified with both of these themes at or before the time of the contract. Should these facts have mattered? If so, why? *See* Mary Jo Frug, *Re-Reading Contracts: A Feminist Analysis of a Contracts Casebook*, 34 AM. U. L. REV. 1065, 1113–1123 (1985).

3.2. More doggerel:

There once was a lawsuit by Shirley
Who thought the defendant quite surly.
Re the movie she missed,
The defense was dismissed
And the judgment for Shirley came early.

Douglass G. Boshkoff, *Selected Poems on The Law of Contracts: Raintree County Memorial Library Occasional Paper No. 1*, 66 N.Y.U. L. REV. 1533, 1542 (1991).

4. **You Be the Lawyer!**

If Ms. McClain had accepted the lead role in "Big Country, Big Man," could she still have recovered from defendant for breach of contract? If so, what would be your argument as to the amount of her expectation damages?

QUESTIONS BEFORE THE CASE

1. Who is in breach in the following case? Why?

2. When reading the case, ask yourself when you would have taken action instead of waiting for the breacher to fix the mess.

R.R. DONNELLEY & SONS CO. V. VANGUARD TRANSP. SYSTEMS, INC.

United States District Court, N.D. Illinois
641 F. Supp. 2d 707 (2009)

JEFFREY COLE, UNITED STATES MAGISTRATE JUDGE.

[Donnelley is a commercial printer; Vanguard is an interstate motor carrier. Donnelley contracted with Vanguard to pay Vanguard $750 to transport brochures for Macy's post-Christmas sale brochures from a Kentucky printer to Donnelly's Atlanta distribution Center by December 16. Vanguard breached. While the Vanguard tractor trailer carrying the materials arrived in Atlanta on December 16, the trailer was left at Vanguard's Atlanta facility. In calls after December 16, Vanguard told Donnelley variously that it would "attempt" to deliver the load, that it was having difficulty getting a driver, and that its computers were down. The brochures were not delivered to Donnelley's distribution center in Atlanta until December 27, 2005—eleven days after the promised date of delivery. By then it was too late to mail the brochures to Macy's customers, and so Macy's did not pay Donnelley for the brochures. Donnelley sued Vanguard for breach of contract, and, at the bench trial, Donnelley sought to recover the cost of the brochures, $81,650. Vanguard contends that Donnelley can not recover because it failed to mitigate damages.]

* * *

Failure to mitigate is an affirmative defense on which Vanguard has the burden of proof. Cates v. Morgan Portable Bldg., 780 F.2d 683, 687 (7th Cir. 1985) * * * The so-called duty to mitigate damages, which is often referred to as a general contractual duty, is a principle of ancient vintage. Referring to mitigation of damages—or as it is called in tort law "avoidable consequences"—in terms of a "duty" is somewhat misleading, because a plaintiff incurs no liability for failing to act. See *Restatement (Second) of Contracts* § 350, Comment b. (1981). Rather the amount of loss that could reasonably have been avoided by stopping performance or making substitute arrangements is simply subtracted from the amount that would otherwise have been recoverable as damages * * *

The victim of the breach must " 'exercise reasonable diligence and ordinary care in attempting to minimize the damages after injury has been inflicted.' " And while he must act with "reasonable dispatch," *Cates*, 780 F.2d at 687, the injured party is not required to take steps that involve "undue risk or burden." But there are instances where the victim of the breach might be lulled by the breaching party into inaction because of assurances that all will be well. "[T]o put this differently, the [breaching party] may not insist on mitigation when by its words or deeds it has led the [non-breaching party] to believe that it has assumed what would otherwise be the buyer's burden of mitigation." *Cates*, 780 F.2d at 687.[10] While that is going on, the duty to mitigate is suspended.

Donnelley contends that is what occurred here, * * * Donnelley is adamant that it could and would have mitigated its damages by retaining a "local cartage company" to deliver the load if only Vanguard had told the truth about not having a driver to redeliver the load and not have misled it on a daily basis. "Think about what mitigation would have occurred if that had happened," Donnelley laments. But Donnelley's claim is unsupportable and is indeed contradicted by not only the evidence at trial, but by the judicial admissions in the Complaint * * * Paragraph 31 charges that Donnelley was trying to "persuade" Vanguard to reschedule, but Vanguard was unresponsive, "claim[ing] variously that its computer was down and that it did not have trucks or drivers available to effect delivery." * * *

Donnelley could not indefinitely operate on the assumption or on the further assumption that the load would be delivered by the 21st. There comes a point at which even unequivocal promises by the breaching party—and there were no such promises by Vanguard—cannot be uncritically relied on. Judge Posner made the point in *Cates* with the tale of the host waiting for the late dinner guest: "If you invite someone to dinner, and hours after he was due he still hasn't arrived, you had better infer that he isn't coming, and start eating. You can't let yourself and your other guests starve merely because there is a slight chance that he will show up days later." *Cates*, 780 F.2d at 687. * * *

Donnelley was perhaps entitled to wait until Tuesday the 20th. It was not, however, entitled to wait beyond that since the brochures would be of no value unless delivered to Donnelley by Wednesday the 21st. * * * By the 20th, it should have been clear to any reasonable and commercially sophisticated person in the industry—and Donnelley was an exceedingly sophisticated consumer of cartage services—that Vanguard's equivocal statement that it would "attempt" delivery on the 21st could not be relied. On the morning of the 21st—which Mr. Janiak described at trial as the "drop dead" date for delivery—the best Vanguard could say was that it "will attempt delivery this AM." At 2:23 p.m. that afternoon, Donnelley was told that the load would not be delivered until the 22nd at 1:00 p.m. * * *

---

[10] This is an application of the broader principle that a party cannot complain about the consequences of his actions. *Cf. R.H. Stearns Co. v. United States*, 291 U.S. 54, 61–62, 54 S.Ct. 325, 78 L.Ed. 647 (1934) (Cardozo, J.) ("He who prevents a thing from being done may not avail himself of the non-performance which he has himself occasioned, for the law says to him in effect 'this is your own act, and therefore you are not damnified. * * *' ").

Normally "[i]t is a nice question, however, just when the [non-breaching party] should have awakened to the fact that [the breaching party]" can no longer be relied on. *Cates*, 780 F.2d at 687. In most cases, there will be no precise time that can be pointed to that marks when the plaintiff's duty to mitigate can no longer be held in suspension. It is often a guess and "no more than a guess [will be] possible." *Id.* In *Cates*, waiting a month to see if the defendant would make the promised repairs was reasonable. In the instant case, there is no guess work involved, and the precise time can be pointed to that marks when the plaintiff's duty to mitigate can no longer be held in suspension. For Donnelley to have allowed December 20th to have passed without having taken remedial steps its Reply Brief admits were cheap and easy was unreasonable. To return to Judge Posner's parable, by December 20th—and surely by the morning of the 21st—Donnelly should have "infer[red] that [Vanguard] [wa]sn't coming," *Cates*, 780 F. 2d at 687, and if it continued to wait for Vanguard to arrive, the soufflé would fall, the candles would go out, and the guest would all be gone. * * *

Donnelley's inaction is mystifying, especially in light of what its post-trial Reply Brief concedes was the minimal time and effort needed for Donnelley to have eliminated any damage. As the Reply Brief acknowledges, all that would have been entailed was the minimal cost of renting a truck from a local cartage company and driving the half hour to the Vanguard lot to pick up the load and delivering it to the Atlanta facility. Mr. Menne, of Vanguard, estimated that the cost would have been about $250. Even if the estimate is low, the cost would have been less than the $750 it cost to haul the load several hundred miles from Kentucky to Georgia.

The fact that Vanguard could have rented another truck or hired a local cartage company does not resolve the question of the whether Donnelley was required to mitigate its damages by making the alternative arrangements it insists Vanguard should have made. "Contract law seeks to preserve the [the non-breaching party's] incentive to consider a wide range of possible methods of mitigation of damages, by imposing a duty to mitigate even if some of the possibilities are equally within the [breaching party's] power." *Cates*, 780 F. 2d at 689. Phrased differently, the breaching party's ability to cure the breach does not excuse the victim of the breach from its duty to mitigate. *Id.*

Beyond pointing out how easy it would have been for Vanguard to have rented a truck from a local company and delivered the brochures, Donnelley's post trial briefs have effectively nothing to say about its own duty to mitigate damages. Its Memorandum of Points and Authorities in Support of Closing Arguments does not mention mitigation at all, even though it was an issue in the pretrial order . . . was a significant issue at trial, and was a prominent feature of Vanguard's closing argument.

The Reply Brief * * * merely emphasized how easy and cheap it would have been for Vanguard to have hired a truck from a local cartage company and delivered the load, and how Donnelley could and would have mitigated its damages if it had only known Vanguard was lying when it promised that it would deliver the load. (Reply, at 6–8). However, as already discussed, Vanguard merely told Donnelley that it would *attempt* to deliver the load, and it was apparent certainly by the morning of the 21st, if by not the afternoon of the 20th, that it was unlikely that the load would be delivered in time. The specific time-sensitivity of the load and Vanguard's repeated failures to have made good on its "attempts" to deliver it made Donnelley's duty to mitigate all the more obvious and urgent * * *

That one cannot rely indefinitely on promises of performance no matter what the accompanying circumstances is a common-sense concept that is not confined to the law of contracts or to questions of mitigation of damages * * * If you can easily get out of the way of that forklift at work, you can't shut your eyes and hope to take your company for enough money to retire early.

All that stood between Donnelley and the fulfillment of this obligations to Continental Web Press and the complete mitigation of its certain damages of $81,000 was about an hour of either its time or that of a local cartage company and a few hundred dollars. Donnelly chose to do nothing, as it had the right to do. But in law as in life, choices have consequences. The consequence here is that the avoidable loss of more than $80,000 cannot be taxed to Vanguard * * *

QUESTIONS

1. Questions about the facts of this case

   1.1. Vanguard had the burden of proof. What fact was most important to Vanguard's meeting its burden?

   1.2. Would the court have reached a different decision if, at noon on December 20th, Vanguard had unequivocally promised delivery by 5 p.m. that day?

2. Questions of law

   2.1. What is this court's position on whether there is a duty to mitigate?

   2.2. Is Judge Posner's dinner party analogy helpful? In light of the quality and quantity of his writings, were you surprised that Judge Posner knows anything about dinner parties and soufflés? *Cf.* https://www.law.uchicago.edu/faculty/posner-r.

3. **You Be the Lawyer!**

You represent Donnelley. If, on December 19, Donnelley had spent $400 to rent a truck and transport the brochures from Vanguard's Atlanta facility to Donnelley's Atlanta distribution center, would you be able to argue that Donnelley should recover the $400 from Vanguard?

---

2. Second Limitation on Money Damages: Foreseeability

Remember the Markell/Ponoroff car wash contract: Ponoroff contracted to wash Markell's car for $10. Markell's expectation was that Ponoroff would perform the contract without breach, that his car would be washed for $10. Damages are generally measured by the expectation interest. Markell gets the amount of damages that would have put him in the same dollar position as he would have been had Ponoroff not breached. So if Epstein is willing to wash Markell's car for $15, it would seem that Markell's damages award should be $5.

But what if the breach relates to the acquisition of a good or service that the non-breaching party was going to use to make money elsewhere? What if Ponoroff was to wash Markell's car by seven on Monday evening, and Ponoroff breached, but:

— Markell had a contract with Epstein to drive Epstein in a clean car starting at 7:30 that night for $1,000 plus expenses. It was imperative that the car be clean because Epstein was planning to wear his white leather Evel Knievel jumpsuit. http://www.leatherwardrobe.com/evel-knievel-white-leather-jumpsuit.html.

— Markell was unable to find anyone else who can wash his car in time for him to pick up Epstein at 7:30. Epstein saw Markell's dirty car and legitimately cancelled the contract, so Markell lost the $1,000 he would have legitimately made had Ponoroff not breached.

Under these facts, can Markell still recover the $5 more that it will cost him to have the car washed the next day? Under these facts, can Markell also recover the $1,000 he lost because of Ponoroff's breach so that Markell will be in the same dollar position as he would have been had Ponoroff not breached?

We need more facts to answer the question of whether Markell can recover the $1,000. As now-retired Justice Souter (when he was a member of the New Hampshire Supreme Court) explained: "*Hadley v. Baxendale*, 156 Eng. Rep. 145 (1854) thus limits damages to those reasonably foreseeable at the time of the contract. To satisfy the foreseeability requirement, the injury for which damages are sought 'must follow the breach in the natural course of events, or the evidence must specifically show that the breaching party had reason to foresee the injury.' *Salem Engineering & Const. Corp. v. Londonderry School Dist.*, 122 N.H. 379, 384, 445 A.2d 1091, 1094 (1982). Thus, peculiar circumstances and particular needs must be made known to the [breaching party] if they are to be considered in determining the foreseeability of damages." *Hydraform Products Corp. v. American Steel & Aluminum Corp.*, 127 N.H. 187, 197, 498 A.2d 339, 345 (1985).

Hadley v. Baxendale, a 19th century case, is an important case, even to men and women of the 21st century. Indeed, *Hadley v. Baxendale* may be the most famous contracts case. We think that *Hadley v. Baxendale* is such an important case that we have included the entire case report—including the reporter's misleading statement of facts. Notice, unlike Justice Souter, neither the reporter nor Baron Alderson uses the word "foreseeable" or the word "foreseeability."

QUESTIONS BEFORE THE CASE

1. Who is the party in breach? What duty did they not perform?
2. The text above refers to the reporter's "misleading statement of facts." What is the difference between what is stated in the prelude to the case and what Baron Alderson recites as the facts?

HADLEY V. BAXENDALE

Court of the Exchequer
9 Exch. 341, 156 Eng.Rep. 145 (1854)

At the trial before Crompton, J., at the last Gloucester Assizes, it appeared that the plaintiffs carried on an extensive business as millers at Gloucester; and that, on the 11th of May, their mill was stopped by a breakage of the crank shaft by which the mill was worked. The steam-engine was manufactured by Messrs. Joyce & Co., the engineers, at Greenwich, and it became necessary to send the shaft as a pattern for a new one to Greenwich. The fracture was discovered on the 12th, and on the 13th the plaintiffs sent one of their servants to the office of the defendants, who are the well known carriers trading under the name of Pickford & Co., for the purpose of having the shaft carried to Greenwich. The plaintiffs' servant told the clerk that the mill was stopped, and that the shaft must be sent immediately; and in answer to the inquiry when the shaft would be taken, the answer was, that if it was sent up by twelve o'clock any day, it would be delivered at Greenwich on the following day. On the following day the shaft was taken by the defendants, before noon, for the purpose of being conveyed to Greenwich, and the sum of 2£. 4s. was paid for its carriage for the whole distance; at the same time the defendants' clerk was told that a special entry, if required, should be made to hasten its delivery. The delivery of the shaft at Greenwich was delayed by some neglect; and the consequence was, that the plaintiffs did not receive the new shaft for several days after they would otherwise have done, and the working of their mill was thereby delayed, and they thereby lost the profits they would otherwise have received.

On the part of the defendants, it was objected that these damages were too remote, and that the defendants were not liable with respect to them. The learned Judge left the case generally to the jury, who found a verdict with 25£. damages beyond the amount paid into Court.

Whateley, in last Michaelmas Term, obtained a rule nisi for a new trial, on the ground of misdirection.

Keating and Dowdeswell showed cause.

ALDERSON, B. We think that there ought to be a new trial in this case; but, in so doing, we deem it to be expedient and necessary to state explicitly the rule which the Judge, at the next trial, ought, in our opinion, to direct the jury to be governed by when they estimate the damages.

It is, indeed, of the last importance that we should do this; for if the jury are left without any definite rule to guide them, it will, in such cases as these, manifestly lead to the greatest injustice. The Courts have done this on several occasions; and, in Blake v. Midland Railway Company (18 Q.B. 93), the Court granted a new trial on this very ground, and the rule had not been definitely laid down to the jury by the learned Judge at Nisi Prius.

"There are certain established rules," this Court says, in Alder v. Keighley, 15 M. & W. 117, "according to which the jury ought to find." And the Court, in that case, adds: "and here there is a clear rule, that the amount which would have been received if the contract had been kept, is the measure of damages if the contract is broken."

Now we think the proper rule in such a case as the present is this:—Where two parties have made a contract which one of them has broken, the damages which the other party ought to receive in respect of such breach of contract should be such as may fairly and reasonably be considered either arising naturally, i.e., according to the usual course of things, from such breach of contract itself, or such as may reasonably be supposed to have been in the contemplation of both parties, at the time they made the contract, as the probable result of the breach of it. Now, if the special circumstances under which the contract was actually made were communicated by the plaintiffs to the defendants, and thus known to both parties, the damages resulting from the breach of such a contract, which they would reasonably contemplate, would be the amount of injury which would ordinarily follow from a breach of contract under these special circumstances so known and communicated. But, on the other hand, if these special circumstances were wholly unknown to the party breaking the contract, he, at the most, could only be supposed to have had in his contemplation the amount of injury which would arise generally, and in the great multitude of cases not affected by any special circumstances, from such a breach of contract. For, had the special circumstances been known, the parties might have specially provided for the breach of contract by special terms as to the damages in that case; and of this advantage it would be very unjust to deprive them. Now the above principles are those by which we think the jury ought to be guided in estimating the damages arising out of any breach of contract. It is said, that other cases, such as breaches of contract in the nonpayment of money, or in the not making a good title to land, are to be treated as exceptions from this, and as governed by a conventional rule. But as, in such cases, both parties must be supposed to be cognisant of that well-known rule, these cases may, we think, be more properly classed under the rule above enunciated as to cases under known special circumstances, because there both parties may reasonably be presumed to contemplate the estimation of the amount of damages according to the conventional rule. Now, in the present case, if we are to apply the principles above laid down, we find that the only circumstances here communicated by the plaintiffs to the defendants at the time the contract was made, were, that the article to be carried was the broken shaft of a mill, and that the plaintiffs were the millers of that mill. But how do these circumstances show reasonably that the profits of the mill must be stopped by an unreasonable delay in the delivery of the broken shaft by the carrier to the third person? Suppose the plaintiffs had another shaft in their possession put up or putting up at the time, and that they only wished to send back the broken shaft to the engineer who made it; it is clear that this would be quite consistent with the above circumstances, and yet the unreasonable delay in the delivery would have no effect upon the intermediate profits of the mill. Or, again, suppose, that, at the time of the delivery to the carrier, the machinery of the mill had been in other respects defective, then, also, the same results would follow. Here it is true that the shaft was actually sent back to serve as a model for a new one, and that the want of a new one was the only cause of the stoppage of the mill, and that the loss of profits really arose from not sending down the new shaft in proper time, and that this arose from the delay in delivering the broken one to serve as a model. But it is obvious that, in the great multitude of cases of millers sending off broken shafts to third persons by a carrier under ordinary circumstances, such consequences would not, in all probability, have occurred; and these special circumstances were here never communicated by the plaintiffs to the defendants. It follows, therefore, that the loss of profits here cannot reasonably be considered such a consequence of the breach of contract as could have been fairly and reasonably contemplated by both the parties when they made this contract. For such loss would neither have flowed naturally from the breach of this contract in the great multitude of such cases occurring under ordinary circumstances, nor were the special circumstances, which, perhaps, would have made it a reasonable and natural consequence of such breach of contract, communicated to or known by the defendants. The Judge ought, therefore to have told the jury that, upon the facts then before them, they ought not to take the loss of profits into consideration at all in estimating the damages. There must therefore be a new trial in this case.

Rule absolute.

QUESTIONS AND NOTES

1. Questions about the facts of this case

   1.1. Where is the *dramatis personae*? Who are the players here, and what are their roles? Who, for example, is "Alderson, B."? Who are Whateley, Keating and Dowdeswell? For that matter, who is Hadley? Where is Baxendale? Well . . . .

      1.1.1 "Alderson, B." is Baron Alderson, a law lord of the Court of the Exchequer. He was one of only fifteen judges with general jurisdiction in all of England at the time of the decision. He is hearing an appeal from a county court, where the case was heard in Assize session.

      1.1.2 Whateley, Keating and Dowdeswell are counsel for the respective parties; the style of English reports from this time period was to include a summary of the arguments of counsel in the opinion; you can see this in early editions of the reports of the United States Supreme Court as well.

      1.1.3 Joseph and Jonah Hadley were the proprietors of City Steam Mills, the flour mill that engaged Pickford & Co. to transport the mill shaft.

      1.1.4 Joseph Baxendale was one of the managing directors of Pickford & Co.; under the rules of agency and company law then-existing in England, managing directors were personally liable for the unpaid debts of their unincorporated businesses. It was not until 1855 that England extended limited liability to companies not chartered by Parliament.

   1.2. What is the relevant time for a party's knowledge? When must the "special circumstances under which the contract was actually made [be] * * * communicated by the plaintiffs to the defendants, and thus known to both parties"?

1.3. What were the "special circumstances" in this case?

1.4. Were these special circumstances communicated by the plaintiffs to the defendants? *Victoria Laundry (Windsor) Ltd. v. Newman Industries, Ltd.* [1949] 2 K.B. 528, 537, 1 All E.R. 997 expressed the opinion that the headnote to *Hadley* is "definitely misleading insofar as it says that the defendants' clerk, who attended at the office, was told that the mill was stopped and that the shaft must be delivered immediately."

2. Questions about the law

2.1. What is the rule of this case according to Baron Alderson? Do you agree with Baron Alderson's application of his rule to the facts of *Hadley v. Baxendale* as stated by Baron Alderson?

2.2. Illustration 1 to *Restatement (Second) of Contracts* section 351 restates the facts of *Hadley v. Baxendale*.* Does *Restatement (Second)* Section 351, set out in pertinent part below, restate the law of *Hadley v. Baxendale*?

§ 351 Unforseeability and Related Limitations on Damages

(1) Damages are not recoverable for loss that the party in breach did not have reason to foresee as a probable result of the breach when the contract was made.

(2) Loss may be foreseeable as a probable result of a breach because it follows from the breach:

(a) in the ordinary course of events, or

(b) as a result of special circumstances, or beyond the ordinary course of events, that the party in breach had reason to know.

2.3. Do you agree with the following, more recent "restatement" of the law of *Hadley v. Baxendale* by the Seventh Circuit: "Hadley v. Baxendale, 9 Ex. 341, 156 Eng. Rep. 145 (1854) * * * bars the recovery of consequential damages in a suit for breach of contract unless the defendant was on notice of what the consequences of a breach would be and agreed to compensate the

* *Illustration:*

1. A, a carrier, contracts with B, a miller, to carry B's broken crankshaft to its manufacturer for repair. B tells A when they make the contract that the crankshaft is part of B's milling machine and that it must be sent at once, but not that the mill is stopped because B has no replacement. Because A delays in carrying the crankshaft, B loses profit during an additional period while the mill is stopped because of the delay. A is not liable for B's loss of profit. That loss was not foreseeable by A as a probable result of the breach at the time the contract was made because A did not know that the broken crankshaft was necessary for the operation of the mill.

plaintiff for them if there was a breach"? *Leister v. Dovetail, Inc.* 546 F.3d 875, 883 (7th Cir. 2008). Would you agree with the *Leister* restatement of *Hadley* if you knew what "consequential damages" are?* What if we told you that *Leister* is a Judge Posner opinion?

2.4. Which of the following clauses do you think would be sufficient to invoke "special circumstances?

a. Seller acknowledges that Buyer needs the widgets being sold hereunder to meet its obligations under a contract with Bamco.

b. Seller agrees and understands that Buyer will use the widgets hereunder to meet its obligations hereunder in Buyer's contract with Bamco. Time is of the essence under the Bamco contract, so any failure by Seller to make timely delivery of widgets under this contract will result in default under the Bamco contract.

c. Time is of the essence for all performance due under this contract.

d. Seller agrees that should it default, Buyer's damages will include any and all lost profits under Buyer's contract with Bamco, and Seller agrees to assume that risk and responsibility.

Which clause is more likely to result in an award of consequential damages? Which clause is more likely to be agreed to by the parties during their negotiations? If you represented the Seller, and the Buyer presented the language found in item (d), what would you advise your client to do? If you represented the Buyer and requested the language in item (d), would you be surprised if the Seller countered with a price increase request?

2.5. What if you need a part to build a product for resale (think nuts and bolts, literally), and the seller knows that? Can you get consequential damages for any foreseeable lost profits from the planned sale of the product if the seller breaches and you can't build the product? Sure. Section 2–715(2) of the Uniform Commercial Code says:

(2) Consequential damages resulting from the seller's breach include

(a) any loss resulting from general or particular requirements and needs of which the seller at the time

---

* "Consequential damages are those which arise from the intervention of 'special circumstances' not ordinarily predictable." *Roanoke Hosp. Ass'n v. Doyle & Russell, Inc.*, 215 Va. 796, 214 S.E.2d 155, 160 (1975). Consequential damages are also referred to as "special damages" and contrasted with "general damages."

of contracting had reason to know and which could not reasonably be prevented by cover or otherwise * * *

Notice that this is an objective standard; it doesn't require actual knowledge, but only that the seller "had reason to know."

Also, note that consequential damages can only be obtained if the lost profits "could not reasonably be prevented by cover or otherwise." Remember "cover" from section 2–712? Look back at page 813.

3. Notes

3.1. *Hadley*'s history is unearthed in Richard Danzig, *Hadley v Baxendale: A Study in the Industrialization of the Law*, 4 J. Legal Stud. 249 (1975). Professor Danzig's article was then substantially incorporated in his excellent book THE CAPABILITY PROBLEM IN CONTRACT LAW 95 (2d ed. 2004).

3.2. The concept of small acts leading to large consequences is common and venerable. See the following from Benjamin Franklin:

For want of a nail the shoe was lost;
For want of a shoe the horse was lost;
And for want of a horse the rider was lost;
For the want of a rider the battle was lost;
For the want of the battle the kingdom was lost;
And all for the want of a horseshoe-nail.

Benjamin Franklin, *Preface: Note to Courteous Readers*, POOR RICHARD'S ALMANACK (1758). The poem, in some form, is attributed to George Herbert (1651), quoted in John Bartlett, FAMILIAR QUOTATIONS 270 (15th ed. 1980).

3.3. Again, more doggerel:

There once was a young man named Hadley
Whose contract of transport went badly.
"My mill shaft is gone,
All my goods are in pawn,
And my business is closed," he said sadly.

Douglass G. Boshkoff, *Selected Poems on The Law of Contracts: Raintree County Memorial Library Occasional Paper No. 1*, 66 N.Y.U. L. REV. 1533, 1542 (1991).

4. **You Be the Lawyer!**

You represent a modern day Pickford & Son named "FedEx." Their slogan is that you should use them "when it absolutely, positively has to be there overnight.™"* After reading *Hadley*, what language would

* FedEx claims that the phrase is trademarked. *See* http://www.fedex.com/cgi-bin/global_legal.cgi?cc=us&sc=/legal/copyright/us.html

you suggest inserting into their standard form contract? Remember, anxious and litigious law students use FedEx to ship résumés to law firms that "absolutely, positively™"* have to have the student's information the next day. Hint: you might want to look at: http://www.fedex.com/us/legal/.

Well, so how special do "special circumstances" have to be? Go back to Question 2.4 under *Hadley*: Do you have to have agreement or just notice of those circumstances? Next case.

QUESTIONS BEFORE THE CASE

1. Who was in breach in the following case? What were the breaches?
2. Did the breach of contract cause the damage? Was it part of the cause of the damage? Try to list all the various acts that lead to the losses described.

SUNNYLAND FARMS, INC. V. CENTRAL NEW MEXICO ELEC. CO-OP., INC.

Supreme Court of New Mexico
301 P.3d 387 (2013)

CHÁVEZ, JUSTICE.

This case comes before us because of a fire that destroyed a hydroponic tomato facility belonging to a new business, Sunnyland Farms, Inc. (Sunnyland). The day before the fire, Sunnyland's electricity had been shut off by its local utility, the Central New Mexico Electrical Cooperative (CNMEC), for nonpayment. Sunnyland's water pumps were powered by electricity, and without power, Sunnyland's facility had no water. Sunnyland sued CNMEC, alleging both that CNMEC had wrongfully suspended service, and if its electrical service had been in place, firefighters and Sunnyland employees would have been able to stop the fire from consuming the facility.

After a bench trial, the trial court found CNMEC liable for negligence and breach of contract. The trial court awarded damages, including lost profits, of over $21 million in contract and tort, but reduced the tort damages by 80% for Sunnyland's comparative fault. It also awarded

---

* They claim a trademark on this phrase too. Sigh. *See id.* (which means see the prior footnote. Same source).

$100,000 in punitive damages. The parties cross-appealed to the Court of Appeals, which (1) reversed the contract judgment * * *

Sunnyland appealed, and we granted certiorari. *Sunnyland Farms v. Cent. N.M.,* 2011–NMCERT–005, 150 N.M. 667, 265 P.3d 718. We affirm the Court of Appeals regarding the contract judgment [and] take this opportunity to re-examine the standard for consequential contract damages in New Mexico.

BACKGROUND

Sunnyland purchased its electricity from CNMEC. On September 8, 2003, CNMEC shut off electrical service to Sunnyland. Prior to disconnecting electricity for nonpayment, CNMEC ordinarily gives its customers notice that they have fifteen days to pay their overdue bills before service is suspended. It did not give Sunnyland this fifteen-day notice. The trial court record indicates a confusing array of possible billing irregularities, but it is not necessary to address them here because CNMEC does not contest the trial court's findings that it was negligent and that it breached its duty to Sunnyland.

On the morning of September 9, 2003, before electrical service was restored, several Sunnyland employees engaged in arc welding near flammable materials, including cardboard boxes. In doing so, they started a fire that ultimately consumed Sunnyland Farms' packhouse and operations building. When Sunnyland's employees initially discovered the fire, they attempted to put it out using ordinary hoses, but without electricity, the Sunnyland facility had no running water, and the fire grew. Sunnyland does not contest that its employees were negligent both in starting the fire and in reacting to it, for example, by failing to use a fire extinguisher.

Someone living on Sunnyland's property called the fire department. Fire trucks arrived, but they were unable to access well water for firefighting because there was no electricity to power the pumps. Sunnyland had also failed to make alternative arrangements for emergency water in the event that power failed. Firefighters attempted to contact CNMEC to restore electricity to the water sources, but CNMEC employees expressed reservations to the emergency dispatcher, and the firefighters interpreted their statements as a threat that the fire department would have to assume liability. Firefighters attempted to use reservoir water and to preserve water by using foam and smaller hoses, but the buildings were nonetheless destroyed.

Sunnyland sued CNMEC in contract and tort, among other causes of action, for damages resulting from the fire, alleging that if CNMEC had taken adequate care prior to disconnecting Sunnyland's electrical service, firefighters and Sunnyland employees would have had access to water and the fire could have been contained. The trial court found CNMEC liable both in contract and in tort. It calculated total consequential damages of over $21 million, of which $13.7 million was the net value of lost crops that the facility would have been able to grow in the absence of the fire. The trial court, * * * in contract, the trial court awarded the entire almost $21.4 million. The trial court allowed plaintiffs to elect a remedy in contract or tort after the resolution of their appeals.

* * *

DISCUSSION

A. CONTRACT DAMAGES

1. *Hadley v. Baxendale* and Restatement (Second) of Contracts state the proper test for consequential damages in New Mexico

This Court has previously stated that in an action for breach of contract, the breaching party "is justly responsible for all damages flowing naturally from the breach." *Camino Real Mobile Home Park P'ship v. Wolfe,* 119 N.M. 436, 443, 891 P.2d 1190, 1197 (1995). Damages "that arise naturally and necessarily as the result of the breach" are "general damages," which give the plaintiff whatever value he or she would have obtained from the breached contract. *Id.* In some circumstances, the plaintiff can also recover for "consequential damages" or "special damages," which "are not based on the capital or present value of the promised performance but upon benefits it can produce or losses that may be caused by its absence." *Id.* (quoting 3 Dan B. Dobbs, *Dobbs Law of Remedies* § 12.2(3), at 41 (2d ed. 1993)) (internal quotation marks omitted).

The classic test for whether a plaintiff may recover consequential damages comes from *Hadley v. Baxendale,* 156 Eng. Rep. 145, 9 Ex. 341 (1854). In that case, a mill was temporarily shut down due to a broken crankshaft. *Id.* at 147, 9 Ex. at 344. The defendants were common carriers who were supposed to ship the broken crankshaft to an engineering company to have a new one built, but the defendants "wholly neglected and refused so to do for the space of seven days," and the mill was shut down for five days longer than should have been necessary. *Id.* at 146, 9 Ex. at 342–43. The jury awarded the mill damages for the profits it lost due to the delay. *Id.* at 147, 9 Ex. at 344–45. The appellate court reversed, holding that in an action for breach of contract, recovery was permitted for consequential damages only "such as may reasonably be supposed to have been in the contemplation of both parties, at the time they made the contract, as the probable result of the breach of it." *Id.* at 151, 9 Ex. at 354.

The *Hadley* standard has been interpreted as an objective foreseeability test: A defendant is liable for losses that were foreseeable at the time of contracting, regardless of whether the defendant actually contemplated or foresaw the loss. Restatement (Second) of Contracts § 351 cmt. a (1981); *see also id.* Illustr. 1 (illustrating that the Restatement standard comes from *Hadley).* This foreseeability standard is more stringent than "proximate cause" in tort law; the loss must have been foreseeable as the *probable* result of breach, not merely as a possibility. *Hadley,* 156 Eng. Rep. at 151, 9 Ex. at 354; Restatement (Second) of Contracts § 351(1), § 351 cmt. a. The Restatement asks whether there were "special circumstances, beyond the ordinary course of events, that the party in breach had reason to know." *Id.* § 351(2)(b); *see also* U.C.C. § 2–715(2)(a) (2010) (allowing buyers consequential damages for "any loss resulting *393 from general or particular requirements and needs of which the seller at the time of contracting had reason to know and which could not reasonably be prevented by cover or otherwise"). In the absence of such circumstances, the breaching party is liable only for general damages. Restatement (Second) of Contracts § 351 cmt. b ("If loss results other than in the ordinary course of events, there can be no recovery for it unless it was foreseeable by the party in breach because of special circumstances that he had reason to know when he made the contract.").

This Court has cited the *Hadley* standard approvingly and described it as the appropriate rule of analysis in New Mexico cases dealing with consequential damages. *See Camino Real,* 119 N.M. at 446, 891 P.2d at 1200 (describing consequential damages standard as "essentially the rule expressed in the seminal case of *Hadley v. Baxendale").* However, we have also stated that "the foreseeability . . . rule anticipates an explicit or tacit agreement by the defendant" that he or she will assume particular damages if he or she breaches. *Camino Real,* 119 N.M. at 446, 891 P.2d at 1200; *see also Wall v. Pate,* 104 N.M. 1, 2, 715 P.2d 449, 450 (1986) (suggesting that the conditions required for an award of special damages must include a "tacit agreement" (citing *Globe Ref. Co. v. Landa Cotton Oil Co.,* 190 U.S. 540, 543–44, 23 S.Ct. 754, 47 L.Ed. 1171 (1903))).

Engaging in an exhaustive analysis of *Camino Real, Wall,* and other cases in his well-written opinion, Judge Sutin synthesized a "New Mexico rule" of consequential damages. *Sunnyland Farms,* 2011–NMCA–049, ¶ 33, 149 N.M. 746, 255 P.3d 324. This rule is similar to the test in Restatement (Second) of Contracts, but it incorporates the requirement that "the nonperforming party must explicitly or tacitly agree to respond in damages for the particular damages understood to be likely in the event of a breach." *Sunnyland Farms,* 2011–NMCA–049, ¶ 33, 149 N.M. 746, 255 P.3d 324. This makes the "New Mexico rule . . . more limited and restrictive than the notion of foreseeability in . . . the Restatement or the UCC." *Id.* ¶ 34; *see also* 11 Joseph M. Perillo, *Corbin on Contracts* § 56.3, at 90 (rev. ed. 2005) (describing tacit agreement test as "a stricter rule than that announced in *Hadley"* (emphasis added)).

We now abandon the "tacit agreement" test. While we suspect that there may not, in fact, be much space between a "tacit agreement" and the special circumstances required to render a defendant liable for consequential damages, our previous emphasis on the tacit agreement test from *Globe Refining* is confusing and antiquated. We hold that the proper test for consequential damages in New Mexico is the *Hadley* standard as interpreted in Restatement (Second) of Contracts Section 351. In a contract action, a defendant is liable only for those consequential damages that were objectively foreseeable as a probable result of his or her breach when the contract was made. To the extent our earlier cases suggest a different standard, they are overruled.

2. There were no special circumstances in this case warranting consequential damages

We review the trial court's application of the law to the facts de novo. *Ponder v. State Farm Mut. Auto. Ins. Co.,* 2000–NMSC–033, ¶ 7, 129 N.M. 698, 12 P.3d 960. The trial court in this case issued very limited conclusions of law regarding the issue of foreseeability and consequential damages. The trial court made one finding of fact stating that "the damages suffered by Plaintiff were foreseeable and a proximate cause [sic—should probably be "result"] of Defendant's Breach of Contract, negligence and negligence per se." However, in its findings, the trial court did not distinguish between the proximate cause required for tort liability and the more stringent foreseeability required for consequential damages in contract. *See* Restatement (Second) of Contracts § 351 cmt. a ("[F]oreseeability is a more severe limitation of liability than is the requirement of substantial or 'proximate' cause in . . . tort."); 11 Perillo § 56.3 at 91 ("Courts have been willing to include in tort actions more remote and less easily foreseeable elements of injury than is the case in contract actions."). The trial transcript reveals that the trial court did consider the *Hadley* standard for special damages in contract:

> [T]he case law generally addresses consequential damages is [sic] that it has to be a contracted damage, generally speaking. It has to be within the contemplation of the parties, best evidence of that is a contractual agreement. In this case, however, since the contract was with one party being the Co-op and the other party being a general body and being no written—well, written agreement but not being any—not being one-to-one and having a third party PRC, you know, you go back to *Baxter v. Hadendale* [sic], that's a contractual [sic]. And I'm worried about the torts [sic] definition of consequential damages.
>
> I've been toying with this, because, like I said, there is no rule in a New Mexico case that would be on all fours with this. And it would seem to me that—and I'm going to rule that the Co-op, in providing electricity and being the expert party to the contract should have been aware of the consequential damages of providing electricity and if electricity—failing to provide

electricity if there was a breach of contract, that there would be consequential damages.

However, despite this sign that the trial court contemplated the appropriate standard, we cannot say that the trial court actually applied the foreseeability standard correctly. To support the conclusion that Sunnyland's damages were foreseeable to CNMEC at the time of contracting, we would expect the trial court to find "special circumstances, beyond the ordinary course of events." Restatement (Second) of Contracts § 351(2)(b). Despite the voluminous findings of fact by the trial court, there were no findings that special circumstances of this type existed.

Sunnyland suggests that it was sufficient that CNMEC knew that Sunnyland was a for-profit enterprise and it depended on electricity. Both of these factual statements are supported by the trial court's findings of fact and by the evidence presented at trial. The trial court found that "CNMEC [e]mployees . . . testified that it was well known within the community that [the Sunnyland] facility was a hydroponic tomato facility." Furthermore, the trial court found that prior to disconnecting electricity, a CNMEC employee allowed a Sunnyland employee to open the windows in the greenhouse to allow venting, which suggests that CNMEC might have known that cutting off electricity could harm Sunnyland's tomato crop.

Taking these findings of fact to indicate the presence of special circumstances is problematic for three reasons. First, although this Court indulges reasonable inferences in favor of the trial court's judgment, *see Tapia v. Panhandle Steel Erectors Co.,* 78 N.M. 86, 89, 428 P.2d 625, 628 (1967), this is simply too speculative. This Court does not speculate about what the fact-finder might have meant to say but did not. *See Econ. Gas Co. v. Bradley,* 472 S.W.2d 878, 880 (Mo.Ct.App.1971) ("[C]onsider[ing] the evidence in the light most favorable to [the prevailing party] . . . does not require or authorize the court to supply missing evidence, or to give him [or her] the benefit of forced, speculative or unreasonable inferences.").

Second, Sunnyland's injury was not directly caused by the lack of electricity. The actual harm was more attenuated: the lack of electricity interrupted Sunnyland's water supply, which, in conjunction with Sunnyland's lack of backup firefighting options, made it difficult for Sunnyland to respond to the fire its employees negligently started. There were no findings that CNMEC should have known that Sunnyland was likely to start fires or was depending on electricity in order to fight any fires that occurred. Even if some damage to the tomato crop was foreseeable from the disconnection of electricity, the particular damage that occurred was not, and consequential damages are only permissible if the particular damage that actually occurred was foreseeable. "The mere circumstance that some loss was foreseeable, or even that some loss of the same general kind was foreseeable, will not suffice if the loss that actually occurred was not foreseeable." Restatement (Second) of Contracts § 351 cmt. (a).

Third, even if CNMEC had reason to know that Sunnyland depended on its electricity to power water in the event of a fire, CNMEC would still not be liable without the presence of additional special circumstances. *Hadley* provides a good example of what does and does not qualify as "special circumstances." 156 Eng. Rep. at 151, 9 Ex. at 355. In *Hadley,* the defendant knew that the crankshaft it was carrying was a broken part of a for-profit mill. *Id.* However, the plaintiff never told the defendant exactly what was at stake, i.e., that there was no backup shaft or other alternative plan to keep the mill running.[1] *Id.* at 151, 9 Ex. at 355–56. Similarly, in this case, CNMEC would have needed to know not only that Sunnyland depended on its electricity for access to water, but that there was no backup power source, or that there was a particularized need for uninterrupted water or power. There is no evidence that CNMEC had reason to know any of this. In particular, CNMEC could not have been expected to know that Sunnyland did not have a separate power source, independent of the power for the main building, for the well that was to be used in the event of a fire. A firefighter's trial testimony agreed that "if it's going to be an approved firefighting source of water, it has to have two separate sources of electricity . . . [a]nd one of them cannot come through the building that's being . . . protected by the pump," and the trial court found that "Sunnyland Farms was negligent in having only one source of power which ran through the support building to energize the exterior well pump." CNMEC cannot have been expected to anticipate Sunnyland's negligence in this regard.

Langley v. Pacific Gas & Electric Co., 41 Cal.2d 655, 262 P.2d 846 (1953) (in bank), provides an instructive example of what a utility company would need to know to render it liable for consequential damages in the event of a power shutoff. The plaintiff ran a trout hatchery that required electricity to oxygenate the water and keep the trout alive. *Id.* at 847. If power was shut off, the fish could survive for only three and a half hours. *Id.* at 847–48. The plaintiff purchased electricity from the utility and explained his situation to its employees, asking whether the utility had 24-hour monitoring and would always be able to tell him before power was

[1] There is some tension between the opinion of the court and the reporter's description of the facts. The *Hadley* court found that "the only circumstances here communicated by the plaintiffs to the defendants at the time the contract was made, were, that the article to be carried was the broken shaft of a mill, and that the plaintiffs were the millers of that mill." 156 Eng. Rep. at 151, 9 Ex. at 355. The court went on to observe that the defendants could not have been expected to know that a shipping delay would shut down the mill. *Id.* at 151, 9 Ex. at 355–56. The reporter's statement of the facts in the same decision says that "[t]he plaintiffs' servant told the clerk that the mill was stopped, and that the shaft must be sent immediately." *Id.* at 147, 9 Ex. at 344. We treat the opinion of the court, rather than the reporter's summary, as the authoritative statement of the *Hadley* case. *Corbin on Contracts* observes that "if the reporter's headnote were correct, the decision would have gone the other way." 11 Perillo § 56.2 at 84 n.4.

shut off. *Id.* at 848. The plaintiff told the utility that if it was not able to make this guarantee, he would put in a backup pump. *Id.* The utility's employees assured the plaintiff that he would be notified any time the power was shut off. *Id.* Several years later, power to the fish hatchery was shut off for several hours, and the utility failed to warn or inform the plaintiff. *Id.* Nearly all of the plaintiff's fish died. *Id.* at 849. The plaintiff sued the utility for breach of contract, *id.* at 847, 849, and the California Supreme Court upheld a jury verdict in his favor, apparently including full consequential damages. *Id.* at 847; *see id.* at 850 (stating that the measure of the damages was identical under tort and breach of contract theories). The court found that the utility "knew that a continuous supply of electric current to plaintiff was imperative," and the utility had an obligation either to provide it or to give the plaintiff notice so that he could make alternative arrangements. *Id.* at 850.

The facts in *Langley* are starkly different from the facts in the present case. In *Langley,* the plaintiff had an unusual and pressing need for uninterrupted service, and he took steps to notify the utility of that need. *Id.* at 848. He also relied on the utility's assurances by choosing not to install backup power, and the utility knew of that fact as well. *Id.* Unlike in *Hadley* and the present case, the utility in *Langley* understood the particular consequences that would *396 result from a breach, and it accepted the contract anyway.

There were no findings in this case that CNMEC should have known of a particular vulnerability to fire on Sunnyland's part, or that Sunnyland had no backup source of power or water. With neither findings nor evidence of special circumstances, we cannot uphold a judgment for consequential damages. Accordingly, we affirm the Court of Appeals' reversal of the trial court's award of contract damages to Sunnyland.

* * *

CONCLUSION

We affirm the Court of Appeals' reversal of the consequential damages in contract . . . .

QUESTIONS

1. Questions about the facts

    1.1. What was CNMEC's breach?

    1.2. Why did the court say the trial court should have said "proximate result" instead of "proximate cause"?

    1.3. Arc welding near hydroponic tomatoes? Neglecting to use a fire extinguisher to put out a fire? An electric company telling firefighters that if the utility restores electricity to allow the pumps to provide the needed water, the fire department will be liable for Sunnyland's overdue bill? You can't make this stuff up.

2. Questions about the law

2.1. What is the difference between objective foreseeability and the tacit agreement test?

2.2. Why does the court indicate that foreseeability is more limiting that proximate cause? What does that mean?

2.3. What are the connections between Sunnyland's negligence in having proper procedures in place for firefighting and the court's denial of consequential damages?

3. **You Be the Lawyer!**

You represent SunnyHigh, a hydroponic marijuana grower in a state in which state law makes such an endeavor legal. After hearing about *Sunnyland*, the owner asks you to send a letter to the electric utility listing all the possible things that could wrong if the electricity is improperly shut off. "That will put them on notice of the damage we could sustain, right?" Is the owner sampling too much of his product?

---

3. Third Limitation on Money Damages: Certainty

> As a general rule of limitation, damages for breach are recoverable only to the extent that the injured party's loss can be established with reasonable certainty. The issue has arisen most frequently in connection with lost profits claims, presumably for the reason that determining the injured party's 'profits' entails projections and predictions that are sometimes speculative and conjectural and are almost always open to debate.

Marvin A. Chirelstein, CONCEPTS AND CASE ANALYSIS IN THE LAW OF CONTRACTS 197 (5th ed. 2006).

This next case is a more modern version of foreseeability and consequential damages, and thus probably belongs in the last section. But it also addresses the problem highlighted by Professor Chirelstein: what constitutes "reasonable certainty" when dealing with those consequential (and foreseeable) damages. So we put it here.

QUESTIONS BEFORE THE CASE

1. What did the court find the value of the machine sold to be?
2. What was the warranty that was breached?
3. What were the losses claimed due to the breach of the warranty?

MANOUCHEHRI V. HEIM

Court of Appeals of New Mexico
123 N.M. 439, 941 P.2d 978 (1997)

HARTZ, CHIEF JUDGE.

Jeff Heim sold Dr. A. H. Manouchehri a used x-ray machine. Manouchehri sued for breach of warranty and was awarded $4400 in damages after a bench trial. Heim appeals, claiming the following errors: * * * (2) direct damages based on the cost of repair should not have been awarded because there was no evidence of such cost; and (3) consequential damages should not have been awarded because (a) Manouchehri could have avoided them by obtaining a replacement machine; (b) they were not foreseeable, and (c) they were not proved with the required certainty. We affirm.

I. BACKGROUND

Manouchehri was the sole witness at trial. Heim presented no evidence other than through cross-examination of Manouchehri. We summarize Manouchehri's testimony.

Manouchehri is a physician in Cedar Crest, New Mexico. Heim, a sales representative of a medical supply company, had previously sold various items to Manouchehri. In December 1991 Heim learned that Manouchehri wanted to buy a used 100/100 x-ray machine. The two numbers refer to the rating of the machine in kilovolts and milliamps, respectively. The rating of the machine affects the quality of the image obtained. A weak machine often will not be able to produce adequate images.

On December 9 Manouchehri purchased a machine from Heim. He paid with a check for $1900 on which he wrote at the top "guaranteed to work (install Continental 100–100 x-ray) without limitation" and wrote on the memo line "purchase and installation of Continental 100–100 x-ray." Heim signed his name on the front of the check after Manouchehri read the notations to him.

During the following weeks Manouchehri realized that the machine was performing as a 100/60 machine. The power was sufficient only for x-rays of small children and thin people. Manouchehri notified Heim and asked him to repair it, offering to pay half the repair costs. Although Heim sent someone to inspect the machine, no repairs were made. Manouchehri continued to talk regularly with Heim about the problem until the lawsuit was filed in September 1994. Heim at first denied knowing that the x-ray machine was a 100/60 machine but later admitted that he knew. At that time he indicated that it was the sort of machine one can buy for only $1900.

Manouchehri initially obtained a default judgment, but it was later set aside. After trial on April 4, 1996 Manouchehri obtained judgment in the amount of $4400. Of the total, $1900 was for direct contract damages and $2500 was for consequential damages. The district court denied Heim's motion for reconsideration and Heim appealed.

* * *

III. DAMAGES

Heim does not dispute the district court's finding that he breached a warranty to provide Manouchehri with a 100/100 x-ray machine. His appeal focuses on the propriety of the award of damages. The decretal language of the court's judgment was as follows:

> IT IS, THEREFORE, ORDERED, ADJUDGED AND DECREED that [Manouchehri] is entitled to judgment against [Heim] in the amount of $1,900.00, for the cost of repair of the X-ray machine and the amount of $2,500.00 for incidental damages for a total of $4,400.00.

A contract for the sale of merchandise is governed by Article 2 of the Uniform Commercial Code. See NMSA 1978, §§ 55–2–102 and –105(1) (Repl. Pamp. 1993). For breach of warranty the buyer may recover direct, incidental, and consequential damages. The statutory provisions applicable to this appeal are NMSA 1978, §§ 55–2–714 and –715 (Repl. Pamp. 1993). The pertinent portions of Section 55–2–714 state:

> (2) The measure of damages for breach of warranty is the difference at the time and place of acceptance between the value of the goods accepted and the value they would have had if they had been as warranted, unless special circumstances show proximate damages of a different amount.
>
> (3) In a proper case any incidental and consequential damages under the next section may also be recovered.

Section 55–2–715 states:

> (1) Incidental damages resulting from the seller's breach include expenses reasonably incurred in inspection, receipt, transportation and care and custody of goods rightfully rejected, any commercially reasonable charges, expenses or commissions in

connection with effecting cover and any other reasonable expense incident to the delay or other breach.

(2) Consequential damages resulting from the seller's breach include:

(a) any loss resulting from general or particular requirements and needs of which the seller at the time of contracting had reason to know and which could not reasonably be prevented by cover or otherwise; and

(b) injury to person or property proximately resulting from any breach of warranty.

Of the $4400 awarded by the district court, $1900 is for direct damages under Section 55–2–714 and $2500 is for damages under Section 55–2–715. Heim challenges both figures. We first discuss direct damages.

A. Direct Damages

The judgment awarded Manouchehri $1900 for the cost to repair the x-ray machine. The cost of repair can be an appropriate measure of direct damages. Although Section 55–2–714(2) sets the measure of direct damages for breach of warranty as the difference between the value of the goods as warranted and the value of the goods as accepted, often that difference can be approximated by the cost to repair the goods so that they conform to the warranty. For example, if it costs $200 to fix the x-ray machine so that it performed as a 100/100 machine, then one could assume that the unrepaired machine (the "goods accepted") was worth $200 less than the repaired machine (the goods "as warranted"). Thus, the cost of repair is commonly awarded as the direct damages. * * *

As pointed out by Heim, however, there was no evidence at trial of the cost to repair the x-ray machine. On the contrary, the evidence at trial was that the machine could not be transformed into a 100/100 machine. Consequently, Manouchehri could not be awarded direct damages based on a cost of repair. As stated in a leading treatise:

> There are many cases in which the goods will be irreparable or not replaceable and therefore the costs of repair or replacement cannot serve as a yardstick of the buyer's damages. In those cases, the court will have to find some other way to measure the difference between the value of the goods as warranted and the value of the goods as accepted.

1 White & Summers, supra, § 10–2, at 557.

Nevertheless, we affirm the award of $1900 as direct damages. When to do so would not be unfair to the appellant, we can affirm a ruling by the trial court on a ground other than what was expressed by that court. * * * Such a course is particularly appropriate in this case because our review of the record indicates that the district court in fact computed the direct damages on a proper ground even though the judgment does not state that ground.

At the hearing on Heim's motion for reconsideration, Heim's attorney properly stated the law, arguing that Manouchehri's direct damages should be limited to the difference between the value of the x-ray machine as warranted and the value of the machine as it was delivered to Manouchehri. He sought to set aside the award of $1900 on the basis that there was insufficient evidence to support it. Acknowledging that the sales price constituted sufficient evidence of the value of the machine as warranted, see 1 White & Summers, supra, § 10–2, at 557 ("The purchase price of the damaged goods may be the best evidence of the value of the goods as warranted."), he focused his argument on the alleged absence of evidence to support a finding regarding the value of the machine delivered to Manouchehri.

The district court did not dispute the contentions of Heim's attorney as to the proper measure of damages, but it rejected the claim that there was insufficient evidence regarding the value of the machine delivered to Manouchehri. Indeed, Finding No. 5 in the district court's decision states: "Any value to [Manouchehri] of the X-Ray machine 'as is' is offset by the cost to [Manouchehri] of having the machine removed from his premises." On appeal Heim has not challenged this finding. As we understand Finding No. 5, the court determined that Manouchehri could not recover any money for the machine; at the conclusion of trial the court had said, "I presume that someone will be willing to remove the machine for its residual value." * * * Hence, we do not find it unfair to affirm the district court's award of $1900 in direct damages as the difference between the value of the x-ray machine as warranted and the value of the machine actually delivered to Manouchehri.

B. Consequential Damages

The district court's judgment awarded "$2500 for incidental damages." Again, the judgment was not prepared with sufficient care. The damage award was clearly for consequential damages, not incidental damages. See § 55–2–715 (defining "incidental" and "consequential" damages). Finding No. 6 of the district court's decision states: "[Manouchehri] has suffered consequential damages in the form of loss of business of at least $2,500.00 during the time [Manouchehri] reasonably waited for [Heim] to repair the X-Ray machine or otherwise perform under the guarantee."

Manouchehri's testimony with respect to consequential damages was straightforward. He said that taking an x-ray would cost him from three to six dollars and he would charge "about $85 to $88" for taking and reading an x-ray. He also claimed that the inadequacy of the machine prevented him from taking at least 30 x-rays a month, although he had no documentation to support his estimate. Using the lowest possible profit per x-ray, Manouchehri contended in closing argument that the monthly loss would be $2370—computed by multiplying $79 net income per x-ray times 30 x-rays a month.

Heim contends that the award is improper for three reasons. First, he contends that Manouchehri failed to present evidence that he could not avoid the damages by renting or buying a substitute machine. Second, he contends that any lost profits were not reasonably foreseeable. Third, he contends that the proof of damages was too indefinite. Each of Heim's arguments has some force. But they must be examined in light of the district court's award of only $2500. It appears that the district court considered the three matters raised by Heim and adjusted the award accordingly. We now examine each of Heim's arguments.

1. Failure to Obtain Replacement Machine

Consequential damages are not recoverable if they could "reasonably be prevented by cover or otherwise." Section 55–2–715(2)(a). Heim argues that Manouchehri needed to present evidence that he could not avoid the damages by renting or buying a substitute machine. On the record before us, we reject the argument.

Manouchehri testified that he asked Heim to have someone repair the machine and that Heim responded that he would have someone come to the office for that purpose. Manouchehri further testified that he talked to Heim on a monthly basis regarding the problem and that until about a month before he filed the lawsuit he believed that Heim would fix the problem.

The UCC requirement to take reasonable steps to prevent consequential damages derives from standard contract law. In particular, guidance in interpreting Section 55–2–715(2)(a) can be found in the *Restatement (Second) of Contracts* § 350 (1981). See 1 White & Summers, supra, § 10–4, at 577 ("Restatement [§ 350] may be regarded as an articulation of the rules embodied in the adverb 'reasonably' in 2–715."). Restatement, supra, Section 350 reads:

> Avoidability as a Limitation on Damages
>
> (1) Except as stated in Subsection (2), damages are not recoverable for loss that the injured party could have avoided without undue risk, burden or humiliation.
>
> (2) The injured party is not precluded from recovery by the rule stated in Subsection (1) to the extent that he has made reasonable but unsuccessful efforts to avoid loss.

The comment to this section states that it may be reasonable to rely on a breaching party's assurances that the breach will be remedied. See id. cmt. g and illus. 19. * * *

We cannot say that it was unreasonable as a matter of law for Manouchehri to delay seeking a replacement machine for a few months. The district court found that Manouchehri "suffered consequential damages in the form of loss of business of at least $2,500.00 during the time [he] reasonably waited for [Heim] to repair the X-Ray machine or otherwise perform under the guarantee." The district court did not state how long it was reasonable for Manouchehri to wait, nor did it state how much business Manouchehri lost in any particular month. Nevertheless, we see no need for mathematical precision in the circumstances of this case. The question is only whether it was rational for the district court to find, on the basis of the evidence presented, that by the time Manouchehri should have stopped relying on Heim's promises, he had lost at least $2500 in profits. Our answer is yes.

2. Foreseeability

Heim next argues that the lost profits cannot be awarded because Manouchehri failed to present any evidence on the issue of foreseeability. He relies on the language in Section 55–2–715(2)(a) that restricts recovery for consequential damages to losses "resulting from general or particular requirements * * * of which the seller at the time of contracting had reason to know. * * *" We are not persuaded.

This was not a sale of a mass-produced item to an anonymous buyer. Heim knew his customer and knew how the x-ray machine was to be used. Any reasonable person in his position would assume that a doctor using such a machine would charge more for its use than the cost of operation and would earn income from it. Moreover, Manouchehri testified to conversations with Heim that at least touched on the economics of the machine. For example, Manouchehri related one occasion when parts from an old failed x-ray machine were in front of his office:

> [Heim] asked that I had that x-ray and what to do with them and how come it was still sitting there. And I told him that this was a failed x-ray and I am stuck with the loss of this much money. And at that time he promised me, quoting from him, that "I know a doctor that has just [the] x-ray that you want. X-ray 100/100 is what you want, and I can get it for you and install in your office for this much money.

On the evidence at trial the district court could properly find that lost income would be a foreseeable consequence of an underpowered x-ray machine. * * * Although Manouchehri did not tell Heim how much income he would earn from use of the machine, he did not need to do so in order to recover consequential damages so long as the consequence of lost income was reasonably foreseeable. The law does not require those who enter into contracts to disclose to other parties the profits they expect to make from the contracts. See Richard A. Posner, Economic Analysis of Law 115 (3d ed. 1986) ("Any other rule would make it difficult for a good bargainer to collect damages unless before the contract was signed he had made disclosures that would reduce the advantage of being a good bargainer—disclosures that would prevent the buyer from appropriating the gains from his efforts to identify a resource that was undervalued in its present use."); * * * Perhaps some limit could be placed on recovery for particularly large lost profits, cf. Restatement, supra, § 351(3) (court may limit damages for foreseeable loss "in order to avoid disproportionate compensation"), but the award of $2500 in this case was within proper bounds.

3. Certainty of Proof of Damages

Finally, Heim argues that the evidence of lost profits was not certain enough. We disagree. We recognize that "when it is possible to present accurate evidence on the amount of damages, the party upon whom the burden rests to prove damages must present such evidence." * * * This requirement must be understood, however, in the context of the amount at stake. What it is "possible" to present in a suit for a million dollars may be an excessive burden for a small claim. Although Manouchehri's evidence was minimal, it was adequate in the circumstances. The absence of detail and documentary corroboration detracted from the weight of the testimony, but the district court could still find it sufficiently credible to support the $2500 award.

IV. CONCLUSION

We affirm the judgment below.

QUESTIONS

1. Questions about the facts of this case

   1.1. What value did the court place on the X-ray machine as delivered?

   1.2. Why do you suppose that Heim did not put on any evidence? If you were Heim's counsel, what evidence would you have introduced?

   1.3. What evidence did Dr. Manouchehri proffer?

   1.4. What was it about Dr. Manouchehri's evidence that was sufficiently certain? Wasn't it just unsupported talk?

2. Questions about the law

   2.1. The cost of the X-ray machine was $1,900. Why did the court award more than the purchase price?

   2.2. Did this court really suggest that Dr. Manouchehri would have needed more proof if the amount at issue had been more? Why? Is that discriminatory justice?

3. **You Be the Lawyer!**

   If you were Manouchehri's counsel (and had Heim's counsel been a better lawyer), what evidence would you have introduced?

In the next case, the amount at issue was more—"exceed millions of dollars." It's just that no one seemed to know how many "millions of dollars."

QUESTIONS BEFORE THE CASE

1. What is a motion in limine?
2. Did Baseball pay ESPN everything it agreed to under the terms of the contract? If so, then what is Baseball complaining about?

ESPN, INC. V. OFFICE OF THE COMMISSIONER OF BASEBALL

U.S. District Court, Southern District of New York
76 F. Supp. 2d 416 (1999)

SHIRA A. SCHEINDLIN, U.S.D.J.:

On October 15, 1999, ESPN, Inc. ("ESPN") and the Office of the Commissioner of Baseball ("Baseball") moved in limine to preclude the admission of certain evidence and argument at their forthcoming trial. Ten separate motions—five by ESPN and five by Baseball—were fully submitted on October 29, 1999. Six of the motions were resolved by opinion dated November 22, 1999 [Eds: which is reprinted above, at page 730]. Three of the motions were resolved from the bench during a hearing on November 23, 1999. The final motion, ESPN's motion in limine to preclude damages evidence, is the subject of this Opinion and Order.

I. ESPN's Motion in Limine to Preclude Damages Evidence

In my November 22 opinion, I ruled that ESPN breached its 1996 telecasting agreement ("1996 Agreement") with Baseball when it preempted six baseball games scheduled for Sunday nights in September 1998 and September 1999 without the prior written approval of Baseball. See ESPN, Inc. v. Office of the Commissioner of Baseball, 76 F. Supp. 2d 383 (S.D.N.Y. 1999). ESPN broadcast NFL football games rather than the previously scheduled baseball games on those six nights.

Baseball claims that it has been damaged in an amount "believed to exceed millions of dollars" as a result of ESPN's breach of the 1996 Agreement. * * * Baseball attributes its damages to an alleged loss of:

(1) national television exposure;

(2) promotional opportunities and ratings;

(3) value of the "Sunday Night Baseball" television package;

(4) prestige;

(5) potential sponsorships; and

(6) the future value of all of Baseball's national telecast packages

* * * Because Baseball received full payment from ESPN under the contract, it may only seek extra-contractual damages stemming from the six preemptions.

By its motion, ESPN seeks to preclude Baseball from introducing testimony or other evidence of its alleged monetary damages. ESPN contends that "there is no factual basis to support any claim for monetary damages arising from these perceived injuries, and that such claims are the product of speculation and guesswork." * * * Baseball argues that it has made the "requisite showing of damage" and therefore it is "entitled to have the opportunity to prove its damages at trial." * * *

II. Legal Standard

It is well-settled under New York law that

> [a] plaintiff seeking compensatory damages has the burden of proof and should present to the court a proper basis for ascertaining the damages [it] seeks to recover. They must be susceptible of ascertainment in some manner other than by mere conjecture or guesswork.

Dunkel v. McDonald, 272 A.D. 267, 70 N.Y.S.2d 653, 656 (1st Dep't 1947), aff'd, 298 N.Y. 586, 81 N.E.2d 323 (1948). * * * Although it is true that "when the existence of damage is certain, and the only uncertainty is as to its amount, the plaintiff will not be denied recovery of substantial damages," but even then the plaintiff must show "a stable foundation for a reasonable estimate" of damages. * * *

With respect to damages for loss of goodwill, business reputation or future profits, the proof requirements are much more stringent. * * * Not only must the claimant prove the fact of loss with certainty, but the "loss must be 'reasonably certain in amount.'" * * * "In other words, the damages may not be merely possible speculative or imaginary but must be reasonably certain and directly traceable to the breach, not remote or the result of other intervening causes." * * *

III. Baseball's Proffered Damages Evidence

During discovery, ESPN served Baseball with interrogatories regarding its claims for monetary damages. Among other things, ESPN asked Baseball to "state the amount of monetary damages you seek in this action and explain the basis for the computation of your claim." ESPN Interrogatory No. 6, Ex. A to Lobenfeld Aff. at 7. Baseball responded as follows:

> Baseball has not quantified the amount of damages it has sustained by reason of ESPN's willful refusal to carry [baseball] games as required by the 1996 Agreement. A quantification of those damages, however real, is extremely complex and for that reason Baseball insisted, and ESPN agreed, in the 1996 Agreement that ESPN would produce and distribute the telecasts and that its failure to do so could be specifically enforced, without regard to the need for Baseball to prove irreparable harm. At its essence the damages, believed to exceed millions of dollars, are attributable to [loss of national television exposure; promotional opportunities and ratings; value of the "Sunday Night Baseball" television package; prestige; potential sponsorships; and the future value of all of Baseball's national telecast packages].

Id. at 7–8.[2] Nowhere in its response does Baseball set forth any specific dollar amount of monetary damages other than its estimate that damages are "believed to exceed millions of dollars." Nor does Baseball set forth any method of calculating its alleged damages.

As the following excerpts demonstrate, Baseball's [designated] witness on the topic of damages, Baseball's President Paul Beeston, was equally speculative and vague regarding the alleged harm caused by ESPN's breach.

---

[2] Baseball's interrogatory response is quite revealing. Baseball concedes that it had agreed that in the event of a breach it would seek "specific[ ] enforcement" without the need to prove "irreparable harm." Baseball's failure to seek that specific enforcement is puzzling and leads one to question whether it really wanted the games aired, or whether it really wanted an excuse to renegotiate a contract which it no longer found sufficiently lucrative. On the other hand, ESPN's behavior is also suspect. In the November 22 opinion, I held that ESPN should not have engaged in self-help but should have sought judicial intervention as to whether Baseball's failure to grant permission to broadcast football in place of baseball games was unreasonable. ESPN's failure leads one to question whether the fear of an adverse ruling, and the accompanying loss of millions of dollars in revenues, caused ESPN to choose the option of intentionally breaching its contract.

> Q: Has Baseball quantified any of the damages it alleges in this case?
>
> A: No, we have not quantified it to the extent of a specific dollar, no.
>
> Q: Has Baseball made any calculations as to any specific element of its alleged damages?
>
> A: We have not.
>
> Q: Is there a reason why Baseball has not done any calculation of its damages in this case?
>
> A: No. We just believe it's significant. We believe that the case speaks for itself at the present time, and we have not worked out what the dollars are of the damages.

9/27/99 Deposition of Paul Beeston ("Beeston Dep.") at 6–7.

* * *

> Q: What's the basis for your belief that Baseball's alleged damages exceed millions of dollars?
>
> A: Based on what we have right here and what we've said what we've got here going forward. I don't have anything specific, as I said.
>
> Q: If somebody suggested to you that they believed you're right, Baseball was damaged but it's only a hundred thousand dollars, would you be able to point me to anything to say it's not a hundred thousand dollars, it's a million dollars?
>
> A: Specifically I won't be able to say this is what it is, try this calculation and that's the way it works out, no.

Id. at 28.

* * *

> Q: Can you point to anything specific as evidence that ESPN's [breach] has made Baseball less valuable in any way?
>
> A: "Specifically, no if you're asking for one example that I could give you. * * *"
>
> Q: You say you think it probably hurt you. Are you able to point to us specifically—
>
> A: No, I said I cannot.

Id. at 10–11. Not once during his deposition did Beeston offer a concrete example of harm or monetary loss stemming from Baseball's breach.

Baseball's expert witness, Robert J. Wussler,* was similarly unable to cite specific examples of loss. During his deposition, Wussler testified as follows:

> Q: Are you aware of any money that Baseball lost as a result of those three games?
>
> A: No I'm not.
>
> Q: And the same thing is true in '99, same question with respect to '99?
>
> A: They've lost in perception. It's very hard to evaluate dollars and perception.
>
> Q: I'm not going to ask you about perception. You are not aware of any dollars lost, correct?
>
> A: I'm not.

10/15/99 Deposition of Robert J. Wussler at 92–93.

* * *

> Q: Again, just so I'm clear, are you aware of 5 cents of advertising revenue that Baseball lost as a result of the three games being [not shown on ESPN]—
>
> A: No I'm not.

Id. at 107.

* * *

> Q: I take it you are not aware of any lost sponsors or lost advertisers; is that correct?
>
> A: That is correct.

Id. at 108.

Finally, on November 23, this Court held oral argument on ESPN's motion to preclude damages evidence. During that argument, this Court specifically asked counsel for Baseball whether Baseball had any "concrete proof of monetary harm.". * * * In response, counsel for Baseball merely reiterated the entirely subjective and speculative assertion that Baseball "feel[s] this was very dilatory [*sic*] to our position and denigrated our product and cost us in the marketplace and otherwise." * * * Counsel for Baseball was unable to show "any loss of sponsorship, any loss of advertising, [or] any loss of ancillary sales or ticket sales." * * * As counsel

* [Mr. Wussler had been President of CBS Sports and then President of CBS Television Network. Eds.]

for Baseball conceded: "We have not shown specific losses your Honor, we agree with you there. What we have said is we believe it did affect us."[3]

IV. Discussion

As the above-quoted testimony and answers to ESPN's interrogatories demonstrate, there can be no question that Baseball has failed to adequately demonstrate either the fact of damages or the amount of damages. Put simply, Baseball's subjective belief that the amount of damages is "significant"—no matter how fervent—does not meet any of the required proofs set forth under New York law. Baseball has not cited a single lost promotional opportunity, sponsor or advertising dollar stemming from ESPN's breach. Nor has Baseball set forth any evidence of a decrease in ratings or box office ticket sales. Although damage to Baseball's prestige and future value are difficult to prove, such difficulty does not allow Baseball to proceed with speculative claims of damages. To the contrary, under New York law, a claim of damages for loss of reputation and future profits must be "reasonably certain." * * *

Baseball's damages claim is based on nothing more than its own vague assertions that it was "hurt." Baseball cites no specific examples of monetary damage, nor does it proffer a method for calculating such damages. The proffered unsupported allegations are simply inadequate to sustain a claim for damages under New York law, and therefore ESPN's motion to preclude damages evidence is granted.

V. Nominal Damages and Materiality

Although Baseball is not entitled to an award of money damages, it may still receive nominal damages. "It is a well-settled tenet of contract law that even if the breach of contract caused no loss or if the amount of the loss cannot be proven with sufficient certainty, the injured party is entitled to recover as nominal damages a small sum fixed without regard to the amount of the loss, if any." * * *[4] Accordingly, I will instruct the jury that if Baseball proves its breach of damages claim, it is entitled to an award of nominal damages.

---

[3] At the end of oral argument, counsel for Baseball set forth, for the very first time, an alternate theory of damages. Baseball proposed that damages be calculated according to the amount it would have sought had ESPN asked Baseball to "sell the right to dump [Baseball] onto [another channel]." 11/23/99 Tr. at 30. In other words, Baseball seeks to calculate damages based on a hypothetical negotiation or sale of the six preempted games.

Regardless of the merits of Baseball's alternate theory, I reject it as a basis for the calculation of damages. Baseball's failure to mention this alternate theory of damages until six days before trial—months after the close of discovery and weeks after the submission of pre-trial motions—bars it from presenting such a theory at trial.

[4] Although unable to prove monetary damage, there is no question that Baseball was harmed by virtue of ESPN's breach. Baseball was entitled to the broadcast of six baseball games during September 1998 and September 1999. When ESPN failed to broadcast those games, ESPN was harmed regardless of whether it can prove any monetary damage.

Baseball's ability to recover only nominal damages does not impede its ability to present testimony and evidence regarding the materiality of ESPN's breach. Materiality goes to the essence of the contract. That is, a breach is material if it defeats the object of the parties in making the contract and "deprive[s] the injured party of the benefit that it justifiably expected." Farnsworth, Contracts § 8.16 (3d ed. 1999). Materiality does not depend upon the amount of provable money damages, it depends upon whether the nonbreaching party lost the benefit of its bargain. Thus, although Baseball is only entitled to nominal damages, it may still present evidence and argument to the effect that ESPN's breach was material. * * *

VII. Conclusion

For the reasons set forth above, Baseball is precluded from presenting damages evidence at trial and is only entitled to seek an award of nominal damages.

QUESTIONS

1. Questions about the facts of this case

   1.1. Did ESPN make all payments to Baseball required under the contract?

   1.2. Did ESPN breach the contract?

   1.3. Do you believe that Baseball was harmed by ESPN's showing NFL games in September instead of baseball games? If so, was the damage to Baseball "nominal"?

2. Questions about the law

   2.1. The court states, "Because Baseball received full payment from ESPN, it may only seek extra-contractual damages." What does the court mean by the phrase "extra-contractual damages"? Are "extra-contractual damages" the same thing as "consequential damages"?

   2.2. What are the merits and "demerits" of Baseball's alternate theory set out in footnote 3?

   2.3. What does "nominal damages" mean? What should be the amount of "nominal" damages in this case? Why do nominal damages even exist? Why not just dismiss the case for failure of proof of an essential element of a breach of contract cause of action; that is, damages?

   2.4. Do you agree with the statement in footnote 2 that "Baseball's failure to seek specific enforcement is puzzling"? If Baseball had filed timely a lawsuit seeking specific performance, would the court have ordered ESPN to show baseball games on Sunday nights in September?

2.5. If you were counsel for Baseball, wouldn't you be embarrassed if your bill exceeded the "nominal" damages awarded? Doesn't Baseball have the resources to hire counsel who should have seen this result coming? What do you think really happened?

3. **You Be the Lawyer!**

How would you have gone about calculating the harm to Baseball from the breach? Would you have consulted with marketing and advertising experts? With baseball fans? Football fans? People who don't like sports?

3. AGREED REMEDIES

We've just marched (trudged?) through the common law of damage remedies, as altered by the U.C.C. Wouldn't it be easier if the parties could just specify the damages if someone breached?

Consider the following hypothetical: Ponoroff agreed to wash Markell's car for $10 on Monday. It is now Tuesday, and Markell's car is still dirty. Epstein's Car Wash will do a nice job for $15—$5 more than Ponoroff agreed to take for the exact same job. Note that, due to the passage of time, it is now impossible for Markell to get exactly what he bargained for—a car wash on Monday.

But it pains Markell that Ponoroff doesn't have to get wet and messy cleaning his car. And going to court to establish money damages doesn't seem fair compensation for the excruciating pain Markell will have to go through listening to Epstein babbling incoherently and inaccurately about how his parts of the Contracts casebook are the best while Markell waits for the car to be washed. Is there a way that Markell can ensure that Ponoroff feels his pain?

Recall this is Contracts, the study of consensual obligations. Can Ponoroff and Markell agree ahead of time what Ponoroff will pay if Ponoroff doesn't do what he promised to do? What if Ponoroff and Markell agree that if the car isn't washed by Monday, and there's no excuse, Ponoroff will pay Markell $500? Can Markell go into court Tuesday, get an order directing Ponoroff to pay him 500 simoleons,* and then brave the hot air at Epstein's

* In an earlier edition of this book, the text used "smackers" instead of simoleons, drawing sardonic cracks from Epstein and Ponoroff. All Markell can say is that, given the intensity of their discussions about how to split casebook royalties, Markell is surprised that there is any synonym for "dollars" that Epstein and Ponoroff don't know. BAM

and pocket the extra $485? Whether Markell can do that is the subject of the this section.

Parties often will stipulate what the amount of damage will be (that is, they will "liquidate" the amount). Such damages are typically called liquidated damages; sometimes they are called agreed remedies. The contract may also specify a certain action other than damages, such as the repair or replacement of an item sold. We'll look at both types of agreed remedies.

A. LIQUIDATED DAMAGES

QUESTIONS BEFORE THE CASE

1. What is the consequence of a borrower's breach under the terms of the contract in the next case? Did the borrower know of them?
2. Can you (or does the court) make principled distinctions between amounts that are penalties and amounts that compensate for intangible injury?

DOBSON BAY CLUB II DD, LLC v. LA SONRISA DE SIENA, LLC

Supreme Court of Arizona
242 Ariz. 108, 393 P.3d 449 (2017)

JUSTICE TIMMER, opinion of the Court:

A liquidated damages contract provision is enforceable if the pre-determined amount for damages seeks to compensate the non-breaching party rather than penalize the breaching party. We here hold that a nearly $1.4 million late fee assessed on a final loan balloon payment constitutes an unenforceable penalty.

I. Background

In 2006, Canadian Imperial Bank of Commerce loaned Dobson Bay Club II DD, LLC and related entities ("Dobson Bay") $28.6 million for Dobson Bay's purchase of four commercial properties. The loan was secured by a deed of trust encumbering those properties. Under the terms of a promissory note, Dobson Bay was to tender interest-only payments to Canadian Imperial Bank until the loan matured in September 2009, when the entire principal would become due—the "balloon" payment. In 2009, the parties extended the loan maturity date to September 2012.

Dobson Bay bore significant consequences for any delay in payment. In addition to continuing to pay regular interest, Dobson Bay was required to pay default interest and collection costs, including reasonable attorney fees, and a 5% late fee assessed on the payment amount. If Canadian

Imperial Bank foreclosed the deed of trust, Dobson Bay was also obligated to pay costs, trustee's fees, and reasonable attorney fees.

As the 2012 loan maturity date approached, the parties negotiated to extend that date but could not reach an agreement. The maturity date passed, and Dobson Bay failed to make the balloon payment.

La Sonrisa de Siena, LLC ("La Sonrisa") bought the note and deed of trust from Canadian Imperial Bank and promptly noticed a trustee's sale of the secured properties. It contended that Dobson Bay owed more than $30 million, including a nearly $1.4 million late fee. Dobson Bay disputed it owed various sums, including the late fee. Litigation ensued. Dobson Bay secured new financing and paid the outstanding principal and undisputed interest in March 2013. (Dobson Bay simultaneously deposited the disputed amounts with the superior court pending the litigation.) The parties filed cross-motions for partial summary judgment on whether the late fee provision in the note was an enforceable liquidated damages provision or, instead, an unenforceable penalty.

The superior court granted partial summary judgment for La Sonrisa, ruling that the late fee was enforceable as liquidated damages. The court of appeals reversed, holding "as a matter of law, that absent unusual circumstances the imposition of a flat 5% late-fee on a balloon payment for a conventional, fixed-interest rate loan is not enforceable as liquidated damages." *Dobson Bay Club II DD, LLC v. La Sonrisa de Siena, LLC*, 239 Ariz. 132, 140 ¶ 22, 366 P.3d 1022, 1030 (App. 2016).

We granted review because the enforceability of late fee provisions in commercial loan agreements presents a legal issue of statewide importance. . . .

II. Discussion

A. Enforceability of liquidated damages provisions

Parties to a contract can agree in advance to the amount of damages for any breach. *See Miller Cattle Co. v. Mattice*, 38 Ariz. 180, 190, 298 P. 640, 643 (1931). Such "liquidated damages" provisions serve valuable purposes. They provide certainty when actual damages would be difficult to calculate, and they alleviate the need for potentially expensive litigation. *Cf. Mech. Air Eng'g Co. v. Totem Constr. Co.*, 166 Ariz. 191, 193, 801 P.2d 426, 428 (App. 1989) (noting that a liquidated damages provision "promotes enterprise by increasing certainty and by decreasing risk-exposure, proof problems, and litigation costs"); Restatement (Second) of Contracts ("Restatement Second") § 356 cmt. a. (Am. Law Inst. 1981) ("The enforcement of such provisions . . . saves the time of courts, juries, parties and witnesses and reduces the expense of litigation.").

Parties, however, do not have free rein in setting liquidated damages. Because "[t]he central objective behind the system of contract remedies is compensatory, not punitive," parties cannot provide a penalty for a breach. Restatement Second § 356 cmt. a; *see also id.* ("Punishment of a promisor for having broken his promise has no justification on either economic or other grounds and a term providing such a penalty is unenforceable on grounds of public policy."). "A [contract] term fixing unreasonably large liquidated damages is unenforceable on grounds of public policy as a penalty." *Id.* § 356(1). The contract remains valid, however, and the non-breaching party can still recover actual damages. *See Gary Outdoor Advert. Co. v. Sun Lodge, Inc.*, 133 Ariz. 240, 243, 650 P.2d 1222, 1225 (1982); *Miller Cattle*, 38 Ariz. at 190, 298 P. at 643.

Arizona courts have used different methods to decide whether stipulated damages provisions are enforceable as liquidated damages or void as penalties. This Court has considered whether the stipulated amounts were reasonably related to actual damages. . . . We have also examined liquidated damages provisions prospectively, considering whether they were reasonable at the time the contracts were created. . . .

* * *

In this case, the court of appeals applied Restatement Second § 356(1), which reframed the Restatement First test in 1981 to harmonize with Uniform Commercial Code ("UCC") § 2–718(1). *See Dobson Bay Club*, 239 Ariz. at 136 ¶ 9 n.2, 366 P.3d at 1026 n.2; Restatement Second § 356 reporter's note. Section 356(1) provides that a liquidated damages provision is enforceable, "but only at an amount that is reasonable in the light of the anticipated or actual loss caused by the breach and the difficulties of proof of loss." This test requires courts to consider (1) the anticipated or actual loss caused by the breach, and (2) the difficulty of proof of loss. Whether a fixed amount is a penalty turns on the relative strengths of these factors. As explained by comment b to § 356:

> If the difficulty of proof of loss is great, considerable latitude is allowed in the approximation of anticipated or actual harm. If, on the other hand, the difficulty of proof of loss is slight, less latitude is allowed in that approximation. If, to take an extreme case, it is clear that no loss at all has occurred, a provision fixing a substantial sum as damages is unenforceable.

La Sonrisa urges us to disavow the Restatement Second § 356(1) test to the extent it "retrospectively" considers actual damages. It contends that this approach undermines the contracting parties' freedom to allocate risk and defeats the purpose of a liquidated damages provision by requiring the non-breaching party to establish actual damages. Not so.

Section 356(1) provides two methods for deciding whether the parties' damages forecast was reasonable. The amount is reasonable if it approximates either the loss anticipated at the time of contract creation (despite any actual loss) or the loss that actually resulted (despite what the parties might have anticipated in other circumstances). *See* Restatement Second § 356 cmt. b. The non-breaching party is not required to prove actual damages to enforce a liquidated damages provision, and a court will respect the parties' agreement if it is "reasonable" in relation to anticipated or actual loss. But if the difficulty of proof of loss is slight and either no loss occurs or the stipulated sum is grossly disproportionate to the loss, the parties' stipulation would be unreasonable and therefore unenforceable as a penalty. *See id.* This approach is consistent with this Court's opinions. . . .

We adopt the Restatement Second § 356(1) to test the enforceability of a stipulated damages provision. First, § 356(1) aligns with UCC § 2–718(1), which Arizona has adopted. *See* A.R.S. § 47–2718(A). Thus, courts can apply the same test to both UCC-governed and non-UCC-governed contracts. Second, the test best accommodates the goal of compensating the non-breaching party for a loss rather than penalizing the breaching party. Under the Restatement Second test, courts have flexibility to respect the parties' right to stipulate to damages for a breach but, when appropriate, prevent imposition of a penalty.

B. Application of Restatement Second § 356(1) to this case

The late fee provision in the promissory note here provides:

> If any installment payable under this Note (including the final installment due on the Maturity Date) is not received by Lender prior to the calendar day after the same is due . . . Borrower shall pay to Lender upon demand an amount equal to the lesser of (a) five percent (5%) of such unpaid sum or (b) the maximum amount permitted by applicable law to defray the expenses incurred by Lender in handling and processing such delinquent payment and to compensate Lender for the loss of the use of such delinquent payment. . . .

La Sonrisa seeks 5% of the late balloon payment; "the maximum amount permitted by applicable law" is not at issue.

Dobson Bay, as the party seeking to avoid enforcement of the late fee provision, has the burden of persuading this Court that the provision imposes an unenforceable penalty. * * *

1. Anticipated or actual damages

Dobson Bay argues that the late fee provision was neither a reasonable forecast of anticipated damages nor reasonably related to actual damages incurred as a result of the untimely balloon payment because La Sonrisa's loss has been compensated already by payment of default interest and collection costs. La Sonrisa asserts that actual damages are irrelevant. It contends that when the loan was made, the 5% late fee was a reasonable forecast of just compensation for harm that could be caused by Dobson Bay's default in timely making the balloon payment.

a. Anticipated damages

The late fee did not reasonably forecast anticipated damages likely to result from an untimely balloon payment.

First, the 5% fee is static, payable on demand whether the payment is one day late or one year late. Five percent of the loan principal is a significant sum of money, which did not likely reflect losses from a short delay in payment. Because the fee did not account for the length of time Canadian Imperial Bank would be deprived of the balloon payment, the fee could not reasonably predict the Bank's loss. * * *

La Sonrisa asserts that the 5% late fee did not necessarily establish a fixed sum of approximately $1.4 million as "[a]t the time the parties formed their agreement, the exact amount of the final installment was unknown because the loan documents provided Dobson Bay with the flexibility to pay all, some, or none of the principal prior to the maturity date." But the note permits Dobson Bay to prepay the loan principal only "in whole" and "not in part," except that any condemnation or casualty insurance proceeds would be applied to pay down the principal. Thus, unless Dobson Bay prepaid the entire principal amount, meaning the late fee provision would not apply, the parties contemplated that the balloon payment would approximate the entire loan principal, requiring a late fee of roughly $1.4 million for an untimely payment.

Second, the late fee either duplicated other fees triggered by a default or was grossly disproportionate to any remaining sums needed to compensate for the anticipated losses identified in the late fee provision. *Cf. United Dairymen of Ariz. v. Schugg*, 212 Ariz. 133, 138 ¶ 16, 128 P.3d 756, 761 (App. 2006) ("The right to recover liquidated damages is limited by the express terms of the parties' agreement."); 11 Joseph M. Perillo, Corbin on Contracts § 58.11 at 457 (rev. ed. 2005) ("The probable injury that the parties had reason to foresee is a fact that largely determines the question whether they made a genuine pre-estimate of that injury. . . .").

The late fee is calculated as the lesser of 5% of the delinquent payment or the maximum amount permitted by law "to defray the expenses incurred by [Canadian Imperial Bank] in handling and processing such delinquent payment and to compensate [Canadian Imperial Bank] for the loss of the use of such delinquent payment." It is debatable whether this quoted language qualifies each calculation method or just the latter one. But it matters not. Requiring an "either-or" comparison to fix the late fee suggests that both calculation methods were intended to compensate for the same categories of loss: (1) the costs in handling and processing a late payment, and (2) the loss of use of the payment. * * *

Both categories of loss identified in the late fee provision are substantially addressed elsewhere in the promissory note and deed of trust. Assuming that "handling and processing" includes actions taken to collect the late payment, those costs would be compensated by Dobson Bay's required payment of "all costs of collection," including reasonable attorney fees, and, in the event of foreclosure, "all expenses incident to such proceeding," including attorney fees and trustee's fees and costs. The loss of use of money would be compensated by continuing payments of regular interest plus default interest. *Cf. Ariz. E.R.R. Co. v. Head*, 26 Ariz. 259, 262, 224 P. 1057, 1058 (1924) ("Interest is the compensation paid for the use of money.").

What's left to compensate by payment of a $1.4 million late fee? La Sonrisa and the dissent rely on an affidavit from Mitchel Medigovich, a commercial lending expert, who opined that a 5% late fee is a reasonable forecast of just compensation for impairment of a bank's economic interests due to an untimely balloon payment. But much of this anticipated impairment falls outside the two categories of loss identified by the parties in the late fee provision. For example, Medigovich states that a predetermined late fee compensates for post-default "reputational risks," "regulatory risks," and the "risk of expense of preserving the collateral." Medigovich addresses the categories of loss identified in the late fee provision by stating that late fees properly subsidize a lender's debt collection practices and compensate for the loss of expected funds. He does not explain, however, what amounts, if any, are reasonably needed to compensate for these expected losses when, as here, the borrower is already obligated to pay all collection costs and interest at both the regular rate and a default rate. Consequently, Medigovich's affidavit does not persuade us that a flat $1.4 million late fee was a reasonable forecast of Canadian Imperial Bank's anticipated losses from a late balloon payment that would not have been compensated by the payment of regular interest, default interest, and collection costs. * * *

In sum, a flat 5% late fee did not reasonably predict the damages that would be sustained by Canadian Imperial Bank for a late balloon payment of the entire loan principal.

b. Actual damages

The $1.4 million late fee did not reasonably approximate either the actual costs of handling and processing the late balloon payment or the loss of use of that payment.

The summary judgment papers did not address the actual losses incurred by Canadian Imperial Bank and La Sonrisa after Dobson Bay's default. Nevertheless, the record reflects that neither lender spent significant time handling and processing the late payment. The only outstanding payment was the last payment, and nothing suggests that either lender had much to "handle and process" before the trustee's sale was initiated. *Cf. In re Mkt. Ctr. E. Retail Prop., Inc.*, 433 B.R. at 364 (concluding that after default on a balloon payment "there would be little or no more administrative expenses in handling and processing delinquent payments" and "[a]ll that is left to do is have the attorneys sue to foreclose"). The note already required Dobson Bay to pay any collection costs, including attorney fees. It is inconceivable that any remaining administrative collection costs approached $1.4 million, particularly in light of the short time between the default and initiation of the trustee's sale—about three months. Thereafter, the deed of trust applied to require Dobson Bay to pay attorney fees and trustee's fees and costs.

La Sonrisa was also compensated for the loss of use of money suffered by it and its assignor, Canadian Imperial Bank, by Dobson Bay's obligation to pay regular and default interest. . . . Dobson Bay was current on the loan until the maturity date. La Sonrisa did not dispute Dobson Bay's representation at oral argument before this Court that La Sonrisa received between $600,000 and $700,000 in default interest alone for the six-month delay in paying the balloon amount.

In sum, nothing indicates that either lender, separately or together, suffered an uncompensated loss that approached $1.4 million.

2. Difficulty of proof of loss

We next consider the difficulty of proving the losses actually sustained by Canadian Imperial Bank and La Sonrisa in handling and processing the late balloon payment and by being deprived of use of that payment. Restatement Second § 356 cmt. b & illus. 2–4. In doing so, we examine the difficulty of either proving that a loss occurred or establishing its amount with certainty. *Id.* § 356 cmt. b.

La Sonrisa would have had no difficulty proving it sustained a loss in handling and processing the late balloon payment, if a loss occurred. (Because La Sonrisa noticed the trustee's sale about a week after acquiring the loan, it may not have expended any resources handling and processing the balloon payment.) It could have produced evidence of the tasks undertaken by it to do so. La Sonrisa would have had slightly more difficulty precisely proving the amount of damages incurred from any such loss depending on what activities constituted "handling and processing" and how it allocated the costs of these activities. *Cf. Garrett v. Coast & S. Fed. Sav. & Loan Ass'n*, 9 Cal.3d 731, 108 Cal.Rptr. 845, 511 P.2d 1197, 1203 (1973) (invalidating a late fee provision and noting that "[t]he lender's charges could be fairly measured by the period of time the money was wrongfully withheld plus the administrative costs reasonably related to collecting and accounting for a late payment").

La Sonrisa would have had no difficulty proving that either lender sustained a loss by being deprived of the use of the balloon payment. Interest on the outstanding amount could have been assessed to compensate for the loss of use of money. *Cf. Ariz. E.R.R. Co.*, 26 Ariz. at 262, 224 P. at 1058. And La Sonrisa would be entitled to collect interest earned when Canadian Imperial Bank was the note payee and the loan was in default. *Cf. K.B.*, 189 Ariz. at 267, 941 P.2d at 1292. Indeed, the promissory note required Dobson Bay to pay regular interest and default interest for that purpose.

In sum, under the circumstances here, the difficulty of proving La Sonrisa's loss as identified in the late fee provision was slight.

3. Consideration of factors

We are persuaded that the late fee is an unenforceable penalty. The difficulty of proving losses attributable to handling and processing the balloon payment was slight. We therefore give less latitude to Canadian Imperial Bank and Dobson Bay's approximation of anticipated or actual harm. *See* Restatement Second § 356 cmt. b.

As explained, the late fee neither reasonably forecasted anticipated damages for the losses identified in the late fee provision nor reasonably approximated the actual losses. In view of Dobson Bay's obligation to pay regular and default interest, collection costs, trustee's fees and costs, and attorney fees as a consequence of the six-month delay in paying the balloon, an approximate $1.4 million late fee is unreasonable and an unenforceable penalty. La Sonrisa is not precluded, however, from seeking actual damages incurred for handling and processing the late balloon payment and for losing use of the payment if La Sonrisa has not already been compensated for that loss by the other fees and costs Dobson Bay is required to pay under the note and deed of trust. *See Gary Outdoor Advert. Co.*, 133 Ariz. at 243, 650 P.2d at 1225.

C. The dissent

Our dissenting colleague colorfully compares our decision to a child's cry of "backsies" to sidestep a promise. Rather than invoking playground rules, however, we apply long-established common law principles that render contractual penalty provisions—even when agreed upon by sophisticated parties—unenforceable as a matter of public policy. This is nothing unique. Courts will likewise disregard the parties' intent and refuse to enforce contract terms that are unconscionable, illegal, or otherwise against public policy. *Cf. Maxwell v. Fidelity Fin. Servs., Inc.*, 184 Ariz. 82, 88, 907 P.2d 51, 57 (1995) ("[E]ven if the contract provisions are consistent with the reasonable expectations of the party they are unenforceable if they are oppressive or unconscionable." (internal quotations and alterations omitted)); *Goodman v. Newzona Inv. Co.*, 101 Ariz. 470, 474, 421 P.2d 318, 322 (1966) (recognizing "the fundamental right of the individual to [have] complete freedom to contract . . . so long as his contract is not illegal or against public policy"). That the dissent prefers to ignore these principles does not affect their applicability. * * *

III. Conclusion

We vacate the court of appeals' opinion, reverse the trial court's partial summary judgment in favor of La Sonrisa on the liquidated damages claim, and remand to that court for further proceedings, including entry of partial summary judgment for Dobson Bay on its declaratory relief claim concerning the late fee. We award Dobson Bay its reasonable attorney fees pursuant to A.R.S. § 12–341.01 subject to its compliance with ARCAP 21(c).

BOLICK, J., dissenting.

As children, we learn that the rules of the playground dictate that if someone makes a promise, no matter how solemnly, it is unenforceable if the person making the promise had his fingers crossed behind his back. As we grow up, we learn instead that many promises are moral and legal obligations, with consequences properly attached to breaking them. Still, some grown-ups prefer the playground rules.

The Court today invalidates a core and unambiguous provision of a contract freely negotiated for mutual benefit between sophisticated parties represented by competent counsel. After Dobson Bay reaped the full benefits of its bargain, it defaulted on its repayment obligation and looked to the courts to avoid significant agreed-upon consequences of that default. The majority determines that the liquidated damages provision agreed to by the parties is an unenforceable penalty, based on its thorough examination of the Restatement (Second) of Contracts. Because I believe that over the course of that journey the majority lost the forest for the trees, I respectfully dissent.

* * *

"The law of liquidated damages is unique within the common law of contracts because it overtly affronts freedom of contract." Larry A. Dimatteo, *A Theory of Efficient Penalty: Eliminating the Law of Liquidated Damages*, 38 Am. Bus. L.J. 633, 634 (2001). That is because it allows courts to displace the intent of the parties by determining that a provision amounts to a penalty. Such discretion should be exercised with great care, for as the majority aptly notes, liquidated damages provisions "serve important purposes," such as providing certainty when actual damages would be difficult to calculate and avoiding the costs and delays of litigation.

Moreover, "a party concerned foremost with performance, especially a timely performance, may use such a clause in the hope that it will provide a further inducement for performance." Dimatteo, 38 Am. Bus. L.J. at 634. Certainly that is the case with the contract here. Dobson Bay sought a considerable loan—$28.6 million—to purchase four commercial properties. Under the contract terms, it would make interest-only payments for a prescribed period, after which it would repay the entire principal in a "balloon" payment. The timely return of the principal is a critical, indeed defining, feature of the loan. The contract underscored that fact by requiring, in addition to other fees described by the majority, a 5% fee for late interest payments or principal repayment. Absent evidence to the contrary by the party properly bearing the burden of proof, we may presume that the substantial loan Dobson Bay sought would not have been made absent this assurance.

The lender was not voracious. Before the balloon payment was originally due in 2009, the parties negotiated a three-year extension. As the new date approached, the parties negotiated over another extension but failed to reach agreement. Thereafter the note was sold to La Sonrisa which then commenced foreclosure proceedings.

The majority applies two factors in determining whether the liquidated damages provision is "reasonable": the anticipated or actual loss caused by the breach, and the difficulty of proof of loss. Proving the provision is reasonable based on actual damages makes little sense in most instances, given that the point of a liquidated damages provision is to avoid litigation that requires proving actual damages. Accordingly, the proper inquiry "is whether the stipulated amount was, when all of the facts are considered, reasonable at the time of the contract and not whether it was reasonable with the benefit of hindsight." *Rampello*, 168 Ariz. at 300, 812 P.2d at 1118. At the same time, citing a comment to Restatement (Second) § 356, the majority notes that if the difficulty of forecasting actual damages is great, considerable latitude is appropriate in assigning liquidated damages. Although the difficulty of forecasting the amount of loss here was great, the majority extends no such latitude.

The majority concludes that the lender is compensated for losses owing to a dilatory final payment elsewhere in the contract; specifically, through collection costs and foreclosure expenses. Further, "[t]he loss of use of money would be compensated by continuing payments of regular interest plus default interest." *Id.* Given that we have no idea the use to which the lender would have put the money had it been returned in a timely manner, that conclusion is conjecture, and illustrates precisely why liquidated damages provisions are preferable to protracted litigation and judicial second-guessing.

The main cost to the lender of failing to recover the loan corpus in a timely fashion, and the most difficult to calculate in advance, is opportunity cost. La Sonrisa produced a declaration from Mitchel Medigovich, who has extensive experience as an Arizona trustee and real estate broker and originator. He attests that when a borrower unilaterally extends the due date of a balloon payment, it imposes costs, including opportunity costs, upon the lender. He likens the situation to a car rental company with a fixed fleet of cars. If a renter unilaterally extends a rental even by one day, it diminishes fleet availability and the ability to provide new rentals, which has economic ripple effects throughout the enterprise.

* * *

Our Court . . . should presume that a liquidated damages provision negotiated by sophisticated parties is valid and conclude that the party bearing the burden of demonstrating its unreasonableness failed to sustain that burden in this case. Instead, we reward the party breaching the contract by removing a critical term to which it assented and, as a necessary consequence adding both insult and injury, require the non-breaching party to pay its attorney fees. Our decision will inevitably have a corrosive effect on the making and enforcement of contracts in Arizona, with predictable and substantial adverse economic consequences, notwithstanding that freedom of contract is enshrined in our organic law. With great respect to my colleagues, I dissent.

QUESTIONS AND NOTE

1. Questions about the facts

   1.1. What do you think La Sonrisa paid Canadian Imperial Bank for the rights to the loan? Do you think it paid a discount from the principal amount, or a premium? Should that matter in terms of the damages incurred?

   1.2. Do you think the final payoff of a loan should be called an "installment"?

   1.3. Would the lender have done better to exclude late payment of the final installment from the liquidated damages clause?

2. Questions about the law

   2.1. The dissent claims the majority is speculating on how a lender would use funds paid to it (and thus gives more certainty to a late fee based on interest, rather than a flat fee). Is that really speculation? Does that mean a successful high-risk lender with a large internal rate of return (fancy finance talk for good profits given the assets at hand) could insist and enforce a larger liquidated damage clause than the corner bank?

   2.2. Is the comparison the majority makes between liquidated damages, on the one hand, and unconscionability, illegality and public policy, on the other, a fair comparison? Does it effectively rebut the dissent's point?

   2.3. Isn't there something called usury that takes care of high interest rates?

2.4. If the loan documents had characterized the 5% amount as a "late payment privilege fee," would that have made any difference in the outcome?

3. Note

The court doesn't mention it, but one of the most common liquidated damage clauses is the good faith or "earnest money" deposit used in contracts to buy real estate. *Black's Law Dictionary* defines "earnest money" as "[a] deposit paid (often in escrow) by a prospective buyer (esp. of real estate) to show a good-faith intention to complete the transaction, *and ordinarily forfeited if the buyer defaults*." (emphasis added). Indeed, the First Circuit has noted that "Massachusetts courts have held that an earnest money deposit of 5% of the purchase price in a contract for the purchase and sale of real estate is reasonable as a matter law." *Kunelius v. Town of Stow*, 588 F.3d 1, 15 (1st Cir. 2009).

How is it that 5% for a land purchase is *per se* reasonable, but unenforceable for a loan to buy the same land?

4. **You Be the Lawyer!**

You are lucky enough to be La Sonrisa's counsel after this case is decided. Sonrisa still wants to purchase troubled loans, but is wary now that the liquidated damages provisions may not be enforceable. What checklist items would you add to your checklist because of this case?

Dobson Bay indicates that Section 356 of the *Restatement (Second) of Contracts* is consistent with the U.C.C. Read the next case and tell us what you think.

QUESTIONS BEFORE THE CASE

1. What was the basis for the trial court's invalidation of the liquidated damages clause. Does it find any basis in the statute?
2. What did the $5 per case figure represent? Anticipated gross revenues? Anticipated profits after accounting Kvassay's time? Before accounting for his time? Something else?

KVASSAY V. MURRAY

Court of Appeals of Kansas
15 Kan.App.2d 426, 808 P.2d 896 (1991)

WALKER, DISTRICT JUDGE, Assigned:

Plaintiff Michael Kvassay, d/b/a Kvassay Exotic Food, appeals the trial court's finding that a liquidated damages clause was unenforceable and from the court's finding that damages for lost profits were not recoverable. Kvassay contends these damages occurred when Great American Foods, Inc., (Great American) breached a contract for the purchase of baklava.

* * *

On February 22, 1984, Kvassay, who had been an independent insurance adjuster, contracted to sell 24,000 cases of baklava to Great American at $19.00 per case. Under the contract, the sales were to occur over a one-year period and Great American was to be Kvassay's only customer. The contract included a clause which provided: "If Buyer refuses to accept or repudiates delivery of the goods sold to him, under this Agreement, Seller shall be entitled to damages, at the rate of $5.00 per case, for each case remaining to be delivered under this Contract."

Problems arose early in this contractual relationship with checks issued by Great American being dishonored for insufficient funds. Frequently one of the Murrays issued a personal check for the amount due. After producing approximately 3,000 cases, Kvassay stopped producing the baklava because the Murrays refused to purchase any more of the product.

* * *

In April 1985, Kvassay filed suit for damages arising from the collapse of his baklava baking business. Great American counterclaimed and, in May 1988, the trial court sustained a defense motion to bifurcate the case. The court conducted bench hearings on the validity of the liquidated damages clause. * * * The trial court ruled that liquidated damages could not be recovered. * * * The court also held "as a matter of law" that Kvassay would not be able to recover damages for lost profits in the action because they were too "speculative and conjectural."

* * *

Kvassay first attacks the trial court's ruling that the amount of liquidated damages sought by him was unreasonable and therefore the liquidated damages clause was unenforceable.

Kvassay claimed $105,000 in losses under the liquidated damages clause of the contract, representing $5 per case for the approximately 21,000 cases of baklava which he was not able to deliver. The trial court determined that Kvassay's use of expected profits to formulate liquidated damages was improper because the business enterprise lacked duration, permanency, and recognition. The court then compared Kvassay's previous yearly income (about $20,000) with the claim for liquidated damages ($105,000) and found "the disparity becomes so great as to make the clause unenforceable."

Since the contract involved the sale of goods between merchants,* the Uniform Commercial Code governs. See K.S.A. 84–2–102 [U.C.C. 2–102]. "The Code does not change the pre-Code rule that the question of the propriety of liquidated damages is a question of law for the court." 4 Anderson, Uniform Commercial Code § 2–718:6, p. 572 (3d ed. 1983). Thus, this court's scope of review of the trial court's ruling is unlimited.

Liquidated damages clauses in sales contracts are governed by K.S.A. 84–2–718, which reads in part:

> (1) Damages for breach by either party may be liquidated in the agreement but only at an amount which is reasonable in the light of the anticipated or actual harm caused by the breach, the difficulties of proof of loss, and the inconvenience or nonfeasibility of otherwise obtaining an adequate remedy. A term fixing unreasonably large liquidated damages is void as a penalty.

To date, the appellate courts have not interpreted this section of the UCC in light of facts similar to those presented in this case. In ruling on this issue, the trial court relied on rules governing liquidated damages as expressed in *U.S.D. No. 315 v. DeWerff*, 6 Kan. App.2d 77, 626 P.2d 1206 (1981). *DeWerff*, however, involved a teacher's breach of an employment contract and was not governed by the UCC. Thus, the rules expressed in that case should be given no effect if they differ from the rules expressed in 84–2–718.

In *DeWerff*, this court held a "stipulation for damages upon a future breach of contract is valid as a liquidated damages clause if the set amount is determined to be reasonable and the amount of damages is difficult to ascertain." 6 Kan.App.2d at 78, 626 P.2d 1206. This is clearly a two-step test: Damages must be reasonable and they must be difficult to ascertain. Under the UCC, however, reasonableness is the only test. K.S.A. 84–2–718. K.S.A. 84–2–718 provides three criteria by which to measure reasonableness of liquidated damages clauses: (1) anticipated or actual harm caused by breach; (2) difficulty of proving loss; and (3) difficulty of obtaining an adequate remedy.

---

* Okay. We can't let this wait until the *Questions and Notes*. Does a transaction have to be "between merchants" to be within the U.C.C.? ***Of Course Not!*** If you don't believe us, reread § 2–102. Your purchase of this casebook was governed by the U.C.C., as was your purchase of the highlighter you're using to note this sentence. Those trained in the classics will have heard the phrase, "Even Homer nods," but here we're not even sure the judge qualifies as a Homer of the prairie. Despite this goof, don't discount the rest of the case. Perhaps the judge took the test from the trial court, who *really* made a hash of § 2–718. And hash and baklava don't mix; trust us. Eds.

In its ruling, the trial court found the liquidated damages clause was unreasonable in light of Kvassay's income before he entered into the manufacturing contract with Great American. There is no basis in 84–2–718 for contrasting income under a previous unrelated employment arrangement with liquidated damages sought under a manufacturing contract. Indeed, the traditional goal of the law in cases where a buyer breaches a manufacturing contract is to place the seller "in the same position he would have occupied if the vendee had performed his contract." *Outcault Adv. Co. v. Citizens' Nat'l Bank*, 118 Kan. 328, 330–31, 234 P. 988 (1925). Thus, liquidated damages under the contract in this case must be measured against the anticipated or actual loss under the baklava contract as required by 84–2–718. The trial court erred in using Kvassay's previous income as a yardstick.

Was the trial court correct when it invalidated the liquidated damages clause, notwithstanding the use of an incorrect test? If so, we must uphold the decision even though the trial court relied on a wrong ground or assigned an erroneous reason for its decision. To answer this question, we must look closer at the first criteria for reasonableness under 84–2–718, anticipated or actual harm done by the breach.

Kvassay produced evidence of anticipated damages at the bench trial showing that, before the contract was signed between Kvassay and Great American, Kvassay's accountant had calculated the baklava production costs. The resulting figure showed that, if each case sold for $19, Kvassay would earn a net profit of $3.55 per case after paying himself for time and labor. If he did not pay himself, the projected profit was $4.29 per case. Nevertheless, the parties set the liquidated damages figure at $5 per case. In comparing the anticipated damages of $3.55 per case in lost net profit with the liquidated damages of $5 per case, it is evident that Kvassay would collect $1.45 per case or about 41 percent over projected profits if Great American breached the contract. If the $4.29 profit figure is used, a $5 liquidated damages award would allow Kvassay to collect 71 cents per case or about 16½% percent over projected profits if Great American breached the contract.

An examination of these pre-contract comparisons alone might well lead to the conclusion that the $5 liquidated damages clause is unreasonable because enforcing it would result in a windfall for Kvassay and serve as a penalty for Great American. A term fixing unreasonably large liquidated damages is void as a penalty under 84–2–718.

A better measure of the validity of the liquidated damages clause in this case would be obtained if the actual lost profits caused by the breach were compared to the $5 per case amount set by the clause. However, no attempt was made by Kvassay during the bench trial to prove actual profits or actual costs of production. Thus, the trial court could not compare the $5 liquidated damages clause in the contract with the actual profits lost by the breach. It was not until the jury trial that Kvassay attempted to prove his actual profits lost as part of his damages. Given the trial court's ruling that lost profits were not recoverable and could not be presented to the jury, it is questionable whether the court would have permitted evidence concerning lost profits at the bench trial.

The trial court utilized an impermissible factor to issue its ruling on the liquidated damages clause and the correct statutory factors were not directly addressed. We reverse the trial court on this issue and remand for further consideration of the reasonableness of the liquidated damages clause in light of the three criteria set out in 84–2–718 and our ruling on recoverability of lost profits which follows.

* * *

The trial court's decisions with respect to liquidated damages and lost profits are reversed and the case is remanded for a new trial on those issues. * * *

QUESTIONS AND NOTE

1. Questions about the facts of this case

   1.1. What is baklava?

   1.2. What evidence did Kvassay introduce? At the new trial, what additional evidence should Kvassay introduce?

2. Questions about the law

   2.1. What are the differences between: (i) the law of liquidated damages under common law as set forth in the *Restatement* and in *La Sonrisa,* and (ii) the law of liquidated damages set forth in U.C.C. § 2–718 and *Kvassay*?

   2.2. Who measures reasonableness? The court or the jury? Do you think the $5 per case was unreasonable?

3. Note

   Another look at liquidated damages and penalties. In *Lake River Corp. v. Carborundum Co.*, 769 F.2d 1284 (7th Cir. 1985), Judge Richard Posner had the following to say about the liquidated damages/penalty distinction:

   > Deep as the hostility to penalty clauses runs in the common law, see Loyd, *Penalties and Forfeitures*, 29 Harv. L. Rev. 117 (1915), we still might be inclined to question, if we thought ourselves free to do so, whether a modern court should refuse to enforce a penalty clause where the signator is a substantial

corporation, well able to avoid improvident commitments. Penalty clauses provide an earnest of performance. The clause here enhanced Carborundum's credibility in promising to ship the minimum amount guaranteed by showing that it was willing to pay the full contract price even if it failed to ship anything. On the other side it can be pointed out that by raising the cost of a breach of contract to the contract breaker, a penalty clause increases the risk to his other creditors; increases (what is the same thing and more, because bankruptcy imposes "deadweight" social costs) the risk of bankruptcy; and could amplify the business cycle by increasing the number of bankruptcies in bad times, which is when contracts are most likely to be broken. But since little effort is made to prevent businessmen from assuming risks, these reasons are no better than makeweights.

A better argument is that a penalty clause may discourage efficient as well as inefficient breaches of contract. Suppose a breach would cost the promisee $12,000 in actual damages but would yield the promisor $20,000 in additional profits. Then there would be a net social gain from breach. After being fully compensated for his loss the promisee would be no worse off than if the contract had been performed, while the promisor would be better off by $8,000. But now suppose the contract contains a penalty clause under which the promisor if he breaks his promise must pay the promisee $25,000. The promisor will be discouraged from breaking the contract, since $25,000, the penalty, is greater than $20,000, the profits of the breach; and a transaction that would have increased value will be forgone.

On this view, since compensatory damages should be sufficient to deter inefficient breaches (that is, breaches that cost the victim more than the gain to the contract breaker), penal damages could have no effect other than to deter some efficient breaches. But this overlooks the earlier point that the willingness to agree to a penalty clause is a way of making the promisor and his promise credible and may therefore be essential to inducing some value-maximizing contracts to be made. It also overlooks the more important point that the parties (always assuming they are fully competent) will, in deciding whether to include a penalty clause in their contract, weigh the gains against the costs—costs that include the possibility of discouraging an efficient breach somewhere down the road—and will include the clause only if the benefits exceed those costs as well as all other costs.

On this view the refusal to enforce penalty clauses is (at best) paternalistic—and it seems odd that courts should display parental solicitude for large corporations. But however this may be, we must be on guard to avoid importing our own ideas of

> sound public policy into an area where our proper judicial role is more than usually deferential. The responsibility for making innovations in the common law of Illinois rests with the courts of Illinois, and not with the federal courts in Illinois. And like every other state, Illinois, untroubled by academic skepticism of the wisdom of refusing to enforce penalty clauses against sophisticated promisors, see, e.g., Goetz & Scott, Liquidated Damages, Penalties and the Just Compensation Principle, 77 Colum. L. Rev. 554 (1977), continues steadfastly to insist on the distinction between penalties and liquidated damages. * * * To be valid under Illinois law a liquidation of damages must be a reasonable estimate at the time of contracting of the likely damages from breach, and the need for estimation at that time must be shown by reference to the likely difficulty of measuring the actual damages from a breach of contract after the breach occurs. If damages would be easy to determine then, or if the estimate greatly exceeds a reasonable upper estimate of what the damages are likely to be, it is a penalty. * * *

Id. at 1288–90.

4. **You Be the Lawyer!**

If you represented Kavassy when the initial contract was signed, but knowing what you know now, what per-case liquidated damages amount would you choose?

PROBLEMS ON LIQUIDATED DAMAGES

1. *Liquidated Damages and Specific Performance*

Despite all advice to the contrary, Epstein, Markell and Ponoroff form a law partnership. Being crafty devils, they place in their partnership agreement a non-compete clause, and set liquidated damages for breach of that non-compete clause at $50,000, a sum everyone agrees is on the high side of reasonable given the nature of the proposed practice.

Unfortunately, a year later, to everyone's surprise, Epstein wins a huge case. His name and picture (with a big, toothy grin) is plastered all over the papers. When Markell and Ponoroff refuse to amend the formula used to allocate partnership profits to give Epstein more of a share, Epstein is silent for a second, checks the partnership agreement, and then says, "G'bye, y'all."

Epstein then sets up shop next door to Markell and Ponoroff and begins competing in direct violation of the non-compete clause. Markell and Ponoroff sue to enjoin Epstein. What result?

If an injunction is not granted, may Markell and Ponoroff show that their real damages from Epstein's blatant violation of the non-compete clause are closer to $200,000, given that Epstein is now sucking all of the legal work in town to his new boutique? Why, or why not?

2. *Scare Tactics*

Many retail stores have signs above the counter that say "$40 charge on returned checks." Putting aside for now the question as to whether this sign becomes part of the contract, if it is, do you think such a term is enforceable? Would you advise a retailer client to rely on such a sign?

3. *Final Problem*

Most construction contracts call for a per day "penalty" or "fee" to be paid if a job is not completed within the agreed time. Assume that Markell Construction Co. agrees with Epstein to build an addition to Epstein's house for $10,000. The contract says that Markell will pay $100 a day for each day he is late in finishing past the agreed due date of July 1. True to form, Markell (as his mother would say) is "slower than molasses running uphill in the month of January." He finishes thirty days late. Can he successfully contest the $3,000 in liquidated damages as a penalty? What more would you want to know before answering? What if Markell is 100 days late? Are Epstein's damages then $10,000 on this $10,000 contract? What if Markell never finishes?

B. LIMITATION OF REMEDIES TO REPAIR, REPLACEMENT, OR RETURN OF MONEY PAID

As we have seen with liquidated damages, parties often try to anticipate the effect of breach and specify its consequences. With the sale of goods, especially goods produced on a mass scale, the parties (or at least the seller) know that a breach to a least some buyers is inevitable. Sellers often attempt to control their costs by providing in contracts governing the sales of their goods that damages are not available as a remedy—that the seller's efforts to repair or replace the defective goods or return of the purchase price will be the only remedies available to an aggrieved buyer. Such provisions in contracts for the sale of goods are governed by U.C.C. § 2–719, entitled "Contractual Modification or Limitation of Remedy":

> (1) Subject to the provisions of subsections (2) and (3) of this section and of the preceding section on liquidation and limitation of damages,
>
> > (a) the agreement may provide for remedies in addition to or in substitution for those provided in this Article and may limit or alter the measure of damages recoverable under this Article, as by limiting the buyer's remedies to return of the goods and repayment of the price or to repair and replacement of non-conforming goods or parts; and

(b) resort to a remedy as provided is optional unless the remedy is expressly agreed to be exclusive, in which case it is the sole remedy.

(2) Where circumstances cause an exclusive or limited remedy to fail of its essential purpose, remedy may be had as provided in this Act

One of the recurring problems in determining if and when a "repair and replacement" remedy has failed its essential purpose within the meaning of § 2–719(2) occurs when the seller fails to effect repairs despite several attempts to do so, or, while individual defects are repaired, unrelated defects keep cropping up. Eventually, the frustrated buyer wants to return the goods or sue for damages. The seller, however, is perfectly happy to continue to offer repair opportunities. Clearly, at some point the remedy has failed, but just how many repair efforts, or how many defects, must the buyer endure?

The reported cases offer very little consistent guidance on this question, so we have not included a case applying § 2–719. Moreover, the federal government and state governments have addressed this problem for consumer buyers through consumer protection statutes which are addressed in second and third year courses in consumer protection.

For this contracts course, it is valuable to distinguish between clauses that limit or modify remedies (as in the last case) and clauses that attempt to disclaim liability. We encountered an example of the latter in Chapter 5 in contracts for the sale of goods where the seller attempts to disclaim liability for breach of warranty. A disclaimer, if effective, eliminates a cause of action altogether and, therefore, eliminates the need to worry about limiting damages. The final sentences of Official Comment 2 to § 2–316 (the warranty disclaimer provision) makes this clear: "If no warranty exists, there is of course no problem of limiting remedies for breach of warranty."

It is also important to see the relationship between remedy limitations and agreed remedies, the topic of the previous subsection.

In "theory," § 2–719 governs when enforceability of a provision under which the parties have agreed to limit or exclude, but not actually fix, damages, while § 2–718 applies where the parties have actually specified what the damaged upon breach will be. As we have seen, the main concern in liquidated damage cases is that the stipulated sum will be unreasonably large. See § 2–718(1). By contrast, the rationale underlying the "essential-purpose" doctrine in § 2–719 is that a seller will use the remedy limitation provision to deprive the buyer of a "minimum adequate remedy." *See* Comment 1 to § 2–719.

In practice, a "clever" lawyer can draft a liquidated damage clause that has the effect of virtually always excluding or limiting the buyer's recovery in the event of a breach. Likewise, a "clever" lawyer can craft a clause stipulating an exclusive remedy to just as easily over-compensate a party as opposed to deprive the other party of an adequate remedy. Because the rules and standards governing enforceability under §§ 2–718 and 2–719 differ, it can make an important difference which section of Article 2 a court chooses to employ in reviewing either or both kinds of remedy provisions.

---

4. NON-MONETARY RELIEF

Often, when there is a material breach, the aggrieved party doesn't want money damages. She just wants the breacher to do what he promised he would do. The remedy here is called specific performance, and we've seen it throughout this book, starting with *Lucy v. Zehmer* on page 44.

In other cases, the aggrieved party just wants to be paid, but also wants to be quit of the breacher. The termination of a contract by one party is typically called cancellation or termination.

We look at both types of non-monetary relief below.

A. SPECIFIC PERFORMANCE: DOING WHAT WAS PROMISED

1. A Short Digression into the History of Equitable Remedies

Before diving into the law of specific performance, a few words about the origins of the remedy are in order. You may have noticed that in most every case we've studied in this book, the winner received a judgment entitling them to money damages. Only in a few cases, and most of those involved the sale of real property, did the court ever compel the breaching party to do what they promised to do.

This should strike you as strange. Why should we let contract breachers—scum of the earth that they are—skate by simply writing a check to cover their perfidy? The answer, in part, lies in the history of how common law courts have enforced promises. In the excerpt below, Professor Allan Farnsworth provides a good summary of the law's development on this point:

> The typical judgment at common law declared that the plaintiff recover from the defendant a sum of money, which in effect imposed on him a new obligation as redress for the breach of the old. The new obligation required no cooperation on his part for its enforcement since, if the sum was not paid, a writ of execution would issue empowering the sheriff to seize and sell so much of

> the defendant's property as was required to pay the plaintiff. . . . The judgment itself was seen as a mere declaration of rights as between the parties, and the process for its execution was directed not at the defendant but at the sheriff, ordering him to put the plaintiff in possession of real or personal property or to seize the defendant's property and sell such of it as was necessary to satisfy a money judgment.
>
> * * *
>
> The most important of the historical limitations [on granting equitable relief] derives from the circumstance that, since the chancellor had first granted equitable relief in order to supply the deficiencies of the common law, equitable remedies were readily characterized as "extraordinary." When, during the long jurisdictional struggle between the two systems of courts, some means of accommodation were needed, an "adequacy" test was developed to prevent encroachment by the chancellor on the powers of the common law judges. Equity would stay its hand if the remedy at law was "adequate." To this test was added the gloss that the money damages awarded by the common law courts were ordinarily "adequate"—a gloss encouraged by the philosophy of free enterprise, since in a market economy money ought to enable an aggrieved promisee to arrange a substitute transaction. As one writer put it:
>
> The law, concerning itself more and more with merchandise bought or sold for money, with things having a definite and calculable exchange value, came to conceive that the money compensation, which was an entirely adequate remedy in the common case, and in many cases the only possible one when once the wrong complained of had been committed, was [generally] the only remedy available for their Use. . . .

E. Allan Farnsworth, *Legal Remedies for Breach of Contract*, 70 Colum. L. Rev. 1145, 1151–52, 1154 (1970). To repeat Justice Holmes' adage: "The duty to keep a contract at common law means a prediction that you must pay damages if you do not keep it—and nothing else." Oliver W. Holmes, *The Path of the Law*, 10 Harv. L. Rev. 457, 462 (1897).

Since Professor Farnsworth wrote, there has been significant debate as to whether the adequacy of remedy rule retains any true vitality. In *The Death of the Irreparable Injury Rule*, 103 Harv. L. Rev. 687 (1990), Professor Douglas Laycock argued at length that courts have essentially vitiated the rule that money damages are an adequate substitute for actual performance. His words: "Courts have escaped the rule by defining adequacy in such a way that damages are never an adequate substitute for plaintiff's loss. Thus, our law embodies a preference for specific relief if plaintiff wants it." *Id.* at 691.

Is that what's going on in the next case?

---

2. Specific Performance at Common Law

QUESTIONS BEFORE THE CASE

1. Is there anything unique or unusual about the property in the following case?
2. Is there anything unique or unusual about the buyer in the following case?

OLIVER V. BALL

Superior Court of Pennsylvania
136 A.3d 162 (2016), *appeal denied,* 145 A.3d 167 (Pa. 2016)

Opinion by STABILE, J.:

Appellant Jerome P. Oliver appeals from the September 26, 2014 judgment entered in the Court of Common Pleas of Butler County ("trial court"), following the denial of his post-trial motion to remove a compulsory nonsuit that the trial court granted at the close of his case-in-chief in this breach of contract action. Upon review, we reverse.

The facts and procedural history underlying this case are undisputed. Appellant entered into a sale of real estate contract with Appellees Larry M. Ball, Danny R. Ball, Larry J. Ball and Mary H. Ball ("Balls") for the purchase of two tracts of land in Cranberry Township, Butler County, containing approximately 71.5 acres ("the Property"). Balls failed to convey the Property. Appellant filed suit against Balls for breach of contract, seeking specific performance and/or monetary damages. * * *

Appellant's claim for specific performance was severed from his claim for damages and proceeded to a non-jury trial. Following testimony on the liability phase, the trial court concluded that a valid and binding contract for the sale of the Property existed between the parties, which Balls breached. The case next proceeded to the damage phase, at which Appellant testified in support of specific performance. In particular, describing the Property, Appellant testified that "[i]t was wood[ed] property with some open fields, some old farm land, with a, like a wet weather stream running through it. It was hilly. Wasn't terribly hilly but it was sloping like all other property in Butler County." N.T. Trial, 6/17/14, at 341. Appellant testified that he planned to purchase the Property for investment purposes. *Id.* at 342. Specifically, he testified that "[m]y plans were to hold it for a long-term investment. At that time I was still in the timber business and there was some timber on [the Property] that I thought could be harvested." *Id.* He also testified:

> [a]s a real estate investor [the Property] had a lot of things I look for. It was big so it possibly could be subdivided in the future for, you know, further development. Of course, it had all the mineral rights coming with it so that was something that I hoped to put into my business in the future.

Id. at 342–43. Appellant testified that the location of the Property was important to him because it "is only maybe five miles as the crow flies from my home so that is important, to try to keep my investments within a reasonable distance from my home and where I work." *Id.* at 343. Explaining why the Property was important to him, Appellant testified:

> It's basically the sum of the parts of this property are much more valuable than the whole. So, again, what I have learned through 26 years of business and what I have been able to do and have learned to do is to take a whole property like this that has valuable parts, subdivide those parts, if you will, and have it become very strong investment.

Id. at 347. On cross-examination, Appellant acknowledged that he owns investment properties located as far away as Westmoreland and Crawford Counties. *Id.* at 348–49.

Following Appellant's testimony, Balls moved for nonsuit, arguing that Appellant failed to establish that he lacked an adequate remedy at law. The trial court agreed, granting Balls' motion for nonsuit and denying Appellant's request for specific performance. * * *

On June 27, 2014, Appellant filed a post-trial motion, seeking the removal of the nonsuit. Appellant argued that he was entitled to specific performance because the Property was unique and, therefore, his remedy at law inadequate. The trial court disagreed, denying Appellant's post-trial motion on September 19, 2014. In so doing, the court observed:

> [Appellant] did not offer evidence that the quality, quantity, or type of timber on the [P]roperty is unique or unavailable elsewhere. [Appellant] did not offer evidence that gas rights are not attainable elsewhere in the [c]ounty. [Appellant] did not offer evidence that damages for the loss of these assets were unquantifiable, such that he does not have an adequate remedy at law. [Appellant] did not offer evidence that he would suffer a significant difference in purchase price for the purchase of similar property in Butler County or that the difference in purchase price is not quantifiable. [Appellant] did not offer evidence that the value of this specific . . . [P]roperty was unique to him. [Appellant]

> did not offer evidence that the [P]roperty's terrain was especially important to him, or that its location, other than being in Butler County and somewhat close to his home, was important to him. In sum, [Appellant] did not offer any evidence that this [P]roperty had any unique characteristics, of import to him, that cannot be found or purchased elsewhere, even within Butler County. Further, [Appellant] did not present any evidence to establish that the value of the [P]roperty was not quantifiable in money damages.

Trial Court Opinion, 9/22/14, at 9. On September 26, 2014, Balls filed a praecipe for entry of judgment in their favor. Appellant timely appealed to this Court.

* * *

With respect to specific performance, our Supreme Court explained in *Payne v. Clark,* 409 Pa. 557, 187 A.2d 769 (1963):

> From the moment an agreement of sale of real estate is executed and delivered it vests in the grantee [(purchaser)] what is known as an equitable title to the real estate. Thereupon the vendor [(seller)] is considered as a trustee of the real estate for the purchaser and the latter becomes a trustee of the balance of the purchase money for the seller. Hence, if the terms of the agreement are violated by the [seller], [the purchaser] may go into a court of equity seeking to enforce the contract and to compel specific performance.

Payne, 187 A.2d at 770–71 (internal citations omitted). In other words, a request for specific performance is an appeal to the court's equitable powers. *See Lackner v. Glosser,* 892 A.2d 21, 31 (Pa.Super.2006). Specific performance generally is described as the surrender of a thing in itself, because that thing is unique and thus incapable—by its nature—of duplication. *See Cimina v. Bronich,* 517 Pa. 378, 537 A.2d 1355, 1357 (1988). "A decree of specific performance is not a matter of right, but of grace." *Barnes v. McKellar,* 434 Pa.Super. 597, 644 A.2d 770, 776 (1994) (citation omitted), *appeal denied,* 539 Pa. 663, 652 A.2d 834 (1994). Such a decree will be granted only if a plaintiff clearly is entitled to such relief, there is no adequate remedy at law, and the trial court believes that justice requires such a decree. *Id.* "Inequity or hardship may be a valid defense in an action for specific performance and such decree refused if in the exercise of a sound discretion it is determined that, under the facts, specific performance would be contrary to equity or justice." *Payne,* 187 A.2d at 771. Mere inadequacy of price, however, will not defeat specific performance, unless grossly disproportionate. *Id.*

Courts in this Commonwealth consistently have determined that specific performance is an appropriate remedy to compel the conveyance of real estate where a seller violates a realty contract and specific enforcement of the contract would not be contrary to justice.[4] *See Borie v. Satterthwaite,* 180 Pa. 542, 37 A. 102 (1897) (affirming specific performance for breach of real estate agreement); *see also Agnew v. Southern Ave. Land Co.,* 204 Pa. 192, 53 A. 752 (1902) (noting that a court may enforce specifically only an agreement for realty whose terms are definite); *Rusiski v. Pribonic,* 511 Pa. 383, 515 A.2d 507, 510 (1986) (affirming only the award of specific performance for breach of a realty agreement); *Petry v. Tanglwood Lakes, Inc.,* 514 Pa. 51, 522 A.2d 1053, 1055 (1987) (noting that real estate contracts "have been traditionally regarded as being specifically enforceable in equity by the buyer"); *Cimina,* 537 A.2d at 1360 (reversing this Court's decision to overrule the trial court's grant of specific performance for a breach of realty agreement). As explained in the second restatement:

> Contracts for the sale of land have traditionally been accorded a special place in the law of specific performance. A specific tract of land has long been regarded as unique and impossible of duplication by the use of any amount of money.

Restatement (Second) of Contracts, § 360 cmt. e. As is obvious, specific performance for the sale of land is available because no two parcels of land are identical. An award of damages will not suffice to allow a plaintiff to acquire the same parcel of land anywhere else. Thus, in the context of realty agreements breached by a seller, "we can assume that [a buyer] has no adequate remedy at law." *Snyder v. Bowen,* 359 Pa.Super. 47, 518 A.2d 558, 560 (1986) (citing 81 C.J.S. Specific Performance § 76 (1977)); *cf. Petry,* 522 A.2d at 1055 ("[W]here Appellant is not claiming the right to have an *estate* in land conveyed to her, an automatic right to compel the remedy of specific performance cannot be successfully maintained.").

Instantly, we note that the parties do not dispute that a valid, enforceable contract for the Property existed and that Balls breached the same by failing to convey the Property. The parties also do not argue that hardship or injustice would ensue if Appellant's request for specific

---

[4] Outside of this Commonwealth, many jurisdictions have espoused a similar view where a sale of realty contract is breached. See, e.g., Pardee v. Jolly, 163 Wash.2d 558, 182 P.3d 967, 973 (2008) (en banc) ("Specific performance is frequently the only adequate remedy for a breach of a contract regarding real property because land is unique and difficult to value.") (citation omitted); Osborn ex rel. Osborn v. Kemp, 991 A.2d 1153 (Del.2010) (recognizing that "real property is unique and often the law cannot adequately remedy a party's refusal to honor a real property contract."); In re Smith Trust, 480 Mich. 19, 745 N.W.2d 754, 759 (2008) ("Land is presumed to have a unique and peculiar value, and contracts involving the sale of land are generally subject to specific performance."); Alba v. Kaufmann, 27 A.D.3d 816, 810 N.Y.S.2d 539, 540 (2006) (noting "the equitable remedy of specific performance is routinely awarded in contract actions involving real property, on the premise that each parcel of real property is unique.").

performance were granted. Rather, the issue on appeal concerns only the adequacy of a remedy at law, and as such, involves a question of law.

Appellant points out that the Property is unique because it had a wet weather stream running through it, was hilly, featured timber and other minerals, and provided opportunities to him for further development. *See* N.T. Trial, 6/17/14, at 341–43. It also was important that the Property was only five miles away from his home so that he could keep his investments within a reasonable distance from home and work. *Id.* Appellant adequately testified to the unique aspects of the Property and to attributes that made the parcel valuable to him. The trial court dismissed this testimony upon the basis that Appellant did not demonstrate that these attributes could not be duplicated elsewhere. Given that all tracts of land long have been regarded as unique, and Appellant further testified to the Property's unique characteristics *vis-á-vis* his needs, we agree with Appellant that a remedy at law is inadequate. Accordingly, we reject the trial court's conclusion that Appellant was not entitled to specific performance because the Property did not have any unique characteristics that could not be found or purchased elsewhere. We conclude that, based on our review of pertinent case law, the trial court erred in denying Appellant's claim for specific performance and granting Balls' motion for nonsuit. As stated, courts in this Commonwealth must enforce specifically realty agreements breached by sellers, except in cases where hardship or injustice would result. *See, Snyder, supra; Petry, supra.*

* * *

In sum, we conclude that the trial court erred in denying Appellant's post-trial motion for removal of nonsuit when the Appellant clearly established that his remedy at law was inadequate under the circumstances of this case.

Judgment reversed. Case remanded for proceedings consistent with this opinion. Jurisdiction relinquished.

QUESTIONS AND NOTES

1. Questions about the facts

   1.1. Is there any question here regarding material breach?

   1.2. Why did Ball think it relevant that there were other similar properties for sale in the area?

2. Questions about the law

   2.1. Would you get the same result if the plaintiff lived in Los Angeles? If there was not a wet weather stream (and just what is a "wet weather" stream anyway)?

2.2. What is an "adequate remedy at law"?

2.3. Would it have mattered if Oliver had lied about his intentions to hold the property as investment, and had instead represented that he was buying the property to preserve it in its pristine state?

3. Notes

3.1. So you get a court order for specific performance? So what? Doesn't the owner have to sign a deed or something before the land records will reflect the change in ownership? Can't they just obdurately sit back and waive a single finger at the victorious plaintiff? Well, no. Rule 70(a) of the Federal Rules of Civil Procedure states that:

> If a judgment requires a party to convey land, to deliver a deed or other document, or to perform any other specific act and the party fails to comply within the time specified, the court may order the act to be done—at the disobedient party's expense—by another person appointed by the court. When done, the act has the same effect as if done by the party.

3.2. What if specific performance requires ongoing compliance, or that one party refrain from doing something? You know, the type of thing that is typically covered by injunctions. To put it more particularly, is specific performance the same thing as an equitable injunction? That was the issue in *Minnesota Vikings Football Stadium, LLC v. Wells Fargo Bank Nat'l Ass'n*, 193 F.Supp.3d 1002 (D. Minn. 2016). There, Wells Fargo agreed not to put an illuminated sign on the roof of a new building it was building as part of the new stadium complex for the Minnesota Vikings football team (the Viking's stadium is named after a competitor of Wells Fargo, U.S. Bank, and U.S. Bank did not want any shots of the stadium from the Goodyear blimp to show a competitor's name—really.)

Wells Fargo blatantly breached the contract, putting up a gaudy illuminated sign. The stadium sued for breach, and asked as a remedy that the sign be taken down, and that Wells Fargo be enjoined from erecting new ones which did not comply with the existing contract. The court agreed. It reasoned as follows:

> When a party breaches a contract, a Court may, in certain circumstances, order specific performance of a contract duty or order an injunction against breach of a contract duty. Restatement (Second) of Contracts § 357 (1981) (updated Mar. 2016). When the duty at issue is to refrain from certain conduct, however, satisfaction of that duty to refrain could be characterized as specific performance of the duty or as an

> injunction against the prohibited conduct. *See id.* § 357 cmt. b (explaining that when performance due under a contract consists of forbearance, an injunction directing a party to refrain from doing a specified act effectively orders specific performance). In addition, the fact that injunctions may be mandatory, as well as prohibitory, undermines any distinction between specific performance and injunctive relief in a contract case. . . .
>
> Perhaps recognizing the difficulty in distinguishing between specific performance and injunctions, courts often characterize requests for specific performance of contract duties as requests for injunctive relief. . . . [Injunctive relief, however, requires "irreparable injury."] [A]lthough Minnesota law does not expressly state that a court must find "irreparable injury" before issuing an order for specific performance, one of the factors courts consider in specific performance cases is whether monetary damages provide an adequate remedy, a question closely tied to the question of irreparable injury. . . . Indeed, in the context of a claim for injunctive relief, the Eighth Circuit has explained that "[i]rreparable harm occurs when a party has no adequate remedy at law, typically because its injuries cannot be fully compensated through an award of damages."

Id. at 1014–15.

4. **You Be the Lawyer!**

   After *Oliver*, would you advise any Pennsylvania seller of land to defend a breach of contract action on the basis that the land was not unique or special?

QUESTIONS BEFORE THE CASE

1. What did the contract in this case require the LLC to do?
2. How much time lapsed between the signing of the contract and the proposed opening of the park? What had the LLC done in the interim with respect to other donors?

REED FOUNDATION, INC. V. FRANKLIN D. ROOSEVELT FOUR FREEDOMS PARK, LLC

New York Supreme Court
37 Misc.3d 1226(A), 964 N.Y.S.2d 62 (2012), *aff'd*, 108 A.D.3d 1, 964 N.Y.S.2d 152 (2013)

CHARLES EDWARD RAMOS, J.

Petitioner, The Reed Foundation, Inc. (the "Foundation"), seeks an order declaring that Respondent Franklin D. Roosevelt Four Freedoms Park LLC (the "LLC") breached its contractual obligations to the Foundation based on the LLC's continuing failure to complete an agreed engraving at the FDR Four Freedoms Park (the "Park").

* * *

BACKGROUND

What follows are the undisputed facts.

The Park was designed in the 1970s by the late architect Louis I. Kahn. The Park consists of a grand staircase, which ascends to a triangular garden of trees and paving stones bordered by a stone promenade, a forecourt area at the point of the triangle that leads to a large bronze bust of Roosevelt housed in a 12 foot-tall granite structure known as the "Threshold," and, just beyond the Threshold, a square granite "Room," which sits at the southernmost tip of Roosevelt Island overlooking the East River.

For over 30 years, efforts to develop the Park were unsuccessful. Then, in 2005, Reed and Jane Gregory Rubin, officers of the Foundation, helped resurrect the long dormant Roosevelt Island project by funding an exhibit on the project at the Cooper Union for the Advancement of Science and Art. The project thereafter gained momentum, with public and private donors displaying interest and ultimately contributing the necessary funds to finance the project.

Consistent with the Rubins' efforts to advance the project, in March 2010, the Foundation contracted to provide the Grant, the express purpose of which was "to support Phase One . . . of construction of the [Park]. . . ." The Grant was among the very first grants made in connection with this project, at a time when there was considerable doubt as to whether the project could be completed. The Grant enabled the LLC to secure public funding from New York State and New York City.

The Agreements

The Grant is governed by a series of interrelated agreements, including the Grant Agreement and the Recognition Agreement. The Grant Agreement and the Recognition Agreement are referred to collectively as the "Foundation-FDR Agreements." These are detailed contracts, drafted by experienced attorneys representing all parties, which carefully documented the parties' mutual agreement at the time of the Foundation's grant.

Under the Grant Agreement, Phase One of the construction of the Park "must include the construction of the Threshold no later than December 31, 2011 (or such later date agreed to in writing by the Foundation)" and that the construction of the Threshold "will include . . . the carving of, and/or other display of, the Threshold Recognition Text and the other text on the Threshold," which is an excerpt of a speech by FDR entitled the Four Freedoms Speech.

The Recognition Agreement sets forth the precise location and wording of the "Threshold Recognition Text," as well as the process for its inscription. The LLC, as developer of the FDR Four Freedoms Park, agreed that the Recognition would be permanently carved on the West-Facing Side of the Threshold as follows:

IN HONOR OF VERA D. RUBIN AND SAMUEL RUBIN THE REED FOUNDATION

The Recognition Agreement went on to specify the manner of carving, size, font and placement reasonably acceptable to the Foundation. It also specified that the Recognition would be designed by The John Stevens Shop under the supervision of Nick Benson, Creative Director, that no other text, signage or similar wording recognizing a donor or other contributor could be placed on the West-Facing Side of the Threshold or the North-Facing Side of the Threshold, and that no other carving, inscription, or other signage may be displayed on the West-Facing Side of the Threshold without the prior written consent of the Foundation.

The Recognition Agreement also provides that a "Default" occurs if "the Threshold has not been installed in the Sculpture Court by December 31, 2011." In addition, the LLC agreed that "the Foundation's remedies at law for a failure to perform, breach or threatened breach of any of Sections 1 and 2 of this Recognition Agreement would be inadequate and the Foundation would suffer irreparable damages as a result of such failure to perform, breach or threatened breach." In recognition of this fact, the LLC agreed that, in the event of the LLC's failure to perform, breach or threatened breach, in addition to any remedies at law, the Foundation, without posting any bond, would be entitled to seek equitable relief in the form of specific performance, temporary restraining order, temporary or permanent injunction or any other equitable remedy which may then be available." (Recognition Agreement, § 6).

Discussion

The LLC seeks to admonish the Foundation, and presumably all of the other donors to and benefactors of the Park whose names are set forth on the monument,[2] by quoting from Maimonides in its memo of law: "Giving is most blessed and most acceptable When the donor remains completely anonymous."

This litigation would not have occurred if the LLC had articulated such a concern to the Foundation before it accepted and spent the Foundation's money.

The Foundation-FDR Agreements are governed by New York law and contain forum selection clauses in which the parties submit to this Court's jurisdiction.

Pursuant to the Grant Agreement, the Foundation paid the Grant to be used to construct Phase One of the Park, including parts of the Threshold.

On June 21, 2012, the Foundation and the LLC confirmed their agreement regarding placement of the Threshold Recognition Text on the West-Facing Side of the Threshold as reflected in a mock-up of the required engraving. On June 21, 2012, the Foundation also consented to a request by the LLC that the lettering for the Threshold Recognition Text be changed from black to gray. This Court has examined the Text and finds it to be understated, low to the ground, in small font, on the West-Facing Side of the Threshold, not facing the bust of FDR.

By July 2012, the LLC had completed the inscription of FDR's speech on the south-facing side of the Threshold but the LLC still had not commenced engraving of the Threshold Recognition Text. At that time, the designated artisan who was responsible for overseeing all engraving on the Threshold, Nick Benson, was on site. The LLC did not apprise the Foundation of its decision not to complete engraving of the Threshold Recognition Text while Mr. Benson was on site.

The LLC asked the Foundation to abdicate its right to the Threshold Recognition Text on the West-Facing Side of the Threshold, and, instead, agree to recognition text on the "grand stair" (where other donors' names would be engraved). The LLC reported complications with other donors and an evolving aesthetic view that the Threshold should not include the Threshold Recognition Text. The Foundation would not consent to relocating the Threshold Recognition Text.

* * *

On October 2, 2012, just over two weeks before the Park's dedication, the LLC advised the Foundation that the LLC will not perform because "[o]ur architects and consultants have told us" that including the Threshold Recognition Text on the Threshold was not the "best aesthetic." The LLC

[2] The LLC has also sought to prominently acknowledge its Chairman, Maimonides' rebuke notwithstanding.

offered to either relocate the engraving or to agree to repay the Foundation's grant, with interest.

Other than the completion of the Threshold Recognition Text on the Threshold in accordance with the Foundation-FDR Agreements, all other phases of construction of the Park and the Threshold are essentially complete.

Specific Performance

The Foundation sought to invoke its rights to specific performance and injunctive relief under the Recognition Agreement and sought an order requiring the LLC to complete the Threshold Recognition Text on or before the Park's dedication on October 17, 2012.

* * *

The LLC has materially breached the Foundation-FDR Agreements by refusing to engrave the Threshold Recognition Text by December 31, 2011, as it is contractually obligated to do.

The construction of an unambiguous contract-such as the Grant Agreement and the Recognition Agreement here-is a matter of law for the court and "the intention of the parties may be gathered from the four corners of the instrument and should be enforced according to its terms" (*Beal Sav. Bank v. Sommer,* 8 NY3d 318, 324 [2007]). It is also a "familiar and eminently sensible proposition of law [ ] that, when parties set down their agreement in a clear, complete document, their writing should . . . be enforced according to its terms' " (*Vermont Teddy Bear Co. v. 538 Madison Realty Co.,* 1 NY3d 470, 475 [2004] *quoting W.W.W. Assocs. v. Giancontieri,* 77 N.Y.2d 157, 162 [1990]).

Under the Recognition Agreement, the LLC acknowledged the Foundation's remedy for breach is specific performance. The LLC agreed that remedies at law were inadequate to redress the LLC's failure to perform and therefore the Foundation "shall be entitled to seek equitable relief in the form of specific performance" (Recognition Agreement, ¶ 6). The LLC's offer to agree to return the gift would negate that term of the Agreement and is hereby rejected. New York courts favor granting equitable relief where, as here, sophisticated parties agree to such remedies "in a clear, complete document" (*Bank of Am., N.A. v. PSW NYC LLC,* 29 Misc.3d 1216(A), 2010 N.Y. Slip Op 51848[U], 10–12 [2010] [granting equitable relief because the parties "agreed that monetary damages would not serve as an adequate remedy at law" and "their writing should . . . be enforced according to its terms" *citing Vermont Teddy Bear Co.* at 475]).

Specific performance is a proper remedy for a breach of contract if money damages would be inadequate to uphold the expectations of the injured party (*see Sokoloff v. Harriman Estates Dev Corp.,* 96 N.Y.2d 409,

415 [2001] *citing Restatement (Second) of Contracts* § 359 [1981]), and when "the subject matter of the particular contract is unique and has no established market value" (*id. quoting Van Wagner Adver. Corp. v. S & M Enters.,* 67 N.Y.2d 186, 193 [1986]; *see also Cho v. 401–403 57th St. Realty Corp.,* 300 A.D.2d 174, 175 [1st Dept 2002] ["[S]pecific performance has been held to be a proper remedy in actions for breach of contract . . . when the uniqueness of the [subject matter] in question makes calculation of money damages too difficult or too uncertain"]).

Here, the Foundation's manifested expectation at the time of the Grant was an engraving of the Threshold Recognition Text on the Threshold in advance of this Park's dedication. By its very nature, such a unique and precise honorary recognition is not subject to monetary valuation. This Court understands that this lasting recognition of the Foundation's role in erecting the Park has significance to the Foundation and its principals. New York courts have granted specific performance in analogous situations involving unique projects and momentous events, with clear uncertainty in valuation (*see Robins v. Zwirner,* 713 F Supp 2d 367, 374–75 [SD N.Y.2010] [seller's refusal to convey "unique works of art" by an artist constitutes irreparable harm to the purchaser]; *Hoffmann v. Springchorn,* No. 95–CV–0579E (Sc), 1997 WL 128352 at *1, 4 [WD N.Y.1997] [granting specific performance to the purchaser of a rare automobile because "there is no doubt that the [automobile] is unique"]; *David Tunick, Inc. v. Kornfeld,* 838 F Supp 848, 851 [SD N.Y.1993] [art collector who contracted to buy a specific Picasso print was not obligated under the UCC to accept a substitute print of the same Picasso painting because, as art prints are "by definition, unique," an art purchaser is entitled to receive the print that "he viewed [ ] as uniquely beautiful"]; *Chabert v. Robert & Co.,* 273 AD 237, 238–39 [1st Dept 1948] [specific performance appropriate to require promisor to sell a rare oil of "special and unascertainable value to the plaintiff" that could not be calculated for a damage award]; *Raftery v. World Film Corp.,* 180 AD 475, 481–83 [1st Dept 1917] [specific performance appropriate to compel the return of photographic prints because of their "unique character" and the impossibility of "estimat[ing] the damage that may come to plaintiff"]; *see also Destiny USA Holdings, LLC v. Citigroup Global Markets Realty Corp.,* No. 09–4157, 2009 WL 2163483, *18–19 [NY Sup Ct, Onondaga County 2009, J. Elfvin], *aff'd as modified by* 69 A.D3d 212 [4th Dept 2009] [promisor required to fund pending loan advances under loan agreement in order to effect promisee's unique expectation interest in a landmark public improvement project]; *Barry v. Dandy, LLC,* No. 602282/07, 2007 WL 2917248, at *2 [NY Sup Ct, New York County 2007, J. Tingling] [ordering event planner to specifically perform obligation to provide promisee a suitable wedding hall]).

The understanding, as carefully set forth in the Agreement, is that the Threshold Recognition Text will be engraved on the Threshold according to contract well in advance of the Park's dedication. The Foundation's right to the agreed recognition was not illusory. It was not subject to the arbitrary whims of the LLC or its consultants. Contract law-and philanthropic custom-require enforcement of an unambiguous undertaking to provide a donor, like the Foundation, the specific recognition it was promised. (*Cf. Capital City Cmty. Urban Redevelopment Corp. v. City of Columbus,* No. 08AP–769, 2009 WL 5062063, at *8 [Ohio Ct App 2009, J. McGrath] [recognizing seller's right to select the "size, text, and location" of a bronze plaque to be installed on the front of a theater despite the City of Columbus' desire to remove the plaque so as not to "eviscerate" the seller's contractual rights by making them "subject to arbitrary rejection" by the city-purchaser]).

This Court is disturbed by the actions of the LLC. No potential donor in this State should be made to fear that its generosity will be diminished by strategically delayed artistic whims of a charity's managers. Public policy and the public's interest in charitable giving require that philanthropy trump fashion.

Perhaps instead of insulting their donors by quoting Maimonides, the members of the LLC should have read Shelley instead:

I met a traveller from an antique land,
Who said—"Two vast and trunkless legs of stone
Stand in the desert. Near them, on the sand,
Half sunk a shattered visage lies, whose frown,
And wrinkled lip, and sneer of cold command,
Tell that its sculptor well those passions read
Which yet survive, stamped on these lifeless things,
The hand that mocked them, and the heart that fed.
And on the pedestal, these words appear:
'My name is Ozymandias, King of Kings;
Look on my Works, ye Mighty, and despair!'
Nothing beside remains. Round the decay
Of that colossal Wreck, boundless and bare
The lone and level sands stretch far away."

This Court expects that the inspiration of the Four Freedoms will far outlive the memory of King Ozymandias but the only path the courts can take to insure [*sic*] that New York's generous custom and practice of philanthropy survives is to require the LLC to honor its obligations that were so carefully articulated in the Agreements. The LLC is directed to complete the Threshold Recognition Text on the Threshold in accordance with the Agreements.

This Court hereby grants the Foundation's Petition.

QUESTIONS

1. Questions about the facts of this case

    1.1. Was there any uncertainty in where and how the text should be displayed? If not, why the lawsuit?

    1.2. Would it have mattered if the parties had not been so specific about the nature of the engraving? What if the agreement had simply said "LLC will honor the Foundation with an engraving on the monument"?

2. Questions about the law

    2.1. The LLC agreed to return all the money, with interest. Why shouldn't that be sufficient to give them victory?

    2.2. Would you get the same result if the issue was putting the name of the artist who drew "Dogs Playing Poker" on prints for commercial sale at Wal-Mart?

    2.3. Who is Shelley? Who is Maimonides? Why are they being quoted in a simple law case from New York? While we're at it, what are the four freedoms?

3. **You Be the Lawyer!**

    You represent the LLC. Your board realizes that agreeing to the "Threshold Recognition Text" was a horrible aesthetic mistake. Other than waiting until the last minute to spring this decision on the Foundation, was there any legal action that The Foundation could have taken to ensure the purity of the sculpture and the recognition of the foundation?

Don't let *Oliver* and *Reed Foundation* fool you. Most contract litigation seeks damages, not specific performance, in large part because lawyers know they can't get specific performance. If Epstein defaults on his contract to paint Markell's house Markell for $1,000, and Ponoroff will paint the same house with the same paint with the same result for $1,100, no court in the land will give Markell specific performance. But what if you get some really good software, that helps you analyze all these complex contracts cases, and then the maker of the software refuses to update or provide service? Read the next case.

---

3. Specific Performance Under the U.C.C.

QUESTIONS BEFORE THE CASE

1. What does i.Lan want as a remedy?
2. What is this court's view on i.Lan's accumulated experience with the software as uniqueness sufficient to invoke Section 2–716 of the U.C.C.?

---

i.LAN SYSTEMS, INC. V. NETSCOUT SERVICE LEVEL CORP.

183 F.Supp.2d 328, 46 UCC Rep.Serv.2d 287 (D. Mass. 2002)

MEMORANDUM

YOUNG, CHIEF JUDGE.

* * *

I. INTRODUCTION

The plaintiff, i.LAN Systems, Inc. ("i.LAN"), helps companies monitor their computer networks. The defendant, NetScout Service Level Corp., formerly known as NextPoint Networks, Inc. ("NextPoint"), sells sophisticated software that monitors networks. In 1998, i.LAN and NextPoint signed a detailed Value Added Reseller ("VAR") agreement whereby i.LAN agreed to resell NextPoint's software to customers. This dispute concerns a transaction that took place in 1999.

i.LAN claims that for $85,231.42 it purchased the unlimited right to use NextPoint's software, replete with perpetual upgrades and support, whereby it effectively could rent, rather than sell, NextPoint's software to customers. In support of its argument, i.LAN points to the purchase order associated with the transaction. NextPoint, in response, points to the 1998 VAR agreement and the clickwrap license agreement contained in the software itself to reach a different conclusion.

The parties continued their relationship for several months without confronting their conflicting interpretations of the 1999 purchase order, but eventually the disagreement erupted into litigation. i.LAN filed a complaint that alleges, among other things, breach of contract * * *.

i.LAN quickly took the offensive and brought a motion for summary judgment, Fed.R.Civ.P. 56(a). i.LAN argued that it should be awarded specific performance—in particular, perpetual upgrades of NextPoint's software and unlimited support.

* * *

II. DISCUSSION

B. What Is at Stake?

1. Specific Performance

More than anything else, i.LAN wants specific performance—in particular, perpetual upgrades of NextPoint's software and unlimited support. Assuming the clickwrap license agreement is enforceable, NextPoint argues that the agreement prohibits specific performance as a remedy. In the alternative, NextPoint argues that specific performance is inappropriate under the UCC.

Section 4 of the clickwrap license agreement states, "NEXTPOINT'S LIABILITY FOR DAMAGES TO LICENSEE FOR ANY CAUSE WHATSOEVER, REGARDLESS OF THE FORM OF ANY CLAIM OR ACTION, SHALL BE LIMITED TO THE LICENSE FEES PAID FOR THE LICENSED PRODUCT." Def.'s App. tab 8. From this provision, NextPoint concludes that money damages are the only possible remedy. An equally plausible reading of the provision, however, is that the limitation only applies to "damages," not equitable remedies. Indeed, section 6 of the agreement states, "[E]ach party shall have the right to institute judicial proceedings against the other party . . . in order to enforce the instituting party's rights hereunder through reformation of contract, specific performance, injunction or similar equitable relief." Id. On balance, sections 4 and 6 cut against NextPoint's argument that the clickwrap license agreement prohibits specific performance as a remedy.

That being said, the law does not permit specific performance simply because a contract does not prohibit it. The UCC provides, in relevant part:

§ 2–716. Buyer's Right to Specific Performance or Replevin.

> (1) Specific performance may be decreed where the goods are unique or in other proper circumstances.
>
> (2) The decree for specific performance may include such terms and conditions as to payment of the price, damages, or other relief as the court may deem just.

UCC § 2–716, Mass. Gen. Laws ch. 106, § 2–716 (emphasis added). Although the UCC also allows specific performance in "other proper circumstances," i.LAN has not argued that the circumstances here are proper. Instead, i.LAN has argued that NextPoint's software is unique, a determination left to the discretion of the Court. See UCC § 2–716 cmt. 1;

cf., e.g., McCarthy v. Tobin, 429 Mass. 84, 89, 706 N.E.2d 629 (1999) (applying common law).

The UCC commentary states that the UCC "seeks to further a more liberal attitude than some courts have shown in connection with the specific performance of contracts of sale." UCC § 2–716 cmt. 1. "Specific performance is no longer limited to goods which are already specific or ascertained at the time of contracting. The test of uniqueness under this section must be made in terms of the total situation which characterizes the contract." Id. cmt. 2. One court has restated the test for specific performance as follows: "Basically courts now determine whether goods are replaceable as a practical matter—for example, whether it would be difficult to obtain similar goods on the open market." Magellan Int'l Corp. v. Salzgitter Handel GmbH, 76 F.Supp.2d 919, 926 (N.D.Ill.1999). * * *

Before turning to the facts of this case, the Court considers the facts of other cases, which are instructive. No published decision in Massachusetts has applied UCC section 2–716, but three decisions are notable. In the first and most recent case, the First Circuit, applying Maine common law but looking to UCC section 2–716 for guidance, awarded specific performance in a case involving a minor-league baseball team. Triple-A Baseball Club Assocs. v. Northeastern Baseball, Inc., 832 F.2d 214 (1st Cir.1987). The First Circuit reasoned that "the Triple-A franchise has no readily ascertainable market value, it cannot be easily obtained from other sources, and it is of special interest to [the appellee]." Id. at 224. In short, "There can be no doubt that what [the appellee] sought, a Triple-A franchise, was unique." Id. In another instructive case, the Massachusetts Supreme Judicial Court many years ago refused to award specific performance in a case involving an automobile whose delivery was delayed by World War II. Poltorak v. Jackson Chevrolet Co., 322 Mass. 699, 79 N.E.2d 285 (1948). The court reasoned:

> The scarcity of automobiles, which went no farther than to occasion considerable delay in delivery, is not sufficient basis for a decree of specific performance in favor of one who sought the completion of a contract for the sale of an ordinary passenger vehicle, and who showed no substantial harm of a kind of character which could not be adequately compensated by an award of damages in an action at law.

Id. at 702, 79 N.E.2d 285. In a third helpful case, the Supreme Judicial Court did allow specific performance in a case involving doors custom-made for an elevator. Dahlstrom Metallic Door Co. v. Evatt Constr. Co., 256 Mass. 404, 152 N.E. 715 (1926). The court reasoned:

> The materials were designed and made for use in the chamber of commerce building; they were limited in number and could not readily be used in any other building; they could not have been

> purchased in the open market. To have had them manufactured elsewhere would have caused serious delay in the construction of the building to the great damage of the contractor as well as of the owners. The contractor would not have an adequate remedy at law.

Id. at 414–15, 152 N.E. 715. Although Poltorak and Dahlstrom predate the UCC, they are significant because the Massachusetts comment to UCC section 2–716 states that the two cases are consistent with the UCC's vision of when specific performance should be allowed. Mass. Gen. Laws ch. 106 § 2–716, cmt.

Turning to the facts of this case, i.LAN makes three arguments why NextPoint's software is unique. First, i.LAN argues that the software is copyrighted and took years to design. The same could be said of any mass-produced item, however, and certainly a mass-produced item is the antithesis of the word "unique." More importantly, NextPoint's software is one of several competing software packages in the market; all run on ordinary computers and perform substantially the same functions. Although these software packages may be copyrighted and the product of intense labor, they are interchangeable as a practical matter and thus none is unique. Second, i.LAN argues that it has tailored its business around NextPoint's software, thus making the software unique to it. The UCC is sensitive to this consideration, but at the same time this Court will not conflate reliance with uniqueness. Much as i.LAN may not want to, it certainly could purchase comparable software on the open market and reconfigure its systems to run that software, just as any person could buy such software and run it. Finally, i.LAN argues that it does not know the number of software licenses it will need in the future to provide its rental services, so money damages would not adequately compensate it. This argument is not that NextPoint's goods are unique, but that i.LAN had struck what it thought to be a unique contract: for a mere $85,231.42 it would have unlimited copies of all of NextPoint's software forever. The UCC, however, looks to the uniqueness of the goods, not the contract.

In sum, even if the clickwrap license agreement permits specific performance, and even if the Court were to enter judgment in favor of i.LAN, NextPoint's software is not unique or irreplaceable as a practical matter, so the Court would not award specific performance.

III. CONCLUSION

For the reasons set forth above, NextPoint's cross-motion for partial summary judgment * * * was ALLOWED on September 28, 2001 with respect to i.LAN's claims for specific performance * * *.

QUESTIONS AND NOTE

1. Questions about the facts

   1.1. What was NextPoint's best fact with respect to its argument that its software was not unique?

   1.2. What does the court mean when it concludes that "The UCC, however, looks to the uniqueness of the goods, not the contract." What would have had to change here to make the software unique?

2. Questions about the law

   2.1. Does the court ever examine whether i.Lan's remedies would be adequate at law? Why not?

   2.2. Does the U.C.C. even apply here? Where is the "transaction[ ] in goods"? U.C.C. § 2–102?

   2.3. Is the court saying that damages will remedy i.Lan's injury? If not, what is it saying?

3. Note

As *i.Lan* notes, the U.C.C. allows specific performance when "the goods are unique or in other proper circumstances."

Well, unique is easy enough to understand. One of a kind, that sort of thing. What about "other proper circumstances"?

How about a contract to buy a dog? In *Houseman v. Dare*, 405 N.J.Super. 538, 966 A.2d 24 (2009) the court awarded specific performance for a dog. Admittedly, it wasn't a normal, commercial situation. The parties had been living together for over a decade, and then split up under less than amicable circumstances. They disputed who got to keep the community pooch. Despite the noncommercial setting, the court found that there was an enforceable oral contract to convey the dog.

But isn't a dog a dog like any other dog? Further, the person seeking the dog had stipulated that the dog's value was $1,500 (that's some dog, we might say). The court dismissed this notion. "The special subjective value of personal property worthy of recognition by a court of equity is sentiment explained by facts and circumstances—such as the party's relationship with the donor or prior associations with the property—that give rise to the special affection." As to the agreed value? "Her stipulation to the dog's intrinsic monetary value cannot be viewed as a concession that the stipulated value was adequate to compensate her for loss of the special value given her efforts to pursue her claim for specific performance at trial."*

Okay, transport this case to a more commercial setting. You represent Bob, who wants to buy a screaming yellow Lamborghini Aventador LP 700–4 from the local dealer. Beyond all reason, he really wants the one on the showroom floor. Would you advise him to write the following on the contract before he signs it: "I am in love with this beautiful car. I cannot imagine living without it." Would this language help Bob to obtain specific performance if the dealer wanted to breach the contract and sell the car to another customer for more money, while he offered the same model, but in igneous orange, to Bob?

4. **You Be the Lawyer!**

Can you get around *i.Lan* if you put in the next contract a clause like that found in *Reed Foundation*; that is, can you draft something like: "NextPoint agrees that i.Lan's remedies in the event of breach of contract will be difficult to calculate, and thus, if NextPoint breaches, i.Lan may obtain relief by way of specific performance"?

Even if you can convince a court that the subject matter of your contract is unique, or that your damages at law are inadequate, can you ensure that a court will order specific performance? In short, no. Remember, it's equity. Equity has all sorts of rules that "law" does not. Some are highlighted in the next note.

SPECIFIC PERFORMANCE AND NEGATIVE INJUNCTIONS

As we have seen, all sorts of equitable considerations play into whether a court will order specific performance. This includes the difficulty in monitoring performance, a problem that is particularly acute in contracts to perform a service. How do you know that the person is really performing as intended, and not just "dogging" it? An early remark of New York's Chancellor Walworth (in 1833!) captures this problem. In a suit against an opera singer seeking specific performance of a contract to perform an opera, he said: "I am not aware that any officer of this court has that perfect knowledge of the Italian language, or possesses that exquisite sensibility in the auricular nerve which is necessary to understand, and to enjoy with a proper zest, the peculiar beauties of the Italian opera, so fascinating to the fashionable world." *DeRivafinoli v. Corsetti*, 4 Paige 263, 270, 3 N.Y.

* Of some note is that the Animal Legal Defense Fund and Lawyers in Defense of Animals both filed a brief as amicus curiae. They urged the court to adopt a rule that required consideration of the best interests of the dog. Really. Oh, and the case never mentions the dog's name.

Ch. Ann. 429, 25 Am.Dec. 532 (N.Y. Ch. 1833). Section 367(1) of the *Restatement (Second)* captures this notion concisely, stating that "A promise to render personal service will not be specifically enforced."

So what do you do when someone agrees to perform a service for you and then breaches and tries to do the same thing for someone else?

The answer is to enjoin them from doing so. The distinction is subtle; you are not forcing them to perform for you. You are just attempting to stop them from performing for others. This can be seen in contracts to provide a service, or license some desirable good. In *Tom Doherty Associates Inc. v. Saban Entertainment Inc.*, 869 F. Supp.2d 1130 (S.D.N.Y. 1994), for example, the owner of the rights to the Power Rangers, Saban Entertainment, granted publishing rights to TOR, a fledgling science fiction publisher. This contract was made before the Power Rangers became the force that they ultimately became. After fame hit, Saban no longer wished to be associated with the lowly publisher, and shopped the Power Ranger rights to others. Smarting from the slight, TOR sued. There was no doubt as to the contract breach, only the remedy. Specific performance regarding the actual writing of the books would not be awarded because the court could not supervise the writing, nor could it determine whether any books so produced were of the quality called for in the contract. (Although if any books were written, the court required Saban to give TOR a first right of refusal on their publication.)

What the court could do, however, was stop the distribution or licensing of Power Rangers books to others. And that it did. The court enjoined "from entering into any further licenses, or in any way expanding or extending any existing licenses, to any party other than TOR, of the right to publish any book based on the Power Rangers." That settles that.

In this, the court was following a venerable line of cases enjoining parties, principally performers, who breach one contract from taking another, usually more profitably, one. In *Lumley v. Wagner*, 1 De G.M. & G. 604, 42 Eng. Rep. 687 (Ch. 1852), for example, an opera singer named Wagner sought to break one performance contract to take another, more profitable, engagement. The court enjoined her from performing at the new venue. It stated:

> Wherever this Court has not proper jurisdiction to enforce specific performance, it operates to bind men's consciences, as far as they can be bound, to a true and literal performance of their agreements; and it will not suffer them to depart from their contracts at their pleasure, leaving the party with whom they have contracted to the mere chance of any damages which a jury may give. The exercise of this jurisdiction has, I believe, had a wholesome tendency towards the maintenance of that good faith which exists in this country to a much greater degree perhaps

> than in any other; and although the jurisdiction is not to be extended, yet a Judge would desert his duty who did not act up to what his predecessors have handed down as the rule for his guidance in the administration of such an equity.
>
> It was objected that the operation of the injunction in the present case was mischievous, excluding the Defendant J. Wagner from performing at any other theatre while this Court had no power to compel her to perform at Her Majesty's Theatre. It is true that I have not the means of compelling her to sing, but she has no cause of complaint if I compel her to abstain from the commission of an act which she has bound herself not to do, and thus possibly cause her to fulfil her engagement. The jurisdiction which I now exercise is wholly within the power of the Court, and being of opinion that it is proper case for interfering, I shall leave nothing unsatisfied by the judgment I pronounce. The effect, too, of the injunction in restraining J. Wagner from singing elsewhere may, in the event of an action being brought against her by the Plaintiff, prevent any such amount of vindictive damages being given against her as a jury might probably be inclined to give if she had carried her talents and exercised them at the rival theatre: the injunction may also, as I have said, tend to the fulfilment of her engagement; though, in continuing the injunction, I disclaim doing indirectly what I cannot do directly.

Lumley v. Wagner, 1 De G.M. & G. 604, 619 42 Eng. Rep. 687, 693 (Ch. 1852).

Although *Lumley* entered a negative injunction, there are plenty of cases in which a court will not. *See, e.g., American Broadcasting Companies, Inc. v. Wolf*, 52 N.Y.2d 394, 420 N.E.2d 363, 438 N.Y.S.2d 482 (1981).

B. RESCISSION AND CANCELLATION

As we have seen, when one party to a contract has materially breached, the non-breaching party has options. One is to accept the breach, and move forward with appropriate compensation for the past breach. We explored that option when we looked at election of remedies. Another is to go to court to seek a remedy—either damages or specific performance—caused by the non-performance or faulty performance. That's what we've studied in this chapter to this point.

If those obligations are gone, can the non-breaching party just seek to recover what the non-breaching party has paid or the value of the services it has performed? In essence, can the non-breaching party just "undo" the transaction and get back to where it once belonged?

Often, this desire is called rescission. In some cases, it can be preferable to damages, especially when the non-breaching party has paid a significant sum for performance it never received. *CanPro Invs. Ltd. v. United States*, 130 Fed. Cl. 320, 340 (2017) elaborates:

> "Rescission has the effect of voiding a contract from its inception, i.e., as if it never existed." Dow Chem. Co. v. United States, 226 F.3d 1334, 1345 (Fed. Cir. 2000). It is "essentially an equitable remedy [and] will not ordinarily be invoked where money damages—in this case damages for breach of contract—will adequately compensate a party to the contract." *Id.*

Section 37(2) of the *Restatement (Third) of Restitution and Unjust Enrichment* (2011) confirms another limitation on the remedy of rescission. "Rescission as a remedy for breach of contract is not available against a defendant whose defaulted obligation is exclusively an obligation to pay money."

But there is yet another concern: what about the non-breaching party's future obligations to the breaching party under the contract? Are they dead and gone? Yup. We saw that with respect to our study of the effects of material breach. And *CanPro Invs. Ltd. v. United States*, 130 Fed. Cl. 320, 340 (2017) confirms this:

> Unlike rescission, contract termination is a remedy generally available under a termination provision in a contract following a material breach by the other contracting party. Id. at 1346; see also McDonnell Douglas Corp. v. United States, 182 F.3d 1319, 1327 (Fed. Cir. 1999) (explaining that a party can choose to terminate a contract upon default by the other party and discussing the government's ability to terminate for convenience). . . . Thus, defendant's observation that rescission and contract termination are different remedies is correct. Accord Restatement (Second) of Contracts § 283 cmt. a (Am. Law Inst. 1981) (differentiating between rescission, termination, and cancellation).

As *CanPro* acknowledges, relief of the non-breacher's unperformed obligations can occur in at least two ways: one is termination under the provisions of the contract; another is explicit cancellation by the non-breaching party.

Is there a difference between termination and cancellation? The U.C.C. thinks so. Section 2–106(3) states that:

> "Termination" occurs when either party pursuant to a power created by agreement or law puts an end to the contract otherwise

> than for its breach. On "termination" all obligations which are still executory on both sides are discharged but any right based on prior breach or performance survives.

So if the contract says that one side can end the contract if the other side is, for example, not properly insured, that is a termination. The contract is at an end, and so are the non-breaching party's unperformed obligations.

How does that compare with cancellation? Again, U.C.C., this time section 2–106(4):

> "Cancellation" occurs when either party puts an end to the contract for breach by the other and its effect is the same as that of "termination" except that the cancelling party also retains any remedy for breach of the whole contract or any unperformed balance.

Under the U.C.C., cancellation is an appropriate remedy for buyers (§ 2–711(1)) and sellers (§ 2–703(f)) when the other side breaches or repudiates.

---

5. ARBITRATION AS A CONTRACTUAL ALTERNATE TO LAWSUITS

There have always been alternatives to resolution of disputes by courts. Especially in commercial matters, parties have often turned to arbitration to resolve their disputes. Indeed, Section 345(f) of the *Restatement (Second) of Contracts* recognizes the "enforcing of an arbitration award" as a judicial remedy available for breach of contract.

What is arbitration? Arbitration is a private dispute resolution process in which the rules of evidence are relaxed, the award is often not subject to any appeal, and the parties can pick the arbiter. Arbitration cases, at least according to conventional wisdom, move faster than do court proceedings.

Small wonder that Congress has given favorable treatment to arbitration. In 1925, it enacted the United States Arbitration Act, found at 9 U.S.C. § 1 *et seq.*, and generally known as the Federal Arbitration Act (FAA). The FAA applies when a transaction contemplated by the parties involves a contract with an arbitration clause, and touches "interstate commerce."

The FAA allows any party to a contract with an arbitration clause to stay litigation commenced contrary to that clause, 9 U.S.C. § 3, and further provides that any party may obtain a court order compelling the other side to submit to arbitration. *Id.* § 4.

The FAA also empowers arbitrators to call third-party witnesses, compel them to appear (and provide any documents they have that are material to the case), and hold such witnesses in contempt if they fail to comply. 9 U.S.C. § 7.

Once an arbitrator enters an award, that award must be "confirmed" in a court. Once confirmed, the award is reduced to a judgment, which may be enforced by the winning party in court, like any other judgment.

Arbitration sometimes gets a bad rap as being too business-friendly. Part of this lore is that arbitrators are less likely to grant large damage awards, or to give aggrieved parties punitive damages. The next case examines one such party who wanted to opt out of the arbitration clause in its contract.

QUESTIONS BEFORE THE CASE

1. What is the difference between a claim that "arises out of" a contract, and one which merely "relates" to a contract?
2. What was the fraud alleged?

JACKSON V. SHAKESPEARE FOUNDATION, INC.

Supreme Court of Florida
108 So.3d 587 (2013)

LEWIS, J.

This case is before the Court for review of the decision of the First District Court of Appeal in *Shakespeare Foundation, Inc. v. Jackson,* 61 So.3d 1194 (Fla. 1st DCA 2011), and concerns whether an action for fraud is within the scope of an arbitration provision in a contract for the purchase and sale of real property. The First District certified that its decision is in conflict with the decision of the Fifth District Court of Appeal in *Maguire v. King,* 917 So.2d 263 (Fla. 5th DCA 2005). We have jurisdiction. *See* art. V, § 3(b)(4), Fla. Const.

FACTS

In 2006, George Jackson, Kerry Jackson, and the Jackson Realty Team, Inc. ("the Jacksons") decided to sell the real property that is the subject of the contract which forms the basis of this dispute. They posted the following advertisement in the Bay County Multiple Listing Service:

> This is a Great affordable housing project. Estimate from North Bay Engineering is $17,500 to get you to Dev order stage. Topography and boundary survey completed recently by Dragon

> Surveying to be included in price. Property is 165′ on Everitt Avenue and 396′ deep, totally cleared and filled except for 10′ around fence line. Zoning per City of PC is MU2, Mixed Use 2, Multi Family duplex, triplex or quadraplex be built on the property. Recently tapped into Panama City Water and Sewer, with new commercial grade pump/lift station on site. Local Engineering company has platted 10 duplexes could fit 6 4 plexes. Zoned 20 units per acre or 30 units total. *Wetlands study verifies No Wetlands.* One of Sellers is Licensed Fl. Realtor.

(Emphasis added.) When the Jacksons posted this advertisement, they had in their possession a Property Report Land Use Planning Analysis, which established, contrary to the advertisement, that 25% of the subject property constituted wetlands.

The Jacksons and the Respondents—the Shakespeare Foundation, Inc., and the Herd Community Development Corp. (collectively the "Shakespeare Foundation" or the "Foundation")—entered into negotiations for the purchase of the real property. During the negotiations, the Shakespeare Foundation advised the Jacksons that they intended to develop the property into a twenty-seven unit low-income housing development. The Shakespeare Foundation relied on the representations set forth in the advertisement and entered into a contract with the Jacksons for the purchase of the real property.

In July 2007, after the Shakespeare Foundation tendered full payment to the Jacksons for the property, the Foundation held an onsite meeting with a builder and engineer. The builder reported that the property might contain wetlands. The Shakespeare Foundation hired an engineering firm to perform a wetlands delineation on the property. The firm provided the Shakespeare Foundation with a report that established that 0.39 acres of the 1.5 acre property was wetlands rendering it unbuildable. The wetlands constituted 26% of the entire tract which was equal to nine of the twenty-seven units that the Shakespeare Foundation had intended to develop.

The Shakespeare Foundation thereafter filed an action against the Jacksons for fraudulent misrepresentation. In the complaint, it was alleged that in the advertisement for the sale of the property, the Jacksons knowingly and falsely misrepresented that the property had no wetlands and that the property was suitable for the construction of thirty units, and the Shakespeare Foundation relied on these misrepresentations when entering into the contract. The Shakespeare Foundation contended that if it had been known that 26% of the property constituted wetlands, the property would have never been purchased because that percentage of wetlands made use of the property "economically unfeasible." The Shakespeare Foundation also asserted that the existence of the wetlands led to a delay in project development. It was alleged that this delay of time caused the Foundation to miss a favorable real estate market in which the subject property could have been sold, and placed them in one of the worst real estate markets in the modern era.

The Jacksons moved to dismiss the Shakespeare Foundation's action. They asserted that the fraud claim arose out of, and was related to, the contract and, therefore, fell within the arbitration provision of the contract. The arbitration provision in the contract, titled "Default and Dispute Resolution," states:

> **14. DISPUTE RESOLUTION:** This Contract will be construed under Florida law. All controversies, claims, and other matters in question arising out of or relating to this transaction or this Contract or its breach will be settled as follows:
>
> **(a) Disputes concerning entitlement to deposits made and agreed to be made:** Buyer and Seller will have 30 days from the date conflicting demands are made to attempt to resolve the dispute through mediation. If that fails, Escrow Agent will submit the dispute, if so required by Florida law, to Escrow Agent's choice of arbitration, a Florida court or the Florida Real Estate Commission. Buyer and Seller will be bound by any resulting award, judgment, or order.
>
> **(b) All other disputes:** Buyer and Seller will have 30 days from the date a dispute arises between them to attempt to resolve the matter through mediation, failing which the parties will resolve the dispute through neutral binding arbitration in the county where the Property is located. The arbitrator may not alter the Contract terms or award any remedy not provided for in this Contract. . . . This clause will survive closing.

(Emphasis added.) The Jacksons contended that the contractual provisions required the Shakespeare Foundation to submit the fraud claim to binding arbitration. It was asserted that this provision required binding arbitration of the fraud claim because the scope of the contractual provision included all claims "arising out of *or relating to* this transaction or this Contract." (Emphasis added.)

The trial court subsequently granted the Jacksons' motion to dismiss, concluding that the arbitration provision in the contract required that the parties submit the fraud claim to arbitration. The Shakespeare Foundation appealed the judgment of dismissal to the First District Court of Appeal. *See Shakespeare Found.*, 61 So.3d at 1196.

Decision of the First District

On appeal, the First District examined whether the trial court erred in dismissing the action. *See id.* at 1197–98. The crux of the appellate court's review was whether the fraud claim of the Shakespeare Foundation was within the scope of the arbitration provision of the contract. *See id.* at 1198.

The district court below concluded that the arbitration provision of the subject contract was broad in scope because its terms were to apply to all claims or controversies "arising out of or relating to" the contract. *See id.* (concluding that the "or relating to" language rendered the arbitration provision broad in scope). The district court then held that a claim falls within a broad arbitration provision if a "significant relationship"—i.e., a "contractual nexus"—exists between the contract and the claim. *See id.*

The district court, however, determined that the fraud claim here did not come within the broad scope of the arbitration provision because the fraud claim arose from a general duty established under the common law; not from an obligation arising under the contract. *See id.* at 1199. More specifically, the district court concluded that the fraud claim did not significantly relate to the contract because determination of this claim required neither reference to nor construction of the contract. *See id.* Rather, the district court held that the claim rested on the alleged false statements in the published advertisement and the general common law duty not to make fraudulent misrepresentations. *See id.* The court further determined that the fraud claim was not within the scope of the arbitration provision because the contract was only incidental to the dispute since the Shakespeare Foundation had the ability, as well as the right, to assert a fraud claim before the parties executed the contract. *See id.* The district court also concluded that the express language of the contract evinced an intent that a fraud claim would not be litigated under the contract and its arbitration provision. *See id.* Specifically, the district court held that the express language of the contract only contemplates remedies for a breach of contract action, and prohibits an arbitrator from providing a remedy not specifically provided for in the provisions of the contract, such as a remedy in the event of a tort or fraud action. *See id.*

The First District ultimately held that the action based on fraud was not a dispute subject to arbitration under the contract, reversed the trial court's order, and certified conflict with the decision of the Fifth District in *Maguire. See id.* at 1201.

* * *

ANALYSIS

* * *

Applicable Rules of Law

Generally, the three fundamental elements that must be considered when determining whether a dispute is required to proceed to arbitration are: (1) whether a valid written agreement to arbitrate exists; (2) whether an arbitrable issue exists; and (3) whether the right to arbitration was waived. *See Seifert v. U.S. Home Corp.,* 750 So.2d 633, 636 (Fla.1999). Arbitration provisions are contractual in nature and remain a matter of contractual interpretation. *See id.* The intent of the parties to a contract, as manifested in the plain language of the arbitration provision and contract itself, determines whether a dispute is subject to arbitration. *See id.* Courts generally favor such provisions, and will try to resolve an ambiguity in an arbitration provision in favor of arbitration. *See id.; see also Qubty v. Nagda,* 817 So.2d 952, 956 (Fla. 5th DCA 2002).

Two basic types of arbitration provisions have emerged: (1) provisions with language and application narrow in scope, and (2) provisions with language and application broad in scope. *See Seifert,* 750 So.2d at 636–37. An arbitration provision that is considered to be narrow in scope typically requires arbitration for claims or controversies "arising out of" the subject contract. *See id.* at 636. This type of provision limits arbitration to those claims that have a direct relationship to a contract's terms and provisions. *See id.* In contrast, an arbitration provision that is considered to be broad in scope typically requires arbitration for claims or controversies "arising out of *or relating to"* the subject contract. *See id.* at 637 (emphasis added). The addition of the words "relating to" broadens the scope of an arbitration provision to include those claims that are described as having a "significant relationship" to the contract—regardless of whether the claim is founded in tort or contract law. *See id.* at 637–38.

A "significant relationship" between a claim and an arbitration provision does not necessarily exist merely because the parties in the dispute have a contractual relationship. *See id.* Rather, a significant relationship is described to exist between an arbitration provision and a claim if there is a "contractual nexus" between the claim and the contract. *See id.* at 638. A contractual nexus exists between a claim and a contract if the claim presents circumstances in which the resolution of the disputed issue requires either reference to, or construction of, a portion of the contract. *See id.* More specifically, a claim has a nexus to a contract and arises from the terms of the contract if it emanates from an inimitable duty created by the parties' unique contractual relationship. *See id.* at 639. In contrast, a claim does not have a nexus to a contract if it pertains to the breach of a duty otherwise imposed by law or in recognition of public policy, such as a duty under the general common law owed not only to the contracting parties but also to third parties and the public. *See id.*

* * *

Instant Case

We hold that the action here based on fraud is within the scope of the arbitration provision because it has a clear contractual nexus with, and thus a significant relationship to, the contract. This relationship exists because: (1) the fraud claim is inextricably intertwined with both the circumstances that surrounded the transaction from which the contract emanated and the contract itself; and (2) resolution of the fraud claim requires the construction and consideration of duties arising under the contract.

In this case, as in *Seifert,* the contract at issue has a broad arbitration provision because it subjects "[a]ll controversies, claims, and other matters in question *arising out of or relating to* this transaction or this Contract or its breach" to binding arbitration. (Emphasis added.) *See Seifert,* 750 So.2d at 637 (holding that an arbitration provision which contains the phrase "arising from or relating to" is considered a broad arbitration provision because of the addition of the "or relating to" language). However, in *Seifert,* this Court concluded that the negligence-type claims at issue did not have a significant relationship to a contract that had a broad arbitration provision because a contractual nexus did not exist between the claims and the contract. *See id.* at 640–42. We held that this was because the claims did not require some reference to or construction of the contract, and pertained to the duty of care imposed by general common law in recognition of public policy. *See id.* at 637, 640–41.

In contrast to *Seifert,* here, although the fraud claim is based on common law fraud, it is inextricably intertwined with both the circumstances that surrounded the transaction from which the contract emanated and the contract itself. As alleged in the complaint as a basis for the action, the genesis of the fraud claim is that the Jacksons knowingly misrepresented facts in the published advertisement that the subject property did not contain wetlands when, in fact, the Jacksons knew of the wetlands' existence through their own previous study which established that wetlands constituted 25% of the property. The Shakespeare Foundation allegedly relied on the misrepresentations in the published advertisement and entered into the contract. The subsequent damages the Shakespeare Foundation allegedly incurred arose from the contract itself, i.e., by entering into the contract, the Foundation suffered the economic damage of owning property it was unable to develop or sell.

Therefore, unlike the negligence-type claims in *Seifert,* the fraud claim at issue here is inextricably intertwined with both the transaction from which the contract arose and the contract itself—the reliance element of the claim emanates from the transaction from which the contract arose, and the damages element of the claim arises from the execution and existence of the contract itself. Accordingly, the fraud claim has a significant relationship to the contract and is within the scope of the contract's broad arbitration provision.

Furthermore, the resolution of the fraud claim requires reference to and construction of both the contract's arbitration provision and its "as is" provision. In particular, the arbitration provision of the contract limits the remedies for disputes arising from the contractual relationship to those provided in the contract, stating that the "arbitrator may not alter the Contract terms or award any remedy not provided for in this Contract." The express remedies in the contract are limited to the parties' rights in the event of a default, and the contract does not mention the parties' remedial rights in the event of a fraud or tort action.

This limitation of remedies in the arbitration provision may have an impact on the contract and the arbitration provision. *See Hialeah Auto., LLC v. Basulto,* 22 So.3d 586, 590–91 (Fla. 3d DCA 2009) (holding as unconscionable an arbitration provision that resulted in the waiver of common law and statutory remedies). However, we do not resolve such questions here as they were not presented for review nor addressed by the district court below. These are issues that remain for consideration below as we address only the initial question concerning whether the arbitration clause may apply.

The adjudication of the fraud action may also require reference to and the construction of the "as is" provision of the contract. More specifically, the resolution of the fraud claim may require a determination as to whether that claim is negated due to an election of the "Feasibility Study" option under the "as is" provision of the contract. By electing this option, the Shakespeare Foundation may have accepted the property "as is" for the intended use and waived any claims. *See Gilman v. Butzloff,* 155 Fla. 888, 22 So.2d 263, 265 (1945) ("A party may waive any right to which he is legally entitled, whether secured by contract, conferred by statute, or guaranteed by the Constitution."). Although the Shakespeare Foundation's election of the option may not result in a waiver of the fraud claim, whether this argument is viable will require reference to, and the construction of, the contract and all other facts. *See, e.g., D & M Jupiter Inc. v. Friedopfer,* 853 So.2d 485, 488–89 (Fla. 4th DCA 2003) (citing *Oceanic Villas Inc. v. Godson,* 148 Fla. 454, 4 So.2d 689, 690 (1941)) (concluding that although a claim for fraudulent inducement of a contract may vitiate an "as is" provision, such a determination requires an examination of the contract and the circumstances surrounding its execution, and a resolution of whether a fraudulent representation occurred).

* * *

CONCLUSION

Accordingly, we conclude that the fraud action here filed by the Shakespeare Foundation has a contractual nexus with, and a significant relationship to, the contract between the Shakespeare Foundation and the Jacksons and is, as a general principle, within the scope of the contract's broad arbitration provision. We do not determine nor do we address any other issue beyond this threshold determination. We, therefore, quash the decision below, remand for further consideration, and approve the decision in *Maguire* to the extent that it is consistent with this opinion.

It is so ordered.

PARIENTE, QUINCE, LABARGA, and PERRY, JJ., concur.

POLSTON, C.J., and CANADY, J., concur in result.

QUESTIONS

1. Questions about the facts

   1.1. What is the conflict between the misstatement in the advertisement and the statement that the property was being sold "as-is"?

   1.2. Why do you suppose Jackson wanted arbitration?

2. Questions about the law

   2.1. Much discretion is vested in the parties regarding the type of arbitration required. Can you articulate how the three simple words "or related to" expanded the scope of the arbitration?

   2.2. If Shakespeare wanted to sue Jackson for fraud related to a representation by Jackson that a neighboring property, also owned by Jackson, wasn't for sale (and it turns out it was), would that dispute have to be sent to arbitration?

3. **You Be the Lawyer!**

   The general counsel of the Shakespeare Foundation is in your office after the above loss. He wants you to explain how they should change the language to ensure their rights to sue in court for common law torts while preserving arbitration for matters covered by the contract. Can you?

---

6. RESTITUTION INTEREST AS AN ALTERNATIVE MEASURE OF DAMAGES

There is a third interest that contract remedies can protect. As stated in *Crown Coal & Coke Co. v. Powhatan Mid-Vol Coal Sales, L.L.C.*, 929 F.Supp.2d 460, 472 (W.D. Pa. 2013):

> Damages under a theory of restitution also can provide an appropriate measure of relief where the injured party's ability to recover is clouded or otherwise not feasible. The objective of this approach "is not the enforcement of contracts through the

> protection of an injured party's expectation or reliance interests, but is instead rooted in common notions of equity through the protection of the injured's restitution interest." * * * 5 Arthur L. Corbin, supra, § 1101, at 548; Restatement, supra, Ch. 16, Topic 4, intro. note, at 199). Under this theory the breaching party must disgorge the benefits received to the party who conferred them. Id. (citing Trosky, 652 A.2d at 817). The propriety of such a recovery generally is governed by the traditional principles of equity, such as those utilized under unjust enrichment or forfeiture.
>
> A party may elect the remedy of restitution but its decision to do so is at the exclusion of the other compensatory remedies. See Smith v. Brink, 385 Pa.Super. 597, 561 A.2d 1253, 1255 (1989) ("the injured party may either rescind the contract and seek restitution, or enforce the contract and recover [compensatory damages]"); * * * The injured party's retention of any benefit received under the contractual undertaking bars rescission.

As rephrased in the *Restatement*, the injured party has a right to damages based on the restitution interest,* "which is his interest in having restored to him any benefit that he has conferred on the other party." *Restatement (Second) Contracts* § 344(c).

This measure of damages makes the most sense when one party has performed, and the other party has not, and the nonbreaching party cannot prove damages under the rules stated above. As stated by the Federal Circuit:

> When proof of expectancy damages fails, the law provides a fall-back position for the injured party—he can sue for restitution. The idea behind restitution is to restore—that is, to restore the non-breaching party to the position he would have been in had there never been a contract to breach. * * * In other words, the objective is to restore the parties to the status quo ante. * * * This is typically not as good as lost profits, from the viewpoint of the non-breacher, but a lot better than nothing.

First Annapolis Bancorp, Inc. v. United States, 89 Fed.Cl. 765, 799 (Ct. Cl. 2009) (quoting *Glendale Federal Bank v. United States*, 239 F.3d 1374, 1380 (Fed. Cir. 2001)).

Think of the following case: Epstein wants to fly to Michigan to see Ponoroff. Epstein chooses BAM Airlines and pays $500 for his ticket. Before

---

* You guessed it! "Restitution interest" is another Fuller and Perdue term: "The court may force the defendant to disgorge the value he received from the plaintiff. The object here may be termed the prevention of gain by the defaulting promisor at the expense of the promisee; more briefly, the prevention of unjust enrichment. The interest protected may be called the restitution interest." Lon L. Fuller & William R. Perdue, Jr., *The Reliance Interest in Contract Damages*, 46 YALE L.J. 52, 53 (1937).

the trip commences, BAM Airlines fails, and Epstein, lucky duck that he is, manages to get another ticket for $450. Does he have any damages for BAM Airlines' failure to fly him to Arizona? No expectancy damages; he is in some sense better off since he got a better deal. No reliance damages; he just paid the price asked. But he does need to get his $500 back. And a court will do that. It will "restore" Epstein to the position he was in before the contract was entered into.

So restitution is easy when there is full payment by one side and total breach by the other, and none of the other damage measures compensate. But what if there is not full payment, but some benefit conferred? Or if the person who conferred the benefit was also in breach? Read on.

QUESTIONS BEFORE THE CASE

1. Who is in breach in the following case?

2. What is the formula that the subcontractor uses to calculate how much money they should receive?

UNITED STATES V. ALGERNON BLAIR, INCORPORATED

U.S. Court of Appeals, Fourth Circuit
479 F.2d 638 (1973)

CRAVEN, CIRCUIT JUDGE:

May a subcontractor, who justifiably ceases work under a contract because of the prime contractor's breach, recover in quantum meruit the value of labor and equipment already furnished pursuant to the contract irrespective of whether he would have been entitled to recover in a suit on the contract? We think so, and, for reasons to be stated, the decision of the district court will be reversed.

The subcontractor, Coastal Steel Erectors, Inc., brought this action under the provisions of the Miller Act, 40 U.S.C.A. § 270a et seq., in the name of the United States against Algernon Blair, Inc., and its surety, United States Fidelity and Guaranty Company. Blair had entered a contract with the United States for the construction of a naval hospital in Charleston County, South Carolina. Blair had then contracted with Coastal to perform certain steel erection and supply certain equipment in conjunction with Blair's contract with the United States. Coastal commenced performance of its obligations, supplying its own cranes for handling and placing steel. Blair refused to pay for crane rental, maintaining that it was not obligated to do so under the subcontract. Because of Blair's failure to make payments for crane rental, and after completion of approximately 28 percent of the subcontract, Coastal terminated its performance. Blair then proceeded to complete the job with a new subcontractor. Coastal brought this action to recover for labor and equipment furnished.

The district court found that the subcontract required Blair to pay for crane use and that Blair's refusal to do so was such a material breach as to justify Coastal's terminating performance. This finding is not questioned on appeal. The court then found that under the contract the amount due Coastal, less what had already been paid, totaled approximately $37,000. Additionally, the court found Coastal would have lost more than $37,000 if it had completed performance. Holding that any amount due Coastal must be reduced by any loss it would have incurred by complete performance of the contract, the court denied recovery to Coastal. While the district court correctly stated the " 'normal' rule of contract damages,"[1] we think Coastal is entitled to recover in quantum meruit.

In United States for Use of Susi Contracting Co. v. Zara Contracting Co., 146 F.2d 606 (2d Cir. 1944), a Miller Act action, the court was faced with a situation similar to that involved here—the prime contractor had unjustifiably breached a subcontract after partial performance by the subcontractor. The court stated:

> For it is an accepted principle of contract law, often applied in the case of construction contracts, that the promisee upon breach has the option to forego any suit on the contract and claim only the reasonable value of his performance.

146 F.2d at 610. The Tenth Circuit has also stated that the right to seek recovery under quantum meruit in a Miller Act case is clear. Quantum meruit recovery is not limited to an action against the prime contractor but may also be brought against the Miller Act surety, as in this case. Further, that the complaint is not clear in regard to the theory of a plaintiff's recovery does not preclude recovery under quantum meruit. Narragansett Improvement Co. v. United States, 290 F.2d 577 (1st Cir. 1961). A plaintiff may join a claim for quantum meruit with a claim for damages from breach of contract.

In the present case, Coastal has, at its own expense, provided Blair with labor and the use of equipment. Blair, who breached the subcontract, has retained these benefits without having fully paid for them. On these facts, Coastal is entitled to restitution in quantum merit.

> The "restitution interest," involving a combination of unjust impoverishment with unjust gain, presents the strongest case for relief. If, following Aristotle, we regard the purpose of justice as

[1] Fuller & Perdue, The Reliance Interest in Contract Damages, 46 Yale L.J. 52 (1937); Restatement of Contracts § 333 (1932).

> the maintenance of an equilibrium of goods among members of society, the restitution interest presents twice as strong a claim to judicial intervention as the reliance interest, since if A not only causes B to lose one unit but appropriates that unit to himself, the resulting discrepancy between A and B is not one unit but two.

Fuller & Perdue, The Reliance Interest in Contract Damages, 46 Yale L. J. 52, 56 (1937).[6]

The impact of quantum meruit is to allow a promisee to recover the value of services he gave to the defendant irrespective of whether he would have lost money on the contract and been unable to recover in a suit on the contract. *Scaduto v. Orlando,* 381 F.2d 587, 595 (2d Cir. 1967). The measure of recovery for quantum meruit is the reasonable value of the performance, Restatement of Contracts § 347 (1932); and recovery is undiminished by any loss which would have been incurred by complete performance. 12 Williston on Contracts § 1485, at 312 (3d ed. 1970). While the contract price may be evidence of reasonable value of the services, it does not measure the value of the performance or limit recovery.

It should be noted, however, that in suits for restitution there are many cases permitting the plaintiff to recover the value of benefits conferred on the defendant, even though this value exceeds that of the return performance promised by the defendant. In these cases it is no doubt felt that the defendant's breach should work a forfeiture of his right to retain the benefits of an advantageous bargain. Fuller & Perdue, *supra* at 77. Rather, the standard for measuring the reasonable value of the services rendered is the amount for which such services could have been purchased from one in the plaintiff's position at the time and place the services were rendered.

Since the district court has not yet accurately determined the reasonable value of the labor and equipment use furnished by Coastal to Blair, the case must be remanded for those findings. When the amount has been determined, judgment will be entered in favor of Coastal, less payments already made under the contract. Accordingly, for the reasons stated above, the decision of the district court is

Reversed and remanded with instructions.

QUESTIONS AND NOTES

1. Questions about the facts of this case

    1.1. Who won in the district court? Who brought the appeal?

---

[6] This case also comes within the requirements of the *Restatements* for recovery in quantum meruit. *Restatement of Restitution* § 107 (1937); *Restatement of Contracts* §§ 347–357 (1932).

1.2. What makes cases like this somewhat unusual? Think about it in these terms. If we have a contract under which one party made a bad deal and is going to lose money, which of the two parties would you guess is most likely to commit a breach?

2. Questions about the law

2.1. If the contract to Coastal would not return a profit, why should it be awarded anything? Doesn't that undermine the expectancy basis of contract damages?

2.2. What amount is the court on remand supposed to calculate? What will it do then?

2.3. So Coastal gets damages even though it would have lost money on the contract? What is to stop the Coastals of this world, every time they enter into a losing contract, from goading the other side into breach so that it can get out of the contract with its costs? Take a look at *Restatement (Second) of Contracts* § 349 and, in particular, the last clause in that section, beginning with "* * * less any loss the party in breach * * *" In what circumstance might that clause apply?

3. Notes

3.1. Section 373(1) of the *Restatement (Second)* expressly provides that "on breach for nonperformance * * * the injured party is entitled to restitution. * * *" This is certainly consistent with the holding in *Algernon Blair*. However, that provision is also made "[s]ubject to the rule stated in Subsection (2)." That rule carves out an exception to the option of the injured party to seek restitution in lieu of enforcement of her claim under the contract. Look at subsection (2) and see if you can figure out what the justification might be for this exception.

3.2. Restitution measures the value of the benefit conferred on the other party, which may or may not be the same as the costs incurred by the non-breaching party—that's the difference between a restitutionary recovery and a reliance recovery; *i.e.,* the former excludes recovery of non-beneficial reliance expenditures. But can recovery based on restitution actually exceed the direct expenditures incurred by the injured party? Epstein agrees to build a house for Ponoroff at a price of $100,000. After Epstein has incurred $70,000 of costs, and would have had to incur an additional $40,000 to complete the construction, Ponoroff repudiates. If Epstein puts on evidence at trial in the form of expert testimony from Markell, another local contractor, that Markell would have charged $75,000 to do just the work that Epstein did up to the point of Ponoroff's breach, can Epstein recover $75,000, and thereby turn what would have been a losing contract into a winner? The answer is that there is authority for both views. So, it is up to you to figure out which is the *right* view!

4. **You Be the Lawyer!**

What if Algernon Blair had put this clause immediately above the signature line of the contract: "Coastal acknowledges that Algernon Blair is relying on Coastal's bid in making its own bid to get the main contract, and thus Coastal shall always bear the consequences of any mistakes regarding the profitability of its contract."?

What if Coastal were in breach instead of Blair? The fact that a person is in breach does not affect the value of the services that he has rendered, does it? Section 373(1) of the *Restatement (Second)*, however, talks about the right of the *injured party* to seek restitution in lieu of suing under the contract. So, if Coastal were in breach, does that mean it would just be out of luck even though it conferred a benefit on Blair for which it was not compensated? Consider that question as you read, and try to make sense of, the next case.

QUESTIONS BEFORE THE CASE

1. How long did Britton work for Turner? How long was he supposed to work for Turner?
2. The court says that Britton is not suing on the contract. So what is he suing on?

BRITTON V. TURNER

Supreme Court of New Hampshire
6 N.H. 481 (1834)

Syllabus:

Assumpsit for work and labour, performed by the plaintiff, in the service of the defendant, from March 9th, 1831, to December 27, 1831.

The declaration contained the common counts, and among them a count in quantum meruit, for the labor, averring it to be worth one hundred dollars.

At the trial in the C. C. Pleas, the plaintiff proved the performance of the labor as set forth in the declaration.

The defence was that it was performed under a special contract—that the plaintiff agreed to work one year, from some time in March, 1831, to

March 1832, and that the defendant was to pay him for said year's labor the sum of one hundred and twenty dollars; and the defendant offered evidence tending to show that such was the contract under which the work was done.

Evidence was also offered to show that the plaintiff left the defendant's service without his consent, and it was contended by the defendant that the plaintiff had no good cause for not continuing in his employment.

There was no evidence offered of any damage arising from the plaintiffs departure, farther than was to be inferred from his non fulfillment of the entire contract.

The court instructed the jury, that if they were satisfied from the evidence that the labor was performed, under a contract to labor a year, for the sum of one hundred and twenty dollars, and if they were satisfied that the plaintiff labored only the time specified in the declaration, and then left the defendant's service, against his consent, and without any good cause, yet the plaintiff was entitled to recover, under his quantum meruit count, as much as the labor he performed was reasonably worth, and under this direction the jury gave a verdict for the plaintiff for the sum of $95.

The defendant excepted to the instructions thus given to the jury.

PARKER, J.

It may be assumed, that the labor performed by the plaintiff, and for which he seeks to recover a compensation in this action, was commenced under a special contract to labor for the defendant the term of one year, for the sum of one hundred and twenty dollars, and that the plaintiff has labored but a portion of that time, and has voluntarily failed to complete the entire contract.

It is clear, then, that he is not entitled to recover upon the contract itself, because the service, which was to entitle him to the sum agreed upon, has never been performed. But the question arises, can the plaintiff, under these circumstances, recover a reasonable sum for the service he has actually performed, under the count in quantum meruit.

* * *

That such rule in its operation may be very unequal, not to say unjust, is apparent * * *.

The case before us presents an illustration. Had the plaintiff in this case never entered upon the performance of his contract, the damage could not probably have been greater than some small expense and trouble incurred in procuring another to do the labor which he had contracted to perform. But having entered upon the performance, and labored nine and a half months, the value of which labor to the defendant as found by the jury is $95, if the defendant can succeed in this defence, he in fact receives nearly five sixths of the value of a whole year's labor, by reason of the breach of contract by the plaintiff a sum not only utterly disproportionate to any probable, not to say possible damage which could have resulted from the neglect of the plaintiff to continue the remaining two and an half months, but altogether beyond any damage which could have been recovered by the defendant, had the plaintiff done nothing towards the fulfillment of his contract.

* * *

We hold then, that where a party undertakes to pay upon a special contract for the performance of labor, or the furnishing of materials, he is not to be charged upon such special agreement until the money is earned according to the terms of it, and where the parties have made an express contract the law will not imply and raise a contract different from that which the parties have entered into, except upon some farther transaction between the parties.

In case of a failure to perform such special contract, by the default of the party contracting to do the service, if the money is not due by the terms of the special agreement he is not entitled to recover for his labor, or for the materials furnished, unless the other party receives what has been done, or furnished, and upon the whole case derives a benefit from it. * * *

But if, where a contract is made of such a character, a party actually receives labor, or materials, and thereby derives a benefit and advantage, over and above the damage which has resulted from the breach of the contract by the other party, the labor actually done, and the value received, furnish a new consideration, and the law thereupon raises a promise to pay to the extent of the reasonable worth of such excess. This may be considered as making a new case, one not within the original agreement, and the party is entitled to "recover on his new case, for the work done, not as agreed, but yet accepted by the defendant." 1 Dane's Abr. 224.

If on such failure to perform the whole, the nature of the contract be such that the employer can reject what has been done, and refuse to receive any benefit from the part performance, he is entitled so to do, and in such case is not liable to be charged, unless he has before assented to and accepted of what has been done, however much the other party may have done towards the performance. He has in such case received nothing, and having contracted to receive nothing but the entire matter contracted for, he is not bound to pay, because his express promise was only to pay on receiving the whole, and having actually received nothing the law cannot and ought not to raise an implied promise to pay. But where the party receives value—takes and uses the materials, or has advantage from the labor, he is liable to pay the reasonable worth of what he has received. * * * And the rule is the same whether it was received and accepted by the assent of the party prior to the breach, under a contract by which, from its nature, he was to receive labor, from time to time until the completion of the whole contract; or whether it was received and accepted by an assent subsequent to the performance of all which was in fact done. If he received it under such circumstances as precluded him from rejecting it afterwards, that does not alter the case—it has still been received by his assent.

* * *

It is easy, if parties so choose, to provide by an express agreement that nothing shall be earned, if the laborer leaves his employer without having performed the whole service contemplated, and then there can be no pretence [*sic*] for a recovery if he voluntarily deserts the service before the expiration of the time.

The amount, however, for which the employer ought to be charged, where the laborer abandons his contract, is only the reasonable worth, or the amount of advantage he receives upon the whole transaction, and, in estimating the value of the labor, the contract price for the service cannot be exceeded. * * *

If a person makes a contract fairly he is entitled to have it fully performed, and if this is not done he is entitled to damages. He may maintain a suit to recover the amount of damage sustained by the non performance.

The benefit and advantage which the party takes by the labor, therefore, is the amount of value which he receives, if any, after deducting the amount of damage; and if he elects to put this in defence he is entitled so to do, and the implied promise which the law will raise, in such case, is to pay such amount of the stipulated price for the whole labor, as remains after deducting what it would cost to procure a completion of the residue of the service, and also any damage which has been sustained by reason of the non fulfillment of the contract.

If in such case it be found that the damages are equal to, or greater than the amount of the labor performed, so that the employer, having a right to the full performance of the contract, has not upon the whole case received a beneficial service, the plaintiff cannot recover.

This rule, by binding the employer to pay the value of the service he actually receives, and the laborer to answer in damages where he does not complete the entire contract, will leave no temptation to the former to drive the laborer from his service, near the close of his term, by ill treatment in order to escape from payment; not to the latter to desert his service before the stipulated time, without a sufficient reason; and it will in most instances settle the whole controversy in one action and prevent a multiplicity of suits and cross actions.

* * *

The defendant sets up a mere breach of contract in defense of the action, but this cannot avail him. He does not appear to have offered evidence to show that he was damnified by such breach, or to have asked that a deduction should be made on that account. The direction to the jury was therefore correct, that the plaintiff was entitled to recover as much as the labor performed was reasonably worth, and the jury appear to have allowed a pro rata compensation, for the time which the plaintiff labored in the defendant's service.

As the defendant has not claimed or had any adjustment of damages, for the breach of the contract, in this action, if he has actually sustained damage he is still entitled to a suit to recover the amount.

* * *

Judgment on the verdict.

QUESTIONS AND NOTE

1. Questions about the facts of this case

   1.1. Why do you think Turner failed to offer any evidence of damages arising from Britton's breach of his employment contract?

   1.2. Was the court concerned with the reasons why Britton left Turner's employ before the end of the one-year? Is that fact relevant to the legal issue in the case?

2. Questions about the law

   2.1. Look at the trial court's instruction to the jury. Did the court permit Britton to recover under the contract?

   2.2. Could you argue that Britton "substantially performed"? How would the analysis and/or the outcome have been different if the court had concluded that there had been substantial performance?

   2.3. What, if anything, would Turner have had to pay to Britton if Turner had been able to show that it cost him $50 to hire someone else to perform Britton's duties for the balance of the contract term? Suppose the cost was only $15?

   2.4. Suppose Turner had been able to show that the contract price was above market rates for similar services or that Britton performed his job in a sloppy manner. Would either of these facts affect the amount Britton should be able to recover in a *quantum meruit* claim?

   2.5. What are the policy issues with which the court was concerned? Does the rule devised by the court in this case advance those policies? How is the rule different from the rule advanced in *Algernon Blair*?

3. Note

Today, in virtually all jurisdictions, employers are required by statute to pay their employees periodically (*i.e.*, bi-weekly or monthly) without regard to either the quality of the employee's work or whether the employee has substantially performed the contract. In effect, employment contracts are made divisible by statute. However, the "net benefit rule" established in *Britton v. Turner* still has enormous viability in other contexts, including construction services and independent contractor arrangements.

4. **You Be the Lawyer!**

Britton comes to you and says he absolutely has to leave his job; Turner is a worse ogre than Epstein. If true, you know you must help this wretch leave his employment and find another job. Before Britton tenders his resignation, what would you advise him to do? How should he handle the resignation; should he just take off as Britton appears to have done in the main case?

CHAPTER 8

WHAT ARE THE ALTERNATIVES TO CONTRACTS AND CONTRACT LAW? (QUASI-CONTRACT AND RESTITUTION)

■ ■ ■

1. NATURE AND ORIGINS OF QUASI-CONTRACT

As we discussed way back in Chapter 1, contract liability is distinguished from other forms of liability in that it is *consensual*. That is to say, a contractual obligation exists because it is voluntarily undertaken by the promisor rather than, as in the case of tort or criminal liability, imposed as a matter of societal judgment about what forms of behavior will be deemed culpable. Our legal regime has, however, devised another form of liability which is neither purely fault-based nor truly promise-based, although, for historical reasons discussed more fully below, the terminology used to describe this type of liability sounds eerily like the terminology used to describe conventional contract liability. In fact, this form of liability has come to bear the appellation of *Quasi-Contract*.

A quasi-contractual claim, which exists somewhere in-between classic contract and classic tort liability, is based neither on an express agreement nor an agreement implied-in-fact. Instead, it is a legal fiction, or an *implied-in-law* agreement, that rests on the proposition or general theory of obligation that one party should not be permitted to be enriched unjustly at the expense of a second party unless the first party makes compensation to the second party for the value of the benefit conferred. In effect, then, the cause of action for quasi-contract is based on the doctrine of *unjust enrichment*. It is a separate theory of liability (distinct from ordinary contract liability) that provides a remedy, namely, *restitution*, in circumstances where no true contract exists.

Restitution is its own area of law, with its own history, its own jurisprudence, and even its own Restatement—*Restatement Third, Restitution and Unjust Enrichment* (2011). You will recall that when we considered how the law enforces a deal in Chapter 6, we looked at "restitutionary" recovery as an alternative to recovery under the contract based on either the expectation or reliance interests. Indeed, the law of restitution pertains to situations wholly unrelated to contract, such as cases involving fraud and conversion, as well as cases that arise in the more typical contractual or quasi-contractual contexts. Thus, the term restitution really has two meanings: it refers to both the substantive legal rules that embody the right of an innocent party to recover for unjust enrichment and the remedy, at law or equity, that is available to redress an unjust enrichment. For present purposes, however, what is critical is that you understand two things: (1) the formal distinction between a genuine contract (whether express or implied-in-fact) and a quasi or implied-in-law contract; and (2) the fundamentally different purposes served by these separate areas of law. To this end, consider the following explanation offered more than a hundred years ago by Professor Maine.

HENRY SUMNER MAINE, *ANCIENT LAW*

3rd AMERICAN ED. 332–33 (1888)

The part of Roman law which has had most extensive influence on foreign subjects of inquiry has been the law of Obligation, or, what comes nearly to the same thing, of Contract and Delict. The Romans themselves were not unaware of the offices which the copious and malleable terminology belonging to this part of their system might be made to discharge, and this is proved by their employment of the peculiar adjunct *quasi* in such expressions as Quasi-Contract and Quasi-Delict. 'Quasi,' so used, is exclusively a term of classification. It has been usual with English critics to identify the quasi-contracts with implied contracts; but this is an error, for implied contracts are true contracts, which quasi-contracts are not. In implied contracts, acts and circumstances are the symbols of the same ingredients which are symbolized, in express contracts, by words; and whether a man employs one set of symbols or the other must be a matter of indifference so far as concerns the theory of agreement. But a quasi-contract is not a contract at all. The commonest sample of the class is the relation subsisting between two persons, one of whom has paid money to the other through mistake. The law, consulting the interests of morality, imposes an obligation on the receiver to refund; but the very nature of the transaction indicates that it is not a contract, inasmuch as the convention, the most essential ingredient of contract, is wanting. This word 'quasi,' prefixed to a term of Roman law, implies that the conception to which it serves as an index is connected with the conception with which the comparison is instituted by a strong superficial analogy or resemblance. It does not denote that the two conceptions are the same, or that they belong to the same genus. On the contrary, it negatives the notion of an identity between them; but it points out that they are sufficiently similar for one to be classed as the sequel to the other, and that the phraseology taken from one department of law may be transferred to the other, and employed without violent straining, in the statement of rules which would otherwise be imperfectly expressed.

In order to understand how claims for unjust enrichment came to be based on a fictional contract, it must be emphasized that early common law lawyers in seeking redress for a particular kind of action thought not in terms of *rights*, as modern lawyers tend to do, but in terms of *remedies*. This was because, in medieval England, a plaintiff seeking relief against a particular defendant was required to fit his claim into a recognized form of action or *writ*. For example, the modern law of contracts was developed through extension of the form of trespass on the case known as *special assumpsit* (literally that the defendant undertook or promised to perform a particular act).* Early on, however, assumpsit, which was really a tort-based remedy, was not available if the action of *Debt*—to recover a sum certain—more neatly fit the facts. But the older action of Debt was still subject to the ancient procedure known as "wager of law," pursuant to which a defendant could avoid liability by producing a number of professional "oath-sayers" who would swear that the defendant was telling the truth. This made the action of Debt easy for the defendant to manipulate in order to avoid a just debt. Therefore, ingenious common law judges,** desirous of providing a remedy in deserving cases, gradually began to permit actions for payment of a sum certain to be brought in assumpsit. However, to circumvent the cumbersome action of Debt, this action was known as *general assumpsit* and, unlike special assumpsit, it did not depend on the existence of a real promise or an actual contract. Instead, it rested on a promise implied in law where one party had already performed but received nothing in return from the party benefitted by that performance. For this reason, in addition to an alternative to either an action of Debt or special assumpsit, this action proved useful when the defendant had received a clear benefit from the plaintiff, but no express promise could be proved or established. In effect, general assumpsit would lie where one party had been unjustly enriched at the expense of another party because the court would indulge the fiction that the benefit was conferred by the plaintiff *at the request* of the defendant and with the attendant obligation to compensate the plaintiff for the value of the benefit conferred. In the parlance of the common law at the time, such claims were said to arise *quasi ex contractu,* and the enduring link between contract law and unjust enrichment was forged.

---

* For more on the history of the development of the writ of assumpsit, *see* A.W.B. SIMPSON, A HISTORY OF THE COMMON LAW OF CONTRACT: THE RISE OF THE ACTION OF ASSUMPSIT (1975); KEVIN M. TEEVEN, A HISTORY OF THE ANGLO-AMERICAN COMMON LAW OF CONTRACT, 27–50 (1990); James Barr Ames, *The History of Assumpsit,* 2 HARV. L. REV. 1 (1888).

** Lord Mansfield is generally credited with bringing quasi-contract into the mainstream of English common law. *See* Moses v. Macferlan, 2 Burr. 1005, 97 Eng. Rep. 676 (K.B. 1760). ("In one word, the gist of this kind of action is, that the defendant, upon the circumstances of the case, is obliged by the ties of natural justice and equity to refund the money" [paid by mistake]).

GEORGE E. PALMER, *LAW OF RESTITUTION*

§ 1 at 2 (1978)

Restitution based upon unjust enrichment cuts across many branches of the law, including contract, tort, and fiduciary relationship, but it also occupies much territory that is its sole preserve.

---

2. ELEMENTS OF A QUASI-CONTRACTUAL CLAIM

A. IN GENERAL

JOHN W. WADE, *RESTITUTION FOR BENEFITS CONFERRED WITHOUT REQUEST*

19 VAND. L. REV. 1183, 1183–84, 1211–12 (1966)

I. Introduction

The principle is now fully recognized in this country that a "person who has been unjustly enriched at the expense of another is required to make restitution to the other." This is the language of the first section of the *Restatement of Restitution*. When one person confers a benefit upon another without the latter's solicitation, the benefit received constitutes an enrichment—a windfall, so to speak. This benefit may take one of several forms. It may involve (1) transferring property to the defendant, (2) saving, preserving or improving his property, (3) rendering personal services for him, or (4) performing for him a duty imposed directly by law by his own contractual arrangements. In any of these situations there is an enrichment, and the principle quoted above comes into play if the enrichment is "unjust." When is it unjust? Obviously, it would not be so characterized if it were intended as a gift; just as obviously, the opposite is true if the plaintiff acted under legal compulsion and against his will. In making the determination, considerable weight is given to the circumstances that the benefit was not requested by the defendant.

The common law has long had a pronounced policy that benefits may not be forced upon a party against his will, so as to require him to pay for them. This idea has been forcefully expressed on a number of occasions. Said the court in the leading English case, "Liabilities are not to be forced upon people behind their backs any more than you can confer a benefit upon a man against his will." Most of the time this idea has been indicated by applying an epithet to the plaintiff. The term most frequently used is that of "volunteer." Applied to the plaintiff, particularly if it carries the adjective "mere," it has played the "kiss of death" and the sure indication that he will not be allowed to recover. Other derogatory terms used include meddler, intermeddler, interloper, mere stranger, mere impertinence. The Restatement uses the adjective "officious," which carries a somewhat more restricted connotation.[1] All of these terms embody the policy that one should not be required to pay for benefits which he did not solicit and does not desire.

. . . .

IV. Conclusion

The restrictions on recovery which have been spelled out at considerable length have all been presented from a negative standpoint.

It may now be possible to summarize them and present a general principle stated in a positive fashion.

Perhaps the following two sentences will prove helpful in this regard:

> One who without intent to act gratuitously, confers a measurable benefit upon another, is entitled to restitution, if he affords the other an opportunity to decline the benefit or else has a reasonable excuse for failing to do so. If the other refuses to receive the benefit, he is not required to make restitution unless the actor justifiably performs for the other a duty imposed upon him by law.

Dean Wade's definition suggests that a mere volunteer, one who confers a benefit gratuitously, is not entitled to restitution under this doctrine. Why not? Can you think of some examples where this limitation would preclude a quasi-contractual recovery? Suppose, without being asked, Markell rushes out and washes Epstein's filthy car. Does Markell have a claim against Epstein for payment? Does it matter if Markell can show that the rear window was so dirty that it was becoming a safety hazard?

QUESTIONS BEFORE THE CASE

1. What is the benefit conferred in this case?
2. On whom is the benefit conferred?

---

[1] "A person who officiously confers a benefit upon another is not entitled to restitution therefor." *Restatement, Restitution* § 2 (1937). "Officiousness means interference in the affairs of others not justified by the circumstances under which the interference takes place." *Id.*, comment a.

PATTERSON V. PATTERSON

Court of Appeals of New York
59 N.Y. 574 (1875)

[This case was filed by the executrix of the estate of William Patterson to foreclose a mortgage executed by the defendant and given to the testator to secure the payment of $1,200 due upon William Patterson's death. By way of counterclaim, the defendant raised his right to set off against this claim, among other amounts, the sum of $180.30, representing the amount paid by the defendant to the undertakers to defray the cost of the testator's funeral expenses. The trial court held in favor of the plaintiff on the basis that, under applicable statutes, the defendant could not setoff a debt arising after the death of the testator against a debt due from the defendant arising during the life of the testator. The defendant appealed].

FOLGER, JUSTICE.

* * *

I have no doubt but that the reasonable and necessary expenses of the interment of the dead body of one deceased, are a charge against his estate, though not strictly a debt due from him. The ground of this is the general right of every one to have decent burial after death; which implies the right to have his body carried, decently covered, from the place where it lies to a cemetery or other proper inclosure, and there put under ground. (*Regina v. Stewart*, 12 Ad. & Ell., 773, citing *Gilbert v. Buzzard*, 2 Hagg. Consist. R., 333; see, also, *Chapple v. Coope*, 13 M. & W., 252.) In the last case, in which an infant, a widow, was held liable on her contract for the funeral expenses of the burial of her deceased husband, it was said, that "there are many authorities which lay it down that decent Christian burial is a part of a man's own rights; and we think it not great extension of the rule to say, that it may be classed as a personal advantage and reasonably necessary to him." This right existing, the law casts upon some one the duty of seeing that it is accorded. So it would seem, at common law, that if a poor person of no estate dies, it is the duty of him under whose roof his body lies, to carry it, decently covered, to the place of burial. The husband surviving is bound to bury the corpse of his wife; and in his absence, another, a relative, with whom she has lived up to her death, having directed the funeral and paid the expense, may recover it of the husband. * * * And where the owner of some estate dies, the duty of the burial is upon the executor. * * * And our Revised Statutes (2 R. S., 71 § 16) recognize this duty, in that the executor is prohibited from any interference with the estate until after probate, except that he may discharge the funeral expenses. From this duty springs a legal obligation, and from the obligation the law implies a promise to him who, in the absence or neglect of the executor, not officiously, but in the necessity of the case, directs a burial and incurs and pays such expense thereof as is reasonable. * * * It is analogous to the duty and obligation of a father to furnish necessaries to a child, and of a husband to a wife, from which the law implies a promise to pay him who does what the father or the husband, in that respect, omits. * * *

No statutory provisions are now in mind which interpose an obstacle. Though our statute of payment of debts and legacies (2 R.S., p. 87 § 27) gives the order in which the executor shall make payment of debts against the estate, and though there is no provision there for a priority of payment of funeral expenses, it is not to be held therefrom that the common-law rule is abrogate. Those expenses are not to be treated as a debt against the estate, but as a charge upon the estate, the same as the necessary expenses of administration. * * * The expenses of probate of will precede the formal authority to the executor, but are allowed to him on an accounting. So should funeral expenses be. The decent burial of the dead is a matter in which the public have concern. It is against the public health if it do not take place at all, and against a proper public sentiment, that it should not take place with decency. * * *

Can the defendant set off these expenses in this action? His cause of action is against the plaintiff on a promise implied by law from her. He had no cause of action therefor, against the testator. As the cause of action against the defendant, arose after the death of the testator, and to the plaintiff, it appears that the two demands are mutual debts respectively due to and from defendant, and to and from the plaintiff in the same capacity. This demand may therefore be set off.

The judgment appealed from, must be modified so as to allow to the defendant, in diminution of the amount of the claim established against him, the sum of $180.30. He is also entitled to the interest thereon.

The judgment so modified, should be affirmed, without costs to either party in this court.

QUESTIONS

1. Questions about the facts of this case

    1.1. What was the relationship between William Patterson and the defendant?

    1.2. The court concludes that William Patterson's estate is liable for the costs incurred by defendant in arranging for the burial of the testator. Did William Patterson, during his life, agree to reimburse the defendant for the costs of paying Mr. Patterson's funeral expenses? Did the executrix agree to reimburse those expenses? If the answer to both questions is "no," then what were the key facts from which this obligation could be said to arise?

2. Questions about the law

   2.1. The court also concludes that the set-off sought by the defendant for funeral expenses was proper because "the two demands are mutual debts respectively due to and from the defendant, and to and from the plaintiff in the same capacity." What does this mean? If mutuality of obligation is a requirement to the right of set-off, did the court properly apply it in this case? Wasn't the defendant's debt owed to William Patterson and his claim against the estate?

   2.2. Under the trial court's reasoning, would the defendant have been able to recover for the $180.30 paid to defray funeral expenses?

3. **You Be the Lawyer!**

   If you had represented the defendant, what steps would you have recommended before paying William Patterson's funeral expenses?

B. AT THE REQUEST OF THE DEFENDANT

QUESTION BEFORE THE CASE

1. Why does the majority conclude that there can be no recovery for breach of contract?
2. How would the majority have ruled on the plaintiff's unjust enrichment claim if the court had concluded that there could be recovery for breach of contract?

SCHOTT V. WESTINGHOUSE ELECTRIC CORPORATION

Supreme Court of Pennsylvania
436 Pa. 279, 259 A.2d 443 (1969)

POMEROY, J.

During the period 1962 to 1965 (the relevant times for the purpose of this case), there was in effect at Westinghouse Electric Corporation (hereinafter "Company") a formalized suggestion program under which its employees were invited to submit to the Company any suggestions they might have for increasing production and reducing costs. The question in this case is whether the Company may have become contractually obligated to one of its employees, appellant herein, by virtue of the actions of both parties pursuant to the program. This appeal is from the sustaining of preliminary objections by the Company in the nature of a demurrer. Consequently, the facts before us are confined to the appellant's complaint, as amended, and the demurrer admits for present purposes every well pleaded material fact set forth in the pleading to which it is addressed, as well as the inferences reasonably deducible therefrom. * * *

The terms of the suggestion program are set forth in the documentary exhibits attached to the complaint. In pertinent part, the basic form of the suggestion system provides as follows:

> "With a view toward increasing production and reducing costs, thereby promoting employment, the Westinghouse Electric Corporation encourages practical suggestions from employees.
>
> "Cash awards ranging from a minimum of $5.00 to a maximum of $15,000 will be paid for each suggestion adopted. * * *
>
> "Suggestions must be submitted on this form. * * * All suggestions will be passed upon as soon as possible, and suggesters will be notified as to the action taken. * * *"

Space was provided for the statement of the employee's suggestion. Beneath that space and immediately above the signature line where the employee-suggester was to sign was the following stipulation:

> "In submitting this suggestion, I agree that the decision of the local Suggestion Committee on all matters pertaining to this suggestion, my eligibility for an award, and the amount of award, if any, will be final. I further understand that if this suggestion is rejected, I have the right to reopen it within 12 months from the date of rejection, or to re-submit it as a new suggestion at any time thereafter.
>
> "Note: If adopted; Minimum Award—$5.00
>
> Maximum Award—$15,000"

In May, 1962, the appellant, an employee of the Company, submitted a suggestion that certain panels used on circuit breakers manufactured by the Company be made from fabricated heavy gauge steel rather than the material then used, cast aluminum. Appellant submitted the suggestion, as required, on the standard form with its stipulation that the decision of the Suggestion Committee should be determinative as to all matters. Thereafter, the Suggestion Committee informed the appellant in writing that his suggestion had been rejected (Exhibit C to the complaint). This communication stated that a change of the panels would necessitate large expenditures for design work, the building of models, and laboratory tests, and that these costs would more than offset any savings which might be realized from the proposed change. Appellant was informed that "If breaker re-design is started for other reasons in the future, this idea will be considered." He was also advised, in the same communication, that his suggestion could be reopened within a year or resubmitted after a year.

In September, 1963, appellant resubmitted his suggestion, again using the Company's prescribed form for his submission; in January, 1964, he was informed that the suggestion had again been rejected. In explaining its action, the Suggestion Committee cited its original reasons, adverted to further problems in the design of the panels resulting from the need to use nonmagnetic materials in the panel, and mentioned that redesign of the panels to include partial nonmagnetic materials was being undertaken as part of an independent cost reduction study.

At this point in the narrative, resort must be had to the complaint itself, as distinguished from the documentary exhibits. The complaint averred, in paragraph 8, that thereafter, probably in 1964, the Company "did adopt and utilize" the recommendations advanced by the suggestion, and the plaintiff (appellant) thereupon requested reconsideration of his suggestion. The Company apparently made such a review and communicated the results thereof to appellant in a letter of May, 1965 (Exhibit F to the complaint). This letter adverts to the Company's "application of the same basic idea [as that contained in appellant's suggestion] in a redesign" and confirms the Company's view that the reason given for the initial rejection of the suggestion in 1962 had been valid at that time. It further states the opinion of the writer (General Manager of the Switchgear Division) that "the action taken [by the Company] in 1964 changing the back plate was the result of independent action taken without knowledge of your [appellant's] suggestion," and reaffirmed the Company's refusal to make an award to appellant.

In November, 1966, appellant filed a complaint which averred that the Company had adopted the appellant's suggestion and prayed for an accounting as to the Company's savings therefrom, and damages equal to 20% thereof. The Company filed preliminary objections, on the ground that the complaint did not set forth a valid claim against the Company on which relief could be granted. In support of this conclusion the objections cited the stipulation that "the decision of the Local Suggestion Committee on all matters pertaining to this suggestion * * * will be final." The lower court in sustaining the Company's objections, found that the suggestion program of the Company was an invitation to its employees to make an offer; that the offer of the appellant was by its terms subject to acceptance or rejection by the Company through its Committees; and that the offer had been duly and consistently rejected by the Company. The court further held: "Plaintiff is bound by the statement to which he agreed that the decision of the Suggestion Committee will be final on all matters pertaining to his suggestion and his eligibility for an award unless there is fraud or deceit practiced by or an unjust enrichment inuring to the defendant and no such allegations are made in this case." Finding that no enforceable contract had been pleaded by appellant, the court sustained defendant's preliminary objections and granted plaintiff leave to amend his complaint.

Thereafter, appellant filed an amended complaint seeking damages both under a theory of contract and under a theory sounding in unjust enrichment, properly set forth in a separate count. The amended complaint alleged no new facts but charged appropriation of plaintiff's valuable idea.

The Company again filed preliminary objections, renewing its position that appellant had failed to state a cause of action sounding in contract and further asserting that no cause of action based on unjust enrichment had been set forth. The lower court (McKenna, Jr., J.) found that the amended complaint added no substantial allegation to the original complaint. Holding that appellant was bound by the adverse determinations of the Suggestion Committee, the court below sustained the objections and dismissed the amended complaint. * * *

The present appeal is from the order of the lower court dismissing appellant's amended complaint. Appellant argues that he was entitled to recover the value of his suggestion, either under a theory of performance of a unilateral contract or under a theory of unjust enrichment.

We agree with the lower court that the appellant cannot recover under a contract theory, but under the facts averred we believe the appellant has stated a cause of action in unjust enrichment. Accordingly, we are obliged to reverse and remand.

I

As we view the first cause of action, we need not decide whether the purported contract was unilateral or bilateral in nature. Whichever interpretation is adopted, it is clear that appellant agreed to abide by the decision of the Suggestion Committee on "all matters" (including the acceptableness of the suggestion itself). The Committee rejected the suggestion, and that rejection bars the appellant's recovery under his first cause of action, not because appellant was thereby made ineligible for an award under a valid contract with the Company, but rather because, in view of the Committee's action, no contract existed between the parties.

* * *

II

Appellant's alternative position is that, relying on the Company's promise in the suggestion invitation, he submitted a valuable idea to the Company in hope of securing a monetary award therefor; that the Company "adopted" or appropriated the idea to its own use and benefit; that the Company has refused to make payment to appellant therefor in accordance with the terms of the suggestion system; that in consequence appellant is entitled to the full value of the saving realized by the Company from its use of his idea. The Company responds that these are but conclusory averments and that no cause of action is set forth. * * *

Returning to the applicable law, we note that this Court has found the quasi-contractual doctrine of unjust enrichment inapplicable when the relationship between parties is founded on a written agreement or express contract. * * * But in the present case, having found that no legal contract bound the parties, it would be manifestly unjust to fail to consider appellant's claim on the ground that there might have been a contract or that the parties had attempted to enter into a contract.

Quasi-contracts, or contracts implied in law, are to be distinguished from express contracts or contracts implied in fact. "[U]nlike true contracts, quasi-contracts are not based on the apparent intention of the parties to undertake the performances in question, nor are they promises. They are obligations created by law for reasons of justice." *Restatement (Second) of Contracts*, § 5, comment b at 24 (Tent. Draft No. 1, 1964). See also Corbin, Contracts, § 19 (1950); * * * Quasi-contracts may be found in the absence of any expression of assent by the party to be charged and may indeed be found in spite of the party's contrary intention. * * * Consequently, the failure of the Company's Suggestion Committee to accept the appellant's suggestion is not determinative of appellant's quasi-contractual cause of action.

* * *

MR. JUSTICE ROBERTS (concurring):

I agree that appellee's preliminary objections should be dismissed and this case should be permitted to go to trial, but I do so because, in my view, appellant's complaint alleges facts which if established would prove that appellee's actions have created a contract.

* * *

I cannot accept, however, the majority's conclusion that appellant can withstand appellee's preliminary objections on an "unjust enrichment" theory. When appellant submitted his suggestion on appellee's form, in accordance with appellee's procedure, in my view he gave up any claim he might have had to unjust enrichment damages. If appellant is to recover at all, it must be within the limitations of appellee's procedure for offering suggestions. I do not believe that it is wise to become entangled in metaphysical notions of whether appellee extended an offer or an invitation to deal, and whether appellant thus tendered an acceptance or an offer. In my view it is enough to say that appellant cannot, under these circumstances, recover outside of appellee's established procedure, a procedure appellant accepted when tendering his suggestion, and thus unjust enrichment in my judgment is not appropriate.

* * *

MR. CHIEF JUSTICE BELL (dissenting):

The Majority admits there was no fraud or deceit by defendant. I am strongly opposed to the doctrine of unjust enrichment. Furthermore, even if the doctrine be judicially adopted by this Court, it cannot be applied in this case in view of the written contract which so clearly prescribes and defines, and thus limits, the rights of the parties.

QUESTIONS AND NOTE

1. Questions about the facts of this case

   1.1. Did the court believe that the company's redesign of the panels was "independent action" taken without knowledge of Schott's earlier suggestion? Does it matter?

   1.2. If the reasons for the company's rejection of Schott's suggestion were valid when made, is it unjust for the company to later use that suggestion, after circumstances change, without compensating Schott?

   1.3. What is the significance of the fact that, at the time of the resubmittal of Schott's suggestion, the company acknowledged that it was undertaking an effort to redesign the panels to include partial nonmagnetic materials?

   1.4. What do you suppose Chief Justice Bell has against the doctrine of unjust enrichment?

2. Questions about the law

   2.1. Why was the dismissal of the plaintiff's breach of contract claim affirmed on appeal?

   2.2. Do you agree with Chief Justice Bell that the parties can, by their contract, preclude the possibility of a claim for restitution?

   2.3. Justice Roberts seems to believe that the existence of a valid contract would preclude a claim for restitution. Do you agree? If Justice Roberts' view had prevailed, what would Schott's argument be on remand to establish the existence of a contract?

   2.4. Note that Schott's complaint prayed for damages equal to 20 percent of the savings realized by the company for use of his suggestion, as determined by an accounting. Was that proper in view of the fact that the suggestion program promised cash awards ranging from $5 to $15,000?

3. Note

   The aim of restitution is to make the defendant account for the value of the benefit conferred on the defendant. Suppose, however, that during the course of contractual negotiations, one party performs work at the request of the other, but those negotiations never ripen into an enforceable contract. If those services do not *benefit* the requesting party, can the person providing the services nevertheless bring a claim for unjust enrichment? *See Earhart v. William Low Co.*, 25 Cal.3d 503, 158 Cal.Rptr. 887, 600 P.2d 1344 (1979).

4. **You Be the Lawyer!**

If you are retained to handle the trial on remand for Mr. Schott, what are the key facts you will seek to establish in order to support your claim for recovery?

C. NOT AT THE REQUEST OF THE DEFENDANT

QUESTION BEFORE THE CASE

Does the fact that the defendant did not request the benefit make it an easier or a harder case for recovery?

CABLEVISION OF BRECKENRIDGE, INC. V. TANNHAUSER CONDOMINIUM ASSOCIATION

Supreme Court of Colorado
649 P.2d 1093 (1982)

LOHR, J.

We granted certiorari to review the decision of the Colorado Court of Appeals in *Cablevision of Breckenridge, Inc. v. Tannhauser Condominium Association*, * * * which reversed the judgment of the Summit County District Court awarding the plaintiff, Cablevision of Breckenridge, Inc. (Cablevision), damages for the wrongful conversion of its subscription cable service. We reverse the decision of the court of appeals and remand for reinstatement of the district court judgment.

I.

This case was tried to the district court under a stipulated set of facts which included those that follow. Cablevision is a corporation engaged in providing cable television and FM radio to its subscribers in areas where the television signals are weak or nonexistent. This is a frequently encountered problem in the vicinity of Breckenridge, Colorado, because the topography of the community and its distance from the originating broadcast stations generally result in an inability to receive a useful broadcast signal when using only the traditional antennas normally employed by individual households.

In order to provide its service, Cablevision constructed several antennas on a mountain peak near Breckenridge, by which it receives six television stations as well as FM radio. At the point of reception, the television signals are strong enough to reproduce a black and white picture, but are too weak to allow color reproduction. Consequently, the signals are fed into a "pre-amp," which magnifies their strength. The signals are then transmitted to a "head-end" building, located near the receiving antennas, where they are passed through a channel processor and mixer for the purpose of improving the clarity of the picture produced by the transmission. From this building, the signals are sent by coaxial cable to the "hub" facility in Breckenridge, and thence through distribution lines to the individual subscribers. Additional amplification of the signals is necessary as they are transmitted through the system, so amplifiers are installed along the distribution lines. Cablevision's capital investment in the transmission system is approximately $450,000.

The stipulated facts further establish that in October 1972 Cablevision entered into an oral agreement for the provision of subscription cable services with Judy Keller, who was acting on behalf of the owners of the condominium units comprising the Tannhauser I development in Breckenridge. The Tannhauser I building consisted of 33 condominium units, and each was to receive the Cablevision service. Pursuant to this agreement Cablevision installed the equipment necessary to provide its service to each of the units. This was accomplished by running a connecting line from the distribution system to an amplifier located inside Tannhauser I. The signals were then transmitted from this amplifier to individual wall plates serving each of the units. From January 1, 1972, through March 1974, Tannhauser I paid for the service to these 33 units at a specified rate per unit.

Effective May 1974, Cablevision ceased billing for service to 33 units and began billing for service to only three units. This was done at the request of Jerry White, whose status is not described in the stipulation but who apparently acted as a representative for the Tannhauser I owners. The stipulation reflects disagreement over the exact events leading to this change in service, but it is undisputed that the Cablevision amplifier inside Tannhauser I was removed; that White then substituted his own amplifier and connected it to the Cablevision line; and that, following May 1, television and FM radio service was still provided to all 33 units of Tannhauser I despite the payment to Cablevision for service to only three of those units. This state of affairs continued from May 1, 1974, to approximately December 1, 1976.

In the fall of 1974 a second building, known as Tannhauser II and comprised of 25 condominium units, was constructed near Tannhauser I. Cablevision was never requested to supply service to Tannhauser II. However, the new building was wired internally for cable television and

FM radio, and in November 1974 White supervised and assisted in the installation of a cable between Tannhauser I and Tannhauser II enabling extension of the Cablevision service to each of the 25 units in Tannhauser II. Tannhauser II began receiving the Cablevision transmission approximately November 30, 1974. Cablevision subsequently discovered the unauthorized use of its transmission by Tannhauser I and II and terminated all service to the condominiums about December 1, 1976.

Thereafter, Cablevision brought the present action, naming the condominium associations for Tannhausers I and II and the owners of the individual condominium units as defendants. Cablevision's amended complaint contained eight claims for relief, including breach of contract, concealment, conversion, various claims of unjust enrichment, and a request for injunctive relief.

However, as part of the pre-trial stipulation of facts summarized above, the parties submitted for judicial resolution the following single stipulated issue:

> Have the Defendants, or any of them, breached any contract with Plaintiff, written or oral, in fact or implied, for which Plaintiff is entitled for damages, actual or punitive?

After a hearing, the trial court entered an oral ruling incorporating the parties' stipulated facts, and holding that the defendants were liable for conversion of Cablevision's service. The parties had originally provided in their stipulation that, in the event of recovery, the damages would be $12,195, plus appropriate interest. However, the defendants advised the court subsequent to entry of the stipulation that they objected to this figure, so a further hearing was held on the question of damages. The court then entered its written judgment. The court again adopted the stipulation of the parties as its findings of fact and concluded:

> The plaintiff's property and services in the furnishing of cable television is a legally protected interest for which it is entitled to charge an appropriate and lawful rate to its subscribers. The defendants, through the actions stated in the Stipulation, have converted those protected interests without fully paying for them.

Based upon the damages hearing, the court entered judgment for actual damages of $11,597.50 plus statutory interest and court costs, and denied the prayer for punitive damages. The defendants then appealed.

The court of appeals reversed. It held that the trial court erred in ruling that the defendants were liable on the basis that they converted Cablevision's property interests because, pursuant to the parties' stipulation, "the only issue before the trial court was whether any defendant breached any contract with [Cablevision]." It further held that, because the stipulation did not establish the essential elements of a contract, Cablevision had not proved its breach of contract claim. Therefore, it directed the trial court to enter judgment for the defendants.

We accepted certiorari to review the court of appeals' decision. * * * [W]e do not address these arguments because we conclude that the judgment of the trial court is supported by an alternative basis of liability raised by the stipulated issue submitted by the parties.

II.

As stipulated by the parties, the issue for decision was whether "the Defendants, or any of them, *breached any contract* with Plaintiff, written or oral, in fact or implied." (Emphasis added.) We read the mention of "implied" contracts as a reference to the doctrine of quasi-contract or unjust enrichment, under which courts imply a contract as a matter of law where necessary to avoid unjust enrichment. This interpretation is based in part upon the apparent intent of parties in distinguishing "implied contracts" and contracts "in fact," and draws further support from the inclusion of unjust enrichment claims in the complaint.

In addressing only the issue of whether the stipulated evidence established a contract in fact, the court of appeals did not consider this alternative basis of liability. We conclude that the facts of this case present an appropriate basis for application of the doctrine of unjust enrichment, and reverse the decision of the court of appeals for that reason.

To recover under a theory of quasi-contract or unjust enrichment, a plaintiff must show (1) that a benefit was conferred on the defendant by the plaintiff, (2) that the benefit was appreciated by the defendant, and (3) that the benefit was accepted by the defendant under such circumstances that it would be inequitable for it to be retained without payment of its value. * * * Application of the doctrine does not depend upon the existence of a contract, express or implied in fact, but on the need to avoid unjust enrichment of the defendant notwithstanding the absence of an actual agreement to pay for the benefit conferred. * * * The scope of this remedy is broad, cutting across both contract and tort law, with its application guided by the underlying principle of avoiding the unjust enrichment of one party at the expense of another. 1 G. Palmer, *The Law of Restitution* § 1.1 (1978); 66 *Am. Jur. 2d Restitution and Implied Contracts, supra*, § 11.

In the present case, we conclude that a benefit was conferred upon the defendants by Cablevision and that the defendants appreciated this benefit. The defendants' initial payment for this service in connection with the 33 Tannhauser I condominium units and their continued payment for service to three of those units amply demonstrate both the beneficial service provided by Cablevision and the appreciation of that service by the defendants. Instructive in this regard is the broad definition of benefit contained in the *Restatement of Restitution* § 1, comment b (1937):

> A person confers a benefit upon another if he gives to the other possession of or some other interest in money, land, chattels, or choses in action, performs services beneficial to or at the request of the other, satisfies a debt or a duty of the other, or in any way adds to the other's security or advantage. He confers a benefit not only where he adds to the property of another, but also where he saves the other from expense or loss. The word "benefit," therefore, denotes any form of advantage.

We also conclude that the defendants have retained this service under such circumstances that it would be inequitable to allow its use without payment for its value. The stipulated facts demonstrate that Cablevision never intended to provide its service to all of Tannhausers I and II in exchange for payment in connection with only three units. Indeed, upon discovery of the unauthorized use of its signals, Cablevision terminated all service to the defendants. Further, the defendants were not innocent or unwilling recipients of this benefit, but actively facilitated its provision.

* * *

The defendants have accepted a service from Cablevision that is customarily paid for and, in fact, was initially paid for by these defendants. The defendants were active participants in obtaining this benefit from Cablevision, and, based on the initial agreement to serve Tannhauser I, their representatives must have acted with the knowledge that Cablevision expected compensation for each Tannhauser unit receiving the Cablevision transmission. Under these facts, restitution is appropriate to avoid unjust enrichment to the defendants. * * *

The damages awarded were based upon the rate prescribed in Cablevision's franchise from Breckenridge, which correspond to the rate paid for the three Tannhauser I units during the period of unauthorized use of the Cablevision signals. This was an appropriate measure of the benefit conferred upon the defendants and the amount of restitution due.

* * *

We reverse the decision of the court of appeals and return the case to that court for remand to the trial court with directions to enter judgment in accordance with the views expressed in this opinion.

QUESTIONS

1. Questions about the facts of this case

    1.1. Why did Cablevision's lawyer agree in the pre-trial stipulation that the only issue to be resolved at trial was the issue of breach of contract? Was that a mistake? Was it malpractice?

1.2. Did the residents of the Tannhauser units know they were getting for free a service that other people pay for? Was that fact important to the court? Should it matter? If an ATM malfunctions and gives you twice as much cash as you requested, without charging your account, is it a good defense to the bank's unjust enrichment claim if you can show that you were unaware of the error?

1.3. How important was the fact that the Tannhauser I units had received and paid for cable service for over two years?

2. Questions about the law

2.1. What was the key difference in the interpretation given to the parties' pre-trial stipulation by the Colorado Court of Appeals and the Colorado Supreme Court? Did the Colorado Supreme Court conclude that there had been a breach of contract in the traditional sense?

2.2. The court awarded damages based on the rate prescribed in Cablevision's franchise from the City of Breckenridge* during the period of the unauthorized use. Was that appropriate? If you represented the defendants, what kind of evidence would you have sought to introduce to justify a lesser recovery?

3. **You Be the Lawyer!**

If you had represented Cablevision at trial, how would you have insisted that the pretrial stipulation be worded?

QUESTIONS BEFORE THE CASE

1. How important is it to the result in this case that the plaintiff's personal and business contributions increased the wealth accumulated during the couple's relationship?

2. What other areas of contract law doctrine that we have studied does this case implicate?

---

* Actually, Breckenridge fancies itself (even if unofficially) a "kingdom," not a city, and, as far as we know, the only such governmental entity in the country. But that's another story.

WATTS V. WATTS

Supreme Court of Wisconsin
137 Wis.2d 506, 405 N.W.2d 303 (1987)

ABRAHAMSON, J.

This is an appeal from a judgment of the circuit court for Dane County, William D. Byrne, Judge, dismissing Sue Ann Watts' amended complaint, pursuant to sec. 802.06(2)(f), Stats. 1985–86, for failure to state a claim upon which relief may be granted. * * *

The case involves a dispute between Sue Ann Evans Watts, the plaintiff, and James Watts, the defendant, over their respective interests in property accumulated during their nonmarital cohabitation relationship which spanned 12 years and produced two children. The case presents an issue of first impression and comes to this court at the pleading stage of the case, before trial and before the facts have been determined.

* * *

We test the sufficiency of the plaintiff's amended complaint by first setting forth the facts asserted in the complaint and then analyzing each of the five legal theories upon which the plaintiff rests her claim for relief.

I.

The plaintiff commenced this action in 1982. The plaintiff's amended complaint alleges the following facts, which for purposes of this appeal must be accepted as true. The plaintiff and the defendant met in 1967, when she was 19 years old, was living with her parents and was working full time as a nurse's aide in preparation for a nursing career. Shortly after the parties met, the defendant persuaded the plaintiff to move into an apartment paid for by him and to quit her job. According to the amended complaint, the defendant "indicated" to the plaintiff that he would provide for her.

Early in 1969, the parties began living together in a "marriage-like" relationship, holding themselves out to the public as husband and wife. The plaintiff assumed the defendant's surname as her own. Subsequently, she gave birth to two children who were also given the defendant's surname. The parties filed joint income tax returns and maintained joint bank accounts asserting that they were husband and wife. The defendant insured the plaintiff as his wife on his medical insurance policy. He also took out a life insurance policy on her as his wife, naming himself as the beneficiary. The parties purchased real and personal property as husband and wife. The plaintiff executed documents and obligated herself on promissory notes to lending institutions as the defendant's wife.

During their relationship, the plaintiff contributed childcare and homemaking services, including cleaning, cooking, laundering, shopping, running errands, and maintaining the grounds surrounding the parties' home. Additionally, the plaintiff contributed personal property to the relationship which she owned at the beginning of the relationship or acquired through gifts or purchases during the relationship. She served as hostess for the defendant for social and business-related events. The amended complaint further asserts that periodically, between 1969 and 1975, the plaintiff cooked and cleaned for the defendant and his employees while his business, a landscaping service, was building and landscaping a golf course.

From 1973 to 1976, the plaintiff worked 20–25 hours per week at the defendant's office, performing duties as a receptionist, typist, and assistant book-keeper. From 1976 to 1981, the plaintiff worked 40–60 hours per week at a business she started with the defendant's sister-in-law, then continued and managed herself after the dissolution of that partnership. The plaintiff further alleges that in 1981 the defendant made their relationship so intolerable that she was forced to move from their home and their relationship was irretrievably broken. Subsequently, the defendant barred the plaintiff from returning to her business.

The plaintiff alleges that during the parties' relationship, and because of her domestic and business contributions, the business and personal wealth of the couple increased. Furthermore, the plaintiff alleges that she never received any compensation for these contributions to the relationship and that the defendant indicated to the plaintiff both orally and through his conduct that he considered her to be his wife and that she would share equally in the increased wealth.

The plaintiff asserts that since the breakdown of the relationship the defendant has refused to share equally with her the wealth accumulated through their joint efforts or to compensate her in any way for her contributions to the relationship.

* * *

The plaintiff's fourth theory of recovery involves unjust enrichment. Essentially, she alleges that the defendant accepted and retained the benefit of services she provided knowing that she expected to share equally in the wealth accumulated during their relationship. She argues that it is unfair for the defendant to retain all the assets they accumulated under these circumstances and that a constructive trust should be imposed on the property as a result of the defendant's unjust enrichment. In his brief, the defendant does not attack specifically either the legal theory or the factual allegations made by the plaintiff.

Unlike claims for breach of an express or implied in fact contract, a claim of unjust enrichment does not arise out of an agreement entered into by the parties. Rather, an action for recovery based upon unjust enrichment is grounded on the moral principle that one who has received a benefit has a duty to make restitution where retaining such a benefit would be unjust. * * *

Because no express or implied in fact agreement exists between the parties, recovery based upon unjust enrichment is sometimes referred to as "quasi contract," or contract "implied in law" rather than "implied in fact." Quasi contracts are obligations created by law to prevent injustice. * * *

In Wisconsin, an action for unjust enrichment, or quasi contract, is based upon proof of three elements: (1) a benefit conferred on the defendant by the plaintiff, (2) appreciation or knowledge by the defendant of the benefit, and (3) acceptance or retention of the benefit by the defendant under circumstances making it inequitable for the defendant to retain the benefit. * * *

The plaintiff has cited no cases directly supporting actions in unjust enrichment by unmarried cohabitants, and the defendant provides no authority against it. * * *

As part of his general argument, the defendant claims that the court should leave the parties to an illicit relationship such as the one in this case essentially as they are found, providing no relief at all to either party. * * *

As we have discussed previously, allowing no relief at all to one party in a so-called "illicit" relationship effectively provides total relief to the other, by leaving that party owner of all the assets acquired through the efforts of both. Yet it cannot seriously be argued that the party retaining all the assets is less "guilty" than the other. Such a result is contrary to the principles of equity. Many courts have held, and we now so hold, that unmarried cohabitants may raise claims based upon unjust enrichment following the termination of their relationships where one of the parties attempts to retain an unreasonable amount of the property acquired through the efforts of both.

In this case, the plaintiff alleges that she contributed both property and services to the parties' relationship. She claims that because of these contributions the parties' assets increased, but that she was never compensated for her contributions. She further alleges that the defendant, knowing that the plaintiff expected to share in the property accumulated, "accepted the services rendered to him by the plaintiff" and that it would be unfair under the circumstances to allow him to retain everything while she receives nothing. We conclude that the facts alleged are sufficient to state a claim for recovery based upon unjust enrichment.

As part of the plaintiff's unjust enrichment claim, she has asked that a constructive trust be imposed on the assets that the defendant acquired during their relationship. A constructive trust is an equitable device created by law to prevent unjust enrichment. * * * To state a claim on the theory of constructive trust the complaint must state facts sufficient to show (1) unjust enrichment and (2) abuse of a confidential relationship or some other form of unconscionable conduct. The latter element can be inferred from allegations in the complaint which show, for example, a family relationship, a close personal relationship, or the parties' mutual trust. These facts are alleged in this complaint or may be inferred. * * * Therefore, we hold that if the plaintiff can prove the elements of unjust enrichment to the satisfaction of the circuit court, she will be entitled to demonstrate further that a constructive trust should be imposed as a remedy.

* * *

You Be the Lawyer!

If Sue Ann Evans had consulted you in 1967, just before moving in with James Watts, would you have advised have recommended that she get a "prenup" from Mr. Watts? By the way, Dr. James W. Watts was a neurosurgeon who advocated and was a prolific practitioner of psychosurgery, and, more specifically, the lobotomy. He is most well known for having performed the lobotomy of Rosemary Kennedy, sister of President John F. Kennedy. Would knowing this information affect in any way your advice to Sue Ann, or would that just be paranoid?

PROBLEM: THE GOOD SAMARITAN AND THE GREEDY DOCTOR

One day, Epstein, an elderly man, was crossing the street when he was hit by a car. Markell, an attorney who had dropped out of medical school several years earlier, witnessed the accident and rushed to Epstein's aid. Able to draw on his prior medical training, Markell saved Epstein's life. Thereafter, he submitted a bill to Epstein for the reasonable value of his services. Epstein balked at paying, so Markell now brought his legal training to bear and filed suit. Should Markell recover? Would it make a difference if Epstein had not survived the accident? How about if Markell were a real doctor? How about if the basis for Epstein's refusal to pay is his strong religious convictions against seeking medical intervention under any circumstances? *See In re Crisan's Estate*, 362 Mich. 569, 107 N.W.2d 907 (1961).

D. AT THE REQUEST OF A THIRD PARTY

QUESTIONS BEFORE THE CASE

1. Did the plaintiff in this case have a contractual promise to pay the amount for which it seeks recovery on a quasi-contract theory?
2. If so, why did that not preclude a quantum meruit recovery?

FLOORING SYSTEMS, INC. V. RADISSON GROUP, INC.

Supreme Court of Arizona
160 Ariz. 224, 772 P.2d 578 (1989)

CORCORAN, JUSTICE.

Plaintiff Flooring Systems, Inc. appeals from summary judgment entered in favor of defendants Radisson Group, Inc. and CSA, Inc. We granted review to consider whether summary judgment was properly granted on Flooring's unjust enrichment claim. * * *

Facts

In July 1985, CSA, as Radisson's agent, invited Flooring to bid on carpeting work for the Scottsdale Radisson Resort. Flooring submitted a bid, which CSA accepted in August 1985.

In October 1985, Radisson chose Five Star Services, Inc. as the general contractor for the renovations and an agreement was executed. Five Star then entered into a subcontract agreement with Flooring for the same carpeting work included in Flooring's bid that CSA accepted. Neither Radisson nor CSA was a party to this subcontract agreement. During renovation, Flooring submitted all payment requests to Five Star, not Radisson.

Although Flooring completed its work, Five Star failed to pay Flooring the full amount due under the subcontract. Because of Five Star's default, Radisson withheld approximately $25,000 due under its general contract with Five Star. Section 6.2 of Radisson's general contract with Five Star permitted Radisson to withhold final payment until Five Star satisfied "all known indebtedness" connected with the work.

Flooring sued Radisson, CSA and Five Star to recover the amount due. Five Star later filed for bankruptcy and was dismissed as a party.

Procedure and Issue

In its complaint, Flooring alleged breach of contract and unjust enrichment. Radisson and CSA moved for summary judgment, arguing that, * * * the existence of a subcontract agreement between Five Star and

Flooring precluded any recovery from Radisson and CSA under an unjust enrichment theory. The trial court granted summary judgment against Flooring. The court of appeals affirmed. * * *

Discussion

Flooring contends that it is entitled to recover on its unjust enrichment claim because it has sold and installed $59,000 worth of carpet, and Radisson has paid no one for at least $25,000 of it. In response, Radisson and CSA rely on *Stratton v. Inspiration Consol. Copper Co.,* 140 Ariz. 528, 683 P.2d 327 (App.1984), and *Advance Leasing & Crane Co. v. Del E. Webb Corp.*, 117 Ariz. 451, 573 P.2d 525 (App.1977).

In *Stratton*, the defendant hired a general contractor to do remodeling. The general contractor subcontracted the painting work to the plaintiff. Defendant approved the general contractor's hiring of plaintiff and inspected the work from time to time, but no contract existed between defendant and plaintiff. Defendant fully paid the general contractor pursuant to the contract and later changed orders, but the general contractor did not pay plaintiff. Attempting to recover from defendant, plaintiff filed a mechanic's lien and sued to foreclose on defendant's property. The complaint also alleged unjust enrichment.

The trial court granted summary judgment in defendant's favor. The court of appeals affirmed, stating that "the doctrine of unjust enrichment has no application to the owner where an explicit contract exists between the subcontractor and the prime contractor." 140 Ariz. at 531, 683 P.2d at 330.

The *Stratton* court relied on *Advance Leasing*, in which the court of appeals also held that a contract between a general contractor and a subcontractor precluded recovery by the subcontractor against the owner. 117 Ariz. at 452, 573 P.2d at 526. In so holding, the court indicated its agreement with *Restatement of Restitution* § 110 (1937), which states:

> § 110 Restitution from Beneficiary of a Contract with Third Person Who Has Failed to Perform.
>
> A person who has conferred a benefit upon another as the performance of a contract with a third person is not entitled to restitution from the other merely because of the failure of performance by the third person.

The facts in *Advance Leasing* were similar to those in *Stratton*: no contract existed between the owner and the subcontractor and, although the owner fully paid the general contractor, the general contractor failed to pay the subcontractor.

In support of its position, Flooring relies on *Commercial Cornice & Millwork, Inc. v. Camel Constr. Serv. Corp.,* 154 Ariz. 34, 739 P.2d 1351

(App.1987), and *Costanzo v. Stewart*, 9 Ariz. App. 430, 453 P.2d 526 (1969). The plaintiff in *Commercial Cornice*, a subcontractor, alleged that the owner had agreed to pay the full amount due under the contract between plaintiff and the general contractor. In fact, the owner had paid a portion of the amount due, but neither the owner nor the general contractor paid the remainder. The trial court granted the owner's motion to dismiss for failure to state a claim because of plaintiff's contract with the general contractor.

The court of appeals held that dismissal was inappropriate, despite the existence of the contract between the subcontractor and the general contractor. The court distinguished *Stratton* and *Advance Leasing* by noting that in both cases the owner had fully paid the general contractor, and thus was not unjustly enriched.

The owner in *Costanzo* had assured the subcontractor that "the money for the job was in escrow and that he would write a check to him and [the general contractor] when the job was finished. * * *" 9 Ariz. App. at 431, 453 P.2d at 527. The subcontractor completed the job, but the bank did not honor the general contractor's check to him. In permitting the subcontractor to recover from the owner on an unjust enrichment claim, the court of appeals commented, "Costanzo [the owner] has paid no one anything for the work done." 9 Ariz. App. at 431, 453 P.2d at 527, citing *Restatement of Restitution* § 40, comment d (1937),[1] the court stated:

> The trial court found, and the testimony shows, that defendant [the owner] knew plaintiff [the subcontractor] was concerned about his payment and he assured him escrow arrangements had been made. These facts establish a good case for restitution. 9 Ariz. App. at 432–33, 453 P.2d at 528–29.

Neither party cites our decision in *Murdock-Bryant Constr., Inc. v. Pearson*, 146 Ariz. 48, 703 P.2d 1197 (1985). In that case, we held that a general contractor's joint venturers were liable for benefits received from a subcontractor, even though they became joint venturers after the general contractor had contracted with the subcontractor. We stated that "a party may be liable to make restitution for benefits received, even though he has committed no tort and is not contractually obligated to the plaintiff." 146 Ariz. at 53, 703 P.2d at 1202. We set forth the following analysis to be used in deciding unjust enrichment claims:

> In determining whether it would be unjust to allow the retention of benefits without compensation, a court need not find that the

---

[1] Restatement of Restitution § 40, comment d (1937) provides:

[W]here a person accepts services from another, having reason to know that the other is under a belief that the recipient or a third person has promised compensation or is otherwise under a duty to pay for them * * * the recipient is liable for the reasonable value of the services irrespective of their value to him.

> defendant intended to compensate the plaintiff for the services rendered or that the plaintiff intended that the defendant be the party to make compensation. This is because the duty to compensate for unjust enrichment is an obligation implied by law without reference to the intention of the parties. 1 S. Williston, Contracts § 3A at 13 (3rd ed. 1957). What is important is that it be shown that it was not intended or expected that the services be rendered or the benefit conferred gratuitously, and that the benefit was not "conferred officiously."

146 Ariz. at 54, 703 P.2d at 1203, *quoting Pyeatte v. Pyeatte,* 135 Ariz. 346, 353, 661 P.2d 196, 203 (App.1982). We explained that the subcontractor's contract with the general contractor

> has importance in considering [the] claim for unjust enrichment because it both evidences [plaintiff's] expectation of compensation and the circumstances which make it unjust to allow [defendant] to retain the benefits.

Id.

Using the above analysis, we find that Radisson and CSA were not entitled as a matter of law to prevail on Flooring's unjust enrichment claim. Flooring clearly did not intend to provide carpeting work gratuitously or officiously; its contract with Five Star evinces its intent to be paid for its services. Although Flooring has completed its work, it has not been paid fully for its services. CSA invited Flooring to bid on the job and accepted Flooring's bid. Radisson obviously knew that Flooring had not been paid and on that basis Radisson withheld final payment from Five Star. Under these circumstances, to permit Radisson and CSA to retain the full benefit of Flooring's work at Flooring's expense may be unjust. We therefore hold that summary judgment in favor of Radisson and CSA on this issue was improper.

Radisson argues that it is merely protecting itself from having to pay an amount in excess of that contracted for, should other subcontractors on the remodeling job also seek payment, and that it will pay the approximately $25,000 retained to Five Star and/or its creditors after the court enters a final, non-appealable judgment in its favor. Radisson may have a remedy through interpleader, requiring all parties with potential claims to the retained funds to bring their claims before a single court for resolution. However, Radisson may not merely retain the money, making promises of disbursement at some future time.

CONCLUSION

We hold that summary judgment was improperly granted on Flooring's unjust enrichment claim and therefore reverse the trial court's judgment on that issue, as well as the trial court's award of attorneys' fees to Radisson and CSA. * * * We vacate that portion of the opinion that is inconsistent with this opinion, including the award of attorneys' fees to Radisson and CSA, and remand the case to the trial court for proceedings consistent with this opinion.

* * *

QUESTIONS AND NOTE

1. Questions about the facts of this case

   1.1. How important in this case was the fact that CSA had solicited Flooring Systems' original bid for the carpeting work?

   1.2. How important was it to the decision in *Flooring Systems* that Radisson had withheld a portion of the contract price due to the general contractor, Five Star Services?

2. Questions about the law

   2.1. Is the court saying that it is always unjust for an owner to retain the benefits of a subcontractor's work without paying?

   2.2. On remand, should Flooring Systems' recovery be limited to the amount withheld ($25,000), even though its claim was for a greater amount ($59,000)? If so, what about other unpaid subcontractors who come along later; are they just out of luck? If not, what should Radisson do? Will the interpleader technique suggested by the court be a viable approach?

3. Note

   In most states, subcontractors, suppliers, and laborers who work on a construction project are protected by statutory mechanic's liens. These statutes differ considerably from state to state in terms of scope and procedure. Generally speaking, however, they allow unpaid suppliers of goods and services on the project to file a *lien* against the owner's property for the amount they are owed by the general contractor. A lien is a charge against the property rather than an *in personam* claim against the owner. Ultimately, the lien must be satisfied through a judicial foreclosure proceeding in which the property is auctioned to the highest bidder and the lienholder is paid with the proceeds. In the typical situation, the owner will already have paid the general contractor the full contract price. However, if the general contractor is dishonest or insolvent, it will not always make payment under its subcontracts with laborers and suppliers, thus giving rise to their lien claims. To avoid the loss of her property, obviously the owner will have to pay the lien. This means the owner will end up having paid twice for the same work and will be left only with what often amounts to a worthless claim against the general contractor. Knowing how these mechanic's liens work, why didn't Flooring Systems seek to enforce a lien against Radisson rather than suing for breach of contract and unjust enrichment? If you are contracting for a major renovation on your house, what steps might you take to ensure that the property does not later become subject to such liens?

4. **You Be the Lawyer!**

   How can a subcontractor like Flooring Systems protect itself from the perfidy or insolvency of a general contractor in circumstances like these?

PROBLEM ON THIRD PARTY BENEFITS

Ponoroff retained Epstein, attorney-at-law, to pursue a claim against the Great South Health Network, Ponoroff's health insurer, for failing to pay expenses incurred by Ponoroff at the Tulane Medical Center ("TMC"). As a result of Epstein's adroit lawyering skills, Great South finally capitulated and agreed to pay the disputed charges. Thereupon, Epstein sued TMC claiming that the latter benefited from his services by virtue of receiving a payment for services from Ponoroff's insurer that Ponoroff never would have paid out of his own pocket. What result? *See generally Lynch v. Deaconess Medical Center,* 113 Wash.2d 162, 776 P.2d 681 (1989).

---

3. PROMISSORY RESTITUTION

WEBB V. MCGOWIN

In *Webb*, *supra*, at 318, the Alabama Court of Appeals recognized, and the Alabama Supreme Court affirmed, that an exception to the general rule that past consideration is not good consideration exists when the promise is made in recognition of an antecedent benefit conferred on the defendant by the plaintiff. As we saw, the so-called "material benefit rule" is now codified in § 86 of the *Restatement (Second) of Contracts.* Take a moment to review § 86 again. It sets forth the elements that must be established in order for a party to recover on a promise even though the benefit which induced the promise occurred before it was made. Do these elements sound familiar? In fact, do they even sound a little bit like the elements for recovery under quasi-contract? The similarity is no accident. There is unquestionably a relationship between the material benefit rule and the doctrine of unjust enrichment. Consider whether, if McGowin had not made the promise to pay Webb $15 every two weeks, Webb could have succeeded in an action for unjust enrichment? Clearly, the benefit conferred was material; McGowin's life, and the exigency of the situation would excuse Webb's failure to give McGowin the opportunity to deny the benefit. So far so good. But was there really an expectation of compensation on Webb's part? Probably not; the act was gratuitous. However, when you add to the mix McGowin's subsequent decision to agree to pay a reasonable amount in recognition of the benefit conferred, the case for enforcement becomes sufficiently compelling, or so the argument goes, to justify the case for enforcement. Professor (later, Judge) Robert Braucher, the first Reporter for the *Restatement (Second) of Contracts*, in commenting on an earlier draft of § 86, stated that the section fairly "bristles with nonspecific concepts." Do you agree? At the same time, however, he also noted that the provision "seeks to draw a distinction between the cases involving moral obligation based on gratitude and sentiment and those cases which are on the borderline of quasi-contract. * * *" Braucher, *Freedom of Contract and the Second Restatement*, 78 YALE L.J. 598, 605 (1969).

Recall in Chapter 3 we examined two other cases (*Harrington v. Taylor*, *supra*, at 278, and *Mills v. Wyman*, *supra*, at 279), in both of which the court rejected the argument that past consideration creates a moral obligation sufficient to support enforcement of a subsequent promise of payment. Instead of asserting the enforceability of the actual promises made by the defendants in *Harrington* and *Mills,* what if the plaintiffs in those cases had brought a claim for restitution based on unjust enrichment? Would either or both of them have prevailed? Why did the court in *Mills* stress the age of the defendant's son? If the son had been a minor or a dependent how would that have helped the case for recovery for breach of contract? For unjust enrichment?

Look again at the elements of § 86, specifically subsection (2), which provides that the promise is *not* binding if (a) the promisee conferred the benefit as a *gift*, or (b) the promisor has not been unjustly enriched. Can an act be gratuitous and still not intended as a gift? We think so. Was Webb making a gift when he decided to fall with the 75-pound pine block? The other limitation in § 86(2) is that the promise will not be enforced to the extent that its value is disproportionate to the benefit. Is there a link to the doctrine of unjust enrichment here, too? In answering that question for yourself, consider the material from Chapter 6 dealing with how to measure the value of the restitutionary interest.

---

4. OTHER REMEDIES FOR UNJUST ENRICHMENT

The idea behind quasi-contract is to prevent the inequitable enrichment of one party at the expense of the other. Thus, the benefit conferred must be restored if equity is to be done. That is to say, the defendant must make *restitution.* But sometimes that can be easier said than done, particularly when the benefit is not an object or commodity that is capable of being physically returned to the plaintiff. Also, as we observed in Chapter 7, when the basis of the plaintiff's claim is an action for restitution, then, unlike in a conventional breach of contract action where the object is to enforce a broken promise, it is not necessarily appropriate to award the plaintiff her "expectation" (*i.e.*, what she would have received had an actual promise been made by the defendant). Instead, in many cases, the court will have to determine the *reasonable value* of the benefit conferred in order to fashion an appropriate remedy. But often value, like beauty, is in the eye of the beholder.

In the next case, the plaintiffs have no contractual claim against the defendants—no claim in law. The plaintiffs do, however, assert the right to recover in equity. Pay particular attention to the way in which the claim is cast by the plaintiffs affects the remedy that the court awards.

QUESTIONS BEFORE THE CASE

1. How does the remedy of an "equitable lien," as discussed in this case, differ from the remedy of a "constructive trust" discussed in *Watts v. Watts, supra*?
2. What features does the equitable lien have in common with the constructive trust?

PULL V. BARNES

Supreme Court of Colorado
142 Colo. 272, 350 P.2d 828 (1960)

PER CURIAM:

The parties appear here in the same order they appeared in the trial court, namely Burnard T. and Margaret H. Pull as plaintiffs, and Margaret Barnes and Mary E. Moffat as defendants. * * *

The action was brought by the plaintiffs in September of 1956 in the district court of Jefferson County to determine the boundary line between properties owned by the plaintiffs and the defendants, for damages and other relief.

In June of 1953 the plaintiffs located a parcel of land about one acre in size in Jefferson County, upon which they desired to build a mountain home and began to search out the owners of it. Just west of the piece of land selected was a line of an old fence which had upon it "No Trespassing" signs. Plaintiffs proceeded to negotiate with and buy from the parties who, in good faith, asserted the title to the land now in question. It later was determined by a survey that the defendants Barnes and Moffat, who owned the land west of the fence line, actually owned most of the land east of the fence line which the plaintiffs believed they had purchased, and upon which they had constructed their cabin.

Prior to constructing their cabin the plaintiffs hired a licensed surveyor to stake out the corners of the cabin site, but did not ask him to survey the land itself to determine the boundary lines between their property and that of the defendants'. Construction of the cabin upon the site, with a concrete slab floor and foundation, was begun in August 1953 and substantially completed by the fall of 1953.

During the construction the defendants several times were on the scene and acted as neighbors-about-to-be. The evidence clearly discloses that neither party knew or even suspected at the time of the construction of the cabin that it was being built upon land belonging to defendants.

After the cabin was completed the defendant Barnes negotiated with plaintiffs for a right-of-way through the land upon which the plaintiffs had built their cabin, and upon being refused hired a surveyor, and for the first time learned that the cabin which the plaintiffs had erected was solely upon her and the defendant Moffatt's land. Thereupon defendants erected a fence excluding the plaintiffs from the cabin and the land until a preliminary injunction was entered in this case some two years later.

Defendants now assert dominion over the cabin, contending that the plaintiffs had no rights therein, it having been built on defendants' land and as a result became a part of the land by operation of law.

Plaintiffs contend that the principles laid down by *Golden Press v. Rylands,* 124 Colo. 122, 235 P. (2d) 592, which permitted relief to a party who had encroached to a small extent on his neighbor's land, should apply. Plaintiffs further contend that the defendants are estopped by reason of their conduct from asserting title to the house.

On the other hand defendants urged that the facts in the present case do not bring it within the rule of *Golden Press, supra,* and further in the light of *Jacobs v. Perry,* 135 Colo. 550, 313 P. (2d) 1008, the doctrine of estoppel cannot apply here.

The trial court held that the boundary line of the property was the line surveyed east of the old fence line, thereby placing the cabin entirely within the land owned by the defendants, and held that the doctrine announced in *Golden Press, supra,* did not apply and that *Jacobs, supra,* forbade the application of the doctrine of estoppel. Judgment was entered for the defendants. In the course of its findings the court said:

"We would be inclined to grant some relief with reference to this building if it were within our power to do so. However, the only suggestion that has been made to us would be relief under the principle as laid down in the case of *Golden Press v. Rylands,* 124 Colo. 122, and we believe that the principle of encroachment set forth in that case is not applicable."

The trial court was correct in determining that *Golden Press, supra,* presented a different fact situation than is presented here; however, it is clear from the trial court's finding that it was searching for an equitable remedy which it could apply and which would prevent the harshness of the ruling.

As an abstract principle of law it is true that the moment a house is built upon land, it belongs to the owner of the land by mere operation of law and he may possess and enjoy it as his own. But this is merely stating the technical rule of law by which the owner seeks to hold what, in a just sense, he never had the slightest title to; that is, the house if it were not attached to the realty. It is not answering the objection by merely and dryly stating that the law so holds; for admitting this to be so, in law, such a situation furnishes a strong ground why equity should and does interpose and grant relief in proper cases.

Here the powers of the trial court were invoked to settle a boundary dispute and the problems arising from the situation in which the plaintiffs and the defendants found themselves without bad faith on the part of any of the parties. The matter having been presented to the court, it was the court's duty to grant the relief in equity which the situation demanded.

We think the applicable rule is stated in *Johnson v. Dunkel (1955)*, 132 Colo. 383, 288 P. (2d) 343, and is peculiarly applicable to the situation before us. In that case the adjoining owner who had in good faith erected improvements on adjoining land, believing it to be his own, was granted the right to remove same if feasible and if not, then was given an equitable lien on the property for the value thereof.

The judgment is accordingly reversed with directions to the trial court to hold a further hearing to determine whether it would be practical and feasible for Pull to remove the improvements from the land in question, and if so to specify the conditions under which it shall be done. If removal of the cabin is not feasible, then the value thereof should be determined and the land subjected to a lien in favor of plaintiffs in an amount equal to the value so determined.

QUESTIONS AND NOTES

1. Questions about the facts of this case

   1.1. What facts are most helpful to the plaintiffs' case?

1.2. What facts are most helpful to support the defendants' contentions?

2. Questions about the law

2.1. What do you understand the court to be saying in this case about the relationship between law and equity?

2.2. On remand, if the trial court in *Pull* determines that removal is not feasible and, therefore, decides to impose an equitable lien on the defendants' property for the value of the cabin constructed on the defendants' land, how should "value" be determined under these circumstances? *See Restatement (Second) of Contracts* § 371. What if the defendants didn't really like the design of the cabin and planned to tear it down because they considered it an eyesore?

2.3. If removal of the cabin were practicable, can plaintiffs recover the costs associated with doing so?

3. Notes

3.1. In *Watts v. Watts, supra*, the plaintiff requested that a *constructive trust* be imposed on the defendant's assets acquired during the course of the relationship. In *Pull v. Barnes*, the Colorado Supreme Court directed that if removing the cabin was not feasible, the defendants' land should be subjected to an *equitable lien* in favor of the plaintiffs for the value of the improvements made on the land. As we noted earlier, a lien creates a charge against the property for the amount owed to the lienholder such that good title to the land cannot be conveyed until the lien is discharged by payment to the lienholder. Most liens, like most trusts, are created by agreement between the parties. In *Pull*, however, the court imposed the lien as a matter of law, rather than as a matter of contract, hence the term *equitable lien*. Similarly, a constructive trust is not a real trust in the conventional sense of the term, but instead is a remedy whereby the party with legal title to certain assets is deemed to hold title for the benefit of the party with a superior claim to such assets. Both constructive trusts and equitable liens are restitutionary remedies that may be employed by the court to prevent unjust enrichment. How would you describe the difference between the two? Why would the constructive trust not have been an appropriate remedy in *Pull*?

3.2. As we have seen, sometimes a court may simply award damages based on the monetary value of what the defendant has unjustly received from the plaintiff. Indeed, this is the traditional remedy at common law for recovery in a quasi-contract action. Historically, an action in quasi-contract was sometimes referred to as a count (cause of action) of *quantum meruit* (literally, "as much as it deserves"), and that terminology still shows up in cases today. We have also seen that such a recovery differs from a recovery under the contract and that, when the benefit conferred consists of something other than money, for example property or services, measuring the value of the restitutionary interest can get tricky. In case you forgot, let the cross-reference to our last case serve as a reminder.

4. **You Be the Lawyer!**

What steps would you have advised the Pulls to take before building their cabin, and perhaps even before purchasing the Jefferson County property? If the trial court's decision in this case had been affirmed, what recourse, if any, would you have advised the Pulls to pursue?

BRITTON V. TURNER

Supreme Court of New Hampshire
6 N.H. 481 (1834)

Supra p. 942.

CHAPTER 9

WHEN DO YOU HAVE RIGHTS AND DUTIES UNDER A CONTRACT THAT YOU DID NOT MAKE?

■ ■ ■

We have now covered the story of a contract from beginning to end. We have considered the questions:

- is there a contract, *i.e.*, an agreement that is legally enforceable?
- if so, what are its terms?
- have the two contracting parties performed pursuant to those terms?
- if not, is the nonperformance excused?
- and, if not, what are the legal remedies?

While we have covered the entire story, it has been a two-character or a two-party story. We now need to consider when third parties have rights or duties under a contract that they did not enter into themselves. More specifically, we need to consider third party beneficiaries, assignees of contract rights, and delegatees of contract duties.

---

1. THIRD PARTY BENEFICIARIES

Issues of third party beneficiary law arise in situations in which a person who is not a party to a contract and who did not provide the consideration for that contract claims that they can enforce the contract because the parties intended for them to benefit from performance of the contract.

The most obvious example of a third party beneficiary contract is a life insurance contract. For example, Epstein enters into a life insurance contract with the Allstate Insurance Company in which Epstein agrees to make annual premium payments of $1,000, and Allstate agrees to pay $25,000 in policy benefits to Sharon Stone on Epstein's death. When Epstein dies, Allstate refuses to pay Sharon Stone, contending that it never contracted with her and never received consideration from her. Even though Sharon Stone was not a party to the Epstein-Allstate contract and provided no consideration to Allstate, she can enforce that life insurance contract. She is a third party beneficiary.

It is important to understand that example and to understand that it is an example based on general contract law rather than special life insurance law. The legal basis for Sharon Stone's rights against Allstate is the general contract law concept of third party beneficiary rather than some special life insurance law rule.

Consider a third party beneficiary example unrelated to life insurance. Gilfoyle owed Ehrlich $300. Gilfoyle later entered into a contract whereby Gilfoyle loaned Dinesh $300 and Dinesh promised to repay that $300 to Ehrlich, thus satisfying Gilfoyle's debt to Ehrlich.

Under these facts, Ehrlich is not a party to the contract between Gilfoyle and Dinesh. Under these facts, Ehrlich did not provide the consideration to Dinesh in exchange for Dinesh's promise to pay him $300. Nonetheless, Ehrlich as an "intended beneficiary" can enforce the promise of the "promisor," Dinesh.

This Gilfoyle/Ehrlich/Dinesh hypothetical is similar to *Lawrence v. Fox*, which is generally regarded as the seminal case recognizing rights of certain third party beneficiaries.

QUESTIONS BEFORE THE CASE

1. When Fox did not pay Lawrence, could Holly successfully sue Fox for breach of contract?
2. When Fox did not pay Lawrence, could Lawrence have collected the $300 from Holly?

LAWRENCE V. FOX

Court of Appeals of New York
20 N.Y. 268 (1859)

APPEAL from the Superior Court of the city of Buffalo. On the trial before Mr. Justice MASTEN, it appeared by the evidence of a bystander, that one Holly, in November, 1857, at the request of the defendant, loaned and advanced to him $300, stating at the time that he owed that sum to the plaintiff for money borrowed of him, and had agreed to pay it to him the then next day; that the defendant in consideration thereof, at the time of receiving the money, promised to pay it to the plaintiff the then next day. Upon this state of facts the defendant moved for a nonsuit, upon three several grounds, viz.: That there was no proof tending to show that Holly was indebted to the plaintiff; that the agreement by the defendant with Holly to pay the plaintiff was void for want of consideration, and that there was no privity between the plaintiff and defendant. The court overruled the motion, and the counsel for the defendant excepted. The cause was then submitted to the jury, and they found a verdict for the plaintiff for the amount of the loan and interest, $344.66, upon which judgment was entered; from which the defendant appealed to the Superior Court, at general term, where the judgment was affirmed, and the defendant appealed to this court.

H. GRAY, J.

[I]t is claimed that [the defendant's promise], * * * was void for the want of consideration. It is now more than a quarter of a century since it was settled by the Supreme Court of this State—in an able and painstaking opinion by the late Chief Justice SAVAGE, in which the authorities were fully examined and carefully analysed—that a promise in all material respects like the one under consideration was valid; and the judgment of that court was unanimously affirmed by the Court for the Correction of Errors. (Farley v. Cleaveland, 4 Cow., 432; same case in error, 9 id., 639.) In that case one Moon owed Farley and sold to Cleaveland a quantity of hay, in consideration of which Cleaveland promised to pay Moon's debt to Farley; and the decision in favor of Farley's right to recover was placed upon the ground that the hay received by Cleaveland from Moon was a valid consideration for Cleaveland's promise to pay Farley, and that the subsisting liability of Moon to pay Farley was no objection to the recovery. The fact that the money advanced by Holly to the defendant was a loan to him for a day, and that it thereby became the property of the defendant, seemed to impress the defendant's counsel with the idea that because the defendant's promise was not a trust fund placed by the plaintiff in the defendant's hands, out of which he was to realize money as from the sale of a chattel or the collection of a debt, the promise although made for the benefit of the plaintiff could not enure to his benefit. The hay which Cleaveland delivered to Moon was not to be paid to Farley, but the debt incurred by Cleaveland for the purchase of the hay, like the debt incurred by the defendant for money borrowed, was what was to be paid.

That case * * * puts to rest the objection that the defendant's promise was void for want of consideration. The report of that case shows that the promise was not only made to Moon but to the plaintiff Farley. In this case the promise was made to Holly and not expressly to the plaintiff; and this difference between the two cases presents the question, raised by the defendant's objection, as to the want of privity between the plaintiff and defendant.

But it is urged that because the defendant was not in any sense a trustee of the property of Holly for the benefit of the plaintiff, the law will not imply a promise. I agree that many of the cases where a promise was implied were cases of trusts, created for the benefit of the promiser. The duty of the trustee to pay the cestuis que trust, according to the terms of the trust, implies his promise to the latter to do so. In this case the defendant, upon ample consideration received from Holly, promised Holly to pay his debt to the plaintiff; the consideration received and the promise to Holly made it as plainly his duty to pay the plaintiff as if the money had been remitted to him for that purpose, and as well implied a promise to do so as if he had been made a trustee of property to be converted into cash with which to pay. The fact that a breach of the duty imposed in the one case may be visited, and justly, with more serious consequences than in the other, by no means disproves the payment to be a duty in both. The principle illustrated by the example so frequently quoted (which concisely states the case in hand) "that a promise made to one for the benefit of another, he for whose benefit it is made may bring an action for its breach," has been applied to trust cases, not because it was exclusively applicable to those cases, but because it was a principle of law, and as such applicable to those cases.

It was also insisted that Holly could have discharged the defendant from his promise, though it was intended by both parties for the benefit of the plaintiff, and therefore the plaintiff was not entitled to maintain this suit for the recovery of a demand over which he had no control. It is enough that the plaintiff did not release the defendant from his promise, and whether he could or not is a question not now necessarily involved * * *.

No one can doubt that he owes the sum of money demanded of him, or that in accordance with his promise it was his duty to have paid it to the plaintiff; nor can it be doubted that whatever may be the diversity of opinion elsewhere, the adjudications in this State, from a very early period, approved by experience, have established the defendant's liability; if, therefore, it could be shown that a more strict and technically accurate application of the rules applied, would lead to a different result (which I by no means concede), the effort should not be made in the face of manifest justice.

The judgment should be affirmed.

QUESTIONS

1. Questions about the facts of this case

   1.1. To whom did the plaintiff Lawrence loan money?

   1.2. From whom is the plaintiff Lawrence trying to collect that debt?

2. Questions about the law

   2.1. Why is the court considering consideration?

   2.2. Is there any question as to whether the defendant Fox received consideration for its promise to pay the plaintiff $300?

   2.3. Did the defendant Fox receive that consideration from the plaintiff Lawrence?

   2.4. What is the purpose of requiring consideration?

   2.5. What is "privity"? Are the plaintiff Lawrence and the defendant Fox in privity?

   2.6. Didn't the defendant Lawrence expressly promise to pay the plaintiff Fox? Why is the court discussing implied promises?

3. **You Be the Lawyer!**

   If you had been the lawyer for the defendant, would you have recommended that defendant pay the $300 instead of litigate?

Our Dinesh/Ehrlich/Gilfoyle hypothetical (and *Lawrence v. Fox*)_ is also similar to Restatement (Second) Contracts section 304 and example 1 thereto

§ 304 Creation of Duty to Beneficiary

A promise in a contract creates a duty in the promisor to any intended beneficiary to perform the promise, and the intended beneficiary may enforce the duty.

Illustrations:

1. A owes C $100. For consideration B promises A to pay the debt. B breaks his contract. C may sue B and obtain judgment for the amount of the debt.

Application of *Restatement (Second) of Contracts* section 304 requires an understanding of two terms in section 304—"promisor" and "intended beneficiary"—and the term "promisee." These terms are defined in the *Restatement (Second)* provisions set out below:

§ 2 Promise; Promisor; Promisee; Beneficiary

(1) A promise is a manifestation of intention to act or refrain from acting in a specified way, so made as to justify a promisee in understanding that a commitment has been made.

(2) The person manifesting the intention is the promisor.

(3) The person to whom the manifestation is addressed is the promisee.

(4) Where performance will benefit a person other than the promisee, that person is a beneficiary.

§ 302 Intended and Incidental Beneficiaries

(1) Unless otherwise agreed between promisor and promisee, a beneficiary of a promise is an intended beneficiary if recognition of a right to performance in the beneficiary is appropriate to effectuate the intention of the parties and either

(a) the performance of the promise will satisfy an obligation of the promisee to pay money to the beneficiary; or

(b) the circumstances indicate that the promisee intends to give the beneficiary the benefit of the promised performance.

(2) An incidental beneficiary is a beneficiary who is not an intended beneficiary.

In example 1 above, A is the "promisee"; B is the "promisor" and C is an "intended beneficiary" under section 302(1)(a). Similarly, Dinesh is the "promisor"; Gilfoyle is the "promisee" and Ehrlich is an "intended beneficiary under section 302(1)(b).

That should be easy. What is hard, as illustrated by the next two cases, is determining who is an "intended beneficiary" under section 302(1)(b).

QUESTIONS BEFORE THE CASE

1. Why did the Stameys and Green Tree enter into a contract?
2. Whose intent was relevant to the Alabama Supreme Court in determining whether Hallmont was an intended beneficiary?

A. WHEN A THIRD PARTY IS AN "INTENDED BENEFICIARY"

EX PARTE STAMEY

Supreme Court of Alabama
776 So.2d 85 (2000)

HOUSTON, JUSTICE.

Gary Stamey and Deborah Stamey, third-party plaintiffs in an action currently pending in the Mobile Circuit Court, petition for a writ of mandamus directing the trial court to vacate its order compelling arbitration of the Stameys' claims against Green Tree Financial Corporation, Hallmont Homes, Inc., and Hallmont employees Jarod Hall and Gaylon Hall. We deny the writ.

In December 1996, the Stameys contracted with Hallmont Homes, Inc., to purchase land and a mobile home. The contract also included assurances that Hallmont would prepare a foundation for the mobile home and would install a septic system and a light pole. The Stameys claim that the septic system and the light pole were never installed. The Stameys had borrowed money from Green Tree to pay for these purchases and installations. Included in the financing agreement between Green Tree and the Stameys was this arbitration provision:

> "ARBITRATION: ALL DISPUTES, CLAIMS OR CONTROVERSIES ARISING FROM OR RELATING TO THIS CONTRACT OR THE PARTIES THERETO SHALL BE RESOLVED BY BINDING ARBITRATION BY ONE ARBITRATOR SELECTED BY YOU WITH MY CONSENT. THIS AGREEMENT IS MADE PURSUANT TO A TRANSACTION IN INTERSTATE COMMERCE AND SHALL BE GOVERNED BY THE FEDERAL ARBITRATION ACT AT 9 U.S.C. SECTION 1. JUDGMENT UPON THE AWARD RENDERED MAY BE ENTERED IN ANY COURT HAVING JURISDICTION. THE PARTIES AGREE AND UNDERSTAND THAT THEY CHOOSE ARBITRATION INSTEAD OF LITIGATION TO RESOLVE DISPUTES. THE PARTIES UNDERSTAND THAT THEY HAVE A RIGHT OR OPPORTUNITY TO LITIGATE DISPUTES IN COURT, BUT THAT THEY PREFER TO RESOLVE THEIR DISPUTES THROUGH ARBITRATION, EXCEPT AS PROVIDED HEREIN. THE PARTIES VOLUNTARILY AND KNOWINGLY WAIVE ANY RIGHT THEY HAVE TO A JURY TRIAL, EITHER PURSUANT TO ARBITRATION UNDER THIS CLAUSE OR PURSUANT TO A COURT ACTION BY YOU (AS PROVIDED HEREIN). THE PARTIES AGREE AND UNDERSTAND THAT ALL DISPUTES ARISING UNDER CASE LAW, STATUTORY LAW AND ALL OTHER LAWS INCLUDING, BUT NOT LIMITED TO, ALL CONTRACT, TORT AND PROPERTY DISPUTES WILL BE SUBJECT TO BINDING ARBITRATION IN ACCORD WITH THIS CONTRACT.

Dr. Bernard Eichold II, in his capacity as health officer of Mobile County, sued for injunctive relief against the Stameys, alleging that their property was in violation of state health laws—specifically, his complaint alleged a violation concerning the septic system on the Stameys' property. The Stameys filed an answer, along with a third-party complaint against Hallmont and Green Tree, alleging conversion, fraud, and breach of contract. The Stameys contend that Hallmont and/or Green Tree caused the problem with the septic system for which the Stameys were sued. Hallmont and Green Tree both moved the trial court to compel arbitration of the claims asserted against them. Hallmont was not a signatory to the arbitration agreement. The trial court granted the motions to compel. * * *

While the Stameys' contract with Green Tree contains an arbitration agreement, neither the sale contract between the Stameys and Hallmont nor any other document to which Hallmont was a signatory contained an arbitration agreement. Hallmont's motion to compel arbitration was based on the arbitration provision in the contract between Green Tree and the Stameys.

Normally, in order to have a valid arbitration provision, there must be an agreement to arbitrate, and if no agreement exists, then a party cannot be forced to submit a dispute to arbitration. The question whether one has assented to an arbitration provision is governed by ordinary principles of a state's common law and statutory law governing the formation of contracts. Assent to arbitrate is usually to be manifested through a party's signature on the contract containing the arbitration provision. However, both Federal courts and Alabama courts have enforced exceptions to this rule, so as to allow a nonsignatory, and even one who is not a party, as to a particular contract, to enforce an arbitration provision within that same contract. * * * If Hallmont is a third-party beneficiary, then it should be able to enforce the arbitration provision included in the contract between the Stameys and Green Tree. Thus, we must determine whether Hallmont is a third-party beneficiary of that contract.

A party claiming to be a third-party beneficiary, "must establish that the contracting parties intended, upon execution of the contract, to bestow a direct, as opposed to an incidental, benefit upon the third party." Weathers Auto Glass, Inc. v. Alfa Mut. Ins. Co., 619 So.2d 1328, 1329 (Ala.1993). In other words, Hallmont must show that the Stameys and Green Tree intended for Hallmont to receive a direct benefit from the financing contract. This issue will be determined with the intent of the parties as indicated by the language used. [W]e look to the language of the entire financing contract between the Stameys and Green Tree. We conclude that they did intend for Hallmont to receive a direct benefit.

The financing contract is a standard contract that provides for a secured transaction in which Green Tree received a security interest in the manufactured home and in which Green Tree would pay Hallmont for the manufactured home on behalf of the Stameys. In other words, this contract allows Green Tree to pay the obligation of the Stameys to Hallmont. The section of the contract entitled "ITEMIZATION OF THE AMOUNT FINANCED" sets out the amounts that were to be "paid on [the Stameys'] behalf." Included in this chart are the amounts that were paid on behalf of the Stameys to Hallmont for the cost of the manufactured home, the cost of the land, and the cost of the installations.

Furthermore, the language of the contract clearly shows that the parties contemplated Hallmont as a third-party beneficiary. The last section of the contract states:

> "WAIVER OF JURY TRIAL: I HEREBY WAIVE ANY RIGHT TO A TRIAL BY JURY THAT I HAVE IN ANY SUBSEQUENT LITIGATION BETWEEN ME AND THE SELLER, OR ME AND ANY ASSIGNEE OF THE SELLER, WHERE SUCH LITIGATION ARISES OUT OF, IS RELATED TO, OR IS IN CONNECTION WITH ANY PROVISION OF THIS AGREEMENT, WHETHER THE AGREEMENT IS ASSERTED AS RELATED TO, OR IS IN CONNECTION WITH ANY PROVISION OF THIS AGREEMENT, WHETHER THE AGREEMENT IS ASSERTED AS THE BASIS FOR A CLAIM, COUNTERCLAIM OR CROSS CLAIM, OR A DEFENSE TO A CLAIM, COUNTERCLAIM OR CROSS CLAIM."

(Emphasis added.) By this section, the Stameys clearly waived the right to a jury trial, not against Green Tree, but against Hallmont—"the seller."

The language of the two sections mentioned in the two preceding paragraphs clearly indicates an intent on behalf of the Stameys and Green Tree to benefit Hallmont through the financing contract. Therefore, we conclude that Hallmont is a third-party beneficiary of the financing contract and that it has all the rights that exist under that contract. As a result, Hallmont can enforce the arbitration agreement set out in that contract. * * *

QUESTIONS

1. Questions about the law

   1.1. According to the Alabama Supreme Court, "the language of the contract *clearly* shows that the parties contemplated Hallmont as a third party beneficiary." (emphasis added) What contract language?

   1.2. Should the question be whether "the parties contemplated Hallmont as a third-party beneficiary" of the contract or whether "the parties contemplated Hallmont as a third-party beneficiary" of the arbitration clause in the contract?

   1.3. How would this case have been decided by the *Restatement (Second)* section 304(1)?

2. **You Be the Lawyer!**

   As attorney for Hallmont, would you recommend to your client that it include mandatory arbitration clauses in its mobile home sale contracts?

Lawrence v. Fox and *Ex parte Stamey* involve consumer contracts that create third party beneficiary rights. The next case involves commercial contracts.

QUESTIONS BEFORE THE CASE

1. Why did PI contract with CMI?
2. Why did CMI include a warranty in its contract with PI?

MIDWEST GRAIN PRODUCTS OF ILLINOIS, INC. V. PRODUCTIZATION, INC. AND CMI CORP.

U.S. Court of Appeals, Seventh Circuit
228 F.3d 784 (2000)

DIANE P. WOOD, CIRCUIT JUDGE.

This case presents a classic contract dispute: A orders a product from B, and B turns to C to manufacture it. When A receives the product, it is not satisfied, and it wants to hold C responsible for the alleged flaws. We must decide whether there is enough evidence of some kind of warranty, either express or as a matter of law, to allow Midwest Grain Products (Company A) to move beyond summary judgment in its action against CMI Corporation (Company C). (Midwest settled its claims against Productization, Inc. (PI) (Company B), and so that actor has not been part of this case for some time.) The district court concluded that Midwest's evidence was lacking and that CMI was entitled to judgment as a matter of law. It also ruled that CMI was not entitled to its attorneys' fees. Each company has appealed from the part of the judgment adverse to it, but, finding no error in the district court's disposition of the action, we affirm.

I.

On January 12, 1993, Midwest Vice President Anthony Petricola sent a letter to PI President Andrew Livingston requesting a quote on grain dryers to be used in Midwest's expansion of its facility in Pekin, Illinois. Livingston responded on January 26 with an offer on PI's behalf to provide two dryers for a total price of $1,515,800. Midwest accepted PI's offer on February 25, through a purchase order sent to Livingston.

With the deal in hand, PI then turned to CMI to manufacture the dryers. On April 29, 1993, it sent CMI a set of specifications for the dryers Midwest wanted. CMI replied with a fax giving price terms and stating that "[a]cceptance of the order will be subject to receipt by CMI of a letter from Midwest Grain agreeing to make payment, with checks made payable jointly to CMI and Productization." * * *

On May 10, Midwest's Petricola sent the requested letter directly to CMI. The letter commits Midwest to "make payment for equipment purchased by Productization, Inc. from CMI Corporation for its [*i.e.*, Midwest's] project in Pekin, Illinois, with check(s) payable jointly to Productization, Inc. and CMI Corporation." It also mentions the shipment, price, and storage terms of the PI/CMI agreement and states that CMI will issue waivers of liens to Midwest upon CMI's receipt of payment.

This was Midwest's only direct appearance into the dealings between PI and CMI. The latter two companies continued to work out the details of their contract. * * *

* * * Paragraph 8 addressed warranties, and said in pertinent part:

> CMI warrants such equipment, accessories, parts and other goods covered by this order and as are manufactured by CMI against defective material or workmanship for a period of six (6) months after date of first delivery or for one thousand (1,000) hours of use, whichever comes first; * * * THIS WARRANTY IS EXPRESSLY IN LIEU OF AND EXCLUDES ALL OTHER WARRANTIES, EXPRESSED OR IMPLIED (INCLUDING ANY WARRANTY OF MERCHANTABILITY AND FITNESS OF ANY PRODUCT OR GOODS FOR A PARTICULAR PURPOSE), AND ALL OTHER OBLIGATIONS OR LIABILITIES ON CMI'S PART, AND CMI NEITHER ASSUMES NOR AUTHORIZES ANY OTHER PERSON TO ASSUME FOR CMI ANY OTHER LIABILITY IN CONNECTION WITH THE SALE OF CMI'S PRODUCTS. THERE ARE NOT ANY WARRANTIES WHICH EXTEND BEYOND THE DESCRIPTION ON THE FACE OF THIS ORDER.
>
> * * *

The first dryer reached Midwest in February 1994, but it was not put into service until 1995. The other dryer was delivered in April 1994 and was put into service two months later. Midwest experienced a variety of problems with both units. Initially, CMI and PI serviced them. Later, still unhappy with PI and CMI, it filed this action.

* * *

We begin with the question whether, under Oklahoma law, Midwest has any claim to third-party beneficiary status to the agreement between CMI and PI.

* * *

Under Oklahoma law, a party may be a third-party beneficiary to an agreement only if the contracting parties intended the benefits of the contract to run to the third party. * * * "[I]t is not necessary that third-party beneficiaries be specifically identified at the time of contracting, but it must appear that the contract was expressly made for the benefit of a class of persons to which the party seeking enforcement belongs."

There are only two pieces of evidence in this record that link the CMI/PI contract to Midwest: first, the fact that CMI knew that PI wanted the dryers so that it could then sell them to Midwest, and second, the fact that CMI insisted that it be paid by checks that Midwest made payable jointly to PI and to itself. Nothing in Oklahoma law the parties have cited, and nothing in Oklahoma law that we have been able to find ourselves, comes close to holding that an ultimate buyer is a third-party beneficiary of every contract its seller enters into with suppliers in order to fulfill the contract. Nor are we referred to, or can we find, any Oklahoma decision indicating that the kind of financial arrangement CMI secured here is enough to give the ultimate buyer third-party beneficiary status. That step was enough to make Midwest a surety for PI, and in that sense it allowed CMI to look not only to PI for payment (a right it had under the basic contract) but also to Midwest. But it did not indicate that the contract was expressly for Midwest's benefit. From CMI's point of view, it was a contract for the sale of goods, and it was not CMI's problem in the final analysis what PI wanted to do with the dryers once it received them.

Indeed, in the section of Midwest's brief entitled "Plaintiff's third-party beneficiary status was ignored or improperly addressed," it cites not a single decision of an Oklahoma court. It refers instead to one Illinois case, *Olson v. Etheridge*, 177 Ill.2d 396, 226 Ill.Dec. 780, 686 N.E.2d 563 (Ill.1997), and one decision from this court in a diversity case governed by Illinois law. States vary in their approach to rules like those governing the recognition and rights of third-party beneficiaries, and we would at least need some reason to conclude that Oklahoma and Illinois take the same approach before these authorities would be persuasive.

If Midwest was not a third-party beneficiary of the CMI/PI contract, which is our best predication of what an Oklahoma court would find, then it has no case. * * *

In the final analysis, the party that Midwest needed to pursue was its seller, PI. Indeed, it did include PI in this action at the outset. The terms of its settlement with PI are not pertinent to its case against CMI and are not in any event a matter of record. We hold only that, under the facts as presented and the governing law, the district court correctly granted summary judgment in the case Midwest wanted to bring against CMI.

QUESTIONS

1. Questions about the facts of this case

   1.1. Who bought what from whom?

   1.2. Why is the buyer, Midwest, suing CMI instead of PI?

   1.3. What facts support Midwest's contention that it is an intended third-party beneficiary of the CMI/PI contract?

2. Questions about the law

   In omitted dictum, Judge Wood stated: "Indeed, as a general matter, the Oklahoma courts do not seem to be inclined to adopt rules from the Contracts *Restatement*, perhaps because Title 15 of the Oklahoma Code is a comprehensive legislative statement of the law of contracts in that state." 238 F.3d at 790. Would Judge Wood have reached a different decision if Oklahoma had been "inclined to adopt rules from the Contracts *Restatement*?"

3. **You Be the Lawyer!**

   If you were the attorney for Midwest would your brief have included 15 Okl.St.Ann. § 29 which provides "A contract, made expressly for the benefit of a third person, may be enforced by him at any time before the parties thereto rescind it."?

Both of the contracts in the *Midwest Grain* case involved sales of goods; both of the contracts are thus governed by Article 2 of the UCC—Article 2 has a provision governing who is a "third party beneficiary"—section 2–318. Actually, Article 2 has three such provisions; Alternative A, Alternative B and Alternative C of section 2–318. Oklahoma has adopted a somewhat modified version of Alternative A.

§ 2–318. Third Party Beneficiaries of Warranties Express or Implied

Third Party Beneficiaries of Warranties Express or Implied.

(1) A seller's warranty whether express or implied extends to any natural person who is in the family or household of his buyer or who is a guest in his home if it is reasonable to expect that such person may use, consume or be affected by the goods and who is injured in person by breach of the warranty.

(2) This section does not displace principles of law and equity that extend a warranty to or for the benefit of a buyer to other persons. . . .

Why didn't Judge Wood, who was on Professor Obama's Supreme Court shortlist* and, more important, a student in Epstein's contracts class at the University of Texas Law School before you were born, discuss section 2–318 in her *Midwest Grain* opinion?

B. CANCELLATION AND MODIFICATION OF THE RIGHTS OF THE THIRD PARTY BENEFICIARY AND DEFENSES AGAINST THE THIRD PARTY BENEFICIARY

The previous three cases focused on the question of whether a third party has any right to enforce a contract entered into by others. That is the primary focus of most of the reported third party beneficiary cases.

The next case deals with: (i) the related question of when the rights of a third party beneficiary can be cancelled or modified—a question raised but not considered in *Lawrence v. Fox,* and (ii) the question of what defenses can be asserted against a third-party beneficiary.

QUESTIONS BEFORE THE CASE

1. At the time the Plaintiffs Olson agreed to sell their business to Etheridge and entered into Agreement I and Note 1 with Etheridge, was Engelhaupt legally obligated to make payments to the Plaintiffs Olson?
2. What are the Plaintiffs Olson legal rights against Engelhaupt and Etheridge after the Supreme Court of Illinois decision in this case?

OLSON V. ETHERIDGE

Supreme Court of Illinois
177 Ill.2d 396, 226 Ill.Dec. 780, 686 N.E.2d 563 (1997)

[Plaintiffs (the third party beneficiaries) sold their John Deere dealership to Etheridge (the promisee) pursuant to Agreement I with annual payments to be made by Etheridge to Plaintiffs pursuant to Note I. Subsequently, in 1983, Etheridge sold one-half of the business to

* http://www.nytimes.com/2009/05/12/us/politics/12wood.html?mtrref=www.google.com&gwh=64A49A4CE6B4FA5B78E9EB1FBD767D1D&gwt=pay

Engelhaupt (the promisor) pursuant to Agreement II with annual payments to be made pursuant to Note II. Agreement II and Note II provided that Engelhaupt's payments were to be made to Plaintiffs to reduce Etheridge's obligation to Plaintiffs under Note 1. In 1986, Etheridge and Engelhaupt and Princeton Bank entered into Agreement III which provided for Engelhaupt to pay the remaining balance of Note II to Princeton Bank to satisfy one of Etheridge's other debts. Engelhaupt made such a payment. Etheridge defaulted on its obligations under Agreement I and Note I. Plaintiffs sued both Etheridge and Engelhaupt for the unpaid balance of Note I.]

JUSTICE BILANDIC delivered the opinion of the court:

Bay v. Williams, 112 Ill. 91, 1 N.E. 340 (1884), established the rule in Illinois that the rights of a third-party beneficiary in a contract are subject to immediate vesting and, once vested, cannot be altered or extinguished through a later agreement of the contracting parties without the assent of the beneficiary. We are here called upon to determine the continued validity of the *Bay* rule.

The four plaintiffs in this case are third-party beneficiaries of a promise contained in a contract entered into by the appellant and another party. The circuit court of Bureau County awarded summary judgment to the plaintiffs based on *Bay*. The appellate court affirmed. We now reverse this award of summary judgment and remand for further proceedings, for the reasons set forth below.

* * *

Engelhaupt's appeal focuses on the appellate court's rejection of his claim that he is not subject to liability to the plaintiffs because all his obligations under Agreement II and Note II were discharged by the actions taken between him, Etheridge, and Princeton Bank on February 10, 1986. The actions pointed to by Engelhaupt are his $83,385 payment to Princeton Bank on Note II, and Princeton Bank's agreement that this constituted full payment; and his $100 payment to Princeton Bank for Agreement II, and Princeton Bank's and Etheridge's assignments of all their interests in Agreement II over to Engelhaupt. Engelhaupt concedes that the vesting rule in Bay commands a contrary conclusion, but argues that the *Bay* rule should be replaced with the vesting rule set forth in section 311 of the *Restatement (Second) of Contracts* (1981). According to Engelhaupt, if section 311 is applied, the summary judgment entered in favor of the plaintiffs was improper because questions of material fact remain to be determined.

* * *

Before addressing the parties' arguments, we briefly summarize third-party beneficiary law. The well-established rule in Illinois is that if a contract is entered into for the direct benefit of a third person, the third person may sue for a breach of the contract in his or her own name, even though the third person is a stranger to the contract and the consideration. This principle of law is widely accepted throughout the United States, because allowing a third-party beneficiary to sue the promisor directly is said to be manifestly just and practical. In cases such as this one, it increases judicial efficiency by removing the privity requirement, under which the beneficiary must sue the promisee, who then in turn must sue the promisor.

An important corollary to this principle is that the promisor may assert against the beneficiary any defense that the promisor could assert against the promisee if the promisee were suing on the contract. This is because the third-party beneficiary's rights stem from a contract to which the beneficiary is not a party. Accordingly, the promisor in this case, Engelhaupt, may assert against the plaintiffs-beneficiaries any defense that he could assert against the promisee, Etheridge, if Etheridge were suing him on Agreement II. Engelhaupt here asserts the defense that all his obligations under Agreement II and Note II were discharged when he made full payment to Princeton Bank on Note II and obtained assignments of both Princeton Bank's and Etheridge's interests in Agreement II.

The plaintiffs maintain, however, that Engelhaupt is not entitled to assert this defense against them because their rights as third-party beneficiaries had "vested." The vesting doctrine is an exception to the above rule that the promisor may assert against the beneficiary any defense that the promisor could assert against the promisee. Under this doctrine, once a third-party beneficiary's rights vest, the original contracting parties cannot modify or discharge those rights without the beneficiary's assent. The "question of vesting arises only where the promisor and the promisee purport to vary or discharge the rights of the beneficiary"; otherwise, "the topic of vesting is irrelevant." Before proceeding, then, we must determine in this case what rights the plaintiffs are asserting under Agreement II, and whether Engelhaupt and Etheridge attempted to vary or discharge those rights.

The plaintiffs here are asserting third-party beneficiary rights in Agreement II. In particular, they claim that they are the beneficiaries of Engelhaupt's promise in Agreement II "to assume" one-half of Etheridge's obligation to pay the plaintiffs under Agreement I and Note I. This assumption by Engelhaupt of one-half of Etheridge's obligation to pay is a classic example of a delegation. Unlike an assignment, which involves only a transfer of rights, a delegation involves the appointment of another to perform one's duties. ("Rights are assigned; duties are delegated"); J. Calamari & J. Perillo, Contracts § 18–1, at 722 (3d ed.1987). When a duty is delegated, the delegating party continues to remain liable for performance. The effects of this delegation are as follows: Etheridge remains liable to the plaintiffs under Agreement I and Note I, while Engelhaupt is liable to the plaintiffs under the third-party beneficiary theory. The plaintiffs therefore have a claim against both Etheridge and Engelhaupt, but are entitled to only one satisfaction. Thus, in count V, the plaintiffs are asserting their rights as third-party beneficiaries to payment from Engelhaupt, as provided for in Agreement II.

* * *

We now turn to the primary issue in this case: how vesting should be defined in this context. The plaintiffs urge application of the vesting rule declared in *Bay*. Engelhaupt, on the other hand, asks us to apply the vesting rule set forth in section 311 of the Second Restatement of Contracts.

In *Bay*, 112 Ill. 91, 1 N.E. 340, Williams sold land to Newman and Sissons in exchange for a down payment and promissory notes payable in installments. Newman and Sissons then sold the land to Bay. The deed tendered to Bay contained an express promise by Bay to pay the balance due on the promissory notes executed by Williams and Newman and Sissons. Bay later obtained a release of his obligation to pay Williams from Sissons. Newman went bankrupt without giving Bay a release. Williams exercised her power of foreclosure and sold the land, but was left being owed $3,559 on the notes. She sued Bay for that amount as third-party beneficiary of the deed between Newman and Sissons and Bay.

Bay argued that he was absolved from his promise to pay the promissory notes by Sissons' release. He proposed three different theories: (1) that third-party beneficiary rights do not vest until suit is brought; (2) that third-party beneficiary rights do not vest until the beneficiary relies upon or accepts the promisor's promise; and (3) that the promisor's promise to pay is a mere indemnity, which cannot be reached until the promisee is insolvent or on some other equitable ground. This court in *Bay* rejected these views, holding:

> "[The promisor's] promise invests the person for whose use it is made with an immediate interest and right, as though the promise had been made to him. This being true, the person who procures the promise has no legal right to release or discharge the person who made the promise, from his liability to the beneficiary. Having the right, it is under the sole control of the person for whose benefit it is made,—as much so as if made directly to him."

Consequently, *Bay* established the rule in Illinois that third-party beneficiary rights vest immediately and cannot be altered or extinguished through a later agreement of the original parties to the contract, unless the beneficiary assents.

Engelhaupt urges us to replace the *Bay* rule with the "modern view" as set forth in section 311 of the Second Restatement. Section 311, entitled "Variation of a Duty to a Beneficiary," stands in direct contrast to *Bay*. It provides that, in the absence of language in a contract making the rights of a third-party beneficiary irrevocable, the parties to the contract "retain power to discharge or modify the duty by subsequent agreement," without the third-party beneficiary's assent, at any time until the third-party beneficiary, without notice of the discharge or modification, materially changes position in justifiable reliance on the promise, brings suit on the promise or manifests assent to the promise at the request of the promisor or promisee. *Restatement (Second) of Contracts* § 311 (1981).

Section 311 now represents the majority view on the subject of vesting. In contrast, the immediate vesting rule as set forth in *Bay* represents the minority view, followed by only a handful of states.

Engelhaupt maintains that we should adopt section 311. He asserts that section 311 represents the majority rule on vesting because it better conforms to modern commercial practices and general principles of contract law. According to Engelhaupt, parties should remain free to modify or discharge their contracts as they see fit, without the assent of a third-party beneficiary, subject only to the three exceptions provided for in section 311. Section 311 makes sense, Engelhaupt contends, because third-party beneficiaries should not be able to enforce contracts for which they do not give any consideration, unless they demonstrate some detriment or act of faith in reliance on the contract.

Engelhaupt asserts that the superiority of the Restatement approach over the *Bay* rule is demonstrated by the facts present in this case. As he explains, the plaintiffs here freely chose to extend credit to Etheridge, who was then bound to pay them under Agreement I and Note I. Etheridge and Engelhaupt then freely contracted with each other that Engelhaupt would make one-half of Etheridge's payments to the plaintiffs, in Agreement II and Note II. The plaintiffs, however, were not bound to accept Engelhaupt's promise to pay in Agreement II and Note II in replacement of Etheridge's promise to pay in Agreement I and Note I, and did not do so. Consequently, the plaintiffs' contractual remedies against Etheridge in the event of Etheridge's nonpayment under Agreement I remained intact. Engelhaupt asserts that, in this situation, he and Etheridge should not be forever barred from modifying or discharging their agreement without the plaintiffs' assent, which is precisely what *Bay* mandates. Rather, Engelhaupt asserts, the third-party beneficiary plaintiffs should be found to have obtained vested rights in his and Etheridge's contract only if they meet one of the circumstances set forth in section 311.

Finding Engelhaupt's arguments persuasive, we hereby adopt the vesting rule set forth in section 311 of the Second Restatement. The rationale underlying section 311's vesting rule is that "parties to a contract should remain free to amend or rescind their agreement so long as there is no detriment to a third party who has provided no consideration for the benefit received." This rationale is compelling. Moreover, we find this rationale to be consistent with the general principles running throughout contract law. Contract law generally favors the freedom to contract. Contract law also allows for equitable remedies where the facts compel such a result.

In contrast, the immediate vesting rule of *Bay* curtails the freedom to contract. It provides, in essence, that every promise which benefits a third-party beneficiary carries with it another term, implied at law, that the parties to the contract are prohibited from modifying or discharging the promise that benefits the beneficiary, without the beneficiary's assent. We do not believe that the modern law of contracts should always imply such a term. To do so can work a great injustice upon the parties involved in a particular case. Although, as the plaintiffs contend, the *Bay* rule is clear and easy to apply, this does not persuade us to retain it. Our concern is that the rule of law we expound best serves the pursuit of justice, not that it is the easiest rule of law for courts to apply.

We note, moreover, that the plaintiffs' argument against adoption of the Restatement rule is not persuasive. They maintain that the Restatement position has fluctuated so much over the past century that it is not stable. We do not agree with this characterization. In fact, the Restatement position regarding creditor beneficiaries, such as the plaintiffs, is essentially the same as it has always been. Under the original Restatement, the rights of creditor beneficiaries vested once the beneficiary brought suit or otherwise materially changed position in reliance on the promise. Restatement of Contracts §§ 142, 143 (1932). Today, creditor beneficiaries are called intended beneficiaries, and their rights vest once the beneficiary brings suit on the promise, materially changes position in justifiable reliance on the promise or manifests assent to the promise at the request of the promisor or promisee. *Restatement (Second) of Contracts* §§ 302, 311 (1981). As to donee beneficiaries, the original Restatement provided that their rights vested immediately. Restatement of Contracts §§ 142, 143 (1932). This was changed after substantial criticism. Now donee beneficiaries are also classified as intended beneficiaries, and their rights vest as in the same manner stated above. *Restatement (Second) of Contracts* §§ 302, 311 (1981). Even were we to agree with the plaintiffs' characterization of the Restatement view as unstable, however, this would not impact our decision. We find the current Restatement position on vesting to be consistent with general principles underlying contract law. This court is free to reject any later revisions of the Restatement.

In conclusion, we adopt the vesting rule set forth in section 311 of the Second Restatement. *Bay* is hereby overruled. The circuit court awarded summary judgment to the plaintiffs based on the *Bay* rule. The circuit court did not consider the plaintiffs' motion for summary judgment in the context of the vesting rule of section 311. We therefore reverse this award of summary judgment for the plaintiffs and remand to the circuit court for further proceedings, consistent with section 311's vesting rule. * * *

QUESTIONS AND NOTE

1. Questions about the facts of this case

   1.1. Who is the third party beneficiary of Agreement II?

   1.2. Who is the promisor in Agreement II?

   1.3. Has the promisor paid all amounts that he promised to pay in Agreement II?

2. Questions about the law

   2.1. At trial, Engelhaupt argued that the Plaintiffs were not intended third-party beneficiaries of Agreement II. The trial court held that the Plaintiffs were intended third-party beneficiaries and Engelhaupt did not challenge that holding on appeal. Do you agree with that decision? Would Judge Wood agree? Recall that this case, *Olson v. Etheridge*, was the one case referred to in the *Midwest Grain Products* case.

   2.2. Would this case have been decided differently if Etheridge was in default under Agreement I after 1985 but Plaintiffs had not foreclosed because of the promised payments from Engelhaupt under Agreement II?

   2.3. What is the practical significance, if any, of the court's statement in this case that "the promisor may assert against the beneficiary any defense that the promisor could assert against the promisee if the promisee were suing on the contract"? What if in *Lawrence v. Fox*, the $300 that Holly "loaned and advanced" to the defendant was counterfeit funds?

   2.4. On January 15, Batman contracts to provide protection to Gotham for the remainder of the year in exchange for Gotham's promise to pay Robin $20,000 on December 31. Notwithstanding this contract, Batman fails to provide any protection to Gotham. Does Gotham still have to pay Robin $20,000 on December 31?

   2.5. Do you agree with the statement in *Olson* that "the vesting doctrine is an exception to the * * * rule that the promisor may assert against the beneficiary any defense that the promisor could assert against the promisee"?

3. Note

"Section 311 of Restatement (Second) reversed the rule of irrevocability to a presumption of revocability subject to a few exceptions. Specifically, the initial counterparties may not modify away third-party rights under three circumstances: (1) the counterparties state at the outset that these rights are not subject to alteration, (2) the third-party beneficiary materially changes her position in justifiable reliance on the promise before the attempt at modification, or (3) the third-party beneficiary manifests assent to her rights at the behest of the promisor or promisee. It is hardly clear why the assent of an outsider to third-party enforcement rights should have legal impact on the modification powers of the initial counterparties." George S. Geis, *Broadcast Contracting*, 106 Nw.U.L.Rev. 1153, 1168–9 (2012).

4. **You Be the Lawyer!**

Assume that you are the lawyer for Engelhaupt. How would you have responded to Engelhaupt's question whether he should appeal from the circuit court's award of summary judgment to the Plaintiffs based on *Bay*?

Do you understand the statement in *Olson* that "the assumption by Engelhaupt of one half of Etheridge's obligation to pay is a classic example of a delegation"? Was *Lawrence v. Fox* also a "classic example of a delegation"? What is the difference between a delegation and a third-party beneficiary transaction? Between a delegation and an assignment?

The next section—the last section of the book—answers those questions about delegation and assignment and more.

---

2. ASSIGNMENT AND DELEGATION

A. INTRODUCTION TO ASSIGNMENT AND DELEGATION: WHAT ARE THEY?

A contract creates both rights and duties. If for example, Markell contracts to buy Epstein's 1973 Cadillac for $400, Markell has a right to obtain Epstein's car and a duty to pay $400. Epstein has a right to be paid $400 and a duty to deliver his 1973 Cadillac.

Similarly, if Epstein contracts with BARBRI to do contracts bar review lectures in California for $10 a lecture, Epstein has a right to be paid $10 and a duty to deliver contracts lectures. BARBRI has a right to Epstein's lectures and a duty to pay $10.

A contracting party's later transfer of his contract rights to a third party is generally referred to as assignment. If, for example, Markell transfers his right to obtain Epstein's car to Ponoroff, that is an "assignment" and, Markell is an assignor, and Ponoroff is an assignee. The *Olson* case above provides another example of an assignment. Recall that in *Olson,* Etheridge assigned the right to payment from Engelhaupt under Agreement II to Princeton Bank. Etheridge is the assignor; Princeton Bank is the assignee; and Engelhaupt is the obligor.

A contracting party's later agreement with a third party to perform their contract duties is generally referred to as a delegation. If, for example, Epstein gets Ponoroff to do the BARBRI contracts bar review lectures in California, that is a delegation, Epstein is a delegator, and Ponoroff is a delegatee. Again, the *Olson* case provides another example of a delegation. Recall that in Agreement II in *Olson*, Etheridge got Engelhaupt to agree to pay one-half of what Etheridge owed to Plaintiffs, *i.e.*, Etheridge delegated that duty to Engelhaupt. Etheridge is the delegator; Emgelhaupt is the delegate; and the Plaintiff Olson is the obligee

As the *Olson* case illustrates, a contracting party can both assign their contract rights and delegate his contract duties. Another example of both assignment and delegation: Epstein and Ponoroff agree that Ponoroff will do the California BARBRI lectures and collect the $10 from BARBRI as provided for in Epstein's earlier contract with BARBRI.

There are three questions about contract assignments and delegations that lawyers and first year law students need to be able to answer:

1. How is an assignment of rights under a contract factually different from a contract intended to benefit a third party? (In other words, when do you look to the law regarding third party beneficiaries and when do you look to the law regarding assignments?)

2. What are the legal consequences of an assignment and/or a delegation?

3. What are the limitations on the making of an assignment and/or a delegation?

You should already be able to answer the first question from the previous material in this section. If Batman contracts with Gotham to provide security services for a year in exchange for Gotham's paying Robin $200,000 then Robin is a third party beneficiary of the Batman/Gotham contract. On the other hand, if Batman contracts with Gotham to provide security services for a year in exchange for Gotham's paying Batman $200,000 and then later Batman transfers his right to payment from Gotham to Robin, then Robin is an assignee of the Batman/Gotham contract.

You should be able to answer the next two questions about legal consequences of assignment and delegation and limitations on assignment and delegation from the following materials in this section.

B. CONSEQUENCES OF AN ASSIGNMENT AND DELEGATION: WHO CAN SUE WHOM?

1. Assignee (But Not the Assignor) Can Sue Obligor

Illustration 1 to *Restatement (Second) Contracts* § 317 illustrates the two legal consequences of an assignment.

> 1. A has a right to $100 against B. A assigns his right to C. A's right is thereby extinguished, and C acquires a right against B to receive $100.

PROBLEMS

1. Markell enters into a contract with Epstein to purchase Epstein's 1973 Cadillac for $400. The contract provides that Markell will pay Epstein for the car within ten days after delivery. Epstein delivers the car to Markell. Epstein then assigns his right to the $400 payment under the Markell contract to Ponoroff. Markell refuses to pay Ponoroff. Can Ponoroff sue Markell for breach of the Cadillac contract even though Ponoroff was not a party to that contract?
2. Under the facts in question 1 above, can Epstein sue Markell for breach of contract?
3. In questions 1 and 2, should it matter whether Ponoroff paid Epstein or Epstein simply made a gift to Ponoroff?
4. Epstein's klezmer band, The Alter Kochers, signs a contract with Bad Boy Records to record "Bubba's Bar Mitzvah." The contract provides for the payment of royalties to Epstein based on sales. Subsequently, Epstein assigns his right to "Bubba's Bar Mitzvah" royalty payments to Markell. To whom should Bad Boy make the royalty payments? What if Bad Boy makes a royalty payment to Epstein after the assignment but before it had been notified of the assignment?

---

2. Obligee Can Sue Delegator

The *Restatement* restates the law with respect to who can sue whom after a delegation of duties to perform under a contract. Please read section

318 of the *Restatement (Second) of Contracts* set out below and apply it in the questions below.

§ 318 Delegation of Performance of Duty

(3) Unless the obligee agrees otherwise, neither delegation of performance nor a contract to assume the duty made with the obligor by the person delegated discharges any duty or liability of the delegating obligor.

Illustrations:

9. A borrows $50,000 from B and contracts to repay it. The contract provides that, if a corporation C is organized and assumes the debt under described conditions, A will be under no further obligation. C is organized and in good faith assumes the debt as provided. A is discharged.

10. A contracts with B to cut the grass on B's meadow. A delegates performance to C, who contracts with A to assume A's duty and perform the work. C begins performance with B's assent, but later breaks the contract. C is liable to B, but A is not discharged.

PROBLEMS

1. Epstein contracts with BARBRI to do bar review lectures in California for $10. Being the kind of friend that he is, Ponoroff agrees to do the lectures for Epstein without charge. And, being the kind of friend that he is, notwithstanding this agreement, Ponoroff does not do the lectures. Can BARBRI sue Epstein for breach of contract?

2. Same facts as question 1. Can BARBRI sue Ponoroff for breach of contract?

3. Would your answers to questions 1 and/or 2 change if Epstein paid Ponoroff $30 to do the lectures? (Hint: Is the following statement doctrine as well as doggerel: "A delegation for consideration results in a third party beneficiary obligation"?)

4. Would your answers to questions 1 and/or 2 change if BARBRI and Epstein and Ponoroff had agreed that Ponoroff could do the lectures instead of Epstein?

5. H enters into a contract with M under which M loans H $50,000 and H grants M a mortgage on H's house. Subsequently, H sells the house to T who assumes the mortgage. If T misses a mortgage payment, can M still sue H? Can M sue T? What, if any, needed facts are missing?

C. LIMITATIONS ON ASSIGNMENT AND DELEGATION

It should be obvious that there are limitations on a contracting party's ability to assign her contract rights and/or delegate her contract duties. If not, consider the following easy questions:

1. Batman enters into a contract with Gotham to provide security services to Gotham for one year in exchange for a payment of $100,000. Why should Batman be able to assign his contract rights to Robin but Gotham should not be able to assign its contract rights to Metropolis?
2. Lebron James contracts to play basketball for the Cleveland Cavaliers*. Can Mr. James delegate his contract performance obligations to Darko Milicic? To Kevin Durant?

As the first question illustrates, there is a common law prohibition on assignments that materially change the duty of the other party. Batman 's assignment of his right to payment to Robin does not materially affect Gotham's contract duties. It is just as easy for Gotham to pay the $100,000 to Robin as to Batman.

It is not however just as easy for Batman to defend Metropolis as Gotham. The primary threat to Gotham is a Joker; Gotham has much more challenging array of villians. The assignment by Gotham of its contract rights to Batman's services would substantially change the obligor Batman's duties and and thus not be valid.

And, as should be obvious from the second illustration, common law does not permit a delegation of work that requires special skill. The Cleveland Cavaliers have a substantial interest in Lebron James himself performing. Thus Mr. James' contract duties are not delegable.

The Uniform Commercial Code section 2–210 governs assignment and delegation of a contract for the sale of goods.

§ 2–210. Delegation of Performance; Assignment of Rights.

(1) A party may perform his duty through a delegate unless otherwise agreed or unless the other party has a substantial interest in having his original promisor perform or control the acts required by the contract. No delegation of performance relieves the party delegating of any duty to perform or any liability for breach.

(2) Unless otherwise agreed all rights of either seller or buyer can be assigned except where the assignment would materially change the duty of the other party, or increase materially the burden or risk

* Remember this book "went to press" in 2018. If you are reading this in 2019, it might be necessary to substitute "Los Angeles Lakers" for "Cleveland Cavaliers."

imposed on him by his contract, or impair materially his chance of obtaining return performance. A right to damages for breach of the whole contract or a right arising out of the assignor's due performance of his entire obligation can be assigned despite agreement otherwise.

(3) Unless the circumstances indicate the contrary a prohibition of assignment of "the contract" is to be construed as barring only the delegation to the assignee of the assignor's performance.

(4) An assignment of "the contract" or of "all my rights under the contract" or an assignment in similar general terms is an assignment of rights and unless the language or the circumstances (as in an assignment for security) indicate the contrary, it is a delegation of performance of the duties of the assignor and its acceptance by the assignee constitutes a promise by him to perform those duties. This promise is enforceable by either the assignor or the other party to the original contract.

(5) The other party may treat any assignment which delegates performance as creating reasonable grounds for insecurity and may without prejudice to his rights against the assignor demand assurances from the assignee (Section 2–609).

The next case "applies" section 2–210. The next case is our last case. It is a great last case. A great case for your

- — reflecting on the concepts that you have learned in this Chapter and elsewhere in the book;
- — comparing the skills you have acquired in distinguishing cases and reading statutes with the skills of the judges on the Seventh Circuit and their law clerks;
- — appreciating the importance of a deal lawyer's knowing contract law;
- — understanding, that notwithstanding the incredible amount that you have learned from this wonderful contracts course, there is a need for more law school courses.

QUESTIONS BEFORE THE CASE

1. Does Judge Cudahy view this as a case involving Nexxus's challenge to Best's assignment of its contract rights to Sally Beauty or a challenge to Best's delegation of its contract duties to Sally Beauty or to challenge to both?

2. Under section 2–210(1), which of the parties in this case is the "party"? The "original promisor"? The "other party"? In this case, what is the "substantial interest in having his original promisor perform"?

SALLY BEAUTY CO., INC. V. NEXXUS PRODUCTS CO., INC.

U.S. Court of Appeals, Seventh Circuit
801 F.2d 1001 (1986)

CUDAHY, CIRCUIT JUDGE.

Nexxus Products Company ("Nexxus") entered into a contract with Best Barber & Beauty Supply Company, Inc. ("Best"), under which Best would be the exclusive distributor of Nexxus hair care products to barbers and hair stylists throughout most of Texas. When Best was acquired by and merged into Sally Beauty Company, Inc. ("Sally Beauty"), Nexxus cancelled the agreement. Sally Beauty is a wholly-owned subsidiary of Alberto-Culver Company ("Alberto-Culver"), a major manufacturer of hair care products and a competitor of Nexxus'. Sally Beauty claims that Nexxus breached the contract by cancelling; Nexxus asserts by way of defense that the contract was not assignable or, in the alternative, not assignable to Sally Beauty. The district court granted Nexxus' motion for summary judgment, ruling that the contract was one for personal services and therefore not assignable. We affirm on a different theory—that this contract could not be assigned to the wholly-owned subsidiary of a direct competitor under section 2–210 of the Uniform Commercial Code.

I.

Only the basic facts are undisputed and they are as follows. Prior to its merger with Sally Beauty, Best was a Texas corporation in the business of distributing beauty and hair care products to retail stores, barber shops and beauty salons throughout Texas. Between March and July 1979, Mark Reichek, Best's president, negotiated with Stephen Redding, Nexxus' vice-president, over a possible distribution agreement between Best and Nexxus. Nexxus, founded in 1979, is a California corporation that formulates and markets hair care products. Nexxus does not market its products to retail stores, preferring to sell them to independent distributors for resale to barbers and beauticians. On August 2, 1979, Nexxus executed a distributorship agreement with Best, in the form of a July 24, 1979 letter from Reichek, for Best, to Redding, for Nexxus:

> Dear Steve:
>
> It was a pleasure meeting with you and discussing the distribution of Nexus Products. The line is very exciting and we feel we can do a substantial job with it—especially as the exclusive distributor in Texas (except El Paso).

If I understand the pricing structure correctly, we would pay $1.50 for an item that retails for $5.00 (less 50%, less 40% off retail), and Nexus will pay the freight charges regardless of order size. This approach to pricing will enable us to price the items in the line in such a way that they will be attractive and profitable to the salons.

* * *

While we feel confident that we can do an outstanding job with the Nexus line and that the volume we generate will adequately compensate you for your continued support, it is usually best to have an understanding should we no longer be distributing Nexus Products—either by our desire or your request. Based on our discussions, cancellation or termination of Best Barber & Beauty Supply Co., Inc. as a distributor can only take place on the anniversary date of our original appointment as a distributor—and then only with 120 days prior notice. If Nexus terminates us, Nexus will buy back all of our inventory at cost and will pay the freight charges on the returned merchandise.

Steve, we feel that the Nexus line is exciting and very promotable. With the program outlined in this letter, we feel it can be mutually profitable and look forward to a long and successful business relationship. If you agree that this letter contains the details of our understanding regarding the distribution of Nexus Products, please sign the acknowledgment below and return one copy of this letter to me.

VERY TRULY YOURS,
/S/ MARK E. REICHEK
PRESIDENT

Acknowledged /s/ Stephen Redding Date 8/2/79. Appellant's Appendix at 2–3.

In July 1981, Sally Beauty acquired Best in a stock purchase transaction and Best was merged into Sally Beauty, which succeeded to Best's rights and interests in all of Best's contracts. Sally Beauty, a Delaware corporation with its principal place of business in Texas, is a wholly-owned subsidiary of Alberto-Culver. Sally Beauty, like Best, is a distributor of hair care and beauty products to retail stores and hair styling salons. Alberto-Culver is a major manufacturer of hair care products and, thus, is a direct competitor of Nexxus in the hair care market.

Shortly after the merger, Redding met with Michael Renzulli, president of Sally Beauty, to discuss the Nexxus distribution agreement. After the meeting, Redding wrote Renzulli a letter stating that Nexxus would not allow Sally Beauty, a wholly-owned subsidiary of a direct competitor, to distribute Nexxus products:

> "As we discussed in New Orleans, we have great reservations about allowing our NEXXUS Products to be distributed by a company which is, in essence, a direct competitor. We appreciate your argument of autonomy for your business, but the fact remains that you are totally owned by Alberto-Culver.
>
> Since we see no way of justifying this conflict, we cannot allow our products to be distributed by Sally Beauty Company."

In August 1983, Sally Beauty commenced this action by filing a complaint in the Northern District of Illinois, claiming that Nexxus had breached the distribution agreement. * * * Nexxus filed a motion for summary judgment on the breach of contract claim the next day.

The district court granted Nexxus' motion for summary judgment. * * *

In ruling on this motion, the district court framed the issue before it as "whether the contract at issue here between Best and Nexxus was of a personal nature such that it was not assignable without Nexxus' consent." It ruled:

> The court is convinced, based upon the nature of the contract and the circumstances surrounding its formation, that the contract at issue here was of such a nature that it was not assignable without Nexxus's consent. First, the very nature of the contract itself suggests its personal character. A distribution agreement is a contract whereby a manufacturer gives another party the right to distribute its products. It is clearly a contract for the performance of a service. In the court's view, the mere selection by a manufacturer of a party to distribute its goods presupposes a reliance and confidence by the manufacturer on the integrity and abilities of the other party. * * * In addition, in this case the circumstances surrounding the contract's formation support the conclusion that the agreement was not simply an ordinary commercial contract but was one which was based upon a relationship of personal trust and confidence between the parties. Specifically, Stephen Redding, Nexxus's vice-president, travelled to Texas and met with Best's president personally for several days before making the decision to award the Texas distributorship to Best. Best itself had been in the hair care business for 40 years and its president Mark Reichek had extensive experience in the industry. It is reasonable to conclude that Stephen Redding and Nexxus would want its distributor to be experienced and knowledgeable in the hair care field and that the selection of Best was based upon personal factors such as these.

* * *

We cannot affirm this summary judgment on the grounds relied on by the district court. * * * Although it might be "reasonable to conclude" that Best and Nexxus had based their agreement on "a relationship of personal trust and confidence," and that Reichek's participation was considered essential to Best's performance, this is a finding of fact. Since the parties submitted conflicting affidavits on this question,[3] the district court erred in relying on Nexxus' view as representing undisputed fact in ruling on this summary judgment motion.

We may affirm this summary judgment, however, on a different ground if it finds support in the record. Sally Beauty contends that the distribution agreement is freely assignable because it is governed by the provisions of the Uniform Commercial Code (the "UCC" or the "Code"), as adopted in Texas. We agree with Sally that the provisions of the UCC govern this contract and for that reason hold that the assignment of the contract by Best to Sally Beauty was barred by the UCC rules on delegation of performance, UCC § 2–210(1).

* * * Texas applies the "dominant factor" test to determine whether the UCC applies to a given contract or transaction: was the essence of or dominant factor in the formation of the contract the provision of goods or services? No Texas case addresses whether a distribution agreement is a contract for the sale of goods, but the rule in the majority of jurisdictions is that distributorships (both exclusive and non-exclusive) are to be treated as sale of goods contracts under the UCC.

Several of these courts note that "a distributorship agreement is more involved than a typical sales contract." This is true of the contract at issue here (as embodied in the July 24, 1979 letter from Reichek to Redding). Most of the agreed-to terms deal with Nexxus' sale of its hair care products to Best. We are confident that a Texas court would find the sales aspect of this contract dominant and apply the majority rule that such a distributorship is a contract for "goods" under the UCC.

---

[3] Reichek stated the following in an affidavit submitted in support of Sally Beauty's Memorandum in Opposition to Nexxus' Motion for Summary Judgment:

> At no time prior to the execution of the Distribution Agreement did Steve Redding tell me that he was relying upon my personal peculiar tastes and ability in making his decision to award a Nexxus distributorship to Best. Moreover, I never understood that Steve Redding was relying upon my skill and ability in particular in choosing Best as a distributor. I never considered the Distribution Agreement to be a personal service contract between me and Nexxus or Stephen Redding. I always considered the Distribution Agreement to be between Best and Nexxus as expressly provided in the Distribution Agreement which was written by my brother and me. At all times I conducted business with Nexxus on behalf of Best and not on my own behalf. In that connection, when I sent correspondence to Nexxus, I invariably signed it as president of Best. Neither Stephen Redding nor any other Nexxus employee ever told me that Nexxus was relying on my personal financial integrity on executing the Distribution Agreement or in shipping Nexxus products to Best * * *

The fact that this contract is considered a contract for the sale of goods and not for the provision of a service does not, as Sally Beauty suggests, mean that it is freely assignable in all circumstances. The delegation of performance under a sales contract (whether in conjunction with an assignment of rights, as here, or not) is governed by UCC section 2–210(1). The UCC recognizes that in many cases an obligor will find it convenient or even necessary to relieve himself of the duty of performance under a contract, *see* Official Comment 1, UCC § 2–210 ("[T]his section recognizes both delegation of performance and assignability as normal and permissible incidents of a contract for the sale of goods."). The Code therefore sanctions delegation except where the delegated performance would be unsatisfactory to the obligee: "A party may perform his duty through a delegate unless otherwise agreed to or unless the other party has a substantial interest in having his original promisor perform or control the acts required by the contract." UCC § 2–210(1). Consideration is given to balancing the policies of free alienability of commercial contracts and protecting the obligee from having to accept a bargain he did not contract for.

We are concerned here with the delegation of Best's duty of performance under the distribution agreement, as Nexxus terminated the agreement because it did not wish to accept Sally Beauty's substituted performance.[6] Only one Texas case has construed section 2–210 in the context of a party's delegation of performance under an executory contract. In *McKinnie v. Milford*, 597 S.W.2d 953 (Tex.Civ.App.1980, writ ref'd, n.r.e.), the court held that nothing in the Texas Business and Commercial Code prevented the seller of a horse from delegating to the buyer a pre-existing contractual duty to make the horse available to a third party for breeding. "[I]t is clear that Milford [the third party] had no particular interest in not allowing Stewart [the seller] to delegate the duties required by the contract. Milford was only interested in getting his two breedings per year, and such performance could only be obtained from McKinnie [the buyer] after he bought the horse from Stewart." *Id.* at 957. In McKinnie, the Texas court recognized and applied the UCC rule that bars delegation of duties if there is some reason why the non-assigning party would find performance by a delegate a substantially different thing than what he had bargained for.

In the exclusive distribution agreement before us, Nexxus had contracted for Best's "best efforts" in promoting the sale of Nexxus products

---

6 If this contract is assignable, Sally Beauty would also, of course, succeed to Best's rights under the distribution agreement. But the fact situation before us must be distinguished from the assignment of contract rights that are no longer executory (*e.g.*, the right to damages for breach or the right to payment of an account), which is considered in UCC section 2–210(2), Tex.Bus. & Com.Code Ann. S 2–210(b) (Vernon 1968), and in several of the authorities relied on by appellants. The policies underlying these two situations are different and, generally, the UCC favors assignment more strongly in the latter. *See* UCC § 2–210(2) (non-executory rights assignable even if agreement states otherwise).

in Texas. UCC § 2–306(2), states that "[a] lawful agreement by either buyer or seller for exclusive dealing in the kind of goods concerned imposes unless otherwise agreed an obligation by the seller to use best efforts to supply the goods and by the buyer to use best efforts to promote their sale." This implied promise on Best's part was the consideration for Nexxus' promise to refrain from supplying any other distributors within Best's exclusive area. *See* Official Comment 5, UCC S 2–306. It was this contractual undertaking which Nexxus refused to see performed by Sally.

In ruling on Nexxus' motion for summary judgment, the district court noted: "Unlike Best, Sally Beauty is a subsidiary of one of Nexxus' direct competitors. This is a significant distinction and in the court's view, it raises serious questions regarding Sally Beauty's ability to perform the distribution agreement in the same manner as Best." We agree with these assessments and hold that Sally Beauty's position as a wholly-owned subsidiary of Alberto-Culver is sufficient to bar the delegation of Best's duties under the agreement.

We do not believe that our holding will work the mischief with our national economy that the appellants predict. We hold merely that the duty of performance under an exclusive distributorship may not be delegated to a competitor in the market place—or the wholly-owned subsidiary of a competitor—without the obligee's consent. We believe that such a rule is consonant with the policies behind section 2–210, which is concerned with preserving the bargain the obligee has struck. Nexxus should not be required to accept the "best efforts" of Sally Beauty when those efforts are subject to the control of Alberto-Culver. It is entirely reasonable that Nexxus should conclude that this performance would be a different thing than what it had bargained for. At oral argument, Sally Beauty argued that the case should go to trial to allow it to demonstrate that it could and would perform the contract as impartially as Best. It stressed that Sally Beauty is a "multi-line" distributor, which means that it distributes many brands and is not just a conduit for Alberto-Culver products. But we do not think that this creates a material question of fact in this case. When performance of personal services is delegated, the trier merely determines that it is a personal services contract. If so, the duty is *per se* nondelegable. There is no inquiry into whether the delegate is as skilled or worthy of trust and confidence as the original obligor: the delegate was not bargained for and the obligee need not consent to the substitution. And so here: it is undisputed that Sally Beauty is wholly owned by Alberto-Culver, which means that Sally Beauty's "impartial" sales policy is at least acquiesced in by Alberto-Culver—but could change whenever Alberto-Culver's needs changed. Sally Beauty may be totally sincere in its belief that it can operate "impartially" as a distributor, but who can guarantee the outcome when there is a clear choice between the demands of the parent-manufacturer, Alberto-Culver, and the competing needs of Nexxus? The risk of an unfavorable outcome is not one which the law can force Nexxus to take. Nexxus has a substantial interest in not seeing this contract performed by Sally Beauty, which is sufficient to bar the delegation under section 2–210. Because Nexxus should not be forced to accept performance of the distributorship agreement by Sally, we hold that the contract was not assignable without Nexxus' consent.

The judgment of the district court is AFFIRMED.

POSNER, CIRCUIT JUDGE, dissenting.

My brethren have decided, with no better foundation than judicial intuition about what businessmen consider reasonable, that the Uniform Commercial Code gives a supplier an absolute right to cancel an exclusive-dealing contract if the dealer is acquired, directly or indirectly, by a competitor of the supplier. I interpret the Code differently.

Nexxus makes products for the hair and sells them through distributors to hair salons and barbershops. It gave a contract to Best, cancellable on any anniversary of the contract with 120 days' notice, to be its exclusive distributor in Texas. Two years later Best was acquired by and merged into Sally Beauty, a distributor of beauty supplies and wholly owned subsidiary of Alberto-Culver. Alberto-Culver makes "hair care" products, too, though they mostly are cheaper than Nexxus's, and are sold to the public primarily through grocery stores and drugstores. * * *

* * * So far as appears, the same people who distributed Nexxus's products for Best (except for Best's president) continued to do so for Sally Beauty. Best was acquired, and continues, as a going concern; the corporation was dissolved, but the business wasn't. Whether there was a delegation of performance in any sense may be doubted. The general rule is that a change of corporate form—including a merger—does not in and of itself affect contractual rights and obligations.

The fact that Best's president has quit cannot be decisive on the issue whether the merger resulted in a delegation of performance. The contract between Nexxus and Best was not a personal-services contract conditioned on a particular individual's remaining with Best. If Best had not been acquired, but its president had left anyway, as of course he might have done, Nexxus could not have repudiated the contract.

* * *

Steel companies both make fabricated steel and sell raw steel to competing fabricators. General Motors sells cars manufactured by a competitor, Isuzu.

* * *

Suppose there had been no merger, but the only child of Best's president had gone to work for Alberto-Culver as a chemist. Could Nexxus have canceled the contract, fearing that Best (perhaps unconsciously) would favor Alberto-Culver products over Nexxus products? That would be an absurd ground for cancellation, and so is Nexxus's actual ground. At most, so far as the record shows, Nexxus may have had grounds for "insecurity" regarding the performance by Sally Beauty of its obligation to use its best efforts to promote Nexxus products, but if so its remedy was not to cancel the contract but to demand assurances of due performance. *See* UCC § 2–609; Official Comment 5 to § 2–306. No such demand was made. An anticipatory repudiation by conduct requires conduct that makes the repudiating party unable to perform. The merger did not do this. At least there is no evidence it did. The judgment should be reversed and the case remanded for a trial on whether the merger so altered the conditions of performance that Nexxus is entitled to declare the contract broken.

QUESTIONS

1. Questions about the facts of this case

   1.1. What fact did the court treat as the most important fact in the case? Do you agree?

   1.2. What facts do you think should be important?

   (a) Was there language in the contract between Nexxus and Best regarding assignment and delegation of the contract? Is that important?

   (b) Is it important that the contract made Best the exclusive distributor for Nexxus' products for most of the State of Texas?

   (c) Is it important that Texas is sometimes referred to as the "Big Hair State" http://www.texasmonthly.com/story/hooray-big-hair

2. Questions about the law

   2.1. What is the court's holding? Did the court hold that the contract could not be delegated, or that the contract could not be delegated to a competitor of the obligee? Would the Seventh Circuit have decided this case differently if Sally Beauty had been owned by Alberto Markell, Bruce Markell's South American cousin, instead of Alberto-Culver, a competitor of Nexxus? Should a court apply section 2–210(1) differently to a sale of Nexxus to Alberto Markell, a cousin of Bruce Markell, than to a sale of Nexxus to Sally Beauty, a subsidiary of Alberto Culver?

   2.2. Why didn't Judge Posner's section 2–609 argument convince the other two Seventh Circuit judges on the *Sally Beauty* panel?

3. **You Be the Lawyer!**

Assume that you are the Sally Beauty attorney negotiating for the acquisition of Best. If the contract between Nexxus and Best had stated "This contract is not assignable," would you recommended to Sally Beauty that it reduce its offer to Best? *Cf.* section 2–210(3).

The *Nexxus* case involves not only the transfer of contract rights but also a stock purchase transaction and a merger—stuff covered in second and third year courses on business associations. (And stuff covered by a casebook that Epstein has co-authored and a student guide that Epstein has authored). Increasingly, the transfer of contract rights are governed by statutes. Articles 3 and 4 of the Uniform Commercial Code deal with the transfer of rights under contracts that are negotiable instruments; Article 9 of the Uniform Commercial Code deals with transferring rights under accounts receivable and other contracts as security for loans courses on the U.C.C. (And stuff covered by a casebook that Epstein has co-authored.) The Bankruptcy Code provides special rules for transfers of contract rights by or to a person who is a debtor in a bankruptcy case—stuff covered in second and third year courses in bankruptcy. (And stuff covered by a casebook that Epstein, Markell and Ponoroff have co-authored and student guides that Epstein has authored and Markell and Ponoroff have co-authored.) Take these courses, buy our books!

FINAL NOTE FROM THE AUTHORS

We hope you enjoyed reading *Making and Doing Deals* as much as we enjoyed writing it. In fact, we hope you enjoyed it so much that you decide to keep it rather than to sell it back to the bookstore! Regardless, we wish you every possible success throughout the remainder of your law school years and beyond!

DGE, BAM, LP

INDEX

References are to Pages

T

U

V

W